Professional VB.N

Third Edition

Professional VB.NET 2003

Third Edition

Bill Evjen

Billy Hollis

Rockford Lhotka

Tim McCarthy

Jonathan Pinnock

Rama Ramachandran

Bill Sheldon

WILEY

Wiley Publishing, Inc.

Professional VB.NET 2003, Third Edition

Published by
Wiley Publishing, Inc.
10475 Crosspoint Boulevard
Indianapolis, IN 46256
www.wiley.com

Library of Congress Cataloging-in-Publication Data

Professional VB.NET 2003 / Bill Evjen ... [et al.].
    p. cm.
Includes index.
ISBN: 0-7645-5992-3 (paper/website)
    1. Microsoft Visual BASIC.   2. BASIC (Computer program language).   3. Microsoft .NET.
I. Evjen, Bill.
    QA76.73.B3P748   2004
    005.2'768—dc22   2004005518

Printed in the United States of America

10 9 8 7 6 5 4 3 2

About the Authors

Bill Evjen

Bill Evjen is an active proponent of the .NET technologies and community-based learning initiatives for .NET. He has been involved with .NET since the first bits were released in 2000 and has since become president of the St. Louis .NET User Group (www.stlnet.org). Bill is also the founder and executive director of the International .NET Association, known as INETA (www.ineta.org), which represents more than 175,000 .NET developers worldwide. Based in St. Louis, Missouri, USA, Bill is an acclaimed author and speaker on ASP.NET and XML Web services. He has written numerous books including *Visual Basic .NET Bible*, *ASP.NET Professional Secrets*, *Web Services Enhancements*, and Wrox's *Professional C#, Third Edition*.

Bill is currently technical director in the Office of the Chief Scientist for Reuters, the global news and information company. He travels the world working with the top financial services companies in assisting them with their applications and architectures. You can contact Bill at evjen@yahoo.com.

To my lovely wife, Tuija, who can with a few words help me see through the smoke and clouds.

Billy Hollis

Billy Hollis is co-author of the first book ever published on Visual Basic. NET, *VB.NET Programming on the Public Beta* (Wrox Press), as well as numerous other books and articles on .NET. Billy is a Microsoft Regional Director and an MVP, and he was selected as one of the original .NET "Software Legends." He writes a monthly column for MSDN Online and is heavily involved in training, consultation, and software development on the Microsoft .NET platform, focusing on smart-client development and commercial packages. He frequently speaks at industry conferences such as Microsoft's Professional Developer Conference (PDC), TechEd, and COMDEX. Billy is a member of the INETA (International .NET Association of user groups) speaker's bureau and speaks at user group meetings all over the United States.

Rockford Lhotka

Rockford Lhotka is Principal Technology Evangelist for Magenic Technologies, a company focused on delivering business value through applied technology and one of the nation's premiere Microsoft Gold Certified Partners. Rockford is the author of several books on .NET development, including *Expert One-on-One Visual Basic .NET Business Objects* (Wrox Press). He is a columnist for MSDN Online and a contributing author for *Visual Studio Magazine*, and he regularly presents at major conferences around the world — including Microsoft PDC, Tech Ed, VS Live!, and VS Connections. Rockford has more than seventeen years' experience in software development and has worked on many projects in various roles, including software architecture, design and development, network administration, and project management.

For my mom and dad, whose love and guidance have been invaluable in my life. Thank you!

Tim McCarthy

Tim McCarthy is a Principal Engineer at InterKnowlogy, where he architects and builds highly scalable n-tier Web and smart-client applications utilizing the latest Microsoft technologies. He has been an author and technical reviewer for several Wrox Press books and has written numerous articles for the Developer .NET Update newsletter. Tim has also developed several packaged presentations for the MSDN Field Content team and has written a white paper for Microsoft on using COM+ services in .NET. Tim has been a regular speaker at Microsoft Developer Days for several years and has delivered several MSDN Webcasts. He can be reached at `timm@interknowlogy.com`.

This book is dedicated to my wife, Miriam; my daughter Jasmine; and my step-children Angie, B.D., and Chris. I am lucky to have such a good family that always supports me in whatever I do.

Jonathan Pinnock

Jonathan Pinnock started programming in Pal III assembler on his school's PDP 8/e with a massive 4K of memory, back in the days before Moore's Law reached the statute books. These days he spends most of his time developing and extending the increasingly successful PlatformOne product set that his company, JPA (`www.jpassoc.co.uk`), markets to the financial services community. He seems to spend the rest of his time writing for Wrox, although he occasionally surfaces to say "Remember me?" to his wife and two children.

Rama Ramachandran

Rama Ramachandran is the software architect at a major hedge fund company. He is a Microsoft Certified Solution Developer and Site-Builder and has excelled in designing and developing Windows and Web applications using .NET, ASP/+, COM, Visual Basic, SQL Server, and Windows 2000. Rama has more than fifteen years' experience with all facets of the software development life cycle and has co-written *Introducing.NET*, *Professional ASP Data Access*, *Professional Visual InterDev 6 Programming* (all Wrox Press), and four books on Visual Basic.

Rama is also the "ASP Pro" at Devx.com, where he maintains ASP-related columns. He teaches Visual Basic and Web Development at Fairfield University and the University of Connecticut. Reach Rama at `ramabeena@hotmail.com`.

This book is dedicated to my wife, Beena, and our children, Ashish and Amit. They make my life whole. I'm great at writing about technology but get tongue-tied trying to say how much I love and care about the three of you. I am grateful to our prayer-answering God for your laughing, mischievous, adoring lives. Thanks for being there, Beens. I love you.

Bill Sheldon

Bill Sheldon is a software architect and engineer originally from Baltimore, Maryland. Holding a degree in Computer Science from the Illinois Institute of Technology (IIT) and a Microsoft Certified Solution Developer (MCSD) qualification, Bill has been employed as an engineer since resigning his commission with the U.S. Navy following the first Gulf War. Bill is involved with the San Diego .NET User Group and writes for *Windows* and *.NET* magazines, including the twice monthly Develop .NET Updates e-mail newsletter. He is also a frequent online presenter for MSDN and speaks at live events such as Microsoft Developer Days. He lives with his wife, Tracie, in Southern California, where he is employed as a Principal Engineer with InterKnowlogy. You can reach Bill at `bills@InterKnowlogy.com`.

I dedicate my contributions to this book to my loving and wonderful wife, Tracie, who has shown great patience in putting up with the long hours and running a household while her husband is in his office.

Credits

Contents

About the Authors v

Acknowledgments xxvii

Introduction 1

Chapter 1: What Is Microsoft .NET? 9

What Is .NET? 9

A Broad and Deep Platform for the Future 10

What's Wrong with DNA and COM? 10

An Overview of the .NET Framework 13

The Common Language Runtime 14

Key Design Goals 15

Metadata 17

Multiple Language Integration and Support 17

A Common Type System 17

Namespaces 18

The Next Layer — The .NET Class Framework 18

What Is in the .NET Class Framework? 18

User and Program Interfaces 19

Windows Forms 20

Web Forms 21

Console Applications 21

Web Services 21

XML as the .NET "Meta-Language" 22

The Role of COM 22

No Internal Use of COM 23

Some Things Never Change . . . 23

.NET Drives Changes in Visual Basic 23

"How Does .NET Affect Me?" 24

A Spectrum of Programming Models 24

Reducing Barriers to Internet Development 24

Libraries of Prewritten Functionality 25

Easier Deployment 25

The Future of .NET 25

Summary 25

Contents

Chapter 2: Introducing VB.NET and VS.NET   **27**

Visual Studio .NET — Startup   **28**

Visual Studio .NET   **29**

The Solution Explorer   30

Namespaces   31

The New Code Window   33

The Properties Window   36

Dynamic Help   37

Working with Visual Basic .NET   **38**

Form Properties Set in Code   38

AssemblyInfo.vb   39

Enhancing the Sample Application   **41**

Add a Control and Event Handler   42

Customizing the Code   43

Build Configurations   47

Building Applications   50

Useful Features of VS.NET   **54**

The Task List   54

The Command Window   55

The Server Explorer   55

Recording and Using Macros in VS.NET   56

Summary   **57**

Chapter 3: The Common Language Runtime   **59**

Elements of a .NET Application   **60**

Assemblies   60

Modules   60

Types   61

Versioning and Deployment   **61**

Better Support for Versioning   62

Better Deployment   63

Memory Management   **63**

Better Garbage Collection   64

Faster Memory Allocation for Objects   68

Garbage Collector Optimizations   70

Cross-Language Integration   **72**

The Common Type System   72

Metadata   73

Better Support for Metadata   74

Attributes 75
The Reflection API 76
IL Disassembler **78**
Summary **79**

Chapter 4: Variables and Type 81

Differences of Value and Reference Types **82**
Value Types (Structures) **83**
Primitive Types 84
Explicit Conversions **92**
Option Strict, Option Explicit, and Option Compare 93
Performing Explicit Conversions 94
Reference Types (Classes) **96**
The Object Class 97
The String Class 98
The DBNull Class 101
Arrays 101
Collections 104
Parameter Passing **106**
Boxing **107**
Retired Keywords and Methods **108**
Elements of VB6 Removed in VB.NET 108
Summary **109**

Chapter 5: Object Syntax Introduction 111

Object-Oriented Terminology **112**
Objects, Classes, and Instances 112
Composition of an Object 113
Working with Objects **116**
Object Declaration and Instantiation 117
Object References 119
Dereferencing Objects 119
Early versus Late Binding 120
Creating Classes **123**
Creating Basic Classes 123
Constructor Methods 141
Termination and Cleanup 142
Advanced Concepts **145**
Overloading Methods 145

Contents

Overloading Constructor Methods 148
Shared Methods, Variables, and Events 149
Delegates 154
Classes versus Components 158
Summary **161**

Chapter 6: Inheritance and Interfaces **163**

Inheritance **164**
Implementing Inheritance 166
Multiple Interfaces **212**
Object Interfaces 212
Secondary Interfaces 213
Summary **220**

Chapter 7: Applying Objects and Components **221**

Abstraction **221**
Encapsulation **224**
Polymorphism **227**
Method Signatures 227
Implementing Polymorphism 227
Inheritance **237**
When to Use Inheritance 237
Inheritance and Multiple Interfaces 242
How Deep to Go? 248
Fragile Base Class Issue 250
Summary **253**

Chapter 8: Namespaces **255**

What Is a Namespace? **256**
Namespaces and References 259
Common Namespaces 261
Importing and Aliasing Namespaces **263**
Importing Namespaces 264
Aliasing Namespaces 266
Creating Your Own Namespaces **266**
Summary **268**

Chapter 9: Error Handling   271

A Quick Overview of Error Handling in VB6   **271**
Exceptions in .NET   **273**
     Properties and Methods of an Exception   273
     How Exceptions Differ from the Err Object in VB6   274
     Commonly Used Exception Types   274
Structured Exception Handling Keywords in VB.NET   **275**
     The Try, Catch, and Finally Keywords   276
     The Throw Keyword   277
     Throwing a New Exception   278
     The Exit Try Statement   279
     Nested Try Structures   280
     The Message Property   282
     The InnerException and TargetSite Properties   282
Error Logging   **288**
     The Event Log   289
     Writing to Trace Files   292
Debugging and Measuring Performance   **295**
     Measuring Performance via the Trace Class   296
Summary   **299**

Chapter 10: Using XML in VB.NET   301

An Introduction to XML   **302**
XML Serialization   **303**
     Source Code Style Attributes   308
System.Xml Document Support   **309**
XML Stream-Style Parsers   **310**
     Writing an XML Stream   311
     Reading an XML Stream   314
     Using the MemoryStream Object   320
     Document Object Model (DOM)   324
XSLT Transforms   **330**
     XSLT Transforming Between XML Standards   334
     Other Classes and Interfaces in System.Xml.Xsl   337
ADO.NET   **337**
     ADO.NET and SQL Server's Built-In XML Features   339
     Typed DataSet Objects   341
     Generating Typed DataSets   342
Summary   **346**

Contents

Chapter 11: Data Access with ADO.NET   **349**

Why Do We Need ADO.NET?   350
The ADO.NET Architecture   **350**
ADO.NET Components   351
Differences Between ADO and ADO.NET   352
.NET Data Providers   **355**
Connection Object   356
Command Object   356
DataReader Object   357
DataAdapter Objects   359
SQL Server .NET Data Provider   361
OLE DB .NET Data Provider   362
The DataSet Component   **362**
DataTableCollection   362
DataRelationCollection   363
ExtendedProperties   363
Creating and Using DataSet Objects   364
ADO.NET DataTable Objects   368
Connection Pooling in ADO.NET   **368**
Using Stored Procedures with ADO.NET   **369**
Creating a Stored Procedure   370
Calling the Stored Procedure   371
Building a Data Access Component   **375**
Constructors   376
Properties   377
Stored Procedure XML Structure   378
Methods   379
Using DataSet Objects to Bind to DataGrids   **391**
Summary   **393**

Chapter 12: Windows Forms   **395**

The Importance of Windows Forms   **395**
The System.Windows.Forms Namespace   **396**
Forms as Classes   **397**
Using Forms via Sub Main   398
What Is a Form in .NET?   399
Forms at Design Time   **399**
The Design Time Grid   399
Setting the Startup Form   400
Form Borders   400

Always on Top—The TopMost Property   401
Owned Forms   402
Startup Location   403
Making Forms Transparent and Translucent   403
Visual Inheritance   405
Setting Limits on the Form Size   405
Scrollable Forms   405
Forms at Runtime   **406**
Controls   **407**
Control Tab Order   407
Control Arrays   408
Automatic Resizing and Positioning Controls   410
Extender Provider Controls   414
Validating Data Entry   416
Menus   418
Toolbars   423
Common Dialogs   425
Drag and Drop   428
Panel and GroupBox Container Controls   430
Summary of Standard Windows.Forms Controls   431
Retired Controls   435
Using ActiveX Controls   435
Other Handy Programming Tips   436
MDI Forms   436
An MDI Example in VB.NET   438
Dialog Forms   439
Summary   **441**

Chapter 13: Creating Windows Controls   **443**

Sources of Controls   **443**
Built-in Controls   444
Existing ActiveX Controls   444
Third-Party Controls   444
Custom Controls   444
Developing Custom Controls in .NET   **445**
Inherit from an Existing Control   445
Build a Composite Control   446
Write a Control from Scratch   446
Inheriting from an Existing Control   **446**
Overview of the Process   447

Contents

Creating a Numeric-Only Text Box   447
Making Changes to a Custom Control   450
Adding Additional Logic to a Custom Control   450
Creating a Property for a Custom Control   451
Other Useful Attributes   454
Defining a Custom Event for the Inherited Control   455
Creating a CheckedListBox that Limits the Number of Selected Items   456
The Control and UserControl Base Classes   **459**
The Control Class   460
The UserControl Class   460
A Composite UserControl   **463**
Creating a Composite UserControl   463
How Does Resize Work?   465
Setting a Minimum Size for Controls   465
Exposing Properties of Sub-Controls   465
Stepping Through the Example   465
Building a Control from Scratch   **469**
Painting a Custom Control with GDI+   470
Attaching an Icon for the Toolbox   **476**
Summary   **477**

Chapter 14: Web Forms   **479**

A Web Form in Action   **479**
Setting Up the Environment   480
The HelloWorld Web Form   480
The Anatomy of a Web Form   **484**
The Template for Presentation   485
The Code Component   486
A More Complex Example   **486**
The Processing Flow of ASP.NET Web Forms   **489**
The Controls Available in Web Forms   **492**
The Concept of Server-Side Controls   493
HTML Server Controls   496
ASP.NET Server Controls   497
Validation Controls   498
User Controls   500
Events in Web Forms   **501**
The Web Form's Lifecycle   502
Event Categories   503
Web Forms Versus ASP   **504**

Transferring Control among Web Forms **505**
A Final Example **506**
Summary **520**

Chapter 15: Creating Web Controls **523**

Why Create Your Own Controls? **524**
When to Create Your Own Controls **524**
Types of Custom Web Controls **525**
    Web User Controls 525
    Subclassed Controls 526
    Composite Controls 526
    Templated Controls 527
When to Use Custom Web Controls **527**
Creating a Web User Control **528**
    Building a Simple Web User Control 528
    Converting a Web Page into a Web User Control 535
    Adding a Web User Control Item to the Project 543
    Reusing Code in a Web User Control 547
    The @ Control Directive 547
    Web User Controls and the @ Register Directive 548
    Reaching Into a Web User Control 549
    Reaching Out of a Web User Control 562
    Other Web User Control Features 563
Creating a Subclassed Control **564**
    Setting Up a Test Bed Project 565
    Subclassed Controls and the Web Custom Control Template 566
    The Render Method 569
    Developing Subclassed Controls 572
Summary **581**

Chapter 16: Data Binding **583**

Presenting Data **583**
    Saving Changes 586
    Profiling the Update Statement 590
Master/Details Data Binding **592**
    Multiple, Related Tables in a Single DataGrid 592
    A More Usable Solution 596
Forms **599**
    Moving Through the Records 602
    Saving Changes 606

Contents

What Data Can Be Data Bound?   **609**
   Lists of Items   610
   Properties of Objects   610
Summary   **612**

Chapter 17: Working with Classic COM and Interfaces   613

Classic COM   **613**
COM and .NET in Practice   **615**
   A Legacy Component   615
   The .NET Application   618
   Trying It All Out   620
   Using TlbImp Directly   620
   Late Binding   622
ActiveX Controls   **627**
   A Legacy ActiveX Control   627
   A .NET Application, Again   629
   Trying It All Out, Again   631
Using .NET Components in the COM World   **631**
   A .NET Component   632
   RegAsm   634
   TlbExp   637
Summary   **638**

Chapter 18: Component Services   639

Transactions   **640**
   The ACID Test   640
Transactional Components   **641**
   An Example of Transactions   642
Other Aspects of Transactions   **658**
   Manual Transactions   658
   Just-In-Time   659
   Object Pooling   659
   Holding Things Up   659
Queued Components   **660**
   An Example of Queued Components   660
   Transactions with Queued Components   667
Summary   **669**

Contents

Chapter 19: Threading   671

What Is a Thread?   671
Processes, AppDomains, and Threads   673
Thread Scheduling   674
Thread Safety and Thread Affinity   677
When to Use Threads   677
Designing a Background Task   678
Implementing Threading   680
A Quick Tour   680
Threading Options   686
Shared Data   692
Canceling a Background Task   711
Summary   717

Chapter 20: Remoting   719

Remoting Overview   720
Basic Terminology   720
SingleCall, Singleton, and Activated Objects   723
Implementing Remoting   727
A Simple Example   727
Using IIS as a Remoting Host   738
Using Activator.GetObject   743
Interface-Based Design   744
Using Generated Proxies   745
Summary   746

Chapter 21: Windows Services   749

Example Windows Services   749
Characteristics of a Windows Service   750
Interacting with Windows Services   751
Creating a Windows Service   752
The .NET Framework Classes for Windows Services   752
Other Types of Windows Service   755
General Instructions to Create a Windows Service with VB.NET   756
Creating a Counter Monitor Service   757
Installing the Service   759
Starting the Service   760
Uninstalling the Service   760

Contents

Monitoring a Performance Counter	**762**
Creating a Performance Counter	762
Integrating the Counter into the Service	763
Changing the Value in the Performance Counter	763
Communicating with the Service	**764**
The ServiceController Class	765
Integrating a ServiceController into the Example	766
More About ServiceController	768
Custom Commands	**768**
Passing Strings to a Service	770
Creating a File Watcher	**770**
Writing Events Using an Eventlog	771
Creating a FileSystemWatcher	771
Debugging the Service	**775**
To Debug a Service	776
Summary	**778**
Chapter 22: Web Services	**781**
Introduction to Web Services	**781**
Early Architectural Designs	**783**
The Network Angle	783
Application Development	783
Merging the Two with the Web	783
The Foundations of Web Services	784
The Problems	785
The Other Players	786
What All the Foundations Missed	786
Building a Web Service	**790**
A Realistic Example	**793**
Using Visual Studio .NET to Build Web Services	795
Returning Rich Sets of Data	**798**
VB .NET and System.Web.Services	**800**
System.Web.Services Namespace	800
System.Web.Services.Description Namespace	801
System.Web.Services.Discovery Namespace	802
System.Web.Services.Protocols Namespace	802
Architecting with Web Services	**803**
Why Web Services?	803
How This All Fits Together	804
Web Service Proxies	804

Contents

State Management for XML Web Services 804
Using DNS as a Model 805
Security in Web Services **808**
The Secure Sockets Layer 809
Directory Level Security 809
Other Types of Security 810
The Down Side **810**
Security 810
State 810
Transactions 810
Speed and Connectivity 810
Where We Go from Here **811**
Summary **811**

Chapter 23: VB.NET and the Internet **813**

Downloading Internet Resources **813**
Sockets **817**
Building the Application 818
Creating Conversation Windows 820
Sending Messages 828
Shutting Down the Application 833
Using Internet Explorer in Your Applications **837**
Internet Explorer Interop Design Pattern 838
Summary **846**

Chapter 24: Security in the .NET Framework **847**

Security Concepts and Definitions **848**
Permissions in the System.Security.Permissions Namespace **850**
Code Access Permissions 852
Role-Based Permissions 853
Identity Permissions 856
Managing Code Access Permissions **856**
Managing Security Policy **861**
Security Tools 873
Cryptography Basics **874**
Hash Algorithms 875
Summary **875**

Contents

Chapter 25: Assemblies and Deployment   897

Assemblies   **897**
The Manifest   **899**
    The Identity Section   900
    Referenced Assemblies   902
Assemblies and Deployment   **903**
    Application-Private Assemblies   904
    Shared Assemblies   904
Versioning Issues   **906**
    Application Isolation   906
    Side-by-Side Execution   907
    Self-Describing   907
    Version Policies   907
    Configuration Files   909
Application Deployment   **912**
    DLL Hell   913
    XCOPY Deployment   914
    Deployment Options Prior to .NET   914
    Application Deployment in Visual Studio .NET   916
Visual Studio .NET Deployment Projects   **916**
    Project Templates   916
    Creating a Deployment Project   918
    Walkthroughs   918
Modifying the Deployment Project   **931**
    Project Properties   933
    The File System Editor   936
    The Registry Editor   941
    The File Types Editor   943
    The User Interface Editor   945
    The Custom Actions Editor   947
    The Launch Conditions Editor   950
Building   **954**
Summary   **954**

Chapter 26: Mobile Application Development   957

Mobile Web Applications   **958**
    Web Services for Mobile Applications   958
    Limitations of the Mobile Web Template   958
    Creating a Mobile Web Application   961
    Differences of Mobile Web and .NET Compact Framework Applications   964

Contents

Introducing the .NET Compact Framework   **966**

    Limitations of the .NET Compact Framework   967

    .NET Compact Framework Specific Namespaces   971

    Mobile Device Emulators   971

A First .NET Compact Framework Application   **973**

Summary   **983**

Appendix A: Upgrading: Using the Visual Basic Compatibility Library   **985**

Index   **999**

Acknowledgments

Bill Evjen: Big thanks go to Sharon Cox for getting me involved with this project. Then special thanks go to Katie Mohr and Eileen Bien Calabro for getting me to the end! The folks at Wiley are an impressive group to work with, and writing for such a great group of people is one of the best things about the job.

Jonathan Pinnock: My heartfelt thanks go to Gail, who first suggested my getting into writing and now suffers the consequences on a fairly regular basis, and to Mark and Rachel, who just suffer the consequences.

Bill Sheldon: My thanks to Tim Huckaby, who got me started down this road of authoring and has been both inspirational and supportive over the past few years.

Introduction

In 2002, Visual Basic took the biggest leap in innovation since it was released, with the introduction of Visual Basic .NET (VB.NET). After more than a decade, Visual Basic was overdue for a major overhaul. But .NET goes beyond an overhaul. It changes almost every aspect of software development. From integrating Internet functionality to creating object-oriented frameworks, VB.NET challenges traditional VB developers to learn dramatic new concepts and techniques.

First, it's necessary to learn the differences between VB.NET and the older versions. In some cases, the same functionality is implemented in a different way. This was not done arbitrarily — there are good reasons for the changes. But you must be prepared to unlearn old habits and form new ones.

Next, you must be open to the new concepts. Full object orientation, new component techniques, new visual tools for both local and Internet interfaces — all of these and more must become part of your skill set to effectively develop applications in VB.NET.

In this book, we cover VB.NET virtually from start to finish. We begin by looking at the .NET Framework and end by looking at the best practices for deploying .NET applications. In between, we look at everything from database access to integration with other technologies such as XML, along with investigating the new features in detail. You will see that VB.NET has emerged as a powerful yet easy to use language that will allow you to target the Internet just as easily as the desktop.

The Importance of Visual Basic

Early in the adoption cycle of .NET, Microsoft's new language, C#, got the lion's share of attention. But as .NET adoption has increased, Visual Basic's continuing importance has also been apparent. Microsoft has publicly stated that they consider VB.NET the language of choice for applications where developer productivity is one of the highest priorities.

Future development of Visual Basic is emphasizing capabilities that enable access to the whole expanse of the .NET Framework in the most productive way, while C# development is emphasizing the experience of writing code. That fits the traditional role of Visual Basic as the language developers use in the real world to create business applications as quickly as possible.

This difference is more than academic. One of the most important advantages of the .NET Framework is that it allows applications to be written with dramatically less code. In the world of business applications, the goal is to concentrate on writing business logic, and to eliminate routine coding tasks as much as possible. The value in this new world is not in churning out lots of code — it is in writing robust, useful applications with *as little code as possible*.

Visual Basic is an excellent fit for this type of development, which makes up the bulk of software development in today's economy. And it will grow to be an even better fit as it is refined and evolved for exactly that purpose.

Who Is This Book for?

This book is written to help experienced developers learn about VB.NET. From those who are just starting the transition from earlier versions to those who have used VB.NET for a while and need to gain a deeper understanding, this book discusses the most common programming tasks and concepts you need.

Professional VB.NET offers a wide-ranging presentation of VB.NET concepts, but the .NET Framework is so large and comprehensive that no single book can cover it all. The most important area in which this book does not attempt to be complete is Web development. While chapters discussing the basics of browser-based programming in VB.NET are included, professional Web developers should instead refer to *Professional ASP.NET* (Wrox Press).

What You Need to Use This Book

Although, it is possible to create VB.NET applications using the command line tools contained in the *.NET Framework SDK*, you will need *Visual Studio .NET 2003* (Professional or higher), which includes the .NET Framework SDK, to get the most out of this book. You may use *Visual Studio .NET 2002* instead, but you will encounter a few instances where the dialog boxes and menus will be slightly different.

In addition:

❑ Some chapters make use of *SQL Server 2000*. However, you can also run the example code using *Microsoft Data Engine* (MSDE), which ships with Visual Studio .NET (VS.NET).

❑ Several chapters make use of *Internet Information Services* (IIS). IIS ships with Windows 2003 Server, Windows 2000 Server, Windows 2000 Professional, and Windows XP, although it is not installed by default.

❑ Chapter 18 makes use of MSMQ to work with queued transactions. MSMQ ships with Windows 2003 Server, Windows 2000 Server, Windows 2000 Professional, and Windows XP, although it is not installed by default.

What Does This Book Cover?

Chapter 1, "What Is Microsoft .NET?" — This chapter explains the importance of .NET, and just how much it changes application development. We gain an understanding of why we need .NET by looking at what's wrong with the current development technologies, including COM and the DNA architectural model. Then, we look at how .NET corrects the drawbacks by using the common language runtime (CLR).

Chapter 2, "Introducing VB.NET and VS.NET" — This chapter provides our first look at a VB.NET application. As we develop this application, we'll take a tour of some of the new features of VS.NET.

Chapter 3, "The Common Language Runtime" — This chapter examines the core of the .NET platform, the common language runtime (CLR). The CLR is responsible for managing the execution of code compiled for the .NET platform. We cover versioning and deployment, memory management, cross-language integration, metadata, and the IL Disassembler.

Chapter 4, "Variables and Data Types" — This chapter introduces many of the types commonly used in VB.NET. The main goal of this chapter is to familiarize you with value and reference types and to help those with a background in VB6 understand some of the key differences in how variables are defined in VB.NET.

Chapter 5, "Object Syntax Introduction" — This is the first of three chapters that explore object-oriented programming in VB.NET. This chapter will define objects, classes, instances, encapsulation, abstraction, polymorphism, and inheritance.

Chapter 6, "Inheritance and Interfaces" — This chapter examines inheritance and how it can be used within VB.NET. We create simple and abstract base classes and understand how to create base classes from which other classes can be derived.

Chapter 7, "Applying Objects and Components" — This chapter puts the theory of Chapters 5 and 6 into practice. The four defining object-oriented concepts (abstraction, encapsulation, polymorphism, inheritance) are discussed, and we explain how these concepts can be applied in design and development to create effective object-oriented applications.

Chapter 8, "Namespaces" — This chapter introduces namespaces and their hierarchical structure. An explanation of namespaces and some common ones is given. In addition, we understand how to create new namespaces, and how to import and alias existing namespaces within projects.

Chapter 9, "Error Handling" — This chapter covers how error handling works in VB.NET by discussing the CLR exception handler and the new `Try...Catch...Finally` structure. We also look at error and trace logging, and how we can use these methods to obtain feedback on how our program is working.

Chapter 10, "Using XML in VB.NET" — This chapter presents the features of the .NET Framework that facilitate the generation and manipulation of XML. We describe the .NET Framework's XML related namespaces, and a subset of the classes exposed by these namespaces is examined in detail. This chapter also touches on a set of technologies that utilize XML, specifically ADO.NET and SQL Server.

Chapter 11, "Data Access with ADO.NET" — This chapter focuses on what you will need to know about the ADO.NET object model in order to be able to build flexible, fast, and scalable data access objects and applications. The evolution of ADO into ADO.NET is explored, and the main objects in ADO.NET that you need to understand in order to build data access into your .NET applications are explained.

Chapter 12, "Windows Forms" — This chapter looks at Windows Forms, concentrating primarily on forms and built-in controls. What is new and what has been changed from the previous versions of Visual Basic are discussed, along with the `System.Windows.Forms` namespace.

Chapter 13, "Creating Windows Controls" — This chapter looks at creating our own Windows controls. In particular, we discuss how to inherit from another control, build a composite control, and write controls from scratch based on the `Control` class.

Chapter 14, "Web Forms" — This chapter explores Web forms and how you can benefit from their use. Using progressively more complex examples, this chapter explains how .NET provides the power of Rapid Application Development (normally associated with Windows applications) for the development of Web applications.

Chapter 15, "Creating Web Controls" — This chapter looks at an entirely new form of Visual Basic control development: custom Web controls. It looks at the various forms of custom Web control development that are available in the .NET Framework. The basic structure of Web user and subclassed controls is examined, along with a look at composite and templated controls.

Chapter 16, "Data Binding" — This chapter examines how data binding in .NET makes the process of associating an underlying data store with controls easier than in the previous versions of Visual Basic. We look at how .NET allows the automatic population of controls with data from an underlying data source and provides a mechanism for updating the underlying data source in response to any changes the user may make within Windows applications.

Chapter 17, "Working with Classic COM and Interfaces" — This chapter discusses COM and .NET component interoperability, and what tools are provided to help link the two technologies.

Chapter 18, "Component Services" — This chapter explores the .NET component services — in particular, transaction processing and queued components.

Chapter 19, "Threading" — This chapter explores threading and explains how the various objects in the .NET Framework enable any of its consumers to develop multithreaded applications. We examine how threads can be created, how they relate to processes, and the differences between multitasking and multithreading.

Chapter 20, "Remoting" — This chapter takes a detailed look at how to use remoting in classic three-tier application design. We look at the basic architecture of remoting and build a basic server and client that uses a singleton object for answering client requests into the business tier. We then look at how to use serialization to return more complex objects from the server to the client and how to use the call context for passing extra data from the client to the server along with each call without having to change the object model.

Chapter 21, "Windows Services" — This chapter examines how VB.NET is used in the production of Windows Services. The creation, installation, running, and debugging of Windows Services are covered.

Chapter 22, "Web Services" — This chapter looks at how to create and consume Web services using VB.NET. The abstract classes provided by the CLR to set up and work with Web services are discussed, as are some of the technologies that support Web services. Finally, some of the disadvantages to using any distributed architecture and the future with Web services are examined.

Chapter 23, "VB.NET and the Internet" — This chapter looks at how to download resources from the Web, how to design our own communication protocols, and how to reuse the Web browser control in our applications.

Chapter 24, "Security in the .NET Framework" — This chapter examines the additional tools and functionality with regard to the security provided by .NET. `Caspol.Exe` and `Permview.exe`, which assist in establishing and maintaining security policies, are discussed. The `System.Security.Permissions` namespace is looked at, and we discuss how it relates to managing permissions. Finally, we examine the `System.Security.Cryptography` namespace and run through some code to demonstrate the capabilities of this namespace.

Chapter 25, "Assemblies and Deployment in .NET" — This chapter examines assemblies and their use within the CLR. The structure of an assembly, what it contains, and the information it contains are examined. In addition, the manifest of the assembly and its role in deployment will be looked at. We also look at what VS.NET and the CLR have to offer us when we come to deploy our applications.

Chapter 26, "Mobile Application Development" — This chapter covers mobile Web applications, differences between Mobile Web and .NET Compact Framework applications, the .NET Compact Framework, and mobile device emulators.

Appendix A, "Using the Visual Basic Compatibility Library" — This appendix looks at the Visual Basic Compatibility Library, which is provided in order to assist in the conversion of the existing code, as well as provide backward compatibility and support for developers who are transitioning to VB.NET.

Conventions

We have used a number of different styles of text and layout in the book to help differentiate between the different kinds of information. Here are examples of the styles we use and an explanation of what they mean:

Bullets appear indented, with each new bullet marked as follows:

- ❑ **Important Words** are in a bold type font
- ❑ Words that appear on the screen in menus like the File or Window are in a similar font to the one that you see on screen
- ❑ Keys that you press on the keyboard, like *Ctrl* and *Enter*, are in italics
- ❑ If you see something like Object, you'll know that it's a filename, object name, or function name

Code in a gray box shows new, important, pertinent code:

```
Dim objMyClass as New MyClass("Hello World")
Debug.WriteLine(objMyClass.ToString)
```

Sometimes you'll see code in a mixture of styles, such as:

```
Dim objVar as Object
objVar = Me
CType(objVar, Form).Text = "New Dialog Title Text"
```

The code with a white background is code we've already looked at and that we don't wish to examine further.

Advice, hints, and background information come in an italicized, indented paragraph like this.

Important pieces of information come in shaded boxes like this.

Customer Support

We always value hearing from our readers, and we want to know what you think about this book: what you liked, what you didn't like, and what you think we can do better next time. You can send us your comments, either by returning the reply card in the back of the book or by e-mail to feedback@wrox.com. Please be sure to mention the book title in your message.

How to Download the Sample Code for the Book

When you visit the Wrox site, www.wrox.com, simply locate the title through our Search facility or by using one of the title lists. Click Download in the Code column, or on Download Code on the book's detail page.

The files that are available for download from our site have been archived using WinZip. When you have saved the attachments to a folder on your hard -drive, you need to extract the files using a decompression program such as WinZip or PKUnzip. When you extract the files, the code is usually extracted into chapter folders. When you start the extraction process, ensure that your software (WinZip, PKUnzip, and so on.) is set to use folder names.

Errata

We've made every effort to make sure that there are no errors in the text or in the code. However, no one is perfect and mistakes do occur. If you find an error in one of our books, like a spelling mistake or a faulty piece of code, we would be very grateful for feedback. By sending in errata, you may save another reader hours of frustration, and of course, you will be helping us provide even higher quality information. Simply e-mail the information to support@wrox.com; your information will be checked and if correct, posted to the errata page for that title, or used in subsequent editions of the book.

To find errata on the Web site, go to www.wrox.com, and simply locate the title through our Advanced Search or title list. Click the Book Errata link, which is below the cover graphic on the book's detail page.

p2p.wrox.com

For author and peer discussion, join the P2P mailing lists. Our unique system provides *programmer to programmer*™ contact on mailing lists, forums, and newsgroups, all in addition to our one-to-one e-mail support system. If you post a query to P2P, you can be confident that it is being examined by the many Wrox authors and other industry experts who are present on our mailing lists. At p2p.wrox.com you will find a number of different lists that will help you, not only while you read this book, but also as you develop your own applications.

> **Particularly appropriate to this book are the vb_dotnet and pro_vb_dotnet lists.**

To subscribe to a mailing list just follow these steps:

1.   Go to http://p2p.wrox.com/.
2.   Choose the appropriate category from the left menu bar.

3. Click the mailing list you wish to join.

4. Follow the instructions to subscribe and fill in your e-mail address and password.

5. Reply to the confirmation e-mail you receive.

6. Use the subscription manager to join more lists and set your e-mail preferences.

You can read messages in the forums without joining P2P, but in order to post your own messages, you must join.

Once you join, you can post new messages and respond to messages other users post. You can read messages at any time on the Web. If you would like to have new messages from a particular forum e-mailed to you, click the Subscribe to this Forum icon by the forum name in the forum listing.

For more information about how to use the Wrox P2P, be sure to read the P2P FAQs for answers to questions about how the forum software works as well as many common questions specific to P2P and Wrox books. To read the FAQs, click the FAQ link on any P2P page.

What Is Microsoft .NET?

New technologies force change, nowhere more so than in computers and software. Occasionally, a new technology is so innovative that it forces us to challenge our most fundamental assumptions. In the computing industry, the latest such technology is the Internet. It has forced us to rethink how software should be created, deployed, and used.

However, that process takes time. Usually, when a powerful new technology comes along, it is first simply strapped onto existing platforms. So it has been for the Internet. Before the advent of Microsoft .NET, we used older platforms with new Internet capabilities "strapped on". The resulting systems worked, but they were expensive and difficult to produce, hard to use, and difficult to maintain.

Realizing this several years ago, Microsoft decided it was time to design a new platform from the ground up specifically for the post-Internet world. The result is called *.NET*. It represents a turning point in the world of Windows software for Microsoft platforms. Microsoft has staked their future on .NET, and publicly stated that henceforth almost all their research and development will be done on this platform. It is expected that, eventually, almost all Microsoft products will be ported to the .NET platform. (However, the name ".NET" will evolve, as we will see at the end of the chapter.)

What Is .NET?

Microsoft's .NET initiative is broad-based and very ambitious. It includes the *.NET Framework*, which encompasses the languages and execution platform, plus extensive class libraries providing rich built-in functionality. Besides the core .NET Framework, the .NET initiative includes protocols (such as the *Simple Object Access Protocol*, commonly known as *SOAP*) to provide a new level of software integration over the Internet, via a standard known as Web services.

Although Web services are important (and are discussed in detail in Chapter 22), the foundation of all .NET-based systems is the .NET Framework. This chapter will look at the .NET Framework from the viewpoint of a Visual Basic developer. Unless you are quite familiar with the Framework already, you should consider this introduction an essential first step in assimilating the information about Visual Basic .NET that will be presented in the rest of this book.

The first released product based on the .NET Framework was *Visual Studio .NET 2002*, which was publicly launched in February of 2002, and included version 1.0 of the .NET Framework. The current version is *Visual Studio .NET 2003*, which was introduced a year later, and included version 1.1 of the .NET Framework. This book assumes you are using VS.NET 2003, but almost all of the examples will work transparently with VS.NET 2002 because the differences in the two versions are minor.

A Broad and Deep Platform for the Future

Calling the .NET Framework a *platform* doesn't begin to describe how broad and deep it is. It encompasses a virtual machine that abstracts away much of the Windows API from development. It includes a class library with more functionality than any yet created. It makes available a development environment that spans multiple languages, and it exposes an architecture that makes multiple language integration simple and straightforward.

At first glance, some aspects of .NET appear similar to previous architectures, such as UCSD Pascal and Java. No doubt some of the ideas for .NET were inspired by these past efforts, but there are also many brand new architectural ideas in .NET. Overall, the result is a radically new approach to software development.

The vision of Microsoft .NET is globally distributed systems, using XML as the universal glue to allow functions running on different computers across an organization or across the world to come together in a single application. In this vision, systems from servers to wireless palmtops, with everything in between, will share the same general platform, with versions of .NET available for all of them, and with each of them able to integrate transparently with the others.

This does not leave out classic applications as we have always known them, though. Microsoft .NET also aims to make traditional business applications much easier to develop and deploy. Some of the technologies of the .NET Framework, such as Windows Forms, demonstrate that Microsoft has not forgotten the traditional business developer. In fact, such developers will find it possible to Internet-enable their applications more easily than with any previous platform.

What's Wrong with DNA and COM?

The pre-.NET technologies used for development on Microsoft platforms encompassed the *COM (Component Object Model) standard* for creation of components, and the *DNA model* for multitier software architectures. As these technologies were extended into larger, more enterprise-level settings, and as integration with the Internet began to be important, several major drawbacks became apparent. These included:

❏ Difficulty in integrating Internet technologies:

　　❏ Hard to produce Internet-based user interfaces

　　❏ No standard way for systems and processes to communicate over the Internet

- ❑ Expensive, difficult, and undependable deployment
- ❑ Poor cross-language integration
- ❑ Weaknesses in the most popular Microsoft tool — Visual Basic:
  - ❑ Lack of full object orientation, which made it impossible to produce frameworks in Visual Basic
  - ❑ One threading model that did not work in some contexts
  - ❑ Poor integration with the Internet
- ❑ Other weaknesses such as poor error handling capabilities

It is important to note that all pre-.NET platforms, such as Java, also have some of these drawbacks, as well as unique ones of their own. The drawbacks related to the Internet are particularly ubiquitous.

Let's take a brief look at these drawbacks to pre-.NET Microsoft technologies before taking up how .NET addresses them.

Difficulty in Integrating Internet Technologies

Starting in late 1995, Microsoft made a dramatic shift toward the Internet. They had to make some serious compromises to quickly produce Internet-based tools and technologies. The main result, *Active Server Pages (ASP)*, was a tool that was not oriented around structured and object-oriented development. Having to design, debug, and maintain such unstructured ASP code is also a headache. While many viable systems were produced with ASP pages, these obvious flaws needed to be addressed.

Later in the evolution of the Internet, it became apparent that communicating with the user via HTTP and HTML was limiting. To get, for example, a stock quote from an Internet server, it was often necessary for a program to pretend to be a user, get an HTML page, and then take it apart to get the information needed. This was fussy development, and the result was quite brittle because of the possibility that the format of the page might change and, thus, need new parsing logic.

Developers needed a standard way for *processes* to communicate over the Internet, rather than the communication being directed only at *users*. DNA and COM lacked any such standard.

Deployment Issues

Microsoft's COM standard was developed for use on small systems with limited memory running Microsoft Windows. The design trade-offs for COM were oriented around sharing memory, and quick performance on hardware we would now consider slow.

This meant that *Dynamic Link Libraries (DLLs)* were shared between applications to save memory, and a binary interface standard was used to ensure good performance. To quickly find the components needed to run an application, DLLs had to register their class IDs to the local Windows Registry.

Besides the registration logistics needed to make DLLs work at all, COM components could be rendered inoperable by versioning issues. The resulting morass of problems related to versioning was colloquially known as "DLL Hell."

The need to register components locally also resulted in other limitations. It was not possible for a COM application to be placed on a CD-ROM or a network drive, and then run from that location without an installation procedure.

Poor Cross-Language Integration

COM/DNA typically required the use of three separate development models. Business components were most often written in Visual Basic, and Visual Basic could also be used for local Win32 user interfaces. Browser-based user interfaces required ASP. System components sometimes required the use of C++.

Each of these languages had difficulties integrating with the others. Getting VB strings properly transferred to and from C++ routines is a challenge. For example, ASP pages required a COM interface with only Variants for data, which negated the strong typing available in Visual Basic and C++. Getting all three languages to work together required several arcane skills.

Weaknesses in Visual Basic in COM/DNA Applications

Visual Basic 6 (VB6) (and earlier versions) was easily the most popular language for developing applications with the DNA model. As noted above, it can be used in two major roles — forms-based VB clients and COM components (on either the client or the server).

There are other options, of course, including C++, J++, and various third-party languages such as Delphi and Perl, but the number of VB developers outnumbers them all put together.

Despite its popularity, VB6 suffered from a number of limitations in the COM/DNA environment. Some of the most serious limitations include:

- ❑ No capability for multithreading
- ❑ Lack of implementation inheritance and other object-oriented features
- ❑ Poor error handling ability
- ❑ Poor integration with other languages such as C++ (as discussed above)
- ❑ No effective user interface for Internet-based applications

Lack of multithreading implies, for example, that VB6 can't be used "out of the box" to write an NT-type service. There are also situations in which the apartment threading used by components created in Visual Basic limits performance.

VB6's limited object-oriented features, in particular the lack of inheritance, made it unsuitable for development of object-based frameworks, and denied design options to VB6 developers that were available to C++ or Java developers.

VB6's archaic error handling becomes especially annoying in a multitier environment. It is difficult in VB6 to track and pass errors through a stack of component interfaces.

Perhaps the biggest drawback to using VB6 became apparent when many developers moved to the Internet. While VB forms for a Win32 client were state-of-the-art, for applications with a browser interface, VB6 was relegated mostly to use in components because it did not have an effective way to do user interfaces for the Web.

Microsoft tried to address this problem in VB6 with Web classes and DHTML pages. Neither caught on because of their inherent limitations.

All of these limitations needed to be addressed, but Microsoft decided to look beyond just Visual Basic and solve these problems on a more global level. All of these limitations are solved in VB.NET through the use of technology in the .NET Framework.

An Overview of the .NET Framework

First and foremost, .NET is a framework that covers all the layers of software development above the operating system. It provides the richest level of integration among presentation technologies, component technologies, and data technologies ever seen on a Microsoft, or perhaps any, platform. Secondly, the entire architecture has been created to make it as easy to develop Internet applications, as it is to develop for the desktop.

The .NET Framework actually "wraps" the operating system, insulating software developed with .NET from most operating system specifics such as file handling and memory allocation. This prepares for a possible future in which the software developed for .NET is portable to a wide variety of hardware and operating system foundations.

VS.NET supports Windows 2003, Windows XP, and all versions of Windows 2000. Programs created for .NET can also run under Windows NT, Windows 98, and Windows Me, though VS.NET does not run on these systems.

The major components of the Microsoft .NET Framework are shown in Figure 1-1.

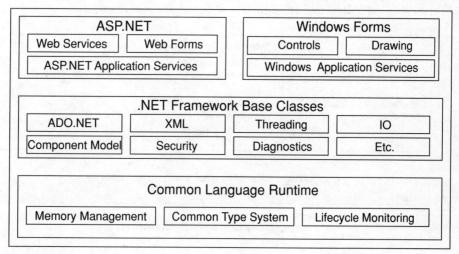

Figure 1-1

The framework starts all the way down at the memory management and component loading level, and goes all the way up to multiple ways of rendering user and program interfaces. In between, there are layers that provide just about any system-level capability that a developer would need.

At the base is the *common language runtime*, often abbreviated to *CLR*. This is the heart of the .NET Framework—it is the engine that drives key functionality. It includes, for example, a common system of datatypes. These common types, plus a standard interface convention, make cross-language inheritance possible. In addition to allocation and management of memory, the CLR also does reference tracking for objects, and handles garbage collection.

The middle layer includes the next generation of standard system services such as classes that manage data and XML. These services are brought under control of the framework, making them universally available and making their usage consistent across languages.

The top layer includes user and program interfaces. *Windows Forms* is a new and more advanced way to do standard Win32 screens (often referred to as "'smart clients"). *Web Forms* provides a new Web-based user interface. Perhaps the most revolutionary is *Web services*, which provides a mechanism for programs to communicate over the Internet, using SOAP. Web services provide an analog of COM and DCOM for object brokering and interfacing, but based on Internet technologies so that allowance is made even for integration to non-Microsoft platforms. Web Forms and Web services, which comprise the Internet interface portion of .NET, are implemented by a part of the .NET Framework referred to as *ASP.NET*.

All of these capabilities are available to any language that is based on the .NET platform, including, of course, VB.NET.

The Common Language Runtime

We are all familiar with runtimes—they go back further than DOS languages. However, the *common language runtime* (CLR) is as advanced over traditional runtimes as a machine gun is over a musket. Figure 1-2 shows a quick diagrammatic summary of the major pieces of the CLR.

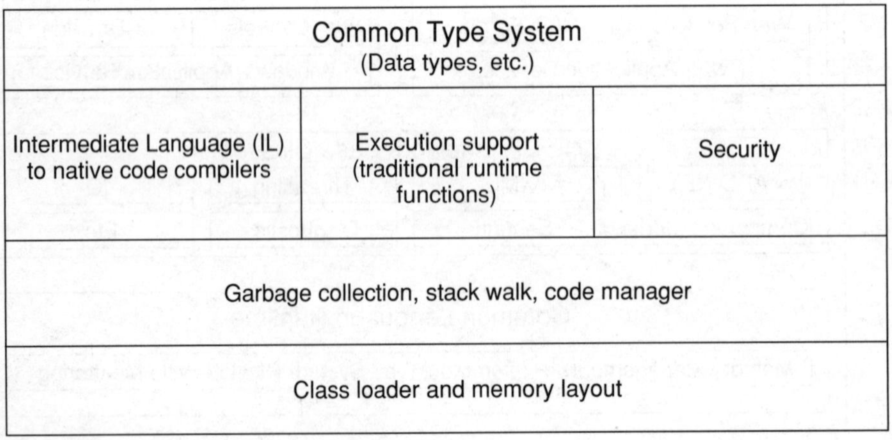

Common Type System (Data types, etc.)		
Intermediate Language (IL) to native code compilers	Execution support (traditional runtime functions)	Security
Garbage collection, stack walk, code manager		
Class loader and memory layout		

Figure 1-2

That small part in the middle of Figure 1-2 called Execution support contains most of the capabilities normally associated with a language runtime (such as the VBRUNxxx.DLL runtime used with Visual Basic). The rest is new, at least for Microsoft platforms.

Key Design Goals

The design of the CLR is based on the following primary goals:

❑   Simpler, faster development

❑   Automatic handling of system-level tasks such as memory management and process communication

❑   Excellent tool support

❑   Simpler, safer deployment

❑   Scalability

Notice that many of these design goals directly address the limitations of COM/DNA. Let's look at some of these in detail.

Simpler, Faster Development

A broad, consistent framework allows developers to write less code, and reuse code more. Less code is possible because the system provides a rich set of underlying functionality. Programs in .NET access this functionality in a standard, consistent way, requiring less "hardwiring" and customization logic to interface with the functionality than is typically needed today.

Programming is also simpler in .NET because of the standardization of datatypes and interface conventions. As will be discussed later, .NET makes knowledge of the intricacies of COM much less important.

The net result is that programs written in VB.NET that take proper advantage of the full capabilities of the .NET Framework typically have significantly less code than equivalent programs written in earlier versions of Visual Basic. Less code means faster development, fewer bugs, and easier maintenance.

Excellent Tool Support

Although much of what the CLR does is similar to operating system functionality, it is very much designed to support development languages. It furnishes a rich set of object models that are useful to tools like designers, wizards, debuggers, and profilers, and since the object models are at the runtime-level, such tools can be designed to work across all languages that use the CLR. It is expected that third parties will produce a host of such tools.

Simpler, Safer Deployment

It is hard for an experienced Windows component developer to see how anything can work without registration, GUIDs, and the like, but the CLR does. Applications produced in the .NET Framework can be designed to install with a simple XCOPY. That's right—just copy the files onto the disk and run the application. This hasn't been seen in the Microsoft world since the days of DOS (and some of us really miss it).

This works because compilers in the .NET Framework embed identifiers (in the form of *metadata*, to be discussed later) into compiled modules, and the CLR manages those identifiers automatically. The identifiers provide all the information needed to load and run modules, and to locate related modules.

As a great by-product, the CLR can manage multiple versions of the same component (even a shared component), and have them run side by side. The identifiers tell the CLR which version is needed for a particular compiled module because such information is captured at compile time. The runtime policy can be set in a module to use the exact version of a component that was available at compile time, to use the latest compatible version, or to specify an exact version. The bottom line is that .NET is intended to eradicate DLL Hell once and for all.

This has implications that might not be apparent at first. For example, if a program needs to run directly from a CD or a shared network drive (without first running an installation program), that was not feasible in Visual Basic after version 3. That capability reappears with VB.NET. This dramatically reduces the cost of deployment in many common scenarios.

Another significant deployment benefit in .NET is that applications only need to install their own core logic. An application produced in .NET does not need to install a runtime, for example, or modules for ADO or XML. Such base functionality is part of the .NET Framework, which is installed separately and only once for each system. The .NET Framework will eventually be included with the operating system and probably with various applications. Those four-disk installs for a VB "Hello world" program will be a thing of the past.

> The .NET Framework, which includes the CLR and the Framework base classes, is
> required on every machine where you want to run .NET applications and code. For
> Windows 2003 and above, the .NET Framework is installed automatically as part of
> the operating systems. For older operating systems, the .NET Framework is a
> separate installation. Deployment of .NET applications is discussed in Chapter 25.

Scalability

Since most of the system-level execution functions are concentrated in the CLR, they can be optimized and architected to allow a wide range of scalability for applications produced in the .NET Framework. As with most of the other advantages of the CLR, this one comes to all applications with little or no effort.

Memory and process management is one area where scalability can be built in. The memory management in the CLR is self-configuring and tunes itself automatically. Garbage collection (reclaiming memory that is no longer being actively used) is highly optimized, and the CLR supports many of the component management capabilities of MTS/COM+ (such as object pooling). The result is that components can run faster, and thus support more users.

This has some interesting side effects. For example, the performance and scalability differences among languages become smaller. All languages compile to a standard bytecode called *Microsoft Intermediate Language (MSIL)*, often referred to simply as *IL*, and there is a discussion later on how the CLR executes IL. With all languages compiling down to similar bytecode, it becomes unnecessary in most cases to look to other languages when performance is an issue. The difference in performance among .NET languages is minor — Visual Basic, for example, gives about the same performance as any of the other .NET languages.

Versions of the CLR are available on a wide range of devices. The vision is for .NET to be running at all levels, from smart palmtop devices all the way up to Web farms. The same development tools work across the entire range — news that will be appreciated by those who have tried to use older Windows CE development kits.

Metadata

The .NET Framework needs lots of information about an application to carry out several automatic functions. The design of .NET requires applications to carry that information within them. That is, applications are *self-describing*. The collected information that describes an application is called *metadata*.

The concept of metadata is not new. For example, COM components use a form of it called a type library, which contains metadata describing the classes exposed by the component and is used to facilitate OLE Automation. A component's type library, however, is stored in a separate file. In contrast, the metadata in .NET is stored in one place — *inside* the component it describes. Metadata in .NET also contains more information about the component, and is better organized.

Chapter 3 on the CLR goes into more information about metadata. For now, the most important point for you to internalize is that metadata is key to the easy deployment in .NET. When a component is upgraded or moved, the necessary information about the component cannot be left behind. Metadata can never get out of sync with a .NET component because it is not in a separate file. Everything the CLR needs to know to run a component is supplied with the component.

Multiple Language Integration and Support

The CLR is designed to support multiple languages and allow unprecedented levels of integration among those languages. By enforcing a common type system, and by having complete control over interface calls, the CLR allows languages to work together more transparently than ever before. The cross-language integration issues of COM simply don't exist in .NET.

It is straightforward in the .NET Framework to use one language to subclass a class implemented in another. A class written in Visual Basic can inherit from a base class written in C#, or in COBOL for that matter. The VB program doesn't even need to know the language used for the base class. .NET offers full implementation inheritance with no problems requiring recompilation when the base class changes.

Chapter 3 also includes more information on the multiple language integration features of .NET.

A Common Type System

A key piece of functionality that enables multiple language support is a *common type system*, in which all commonly used datatypes, even base types such as `Long` and `Boolean`, are actually implemented as objects. Coercion among types can now be done at a lower level for more consistency between languages. Also, since all languages are using the same library of types, calling one language from another doesn't require type conversion or weird calling conventions.

This results in the need for some readjustment, particularly for VB developers. For example, what we called an `Integer` in VB6 and earlier, is now known as a `Short` in VB.NET. The adjustment is worth it to bring Visual Basic in line with everything else, though, and, as a by-product, other languages get the same support for strings that Visual Basic has always had.

The CLR enforces the requirement that all datatypes satisfy the common type system. This has important implications. For example, it is not possible with the common type system to get the problem known in COM as a buffer overrun, which is the source of many security vulnerabilities. Programs written on .NET should therefore have fewer such vulnerabilities, because .NET is not dependent on the programmer to constantly check passed parameters for appropriate type and length. Such checking is done by default.

Chapter 4 goes into detail about the new type system in .NET.

Namespaces

One of the most important concepts in Microsoft .NET is *namespaces*. Namespaces help organize object libraries and hierarchies, simplify object references, prevent ambiguity when referring to objects, and control the scope of object identifiers. The namespace for a class allows the CLR to unambiguously identify that class in the available .NET libraries that it can load.

Namespaces are discussed briefly in Chapter 2 and in more detail in Chapter 8. Understanding the concept of a namespace is essential for your progress in .NET, so do not skip those sections if you are unfamiliar with namespaces.

The Next Layer — The .NET Class Framework

The next layer up in the framework provides the services and object models for data, input/output, security, and so forth. It is called the *.NET Class Framework*, sometimes referred to as the *.NET base classes*. For example, the next generation of ADO, called ADO.NET, resides here. Some of the additional functionality in the .NET Class Framework is listed below.

You might be wondering why .NET includes functionality that is, in many cases, duplication of existing class libraries. There are several good reasons:

❑ The .NET Class Framework libraries are implemented in the .NET Framework, making them easier to integrate with .NET-developed programs.

❑ The .NET Class Framework brings together most of the system class libraries needed into one location, which increases consistency and convenience.

❑ The class libraries in the .NET Class Framework are much easier to extend than older class libraries, using the inheritance capabilities in .NET.

❑ Having the libraries as part of the .NET Framework simplifies deployment of .NET applications. Once the .NET Framework is on a system, individual applications don't need to install base class libraries for functions like data access.

What Is in the .NET Class Framework?

The .NET Class Framework contains literally thousands of classes and interfaces. Here are just some of the functions of various libraries in the .NET Class Framework:

❑ Data access and manipulation

❑ Creation and management of threads of execution

❑ Interfaces from .NET to the outside world — Windows Forms, Web Forms, Web services, and console applications

❑ Definition, management, and enforcement of application security

- ❑ Encryption, disk file I/O, network I/O, serialization of objects, and other system-level functions
- ❑ Application configuration
- ❑ Working with directory services, event logs, performance counters, message queues, and timers
- ❑ Sending and receiving data with a variety of network protocols
- ❑ Accessing metadata information stored in assemblies

Much of the functionality that a programmer might think of as being part of a language has been moved to the base classes. For example, the VB keyword Sqr for extracting a square root is no longer available in .NET. It has been replaced by the System.Math.Sqrt() method in the framework classes.

It's important to emphasize that all languages based on the .NET Framework have these framework classes available. That means that COBOL, for example, can use the same function mentioned above for getting a square root. This makes such base functionality widely available and highly consistent across languages. All calls to Sqrt look essentially the same (allowing for syntactical differences among languages) and access the same underlying code. Here are examples in VB.NET and C#:

```
' Example using Sqrt in Visual Basic .NET
Dim dblNumber As Double = 200
Dim dblSquareRoot As Double
dblSquareRoot = System.Math.Sqrt(dblNumber)
Label1.Text = dblSquareRoot.ToString


' Same example in C#
Double dblNumber = 200;
Double dblSquareRoot = System.Math.Sqrt(dblNumber);
dblSquareRoot = System.Math.Sqrt(dblNumber);
label1.Text = dblSquareRoot.ToString;
```

Notice that the line using the Sqrt() function is exactly the same in both languages.

As a side note, a programming shop can create its own classes for core functionality, such as globally available, already compiled functions. This custom functionality can then be referenced in code the same way as built-in .NET functionality.

Much of the functionality in the base framework classes resides in a vast namespace called System. The System.Math.Sqrt() method was just mentioned. Here are a few other examples of the subsections of the System namespace, which actually contains dozens of such subcategories:

This list merely begins to hint at the capabilities in the System namespace. Some of these namespaces are used in later examples in other chapters throughout the book.

User and Program Interfaces

At the top layer, .NET provides three ways to render and manage user interfaces:

- ❑ *Windows Forms*
- ❑ *Web Forms*
- ❑ *Console applications*

Namespace	What It Contains	Example Classes and Sub-namespaces
System.Collections	Creation and management of various types of collections	Arraylist, Hashtable, SortedList
System.Data	Classes and types related to basic database management (see Chapter 11 for details)	DataSet, DataTable, DataColumn,
System.Diagnostics	Classes to debug an application and to trace the execution of code	Debug, Trace
System.IO	Types which allow reading and writing to files and other data streams	File, FileStream, Path, StreamReader, StreamWriter
System.Math	Members to calculate common mathematical quantities, such as trigonometric and logarithmic functions	Sqrt (square root), Cos (cosine), Log (logarithm), Min (minimum)
System.Reflection	Capability to inspect metadata	Assembly, Module
System.Security	Types that enable security capabilities (see Chapter 24 for details)	Cryptography, Permissions, Policy

and one way to handle interfaces with remote components:

❑ *Web services*

Windows Forms

Windows Forms is a more advanced and integrated way to do standard Win32 screens. All languages that work on the .NET Framework, including new versions of Visual Studio languages, use the Windows Forms engine, which duplicates the functionality of the VB forms engine. It provides a rich, unified set of controls and drawing functions for all languages, as well as a standard API for underlying Windows services for graphics and drawing. It effectively replaces the Windows graphical API, wrapping it in such a way that the developer normally has no need to go directly to the Windows API for any graphical or screen functions.

In Chapter 12, we will look at Windows Forms in more detail and note significant changes in Windows Forms versus older VB forms. Chapter 13 continues discussing Windows Forms technologies by describing in detail the various methods for creating a Windows Forms control.

Client Applications versus Browser-Based Applications

Before .NET, many internal corporate applications were made browser-based simply because of the cost of installing and maintaining a client application on hundreds or thousands of workstations. Windows Forms and the .NET Framework change the economics of these decisions. A Windows Forms application is much easier to install and update than an equivalent VB6 desktop application. With a simple XCOPY deployment and no registration issues, installation and updating become much easier.

That means "smart client" applications with a rich user interface are more practical under .NET, even for a large number of users. It may not be necessary to resort to browser-based applications just to save installation and deployment costs. .NET even has the capability to deploy these "smart client" applications over the Internet from a Web server, with automatic updating of changed modules on the client.

This means you should not dismiss Windows Forms applications as merely replacements for earlier VB6 desktop applications. Instead, you should examine applications in .NET and explicitly decide what kind of interface makes sense in a given case. In some cases, applications that you might have assumed should be browser-based simply because of a large number of users and wide geographic deployment instead can be smart-client-based, which can improve usability, security, and productivity.

Web Forms

The part of .NET that handles communications with the Internet is called ASP.NET. It includes a forms engine called Web Forms, which can be used to create browser-based user interfaces.

Divorcing layout from logic, Web Forms consist of two parts:

❑ A *template*, which contains HTML-based layout information for all user interface elements

❑ A *component*, which contains all logic to be hooked to the user interface

It is as if a standard Visual Basic form were split into two parts, one containing information on controls and their properties and layout, and the other containing the code. Just as in Visual Basic, the code operates "behind" the controls, with events in the controls activating event routines in the code.

As with Windows Forms, Web Forms will be available to all languages. The component handling logic for a form can be in any language that supports .NET. This brings complete, flexible Web interface capability to a wide variety of languages. Chapters 14 and 15 go into detail on Web Forms and the controls that are used on them.

Console Applications

Although Microsoft doesn't emphasize the ability to write character-based applications, the .NET Framework does include an interface for such console applications. Batch processes, for example, can now have components integrated into them that are written to a console interface.

As with Windows Forms and Web Forms, this console interface is available for applications written in any .NET language. Writing character-based applications in previous versions of Visual Basic, for example, has always been a struggle because it was completely oriented around a GUI. VB.NET can be used for true console applications.

Web Services

Application development is moving into the next stage of decentralization. The oldest idea of an application is a piece of software that accesses basic operating system services, such as the file system and graphics system. Then we moved to applications that used lots of base functionality from other system-level applications, such as a database — this type of application added value by applying generic functionality to specific problems. The developer's job was to focus on adding business value, not on building the foundation.

Web services represent the next step in this direction. In Web services, software functionality becomes exposed as a service that doesn't care what the consumer of the service is (unless there are security considerations). Web services allow developers to build applications by combining local and remote resources for an overall integrated and distributed solution.

In .NET, Web services are implemented as part of ASP.NET (see Figure 1-1), which handles all Web interfaces. It allows programs to talk to each other directly over the Web, using the SOAP standard. This has the capacity to dramatically change the architecture of Web applications, allowing services running all over the Web to be integrated into a local application.

Chapter 22 contains a detailed discussion of Web services.

XML as the .NET "Meta-Language"

Much of the underlying integration of .NET is accomplished with XML. For example, Web services depend completely on XML for interfacing with remote objects. Looking at metadata usually means looking at an XML version of it.

ADO.NET, the successor to ADO, is heavily dependent on XML for remote representation of data. Essentially, when ADO.NET creates what it calls a *dataset* (a more complex successor to a recordset), the data is converted to XML for manipulation by ADO.NET. Then, the changes to that XML are posted back to the datastore by ADO.NET when remote manipulation is finished.

> **Chapter 10 discusses XML in .NET in more detail, and, as previously mentioned, Chapter 8 contains a discussion of ADO.NET.**

With XML as an "entry point" into so many areas of .NET, integration opportunities are multiplied. Using XML to expose interfaces to .NET functions allows developers to tie components and functions together in new, unexpected ways. XML can be the glue that ties pieces together in ways that were never anticipated, both to Microsoft and non-Microsoft platforms.

The Role of COM

When the .NET Framework was introduced, some uninformed journalists interpreted it as the death of COM. That is completely incorrect. COM is not going anywhere for a while. In fact, Windows will not boot without COM.

.NET integrates very well with COM-based software. Any COM component can be treated as a .NET component by native .NET components. The .NET Framework wraps COM components and exposes an interface that .NET components can work with. This is absolutely essential to the quick acceptance of .NET, because it makes .NET interoperable with a tremendous amount of older COM-based software.

Going in the other direction, the .NET Framework can expose .NET components with a COM interface. This allows older COM components to use .NET-based components as if they were developed using COM.

Chapter 17 discusses COM interoperability in more detail.

No Internal Use of COM

It is important, however, to understand that native .NET components *do not* interface using COM. The CLR implements a new way for components to interface, one that is not COM-based. Use of COM is only necessary when interfacing with COM components produced by non-.NET tools.

Over a long span of time, the fact that .NET does not use COM internally may lead to the decline of COM, but for any immediate purposes, COM is definitely important.

Some Things Never Change . . .

Earlier in the chapter, we discussed the limitations of the pre-.NET programming models. However, those models have many aspects that still apply to .NET development. Tiered layers in software architecture, for example, were specifically developed to deal with the challenges in design and development of complex applications, and are still appropriate. Many persistent design issues, such as the need to encapsulate business rules, or to provide for multiple user-interface access points to a system, do not go away with .NET.

Applications developed in the .NET Framework will still, in many cases, use a tiered architecture. However, the tiers will be a lot easier to produce in .NET. The presentation tier will benefit from the new interface technologies, especially Web Forms for Internet development. The middle tier will require far less COM-related headaches to develop and implement. And richer, more distributed middle tier designs will be possible by using Web services.

The architectural skills that experienced developers have learned in earlier models are definitely still important and valuable in the .NET world.

.NET Drives Changes in Visual Basic

We previously covered the limitations of Visual Basic in earlier versions. To recap, they are:

- ❏ No capability for multithreading
- ❏ Lack of implementation inheritance and other object features
- ❏ Poor error handling ability
- ❏ Poor integration with other languages such as C++
- ❏ No effective user interface for Internet-based applications

Since VB.NET is built on top of the .NET Framework, all of these shortcomings have been eliminated. In fact, Visual Basic gets the most extensive changes of any existing language in the VS.NET suite. These changes pull Visual Basic in line with other languages in terms of datatypes, calling conventions, error handling, and, most importantly, object orientation. Chapters 5, 6, and 7 go into detail about object-oriented concepts in VB.NET, and Chapter 9 discusses error handling.

"How Does .NET Affect Me?"

One of the reasons you are probably reading this book is because you want to know how VB.NET will affect you as an existing Visual Basic developer. Here are some of the most important implications.

A Spectrum of Programming Models

In previous Microsoft-based development tools, there were a couple of quantum leaps required to move from simple to complex. A developer could start simply with ASP pages and VBScript, but when those became cumbersome, it was a big leap to learn component-based, three-tier development in Visual Basic. And it was another quantum leap to become proficient in C++, ATL, and related technologies for system-level work.

A key benefit of VB.NET and the .NET Framework is that there exists a more gradual transition in programming models from simple to full power. ASP.NET pages are far more structured than ASP pages, and code used in them is often identical to equivalent code used in a Windows Forms application. Internet development can now be done using real Visual Basic code instead of VBScript.

Visual Basic itself becomes a tool with wider applicability, as it becomes easy to do a Web interface with Web Forms, and it also becomes possible to do advanced object-oriented designs. Even system-level capabilities, such as Windows services can be done with VB.NET (see Chapter 21). Old reasons for using another language, such as lack of performance or flexibility, are mostly gone. Visual Basic will do almost anything that other .NET languages can do.

This increases the range of applicability of Visual Basic. It can be used all the way from "scripts" (which are actually compiled on the fly) written with a text editor, up through sophisticated component and Web programming in one of the most advanced development environments available.

Reducing Barriers to Internet Development

With older tools, programming for the Internet requires a completely different programming model than programming systems that will be run locally. The differences are most apparent in user-interface construction, but that's not the only area of difference. Objects constructed for access by ASP pages, for example, must support `Variant` parameters, but objects constructed for access by Visual Basic forms can have parameters of any datatype. Accessing databases over the Internet requires using technologies like RDS instead of the ADO connections that local programming typically uses.

The .NET Framework erases many of these differences. Programming for the Internet and programming for local systems are much more alike in .NET than with today's systems. Differences remain — Web Forms still have significant differences from Windows Forms, for example, but many other differences, such as the way data is handled, are much more unified under .NET.

A big result of this similarity of programming models is to make Internet programming more practical and accessible. With functionality for the Internet designed in from the start, developers don't have to know as much or do as much to produce Internet systems with the .NET Framework.

Libraries of Prewritten Functionality

The evolution of Windows development languages, including Visual Basic, has been in the direction of providing more and more built-in functionality so that developers can ignore the foundations and concentrate on solving business problems. The .NET Framework continues this trend.

One particularly important implication is that the .NET Framework extends the trend of developers spending less time writing code and more time discovering how to do something with prewritten functionality. Mainframe COBOL programmers could learn everything they ever needed to know about COBOL in a year or two, and very seldom need to consult reference materials after that. In contrast, today's Visual Basic developers already spend a significant portion of their time digging through reference material to figure out how to do something that they may never do again. The sheer expanse of available functionality, plus the rapidly changing pace, makes it imperative for an effective developer to be a researcher also. .NET accelerates this trend, and will probably increase the ratio of research time to coding time for a typical developer.

Easier Deployment

A major design goal in Microsoft .NET is to simplify installation and configuration of software. With "DLL Hell" mostly gone, and with installation of compiled modules a matter of a simple file copy, developers should be able to spend less time worrying about deployment of their applications, and more time concentrating on the functionality of their systems. The budget for the deployment technology needed by a typical application will be significantly smaller.

The Future of .NET

At the Professional Developer's Conference (PDC) in Los Angeles in October of 2003, Microsoft gave the first public look at their next generation operating system, code-named Longhorn. It was clear from even this early glimpse that .NET is at the heart of Microsoft's operating system strategy going forward.

However, the naming of what we now know as .NET is going to change. While Web services and related technologies may still carry the .NET label going forward, the .NET Framework is called WinFX in Longhorn. This may cause some confusion in names going forward, but be assured that what you learn today about the .NET Framework and VB.NET will be important for years to come in the world of Microsoft applications.

Summary

VB.NET is not like other versions of Visual Basic. It is built with completely different assumptions, on a new platform that is central to Microsoft's entire product strategy. In this chapter, we have discussed the reasons Microsoft has created this platform, and how challenges in earlier, pre-Internet technologies have been met by .NET.

This chapter has also discussed in particular how this will affect VB developers. .NET presents many new challenges for developers, but simultaneously provides them with greatly enhanced functionality. In particular, Visual Basic developers now have the ability to develop object-oriented and Web-based applications far more easily and cheaply.

In the next chapter, we move on to take a closer look at the VS.NET IDE, and discuss the basics of doing applications in VB.NET.

2

Introducing VB.NET and VS.NET

Chapter 1 introduced .NET and explained why it is an important and necessary step in the evolution of programming on the Windows platform. This chapter takes a practical look at how .NET changes the way applications are created. It starts with the creation of the standard "Hello World" Windows application using *Visual Studio .NET 2003* (VS.NET). After creating the initial application, you can step through simple additions to this first application. You can compare your code at each stage to understand the changes that have been made.

The chapter also covers several introductory topics associated with becoming familiar with VS.NET and creating a simple application, including:

- ❑ Project types
- ❑ References
- ❑ Code regions
- ❑ Forms as classes
- ❑ Class constructors
- ❑ Setting form properties
- ❑ Selecting a runtime environment
- ❑ VS.NET environment

This chapter will provide only a brief introduction to Visual Basic .NET (VB.NET) Windows Form applications. It will step you through creating your first .NET project and review many of the elements that are common to every .NET application. The discussion of several other project types, such as Web projects, will be covered in later chapters.

If you are familiar with Visual Studio .NET 2002 and the .NET Framework version 1.0, note that the updates to Visual Studio 2003 are minor and you may want to skip to the end of this chapter and review selecting the runtime environment.

Visual Studio .NET — Startup

One of the first things that you will notice when you go to start VS.NET 2003 is that there is only one entry for VS.NET in the Start menu — there are no separate entries for Visual Basic, Visual C++, or Visual C#. This is the first physical hint of the common language runtime (CLR) at work. All of the Visual Studio languages share the same integrated development environment (IDE).

> Since all .NET languages are tied to the .NET Framework, and the .NET Framework is actually separate from VS.NET, you don't need to use VS.NET to develop applications. You could simply use your favorite text editor to create the source files and use the command line compilers provided by the framework, or a tool, such as the ASP.NET Web matrix to create a Web project. However, Visual Studio provides several built-in tools to make developers more productive. Debugging, code generation, an integrated help system, advanced editing (IntelliSense) and help system all provide a robust development environment. This book uses VS.NET throughout.

When *VS.NET* is started, the window shown in Figure 2-1 is displayed to permit you to configure your custom profile.

By default, when you first access VS.NET you are taken to the My Profile tab of the VS.NET Start Page. You can use the settings in the main portion of the window to select an appropriate profile in order to adapt the environment to your needs. For most developers the defaults are appropriate. However, if you have experience developing with Visual Basic 6 or some other tool, you may find the development experience more familiar by changing the default settings in this page. Selecting, for example, Visual Basic 6 as your profile enables a set of keyboard shortcuts that differ slightly from the new default settings.

When a profile is chosen, such as the Visual Basic Developer profile, from the drop-down list, several aspects of the IDE are customized at once, such as the position of the Code window and Properties window, as well as which windows take precedence in the environment. Alternatively, you can leave the default of Visual Studio Developer selected as your profile and instead choose to customize only the keyboard shortcuts or the display area using the Keyboard Layout and Window Layout drop-down boxes.

Although separated by a horizontal line, there are two separate options related to help in your profile. In answer to a long-standing gripe about Visual Studio 6, the help system can be filtered to offer help for particular languages and subjects. The My Profile page contains a Help Filter drop-down box. When VS.NET is installed, it is set to No filter. This is the appropriate setting if you will be working with multiple .NET languages. However, if you will be working exclusively with VB.NET you might find it useful to change this to Visual Basic.

Second, VS.NET provides an option of showing help within the IDE (as a tabbed window in the same display area where code is shown), or outside the IDE (as a separate window that can be positioned and manipulated independently).

Finally, your profile allows you to indicate how you would like VS.NET to open. By default, you can start on the standard start page, which will list your most recent projects, or you can choose to automatically open the project you were last working on. In either case, the choice is yours.

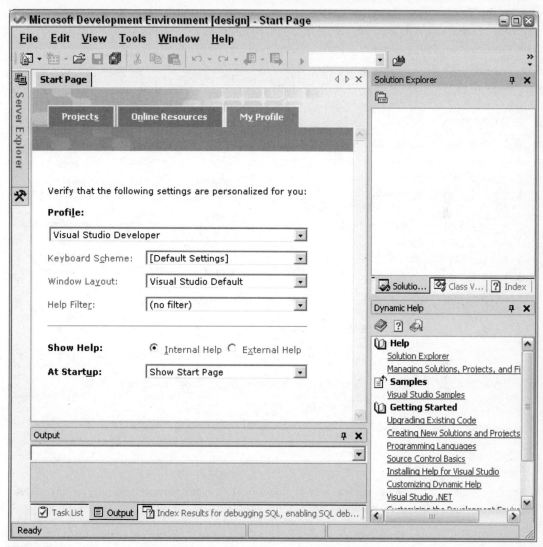

Figure 2-1

Visual Studio .NET

Once you have set up your profile, the next step is to create your first project. Selecting File ➪ New Project opens the New Project Dialog window, shown in Figure 2-2. You may notice that this window separates project types into a series of categories. While the top three project types are language-based, notice that the bottom three are more generic categories that are not language specific. The Visual Basic (VB) project templates differ from those of the COM world exposed in Visual Basic 6. The .NET Framework runs in the CLR environment, and as a result there is no need to create COM interfaces. The CLR exposes a common metadata environment that allows applications to pass data between environments, instead of building to a binary protocol such as COM. Keep in mind that you can, and should, still create dynamic link libraries (DLLs) by using a Class Library or Web service project template. These types of projects will be discussed at length in later chapters. For now, you can select a Windows Application project template.

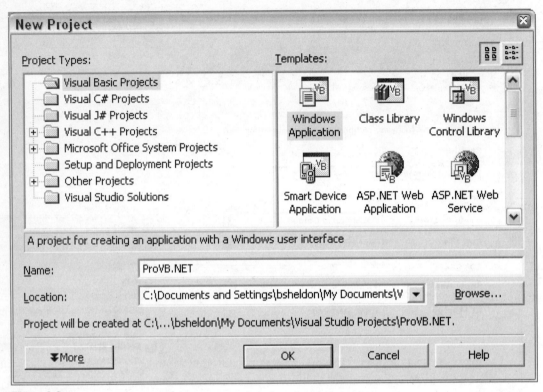

Figure 2-2

For this example, you can use `ProVB.NET` as the project name, and then click the OK button. VS.NET then takes over and uses the Windows Application template to create a new Windows Forms project. The project contains a blank form which can be customized and a variety of other elements that you can explore. Before you start customizing any code, let's first look at the elements of this new project.

The Solution Explorer

On the right-hand side of the VS.NET display is the Solution Explorer window. As shown in isolation in Figure 2-3, this window provides a central location for all of the files in your project. Different project templates create different initial setups in this window — for example, Web forms start with a default ASPX page, while Web service projects start with a default ASMX page, and Class Library projects start with a default .VB file. For a Windows Forms application, two source code files, `Form1.vb` and `AssemblyInfo.vb`, are added to the project. Note that there is only one file extension for VB source files (`.vb`). There is no longer one extension for a class module and a different one for a form; differences of implementation are kept within the source file.

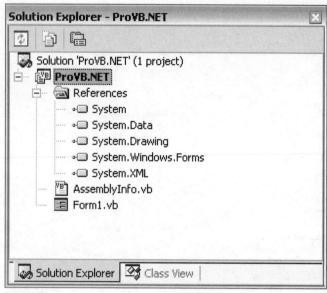

Figure 2-3

Those of you familiar with previous Microsoft development tools will find a solution similar to a project group. However, a .NET Solution can contain projects of any .NET language and also allows inclusion of the database, testing, and installation projects as part of the overall solution.

Addition, Figure 2-3 shows that the project is not made up of only the two source files. The figure shows an expanded view of the References section of the project. References are an important tool for managing complexity within .NET projects. Similar to how you can reference COM components in a traditional Windows application, .NET allows you to create references to other components (both those implemented with a .NET language and COM) to extend the capabilities of your application.

Namespaces

In addition to the Solution Explorer, you can review the namespaces which make up an application using the Object Browser. To open the Object Browser you can use the default key combination of *Ctrl-Alt-J* or access the View menu and select the Object Browser.

As shown in Figure 2-4, the Object Browser is split into two panes. The pane to the left lists the namespaces that are available to the application. You can expand the namespace nodes to reveal the classes, structures, and other types that are contained within each namespace. As shown in the figure, the `System.Drawing` namespace has been selected and you can see that it is related to the `System.Drawing.DLL`, which is part of the .NET Framework. This namespace contains a collection of classes that have been further nested into additional tiers. If you select a class or other type from the left-hand pane, the member functions and properties of that class will be listed in the right-hand pane.

Namespaces, which are covered in more detail in Chapter 8, can also be nested inside other namespaces. This nesting helps to organize classes into a more logical structure, which reduces confusion and aids the

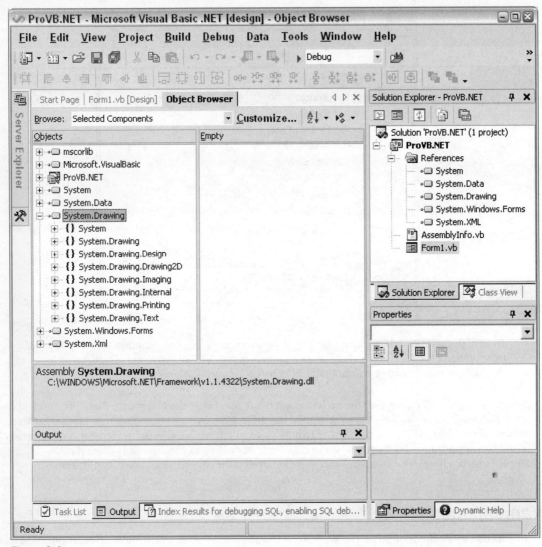

Figure 2-4

developer. For example, in the System.Drawing namespace, the Imaging namespace is a child of (is nested within) the System.Drawing namespace. Similar to the default code files that are created with a new project, each project has a default set of referenced libraries. Just as with COM components, it's a good idea to create your own root namespace and then build your custom classes under that root. For Windows Forms applications, the list of default namespaces is fairly short and shown in the following table.

It's possible to add additional references as part of your project. Right-click the References node in the Solution Explorer and select Add Reference to open the Add References dialog box. From this dialog box, you can select other .NET class libraries and applications, as well as COM components. There is even a shortcut tab for selecting classes defined within other projects of your current solution.

Reference	Description
System	Often referred to as the root namespace. All the base data types (String, Object, and so on) are contained within the System namespace. This namespace also acts as the root for all other System classes.
System.Data	Classes used to implement ADO.NET. This namespace is covered in more detail in Chapter 11.
System.Drawing	Provides access to the GDI+ graphics functionality.
System.Windows.Forms	Classes used to create traditional Windows-based applications. This namespace is covered in more detail in Chapter 12.
System.XML	Classes used for processing XML. This namespace is covered in more detail in Chapter 10.

The New Code Window

The Form Designer is open by default when a new project is created. If you have closed it you can easily reopen it by right-clicking Form1.vb in the Solution Explorer and selecting View Designer from the pop-up menu. From this window you can also bring up the code view for this form. This can be done either by right-clicking Form1.vb in the Solution Explorer and selecting code view, or by right-clicking the form in the Designer and selecting View Code from the pop-up menu. At this point you will have a display similar to the one shown in Figure 2-5.

By default you can see that the initial display of the form looks very simple. The Code Editor window should be familiar from previous development environments, such as the one for Visual Basic 6, except for the gray line on the left with the plus and minus signs. It appears there is almost no code in the Form1.vb file. However, if you expand the region associated with the Windows Form Designer Generated Code, you'll see that there is quite a bit of custom code generated by VS.NET already in your project. Modules inside source files in VS.NET can be hidden on the screen, a feature known as outlining. By default there is a minus sign next to every method (sub or function). This makes it easy to hide or show code on a method-by-method basis. If the code for a method is hidden, the method declaration is still shown, and has a plus sign next to it to indicate that the body code is hidden. This feature is very useful when a developer is working on a few key methods in a module, and wishes to avoid scrolling through many screens of code that are not relevant to the current task.

It is also possible to hide custom regions of code. The #Region directive is used for this within the IDE, though it has no effect on the actual application. A region of code is demarcated by the #Region directive at the top and the #End Region directive at the end. The #Region directive used to begin a region should include a description. The description will appear next to the plus sign shown when the code is minimized. For example, the Windows Form Designer Generated Code section is a custom region with a descriptive label.

The outlining enhancement was probably inspired by the fact that the VS.NET designers generate a lot of code when a project is started. Items that were hidden in Visual Basic 6 (such as the logic which sets initial form properties) are actually inside the generated code in VS.NET. However, seeing all of these functions

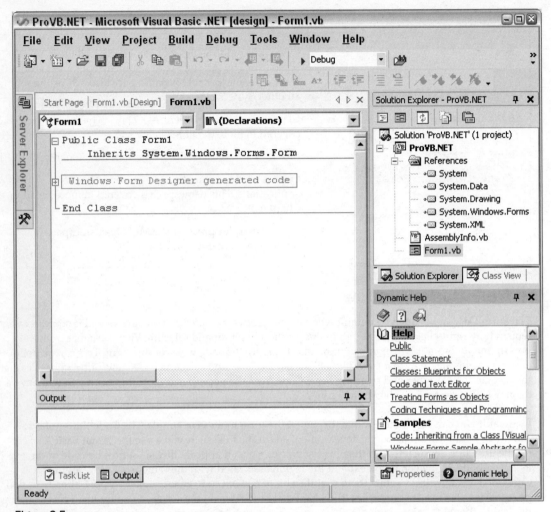

Figure 2-5

in the code is an improvement because it is easier for the developer to understand what is happening, and possibly to manipulate the process in special cases.

Outlining can also be turned off by selecting Edit ➪ Outlining ➪ Stop Outlining from the Visual Studio menu. This menu also contains some other useful functions. A section of code can be temporarily hidden by highlighting it and selecting Edit ➪ Outlining ➪ Hide Selection. The selected code will be replaced with an ellipsis with a plus sign next to it, as if you had dynamically identified a region within the source code. Clicking the plus sign displays the code again.

Tabs versus MDI

You may have noticed in Figure 2-5 that the code view and form designer windows opened in a tabbed environment. This tabbed environment is the default for working with the code windows insideVS.NET. However, it is possible to toggle this setting, allowing you to work with a more traditional MDI-based interface. Such an interface opens each code window within a separate frame instead of anchoring it to the tabbed display of the IDE.

To change the arrangement that is used between the tabbed and MDI interface, use the Options dialog box (accessible via Tools ⇨ Options). You can also force the development environment to use the MDI as opposed to the tabbed interface by using the command line option /mdi when VS.NET is started.

Customizing the Text Editor

VS.NET has a rich set of customizations related to the Text Editor. Go to the Tools menu and select Options to open the Options dialog box, shown in Figure 2-6. Within the dialog box, select the Text Editor folder, and then select the All Languages folder. This section allows you to make changes to the text editor which are applied across every supported development language. Additionally, you can select the Basic folder. Doing so will allow you to make changes that are specific to how the text editor will behave when you are editing VB source code.

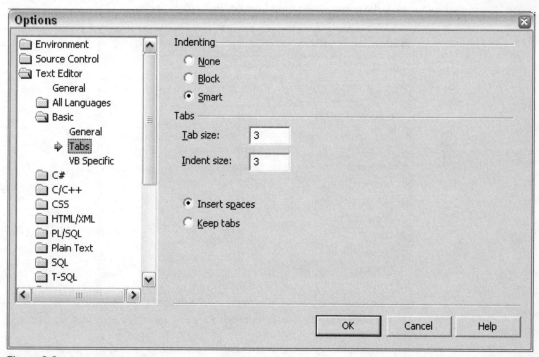

Figure 2-6

From this dialog box it is possible to modify the number of spaces each tab will insert into your source code and to manage several other elements of your editing environment. One little-known capability of the text editor that can be useful is line numbering. Checking the line numbers check box will cause the editor to number all lines, which provides an easy way to unambiguously reference lines of code.

Extended IntelliSense

IntelliSense has always been a popular feature of Microsoft tools and applications. IntelliSense has been enhanced in VS.NET allowing you to not only work with the methods of a class, but automatically displaying the list of possible values associated when an enumerated list of properties has been defined.

IntelliSense also provides a tool-tip–like list of parameter definitions when you are making a method call. You'll see an example of this feature later in this chapter.

Additionally, if you type `Exit` and a space, IntelliSense displays a list of keywords in a drop-down list which could follow `Exit`. Other keywords that have drop-down lists to present available options include `Goto`, `Implements`, `Option`, and `Declare`. IntelliSense generally displays more tool-tip information in the environment than before and helps the developer match up pairs of parentheses, braces, and brackets.

The Properties Window

The Properties window, shown in Figure 2-7, is by default placed in the lower right corner of the Visual Studio display. Like many of the other windows in the IDE, if you close it, it can be accessed through the View menu. Alternatively, the *F4* key is a shortcut to reopen this window. The Properties window is similar to the one with which you are probably familiar from previous development environments. It is used to set the properties of the currently selected item control in the display.

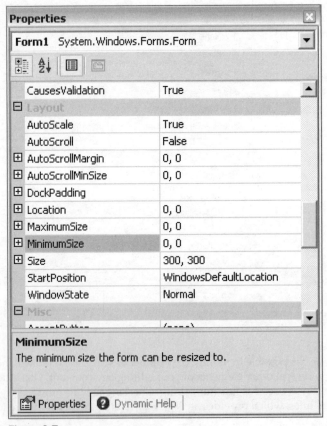

Figure 2-7

For example, in the design view select your form. You'll see the Properties window adjust to display the properties of Form1, as shown in Figure 2-8. This is the list of properties associated with your form. For example, if you want to limit how small a user can reduce the display area of your form, you can now

Figure 2-8

define this as a property. For your sample go to the Text property and change the default of Form1 to "Profession VB.NET Intro." You'll see that once you have accepted the property change, the new value is displayed as the caption of your form. Later in the section on setting form properties in code, you'll see that unlike other environments where properties you edit through the user interface are hidden in some binary or proprietary portion of the project, .NET properties are defined within your source file. Thus, while the Properties window may look similar to other environments, such as Visual Basic 6, you'll find that it is far more powerful under VS.NET.

Dynamic Help

The Properties window may not have changed much from Visual Basic 6, but the Dynamic Help tab below the Properties window is new. Dynamic Help makes a guess at what you might be interested in looking at, based on what you have done recently. The options in the Dynamic Help window are categorized into three areas. The top category, entitled Help, gives a best guess on the features that the environment thinks you might be trying to use. This best guess is the same as if you pressed *F1* while highlighting a keyword within your code.

Just below that is a section called Samples, and it points to a Help page that lists a variety of sample applications. The third section is a category called Getting Started, which contains a variety of help options on introductory material. One of the options in the Getting Started category is Visual Studio Walkthroughs. This contains step-by-step guides on how to perform the basic tasks for the different types of projects that can be created in VS.NET.

Working with Visual Basic .NET

By now you should be reasonably familiar with some of the key windows available to you in VS.NET. The next step is to look at the code in your sample form. The following lines start the declaration for your form:

```
Public Class Form1
    Inherits System.Windows.Forms.Form
```

The first line declares a new class called `Form1`. In VB.NET, you can declare classes in any source file. This is a change from previous versions of Visual Basic which required that classes be defined in a class module (`.cls`). You can also declare any number of classes in a single source file, since classes are not defined by their source file. The second line of the class declaration specifies the parent for your class. In the above case, your sample `Form1` class is based on the `Form` class contained in the `System.Windows.Forms` namespace.

Forms are classes that derive from the `System.Windows.Forms.Form` class. This class is used to create dialog boxes and windows for traditional Windows-based applications. Chapters 5, 6, and 7 focus on many of the new object-oriented keywords, such as Inherits, that you will use when developing more robust VB.NET applications.

As noted, the name of your class and the file in which it exists are not tightly coupled. Thus when referencing your form from code, it will be referenced as Form1, unless you modify the name used in the class declaration. Similarly, you can rename the file that contains the class without changing the actual name of the class.

One of the powerful results of forms being implemented as classes is that you can now derive one form from another form. This technique is called *visual inheritance*, although the elements that are actually inherited may not be displayed. This concept is covered in much more detail in Chapter 12.

Form Properties Set in Code

As noted in the section discussing the Properties window, VS.NET keeps every object's custom property values in the source code. To do this, VS.NET adds a method to your form class called `InitializeComponent`. As the name suggests, this handles the initialization of the components contained on the form. A comment before the procedure warns you that the form designer modifies the code contained in the procedure and that you should not modify the code directly. This module is stored in the Generated Code Region of your source file, and VS.NET updates this section as changes are made through the IDE.

```
'NOTE: The following procedure is required by the Windows Form Designer
'It can be modified using the Windows Form Designer.
'Do not modify it using the code editor.
<System.Diagnostics.DebuggerStepThrough()> Private Sub _
        InitializeComponent()
'
```

```
'Form1
'
    Me.AutoScaleBaseSize = New System.Drawing.Size(5, 13)
    Me.ClientSize = New System.Drawing.Size(292, 273)
    Me.Name = "Form1"
    Me.Text = "Professional VB.NET Intro"

  End Sub
```

The four lines of the `InitializeComponent` procedure assign values to the properties of your `Form1` class. All the properties of the form and controls are now set directly in code. When you change the value of a property of the form or a control through the Properties window an entry will be added to `InitializeComponent` that will assign that value to the property. Previously, while examining the Properties window you set the `Text` property of the form to Professional VB.NET Intro, which caused the following line of code to be added automatically.

```
    Me.Text = "Professional VB.NET Intro"
```

The code accessing the properties of the form uses the Me keyword. The Me keyword acts as a variable that refers to the instance of the current class in which it is used. When you are working within a control that is used by your form, the Me keyword will refer to the control if the method you are working on is part of the control classes definition, even though that method may be called by your form class. The Me keyword isn't necessary but it aids in the understanding of the code, so that you immediately recognize that the property references are not simply local variables. The other three properties of the form class that are set in `InitializeComponent` by default are shown in the following table.

Property	Description
AutoScaleBaseSize	Initializes the size of the font used to layout the form at design time. At runtime, the font that is actually rendered is compared with this property and the form is scaled accordingly.
ClientSize	Sets the area in which controls can be placed (the client area). It is the size of the form minus the size of the title bar and form borders.
Name	This property is used to set the textual name of the form.

AssemblyInfo.vb

The second file generated for your new project is common to each new project template. `AssemblyInfo.vb` contains just what you would expect, common settings related to your project. Within this file it is possible to define file properties, such as your company's name and versioning information, which will be embedded into the operating system's file attributes for your project's output. The frame of the assembly file shows that by default it contains several standard values.

```
Imports System.Reflection
Imports System.Runtime.InteropServices

' General Information about an assembly is controlled through
' the following set of attributes. Change these attribute values
```

```
' to modify the information associated with an assembly.

' Review the values of the assembly attributes

<Assembly: AssemblyTitle("")>
<Assembly: AssemblyDescription("")>
<Assembly: AssemblyCompany("")>
<Assembly: AssemblyProduct("")>
<Assembly: AssemblyCopyright("")>
<Assembly: AssemblyTrademark("")>
<Assembly: CLSCompliant(True)>

'The following GUID is for the ID of the typelib if this project
'is exposed to COM
<Assembly: Guid("6CCAA661-F174-454C-948E-D3E25426484C")>

' Version information for an assembly consists of the following
' four values:
'
        ' Major Version
        ' Minor Version
        ' Build Number
        ' Revision
'
' You can specify all the values or you can default the Build
' and Revision Numbers by using the '*' as shown below:

<Assembly: AssemblyVersion("1.0.*")>
```

The information and properties created in the `AssemblyInfo` file are set using *attributes*. These attributes are then embedded into your assembly's compiled file. Additionally, if you are working to sign an assembly you add this attribute to the `AssemblyInfo` file. There are several reasons you might sign a file—for example, to provide strong naming for COM interoperability or to allow users to grant your assembly additional security privileges. Assembly signing is beyond the scope of this chapter.

Assembly Attributes

The `AssemblyInfo.vb` file contains attribute blocks, which are used to set information about the assembly. Each attribute block has an *assembly modifier*, for example,

```
<Assembly: AssemblyTitle("")>
```

All the attributes set within this file provide information that is contained within the assembly metadata. Most of these properties can be seen by right-clicking the file within Windows Explorer and selecting Properties. Different properties are displayed on different tabs of the Properties dialog box. The attributes contained within the file are summarized in the following table.

Running ProVB.NET

Now that you've reviewed the elements of your generated project, let's test the code before you continue. To run an application from within Visual Studio, there are several options. The first is to click the Start

Attribute	Description
AssemblyCompany	Sets the name of the company that produced the assembly. The name set here appears within the version tab of the file properties.
AssemblyCopyright	The copyright information of the assembly, this value appears on the version tab of the file properties.
AssemblyDescription	This attribute is used to provide a textual description of the assembly, which is added to the comments property for the file.
AssemblyProduct	Sets the product name of the resulting assembly. The product name will appear within the version tab of the file properties.
AssemblyTitle	Sets the name of the assembly, which appears within the file properties of the compiled file as the Description.
AssemblyTrademark	Used to assign any trademark information to the assembly. This information appears within the version tab of the file properties.
AssemblyVersion	This attribute is used to set the version number of the assembly. Assembly version numbers can be generated, which is the default setting for .NET applications and are covered in more detail in Chapter 25.
CLSCompliant	This attribute is used to indicate whether this assembly is compliant with the Common Language Specification (CLS). The CLS is a subset of the common language runtime (see Chapter 3 for more information).
Guid	If the assembly is to be exposed as a traditional COM object then the value of this attribute will become the ID of the resulting type library.

button, which looks like the play button on a tape recorder. Alternatively, you can go to the Debug menu and select Start. Finally, the most common way of launching applications is to press *F5*.

Once the application starts, you will see an empty form display with the standard control buttons from which you can control the application. The form name should be the Professional VB.NET Intro that you applied earlier. At this point, the sample doesn't have any custom code to examine, so the next step is to add some simple elements to this application.

Enhancing the Sample Application

To start enhancing the application, you are going to use the control *toolbox*. The Toolbox window is available whenever a form is in design mode. By default, the Toolbar, shown in Figure 2-8, lives on the left-hand side of VS.NET as a tab. When you click this tab, the control window expands and you can then drag controls onto your form. Alternatively, if you have closed the Toolbox tab, you can go to the View menu and select Toolbox.

If you haven't set up the toolbox to be permanently visible, it will slide out of the way and disappear whenever focus is moved away from it. This is a new feature of the IDE that has been added to help maximize the available screen real estate. If you don't like this feature and would like the toolbox to be permanently visible, all you need to do is click the pushpin icon on the toolbox's title bar.

Add a Control and Event Handler

Once you have the toolbox open you can drag any of the available controls onto your form. For this walkthrough, I recommend using a button control as it allows you to add an event handler that will respond to a button click. Dragging a button onto your form should give you a display that looks similar to the one shown in Figure 2-9.

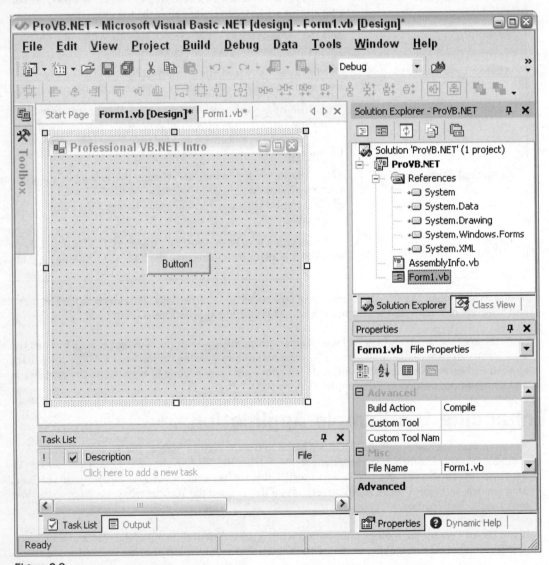

Figure 2-9

The button you've dragged onto the form is ready to go in all respects. However, VS.NET has no way of knowing how you want to customize it. Start by going to the Properties window and changing its text property to "Hello World." You can then change the button's name property to `btnHelloWorld`. Having made these changes, double-click the button in the display view. Double-clicking tells Visual Studio that you want to add an event handler to this control, and by default Visual Studio adds an `On_Click` event handler for buttons. The IDE then shifts the display to the code view so that you can customize this handler.

While the event handler can be added through the designer, it is also possible to add event handlers from the code view. Notice that when your display shifts to the code view the drop-down boxes on the top of your window indicate your command on the left and the Click event on the right. It is possible to add new event handlers using these drop-down lists.

The drop-down box on the left-hand side lists the objects for which event handlers can be added. The drop-down box on the right-hand side lists all the events for the selected object. This is similar to the previous versions of Visual Basic, apart from an enhancement thatallows us to handle the events of the classes that have been overridden. For now however, you have created a new handler for your button's click event, and it's time to look at customizing the code associated with this event.

Customizing the Code

By default, the Code window will open to the newly added event handler for the "Hello World" button. Adding a handler to a control involves two elements of generated code. Visual Studio adds a line to the Generated Code section of your application linking the control for which a handler is being generated with the generated name of the handler. It then adds a default method implementation to the editable portion of your source code.

While the method declaration can be changed, keep in mind that any changes to the name of this method must be reflected in the generated code that binds the control's event to this method. Before you start adding new code to this method handler however, you may want to reduce the complexity of finding some of the `Windows.Forms` enumerations that will be used in your custom code. To do this, you need to Import a local reference to the `System.Windows.Forms` namespace.

Working with the Imports Statement

Go to the very first line of your code and add Imports statements to the generated code. The Imports statement is similar to a file-based reference for local access to the classes contained in that namespace. By default, to reference a class you need to provide its full namespace. However, when a namespace is imported into a source file you can instead reference that class by its short name. This topic will be covered in more detail in Chapter 8. For now, you can just add the following reference to the top of `Form1.vb`.

```
Imports System.Windows.Forms
```

This line of code means that if you want the list of possible MessageBox button values all you need to reference is the enumeration `MessageBoxButtons`. Without this statement you would need to reference `System.Windows.Forms.MessageBoxButtons` in order to use the same enumeration. An example of this is shown in the next section where you customize the event handler. The Imports statement has additional capabilities to make it easy for you to work with the wide array of available namespaces in .NET. The statement is covered in more detail in Chapter 8.

Customize the Event Handler

Now customize the code for the button handler. By default this method doesn't actually do anything. To change this, add a command to open a message box and show the "Hello World" message. Use the `System.Windows.Forms.MessageBox` class. Fortunately, since you've imported that namespace you can reference the `MessageBox.Show` method directly. The Show method has several different parameters and as you see in Figure 2-10, not only does Visual Studio provide a tool tip for the list of parameters on this function, but it also provides help on the appropriate value for individual parameters.

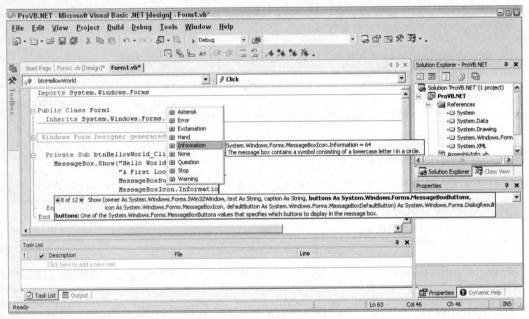

Figure 2-10

The completed call to show should look similar to the following code snippet. Note that the underscore character has been used to continue the command across multiple lines. Also note that unlike previous versions of Visual Basic where parentheses were sometimes not needed, in VS.NET the syntax now always expects parenthesis for every method call.

```
MessageBox.Show("Hello World", _
                "A First Look at VB.NET", _
                MessageBoxButtons.OK, _
                MessageBoxIcon.Information)
```

Once you have entered this line of code, you may notice a squiggly line underneath some portion of your text. This occurs if there is an error in the line you have typed. In previous versions of Visual Basic the development environment would interrupt your progress with a dialog box, but with VS.NET the IDE works more like the latest version of Word. Instead of interrupting your progress, it highlights the problem and allows you to continue working on your code.

Review the Code

Now that you have created a simple Windows application, let's review the elements of the code that have been added by Visual Studio. Below is the entire Form1.vb source listing. Highlighted in this listing are the lines of code that have changed since the original template was used to generate this project.

```
Imports System.Windows.Forms
Public Class Form1
    Inherits System.Windows.Forms.Form
#Region "Windows Form Designer generated code"

    Public Sub New()
        MyBase.New()

        'This call is required by the Windows Form Designer.
        InitializeComponent()

        'Add any initialization after the InitializeComponent() call

    End Sub

    `Form overrides dispose to clean up the component list.
    Protected Overloads Overrides Sub Dispose(ByVal disposing As Boolean)

        If disposing Then
            If Not (components Is Nothing) Then
                components.Dispose()
            End If
        End If
        MyBase.Dispose(disposing)
    End Sub

    'Required by the Windows Form Designer
    Private components As System.ComponentModel.Icontainer
    'NOTE: The following procedure is required by the Windows Form Designer
    'It can be modified using the Windows Form Designer.
    'Do not modify it using the code editor.
    Friend WithEvents btnHelloWorld As System.Windows.Forms.Button
    <System.Diagnostics.DebuggerStepThrough()> _
    Private Sub InitializeComponent()
      Me.btnHelloWorld = New System.Windows.Forms.Button()
      Me.SuspendLayout()
      '
      `btnHelloWorld
      '
      Me.btnHelloWorld.Location = New System.Drawing.Point(112, 112)
      Me.btnHelloWorld.Name = "btnHelloWorld"
      Me.btnHelloWorld.TabIndex = 0
      Me.btnHelloWorld.Text = "Hello World"
      '
      'Form1
      '
      Me.AutoScaleBaseSize = New System.Drawing.Size(5, 13)
      Me.ClientSize = New System.Drawing.Size(292, 273)
```

```
    Me.Controls.AddRange(New System.Windows.Forms.Control()
{Me.btnHelloWorld })

    Me.Name = "Form1"

    Me.Text = "Professional VB.NET Intro"
    Me.ResumeLayout(False)
```

```
End Sub
```

```
#End Region
```

```
Private Sub btnHelloWorld _Click(ByVal sender As System.Object, _
                    ByVal e As System.EventArgs) _
                    Handles btnHelloWorld.Click
    System.Windows.Forms.MessageBox.Show("Hello World", _
                        "A First Look at VB.NET", _
                        MessageBoxButtons.OK, _
                        MessageBoxIcon.Information)
```

```
    End Sub
```

```
    End Class
```

After the Imports statement, the first change that has been made to the code is the addition of a new variable to represent the new button:

```
    Friend WithEvents btnHelloWorld As System.Windows.Forms.Button
```

When any type of control is added to the form, a new variable will be added to the form class. Controls are represented by variables and, just as form properties are set in code, form controls are added in code. The Button class in the System.Windows.Forms namespace implements the button control on the toolbox. Each control that is added to a form has a class that implements the functionality of the control. For the standard controls these classes are usually found in the System.Windows.Forms namespace. The WithEvents keyword has been used in the declaration of the new variable so that it can respond to events raised by the button.

The bulk of the code changes are in the InitializeComponent procedure. Eight lines of code have been added to help set up and display the button control. The first addition to the procedure is a line that creates a new instance of the Button class and assigns it to the button variable:

```
    Me.btnHelloWorld = New System.Windows.Forms.Button()
```

Before a button is added to the form, the form's layout engine must be paused. This is done using the next line of code:

```
    Me.SuspendLayout()
```

The next four lines of code set properties of the button. The Location property of the Button class sets the location of the top left corner of the button within the form:

```
    Me.btnHelloWorld.Location = New System.Drawing.Point(112, 112)
```

The location of a control is expressed in terms of a `Point` structure. Next the `Name` property of the button is set:

```
Me.btnHelloWorld.Name = "btnHelloWorld"
```

The `Name` property acts in exactly the same way as it did for the form, setting the textual name of the button. The `Name` property has no effect on how the button is displayed on the form, but is used to recognize the button's context within the source code. The next two lines of code assign values to the `TabIndex` and `Text` properties of the button:

```
Me.btnHelloWorld.TabIndex = 0
Me.btnHelloWorld.Text = "Hello World"
```

The `TabIndex` property of the button is used to set the order in which the control will be selected when the user cycles through the controls on the form using the *Tab* key. The higher the number, the later the control will get focus. Each control should have a unique number for its `TabIndex` property. The `Text` property of a button sets the text that appears on the button.

Once the properties of the button have been set, it needs to be added to the form. This is accomplished with the next line of code:

```
    Me.Controls.AddRange(New System.Windows.Forms.Control()
{Me.btnHelloWorld})
```

This line of code adds the button to the collection of child controls for the form. The `System.Windows.Forms.Form` class (from which your `Form1` class is derived) has a property called `Controls` that keeps track of all of the child controls of the form. Whenever you add a control to a form, a line similar to the one above is added automatically to the Form's initialization process.

Finally, near the bottom of the initialization logic is the final code change. The form is given permission to resume the layout logic:

```
Me.ResumeLayout(False)
```

The final code change is the event handler added for the button. The code contained in the handler was already covered, with the exception of the naming convention for event handlers. Event handlers have a similar naming convention to that of previous versions of Visual Basic: the control name is followed by an underscore and then the event name. The event itself may also have a standard set of parameters. At this point you can test the application, but first perhaps a review of build options is appropriate.

Build Configurations

In previous versions of Visual Basic, a project had only one set of properties. There was no way to have one set of properties for a debug build and a separate set for a release build. The result was that you had to manually change any properties that were environment-specific before you built the application. This has changed with the introduction of build configurations, which allow us to have different sets of project properties for debug and release builds. VS.NET also does not limit you to only two build configurations, it is possible to create additional custom configurations. The properties that can be set for a project have been split into two groups: those that are independent of build configuration and therefore apply to all build configurations, and those that apply to only the active build configuration. For example, the Project Name and Project Location properties are the same irrespective of what build configuration is active, whereas the code optimization options differ depending on the active build configuration. This isn't a new concept and has been available to Visual C++ developers for some time, but it is the first time it has been available for VB developers.

The advantage of multiple configurations is that it is possible to turn off optimization while an application is in development and add symbolic debug information that will help locate and identify errors. When you are ready to ship the application, a single switch to the release configuration results in an executable that is optimized. The settings associated with the various build configurations are stored in the project properties. Unlike the display properties which show up in the window discussed earlier in this chapter, project properties are accessed through a set of Property Pages. To access a project's Property Pages dialog box, right-click the project in the Solution Explorer and select Properties from the pop-up menu. Alternatively, it is possible to open the project Property Pages dialog box by selecting Properties from the Project menu in Visual Studio.

On the left side of the dialog box are two folders that represent the two groups of project properties (see Figure 2-11). Each folder contains a number of sections that logically group properties together further. The first, called Common Properties, is where properties that are independent of build configuration are set.

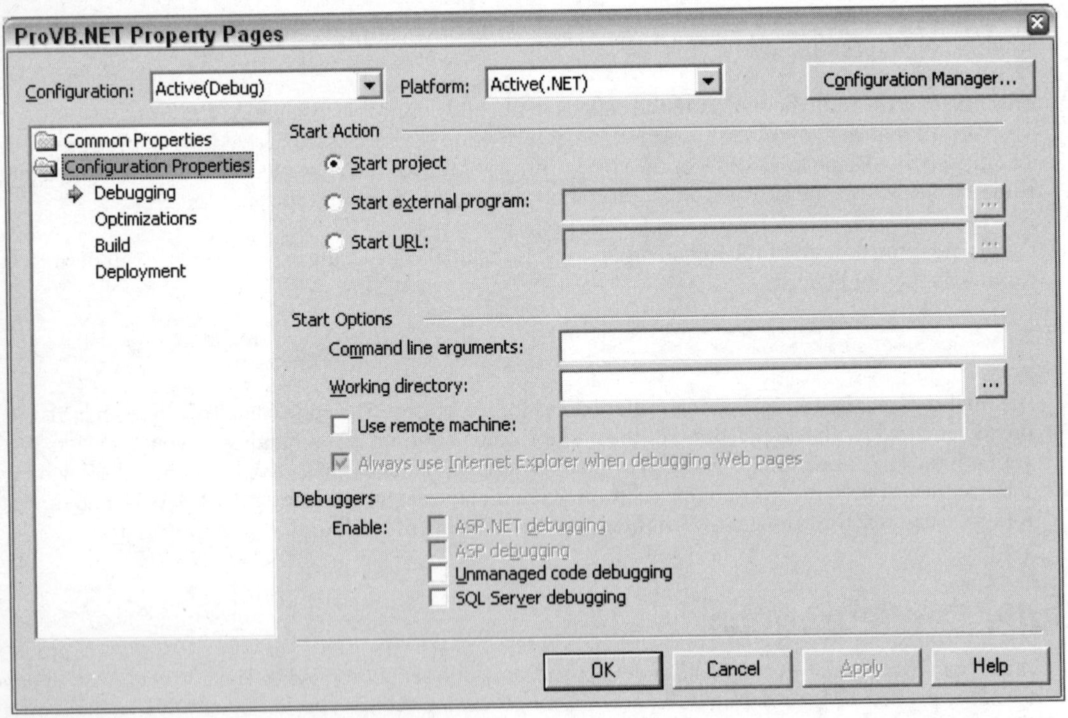

Figure 2-11

The second folder, called Configuration Properties, contains sections where properties that are dependent on the active build configuration are set. When a section from the Configuration Properties folder is selected, the configuration drop-down box, shown at the top of the dialog box in Figure 2-11, becomes enabled. This drop-down box allows us to select a build configuration to edit. The configuration currently selected as the build configuration will be listed as Active, with the configuration name in brackets. The second drop-down box, labeled Platform, allows selection of a target platform for the project. Note that for .NET applications this platform isn't defined at the machine level but at the runtime environment. For example, the CLR environment is the default for all .NET applications.

If there is more than one project in the current solution, it is possible to customize which projects are included in each build configuration. Projects are assigned to build configurations through the Configuration Manager. It is possible to open the Configuration Manager from the project Property Pages dialog box by clicking the button shown in the upper right-hand corner of Figure 2-11. Alternatively, the Configuration Manager, shown in Figure 2-12, can be opened using the drop-down list box to the right of the run button on the VS.NET toolbar. The active configuration drop-down box contains the following options: Debug, Release, and Configuration Manager. The first two default options are the current available configurations. However, selecting the bottom option, Configuration Manager, opens the dialog box shown in Figure 2-12.

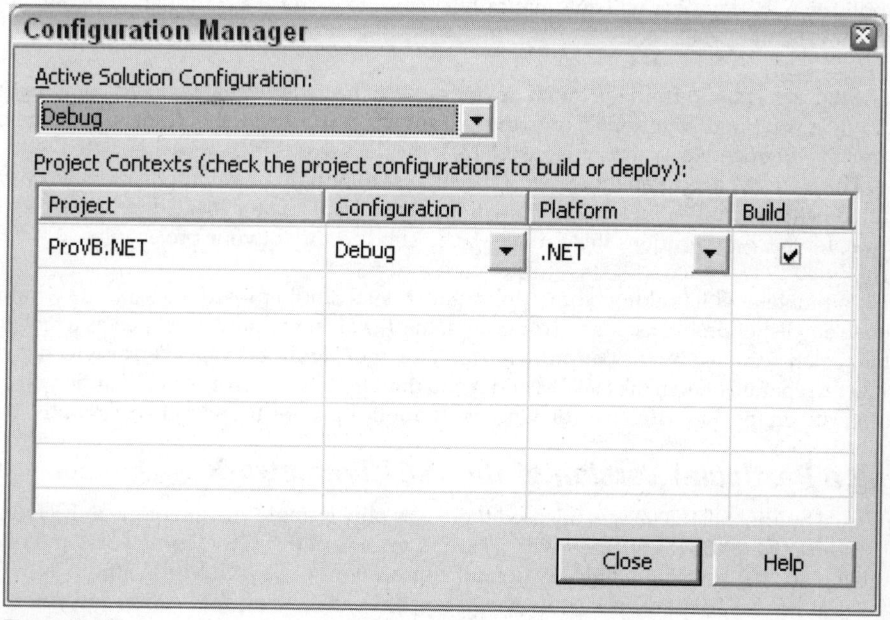

Figure 2-12

The Configuration Manager, shown in Figure 2-12, contains an entry for each project in the current solution. It is possible to include or exclude a project from the selected configuration by clearing the check box in the column of the grid labeled Build. This is a valuable capability when a solution has multiple projects so that time isn't spent waiting while a project that isn't being worked on is recompiled. A common example of using the build configuration is when a Setup project is added to a solution. The normal plan is to only rebuild the Setup package when a release version of the actual application project is created. It's important to note that regardless of the build configuration, it is possible to build any assembly by right-clicking that project and selecting the Build option from the popup menu.

Building Applications

For this example it is best to just build your sample application using the Debug build configuration. The first step is to make certain that the configuration drop-down list box discussed in the previous section has Debug selected as the active configuration. Visual Studio provides an entire Build menu with the various options available for how to build an application. There are essentially two options for building applications:

❑ Build — Use the currently active build configuration to build the project

❑ Rebuild — Clean all intermediate files (object files) and the output directory before building the project using the active build configuration

The Build menu supports doing each of these for either the current configuration or for only the currently selected project. Thus, you can choose to only build a single project in your solution, to rebuild all of the supporting files for a single project, or to use the current configuration and build or rebuild all of the projects which have been defined as part of that configuration. Of course, anytime you choose to test run your application the compiler will automatically attempt to perform a compilation so that you run the most recent version of your code.

You can either select Build from the menu or you can use the *Ctrl-Shift-B* keyboard combination to initiate a build. When you build your application, the Output window along the bottom edge of the development environment will open. As shown in Figure 2-13, it displays status messages associated with the build process. This window acts as an indicator of the success of building your application. Once your application has been built successfully you will find the executable file located in the targeted directory. By default, for .NET applications this is the '\bin' subdirectory of your project files.

If there is a problem with building your application, Visual Studio provides a separate window to help coordinate any list of problems. If an error occurs, the Task List window will open as a tabbed window in the same region occupied by the Output window shown in Figure 2-13. Each error which is encountered will trigger a separate item in the task list and if you double-click an error, Visual Studio will automatically reposition you on the line with an error. Once your application has been built successfully, you can run it.

Targeting a Particular Version of the .NET Framework

When Visual Studio .NET 2002 was released there was only a single version of the .NET Framework. Visual Studio .NET 2003 was released with a second version of the .NET Framework, and of course, not everything is 100 percent compatible. By default, applications built with Visual Studio .NET 2003 target version 1.1 of the .NET Framework. However, if you have an existing application and you need to ensure that it will continue to run on a specific version of .NET, it is possible to do this by updating your project's build settings. However, this action is neither necessary nor recommended in most cases. After all, it is possible to run Visual Studio .NET 2002 and Visual Studio .NET 2003 side by side, with each targeting the accompanying version of the .NET Framework. The only challenge with this is that when version 1.1 of the .NET Framework is installed, all ASP.NET applications automatically run in the updated environment.

To target an application to a specific version of the .NET Framework, you must have both version 1.1 and version 1.0 of the .NET Framework installed on your computer. Right-click your project and select Properties to open the Properties window. Within the Common Properties folder select the build options. On the bottom half of the build options display you will see a note indicating that by default applications built with Visual Studio 2003 target the .NET Framework version 1.1. Alongside this note is a Change

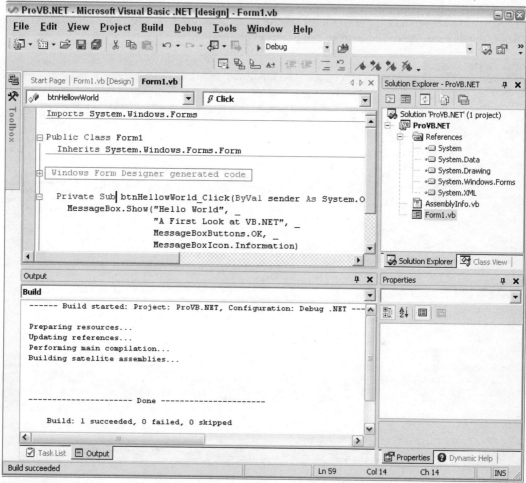

Figure 2-13

button. Selecting the Change button will allow you to target either both version 1.0 and version 1.1 of the .NET Framework or only version 1.0 of the .NET Framework.

Running an Application in the Debugger

As was discussed earlier, there are several ways to start your application. Starting your application launches a series of events. First, Visual Studio looks for any modified files, and saves these files automatically. It then verifies the build status of your solution, and rebuilds any project which does not have an updated binary, including dependencies. Finally, it initiates a separate process space and starts up your application with the Visual Studio debugger preattached to that process.

Once your application is running, the look and feel of VS.NET's IDE changes. New windows and button bars associated with debugging become visible. While your solution and code remain visible, the IDE is displaying additional windows such as the Autos, Locals, and Watch windows, shown on the lower right-hand side of Figure 2-14. These windows are used by the debugger for reviewing the current value of variables within your code. On the lower right-hand side of VS.NET, the Call Stack, Breakpoints, Command window, and Output windows open to provide feedback on what your application is doing. These windows are discussed in more detail later in this chapter.

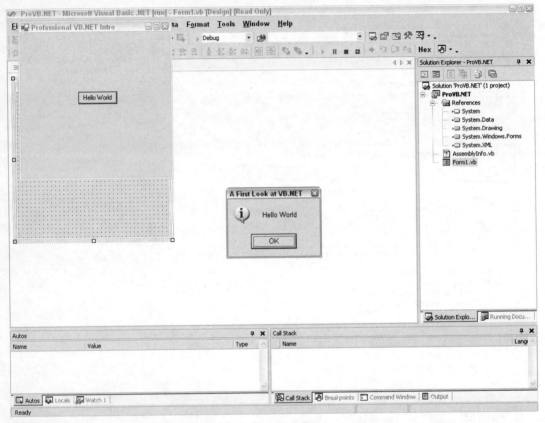

Figure 2-14

With your application running, select Visual Studio as the active window. Then click in the border alongside the line of code you added to open a message box when the "Hello World" button is clicked. Doing this will create a breakpoint on the selected line. If you return to your application and click the "Hello World" button you will see that VS.NET takes the active focus and that within your code window the line with your breakpoint is now selected.

While in break mode, it is possible to update the applications running values and view the current status of your application. Chapter 9, which focuses on error handling, delves into many of the more advanced capabilities of the VS.NET debugger. At this point you should have a basic understanding of how to work in the VS.NET environment. However, there are a few other elements of this environment which you will use as you develop more complex applications.

Other Debug-Related Windows

As noted earlier in this chapter, when you run an application in debug mode, Visual Studio .NET 2003 opens up a series of windows. Each of these windows provides a view of a limited set of the overall environment in which your application is running. From these windows it is possible to find things like the list of calls used to get to the current line of code, or the present value of all of the variables that are currently available. VS.NET has a powerful debugger that is fully supported with IntelliSense and these windows extend the debugger.

Output

As noted earlier, the build process puts progress messages in this window. Similarly, your program can also place messages in it. There are several options for accessing this window that will be discussed in later chapters, but at the simplest level, the `Console` object will echo its output to this window during a debug session. For example, the following line of code can be added to your sample application.

```
Console.WriteLine("This is printed in the Output Window")
```

This line of code will cause the string `This is printed in the Output Window` to appear in the Output window when your application is running. You can verify this by adding this line in front of the command to open the message box and then running your application and having the debugger stop on the line where the message box is opened. Examining the contents of the Output window you will find your string has been displayed.

Anything written to the Output window is shown only while running a program from the environment. During execution of the compiled module, no Output window is present, so nothing can be written to it. This is the basic concept behind other objects such as the Debug and Trace objects, which are covered in more detail in Chapter 9.

Call Stack

The Call Stack window lists the procedures that are currently calling other procedures and waiting for their return. The call stack represents the path through your code that has led to the current executing command. This can be a valuable tool when you are trying to determine what code is executing a line of code that you didn't expect to execute. This was accessed in Visual Basic 6 with a menu option on the View menu.

Breakpoints

The Breakpoints window is an enhanced breakpoint handler in which breakpoints can be defined and monitored. Earlier you saw that you can add breakpoints directly in your code by simply selecting a line. It is also possible to add specific properties to your breakpoints, defining that a given breakpoint should only execute if a certain value is defined (or undefined) or only after it has been executed several times. This is useful for debugging problems that occur only after a certain number of iterations of a routine. (Note that breakpoints are saved when a solution is saved by the IDE.) The breakpoint handler in VS.NET is significantly enhanced from previous versions of Visual Basic.

Locals

The Locals window is used to monitor the value of all variables that are currently in scope. This is a fairly self-explanatory window in that it shows a list of the current local variables and next to each item is the value of the variable. As in pervious versions of Visual Studio, this display supports examining the contents of object and array via a tree-control interface.

Autos

The Autos window displays variables used in the statement currently being executed and the statement just before it. These variables are identified and listed for you automatically, hence the window name. This window will show more than just your local variables. For example, if you are in the debugger mode on the line to open the MessageBox in the ProVB.NET sample, you will see that the MessageBox constants which are referenced on this line are shown in this window. This window allows you to see the content of every variable involved in the currently executing command.

Watch Windows

There are four Watch windows, called Watch 1 to Watch 4. Each window can hold a set of variables or expressions for which you want to monitor the value. It is also possible to modify the value of a variable from within a Watch window. The display can be set to show variable values in decimal or in hexadecimal format. To add a variable to a Watch window, right-click the variable in the code editor and then select "Add Watch" from the popup menu.

Useful Features of VS.NET

The focus of most of this chapter has been on creating a simple application. When you are working with a tool such as Visual Studio .NET 2003, often your task will require some features and not require others. In the case of the preceding example, there are four in particular that are worth covering:

❑ The Task List

❑ The Command window

❑ The Server Explorer

❑ Macros in Visual Studio

The Task List

The Task List is a great productivity tool that tracks not only errors, but pending changes and additions. It's also a good way for the VS.NET environment to communicate information that the developer needs to know, such as any current errors. The Task List is displayed by selecting the Task List from the Other Windows option of the View menu, or if there are errors found during a build of your solution, the window opens automatically.

Although it isn't immediately obvious, the task list has several options. The quickest way to get a list of these options is to go to the View menu and select the Show Tasks option. This will provide a list of the different types of tasks that can be organized in the Task List. By default the Task List displays All tasks. However, it is possible to change this default and screen the tasks that are displayed.

The Comment option is for tasks embedded into code comments. This is done by creating a standard comment with the apostrophe, and then starting the comment with the VS.NET keyword TODO:. The keyword can be followed with any text that then describes what needs to be done. Once entered, the text of these comments shows up in the Task List if either the Comment option or the All option is selected. Note that a user can create his or her own comment tokens in the options for Visual Studio via the Tools ➪ Options ➪ Environment ➪ Task List menu.

Besides helping developers track these tasks, embedding the tasks in code results in another benefit. Just as with errors, clicking a task in the Task List causes the code editor to jump right to the location of the task without hunting through the code for it.

Finally, it is possible to enter tasks into the Task List manually. By Selecting an open row of the task list, you can add additional tasks that might be needed but which may not be associated with a particular spot in your source code. These user-entered tasks are displayed both when the View ➪ Show Tasks ➪ User option is selected, and when all tasks are displayed.

The Command Window

The Command window is one of the windows that are displayed while in debug mode. It is also possible to open this window from the Other Windows section of the View menu. When opened, the window displays a prompt of ">". This is a command prompt at which you can execute commands.

The Command window can be used to access VS.NET menu options and commands by typing them in instead of selecting them in the menu structure. For example, if you type `File.AddNewProject` and press *Enter*, the dialog box to add a new project will appear. Note that IntelliSense is available to help enter commands in the Command window.

The Command window also has an immediate mode in which expressions can be evaluated. This mode is accessed by typing Immed at the prompt. In this mode, the window title changes to indicate that the immediate mode is active. The key difference between modes of the Command window is how the equal sign behaves. Normally, the equal sign is used as a comparison operator in the Command window. Thus the statement $a=b$ is used to determine whether the value a is the same as b. In immediate mode, the statement $a=b$ attempts to assign the value of b to a. This can be very useful if you are working in the debugger mode and need to modify a value that is part of a running application. To return to the command mode, type `'>cmd'`.

In the immediate mode, the Command window behaves very similar to the Immediate window in Visual Basic 6.

The Server Explorer

As development has become more server-centric, developers have a greater need to discover and manipulate services on the network. The Server Explorer is a feature in VS.NET that makes this easier. Visual Interdev started in this direction with a Server Object section in the Interdev Toolbox. The Server Explorer in VS.NET is more sophisticated in that it allows you to explore and even alter your applications database or your local registry values. With the assistance of a SQL Database project template (part of the Other Project types) it is possible to fully explore and alter a SQL Server database. You can define the tables, stored procedures, and other database objects that you might have previously done with the SQL Enterprise Manager.

However, the Server Explorer is not specific to databases. You open the Server Explorer similar to how you open the control Toolbox. When you hover over or click the Server Explorer's tab, the window will expand from the left-hand side of the IDE. Once open, you will have a display similar to the one shown in Figure 2-15.

It might at first seem as if this window is specific to only SQL Server, but if you expand the list of available servers, as shown in Figure 2-15, you will see that you have access to several server resources. The Server Explorer even provides the ability to stop and restart services on the server. Notice the wide variety of server resources that are available for inspection, or for use in the project. Having the Server

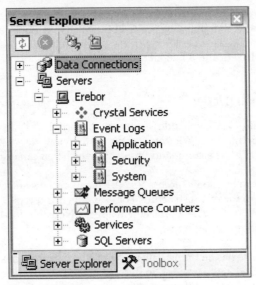

Figure 2-15

Explorer available means that you don't have to go to an outside resource to find, for example, what message queues are available.

By default you have access to the resources on your local machine. However, if you are in a domain it is possible to add other machines, such as your Web server, to your display. The Add Server option allows a new server to be selected and inspected. To explore the event logs and registry of a server, you need to add this server to your display. Use the Add Server button shown in Figure 2-15 to open the Add Server dialog box. In this dialog box, provide just the name of your server and select the OK button. This will add the new server to your display.

Recording and Using Macros in VS.NET

C++ developers have long had one feature that many VB developers craved — *macros*. In VS.NET, macros become part of the environment and are available to any language. However, as with the Microsoft Office suite (prior to Office 2003), macros can be written only with VB syntax.

Macro options are accessible from the Tools-Macros menu. The concept of macros is simple: the idea is to record a series of keystrokes and/or menu actions, and then play them back by pressing a certain keystroke combination.

For example, suppose one particular function call with a complex set of arguments is constantly being called on in code, and the function call usually looks about the same except for minor variations in the arguments. The keystrokes to code the function call could be recorded and played back as necessary, which would insert code to call the function that could then be modified as necessary.

Macros can be far more complex than this, containing logic as well as keystrokes. The macro capabilities of VS.NET are so comprehensive that macros have their own IDE (accessed using Tools ⇨ Macros ⇨ Macros IDE).

Macros can be developed from scratch in this environment, but more commonly they are recorded using the Record Temporary Macro option on the Macros menu, and then renamed and modified in the above development environment. Here is an example of recording and modifying a macro:

1. Start a new window Application project.

2. In the new project, add a button to the `Form1` that was created with the project.

3. Double-click the button to get to its `Click` event routine.

4. Select Tool‗Macros‗Record Temporary Macro. A small toolbar will appear on top of the IDE with button to control recording of macro (Pause, Stop, and Cancel).

5. Press the *Enter* key and then type in the following line of code:

```
Console.WriteLine("Macro test")
```

6. Press the *Enter* key agian.

7. In the small toolbar, press the Stop button.

8. Select Tool ⇨ Macros ⇨ Record Temporary Macro. The Macro Explorer will appear (in the location normally occupied by the Solution Explorer), and new macro will be in it, You can name the macro anything you like.

9. Right-click the macro and select Edit to get to the macro editor. You will see following code in your macro:

```
DTE.ActiveDocument.Selection.NewLine()
DTE.ActiveDocument.Selection.Text = "Console.WriteLine(""A macro test"")"
DTE.ActiveDocument.Selection.NewLine()
```

The code that appears in step 9 can vary depending on how you typed in the line. If you made a mistake and backspaced, for example, those actions will have their own corresponding lines of code. As a result after you record a macro it is often worthwhile to examine the code and remove any unnecessary lines.

The code in a macro recorded this way is just standard VB.NET code, and it can be modified as desired. However, there are some restrictions on what you can do inside the macro IDE. For example, you cannot refer to the namespace for setting up database connections as this might constitute a security violation.

To run a macro, you can just double-click it in the Macro Explorer, or select Tools ⇨ Macros ⇨ Run Macro. You can also assign a keystroke to a macro in the Keyboard dialog box in the Tools ⇨ Options ⇨ Environment folder.

Summary

In this chapter, you have created your first sample VB.NET application. Creating this example has helped you to explore the new VS.NET IDE, and to show how powerful the features of the IDE are. Some of the key points that were covered in this chapter include:

❑   How to create projects and the different project templates available

❑   Code regions and how the form designer uses them to conceal code that it doesn't want the developer to change

- ❏ Namespaces and how to import them into applications
- ❏ How forms are classes, and how the properties of forms are set in code
- ❏ Some of the new object-oriented features of Visual Basic
- ❏ Build configurations and how to modify the build configuration of your project
- ❏ Running an application in debug mode and how to set a breakpoint

With .NET, Microsoft has for the first time brought different development languages and paradigms into a single development environment, and it is a powerful one. Users of previous versions of Visual Basic, Visual Interdev, and Visual Studio will generally find this environment familiar. The IDE offers many new features over previous development tools to help boost developer productivity.

You've also seen that VS.NET is customizable. Various windows can be hidden, docked, or undocked, layered in tabs, and can be moved within the IDE. There are many tools in VS.NET at your disposal and it's worth the effort to learn how to use them effectively.

3

The Common Language Runtime

The architects of .NET realized that all procedural languages require certain base functionality. For example, many languages ship with their own runtime that provides features, such as memory management. But what if instead of each language shipping with its own runtime implementation, all languages used a common runtime? This would provide languages with a standard environment and access to all of the same features. This is exactly what the common language runtime (CLR) provides.

The CLR manages the execution of code on the .NET platform. In some ways VB developers can view the CLR as a better VB runtime. In this chapter, we'll discuss how the previous VB specific runtime environment has been replaced and enhanced by the CLR.

The functionality exposed by the CLR is available to all .NET languages; more importantly, all of the features available to other .NET languages via the CLR are available to VB developers. For some time, VB developers have been asking for better support for many advanced features, including operator overloading, implementation inheritance, threading, and the ability to marshal objects. Building such features into a language is not trivial, but as the CLR supports them and as Visual Basic .NET is built on top of the CLR, VB.NET can use these features, eliminating many of the shortcomings of the previous versions of Visual Basic.

In this chapter, we'll examine the features provided to .NET applications by the CLR. This chapter gets down into the weeds of the application runtime environment as you look at:

❑ Elements of a .NET application

❑ Versioning and deployment

❑ Memory management and the Garbage Collector (GC)

❑ Integration across .NET languages

However, since in the last chapter you explored how to create a VB.NET application, the first step is to ensure that you are familiar with how to describe the major elements that make up a typical .NET application.

Elements of a .NET Application

A .NET application is composed of three primary entities:

❑ Assemblies — the primary unit of deployment of a .NET application

❑ Modules — the individual files that make up an assembly

❑ Classes — the basic units that encapsulate data and behavior

Assemblies

An assembly is the primary unit of deployment for .NET applications — it is either a dynamic link library (DLL) or an executable (EXE). An assembly is composed of a manifest, one or more modules, and (optionally) other files, such as .config, .ASPX, .ASMX, images, and so on.

The manifest of an assembly contains:

❑ Information about the identity of the assembly, including its textual name and version number.

❑ If the assembly is public, the manifest will contain the assembly's public key. The public key is used to help ensure that types exposed by the assembly reside within a unique namespace. It may also be used to uniquely identify the source of an assembly.

❑ A declarative security request that describes the assembly's security requirements (the assembly is responsible for declaring the security it requires). Requests for permissions fall into three categories: required, optional, and denied. The identity information may be used as evidence by the CLR in determining whether or not to approve security requests.

❑ A list of other assemblies that the assembly depends on. The CLR uses this information to locate an appropriate version of the required assemblies at runtime. The list of dependencies also includes the exact version number of each assembly at the time the assembly was created.

❑ A list of all types and resources exposed by the assembly. If any of the resources exposed by the assembly are localized, the manifest will also contain the default culture (language, currency, date/time format, and so on) that the application will target. The CLR uses this information to locate specific resources and types within the assembly.

The manifest can be stored in a separate file or in one of the modules, but by default for most applications it will be part of the .DLL or .EXE file which is compiled by Visual Studio. For web applications, you will find that although there are a collection of .ASPX pages, the actual assembly information is located in a DLL that is referenced by those ASPX pages.

Modules

A module contains Microsoft Intermediate Language (MSIL, often abbreviated to IL) code, associated metadata, and the assembly's manifest. By default, the VB.NET compiler will create an assembly that is composed of a single module having both the assembly code and manifest.

IL is a platform independent way of representing managed code within a module. Before IL can be executed, the CLR must compile it into the native machine code. The default method is for the CLR to use the JIT(just-in-time)compiler to compile the IL on a method-by-method basis. At runtime, as each method is called by an application for the first time, it is passed through the JIT compiler for compilation to machine code. Similarly, for an ASP.NET application each page is passed through the JIT compiler the first time that it is requested to create an in-memory representation of the machine code that represents that page.

Additional information about the types declared in the IL is provided by the associated metadata. The metadata contained within the module is used extensively by the CLR. For example, if a client and an object reside within two different processes, the CLR will use the type's metadata to marshal data between the client and the object.

Types

The type system provides a template that is used to describe the encapsulation of data and an associated set of behaviors. It is this common template for describing data that provides the basis for the metadata that .NET uses when applications interoperate. Unlike COM, which is scoped at the machine level, types are scoped at the assembly level, but are based on a common system that is used across all .NET languages.

There are two kinds of types: reference and value. The differences between these two types are discussed further in Chapter 4, but for the time being you can think (loosely) of reference types as classes and value types as structures (which have replaced the user-defined types of VB6).

A type has fields, properties, and methods:

❑ Fields — are variables that are scoped to the type. For example, a Pet class could declare a field called Name that holds the pet's name.

❑ Properties — look like fields to clients of the type, but can have code behind them (that usually performs some sort of data validation). For example, a Dog data type could expose a property to set its gender. Code could then be placed behind the property so that it can only be set to "male" or "female," and then this property too could be saved internally to one of the fields in the dog class.

❑ Methods — define behaviors exhibited by the type. For example, the Dog data type could expose a method called Sleep which would suspend the activity of the Dog.

The preceding elements make up each application. Once you have an application the next challenge is to know which version of that application you have. One of the advantages of .NET is that it is possible to keep several different versions of the same application operational on the same machine.

Versioning and Deployment

Components and their clients are often installed at different times by different vendors. For example, a VB application might rely on a third-party grid control to display data. Runtime support for versioning is crucial in ensuring that an incompatible version of the grid control does not cause problems for the VB application.

In addition to this issue of compatibility, the deployment of applications written in previous versions of Visual Basic was problematic. Fortunately, .NET provides major improvements over the versioning and deployment offered by COM and the previous versions of Visual Basic.

Better Support for Versioning

Managing the version of components was challenging in the previous versions of Visual Basic. The version number of the component could be set, but this version number was not used by the runtime. COM components are often referenced by their ProgID, but Visual Basic does not provide any support for appending the version number on the end of the ProgID.

For those of you who are unfamiliar with the term ProgID, suffice to know that ProgIDs are developer friendly strings used to identify a component. For example, `Word.Application` describes Microsoft Word. ProgIDs can be fully qualified with the targeted version of the component, for example, `Word.Application.10`, but this is a limited capability and relies on both the application and whether the person consuming it chooses to use this optional addendum. As we'll see in Chapter 8, Namespace is built on the basic elements of a ProgID, but provides a more robust naming system.

For many applications, .NET has removed the need to identify the version of each assembly in a central registry on a machine. However, some assemblies will be installed once and used by multiple applications. .NET provides a Global Assembly Cache (GAC) which is used to store assemblies that are intended for use by multiple applications. The CLR provides versioning support for all components that are loaded in the GAC.

The CLR provides two features for assemblies installed within the GAC:

❑ Side-by-side versioning — multiple versions of the same component can be simultaneously stored in the GAC.

❑ Automatic QFE (hotfix) support — if a new version of a component, which is still compatible with the old version, is available in the GAC, the CLR will load the updated component. The version number, which is maintained by the developer who created the referenced assembly, drives this behavior.

The assembly's manifest contains the version numbers of referenced assemblies. The CLR uses this list at runtime to locate a compatible version of a referenced assembly. The version number of an assembly takes the following form:

```
Major.Minor.Build.Revision
```

Changes to the major and minor version numbers of the assembly indicate that the assembly is no longer compatible with the previous versions. The CLR will not use versions of the assembly that have a different major or minor number unless it is explicitly told to do so. For example, if an assembly was originally compiled against a referenced assembly with a version number of 3.4.1.9, the CLR will not load an assembly stored in the GAC unless it has a major and minor number of 3 and 4.

Incrementing the revision and build numbers indicates that the new version is still compatible with the previous version. If a new assembly that has an incremented revision or build number is loaded into the GAC, the CLR can still load this assembly for clients that were compiled against a previous version. Versioning is discussed in greater detail in Chapter 25, i.e. Assemblies and Deployment in .NET.

Better Deployment

Applications written using the previous versions of VB and COM were often complicated to deploy. Components referenced by the application needed to be installed and registered, and for VB components the correct version of the VB runtime needed to be available. The Component Deployment tool helped in the creation of complex installation packages, but applications could be easily broken if the dependent components were inadvertently replaced by incompatible versions on the client's computer during the installation of an unrelated product.

In .NET, most components do not need to be registered. When an external assembly is referenced, the application makes a decision on using a global copy (which must be in the GAC on the developer's system) or on copying a component locally. For most references, the external assemblies are referenced locally which means they are carried in the application's local directory structure. Using local copies of external assemblies allow the CLR to support the side-by-side execution of different versions of the same component. As noted earlier, to reference a globally registered assembly, that assembly must be located in the GAC. The GAC provides a versioning system that is robust enough to allow different versions of the same external assembly to exist side-by-side. For example, an application could use a newer version of ADO.NET without adversely affecting another application that relies on a previous version.

So long as the client has the .NET runtime installed (which has to be done only once), a .NET application can be distributed using a simple command like this:

```
xcopy \\server\appDirectory "C:\Program Files\appDirectory" /E /O /I
```

The preceding command would copy all of the files and subdirectories from `\\server\appDirectory` to `C:\ Program Files\appDirectory`, and would also transfer the file's Access Control Lists (ACLs).

Besides the ability to XCopy applications, Visual Studio .NET provides a built-in tool for constructing simple .MSI installations. These projects can be added to your project solution allowing you to integrate the deployment project with your application output.

Finally, .NET provides an entirely new method of deployment referred to as Smart Client deployment. In the smart client model your application is placed on a central server from which the clients accesses the application files. Smart client deployment builds on the XML Web services architecture about which you are learning. It has the advantages of central application maintenance combined with a richer client interface and fewer server communication requirements that you have become familiar with in Windows forms applications. Deployment is discussed in greater detail in Chapter 25.

Memory Management

One of the benefits of the CLR, memory management, fixes the shortcomings of the VB runtime's memory management. VB developers are accustomed to only worrying about memory management in an abstract sense. The basic rule was that every object created needed to be destroyed. The CLR introduces a Garbage

Collector (GC) which simplifies this paradigm even further. Gone are the days where a misbehaving component that fails to properly dispose of its object references can crash a Web server.

Better Garbage Collection

The VB6 runtime provides limited memory management by automatically releasing references to objects when they are no longer referenced by the application. Once all of the references are released on an object, the runtime will automatically release the object from memory. For example, consider the following VB6 code that uses the `Scripting.FileSystem` object to write an entry to a log file:

```
' Requires a reference to Microsoft Scripting Runtime (scrrun.dll)
Sub WriteToLog(strLogEntry As String)
 Dim objFSO As Scripting.FileSystemObject
 Dim objTS As Scripting.TextStream

 objTS = objFSO.OpenTextFile("C:\temp\AppLog.log", ForAppending)
 Call objTS.WriteLine(Date & vbTab & strLogEntry)
End Sub
```

`WriteToLog` creates two objects, a `FileSystemObject` and a `TextStream`, which are used to create an entry in the log file. Because these are COM objects they may live either within the current application process or in their own process. Once the routine exits, the VB runtime will dereference the objects, which results in both the objects being deactivated. However, there are situations in which objects that are no longer referenced by an application will not be properly cleaned up by the VB6 runtime. One cause of this is the cyclical reference.

Cyclical References

One of the most common situations in which the VB runtime is unable to ensure that objects no longer referenced by the application is when objects contain a cyclical reference. An example of a cyclical reference is when object A holds a reference to object B and object B holds a reference to object A.

Cyclical references are problematic because the VB runtime relies on the reference counting mechanism of COM to determine whether an object can be deactivated. Each COM object is responsible for maintaining its own reference count and for destroying itself once the reference count reaches zero. Clients of the object are responsible for updating the reference count appropriately, by calling the `AddRef` and `Release` methods on the object's `IUnknown` interface. However, in this scenario, object A continues to hold a reference to object B, and vice versa, and thus the internal cleanup logic of these components is not triggered.

In addition, problems can occur if the clients do not properly maintain the COM object's reference count. For example, an object will never get deactivated if a client forgets to call `Release` when the object is no longer referenced (and no other clients call `Release` too many times). To avoid this, the VB6 runtime takes care of updating the reference count for us; but the object's reference count can be an invalid indicator of whether or not the object is still being used by the application. As an example, consider the references that objects A and B hold.

The application can invalidate its references to A and B by setting the associated variables equal to `Nothing`. However, even though objects A and B are no longer referenced by the application, the VB runtime cannot ensure that the objects get deactivated because A and B still reference each other. Consider the following (VB6) code:

```
' Class:  CCyclicalRef

' Reference to another object.
Dim m_objRef As Object

Public Sub Initialize(objRef As Object)
   Set m_objRef = objRef
End Sub

Private Sub Class_Terminate()
   Call MsgBox("Terminating.")
   Set m_objRef = Nothing
End Sub
```

The CCyclicalRef class implements an Initialize method that accepts a reference to another object, and saves it as a member variable. Notice that the class does not release any existing reference in the m_objRef variable before assigning a new value. The following code demonstrates how to use this CCyclicalRef class to create a cyclical reference:

```
Dim objA As New CCyclicalRef
Dim objB As New CCyclicalRef

Call objA.Initialize(objB)
Call objB.Initialize(objA)

Set objA = Nothing
Set objB = Nothing
```

We create two instances (objA and objB) of CCyclicalRef, both of which have a reference count of one. We then call the Initialize method on each object by passing it a reference to the other. Now each of the object's reference counts is equal to two: one held by the application and one held by the other object. Next, explicitly set objA and objB to Nothing, which decrements each object's reference count by one. However, since the reference count for both instances of CCyclicalRef is still greater than zero, the objects will not be released from memory until the application is terminated. The CLR Garbage Collector solves the problem of cyclical references.

The CLR Garbage Collector

The .NET garbage collection mechanism is a very complex software, and the details of its inner workings are beyond the scope of this book. However, it is important to understand the principles behind its operation. The GC is responsible for collecting objects that are no longer referenced. The GC takes a completely different approach to that of the VB runtime to accomplish this. At certain times, and based on internal rules, a task will run through all the objects looking for those that no longer have any references. Those objects may then be terminated; the garbage is collected.

As long as all references to an object are either implicitly or explicitly released by the application, the GC will take care of freeing the memory allocated to it. Unlike COM objects, managed objects in .NET are not responsible for maintaining their reference count, and they are not responsible for destroying themselves. Instead, the GC is responsible for cleaning up objects that are no longer referenced by the application. The

GC will periodically determine which objects need to be cleaned up by leveraging the information the CLR maintains about the running application. The GC obtains a list of objects that are directly referenced by the application. Then, the GC discovers all the objects that are referenced (both directly and indirectly) by the application's "root" objects. Once the GC has identified all the referenced objects, it is free to clean up any remaining objects.

The GC relies on references from an application to objects, thus, when it locates an object which is unreachable from any of the root objects it can clean up that object. Any other references to that object will be from other objects that are also unreachable. Thus, the GC will automatically clean up objects that contain cyclical references.

In some environments, such as COM, objects are destroyed in a deterministic fashion. Once the reference count reaches zero the object will destroy itself, which means that you can tell *exactly* when the object will be terminated. However, with garbage collection, you can't tell exactly when an object will be destroyed. Just because you eliminate all references to an object doesn't mean it will be terminated immediately. It will just remain in memory until the garbage collection process gets around to locating and destroying it. This is called nondeterministic finalization.

This nondeterministic nature of CLR garbage collection provides a performance benefit. Rather than expending the effort to destroy objects as they are dereferenced, the destruction process can occur when the application is otherwise idle — often decreasing the impact on the user. Of course, if garbage collection must occur when the application is active, the system may see a slight performance fluctuation as the collection is accomplished.

It is possible to explicitly invoke the GC by calling the System.GC.Collect method. However, this process takes time, so it is not the sort of thing that should be done in a typical application. For example, you could call this method each time you set an object variable to Nothing, so that the object would be destroyed almost immediately. However, this forces the GC to scan all the objects in your application — a very expensive operation in terms of performance.

It's far better to design applications so that it's acceptable for unused objects to sit in the memory for some time before they are terminated. That way, the Garbage Collector too can run based on its optimal rules — collecting many dereferenced objects at the same time. This means that you need to design objects that don't maintain expensive resources in instance variables. For example, database connections, open files on disk, and large chunks of memory (such as an image) are all examples of expensive resources. If you rely on the destruction of the object to release this type of resource, the system might be keeping the resource tied up for a lot longer than you expect; in fact, on a lightly utilized Web server it could literally be days.

The first principle is working with object patterns that incorporate cleaning up such pending references before the object is released. Examples of this include calling the close method on an open database connection or file handle. In most cases it is possible for applications to create classes that do not risk keeping these handles open. However, certain requirements can even with the best object design create a risk that a key resource will not be cleaned up correctly. In such an event, there are two occasions where the object could attempt to perform this cleanup: when the final reference to the object is released and immediately before the GC destroys the object.

One option is to implement the IDisposable interface. When implemented, this interface is used to ensure that persistent resources are released. This is the preferred method for releasing resources and is discussed further in Chapter 5. The second option is to add a method to your class that the system will run immediately before an object is destroyed.

The Finalize Method

Conceptually, the GC calls an `Object`'s `Finalize` method immediately before it collects an object that is no longer referenced by the application. Classes can override the `Finalize` method to perform any necessary cleanup. The basic concept is to create a method that acts as what is in other object-oriented languages referred to as a destructor. Similarly, the `Class_Terminate` available in the previous versions of Visual Basic does not have a functional equivalent in .NET. Instead, it is possible to create a Finalize method which will be recognized by the GC and that will prevent a class from being cleaned up until after the finalization method is completed. An example of the structure of the Finalize method is:

```
Protected Overrides Sub Finalize()
  ' clean up code goes here
  MyBase.Finalize()
End Sub
```

This code uses both Protected scope and the `Overrides` keyword — concepts that are discussed in detail in Chapter 6. For now, it's sufficient to know that these key-words are needed to create the `Finalize` method in a class. Notice that not only does custom cleanup code go here (as indicated by the comment), but this method also calls `MyBase.Finalize()`, which causes any finalization logic in the base class to be executed as well.

Be careful however, not to treat the `Finalize` method as if it were a destructor. A destructor is based on a deterministic system where the method is called when the object's last reference is removed. In the GC system there are key differences in how a finalizer works:

❑ The GC doesn't actually run Finalize methods. When the GC finds a Finalize method it queues the object up for the Finalizer to execute the object's method. This means that an object is not cleaned up during the current GC pass. Because of how the GC is optimized, this can result in the object remaining in memory for a much longer period.

❑ Since the GC is optimized to only clean up memory when necessary, there will be a delay between when the object is no longer referenced by the application and when the GC collects it. Because of this, the same expensive resources that are released in the `Finalize` method may stay open longer than they need to be.

❑ The GC will usually be triggered when the available memory is running low. As a result, execution of the object's `Finalize` method is likely to incur performance penalties. Therefore, the code in the `Finalize` method should be as short and quick as possible.

❑ There's no guarantee that a service you require is still available. For example, if the system is closing and you have a file open, .NET may have unloaded the various bits and pieces required to close the file.

All cleanup activities should be placed in the `Finalize` method. However, objects that require timely cleanup should implement either a `Dispose` method that can then be called by the client application just before setting the reference to `Nothing`. For example:

```
Class DemoDispose
   Private m_disposed As Boolean = False

   Public Sub Dispose()
      If (Not m_disposed) Then
         ' Call cleanup code in Finalize.
         Finalize()

         ' Record that object has been disposed.
         m_disposed = True

         ' Finalize does not need to be called.
         GC.SuppressFinalize(Me)
      End If
   End Sub

   Protected Overrides Sub Finalize()
      ' Perform cleanup here ...
   End Sub
End Class
```

The DemoDispose class overrides the Finalize method and implements the code to perform any necessary cleanup. This class places the actual cleanup code within the Finalize method. To ensure that the Dispose method only calls Finalize once, the value of the private m_disposed field is checked. Once Finalize has been run, this value is set to True. The class then calls GC.SuppressFinalize to ensure that the GC does not call the Finalize method on this object when the object is collected. If you need to implement a Finalize method, this is the preferred implementation pattern.

This example implements all of the object's cleanup code in the Finalize method to ensure that the object will be cleaned up properly before the GC collects it. The Finalize method still serves as a safety net in case the Dispose or Close methods were not called before the GC collects the object.

Faster Memory Allocation for Objects

The CLR introduces the concept of a managed heap. Objects are allocated on the managed heap and the CLR is responsible for controlling access to these objects in a type-safe manner. One of the advantages of the managed heap is that memory allocations on it are very efficient. When unmanaged code (such as VB6 or C++) allocates memory on the unmanaged heap, it typically scans through some sort of data structure in search of a free chunk of memory that is large enough to accommodate the allocation. The managed heap maintains a reference to the end of the most recent heap allocation. When a new object needs to be created on the heap, the CLR allocates memory on the top of memory that has previously been allocated and then increments the reference to the end of heap allocations accordingly. Figure 3-1 is a simplification of what takes place in the managed heap for .NET.

❏   State 1: Shows a compressed memory heap with a reference to the end point on the heap.

❏   State 2: Object B, although no longer referenced, remains in its current memory location. The memory has not been freed and does not alter the allocation of memory or of other objects on the heap.

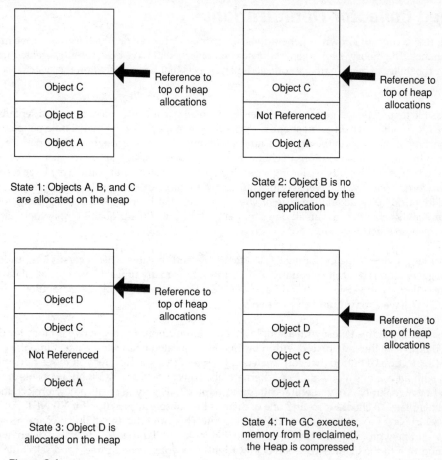

Figure 3-1

- ❑ State 3: Even though now there is a gap between the memory allocated for object A and object C, the memory allocation for D still occurs on the top of the heap. The unused fragment of memory on the managed heap is ignored at allocation time.

- ❑ State 4: After one or more allocations, before there is an allocation failure, the Garbage Collector runs. It reclaims the memory that was allocated to B and repositions the remaining valid objects. This compresses the active objects to the bottom of the heap creating more space for additional object allocations.

This is where the power of the GC really shines. Before the CLR is unable to allocate memory on the managed heap, the GC is invoked. The GC is responsible for collecting objects that are no longer referenced by the application and for compacting the heap. Thus, not only does the GC reclaim the memory associated with objects that are no longer referenced, it also compacts the remaining objects. The GC effectively squeezes out all of the spaces between the remaining objects, freeing up another large managed heap for new object allocations.

Garbage Collector Optimizations

The GC uses a concept known as generations, the primary purpose of which is to improve its performance. The theory behind generations is that objects that have been recently created tend to have a higher probability of being garbage collected than objects that have existed on the system for a longer time.

It is possible to understand generations in terms of a mall parking lot where cars represent objects created by the CLR. People have different shopping patterns when they visit the mall. Some people will spend a good portion of their day in the mall and others will only stop long enough to pick up an item or two. Applying the theory of generations in trying to find an empty parking space for a car yields a situation where the highest probability of finding a parking space is a place where other cars have recently parked. In other words, spaces which were occupied recently are more likely to be held by someone who just needed to quickly pick up an item or two. The longer a car has been parked in the parking lot, the higher is the probability that they are an all-day shopper and the lower the probability that their parking space will be freed up any time soon.

Generations provides a means for the GC to identify recently created objects versus long-lived objects. An object's generation is basically a counter that indicates how many times it has successfully avoided garbage collection. In versions 1.0 and 1.1 of the .NET Framework, an object's generation counter starts at zero and can have a maximum value of two.

It is possible to put this to test with a simple VB.NET application. There are two options for this simple code, you can take the code placed within the Sub Main located below and paste it into the event handler for the `Hello World` button that you created in Chapter 2. This will allow you to see how this code works, without creating a new project. Alternatively, you can add a new VB.NET console application project to your solution. As you will recall from Chapter 2, when you create a new project, there are several templates to choose from and one of them is the console application for VB.NET. From the File menu, select New Project from the Add Project menu. This will open the dialog box and after you have created your new project you will have a frame that looks similar to the code below. Then, within the Main module add the highlighted code below. Right-click your second project and select the "Set as Startup Project" option so that when you run your solution your new project is automatically started.

```
Module Module1

    Sub Main()
      Dim myObject As Object = New Object()
      Dim i As Integer

        For i = 0 To 3
          Console.WriteLine(String.Format("Generation = {0}", _
                            GC.GetGeneration(myObject)))
          GC.Collect()
          GC.WaitForPendingFinalizers()
      Next i
    End Sub


End Module
```

Regardless of the project you use, this code sends its output to the .NET console. For a Windows application, this console defaults to the VS.NET Output Window. When you run this code it creates an instance of an object and then iterates through a loop four times. For each loop, it displays the current generation count of myObject and then calls the GC. The `GC.WaitForPendingFinalizers` method blocks execution until the garbage collection has been completed.

As shown in Figure 3-2, each time the GC was run the generation counter was incremented for myObject, up to a maximum of 2.

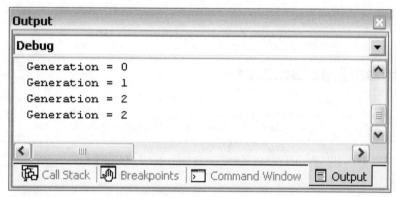

Figure 3-2

Each time the GC is run, the managed heap is compacted and the reference to the end of the most recent memory allocation is updated. After compaction, objects of the same generation will be grouped together. Generation two objects will be grouped at the bottom of the managed heap and generation one objects will be grouped next. Since new generation zero objects are placed on top of the existing allocations, they will be grouped together as well.

This is significant because recently allocated objects have a higher probability of having shorter lives. Since objects on the managed heap are ordered according to generations, the GC can opt to collect newer objects. Running the GC over a limited portion of the heap will be quicker than running it over the entire managed heap.

It's also possible to invoke the GC with an overloaded version of the `Collect` method that accepts a generation number. The GC will then collect all objects no longer referenced by the application that belong to the specified (or younger) generation. The version of the `Collect` method that accepts no parameters collects objects that belong to all generations.

Another hidden GC optimization is that a reference to an object may implicitly go out of scope and can therefore be collected by the GC. It is difficult to illustrate how the optimization occurs only if there are no additional references to the object, and the object does not have a Finalizer. However, if an object is declared and used at the top of a module and then not referenced again in a method, then in the release mode the metadata will indicate that the variable is not referenced in the later portion of the code. Once the last reference to the object is made its logical scope ends, and if the Garbage Collector runs, the memory for that object which will no longer be referenced can be reclaimed before it has gone out of its physical scope.

Cross-Language Integration

In the previous versions of Visual Basic, interoperating with the code written in other languages was challenging. There were pretty much two options for reusing functionality developed in other languages: COM interfaces or DLLs with exported C functions. As for exposing functionality written in Visual Basic, the only option was to create COM interfaces.

Since VB.NET is built on top of the CLR, it's able to interoperate with the code written in other .NET languages. It's even able to derive from a class written in another language. In order to support this type of functionality, the CLR relies on a common way of representing types, as well as rich metadata that can describe these types.

The Common Type System

Each programming language seems to bring its own island of data types with it. For example, previous versions of Visual Basic represent strings using the BSTR struct (which is the internal representation of the VB String data type), C++ offers char and wchar data types, and MFC offers the CString class. And the fact that the C++ int data type is a 32-bit value whereas the VB6 Integer data type is a 16-bit value makes it difficult to pass parameters between applications written using different languages.

To help resolve this problem, C has become the lowest common denominator for interfacing between programs written in multiple languages. An exported function written in C that exposes simple C data types can be consumed by Visual Basic, Java, Delphi, and a variety of other programming languages. In fact, the Windows API is exposed as a set of C functions.

Unfortunately, in order to access a C interface, you must explicitly map C data types to a language's native data types. For example, a VB developer would use the following statement to map the GetUserNameA Win32 function (GetUserNameA is the ANSI version of the GetUserName function):

```
' Map GetUserName to the GetUserNameA exported function
' exported by advapi32.dll.
'    BOOL GetUserName(
'       LPTSTR lpBuffer, // name buffer
'       LPDWORD nSize    // size of name buffer
'    );
Public Declare Function GetUserName Lib "advapi32.dll" _
Alias "GetUserNameA" (ByVal strBuffer As String, nSize As Long) As Long
```

This code explicitly mapped the lpBuffer C character array data type to the strBuffer VB String parameter. This is not only cumbersome, but also error prone. Accidentally mapping a variable declared as Long to lpBuffer wouldn't generate any compilation errors. However, calling the function would more than likely result in a difficult to diagnose, intermittent access violation at runtime.

COM provides a more refined method of interoperation between languages. Visual Basic introduced a Common Type System (CTS) for all languages that supported COM — variant compatible data types. However, variant data types are as cumbersome to work with for non-VB developers as the underlying C data structures that make up the variant data types (such as BSTR and SAFEARRAY) for VB developers. The result is that interfacing between unmanaged languages is still more complicated than it needs to be.

The CTS provides a set of common data types for use across all programming languages. The CTS provides every language running on top of the .NET platform with a base set of types, as well as mechanisms for extending those types. These types may be implemented as Classes or as Structs, but in either case they are derived from a common `System.Object` class definition.

Since every type supported by the CTS is derived from `System.Object`, every type supports a common set of methods.

Method	Description
`Boolean Equals(`*Object*`)`	Used to test equality with another object. Reference types should return `True` if the *Object* parameter references the same object. Value types should return `True` if the *Object* parameter has the same value. (Reference and value types will be discussed in Chapter 4.)
`Int32 GetHashCode()`	Generates a number corresponding to the value of an object. If two objects of the same type are equal, then they must return the same hash code.
`Type GetType()`	Gets a `Type` object that can be used to access metadata associated with the type. It also serves as a starting point for navigating the object hierarchy exposed by the Reflection API (which we'll discuss shortly).
`String ToString()`	The default implementation returns the fully qualified name of the class of the object. This method is often overridden to output data that is more meaningful to the type. For example, all base types return their value as a string.

Metadata

Metadata is the information that enables components to be self describing. Metadata is used to describe many aspects of a .NET component including classes, methods and fields, and the assembly itself. Metadata is used by the CLR to facilitate all sorts of things, such as validating an assembly before it is executed or performing garbage collection while managed code is being executed.

VB developers have used metadata for years while developing and using components within their applications.

❑ VB developers use metadata to instruct the VB runtime on how to behave. For example, you can set the Unattended Execution property to determine whether unhandled exceptions are shown on the screen in a message box or are written to the Event Log.

❑ COM components refered within VB applications have accompanying type libraries that contain metadata about the components, their methods, and their properties. You can use the Object Browser to view this information. (The information contained within the type library is what is used to drive IntelliSense.)

❑ Additional metadata can be associated with a component by installing it within COM+. Metadata stored in COM+ is used to declare the support a component needs at runtime, including transactional support, serialization support, and object pooling.

Better Support for Metadata

Metadata associated with a VB6 component was scattered in multiple locations and stored using multiple formats:

❑ Metadata instructing the VB runtime how to behave (such as the Unattended Execution property) is compiled into the VB generated executable

❑ Basic COM attributes (such as the required threading model) are stored in the registry

❑ COM+ attributes (such as the transactional support required) are stored in the COM+ catalog

.NET refines the use of metadata within applications in three significant ways:

❑ .NET consolidates the metadata associated with a component

❑ Since a .NET component does not have to be registered, installing and upgrading the component is easier and less problematic

❑ .NET makes a much clearer distinction between attributes that should only be set at compile time and those that can be modified at runtime

> **All attributes associated with VB.NET components are represented in a common format and consolidated within the files that make up the assembly.**

Since much of a COM/COM+ component's metadata is stored separately from the executable, installing and upgrading components can be problematic. COM/COM+ components must be registered to update the registry/COM+ catalog before they can be used and the COM/COM+ component executable can be upgraded without upgrading its associated metadata.

The process of installing and upgrading a .NET component is greatly simplified. Since all metadata associated with a .NET component must reside within the file that contains the component, no registration is required. Once a new component is copied into an application's directory, it can be used immediately. Since the component and its associated metadata cannot get out of sync, upgrading the component becomes much less problematic.

Another problem with COM+ is that attributes that should only be set at compile time may be reconfigured at runtime. For example, COM+ can provide serialization support for neutral components. A component that does not require serialization must be designed to accommodate multiple requests from multiple clients simultaneously. You should know at compile time whether or not a component requires support for serialization from the runtime. However, under COM+, the attribute describing whether or not client requests should be serialized can be altered at runtime.

.NET makes a much better distinction between attributes that should be set at compile time versus those that should be set at runtime. For example, whether a .NET component is serializable is determined at compile time. This setting cannot be overridden at runtime.

Attributes

Attributes are used to decorate entities such as assemblies, classes, methods, and properties with additional information. Attributes can be used for a variety of purposes. It can provide information, request a certain behavior at runtime, or even invoke a particular behavior from another application. An example of this can be shown by using the Demo class defined in the following code block:

```
Module Module1

  <Serializable()> Public Class Demo

    <Obsolete("Use Method2 instead.")> Public Sub Method1()
      ' Old implementation ...
    End Sub

    Public Sub Method2()
      ' New implementation ...
    End Sub

  End Class

  Public Sub Main()
    Dim d As Demo = New Demo()
    d.Method1()
  End Sub
End Module
```

The sample class can be added to the Form1 file that you created as part of your sample application in Chapter 2. Then you can add the two lines which will create an instance of this class and call Method1 to your event handler for your Hello World button.

The first attribute on the Demo class marks the class with the Serializable attribute. The base class library will provide serialization support, for instances, of the Demo type. For example, the ResourceWriter type can be used to stream an instance of the Demo type to disk.

The second attribute is associated with Method1. Method1 has been marked as obsolete, but has not been made unavailable. When a method is marked as obsolete there are two options, one is that Visual Studio should prevent applications from compiling. However, a better strategy for large applications is to first mark a method or class as obsolete and then prevent its use in the next release. The code shown above will cause VS.NET to display an IntelliSense warning if Method1 is referenced within the application, as shown in Figure 3-3. As you can see, not only does the line with Method1 have a visual hint of the issue, but a task has been automatically added to the Task window.

If the developer leaves this code unchanged and then compiles, the application will compile correctly. As you see in Figure 3-4, the compilation is complete, but the developer is given a warning with a meaningful message that they need to change this code to use the correct method.

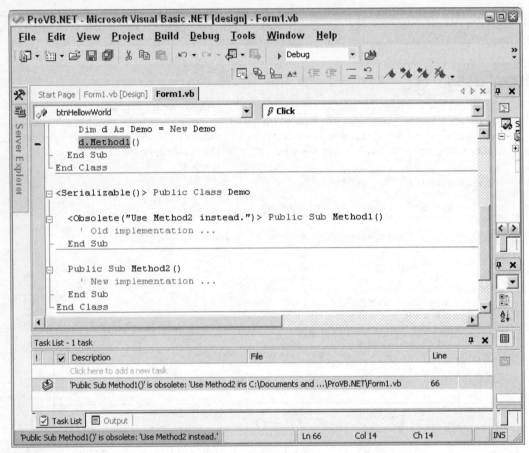

Figure 3-3

There are also times when you might need to associate multiple attributes with an entity. The following code shows an example of using both of the attributes from the previous code at the class level. Note that in this case the Obsolete attribute has been modified to cause a compilation error by setting its second parameter to True:

```
<Serializable(), Obsolete("No longer used.", True)> Public Class Demo
    ' Implementation ...
End Class
```

Attributes play an important role in the development of .NET applications, particularly XML Web services. As you'll see in Chapter 22, the declaration of a class as a Web service and of particular methods as Web methods is all handled through the use of attributes.

The Reflection API

The .NET Framework provides the Reflection API for accessing metadata associated with managed code. You can use the Reflection API to examine the metadata associated with an assembly and its types, and even to examine the currently executing assembly.

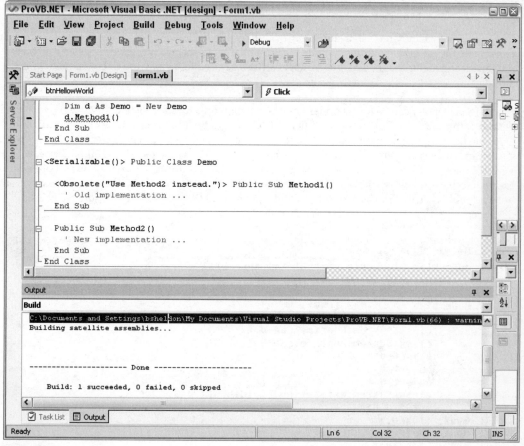

```
Dim d As Demo = New Demo
    d.Method1()
    End Sub
End Class

<Serializable()> Public Class Demo

    <Obsolete("Use Method2 instead.")> Public Sub Method1()
        ' Old implementation ...
    End Sub

    Public Sub Method2()
        ' New implementation ...
    End Sub
End Class
```

Figure 3-4

The `Assembly` class in the `System.Reflection` namespace can be used to access the metadata in an assembly. The `LoadFrom` method can be used to load an assembly and the `GetExecutingAssembly` method can be used to access the currently executing assembly. The `GetTypes` method can then be used to obtain the collection of types defined in the assembly.

It's also possible to access the metadata of a type directly from an instance of that type. Since every object derives from `System.Object`, every object supports the `GetType` method, which returns a `Type` object that can be used to access the metadata associated with the type.

The `Type` object exposes many methods and properties for obtaining the metadata associated with a type. For example, you can obtain a collection of properties, methods, fields, and events exposed by the type by calling the `GetMembers` method. The `Type` object for the object's base type can also be obtained by calling the `DeclaringType` property.

> A good tool that demonstrates the power of Reflection is Lutz Roeder's Reflector for .NET. Check out **www.aisto.com/roeder/dotnet/**.

IL Disassembler

One of the many handy tools that ships with VS.NET is the *IL Disassembler* (ildasm.exe). It can be used to navigate the metadata within a module including the types the module exposes, as well as their properties and methods. The IL Disassembler can also be used to display the IL contained within a module.

The IL Disassembler can be found under your installation directory for Visual Studio 2003, with the default path being: "C:\Program Files\Microsoft Visual Studio .NET 2003\SDK\v1.1\Bin\ILDasm.exe." Once the IL Disassembler has been started, select File and then Open. Open mscorlib.dll, which is located in your system directory under the default path of "C:\Windows\Microsoft.NET\Framework\ V1.1.4322\mscorlib.dll". Once mscorlib.dll has been loaded ILDasm will display a set of folders for each namespace in this assembly. Expand the System namespace, then the ValueType namespace, and finally double-click the Equals method. A window similar to the one shown in Figure 3-5 will be displayed.

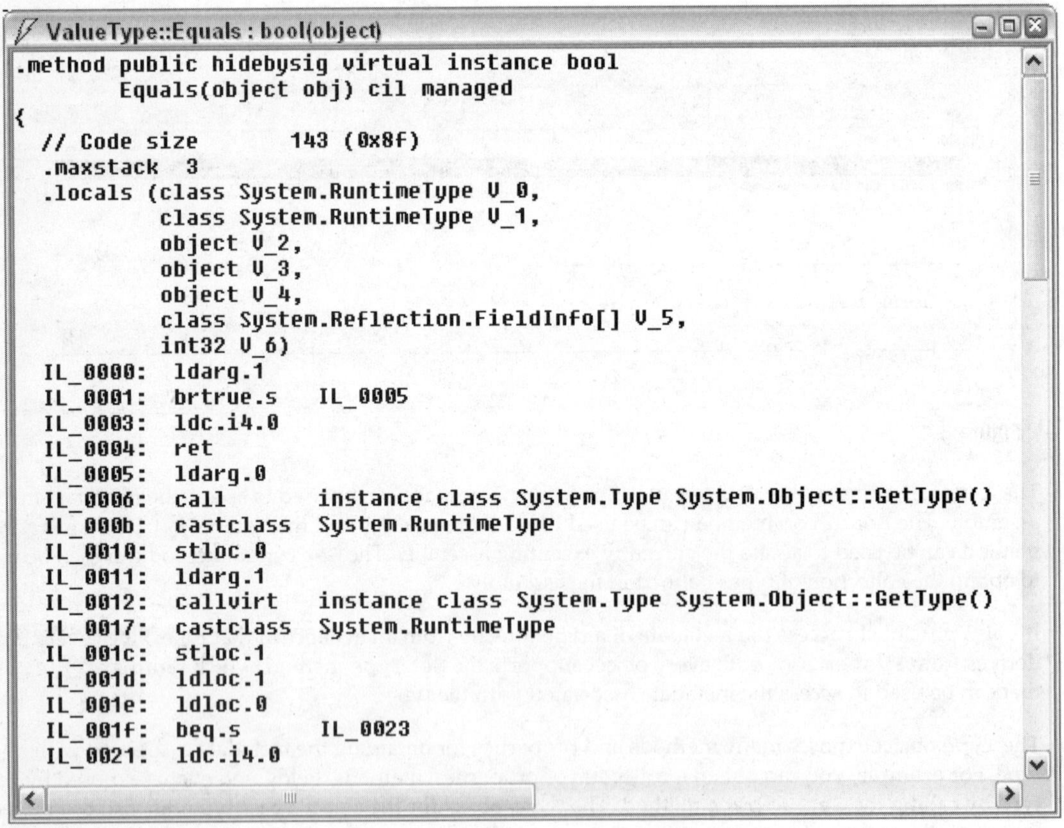

```
ValueType::Equals : bool(object)
.method public hidebysig virtual instance bool
        Equals(object obj) cil managed
{
  // Code size       143 (0x8f)
  .maxstack  3
  .locals (class System.RuntimeType V_0,
           class System.RuntimeType V_1,
           object V_2,
           object V_3,
           object V_4,
           class System.Reflection.FieldInfo[] V_5,
           int32 V_6)
  IL_0000:  ldarg.1
  IL_0001:  brtrue.s   IL_0005
  IL_0003:  ldc.i4.0
  IL_0004:  ret
  IL_0005:  ldarg.0
  IL_0006:  call       instance class System.Type System.Object::GetType()
  IL_000b:  castclass  System.RuntimeType
  IL_0010:  stloc.0
  IL_0011:  ldarg.1
  IL_0012:  callvirt   instance class System.Type System.Object::GetType()
  IL_0017:  castclass  System.RuntimeType
  IL_001c:  stloc.1
  IL_001d:  ldloc.1
  IL_001e:  ldloc.0
  IL_001f:  beq.s      IL_0023
  IL_0021:  ldc.i4.0
```

Figure 3-5

Figure 3-5 shows the IL for the Equals method. Notice how the Reflection API is used to navigate through the instance of the value type's fields in order to determine if the values of the two objects being compared are equal.

The IL Disassembler is a very useful tool for learning how a particular module is implemented, but on the other hand, it could jeopardize your company's proprietary logic. After all, what is to prevent someone from using it to reverse engineer your code. The answer is that VS.NET 2003 ships with a third party tool called an obfuscator. The role of the obfuscator is to make it so that the IL Disassembler cannot build a meaningful representation of your application logic.

It is beyond the scope of this chapter to completely cover the obfuscator that ships with VS.NET 2003. However, in order to access this tool, you go to the Tools menu and select the Dotfuscator Community Edition menu item to start the obfuscator. The obfuscator runs against your compiled application taking your IL file and stripping out many of the items that are embedded by default during the compilation process.

Summary

This chapter introduced the CLR and compared and contrasted it with the VB6 runtime. It discussed the memory management features of the CLR and how they compare to the VB6 runtime, including how the CLR eliminates the circular reference problem that has plagued VB6 developers. Next, the chapter examined the `Finalize` method and understood why it should not be treated like the `Class_Terminate` method. Specifically, topics covered in this chapter include:

❑   Whenever possible, do not implement the `Finalize` method in a class.

❑   If the `Finalize` method is used to perform necessary cleanup, make the code for the `Finalize` method as short and quick as possible.

❑   There is no way to accurately predict when the GC will collect an object that is no longer referenced by the application (unless the GC is invoked explicitly).

❑   If the `Finalize` method is implemented, also implement either a `Dispose` or a `Close` method that can be called by the client when the object is no longer needed.

❑   The order in which the GC collects objects on the managed heap is nondeterministic. This means that the `Finalize` method should not call methods on other objects referenced by the object being collected.

This chapter also examined the value of a common runtime and type system that can be targeted by multiple languages. The chapter then looked at how the CLR offers better support for metadata. Metadata is used to make types "self describing", and is used for language elements such as attributes. There were examples of how metadata is used by the CLR and the .NET Class Library and the chapter showed you how to extend metadata by creating your own attributes. Finally, there was a brief review of the Reflection API and the IL Disassembler utility (`ildasm.exe`) which can display the IL contained within a module.

Variables and Type

The previous chapter introduced the Common Type System, which provides a common set of types across .NET languages. This chapter will examine exactly what these types are and how to use them.

Experienced developers generally consider integers, characters, Booleans, and strings to be the basic building blocks of any language. In .NET, all objects share a logical inheritance from the base `Object` class. The advantage of this common heritage is the ability to rely on certain common methods of every variable. However, this logical inheritance does not require a common physical implementation for all variables. For example, what most programmers see as some of the basic underlying types, such as `Integer`, `Long`, `Character`, and even `Byte`, are not implemented as classes. Instead .NET has a base type of object and then allows simple structures to inherit from this base class. While everything in .NET is based on the `Object` class, under the covers .NET has two major variable types, value and reference.

❑ Value types represent simple data storage located on the stack. They are what VB6 (Visual Basic 6) developers would often refer to as datatypes.

❑ Reference types are based complex classes with implementation inheritance from their parent classes, and custom storage on the managed heap.

Value and reference types are treated differently within assignment statements, and their memory management is handled differently. It is important to understand how theses differences affect the software you will write in Visual Basic .NET (VB.NET). Understanding the foundations of how data is manipulated in the .NET Framework will enable you to build more reliable and better performing applications.

The main goal of this chapter is to get familiar with value and reference types and to understand some of the key differences in how variables are defined in VB.NET as compared with VB6. The chapter begins by looking at value types, followed by a clear definition of a logical grouping called primitive types. It then examines classes, how they work, and how some of the basic classes are used. Specifically, this chapter covers:

- Value vs. reference types
- Value types (structures)
- Primitive types
- Reference types (classes)
- Explicit conversions
- `Option Strict` and `Option Explicit`
- Parameter passing `ByVal` and `ByRef`
- Boxing
- Retired keywords and functions

Differences of Value and Reference Types

When you start looking into the .NET Framework's underlying type systems, you'll often hear a conflicting set of statements. On the one hand you are told that all types inherit from the `Object` class, and on the other hand you are told to beware when transitioning between value types and reference types. The key is that while every type, whether it is a built-in structure such as an integer or string or a custom class such as `MyEmployee`, does in fact inherit from the `Object` class. The difference between value and reference types is an underlying implementation difference.

The difference between value types and reference types is an excellent place to start, because it is a relatively simple difference. More important, as a .NET developer you generally don't need to be concerned with this difference, except in certain performance-related situations. Value and reference types behave differently when data is assigned to them:

- When data is assigned to a value type the actual data is stored in the variable on the stack.
- When data is assigned to a reference type only a reference is stored in the variable. The actual data is stored on the managed heap.

It is important to understand the difference between the stack and the heap. The stack is a comparatively small memory area in which processes and threads store data of fixed size. An integer or decimal value will need the same number of bytes to store their data, regardless of their actual value. This means that the location of such variables on the stack can be efficiently determined. (When a process needs to retrieve a variable it has to search the stack. If the stack contained variables that had dynamic memory sizes, such a search could take a long time.)

Reference types do not have a fixed size. For example, a string could vary in size from 2 bytes to close to all the memory available on a system. The dynamic size of reference types means that the data they contain is stored on the heap rather than the stack. However, the address of the reference type (that is, the location of the data on the heap) does have a fixed size, and so can be stored on the stack. By only storing a reference on the stack, the program as a whole runs much quicker since the process can quickly locate the data associated with a variable.

Storing the data contained in fixed and dynamically sized variables in different places results in differences in the way that variables behave. This can be illustrated by comparing the behavior of the

`System.Drawing.Point` structure (a value type) and the `System.Text.StringBuilder` class (a reference type).

The Point structure is used as part of the .NET graphics library that is part of the `System.Drawing` namespace. The `StringBuilder` class is part of the `System.Text` namespace and is used to improve performance when we're editing strings. Namespaces are covered in detail in Chapter 8.

First, here is an example of how the `System.Drawing.Point` structure is used:

```
Dim ptX As New System.Drawing.Point(10, 20)
Dim ptY As New System.Drawing.Point

ptY = ptX
ptX.X = 200

Console.WriteLine(ptY.ToString())
```

The output from this operation will be $\{X = 10, Y = 20\}$, which seems logical. When the code copies `ptX` into `ptY`, the data contained in `ptX` is copied into the location on the stack that is associated with `ptY`. When later the value of `ptX` is changed, only the memory on the stack that is associated with `ptX` is altered. Altering the value of `ptX` had no effect on `ptY`. This is not the case with reference types. Consider the following code, which uses the `System.Text.StringBuilder` class:

```
Dim objX As New System.Text.StringBuilder("Hello World")
Dim objY As System.Text.StringBuilder

objY = objX
objX.Replace("World", "Test")

Console.WriteLine(objY.ToString())
```

The output from this operation will be "Hello Test", not "Hello World". The previous example using points demonstrated that when one value type is assigned to another, the data stored on the stack is copied. Similarly, this example demonstrates that when `objY` is assigned to `objX`, the data associated with `objX` on the stack is copied to the data associated with `objY` on the stack. However, what is copied in this case isn't the actual data, but rather the address on the managed heap where the data is actually located. This means that `objY` and `objX` now reference the same data. When the data on the heap is changed, the data associated with every variable that holds a reference to that memory is changed. This is the default behavior of reference types and is known as a shallow copy. Later in this chapter, we'll see how this behavior has been overridden for strings (which perform a deep copy).

The differences between value types and reference types go beyond how they behave when copied, and we'll encounter some of the other features provided by objects later in this chapter. First though, we're going to take a closer look at some of the most commonly used value types, and understand how .NET works with them.

Value Types (Structures)

Value types aren't as versatile as reference types, but they can provide better performance in many circumstances. The core value types (which include the majority of primitive types) are `Boolean`, `Byte`,

`Char`, `DateTime`, `Decimal`, `Double`, `Guid`, `Int16`, `Int32`, `Int64`, `SByte`, `Single`, and `TimeSpan`. These are not the only value types, but rather the subset with which most VB.NET developers will consistently work. As we've seen, by definition value types store data on the stack.

Value types can also be referred to by their proper name: Structures. Previous versions of Visual Basic supported the userdefined type (UDT). The UDT framework has been replaced by the ability to create custom structures. The underlying principles and syntax of creating custom structures mirrors that of creating classes, which we will cover in the next chapter. This section is going to focus on some of the built-in types that are provided by the .NET Framework, and in particular, a special group of these built-in types known as primitives.

Primitive Types

VB.NET, in common with other development languages, has a group of elements such as integers and strings that are termed primitive types. These primitive types are identified by keywords like `String`, `Long`, and `Integer`, which are aliases for types defined by the .NET class library. This means the line

```
Dim i As Long
```

is equivalent to the line

```
Dim i As System.Int64
```

The following table lists the primitive types that VB.NET defines and the structures or classes that they map to.

Primitive Type	.NET Class or Structure
Byte	System.Byte (structure)
Short	System.Int16 (structure)
Integer	System.Int32 (structure)
Long	System.Int64 (structure)
Single	System.Single (structure)
Double	System.Double (structure)
Decimal	System.Decimal (structure)
Boolean	System.Boolean (structure)
Date	System.DateTime (structure)
Char	System.Char (structure)
String	System.String (class)

> The `string` primitive type stands out from the other primitives. Strings are implemented as a class, not a structure. Strings are the one primitive type that is a reference type.

There are certain operations you can perform on primitive types that you cannot perform on other types. For example, you can assign a value to a primitive type using a literal:

```
Dim i As Integer = 32
Dim str As String = "Hello"
```

It is also possible to declare primitive types as constant using the `Const` keyword. For example,

```
Dim Const str As String = "Hello"
```

The value of the variable `str` in the line of code above cannot be changed elsewhere in the application containing this code at runtime. These two simple examples illustrate the key properties of primitive types. As noted, most primitive types are in fact value types. So the next step is to take a look at the specific behavior of some of the common value types in VB.NET.

Boolean

The .NET `Boolean` type has been implemented with three values, two for `True`, and one for `False`. Two `True` values have been implemented for backward compatibility because, in contrast to most languages (in which Boolean `True` equates to 1), Visual Basic converts a value of `True` to –1. This is one of the few (but not the only) legacy carry-over from VB6. The reason this was done was to save developers from needing to examine every Boolean expression to ensure valid return values. Of course, at the lowest level all .NET languages operate on the basis that 0 is `False` and a nonzero value will be converted to `True`. Of course, VB.NET works as part of a multilanguage environment, with metadata-defining interfaces. Fortunately, Microsoft implemented VB.NET such that while –1 is supported within VB.NET, the .NET standard of 1 is exposed from VB.NET methods to other languages.

Of course, this compromise involves making some decisions that add complexity to `True` or `False` evaluations. While a `True` value in a Boolean expression equates to –1, if converted to any other format, it equates to 1. This is best illustrated by some sample VB.NET code. Keep in mind though that this code follows poor programming practice as it references Boolean values as integers (and does so with implicit conversions):

```
Dim blnTrue As Boolean = True
Dim blnOne As Boolean = 1
Dim blnNegOne As Boolean = -1
Dim blnFalse As Boolean = False
```

The following condition, which is based on the implicit conversion of the `Boolean`, works even though the `blnOne` variable was originally assigned a value of 1.

```
If blnOne = -1 Then
    Console.WriteLine(blnTrue)
    Console.WriteLine(blnOne.ToString)
    Console.WriteLine(Convert.ToString(Convert.ToInt32(blnNegOne)))
End If
```

The key is that implicit conversions such as the one in the preceding example work differently from explicit conversions. If you add sample code to explicitly convert the value of a `Boolean` type to an `Integer` type, and then test the result, the integer will be a positive 1. The implicit and explicit conversion of Boolean values is not consistent in VB.NET. Converting blnNegOne to an integer results in a positive value, regardless of what was originally assigned.

```
If Convert.ToInt16(blnNegOne) = 1 Then
    Console.WriteLine(blnFalse)
    Console.WriteLine(Convert.ToString(Convert.ToInt32(blnFalse)))
End If
```

This code will not compile if you are using `Option Strict` (more on this later) but it is a good illustration of what you should expect when casting implicitly rather than explicitly. The output from this code is shown in Figure 4-1.

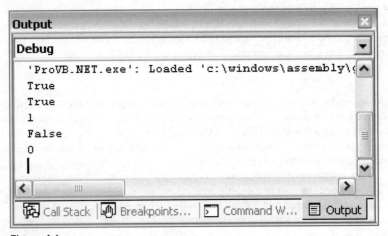

Figure 4-1

Figure 4-1 illustrates the output when the two preceding conditionals are run as part of a test program such as the ProVB.NET sample you created in Chapter 2. The first conditional expression demonstrates that if casting is performed between a Boolean and an integer value then, regardless of how a Boolean in VB.NET is initialized, `True` is implicitly evaluated as −1. The three write statements associated with this display the string representation (`True`) of a Boolean, both implicitly and explicitly, as well as the explicitly converted value.

The second conditional expression performs an explicit cast from a Boolean to an integer value. Since this condition succeeds, it demonstrates that the conversion results in a value of 1. Behind the scenes, the reason for this is that the code used to do the explicit cast is part of the .NET Framework and, in the framework the value of `True` is 1. The result is that the code displays the string and converted values for a Boolean `False`.

This demonstrates the risk involved in relying on implicitly converted values. If at some point the default value associated with `True` were to change, this code would execute differently. The difference between an explicit and implicit conversion is subtle, and there are two steps to take in order to avoid difficulty:

❑   Always use the `True` and `False` constants in code.

❑   If there is any doubt as to how the return value from a method will be handled, it should be assigned to a Boolean variable. That Boolean variable can then be used in conditional expressions.

The final area where this can be an issue is across languages. Now you need to consider the behavior of a referenced component within your VB.NET code. You can look at a hypothetical class called `MyCSharpClass` that might have a single method `TestTrue()`. The method doesn't need any parameters, it simply returns a Boolean which is always `True`.

From your VB.NET example you can create an instance of `MyCSharpClass` and make calls to the `TestTrue()` method:

```
Dim objMyClass as New MyCSharpClass.MyCSharpClass()

If objMyClass.TestTrue() = 1 Then
    Console.WriteLine("CSharp uses a 1 for true but does it" & _
                " implicitly convert to a 1 in VB?")
Else
    Console.WriteLine("Even classes implemented in other .NET languages" & _
                " are evaluated implicitly as -1 in VB.NET")
End If

If objMyClass.TestTrue() = True Then
    Console.WriteLine("CSharp True always converts to Visual Basic True.")
End If
```

It's probably unclear if the first conditional in this code will ever work, after all, C# uses a value of 1 to represent `True`. However, this code is running in VB.NET, therefore the rules of VB.NET apply. Even when you return a Boolean from a .NET language that uses 1, not –1, to represent `True`, the VB.NET compiler will ensure that the value of `True` is implicitly interpreted as –1. Figure 4-2 illustrates that the behavior of the second conditional is both clear and safe from future modifications of the VB language. If VB.NET is modified at some future date to no longer use –1 to equate to `True`, statements that instead compare to the Boolean `True` will remain unaffected.

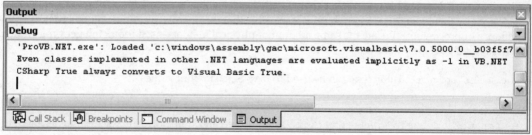

Figure 4-2

To create reusable code it is always better to avoid implicit conversions. In the case of Booleans, if the code needs to check for an integer value, you should explicitly evaluate the Boolean and create an appropriate integer — this code will be far more maintainable and prone to fewer unexpected results. Now that

Booleans have been covered in depth, the next step is to examine the integer types that are part of VB.NET.

The Integer Types

In VB6, there were two types of integer values: the Integer type was limited to a maximum value of 32767 and the Long type supported a maximum value of 2147483647. The .NET Framework adds a new integer type, the Short. The Short is the equivalent of the Integer value from VB6, the integer has been promoted to support the range previously supported by the Long type, and the Long type is bigger than ever. In addition, each of these types also has two alternative types. In all, VB.NET supports nine integer types.

Type	Allocated Memory	Minimum Value	Maximum Value
Short	2 bytes	−32768	32767
Int16	2 bytes	−32768	32767
UInt16	2 bytes	0	65535
Integer	4 bytes	−2147483648	2147483647
Int32	4 bytes	−2147483648	2147483647
UInt32	4 bytes	0	4294967295
Long	8 bytes	−9223372036854775808	9223372036854775807
Int64	8 bytes	−9223372036854775808	9223372036854775807
UInt64	8 bytes	0	18446744073709551615

Short

A Short value is limited to the maximum value that can be stored in 2 bytes. This means there are 16 bits and that the value can range between −32768 and 32767. This limitation may or may not be based on the amount of memory physically associated with the value; it is a definition of what must occur in the .NET Framework. This is important, because there is no guarantee that the implementation will actually use less memory than using an integer value. It is possible that the operating system will, in order to optimize memory or processing, allocate the same amount of physical memory used for an integer type and then just limit the possible values.

The Short (or Int16) value type can be used to map SQL smallint values.

Integer

An Integer is defined as a value that can be safely stored and transported in 4 bytes (not as a 4-byte implementation). This gives the Integer and Int32 value types a range from −2147483648 to 2147483647. This range is more than adequate to handle most tasks.

The main reason to use an Int32 in place of an integer value is to ensure future portability with interfaces. For example, the Integer value in VB6 was limited to a 2-byte value, but is now a 4-byte value. In future 64-bit platforms, the Integer value will be an 8-byte value. Problems could occur if an interface used a 64-bit integer with an interface that expected a 32-bit integer value. The solution is to use `Int32`, which would remain a 32-bit value, even on a 64-bit platform.

The new `Integer` value type matches the size of an integer value in SQL Server, which means that you can easily align the column type of a table with the variable type in your programs.

Long

The `Long` type is aligned with the `Int64` value. `Long`'s have an 8-byte range, which means that their value can range from −9223372036854775808 to 9223372036854775807.

This is a big range, but if you need to add or multiply integer values then you will often need a large value to contain the result. It's common while doing math operations on one type of integer to use a larger type to capture the result if there's a chance that the result could exceed the limit of the types being manipulated.

The `Long` value type matches the bigint type in SQL.

Unsigned Types

Another way to gain additional range on the positive side of an integer type is to use one of the unsigned types. The unsigned types provide a useful buffer that will hold a result that might exceed an operation by a small amount, but that isn't the main reason they exist. The `UInt16` type happens to have the same characteristics as the `Character` type, while the `UInt32` type has the same characteristics as a system memory pointer on a 32-byte system. Be forewarned that on a 64-bit system this changes to the `UInt64` type. These types are used to interface with software that expects these values, and are the underlying implementation for other value types.

The Decimal Types

Just as there are a number of types to store integer values, there are three implementations of value types to store real number values. The `Single` and `Double` types work the same way in VB.NET as they did in VB6. The difference is the VB6 `Currency` type (which was a specialized version of a `Double` type) which is nowobsolete and a new `Decimal` value type takes its place for very large real numbers.

Type	Allocated Memory	Negative Range	Positive Range
Single	4 bytes	−3.402823E38 to −1.401298E-45	1.401298E-45 to 3.402823E38
Double	8 bytes	−1.79769313486231E308 to −4.94065645841247E-324	4.94065645841247E-324 to 1.79769313486232E308
Currency	Obsolete	—	—
Decimal	16 bytes	−79228162514264337593543950335 to 0.0000000000000000000000000001	0.000000000000000000000000001 to 79228162514264337593543950335

Single

The `Single` type contains 4 bytes of data and its precision can range anywhere from 1.401298E-45 to 3.402823E38 for positive values and from −3.402823E38 to −1.401298E-45 for negative values.

It can seem strange that a value which is stored using 4 bytes (the same as the `Integer` type) can store a number that is larger than even the `Long` type. This is possible because of the way the numbers are stored — a real number can be stored with different levels of precision. Notice that there are six digits after the decimal point in the definition of the `Single` type. When a real number gets very large, or very small, the stored value will contain fewer significant places.

For example, while it is possible to represent a `Long` with the value of 9223372036854775805, the `Single` type rounds this value to 9.223372E18. This seems like a reasonable action to take, but it isn't a reversible action. The following code demonstrates how this loss of data can result in errors:

```
Dim l As Long
Dim s As Single

l = Long.MaxValue
Console.WriteLine(l)

s = Convert.ToSingle(l)
s -= 1000000000000
l = Convert.ToInt64(s)

Console.WriteLine(l)
```

This code creates a `Long` that has the maximum value possible and outputs this value. Then it stores the value in a `Single`, subtracts 1000000000000, stores the value of the `Single` in the `Long`, and outputs the results, as seen in Figure 4-3, Notice that the results aren't consistent with what you might expect.

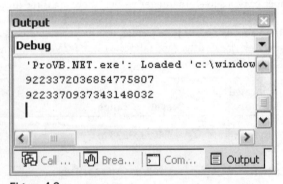

Figure 4-3

Double

The behavior of the previous example changes dramatically if you replace the value type of `Single` with `Double`. A `Double` uses 8 bytes to store values and as a result has a greater precision and range. The range for a `Double` is from 4.94065645841247E-324 to 1.79769313486232E308 for positive values and from −1.79769313486231E308 to −4.94065645841247E-324 for negative values. The precision has increased so that a number can contain 15 digits before the rounding begins. This greater level of precision makes the

Double value type a much more reliable variable for use in math operations. It's possible to represent most operations with complete accuracy with this value.

Double wasn't the only 8-byte decimal value in VB6. One of the other variable types, Currency, is now obsolete. The Currency type was a specialized version of the Double type, and was designed to support numbers using 19 available digits. While this was certainly better precision than the 15-digit precision available with the Double type, it pales in comparison to the new 28-digit Decimal type available in the .NET Framework.

Decimal

The Decimal type (new in VB.NET) is a hybrid that consists of a 12-byte integer value combined with two additional 16-bit values that control the location of the decimal point and sign of the overall value. A Decimal value will consume 16 bytes in total, and can store a maximum value of 79228162514264337593543950335. This value can then be manipulated by adjusting where the decimal place is located. For example, the maximum value while accounting for four decimal places is 7922816251426433759354395.0335. This is because a Decimal isn't stored as a traditional number, but is rather stored as a 12-byte integer value, and the location of the decimal in relation to the available 28 digits. This means that a Decimal does not inherently round numbers the way a Double does.

As a result of the way values are stored, the closest precision to zero that a Decimal supports is 0.0000000000000000000000000001. And as the location of the decimal point is stored separately, it also stores a value that indicates whether its value is positive or negative. This means that the positive and negative ranges are exactly the same, regardless of the number of decimal places.

Thus the system makes a tradeoff where the need to store a larger number of decimal places reduces the maximum value that can be kept at that level of precision. This tradeoff makes a lot of sense. After all, it's not often that you will need to store a number with 15 digits on both sides of the decimal point, and for those cases you can create a custom class that manages the logic and leverages one or more decimal values as its properties.

Char and Byte

The default character set under VB.NET is Unicode. So when a variable is declared as type Char it creates a 2-byte value, since, by default, all characters in the Unicode character set require 2 bytes. VB.NET supports the declaration of a character value in three ways. Placing a *c* following a literal string informs the compiler that the value should be treated as a character, or with the use of the Chr and ChrW methods. The following code snippet shows that all three of these options work similarly, with the difference between the Chr and ChrW methods being the range of valid input values that are available. The ChrW method allows for a broader range of values based on wide character input.

```
Dim chrLtr_a As Char = "a"c
Dim chrAsc_a As Char = Chr(97)
Dim chrAsc_b as Char = ChrW(98)
```

To convert characters into a string that was suitable for an ASCII interface, the runtime library would need to validate each character's value to ensure it is within a valid range. This could have a performance impact for certain serial arrays. Fortunately, VB.NET supports the Byte value type. This type contains a value between 0 and 255 that exactly matches the range of the ASCII character set. When interfacing with a system that uses ASCII it is best to use a Byte array. The runtime knows that there is no need to perform a Unicode to ASCII conversion for a `Byte` array, so the interface between the systems will operate significantly faster.

In VB.NET the `Byte` value type expects a numeric value. Thus, in order to assign the letter "a" to a `Byte`, you must use the appropriate character code. One option to get the numeric value of a letter is by using the `Asc` method, as shown in the following line of code:

```
Dim bytLtrA as Byte = Asc("a")
```

DateTime

The Visual Basic `Date` keyword has always supported a structure of both date and time. Under VB.NET, the Date structure has all of the same capabilities it had in VB6 but is now implemented as part of the DateTime structure. You can, in fact, declare data values using both the `DateTime` and `Date` types. Of note, internally VB.NET does not store date values as doubles, it provides key methods for converting the new internal date representation to the VB6 `Double` type. The `ToOADate` and `FromOADate` methods support backward compatibility during migration from previous versions of Visual Basic.

VB.NET also provides a set of shared methods which provide some common dates. The concept of shared methods is covered in more detail in the next chapter on Object Syntax, but, in short, shared methods are available even when you don't create an instance of a class. For the `DateTime` structure, the `Now()` method returns a Date value with the local date and time. This method has not been changed from VB6, but `Today()` and `UtcNow()` methods have also been added. These methods can be used to initialize a Date object with the current local date, or the date and time based on Universal Coordinated Time (also known as Greenwich Mean Time) respectively. You can use these shared methods to initialize your classes, as shown in the following code sample:

```
Dim dteNow as Date = Now()
Dim dteToday as Date = Today()
Dim dteGMT as DateTime = DateTime.UtcNow()
```

Explicit Conversions

So far this chapter has focused primarily on implicit conversions. With implicit conversions it is safe, for example, to assign the value of a smaller type into a larger type. For example, in the following code the value of a `Short` is assigned to a `Long`.

```
Dim shtShort As Short = 32767
Dim lnhLong As Long = shtShort
```

However, the reverse of this will result in a compilation error, since the compiler doesn't have any safe way of handling the assignment when the larger value is outside the range of the smaller value. It is still possible to cast a value from a larger type to a smaller type, as shown earlier in this chapter. Using the `CType` method it is possible to assign specific values. However, another of VB.NET's legacy carry-overs is the ability to implicitly cast across types that don't fit the traditional implicit casting boundaries.

The best way to understand how VB.NET has maintained this capability is to understand one of the new options in VB.NET. Under VB6 it was possible to define that a module should follow the rules defined by `Option Explicit`. This capability remains under VB.NET, but now `Option Explicit` is the default.

Similarly, VB.NET now provides a new option called `Option Strict`. It defines the support that your code should provide at compile time for implicit type conversions.

Option Strict, Option Explicit, and Option Compare

When `Option Strict` is turned on, the compiler must be able to determine the type of each variable. And if an assignment between two variables requires a type conversion—for example, from `Integer` to `Boolean`—the conversion between the two types must be expressed explicitly.

This setting can be edited in two ways. The first is by adding an `Option Strict` declaration to the top of your source code file. The statement will apply to all of the code entered in that source file, but only to the code in the file. The more consistent application of this setting is to edit the setting for an entire project, for which you need to open the Properties window of your project. You can access this screen by right-clicking the project in the Solution Explorer and selecting Properties from the context menu. The left-hand side of the resulting window contains a tree section that defaults to Common Properties. If you select the Build node you should see a window similar to the one shown in Figure 4-4.

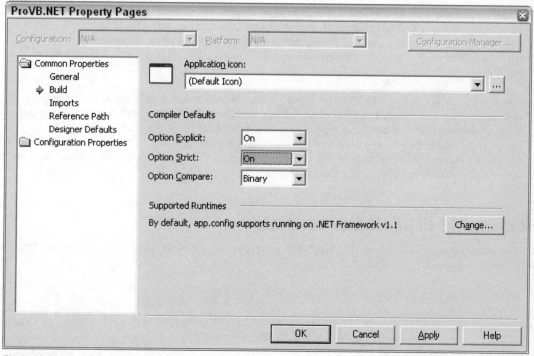

Figure 4-4

In addition to setting `Option Strict` on this screen it is possible to set two other project wide settings in this screen. These settings don't require detailed coverage but are mentioned here for completeness.

❑   `Option Explicit`—This option has not changed from VB6. When turned on it ensures that any variable name is declared. Of course, if you are using `Option Strict`, then this setting does not matter since the compiler would not recognize the type of an undeclared variable. There is, to my knowledge, no good reason to *ever* turn this option off.

❑ Option Compare — This option determines whether strings should be compared as binary strings or if the array of characters should be compared as text. In most cases leaving this as binary is appropriate. Doing a text comparison requires the system to convert the binary values that are stored internally prior to comparison. However, the advantage of a text-based comparison is that the character "A" is equal to "a" because the comparison is case-insensitive. This allows you to perform comparisons that don't require an explicit case conversion of the compared strings. In most cases, however, this conversion will still occur, so it's better to use binary comparison and explicitly convert case as required.

Most experienced developers agree that using Option Strict and being forced to recognize when type conversions are occurring is a good thing. Certainly, when developing software that will be deployed in a production environment, anything that can be done which will help prevent runtime errors is a good thing. However, Option Strict can slow the development of a program because you are forced to explicitly define each conversion that needs to occur. If you are developing a prototype or demo component that has a limited life you might find this option limiting.

If that were the end of the argument, then many developers would simply turn the option off — as it currently defaults — and forget about it. However, Option Strict has a runtime benefit. When type conversions are explicitly identified, the system does them faster. Implicit conversions require the runtime system to first identify the types involved in a conversion and then obtain the correct handler.

Another advantage of Option Strict is that during implementation developers are forced to consider that everywhere a conversion might occur. Perhaps the development team didn't realize that some of the assignment operations resulted in a type conversion. Setting up projects which require explicit conversions means that the resulting code tends to have type consistency to avoid conversions and thus reduce the number of conversions in the final code. The result is not only conversions that run faster, but hopefully a smaller number of conversions as well.

Performing Explicit Conversions

The following code is an example of how to convert between different integer types when Option Strict is enabled.

```
Dim shrShort As Short
Dim shrUInt16 As UInt16
Dim shrInt16 As Int16
Dim intInteger As Integer
Dim intUInt32 As UInt32
Dim intInt32 As Int32
Dim lngLong As Long
Dim lngInt64 As Int64

shrShort = 0
shrUInt16 = Convert.ToUInt16(shrShort)
shrInt16 = shrShort
intUInt32 = Convert.ToUInt32(shrShort)
```

```
intInt32 = shrShort
lngInt64 = shrShort

lngLong = lngLong.MaxValue
If lngLong < Short.MaxValue Then
  shrShort = Convert.ToInt16(lngLong)
End If
intInteger = CInt(lngLong)
```

The preceding snippet provides some excellent examples of what might not be intuitive behavior. The first thing to note is that you can't implicitly cast from Short to UInt16, or any of the other unsigned types for that matter. That is because with Option Strict the compiler will not allow an implicit conversion that might result in a value out of range or in loss of data. Your first thought is that an unsigned Short has a maximum that is twice the maximum of a signed Short, but in this case, if the variable shrShort contained a -1 then the value wouldn't be in the allowable range for an unsigned type.

The second item illustrated in this code is the shared method MaxValue. All of the integer and decimal types have this method. As the name indicates, it returns the maximum value for the specified type. There is a matching MinValue method for getting the minimum value. As shared methods, the methods can be called on either an instance of the class (LngLong.MaxValue) or by referencing the class (Short.MaxValue).

One fact that isn't apparent in the code above is that whenever possible, conversions should be avoided. Each of the Convert.MethodName methods has been overloaded to accept various types. However, the CInt method (which most VB6 programmers are familiar with) is defined to accept a parameter of type Object. This is important because it involves boxing the value type. As is noted later in this chapter, repeated boxing of value types has performance implications.

Finally, although this code will compile, it will not always execute correctly. It illustrates a classic intermittent error in that the final conversion statement does not check to ensure that the value being assigned to intInteger is within the maximum range for an integer type. On those occasions where LngLong is larger than the maximum allowed, this code will throw an exception.

VB.NET has many ways to convert values. Some of them are updated versions of techniques familiar from VB6. Others, such as the ToString method, are an inherent part of every class (although the .NET specification does not guarantee how a ToString class is implemented for each type).

The following set of conversion methods are based on the conversions supported by VB6. They coincide with the primitive datatypes described earlier.

CBool()	CByte()	CChar()	CDate()
CDbl()	CDec()	CInt()	CLng()
CObj()	CShort()	CSng()	CStr()

Each of these methods has been designed to accept the input of the other primitive datatypes (as appropriate) and to convert that item to the type indicated by the method name. Thus, the CStr class is used to convert a primitive type to a String. The disadvantage of these methods is that they have been designed to support any object. This means that if a primitive type is used, the method automatically boxes the parameter prior to getting the new value. This results in a loss of performance. Finally, although these are available as methods within the VB language, they are actually implemented in a class (as with everything in the .NET Framework). Because the class uses a series of type-specific overloaded methods, the conversions run faster when the members of the Convert class are called explicitly.

```
Dim intMyShort As Integer = 200
Convert.ToInt32(intMyShort)
Convert.ToDateTime("9/9/2001")
```

The classes that are part of System.Convert implement not only the conversion methods listed above but other common conversions as well. These additional methods include standard conversions for things like unsigned integers and pointers.

All of the preceding type conversions are great for value types and the limited number of classes to which they apply. However, these implementations are oriented around a limited set of known types. It is not possible to convert a custom class to an Integer using these classes. More importantly, there should be no reason to have such a conversion. Instead, a particular class should provide a method that returns the appropriate type—no type conversion will be required. However, when Option Strict is enabled, the compiler will require you to cast an object to an appropriate type before triggering an implicit conversion. But the Convert method isn't the only way to indicate that a given variable can be treated as another type.

The CType Method

The CType method accepts two parameters. The first parameter is the object which is having its type cast, and the second parameter is the name of the object to which it is being cast. This system allows us to cast objects from parent to child or from child to parent types. There is a limitation in the second parameter in that it can't be a variable containing the name of the casting target. Casting occurs at compile time, and any form of dynamic name selection would need to occur at runtime. An example of casting is shown as part of the discussion of working with the Object class later in this chapter.

Support for a runtime determination of object types is based on treating variables as objects and using the object metadata and the TypeOf operator to verify that an object supports various method and property calls. Alternatively, in VB.NET it is possible to turn off Option Strict and as noted later in this chapter, your application will automatically treat objects as objects allowing for a great deal of runtime casting.

Reference Types (Classes)

A lot of the power of VB.NET is harnessed in objects. An object is defined by its class, which describes what data, methods, and other attributes an instance of that class will support. There are thousands of classes provided in the .NET Framework class library.

When code instantiates an object from a class, the object created is a reference type. You may recall earlier in the section Value vs. Reference Types, how the data contained in value and reference types is stored in different locations, but this is not the only difference between them. A class (which is the typical way to refer to a reference type) has additional capabilities, such as support for protected methods and properties, enhanced event handling capabilities, constructors, finalizers, and can be extended with a custom base class via inheritance. Classes can also be used to define how operators such as "=" and "+" work on an instance of the class.

The intention of this chapter is to introduce you to some commonly used classes, in order to complement your knowledge of the common value types we've already covered. Chapters 5, 6, and 7 contain a detailed look at object-orientation in VB.NET. In this chapter, we'll take a look at the features of the Object, String, DBNull, and Array classes, as well as the Collection classes found in the System.Collections namespace.

The Object Class

The Object class is the base class for every type in .NET—both value and reference types. At their core, every variable is an object and can be treated as such. The VB6 runtime environment managed the interpretation of Variant objects for VB programmers. This is good in some ways because it supported a situation where the contents of the variant could be assumed and the developer just worked as if they would be present. So long as the content of the memory area was an object of the appropriate type then the call to a method on that object would succeed. While this was simple to do, it left VB6 programs open to some unusual runtime errors that are generally harder to diagnose and debug. At the same time, in ASP pages and other scripted code, Variants were a requirement because of the way these loosely typed languages worked. Of course, this runtime type evaluation came with its own performance implications, but this was secondary to the ease of development.

You can think of the Object class (in some ways) as the replacement for the Variant type from VB6, but take care. In VB6 a Variant type represents a variant memory location, in VB.NET an Object type represents a reference to an instance of the Object class. In VB6 a Variant was implemented to provide a reference to a memory area on the heap, but its definition didn't define any specific ways of accessing this data area.

The following lines can work equally well in VB6 and VB.NET (so long as Option Strict is not enabled in your VB.NET project):

```
Dim varObj
Dim objVar
```

Interestingly enough, when not using Option Strict, the behavior of a VB6 Variant and a VB.NET Object is almost identical. Since the Object class is the basis of all types, you can assign any variable to an object. Reference types will maintain their current reference and implementation but will be generically handled, while value types will be packaged into a box and placed into the memory location associated with the Object. The new Object supports all of the capabilities that were available from the Variant type but it goes beyond the VB6 variant type in its support for methods. For example, there are instance methods that are available on Object, such as ToString. This method will, if implemented, return a string representation of an instance value. Since the Object class defines it, it can be called on any object.

```
Dim objMyClass as New MyClass("Hello World")

Console.WriteLine(objMyClass.ToString)
```

Which brings up the question of how does the Object class know how to convert custom classes to String objects? The answer to this question is that it doesn't. For this method to actually return the data in an instance of a `String`, a class must override this method. Otherwise, when this code is run, the default version of this method defined at the `Object` level will return the name of the current class (`MyClass`) as its string representation.

The `Object` class continues to fill the role of the `Variant` class even when `Object Strict` is enabled. The declaration is more explicit, anything that can be done with `Object Strict` disabled can be done with it enabled. The difference is that with `Option Strict` code must explicitly define the type of object whose property or method it plans to access. Thus, if you don't want to access only those methods available from the base `Object` class, you need to specify the actual type of the object to be used. An example of this using the `CType` variable to explicitly cast an object and call a method is as follows:

```
Dim objVar as Object

objVar = Me

CType(objVar, Form).Text = "New Dialog Title Text"
```

This snippet shows how to create a generic object under the `Option Strict` syntax. It is then assigned a copy of the current instance of a VB.NET form. The name `Me` is reserved in Visual Basic and its use will be described further in Chapter 6. Once it has been assigned, in order to access the Text property of this class it must be cast from its base `Object` definition to a type that supports a Text property. The `CType` command (covered earlier) accepts the object as its first parameter and the class name (without quotes) as its second parameter. In this case the current instance variable is of type Form, and by casting this variable the code can reference the Text property of the current form.

The String Class

Another class that will play a large role in most development projects is the `String` class. Having Strings defined as a class is more powerful than the VB6 datatype of `String` with which you may be familiar. The `String` class is special within .NET because it is the one primitive type that is not a value type. In order to make `String` objects compatible with some of the underlying behavior in .NET, they have some interesting characteristics.

The following table lists a subset of the shared methods that are available from the `String` class.

These methods are shared, which means that the methods are not specific to any instance of a `String`. The `String` class also contains several other methods that are called based on an instance of a specific `String` object. The methods on the `String` class replace the functions that VB6 had as part of the language for string manipulation and perform operations such as inserting strings, splitting strings, and searching strings.

The String() Method

The `String()` method, which in VB6 allows for the creation of a `String` with a set length and populated with a specific character, no longer exists in VB.NET. This is because `String` is a class and has a constructor. In fact, the `String` class has several different constructors:

```
Dim strConstant as String = "ABC"
Dim strRepeat as New String("A"c, 20)
```

Shared Methods	Description
Empty	This is actually a property. It can be used when an empty String is required. It can be used for comparison or initialization of a String
Compare	Compares two objects of type String
CompareOrdinal	Compares two Strings, without considering the local national language or culture
Concat	Concatenates one or more Strings
Copy	Creates a new String with the same value as an instance provided
Equals	Determines whether two Strings have the same value
Equality operator (=)	An overloaded version of the equality operator that compares two String objects
Inequality operator (op_Inequality)	A method that accepts two String objects for comparison. The method returns True if the objects are not equal

The second example of constructing a new string imitates the VB6 String() method. Not only have creation methods been encapsulated, but other string-specific methods, such as character and substring searching, and case changes are now available from String objects.

The SubString Method

Although not removed, the Left, Right, and Mid methods are deprecated in VB.NET. This is largely due to the fact that the .NET String class has a method called SubString. This single method replaces the three methods that VB6 programmers are accustomed to using to create substrings. Thanks to overloading, which is covered in Chapter 5, there are two versions of this method: the first accepts a starting position and the number of characters to retrieve, while the second accepts simply the starting location. The following code shows examples of using both of these methods on an instance of a string.

```
Dim strMyString as String = "Hello World"

Console.WriteLine(strMystring.SubString(0,5))
Console.WriteLine(strMyString.SubString(6))
```

The PadLeft and PadRight Methods

The LSet and RSet statements from previous versions of Visual Basic have been removed. These functions have been replaced by the PadLeft and PadRight methods. These methods allow us to justify a String so that it is left or right justified. As with SubString, the PadLeft and PadRight methods are overloaded. The first version of these methods requires only a maximum length of the String, and then uses spaces to pad the String. The other version requires two parameters, the length of the returned

String and the character that should be used to pad the original String. An example of working with the PadLeft method is as follows:

```
Dim strMyString as String = "Hello World"

Console.WriteLine(strMyString.PadLeft(30))
Console.WriteLine(strMyString.PadLeft(20,"."c))
```

The String Class Is Immutable

The VB.NET String class isn't entirely different from the String type that VB programmers have used for years. The majority of String behaviors remain unchanged, and the majority of methods are now available as methods. However, in order to support the default behavior that people associate with the String primitive type, the String class isn't declared the same way several other classes are. Strings in .NET do not allow editing of their data. When a portion of a String is changed or copied, the operating system allocates a new memory location and copies the resulting String to this new location. This ensures that when a String is copied to a second variable, the new variable references its own copy.

To support this behavior in .NET, the String class is defined as an immutable class. This means that each time a change is made to the data associated with a String, a new instance is created, and the original referenced memory is released for garbage collection. This is an expensive operation, but the result is that the String class behaves as people expect a primitive type to behave. Additionally, when a copy of a String is made, the String class forces a new version of the data into the referenced memory. This ensures that each instance of a String will reference only its own memory. Consider the following code.

```
Dim strMyString as String
Dim intLoop as Integer

For intLoop = 1 to 1000
    strMyString = strMyString & "A very long string"
Next
Console.WriteLine(strMyString)
```

This code does not perform well. For each assignment operation on the strMyString variable, the system allocates a new memory buffer based on the size of the new string, and copies both the current value of strMyString and the new text that is to be appended. The system then frees the previous memory that must be reclaimed by the Garbage Collector. As this loop continues, the new memory allocation requires a larger chunk of memory. The result is that operations such as this can take a long time. However, .NET offers an alternative in the System.Text.StringBuilder object shown in the following sample code.

```
Dim objMyStrBldr as New System.Text.StringBuilder()
Dim intLoop as Integer

For intLoop = 1 to 1000
    ObjMyStrBldr.Append("A very long string")
Next
Console.WriteLine(objMyStrBldr.ToString())
```

The preceding code works with strings but does not use the String class. The .NET class library contains a class called System.Text.StringBuilder, which performs better when strings will be edited repeatedly. This class does not store a string in the conventional manner — editing or appending more characters does not involve allocating new memory for the entire string. Since the preceding code snippet does not need to reallocate the memory used for the entire string, each time another set of characters is appended it performs significantly faster. In the end, an instance of the `String` class is never explicitly needed because the `StringBuilder` class implements the `ToString` method to roll up all of the characters into a string. While the concept of the `StringBuilder` class isn't new, the fact that it is now available as part of the VB.NET implementation means developers no longer need to create their own string memory managers.

The DBNull Class

The `IsNull` and `IsEmpty` functions from VB6 are now obsolete. VB.NET provides an alternative way of determining if a variable has not been initialized, `IsDBNull()`. The `IsDBNull` method accepts an object as its parameter and returns a Boolean that indicates if the variable has been initialized. In addition to this method, VB.NET has access to the `DBNull` class. The class is part of the `System` namespace and in order to use it you declare a local variable with the `DBNull` type. This variable is then used with an `is` comparison operator to determine if a given variable has been initialized.

```
Dim sysNull As System.DBNull
Dim strMyString As String

If strMyString Is sysNull Then
   strMyString = "Initialize my String"
End If
If Not IsDBNull(strMyString) Then
   Console.WriteLine(strMyString)
End If
```

In this code the `strMyString` variable is declared but not yet initialized, making its value null. The first conditional is evaluated to `True` and as a result the string is initialized. The second conditional then ensures that the declared variable has been initialized. Since this was accomplished in the preceding code, this condition is also true. In both cases, the `sysNull` value is used not to verify the type of the object, but to verify that it has not yet been instantiated with a value.

Arrays

When VB.NET was first announced, a lot of significant changes were planned to the way that arrays worked. A major reason for these changes involved getting rid of the `Variant_Array` structure. This structure, introduced with COM, was hidden from most VB programmers, but was nevertheless ever present. It was necessary because Visual Basic defined arrays in a unique way. The variant array has been removed not only from Visual Basic but from every .NET language. The reason it was removed is that under .NET, arrays are handled in a consistent way. All .NET arrays at an index of zero have a defined number of elements. However, the way that an array is declared in VB.NET varies slightly from other .NET languages like C#.

When VB.NET was announced it was said that arrays would always begin at 0 and that they would be defined based on the number of elements in the array. However, in VB6 the `Option Base` statement allowed arrays to be declared as starting at 1 or any other specified value. This meant that arrays were defined based on their upper limit. The VB6 Option Base This = statement resulted in a problem when converting existing code to VB.NET. To resolve this issue the engineers at Microsoft decided on a compromise. All arrays in .NET will begin at 0, but when an array is declared in VB.NET the definition is based on the upper limit of the array, not the number of elements. The main result of this upper limit declaration is that arrays defined in VB.NET have one more entry by definition than those defined with other .NET languages.

Overall, the result in the change in how arrays work means that some of the more esoteric declarations that were available in VB6, such as Dim intMyArr(15 to 30), are no longer supported. Still the majority of capabilities for arrays remain unchanged. It is still possible to declare an array with multiple indices. It is also possible to declare any type as an array of that type. Since an array is a modifier of another type, the basic Array class is never explicitly declared for a variable's type. The System.Array class that serves as the base for all arrays is defined such that it cannot be created, but must be inherited. As a result, to create an Integer array a set of parentheses is added to the declaration of the variable. These parentheses indicate that the system should create an array of the type specified. The parentheses used in the declaration may be empty or may contain the size of the array. An array can be defined as having a single dimension using a single number, or as having multiple dimensions.

The following code illustrates some simple examples to demonstrate five different ways of creating arrays using a simple integer array as the basis for the comparison.

```
Dim arrMyIntArray1(20) as Integer
Dim arrMyIntArray2() as Integer = {1, 2, 3, 4}
Dim arrMyIntArray3(4,2) as Integer
Dim arrMyIntArray4( , ) as Integer = _
    { {1, 2, 3, 4},{5, 6, 7, 8},{9, 10, 11, 12},{13, 14 , 15 , 16} }
Dim arrMyIntArray5() as Integer
```

In the first case, the code defines an array of integers that spans from arrMyIntArray1(0) to arrMyIntArray1(20). This is a 21-element array, because all arrays start at 0 and end with the value defined in the declaration as the upper bound. The second statement creates an array with four elements numbered 0 through 3 containing the values 1 to 4. The third statement creates a multidimensional array containing five elements at the first level and with each of those elements containing three child elements. The challenge, of course, is that you have to remember that all subscripts go from 0 to the upper bound, meaning that each array contains one more element than its upper bound. The result is an array with 15 elements. The next line of code, the fourth, shows an alternative way of creating the same array, but in this case there are four elements each containing four elements with subscripts from 0 to 3 at each level. Finally, the last line demonstrates it is possible to simply declare a variable and indicate that the variable will be an array without specifying the number of elements in that array.

The UBound Function

Continuing to reference the arrays defined earlier, the declaration of arrMyIntArray2 actually defined an array that spans from arrMyIntArray2(0) to arrMyIntArray1(3). This is because when you declare an array by specifying the set of values it still starts at 0. However, in this case you are not specifying the upper bound, but rather initializing the array with a set of values. If this set of values came from a database or other source it might not be clear what the upper limit on the array was. In order to verify the upper bound of an array a call can be made to the UBound function:

```
Console.Writeline CStr(UBound(ArrMyIntArray2))
```

The UBound function has a companion called LBound. The LBound function computes the lower bound for a given array. However, since all arrays in VB.NET are 0-based, it doesn't have much value anymore.

Multidimensional Arrays

As shown earlier in the sample array declarations, the definition of arrMyIntArray3 is as a multidimensional array. This declaration creates an array with 15 elements (five in the first range, each containing three elements) ranging from arrMyIntArray3(0,0) through arrMyIntArray3(2,1) to arrMyIntArray3(4,2). As with all elements of an array, when it is created without specific values, the values of each of these elements is created with the default value for that type. This case also demonstrates that the size of the different dimensions can vary. It is also possible to nest deeper than two levels, but this should be done with care as such code is difficult to maintain.

The fourth declaration shown previously creates arrMyIntArray4(,) with predefined values. The values are mapped based on the outer set being the first dimension and the inner values being associated with the next inner dimension. For example, the value of arrMyIntArray4(0,1) is 2 while the value of arrMyIntArray4(2,3) is 12. The following code snippet illustrates this using a set of nested loops to traverse the array. Additionally, it provides an example of calling the UBound method with a second parameter to specify that you are interested in the upper bound for the second dimension of the array:

```
Dim intLoop1 as Integer
Dim intLoop2 as Integer
For intLoop1 = 0 to UBound(arrMyIntArray4)
  For intLoop2 = 0 to UBound(arrMyIntArray4, 2)
    Console.WriteLine arrMyIntArray4(intLoop1, intLoop2).ToString
  Next
Next
```

The ReDim Statement

The final declaration demonstrated previously is for arrMyIntArray5(). This is an example of an array which has not yet been instantiated. If an attempt were made to assign a value into this array, it would trigger an exception. The solution to this is to use the ReDim keyword. Although ReDim was part of VB6, it has changed slightly in VB.NET. The first change is that code must first Dim an instance of the variable; it is not acceptable to declare an array using the ReDim statement. The second change is that code cannot change the number of dimensions in an array. For example, an array with three dimensions cannot grow to an array of four dimensions and nor can it be reduced to only two dimensions. To further extend the example, code associated with arrays consider the following code that manipulates some of the arrays previously declared.

```
Dim arrMyIntArray5() as Integer
```

```
' The statement below would compile but would cause a runtime exception.
'arrMyIntArray5(0) = 1

ReDim arrMyIntArray5(2)
ReDim arrMyIntArray3(5,4)
ReDim Preserve arrMyIntArray4(UBound(arrMyIntArray4),2)
```

The ReDim of arrMyIntArray5 instantiates the elements of the array so that values can be assigned to each element. The second statement redimensions the arrMyIntArray3 variable defined earlier. Note that it is changing the size of both the first and the second dimension. While it is not possible to change the number of dimensions in an array, it is possible to resize any of an array's dimensions. This capability is required if declarations such as *Dim arrMyIntArray6 (, , ,) As Integer* are to be legal.

The Preserve Keyword

The last item in the code snippet in the preceding section illustrates an additional keyword associated with redimensioning. The `Preserve` keyword indicates that the data that is stored in the array prior to redimensioning it should be transferred to the newly created array. If this keyword is not used, then the data that was stored in an array is lost. Additionally, in the example above, the `ReDim` statement actually reduces the second dimension of the array. While this is a perfectly legal statement it should be noted that this means that even though you have asked to preserve the data, the data values 4, 8, 12, and 16 that were assigned in the original definition of this array will be discarded. These are lost because they were assigned in the highest index of the second array. Since `arrMyIntArray4(1,3)` is no longer valid, the value that resided at this location has been lost.

Arrays continue to be very powerful in VB.NET. However, the basic array class is just that, basic. While it provides a powerful framework it does not provide a lot of other features that would allow for more robust logic built into the array. To accomplish more advanced features, such as sorting and dynamic allocation, the base `Array` class has been inherited by the classes that make up the `Collections` namespace.

Collections

The `Collections` namespace is part of the `System` namespace and provides a series of classes that implement advanced array features. While being able to make an array of existing types is powerful, sometimes more power is needed in the array itself. The ability to inherently sort or dynamically add dissimilar objects in an array is provided by the classes of the `Collections` namespace. This namespace contains a specialized set of objects that can be instantiated for additional features when working with a collection of similar objects. The following table defines several of the objects that are available as part of the `System.Collections` namespace.

Class	Description
ArrayList	Implements an array whose size increases automatically as elements are added
BitArray	Manages an array of Booleans that are stored as bit values
Hashtable	Implements a collection of values organized by key. Sorting is done based on a hash of the key
Queue	Implements a first-in-first-out collection
SortedList	Implements a collection of values with associated keys. The values are sorted by key, and are accessible by key or index
Stack	Implements a last-in-first-out collection

Each of the objects listed is focused on storing a collection of objects. This means that in addition to the special capabilities each provides it also provides one additional capability not available to objects created based on the `Array` class. In short, since every variable in .NET is based on the `Object` class, it is possible to have a collection defined, as one of these objects contain elements that are defined with different types. This is because each stores an array of objects, and since all classes are of type object a string could be stored alongside an integer value. The result is that it's possible within the collection classes for the actual objects being stored to be different. Consider the following example code.

```
Dim objMyArrList As New System.Collections.ArrayList()
Dim objItem As Object
Dim intLine As Integer = 1
Dim strHello As String = "Hello"
Dim objWorld As New System.Text.StringBuilder("World")

' Add an integer value to the array list.
objMyArrList.Add(intLine)

' Add an instance of a string object
objMyArrList.Add(strHello)

' Add a single character cast as a character
objMyArrList.Add(" "c)

' Add an object that isn't a primitive type
objMyArrList.Add(objWorld)

' To balance the string, insert a break between the line
' and the string "Hello", by inserting a string constant
objMyArrList.Insert(1, ". ")

For Each objItem In objMyArrList
   ' Output the values...
   Console.Write(objItem.ToString())
Next
```

The preceding code is an example of implementing the new `ArrayList` collection class. The collection classes, as this example shows, are more versatile than any similar structures in VB6. The preceding code creates a new instance of an ArrayList, along with some related variables to support the demonstration. The code then shows four different types of variable being inserted into the same ArrayList. The code then inserts another value into the middle of the list. At no time has the size of the array been declared nor has a redefinition of the array size been required.

Part of the reason for this is that the Add and Insert methods on the `ArrayList` class are defined to accept a parameter of type `Object`. This means that the `ArrayList` object can literally accept any value in .NET. This comes at a slight performance cost for those variables that are value types because of boxing.

The System.Collections.Specialized Namespace

VB.NET has additional classes available as part of the `System.Collections.Specialized` namespace. These classes tend to be oriented around a specific problem. For example, the `ListDictionary` class is designed to take advantage of the fact that while a hash table is very good at storing and retrieving a large number of items, it can be costly when there are only a few items. Similarly, the `StringCollection` and `StringDictionary` classes are defined so that when working with strings the time spent interpreting the type of object is reduced and overall performance is improved.

Class	Description
ListDictionary	A singly linked list that allows a small number of elements to be accessed faster than other collection implementations. This collection should not be used for a large number of elements
StringCollection	Implements a collection of strings
StringDictionary	Implements a hash table, but the key is strongly typed as a string rather than as a base object

Parameter Passing

When an object's methods or an assembly's procedures and methods are called, it's often appropriate to provide input for the data to be operated on by the code. VB.NET has changed the way that functions, procedures, and methods are called and how those parameters are passed. The first change actually makes writing such calls more consistent. Under VB6, the parameter list for a procedure call didn't require parentheses. On the other hand, a call to a method did require parentheses around the parameter list. In VB.NET, the parentheses are always required and the Call keyword is obsolete.

Another change in VB.NET is the way parameters with default values are handled. As with VB6 it is possible to define a function, procedure, or method that provides default values for the last parameter(s). This way it is possible to call a method such as PadRight passing either with a single parameter defining the length of the string and using a default of space for the padding character, or with two parameters, the first still defining the length of the string, but the second now replacing the default of space with a dash.

```
Public Function PadRight(ByVal intSize as Integer, _
                    Optional ByVal chrPad as Char = " "c)
End Function
```

To use default parameters it is necessary to make them the last parameters in the function declaration. VB.NET also requires that every Optional parameter have a default value. It is not acceptable to just declare a parameter and assign it the Optional keyword. In VB.NET, the Optional keyword must be accompanied by a value that will be assigned if the parameter is not passed in.

The most important change related to parameters in VB.NET is how the system handles them. In VB6 the default was that parameters were passed by reference. Passing a parameter by reference means that if changes are made to the value of a variable passed to a method, function, or procedure call, these changes were to the actual variable and therefore available to the calling routine.

Passing a parameter by reference sometimes results in unexpected changes being made to a parameter's value. It is partly becauseof this that parameters default to passing by value in VB.NET. The advantage of passing by value is that regardless of what a function might do to a variable while it is running, when the function completes, the calling code still has the original value. Making this the default results in safer code.

Under version 1.0 of the .NET Framework there was an additional performance advantage for passing parameters by value. With the release of version 1.1 of the .NET Framework, passing by reference is implemented as you would expect. Instead of passing an entire copy of the data in an object, when passed by reference only a pointer to the data located on the managed heap is passed. The result is faster calls when objects are passed by reference. However, keep in mind that this performance gain comes at the risk of a procedure modifying your copy of the data.

Boxing

Normally when a conversion (implicit or explicit) occurs, the original value is read from its current memory location and then the new value is assigned. For example, to convert a Short to a Long, the system reads the 2 bytes of Short data, and writes them to the appropriate bytes for the Long variable. However, under VB.NET if a value type needs to be managed as an object, then the system will perform an intermediate step. This intermediate step involves taking the value that is on the stack and copying it to the heap, a process referred to as boxing. As noted earlier, the Object class is implemented as a reference type. Therefore, the system needs to convert value types into reference types for them to be objects. This doesn't cause any problems or require any special programming, as boxing isn't something you declare or directly control. However, it does have an impact on performance.

In a situation where you are copying the data for a single value type this is not a significant cost. However, if you are processing an array that contains thousands of values, the time spent moving between a value type and a temporary reference type can be significant.

There are ways to limit the amount of boxing that occurs. One method that has been shown to work well is to create a class based on the value type you need to work with. On first thought this seems counter-intuitive because it costs more to create a class. The key is how often you reuse the data that is contained in the class. By repeatedly using this object to interact with other objects, you will save on the creation of a temporary boxed object.

There are two important areas to examine with examples to better understand boxing. The first involves the use of arrays. When an array is created, the portion of the class which tracks the element of the array is created as a reference object, but each of the elements of the array is created directly. Thus an array of integers consists of the array object and a set of integer value types. When you update one of these values with another integer value there is no boxing involved:

```
Dim arrInt(20) as Integer
Dim intMyValue as Integer = 1

arrInt(0) = 0
arrInt(1) = intMyValue
```

Neither of the above assignments of an integer value into the integer array that was defined previously requires boxing. In each case, the array object identifies which value on the stack needs to be referenced and the value is assigned to that value type. The point here is that just because you have referenced an object doesn't mean you are going to box a value. The boxing only occurs when the values being assigned are being transitioned from a value to reference type:

```
Dim objStrBldr as New System.Text.StringBuilder()
Dim objSortedList as New System.Collections.SortedList()
Dim intCount as Integer
```

```
For intCount = 1 to 100
  objStrBldr.Append(intCount)
  objSortedList.Add(intCount, intCount)
Next
```

The preceding snippet illustrates two separate calls to object interfaces. One of these calls requires boxing of the value `intCount`, while the other does not. There is nothing in the code to indicate which call is which. The answer is that the `Append` method of `StringBuilder` has been overridden to include a version that accepts an `Integer`, while the `Add` method of `SortedList` collection expects two objects. While the integer values can be recognized by the system as objects, doing so requires the runtime library to box up these values so that they can be added to the sorted list.

The key to boxing isn't that you are working with objects as part of an action, but that you are passing a value to a parameter that expects an object, or are taking an object and converting it to a value type. However, one time that boxing does not occur is when you call a method on a value type. There is no conversion to an object, so if you need to assign an `Integer` to a string using the `ToString` method, there is no boxing of the integer value as part of the creation of the string. On the other hand, you are explicitly creating a new string object so the cost is similar.

Retired Keywords and Methods

This chapter has covered several changes from VB6 that are part of VB.NET. They include the removal of the `Currency` type, `String` function, `Rset`, and `Lset` functions. Other functions such as Left, Right, and Mid have been discussed as becoming obsolete although they may still be supported. Functions such as IsEmpty and IsNull have been replaced with new versions. Additionally, this chapter has looked at some of the differences in how VB.NET works with arrays.

VB.NET has removed many keywords that won't be missed. For example, the `DefType` statement has been removed. This statement was a throwback to Fortran, allowing a developer to indicate, for example, that all variables starting with the letters I, J, K, L, M, N would be integers. Most programmers have probably never used this function and it doesn't have a logical replacement in VB.NET.

One of the real advantages of VB.NET is the way that it removed some of the more esoteric and obsolete functions from Visual Basic. The following list contains the majority of such functions. As with others that have already been discussed, some have been replaced; for example, the math functions are now part of the `System.Math` library, while others such as IsObject really don't have much more meaning than LBound in the context of .NET, where everything is an object and the lower bound of all arrays is 0.

Elements of VB6 Removed in VB.NET

Also as previously noted, the UDT has also been removed from the Visual Basic vocabulary. Instead, the ability to create a user-defined set of variables as a type has been replaced with the ability to create custom structures and classes in VB.NET.

> Remember that VB.NET isn't Visual Basic 7. It is an entirely new language based on the .NET Framework and the syntax of Visual Basic.

`As Any`	`Now` function
`Atn` function	`Null` keyword
`Calendar` property	`On ... GoSub`
`Circle` statement	`On ... GoTo`
`Currency`	`Option Base`
`Date` function and statement	`Option Private Module`
`Date$` function	`Property Get`, `Property Let`, and `Property Set`
`Debug.Assert` method	`PSet` method
`Debug.Print` method	`Rnd` function
`DefType`	`Round` function
`DoEvents` function	`Rset`
`Empty`	`Scale` method
`Eqv` operator	`Set` statement
`GoSub` statement	`Sgn` function
`Imp` operator	`Sqr` function
`Initialize` event	`String` function
`Instancing` property	`Terminate` event
`IsEmpty` function	`Time` function and statement
`IsMissing` function	`Time$` function
`IsNull` function	`Timer` function
`IsObject` function	`Type` statement
`Let` statement	`Variant` datatype
`Line` statement	`VarType` function
`Lset`	`Wend` keyword

Summary

This chapter looked at many of the basic building blocks of VB.NET that are used throughout project development. Understanding how they work will help you to write more stable and better performing software. There are five specific points to take note of:

❑　Beware of array sizes; all arrays start at 0 and are defined not by size but by the highest index

❑　Remember to use the `StringBuilder` class for string manipulation

❑　Use `Option Strict`; it's not just about style, it's about performance

Chapter 4

❑   Beware of parameters that are passed `ByValue` so changes are not returned

❑   Take advantage of the new collection classes

While this chapter covered many other items such as how the new `Decimal` type works and how boxing works, these five items are really the most important. Whether you are creating a new library of methods or a new user interface, these five items will consistently turn up in some form. While .NET provides a tremendous amount of power, this chapter has hopefully provided information on places where that power comes at a significant performance cost.

5

Object Syntax Introduction

Visual Basic has had powerful object-oriented capabilities since the introduction of version 4.0. Visual Basic .NET (VB.NET) carries that tradition forward. VB.NET simplifies some of the syntax and greatly enhances these capabilities, and it now supports the four major defining concepts required for a language to be fully object-oriented:

❑ *Abstraction* — Visual Basic has supported abstraction since VB4. Abstraction is merely the ability of a language to create "black box" code, to take a concept and create an abstract representation of that concept within a program. A `Customer` object, for instance, is an abstract representation of a real-world customer. A `Recordset` object is an abstract representation of a set of data.

❑ *Encapsulation* — This has also been with us since version 4.0. It's the concept of a separation between interface and implementation. The idea is that we can create an interface (`Public` methods in a class), and, as long as that interface remains consistent, the application can interact with our objects. This remains true even if we entirely rewrite the code within a given method — thus the interface is independent of the implementation.

Encapsulation allows us to hide the internal implementation details of a class. For example, the algorithm we use to compute Pi might be proprietary. We can expose a simple API to the end user, but we hide all of the logic used by our algorithm by encapsulating it within our class.

❑ *Polymorphism* — Likewise, polymorphism was introduced with VB4. Polymorphism is reflected in the ability to write one routine that can operate on objects from more than one class — treating different objects from different classes in exactly the same way. For instance, if both `Customer` and `Vendor` objects have a `Name` property, and we can write a routine that calls the `Name` property regardless of whether we're using a `Customer` or `Vendor` object, then we have polymorphism.

Visual Basic, in fact, supports polymorphism in two ways — through late binding (much like Smalltalk, a classic example of a true object-orientated language) and through the implementation of multiple interfaces. This flexibility is very powerful and is preserved within VB.NET.

❑ *Inheritance* — VB.NET is the first version of Visual Basic that supports inheritance, the idea that a class can gain the pre-existing interface and behaviors of an existing class. This is done by inheriting these behaviors from the existing class through a process known as subclassing. With the introduction of full inheritance, Visual Basic is now a fully *object-oriented* language by any reasonable definition.

We'll discuss these concepts in detail in Chapter 7, using this chapter and Chapter 6 to focus on the syntax that enables us to utilize these concepts.

In addition, because VB.NET is a component-based language, we have some other capabilities available to us in the language. They are closely related to the traditional concepts of object-orientation.

❑ *Multiple interfaces* — Each class in VB.NET defines a primary interface (also called the default or native interface) through its `Public` methods, properties, and events. Classes can also implement other, secondary interfaces in addition to this primary interface. An object based on this class then has multiple interfaces, and a client application can choose by which interface it will interact with the object.

❑ *Assembly (component) level scoping* — Not only can we define our classes and methods to be `Public` (available to anyone), `Protected` (available through inheritance), and `Private` (available locally only), but we can also define them as `Friend` — meaning they are available only within the current assembly or component. This is not a traditional object-oriented concept, but is very powerful when designing component-based applications.

In this chapter, we'll explore the creation and use of classes and objects in VB.NET. We will get too deep into code. However, it is important that we spend a little time familiarizing ourselves with basic object-oriented terms and concepts.

Object-Oriented Terminology

To start with, let's take a look at the word *object* itself, along with the related *class* and *instance* terms. Then we'll move on to discuss the four terms that define the major functionality in the object-oriented world — encapsulation, abstraction, polymorphism, and inheritance.

Objects, Classes, and Instances

An *object* is a code-based abstraction of a real-world entity or relationship. For instance, we might have a `Customer` object that represents a real-world customer, such as customer number 123, or we might have a `File` object that represents `C:\config.sys` on our computer's hard drive.

A closely related term is *class*. A class is the code that defines our object, and all objects are created based on a class. A class is an abstraction of a real-world concept, and it provides the basis from which we create instances of specific objects. For example, in order to have a `Customer` object representing customer number 123, we must first have a `Customer` class that contains all of the code (methods, properties, events, variables, and so on) necessary to create `Customer` objects. Based on that class, we can create any number of objects, each one an *instance* of the class. Each object is identical to the others, except that it may contain different data.

We may create many instances of `Customer` objects based on the same `Customer` class. All of the `Customer` objects are identical in terms of what they can do and the code they contain, but each one contains its own unique data. This means that each object represents a different physical customer.

Composition of an Object

We use an *interface* to get access to an object's data and behavior. The object's data and behaviors are contained within the object, so a client application can treat the object like a black box accessible only through its interface. This is a key object-oriented concept called *encapsulation*. The idea is that any program that makes use of this object won't have direct access to the behaviors or data; rather, those programs must make use of our object's interface.

Let's walk through each of the three elements in detail.

Interface

The interface is defined as a set of methods (`Sub` and `Function` routines), properties (`Property` routines), events, and fields (variables or attributes) that are declared `Public` in scope.

> *The word* attribute *means one thing in the general object-oriented world, and something else in .NET. The OO world often refers to an object's variables as attributes, while in .NET an attribute is a coding construct that we can use to control compilation, the IDE, and so on.*

We can also have `Private` methods and properties in our code. While these methods can be called by code within our object, they are not part of the interface and cannot be called by programs written to use our object. Another option is to use the `Friend` keyword, which defines the scope to be our current project, meaning that any code within our project can call the method, but no code outside of our project (that is, from a different .NET assembly) can call the method. To complicate things a bit, we can also declare methods and properties as `Protected`, which are available to classes that inherit from our class. We'll discuss `Protected` in Chapter 6 along with inheritance.

For example, we might have the following code in a class:

```
Public Function CalculateValue() As Integer

End Function
```

Since this method is declared with the `Public` keyword, it is part of our interface and can be called by client applications that are using our object. We might also have a method such as this:

```
Private Sub DoSomething()

End Sub
```

This method is declared as being `Private`, and so it is not part of our interface. This method can only be called by code within our class—not by any code outside of our class, such as the code in a program that is using one of our objects.

On the other hand, we can do something like this:

```
Public Function CalculateValue() As Integer
   DoSomething()
End Function
```

In this case, we're calling the `Private` method from within a `Public` method. While code using our objects can't directly call a `Private` method, we will frequently use `Private` methods to help structure the code in our class to make it more maintainable and easier to read.

Finally, we can use the `Friend` keyword:

```
Friend Sub DoSomething()

End Sub
```

In this case, the `DoSomething` method can be called by code within our class, or from other classes or modules within our current VB.NET project. Code from outside our project will not have access to the method.

The `Friend` scope is very similar to the `Public` scope, in that it makes methods available for use by code outside of our object itself. However, unlike `Public`, the `Friend` keyword restricts access to code within our current VB.NET project, preventing code in other .NET assemblies from calling the method.

> *This is very unlike the C++ Friend keyword, which implements a form of tight coupling between objects and which is generally regarded as a bad thing to do. Instead, this is the same Friend keyword that Visual Basic has had for many years and which was later adopted by Java to provide component-level scoping in that language as well. It is equivalent to the internal keyword in C#.*

Implementation or Behavior

The code inside of a method is called the *implementation*. Sometimes it is also called *behavior*, since it is this code that actually makes the object do useful work.

For instance, we may have an `Age` property as part of our object's interface. Within that method, we may have some code (perhaps written by an inexperienced developer, since it is just returning a noncalculated value):

```
Private mintAge As Integer

Public ReadOnly Property Age() As Integer
   Get
      Return mintAge
   End Get
End Sub
```

In this case, the code is returning a value directly out of a variable, rather than doing something better like calculating the value based on a birth date. However, this kind of code is often written in applications, and it seems to work fine for a while.

The key concept here is to understand that client applications can use our object even if we change the implementation, as long as we don't change the interface. As long as our method name and its parameter list and return data type remain unchanged, we can change the implementation any way we want.

The code necessary to call our `Age` property would look something like this:

```
theAge = MyObject.Age
```

The result of running this code is that we get the `Age` value returned for our use. While our client application will work fine, we'll soon discover that hard coding the age into the application is a problem and so, at some point, we'll want to improve this code. Fortunately, we can change our implementation without changing the client code:

```
Private mdtBirthDate As Date

Public ReadOnly Property Age() As Integer
  Get
    Return DateDiff(DateInterval.Year, mdtBirthDate, Now())
  End Get
End Sub
```

We've changed the implementation behind the interface, effectively changing how it behaves, without changing the interface itself. Now, when we run our client application, we'll find that the `Age` value returned is accurate over time whereas with the previous implementation it was not.

It is important to keep in mind that encapsulation is a syntactic tool — it allows our code to continue to run without change. However, it is not semantic, meaning that just because our code continues to run, that doesn't mean it continues to do what we actually wanted it to do.

In this example, our client code may have been written to overcome the initial limitations of the implementation in some way, and thus might not only rely on being able to retrieve the `Age` value, but the client code might be counting on the result of that call being a fixed value over time.

While our update to the implementation won't stop the client program from running, it may very well prevent the client program from running correctly.

Member or Instance Variables

The third key part of an object is its data, or *state*. In fact, it might be argued that the only important part of an object is its data. After all, every instance of a class is absolutely identical in terms of its interface and its implementation; the only thing that can vary at all is the data contained within that particular object.

Member variables are those that are declared so that they are available to all code within our class. Typically, member variables are `Private` in scope, available only to the code in our class itself. They are also sometimes referred to as *instance variables* or as *attributes*. The .NET Framework also refers to them as fields.

We shouldn't confuse instance variables with *properties*. In Visual Basic, a `Property` is a type of method that is geared to retrieving and setting values, while an instance variable is a variable within the class that may *hold* the value exposed by a `Property`.

For instance, we might have a class that has instance variables:

```
Public Class TheClass

    Private mstrName As String
    Private mdtBirthDate As Date

End Class
```

Each instance of the class — each object — will have its own set of these variables in which to store data. Because these variables are declared with the `Private` keyword, they are only available to code within each specific object.

While member variables *can* be declared as `Public` in scope, this makes them available to any code using our objects in a manner we can't control. Such a choice directly breaks the concept of encapsulation, since code outside our object can directly change data values without following any rules that might otherwise be set in our object's code.

If we want to make the value of an instance variable available to code outside of our object, we should use a *property*:

```
Public Class TheClass
    Private mstrName As String
    Private mdtBirthDate As Date

    Public ReadOnly Property Name() As String
      Get
        Return mstrName
      End Get
    End Property

End Class
```

Since the `Name` property is a method, we are not directly exposing our internal variables to client code, so we preserve encapsulation of our data. At the same time, through this mechanism we are able to safely provide access to our data as needed.

Member variables can also be declared with `Friend` scope, which means they are available to all code in our project. Like declaring them as `Public`, this breaks encapsulation and is strongly discouraged.

Now that we have a grasp of some of the basic object-oriented terminology, we're ready to explore the creation of classes and objects. First, we'll see how Visual Basic allows us to interact with objects, and then we'll dive into the actual process of authoring those objects.

Working with Objects

In the .NET environment, and within Visual Basic in particular, we use objects all the time without even thinking about it. Every control on a form — in fact, every form — is an object. When we open a file or interact with a database, we are using objects to do that work.

Object Declaration and Instantiation

Objects are created using the New keyword, indicating that we want a new instance of a particular class. There are a number of variations on how or where we can use the New keyword in our code. Each one provides different advantages in terms of code readability or flexibility.

> *Unlike previous versions of Visual Basic, VB.NET doesn't use the CreateObject statement for object creation. CreateObject was an outgrowth of VB's relationship with COM and, since VB.NET doesn't use COM, it has no use for CreateObject. The CreateObject method still exists to support COM interoperability, but it is not used to access .NET objects.*

The most obvious way to create an object is to declare an object variable and then create an instance of the object:

```
Dim obj As TheClass
obj = New TheClass()
```

The result of this code is that we have a new instance of TheClass ready for our use. To interact with this new object, we will use the obj variable that we declared. The obj variable contains a reference to the object, a concept we'll explore later.

We can shorten this by combining the declaration of the variable with the creation of the instance:

```
Dim obj As New TheClass()
```

> *In previous versions of Visual Basic this was a very poor thing to do, as it had both negative performance and maintainability effects. However, in VB.NET, there is no difference between our first example and this one, other than that our code is shorter.*

This code both declares the variable obj as data type TheClass and also creates an instance of the class, immediately creating an object that we can use from our code.

Another variation on this theme is:

```
Dim obj As TheClass = New TheClass()
```

Again, this both declares a variable of data type TheClass and creates an instance of the class for our use.

This third syntax provides a great deal of flexibility while remaining compact. Though it is a single line of code, it separates the declaration of the variable's data type from the creation of the object.

Such flexibility is very useful when working with inheritance or with multiple interfaces. We might declare the variable to be of one type — say, an interface — and instantiate the object based on a class that implements that interface. We'll cover interfaces in detail in Chapter 6, but as an example here, let's create an interface named ITheInterface:

```
Public Interface ITheInterface
    Sub DoSomething()
End Interface
```

Our class can then implement that interface, meaning that our class now has its own native interface and also a secondary interface — ITheInterface:

```
Public Class TheClass
   Implements ITheInterface

   Public Sub DoSomething() Implements ITheInterface.DoSomething
      ' implementation goes here
   End Sub
End Class
```

We can now create an instance of TheClass, but reference it via the secondary interface by declaring the variable to be of type ITheInterface:

```
Dim obj As ITheInterface = New TheClass()
```

We can also do this using two separate lines of code:

```
Dim obj As ITheInterface
obj = New TheClass()
```

Either technique works fine and achieves the same result, which is that we have a new object of type TheClass, being accessed via its secondary interface. We'll discuss multiple interfaces in more detail in Chapter 6.

So far we've been declaring a variable for our new objects. However, sometimes we may simply need to pass an object as a parameter to a method, in which case we can create an instance of the object right in the call to that method:

```
DoSomething(New TheClass())
```

This calls the DoSomething method, passing a new instance of TheClass as a parameter.

This can be even more complex. Perhaps, instead of needing an object reference, our method needs an Integer. We can provide that Integer value from a method on our object:

```
Public Class TheClass
   Public Function GetValue() As Integer
      Return 42
   End Function
End Class
```

We can then instantiate the object and call the method all in one shot, thus passing the value returned from the method as a parameter:

```
DoSomething(New TheClass().GetValue())
```

Obviously, we need to carefully weigh the readability of such code against its compactness. At some point, having more compact code can detract from readability rather than enhance it.

Notice that nowhere do we use the `Set` statement when working with objects. In VB6, any time we worked with an object reference we had to use the `Set` command to differentiate objects from any other data type in the language.

> **In VB.NET, objects are not treated differently from any other data type, and so we can use direct assignment for objects just as we do with Integer or String data types. The Set command is no longer valid in VB.NET.**

Object References

Typically, when we work with an object we are using a *reference* to that object. On the other hand, when we are working with simple data types, such as `Integer`, we are working with the actual value rather than with a reference. Let's explore these concepts and see how they work and interact.

When we create a new object using the `New` keyword, we store a reference to that object in a variable. For instance:

```
Dim obj As New TheClass()
```

This code creates a new instance of `TheClass`. We gain access to this new object via the `obj` variable. This variable holds a reference to the object. We might then do something like this:

```
Dim another As TheClass
another = obj
```

Now, we have a second variable, `another`, which also has a reference to the same object. We can use either variable interchangeably, since they both reference the exact same object. We need to remember that the variable we have is not the object itself but is just a reference or pointer to the object.

Dereferencing Objects

When we are done working with an object, we can indicate that we're through with it by dereferencing the object.

To dereference an object, we need to simply set our object reference to `Nothing`:

```
Dim obj As TheClass

obj = New TheClass()
obj = Nothing
```

This code has no impact on our object. In fact, the object may remain blissfully unaware for some time that it has been dereferenced.

Once any or all variables that reference an object are set to `Nothing`, the .NET runtime can tell that we no longer need that object. At some point, the runtime will destroy the object and reclaim the memory and resources consumed by the object.

Between the time that we dereference the object and the time that the .NET Framework gets around to actually destroying it, the object simply sits in the memory, unaware that it has been dereferenced. Right before .NET destroys the object, the framework will call the `Finalize` method on the object (if it has one). We discussed the `Finalize` method in Chapter 3.

Early versus Late Binding

One of the strengths of Visual Basic has long been that we had access to both early and late binding when interacting with objects.

Early binding means that our code directly interacts with the object by directly calling its methods. Since the Visual Basic compiler knows the object's data type ahead of time, it can directly compile code to invoke the methods on the object. Early binding also allows the IDE to use IntelliSense to aid our development efforts; it allows the compiler to ensure that we are referencing methods that do exist and that we are providing the proper parameter values.

> *In previous versions of Visual Basic, early binding was also known as vtable binding. The vtable was an artifact of COM, providing a list of the addresses for all the methods on an object's interface. In .NET, things are simpler and there is no real vtable. Instead, the compiler is able to generate code to directly invoke the methods on an object. From a VB coding perspective this makes no difference, but it is quite a change behind the scenes.*

Late binding means that our code interacts with an object dynamically at runtime. This provides a great deal of flexibility since our code literally doesn't care what type of object it is interacting with as long as the object supports the methods we want to call. Because the type of the object isn't known by the IDE or compiler, neither IntelliSense nor compile-time syntax checking is possible, but in exchange we get unprecedented flexibility.

If we enable strict type checking by using `Option Strict On` at the top of our code modules, then the IDE and compiler will enforce early binding behavior. By default, `Option Strict` is turned off and so we have easy access to the use of late binding within our code. We discussed `Option Strict` in Chapter 4.

Implementing Late Binding

Late binding occurs when the compiler can't determine the type of object that we'll be calling. This level of ambiguity is achieved through the use of the `Object` data type. A variable of data type `Object` can hold virtually any value, including a reference to any type of object. Thus, codesuch as the following could be run against any object that implements a `DoSomething` method that accepts no parameters:

```
Option Strict Off

Module LateBind
   Public Sub DoWork(ByVal obj As Object)
     obj.DoSomething()
   End Sub
End Module
```

If the object passed into this routine does not have a DoSomething method that accepts no parameters, then a runtime error will result. Thus, it is recommended that any code that uses late binding always provide error trapping:

```
Option Strict Off

Module LateBind
   Public Sub DoWork(ByVal obj As Object)
      Try
         obj.DoSomething()
      Catch ex As Exception When Err.Number = 438
         ' do something appropriate given failure to call the method
      End Try
   End Sub
End Module
```

Here, we've put the call to the DoSomething method in a Try block. If it works, then the code in the Catch block is ignored but, in the case of a failure, the code in the Catch block is run. We would need to write code in the Catch block to handle the case that the object did not support the DoSomething method call. This Catch block, in fact, catches only error number 438, which is the error indicating that the method doesn't exist on the object.

While late binding is flexible, it can be error prone and is slower than early bound code. To make a late bound method call, the .NET runtime must dynamically determine if the target object actually has a method that matches the one we're calling. It must then invoke that method on our behalf. This takes more time and effort than an early bound call where the compiler knows ahead of time that the method exists and can compile our code to make the call directly. With a late bound call, the compiler has to generate code to make the call dynamically at runtime.

Use of the CType Function

Whether we are using late binding or not, it can be useful to pass object references around using the Object data type, converting them to an appropriate type when we need to interact with them. This is particularly useful when working with objects that use inheritance or implement multiple interfaces, concepts that we'll discuss in Chapter 6.

If Option Strict is turned off, which is the default, we can write code that allows us to use a variable of type Object to make an early bound method call:

```
Module LateBind
   Public Sub DoWork(obj As Object)

      Dim local As TheClass
      local = obj
      local.DoSomething()
   End Sub
End Module
```

We are using a strongly typed variable, local, to reference what was a generic object value. Behind the scenes, VB.NET converts the generic type to a specific type so it can be assigned to the strongly typed variable. If the conversion can't be done we'll get a trappable runtime error.

The same thing can be done using the CType function. If Option Strict is enabled, then the previous approach will not compile and the CType function must be used. Here is the same code making use of CType:

```
Module LateBind
    Public Sub DoWork(obj As Object)

        Dim local As TheClass

        local = CType(obj, TheClass)
        local.DoSomething()
    End Sub
End Module
```

Here, we've declared a variable of type TheClass, which is an early bound data type that we want to use. The parameter we're accepting, though, is of the generic Object data type, and so we use the CType() method to gain an early bound reference to the object. If the object isn't of type TheClass, the call to CType() will fail with a trappable error.

Once we have a reference to the object, we can call methods by using the early bound variable, local.

Since all the method calls with CType( ) are early bound, this code will work even if we override the default and set Option Strict On.

This code can be shortened to avoid the use of the intermediate variable. Instead, we can simply call methods directly from the data type:

```
Module LateBind
    Public Sub DoWork(obj As Object)
        CType(obj, TheClass).DoSomething()
    End Sub
End Module
```

Even though the variable we're working with is of type Object and, thus, any calls to it will be late bound, we are using the CType method to temporarily convert the variable into a specific type — in this case, the type TheClass.

> If the object passed as a parameter is not of type TheClass, we will get a trappable error, so it is always wise to wrap this code in a Try...Catch block.

The CType function can be very useful when working with objects that implement multiple interfaces, since we can reference a single object variable through the appropriate type as needed. For instance, as we discussed earlier, if we have an object of type TheClass that also implements ITheInterface, we can use that interface with the following code:

```
Dim obj As TheClass

obj = New TheClass
CType(obj, ITheInterface).DoSomething()
```

In this way, we can make early bound calls to other interfaces on an object without needing to declare a new variable of the interface type. We'll discuss multiple interfaces in detail in Chapter 6.

Use of the DirectCast Function

Another function that is very similar to CType is DirectCast. DirectCast also converts values of one type into another type. It is more restrictive in its working than Ctype, but the tradeoff is that it can be somewhat faster than CType. DirectCast is used like the following code:

```
Dim obj As TheClass

obj = New TheClass
DirectCast(obj, ITheInterface).DoSomething()
```

This is similar to the last example with CType, illustrating the parity between the two functions. There are differences, however. First, DirectCast works only with reference types, while CType accepts both reference and value types. For instance, with CType we can use the following code:

```
Dim int As Integer = CType(123.45, Integer)
```

Trying to do the same thing with DirectCast would result in a compiler error, since the value 123.45 is a value type, not a reference type.

The other difference is that DirectCast is not as aggressive about converting types as CType can be. CType can be viewed as an intelligent combination of all the other conversion functions (such as CInt, CStr, etc.). DirectCast on the other hand, assumes that the source data is directly convertible and it won't take extra steps to convert the data.

As an example, consider the following code:

```
Dim obj As Object = 123.45

Dim int As Integer = DirectCast(obj, Integer)
```

If we were using CType this would work, since CType would use CInt-like behavior to convert the value to an Integer. DirectCast, however, will throw an exception because the value is not directly convertible to Integer.

Creating Classes

Using objects is fairly straightforward and intuitive. It is the kind of thing that even the most novice programmers pick up and accept rapidly. Creating classes and objects is a bit more complex and interesting, and that is what we'll cover through the rest of the chapter.

Creating Basic Classes

As we discussed earlier, objects are merely instances of a specific template (a class). The class contains the code that defines the behavior of its objects, as well as defining the instance variables that will contain the object's individual data.

Classes are created using the Class keyword, and include definitions (declaration) and implementations (code) for the variables, methods, properties, and events that make up the class. Each object created based on this class will have the same methods, properties, and events, and will have its own set of data defined by the variables in our class.

The Class Keyword

If we wanted to create a class that represents a person—a `Person` class—we could use the `Class` keyword like this:

```
Public Class Person

    ' implementation code goes here
End Class
```

As we know, VB.NET projects are composed of a set of files with the `.vb` extension. Each file can contain multiple classes. This means that, within a single file, we could have something like this:

```
Public Class Adult
    ' implementation code goes here
End Class

Public Class Senior
    ' implementation code goes here
End Class

Public Class Child
    ' implementation code goes here
End Class
```

The most common approach is to have a single class per file. This is because the Visual Studio .NET (VS.NET) Solution Explorer and the code-editing environment are tailored to make it easy to navigate from file to file to find our code. For instance, if we create a single class file with all these classes, the Solution Explorer simply shows a single entry as shown in Figure 5-1.

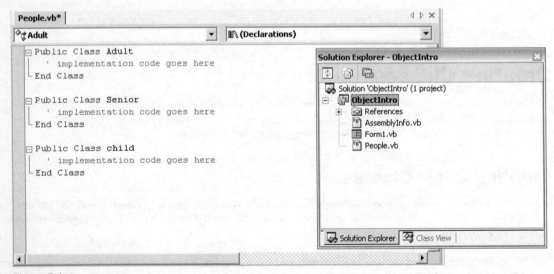

Figure 5-1

However, the VS.NET IDE does provide the Class View window. If we do decide to put multiple classes in each physical .vb file, we can make use of the Class View window to quickly and efficiently navigate through our code, jumping from class to class without having to manually locate those classes in specific code files as shown in Figure 5-2.

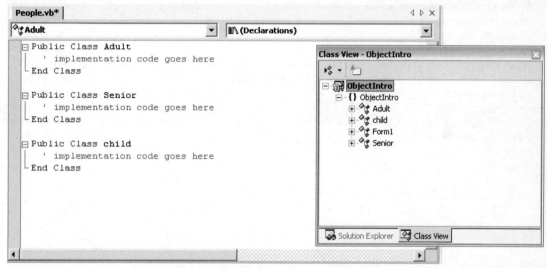

Figure 5-2

> **The Class View window is incredibly useful even if we keep to one class per file, since it still provides us with a class-based view of our entire application.**

In this chapter, we'll stick with one class per file, as it is the most common approach. Open the VS.NET IDE and create a new Windows Application project. Name it ObjectIntro. Choose the Project ⇨ Add Class menu option to add a new class module to the project. You'll be presented with the standard Add New Item dialog box. Change the name to Person.vb and click Open. The result will be the following code that defines our Person class:

```
Public Class Person

End Class
```

It is worth noting that all VB.NET source files end in a .vb extension, regardless of which type of VB source file we choose (form, class, module, etc.) when we are adding the file to our project. In fact, any forms, classes, components, or controls that we add to our project are actually class modules — they are just specific types of classes that provide the appropriate behaviors. Typically, these behaviors come from another class via inheritance, which we'll discuss in Chapter 6.

The exception is the Module, which is a special construct that allows us to include code within our application that is not directly contained within any class. As with previous versions of Visual Basic, methods placed in a Module can be called directly from any code within our project.

With our `Person` class created, we're ready to start adding code to declare our interface, implement our behaviors, and declare our instance variables.

Member Variables

Member or instance variables are variables declared in our class that will be available to each individual object when our application is run. Each object gets its own set of data—basically, each object gets its own copy of the variables.

At the beginning of the chapter, we discussed how a class is simply a template from which we create specific objects. Variables that we define within our class are also simply templates—and each object gets its own copy of those variables in which to store its data.

Declaring member variables is as easy as declaring variables within the `Class` block structure. Add the following code to our `Person` class:

```
Public Class Person

  Private mstrName As String
  Private mdtBirthDate As Date

End Class
```

We can control the scope of our variables by using the following keywords:

❑ `Private`—available only to code within our class

❑ `Friend`—available only to code within our project/component

❑ `Protected`—available only to classes that inherit from our class (discussed in detail in Chapter 6)

❑ `Protected Friend`—available to code within our project/component and classes that inherit from our class whether in our project or not (discussed in detail in Chapter 6)

❑ `Public`—available to code outside our class and to any projects that reference our assembly

Typically, member variables are declared using the `Private` keyword, making them available only to code within each instance of our class. Choosing any other option should be done with great care, as all the other options allow code *outside* our class to directly interact with the variable, meaning that the value could be changed and our code would never know that a change took place.

> One common exception to making variables Private is the use of the Protected keyword, as we'll discuss in Chapter 6.

Methods

Objects typically need to provide services (or functions) that we can call when working with the object. Using their own data or data passed as parameters to the method, they manipulate information to yield a result or to perform a service.

Methods declared as `Public`, `Friend`, or `Protected` in scope define the interface of our class. Methods that are `Private` in scope are available to the code only within the class itself and can be used to provide structure and organization to our code. As we discussed earlier, the actual code within each method is called *implementation*, while the declaration of the method itself is what defines our interface.

Methods are simply routines that we code within the class to implement the services that we want to provide to the users of our object. Some methods return values or provide information back to the calling code. These are called *interrogative methods*. Others, called *imperative methods*, just perform a service and return nothing to the calling code.

In VB.NET, methods are implemented using `Sub` (for imperative methods) or `Function` (for interrogative methods) routines within the class module that defines our object. `Sub` routines may accept parameters, but they don't return any result value when they are complete. `Function` routines can also accept parameters, and they always generate a result value that can be used by the calling code.

A method declared with the `Sub` keyword is merely one that returns no value. Add the following code to our `Person` class:

```
Public Sub Walk()
  ' implementation code goes here
End Sub
```

The `Walk` method would presumably contain some code that performed some useful work when called but has no result value to return when it is complete.

To use this method, we might write code such as:

```
Dim myPerson As New Person()
myPerson.Walk()
```

Once we've created an instance of the `Person` class, we can simply invoke the `Walk` method.

Methods that Return Values

If we have a method that does generate some value that should be returned, we need to use the `Function` keyword:

```
Public Function Age() As Integer
  Return DateDiff(DateInterval.Year, mdtBirthDate, Now())
End Function
```

Notice that we need to indicate the data type of the return value when we declare a `Function`. In this example, we are returning the calculated age as a result of the method. We can return any value of the appropriate data type by using the `Return` keyword.

We can also return the value without using the `Return` keyword, by setting the value of the function name itself:

```
Public Function Age() As Integer
  Age = DateDiff(DateInterval.Year, mdtBirthDate, Now())
End Function
```

This is functionally equivalent to the previous code. Either way, we can use this method with code similar to the following:

```
Dim myPerson As New Person()
Dim intAge As Integer

intAge = myPerson.Age()
```

The `Age` method returns an `Integer` data value that we can use in our program as required; in this case, we're just storing it into a variable.

Indicating Method Scope

Adding the appropriate keyword in front of the method declaration indicates the scope:

```
Public Sub Walk()
```

This indicates that `Walk` is a `Public` method and is thus available to code outside our class and even outside our current project. Any application that references our assembly can use this method. By being `Public`, this method becomes part of our object's interface.

On the other hand, we might choose to restrict the method somewhat:

```
Friend Sub Walk()
```

By declaring the method with the `Friend` keyword, we are indicating that it should be part of our object's interface only for code inside our project, any other applications or projects that make use of our assembly will not be able to call the `Walk` method.

```
Private Function Age() As Integer
```

The `Private` keyword indicates that a method is only available to the code within our particular class. `Private` methods are very useful to help us organize complex code within each class. Sometimes our methods will contain very lengthy and complex code. In order to make this code more understandable, we may choose to break it up into several smaller routines, having our main method call these routines in the proper order. Moreover, we may use these routines from several places within our class and so, by making them separate methods, we enable reuse of the code. These subroutines should never be called by code outside our object, and so we make them `Private`.

Method Parameters

We will often want to pass information into a method as we call it. This information is provided via parameters to the method. For instance, in our `Person` class, perhaps we want our `Walk` method to track the distance the person walks over time. In such a case, the `Walk` method would need to know how far the person is to walk each time the method is called. Add the following code to our `Person` class:

```
Public Class Person
   Private mstrName As String
   Private mdtBirthDate As Date
   Private mintTotalDistance As Integer
```

```
Public Sub Walk(ByVal Distance As Integer)
   mintTotalDistance += Distance
End Sub

Public Function Age() As Integer
   Return DateDiff(DateInterval.Year, mdtBirthDate, Now())
End Function
End Class
```

With this implementation, a `Person` object will sum up all of the distances walked over time. Each time the `Walk` method is called, the calling code must pass an `Integer` value indicating the distance to be walked. Our code to call this method would be similar to the following code:

```
Dim myPerson As New Person()
myPerson.Walk(12)
```

The parameter is accepted using the `ByVal` keyword. This indicates that the parameter value is a *copy* of the original value. This is the default way by which VB.NET accepts all parameters. Typically, this is desirable because it means that we can work with the parameter inside our code, changing its value with no risk of accidentally changing the original value back in the calling code.

If we do want to be able to change the value in the calling code, we can change the declaration to pass the parameter by reference by using the `ByRef` qualifier:

```
Public Sub Walk(ByRef Distance As Integer)
```

In this case, we'll get a reference (or pointer) back to the original value rather than receiving a copy. This means that any change we make to the `Distance` parameter will be reflected back in the calling code, very similar to the way object references work, as we discussed earlier in Chapter 4.

> **Using this technique can be dangerous, since it is not explicitly clear to the caller of our method that the value will change. Such unintended side effects can be hard to debug and should be avoided.**

Properties

The .NET environment provides for a specialized type of method called a *property*. A property is a method specifically designed for setting and retrieving data values. For instance, we declared a variable in our `Person` class to contain a name, so our `Person` class may include code to allow that name to be set and retrieved. This could be done using regular methods:

```
Public Sub SetName(ByVal Name As String)
   mstrName = Name
End Sub

Public Function GetName() As String
   Return mstrName
End Function
```

Using methods like these, we would write code to interact with our object, such as:

```
Dim myPerson As New Person()

myPerson.SetName("Jones")
MsgBox(myPerson.GetName())
```

While this is perfectly acceptable, it is not as nice as it could be through the use of a property. A `Property` style method consolidates the setting and retrieving of a value into a single structure, and also makes the code within our class overall smoother. We can rewrite these two methods into a single property. Add the following code to the `Person` class:

```
Public Property Name() As String
  Get
      Return mstrName
  End Get
  Set(ByVal Value As String)
    mstrName = Value
  End Set
End Property
```

By using a property method instead, we can make our client code much more readable:

```
Dim myPerson As New Person()

myPerson.Name = "Jones"
MsgBox(myPerson.Name)
```

The `Property` method is declared with both a scope and a data type:

```
Public Property Name() As String
```

In this example, we've declared the property as `Public` in scope, but it can be declared using the same scope options as any other method — `Public`, `Friend`, `Private`, or `Protected`.

As with other methods, a `Public` property is accessible to any code outside our class, including code in other assemblies that reference our assembly. `Friend` is available outside our class, but only to code within our VB project. `Protected` properties are available through inheritance, as we'll discuss in Chapter 6, and `Private` properties are only available to code within our class.

The return data type of this property is `String`. A property can return virtually any data type as appropriate for the nature of the value. In this regard, a property is very similar to a method declared using the `Function` keyword.

Though a `Property` method is a single structure, it is divided into two parts: a getter and a setter. The getter is contained within a `Get...End Get` block and is responsible for returning the value of the property on demand:

```
Get
   Return mstrName
End Get
```

Though the code in this example is very simple, it could be more complex, perhaps calculating the value to be returned or applying other business logic to change the value as it is returned.

Likewise, the code to change the value is contained within a Set ... End Set block:

```
Set(ByVal Value As String)
    mstrName = Value
End Set
```

The Set statement accepts a single parameter value that stores the new value. Our code in the block can then use this value to set the property's value as appropriate. The data type of this parameter must match the data type of the property itself. By having the parameter declared in this manner, we can change the variable name used for the parameter value if needed.

By default, the parameter is named Value. However, if we dislike the name Value, we can change the parameter name to something else, for example:

```
Set(ByVal NewName As String)
   mstrName = NewName
End Set
```

In many cases, we may apply business rules or other logic within this routine to ensure that the new value is appropriate before we actually update the data within our object.

Parameterized Properties

The Name property we created is an example of a single-value property. We can also create property arrays or parameterized properties. These properties reflect a range, or array, of values. As an example, a person will often have several phone numbers. We might implement a PhoneNumber property as a parameterized property, storing not only phone numbers, but also a description of each number. To retrieve a specific phone number we'd write code such as:

```
Dim myPerson As New Person()
Dim strHomePhone As String

strHomePhone = myPerson.Phone("home")
```

Or, to add or change a specific phone number, we'd write the following code:

```
myPerson.Phone("work") = "555-9876"
```

Not only are we retrieving and updating a phone number property, but we're also updating some specific phone number. This implies a couple of things. First, we're no longer able to use a simple variable to hold the phone number, since we are now storing a list of numbers and their associated names. Secondly, we've effectively added a parameter to our property. We're actually passing the name of the phone number as a parameter on each property call.

To store the list of phone numbers we can use the Hashtable class. The Hashtable is very similar to the standard VB Collection object, but it is more powerful — allowing us to test for the existence of an existing element. Add the following declaration to the Person class:

```
Public Class Person
   Private mstrName As String
```

```
Private mdtBirthDate As Date
Private mintTotalDistance As Integer

Private colPhones As New Hashtable()
```

We can implement the `Phone` property by adding the following code to our `Person` class:

```
Public Property Phone(ByVal Location As String) As String
  Get
    Return CStr(colPhones.Item(Location))
  End Get
  Set(ByVal Value As String)
    If colPhones.ContainsKey(Location) Then
      colPhones.Item(Location) = Value
    Else
      colPhones.Add(Location, Value)
    End If
  End Set
End Property
```

The declaration of the `Property` method itself is a bit different from what we've seen:

```
Public Property Phone(ByVal Location As String) As String
```

In particular, we've added a parameter, `Location`, to the property itself. This parameter will act as the index into our list of phone numbers and must be provided both when setting or retrieving phone number values.

Since the `Location` parameter is declared at the `Property` level, it is available to all code within the property, including both the `Get` and `Set` blocks.

Within our `Get` block, we use the `Location` parameter to select the appropriate phone number to return from the `Hashtable`:

```
Get
  Return colPhones.Item(Location)
End Get
```

With this code, if there is no value stored matching the `Location`, we'll get a trappable runtime error.

Similarly, in the `Set` block, we use the `Location` to update or add the appropriate element in the `Hashtable`. In this case, we're using the `ContainsKey` method of `Hashtable` to determine whether the phone number already exists in the list. If it does, we'll simply update the value in the list; otherwise, we'll add a new element to the list for the value:

```
Set(ByVal Value As String)
  If colPhones.ContainsKey(Location) Then
    colPhones.Item(Location) = Value
  Else
    colPhones.Add(Location, Value)
  End If
End Set
```

In this way, we're able to add or update a specific phone number entry based on the parameter passed by the calling code.

Read-Only Properties

There are times when we may want a property to be read-only, so that it can't be changed. In our Person class, for instance, we may have a read–write property for BirthDate, but just a read-only property for Age. In such a case, the BirthDate property is a normal property, as follows:

```
Public Property BirthDate() As Date
  Get
    Return mdtBirthDate
  End Get
  Set(ByVal Value As Date)
   mdtBirthDate = Value
  End Set
End Property
```

The Age value, on the other hand, is a derived value based on BirthDate. This is not a value that should ever be directly altered and, thus, is a perfect candidate for read-only status.

We already have an Age method implemented as a Function. Remove that code from the Person class, as we'll be replacing it with a Property routine instead.

The difference between a Function routine and a ReadOnly Property is quite subtle. Both return a value to the calling code and, either way, our object is running a subroutine defined by our class module to return the value.

The difference is less a programmatic one than a design choice. We could create all our objects without any Property routines at all, just using methods for all interactions with the object. However, Property routines are obviously attributes of the object, while a Function might be an attribute or a method. By carefully implementing all attributes as ReadOnly Property routines, and any interrogative methods as Function routines, we will create more readable and understandable code.

To make a property read-only, we use the ReadOnly keyword and only implement the Get block:

```
Public ReadOnly Property Age() As Integer
  Get
    Return CInt(DateDiff(DateInterval.Year, mdtBirthDate, Now()))
  End Get
End Property
```

Since the property is read-only, we'll get a syntax error if we attempt to implement a Set block.

Write-Only Properties

As with read-only properties, there are times when a property should be write-only, where the value can be changed, but not retrieved.

Many people have allergies, so perhaps our Person object should have some understanding of the ambient allergens in the area. This is not a property that should be read from the Person object since allergens come from the environment rather than from the person, but it is data that the `Person` object needs in order to function properly. Add the following variable declaration to our class:

```
Public Class Person
    Private mstrName As String
    Private mdtBirthDate As Date
    Private mintTotalDistance As Integer
    Private colPhones As New Hashtable()
    Private mintAllergens As Integer
```

We can implement an `AmbientAllergens` property as follows:

```
Public WriteOnly Property AmbientAllergens() As Integer
    Set(ByVal Value As Integer)
        mintAllergens = Value
    End Set
End Property
```

To create a write-only property, we use the `WriteOnly` keyword and only implement a `Set` block in our code. Since the property is write-only, we'll get a syntax error if we attempt to implement a `Get` block.

The Default Property

Objects can implement a default property if desired. A default property can be used to simplify the use of our object at times, by making it appear as if our object has a native value. A good example of this behavior is the `Collection` object, which has a default property called `Item` that returns the value of a specific item, allowing us to write code similar to:

```
Dim colData As New Collection()

Return colData(Index)
```

Default properties *must be* parameterized properties. A property without a parameter cannot be marked as the default. This is a change from previous versions of Visual Basic, where any property could be marked as the default.

Our `Person` class has a parameterized property — the `Phone` property we built earlier. We can make this the default property by using the `Default` keyword:

```
Default Public Property Phone(ByVal Location As String) As String
    Get
        Return colPhones.Item(Location)
    End Get
    Set(ByVal Value As String)
        If colPhones.ContainsKey(Location) Then
            colPhones.Item(Location) = Value
        Else
            colPhones.Add(Location, Value)
        End If
    End Set
End Property
```

Prior to this change, we would need code such as the following to use the `Phone` property:

```
Dim myPerson As New Person()

MyPerson.Phone("home") = "555-1234"
```

But now, with the property marked as `Default`, we can simplify our code:

```
myPerson("home") = "555-1234"
```

By picking appropriate default properties, we can potentially make the use of our objects more intuitive.

Events

Both methods and properties allow us to write code that interacts with our objects by invoking specific functionality, as needed. It is often useful for our objects to provide notification as certain activities occur during processing. We see examples of this all the time with controls, where a button indicates it was clicked via a `Click` event, or a textbox indicates its contents have changed via the `TextChanged` event.

Our objects can raise events of their own, providing a powerful and easily implemented mechanism by which objects can notify our client code of important activities or events. In VB.NET, events are provided using the standard .NET mechanism of *delegates*. We'll discuss delegates after we explore how to work with events in Visual Basic.

Handling Events

We are all used to seeing code in a form to handle the `Click` event of a button, such as the following code:

```
Private Sub button1_Click (ByVal sender As System.Object, _
    ByVal e As System.EventArgs) Handles button1.Click
End Sub
```

Typically, we write our code in this routine without paying a lot of attention to the code created by the VS.NET IDE. However, let's take a second look at that code, since there are a couple of important things to note here.

First, notice the use of the `Handles` keyword. This key word specifically indicates that this method will be handling the `Click` event from the `button1` control. Of course, a control is just an object, so what we're indicating here is that this method will be handling the `Click` event from the `button1` object.

Also notice that the method accepts two parameters. The Button control class defines these parameters. It turns out that any method that accepts two parameters with these data types can be used to handle the `Click` event. For instance, we could create a new method to handle the event:

```
Private Sub MyClickMethod(ByVal s As System.Object, _
    ByVal args As System.EventArgs) Handles button1.Click

End Sub
```

Even though we've changed the method name, and the names of the parameters, we are still accepting parameters of the same data types and we still have the `Handles` clause to indicate that this method will handle the event.

Handling Multiple Events

The `Handles` keyword offers even more flexibility. Not only can the method name be anything we choose, but also a single method can handle multiple events if we desire. Again, the only requirement is that the method and all the events being raised must have the same parameter list.

This explains why all the standard events raised by the .NET system class library have exactly two parameters — the sender and an `EventArgs` object. By being so generic, it is possible to write very generic and powerful event handlers than can accept virtually any event raised by the class library.

One common scenario where this is useful is where we have multiple instances of an object that raises events, such as two buttons on a form:

```
Private Sub MyClickMethod(ByVal sender As System.Object, _
    ByVal e As System.EventArgs) _

    Handles button1.Click, button2.Click

End Sub
```

Notice that we've modified the `Handles` clause to have a comma-separated list of events to handle. Either event will cause our method to run, giving us a central location to handle these events.

The WithEvents Keyword

The `WithEvents` keyword tells Visual Basic that we want to handle any events raised by the object within our code. For example:

```
Friend WithEvents button1 As System.Windows.Forms.Button
```

The `WithEvents` keyword makes any events from an object available for our use, while the `Handles` keyword is used to link specific events to our methods so we can receive and handle them. This is true not only for controls on forms, but also for any objects that we create.

The `WithEvents` keyword cannot be used to declare a variable of a type that doesn't raise events. In other words, if the `Button` class didn't contain code to raise events, we'd get a syntax error when we attempt to declare the variable using the `WithEvents` keyword.

The compiler can tell which classes will and won't raise events by examining their interface. Any class that will be raising an event will have that event declared as part of its interface. In VB.NET, this means that we will have used the `Event` keyword to declare at least one event as part of the interface for our class.

Raising Events

Our objects can raise events just like a control, and the code using our object can receive these events by using the `WithEvents` and `Handles` keywords. Before we can raise an event from our object, however, we need to declare the event within our class by using the `Event` keyword.

In our `Person` class, for instance, we may want to raise an event any time the `Walk` method is called. If we call this event `Walked`, we can add the following declaration to our `Person` class:

```
Public Class Person
    Private mstrName As String
```

```
Private mdtBirthDate As Date
Private mintTotalDistance As Integer
Private colPhones As New Hashtable()
Private mintAllergens As Integer
```

```
Public Event Walked()
```

Our events can also have parameters, values that are provided to the code receiving the event. A typical button's `Click` event receives two parameters, for instance. In our `Walked` method, perhaps we want to also indicate the distance that was walked. We can do this by changing the event declaration:

```
Public Event Walked(ByVal Distance As Integer)
```

Now that our event is declared, we can raise that event within our code where appropriate. In this case, we'll raise it within the `Walk` method. So any time that a `Person` object is instructed to walk, it will fire an event indicating the distance walked. Make the following change to the `Walk` method:

```
Public Sub Walk(ByVal Distance As Integer)
   mintTotalDistance += Distance
   RaiseEvent Walked(Distance)
End Sub
```

The `RaiseEvent` keyword is used to raise the actual event. Since our event requires a parameter, that value is passed within parentheses and will be delivered to any recipient that handles the event.

In fact, the `RaiseEvent` statement will cause the event to be delivered to all code that has our object declared using the `WithEvents` keyword with a `Handles` clause for this event, or any code that has used the `AddHandler` method.

If more than one method will be receiving the event, the event will be delivered to each recipient one at a time. The order of delivery is not defined—meaning that we can't predict the order in which the recipients will receive the event—but the event will be delivered to all handlers. Note that this is a serial, synchronous process. The event is delivered to one handler at a time, and it is not delivered to the next handler until the current handler is complete. Once we call the `RaiseEvent` method, the event will be delivered to all listeners one after another until it is complete; there is no way for us to intervene and stop the process in the middle.

Receiving Events with WithEvents

Now that we've implemented an event within our `Person` class, we can write client code to declare an object using the `WithEvents` keyword. For instance, in our project's `Form1` code module, we can write the following code:

```
Public Class Form1
   Inherits System.Windows.Forms.Form

   Private WithEvents mobjPerson As Person
```

By declaring the variable `WithEvents`, we are indicating that we want to receive any events raised by this object.

We can also choose to declare the variable without the `WithEvents` keyword, though, in that case, we would not receive events from the object as described here. Instead, we would use the `AddHandler` method, which we'll discuss after we cover the use of `WithEvents`.

We can then create an instance of the object, as the form is created, by adding the following code:

```
Private Sub Form1_Load(ByVal sender As System.Object, _
    ByVal e As System.EventArgs) Handles MyBase.Load

  mobjPerson = New Person()

End Sub
```

At this point, we've declared the object variable using `WithEvents`, and have created an instance of the `Person` class so we actually have an object with which to work. We can now proceed to write a method to handle the `Walked` event from the object by adding the following code to the form. We can name this method anything we like, it is the `Handles` clause that is important as it links the event from the object directly to this method, so it is invoked when the event is raised:

```
Private Sub OnWalk(ByVal Distance As Integer) Handles mobjPerson.Walked
  MsgBox("Person walked " & Distance)
End Sub
```

We're using the `Handles` keyword to indicate which event should be handled by this method. We're also receiving an `Integer` parameter. If the parameter list of our method doesn't match the list for the event, we'll get a compiler error indicating the mismatch.

Finally, we need to call the `Walk` method on our `Person` object. Add a button to the form and write the following code for its `Click` event:

```
Private Sub Button1_Click(ByVal sender As System.Object, _
    ByVal e As System.EventArgs) Handles button1.Click

  mobjPerson.Walk(42)

End Sub
```

When the button is clicked, we'll simply call the `Walk` method, passing an `Integer` value. This will cause the code in our class to be run, including the `RaiseEvent` statement. The result will be an event firing back into our form, since we declared the `mobjPerson` variable using the `WithEvents` keyword. Our `OnWalk` method will be run to handle the event, since it has the `Handles` clause linking it to the event.

The diagram in Figure 5-3 illustrates the flow of control.

The diagram illustrates how the code in the button's click event calls the `Walk` method, causing it to add to the total distance walked and then to raise its event. The `RaiseEvent` causes the `OnWalk` method in the form to be invoked and, once it is done, control returns to the `Walk` method in the object. Since we have no code in the `Walk` method after we call `RaiseEvent`, the control returns to the `Click` event back in the form, and then we're all done.

Many people have the misconception that events use multiple threads to do their work. This is not the case. Only one thread is involved in this process. Raising an event is much like making a method call, in that our

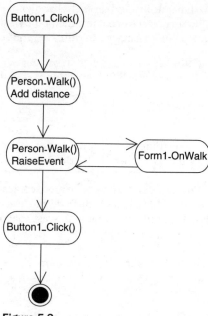

Figure 5-3

existing thread is used to run the code in the event handler. This means our application's processing is suspended until the event processing is complete.

Receiving Events with AddHandler

Now that we've seen how to receive and handle events using the `WithEvents` and `Handles` keywords, let's take a look at an alternative approach. We can use the `AddHandler` method to dynamically add event handlers through our code and `RemoveHandler` to dynamically remove them.

`WithEvents` and the `Handles` clause require that we declare both the object variable and event handler as we build our code, effectively creating a linkage that is compiled right into our code. `AddHandler`, on the other hand, creates this linkage at runtime, which can provide us with more flexibility. However, before we get too deep into that, let's see how `AddHandler` works.

In `Form1`, we can change the way our code interacts with the `Person` object, first, by eliminating the `WithEvents` keyword:

```
Private mobjPerson As Person
```

and then also eliminating the `Handles` clause:

```
Private Sub OnWalk(ByVal Distance As Integer)
   MsgBox("Person walked " & Distance)
End Sub
```

With these changes, we've eliminated all event handling for our object and so our form will no longer receive the event, even though the `Person` object raises it.

Now we can change the code to dynamically add an event handler at runtime by using the AddHandler method. This method simply links an object's event to a method that should be called to handle that event. Any time after we've created our object, we can call AddHandler to set up the linkage:

```
Private Sub Form1_Load(ByVal sender As System.Object, _
    ByVal e As System.EventArgs) Handles MyBase.Load
  mobjPerson = New Person()
  AddHandler mobjPerson.Walked, AddressOf OnWalk
End Sub
```

This single line of code does the same thing as our earlier use of WithEvents and the Handles clause, causing the OnWalk method to be invoked when the Walked event is raised from our Person object.

However, this linkage is done at runtime, and so we have more control over the process than we would have otherwise. For instance, we could have extra code to decide *which* event handler to link up. Suppose we have another possible method to handle the event in the case that a message box is not desirable. Add this code to Form1:

```
Private Sub LogOnWalk(ByVal Distance As Integer)
    System.Diagnostics.Debug.WriteLine("Person walked " & Distance)
End Sub
```

Rather than popping up a message box, this version of the handler logs the event to the Output window in the IDE.

Now we can enhance our AddHandler code to decide which handler should be used dynamically at runtime:

```
Private Sub Form1_Load(ByVal sender As System.Object, _
    ByVal e As System.EventArgs) Handles MyBase.Load
  mobjPerson = New Person()
  If Microsoft.VisualBasic.Command = "nodisplay" Then
    AddHandler mobjPerson.Walked, AddressOf LogOnWalk
  Else
    AddHandler mobjPerson.Walked, AddressOf OnWalk
  End If
End Sub
```

If the word nodisplay is on the command line when our application is run, the new version of the event handler will be used, otherwise we'll continue to use the message box handler.

The counterpart to AddHandler is RemoveHandler. RemoveHandler is used to detach an event handler from an event. One example of where this is useful is if we ever want to set the mobjPerson variable to Nothing or to a new Person object. The existing Person object has its events attached to handlers, and before we get rid of our reference to the object we must release those references:

```
If Microsoft.VisualBasic.Command = "nodisplay" Then
    RemoveHandler mobjPerson.Walked, AddressOf LogOnWalk
Else
    RemoveHandler mobjPerson.Walked, AddressOf OnWalk
  mobjPerson = New Person
```

If we don't detach the event handlers, the old `Person` object would remain in memory as each event handler would still maintain a reference to the object even after `mobjPerson` no longer points to the object.

This illustrates one key reason why the `WithEvents` keyword and `Handles` clause are preferable in most cases. `AddHandler` and `RemoveHandler` must be used in pairs and failure to do so can cause memory leaks in our application, while the `WithEvents` keyword handles these details for us automatically.

Constructor Methods

In VB.NET, classes can implement a special method that is always invoked as an object is being created. This method is called the constructor and it is always named `New`.

The constructor method is an ideal location for such initialization code, since it is always run before any other methods are ever invoked, and it is only ever run once for an object. Of course, we can create many objects based on a class, and the constructor method will be run for each object that is created.

> *The constructor method of a VB.NET class is similar to the Class_Initialize event in previous versions of Visual Basic, but is far more powerful in VB.NET since we can accept parameter values as input to the method.*

We can implement a constructor in our classes as well, using it to initialize our objects as needed. This is as easy as implementing a `Public` method named `New`. Add the following code to our `Person` class:

```
Public Sub New()
    Phone("home") = "555-1234"
    Phone("work") = "555-5678"
End Sub
```

In this example, we're simply using the constructor method to initialize the home and work phone numbers for any new `Person` object that is created.

Parameterized Constructors

We can also use constructors to allow parameters to be passed to our object as it is being created. This is done by simply adding parameters to the `New` method. For example, we can change the `Person` class as follows:

```
Public Sub New(ByVal Name As String, ByVal BirthDate As Date)
    mstrName = Name
    mdtBirthDate = BirthDate

    Phone("home") = "555-1234"
    Phone("work") = "555-5678"
End Sub
```

With this change, any time a `Person` object is created, we'll be provided with values for both the name and birth date. This, however, changes how we can create a new `Person` object. Where we used to having code such as:

```
Dim myPerson As New Person()
```

now we will have code such as:

```
Dim myPerson As New Person("Peter", "1/1/1960")
```

In fact, since our constructor expects these values, they are mandatory—any code wishing to create an instance of our `Person` class *must* provide these values. Fortunately, there are alternatives in the form of optional parameters and method overloading (which allows us to create multiple versions of the same method, each accepting a different parameter list. We'll discuss these topics later in the chapter).

Termination and Cleanup

In the .NET environment, an object is destroyed and the memory and resources it consumes are reclaimed when there are no references remaining for the object.

As we discussed earlier in the chapter, when we are using objects, our variables actually hold a reference or pointer to the object itself. If we have code such as:

```
Dim myPerson As New Person()
```

we know that the `myPerson` variable is just a reference to the `Person` object we created. If we also have code like this:

```
Dim anotherPerson As Person
anotherPerson = myPerson
```

we know that the `anotherPerson` variable is also a reference to *the same object*. This means that this specific `Person` object is being referenced by two variables.

When there are *no* variables left to reference an object, it can be terminated by the .NET runtime environment. In particular, it is terminated and reclaimed by a mechanism called garbage collection, which we'll discuss shortly.

> Unlike COM (and thus VB6), the .NET runtime does not use reference counting to determine when an object should be terminated. Instead, it uses a scheme known as garbage collection to terminate objects. This means that, in VB.NET, we do not have deterministic finalization, so it is not possible to predict exactly when an object will be destroyed.

Before we get to garbage collection, however, let's review how we can eliminate references to an object. We can explicitly remove a reference by setting our variable equal to `Nothing`, with the following code:

```
myPerson = Nothing
```

There are two schools of thought as to whether we should still explicitly set variables to `Nothing` even when they fall out of scope. On one hand, we can save writing extra lines of code by allowing the variable to automatically be destroyed, but on the other hand, we can explicitly show our intent to destroy the object by setting it to `Nothing` manually.

Perhaps the most important fact is that the garbage collection mechanism will sometimes reclaim our objects in the middle of our processing. This can only happen if our code doesn't use the object later in the method. Setting the variable to `Nothing` at the end of the method will prevent the garbage collection mechanism from proactively reclaiming our objects.

We can also remove a reference to an object by changing the variable to reference a different object. Since a variable can only point to one object at a time, it follows naturally that changing a variable to point at another object must cause it to no longer point to the first one. This means we can have code such as in the following:

```
myPerson = New Person()
```

This causes the variable to point to a brand new object, thus releasing this reference to the prior object.

These are examples of *explicit* dereferencing. VB.NET also provides facilities for implicit dereferencing of objects when a variable goes out of scope. For instance, if we have a variable declared within a method, when that method completes the variable will be automatically destroyed, thus dereferencing any object to which it may have pointed. In fact, any time a variable referencing an object goes out of scope, the reference to that object is automatically eliminated. This is illustrated by the following code:

```
Private Sub DoSomething()
  Dim myPerson As Person

  myPerson = New Person()
End Sub
```

Even though we didn't explicitly set the value of myPerson to Nothing, we know that the myPerson variable will be destroyed when the method is complete, since it will fall out of scope. This process implicitly removes the reference to the Person object created within the routine.

Of course, another scenario where objects become dereferenced is when the application itself completes and is terminated. At that point, all variables are destroyed and so, by definition, all object references go away as well.

We discussed garbage collection and the Finalize method in Chapter 3. When we discussed these concepts, we mentioned that there was no automatic way to perform the cleanup when the final reference to an object is released, although implementing the IDisposable interface provides one solution. We'll investigate that solution now.

The IDisposable Interface

In some cases the Finalize behavior is not acceptable. If we have an object that is using some expensive or limited resource, such as a database connection, a file handle, or a system lock, we might need to ensure that the resource is freed as soon as the object is no longer in use.

To accomplish this, we can implement a method to be called by the client code to force our object to clean up and release its resources. This is not a perfect solution, but it is workable. We should remember that this method is not called automatically by the .NET runtime environment, instead, must be called directly by the code using the object.

The .NET Framework provides the IDisposable interface that formalizes the declaration of this cleanup method. We'll discuss creating and working with multiple interfaces in detail later so, for now, we'll just focus on the implementation of the Dispose method from a cleanup perspective.

Any class that derives from System.ComponentModel.Component automatically gains the IDisposable interface. This includes all of the forms and controls that are used in a Windows Forms UI, as well as various other classes within the .NET Framework. For most of our custom classes, however, we'll need to implement the interface ourselves.

We can implement it in our `Person` class by adding the following code to the top of the class:

```
Public Class Person
   Implements IDisposable
```

This interface defines a single method—`Dispose`—that we need to implement in our class. It is implemented by adding the following code to the class:

```
Public Sub Dispose() Implements IDisposable.Dispose
   colPhones = Nothing
End Sub
```

In this case, we're using this method to release our reference to the `HashTable` object that the `colPhones` variable points to. While not strictly necessary, this illustrates how our code can release other objects when the `Dispose` method is called.

It is up to our client code to call this method at the appropriate time to ensure that cleanup occurs. Typically, we'll want to call the method as soon as we're done using the object.

This is not always as easy as it might sound. In particular, an object may be referenced by more than one variable and just because we're dereferencing the object from *one* variable doesn't mean it has been dereferenced by *all* the other variables. If we call the `Dispose` method while other references remain, our object may become unusable and may cause errors when invoked via those other references. There is no easy solution to this problem so careful design is required in the case that we choose to use the `IDispose` interface.

In our application's `Form1` code, we use the `OnLoad` method of the form to create an instance of the `Person` object. In the form's `OnClosed` method, we may want to make sure to clean up by disposing of the `Person` object. To do this, add the following code to the form:

```
Private Sub Form1_Closed(ByVal sender As Object, _
    ByVal e As System.EventArgs) Handles MyBase.Closed

  mobjPerson.Dispose()

End Sub
```

The `OnClosed` method runs as the form is being closed, and so it is an appropriate place to do cleanup work.

Before we can dereference the `Person` object, however, we can now call its `Dispose` method. Since this method is part of a secondary interface (something we'll discuss more later), we need to use the `CType()` method to access that specific interface in order to call the method:

```
CType(mobjPerson, IDisposable).Dispose()
```

`CType()` allows us to indicate the specific interface by which we want to access the object, in this case, the `IDisposable` interface. Once we're using that interface, we can call the `Dispose` method to cause the object to do any cleanup before we release our reference:

```
mobjPerson = Nothing
```

Note that if we opt to implement `IDisposable` we should always also implement a `Finalize` method as described in Chapter 3. There is never a guarantee that our `Dispose` method will be called, so it is critical that `Finalize` trigger our cleanup code if it was not already executed.

This way, once we've released an object reference, we know that the garbage collection mechanism will eventually find and terminate the object, thus running its `Finalize` method. In the meantime, however, we've forced the object to do any cleanup immediately, so its resources are not consumed during the time between our release of the reference and the garbage collection terminating the object.

Advanced Concepts

So far we've seen how to work with objects, how to create classes with methods, properties, and events, and how to use constructors. We've also discussed how objects are destroyed within the .NET environment and how we can hook into that process to do any cleanup required by our objects.

Now let's move on to discuss some more complex topics and variations on what we've discussed so far. First, we'll cover some advanced variations in terms of the methods we can implement in our classes, including an exploration of the underlying technology behind events.

From there we'll move on to delegates, the difference between components and classes, and .NET attributes as they pertain to classes and methods.

Overloading Methods

Methods often accept parameter values. Our `Person` object's `Walk` method, for instance, accepts an `Integer` parameter:

```
Public Sub Walk(ByVal Distance As Integer)
  mintTotalDistance += Distance
  RaiseEvent Walked(Distance)
End Sub
```

Sometimes we might not require the parameter. To solve this issue we can use the `Optional` keyword to make the parameter optional:

```
Public Sub Walk(Optional ByVal Distance As Integer = 0)
  mintTotalDistance += Distance
  RaiseEvent Walked(Distance)
End Sub
```

This doesn't provide us with a lot of flexibility, however, since the optional parameter or parameters must always be the last ones in the list. In addition, all this allows us to do is choose to pass or not to pass the parameter. Suppose we want to do something fancier, such as allow different data types, or even entirely different lists of parameters.

Method *overloading* provides exactly those capabilities. By overloading methods, we can create several methods of the *same name*, with each one accepting a different set of parameters or parameters of different data types.

As a simple example, instead of using the `Optional` keyword in our `Walk` method, we could use overloading. We'll keep our original `Walk` method, but we'll also add *another* `Walk` method that accepts a different parameter list. Change the code in our `Person` class back to:

```
Public Sub Walk(ByVal Distance As Integer)
  mintTotalDistance += Distance
  RaiseEvent Walked(Distance)
End Sub
```

Then we can create another method with the same name, but with a different parameter list (in this case no parameters). Add this code to the class, without removing or changing the existing `Walk` method:

```
Public Sub Walk()
   RaiseEvent Walked(0)
End Sub
```

At this point we have *two* `Walk` methods. The only way to tell them apart is by the list of parameters each accepts, the first requiring a single Integer parameter, the second having no parameter.

There is an Overloads keyword as well. This keyword is not needed for simple overloading of methods as described here, but is required when combining overloading and inheritance. We'll discuss this in Chapter 6.

Now we have the option of calling our `Walk` method in a couple of different ways. We can call it with a parameter:

```
objPerson.Walk(42)
```

or without a parameter:

```
objPerson.Walk()
```

We can have any number of `Walk` methods in our class as long as each individual `Walk` method has a different *method signature*.

Method Signatures

All methods have a signature, which is defined by the method name and the data types of its parameters.

```
Public Function CalculateValue() As Integer

End Sub
```

In this example, the signature is $f()$. The letter f is often used to indicate a method or function. It is appropriate here, because we don't care about the *name* of our function, only its parameter list is important.

If we add a parameter to the method, the signature will change. For instance, we could change the method to accept a `Double`:

```
Public Function CalculateValue(ByVal Value As Double) As Integer
```

Then the signature of the method is $f(\text{Double})$.

Notice that in VB.NET the return value is not part of the signature. We can't overload a `Function` routine by just having its return value's data type vary. It is the data types in the parameter list that must vary to utilize overloading.

Also make note that the *name* of the parameter is totally immaterial, only the data type is important. This means that the following methods have identical signatures:

```
Public Sub DoWork(ByVal X As Integer, ByVal Y As Integer)

Public Sub DoWork(ByVal Value1 As Integer, ByVal Value2 As Integer)
```

In both cases the signature is f(Integer, Integer).

The data types of the parameters define the method signature, but whether the parameters are passed ByVal or ByRef does not. Changing a parameter from ByVal to ByRef will not change the method signature.

Combining Overloading and Optional Parameters

Overloading is more flexible than using optional parameters, but optional parameters have the advantage that they can be used to provide default values as well as making a parameter optional.

We can combine the two concepts, overloading a method and also having one or more of those methods utilize optional parameters. Obviously, this sort of thing could get very confusing if overused, since we're employing two types of method "overloading" at the same time.

The Optional keyword causes a single method to effectively have two signatures. This means that a method declared as:

```
Public Sub DoWork(ByVal X As Integer, Optional ByVal Y As Integer = 0)
```

has two signatures at once: f(Integer, Integer) and f(Integer).

Because of this, when we use overloading along with optional parameters, our other overloaded methods cannot match *either* of these two signatures. However, as long as our other methods don't match either signature, we can use overloading as we discussed earlier. For instance, we could implement methods with the following different signatures:

```
Public Sub DoWork(ByVal X As Integer, _
     Optional ByVal Y As Integer = 0)
```

and

```
Public Sub DoWork(ByVal Data As String)
```

since there are no conflicting method signatures. In fact, with these two methods, we've really created three signatures:

- ❏ f(Integer, Integer)
- ❏ f(Integer)
- ❏ f(String)

The IntelliSense built into the VS.NET IDE will show that we have two overloaded methods, one of which has an optional parameter. This is different from if we had created three different overloaded methods to match these three signatures in which case the IntelliSense would list three variations on the method from which we can choose.

Overloading Constructor Methods

In many cases, we may want our constructor to accept parameter values for initializing new objects, but we also want to have the ability to create objects without providing those values. This is possible through method overloading, which we'll discuss later or through the use of optional parameters.

Optional parameters on a constructor method follow the same rules as optional parameters for any other Sub routine; they must be the last parameters in the parameter list and we must provide default values for the optional parameters.

For instance, we can change our Person class as shown:

```
Public Sub New(Optional ByVal Name As String = "", _
    Optional ByVal BirthDate As Date = #1/1/1900#)
  mstrName = Name
  mdtBirthDate = BirthDate

  Phone("home") = "555-1234"
  Phone("work") = "555-5678"
End Sub
```

Here we've changed both the Name and BirthDate parameters to be optional, and we are providing default values for both of them. Now we have the option of creating a new Person object with or without the parameter values:

```
Dim myPerson As New Person("Peter", "1/1/1960")
```

or

```
Dim myPerson As New Person()
```

If we don't provide the parameter values then the default values of an empty String and 1/1/1900 will be used and our code will work just fine.

Overloading the Constructor Method

We can combine the concept of a constructor method with method overloading to allow for different ways of creating instances of our class. This can be a very powerful combination, as it allows a great deal of flexibility in object creation.

We've already explored how to use optional parameters in the constructor. Now let's change our implementation in the Person class to make use of overloading instead. Change the existing New method as follows:

```
Public Sub New(ByVal Name As String, ByVal BirthDate As Date)
  mstrName = Name
  mdtBirthDate = BirthDate
```

```
      Phone("home") = "555-1234"
      Phone("work") = "555-5678"
   End Sub
```

With this change, we require the two parameter values to be supplied.

Now add that second implementation as shown:

```
   Public Sub New()
      Phone("home") = "555-1234"
      Phone("work") = "555-5678"
   End Sub
```

This second implementation accepts no parameters, meaning that we can now create `Person` objects in two different ways — either with no parameters or by passing the name and birth date:

```
   Dim myPerson As New Person()
```

or

```
   Dim myPerson As New Person("Fred", "1/11/60")
```

This type of capability is very powerful, as it allows us to define the various ways in which applications can create our objects. In fact, the VS.NET IDE takes this into account so, when we are typing the code to create an object, the IntelliSense tool tip will display the overloaded variations on the method, providing a level of automatic documentation for our class.

Shared Methods, Variables, and Events

So far, all of the methods we've built or used have been *instance methods*, methods that require us to have an actual instance of the class before they can be called. These methods have used instance variables or member variables to do their work, which means that they have been working with a set of data that is unique to each individual object.

VB.NET allows us to create variables and methods that belong to the *class* rather than to any specific *object*. Another way to say this is that these variables and methods belong to *all* objects of a given class and are shared across all the instances of the class.

We can use the `Shared` keyword to indicate which variables and methods belong to the class rather than to specific objects. For instance, we may be interested in knowing the total number of `Person` objects created as our application is running — kind of a statistical counter.

Shared Variables

Since regular variables are unique to each individual `Person` object, they don't allow us to easily track the total number of `Person` objects ever created. However, if we had a variable that had a common value *across* all instances of the `Person` class, we could use that as a counter. Add the following variable declaration to our `Person` class:

```
   Public Class Person
      Implements IDisposable

      Private Shared sintCounter As Integer
```

By using the Shared keyword, we are indicating that this variable's value should be shared across all Person objects within our application. This means that if one Person object makes the value be 42, all other Person objects will see the value as 42, it is a shared piece of data.

We are using the letter "s" as a prefix to this variable rather than "m." The letter "m" is commonly used for member variables (or module variables), but this variable is not a member variable, it is a shared variable. Using a different prefix can help distinguish between member and shared variables within our code.

We can now use this variable within our code. For instance, we can add code to the constructor method, New, to increment the variable so it acts as a counter — adding 1 each time a new Person object is created. Change the New methods as shown:

```
Public Sub New()
   Phone("home") = "555-1234"
   Phone("work") = "555-5678"
   sintCounter += 1
End Sub

Public Sub New(ByVal Name As String, ByVal BirthDate As Date)
   mstrName = Name
   mdtBirthDate = BirthDate

   Phone("home") = "555-1234"
   Phone("work") = "555-5678"
   sintCounter += 1
End Sub
```

The sintCounter variable will now maintain a value indicating the total number of Person objects created during the life of our application. We may want to add a property routine to allow access to this value by writing the following code:

```
Public ReadOnly Property PersonCount() As Integer
   Get
      Return sintCounter
   End Get
End Property
```

Notice that we're creating a regular property that returns the value of a shared variable. This is perfectly acceptable. As we'll see shortly, we could also choose to create a shared property to return the value.

Now, we could write code to use our class as follows:

```
Dim myPerson As Person

myPerson = New Person()
myPerson = New Person()
myPerson = New Person()

MsgBox(myPerson.PersonCount)
```

The resulting display would show 3, since we've created three instances of the Person class.

Shared Methods

We can not only share variables across all instances of our class, but we can also share methods. Where a regular method or property belongs to each specific object, a shared method or property is common across all instances of the class. There are a couple of ramifications to this approach.

First, since shared methods don't belong to any specific object, they can't access any instance variables from any objects. The only variables available for use within a shared method are shared variables, parameters passed into the method, or variables declared locally within the method itself. If we attempt to access an instance variable within a shared method, we'll get a compiler error.

Also, since shared methods are actually part of the *class* rather than any *object*, we can write code to call them directly from the class without having to create an instance of the class first.

For instance, a regular instance method is invoked from an object:

```
Dim myPerson As New Person()

myPerson.Walk(42)
```

but a shared method can be invoked directly from the class itself:

```
Person.SharedMethod()
```

This saves the effort of creating an object just to invoke a method, and can be very appropriate for methods that act on shared variables, or methods that act only on values passed in via parameters. We can also invoke a shared method from an object just like a regular method. Shared methods are flexible in that they can be called with or without creating an instance of the class first.

To create a shared method we again use the `Shared` keyword. For instance, the `PersonCount` property we created earlier could easily be changed to become a shared method instead:

```
Public Shared ReadOnly Property PersonCount() As Integer
   Get
      Return sintCounter
   End Get
End Property
```

Since this property returns the value of a shared variable, it is perfectly acceptable for it to be implemented as a shared method. With this change, we can now find out how many `Person` objects have ever been created without having to actually create a `Person` object first:

```
MsgBox(Person.PersonCount)
```

As another example, in our `Person` class we could create a method that compares the ages of two people. Add a shared method with the following code:

```
Public Shared Function CompareAge(ByVal Person1 As Person, _
     ByVal Person2 As Person) As Boolean

   Return Person1.Age > Person2.Age
End Function
```

This method simply accepts two parameters—each a `Person`—and returns `True` if the first is older than the second. The use of the `Shared` keyword indicates that this method doesn't require a specific instance of the `Person` class for us to use it.

Within this code, we are invoking the `Age` property on two separate objects, the objects passed as parameters to the method. It is important to recognize that we're not *directly* using any instance variables within the method, rather are accepting two objects as parameters and are invoking methods on those objects. To use this method, we can call it directly from the class:

```
If Person.CompareAge(myPerson1, myPerson2) Then
```

Alternately, we can also invoke it from any `Person` object:

```
Dim myPerson As New Person()

If myPerson.CompareAge(myPerson, myPerson2) Then
```

Either way, we're invoking the same shared method and we'll get the same behavior, whether we call it from the class or a specific instance of the class.

Shared Properties

As with other types of methods, we can also have shared property methods. Properties follow the same rules as regular methods. They can interact with shared variables, but not member variables, and they can invoke other shared methods or properties, but can't invoke instance methods without first creating an instance of the class. We can add a shared property to our `Person` class with the following code:

```
Public Shared ReadOnly Property RetirementAge() As Integer
  Get
     Return 62
  End Get
End Property
```

This simply adds a property to our class that indicates the global retirement age for all people. To use this value, we can simply access it directly from the class:

```
MsgBox(Person.RetirementAge)
```

Alternately, we can also access it from any `Person` object:

```
Dim myPerson As New Person()

MsgBox(myPerson.RetirementAge)
```

Either way, we're invoking the same shared property.

Shared Events

As with other interface elements, events can also be marked as `Shared`. For instance, we could declare a shared event in the `Person` class, such as:

```
Public Shared Event NewPerson()
```

Shared events can be raised from both instance methods and shared methods. Regular events cannot be raised by shared methods. Since shared events can be raised by regular methods, we can raise this one from the constructors in the `Person` class:

```
Public Sub New()
  Phone("home") = "555-1234"
  Phone("work") = "555-5678"
  sintCounter += 1
  RaiseEvent NewPerson()
End Sub

Public Sub New(ByVal Name As String, ByVal BirthDate As Date)
  mstrName = Name
  mdtBirthDate = BirthDate

  Phone("home") = "555-1234"
  Phone("work") = "555-5678"
  sintCounter += 1
  RaiseEvent NewPerson()
End Sub
```

The interesting thing about receiving shared events is that we can get them from either an object, like a normal event, or from the *class* itself. For instance, we can use the `AddHandler` method in our form's code to catch this event directly from the `Person` class.

First, let's add a method to the form to handle the event:

```
Private Sub OnNewPerson()
  MsgBox("new person " & Person.PersonCount)
End Sub
```

Then, in the form's `Load` event, add a statement to link the event to this method:

```
Private Sub Form1_Load(ByVal sender As System.Object, _
    ByVal e As System.EventArgs) Handles MyBase.Load

  AddHandler Person.NewPerson, AddressOf OnNewPerson

  mobjPerson = New Person()
  If Microsoft.VisualBasic.Command = "nodisplay" Then
    AddHandler mobjPerson.Walked, AddressOf LogOnWalk
  Else
    AddHandler mobjPerson.Walked, AddressOf OnWalk
  End If
End Sub
```

Notice that we are using the *class* rather than any specific object in the `AddHandler` statement. We could use an object as well, treating this like a normal event, but this illustrates how a class itself can raise an event.

When we run the application now, any time a `Person` object is created we'll see this event raised.

Delegates

There are times when it would be nice to be able to pass a procedure as a parameter to a method. The classic case is when building a generic sort routine, where we not only need to provide the data to be sorted, but we need to provide a comparison routine appropriate for the specific data.

It is easy enough to write a sort routine that sorts Person objects by name, or to write a sort routine that sorts SalesOrder objects by sales date. However, if we want to write a sort routine that can sort any type of object based on arbitrary sort criteria, that gets pretty difficult. At the same time, since some sort routines can get very complex it would be nice to reuse that code without having to copy and paste it for each different sort scenario.

By using delegates we can create such a generic routine for sorting, and in so doing we can see how delegates work and can be used to create many other types of generic routines.

The concept of a *delegate* formalizes the process of declaring a routine to be called and calling that routine.

> *The underlying mechanism used by the .NET environment for callback methods is the delegate. VB.NET uses delegates behind the scenes as it implements the Event, RaiseEvent, WithEvents, and Handles keywords.*

Declaring a Delegate

In our code, we can declare what a delegate procedure must look like from an interface standpoint. This is done using the Delegate keyword. To see how this can work, let's create a routine to sort any kind of data.

To do this, we'll declare a delegate that defines a method signature for a method that compares the value of two objects and returns a Boolean indicating whether the first object has a larger value than the second object. We'll then create a sort algorithm that uses this generic comparison method to sort data. Finally, we'll create an actual method that *implements* the comparison and we'll pass the address of that method to the sort routine.

Add a new module to our project by choosing the Project ⇨ Add Module menu option. Name the module Sort.vb and then add the following code:

```
Module Sort

    Public Delegate Function Compare(ByVal v1 As Object, ByVal v2 As Object) _
        As Boolean

End Module
```

This line of code does something interesting. It actually defines a method signature as a *data type*. This new data type is named Compare and it can be used within our code to declare variables or parameters that will be accepted by our methods. A variable or parameter declared using this data type can actually hold the address of a method that matches the defined method signature, and we can then invoke that method by using the variable.

Any method with the signature:

$$f(Object, Object)$$

can be viewed as being of type Compare.

Using the Delegate Data Type

We can write a routine that accepts this data type as a parameter; meaning that anyone calling our routine must pass us the address of a method that conforms to this interface. Add the following sort routine to the code module:

```
Public Sub DoSort(ByVal theData() As Object, ByVal GreaterThan As Compare)
    Dim outer As Integer
    Dim inner As Integer
    Dim temp As Object

    For outer = 0 To UBound(theData)
    For inner = outer + 1 To UBound(theData)
      If GreaterThan.Invoke(theData(outer), theData(inner)) Then
        temp = theData(outer)
        theData(outer) = theData(inner)
        theData(inner) = temp
      End If
    Next
    Next
End Sub
```

The `GreaterThan` parameter is a variable that holds the address of a method matching the method signature defined by our `Compare` delegate. The address of any method with a matching signature can be passed as a parameter to our `Sort` routine.

Note the use of the `Invoke` method, which is the way a delegate is called from our code. Also note that the routine deals entirely with the generic `System.Object` data type rather than with any specific type of data. The specific comparison of one object to another is left to the delegate routine that is passed in as a parameter.

Implementing a Delegate Method

All that remains is to actually create the implementation of the delegate routine and call our sort method. On a very basic level, all we need to do is create a method that has a matching method signature. For instance, we could create a method such as:

```
Public Function PersonCompare(ByVal Person1 As Object, _
    ByVal Person2 As Object) As Boolean

End Function
```

The method signature of this method exactly matches that which we defined by our delegate earlier:

```
Compare(Object, Object)
```

In both cases, we're defining two parameters of type `Object`.

Of course, there's more to it than simply creating the stub of a method. We know that the method needs to return a value of `True` if its first parameter is greater than the second parameter. Otherwise, it should be written to deal with some specific type of data.

The `Delegate` statement defines a data type based on a specific method interface. To call a routine that expects a parameter of this new data type, it must pass us the address of a method that conforms to the defined interface.

To conform to the interface, a method must have the same number of parameters with the same data types as we've defined in our `Delegate` statement. In addition, the method must provide the same return type as defined. The actual name of the method doesn't matter; it is the number, order, and data type of the parameters and the return value that count.

To find the address of a specific method, we can use the `AddressOf` operator. This operator returns the address of any procedure or method, allowing us to pass that value as a parameter to any routine that expects a delegate as a parameter.

Our `Person` class already has a shared method named `CompareAge` that generally does what we want. Unfortunately, it accepts parameters of type `Person` rather than of type `Object` as required by the `Compare` delegate. We can use method overloading to solve this problem.

Create a second implementation of `CompareAge` that accepts parameters of type `Object` as required by the delegate, rather than of type `Person` as we have in the existing implementation:

```
Public Shared Function CompareAge(ByVal Person1 As Object, _
    ByVal Person2 As Object) As Boolean

  Return CType(Person1, Person).Age > CType(Person2, Person).Age

End Function
```

This method simply returns `True` if the first `Person` object's age is greater than the second. The routine accepts two `Object` parameters rather than specific `Person` type parameters, so we have to use the `CType()` method to access those objects as type `Person`. We accept the parameters as type `Object` because that is what is defined by the `Delegate` statement. We are matching its method signature:

f(Object, Object)

Since this method's parameter data types and return value match the delegate, we can use it when calling the sort routine. Place a button on the form and write the following code behind that button:

```
Private Sub Button2_Click(ByVal sender As System.Object, _
    ByVal e As System.EventArgs) Handles button2.Click

  Dim myPeople(4) As Person

  myPeople(0) = New Person("Fred", #7/9/1960#)
  myPeople(1) = New Person("Mary", #1/21/1955#)
  myPeople(2) = New Person("Sarah", #2/1/1960#)
  myPeople(3) = New Person("George", #5/13/1970#)
  myPeople(4) = New Person("Andre", #10/1/1965#)

  DoSort(myPeople, AddressOf Person.CompareAge)
End Sub
```

This code creates an array of `Person` objects and populates them. It then calls the `DoSort` routine from our module, passing the array as the first parameter and the address of our shared `CompareAge` method as the second. To display the contents of the sorted array in the IDE's output window, we can add the following code:

```
Private Sub button2_Click(ByVal sender As System.Object, _
    ByVal e As System.EventArgs) Handles button2.Click

  Dim myPeople(4) As Person

  myPeople(0) = New Person("Fred", #7/9/1960#)
  myPeople(1) = New Person("Mary", #1/21/1955#)
  myPeople(2) = New Person("Sarah", #2/1/1960#)
  myPeople(3) = New Person("George", #5/13/1970#)
  myPeople(4) = New Person("Andre", #10/1/1965#)

  DoSort(myPeople, AddressOf Person.CompareAge)

  Dim myPerson As Person

  For Each myPerson In myPeople
    System.Diagnostics.Debug.WriteLine(myPerson.Name & " " & myPerson.Age)
  Next
End Sub
```

When we run the application and click the button, the output window will display a list of the people, sorted by age as shown in Figure 5-4.

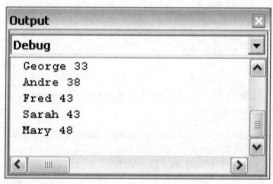

Figure 5-4

What makes this whole thing very powerful is that we can change the comparison routine without changing the sort mechanism. Simply add another comparison routine to the `Person` class:

```
Public Shared Function CompareName(ByVal Person1 As Object, _
    ByVal Person2 As Object) As Boolean

  Return CType(Person1, Person).Name > CType(Person2, Person).Name

End Function
```

and then change the code behind the button on the form to use that alternate comparison routine:

```
Private Sub button2_Click(ByVal sender As System.Object, _
    ByVal e As System.EventArgs) Handles button2.Click

Dim myPeople(4) As Person

myPeople(0) = New Person("Fred", #7/9/1960#)
myPeople(1) = New Person("Mary", #1/21/1955#)
myPeople(2) = New Person("Sarah", #2/1/1960#)
myPeople(3) = New Person("George", #5/13/1970#)
myPeople(4) = New Person("Andre", #10/1/1965#)

DoSort(myPeople, AddressOf Person.CompareName)

Dim myPerson As Person

For Each myPerson In myPeople
    System.Diagnostics.Debug.WriteLine(myPerson.Name & " " & myPerson.Age)
Next
End Sub
```

When we run this updated code, we'll find that our array contains a set of data sorted by name rather than by age as shown in Figure 5-5.

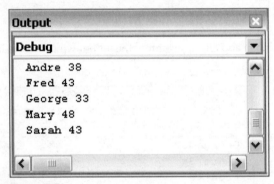

Figure 5-5

By simply creating a new compare routine and passing it as a parameter, we can entirely change the way that the data is sorted. Better still, this sort routine can operate on any type of object, as long as we provide an appropriate delegate method that knows how to compare that type of object.

Classes versus Components

VB.NET has another concept that is very similar to a class, the component. In fact, we can pretty much use a component and a class interchangeably, though there are some differences that we'll discuss.

A component is really little more than a regular class, but it is one that supports a graphical designer within the VB.NET IDE. This means we can use drag-and-drop to provide the code in our component with access to items from the Server Explorer or from the Toolbox.

To add a component to a project, select the Project ⇨ Add Component menu option, give the component a name, and click Open in the Add New Item dialog box.

When we add a class to our project we are presented with the code window. When we add a *component* on the other hand, we are presented with a graphical designer surface, much like what we'd see when adding a Web form to the project.

If we switch to the code view (by right-clicking in the designer view and choosing View Code), we will see the code that is created for us automatically, just like it is with a Windows form, Web form or regular class, see Figure 5-6.

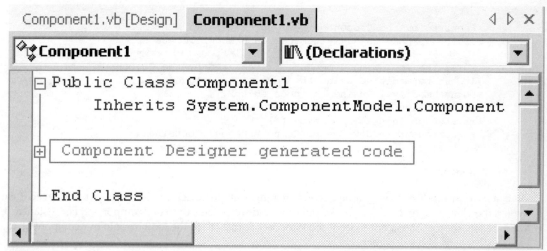

Figure 5-6

This isn't a lot more code than we'd see with a regular class, though there certainly are differences. First, this class inherits from `System.ComponentModel.Component`. While we'll discuss the concepts of inheritance in Chapters 6 and 7, it is important to note here that this `Inherits` line is what brings in all the support for the graphical designer in VS.NET.

There's also a collapsed region of code in a component. This region contains code generated by the graphical designer. Here's a quick look at what is included by default:

```
#Region " Component Designer generated code "

    Public Sub New(Container As System.ComponentModel.IContainer)
        MyClass.New()

        'Required for Windows.Forms Class Composition Designer support
        Container.Add(me)
    End Sub

    Public Sub New()
        MyBase.New()

        'This call is required by the Component Designer.
        InitializeComponent()

        'Add any initialization after the InitializeComponent() call

    End Sub
```

```
'Component overrides dispose to clean up the component list.
Protected Overloads Overrides Sub Dispose(ByVal disposing As Boolean)
    If disposing Then
        If Not (components Is Nothing) Then
            components.Dispose()
        End If
    End If
    MyBase.Dispose(disposing)
End Sub

'Required by the Component Designer
Private components As System.ComponentModel.IContainer

'NOTE: The following procedure is required by the Component Designer
'It can be modified using the Component Designer.
'Do not modify it using the code editor.
<System.Diagnostics.DebuggerStepThrough()> _
Private Sub InitializeComponent()
    components = New System.ComponentModel.Container()
End Sub

#End Region
```

As it stands, this code does very little beyond creating a single `Container` class object. However, if we switch the view back to the designer, we can drag-and-drop items onto our component. For instance, if we drag and drop a Timer control from the Windows Forms tab of the toolbox onto our component, it will be displayed in the designer.

From here, we can set its properties using the standard Properties window in the IDE, just like we would for a control on a form. Using the Properties window, set the `Name` property to `theTimer`.

If we now return to the code window and look at the automatically generated code, we'll see that the region now includes code to declare, create, and initialize the `Timer` object:

```
Friend WithEvents theTimer As System.Windows.Forms.Timer
<System.Diagnostics.DebuggerStepThrough()> Private Sub InitializeComponent()
    Me.components = New System.ComponentModel.Container
    Me.theTimer = New System.Windows.Forms.Timer(Me.components)

End Sub

#End Region
```

Normally, we don't really care about the fact that this code was generated. Rather, what is important is that we now automatically, simply by dragging and dropping and setting some properties, have access to a `Timer` object named `theTimer`.

This means that we can write code within our component, just like we might in a class, to use this object:

```
Public Sub Start()

   theTimer.Enabled = True

End Sub
```

```
Public Sub [Stop]()

  theTimer.Enabled = False

End Sub

Private Sub theTimer_Tick( _
  ByVal sender As System.Object, _
  ByVal e As System.EventArgs) Handles theTimer.Tick

  ' do work

End Sub
```

Here we can see that, with a simple drag-and-drop operation, we've gained access to a variable called `theTimer` referencing a `Timer` object, and we are able to create methods that interact with and use that object much like we would with a control dropped onto a form.

For the most part, we can use a component interchangeably with a basic class, but the use of a component incurs some extra overhead that a basic class does not, since it inherits all the functionality of `System.ComponentModel.Component`.

Summary

VB.NET offers us a fully object-oriented language with all the capabilities we would expect. In this chapter, we've explored the basic concepts around classes and objects, as well as the separation of interface from implementation and data.

We've seen how to use the `Class` keyword to create classes, and how those classes can be instantiated into specific objects, each one an instance of the class. These objects have methods and properties that can be invoked by the client code, and can act on data within the object stored in member or instance variables.

We also explored some more advanced concepts, including method overloading, shared or static variables and methods, and the use of delegates. Finally, we wrapped up with a brief discussion of attributes and how they can be used to affect the interaction of our class or our methods with the .NET environment.

In Chapter 6, we'll continue our discussion of object syntax as we explore the concept of inheritance and all the syntax that enables inheritance within VB.NET. We will also walk through the creation, implementation, and use of multiple interfaces — a powerful concept that allows our objects to be used in different ways depending on the interface chosen by the client application.

Then, in Chapter 7, we'll wrap up our discussion of objects and object-oriented programming by applying all of this syntax. We'll discuss the key object-oriented concepts of abstraction, encapsulation, polymorphism, and inheritance and see how they all tie together to provide a powerful way of designing and implementing applications.

6

Inheritance and Interfaces

Visual Basic .NET (VB.NET) is a fully object-oriented language. In Chapter 5 we covered the basics of creating classes and objects, including the creation of methods, properties, events, and instance variables. We've seen the basic building blocks for abstraction, encapsulation, and polymorphism— concepts we'll discuss in more detail in Chapter 7. The final major techniques we need to cover are inheritance and the use of multiple interfaces.

Inheritance is the idea that we can create a class that reuses methods, properties, events, and variables from another class. We can create a class with some basic functionality, then use that class as a base from which to create other, more detailed, classes. All these classes will have the same common functionality as that base class, along with new, enhanced or even completely changed functionality.

In this chapter, we'll cover the syntax that supports inheritance within VB.NET. This includes creating the base classes from which other classes can be derived, as well as creating those derived classes.

VB.NET also supports a related concept, multiple interfaces. We've already seen in Chapter 5 that all objects have a native or default interface, which is defined by the public methods, properties, and events declared in the class. In the .NET environment an object can have other interfaces in addition to this native interface, in other words, .NET objects can have multiple interfaces.

These secondary interfaces define alternate ways in which our object can be accessed by providing clearly defined sets of methods, properties, and events. Like the native interface, these secondary interfaces define how the client code can interact with our object, essentially providing a "contract" that allows the client to know exactly what methods, properties, and events the object will provide. When we write code to interact with an object, we can choose which of the interfaces we want to use, basically we're choosing how we want to view or interact with that object.

We'll be using relatively basic code examples so that we can focus right in on the technical and syntactic issues surrounding inheritance and multiple interfaces. In Chapter 7, we'll revisit these concepts using a more sophisticated set of code as we continue to explore object-oriented programming and how to apply inheritance and multiple interfaces in a practical manner.

Inheritance

Inheritance is the concept that a new class can be based on an existing class, inheriting its interface and functionality from the original class. In Chapter 5, we explored the relationship between a class and an object, where the class is essentially a template from which objects can be created.

While this is very powerful, it doesn't provide all the capabilities we might like. In particular, there are many cases where a class only *partially* describes what we need for our object. We may have a class called Person, for instance, which has all the properties and methods that apply to all types of people, things like first name, last name and birth date. While useful, this class probably doesn't have everything we need to describe a *specific* type of person, such as an employee or a customer. An employee would have a hire date and a salary that are not included in Person, while a customer would have a credit rating, something neither the Person nor Employee classes would need.

Without inheritance, we'd probably end up replicating the code from the Person class into both the Employee and Customer classes so they'd have that same functionality as well as the ability to add new functionality of their own.

Inheritance makes it very easy to create classes for Employee, Customer, and so forth. We don't have to recreate that code for an employee to be a person; it automatically gets any properties, methods, and events from the original Person class.

We can think of it this way. When we create an Employee class, which inherits from a Person class, we are effectively merging these two classes together. If we then create an object based on the Employee class, it not only has the interface (properties, methods, and events) and implementation from the Employee class, but it also has those from the Person class.

While an Employee object represents the merger between the Employee and Person classes, it is important to realize that the variables and code contained in each of those classes remain independent. There are two perspectives we need to understand.

From the outside, the client code that interacts with the Employee object will see a single, unified object that represents the merger of the Employee and Person classes.

From the inside, the code in the Employee class and the code in the Person class aren't totally intermixed. Variables and methods that are Private are only available within the class where they were written. Variables and methods that are Public in one class can be called from the other class. Variables and methods that are declared as Friend are only available between classes if both classes are in the same VB.NET project. As we'll discuss later in the chapter, there is also a Protected scope that is designed to work with inheritance, but again, this provides a controlled way for one class to interact with the variables and methods in the other class.

There is a standard notation called the *Universal Modeling Language* (UML) that is typically used to diagram the relationships between classes, objects, and other object-oriented concepts. We can model the relationship between the Person, Employee, and Customer classes using UML, as shown in Figure 6-1.

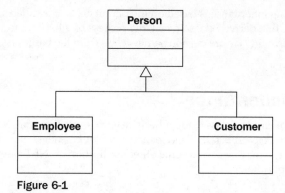

Figure 6-1

Each box in this diagram represents a class, in this case, we have Person, Employee, and Customer classes. The line from Employee back up to Person, terminating in a triangle, indicates that Employee is derived from, or inherits from, Person. The same is true for the Customer class. We'll use UML through the rest of the chapter, as it is a standard diagramming notation for working with classes and objects.

> *If you'd like to learn more about UML, see* Instant UML *(Wiley, 2002).*

In Chapter 7, we'll discuss in more detail when and how inheritance should be used in software design. In this chapter, we'll cover the syntax and programming concepts necessary to implement inheritance. We'll create a base Person class, and then use that class to create both Employee and Customer classes that inherit behavior from Person.

Before we get into the implementation, however, we need to define some basic terms associated with inheritance. And there are a lot of terms, partly because there are often several ways to say the same thing, and the various terms are all used quite frequently and interchangeably.

> **Though we'll try to be consistent in our use of terminology in this book, it is important to note that in other books, articles, and online all these various terms are used in all their various permutations.**

Inheritance, for instance, is also sometimes referred to as *generalization*. This is because the class from which we are inheriting our behavior is virtually always a more general form of our new class. A person is more general than an employee, for instance.

The inheritance relationship is also referred to as an *"is-a" relationship*. When we create a Customer class that inherits from a Person class, that customer is a person. The employee is a person as well. Thus, we have this "is-a" relationship. As we'll see later in this chapter, multiple interfaces can be used to implement something similar to the "is-a" relationship, the "act-as" relationship.

When we create a class using inheritance, we are inheriting behaviors and data from an existing class. That existing class is called the *base class*. It is also often referred to as a superclass or a parent class.

The class we create using inheritance is based on the parent class. It is called a *subclass*. Sometimes it is also called a child class or a derived class. In fact, the process of inheriting from a base class to a subclass is often referred to as *deriving*. We are deriving a new class from the base class. The process is also often called *subclassing*.

Implementing Inheritance

When we set out to implement a class using inheritance, we must first start with an existing class from which we will derive our new subclass. This existing class, or base class, may be part of the .NET system class library framework, it may be part of some other application or .NET assembly, or we may create it as part of our existing application.

Once we have a base class, we can then implement one or more subclasses based on that base class. Each of our subclasses will automatically have all of the methods, properties, and events of that base class — including the implementation behind each method, property and event. Our subclass can add new methods, properties, and events of its own, extending the original interface with new functionality. In addition, a subclass can replace the methods and properties of the base class with its own new implementation — effectively overriding the original behavior and replacing it with new behaviors.

Essentially inheritance is a way of merging functionality from an existing class into our new subclass. Inheritance also defines rules for how these methods, properties, and events can be merged, including control over how they can be changed or replaced, and how the subclass can add new methods, properties, and events of its own. This is what we'll explore as we go forward — what these rules are and what syntax we use in VB.NET to make it all work.

Creating a Base Class

Virtually any class we create can act as a base class from which other classes can be derived. In fact, unless we specifically indicate in the code that our class *cannot* be a base class, we can derive from it (we'll come back to this later).

Create a new Windows Application project in VB.NET. Then add a class to the project using the Project ⇨ Add Class menu option and name it `Person.vb`.

We start with the following code:

```
Public Class Person

End Class
```

At this point, we technically have a base class, since it is possible to inherit from this class even though it doesn't do or contain anything.

We can now add methods, properties, and events to this class as we normally would. All of those interface elements would be inherited by any class we might create based on `Person`. For instance, add the following code:

```
Public Class Person
  Private mstrName As String
  Private mdtBirthDate As Date
```

```
Public Property Name() As String
  Get
    Return mstrName
  End Get
  Set(ByVal Value As String)
    mstrName = Value
  End Set
End Property

Public Property BirthDate() As Date
  Get
    Return mdtBirthDate
  End Get
  Set(ByVal Value As Date)
    mdtBirthDate = Value
  End Set
End Property
```

```
End Class
```

This gives us a simple method we can use to illustrate how basic inheritance works. This class can be represented by the following UML (see Figure 6-2).

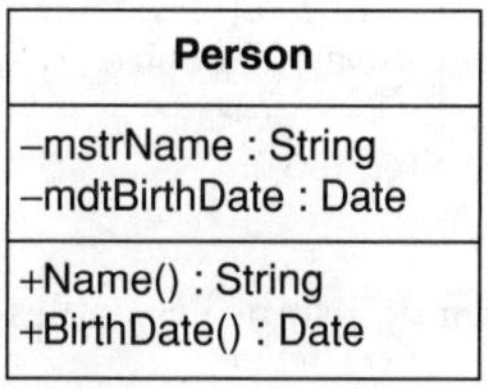

Person
−mstrName : String −mdtBirthDate : Date
+Name() : String +BirthDate() : Date

Figure 6-2

The overall box represents the Person class. In the top section we have the name of the class. In the middle section is a list of the instance variables, or attributes, of the class with their scope marked as Private due to the minus (−) symbol in front of each attribute. In the bottom section are the methods that make up the interface of the class, both marked as Public in scope due to the plus (±) symbol in front of each method.

Creating a Subclass

To implement inheritance we need to add a new class to our project. Use the Project ➪ Add Class menu option and add a new class named Employee.vb. We'll start with the following code.

```
Public Class Employee
  Private mdtHireDate As Date
  Private mdblSalary As Double

  Public Property HireDate() As Date
    Get
      Return mdtHireDate
    End Get
```

```
      Set(ByVal Value As Date)
         mdtHireDate = Value
      End Set
   End Property

   Public Property Salary() As Double
      Get
         Return mdblSalary
      End Get
      Set(ByVal Value As Double)
         mdblSalary = Value
      End Set
   End Property
End Class
```

This is a regular stand-alone class with no explicit inheritance. It can be represented by the following UML (see Figure 6-3).

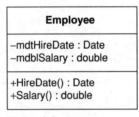

Employee
–mdtHireDate : Date –mdblSalary : double
+HireDate() : Date +Salary() : double

Figure 6-3

Again, we can see the class name, its list of instance variables and the methods it includes as part of its interface.

It turns out that, behind the scenes, this class inherits some capabilities from System.Object. In fact, every class in the entire .NET platform ultimately inherits from System.Object either implicitly or explicitly. This is why all .NET objects have a basic set of common functionality including most notably the GetType method. We'll discuss this in detail later in the chapter.

While having an Employee object with a hire date and salary is useful, it should also have Name and BirthDate properties just like we implemented for our Person class. Without inheritance, we'd probably just copy and paste the code from Person directly into the new Employee class, but with inheritance we can directly reuse the code from the Person class. Let's make our new class inherit from Person.

The Inherits Keyword

To make Employee a subclass of Person we just need to add a single line of code:

```
Public Class Employee
   Inherits Person
```

The Inherits keyword is used to indicate that a class should derive from an existing class, inheriting interface and behavior from that class. We can inherit from almost any class in our project, or from the .NET system class library or from other assemblies. It is possible to *prevent* inheritance, something we'll discuss later in the chapter. When using the `Inherits` keyword to inherit from classes outside our current project we need to either specify the namespace that contains that class or have an `Imports` statement at the top of the class to import that namespace for our use.

The following UML diagram (Figure 6-4) illustrates the fact that our `Employee` class is now a subclass of `Person`.

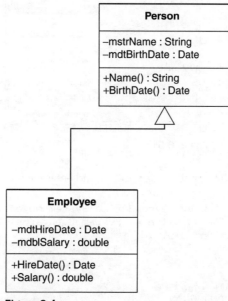

Figure 6-4

The line running from `Employee` back up to `Person` ends in an open triangle, which is the UML symbol for generalization, or inheritance. It is this line that indicates that the `Employee` class also includes all the functionality and the interface from `Person`.

This means that an object created based on the `Employee` class will not only have the methods `HireDate` and `Salary`, but will also have `Name` and `BirthDate`.

To test this, bring up the designer for `Form1` (which is automatically part of our project since we created a Windows Application project) and add the following TextBox controls along with a button to the form.

Control Type	Name	Text Value
TextBox	txtName	<blank>
TextBox	TxtBirthDate	<blank>
TextBox	TxtHireDate	<blank>
TextBox	txtSalary	<blank>
button	btnOK	OK

We can also add some labels to make the form more readable. Our form designer should now look something like Figure 6-5.

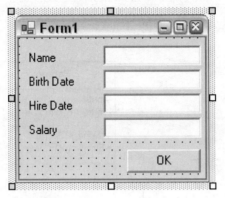

Figure 6-5

Double-click the button to bring up the code window and enter the following code.

```
Private Sub btnOK_Click(ByVal sender As System.Object, _
                        ByVal e As System.EventArgs) Handles btnOK.Click
  Dim objEmployee As New Employee()

  With objEmployee
    .Name = "Fred"
    .BirthDate = #1/1/1960#
    .HireDate = #1/1/1980#
    .Salary = 30000

    txtName.Text = .Name
    txtBirthDate.Text = Format(.BirthDate, "Short date")
    txtHireDate.Text = Format(.HireDate, "Short date")
    txtSalary.Text = Format(.Salary, "$0.00")
  End With

End Sub
```

Even though `Employee` doesn't directly implement `Name` or `BirthDate` methods, they are available for our use through inheritance. If we run this application and click the button, our controls will be populated with the values from the `Employee` object.

When the code in `Form1` invokes the `Name` property on our `Employee` object, the code from the `Person` class is executed, since the `Employee` class has no such method built-in. However, when the `HireDate` property is invoked on the `Employee` object, the code from the `Employee` class *is* executed since it does have that method as part of its code.

From the form's perspective it doesn't matter whether a method is implemented in the `Employee` class or the `Person` class, they are all simply methods of the `Employee` object. Also, since the code in these classes is merged together to create the `Employee` object, there is no performance difference between calling a method implemented by the `Employee` class or a method implemented by the `Person` class.

Overloading Methods

Although our `Employee` class automatically gained the `Name` and `BirthDate` methods through inheritance, it also has methods of its own — `HireDate` and `Salary`. This shows how we've extended the base `Person` interface by adding methods and properties to the `Employee` subclass.

We can add new properties, methods and events to the `Employee` class and they will be part of any object created based on `Employee`. This has no impact on the `Person` class whatsoever, only on the `Employee` class and `Employee` objects.

We can even extend the functionality of the base class by adding methods to our subclass that have the same name as methods or properties in the base class, as long as those methods or properties have different parameter lists. We are effectively overloading the existing methods from the base class. It is essentially the same thing as overloading regular methods as we discussed in Chapter 5.

For example, our `Person` class is currently providing our implementation for the `Name` property. Employees may have other names we also want to store, perhaps an informal name and a very formal name in addition to their normal name. One way to accommodate this requirement is to change the `Person` class itself to include an overloaded `Name` property that supports this new functionality. However, we're really only trying to enhance the `Employee` class, not the more general `Person` class. So what we want is a way to add an overloaded method to the `Employee` class itself, even though we're overloading a method from its base class.

Overloading a method from a base class is done by using the `Overloads` keyword. The concept is the same as we discussed in Chapter 5, but in this case an extra keyword is involved. To overload the `Name` property, for instance, we can add a new property to the `Employee` class. First though, let's define an enumerated type using the `Enum` keyword. This `Enum` will list the different types of name we want to store. Add this `Enum` to the `Employee.vb` file, before the declaration of the class itself:

```
Public Enum NameTypes
  Informal = 1
  Formal = 2
End Enum
```

```
Public Class Employee
```

We can then add an overloaded `Name` property to the `Employee` class itself:

```
Public Class Employee
  Inherits Person

  Private mdtHireDate As Date
  Private mdblSalary As Double
```

```
  Private mcolNames As New Hashtable()

  Public Overloads Property Name(ByVal Type As NameTypes) As String
    Get
      Return mcolNames(Type)
    End Get
    Set(ByVal Value As String)
```

```
      If mcolNames.ContainsKey(Type) Then
         mcolNames.Item(Type) = Value
      Else
         mcolNames.Add(Type, Value)
      End If
   End Set
End Property
```

This Name property is actually a property array, allowing us to store multiple values via the same property. In this case, we're storing the values in a Hashtable object, which is indexed by using the Enum value we just defined.

> *If we omit the Overloads keyword here, our new implementation of the Name method will shadow the original implementation. Shadowing is a very different thing from overloading and is a topic we'll cover later in the chapter.*

Though this method has the same name as the method in the base class, the fact that it accepts a different parameter list allows us to use overloading to implement it here. The original Name property as implemented in the Person class remains intact and valid, but now we've added a new variation with this second Name property. This is shown by the following UML diagram (see Figure 6-6).

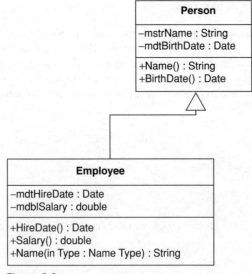

Figure 6-6

The diagram clearly indicates that the Name method in the Person class and the Name method in the Employee class both exist, and have different method signatures.

We can now change Form1 to make use of this new version of the Name property. First off, add a couple of new text box controls and associated labels. The text box controls should be named txtFormal and txtInformal and the form should now look like the one shown in Figure 6-7.

Now double-click the button to bring up the code window and add code to work with the overloaded version of the Name property:

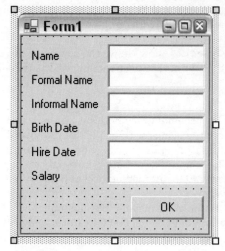

Figure 6-7

```
Private Sub btnOK_Click(ByVal sender As System.Object, _
    ByVal e As System.EventArgs) Handles btnOK.Click
  Dim objEmployee As New Employee()

  With objEmployee
    .Name = "Fred"
    .Name(NameTypes.Formal) = "Mr. Frederick R. Jones, Sr."
    .Name(NameTypes.Informal) = "Freddy"
    .BirthDate = #1/1/1960#
    .HireDate = #1/1/1980#
    .Salary = 30000

    txtName.Text = .Name
    txtFormal.Text = .Name(NameTypes.Formal)
    txtInformal.Text = .Name(NameTypes.Informal)
    txtBirthDate.Text = Format(.BirthDate, "Short date")
    txtHireDate.Text = Format(.HireDate, "Short date")
    txtSalary.Text = Format(.Salary, "$0.00")
  End With
End Sub
```

As we can see, the code still interacts with the original Name property as implemented in the Person class, but we are now also invoking the overloaded version of the property that is implemented in the Employee class.

Overriding Methods

So far we've seen how to implement a base class, and then use it to create a subclass. Finally, we extended the interface by adding methods. We've also explored how to use overloading to add methods that have the same name as methods in the base class, but with different parameters.

However, there are times when we may not only want to extend the original functionality, but to actually change or entirely replace the functionality from the base class. Instead of leaving the existing

173

functionality and just adding new methods or overloaded versions of those methods, we might want to entirely *override* the existing functionality with our own.

We can do exactly this. If the base class allows it, we can substitute our own implementation of a method in the base class — meaning that our new implementation will be used instead of the original.

The Overridable Keyword

By default we can't override the behavior of methods on a base class. The base class must be coded specifically to allow this to occur by using the `Overridable` keyword. This is important, since we may not always want to allow a subclass to entirely change the behavior of the methods in our base class. However, if we do wish to allow the author of a subclass to replace our implementation, we can do so by adding the `Overridable` keyword to our method declaration.

Returning to our `Employee` example, we may not like the implementation of the `BirthDate` method as it stands in the `Person` class. Say, for instance, that we can't employ anyone younger than 16 years of age, so any birth date value more recent than 16 years ago is invalid for an employee.

To implement this business rule, we need to change the way the `BirthDate` property is implemented. While we could make this change directly in the `Person` class, that would not be ideal. It is perfectly acceptable to have a person under age 16, just not an employee.

Open the code window for the `Person` class and change the `BirthDate` property to include the `Overridable` keyword.

```
Public Overridable Property BirthDate() As Date
    Get
        Return mdtBirthDate
    End Get
    Set(ByVal Value As Date)
        mdtBirthDate = Value
    End Set
End Property
```

This change allows any class that inherits from `Person` to entirely replace the implementation of the `BirthDate` property with a new implementation.

By adding the `Overridable` keyword to our method declaration we are indicating that we want to allow any subclass to override the behavior provided by this method. This means that we are giving permission for a subclass to totally ignore our implementation, or to extend our implementation by doing other work before or after our implementation is run.

If the subclass doesn't override this method, the method will work just like a regular method and will be automatically included as part of the subclass's interface. Putting the `Overridable` keyword on a method simply allows a subclass to override the method if we choose to do so.

The Overrides Keyword

In a subclass we override a method by implementing a method of the same name, and with the same parameter list as the base class and then using the `Overrides` keyword to indicate that we are overriding that method.

This is different from overloading, since when we *overload* a method we're adding a new method with the same name but a different parameter list. When we *override* a method we're actually replacing the original method with a new implementation.

Without the `Overrides` keyword we'll get a compilation error when we implement a method with the same name as one from the base class.

Open the code window for the `Employee` class and add a new `BirthDate` property:

```
Public Class Employee
   Inherits Person
Private mdtHireDate As Date
Private mdblSalary As Double
Private mdtBirthDate As Date

Private mcolNames As New Hashtable()

Public Overrides Property BirthDate() As Date
   Get
     Return mdtBirthDate
   End Get
   Set(ByVal Value As Date)
     If DateDiff(DateInterval.Year, Value, Now()) >= 16 Then
       mdtBirthDate = Value
     Else
       Throw New ApplicationException( _
         "An employee must be at least 16 years old")
     End If
   End Set
End Property
```

Since we're implementing our own version of the property, we have to declare a variable to store that value within the `Employee` class. This is not ideal, and there are a couple of ways around it, including the `MyBase` keyword and the `Protected` scope.

Notice also, that we've enhanced the functionality in the `Set` block so it now raises an error if the new birth date value would make the employee be less than 16 years of age. With this code we've now entirely replaced the original `BirthDate` implementation with a new one that enforces our business rule. This is shown by the following UML diagram (see Figure 6-8).

The diagram now includes a `BirthDate` method in the `Employee` class that has the same method signature as the `BirthDate` method in the `Person` class. While perhaps not entirely intuitive, this is how UML indicates that we've overridden the method.

If we now run our application and click the button on the form, everything should work as it did before. This is because the birth date we're supplying conforms to our new business rule. However, we can change the code in our form to use an invalid birth date.

```
With objEmployee
   .Name = "Fred"
   .Name(NameTypes.Formal) = "Mr. Frederick R. Jones, Sr."
   .Name(NameTypes.Informal) = "Freddy"
   .BirthDate = #1/1/2000#
```

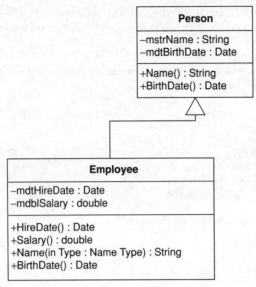

Figure 6-8

When we run the application (from within Visual Studio .NET) and click the button we'll get an error indicating that the birth date is invalid. This proves that we are now using the implementation of the `BirthDate` method from the `Employee` class rather than the one from the `Person` class.

Change the date value in the form back to a valid value so that our application runs properly.

The MyBase Keyword

We've just seen how we can entirely replace the functionality of a method in the base class by overriding it in our subclass. However, this can be somewhat extreme, sometimes it would be preferable to override methods such that we extend the base functionality rather than replacing the functionality.

To do this we need to override the method using the `Overrides` keyword like we just did, but within our new implementation we can still invoke the original implementation of the method. This allows us to add our own code before or after the original implementation is invoked — meaning we can extend the behavior, while still leveraging the code in the base class.

To invoke methods directly from the base class we can use the `MyBase` keyword. This keyword is available within any class, and it exposes all the methods of the base class for our use.

> *Even a base class like Person is an implicit subclass of System.Object, and so it can use MyBase to interact with its base class as well.*

This means that within the `BirthDate` implementation in `Employee`, we can invoke the `BirthDate` implementation in the base `Person` class. This is ideal, since it means we can leverage any existing functionality provided by `Person`, while still enforcing our `Employee`-specific business rules.

To take advantage of this, we can enhance the code in the `Employee` implementation of `BirthDate`. First off, remove the declaration of `mdtBirthDate` from the `Employee` class. We won't need this variable any longer, since the `Person` implementation will keep track of the value on our behalf. Then, change the `BirthDate` implementation in the `Employee` class as follows:

```
Public Overrides Property BirthDate() As Date
  Get
    Return MyBase.BirthDate
  End Get
  Set(ByVal Value As Date)
    If DateDiff(DateInterval.Year, Value, Now()) >= 16 Then
      MyBase.BirthDate = Value
    Else
      Throw New ApplicationException( _
        "An employee must be at least 16 years old")
    End If
  End Set
End Property
```

We can now run our application and we'll see that it works just fine even though the `Employee` class no longer contains any code to actually keep track of the birth date value. We've effectively merged the `BirthDate` implementation from `Person` right into our enhanced implementation in `Employee`, creating a hybrid version of the property.

We'll discuss the `MyBase` keyword in some more depth later in the chapter. Here, we've seen how it can be used to allow us to enhance or extend the functionality of the base class by adding our own code in the subclass, but still invoking the base class method when appropriate.

Virtual Methods

The `BirthDate` method is an example of a *virtual method*. Virtual methods are those that can be overridden and replaced by subclasses.

Virtual methods are more complex to understand than regular nonvirtual methods. With a nonvirtual method there is only one implementation that matches any given method signature, so there's no ambiguity about which specific method implementation will be invoked. With virtual methods, however, there may be several implementations of the same method, with the same method signature and so we need to understand the rules that govern which specific implementation of that method will be called.

When working with virtual methods we need to keep in mind that the data type of the *object* is used to determine the implementation of the method to call, rather than the type of the *variable* that refers to the object.

If we look at the code we've written in our form, we see that we're declaring an object variable of type `Employee` and we are then creating an `Employee` object that we can reference via that object.

```
Dim objEmployee As New Employee()
```

It is not surprising, then, that we are able to invoke any of the methods that are implemented as part of the `Employee` class, and through inheritance any of the methods implemented as part of the `Person` class:

```
With objEmployee
  .Name = "Fred"
  .Name(NameTypes.Formal) = "Mr. Frederick R. Jones, Sr."
```

```
.Name(NameTypes.Informal) = "Freddy"
.BirthDate = #1/1/1960#
.HireDate = #1/1/1980#
.Salary = 30000
```

When we call the `BirthDate` property we know that we're invoking the implementation contained in the `Employee` class, which makes sense since we know that we're using a variable of type `Employee` to refer to an object of type `Employee`.

However, because our methods are virtual methods, we can experiment with some much more interesting scenarios. For instance, suppose that we change the code in our form to interact directly with an object of type `Person` instead of one of type `Employee`.

```
Private Sub btnOK_Click(ByVal sender As System.Object, _
    ByVal e As System.EventArgs) Handles btnOK.Click

  Dim objPerson As New Person()

  With objPerson
    .Name = "Fred"
    .BirthDate = #1/1/1960#

    txtName.Text = .Name
    txtBirthDate.Text = Format(.BirthDate, "Short date")
  End With

End Sub
```

We can no longer call the methods implemented by the `Employee` class, because they don't exist as part of a `Person` object, but only as part of an `Employee` object. However, we can see that both the `Name` and `BirthDate` properties continue to function as we'd expect. When we run the application now it will work just fine. We can even change the birth date value to something that would be invalid for `Employee`.

```
.BirthDate = #1/1/2000#
```

The application will now accept it and work just fine, since the `BirthDate` method we're invoking is the original version from the `Person` class.

These are the two simple scenarios, where we have a variable and object of type `Employee` or a variable and object of type `Person`. However, since `Employee` is derived from `Person`, we can do something a bit more interesting. We can use a variable of type `Person` to hold a reference to an `Employee` object.

Because of this, we can change the code in `Form1` as follows:

```
Private Sub btnOK_Click(ByVal sender As System.Object, _
    ByVal e As System.EventArgs) Handles btnOK.Click

  Dim objPerson As Person
  objPerson = New Employee()
```

```
      With objPerson
        .Name = "Fred"
        .BirthDate = #1/1/2000#

        txtName.Text = .Name
        txtBirthDate.Text = Format(.BirthDate, "Short date")
      End With
    End Sub
```

What we're doing now is declaring our variable to be of type `Person`, but the object itself is an instance of the `Employee` class. We've done something a bit complex here, since the data type of the variable is not the same as the data type of the object itself. It is important to remember that a variable of a base class type can always hold a reference to an object of any subclass.

> This is the reason that a variable of type **System.Object** can hold a reference to literally anything in .NET Framework, because all classes are ultimately derived from **System.Object**.

This technique is very useful when creating generic routines and makes use of an object-oriented concept called polymorphism that we'll discuss more thoroughly in Chapter 7. This technique allows us to create a more general routine that populates our form for any object of type `Person`. Add this code to the form:

```
    Private Sub DisplayPerson(ByVal ThePerson As Person)
      With ThePerson
        txtName.Text = .Name
        txtBirthDate.Text = Format(.BirthDate, "Short date")
      End With
    End Sub
```

Now, we can change the code behind the button to make use of this generic routine:

```
    Private Sub btnOK_Click(ByVal sender As System.Object, _
        ByVal e As System.EventArgs) Handles btnOK.Click

      Dim objPerson As Person
      objPerson = New Employee()

      With objPerson
        .Name = "Fred"
        .BirthDate = #1/1/2000#
      End With

      DisplayPerson(objPerson)
    End Sub
```

The benefit here is that we can pass a `Person` object, or an `Employee` object to `DisplayPerson` and the routine will work the same either way.

When we run the application now, things get interesting. We'll get an error when we attempt to set the `BirthDate` property because it breaks our 16-year old business rule which is implemented in the `Employee` class. How can this be when our `objPerson` variable is of type `Person`?

This clearly demonstrates the concept of a virtual method. It is the data type of the object, in this case `Employee`, that is important. The data type of the variable is not the deciding factor when choosing which implementation of an overridden method is invoked.

The following table shows which method is actually invoked based on the variable and object data types when working with virtual methods.

Variable Type	Object Type	Method Invoked
Base	Base	Base
Base	Subclass	Subclass
Subclass	Subclass	Subclass

Virtual methods are very powerful and useful when we go to implement polymorphism using inheritance. A base class data type can hold a reference to any subclass object, but it is the type of that specific object which determines the implementation of the method. Because of this we can write generic routines that operate on many types of object as long as they derive from the same base class. We'll discuss how to make use of polymorphism and virtual methods in more detail in Chapter 7.

Overriding Overloaded Methods

Earlier, we wrote code in our `Employee` class to overload the `Name` method in the base `Person` class. This allowed us to keep the original `Name` functionality, but also extend it by adding another `Name` method that accepted a different parameter list.

We've also overridden the `BirthDate` method. The implementation in the `Employee` class replaced the implementation in the `Person` class. Overriding is a related, but different concept from overloading. It is also possible to both overload and override a method at the same time.

In our earlier overloading example we added a new `Name` property to the `Employee` class, while retaining the functionality present in the base `Person` class. We may decide that we not only want to have our second overloaded implementation of the `Name` method, but we also want to replace the existing one by overriding the existing method provided by the `Person` class.

In particular, we may want to do this so that we can store the `Name` value in the `Hashtable` object along with our `Formal` and `Informal` names.

Before we can override the `Name` method we need to add the `Overridable` keyword to the base implementation in the `Person` class.

```
Public Overridable Property Name() As String
   Get
      Return mstrName
   End Get
   Set(ByVal Value As String)
      mstrName = Value
   End Set
End Property
```

With that done, the Name method can now be overridden by any derived classes. In the Employee class, we can now override the Name method, replacing the functionality provided by the Person class. First, we'll add a Normal option to the Enum that controls the types of Name value we can store.

```
Public Enum NameTypes
   Informal = 1
   Formal = 2
   Normal = 3
End Enum
```

Then, we can add code to the Employee class to implement a new Name property. This is in addition to the existing Name property already implemented in the Employee class:

```
Public Overloads Overrides Property Name() As String
   Get
      Return Name(NameTypes.Normal)
   End Get
   Set(ByVal Value As String)
      Name(NameTypes.Normal) = Value
   End Set
End Property
```

Notice that we're using both the Overrides keyword to indicate that we're overriding the Name method from the base class, and also the Overloads keyword to indicate that we're overloading this method in the subclass.

This new Name property merely delegates the call to the existing version of the Name property that handles the parameter-based names. To complete the linkage between this implementation of the Name property and the parameter-based version we need to make one more change to that original overloaded version:

```
Public Overloads Property Name(ByVal Type As NameTypes) As String
   Get
      Return mcolNames(Type)
   End Get
   Set(ByVal Value As String)
      If mcolNames.ContainsKey(Type) Then
         mcolNames.Item(Type) = Value
      Else
         mcolNames.Add(Type, Value)
      End If
      If Type = NameTypes.Normal Then
         MyBase.Name = Value
      End If
   End Set
End Property
```

This way, if the client code were to set the Name property by providing the Normal index, we are still updating the name in the base class as well as in the Hashtable object maintained by the Employee class.

Shadowing

Overloading allows us to add new versions of the existing methods as long as their parameter lists are different. Overriding allows our subclass to entirely replace the implementation of a base class method with a new method that has the same method signature. As we've just seen, we can even combine these concepts to not only replace the implementation of a method from the base class, but also to simultaneously overload that method with other implementations which have different method signatures.

However, any time we override a method using the `Overrides` keyword, we are subject to the rules governing virtual methods—meaning that the base class must give us permission to override the method. If the base class doesn't use the `Overridable` keyword, we can't override the method. Sometimes we may need to override a method that is not marked as `Overridable`, and shadowing allows us to do just that.

The `Shadows` keyword can also be used to entirely change the nature of a method or other interface element from the base class, although that is something which should be done with great care since it can seriously reduce the maintainability of our code. Normally, when we create an `Employee` object, we expect that it can only act as an `Employee`, but also as a `Person` since `Employee` is a subclass of `Person`. However, with the `Shadows` keyword we can radically alter the behavior of an `Employee` class so it doesn't act like a `Person`. This sort of radical deviation from what is normally expected invites bugs and makes code hard to understand and maintain.

We'll explore that in more detail later. First, let's see how `Shadows` can be used to override nonvirtual methods.

Overriding Nonvirtual Methods

Earlier in the chapter, we discussed virtual methods and how they are automatically created in VB.NET when the `Overrides` keyword is employed. We can also implement *non-virtual methods* in VB.NET. Nonvirtual methods are methods that cannot be overridden and replaced by subclasses, and so most methods we implement are nonvirtual.

> **If we don't use the Overridable keyword when declaring a method, it is nonvirtual.**

In the typical case, nonvirtual methods are easy to understand. Since they can't be overridden and replaced, we know that there's only one method by that name, with that method signature, so when we invoke it there is no ambiguity about which specific implementation will be called. The reverse is true with virtual methods, where there may be more than one method of the same name, with the same method signature, and we need to understand the rules governing which implementation will be invoked.

Of course, nothing is simple, and it turns out that we *can* override nonvirtual methods by using the `Shadows` keyword. In fact, we can use the `Shadows` keyword to override methods regardless of whether or not they have the `Overridable` keyword in the declaration.

> **The Shadows keyword allows us to replace methods on the base class that the base class designer didn't intend to be replaced.**

Obviously, this can be *very* dangerous. The designer of a base class must be careful when marking a method as `Overridable`, ensuring that the base class will continue to operate properly even when that method is replaced by another code in a subclass. Designers of base classes typically just assume that if they *don't* mark a method as `Overridable` it *will* be called and not overridden. Thus, overriding a nonvirtual method by using the `Shadows` keyword can have unexpected and potentially dangerous side effects since we are doing something that the base class designer assumed would never happen.

If that isn't enough complexity, it turns out that shadowed methods follow different rules from virtual methods when they are invoked. In other words, they don't act like regular overridden methods, instead they follow a different set of rules to determine which specific implementation of the method will be invoked. In particular, when we call a nonvirtual method, it is the data type of the *variable* that refers to the object that indicates which implementation of the method is called, not the data type of the *object* as with virtual methods.

To override a nonvirtual method we can use the `Shadows` keyword instead of the `Overrides` keyword. To see how this works, let's add a new property to our base `Person` class:

```
Public ReadOnly Property Age() As Integer
  Get
    Return CInt(DateDiff(DateInterval.Year, Now(), BirthDate()))
  End Get
End Property
```

We've added a new method to our base class, and thus automatically to our subclass, called `Age`.

This code has a bug, introduced on purpose for illustration. The `DateDiff` parameters are in the wrong order, so we'll get negative age values from this routine. We introduced a bug because sometimes there are bugs in base classes that we didn't write and can't fix because we don't have the source code. In this case, we'll walk through the use of the `Shadows` keyword to help address a bug in our base class, acting under the assumption that for some reason we can't actually fix the code in the `Person` class.

Notice that we're not using the `Overridable` keyword on this method, so any subclass is prevented from overriding the method by using the `Overrides` keyword. The obvious intent and expectation of this code is that all subclasses will use this implementation and will not override it with their own.

However, the base class cannot prevent a subclass from shadowing a method, and so it doesn't matter whether we use `Overridable` or not, either way works fine for shadowing.

Before we shadow the method, let's see how it works as a regular nonvirtual method. First, we need to change our form to use this new value. Add a text box named `txtAge` and a related label to the form. Next, let's change the code behind the button to use the `Age` property. We'll also include the code to display the data on the form right here to keep things simple and clear:

```
Private Sub btnOK_Click(ByVal sender As System.Object, _
    ByVal e As System.EventArgs) Handles btnOK.Click

  Dim objPerson As Employee = New Employee()

  With objPerson
    .Name = "Fred"
```

```
      .BirthDate = #1/1/1960#

    txtName.Text = .Name
    txtBirthDate.Text = Format(.BirthDate, "Short date")
    txtAge.Text = .Age
  End With

  End Sub
```

Don't forget to change the birth date value to something that will be valid for an `Employee`.

At this point we can run the application and the age field should appear in our display as expected, though with a negative value due to the bug we introduced. There's no magic or complexity here. This is basic programming with objects and basic use of inheritance as we discussed at the beginning of this chapter.

Of course, we don't want a bug in our code, but if we assume we don't have access to the `Person` class, and since the `Person` class doesn't allow us to override the `Age` method, what are we to do? The answer lies in the `Shadows` keyword, which allows us to override the method anyway.

Let's shadow the `Age` method within the `Employee` class, overriding and replacing the implementation in the `Person` class even though it is not marked as `Overridable`. Add the following code to `Employee` class:

```
Public Shadows ReadOnly Property Age() As Integer
  Get
    Return CInt(DateDiff(DateInterval.Year, BirthDate(), Now()))
  End Get
End Property
```

In many ways this looks very similar to what we've seen with the `Overrides` keyword, in that we're implementing a method in our subclass with the same name and parameter list as a method in the base class. In this case, however, we'll find some different behavior when we interact with the object in different ways.

Technically, the `Shadows` keyword is not required here. Shadowing is the default behavior when a subclass implements a method that matches the name and method signature of a method in the base class. However, if we omit the `Shadows` keyword the compiler will give us a warning indicating that the method is being shadowed so it is always better to include the keyword, both to avoid the warning and to make it perfectly clear that we knew what we were doing when we chose to shadow the method.

Remember that our code in the form is currently declaring a variable of type `Employee` and is creating an instance of an `Employee` object:

```
Dim objPerson As Employee = New Employee()
```

This is a simple case, and not surprisingly when we run the application now we'll see that the value of the age field is correct, indicating that we just ran the implementation of the `Age` property from the `Employee` class. At this point, we're seeing the same behavior that we got from overriding with the `Overrides` keyword.

Let's take a look at the other simple case where we're working with a variable and object that are both of data type Person. Change the code in Form1 as follows:

```
Private Sub btnOK_Click(ByVal sender As System.Object, _
    ByVal e As System.EventArgs) Handles btnOK.Click

  Dim objPerson As Person = New Person()

  With objPerson
    .Name = "Fred"
    .BirthDate = #1/1/1960#

    txtName.Text = .Name
    txtBirthDate.Text = Format(.BirthDate, "Short date")
    txtAge.Text = .Age
  End With
End Sub
```

Now we have a variable of type Person and an object of that same type. We would expect that the implementation in the Person class would be invoked in this case, and that is exactly what happens, the age field will display the original negative value, indicating that we're invoking the buggy implementation of the method directly from the Person class. Again, this is exactly the behavior we'd expect from a method overridden via the Overrides keyword.

This next one is where things get truly interesting. Change the code in Form1 as follows:

```
Private Sub btnOK_Click(ByVal sender As System.Object, _
    ByVal e As System.EventArgs) Handles btnOK.Click

  Dim objPerson As Person = New Employee()

  With objPerson
    .Name = "Fred"
    .BirthDate = #1/1/1960#

    txtName.Text = .Name
    txtBirthDate.Text = Format(.BirthDate, "Short date")
    txtAge.Text = .Age
  End With
End Sub
```

Now we are declaring the variable to be of type Person, but we are creating an object that is of data type Employee. We did this earlier in the chapter when exploring the Overrides keyword as well, and in that case we discovered that the version of the method that was invoked was based on the data type of the object. The BirthDate implementation in the Employee class was invoked.

If we run the application now we will find that the rules are different when the Shadows keyword is used. In this case, the implementation in the Person class is invoked, giving us the buggy negative value. When the implementation in the Employee class is ignored, we get the exact opposite behavior to what we got with Overrides.

The following table summarizes which method implementation is invoked based on the variable and object data types when using shadowing.

Variable	Object	Method Invoked
Base	Base	Base
Base	Subclass	Base
Subclass	Subclass	Subclass

In most cases, the behavior we'll want for our methods is accomplished by the Overrides keyword and virtual methods. However, in those cases where the base class designer doesn't allow us to override a method and we want to do it anyway, the Shadows keyword provides us with the needed functionality.

Shadowing Arbitrary Elements

The Shadows keyword can be used not only to override nonvirtual methods, but it can be used to totally replace and change the nature of a base class interface element. When we override a method we are providing a replacement implementation of that method with the same name and method signature. Using the Shadows keyword we can do more extreme things, such as changing a method into an instance variable or changing a Property into a Function.

However, this can be very dangerous, since any code written to use our objects will naturally assume that we implement all the same interface elements and behaviors as our base class, because that is the nature of inheritance.

> **By totally changing the nature of an interface element, we can cause a great deal of confusion for programmers who will be interacting with our class in the future.**

To see how we can replace an interface element from the base class, let's entirely change the nature of the Age property. In fact, let's change it from being a read-only property to being a read–write property. We could get even more extreme — changing it to a Function or Sub.

To do this, remove the Age property from the Employee class and add the following code:

```
Public Shadows Property Age() As Integer
  Get
    Return CInt(DateDiff(DateInterval.Year, BirthDate(), Now()))
  End Get
  Set(ByVal Value As Integer)
    BirthDate() = DateAdd(DateInterval.Year, -Value, Now())
  End Set
End Property
```

With this change, the very nature of the Age method has changed. It is no longer a simple read-only property, now it is a read–write property that includes code to calculate an approximate birth date based on the age value supplied.

As it stands, our application will continue to run just fine. This is because we're only using the read-only functionality of the property in our form. We can change the form to make use of the new read–write functionality:

```
Private Sub btnOK_Click(ByVal sender As System.Object, _
    ByVal e As System.EventArgs) Handles btnOK.Click

  Dim objPerson As Person = New Employee()

  With objPerson
    .Name = "Fred"
    .BirthDate = #1/1/1960#
    .Age = 20

    txtName.Text = .Name
    txtBirthDate.Text = Format(.BirthDate, "Short date")
    txtAge.Text = .Age
  End With
End Sub
```

This will, however, leave us with a syntax error. The variable we're working with, objPerson, is of data type Person, and that data type does not provide a writable version of the Age property. This means that in order to use our enhanced functionality, we must be using a variable and object of type Employee:

```
Dim objPerson As Employee = New Employee()
```

If we now run the application and click the button we'll see that the Age is displayed as 20, and the birth date is now a value calculated based on that age value, indicating that we are now running the shadowed version of the Age method as implemented in the Employee class.

As if that wasn't odd enough, we can do some even more strange and dangerous things. We can change Age into a *variable* and we can even change its scope. For instance, we can comment out the Age property code in the Employee class and replace it with the following code.

```
Private Shadows Age As String
```

At this point we've changed everything. Age is now a String instead of an Integer. It is a variable instead of a Property or Function. It has Private scope instead of Public scope. Our Employee object is totally incompatible with the Person data type, something that shouldn't occur normally when using inheritance.

This means that the code we wrote in Form1 will no longer work. The Age property is no longer accessible and can no longer be used and so our project will no longer compile. This directly illustrates the danger in shadowing a base class element such that its very nature or scope is changed by the subclass.

Since this change prevents our application from compiling, remove the line in the Employee class that shadows Age as a String variable, and uncomment the shadowed Property routine:

```
Public Shadows Property Age() As Integer
  Get
    Return CInt(DateDiff(DateInterval.Year, BirthDate(), Now()))
  End Get
  Set(ByVal Value As Integer)
    BirthDate() = DateAdd(DateInterval.Year, -Value, Now())
  End Set
End Property
```

This will restore our application to a working state and we can move on.

Levels of Inheritance

So far we've created a single base class and a single subclass, thus demonstrating that we can implement inheritance that is single level deep. However, we can create inheritance relationships that are several levels deep. These are sometimes referred to as chains of inheritance.

> *In reality, we've been creating a two-level inheritance hierarchy so far because we know that our base class actually derived from* System.Object, *but for most purposes it is easiest to simply ignore that fact and treat only our classes as part of the inheritance hierarchy.*

Multiple Inheritance

Don't confuse multilevel inheritance with multiple inheritance, which is an entirely different concept that is not supported by either VB.NET or the .NET platform itself. The idea behind *multiple inheritance* is that we can have a single subclass that inherits from two base classes all at the same time.

For instance, we may have an application that has a class for Customer and another class for Vendor. It is quite possible that some customers are also vendors, so we might want to combine the functionality of these two classes into a CustomerVendor class. This new class would be a combination of both Customer and Vendor, so it would be nice to inherit from both of them at once, something like the following UML diagram might indicate (see Figure 6-9).

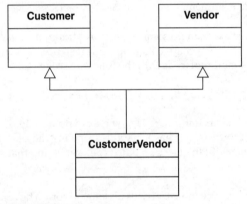

Figure 6-9

Here we see the line running from CustomerVendor back up into both Customer and Vendor and terminating in an open triangle in both cases. This indicates that CustomerVendor inherits from both of those classes.

While a useful concept, multiple inheritance is complex and somewhat dangerous. Within the object-oriented community there is continual debate as to whether the advantages of code reuse outweigh the complexity that comes along for the ride.

Multiple inheritance is not supported by the .NET Framework, and so it is likewise not supported by VB.NET. However, we can use multiple interfaces to achieve an effect similar to multiple inheritance, a topic we'll discuss later in the chapter when we talk about implementing multiple interfaces.

Multilevel Inheritance

We've seen how a subclass derives from a base class with our `Person` and `Employee` classes. However, there's nothing to stop the `Employee` subclass from being the base class for yet another class, a sub-subclass so to speak. This is not at all uncommon. In our example, we may find that we have different kinds of employees, some who work in the office and others who travel.

To accommodate this, we may want to have `OfficeEmployee` and `TravelingEmployee` classes. Of course, these are both examples of an employee and should share the functionality already present in the `Employee` class. The `Employee` class already reuses the functionality from the `Person` class. The following UML illustrates how these classes are interrelated (see Figure 6-10).

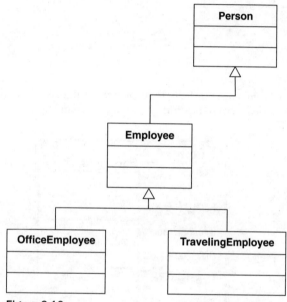

Figure 6-10

We can see that the `Employee` is a subclass of `Person`, and our two new classes are both subclasses of `Employee`. While both `OfficeEmployee` and `TravelingEmployee` are employees, and thus also people, they are each unique. An `OfficeEmployee` almost certainly has a cube or office number, while a `TravelingEmployee` will keep track of the number of miles traveled.

Add a new class to our project and name it `OfficeEmployee`. To make this class inherit from our existing `Employee` class, add the following code to the class:

```
Public Class OfficeEmployee
   Inherits Employee

End Class
```

With this change, the new class now has `Name`, `BirthDate`, `Age`, `HireDate`, and `Salary` methods. Notice that methods from both `Employee` and `Person` are inherited. A subclass always gains all the methods, properties and events of its base class.

We can now extend the interface and behavior of OfficeEmployee by adding a property to indicate which cube or office number the employee occupies:

```
Public Class OfficeEmployee
  Inherits Employee

  Private mstrOffice As String

  Public Property OfficeNumber() As String
    Get
      Return mstrOffice
    End Get
    Set(ByVal Value As String)
      mstrOffice = Value
    End Set
  End Property

End Class
```

To see how this works, let's enhance our form to display this value. Add a new text box control named txtOffice and an associated label so our form looks as shown in Figure 6-11.

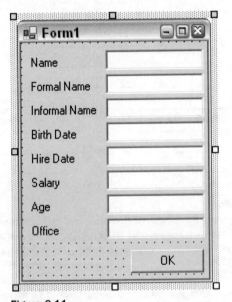

Figure 6-11

Now, change the code behind the button to make use of the new property:

```
Private Sub btnOK_Click(ByVal sender As System.Object, _
    ByVal e As System.EventArgs) Handles btnOK.Click

  Dim objPerson As OfficeEmployee = New OfficeEmployee()

  With objPerson
    .Name = "Fred"
```

```
      .BirthDate = #1/1/1960#
      .Age = 20
      .OfficeNumber = "A42"

      txtName.Text = .Name
      txtBirthDate.Text = Format(.BirthDate, "Short date")
      txtAge.Text = .Age
      txtOffice.Text = .OfficeNumber
    End With
  End Sub
```

We've changed the routine to declare and create an object of type OfficeEmployee — thus allowing us to make use of the new property — as well as all existing properties and methods from Employee and Person since they've been "merged" into the OfficeEmployee class via inheritance.

If we now run the application we'll see that the name, birth date, age, and office values are displayed in the form.

Inheritance like this can go many levels deep, with each level extending and changing the behaviors of the previous levels. In fact, there is no specific technical limit to the number of levels of inheritance we can implement in VB.NET. Very deep inheritance chains are typically not recommended and are often viewed as a design flaw, something we'll discuss in more detail in Chapter 7.

Interacting with the Base Class, Our Class, and Our Object

We've already seen how we can use the MyBase keyword to call methods on the base class from within a subclass. The MyBase keyword is one of three special keywords that allows us to interact with important object and class representations:

- ❑ Me
- ❑ MyBase
- ❑ MyClass

The Me Keyword

The Me keyword provides us with a reference to our current object instance. Typically, we don't need to use the Me keyword, since any time we want to invoke a method within our current object we can just call that method directly.

To see clearly how this works, let's add a new method to the Person class that returns the data of the Person class in the form of a String. This will be a bit interesting in and of itself, since the base System.Object class defines the ToString method for this exact purpose. Remember that all classes in the .NET Framework ultimately derive from System.Object, even if we don't explicitly indicate it with an Inherits statement.

This means we can simply override the ToString method from the Object class within our Person class by adding the following code:

```
Public Overrides Function ToString() As String
  Return Name
End Function
```

191

This implementation will return the person's `Name` property as a result when `ToString` is called.

> *By default, ToString returns the class name of the class. Up to now, if we had called the ToString method on a Person object we would have gotten a result of InheritanceAndInterfaces.Person.*

Notice that the `ToString` method is calling another method within our same class, in this case the `Name` method.

We could also write this routine using the `Me` keyword:

```
Public Overrides Function ToString() As String
   Return Me.Name
End Function
```

However, this is redundant since `Me` is the default for all method calls in a class. These two implementations are identical, so typically the `Me` keyword is simply left off to avoid that extra typing.

To see how the `ToString` method now works, we can change our code in `Form1` to use this value instead of the `Name` property:

```
Private Sub btnOK_Click(ByVal sender As System.Object, _
     ByVal e As System.EventArgs) Handles btnOK.Click
   Dim objPerson As OfficeEmployee = New OfficeEmployee()

   With objPerson
     .Name = "Fred"
     .BirthDate = #1/1/1960#
     .Age = 20
     .OfficeNumber = "A42"

     txtName.Text = .ToString
     txtBirthDate.Text = Format(.BirthDate, "Short date")
     txtAge.Text = .Age
     txtOffice.Text = .OfficeNumber
   End With
End Sub
```

When we run the application we'll see that the person's name is displayed appropriately, which makes sense since the `ToString` method is simply returning the result from the `Name` property.

Earlier, we discussed virtual methods and how they work. Since either calling a method directly or calling it using the `Me` keyword invokes the method on the current object this means that the method calls conform to the same rules as an external method call. In other words, our `ToString` method may not actually end up calling the `Name` method in the `Person` class if that method was overridden by a class further down the inheritance chain such as the `Employee` or `OfficeEmployee` classes.

For example, we could override the `Name` property in our `OfficeEmployee` class such that it always returns the informal version of the person's name rather than the regular name. We can override the `Name` property by adding this method to the `OfficeEmployee` class:

```
Public Overloads Overrides Property Name() As String
  Get
    Return MyBase.Name(NameTypes.Informal)
  End Get
  Set(ByVal Value As String)
    MyBase.Name = Value
  End Set
End Property
```

This new version of the `Name` method relies on the base class to actually store the value, but instead of returning the normal name on request, now we are always returning the informal name:

```
Return MyBase.Name(NameTypes.Informal)
```

Before we can test this, we need to enhance the code in our form to actually provide a value for the informal name. Make the following change to that code:

```
Private Sub btnOK_Click(ByVal sender As System.Object, _
    ByVal e As System.EventArgs) Handles btnOK.Click
  Dim objPerson As OfficeEmployee = New OfficeEmployee()

  With objPerson
    .Name = "Fred"
    .Name(NameTypes.Informal) = "Freddy"
    .BirthDate = #1/1/1960#
    .Age = 20
    .OfficeNumber = "A42"

    txtName.Text = .ToString
    txtBirthDate.Text = Format(.BirthDate, "Short date")
    txtAge.Text = .Age
    txtOffice.Text = .OfficeNumber
  End With
End Sub
```

When we run the application, we'll find that the name field displays the informal name. Even though the `ToString` method is implemented in the `Person` class, it is invoking the implementation of `Name` from the `OfficeEmployee` class. This is because method calls *within* a class follow the same rules for calling virtual methods as code *outside* a class, such as our code in the form.

We'll see this behavior with or without the `Me` keyword, since the default behavior for method calls is to implicitly call them via the current object.

While methods called from within a class follow the same rules for virtual methods, this is not the case for shadowed methods. Here we'll find that the rules for calling a shadowed method from within our class are different from those outside our class.

To see how this works, let's make the `Name` property in `OfficeEmployee` a shadowed method instead of an overridden method:

```
Public Shadows Property Name() As String
  Get
    Return MyBase.Name(NameTypes.Informal)
```

```
      End Get
      Set(ByVal Value As String)
         MyBase.Name = Value
      End Set
   End Property
```

Before we can run our application, we'll have to adjust some code in the form. Because we've overridden the `Name` property in `OfficeEmployee`, we'll find that the version of `Name` from `Employee` that acts as a property array is now invalid.

> **Shadowing a method replaces *all* implementations from higher in the inheritance chain, regardless of their method signature.**

To make our application operate we'll need to change the variable declaration and object creation to declare a variable of type `Employee` so we can access the property array while still creating an instance of `OfficeEmployee`:

```
   Dim objPerson As Employee = New OfficeEmployee()
```

Since our variable is now of type `Employee`, we also need to comment out the lines that refer to the `OfficeNumber` property, since it is no longer available:

```
   With objPerson
      .Name = "Fred"
      .Name(NameTypes.Informal) = "Freddy"
      .BirthDate = #1/1/1960#
      .Age = 20
      '.OfficeNumber = "A42"

      txtName.Text = .ToString
      txtBirthDate.Text = Format(.BirthDate, "Short date")
      txtAge.Text = .Age
      'txtOffice.Text = .OfficeNumber
   End With
```

When we run the application now, we'll find that it displays the name Fred rather than Freddy, meaning it is *not* calling the `Name` method from `OfficeEmployee`, instead it is calling the implementation provided by the `Employee` class. Remember that the code to make this call still resides in the `Person` class, but it now ignores the shadowed version of the `Name` method.

Shadowed implementations in subclasses are ignored when calling the method from *within* a class higher in the inheritance chain.

We'll get this same behavior with or without the `Me` keyword. So the `Me` keyword, or calling methods directly, follows the same rules for overridden methods as any other method call. For shadowed methods, however, any shadowed implementations in subclasses are ignored and the method is called from the current level in the inheritance chain.

So why does the Me keyword exist? Primarily to allow us to pass a reference to the current object as a parameter to other objects or methods. As we'll see when we look at the MyBase and MyClass keywords, things can get very confusing and there may be value in using the Me keyword when working with MyBase and MyClass to ensure that it is always clear which particular implementation of a method we intended to invoke.

The MyBase Keyword

While the Me keyword allows us to call methods on the current object instance, there are times we might want to explicitly call into methods in our parent class. Earlier we saw an example of this when we called back into the base class from an overridden method in the subclass.

The MyBase keyword references only the immediate parent class, and it works like an object reference. This means we can call methods on MyBase, knowing that they are being called just like we had a reference to an object of our parent class's data type.

> **There is no way to directly navigate up the inheritance chain beyond our immediate parent.**

The MyBase keyword can be used to invoke or use any Public, Friend, or Protected element from the parent class. This includes all of those elements directly on the base class, and also any elements the base class inherited from other classes higher in the inheritance chain.

We've already used MyBase to call back into the base Person class as we implemented the overridden Name property in the Employee class.

> **Any code within a subclass can call any method on the base class by using the MyBase keyword.**

We can also use MyBase to call back into the base class implementation even if we've shadowed a method. Though we didn't remark on it at the time, we've already done this in our shadowed implementation of the Name property in the OfficeEmployee class. The highlighted lines indicate where we're calling into the base class from within a shadowed method.

```
Public Shadows Property Name() As String
  Get
    Return MyBase.Name(NameTypes.Informal)
  End Get
  Set(ByVal Value As String)
    MyBase.Name = Value
  End Set
End Property
```

The MyBase keyword allows us to merge the functionality of the base class into our subclass code as we deem fit.

The MyClass Keyword

As we've seen, when we use the Me keyword or call a method directly, our method call follows the rules for calling both virtual and nonvirtual methods. In other words, as we discovered earlier with the Name property, a call to Name from our code in the Person class actually invoked the overridden version of Name located in the OfficeEmployee class.

While this behavior is useful in many cases, there are also cases where we'll want to ensure that we really are running the specific implementation from our class, where even if a subclass overrode our method we still want to ensure we're calling the version of the method that is directly in our class.

Maybe we decide that our ToString implementation in Person should always call the Name implementation that we write in the Person class, totally ignoring any overridden versions of Name in any subclasses.

This is where the MyClass keyword comes into play. This keyword is much like MyBase, in that it provides us with access to methods as though it were an object reference, in this case, a reference to an instance of the class that contains the code we're writing when using the MyClass keyword. This is true even if the instantiated object is an instance of a class derived from our class.

We've seen that a call to ToString from within Person will actually invoke the implementation in Employee or OfficeEmployee if our object is an instance of either of those types. Let's restore the Name property in OfficeEmployee to be an overridden method rather than a shadowed method to see how this works.

```
Public Overloads Overrides Property Name() As String
  Get
    Return MyBase.Name(NameTypes.Informal)
  End Get
  Set(ByVal Value As String)
    MyBase.Name = Value
  End Set
End Property
```

With this change, and based on our earlier testing, we know that the ToString implementation in Person will automatically call this overridden version of the Name property, since the call to the Name method will follow the normal rules for virtual methods. In fact, if we run the application now we'll find that the name field on the form displays Freddy, the informal name of the person.

We can force the use of the implementation in our current class through the use of MyClass. Change the ToString method in Person as follows:

```
Public Overrides Function ToString() As String
  Return MyClass.Name
End Function
```

We are now calling the Name method, but we're doing it using the MyClass keyword. When we run the application and click the button we'll find that the name field in the form displays Fred rather than Freddy, proving that the implementation from Person was invoked even though the data type of the object itself is OfficeEmployee.

The `ToString` method is invoked from `Person`, since neither `Employee` nor `OfficeEmployee` provide an overridden implementation. Then, because we're using the `MyClass` keyword, the `Name` method is invoked directly from `Person`, explicitly defeating the default behavior we'd normally expect.

Constructors

As we discussed in Chapter 5, we can provide a special constructor method, named `New`, on a class and it will be the first code run when an object is instantiated. We can also receive parameters via the constructor method. allowing the code that creates our object to pass data into the object during the creation process.

Constructor methods are affected by inheritance differently from regular methods. A normal `Public` method, such as `BirthDate` on our `Person` class, is automatically inherited by any subclass. From there we can overload, override, or shadow that method as we've discussed so far in this chapter.

Simple Constructors

Constructors don't quite follow the same rules. To explore the differences, let's implement a simple constructor method in our `Person` class:

```
Public Sub New()
  Debug.WriteLine("Person constructor")
End Sub
```

If we now run the application, we'll see the text displayed in the Output window in the IDE. This occurs even though the code in our form is creating an object of type `OfficeEmployee`:

```
Dim objPerson As Employee = New OfficeEmployee()
```

As we might expect, the `New` method from our base `Person` class is invoked as part of the construction process of the `OfficeEmployee` object, simple inheritance at work. However, interesting things occur if we implement a `New` method in the `OfficeEmployee` class itself:

```
Public Sub New()
  Debug.WriteLine("OfficeEmployee constructor")
End Sub
```

Notice that we are not using the `Overrides` keyword, nor did we mark the method in `Person` as `Overridable`. These keywords have no use in this context and in fact, will cause syntax errors if we attempt to use them on constructor methods.

When we run the application now we'd probably expect that only the implementation of `New` in `OfficeEmployee` would be invoked. Certainly, that is what would occur with a normal overridden method. But, of course, `New` isn't overridden so when we run the application we'll find that both implementations are run. Both strings are output into the Output window in the IDE.

It is important to note that the implementation in the `Person` class ran first, followed by the implementation in the `OfficeEmployee` class. This occurs because, as an object is created, all the constructors for the classes in the inheritance chain are invoked, starting with the base class and working out through all the subclasses one by one. In fact, if we implement a `New` method in the `Employee` class we can see that it too is invoked:

```
Public Sub New()
    Debug.WriteLine("Employee constructor")
End Sub
```

When the application is run and the button clicked we'll see all three strings in the Output window. All three constructor methods were invoked, starting with the `Person` class and working down to the `OfficeEmployee` class.

Constructors in More Depth

The rules governing constructors without parameters are pretty straightforward. However, things get a bit more interesting if we start requiring parameters on our constructors.

To understand what is going on, we need to get a slightly better understanding of how even our simple constructors are being invoked. While we see them as being invoked from the base class down through all subclasses to our final subclass, what is really happening is a bit different.

In particular, it is the subclass `New` method that is invoked first. However, VB.NET is automatically inserting a line of code into our routine at compile time. For instance, in our `OfficeEmployee` class we have a constructor:

```
Public Sub New()
    Debug.WriteLine("OfficeEmployee constructor")
End Sub
```

Behind the scenes, VB.NET inserts what is effectively a call to constructor of our parent class on our behalf. We could do this manually by using the `MyBase` keyword with the following change:

```
Public Sub New()
    MyBase.New()
    Debug.WriteLine("OfficeEmployee constructor")
End Sub
```

This call is required to be the first line in our constructor. If we put any other code before this line we'll get a syntax error indicating that our code is invalid. Since the call is always required, and since it always must be the first line in any constructor, VB.NET simply inserts it for us automatically.

It is also worth noting that if we don't explicitly provide a constructor on a class by implementing a `New` method, VB.NET creates one for us behind the scenes. The automatically created method simply has one line of code:

```
MyBase.New()
```

All classes have constructor methods, either created explicitly by us as we write a `New` method, or created implicitly by VB.NET as the class is compiled.

Constructor methods are sometimes called a ctor, short for constructor.

By always calling `Mybase.New()` as the first line in every constructor, we are guaranteed that it is the implementation of `New` in our top-level base class that will actually run first. Every subclass invokes the parent class implementation all the way up the inheritance chain until only the base class remains. Then its code runs, followed by each individual subclass as we've already seen.

Constructors with Parameters

This works great when our constructors don't require parameters. However, if our constructor does require a parameter, then it becomes impossible for VB.NET to automatically make that call on our behalf. After all, how would VB.NET know what values we want to pass as parameters?

To see how this works, let's change the `New` method in the `Person` class to require a `Name` parameter. We can use that parameter to initialize the object's `Name` property:

```
Public Sub New(ByVal Name As String)
  Me.Name = Name
  Debug.WriteLine("Person constructor")
End Sub
```

Now our constructor requires a `String` parameter and uses it to initialize the `Name` property.

We are using the `Me` keyword to make our code easier to read. Interestingly enough, the compiler will actually understand and correctly compile the following code:

```
Name = Name
```

But that is not at all clear to a developer reading the code. By prefixing the property name with the `Me` keyword we've made it clear that we're invoking a property on the object and providing it with the parameter value.

At this point we'll find that our application won't compile. This is because there is an error in the `New` method of our `Employee` class. In particular, VB.NET's attempt to automatically invoke the constructor on the `Person` class is no longer workable, since it has no idea what data value to pass for this new `Name` parameter.

There are three ways we can address this error:

- ❑ We can make the `Name` parameter `Optional`
- ❑ We can overload the `New` method with another implementation that requires no parameter
- ❑ We can manually provide the `Name` parameter value from within the `Employee` class

If we make the `Name` parameter `Optional`, we're indicating that the `New` method can be called with or without a parameter. This means that one viable option is to call the method with no parameters. So VB.NET's default of calling it with no parameters will work just fine.

If we overload the `New` method, we can implement a second `New` method that doesn't accept any parameters, again allowing VB.NET's default behavior to work as we've seen. Keep in mind that this solution would only invoke the overloaded version of `New` with no parameter, the version that requires a parameter would not be invoked.

The final way we can fix the error is by simply providing a parameter value ourselves from within the New method of the Employee class. To do this, change the Employee class:

```
Public Sub New()
  MyBase.New("George")
  Debug.WriteLine("Employee constructor")
End Sub
```

By explicitly calling the New method of our parent class, we are able to provide it with the required parameter value. At this point our application will compile, but it won't run.

Constructors, Overloading, and Variable Initialization

What isn't clear from this code is that we've now introduced a very insidious bug. The constructor in the Person class is using the Name property to set the value:

```
Public Sub New(ByVal Name As String)
  Me.Name = Name
  Debug.WriteLine("Person constructor")
End Sub
```

But the Name property is overridden by the Employee class, so it is that implementation which will be run. Unfortunately, that implementation makes use of a Hashtable object which isn't available yet! It turns out that any member variables declared in a class with the New statement, such as our Hashtable object in Employee:

```
Private mcolNames As New Hashtable()
```

won't be initialized until after the constructor for that class has completed. Since we are still in the constructor for Person, there's no way the constructor for Employee can be complete. To resolve this, we need to change the Employee class a bit so it doesn't rely on the Hashtable being created in this manner. Instead, we'll add code to create it when needed.

First, change the declaration of the variable in the Employee class:

```
Private mcolNames As Hashtable
```

Then, update the Name property so it creates the Hashtable object if needed:

```
Public Overloads Property Name(ByVal Type As NameTypes) As String
  Get
    If mcolNames Is Nothing Then mcolNames = New Hashtable()
    Return mcolNames(Type)
  End Get
  Set(ByVal Value As String)
    If mcolNames Is Nothing Then mcolNames = New Hashtable()
    If mcolNames.ContainsKey(Types) Then
      mcolNames.Item(Types) = Value
    Else
      mcolNames.Add(Type, Value)
    End If
```

```
        If Type = NameTypes.Normal Then
           MyBase.Name = Value
        End If
     End Set
  End Property
```

This will ensure that a `Hashtable` object is created in the `Employee` class code even though its constructor hasn't yet completed.

More Constructors with Parameters

Obviously, we probably don't really want to hard-code a value in a constructor like we did in the `Employee` class, so we may choose instead to change this constructor to also accept a `Name` parameter. Change the `Employee` class constructor as shown:

```
Public Sub New(ByVal Name As String)
  MyBase.New(Name)
  Debug.WriteLine("Employee constructor")
End Sub
```

Of course, this just pushed the issue deeper and now we'll find that the `OfficeEmployee` class has a compile error in its `New` method. Again, we can fix it by having that method accept a parameter so it can provide it up the chain as required. Make the following change to `OfficeEmployee`:

```
Public Sub New(ByVal Name As String)
  MyBase.New(Name)
  Debug.WriteLine("OfficeEmployee constructor")
End Sub
```

Finally, the code in our form is no longer valid. We're attempting there to create an instance of `OfficeEmployee` without passing a parameter value. Let's update that code and then we can run the application:

```
Private Sub btnOK_Click(ByVal sender As System.Object, _
     ByVal e As System.EventArgs) Handles btnOK.Click

  Dim objPerson As Employee = New OfficeEmployee("Mary")

  With objPerson
    '.Name = "Fred"
```

We're passing a `Name` value to the constructor of `OfficeEmployee`. Also, we've commented out the line of code that sets the `Name` property directly—meaning that the value we've passed in the constructor will be displayed in our form.

The Protected Scope

We've seen how a subclass automatically gains all the `Public` methods and properties that comprise the interface of the base class. This is also true of `Friend` methods and properties, they are inherited as well, and are available only to other code in the same project as the subclass.

`Private` methods and properties are not exposed as part of the interface of the subclass, meaning that our code in the subclass cannot call those methods, nor can any code using our objects. These methods are only available to the code within the base class itself. This can get confusing, since the *implementation* contained in the `Private` methods are inherited and are used by any code in the base class, it is just that they aren't available to be called by any other code, including code in our subclass.

There are times when we want to create methods in our base class that *can* be called by a subclass as well as the base class, but not by code outside of those classes. Basically, we want a hybrid between `Public` and `Private` — methods that are private to the classes in our inheritance chain, but are usable by any subclasses that might be created within the chain. This functionality is provided by the `Protected` scope.

`Protected` methods are very similar to `Private` methods, in that they are not available to any code that calls our objects. Instead, these methods are available to code within the base class *and* to code within any subclass. The following table lists all the available scope options.

Scope	Description
Private	Available only to code within our class
Protected	Available only to classes that inherit from our class
Friend	Available only to code within our project/component
Protected Friend	Available to classes that inherit from our class (in any project) and to code within our project/component. This is a combination of `Protected` and `Friend`
Public	Available to code outside our class

The `Protected` scope can be applied to `Sub`, `Function`, and `Property` methods. To see how the `Protected` scope works, let's add an `Identity` field to the `Person` class:

```
Public Class Person
    Private mstrName As String
    Private mdtBirthDate As String
    Private mstrID As String

    Protected Property Identity() As String
      Get
        Return mstrID
      End Get
      Set(ByVal Value As String)
        mstrID = Value
      End Set
    End Property
```

This data field represents some arbitrary identification number or value assigned to a person. This might be a social security number, an employee number, or whatever is appropriate.

The interesting thing about this value is that it is not currently accessible *outside* our inheritance chain. For instance, if we try to use it from our code in the form we'll discover that there is no `Identity` property on our `Person`, `Employee`, or `OfficeEmployee` objects.

However, there is an `Identity` property now available inside our inheritance chain. The `Identity` property is available to the code in the `Person` class just like any other method. The interesting thing is that even though `Identity` is not available to the code in our form, it is available to the code in the `Employee` and `OfficeEmployee` classes. This is because they are both subclasses of `Person`. `Employee` is directly a subclass, and `OfficeEmployee` is indirectly a subclass of `Person` because it is a subclass of `Employee`.

Thus, we can enhance our `Employee` class to implement an `EmployeeNumber` property by using the `Identity` property. To do this, add the following code to the `Employee` class:

```
Public Property EmployeeNumber() As Integer
  Get
    Return CInt(Identity)
  End Get
  Set(ByVal Value As Integer)
    Identity = CStr(Value)
  End Set
End Property
```

This new property exposes a numeric identity value for the employee, but it uses the internal `Identity` property to manage that value.

We can override and shadow `Protected` elements just as we do with elements of any other scope.

Protected Variables

Up to this point we've focused on methods and properties and how they interact through inheritance. Inheritance, and in particular, the `Protected` scope, also has an impact on instance variables and how we work with them.

Though it is not recommended, we can declare variables in a class using `Public` scope. This makes the variable directly available to code both within and outside of our class, allowing any code that interacts with our objects to directly read or alter the value of that variable.

Variables can also have `Friend` scope, which likewise allows any code in our class or anywhere within our project to read or alter the value directly. This is also generally not recommended as it breaks encapsulation.

> Rather than declaring variables with Public or Friend scope, it is better to expose the value using a Property method so that we can apply any of our business rules to control how the value is altered as appropriate.

Of course, we know that variables can be of `Private` scope, and this is typically the case. This makes the variables accessible only to the code within our class and is the most restrictive scope.

As with methods however, we can also use the `Protected` scope when declaring variables. This makes the variable accessible to the code in our class, and to the code in any class that derives from our class—all the way down the hierarchy chain.

There are times when this is useful, as it allows us to provide and accept data from subclasses, but act on that data from code in the base class. At the same time, exposing variables to subclasses is typically not ideal and we should use `Property` methods with `Protected` scope for this instead, since they allow our base class to enforce any business rules that are appropriate for the value, rather than just hoping that the author of the subclass only provides us with good values.

Events and Inheritance

So far we've discussed methods, properties, and variables in terms of inheritance — seeing how they can be added, overridden, extended, and shadowed. In VB.NET, events are also part of the interface of an object and they are impacted by inheritance as well.

Inheriting Events

In Chapter 5, we discussed how to declare, raise and receive events from objects. We can add such an event to our `Person` class by declaring it at the top of the class:

```
Public Class Person
    Private mstrName As String
    Private mdtBirthDate As String
    Private mstrID As String

    Public Event NameChanged(ByVal NewName As String)
```

Then, we can raise this event within the class any time the person's name is changed:

```
Public Overridable Property Name() As String
  Get
     Return mstrName
  End Get
  Set(ByVal Value As String)
    mstrName = Value
    RaiseEvent NameChanged(mstrName)
  End Set
End Property
```

At this point, we can receive and handle this event within our form any time we're working with a `Person` object. The nice thing about this is that our events are inherited automatically by subclasses — meaning that our `Employee` and `OfficeEmployee` objects will also raise this event. Thus, we can change the code in our form to handle the event, even though we're working with an object of type `OfficeEmployee`.

First, we can add a method to handle the event to `Form1`:

```
Private Sub OnNameChanged(ByVal NewName As String)
  MsgBox("New name: " & NewName)
End Sub
```

Note that we're not using the `Handles` clause here. In this case, for simplicity, we'll use the `AddHandler` method to dynamically link the event to this method. However, we could have also chosen to use the `WithEvents` and `Handles` keywords as described in Chapter 5 — either way works.

With the handler built, we can use the `AddHandler` method to link this method to the event on our object:

```
Private Sub btnOK_Click(ByVal sender As System.Object, _
    ByVal e As System.EventArgs) Handles btnOK.Click

  Dim objPerson As Employee = New OfficeEmployee("Mary")
  AddHandler objPerson.NameChanged, AddressOf OnNameChanged

  With objPerson
    .Name = "Fred"
```

Also note that we're uncommenting the line that changes the `Name` property. With this change, we know that the event should fire when the name is changed.

When we run the application now, we'll see a message box indicating that the name has changed, and proving that the `NameChanged` event really is exposed and available even though our object is of type `OfficeEmployee` rather than of type `Person`.

Raising Events from Subclasses

One caveat we need to keep in mind is that while a subclass exposes the events of its base class, the code in the subclass cannot raise the event.

In other words, we cannot use the `RaiseEvent` method in `Employee` or `OfficeEmployee` to raise the `NameChanged` event. Only code directly in the `Person` class can raise the event.

To see this in action, let's add another event to the `Person` class, an event that can indicate the change of other arbitrary data values:

```
Public Class Person
  Private mstrName As String
  Private mdtBirthDate As String
  Private mstrID As String

  Public Event NameChanged(ByVal NewName As String)
  Public Event DataChanged(ByVal Field As String, ByVal NewValue As Object)
```

We can then raise this event when the `BirthDate` is changed:

```
Public Overridable Property BirthDate() As Date
  Get
    Return mdtBirthDate
  End Get
  Set(ByVal Value As Date)
    mdtBirthDate = Value
    RaiseEvent DataChanged("BirthDate", Value)
  End Set
End Property
```

It would also be nice to raise this event from the `Employee` class when the `Salary` value is changed. Unfortunately, we can't use the `RaiseEvent` method to raise the event from a base class, so the following code won't work (don't enter this code):

```
Public Property Salary() As Double
  Get
    Return mdblSalary
  End Get
  Set(ByVal Value As Double)
    mdblSalary = Value

    RaiseEvent DataChanged("Salary", Value)
  End Set
End Property
```

Fortunately there is a relatively easy way to get around this limitation. We can simply implement a `Protected` method in our base class that allows any derived class to raise the method. In the `Person` class we can add such a method:

```
Protected Sub RaiseDataChanged(ByVal Field As String, _
    ByVal NewValue As Object)
  RaiseEvent DataChanged(Field, NewValue)
End Sub
```

Then we can use this method from within the `Employee` class to indicate that `Salary` has changed:

```
Public Property Salary() As Double
  Get
    Return mdblSalary
  End Get
  Set(ByVal Value As Double)
    mdblSalary = Value
    RaiseDataChanged("Salary", Value)
  End Set
End Property
```

Notice that the code in `Employee` is *not* raising the event, it is simply calling a `Protected` method in `Person`. It is the code in the `Person` class that actually raises the event, meaning that all will work as we desire.

We can enhance the code in `Form1` to receive the event. First off, we need to create a method to handle the event:

```
Private Sub OnDataChanged(ByVal Field As String, ByVal NewValue As Object)
  MsgBox("New " & Field & ": " & CStr(NewValue))
End Sub
```

Then, we can link this handler to the event using the `AddHandler` method:

```
Private Sub btnOK_Click(ByVal sender As System.Object, _
    ByVal e As System.EventArgs) Handles btnOK.Click
  Dim objPerson As Employee = New OfficeEmployee("Mary")
  AddHandler objPerson.NameChanged, AddressOf OnNameChanged
  AddHandler objPerson.DataChanged, AddressOf OnDataChanged
```

Finally, we need to make sure we are changing and displaying the `Salary` property:

```
With objPerson
  .Name = "Fred"
  .Name(NameTypes.Informal) = "Freddy"
  .BirthDate = #1/1/1960#
  .Age = 20
  .Salary = 30000
  txtName.Text = .ToString
  txtBirthDate.Text = Format(.BirthDate, "Short date")
  txtAge.Text = .Age
  txtSalary.Text = Format(.Salary, "0.00")
End With
```

When we run the application and click the button now, we'll get message boxes displaying the changes to the `Name` property, the `BirthDate` property (twice, once for the `BirthDate` property and once for the `Age` property, which changes the birth date), and now the `Salary`.

Shared Methods

In Chapter 5, we explored shared methods and how they work, providing a set of methods that can be invoked directly from the class rather than requiring that we create an actual object.

Shared methods are inherited just like instance methods and so are automatically available as methods on subclasses just as they are on the base class. If we implement a shared method in `BaseClass`, we can call that method using any class derived from `BaseClass`.

Like a regular method, shared methods can be overloaded and shadowed. They cannot, however, be overridden. If we attempt to use the `Overridable` keyword when declaring a `Shared` method we will get a syntax error.

For instance, we can implement a method in our `Person` class to compare two `Person` objects:

```
Public Shared Function Compare(ByVal Person1 As Person, _
    ByVal Person2 As Person) As Boolean

  Return (Person1.Name = Person2.Name)

End Function
```

To test this method, let's add another button to our form, name it `btnCompare` and set its `Text` value to `Compare`. Double-click the button to bring up the code window and enter the following code:

```
Private Sub btnCompare_Click(ByVal sender As System.Object, _
    ByVal e As System.EventArgs) Handles btnCompare.Click
  Dim emp1 As New Employee("Fred")
  Dim emp2 As New Employee("Mary")

  MsgBox(Employee.Compare(emp1, emp2))
End Sub
```

This code simply creates two `Employee` objects and compares them. Note though, that the code uses the `Employee` class to invoke the `Compare` method, displaying the result in a message box. This establishes that the `Compare` method implemented in the `Person` class is inherited by the `Employee` class as we'd expect.

Overloading Shared Methods

Shared methods can be overloaded using the `Overloads` keyword in the same manner as we overload an instance method. This means our subclass can add new implementations of the shared method as long as the parameter list differs from the original implementation.

For example, we can add a new implementation of the `Compare` method to `Employee`:

```
Public Overloads Shared Function Compare(ByVal Employee1 As Employee, _
    ByVal Employee2 As Employee) As Boolean

  Return (Employee1.EmployeeNumber = Employee2.EmployeeNumber)

End Function
```

This new implementation compares two `Employee` objects rather than two `Person` objects, and in fact, compares them based on the employee number rather than by name.

We can enhance the code behind `btnCompare` in the form to set the `EmployeeNumber` properties:

```
Private Sub btnCompare_Click(ByVal sender As System.Object, _
    ByVal e As System.EventArgs) Handles btnCompare.Click
  Dim emp1 As New Employee("Fred")
  Dim emp2 As New Employee("Mary")

  emp1.EmployeeNumber = 1
  emp2.EmployeeNumber = 1

  MsgBox(Employee.Compare(emp1, emp2))
End Sub
```

While it might make little sense for these two objects to have the same `EmployeeNumber` value, it will prove a point. When we run the application now, even though the `Name` values of the objects are different, our `Compare` routine will return `True`, proving that we're invoking the overloaded version of the method that expects two `Employee` objects as parameters.

The overloaded implementation is available on the `Employee` class or any classes derived from `Employee` such as `OfficeEmployee`. The overloaded implementation is not available if called directly from `Person`, since that class only contains the original implementation.

Shadowing Shared Methods

Shared methods can also be shadowed by a subclass. This allows us to do some very interesting things, including converting a shared method into an instance method or vice versa. We can even leave the method as shared, but change the entire way it works and is declared. In short, just as with instance methods, we can use the `Shadows` keyword to entirely replace and change a shared method in a subclass.

To see how this works, we can use the `Shadows` keyword to change the nature of the `Compare` method in `OfficeEmployee`:

```
Public Shared Shadows Function Compare(ByVal Person1 As Person, _
    ByVal Person2 As Person) As Boolean

  Return (Person1.Age = Person2.Age)

End Function
```

Notice that this method has the same signature as the original `Compare` method we implemented in the `Person` class, but instead of comparing by name, here we're comparing by age. With a normal method we could have done this by overriding, but since `Shared` methods can't be overridden the only thing we can do is shadow it.

Of course, the shadowed implementation is only available via the `OfficeEmployee` class. Neither the `Person` nor `Employee` classes, which are higher up the inheritance chain, are aware that this shadowed version of the method exists.

To use this from our `Form1` code we can change the code for `btnCompare` as follows:

```
Private Sub btnCompare_Click(ByVal sender As System.Object, _
    ByVal e As System.EventArgs) Handles btnCompare.Click
  Dim emp1 As New Employee("Fred")
  Dim emp2 As New Employee("Mary")

  emp1.Age = 20
  emp2.Age = 25

  MsgBox(OfficeEmployee.Compare(emp1, emp2))
End Sub
```

Instead of setting the `EmployeeNumber` values, we're now setting the `Age` values on our objects. More importantly, notice that we're now calling the `Compare` method via the `OfficeEmployee` class rather than via `Employee` or `Person`. This causes the invocation of our new version of the method and the ages of the objects are compared.

Shared Events

As we discussed in Chapter 5, we can create shared events, events that can be raised by shared or instance methods in a class, whereas regular events can only be raised from within instance methods.

When we inherit from a class that defines a shared event, our new subclass automatically gains that event just like it does with regular events as we discussed earlier in this chapter.

As with instance events, a shared event cannot be raised by code within our subclass, it can only be raised using the `RaiseEvent` keyword from code in the class where the event is declared. If we want to be able to raise the event from methods in our subclass, we need to implement a `Protected` method on the base class that actually makes the call to `RaiseEvent`.

This is no different from what we discussed earlier in the chapter other than to note that with a shared event we can use a method with protected scope that is marked as shared to raise the event rather than using an instance method.

Creating an Abstract Base Class

So far, we've seen how to inherit from a class, how to overload and override methods, and how virtual methods work. In all of our examples so far, the parent classes have been useful in their own right and could be instantiated and do some meaningful work. Sometimes, however, we want to create a class such that it can only be used as a base class for inheritance.

MustInherit Keyword

Our current `Person` class is not only being used as a base class, but it can also be instantiated directly to create an object of type `Person`. Likewise, our `Employee` class is also being used as a base class for the `OfficeEmployee` class we created that derives from it.

If we want to make a class *only* act as a base class we can use the `MustInherit` keyword, thereby preventing anyone from creating objects based directly on the class and requiring them instead to create a subclass and then create objects based on that subclass.

This can be very useful when we are creating object models of real world concepts and entities. We'll discuss ways to leverage this capability in Chapter 7. We can change `Person` to use the `MustInherit` keyword:

```
Public MustInherit Class Person
```

This has no effect on the code within `Person` or any of the classes that inherit from it. However, it does mean that no code can instantiate objects directly from the `Person` class, instead we can only create objects based on `Employee` or `OfficeEmployee`.

Keep in mind that this doesn't prevent us from declaring variables of type `Person`, it merely prevents us from creating an object by using `New Person()`. We can also continue to make use of `Shared` methods from the `Person` class without any difficulty.

MustOverride Keyword

Another option we have is to create a method (`Sub`, `Function`, or `Property`) that must be overridden by a subclass. We might want to do this when we are creating a base class that provides some behaviors, but relies on subclasses to also provide some behaviors in order to function properly. This is accomplished by using the `MustOverride` keyword on a method declaration.

If a class contains any methods marked with `MustOverride`, the class itself must also be declared with the `MustInhert` keyword or we'll get a syntax error:

```
Public MustInherit Class Person
```

This makes sense, if we're requiring that a method be overridden in a subclass it only stands to reason that our class can't be directly instantiated, rather must be subclassed to be useful.

Let's see how this works by adding a `LifeExpectancy` method in `Person` that has no implementation and must be overridden by a subclass:

```
Public MustOverride Function LifeExpectancy() As Integer
```

Notice that there is no `End Function` or any other code associated with the method.

When using `MustOverride`, we cannot provide any implementation for the method in our class. Such a method is called an *abstract method* or *pure virtual function*, since it only defines the interface and no implementation.

Methods declared in this manner *must* be overridden in any subclass that inherits from our base class. If we don't override one of these methods, we'll generate a syntax error in the subclass and it won't compile. This means we need to alter the `Employee` class to provide an implementation for this method:

```
Public Overrides Function LifeExpectancy() As Integer
   Return 90
End Function
```

Our application will compile and run at this point, since we are now overriding the `LifeExpectancy` method in `Employee` and so the required condition is met.

Abstract Base Classes

We can combine these two concepts, using both `MustInherit` and `MustOverride`, to create something called an *abstract base class*. Sometimes this is also referred to as a *virtual class*.

This is a class that provides no implementation, only the interface definitions from which a subclass can be created, for example:

```
Public MustInherit Class AbstractBaseClass
   Public MustOverride Sub DoSomething()
   Public MustOverride Sub DoOtherStuff()
End Class
```

This technique can be very useful when creating frameworks or the high-level conceptual elements of a system. Any class that inherits `AbstractBaseClass` must implement both `DoSomething` and `DoOtherStuff` or a syntax error will result.

In some ways an abstract base class is very comparable to defining an interface using the `Interface` keyword. We'll discuss the `Interface` keyword in detail later in this chapter. We could define the same interface as shown in this example with the following code:

```
Public Interface IAbstractBaseClass
   Sub DoSomething()
   Sub DoOtherStuff()
End Interface
```

Any class that implements the `IAbstractBaseClass` interface must implement both `DoSomething` and `DoOtherStuff` or a syntax error will result, and in that regard this technique is similar to an abstract base class.

Preventing Inheritance

If we want to prevent a class from being used as a base class we can use the `NotInheritable` keyword. For instance, we can change our `OfficeEmployee` as follows:

```
Public NotInheritable Class OfficeEmployee
```

At this point it is no longer possible to inherit from this class to create a new class. Our OfficeEmployee class is now *sealed*, meaning that it cannot be used as a base from which to create other classes.

If we attempt to inherit from OfficeEmployee we'll get a compile error indicating that it cannot be used as a base class. This has no effect on Person or Employee, we can continue to derive other classes from them.

Typically, we'll want to design our classes such that they can be subclassed, as that provides the greatest long-term flexibility in our overall design. There are times, however, when we will want to make sure that our class cannot be used as a base class and the NotInheritable keyword addresses that issue.

Multiple Interfaces

In VB.NET our objects can have one or more interfaces. All objects have a primary or native interface, which is composed of any methods, properties, events, or member variables declared using the Public keyword. Objects can also implement secondary interfaces in addition to their native interface by using the Implements keyword.

VB6 also had the concept of multiple interfaces, though the way we implemented them was not particularly intuitive or clear. The concept remains the same in VB.NET, but the syntax we use to define and implement interfaces is very clear and understandable.

Object Interfaces

The native interface on any class is composed of all the methods, properties, events, or even variables that are declared as anything other than Private. Though this is nothing new, let's quickly review what is included in the native interface to set the stage for discussing secondary interfaces.

To include a method as part of our interface, we can simply declare a Public routine:

```
Public Sub AMethod()

End Sub
```

Notice that there is no code in this routine. Any code would be *implementation* and is not part of the interface. Only the declaration of the method is important when we're discussing interfaces. This can seem confusing at first, but it is an important distinction since the separation of the interface from its implementation is at the very core of object-oriented programming and design.

Since this method is declared as Public it is available to any code outside our class, including other applications that may make use of our assembly.

If our method has a property we can declare it as part of our interface by using the Property keyword:

```
Public Property AProperty() As String

End Property
```

We can also declare events as part of our interface by using the Event keyword:

```
Public Event AnEvent()
```

Finally, we can include actual variables, or attributes, as part of our interface:

```
Public AnInteger As Integer
```

This is strongly discouraged, as it directly exposes our internal variables for use by code outside our class. Since the variable is directly accessible from other code, we give up any and all control over the way the value may be changed or by which code may be accessed.

Rather than making any variable Public, it is far preferable to make use of a Property method to expose the value. In that way we can implement code to ensure that our internal variable is only set to valid values and that only the appropriate code has access to the value based on our application's logic.

Using the Native Interface

In the end, the *native* (or primary) *interface* for any class is defined by looking at all the methods, properties, events, and variables that are declared as anything other than Private in scope. This includes any methods, properties, events or variables that are inherited from a base class.

We're used to interacting with the default interface on most objects, and so this will seem pretty straightforward. Consider a simple class:

```
Public Class TheClass
  Public Sub DoSomething()

  End Sub

  Public Sub DoSomethingElse()

  End Sub
End Class
```

This defines a class and by extension, also defines the native interface that is exposed by any objects we instantiate based on this class. The native interface defines two methods, DoSomething and DoSomethingElse. To make use of these methods, we simply call them:

```
Dim myObject As New TheClass()

myObject.DoSomething()

myObject.DoSomethingElse()
```

This is the same thing we've been doing in Chapter 5 and so far in this chapter. However, let's take a look at creating and using secondary interfaces, as they are a bit different.

Secondary Interfaces

Sometimes it can be helpful for an object to have more than one interface, thus allowing us to interact with the object in different ways.

Inheritance allows us to create subclasses that *are* a specialized case of the base class. For example, our `Employee` *is-a* `Person`.

However, there are times when we have a group of objects that are not the same thing, but we want to be able to treat them as though they were the same. We want all these objects to *act-as* the same thing, even though they are all different.

For instance, we may have a series of different objects in an application, product, customer, invoice and so forth. Each of these would have default interfaces appropriate to each individual object — and each of them *is-a* different class — there's no natural inheritance relationship implied between these classes. At the same time, we may need to be able to generate a printed document for each type of object. So we'd like to make them all *act-as* a printable object.

> *We'll discuss the* is-a *and* act-as *relationships in more detail in Chapter 7.*

To accomplish this we can define a generic interface that would enable generating such a printed document. We can call it `IPrintableObject`.

> **By convention, this type of interface is typically prefixed with a capital I to indicate that it is a formal interface.**

Each of our application objects can choose to implement the `IPrintableObject` interface. Every object that implements this interface must provide code to provide actual *implementation* of the interface, which is unlike inheritance, where the code from a base class is automatically reused.

By implementing this common interface, however, we are able to write a routine that accepts any object that implements the `IPrintableObject` interface and print it — totally oblivious to the "real" data type of the object or the methods its native interface might expose.

Before we see how to use an interface in this manner, let's walk through the process of actually defining an interface.

Defining the Interface

We define a formal interface using the `Interface` keyword. This can be done in any code module in our project, but a good place to put this type of definition is in a standard module. An interface defines a set of methods (`Sub`, `Function`, or `Property`) and events that must be exposed by any class that chooses to implement the interface.

Add a module to the project using Project ➪ Add Module and name it `Interfaces.vb`. Then, add the following code to the module, outside the `Module` code block itself:

```
Public Interface IPrintableObject

End Interface

Module Interfaces

End Module
```

A code module can contain a number of interface definitions, and these definitions must exist outside any other code block. Thus, they don't go within a `Class` or `Module` block, they are at a peer level to those constructs.

Interfaces must be declared using either `Public` or `Friend` scope. Declaring a `Private` or `Protected` interface will result in a syntax error.

Within the `Interface` block of code, we can define the methods, properties and events that will make up our particular interface. Since the scope of the interface is defined by the Interface declaration itself, we can't specify scopes for individual methods and events, they are all scoped the same as the interface itself.

For instance, add the following code:

```
Public Interface  IPrintableObject
   Function Label(ByVal Index As Integer) As String
   Function Value(ByVal Index As Integer) As String
   ReadOnly Property Count() As Integer

End Interface
```

This defines a new data type, somewhat like creating a class or structure, that we can use when declaring variables.

For instance, we can now declare a variable of type `IprintableObject`:

```
Private objPrintable As IPrintableObject
```

We can also have our classes implement this interface, which will require each class to provide implementation code for each of the three methods defined on the interface.

Before we implement the interface in a class, let's see how we can make use of the interface to write a generic routine that can print any object that does implement `IPrintableObject`.

Using the Interface

Interfaces define the methods and events (including parameters and data types), which an object is required to implement if they choose to support the interface. This means that, given just the interface definition, we can easily write code that can interact with *any* object that implements the interface, even though we don't know what the native data types of those objects will be.

To see how we can write such code, let's create a simple routine in our form that can display data to the Output window in the IDE from any object that implements `IPrintableObject`. Bring up the code window for our form and add the following routine:

```
Public Sub PrintObject(TheObject As  IPrintableObject)
  Dim intIndex As Integer

  For intIndex = 1 To TheObject.Count
    Debug.Write(TheObject.Label(intIndex) & ": ")
    Debug.WriteLine(TheObject.Value(intIndex))
  Next
End Sub
```

Notice that we're accepting a parameter of type `IPrintableObject`. This is how secondary interfaces are used, by treating an object of one type as though it was actually of the interface type. As long as the object passed to this routine implements the `IPrintableObject` interface, our code will work fine.

Within the `PrintObject` routine we're assuming that the object will implement three elements — `Count`, `Label`, and `Value` — as part of the `IPrintableObject` interface. Secondary interfaces can include methods, properties, and events, much like a default interface, but the interface itself is defined and implemented using some special syntax.

Now that we have a generic printing routine, we need a way to call it. Bring up the designer for `Form1` and add a button and name it `btnPrint`. Double-click the button and put this code behind it:

```
Private Sub btnPrint_Click(ByVal sender As System.Object, _
    ByVal e As System.EventArgs) Handles btnPrint.Click
  Dim obj As New Employee("Andy")

  obj.EmployeeNumber = 123
  obj.BirthDate = #1/1/1980#
  obj.HireDate = #1/1/1996#

  PrintObject(obj)
End Sub
```

This code simply initializes an `Employee` object and calls the `PrintObject` routine.

Of course, when we try to run this code we'll get a runtime error when trying to call `PrintObject` . `PrintObject` is expecting a parameter that implements `IPrintableObject` and `Employee` implements no such interface.

If we use Option Strict On this will show up as a compile-time error, allowing us to catch the problem earlier in the development cycle.

Let's move on and implement that interface in `Employee` so that we can see how it works.

Implementing the Interface

Any class (other than an abstract base class) can implement an interface by using the `Implements` keyword. For instance, we can implement our `IPrintableObject` interface in `Employee` by adding the following line:

```
Public Class Employee
  Inherits Person
  Implements IPrintableObject
```

This will cause the interface to be exposed by any object created as an instance of `Employee`. Of course, this doesn't actually implement the interface, it just declares that we will implement it. In fact, we now have a compile error showing in the IDE, because we haven't implemented the methods and properties defined by the interface.

> To implement an interface, we must implement *all* the methods and properties defined by that interface.

Before we actually implement the interface, however, let's create an array to contain the labels for our data fields so that we can return them via our `IPrintableObject` interface. Add the following code to the `Employee` class:

```
Public Class Employee
    Inherits Person
    Implements IPrintableObject

    Private marLabels() As String = {"ID", "Age", "HireDate"}
    Private mdtHireDate As Date
    Private mdblSalary As Double
```

To implement the interface we need to create methods and properties with the same parameter and return data types as those defined in the interface. The actual names of each method or property don't matter, because we'll be using the `Implements` keyword to link our internal method names to the external method names defined by the interface. As long as the method signatures match we are all set.

This applies to scope as well. Although the interface and its methods and properties are publicly available, we don't have to declare our actual methods and properties as `Public`. In many cases, we may implement them as `Private` so they don't become part of our native interface and are only exposed via the secondary interface.

However, if we do have a `Public` method with a method signature we can use it to implement a method from the interface. This has the interesting side effect of having this method provide implementation for both a method on the object's native interface *and* on the secondary interface.

In this case, we'll use a `Private` method so it is only providing implementation for the `IPrintableObject` interface. We can implement the `Label` method by adding the following code to `Employee`:

```
Private Function Label(ByVal Index As Integer) As String _
    Implements IPrintableObject.Label
    Return marLabels(Index - 1)
End Function
```

This is just a regular `Private` method that returns a `String` value. We're subtracting 1 from the `Index` value to make it appear as though our data set is 1-based rather than 0-based.

The interesting thing is that we've added the `Implements` clause to the method declaration.

```
Private Function Label(ByVal Index As Integer) As String _
    Implements IPrintableObject.Label
```

By using the `Implements` keyword in this fashion, we're indicating that this particular method is the implementation for the `Label` method on the `IPrintableObject` interface. The actual name of our private method could be anything. It is the use of the `Implements` clause that makes this work. The only requirement is that the parameter data types and the return value data type must match those defined by the `IPrintableObject` interface.

This is very similar to using the `Handles` clause to indicate which method should handle an event. In fact, like the `Handles` clause, the `Implements` clause allows us to have a comma-separated list of interface methods that should be implemented by this one function.

We can then move on to implement the other two elements defined by the `IPrintableObject` interface by adding this code to `Employee`:

```
Private Function Value(ByVal Index As Integer) As String _
    Implements IPrintableObject.Value
  Select Case Index
    Case 1
      Return EmployeeNumber()
    Case 2
      Return Age()
    Case 3
      Return Format(HireDate(), "Short date")
  End Select
End Function

Private ReadOnly Property Count() As Integer _
    Implements IPrintableObject.Count
  Get
    Return UBound(marLabels) + 1
  End Get
End Property
```

The `Value` method returns the value based on the `Index` value, while `Count` returns the number of data elements available, again adding 1 to make it appear that our data list is 1-based like a Collection.

We can now run this application and click the button. The Output window in the IDE will display our results, showing the ID, age, and hire date values as appropriate.

Any object could create a similar implementation behind the `IPrintableObject` interface, and the `PrintObject` routine in our form would continue to work regardless of the native data type of the object itself.

Reusing Common Implementation

Secondary interfaces provide a guarantee that all objects implementing a given interface will have exactly the same methods and events, including the same parameters.

The `Implements` clause links our actual implementation to a specific method on an interface. For instance, our `Value` method is linked to `IPrintableObject.Value` using the following clause:

```
Private Function Value(ByVal Index As Integer) As String _
    Implements IPrintableObject.Value
```

Sometimes our method might be able to serve as the implementation for more than one method, either on the same interface or on different interfaces.

Add the following interface definition to `Interfaces.vb`:

```
Public Interface IValues
   Function GetValue(ByVal Idx As Integer) As String
End Interface
```

This interface defines just one method, `GetValue`. Notice that it defines a single `Integer` parameter and a return type of `String`, the same as the `Value` method from `IPrintableObject`. Even though the method name and parameter variable name don't match, what counts here is that the parameter and return value data types do match.

Now bring up the code window for `Employee`. We'll have it implement this new interface in addition to the `IPrintableObject` interface:

```
Public Class Employee
   Inherits Person
   Implements IPrintableObject
   Implements IValues
```

We already have a method that returns values. Rather than reimplementing that method, it would be nice to just link this new `GetValues` method to our existing method. We can easily do this because the `Implements` clause allows us to provide a comma-separated list of method names:

```
Private Function Value(ByVal Index As Integer) As String _
    Implements IPrintableObject.Value, IValues.GetValue
  Select Case Index
    Case 1
      Return EmployeeNumber()
    Case 2
      Return Age()
    Case 3
      Return Format(HireDate(), "Short date")
  End Select
End Function
```

This is very similar to the use of the `Handles` keyword as discussed in Chapter 5. A single method within our class, regardless of scope or name, can be used to implement any number of methods as defined by other interfaces as long as the data types of the parameters and return values all match.

Combining Interfaces and Inheritance

We can combine implementation of secondary interfaces and inheritance at the same time.

When we inherit from a class that implements an interface, our new subclass automatically gains the interface and the implementation from the base class. If we specify that our base class methods are overridable, then the subclass can override those methods. This will not only override the base class implementation for our native interface, but will also override the implementation for the interface. For instance, we could declare the Value method as follows:

```
Public Overridable Function Value(ByVal Index As Integer) As String _
    Implements IPrintableObject.Value, IValues.GetValue
```

Now it is `Public`, so it is available on our native interface, and it is part of both the `IPrintableObject` and `IValues` interfaces. This means we can access the property three ways in client code:

```
Dim emp As New Employee()
Dim printable As IPrintableObject = emp
Dim values As IValues = emp

Debug.WriteLine(emp.Value(0))
Debug.WriteLine(printable.Value(0))
Debug.WriteLine(values.GetValue(0))
```

Note that we're also now using the `Overrides` keyword in the declaration. This means that a subclass of `Employee`, such as `OfficeEmployee`, can override the `Value` method. The overridden method will be the one invoked regardless of whether we call the object directly or via an interface.

Combining the implementation of an interface in a base class along with overridable methods can provide a very flexible object design.

Summary

In this chapter and in Chapter 5, we've seen how VB.NET allows us to create and work with classes and objects. VB.NET provides the building blocks for abstraction, encapsulation, polymorphism, and inheritance.

In this chapter we've seen how to create both simple base classes as well as abstract base classes. We've also explored how we can define formal interfaces, a concept quite similar to an abstract base class in many ways.

We've also walked through the process of subclassing, creating a new class that derives both interface and implementation from a base class. The subclass can be extended by adding new methods or altering the behavior of existing methods on the base class.

VB.NET provides us with all the capabilities we need to build robust and sophisticated object-oriented applications. In the next chapter, we'll pull this all together by discussing abstraction, encapsulation, polymorphism, and inheritance as they pertain to building practical software.

7

Applying Objects and Components

In Chapters 5 and 6, we explored the syntax provided by Visual Basic .NET (VB.NET) for working with objects, creating classes, and implementing both inheritance and multiple interfaces. These are all powerful tools, providing us with the ability to create very maintainable and readable code—even for extremely complex applications.

However, just knowing the syntax and learning the tools is not enough to be successful. Successfully applying the object-oriented capabilities of VB.NET to create applications requires an understanding of object-oriented programming, which is the application of the theory we've covered in Chapters 5 and 6.

In this chapter, we'll take the syntax that we discussed in Chapters 5 and 6 and see how it allows us to build object-oriented applications. We'll further discuss the four major object-oriented concepts—abstraction, encapsulation, polymorphism, and inheritance—that we defined in Chapter 5. We'll understand how these concepts can be applied in our design and development to create effective object-oriented applications.

Abstraction

Abstraction, which Visual Basic has supported since version 4, is the process by which we can think about specific properties or behaviors without thinking about a particular object that has those properties or behaviors. Abstraction is merely the ability of a language to create "black box" code, to take a concept and create an abstract representation of that concept within a program.

A `Customer` object, for example, is an abstract representation of a real-world customer. A `DataSet` object is an abstract representation of a set of data.

Abstraction allows us to recognize how things are similar and to ignore differences, to think in general terms and not the specifics. A text box control is an abstraction, because we can place it on a form, and then tailor it to our needs by setting properties. Visual Basic allows us to define abstractions using classes.

Any language that allows a developer to create a class from which objects can be instantiated meets this criterion, and Visual Basic is no exception. We can easily create a class to represent a customer, essentially providing an abstraction. We can then create instances of that class, where each object can have its own attributes such that it represents a specific customer.

In VB.NET we implement abstraction by creating a class using the `Class` keyword. Bring up Visual Studio .NET (VS.NET), and create a new VB.NET Windows Application project. Once the project is open, add a new class to the project using the Project ⇨ Add Class menu option. Name the new class `Customer` and add some code to make this class represent a real-world customer in an abstract sense:

```
Public Class Customer
  Private mgID As Guid = Guid.NewGuid
  Private mstrName As String
  Private mstrPhone As String

  Public Property ID() As Guid
    Get
      Return mgID
    End Get
    Set(ByVal Value As Guid)
      mgID = Value
    End Set
  End Property

  Public Property Name() As String
    Get
      Return mstrName
    End Get
    Set(ByVal Value As String)
      mstrName = Value
    End Set
  End Property

  Public Property Phone() As String
    Get
      Return mstrPhone
    End Get
    Set(ByVal Value As String)
      mstrPhone = Value
    End Set
  End Property
End Class
```

We know that a real customer is a lot more complex than an ID, name, and phone number. Yet at the same time, we know that in an abstract sense, our customers really do have names and phone numbers, and that we assign them unique ID numbers to keep track of them. In this case we're using a globally unique identifier (Guid) as a unique ID. Thus, given an ID, name, and phone number, we know which customer we're dealing with and so we have a perfectly valid abstraction of a customer within our application.

We can then use this abstract representation of a customer from within our code. To do this, open the designer for `Form1` and add three text box controls to the form. Then, add the following code to the form. First , we'll declare a variable and create a `Customer` object:

```
Public Class Form1
    Inherits System.Windows.Forms.Form

    Private mobjCustomer As New Customer
```

Then, when the form is loaded we'll display the customer data in the text box controls:

```
Private Sub Form1_Load(ByVal sender As System.Object, _
    ByVal e As System.EventArgs) Handles MyBase.Load

  TextBox1.DataBindings.Add("Text", mobjCustomer, "ID")
  TextBox2.DataBindings.Add("Text", mobjCustomer, "Name")
  TextBox3.DataBindings.Add("Text", mobjCustomer, "Phone")

End Sub
```

We're using the ability of Windows Forms to data bind to a property on an object. In this case, we're binding our three text box controls' `Text` properties to the `ID`, `Name`, and `Phone` properties of our `mobjCustomer` object. (We'll learn more about data binding in Chapter 16.)

This code should work, but we will get a null exception error when we run the application. This is because our `String` variables are references to `Nothing`. They need to be initialized to `" "` or `String.Empty` as they are declared.

```
Private mstrName As String = ""
Private mstrPhone As String = ""
```

Now, we have a simple UI that both displays and updates the data in our `Customer` object; with that object providing the UI developer with an abstract representation of the customer. When we run the application we'll see a display similar to what is shown in Figure 7-1.

Figure 7-1

Here we've displayed the pre-generated ID value, and have entered values for Name and Phone directly into the form.

Encapsulation

Perhaps the most important of the object-oriented concepts is that of *encapsulation*. Encapsulation is the concept that an object should totally separate its interface from its implementation. All the data and implementation code for an object should be entirely hidden behind its interface. Another way to put this is that an object should be a *black box*.

The idea is that we can create an interface (by creating public methods in a class) and, as long as that interface remains consistent, the application can interact with our objects. This remains true even if we entirely rewrite the code within a given method. The interface is independent of the implementation.

Encapsulation allows us to hide the internal implementation details of a class. For example, the algorithm we use to find prime numbers might be proprietary. We can expose a simple API to the end user, but we hide all of the logic used in our algorithm by encapsulating it within our class.

This means that an object should completely contain any data it requires, and that it should also contain all the code required to manipulate that data. Programs should interact with an object through an interface, using the properties and methods of the object. Client code should never work directly with the data owned by the object.

> Programs interact with objects by sending messages to the object that indicate which method or property they'd like to have invoked. These messages are generated by other objects, or by external sources such as the user. The object reacts to these messages through methods or properties.

Visual Basic has provided full support for encapsulation through class modules since version 4.0. Using these modules, we can create classes that entirely hide their internal data and code, providing a well-established interface of properties and methods to the outside world.

Let's look at the following example. Add the following class to our project, the code defines its native interface:

```
Public Class Encapsulation
    Public Function DistanceTo(ByVal X As Single, Y As Single) As Single

    End Function
    Public Property CurrentX() As Single
        Get

        End Get
        Set(ByVal Value As Single)

        End Set
    End Property
```

```
      Public Property CurrentY() As Single
        Get
        End Get
        Set(ByVal Value As Single)

        End Set
      End Property
  End Class
```

This creates an interface for the class. At this point, we can write client code to interact with the class, since from a client perspective all we care about is the interface. Bring up the designer for Form1 and add a button to the form, then write the following code behind the button:

```
Private Sub Button1_Click(ByVal sender As System.Object, _
                          ByVal e As System.EventArgs) _
                          Handles button1.Click
  Dim obj As New Encapsulation
  MsgBox(obj.DistanceTo(10, 10))
End Sub
```

Even though we have no actual code in our Encapsulation class, we can still write code to *use* that class because the interface is defined.

This is a powerful idea, since it means that we can rapidly create class interfaces against which other developers can create the UI or other parts of the application, while we are still creating the implementation behind the interface.

From here, we could do virtually anything we like in terms of implementing the class. For example, we could use the values to calculate a direct distance:

```
Imports System.Math

Public Class Encapsulation
  Private msngX As Single
  Private msngY As Single

  Public Function DistanceTo(ByVal X As Single, Y As Single) As Single
    Return CSng(Sqrt((X - msngX) ^ 2 + (Y - msngY) ^ 2))
  End Function

  Public Property CurrentX() As Single
    Get
      Return msngX
    End Get
    Set(ByVal Value As Single)
      msngX = Value
    End Set
  End Property

  Public Property CurrentY() As Single
    Get
      Return msngY
    End Get
```

```
      Set(ByVal Value As Single)
         msngY = Value
      End Set
   End Property
End Class
```

Now, when we run the application and click the button we'll get a meaningful value as a result (see Figure 7-2).

Figure 7-2

Where encapsulation comes to the fore, however, is that we can change the *implementation* without changing the *interface*. For example, we can change the distance calculation to find the distance between the points (assuming no diagonal travel is allowed).

```
   Public Function DistanceTo(ByVal X As Single, ByVal Y As Single) As Single
      Return Abs(X - msngX) + Abs(Y - msngY)
   End Function
```

This results in the following outcome being displayed if the program is run and we click the button as shown in Figure 7-3.

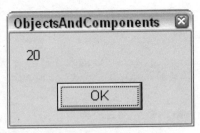

Figure 7-3

We haven't changed the interface of the class, and so our working client program has no idea that we have switched from one implementation to the other. We have achieved a total change of behavior without any change to the client code. This is the essence of encapsulation.

Of course, the user might have a problem if we made such a change to our object. If applications were developed expecting the first set of behaviors, and then we changed to the second, there could be some interesting side effects. However, the key point is that the client programs would continue to function, even if the results were quite different from when we started.

Polymorphism

Polymorphism is often considered to be directly tied to inheritance (which we'll discuss next). In reality, however, it's largely independent. Polymorphism means that we can have two classes with different implementations or code, but with a common set of methods, properties, or events. We can then write a program which operates upon that interface and doesn't care about which type of object it operates at runtime.

Method Signatures

To properly understand polymorphism, we need to explore the concept of a *method signature*, sometimes also called a prototype. All methods have a signature, which is defined by the method's name and the data types of its parameters. We might have code such as this:

```
Public Function CalculateValue() As Integer

End Sub
```

In this example, the signature is

f()

If we add a parameter to the method the signature will change. For example, we could change the method to accept a `Double`:

```
Public Function CalculateValue(Value As Double) As Integer
```

Then, the signature of the method is

f(Double)

Polymorphism merely says that we should be able to write some client code that calls methods on an object, and as long as the object provides our methods with the method signatures we expect, we don't care which class the object was created from. Let's look at some examples of polymorphism within VB.NET.

Implementing Polymorphism

We can use several techniques to achieve polymorphic behavior:

- ❑ Late binding
- ❑ Multiple interfaces
- ❑ .NET reflection
- ❑ Inheritance

Late binding actually allows us to implement "pure" polymorphism, although at the cost of performance and ease of programming. Through multiple interfaces and inheritance we can also achieve polymorphism with much better performance and ease of programming. Reflection allows us to use either late binding or multiple interfaces, but against objects created in a very dynamic way, even going so far as to dynamically load a DLL into our application at runtime so that we can use its classes.

We'll walk through each of these options to see how they are implemented and to explore their pros and cons.

Polymorphism through Late Binding

Typically, when we interact with objects in VB.NET, we are interacting with them through strongly typed variables. For example, in Form1 we interacted with the Encapsulation object with the following code:

```
Private Sub Button1_Click(ByVal sender As System.Object, _
    ByVal e As System.EventArgs) Handles button1.Click

  Dim obj As New Encapsulation

  MsgBox(obj.DistanceTo(10, 10))
End Sub
```

The obj variable is declared using a specific type (Encapsulation)—meaning it is strongly typed or *early bound*.

We can also interact with objects that are *late bound*. Late binding means that our object variable has no specific data type, but rather is of type Object. VB.NET treats the Object data type in a special way, allowing us to attempt arbitrary method calls against the object even though the Object data type doesn't implement those methods.

For example, we could change the code in Form1 to be late bound as follows:

```
Private Sub Button1_Click(ByVal sender As System.Object, _
    ByVal e As System.EventArgs) Handles Button1.Click

  Dim obj As Object = New Encapsulation

  MsgBox(obj.DistanceTo(10, 10))
End Sub
```

When this code is run, we'll get the same result as we did before, even though the Object data type has no DistanceTo method as part of its interface. The late binding mechanism, behind the scenes, dynamically determines the real type of our object and invokes the appropriate method.

> This code requires Option Strict Off in the file containing the code that is calling the objects. This is the case by default, but is required when using late binding.

When we work with objects through late binding, neither the VB.NET IDE nor the compiler can tell whether we are calling a valid method or not. In this case, there is no way for the compiler to know that the object referenced by our `obj` variable actually has a `DistanceTo` method. It just assumes we know what we're talking about and compiles the code.

Then at runtime, when the code is actually invoked it will attempt to dynamically call the `DistanceTo` method. If that is a valid method our code will work, if it is not we'll get an error.

Obviously, there is a level of danger when using late binding, since a simple typo can introduce errors that can only be discovered when the application is actually run. However, there is also a lot of flexibility, since code that makes use of late binding can talk to *any* object from *any* class as long as those objects implement the methods we require.

There is also a substantial performance penalty for using late binding. The existence of each method is discovered dynamically at runtime, and that discovery takes time. Moreover, the mechanism used to invoke a method through late binding is not nearly as efficient as the mechanism used to call a method that is known at compile time.

To make this clearer, we can change the code in `Form1` by adding a generic routine that displays the distance:

```
Private Sub Button1_Click(ByVal sender As System.Object, _
    ByVal e As System.EventArgs) Handles Button1.Click

  Dim obj As New Encapsulation
  ShowDistance(obj)
End Sub
```

```
Private Sub ShowDistance(ByVal obj As Object)
  MsgBox(obj.DistanceTo(10, 10))
End Sub
```

Remember that since we're using late binding, `Form1` must also use `Option Strict Off`. Without this, late binding is not available.

Notice that the new `ShowDistance` routine accepts a parameter using the generic `Object` data type—so we can pass it literally any value—`String`, `Integer`, or one of our objects. It will throw an exception at runtime, however, unless the object we pass into the routine has a `DistanceTo` method that matches the required method signature.

We know our `Encapsulation` object has a method matching that signature, so our code works fine. However, let's add another simple class to demonstrate polymorphism. Add a new class to the project and name it `Poly.vb`:

```
Public Class Poly
  Public Function DistanceTo(ByVal X As Single, ByVal Y As Single) As Single
    Return X + Y
  End Function
End Class
```

This class is about as simple as we can get. It exposes a `DistanceTo` method as part of its interface and provides a very basic implementation of that interface.

We can use this new class in place of the Encapsulation class without changing the ShowDistance method by using polymorphism. Return to the code in Form1 and make the following change:

```
Private Sub Button1_Click(ByVal sender As System.Object, _
    ByVal e As System.EventArgs) Handles button1.Click

  Dim obj As New Poly

  ShowDistance(obj)
End Sub
```

Even though we changed the class of object we're passing to ShowDistance to one with a different overall interface and different implementation, the method called within ShowDistance remains consistent so our code will run.

Polymorphism with Multiple Interfaces

Late binding is nice, because it is flexible and easy. However, it is not ideal because it defeats the IDE and compiler type checking that allows us to fix bugs due to typos during the development process, and because it has a negative impact on performance.

Fortunately, VB.NET not only provides this late binding ability, but also implements a stricter form of polymorphism through its support of multiple interfaces. (We discussed multiple interfaces in Chapter 6, including the use of the Implements keyword and how to define interfaces.)

With late binding we've seen how to treat all objects as equals by making them all appear using the Object data type. With multiple interfaces, we can treat all objects as equals by making them all implement a common data type or interface.

This approach has the benefit that it is strongly typed, meaning that the IDE and compiler can help us find errors due to typos, since the name and data types of all methods and parameters are known at design time. It is also fast in terms of performance; since the compiler knows all about the methods, it can use optimized mechanisms for calling them, especially, as compared to the dynamic mechanisms used in late binding.

Let's return to the project and implement polymorphism with multiple interfaces. First, add a module to the project using the Project ⇨ Add Module menu option and name it Interfaces.vb. Replace the Module code block with an Interface declaration:

```
Public Interface IShared
    Function CalculateDistance(ByVal X As Single, ByVal Y As Single) As Single
End Interface
```

Now we can make both the Encapsulation and Poly classes implement this interface. First, in the Encapsulation class add the following code:

```
Public Class Encapsulation
  Implements IShared

  Private msngX As Single
  Private msngY As Single
```

```
Public Function DistanceTo(ByVal X As Single, ByVal Y As Single) _
   As Single Implements IShared.CalculateDistance

  Return CSng(Sqrt((X - msngX) ^ 2 + (Y - msngY) ^ 2))
End Function
...
```

We can see that we're implementing the `IShared` interface, and since the `CalculateDistance` method's signature matches that of our existing `DistanceTo` method, we're simply indicating that it should act as the implementation for `CalculateDistance`.

We can make a similar change in the `Poly` class:

```
Public Class Poly
  Implements IShared

  Public Function DistanceTo(ByVal X As Single, ByVal Y As Single) As Single _
      Implements IShared.CalculateDistance

    Return X + Y
  End Function
End Class
```

Now this class also implements the `IShared` interface, and we're ready to see polymorphism implemented in our code.

Bring up the code window for `Form1` and change our `ShowDistance` method as follows:

```
Private Sub ShowDistance(ByVal obj As IShared)
  MsgBox(obj.CalculateDistance(10, 10))
End Sub
```

Now that we're no longer using late binding, `Form1` can use `Option Strict On` to provide better compiler type checking of our code.

Notice that instead of accepting the parameter using the generic `Object` data type, we are now accepting an `IShared` parameter—a strong data type known by both the IDE and the compiler. Within the code itself we are now calling the `CalculateDistance` method as defined by that interface.

This routine can now accept any object that implements `IShared`, regardless of what class that object was created from, or what other interfaces that object may implement. All we care about here is that it implements `IShared`.

Polymorphism through .NET Reflection

We've seen how to use late binding to invoke a method on any arbitrary object, as long as that object has a method matching the method signature we're trying to call. We've also walked through the use of multiple interfaces which allows us to achieve polymorphism through a faster, early bound technique. The challenge with these techniques is that late binding can be slow and hard to debug, and multiple interfaces can be somewhat rigid and inflexible.

We can use the concept of *reflection* within .NET to overcome some of these limitations. Reflection is a technology built into .NET that allows us to write code that interrogates a .NET assembly to dynamically determine the classes and data types it contains. We can then use reflection to load the assembly into our process, create instances of those classes and invoke their methods.

When we use late binding, VB.NET makes use of the .NET System.Reflection namespace behind the scenes on our behalf. We can choose to manually use reflection as well. which allows us even more flexibility in how we interact with objects.

For example, suppose the class we want to call is located in some other assembly on disk—an assembly we didn't specifically reference from within our project when we compiled it. How can we dynamically find, load, and invoke such an assembly? Reflection allows us to do this, assuming that the assembly is polymorphic. In other words, it has either an interface we expect, or a set of methods we can invoke via late binding.

To see how reflection works with late binding, let's create a new class in a separate assembly (project) and use it from within our existing application. Choose File ⇨ Add Project ⇨ New Project to add a new Class Library project to our solution. Name it Objects. It will start with a single class module that we can use as a starting point. Change the code in that module to the following:

```
Public Class External
    Public Function DistanceTo(ByVal X As Single, ByVal Y As Single) As Single
        Return X * Y
    End Function
End Class
```

Now compile the assembly by choosing the Build ⇨ Build Objects menu option. Next, bring up the code window for Form1. Add an Imports statement at the top:

```
Imports System.Reflection
```

Remember that since we're using late binding, Form1 also must use Option Strict Off. Without this, late binding is not available.

Then, change the code behind the button to the following:

```
Private Sub Button1_Click(ByVal sender As System.Object, _
    ByVal e As System.EventArgs) Handles button1.Click

    Dim obj As Object
    Dim myDll As [Assembly]

    myDll = [Assembly].LoadFrom("..\..\ Objects\bin\Objects.dll")

    obj = myDll.CreateInstance("Objects.External")
    MsgBox(obj.DistanceTo(10, 10))
End Sub
```

> Assembly is a reserved word in VB.NET, and we surround it with square brackets so that we can use the class name without conflicting with the reserved word.

There's a lot going on here, so let's walk through it a bit. First, notice that we're reverting to late binding, our obj variable is declared as type Object. We'll take a look at using reflection and multiple interfaces in a moment, but to start with we'll use late binding.

Next, we've declared a myDll variable as type Reflection.Assembly. This variable will contain a reference to the Objects assembly that we'll be dynamically loading through our code. Note that we are *not* adding a reference to this assembly via Project ➪ Add References, we'll get access to the assembly at runtime.

We then load the external assembly dynamically by using the Assembly.LoadFrom method:

```
myDll = [Assembly].LoadFrom("..\ ..\Objects\bin\Objects.dll")
```

This causes the reflection library to load our assembly from a file on disk at the location we specify. Once the assembly is loaded into our process, we can use the myDll variable to interact with it, including interrogating it to get a list of the classes it contains or to create instances of those classes.

> *We can also use the [Assembly].Load method, which will scan the directory where our application's EXE file is located (and the .NET global assembly cache) for any EXE or DLL containing the Objects assembly. When it finds the assembly, it loads it into memory, making it available for our use.*

We can then use the CreateInstance method on the assembly itself to create objects based on any class in that assembly. In our case, we're creating an object based on the External class:

```
obj = myDll.CreateInstance("Objects.External")
```

Now, we have an actual object to work with, so we can use late binding to invoke its DistanceTo method. At this point our code is really no different from our earlier late binding example; other than that the assembly and object were created dynamically at runtime rather than being referenced directly by our project.

At this point we should be able to run the application and have it dynamically invoke the assembly at runtime.

Polymorphism through .NET Reflection and Multiple Interfaces

We can also use both reflection and multiple interfaces together. We've seen how multiple interfaces allow us to have objects from different classes implement the same interface and thus be treated identically. We've also seen how reflection allows us to load an assembly and class dynamically at runtime.

We can combine these concepts by using an interface that is common between our main application and our external assembly, and also using reflection to load that external assembly dynamically at runtime.

First, we need to create the interface that will be shared across both application and assembly. To do this, add a new Class Library project to our solution named Interfaces. Once it is created, drag and drop the Interfaces.vb module from our original application into the new project. This makes the IShared interface part of that project and no longer part of our base application.

Of course, our base application still uses IShared, so we'll want to reference the Interfaces project from our application to gain access to the interface. Do this by right-clicking ObjectsAndComponents in the Solution Explorer window and selecting the Add Reference menu option. Then, add the reference as shown in Figure 7-4.

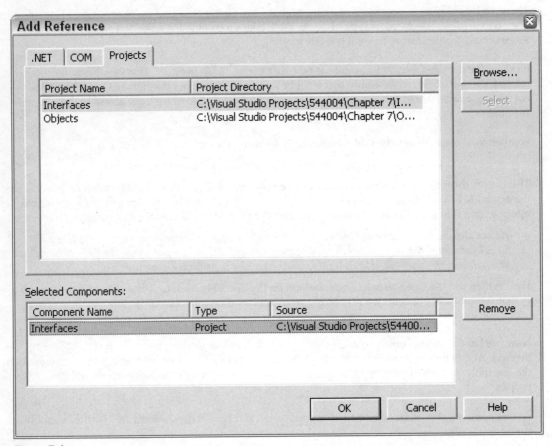

Figure 7-4

Since the IShared interface is now part of a separate assembly, we'll need to add an Imports statement to Form1, Encapsulation, and Poly so they are able to locate the IShared interface.

```
Imports Interfaces
```

Make sure to add this to the top of all three code modules.

We also need to have the Objects project reference Interfaces, so right-click Objects in the Solution Explorer and choose Add Reference there as well. Add the reference to Interfaces and click OK. At this point, both our original application and our external assembly have access to the IShared interface.

We can now enhance the code in `Objects` by changing the `External` class:

```
Imports Interfaces

Public Class External
  Implements IShared
  Public Function DistanceTo(ByVal X As Single, ByVal Y As Single) _
      As Single Implements IShared.CalculateDistance

    Return X * Y
  End Function
End Class
```

With both the main application and external assembly using the same data type, we are now ready to implement the polymorphic behavior using reflection.

Bring up the code window for `Form1` and change the code behind the button to take advantage of the `IShared` interface:

```
Private Sub Button1_Click(ByVal sender As System.Object, _
    ByVal e As System.EventArgs) Handles button1.Click

  Dim myDll As Reflection.Assembly
  Dim obj As IShared
  myDll = System.Reflection.Assembly.LoadFrom( _
    "..\ ..\Objects\bin\Objects.dll")
  obj = CType(myDll.CreateInstance("Objects.External"), IShared)
  ShowDistance(obj)
End Sub
```

Now that we're no longer using late binding, `Form1` can use `Option Strict On` to provide better compiler type checking of our code.

All we've done here is to change the code so that we can pass our dynamically created object to the `ShowDistance` method, which we know requires a parameter of type `IShared`. Since our class implements the same `IShared` interface (from `Interfaces`) as is used by the main application this will work perfectly. Rebuild and run the solution to see this in action.

This technique is very nice, since the code in `ShowDistance` is strongly typed, providing all the performance and coding benefits, but both the DLL and the object itself are loaded dynamically, providing a great deal of flexibility to our application.

Polymorphism with Inheritance

Inheritance, which we discussed in Chapter 6, can also be used to enable polymorphism. The idea here is very similar to that of multiple interfaces, since a subclass can always be treated as though it were the data type of the parent class.

Many people consider the concepts of inheritance and polymorphism to be tightly intertwined. As we've seen, however, it is perfectly possible to use polymorphism without inheritance, a fact that VB developers have understood since Visual Basic 4.0.

At the moment, both our `Encapsulation` and `Poly` classes are implementing a common interface named `IShared`. We are able to use polymorphism to interact with objects of either class via that common interface. The same is true if these are child classes based on the same base class through inheritance. Let's see how this works.

In the `ObjectsAndComponents` project, add a new class named `Parent`. Insert the following code into that class:

```
Public MustInherit Class Parent
    Public MustOverride Function DistanceTo(ByVal X As Single, _
        ByVal Y As Single) As Single
End Class
```

As we discussed in Chapter 6, this is an abstract base class, a class with no implementation of its own. The purpose of an abstract base class is to provide a common base from which other classes can be derived.

To implement polymorphism using inheritance, we do not need to use an abstract base class. Any base class that provides overridable methods (using either `MustOverride` or `Overridable` keywords) will work fine, since all its subclasses are guaranteed to have that same set of methods as part of their interface and yet the subclasses can provide custom implementation for those methods.

In this example we're simply defining the `DistanceTo` method as being a method that must be overridden and implemented by any subclass of `Parent`. Now we can bring up the `Encapsulation` class and change it to be a subclass of `Parent`:

```
Public Class Encapsulation
    Inherits Parent
    Implements IShared
```

We don't need to quit implementing the `IShared` interface just because we're inheriting from `Parent`; inheritance and multiple interfaces coexist nicely. We do, however, have to override the `DistanceTo` method from the `Parent` class.

The `Encapsulation` class already has a `DistanceTo` method with the proper method signature, so we can simply add the `Overrides` keyword to indicate that this method will override the declaration in the `Parent` class:

```
Public Overrides Function DistanceTo(ByVal X As Single, _
                            ByVal Y As Single) _
    As Single Implements IShared.CalculateDistance
```

At this point, our `Encapsulation` class not only implements the common `IShared` interface and its own native interface, but it also can be treated as though it were of type `Parent` since it is a subclass of `Parent`. We can do the same thing to the `Poly` class:

```
Public Class Poly
    Inherits Parent
    Implements IShared

    Public Overrides Function DistanceTo(ByVal X As Single, _
                                ByVal Y As Single) _
        As Single Implements IShared.CalculateDistance
```

```
        Return X + Y
      End Function
    End Class
```

Finally, we can see how polymorphism works by altering the code in Form1 to take advantage of the fact that both classes can be treated as though they were of type Parent. First, we can change the ShowDistance method to accept its parameter as type Parent, and to call the DistanceTo method:

```
    Private Sub ShowDistance(ByVal obj As Parent)
      MsgBox(obj.DistanceTo(10, 10))
    End Sub
```

Then, we can change the code behind our button to create an object of either type Encapsulation or Poly and pass it as a parameter to the method:

```
    Private Sub Button1_Click(ByVal sender As System.Object, _
                              ByVal e As System.EventArgs) _
                              Handles button1.Click
      ShowDistance(New Poly)
      ShowDistance(New Encapsulation)
    End Sub
```

Polymorphism Summary

Polymorphism is a very important concept in object-oriented design and programming, and VB.NET provides us with ample techniques through which it can be implemented.

The following table summarizes the different techniques, their pros and cons and provides some high level guidelines about when to use each.

Inheritance

Inheritance is the concept that a new class can be based on an existing class, inheriting its interface and functionality from the original class. We discussed the mechanics and syntax of inheritance in Chapter 6, so we won't rehash them here. However, in Chapter 6 we really didn't discuss inheritance from a practical perspective, and that will be the focus of this section.

When to Use Inheritance

Inheritance is one of the most powerful object-oriented features a language can support. At the same time, inheritance is one of the most dangerous and misused object-oriented features.

Properly used, inheritance allows us to increase the maintainability, readability, and reusability of our application by offering us a clear and concise way to reuse code, both via interface and implementation. Improperly used, inheritance allows us to create applications that are very fragile, where a change to a class can cause the entire application to break or require changes.

Inheritance allows us to implement an *is-a* relationship. In other words, it allows us to implement a new class that *is a* more specific type of its base class. This means that properly used, inheritance allows us to create child classes that really are the same as the base class.

Technique	Pros	Cons	Guidelines
Late binding	Flexible, "pure" polymorphism	Slow, hard to debug, no IntelliSense	Use to call arbitrary methods on literally any object, regardless of data type or interfaces Useful when we can't control the interfaces that will be implemented by the authors of our classes
Multiple interfaces	Fast, easy to debug, full IntelliSense	Not totally dynamic or flexible, requires class author to implement formal interface	Use when we are creating code that interacts with clearly defined methods that can be grouped together into a formal interface Useful when we control the interfaces that will be implemented by the classes used by our application
Reflection and late binding	Flexible, "pure" polymorphism, dynamically load arbitrary assemblies from disk	Slow, hard to debug, no IntelliSense	Use to call arbitrary methods on objects, where we don't know at design time which assemblies we will be using
Reflection and multiple interfaces	Fast, easy to debug, full IntelliSense, dynamically load arbitrary assemblies from disk	Not totally dynamic or flexible, requires class author to implement formal interface	Use when we are creating code that interacts with clearly defined methods that can be grouped together into a formal interface, but where we don't know at design time which assemblies we will be using
Inheritance	Fast, easy to debug, full IntelliSense, inherits behaviors from base class	Not totally dynamic or flexible, requires class author to inherit from common base class	Use when we are creating objects that have an *is-a* relationship, where we have subclasses that are naturally of the same data type as a base class Polymorphism through inheritance should occur because inheritance makes sense, *not* because we are attempting to merely achieve polymorphism

Perhaps a quick example is in order. Take a duck. We know that a duck *is a* bird. However, a duck can also be food, though that is not its primary identity. Proper use of inheritance would allow us to create a `Bird` base class from which we can derive our `Duck` class. We would *not* create a `Food` class and subclass `Duck` from `Food`, since a duck isn't *really* just food, it merely acts as food sometimes.

This is the challenge. Inheritance is *not* just a mechanism for code reuse. It is a mechanism to create classes that flow naturally from some other class. If we use it anywhere we want code reuse, we'll end up with a real mess on our hands. If we use it anywhere we just want a common interface, but where the child class is not really the same as the base class, then we should be using multiple interfaces—something we'll discuss shortly.

> The question we must ask, when using inheritance, is whether the child class *is a* more specific version of the base class.

For example, we might have different types of products in our organization. All of these products will have some common data and behaviors, they'll all have a product number, description, and a price. However, if we have an agricultural application we might have chemical products, seed products, fertilizer products and retail products. These are all different—each having its own data and behaviors—and yet there is no doubt that each one of them really is a product. We can use inheritance to create this set of products as illustrated by the UML diagram in Figure 7-5.

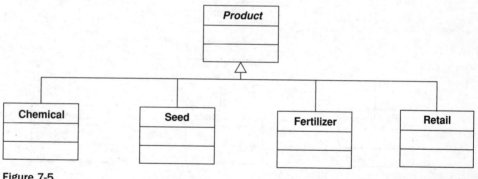

Figure 7-5

This diagram shows that we have an abstract base `Product` class, from which we derive the various types of product our system will actually use. This is an appropriate use of inheritance, because the child classes are obviously each a more specific form of the general `Product` class.

On the other hand, we might try to use inheritance just as a code sharing mechanism. For example, we may look at our application, which has `Customer`, `Product`, and `SalesOrder` classes, and decide that all of them need to be designed so they can be printed to a printer. The code to handle the printing will all be somewhat similar, so to reuse that printing code we create a base `PrintableObject` class. This would result in the UML as shown in Figure 7-6.

Intuitively we know that this doesn't represent an *is-a* relationship. While a `Customer` can be printed, and we are getting code reuse, a customer isn't really a specific case of a printable object. Implementing a

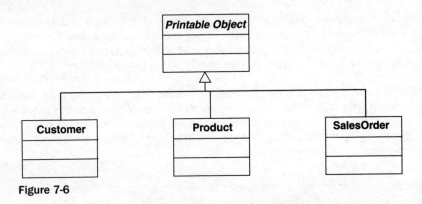

Figure 7-6

system following this design will result in a fragile design and application. This is a case where multiple interfaces are a far more appropriate technology, as we'll discuss later.

To illustrate this point, we might later discover that we have other entities in our organization that are similar to a customer, but are not quite the same. Upon further analysis, we may determine that Employee, Customer, and Contact are all related because they are specific cases of a Person class. The Person class provides commonality in terms of data and behavior across all these other classes (see Figure 7-7).

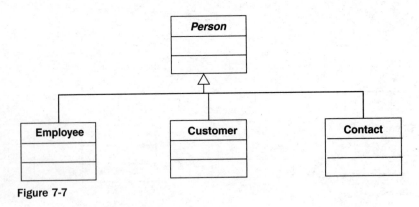

Figure 7-7

But now our Customer is in trouble, we've said it *is-a* PrintableObject, and we're now saying it *is-a* Person.

We *might* be able to just derive Person from PrintableObject (Figure 7-8).

The problem with this is that now Employee and Contact are also of type PrintableObject, even if they shouldn't be. But we're stuck, since we unfortunately had decided early on to go against intuition and say that a Customer *is-a* PrintableObject.

This is a problem that could be solved by *multiple inheritance*, which would allow Customer to be a subclass of more than one base class, in this case, of both Person and PrintableObject. However, the .NET platform and thus VB.NET don't support multiple inheritance in this way. Our alternative is to use

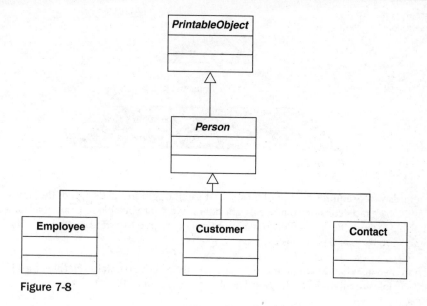

Figure 7-8

inheritance for the *is-a* relationship with `Person`, and use multiple interfaces to allow the `Customer` object to *act as* a `PrintableObject` by implementing an `IPrintableObject` interface.

Application versus Framework Inheritance

What we've just seen is how inheritance can accidentally cause reuse of code where no reuse was desired.

However, we can take a different view of this model by separating the concept of a framework from our actual application. The way we use inheritance in the design of a framework is somewhat different from how we use inheritance in the design of an actual application.

In this context, the word *framework* is being used to refer to a set of classes that provide base functionality that is not specific to our application, but rather may be used across a number of applications within our organization, or perhaps even beyond our organization. The .NET Framework class library is an example of a very broad framework we use when building our applications.

The `PrintableObject` class we discussed earlier, for example, may have little to do with our specific application, but may be the type of thing that is used across many applications. If so, it is a natural candidate for being part of a framework, rather than being considered part of our actual application.

Framework classes exist at a lower level than application classes. For example, the .NET system class library is a framework on which all .NET applications are built. We can layer our own framework on top of the .NET Framework as well (Figure 7-9).

If we take this view, then the `PrintableObject` class wouldn't be part of our application at all, but rather would be part of a framework on which our application is built. In such a case, the fact that `Customer` is not a specific case of `PrintableObject` doesn't matter as much, since we're not saying it is such a thing, but rather we're saying that it is leveraging that portion of the framework functionality.

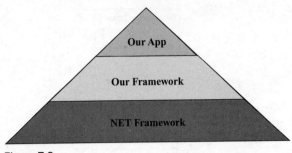

Figure 7-9

To make all this work requires a lot of planning and forethought in the design of the framework itself. To see the dangers we face, consider that we might not only want to be able to print objects, we might also want to be able to store them in a file. So we might not only have PrintableObject, but we might also have SavableObject as a base class.

The question then is, what do we do if Customer should be both printable *and* savable? If all printable objects are savable we might have the result as shown in Figure 7-10.

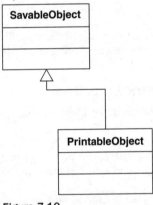

Figure 7-10

Or, if all savable objects are printable we might have the result as shown in Figure 7-11.

But really neither of these provides a decent solution, since the odds are that the concept of being printable and the concept of being savable are different and not interrelated in either of these ways.

When faced with this sort of issue, it is best to avoid using inheritance, and rather rely on multiple interfaces.

Inheritance and Multiple Interfaces

While inheritance is powerful, it is really geared around implementing the is-a relationship. Sometimes we will have objects that need to have a common interface, even though they aren't really a specific case of some base class that provides that interface. We've just been exploring that issue in our discussion of the PrintableObject, SavableObject, and Customer classes.

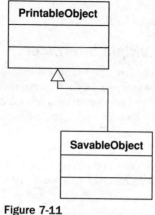

Figure 7-11

Sometimes multiple interfaces are a better alternative than inheritance. We discussed the syntax for creating and using secondary and multiple interfaces in Chapter 6.

Multiple interfaces can be viewed as another way of implementing the *is-a* relationship. It is often better, however, to view inheritance as an *is-a* relationship and to view multiple interfaces as a way of implementing an *act-as* relationship.

To think about this further, we can say that our `PrintableObject` concept could perhaps be better expressed as an interface—`IPrintableObject`.

When our class implements a secondary interface such as `IPrintableObject`, we're not really saying that our class *is-a* printable object, we're saying that it can *act as* a printable object. A `Customer` *is-a* `Person`, but at the same time it can *act as* a printable object. This is illustrated in the following UML (see Figure 7-12).

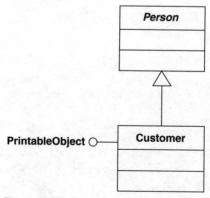

Figure 7-12

The drawback to this approach is that we get no inherited *implementation* when we implement `IPrintableObject`. In Chapter 6, we discussed how to reuse common code as we implement an interface across multiple classes. While not as automatic or easy as inheritance, it is possible to reuse implementation code with a bit of extra work.

Applying Inheritance and Multiple Interfaces

Perhaps the best way to see how inheritance and multiple interfaces interact is to look at an example. In the following ObjectsAndComponents project we'll combine inheritance and multiple interfaces to create an object that has both an *is-a* and *act-as* relationship at the same time. As an additional benefit, we'll be using the .NET Framework's ability to print to a printer or print preview dialog.

Creating the Person Base Class

We already have a simple Customer class in the project, so now let's add a Person base class. Choose Project ➪ Add Class and add a class named Person. Write the following code:

```
Public MustInherit Class Person
  Private mgID As Guid = Guid.NewGuid
  Private mstrName As String = ""

  Public Property ID() As Guid
    Get
      Return mgID
    End Get
    Set(ByVal Value As Guid)
      mgID = Value
    End Set
  End Property

  Public Property Name() As String
    Get
      Return mstrName
    End Get
    Set(ByVal Value As String)
      mstrName = Value
    End Set
  End Property
End Class
```

Subclassing Person

Now we can make the Customer class inherit from this base class, since it *is-a* Person. Also, since our base class now implements both the ID and Name properties, we can simplify the code in Customer by removing those properties and their related variables:

```
Public Class Customer
  Inherits Person

  Private mstrPhone As String = ""

  Public Property Phone() As String
    Get
      Return mstrPhone
    End Get
```

```
        Set(ByVal Value As String)
          mstrPhone = Value
        End Set
      End Property
    End Class
```

This shows the benefit of subclassing `Customer` from `Person`, since we're now sharing the `ID` and `Name` code across all other types of `Person` as well.

Implementing IPrintableObject

However, we also know that a `Customer` should be able to *act-as* a printable object. To do this in such a way that the implementation is reusable requires a bit of thought. First though, we need to define the `IPrintableObject` interface.

We'll use the standard printing mechanism provided by .NET from the `System.Drawing` namespace, and so we'll need to add a reference to `System.Drawing.dll` to the `Interfaces` project before we can define our new interface. With that done, bring up the code window for `Interfaces.vb` in the `Interfaces` project and add the following code:

```
Imports System.Drawing

Public Interface IPrintableObject
  Sub Print()
  Sub PrintPreview()
  Sub RenderPage(ByVal sender As Object, _
      ByVal ev As System.Drawing.Printing.PrintPageEventArgs)
End Interface
```

This interface ensures that any object implementing `IPrintableObject` will have `Print` and `PrintPreview` methods so we can invoke the appropriate type of printing. It also ensures the object will have a `RenderPage` method, which can be implemented by that object to render the object's data onto the printed page.

At this point, we could simply implement all the code needed to handle printing directly within the `Customer` object. This isn't ideal, however, since some of the code will be common across any objects that want to implement `IPrintableObject`, and it would be nice to find a way to share that code.

To do this, let's create a new class, `ObjectPrinter`. This is a framework-style class, in that it has nothing to do with any particular application, but can be used across any application where `IPrintableObject` will be used.

Add a new class named `ObjectPrinter` to the `ObjectsAndComponents` project. This class will contain all the code common to printing any object. It makes use of the built-in printing support provided by the .NET Framework class library. To use this, we need to import a couple of namespaces, so add this code to the new class:

```
Imports System.Drawing
Imports System.Drawing.Printing
Imports Interfaces
```

We can then define a `PrintDocument` variable, which will hold the reference to our printer output. We'll also declare a variable to hold a reference to the actual object we'll be printing. Notice that we're using the `IPrintableObject` interface data type for this variable:

```
Public Class ObjectPrinter

  Private WithEvents MyDoc As PrintDocument
  Private printObject As IPrintableObject
```

Now we can create a routine to kick off the printing process for any object implementing `IPrintableObject`. This code is totally generic, we'll write it here so it can be reused across any number of other classes:

```
Public Sub Print(ByVal obj As IPrintableObject)
   printObject = obj

   MyDoc = New PrintDocument()
   MyDoc.Print()
End Sub
```

Likewise, we can implement a method to show a print preview display of our object. Again, this code is totally generic, so we'll put it here for reuse:

```
Public Sub PrintPreview(ByVal obj As IPrintableObject)
   Dim PPdlg As PrintPreviewDialog = New PrintPreviewDialog()

   printObject = obj

   MyDoc = New PrintDocument()
   PPdlg.Document = MyDoc
   PPdlg.ShowDialog()
End Sub
```

Finally, we need to catch the `PrintPage` event that is automatically raised by the .NET printing mechanism. This event is raised by the `PrintDocument` object whenever the document determines that it needs data rendered onto a page. Typically, it is in this routine that we'd put the code to draw our text or graphics onto the page surface. However, since this is a generic framework class, we won't do that here, instead we'll delegate the call back into the actual application object that we want to print.

```
Private Sub PrintPage(ByVal sender As Object, _
    ByVal ev As System.Drawing.Printing.PrintPageEventArgs)
    Handles MyDoc.PrintPage

  printObject.RenderPage(sender, ev)
End Sub

End Class
```

This allows the application object itself to determine how its data should be rendered onto the output page. Let's see how we can do that by implementing the `IPrintableObject` interface on our

Customer class:

```
Imports Interfaces

Public Class Customer
   Inherits Person
   Implements IPrintableObject
```

By adding this code, we require that our `Customer` class implement the `Print`, `PrintPreview`, and `RenderPage` methods. To avoid wasting paper as we test, let's make both the `Print` and `PrintPreview` methods the same and have them just do a print preview display:

```
Private Sub Print() _
    Implements IPrintableObject.Print, IPrintableObject.PrintPreview

   Dim p As New ObjectPrinter()
   p.PrintPreview(Me)
End Sub
```

Notice that we're using an `ObjectPrinter` object to handle the common details of doing a print preview. In fact, any class we ever create that implements `IPrintableObject` will have this exactly same code to implement a print preview function, relying on our common `ObjectPrinter` to take care of the details.

We also need to implement the `RenderPage` method, which is where we actually put our object's data onto the printed page:

```
Private Sub RenderPage(ByVal sender As Object, _
    ByVal ev As System.Drawing.Printing.PrintPageEventArgs) _
    Implements IPrintableObject.RenderPage

   Dim PrintFont As New Font("Arial", 10)
   Dim LineHeight As Single = PrintFont.GetHeight(ev.Graphics)
   Dim LeftMargin As Single = ev.MarginBounds.Left
   Dim yPos As Single = ev.MarginBounds.Top

   ev.Graphics.DrawString("ID: " & ID.ToString, PrintFont, Brushes.Black, _
     LeftMargin, yPos, New StringFormat())

   yPos += LineHeight
   ev.Graphics.DrawString("Name: " & Name, PrintFont, Brushes.Black, _
     LeftMargin, yPos, New StringFormat())

   ev.HasMorePages = False
End Sub
```

All of this code is unique to our object, which makes sense since we're rendering our specific data to be printed. However, we don't need to worry about the details of whether we're doing printing to paper or print preview, that is handled by our `ObjectPrinter` class, which in turn uses the .NET Framework. This allows us to just focus on generating the output to the page within our application class.

By generalizing the printing code in `ObjectPrinter`, we've achieved a level of reuse that we can tap into via the `IPrintableObject` interface. Any time we want to print a `Customer` object's data, we can have it *act-as* an `IPrintableObject` and call its `Print` or `PrintPreview` method. To see this work, let's change the code behind the button control on `Form1`:

```
Private Sub Button1_Click(ByVal sender As System.Object, _
    ByVal e As System.EventArgs) Handles Button1.Click

    Dim obj As New Customer
    obj.Name = "Douglas Adams"
    CType(obj, IPrintableObject).PrintPreview()
End Sub
```

This code creates a new `Customer` object and sets its `Name` property. We then use the `CType()` method to access the object via its `IPrintableObject` interface to invoke the `PrintPreview` method.

When we run the application and click the button, we'll get a print preview display showing the object's data (see Figure 7-13).

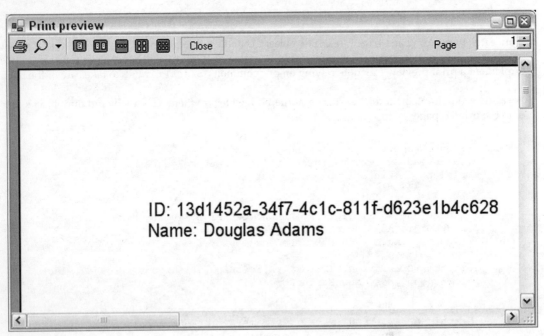

Figure 7-13

How Deep to Go?

Most of the examples we've discussed so far have illustrated how we can create a child class based on a single parent class. That is called single-level inheritance. However, inheritance can be many levels deep. For example, we might have a deep hierarchy as shown in Figure7-14.

From the root of System.Object down to the NAFTACustomer we have four levels of inheritance. This can be described as a four-level inheritance chain.

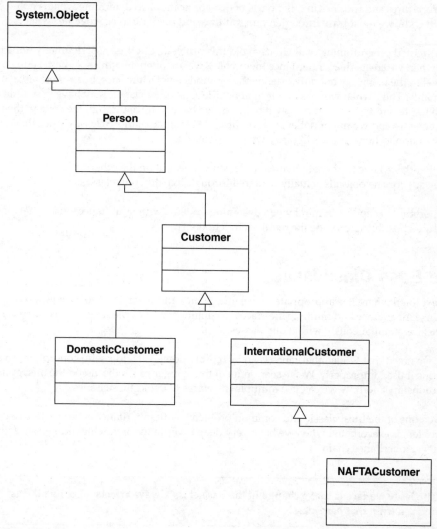

Figure 7-14

There is no hard and fast rule about how deep inheritance chains should go, but conventional wisdom and general experience with inheritance in other languages such as Smalltalk and C++ indicate that the deeper an inheritance chain becomes, the harder it is to maintain an application.

This happens for two reasons. First is the fragile base class or fragile superclass issue, which we'll discuss shortly. The second reason is that a deep inheritance hierarchy tends to seriously reduce readability of our code by scattering the code for an object across many different classes, all of which are combined together by the compiler to create our object.

One of the reasons for adopting object-oriented design and programming is to avoid the so-called spaghetti code where any bit of code we might look at does almost nothing useful, instead calls various other procedures and routines in other parts of our application. To determine what is going on with spaghetti code, we must trace through many routines and mentally piece together what is going on.

Object-oriented programming *can* help us avoid this problem, but it is most definitely not a magic bullet. In fact, when we create deep inheritance hierarchies, we are often creating spaghetti code. This is because each level in the hierarchy not only extends the previous level's interface, but almost always also adds functionality. Thus, when we look at our final NAFTACustomer class it may have very little code. In order to figure out what it does or how it behaves, we have to trace through the code in the previous four levels of classes and we might not even have the code for some of those classes, since they may come from other applications or class libraries we've purchased.

On one hand, we have the benefit that we're reusing code, but on the other hand, we have the drawback that the code for one object is actually scattered through five different classes.

It is important to keep this in mind when designing systems with inheritance—use as few levels in the hierarchy as possible to provide the required functionality.

Fragile Base Class Issue

We've explored where it is appropriate to use inheritance and where it is not. We've also explored how we can use inheritance and multiple interfaces in conjunction to implement both *is-a* and *act-as* relationships simultaneously within our classes.

Earlier, we noted that while inheritance is an incredibly powerful and useful concept, it can also be very dangerous if used improperly. We've seen some of this danger as we discussed the misapplication of the *is-a* relationship, and how we can use multiple interfaces to avoid those issues.

However, one of the most classic and common problems with inheritance is the *fragile base class* problem. This problem is exacerbated when we have very deep inheritance hierarchies, but exists even in a single-level inheritance chain.

> The issue we face is that a change in the base class always affects all child classes derived from that base class.

This is a double-edged sword. On one hand, we get the benefit of being able to change code in one location and have that change automatically cascade out through all derived classes. On the other hand, a change in behavior can have unintended or unexpected consequences further down the inheritance chain, and that can make our application very fragile and hard to change or maintain.

Interface Changes

There are obvious changes we might make, that require immediate attention. For example, we might change our Person class to have FirstName and LastName instead of simply Name as a property. In the Person class, replace the mstrName variable declaration with the following code:

```
Private mstrFirstName As String = ""
Private mstrLastName As String = ""
```

Now replace the `Name` property with the following code:

```
Public Property FirstName() As String
   Get
      Return mstrFirstName
   End Get
   Set(ByVal Value As String)
      mstrFirstName = Value
   End Set
End Property

Public Property LastName() As String
   Get
      Return mstrLastName
   End Get
   Set(ByVal Value As String)
      mstrLastName = Value
   End Set
End Property
```

At this point, the Task List window in the IDE will show a list of locations where we need to alter our code to compensate for the change. This is a graphic illustration of a base class change that causes cascading changes throughout our application. In this case, we've changed the base class interface, thus changing the interface of all subclasses in the inheritance chain.

To avoid having to fix code throughout our application, we should always strive to keep as much consistency in our base class interface as possible. In this case, we can implement a read-only `Name` property that returns the full name of the `Person`:

```
Public ReadOnly Property Name() As String
   Get
      Return mstrFirstName & " " & mstrLastName
   End Get
End Property
```

This resolves most of the items in the Task List window. We can fix any remaining issues by using the `FirstName` and `LastName` properties. For example, in `Form1` we can change the code behind our button to the following:

```
Private Sub Button1_Click(ByVal sender As System.Object, _
    ByVal e As System.EventArgs) Handles button1.Click

  Dim obj As New Customer()
  obj.FirstName = "Douglas"
  obj.LastName = "Adams"
  CType(obj, Interfaces.IPrintableObject).Print()
End Sub
```

Any change to a base class interface is likely to cause problems, so we must think carefully before making such a change.

Implementation Changes

Unfortunately, there's another, more subtle type of change that can wreak more havoc on our application, and that is an implementation change. This is the core of the fragile base class problem.

Encapsulation provides us with separation of interface from implementation. However, keeping our interface consistent is merely a *syntactic* concept. If we change the implementation we are making a *semantic* change, a change that doesn't alter any of our syntax, but can have serious ramifications on the real behavior of the application.

In theory, we can change the implementation of a class, and as long as we don't change its interface any client applications using objects based on that class will continue to operate without change. Of course, reality is never as nice as theory, and more often than not a change to implementation will have some consequences in the behavior of a client application.

For example, we might use a `SortedList` to sort and display some `Customer` objects. To do this, change the code behind our button on `Form1` as follows:

```
Private Sub Button1_Click(ByVal sender As System.Object, _
    ByVal e As System.EventArgs) Handles button1.Click

    Dim col As New SortedList()
    Dim obj As Customer

    obj = New Customer()
    obj.FirstName = "Douglas"
    obj.LastName = "Adams"
    col.Add(obj.Name, obj)

    obj = New Customer()
    obj.FirstName = "Andre"
    obj.LastName = "Norton"
    col.Add(obj.Name, obj)

    Dim i As DictionaryEntry
    For Each i In col
        obj = CType(i.Value, Customer)
        System.Diagnostics.Debug.WriteLine(obj.Name)
    Next
End Sub
```

This code simply creates a couple of `Customer` objects, sets their `FirstName` and `LastName` properties and inserts them into a `SortedList` collection object from the `System.Collections` namespace.

Items in a `SortedList` are sorted based on their key value and we are using the `Name` property to provide that key, meaning that our entries will be sorted by name. Since our `Name` property is implemented to return first name first and last name second, our entries will be sorted by first name.

If we run the application, the Output window in the IDE will display the following:

```
Andre Norton
Douglas Adams
```

However, we can change the implementation of our `Person` class— not directly changing or impacting either the `Customer` class or our code in `Form1`—to return last name first and first name second as shown:

```
Public ReadOnly Property Name() As String
  Get
     Return mstrLastName & ", " & mstrFirstName
  End Get
End Property
```

While no other code requires changing, and no syntax errors are flagged, the behavior of our application is changed. When we run it our output will now be

```
Adams, Douglas
Norton, Andre
```

Maybe this change is inconsequential. Maybe it totally breaks the required behavior of our form. The developer making the change in the `Person` class might not even know that someone was using that property for sort criteria.

This illustrates how dangerous inheritance can be. Changes to implementation in a base class can cascade out to countless other classes in countless applications, having unforeseen side effects and consequences of which the base class developer is totally unaware.

Summary

Over the past three chapters we've seen how object-oriented programming flows from the four basic concepts of abstraction, encapsulation, polymorphism, and inheritance. In this chapter we've provided some basic discussion of each concept and demonstrated how to implement them using VB.NET.

We have understood how (when properly applied) object-oriented design and programming can allow us to create very large and complex applications that remain maintainable and readable over time. However, this is no magic bullet and these technologies and concepts can, if improperly applied, create the same hard-to-maintain code that we might create using procedural or modular design techniques.

It is not possible to fully cover all aspects of object-oriented programming in a single chapter. Before launching into a full-blown object-oriented project, I highly recommend going through other books specifically geared toward object-oriented design and programming.

8

Namespaces

Even if you didn't realize it, you've been using *namespaces* since Chapter 2. For example, `System`, `System.Diagnostics`, and `System.Windows.Forms` are all namespaces contained within the .NET Framework. Namespaces are an easy concept to understand, but in this chapter, we'll put the ideas behind them on a firm footing — and clear up any misconceptions you might have about how they are used and organized.

If you're familiar with COM, you'll find that the concept of namespaces is the logical extension of programmatic identifier (ProgID) values. For example, the functionality of Visual Basic 6's `FileSystemObject` is now mostly encompassed in the .NET's `System.IO` namespace, though this is not a one-to-one mapping. However, namespaces are about more than a change in name; they represent the logical extension of the COM naming structure, expanding its ease of use and extensibility.

In this chapter we'll cover:

❑   What namespaces are

❑   Which namespaces are used in Visual Studio .NET (VS.NET) projects by default

❑   How we can reference namespaces and use the `Imports` statement

❑   How the compiler searches for class references

❑   How we can alias namespaces

❑   How we can create our own namespaces

Let's begin this chapter by defining what a namespace is (and isn't).

What Is a Namespace?

Namespaces are a way of organizing the vast amount of classes, structures, enumerations, delegates, and interfaces that the .NET Framework class library provides. Namespaces are a hierarchically structured index into a class library which are available to all of the .NET languages and not only Visual Basic .NET. The namespaces, or object references, are typically organized by *function*. For example, the System.IO namespace contains classes, structures, and interfaces for working with input/output streams and files. These classes in this namespace *do not* necessarily inherit from the same base classes (apart from Object, of course).

A namespace is a combination of a naming convention and an assembly, which organizes collections of objects and prevents ambiguity in object references. A namespace can be, and often is, implemented across several physical assemblies but, from the reference side, it is the namespace that ties these assemblies together. A namespace consists of not only classes but other (child) namespaces too. For example, IO is a child namespace of the System namespace.

Namespaces provide identification beyond the component name. With a namespace, it is possible to put a more meaningful title (for example, System) followed by a grouping (for example, Text) to group together a collection of classes that contain similar functions. For example, the System.Text namespace contains a powerful class called StringBuilder. To reference this class, we can use the fully qualified namespace reference of System.Text.StringBuilder, as shown here.

```
Dim sb As New System.Text.StringBuilder
```

The structure of a namespace is not a reflection of the physical inheritance of classes that make up a namespace. For example, the System.Text namespace contains another child namespace called RegularExpressions. This namespace contains several classes, but they do not inherit or otherwise reference the classes that make up the System.Text namespace.

Figure 8-1 shows how the System namespace contains the Text child namespace, which also has a child namespace called RegularExpressions.

Both of these child namespaces, Text and RegularExpressions–, contain a number of objects, shown here (Figure 8-1) in the inheritance model for these classes.

As you can see in the figure, while some of the classes in each namespace do inherit from each other, and while all of the classes eventually inherit from the generic Object, the classes in System.Text.RegularExpressions do not inherit from the classes in System.Text.

You might be wondering at this point what all the fuss is about. To emphasize the usefulness of namespaces, we can draw another good example from this figure. If you make a reference to System.Drawing.Imaging.Encoder in your application, you are making a reference to a completely different Encoder class than the namespace that is shown in Figure 8-1 — System.Text.Encoder. Being able to clearly identify classes that have the same name though very different functions and disambiguate them is yet another advantage of namespaces.

If you are an experienced COM developer, you may note that unlike a ProgID which is a one-level relationship between the project assembly and class, a single namespace can use child namespaces to extend the meaningful description of a class. The System namespace, imported by default as part of every project, contains not only the default Object class, but also many other classes that are used as the basis for every .NET language.

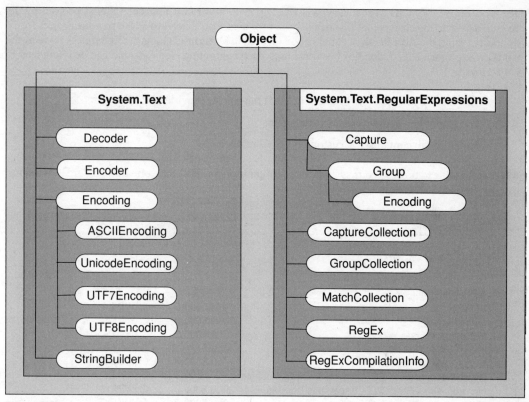

Figure 8-1

However, what if a class you need isn't available in your project? The problem may be with the references in your project. For example, by default the `System.DirectoryServices` namespace, used for getting programmatic access to the Active Directory objects, isn't part of your project's assembly. Using it requires adding a *reference* to the project assembly. The concept of referencing a namespace is very similar to the ability to reference a COM object in VB6.

In fact, with all this talk about referencing, it's probably a good idea to look at an example of adding an additional namespace to a project. Before we do that, we need to know a little bit about how a namespace is implemented.

Namespaces are implemented in .NET assemblies. The `System` namespace is implemented in an assembly called `System.dll` provided with Visual Studio. By referencing this assembly, the project gains the ability to reference all of the child namespaces of `System` that happen to be implemented in this assembly. Using the preceding table, the project can import and use the `System.Text` namespace because its implementation is in the `System.dll` assembly. However, although it is listed above, the project cannot import or use the `System.Data` namespace unless it references the assembly that implements this child of the `System` namespace, `System.Data.dll`.

Let's create a sample project so that we can examine the role that namespaces play within it. Using VS.NET, create a new VB.NET Windows Application project called Namespace_Sampler.

The `Microsoft.VisualBasic.Compatibility.VB6` library isn't part of VB.NET projects by default. To gain access to the classes that this namespace provides, you'll need to add it to your project. You can do this by using the Add Reference dialog box (available by right-clicking the References node in the Solution Explorer). This dialog box has three tabs, each containing elements that can be referenced from your project:

❑ The first tab contains .NET assemblies that have been provided by Microsoft

❑ The second tab contains COM components

❑ The third tab contains any custom .NET assemblies

It is also possible to browse your system for other component files if the one that you are looking for isn't listed, as shown in Figure 8-2.

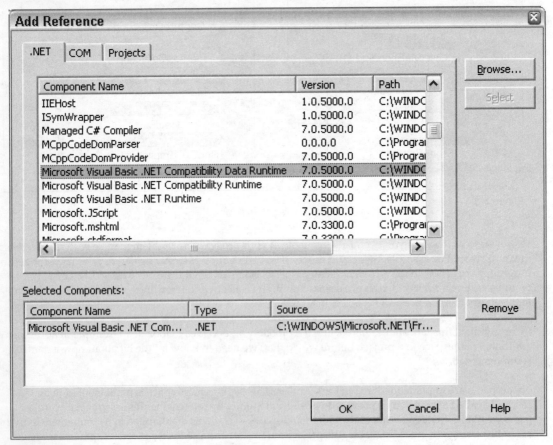

Figure 8-2

The available .NET namespaces are listed by a component name. This is *not* the same as the namespace name. Selecting the Microsoft Visual Basic .NET Compatibility Data Runtime component will add the desired `Microsoft.VisualBasic.Compatibility.VB6` namespace. Although the lower window doesn't have enough space to fully display the path, the file name for this namespace is `Microsoft`

.VisualBasic.Compatibility.Data.dll. The Microsoft Visual Basic .NET Compatibility Runtime component is another compatibility library that is available for you to reference. This will add the assembly, Microsoft.VisualBasic.Compatibility.dll, to your project. This reference contains the second half of the compatibility library.

This implementation, while a bit surprising at first, is very powerful. Firstly, it shows the extensibility of namespaces — the single Microsoft.VisualBasic.Compatibilty.VB6 namespace is implemented in two separate assemblies. Secondly, it allows us to include only the classes that we need — in this case, those that are related to the VB6 (Visual Basic 6) environment or to database tools, or both types.

There are some interesting points about the Microsoft.VisualBasic namespace that you should be aware of. First, this namespace gives you access to all those functions that VB6 developers have had for years. Microsoft has implemented these on .NET and have made them available for your use within your .NET projects. Since these functions have been implemented on .NET, there is no performance hit for using them, but you will most likely find the functionality that they provide available to you in newer .NET namespaces. One big point is that contrary to what the name of the namespace suggests, this namespace is available for use by all of the .NET languages. So this means that a C# developer could also use the Microsoft.VisualBasic namespace if he or she so desired.

Namespaces and References

Highlighting their importance to every project, references (including namespaces) are no longer hidden from view — available only after opening a dialog box as they were in VB6. As shown in the Solution Explorer window in Figure 8-3, every new project comes with a set of referenced namespaces.

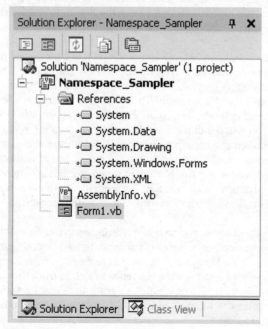

Figure 8-3

The list of default references changes based on the type of project. The example from the left image of Figure 8-3 is the default references for a Windows Forms project in Visual Studio .NET 2002 or Visual Studio .NET 2003. If the project type is an ASP.NET Web Application (shown in the right image of Figure 8-3), the list of references changes appropriately—the reference to the System.Windows.Forms namespace assembly changes and is replaced by a reference to System.Web. If the project type is an ASP.NET Web service (not shown), then the System.Windows.Forms namespace is replaced by references to the System.Web and System.Web.Services namespaces.

In addition to making the namespaces available, references play a second important role in your project. One of the advantages of .NET is using services and components built on the common language runtime (CLR) that allow you to avoid DLL conflicts. The various problems that can occur related to DLL versioning, commonly referred to as DLL Hell, involve two types of conflict.

The first situation occurs when you have a component that requires a minimum DLL version and an older version of the same DLL causes your product to break. The alternative situation is when you require an older version of a DLL and a new version is incompatible. In either case, the result is that a shared file, outside of your control, creates a system-wide dependency that impacts your software. As part of .NET, it is possible, but not required, to indicate that a DLL should be shipped as part of your project to avoid an external dependency.

In order to indicate that a referenced component should be included locally, you can select the reference in the Solution Explorer and then examine the properties associated with that reference. One editable property is called Copy Local. You will see this property and its value in the Properties window within VS.NET. For those assemblies that are part of a VS.NET installation, this value defaults to False. However, for custom references, this property will default to True to indicate that the referenced DLL should be included as part of the assembly. Changing this property to True changes the path associated with the assembly. Instead of using the path to the referenced file's location on the system, the project creates a subdirectory based on the reference name and places the files required for the implementation of the reference in this subdirectory, as shown in Figure 8-4.

The benefit of this is that even if another version of the DLL is later placed on the system, your project's assembly will continue to function. However, this protection from a conflicting version comes at a price. Future updates to the namespace assembly to fix flaws will be in the system version but not in the private version that is part of your project's assembly. To resolve this, Microsoft's solution is to place new versions in directories based on their version information. If you examine the path information for all of the VS.NET references, you will see that it includes a version number. As new versions of these DLLs are released, they will be installed in a separate directory. This method allows for both an escape from DLL Hell, by keeping new versions from stomping on old versions, but also allows for old versions to be easily located for maintenance updates. For this reason, in many cases, it is better to leave alone the default behavior of VS.NET to only copy locally custom components, until your organization implements a directory structure with version information similar to that of Microsoft.

The VB.NET compiler will not allow you to add a reference to your assembly if the targeted implementation includes a reference, which isn't also referenced in your assembly. The good news is that the compiler will help. If, after adding a reference, that reference doesn't appear in the IntelliSense list generated by VS.NET, go ahead and type the reference to a class from that reference. The compiler will flag it with one of its Microsoft Word-like spelling or grammar error underlines. Then by clicking the underlined text, the compiler will tell you which other assemblies need to be referenced in the project in order to use the class in question.

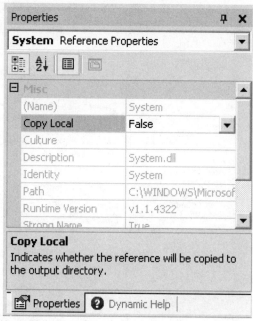

Figure 8-4

Common Namespaces

The generated list of references shown in the Solution Explorer for the newly created Namespace_ Sampler project includes most, but not all, of the namespaces that are part of your Windows Application project. For example, one namespace not displayed as a reference is Microsoft.VisualBasic and the accompanying Microsoft.VisualBasic.dll. Every VB.NET project includes the namespace Microsoft.VisualBasic. This namespace is part of the Visual Studio project templates for VB.NET and is, in short, .what makes VB.NET different from C# or any other .NET language. The implicit inclusion of this namespace is the reason that you can call IsDBNull and other methods of VB.NET directly. The only difference in the default namespaces that are included with VB.NET and C# Windows Application projects is that the former use Microsoft.VisualBasic and the latter use Microsoft.CSharp.

In order to see all of the namespaces that are imported automatically, such as the Microsoft.VisualBasic namespace, right-click the project name in the Solution Explorer and select Properties from the context menu. This will open the project Properties dialog box. Select the Imports node that is under the Common Properties node and you will see Microsoft.VisualBasic at the top of the list. This is illustrated in Figure 8-5.

When looking at the project's global list of imports, you can see that in addition to the Microsoft.VisualBasic namespace, the System.Collections and System.Diagnostics namespaces are also imported into the project. Unlike the other namespaces in the list, these namespaces are not listed as references. That is because the implementation of the System.Collections and System.Diagnostics namespaces is part of the referenced System.dll. Similar to Microsoft.VisualBasic, importing these namespaces allows references to the associated classes,

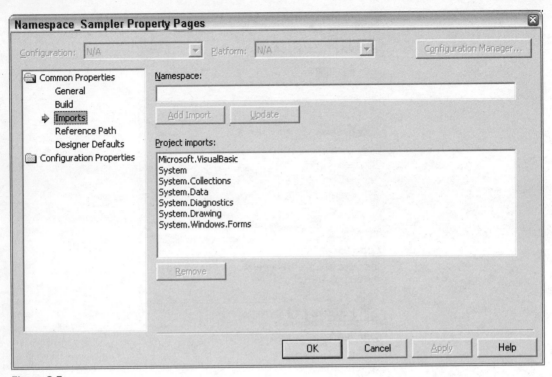

Figure 8-5

such that a fully qualified path is not required. Since these namespaces contain commonly used classes, it is worthwhile to always include them at the project level.

The following listing brings together brief descriptions of some of the namespaces commonly used in VB.NET projects:

❑   System.Collections—Contains the classes that support various feature-rich object collections. Included automatically, it has classes for arrays, lists, dictionaries, queues, hash tables, etc.

❑   System.Data—Included in all VB.NET projects; contains the classes to support the core features of ADO.NET.

❑   System.Diagnostics—Included .in all VB.NET projects, this namespace includes the debugging classes. The Trace and Debug classes provide the primary capabilities but the namespace contains dozens of classes to support debugging.

❑   System.Drawing—Simple drawing classes to support Windows Application projects.

❑   System.EnterpriseServices—Not included automatically, the System. EnterpriseServices implementation must be referenced to make it available. This namespace contains the classes that interface .NET assemblies with COM+.

❑   System.IO—This namespace contains important classes that allow you to read and write to files as well as data streams.

❑ System.Text — This commonly used namespace allows you to work with text in a number of different ways, usually in regards to string manipulation. One of the more popular objects that this namespace offers is the StringBuilder object.

❑ System.Threading — With the release of VB.NET in 2002, you could for the first time create multithreaded applications with ease. This namespace contains the objects to work with and manipulate threads within your application.

❑ System.Web — This is the namespace that deals with one of the more exciting features of the .NET Framework — ASP.NET. This namespace provides the objects that deal with browser–server communications. Two of the main objects include the HttpRequest object, which deals with the request from the client to the server, as well as the HttpResponse object, which deals with the response from the server to the client.

❑ System.Web.Services — This is the main namespace you use when you are creating XML Web services, one of the more powerful capabilities that is provided with the .NET Framework. This namespace provides you with the classes that deal with SOAP messages and the manipulation of these messages.

❑ System.Windows.Forms — The classes to create Windows Forms in Windows Application projects. This namespace contains the form elements.

Of course, to really make use of the classes and other objects in the above listing, you really need more detailed information. In addition to resources such as VS.NET's help files, the best source of information is the Object Browser. It is available directly in the VS.NET IDE. You will find it by selecting View ➪ Object Browser if you are using Visual Studio .NET 2003 or View ➪ Other Windows ➪ Object Browser if you are using Visual Studio .NET 2002. The Visual Studio .NET 2003 Object Browser is shown in Figure 8-6.

The Object Browser displays each of the referenced assemblies and allows you to drill down into the various namespaces. The previous screenshot illustrates how the System.dll implements a number of namespaces, including some that are part of the System namespace. By drilling down into a namespace, it is possible to see some of the classes available. By further selecting a class, the browser shows not only the methods and properties associated with the selected class but also a brief outline of what that class does.

Using the Object Browser is an excellent way to gain insight, not only into which classes and interfaces are available via the different assemblies included in your project, but also into how they work. As you can guess, the ability to actually see not only which classes are available but what and how to use them is important in being able to work efficiently. To work effectively in the .NET CLR environment requires finding the right class for the task.

Importing and Aliasing Namespaces

Not all namespaces should be imported at the global level. Although we have looked at namespaces that are included at this level, it is much better to import namespaces only in the module where they will be used. Importing a namespace at the module level does not change setting the reference, but does mean that you don't add it into the list of imports on the project's property page. Similar to variables used in a project, it is possible to define a namespace at the module level. The advantage of this is similar to the use of local variables in that it helps to prevent different namespaces from interfering with each other. As this section will show, it is possible for two different namespaces to contain classes or even child namespaces with the same name.

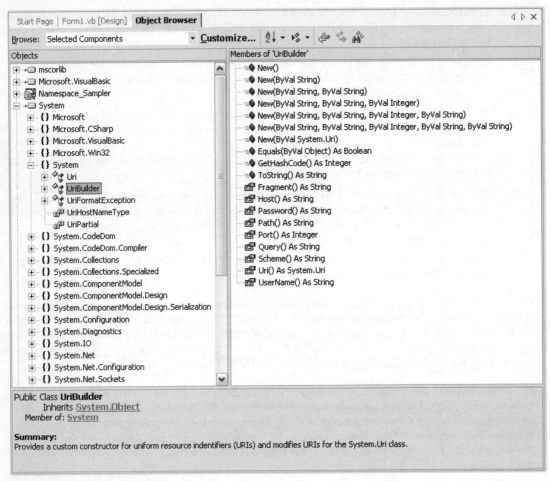

Figure 8-6

Importing Namespaces

The development environment and compiler need a way to prioritize the order that namespaces should be checked when a class is referenced. It is always possible to unequivocally specify a class by stating its complete namespace path. This is referred to as fully qualifying your declaration. Here is an example of fully qualifying a `StringBuilder` object.

```
Dim sb As New System.Text.StringBuilder
```

However, if every reference to every class needed its full namespace declaration, that would make VB.NET and every other .NET language difficult to program in. After all, who would want to type `System.Collections.ArrayList` each time they wanted an instance of the `ArrayList` class. If you review the global references, you'll see the `System.Collections` namespace. Thus, you can just type `ArrayList` whenever you need an instance of this class.

In theory, another way to reference the StringBuilder class is to use Text.StringBuilder but, with all namespaces imported globally, there is a problem with this. The problem is caused by what is known as *namespace crowding*. Because there is a second namespace, System.Drawing, which has a child called Text, the compiler doesn't have a clear location for the Text namespace and therefore cannot resolve the StringBuilder class. The solution to this problem is to make it so that only a single version of the Text child namespace is found locally. Then the compiler will use this namespace regardless of the global availability of the System.Drawing.Text namespace.

Imports statements specify to the compiler those namespaces that the code will use.

```
Imports Microsoft.Win32
Imports System
Imports SysDraw = System.Drawing
```

Once imported into the file, you are then not required to fully qualify your object declarations in your code. For instance, if you imported the System.Data.SqlClient namespace into your file, you would then be able to create a SqlConnection object in the following manner.

```
Dim conn As New SqlConnection
```

Each of these Imports statements from above illustrates a different facet of importing namespaces. The first, Imports Microsoft.Win32, is a namespace that is not imported at the global level. Looking at the reference list, you may not see the Microsoft assembly referenced directly. However, opening the Object Browser reveals that this namespace is actually included as part of the System.dll.

As noted earlier, the StringBuilder references become ambiguous because both System.Text and System.Drawing.Text are valid namespaces at the global level. As a result, the compiler has no way to distinguish which Text child namespace is being referenced. Without any clear indication, the compiler flags Text.StringBuilder declarations in the command handler. However, using the Imports System declaration in the module tells the compiler that, before checking namespaces imported at the global level, it should attempt to match incomplete references at the module level. Since the System namespace is declared at this level, while System.Drawing (for the moment) is not, there is no ambiguity as to which child namespace Text.StringBuilder belongs to.

This demonstrates how the compiler looks at each possible declaration:

❑ First, see if the item is a complete reference such as System.Text.StringBuilder

❑ If the declaration does not match a complete reference, then the compiler tries to see if the declaration is from a child namespace of one of the module level imports

❑ Finally, if a match has not been found, the compiler looks at the global level imports to see if the declaration can be associated with a namespace imported for the entire assembly

While the preceding logical progression of moving from a full declaration through module to global level imports does resolve the majority of issues, it does not handle all possibilities. Specifically, if we imported System.Drawing at the module level, the *namespace collision* would return. This is where the third import statement becomes important — this import statement uses an *alias*.

Aliasing Namespaces

Aliasing has two benefits in .NET. The first is that aliasing allows a long namespace such as System .EnterpriseServices to be replaced with a shorthand name such as COMPlus. The second is that it adds a way to prevent ambiguity of child namespaces at the module level.

As noted earlier, the System and System.Drawing namespaces both contain a child namespace of Text. Since we will be using a number of classes from the System.Drawing namespace, it follows that this namespace should be imported into the form's module. However, were this namespace imported along with the System namespace, the compiler would once again find references to the Text child namespace to be ambiguous. However, by aliasing the System.Drawing namespace to SysDraw, the compiler knows that it should only check the System.Drawing namespace when a declaration begins with that alias. The result is that although multiple namespaces with the same child namespace are now available at the module level, the compiler knows that one (or more) of them should only be checked at this level when they are explicitly referenced.

Creating Your Own Namespaces

Every assembly created in .NET is part of some root namespace. By default, this logic actually mirrors COM in that assemblies are assigned a namespace that matches the project name. However, unlike COM, in .NET it is possible to change this default behavior. In this way, just as Microsoft has packaged the system level and CLR classes using well-defined names, it is possible for us to create our own namespaces. Of course, it's also possible to create projects that match existing namespaces and extend those namespaces, but that is very poor programming practice.

Creating an assembly in a custom namespace can be done at one of two levels. However, unless you want the same name for each assembly that will be used in a large namespace, you will normally reset the root namespace for the assembly. This is done through the assembly's project pages, reached by right-clicking the solution name in the Solution Explorer window and selecting the General tab within the Common Properties folder, as shown in Figure 8-7.

The next step is optional but, depending on whether you want to create a class at the top level or at a child level, you can add a Namespace command to your code. There is a trick to being able to create top-level namespaces, or multiple namespaces within the modules that make up an assembly. Instead of replacing the default namespace with another name, we can delete the default namespace and only define the namespaces in the modules using the Namespace command.

The Namespace command is accompanied by an End Namespace command. This End Namespace command must be placed after the End Class tag for any classes that will be part of the namespace. The following code demonstrates the structure used to create a MyMetaNamespace namespace, which contains a single class.

```
Namespace MyMetaNamespace
    Class MyClass1
        'Code
    End Class
End Namespace
```

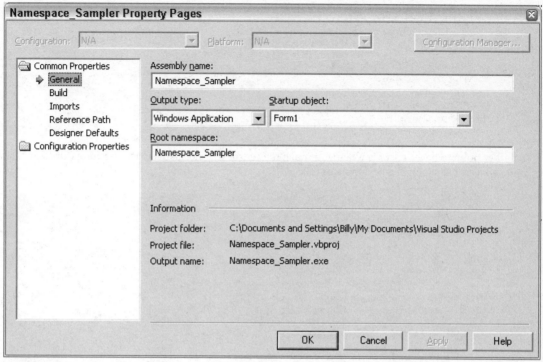

Figure 8-7

You can then utilize the `MyClass1` object by simply referencing its namespace, `MyMetaNamespace.MyClass1`. It is also possible to have multiple namespaces in a single file as shown here.

```
Namespace MyMetaNamespace1
    Class MyClass1
        'Code
    End Class
End Namespace

Namespace MyMetaNamespace2
    Class MyClass2
        'Code
    End Class
End Namespace
```

By using this kind of structure, if you want to utilize `MyClass1` you would get at it through the namespace `MyMetaNamespace.MyClass1`. This *would not* give you access to `MyMetaNamespace2` and the objects that it offers, but instead you would have to make a separate reference to `MyMetaNamespace2.MyClass2`.

The `Namespace` command can also be nested. Using nested `Namespace` commands is how child namespaces are defined. The same rules apply — each `Namespace` must be paired with an `End Namespace` and must fully encompass all of the classes that are part of that namespace. In this example, the `MyMetaNamespace` has a child namespace called `MyMetaNamespace.MyChildNamespace`.

```
Namespace MyMetaNamespace
    Class MyClass1
        'Code
    End Class
    Namespace MyChildNamespace
        Class MyClass2
            'Code
        End Class
    End Namespace
End Namespace
```

Another point to be aware of is when you make references to other namespaces within your own custom namespaces. Let's look at an example of this.

```
Imports System
Imports System.Data
Imports System.Data.SqlClient

Namespace MyMetaNamespace1
    Class MyClass1
        'Code
    End Class
End Namespace

Namespace MyMetaNamespace2
    Imports System.IO

    Class MyClass2
        'Code
    End Class
End Namespace
```

In this example, there are a number of different namespaces referenced in the file. The three namespaces referenced at the top of the code listing,– the System, System.Data, and System.Data.SqlClient namespace references, are available to each and every namespace that is developed in the file. This is because these three references are sitting outside of any particular namespace declarations. However, this is quite different for the System.IO namespace reference. Because this reference is made within the MyMetaNamespace2 namespace, it is therefore unavailable to any other namespace in the file.

> When you create your own namespaces, Microsoft recommends that you use a convention of **CompanyName.TechnologyName**, for example, **Wrox.Books**. This helps to ensure that all libraries are organized in a consistent way.

Summary

The introduction of namespaces with the .NET Framework provides a powerful tool that helps to abstract the logical capabilities from their physical implementation. While there are differences in the syntax of referencing objects from a namespace, as opposed to referencing the same object from a COM style component implementation, overall there are several similarities. This chapter introduced namespaces and their hierarchical structure, and demonstrated:

- ❏ How namespace hierarchies are not related to class hierarchies
- ❏ How to review and add references to a project
- ❏ How to import and alias namespaces at the module level
- ❏ How to create custom namespaces

Namespaces play an important role in enterprise software development. By allowing you to separate the implementation of related functional objects, while retaining the ability to still group these objects, you improve the overall maintainability of your code. Everyone who has ever worked on a large project has been put in the situation where a fix to a component is delayed because of the potential impact on other components in the same project. Regardless of the logical separation of components in the same project, those who watched the development process worried about testing. With totally separate implementations for related components, it is not only possible to alleviate this concern, but it is easier than ever before for a team of developers to work on different parts of the same project.

9

Error Handling

Error handling is an important topic in any programming language. If a program does not handle errors and unexpected conditions properly, it cannot carry out its function.

In this chapter, we will cover how error handling works in Visual Basic .NET (VB.NET). There are many improvements over earlier versions of Visual Basic. We will discuss the common language runtime (CLR) exception handler in detail and the programming methods that are most efficient in catching errors. Specifically, we will discuss:

❑ Error handling in Visual Basic 6 (VB6)

❑ The general principles behind error handling

❑ The `Try...Catch...Finally` structure, the `Exit Try` statement, and nested `Try` structures

❑ The exception handler's methods and properties

❑ Error handling between managed and unmanaged code, and how VB.NET assists us in that area

❑ Error and trace logging and how we can use these methods to obtain feedback on how our program is working

We'll begin with a quick review of error handling in previous versions of Visual Basic, to use as a reference point. Then we will look at the new ways of handling exceptions in .NET.

A Quick Overview of Error Handling in VB6

Error handling in earlier versions of Visual Basic is descended from syntax first developed in DOS versions of BASIC. The `On Error` construct was created in an era when line labels and `GoTo` statements were commonly used.

As a result, the error handling in VB6 and earlier is difficult to use and has limited functionality compared to the error handling capabilities in more modern languages. VB.NET adds these modern error handling capabilities. One way to understand these new capabilities is to compare them to the older error handling syntax. In VB6, a typical routine with error handling code looks like this:

```
Private Function OpenFile(sFileName As String) As Boolean

On Error GoTo ErrHandler:
Open sFileName For Random As #1
OpenFile = True
Exit Sub

ErrHandler:
Select Case Err.Number
    Case 53 ' File not found
        MessageBox.Show "File not found"
    Case Else
        MessageBox.Show "Other error"
End Select
OpenFile = False

End Function
```

The top of the routine points to a section of code called an *error handler*, which is usually placed at the bottom of the routine. The error handler gets control as soon as an error is detected in the routine, and it looks at the error number to see what to do. The error number is available as a property of the Err object, which is a globally available object that holds error information in VB6.

If the error handler can take care of the error without breaking execution, it can resume execution with the line of code that generated the error (Resume) or the one after that (Resume Next) or at a particular location (Resume {LineLabel}).

This structure becomes more complex if the error handling needs to vary in the routine. Multiple On Error GoTo . . . statements must be used to send errors to various error handlers, like this:

```
Private Function OpenFile(sFileName As String) As Boolean

On Error GoTo ErrHandler1
' Do calculations here
Dim i As Integer
i = Len(sFileName)
Dim j As Integer
j = 100 \ i

On Error GoTo ErrHandler2
Open sFileName For Random As #1
OpenFile = True
Exit Function

ErrHandler1:
Select Case Err.Number
    Case 6 ' Overflow
        MessageBox.Show "Overflow"
    Case Else
        MessageBox.Show "Other error"
End Select
```

```
    OpenFile = False
    Exit Function

ErrHandler2:
Select Case Err.Number
    Case 53 ' File not found
        MessageBox.Show "File not found"
    Case Else
        MessageBox.Show "Other error"
End Select
OpenFile = False

End Function
```

With this type of error handling, it is easy to get confused about what should happen under various conditions. You have to remember to change the error handling pointer as necessary, or errors will be incorrectly processed. There is very little information available about the error during the process, except for the error number. You can't tell, for example, the line number on which the error was generated without single stepping through the code.

This is only one way that the On Error capability could be used in VB6. Detailed error handling techniqes have, in the past, been very much left up to developers, who derived a wide variety of different approaches. This sometimes caused inadequate error handling, and also resulted in multiple, inconsistent ways of coding error handling.

VB.NET still supports these old error handling techniques, but that's really for compatibility with old code. There's a much better way to manage errors in VB.NET called "structured exception handling."

Exceptions in .NET

.NET implements a system-wide, comprehensive approach to error handling. The concept of an error is expanded to the concept of an *exception*, which is an object that contains a set of information relevant to the error. Such an object is an instance of a class that derives from a class named System.Exception.

Properties and Methods of an Exception

The Exception class has properties that contain useful information about the exception.

Property	Description
HelpLink	A string indicating the link to the help for this exception
InnerException	Returns the exception object reference to an inner (nested) exception
Message	A string that contains a description of the error, suitable for display to users
Source	A string containing the name of an object that generated the error
StackTrace	A read-only property that holds the stack trace as a text string
TargetSite	A read-only string property that holds the method that threw the exception

The `Exception` class has the following methods:

Method	Description
Equals	Determines if one exception object is equal to another
GetBaseException	Returns the first exception in the chain
GetHashCode	Similar to a hash table, serves as a hash function
GetObjectData	Used to hold the data in the `Exception` object when serializing it
GetType	Gets the type of the object which caused the exception
ToString	Returns the error string, which might include as much information as the error message, the inner exceptions, and stack trace depending on the error

We will see these properties and methods used in the code examples given later, once we have covered the syntax for detecting and handling exceptions.

How Exceptions Differ from the Err Object in VB6

Because an exception contains all of the information needed about an error, structured exception handling does not use error numbers and the `Err` object. In .NET, errors in code cause an object to be generated. The object is called an *exception*, and it loosely corresponds to the `Err` object in VB6.

However, where there is only one global `Err` object in VB6, there are many types of exception objects in VB.NET. For example, if a divide-by-zero is done in code, then an `OverflowException` is generated. There are several dozen types of exception classes in VB.NET, and in addition to using the ones that are available in the .NET Framework, you can inherit from a class called `ApplicationException` and then create your own exception classes (see Chapter 6 for a discussion of inheritance).

Commonly Used Exception Types

In .NET, all exceptions inherit from `System.Exception`. Special-purpose exception classes can be found in many namespaces. The following table lists some of the most common classes that extend `Exception`.

The `System` namespace holds many of the classes that represent exceptions that happen on a routine basis in our applications. The following table describes some of the exception classes that exist within the `System` namespace and their descriptions:

Having many types of exceptions in VB.NET enables different types of errors to be trapped with different error handlers. This is a major advance over VB6. The syntax to do that is discussed as follows.

Namespace	Class
System	ApplicationException SystemException
System.Data	InvalidConstraintException
System.IO	IOException
System.Runtime.InteropServices	COMException
System.Web.Services.Protocols	SoapException
System.XML	XmlException

Class	Description
ApplicationException	Occurs when a nonfatal application error occurs
ArgumentNullException	Occurs when a Null argument is passed and cannot be accepted as Null
DivideByZeroException	Occurs when a 0 is used as a divisor in an arithmetic routine
MissingFieldException	Occurs in an attempt to access a nonexistent field
MissingMemberException	Indicates a DLL versioning problem
OutofMemoryException	Occurs when there is not enough memory to continue
OverflowException	Occurs in an arithmetic overflow situation
SystemException	Occurs when a recoverable exception occurs
Vb6Exception	Occurs when an exception occurs with a function within the VB6 compatibility library

Structured Exception Handling Keywords in VB.NET

Structured exception handling depends on several new keywords in VB.NET. They are:

❑ *Try*. Begin a section of code in which an error might occur. This section of code is often called a "Try block." In some respects, this would be the equivalent of an On Error statement in VB6, though a Try statement does not indicate where a trapped error should be routed as an On Error statement does. Instead, the trapped error is routed to a Catch statement.

❑ *Catch*. Begin an error handler. Catch comes after a Try block, and it receives control when an error is encountered in the Try block. A Try structure can have more than one Catch block, with each one catching a different type of exception. A Catch statement is analagous to the line label used in a VB6 On Error statement, but the ability to route different types of errors to different Catch statements is a radical improvement over VB6.

❑ *Finally.* Contains code that runs when the Try block finishes normally, or if the Catch block receives control and then finishes. That is, the code in the Finally block always runs, regardless of whether an error was detected. There is no equivalent of a Finally in VB6.

❑ *Throw.* Generate an error. This is similar to Err.Raise in VB6. It's usually done in a Catch block when the error should be kicked back to a calling routine.

The Try, Catch, and Finally Keywords

Here is an example showing some typical simple structured exception handling code in VB.NET. In this case, the most likely source of an error is the iItems argument. If it has a value of zero, this would lead to dividing by zero, which would generate an exception.

```
Private Function GetAverage(iItems As Integer, iTotal As Integer) as Single
    ' Code that might throw an exception is wrapped in a Try block
    Try
        Dim sngAverage As Single

        ' This will cause an exception to be thrown if iItems = 0
        sngAverage = CSng(iTotal \ iItems)

        ' This only executes if the line above generated no error
        MessageBox.Show("Calculation successful")
        Return sngAverage

    Catch excGeneric As Exception
        ' If the calculation failed, we get here
        MessageBox.Show("Calculation unsuccessful - exception caught")
        Return 0
    End Try

End Function
```

In this code, we are trapping all the errors with a single generic exception type, and we don't have any Finally logic. Here is a more complex example that traps the divide-by-zero exception explicitly:

```
Private Function GetAverage(iItems As Integer, iTotal As Integer) as Single
    ' Code that might throw an exception is wrapped in a Try block
    Try
        Dim sngAverage As Single

        ' This will cause an exception to be thrown
        sngAverage = CSng(iTotal \ iItems)

        ' This only executes if the line above generated no error
        MessageBox.Show("Calculation successful")
        Return sngAverage
```

```
Catch excDivideByZero As DivideByZeroException
    ' We'll get here with an DivideByZeroException in the Try block
    MessageBox.Show("Calculation generated DivideByZero Exception")
    Return 0

Catch excGeneric As Exception
    ' We'll get here when any exception is thrown and not caught in
    ' a previous Catch block
    MessageBox.Show("Calculation failed - generic exception caught")
    Return 0
Finally
    ' Code in the Finally block will always run.
    MessageBox.Show("We always get here, with or without an error")
End Try
End Function
```

In this code, there are multiple Catch blocks for different types of exceptions. If an exception is generated, .NET will go down the Catch blocks looking for a matching exception type. That means the Catch blocks should go from specific types first to more generic types later.

You'll understand more about structured exception handling if you see it in action. To do that, you can type in the code in the previous listing and run it. Set a breakpoint early in the code and then step through the code line by line.

The Throw Keyword

Sometimes a Catch block is unable to handle an error. Some exceptions are so unexpected that they should be "sent back up the line" to the calling code, so that the problem can be promoted to code that can decide what to do with it. A Throw statement is used for that purpose.

A Throw statement, like an Err.Raise, ends execution of the error handler — that is, no more code in the Catch block after the Throw statement is executed. However, Throw does not prevent code in the Finally block from running. That code still runs before the error is kicked back to the calling routine.

You can see the Throw statement in action by changing the earlier code to look like this:

```
Private Function GetAverage(iItems As Integer, iTotal as Integer) as Single
    ' Code that might throw an exception is wrapped in a Try block
    Try
        Dim sngAverage As Single

        ' This will cause an exception to be thrown
        sngAverage = CSng(iTotal \ iItems)

        ' This only executes if the line above generated no error
        MessageBox.Show("Calculation successful")
        Return sngAverage

    Catch excDivideByZero As DivideByZeroException
        ' We'll get here with an DivideByZeroException in the Try block
        MessageBox.Show("Calculation generated DivideByZero Exception")
```

```
            Throw excDivideByZero
            MessageBox.Show("More logic after the throw -- never executed")

        Catch excGeneric As Exception
            ' We'll get here when any exception is thrown and not caught in
            ' a previous Catch block
            MessageBox.Show("Calculation failed - generic exception caught")
            Throw excGeneric
        Finally
            ' Code in the Finally block will always run, even if
            ' an exception was thrown in a Catch block
            MessageBox.Show("We always get here, with or without an error")
        End Try
    End Function
```

Here is some typical code to call the aforementioned subroutine. You can place this code in a button's click event to test it out.

```
Try
    Dim sngAvg As Single
    sngAvg = GetAverage(0, 100)
Catch exc As Exception
    MessageBox.Show("Back in the click event after an error")
Finally
    MessageBox.Show("Finally block in click event")
End Try
```

Throwing a New Exception

Throw can also be used with exceptions that are created on the fly. For example, we might like our earlier function to generate an ArgumentException, since we can consider a value of iItems of zero to be an invalid value for that argument.

In such a case, a new exception must be instantiated. The constructor allows us to place our own custom message into the exception. To show how this is done, let's change the aforementioned example to throw our own exception instead of the one caught in the Catch block.

```
Private Function GetAverage(iItems As Integer, iTotal as Integer) as Single
    ' Code that might throw an exception is wrapped in a Try block
    Try
        Dim sngAverage As Single

        ' This will cause an exception to be thrown
        sngAverage = CSng(iTotal \ iItems)

        ' This only executes if the line above generated no error
        MessageBox.Show("Calculation successful")
        Return sngAverage

    Catch excDivideByZero As DivideByZeroException
        ' We'll get here with an DivideByZeroException in the Try block
        MessageBox.Show("Calculation generated DivideByZero Exception")
        Throw excDivideByZero
```

```
            MessageBox.Show("More logic after the thrown - never executed")
        Catch excGeneric As Exception
            ' We'll get here when any exception is thrown and not caught in
            ' a previous Catch block
            Dim excOurOwnException As New _
                ArgumentException("Number of items cannot be zero")

            Throw excOurOwnException
        Finally
            ' Code in the Finally block will always run, even if
            ' an exception was thrown in a Catch block
            MessageBox.Show("We always get here, with or without an error")
        End Try
    End Function
```

This technique is particularly well suited to dealing with errors in property procedures. Property Set procedures often do checking to make sure the property is about to be assigned a valid value. If not, throwing a new `ArgumentException` (instead of assigning the property value) is a good way to inform the calling code about the problem.

The Exit Try Statement

The `Exit Try` statement will, under a given circumstance, break out of the `Try` or `Catch` block and continue at the `Finally` block. In the following example, we are going to exit a `Catch` block if the value of `iItems` is 0 because we know that our error was caused by that problem.

```
    Private Function GetAverage(iItems As Integer, iTotal as Integer) As Single
        ' Code that might throw an exception is wrapped in a Try block
        Try
            Dim sngAverage As Single

            ' This will cause an exception to be thrown
            sngAverage = CSng(iTotal \ iItems)

            ' This only executes if the line above generated no error
            MessageBox.Show("Calculation successful")
            Return sngAverage

        Catch excDivideByZero As DivideByZeroException
            ' We'll get here with an DivideByZeroException in the Try block
            If iItems = 0 Then
                Exit Try
            Else
                MessageBox.Show("Error not caused by iItems")
            End If
            Throw excDivideByZero
            MessageBox.Show("More logic after the thrown - never executed")

        Catch excGeneric As Exception
            ' We'll get here when any exception is thrown and not caught in
            ' a previous Catch block
            MessageBox.Show("Calculation failed - generic exception caught")
```

```
        Throw excGeneric
    Finally
        ' Code in the Finally block will always run, even if
        ' an exception was thrown in a Catch block
        MessageBox.Show("We always get here, with or without an error")
    End Try
End Sub
```

In our first `Catch` block we have inserted an `If` block, so that we can exit the block given a certain condition (in this case that the overflow exception was caused by the value of `intY` being 0). The `Exit Try` goes immediately to the `Finally` block and completes the processing there:

```
If iItems = 0 Then
    Exit Try
Else
    MessageBox.Show("Error not caused by iItems")
End If
```

Now, if the overflow exception is caused by something other than a divide-by-zero, we'll get a message box displaying Error not caused by iItems.

Nested Try Structures

In some cases, particular lines in a `Try` block may need special exception processing. Also, errors can occur within the `Catch` portion of the `Try` structures, and cause further exceptions to be thrown. For both of these scenarios, nested `Try` structures are available. We can alter the example under the section The Throw Keyword to demonstrate the following code:

```
Private Function GetAverage(ByVal iItems As Integer, ByVal iTotal As Integer)_
    As Single
    ' Code that might throw an exception is wrapped in a Try block
    Try
        Dim sngAverage As Single

        ' Do something for performance testing...
        Try
            LogEvent("GetAverage")
        Catch exc As Exception
            MessageBox.Show("Logging function unavailable")
        End Try

        ' This will cause an exception to be thrown
        sngAverage = CSng(iTotal \ iItems)

        ' This only executes if the line above generated no error
        MessageBox.Show("Calculation successful")
        Return sngAverage

    Catch excDivideByZero As DivideByZeroException
        ' We'll get here with an DivideByZeroException in the Try block
        MessageBox.Show("Error not divide by 0")
        Throw excDivideByZero
        MessageBox.Show("More logic after the thrown - never executed")
```

```
Catch excGeneric As Exception
    ' We'll get here when any exception is thrown and not caught in
    ' a previous Catch block
    MessageBox.Show("Calculation failed - generic exception caught")
    Throw excGeneric
Finally
    ' Code in the Finally block will always run, even if
    ' an exception was thrown in a Catch block
    MessageBox.Show("We always get here, with or without an error")
End Try
End Function
```

In this example, we are assuming that a function exists to log an event. This function would typically be in a common library, and might log the event in various ways. We will actually discuss logging of exceptions in detail later in the chapter, but a simple LogEvent function might look like this:

```
Public Function LogEvent(ByVal sEvent As String)
    FileOpen(1, "logfile.txt", OpenMode.Append)
    Print(1, DateTime.Now & "-" & sEvent & vbCrLf)
    FileClose(1)

End Function
```

In this case, we don't want a problem logging an event, such as a "disk full" error, to crash the routine. The code for the GetAverage function puts up a message box to indicate trouble with the logging function.

A Catch block can be empty. In that case, it has a similar effect as On Error Resume Next in VB6. The exception is ignored. However, execution does not pick up with the line after the line that generated the error, but instead picks up with either the Finally block or the line after the End Try if no Finally block exists.

Using Exception Properties

The earlier examples have displayed hard-coded messages into message boxes, and this is obviously not a good technique for production applications. Instead, a message box describing an exception should give as much information as possible concerning the problem. To do this, various properties of the exception can be used.

The most brutal way to get information about an exception is to use the ToString method of the exception. Suppose we modify the earlier example to change the displayed information about the exception like this:

```
Private Function GetAverage(ByVal iItems As Integer, ByVal iTotal As Integer) _
    As Single
    ' Code that might throw an exception is wrapped in a Try block
    Try
        Dim sngAverage As Single

        ' This will cause an exception to be thrown
        sngAverage = CSng(iTotal \ iItems)
        ' This only executes if the line above generated no error
```

```
        MessageBox.Show("Calculation successful")
        Return sngAverage

    Catch excDivideByZero As DivideByZeroException
        ' We'll get here with an DivideByZeroException in the Try block
        MessageBox.Show(excDivideByZero.ToString)
        Throw excDivideByZero
        MessageBox.Show("More logic after the thrown - never executed")

    Catch excGeneric As Exception
        ' We'll get here when any exception is thrown and not caught in
        ' a previous Catch block
        MessageBox.Show("Calculation failed - generic exception caught")
        Throw excGeneric
    Finally
        ' Code in the Finally block will always run, even if
        ' an exception was thrown in a Catch block
        MessageBox.Show("We always get here, with or without an error")
    End Try
End Function
```

When the function is accessed with iItems = 0, a message box similar to the one in Figure 9-1 will be displayed.

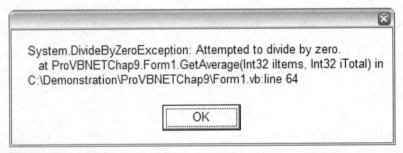

System.DivideByZeroException: Attempted to divide by zero.
   at ProVBNETChap9.Form1.GetAverage(Int32 iItems, Int32 iTotal) in
C:\Demonstration\ProVBNETChap9\Form1.vb:line 64

OK

Figure 9-1

The Message Property

The message in the aforementioned box is helpful to a developer, because it contains a lot of information. But it's not something you would typically want a user to see. Instead, the user normally needs to see a short description of the problem, and that is supplied by the Message property.

If the previous code is changed so that the Message property is used instead of ToString, then the message box will change to look something like Figure 9-2.

The InnerException and TargetSite Properties

The InnerException property is used to store an exception trail. This comes in handy when multiple exceptions occur. It's quite common for an exception to occur that sets up circumstances whereby further exceptions are raised. As exceptions occur in a sequence, we can choose to *stack* our exceptions for later

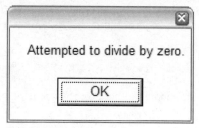

Figure 9-2

reference by use of the `InnerException` property of our `Exception` object. As each exception joins the stack, the previous `Exception` object becomes the inner exception in the stack.

For simplicity, we'll start a new code sample, with just a subroutine that generates its own exception. We'll include code to add a reference to an `InnerException` object to the exception we are generating with the `Throw` method.

Our example will also include a message box to show what's stored in the exception's `TargetSite` property. As we'll see in the results, `TargetSite` will contain the name of the routine generating the exception, in this case `HandlerExample`. Here's the code:

```
Sub HandlerExample()
   Dim intX As Integer
   Dim intY As Integer
   Dim intZ As Integer
   intY = 0
   intX = 5
   ' First Required Error Statement.
   Try
      ' Cause a "Divide by Zero"
      intZ = CType((intX \ intY), Integer)
   ' Catch the error.
   Catch objA As System.DivideByZeroException
      Try
         Throw (New Exception("0 as divisor", objA))
      Catch objB As Exception
         Messagebox.Show(objB.Message)
         Messagebox.Show(objB.InnerException.Message)
         Messagebox.Show(objB.TargetSite.Name)
      End Try
   Catch
      Messagebox.Show("Caught any other errors")
   Finally
      Messagebox.Show(Str(intZ))
   End Try
End Sub
```

As before, we catch the divide-by-zero error in the following statement, which stores our exception in `objA` so that we can reference its properties later.

```
Catch objA As System.DivideException
```

We throw a new exception with a more general message ("0 as divisor") that is easier to interpret and we build up our stack by appending objA as the InnerException object at the end of our New Exception statement:

```
Throw (New Exception("0 as divisor", objA))
```

We catch our newly thrown exception in another Catch statement. Note how it does not catch a specific type of error:

```
Catch objB As Exception
```

Then we display three message boxes:

```
Messagebox.Show(objB.Message)
Messagebox.Show(objB.InnerException.Message)
Messagebox.Show(objB.TargetSite.Name)
```

The message box that is produced by our custom error, which is held in the objB variable, is shown in Figure 9-3.

Figure 9-3

The InnerException property holds the exception object that was generated first. The Message property of the InnerException is shown in Figure 9-4.

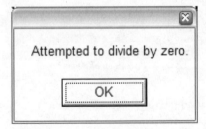

Figure 9-4

As mentioned earlier, the TargetSite property gives us the name of the method that threw our exception. This information comes in handy when troubleshooting and could be integrated into the error message so that the end user could report the method name back to us. Figure 9-5 shows a message box displaying the TargetSite from the previous example.

Figure 9-5

Source and StackTrace

The `Source` and `StackTrace` properties provide the user with information regarding where the error occurred. This supplemental information can be invaluable for the user to pass on to the troubleshooter in order to help get errors resolved more quickly. The following example uses these two properties and shows the feedback when the error occurs.

```
Sub HandlerExample2()
    Dim intX As Integer
    Dim intY As Integer
    Dim intZ As Integer
    intY = 0
    intX = 5
    ' First Required Error Statement.
    Try
        ' Cause a "Divide by Zero"
        intZ = CType((intX \ intY), Integer)
    ' Catch the error.
    Catch objA As System.DivideByZeroException
        objA.Source = "HandlerExample2"
        Messagebox.Show("Error Occurred at :" & _
            objA.Source & objA.StackTrace)
    Finally
        Messagebox.Show(Str(intZ))
    End Try
End Sub
```

The output from our `Messagebox` statement is very detailed and gives the entire path and line number where our error occurred, as shown in Figure 9-6.

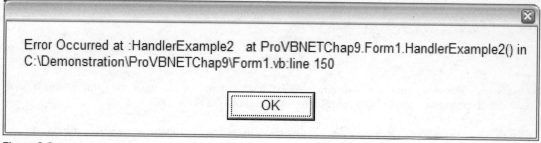

Figure 9-6

Notice that this information was also included in the `ToString` method that was examined earlier (see Figure 9-1).

GetBaseException, GetHashCode, and Equals

The `GetBaseException` method comes in very handy when we are deep in a set of thrown exceptions. This method returns the originating exception, which makes debugging easier and helps keep the troubleshooting process on track by sorting through information that can be misleading.

The `GetHashCode` method allows a programmer to generate a unique number for assignment to an object. An object will always return the same result to the `GetHashCode` method, and so can be used in comparing to see if two reference type objects are the same.

The `Equals` method will evaluate whether one exception is identical to another. Here are examples of each of these methods.

```
Sub HandlerExample3()
   Dim intX As Integer
   Dim intY As Integer
   Dim intZ As Integer
   intY = 0
   intX = 5
   ' First Required Error Statement.
   Try
      ' Cause a "Divide by Zero"
      intZ = CType((intX \ intY), Integer)
   ' Catch the error.
   Catch objA As System.DivideByZeroException
      Try
         Throw (New Exception("0 as divisor", objA))
      Catch objB As Exception
         Messagebox.Show(str(objB.GetHashCode))
      If objA.Equals(objB.InnerException) Then
         Messagebox.Show("Exceptions the same")
      End If
      Try
         Throw (New Exception("New error", objB))
      Catch objC As Exception
         Messagebox.Show(objC.GetBaseException.Message)
      End Try
      End Try
   Finally
      Messagebox.Show(Str(intZ))
   End Try
End Sub
```

In the code where we have used `GetHashCode`, the system generates a hash code and returns it, so that we can display it in a message box similar to the one shown in Figure 9-7.

The hash code generated will vary on different computers and at different instances of the object. Hashcode generation is truly unique for each computer and instance of an object on each computer.

Figure 9-7

We can also evaluate whether objA is the same as the InnerException object of another exception, in this case objB.

```
If objA.Equals(objB.InnerException) Then
   Messagebox.Show("Exceptions the same")
End If
```

The two exception objects are evaluated to be the same, and a message box similar to the one shown in Figure 9-8 will be displayed.

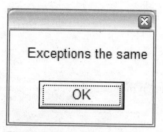

Figure 9-8

The InnerException property provides the information that the GetBaseException method needs, so as our example executes the Throw statements, it sets up the InnerException property. The purpose of the GetBaseException method is to provide the properties of the initial exception in the chain that was produced. Hence, objC.GetBaseException.Message returns the Message property of the original OverflowException message even though we've thrown multiple errors since the original error occurred:

```
Messagebox.Show(objC.GetBaseException.Message)
```

To put it another way, the code traverses back to the exception caught as objA, and displays the same message as the objA.Message property would, as shown in Figure 9-9.

HelpLink

The HelpLink property sets the help link for a specific Exception object to a string. The following example shows the syntax for the HelpLink property:

```
Sub HandlerExample4()
   Dim intX As Integer
   Dim intY As Integer
```

287

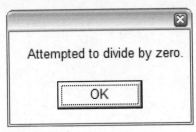

Figure 9-9

```
Dim intZ As Integer
intY = 0
intX = 5
' First Required Error Statement.
Try
    ' Cause a "Divide by Zero"
    intZ = CType((intX / intY), Integer)
' Catch the error.
Catch objA As System.OverflowException
    objA.HelpLink = ("file:///C:/test/help.html")
    Messagebox.Show(objA.HelpLink)
Finally
    Messagebox.Show(Str(intZ))
End Try
End Sub
```

This results in the message box shown in Figure 9-10.

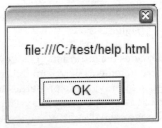

Figure 9-10

Error Logging

Error logging is important in many applications as an alternative way to decipher what exactly is going on when errors occur. It is common for end users of the applications to not remember what the error said exactly and so we can trap specific errors in a log for ease of finding in such situations that we don't want to recreate the error in order to get the specific error message.

While error logging is very important, we only want to use it to trap specific levels of errors, as it carries overhead and can reduce the performance of our application. In general, the overhead it carries is writing the events to the log on a hard disk, which is an extra step in our application that isn't always necessary. The impact to our program will vary, as the hard disk speed varies on each system that the program is running on. We want to only log errors that will be critical to our application integrity, for instance, an error that would cause the data that the application is working with to become invalid.

There are two main approaches to error logging:

❑ Many programmers use a trace-file-based approach, which would write any information in a free-form style to a simple text file located in a strategic location.

❑ We can also take advantage of the event log that is available on NT and Windows 2000 based machines. VB.NET now provides a component that can be used to write and read from the system, application, and security logs on any given machine.

The type of logging you choose depends on the categories of errors you wish to trap and the types of machines you will run your application on. If you choose to write to the event log, you need to categorize the errors and write them in the appropriate log file. Resource-, hardware-, and system-level errors would best fit into the system event log. Data access errors would fit best into the application event log. Permission errors would best fit into the security event log.

> Note that event logs are not available on Windows 98 or Windows ME, even though .NET supports these systems. If you expect to support these operating systems on client machines, you will not be able to use the built-in event log classes shown herein. Logging on these systems will require building your own custom log.

The Event Log

There are three event logs available: the system, application, and security logs.

The event logging operations are available through an event log component that allows a programmer both read and write capabilities with all of the available logs on a machine. The EventLog component is part of the System.Diagnostics namespace and is accessed through adding the namespace as a reference to the VB.NET project. The component is what provides us with functionality such as adding and removing custom event logs, reading and writing from the standard Windows event logs, and creating customized event log entries.

Event logs can get full, as they have a limited amount of space, so we only want to write critical information to our event logs. We can customize each of our system event log's properties by changing the log size and determining how the system will handle events that occur when the log is full. We can configure the log to overwrite when it is full, or overwrite all events older than a given number of days. It is important to remember that the event log that is written to is based on where the code is running from, so that if there are many tiers, we can locate the proper event log information to research the error further.

There are five types of event log entries we can make. These five types are divided into *event type entries* and *audit type entries*.

Event type entries are:

❑ *Information* — added when events such as a service starting or stopping occurs

❑ *Warning* — occurs when a noncritical event occurs that might cause future problems, such as disk space getting low

❑ *Error*—should be logged when something occurs that will prevent normal processing, such as a startup service not being able to start

Audit type entries will usually go into the security log and can be either:

❑ *Success audit*—for example, a success audit might be a successful login through an application to a SQL Server, or

❑ *Failure audit*—a failure audit might come in handy if a user doesn't have access to create an output file on a certain file system

If we don't specify the type of event log entry, an information type entry is generated.

Each entry in an event log has a `Source` property. The `Source` property is required, and is a programmer-defined string that is assigned to an event that helps categorize the events in a log. A new `Source` must be defined prior to being used in an entry in an event log. The `SourceExists` method is used to determine if a particular source already exists on the given computer. We recommend that you use a string that is easily sorted based on where the error originated such as the component name, or a programmer-defined grouping for the source. For instance, packaged software often uses the software name as the Source in the application log. As shown in the screenshot in Figure 9-11, this helps group errors that occur by any given software package.

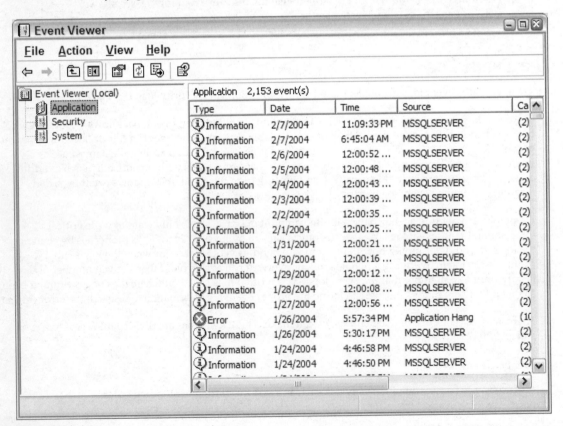

Figure 9-11

The EventLog object model is based on the System.Diagnostics namespace. Therefore, in order to use the EventLog component, you need to include an Imports System.Diagnostics statement in the declarations section of your code.

> **Certain security rights must be obtained in order to manipulate event logs. Ordinary programs can read all of the event logs and write to the application event log. Special privileges, on the administrator level, are required to perform tasks such as clearing and deleting event logs.**

The most common events, methods, and properties are listed and described in the following tables.

Events

Event	Description
EntryWritten	Generated when an event is written to a log

Methods

Methods	Description
CreateEventSource	Creates an event source in the specified log
DeleteEventSource	Deletes an event source and associated entries
WriteEntry	Writes a string to a specified log
Exists	This can be used to determine if a specific event log exists
Methods	Description
SourceExists	Used to determine if a specific source exists in a log
GetEventLogs	Retrieves a list of all event logs on a particular computer
Delete	Deletes an entire event log — *use this method with care*

Properties

Properties	Description
Source	Specifies the source of the entry to be written
Log	Used to specify a log to write to. The three logs are system, application, and security. The system log is the default if not specified

Here is an example that illustrates some of these methods and properties:

```
Sub LoggingExample1()
   Dim objLog As New EventLog()
   Dim objLogEntryType As EventLogEntryType
   Try
      Throw (New EntryPointNotFoundException())
   Catch objA As System.EntryPointNotFoundException
      If Not objLog.SourceExists("Example") Then
         objLog.CreateEventSource("Example", "System")
      End If
      objLog.Source = "Example"
      objLog.Log = "System"
      objLogEntryType = EventLogEntryType.Information
      objLog.WriteEntry("Error: " & objA.Message, objLogEntryType)
   End Try
End Sub
```

We have declared two variables — one to instantiate our log and one to hold our entry's type information. Note that we need to check for the existence of a source prior to creating it. These two lines of code accomplish this.

```
If Not objLog.SourceExists("Example") Then
   objLog.CreateEventSource("Example", "System")
```

Once we have verified or created our source, we can set the `Source` property of the `EventLog` object, set the `Log` property to specify which log we want to write to, and `EventLogEntryType` to `Information` (other choices are `Warning`, `Error`, `SuccessAudit`, and `FailureAudit`). If we attempt to write to a source that does not exist in a specific log, we will get an error. After we have set these three properties of our `EventLog` object, we can then write our entry. In our example, we concatenated the word `Error` with the actual exception's `Message` property to form our string to write to our log:

```
objLog.Source = "Example"
objLog.Log = "System"
objLogEntryType = EventLogEntryType.Information
objLog.WriteEntry("Error: " & objA.Message, objLogEntryType)
```

The following is the copy of the event log that was generated from our example:

Event type:	Information
Event source:	Example
Event category:	None
Event ID:	0
Date:	2/2/2002
Time:	9:42:54 AM
User:	N/A
Computer:	Computer01
Description:	Error: Entry point was not found

Writing to Trace Files

As an alternative for platforms that don't support event logging, or if we can't get direct access to the event log, we can write our debugging and error information to trace files. A *trace file* is a text-based file that we generate in our program to track detailed information about an error condition. Trace files are also a good way to supplement our event logging if we wish to track detailed information that would potentially fill the event log.

A more detailed explanation of the variety of trace tools and uses in debugging follows in *Measuring Performance via the Trace Class*, but we will cover some of the techniques for using the StreamWriter interface in our development of a trace file in this section.

The concepts involved in writing to text files include setting up *streamwriters* and *debug listeners*. The StreamWriter interface is handled through the System.IO namespace and allows us to interface with the files in the file system on a given machine. The Debug class interfaces with these output objects through listener objects. The job of any listener object is to collect, store up, and send the stored output to text files, logs, and the Output window. In our example, we will use the TextWriterTraceListener interface.

As we will see, the StreamWriter object opens an output path to a text file, and by binding the StreamWriter object to a listener object we can direct debug output to a text file.

Trace listeners are output targets and can be a TextWriter, an EventLog, or can send output to the default Output window (which is DefaultTraceListener). The TextWriterTraceListener accommodates the WriteLine method of a Debug interface by providing an output object that stores up information to be flushed to the output stream, which we set up by the StreamWriter interface.

The following table lists some of the commonly used methods from the StreamWriter object:

Method	Description
Close	Closes the StreamWriter
Flush	Flushes all content of the StreamWriter to the output file designated upon creation of the StreamWriter
Write	Writes byte output to the stream. Optional parameters allow designation of where in the stream (offset)
WriteLine	Writes characters followed by a line terminator to the current stream object

The following table lists some of the methods associated with the Debug object, which provides the output mechanism for our text file example to follow.

The following example shows how we can open an existing file (called mytext.txt) for output and assign it to the Listeners object of the Debug object so it can catch our Debug.WriteLine statements.

```
Sub LoggingExample2()
  Dim objWriter As New _
      IO.StreamWriter("C:\mytext.txt", True)
  Debug.Listeners.Add(New TextWriterTraceListener(objWriter))
  Try
```

Method	Description
Assert	Checks a condition and displays a message if `False`
Close	Executes a flush on the output buffer and closes all listeners
Fail	Emits an error message in the form of an Abort/Retry/Ignore message box
Flush	Flushes the output buffer and writes it to the listeners
Write	Writes bytes to the output buffer
WriteLine	Writes characters followed by a line terminator to the output buffer
WriteIf	Writes bytes to the output buffer if a specific condition is `True`
WriteLineIF	Writes characters followed by a line terminator to the output buffer if a specific condition is `True`

```
        Throw (New EntryPointNotFoundException())
    Catch objA As System.EntryPointNotFoundException
        Debug.WriteLine(objA.Message)
        objWriter.Flush()
        objWriter.Close()
        objWriter = Nothing
    End Try
End Sub
```

Looking in detail at this code, we first create a `StreamWriter` that is assigned to a file in our local file system:

```
Dim objWriter As New _
    IO.StreamWriter("C:\mytext.txt", True)
```

We then assign our `StreamWriter` to a debug listener by using the `Add` method:

```
Debug.Listeners.Add(New TextWriterTraceListener (objWriter))
```

In this example, we force an exception and catch it, writing the `Message` property of the `Exception` object (which is `Entry point was not found.`) to the debug buffer through the `WriteLine` method:

```
Debug.WriteLine(objA.Message)
```

We finally flush the listener buffer to the output file and free our resources.

```
objWriter.Flush()
objWriter.Close()
objWriter = Nothing
```

Debugging and Measuring Performance

The .NET Framework has enhanced the capabilities we have to debug and measure the performance of our applications.

The debug capabilities have been expanded not only by the use of the Debug object as we illustrated earlier, but with some system events that we can generate. Debugging our application will always go beyond the development stage, as we can never anticipate everything that users will do with an application.

We discussed and illustrated in the previous logging and trace file examples how we can use the Debug statements in the VS.NET environment to develop output to event logs and files. In this section, we'll expand that capability by coupling it with the use of the Trace class. We can now trace the performance of our application via the use of this class. It is important that an application have the ability to have its performance measured so that we can make improvements as our application environment changes, as it always will over time.

The major difference between what we have seen with using our Debug statements and using tracing techniques is in their respective purpose. The Debug class is primarily used to write information to log files after an error has occurred or in order to be able to track information during program execution about variables. The use of the Trace class and tracing techniques described in this section allows us to see how well a piece of code or an entire application is performing. The two classes have many of the same properties and methods, and both even use listener objects to accomplish output. The biggest difference is that Trace class statements are compiled into release versions of code while Debug statements are not.

The topic of debugging and measuring performance brings up the subject of *instrumentation*. Instrumentation is a widely used term, which simply means that an application has a built-in ability to give the programmer feedback on what's going on within it as it runs. It is important to build these features into our programs, but at the same time, we must consider the overhead of doing the instrumentation constantly. This consideration brings up two points—first, that we must strategically place our instrumentation and second, that we should use conditional compilation statements and trace switches to trigger our instrumentation activity.

Conditional compilation statements have been around for quite a while, and come in quite handy when we want to run code only if certain conditions are met. Basically, a piece of code that is included in a conditional compilation section is surrounded by an #If ... #End If block. If the condition within the #If is met then the code is executed, otherwise it is skipped. There are two ways of setting up conditions to be tested in our #If statements: #Const directives and trace switches:

❑ A #Const directive is simply setting up a constant in the code with a #CONST statement. For instance, if we wanted to test for whether the version of code we had was the English version, we would include a #Const EnglishVersion at the top of our code and then we could use an #If EnglishVersion within our code.

❑ Trace switches are objects we set up in our code that allow us to check a condition and generate our tracing output based on that condition. Our examples in this section will illustrate the use of trace switches and conditional compilation tests further.

Measuring Performance via the Trace Class

The trace tools in the .NET Framework evolve around the `Trace` class, which provides properties and methods that help us trace the execution of our code. By default, tracing is enabled in VB.NET, so not unlike our previous debug discussion, all we have to do is set up the output and utilize its capabilities.

We can specify the detail level we want to perform for our tracing output by configuring trace switches. Trace switches can be either `BooleanSwitch` or `TraceSwitch`. `BooleanSwitch` has a value of either 0 or 1, and is used to determine if tracing is off or on respectively; while `TraceSwitch` allows us to specify a level of tracing based on five enumerated values. We can manage a `BooleanSwitch` or `TraceSwitch` as an environment variable. Once a switch is established, we can create and initialize it in code and use it with either trace or debug.

A `TraceSwitch` can have five enumerated levels that can be read as 0–4 or checked with four properties provided in the switch class interface. The four properties return a Boolean value based on whether the switch is set to a certain level or higher. The five enumerated levels for `TraceSwitch` are as follows:

Level	Description
0	None
1	Only error messages
2	Warning and error messages
3	Information, warning, and error messages
4	Verbose, information, warning, and error messages

The four properties are `TraceError`, `TraceWarning`, `TraceInfo`, and `TraceVerbose`. For example, if our switch was set at number 2 and we asked for the `TraceError` or `TraceWarning` properties, they would return `True`, while the `TraceInformation` and `TraceVerbose` properties would return `False`.

An environment variable is either managed via the command line or under My computer ⇨ Properties ⇨ Advanced within the Environment Variables button.

Within the Environment Variables button, you add a new User variable, giving it the SwitchName and Value for that switch.

From the command line, type

```
Set _Switch_ MySwitch = 0
```

The value on the left of the "=" symbol is the name of the switch, and the value on its right is either 0 or 1 for a `BooleanSwitch` or 0–4 for a `TraceSwitch`. Note that there is a space between the word `Set` and the leading underscore of _Switch. Once you have typed this line, if you follow that by the plain `SET` command at the command line, it will show your new switch as an environment variable, as shown in the sample screen in Figure 9-12.

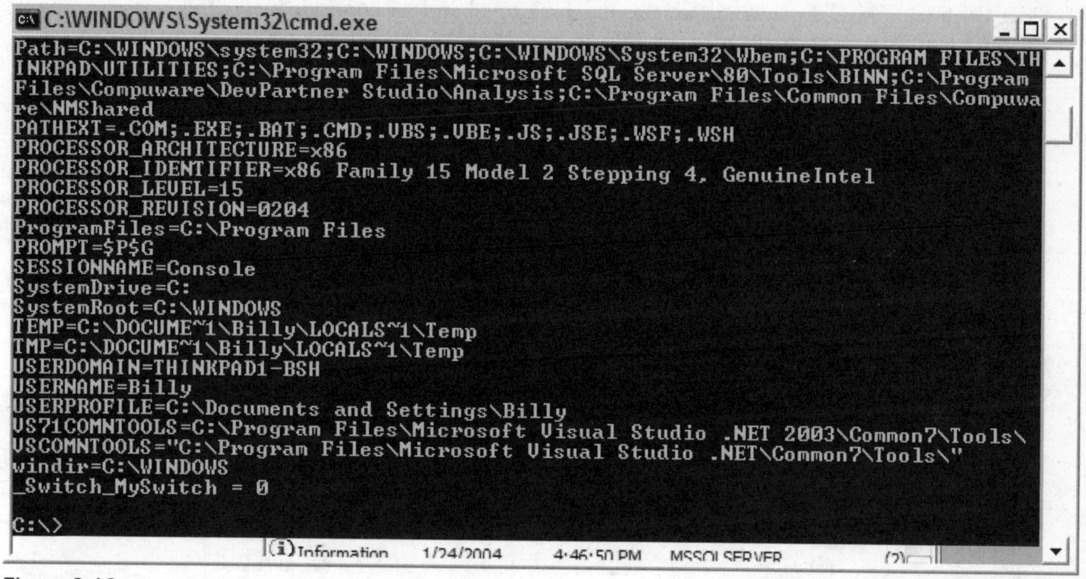

Figure 9-12

For the example that follows, we have the output directed to the default Output window:

```
Sub TraceExample1()
  Dim objTraceSwitch As TraceSwitch
  objTraceSwitch = New TraceSwitch("ExampleSwitch", "Test Trace Switch")
  objTraceSwitch.Level = TraceLevel.Error
  Try
    Throw (New EntryPointNotFoundException())
  Catch objA As System.EntryPointNotFoundException
    Trace.WriteLineIf(objTraceSwitch.TraceVerbose, _
        "First Trace " & objA.Source)
    Trace.WriteLineIf(objTraceSwitch.TraceError, _
        "Second Trace " & objA.Message)
  End Try
End Sub
```

We begin by assigning our switch to an existing registry entry and set its level:

```
objTraceSwitch = New TraceSwitch("ExampleSwitch", "Test Trace Switch")
objTraceSwitch.Level = TraceLevel.Error
```

After we throw our exception, we first cause our trace output listener to catch the Source property of our Exception object based on whether the value of our switch is TraceVerbose or better:

```
Trace.WriteLineIf(objTraceSwitch.TraceVerbose, _
    "First Trace " & objA.Source)
```

Since the tracing level is set to `Error`, this line is skipped and we continue by writing a trace to the Output window to include the message information if the level is set to `Error`:

```
Trace.WriteLineIf(objTraceSwitch.TraceError, _
    "Second Trace " & objA.Message)
```

As we can see in our Output window shown, we successfully wrote only the second trace line based on the level being `Error` on our trace switch, as can be seen in Figure 9-13.

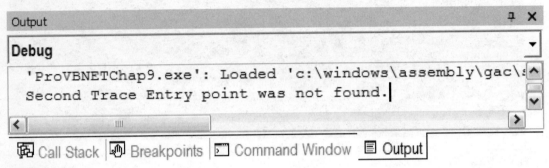

Figure 9-13

The other thing we want the ability to do is to determine the performance of our application. Overall, our application might appear to be working fine, but it is always a good thing to be able to measure the performance of our application so that environment changes or degradation over time can be counteracted. The basic concept here is to use conditional compilation so that we can turn on and off our performance-measuring code:

```
Sub TraceExample2()
    Dim connInfo As New Connection()
    Dim rstInfo As New Recordset()
    #Const bTrace = 1
    Dim objWriter As New _
        IO.StreamWriter(IO.File.Open("c:\mytext.txt", IO.FileMode.OpenOrCreate))
    connInfo.ConnectionString = "Provider = sqloledb.1" & _
        ";Persist Security Info = False;" & "Initial Catalog = Northwind;" & _
        "DataSource = LocalServer"
    connInfo.Open(connInfo.ConnectionString, "sa")
    Trace.Listeners.Add(New TextWriterTraceListener(objWriter))
    #If bTrace Then
        Trace.WriteLine("Begun db query at " & now())
    #End If
    rstInfo.Open("SELECT CompanyName, OrderID, " & _
        "OrderDate FROM Orders AS a LEFT JOIN Customers" & _
        " AS b ON a.CustomerID = b.CustomerID WHERE " & _
        "a.CustomerID = 'Chops'", connInfo, _
        CursorTypeEnum.adOpenForwardOnly, _
        LockTypeEnum.adLockBatchOptimistic)
```

```
   #If bTrace Then
     Trace.WriteLine("Ended db query at " & now())
   #End If
   Trace.Listeners.Clear()
   objWriter.Close()
   rstInfo.Close()
   connInfo.Close()
   rstInfo = Nothing
   connInfo = Nothing
End Sub
```

> This subroutine uses ADO, so be sure to add a reference to an ADO library and an Imports ADODB statement in the declarations section of the module.

In this simple example, we are trying to measure the performance of a database query using a conditional constant defined as bTrace by the following code:

```
#Const bTrace = 1
```

We establish our database connection strings, then right before we execute our query we write to a log file based on whether we are in tracing mode or not:

```
#If bTrace Then
  Trace.WriteLine("Begun db query at " & now())
#End If
```

Again, after our query returns we'll write to our log only if we are in tracing mode:

```
#If bTrace Then
  Trace.WriteLine("Ended db query at" & now())
#End If
```

It is always important to remember that tracing will potentially slow the application down, so we want to use this functionality only when troubleshooting and not let it run all the time.

Summary

As mentioned in Chapter 1, a major weakness of pre-.NET versions of Visual Basic was limited error handling capabilities. As we've seen in this chapter, this problem has been thoroughly addressed. Errors and unexpected conditions are now packaged as *exceptions*, and these exception objects have special syntax to detect and manage them. The Try...Catch...Finally...End Try construct brings VB.NET's error handling capabilities on par with other advanced languages.

In this chapter, we reviewed the exception object and all the syntax that is available to work with exceptions. We've looked at the various properties of exceptions and discussed how to use the exposed information. We've also covered how to promote exceptions to consuming code using the `Throw` statement.

We also covered some other topics related to error handling, such as:

❑   Error logging to event logs and trace files

❑   Instrumentation and measuring performance

❑   Tracing techniques

Using the full capabilities for error handling that are now available in VB.NET can make your applications more reliable and help you diagnose problems faster when they do occur. Proper use of tracing and instrumentation can also help you tune your application for better performance.

10

Using XML in VB.NET

In this chapter we'll look at how we can generate and manipulate *Extensible Markup Language (XML)* using Visual Basic .NET (VB.NET). However, using XML in VB.NET is a vast area to cover (more than possibly could be covered in this chapter). The .NET Framework exposes five XML specific namespaces that contain over a hundred different classes. In addition, there are dozens of other classes that support and implement XML-related technologies, such as ADO.NET, SQL Server, and BizTalk. Consequently, we'll concentrate on the general concepts and the most important classes.

VB.NET relies on the classes exposed in the following XML-related namespaces in order to transform, manipulate, and stream XML documents.

- ❑ `System.Xml` provides core support for a variety of XML standards (including DTD, namespace, DOM, XDR, XPath, XSLT, and SOAP).

- ❑ `System.Xml.Serialization` provides the objects used to transform objects to and from XML documents or streams using serialization.

- ❑ `System.Xml.Schema` provides a set of objects that allow schemas to be loaded, created, and streamed. This support is achieved using a suite of objects that support the in-memory manipulation of the entities that compose an XML schema.

- ❑ `System.Xml.XPath` provides a parser and evaluation engine for the *XML Path Language (XPath)*.

- ❑ `System.Xml.Xsl` provides the objects necessary when working with *Extensible Stylesheet Language (XSL)* and *XSL Transformations (XSLT)*.

The XML-related technologies utilized by VB.NET include other technologies that generate XML documents and allow XML documents to be managed as a data source:

- ❑ *ADO* — The legacy COM objects provided by ADO have the ability to generate XML documents in stream or file form. ADO can also retrieve a previously persisted XML document and manipulate it. (Although ADO will not be used in this chapter, ADO and other legacy COM APIs can be accessed seamlessly from VB.NET.)

❑ *ADO.NET*—This uses XML as its underlying data representation: the in-memory data representation of the ADO.NET `DataSet` object is XML; the results of data queries are represented as XML documents; XML can be imported into a `DataSet` and exported from a `DataSet`. (ADO.NET will be covered in Chapter 11.)

❑ *SQL Server 2000*—XML-specific features were added to SQL Server 2000 (`FOR XML` queries to retrieve XML documents and `OPENXML` in order to represent an XML document as a rowset). VB.NET can use ADO.NET in order to access SQL Server's XML-specific features (the documents generated and consumed by SQL Server can then be manipulated programmatically). Recently, Microsoft also released SQLXML which provides your SQL Server 2000 database with some excellent XML capabilities, such as the ability to query a database using XQuery, get back XML result sets from a database, work with data just as if it was XML, the ability to take huge XML files and have SQLXML convert them to relational data, and much more. SQLXML allows you to do these functions and more via a set of managed .NET classes. You can download SQLXML for free from the Microsoft SQLXML Web site at `http://msdn.micrsoft.com/sqlxml`.

In this chapter, we'll make sense of this range of technologies by introducing some basic XML concepts and demonstrating how VB.NET, in conjunction with the .NET Framework, can make use of XML. Specifically, we will:

❑ Understand the rationale behind XML

❑ Look at the namespaces within the .NET Framework class library that deal with XML and XML-related technologies

❑ Take a closer look at some of the classes contained within these namespaces

❑ Gain an overview of some of the other Microsoft technologies that utilize XML, particularly SQL Server and ADO.NET

At the end of this chapter, you will be able to generate, manipulate, and transform XML using VB.NET.

An Introduction to XML

XML is a tagged markup language similar to HTML. In fact, both XML and HTML are distant cousins and have their roots in the Standard Generalized Markup Language (SGML). This means that XML leverages one of the most useful features of HTML—readability. However, XML differs from HTML in that XML *represents* data while HTML is a mechanism for *displaying* data. The tags in XML *describe* the data, for example

```
<?xml version="1.0" encoding="utf-8"?>
<prescriptions>
  <WXClientPrescription dentistName="Dr. Jam" medicationID="1"
                        quantity="21">
  </WXClientPrescription>
  <WXClientPrescription dentistName="Dr. Jam" medicationID="2"
                        quantity="22">
  </WXClientPrescription>
</prescriptions>
```

This XML document is used to represent a set of medical prescriptions written by a dentist. The standard used to represent a prescription would be useful to dentists, doctors, insurance companies, government-run medical systems, and pharmacies. This information can be shared using XML because:

❑ The data tags in XML are self-describing

❑ XML is an open standard and supported on most platforms today

XML supports the parsing of data by applications not familiar with the contents of the XML document. XML documents can also be associated with a description (a *schema*) that informs an application as to the structure of the data within the XML document.

At this stage, XML looks simple — it's just a human readable way to exchange data in a universally accepted way. The essential points that you should understand about XML are:

❑ XML data can be stored in a plain text file.

❑ A document is said to be *well formed* if it adheres to the XML standard.

❑ Tags are used to specify the contents of a document, for example, `<WXClientPrescription>`.

❑ XML *elements* (also called *nodes*) can be thought of as the objects within a document.

❑ Elements are the basic building blocks of the document. Each element contains a start tag and end tag. A tag can be both a start and an end tag, for example, `<WXClientPrescription/>`. Such a tag is said to be *empty*.

❑ Data can be contained in the element (the element content) or within *attributes* contained in the element.

❑ XML is hierarchical. One document can contain multiple elements, which can themselves contain child elements, and so on. However, an XML document can only have one *root element*.

This last point means that the XML document hierarchy can be thought of as a tree containing nodes:

❑ Our example document has a root node, `<prescriptions>`

❑ The branches of the root node are elements of type `<WXClientPrescription>`

❑ The leaves of the XML element, `<WXClientPrescription>`, are its attributes: `dentistName`, `quantity`, and `medicationID`

Of course, we're interested in the practical use of XML by VB.NET. A practical manipulation of our example XML would be to display for the staff of the dental clinic a particular prescription in some application so that a pharmacy could fill the prescription, and then save the information to a database. In this chapter, we'll look at how we can perform such tasks using the functionality provided by the .NET Framework class library.

XML Serialization

The simplest way to demonstrate VB.NET's support for XML is not with a complicated technology, such as SQL Server or ADO.NET. Instead, we will demonstrate a practical use of XML by serializing a class.

The *serialization* of an object means that it is written out to a stream, such as a file or a socket (this is also known as *dehydrating* an object). The reverse process can also be performed, an object can be deserialized (or rehydrated) by reading it from a stream.

> **The type of serialization we are discussing in this chapter is XML serialization, where XML is used to represent a class in serialized form.**

In order to understand XML serialization, let's examine a class named WXClientPrescription (which can be found in the code download from www.wrox.com). This class is implemented in VB.NET and is used by a dentist in order to write a prescription for medication. This class could be instantiated on a dentist's PDA, laptop, or even mobile phone (so long as the .NET Framework was installed).

An instance of WXClientPrescription corresponding to each prescription could be serialized to XML and sent over a socket using the PDA's cellular modem. (If the dentist's PDA did not have a cellular modem, the instance of WXClientPrescription could be serialized to a file.) The prescription could then be processed when the PDA was dropped into a docking cradle and synced. What we are talking about here is data in a propriety form, an instance of WXClientPrescription being converted into a generic form — XML — that can be universally understood.

The System.Xml.Serialization namespace contains classes and interfaces that support the serialization of objects to XML and the deserialization of objects from XML. Objects are serialized to documents or streams using the XmlSerializer class. Let's look at how we can use XmlSerializer. First, we need to define an object that implements a default constructor, such as WXClientPrescription:

```
Public Class WXClientPrescription

    ' These are Public because we have yet to implement
    ' properties to provide program access

    Public dentistName As String
    Public medicationID As Integer
    Public quantity As Integer

    Public Sub New()
    End Sub

    Public Sub New(ByVal dentistName As String, _
                ByVal medicationID As Integer, _
                ByVal quantity As Integer)
        Me.dentistName = dentistName
        Me.medicationID = medicationID
        Me.quantity = quantity
    End Sub

End Class
```

Then create an instance of XmlSerializer, specifying the object to serialize and its type in the constructor:

```
Dim serialize As XmlSerializer = _
   New XmlSerializer(GetType(WXClientPrescription))
```

Create an instance of the same type as was passed as parameter to the constructor of `XmlSerializer`:

```
Dim prescription As WXClientPrescription = _
   New WXClientPrescription("Dr. Jam", 101, 10)
```

Call the `Serialize` method of the `XmlSerializer` instance and specify the stream to which the serialized object is written (parameter one, `Console.Out`) and the object to be serialized (parameter two, `prescription`):

```
serialize.Serialize(Console.Out, prescription)
Console.Out.WriteLine()
```

The output generated by this code is as follows:

```
<?xml version="1.0" encoding="IBM437"?>
<WXClientPrescription xmlns:xsd="http://www.w3.org/2001/XMLSchema"
                     xmlns:xsi="http://www.w3.org/2001/XMLSchema-instance">
  <dentistName>Dr. Jam</dentistName>
  <medicationID>101</medicationID>
  <quantity>10</quantity>
</WXClientPrescription>
```

This output demonstrates the default way that the `Serialize` method serializes an object:

❏   Each object serialized is represented as an element with the same name as the class, in this case `WXClientPrescription`.

❏   The individual data members of the class serialized are contained in elements named for each data member, in this case `dentistName`, `medicationID`, and `quantity`.

Also generated is:

❏   The specific version of XML generated, in this case `1.0`

❏   The encoding used, in this case `IBM437`

❏   The schemas used to describe our serialized object, in this case `www.w3.org/2001/XMLSchema-instance` and `www.w3.org/2001/XMLSchema`

A schema can be associated with an XML document and describes the data it contains (name, type, scale, precision, length, and so on). Either the actual schema or a reference to where the schema resides can be contained in the XML document. In either case, an XML schema is a standard representation that can be used by all applications that consume XML. This means that applications can use the supplied schema to validate the contents of an XML document generated by the `Serialize` method of `XmlSerializer`.

Our code snippet that demonstrated the `Serialize` method of `XmlSerializer` displayed the XML generated to `Console.Out`. Clearly, we do not expect an application to use `Console.Out` when it would like to access a `WXClientPrescription` object in XML form. The basic idea shown was how serialization can be performed in just two lines of code (one call to a constructor and one call to method). The entire section of code responsible for serializing the instance of `WXClientPrescription` is

```
Try
    Dim serialize As XmlSerializer = _
                New XmlSerializer(GetType(WXClientPrescription))
    Dim prescription As WXClientPrescription = _
            New WXClientPrescription("Dr. Jam", 101, 10)

    serialize.Serialize(Console.Out, prescription)
    Console.Out.WriteLine()
Catch ex As Exception
    Console.Error.WriteLine(ex.ToString())
End Try
```

The Serialize method's first parameter is overridden so that it can serialize XML to a file (the filename is given as type String), a Stream, a TextWriter, or an XmlWriter. When serializing to Stream, TextWriter, or XmlWriter, a third parameter to the Serialize method is permissible. This third parameter is of type XmlSerializerNamespaces and is used to specify a list of namespaces that qualify the names in the XML generated document. The permissible overrides of the Serialize method are

```
Public Sub Serialize(Stream, Object)
Public Sub Serialize(TextWriter, Object)
Public Sub Serialize(XmlWriter, Object)
Public Sub Serialize(Stream, Object, XmlSerializerNamespaces)
Public Sub Serialize(TextWriter, Object, XmlSerializerNamespaces)
Public Sub Serialize(XmlWriter, Object, XmlSerializerNamespaces)
```

An object is reconstituted using the Deserialize method of XmlSerializer. This method is overridden and can deserialize XML presented as a Stream, a TextReader, or an XmlReader. The overloads for Deserialize are

```
Public Function Deserialize(Stream) As Object
Public Function Deserialize(TextReader) As Object
Public Function Deserialize(XmlReader) As Object
```

Before demonstrating the Deserialize method, we will introduce a new class, WXClientMultiPrescription. This class contains an array of prescriptions (an array of WXClientPrescription objects). WXClientMultiPrescription is defined as follows:

```
Public Class WXClientMultiPrescription

    Public prescriptions() As WXClientPrescription

    Public Sub New()
    End Sub

    Public Sub New(ByVal prescriptions() As WXClientPrescription)
        Me.prescriptions = prescriptions
    End Sub
End Class
```

The WXClientMultiPrescription class contains a fairly complicated object, an array of WXClientPrescription objects. The underlying serialization and deserialization of this class is more complicated than that of a single instance of a class that contains several simple types. However, the programming effort involved on our part is just as simple as before. This is one of the great ways in which the .NET Framework makes it easy for us to work with XML data, no matter how it is formed.

The following code demonstrates an object of type WXClientMultiPrescription being deserialized (or rehydrated) from a file, justaddwater.xml. This object is deserialized using this file in conjunction with the Deserialize method of XmlSerializer:

```
' Open file, ..\ justaddwater.xml
Dim dehydrated As FileStream = _
    New FileStream("..\ justaddwater.xml", FileMode.Open)

' Create an XmlSerializer instance to handle deserializing,
' WXClientMultiPrescription
Dim serialize As XmlSerializer = _
            New XmlSerializer(GetType(WXClientMultiPrescription))

' Create an object to contain the deserialized instance of the object
Dim prescriptions As WXClientMultiPrescription = _
        New WXClientMultiPrescription

' Deserialize object
prescriptions = serialize.Deserialize(dehydrated)
```

Once deserialized, the array of prescriptions can be displayed:

```
Dim prescription As WXClientPrescription

For Each prescription In prescriptions.prescriptions
    Console.Out.WriteLine("{0}, {1}, {2}", _
                          prescription.dentistName, _
                          prescription.medicationID, _
                          prescription.quantity)
Next
```

The file, justaddwater.xml, was created using code found in VBNetXML03, which is available in the code download. It is just code that serializes an instance of type, WXClientMultiPrescription. The output generated by displaying our deserialized object containing an array of prescriptions is as follows:

```
Dr. Jam, 1, 11
Dr. Jam, 2, 12
Dr. Jam, 3, 13
Dr. Jam, 4, 14
```

XmlSerializer also implements a CanDeserialize method. The prototype for this method is

```
Public Overridable Function CanDeserialize(ByVal xmlReader As XmlReader) _
    As Boolean
```

If CanDeserialize returns True, then the XML document specified by the xmlReader parameter can be deserialized. If the return value of this method is False, then the specified XML document cannot be deserialized.

The `FromTypes` method of `XmlSerializer` facilitates the creation of arrays that contain `XmlSerializer` objects. This array of `XmlSerializer` objects can be used in turn to process arrays of the type to be serialized. The prototype for `FromTypes` is:

```
Public Shared Function FromTypes(ByVal types() As Type) As XmlSerializer()
```

Before we further explore the `System.Xml.Serialization` namespace, we need to take a moment to consider the various uses of the term "attribute."

Source Code Style Attributes

Thus far we have seen attribute applied to a specific portion of an XML document. Visual Basic has its own flavor of attribute, as does C# and each of the other .NET languages. These attributes refer to annotations to the source code that specify information that can be used by other applications accessing the original code. We will call such attributes *Source Code Style* attributes.

In the context of the `System.Xml.Serialization` namespace, Source Code Style attributes can be used to change the names of the elements generated for the data members of a class or to generate XML attributes instead of XML elements for the data members of a class. In order to demonstrate this we will use a class called `WXPotilasResepti`, which contains data members named `dentistName`, `medicationID`, and `quantity`. It just so happens that the default XML generated when serializing this class is not in a form that can be readily consumed by our external application. For an example of this, let's assume a Finnish development team has written this external application and hence the XML element and attribute names are in Finnish (minus the umlauts) rather than in English.

In order to rename the XML generated for data member, `dentistName`, a Source Code Style attribute will be used. This Source Code Style attribute would specify that when `WXLaClientLaPrescription` is serialized, the `dentistName` data member would be represented as an XML element, `<HammaslaakariNimi>`. The actual Source Code Style attribute that specifies this is

```
<XmlElementAttribute("HammaslaakariNimi")> Public dentistName As String
```

`WXPotilasResepti` also contains other Source Code Style attributes:

❑   `<XmlAttributeAttribute("LaakitysID")>` — specifies that `medicationID` is to be serialized as an XML attribute named `LaakitysID`.

❑   `<XmlAttributeAttribute("Maara")>` — specifies that `quantity` is to be serialized as an XML attribute named `Maara`.

`WXPotilasResepti` is defined as follows:

```
Public Class WXPotilasResepti

    ' These are Public because we have yet to implement
    ' properties to provide program access
    <XmlElementAttribute("HammaslaakariNimi")> Public dentistName As String
    <XmlAttributeAttribute("LaakitysID")> _
```

```
          Public medicationID As Integer
      <XmlAttributeAttribute("Maara")> Public quantity As Integer

      Public Sub New()
      End Sub

      Public Sub New(ByVal dentistName As String, _
                   ByVal medicationID As Integer, _
                   ByVal quantity As Integer)
          Me.dentistName = dentistName
          Me.medicationID = medicationID
          Me.quantity = quantity
      End Sub
  End Class
```

WXPotilasResepti can be serialized as follows:

```
Dim serialize As XmlSerializer = _
    New XmlSerializer(GetType(WXPotilasResepti))
Dim prescription As WXPotilasResepti = _
    New WXPotilasResepti("Dr. Jam", 101, 10)

serialize.Serialize(Console.Out, prescription)
```

The output generated by this code reflects the Source Code Style attributes associated with class WXPotilasResepti:

```
<?xml version="1.0" encoding="IBM437"?>
<WXPotilasResepti xmlns:xsd="http://www.w3.org/2001/XMLSchema"
                  xmlns:xsi="http://www.w3.org/2001/XMLSchema-instance"
                  LaakitysID="101" Maara="10">
  <HammaslaakariNimi>Dr. Jam</HammaslaakariNimi>
</WXPotilasResepti>
```

The value of medicationID is contained in an XML attribute, LaakitysID, and the value of quantity is contained in an XML attribute, Maara. The value of dentistName is contained in an XML element, HammaslaakariNimi.

Our example has only demonstrated the Source Code Style attributes exposed by the XmlAttributeAttribute and XmlElementAttribute classes in the System.Xml .Serialization namespace. A variety of other Source Code Style attributes exist in this namespace that also control the form of XML generated by serialization. The classes associated with such Source Code Style attributes include XmlTypeAttribute, XmlTextAttribute, XmlRootAttribute, XmlIncludeAttribute, XmlIgnoreAttribute, and XmlEnumAttribute.

System.Xml Document Support

The System.Xml namespace implements a variety of objects that support standards-based XML processing. The XML-specific standards facilitated by this namespace include XML 1.0, Document Type Definition (DTD) Support, XML namespaces, XML schemas, XPath, XSL/T, DOM Level 1 and DOM Level 2 (Core implementations), as well as SOAP 1.1, SOAP Contract Language, and SOAP Discovery.

The `System.Xml` namespace exposes over 30 separate classes in order to facilitate this level of XML standard's compliance.

With respect to generating and navigating XML documents, there are two styles of access:

❑ *Stream-based* — `System.Xml` exposes a variety of classes that read XML from and write XML to a stream. This approach tends to be a fast way to consume or generate an XML document because it represents a set of serial reads or writes. The limitation of this approach is that it does not view the XML data as a document composed of tangible entities, such as nodes, elements, and attributes. An example of where a stream could be used would be when receiving XML documents from a socket or a file.

❑ *Document Object Model (DOM)-based* — `System.Xml` exposes a set of objects that access XML documents as data. The data is accessed using entities from the XML document tree (nodes, elements, and attributes). This style of XML generation and navigation is flexible but may not yield the same performance as stream-based XML generation and navigation. DOM is an excellent technology for editing and manipulating documents. For example, the functionality exposed by DOM might make merging your checking, savings, and brokerage accounts simpler.

XML Stream-Style Parsers

When demonstrating XML serialization we alluded to XML stream-style parsers. After all, when an instance of an object was serialized to XML it had to be written to a stream, and when deserialized it was read from a stream. When an XML document is parsed using a stream parser, the parser always points to the current node in the document. The basic architecture of stream parsers is shown in Figure 10-1.

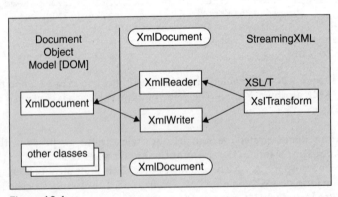

Figure 10-1

The classes that access a stream of XML (read XML) and generate a stream of XML (write XML) are contained in the `System.Xml` namespace and are as follows:

❑ `XmlWriter` — This abstract class specifies a noncached, forward-only stream that writes an XML document (data and schema).

❑ `XmlReader` — This abstract class specifies a noncached, forward-only stream that reads an XML document (data and schema).

Our diagram of the classes associated with the XML stream-style parser referred to one other class, `XslTransform`. This class is found in the `System.Xml.Xsl` namespace and is not an XML stream-style parser. Rather, it is used in conjunction with `XmlWriter` and `XmlReader`. This class will be reviewed in detail later.

The `System.Xml` namespace exposes a plethora of additional XML manipulation classes in addition to those shown in the architecture diagram. The classes shown in the diagram include:

❑ `XmlResolver` — This abstract class resolves an external XML resource using a Uniform Resource Identifier (URI). `XmlUrlResolver` is an implementation of an `XmlResolver`.

❑ `XmlNameTable` — This abstract class provides a fast means by which an XML parser can access element or attribute names.

Writing an XML Stream

An XML document can be created programmatically in .NET. One way to perform this task is by writing the individual components of an XML document (schema, attributes, elements, and so on) to an XML stream. Using a unidirectional write-stream means that each element and its attributes must be written in order — the idea is that data is always written at the head of the stream. In order to accomplish this we would use a writable XML stream class (a class derived from `XmlWriter`). Such a class ensures that the XML document we generate correctly implements the W3C *Extensible Markup Language (XML) 1.0* specification and the *Namespaces in XML* specification.

But why would this be necessary since we have XML serialization? We need to be very careful here to separate interface from implementation. XML serialization worked for a specific class, `WXPotilasResepti`. The class is a proprietary implementation and not the format in which data is exchanged. For this one specific case the XML document generated when `WXPotilasResepti` is serialized just so happens to be the XML format used when generating a prescription. `WXPotilasResepti` was given a little help from Source Code Style attributes in order to conform to a standard XML representation of a prescription.

In a different application, if the software used to manage the entire dental practice wants to generate prescriptions, it will have to generate a document of the appropriate form. Our dental practice management software will achieve this by using an XML stream writer, `XmlTextWriter`. This class is derived from our XML stream writing class, `XmlWriter`, as follows:

```
Object
    XmlWriter
        XmlTextWriter
```

Before reviewing the subtleties of `XmlTextWriter`, it is important to note that this class exposes over 40 methods and properties. The example presented in this section will provide an overview that touches on a subset of these methods and properties. This subset will allow an XML document that corresponds to a medical prescription to be generated.

The code that generates an XML document corresponding to a medical prescription is found in application `VBNetXML02`, which is included in the code download from the Wrox Web site. Ultimately, our instance of `XmlTextWriter`, `prescriptionTextWriter`, is a file on a disk. This means that the

XML document generated is streamed to this file. Since the `prescriptionTextWriter` variable represents a file it must be:

- ❑ Created — the instance of `XmlTextWriter prescriptionTextWriter` is created using the keyword `New`

- ❑ Opened — the file the XML is streamed to, `PrescriptionsProgrammatic.xml`, is opened by passing the filename to the constructor associated with `XmlTextWriter`

- ❑ Generated — the process of generating the XML document is described in detail at the end of this section

- ❑ Closed — the file (the XML stream) is closed using the `Close` method of `XmlTextWriter`

The basic infrastructure for managing the file (the XML text stream) is as follows:

```
Dim prescriptionTextWriter As XmlTextWriter = Nothing

prescriptionTextWriter = _
    New XmlTextWriter("..\ PrescriptionsProgrammatic.XML", Nothing)

prescriptionTextWriter.Close()
```

Before writing the actual elements and attributes of our XML document, certain properties of `XmlTextWriter` will be specified in order to make our document esthetically pleasing. Specifically, we will set the `Formatting` property to `Formatting.Indent`. This setting allows child elements of the XML document to be indented. We will also set `IndentChar` to the space character and the value of property `Indentation` to 4. These settings mean that the character used in child element indentation is the space character and the number of spaces indented is four. The code responsible for configuring our XML text stream in this manner is as follows:

```
prescriptionTextWriter.Formatting = Formatting.Indented
prescriptionTextWriter.Indentation = 4
prescriptionTextWriter.IndentChar = " "
```

With the preliminaries completed (file created and formatting configured), the process of writing the actual attributes and elements of our XML document can begin. The sequences of steps used to generate our XML document is as follows:

- ❑ Call the `WriteStartDocument` method in order to write the XML declaration and specify version 1.0. The XML generated by this method is

```
<?xml version="1.0" standalone="no" ?>
```

- ❑ Write an XML comment using the `WriteComment` method. This comment describes from whence the concept for this XML document originated and generates the following code:

```
<!-- Same as generated by serializing, WXClientPrescription -->
```

- ❑ Begin writing the XML element, `<WXPotilasResepti>`, by calling the `WriteStartElement` method. We can only begin writing this element because its attributes and child elements must be written before the element can be ended with a corresponding </WXPotilasResepti>. The XML generated by the `WriteStartElement` method is

```
<WXPotilasResepti
```

❑ Write the attributes associated with `<WXPotilasResepti>` by calling the `WriteAttributeString` method twice. The XML generated by calling the `WriteAttributeString` method twice adds to our `WXPotilasResepti` XML element that is currently being written to

```
<WXPotilasResepti LaakitysID="101" Maara="10"
```

❑ Using the `WriteElementString` method, write the child XML element `<HammaslaakariNimi>` contained in the XML element, `<WXPotilasResepti>`. The XML generated by calling this method is

```
<HammaslaakariNimi>Dr. Jam</HammaslaakariNimi>
```

❑ Complete writing the `<WXPotilasResepti>` parent XML element by calling the `WriteEndElement` method. The XML generated by calling this method is

```
</WXPotilasResepti>
```

Let's put all this together:

```
Dim prescriptionTextWriter As XmlTextWriter = Nothing

prescriptionTextWriter = _
    New XmlTextWriter("..\ PrescriptionsProgrammatic.XML", Nothing)

With prescriptionTextWriter
  .Formatting = Formatting.Indented
  .Indentation = 4
  .IndentChar = " "
  .WriteStartDocument(False)
  .WriteComment( _
      " Same as generated by serializing, WXPotilasResepti ")
  .WriteStartElement("WXPotilasResepti")
  .WriteAttributeString("LaakitysID", "101")
  .WriteAttributeString("Maara", "10")
  .WriteElementString("HammaslaakariNimi", "Dr. Jam")
  .WriteEndElement() ' End WXPotilasResepti

  .Close()
End With
```

The XML document generated is persisted to a filename `PrescriptionsProgrammatic.XML`. The content of this file is as follows:

```
<?xml version="1.0" standalone="no" ?>
<!-- Same as generated by serializing, WXLaClientLaPrescription -->
```

```
<WXPotilasResepti LaakitysID="101" Maara="10">
    <HammaslaakariNimi>Dr. Jam</HammaslaakariNimi>
</WXPotilasResepti>
```

The previous XML document is the same in form as the XML document generated by serializing the WXPotilasResepti class. Notice how in the previous XML document the <HammaslaakariNimi> element is indented four characters. This was achieved using the Formatting, Indentation, and IndentChar properties of the XmlTextWriter class.

Our sample application, VBNetXML02, covered only a quarter of the methods and properties exposed by the XML stream writing class, XmlTextWriter. Other methods implemented by this class include methods that manipulate the underlying file, such as the Flush method, and methods that allow XML text to be written directly to the stream, such as the WriteRaw method.

The XmlTextWriter class also exposes a variety of methods that write a specific type of XML data to the stream. These methods include WriteBinHex, WriteCData, WriteString, and WriteWhiteSpace.

We can now generate the same XML document in two different ways. We have used two different applications that took two different approaches to generating a document that represents a standardized medical prescription. However, there are even more ways to generated XML depending on circumstance. For example, we could receive a prescription from a patient's doctor and this prescription would have to be transformed from the XML format used by the doctor's office to our own prescription format.

Reading an XML Stream

In .NET, XML documents can be read from a stream. The way a readable stream works is that data is traversed in the stream in order (first XML element, second XML element, and so on). This traversal is very quick because the data is processed in one direction and features, such as write and move backwards in the traversal, are not supported. At any given instance, only data at the current position in the stream can be accessed.

Before exploring how an XML stream can be read, we need to understand why it should be read in the first place. To answer this question, let's return to our dental office. Imagine that the application that manages the dental practice can generate a variety of XML documents corresponding to prescriptions, appointments, and laboratory work, such as the making of crowns and dentures. All the documents (prescription, appointment, and laboratory work) can be extracted in stream form and processed by a report-generating application. This application prints up the schedule of appointments for a given day, the prescriptions that are outstanding for the scheduled patients, and the laboratory work required to treat the patients scheduled. The report generating application processes the data by reading in and parsing a stream of XML.

One class that can be used to read and parse such an XML stream is XmlTextReader. This class is derived from XmlReader. An XmlTextReader can read XML from a file (specified by a string corresponding to the file's name), a Stream, or an XmlReader. For demonstration purposes, we will use an XmlTextReader to read an XML document contained in a file. The application that will demonstrate this is VBNetXML01 (again, contained in the code download). Reading XML from a file and writing it to a file is not the norm when it comes to XML processing but a file is the simplest way to access XML data. This simplified access allows us to focus more on XML-specific issues.

The first step in accessing a stream of XML data is to create an instance of the object that will open the stream (the `readOfficeInfo` variable of type `XmlTextReader`) and then to open the stream itself. Our application performs this as follows (where `DentalManage.xml` is the name of the file containing the XML document):

```
Dim readOfficeInfo As XmlTextReader

readOfficeInfo = New XmlTextReader("..\ DentalManage.xml")
```

The basic mechanism for traversing each stream is to traverse from node to node using the `Read` method. Node types in XML include *element* and *white space*. Numerous other node types are defined, but for the sake of our example we will focus on traversing XML elements and the white space that is used to make the elements more readable (carriage returns, linefeeds, and indentation spaces). Once the stream is positioned at a node, the `MoveToNextAttribute` method can be called to read each attribute contained in an element. The `MoveToNextAttribute` method will only traverse attributes for nodes that contain attributes (nodes of type element). An example of an `XmlTextReader` traversing each node and then traversing the attributes of each node is as follows:

```
While readOfficeInfo.Read()
  ' Process node here
  While readOfficeInfo.MoveToNextAttribute()
  ' Process attribute here
  End While
End While
```

This code, which reads the contents of the XML stream, does not utilize any knowledge of the stream's contents. However, a great many applications know exactly how the stream they are going to traverse is structured. Such applications can use `XmlReadText` in a more deliberate manner and not simply traverse the stream without foreknowledge.

Once our example stream has been read, it can be closed using the `Close` method:

```
readOfficeInfo.Close()
```

The code that traverses an XML document is found in a subroutine named `WXReadXML`. This subroutine takes the filename containing the XML to read as a parameter. The code for subroutine is as follows and is basically the code we just outlined:

```
Private Sub WXReadXML(ByVal fileName As String)
  Dim readOfficeInfo As XmlTextReader

  readOfficeInfo = New XmlTextReader(fileName)
  While readOfficeInfo.Read()
    WXShowXMLNode(readOfficeInfo)
    While readOfficeInfo.MoveToNextAttribute()
      WXShowXMLNode(readOfficeInfo)
    End While
  End While
  readOfficeInfo.Close()
End Sub
```

For each node encountered after a call to the Read method, WXReadXML calls the WXShowXMLNode subroutine. Similarly for each attribute traversed, the WXShowXMLNode subroutine is called. This subroutine breaks down each node into its subentities.

❏ Depth — The Depth property of XmlTextReader determines the level at which a node resides in the XML document tree. To understand depth, consider the following XML document composed solely of elements: \<A\>\<B\>\</B\>\<C\>\<D\>\</D\>\</C\>\</A\>. Element \<A\> is the root element and when parsed would return a Depth of 0. Elements \<B\> and \<C\> are contained in \<A\> and are hence a Depth value of 1. Element \<D\> is contained in \<C\>. The Depth property value associated with \<D\> (depth of 2) should therefore be one more than the Depth property associated with \<C\> (depth of 1).

❏ Type — The type of each node is determined using the NodeType property of XmlTextReader. The node returned is of enumeration type, XmlNodeType. Permissible node types include Attribute, Element, and Whitespace. (Numerous other node types can also be returned including CDATA, Comment, Document, Entity, and DocumentType.)

❏ Name — The type of each node is retrieved using the Name property of XmlTextReader. The name of the node could be an element name, such as \<WXPotilasResepti\>, or an attribute name, such as LaakitysID.

❏ Attribute Count — The number of attributes associated with a node is retrieved using the AttributeCount property of XmlTextReader's NodeType.

❏ Value — The value of a node is retrieved using the Value property of XmlTextReader. For example, the element node \<HammaslaakariNimi\> contains a value of Dr. Jam.

Subroutine WXShowXMLNode is implemented as follows:

```
Private Sub WXShowXMLNode(ByVal reader As XmlReader)

    If reader.Depth > 0 Then
        For depthCount As Integer = 1 To reader.Depth
            Console.Write(" ")
        Next
    End If

    If reader.NodeType = XmlNodeType.Whitespace Then
        Console.Out.WriteLine("Type: {0} ", reader.NodeType)
    ElseIf reader.NodeType = XmlNodeType.Text Then
        Console.Out.WriteLine("Type: {0}, Value: {1} ", _
                        reader.NodeType, _
                        reader.Value)
    Else
        Console.Out.WriteLine("Name: {0}, Type: {1}, " & _
                        "AttributeCount: {2}, Value: {3} ", _
                        reader.Name, _
                        reader.NodeType, _
                        reader.AttributeCount, _
                        reader.Value)
    End If
End Sub
```

Within the `WXShowXMLNode` subroutine, each level of node depth adds two spaces to the output generated:

```
If reader.Depth > 0 Then
  For depthCount As Integer = 1 To reader.Depth
    Console.Write(" ")
  Next
End If
```

We add these spaces in order to make the output generated human-readable (so we can easily determine the depth of each node displayed). For each type of node, `WXShowXMLNode` displays the value of the `NodeType` property. The `WXShowXMLNode` subroutine makes a distinction between nodes of type `Whitespace` and other types of nodes. The reason for this is simple: a node of type `Whitespace` does not contain a name or attribute count. The value of such a node is any combination of white-space characters (space, tab, carriage return, and so on). Therefore, it does not make sense to display the properties if the `NodeType` is `XmlNodeType.WhiteSpace`. Nodes of type `Text` have no name associated with them and so for this type, subroutine `WXShowXMLNode` only displays the properties, `NodeType` and `Value`. For all other node types, the `Name`, `AttributeCount`, `Value`, and `NodeType` properties are displayed.

A portion of the output generated is as follows:

```
Name: DentalManageDump, Type: Element, AttributeCount: 0, Value:
  Type: Whitespace
  Name: WXClientMultiPrescription, Type: Element, AttributeCount: 0, Value:
    Type: Whitespace
    Name: prescriptions, Type: Element, AttributeCount: 0, Value:
     Type: Whitespace
```

This example managed to use three methods and five properties of `XmlTextReader`. The output generated was informative but far from practical. `XmlTextReader` exposes over 50 methods and properties, which means that we have only scratched the surface of this highly versatile class. The remainder of this section will introduce a more realistic use of `XmlTextReader` and demonstrate how the classes of `System.Xml` handle errors.

Traversing XML Using XmlTextReader

An application can easily use `XmlTextReader` in order to traverse a document that is received in a known format. The document could thus be traversed in a deliberate manner. Recall we implemented a class that serialized arrays of prescriptions. Our next example will take an XML document containing multiple XML documents of that type and traverse them. Each prescription will be forwarded to the pharmacy by sending a fax. The document will be traversed as follows:

```
Read root element: <DentalManageDump>
    Process each <WXClientMultiPrescription> element
        Read <prescriptions> element
            Process each <WXClientPrescription>
                Send fax for each prescription here
```

The basic outline for our program's implementation is to open a file containing the XML document to parse and to traverse from element to element within this document.

```
Dim readOfficeInfo As XmlTextReader
Dim drName, medication, quantity As String

readOfficeInfo = New XmlTextReader(fileName)
readOfficeInfo.Read()
readOfficeInfo.ReadStartElement("DentalManageDump")
Do While (True)
    '*******************************************************
    ' * Process WXClientMultiPrescription elements here *
    '*******************************************************
Loop
readOfficeInfo.ReadEndElement() ' </DentalManageDump>
readOfficeInfo.Close()
```

The previous code opened the file using the constructor of XmlTextReader and closed the file using the Close method of this class. The previous code also introduced two methods of the XmlTextReader class:

❑ ReadStartElement(String) — verifies that the current in the stream is an element and that the element's name matches the string passed to method, ReadStartElement. If the verification is successful, the stream is advanced to the next element.

❑ ReadEndElement() — verifies that the current element is an end tab and if the verification is successful the stream is advanced to the next element.

The application knows that an element, <DentalManageDump>, will be found at a specific point in the document. The ReadStartElement method verifies this foreknowledge of the document format. Once all the elements contained in element <DentalManageDump> have been traversed, the stream should point to the end tag </DentalManageDump>. The ReadEndElement method verifies this.

The code that traverses each element of type <WXClientMultiPrescription> similarly uses the ReadStartElement and ReadEndElement methods to indicate the start and end of the <WXClientMultiPrescription> and <prescriptions> elements. The code that ultimately parses the list of prescription and faxes the pharmacy (using the WXFranticallyFaxThePharmacy subroutine) is as follows:

```
Dim readOfficeInfo As XmlTextReader
Dim drName, medication, quantity As String

readOfficeInfo = New XmlTextReader(fileName)
readOfficeInfo.Read()
readOfficeInfo.ReadStartElement("DentalManageDump")
Do While (True)
    readOfficeInfo.ReadStartElement("WXClientMultiPrescription")
    readOfficeInfo.ReadStartElement("prescriptions")
    Do While (True)
        readOfficeInfo.ReadStartElement("WXClientPrescription")
        drName = readOfficeInfo.ReadElementString()
        medication = readOfficeInfo.ReadElementString()
        quantity = readOfficeInfo.ReadElementString()
        readOfficeInfo.ReadEndElement() ' clear </WXClientPrescription>
        WXFranticallyFaxThePharmacy(drName, medication, quantity)
        ' Should read next WXClientPrescription node
```

```
            ' else we quit
            readOfficeInfo.Read()
            If ("WXClientPrescription" <> readOfficeInfo.Name) Then
                Exit Do
            End If
        Loop

        readOfficeInfo.ReadEndElement() ' clear </prescriptions>
        readOfficeInfo.ReadEndElement() ' clear </WXClientMultiPrescription>
        ' Should read next WXClientMultiPrescription node
        ' else we quit
        readOfficeInfo.Read() ' clear </DentalManageDump>
        If ("WXClientMultiPrescription" <> readOfficeInfo.Name) Then
            Exit Do
        End If
    Loop
    readOfficeInfo.ReadEndElement() ' </DentalManageDump>
    readOfficeInfo.Close()
```

Three lines within the previous code contain a call to the `ReadElementString` method:

```
drName = readOfficeInfo.ReadElementString()
medication = readOfficeInfo.ReadElementString()
quantity = readOfficeInfo.ReadElementString()
```

While parsing the stream, it was known that an element named `<dentistName>` existed and that this element contained the name of the dentist. Rather than parsing the start tag, getting the value, and parsing the end tag, it was easier just to get the data using the `ReadElementString` method. This method retrieves the data string associated with an element and advances the stream to the next element. The `ReadElementString` method was also used to retrieve the data associated with the XML elements `<medicationID>` and `<quantity>`.

The output of this example was a fax, which we won't show as the emphasis of this example was to show that it is simpler to traverse a document when its form is known. The format of the document is still verified by `XmlTextReader` as it is parsed.

The `XmlTextReader` class also exposes properties that give more insight into the data contained in the XML document and the state of parsing: `IsEmptyElement`, `EOF`, and `IsStartElement`. This class also allows data in a variety of forms to be retrieved using methods such as `ReadBase64`, `ReadHex`, and `ReadChars`. The raw XML associated with the document can also be retrieved using `ReadInnerXml` and `ReadOuterXml`. Once again, we have only scratched the surface of the `XmlTextReader` class. You will find this class to be quite rich in functionality.

Handling Exceptions

XML is text and could easily be read using mundane methods such as `Read` and `ReadLine`. A key feature of each class that reads and traverses XML is inherent support for error detection and handling. To demonstrate this, consider the following malformed XML document found in the file named `malformed.XML`:

```
<?xml version="1.0" encoding="IBM437" ?>
<WXPotilasResepti LaakitysID="101", Maara="10">
    <HammaslaakariNimi>Dr. Jam</HammaslaakariNimi>
<WXPotilasResepti>
```

This document may not immediately appear to be malformed. By wrapping a call to the method we developed (WXReadXML) we can see what type of exception is raised when XmlTextReader detects the malformed XML within this document:

```
Try
    WXReadXML("..\ Malformed.xml")
Catch xmlEx As XmlException
    Console.Error.WriteLine("XML Error: " + xmlEx.ToString())
Catch ex As Exception
    Console.Error.WriteLine("Some other error: " + ex.ToString())
End Try
```

The methods and properties exposed by the XmlTextReader class raise exceptions of type System.Xml.XmlException. In fact, every class in the System.Xml namespace raises exceptions of type XmlException. Although this is a discussion of errors using an instance of type XmlTextReader, the concepts reviewed apply to all errors generated by classes found in the System.Xml namespace.

The properties exposed by XmlException include:

❑ LineNumber — the number of the line within an XML document where the error occurred.

❑ LinePosition — the position within the line specified by LineNumber where the error occurred.

❑ Message — the error message that corresponds to the error that occurred. This error took place at the line in the XML document specified by LineNumber and within the line at the position specified by LinePostion

The error displayed when subroutine WXReadXML processes malformed.xml is as follows:

```
XML Error: System.Xml.XmlException: The ',' character, hexadecimal value 0x2C,
    cannot begin a name. Line 2, position 49.
```

Looking closely at our document there is a comma separating the attributes in element, <WXPotilasResepti> (LaakitysID="101", Maara="10"). This comma is invalid. Removing the comma and running the code again gives the following output:

```
XML Error: System.Xml.XmlException: This is an unexpected token. Expected
    'EndElement'. Line 5, position 27.
```

Once again, we can recognize the precise error. In this case, we do not have an end element, </WXPotilasResepti>, but we do have an opening element, <WXPotilasResepti>.

The properties provided by the XmlException class (LineNumer, LinePosition, and Message) provide a useful level of precision when tracking down errors. The XmlTextReader class also exposes a level of precision with respect to the parsing of the XML document. This precision is exposed by the XmlTextReader through properties such as LineNumber and LinePosition.

Using the MemoryStream Object

A very useful class that can greatly help us when working with XML is System.IO.MemoryStream. Rather than needing a network or disk resource backing the stream (as in System.Net.Sockets.NetworkStream and System.IO.FileStream), MemoryStream backs itself onto a block of memory. Imagine we want to generate an XML document and e-mail it. The built-in classes for sending e-mail rely on having a `System.String` containing a block of text for the message body. But, if we want to generate an XML document, we need a stream.

If the document is reasonably sized, we should write the document directly to memory and copy that block of memory to the e-mail. This is good from a performance and reliability perspective because we don't have to open a file, write it, rewind it, and read the data back in again. However, you must consider scalability in this situation because if the file is very large, or you have a great number of smaller files, you could run out of memory (in which case you'll have to go the "file" route).

In this section, we'll demonstrate how to generate an XML document to a `MemoryStream` object. We'll read the document back out again as a `System.String` value and e-mail it. What we'll do is create a new class called `EmailStream` that extends `MemoryStream`. This new class will contain an extra method called `CloseAndSend` that, as its name implies, will close the stream and send the e-mail message.

First off, we'll create a new Console Application project called `EmailStream`. The first job is to create a basic `Customer` object that contains a few basic members and that can be automatically serialized by .NET through use of the `SerializableAttribute` attribute:

```
<Serializable()> Public Class Customer

    ' members...
    Public Id As Integer
    Public FirstName As String
    Public LastName As String
    Public Email As String

End Class
```

The fun part now is the `EmailStream` class itself. This needs access to the `System.Web.Mail` namespace, so you'll need to add a reference to the `System.Web` assembly. The new class should also extend `System.IO.MemoryStream`, as shown here:

```
Imports System.IO
Imports System.Web.Mail

Public Class EmailStream
    Inherits MemoryStream
```

The first job of `CloseAndSend` is to start putting together the mail message. This is done by creating a new `System.Web.Mail.MailMessage` object and configuring the sender, recipient, and the subject.

```
' CloseAndSend - close the stream and send the e-mail...
Public Sub CloseAndSend(ByVal fromAddress As String, _
                        ByVal toAddress As String, _
                        ByVal subject As String)

    ' create the new message...
    Dim message As New MailMessage
    message.From = fromAddress
    message.To = toAddress
    message.Subject = subject
```

This method will be called once the XML document has been written to the stream, so we can assume at this point that the stream contains a block of data. To read the data back out again, we have to rewind the stream and use a `System.IO.StreamReader`. Before we do this, the first thing we should do is call `Flush`. Traditionally, streams have always been buffered, that is, the data is not sent to the final destination (the memory block in this case, but a file in the case of a `FileStream` and so on) each and every time the stream is written. Instead, the data is written in (pretty much) a nondeterministic way. Because we need all the data to be written, we call `Flush` to ensure that all the data has been sent to the destination and that the buffer is empty.

In a way, `EmailStream` is a great example of buffering. All of the data is held in a memory "buffer" until we finally send the data on to its destination in a response to an explicit call to this method:

```
' flush and rewind the stream...
Flush()
Seek(0, SeekOrigin.Begin)
```

Once we've flushed and rewound the stream, we can create a `StreamReader` and dredge all the data out into the `Body` property of the `MailMessage` object:

```
' read out the data...
Dim reader As New StreamReader(Me)
message.Body = reader.ReadToEnd()
```

After we've done that, we close the stream by calling the base class method:

```
' close the stream...
Close()
```

Finally, we send the message:

```
    ' send the message...
   SmtpMail.Send(message)

End Sub
```

To call this method, we need to add some code to the `Main` method. First, we create a new `Customer` object and populate it with some test data:

```
Imports System.Xml.Serialization

Module Module1

  Sub Main()

    ' create a new customer...
    Dim customer As New Customer
    customer.Id = 27
    customer.FirstName = "Bill"
    customer.LastName = "Gates"
    customer.Email = "bill.gates@microsoft.com"
```

After we've done that, we can create a new `EmailStream` object. We then use `XmlSerializer` to write an XML document representing the newly created `Customer` instance to the block of memory that `EmailStream` is backing to:

```vb
    ' create a new e-mail stream...
    Dim stream As New EmailStream

    ' serialize...
    Dim serializer As New XmlSerializer(customer.GetType())
    serializer.Serialize(stream, customer)
```

At this point, the stream will be filled with data, and after all the data has been flushed the block of memory that `EmailStream` backs on to will contain the complete document. Now we can call `CloseAndSend` to e-mail the document.

```vb
    ' send the e-mail...
    stream.CloseAndSend("evjen@yahoo.com", _
        "evjen@yahoo.com", "XML Customer Document")

   End Sub

End Module
```

You probably already have Microsoft SMTP Service properly configured — this service is necessary to send e-mail. You also need to make sure that the e-mail addresses used in your code goes to your e-mail address! Run the project, check your e-mail, and you should see something, as shown in Figure 10-2.

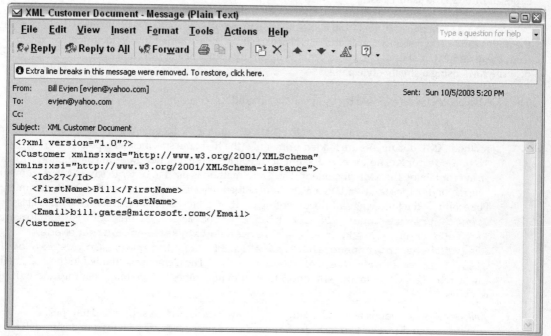

Figure 10-2

Document Object Model (DOM)

The classes of the System.Xml namespace that support the Document Object Model (DOM) interact as illustrated in Figure 10-3.

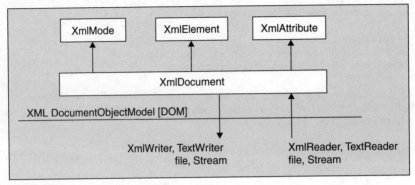

Figure 10-3

Within this diagram, an XML document is contained in a class named XmlDocument. Each node within this document is accessible and managed using XmlNode. Nodes can also be accessed and managed using a class specifically designed to process a specific node's type (XmlElement, XmlAttribute, and so on). XML documents are extracted from XmlDocument using a variety of mechanisms exposed through such classes as XmlWriter, TextWriter, Stream, and a file (specified by filename of type String). XML documents are consumed by an XmlDocument using a variety of load mechanisms exposed through the same classes.

Where a DOM-style parser differs from a stream-style parser is with respect to movement. Using DOM, the nodes can be traversed forwards and backwards. Nodes can be added to the document, removed from the document, and updated. However, this flexibility comes at a performance cost. It is faster to read or write XML using a stream-style parser.

The DOM-specific classes exposed by System.Xml include:

❑ *XmlDocument*—corresponds to an entire XML document. A document is loaded using the Load method. XML documents are loaded from a file (the filename specified as type String), TextReader or XmlReader. A document can be loaded using LoadXml in conjunction with a string containing the XML document. The Save method is used in order to save XML documents. The methods exposed by XmlDocument reflect the intricate manipulation of an XML document. For example, the following self-documenting creation methods are implemented by this class: CreateAttribute, CreateCDataSection, CreateComment, CreateDocumentFragment, CreateDocumentType, CreateElement, CreateEntityReference, CreateNode, CreateProcessingInstruction, CreateSignificantWhitespace, CreateTextNode, CreateWhitespace, and CreateXmlDeclaration. The elements contained in the document can be retrieved. Other methods support the retrieving, importing, cloning, loading, and writing of nodes.

❑ *XmlNode*—corresponds to a node within the DOM tree. This class supports datatypes, namespaces, and DTDs. A robust set of methods and properties are provided to create, delete, and replace nodes: AppendChild, CloneNode, InsertAfter, InsertBefore, PrependChild, RemoveAll, RemoveChild, and ReplaceChild. The contents of a node can similarly be traversed in a variety of ways: FirstChild, LastChild, NextSibling, ParentNode, and PreviousSibling.

❑ *XmlElement* — corresponds to an element within the DOM tree. The functionality exposed by this class contains a variety of methods used to manipulate an element's attributes: GetAttribute, GetAttributeNode, RemoveAllAttributes, RemoveAttributeAt, RemoveAttributeNode, SetAttribute, and SetAttributeNode.

❑ *XmlAttribute* — corresponds to an attribute of an element (XmlElement) within the DOM tree. An attribute contains data and lists of subordinate data. For this reason it is a less complicated object than an XmlNode or an XmlElement. An XmlAttribute can retrieve its owner document (property, OwnerDocument), retrieve its owner element (property, OwnerElement), retrieve its parent node (property, ParentNode), and retrieve its name (property, Name). The value of an XmlAttribute is available via a read–write property named Value.

Given the diverse number of methods and properties (and there are many more than those listed here) exposed by XmlDocument, XmlNode, XmlElement, and XmlAttribute, it should be clear that any XML 1.0 compliant document can be generated and manipulated using these classes. In comparison to their XML stream counterparts, these classes afford more flexible movement within, and editing of XML documents.

A similar comparison could be made between DOM and data serialized and deserialized using XML. Using serialization, the type of node (for example, attribute or element) and the node name are specified at compile time. There is no on-the-fly modification of the XML generated by the serialization process.

Other technologies that generate and consume XML are not as flexible as DOM. This includes ADO.NET and ADO, which generate XML of a particular form. Out of the box, SQL Server does expose a certain amount of flexibility when it comes to the generation (FOR XML queries) and consumption of XML (OPENXML). The choice between using classes within DOM and using SQL Server is a choice between using a language, such as VB.NET, to manipulate objects or requiring SQL Server be installed and perform most XML manipulation in SQL.

DOM Traversing Raw XML Elements

Our first DOM example will load an XML document into an XmlDocument object using a string that contains the actual XML document. This scenario is typical of an application that uses ADO.NET to generate XML but then uses the objects of DOM to traverse and manipulate this XML. ADO.NET's DataSet object contains the results of ADO.NET data access operations. The DataSet class exposes a GetXml method. This method retrieves the underlying XML associated with the DataSet. The following code demonstrates how the contents of the DataSet are loaded into the XmlDocument:

```
Dim xmlDoc As New XmlDocument
Dim ds As New DataSet

' set up ADO.NET DataSet() here
xmlDoc.LoadXml(ds.GetXml())
```

This example will simply traverse each XML element (XmlNode) in the document (XmlDocument) and display the data accordingly. The data associated with this example will not be retrieved from a DataSet but will instead be contained in a string, rawData. This string is initialized as follows

```
Dim rawData As String = _
    "<prescriptions>" & _
    "   <WXClientPrescription>" & _
    "      <dentistName>Dr. Jam</dentistName>" & _
    "      <medicationID>1</medicationID>" & _
    "      <quantity>11</quantity>" & _
    "   </WXClientPrescription>" & _
    "   <WXClientPrescription>" & _
    "      <dentistName>Dr. Jam</dentistName>" & _
    "      <medicationID>2</medicationID>" & _
    "      <quantity>22</quantity>" & _
    "   </WXClientPrescription>" & _
    "</prescriptions>"
```

The XML document in rawData is a portion of the XML hierarchy associated with a prescription written at our dental office. The basic idea in processing this data is to traverse each <WXClientPrescription> element in order to display the data it contains. Each node corresponding to a <WXClientPrescription> element can be retrieved from our XmlDocument using the GetElementsByTagName method (specifying a tag name of WXClientPrescription). The GetElementsByTagName method returns a list of XmlNode objects in the form of a collection of type XmlNodeList. Using the For Each statement to construct this list, the XmlNodeList (clientPrescriptionNodes) can be traversed as individual XmlNode elements (clientPrescriptionNode). The code for handling this is as follows:

```
Dim xmlDoc As New XmlDocument
Dim clientPrescriptionNodes As XmlNodeList
Dim clientPrescriptionNode As XmlNode

xmlDoc.LoadXml(rawData)
' Traverse each <WXClientPrescription>
clientPrescriptionNodes = _
    xmlDoc.GetElementsByTagName("WXClientPrescription")
For Each clientPrescriptionNode In clientPrescriptionNodes
    '************************************************************
    ' Process <dentistName>, <medicationID> and <quantity> here
    '************************************************************
Next
```

Each XmlNode can then have its contents displayed by traversing the children of this node using the ChildNodes method. This method returns an XmlNodeList (baseDataNodes) that can be traversed one XmlNode list element at a time:

```
Dim baseDataNodes As XmlNodeList
Dim bFirstInRow As Boolean

baseDataNodes = clientPrescriptionNode.ChildNodes
bFirstInRow = True
```

```
For Each baseDataNode As XmlNode In baseDataNodes
  If (bFirstInRow) Then
    bFirstInRow = False
  Else
    Console.Out.Write(", ")
  End If
  Console.Out.Write(baseDataNode.Name & ": " & baseDataNode.InnerText)
Next
Console.Out.WriteLine()
```

The bulk of the previous code retrieves the name of the node using the `Name` property and the `InnerText` property of the node. The `InnerText` property of each `XmlNode` retrieved contains the data associated with the XML elements (nodes) `<dentistName>`, `<medicationID>`, and `<quantity>`. Our example displays the contents of the XML elements using `Console.Out`. Our XML document is displayed as follows:

```
dentistName: Dr. Jam, medicationID: 1, quantity: 11
dentistName: Dr. Jam, medicationID: 2, quantity: 22
```

Other, more practical, methods for using this data could have been implemented, including:

❑   The contents could have been directed to an ASP.NET `Response` object. The data retrieved could have been used to create an HTML table (`<table>` table, `<tr>` row, and `<td>` data) that would be written to the `Response` object.

❑   The data traversed could have been directed to a `ListBox` or `ComboBox` Windows Forms control. This would allow the data returned to be selected as part of a GUI application.

❑   The data could have been edited as part of our application's business rules. For example, we could have used the traversal to verify that the `<medicationID>` matched the `<quantity>`. For example, if a medication must be taken three times a day then the quantity prescribed must be a multiple of three.

Our example in its entirety is as follows:

```
Dim rawData As String = _
    "<prescriptions>" & _
    "  <WXClientPrescription>" & _
    "    <dentistName>Dr. Jam</dentistName>" & _
    "    <medicationID>1</medicationID>" & _
    "    <quantity>11</quantity>" & _
    "  </WXClientPrescription>" & _
    "  <WXClientPrescription>" & _
    "    <dentistName>Dr. Jam</dentistName>" & _
    "    <medicationID>2</medicationID>" & _
    "    <quantity>22</quantity>" & _
    "  </WXClientPrescription>" & _
    "</prescriptions>"
Dim xmlDoc As New XmlDocument
Dim clientPrescriptionNodes As XmlNodeList
Dim baseDataNodes As XmlNodeList
Dim bFirstInRow As Boolean

xmlDoc.LoadXml(rawData)
' Traverse each <WXClientPrescription>
```

```
    clientPrescriptionNodes = xmlDoc.GetElementsByTagName("WXClientPrescription")
    For Each clientPrescriptionNode As XmlNode In clientPrescriptionNodes
        baseDataNodes = clientPrescriptionNode.ChildNodes
        bFirstInRow = True
        For Each baseDataNode As XmlNode In baseDataNodes
            If (bFirstInRow) Then
                bFirstInRow = False
            Else
                Console.Out.Write(", ")
            End If
            Console.Out.Write(baseDataNode.Name & ": " & baseDataNode.InnerText)
        Next
        Console.Out.WriteLine()
    Next
```

DOM Traversing XML Attributes

This next example will demonstrate how to traverse data contained in attributes and how to update the attributes based on a set of business rules. In this example, the Xml Document object is populated by retrieving an XML document from a file. After the business rules edit the object, the data will be persisted back to the file.

```
Dim xmlDoc As New XmlDocument

xmlDoc.Load("..\ DentalOfficeReadyPrescriptionsV2.xml")
'************************************************
' Business rules process document here
'************************************************
xmlDoc.Save("..\ DentalOfficeReadyPrescriptionsV2.xml")
```

The data contained in the file, DentalOfficeReadyPrescriptionsV2.xml, is a variation of the dental prescription. We have altered our rigid standard (for the sake of example) so that the data associated with individual prescriptions is contained in XML attributes instead of XML elements. An example of this prescription data is as follows:

```
<WXClientPrescription dentistName="Dr. Jam" medicationID="1" quantity="11">
```

We have already demonstrated how to traverse the XML elements associated with a document, so let's assume that we have successfully retrieved the XmlNode associated with the <WXClientPrescription> element.

```
Dim attributes As XmlAttributeCollection
Dim medicationID As Integer
Dim quantity As Integer

attributes = node.Attributes()
For Each attribute As XmlAttribute In attributes
    If 0 = String.Compare(attribute.Name, "medicationID") Then
        medicationID = attribute.InnerXml
    ElseIf 0 = String.Compare(attribute.Name, "quantity") Then
        quantity = attribute.InnerXml
    End If
Next
```

The previous code traverses the attributes of an `XmlNode` by retrieving a list of attributes using the `Attributes` method. The value of this method is used to set the attributes object (datatype, `XmlAttributeCollection`). The individual `XmlAttribute` objects (variable, `attribute`) contained in attributes are traversed using a `For Each` loop. Within the loop the contents of the `medicationID` and the `quantity` attribute are saved for processing by our business rules.

Our business rules execute an algorithm that ensures that the medication in the prescription is provided in the correct quantity. This rule is that the medication associated with `MedicationID=1` must be dispensed 21 tablets at a time. In the event of an invalid quantity, the code for enforcing this business rule uses the `ItemOf` property to look up the `XmlAttribute` object associated with the `quantity` attribute. The `Value` property of the `XmlAttribute` object is used to set the correct value of the medication's quantity. The code performing this business rule is as follows:

```
If medicationID = 1 Then
    ' medication must be taken 3 times a day for a week (21 times)
    If quantity <> 21 Then
        attributes.ItemOf("quantity").Value = "21"
    End If
End If
```

What is elegant about this example is that the list of attributes was traversed using `For Each`. Then `ItemOf` was used to look up a specific attribute that had already been traversed. This would not have been possible if reading an XML stream with an object derived from the XML stream reader class, `XmlReader`.

We can use this code as follows:

```
Sub WXTraverseAttributes(ByRef node As XmlNode)
    Dim attributes As XmlAttributeCollection
    Dim medicationID As Integer
    Dim quantity As Integer

    attributes = node.Attributes()
    For Each attribute As XmlAttribute In attributes
        If 0 = String.Compare(attribute.Name, "medicationID") Then
            medicationID = attribute.InnerXml
        ElseIf 0 = String.Compare(attribute.Name, "quantity") Then
            quantity = attribute.InnerXml
        End If
    Next

    If medicationID = 1 Then
        ' medication must be taken 3 times a day for a week (21 times)
        If quantity <> 21 Then
            attributes.ItemOf("quantity").Value = "21"
        End If
    End If
End Sub

Sub WXReadDentalDOM()
    Dim xmlDoc As New XmlDocument
    Dim clientPrescriptionNodes As XmlNodeList
```

```
xmlDoc.Load("..\ DentalOfficeReadyPrescriptionsV2.xml")
' Traverse each <WXClientPrescription>
clientPrescriptionNodes = _
    xmlDoc.GetElementsByTagName("WXClientPrescription")
For Each clientPrescriptionNode As XmlNode In clientPrescriptionNodes
    WXTraverseAttributes(clientPrescriptionNode)
Next

xmlDoc.Save("..\ DentalOfficeReadyPrescriptionsV2.xml")
End Sub
```

XSLT Transforms

XSLT is a language that is used to transform XML documents so that they can be presented visually. We have performed a similar task before. When working with XML serialization we rewrote the `WXClientPrescription` class. This class was used to serialize a prescription object to XML using nodes that contained English-language names. The rewritten version of this class, `WXPotilasResepti`, serialized XML nodes containing Finnish names. Source Code Style attributes were used in conjunction with the `XmlSerializer` class in order to accomplish this transformation. Two words in this paragraph send chills down the spine of any experienced developer: *rewrote* and *rewritten*. The point of an XSL Transform is to use an alternate language (XSLT) to transform the XML rather than rewriting the source code, SQL commands, or some other mechanism used to generate XML.

Conceptually, XSLT is straightforward. A file with an `.xslt` extension describes the changes (transformations) that will be applied to a particular XML file. Once this is completed an XSLT processor is provided with the source XML file and the XSLT file, and performs the transformation. The `System.Xml.Xsl.XslTransform` class is such an XSLT processor.

The XSLT file is itself an XML document, although certain elements within this document are XSLT specific commands. There are dozens of XSLT commands that can be used in writing an XSLT file. In our first example, we will explore the following XSLT elements (commands):

❏ *stylesheet* — This element indicates the start of the stylesheet (XSL) in the XSLT file.

❏ *template* — This element denotes a reusable template for producing specific output. This output is generated using a specific node type within the source document under a specific context. For example, the text `<xsl: template match="/">` selects all root notes ("/") for the specific transform template.

❏ *for-each* — This element applies the same template to each node in the specified set. Recall that we demonstrated a class (`WXClientMultiPrescription`) that could be serialized. This class contained an array of prescriptions. Given the XML document generated when a `WXClientMultiPrescription` is serialized, each prescription serialized could be processed using `<xsl:for-each select = "WXClientMultiPrescription/prescriptions/ WXClientPrescription">`.

❏ *value-of* — This element retrieves the value of the specified node and inserts it into the document in text form. For example, `<xsl:value-of select="dentistName" />` would take the value of XML element, `<dentistName>`, and insert it into the transformed document.

The `WXClientMultiPrescription` class when serialized generates XML such as the following (where ... indicates where additional `<WXClientPrescription>` elements may reside):

```
<?xml version="1.0" encoding="us-ascii" ?>
<WXClientMultiPrescription>
    <prescriptions>
        <WXClientPrescription>
            <dentistName>Dr. Jam</dentistName>
            <medicationID>1</medicationID>
            <quantity>11</quantity>
        </WXClientPrescription>
        ...
    </prescriptions>
</WXClientMultiPrescription>
```

The previous XML document is used to generate a report that is viewed by the dental practice's managing doctor. This report is in HTML form, so it can be viewed via the Web. The XSLT elements we previously reviewed (`stylesheet`, `template`, and `for-each`) are all the XSLT elements required to transform our XML document (in which data is stored) into an HTML file (show that the data can be displayed). An XSLT file, `WXDisplayThatPuppy.xslt`, contains the following text that is used to transform a serialized version, `WXClientMultiPrescription`:

```
<?xml version="1.0" encoding="UTF-8" ?>
<xsl:stylesheet xmlns:xsl="http://www.w3.org/1999/XSL/Transform"
    version="1.0">
    <xsl:template match="/">
      <HTML>
      <TITLE>Who's prescribing what</TITLE>
      <BODY>
          <TABLE BORDER="1">
            <TR>
              <TD><B>Dentist</B></TD>
              <TD><B>Medication ID</B></TD>
              <TD><B>Quantity</B></TD>
            </TR>
            <xsl:for-each select=
             "WXClientMultiPrescription/prescriptions/WXClientPrescription">
            <TR>
              <TD><xsl:value-of select="dentistName" /></TD>
              <TD><xsl:value-of select="quantity" /></TD>
              <TD><xsl:value-of select="medicationID" /></TD>
            </TR>
            </xsl:for-each>
          </TABLE>
      </BODY>
      </HTML>
    </xsl:template>
</xsl:stylesheet>
```

In the previous XSLT file, the XSLT elements are marked in boldface. These elements perform operations on the source XML file containing a serialized `WXClientMultiPrescription` object and generate the appropriate HTML file. Our file contains a table (marked by the table tag, `<TABLE>`) that contains a set of rows (each row marked by a table row tag, <TR>). The columns of the table are contained in table data tags, <TD>. The previous XSLT file contains the header row for the table:

```
<TR>
    <TD><B>Dentist</B></TD>
    <TD><B>Medication ID</B></TD>
    <TD><B>Quantity</B></TD>
</TR>
```

Each row containing data (an individual prescription from the serialized object, WXClientMultiPrescription) is generated using the XSLT element, for-each, to traverse each <WXClientPrescription> element within the source XML document:

```
<xsl:for-each select=
    "WXClientMultiPrescription/prescriptions/WXClientPrescription">
```

The individual columns of data are generated using the value-of XSLT element, in order to query the elements contained within each <WXClientPrescription> element (<dentistName>, <quantity>, and <medicationID>):

```
<TR>
    <TD><xsl:value-of select="dentistName" /></TD>
    <TD><xsl:value-of select="quantity" /></TD>
    <TD><xsl:value-of select="medicationID" /></TD>
</TR>
```

The code to create a displayable XML file using the System.Xml.Xsl namespace is as follows:

```
Dim myXslTransform As XslTransform = New XslTransform
Dim myResolver As XmlUrlResolver = New XmlUrlResolver
myResolver.Credentials = System.Net.CredentialCache.DefaultCredentials

Dim destFileName As String = "..\ ShowIt.html"

myXslTransform.Load("..\ WXDisplayThatPuppy.xslt")
myXslTransform.Transform("..\ OneWXClientMultiPrescriptions.xml", _
                    destFileName, myResolver)
System.Diagnostics.Process.Start(destFileName)
```

This consists of only seven lines of code with the bulk of the coding taking place in the XSLT file. Our previous code snippet created an instance of a System.Xml.Xsl.XslTransform object named myXslTransform. The Load method of this class is used to load the XSLT file we previously reviewed, WXDisplayThatPuppy.xslt. The Transform method takes a source XML file as the first parameter which in our case was a file containing a serialized WXClientMultiPrescription object. The second parameter is the destination file that will be created by the transform (filename, ..\ShowIt.html). While the third parameter is the XmlResolver that we are using, which in our case is an XmlUrlResolver object. The Start method of the Process class is used to display HTML file. The Start method launches a process that is most suitable for displaying the file provided. Basically, the extension of the file dictates which application will be used to display the file. On a typical Windows machine, the program used to display this file is Internet Explorer, as shown in Figure 10-4.

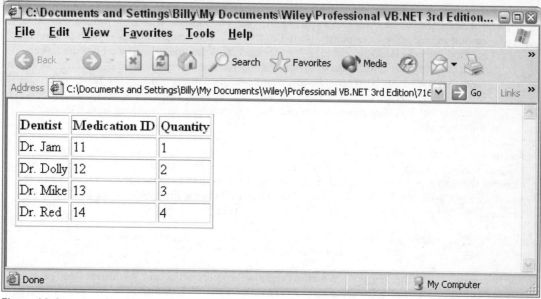

Figure 10-4

Do not confuse displaying this HTML file with ASP.NET. Displaying an HTML file in this manner takes place on a single machine without the involvement of a Web server. ASP.NET is more complex than displaying an HTML page in the default browser.

As was demonstrated, the backbone of the `System.Xml.Xsl` namespace is the `XslTransform` class. This class uses XSLT files to transform XML documents. `XslTransform` exposes the following methods and properties.

❑ *XmlResolver* — This get/set property is used to specify a class (abstract base class, `XmlResolver`) that is used to handle external references (import and include elements within the style sheet). These external references are encountered when a document is transformed (method, `Transform`, is executed). The `System.Xml` namespace contains a class `XmlUrlResolver`, which is derived from `XmlResolver`. The `XmlUrlResolver` class resolves external resource based on a URI.

❑ *Load* — This overloaded method loads an XSLT style sheet to be used in transforming XML documents. It is permissible to specify the XSLT style sheet as a parameter of type: `XPathNavigator`, filename of XSLT file (specified as parameter type, `String`), `XmlReader`, or `IXPathNavigable`. For each of type of XSLT supported, an overloaded member is provided that allows an `XmlResolver` to also be specified. For example, it is possible to call `Load(String, XmlResolver)` where `String` corresponds to a filename and `XmlResolver` is an object that handles references in the style sheet of type `xsl:import` and `xsl:include`. It would also be permissible to pass in a value of `Nothing` for the second parameter of the `Load` method (so no `XmlResolver` would be specified). Note that there have been considerable changes to the parameters that the `Load` method takes between versions 1.0 and 1.1 of the .NET Framework. Look at the SDK documentation for details on the breaking changes that you might encounter when working with the `XslTransform` class.

❑   *Transform* — This overloaded method transforms a specified XML document using the previously specified XSLT style sheet and an `XmlResolver`. The location where the transformed XML is to be output is specified as a parameter to this method. The first parameter of each overloaded method is the XML document to be transformed. This parameter can be represented as an `IXPathNavigable`, XML filename (specified as parameter type, `String`), or `XPathNavigator`. Note that there have been considerable changes to the parameters that the `Transform` method takes between versions 1.0 and 1.1 of the .NET Framework. Look at the SDK documentation for details on the breaking changes that you might encounter when working with the `XslTransform` class.

The most straightforward variant of the `Transform` method is `Transform(String, String, XmlResolver)`. In this case, a file containing an XML document is specified as the first parameter, and a filename that receives the transformed XML document is specified as the second parameter and the `XmlResolver` used as the third parameter. This is exactly how the first XSLT example utilized the `Transform` method:

```
myXslTransform.Transform("..\ OneWXClientMultiPrescriptions.xml", _
                    destFileName, myResolver)
```

The first parameter to the `Transform` method can also be specified as an `IXPathNavigable` or `XPathNavigator`. Either of these parameter types allows the XML output to be sent to an object of type `Stream`, `TextWriter`, or `XmlWriter`. When these two flavors of input are specified, a parameter containing an object of type `XsltArgumentList` can be specified. An `XsltArgumentList` object contains a list of arguments that are used as input to the transform.

XSLT Transforming Between XML Standards

Our first example used four XSLT elements in order to transform an XML file into an HTML file. Such an example has merit, but it does not demonstrate an important use of XSLT. Another major application of XSLT is to transform XML from one standard into another standard. This may involve renaming elements/attributes, excluding elements/attributes, changing datatypes, altering the node hierarchy, and representing elements as attributes and vice versa.

A case of differing XML standards could easily happen to our software that automates dental offices. Imagine that the software including its XML representation of a medical prescription is so successful that we sell 100,000 copies. However, just as we're celebrating, a consortium of the largest pharmacies announces that they will no longer be accepting faxed prescriptions and that they are introducing their own standard for the exchange of prescriptions between medical/dental offices and pharmacies.

Rather than panic, we simply ship an upgrade that comes complete with an XSLT file. This upgrade (a bit of extra code plus the XSLT file) transforms our XML representation of a prescription into the XML representation dictated by the consortium of pharmacies. By using an XSLT file, we can ship the upgrade immediately. If the consortium of pharmacies revises their XML representation, we are not obliged to change our source code. Instead, we can simply ship the upgraded XSLT file that will ensure each dental office is compliant.

The specific source code that executes the transform is as follows:

```
Dim myXslTransform As XslTransform = New XslTransform
Dim myResolver As XmlUrlResolver = New XmlUrlResolver
```

```
myResolver.Credentials = System.Net.CredentialCache.DefaultCredentials

myXslTransform.Load("..\ ConvertLegacyToNewStandard.xslt")
myXslTransform.Transform("..\ DentalOfficeReadyPrescriptions.xml", _
                         "..\ PharmacyReadyPrescriptions.xml", myResolver)
```

The five lines of code are

1. Create an `XslTransform` object

2. Create an `XmlResolver` object

3. Tell the `XmlResolver` object to use the default credentials

4. Use the `Load` method to load an XSLT file (`ConvertLegacyToNewStandard.xslt`)

5. Use the `Transform` method to transform a source XML file
   (`DentalOfficeReadyPrescriptions.xml`) into a destination XML file
   (`PharmacyReadyPrescriptions.xml`) along with the assigned `XmlResolver`

Recall that the input XML document (`DentalOfficeReadyPrescriptions.xml`) does not match the format required by our consortium of pharmacies. The content of this source XML file is as follows:

```
<?xml version="1.0" encoding="utf-8" ?>
<DentalManageDump>
    <WXClientMultiPrescription>
        <prescriptions>
            <WXClientPrescription>
                <dentistName>Dr. Jam</dentistName>
                <medicationID>1</medicationID>
                <quantity>11</quantity>
            </WXClientPrescription>
            <!-- additional <WXClientPrescription>'s specified here -->
        </prescriptions>
    </WXClientMultiPrescription>
    <!-- additional </WXClientMultiPrescription>'s specified here -->
</DentalManageDump>
```

In this XML document, there are two XML comments included (as specified by `<!-- comment -->`). The comments indicate where more `<WXClientPrescription>` elements can be placed in the document and where more `<WXClientMultiPrescription>` elements can be placed in the document.

The format exhibited in the previous XML document does not match the format of the consortium of pharmacies. To be assimilated by the collective of pharmacies we must transform the document as follows:

❑ Rename element `<DentalManageDump>` to `<Root>`

❑ Remove element `<WXClientMultiPrescription>`

❑ Remove element `<prescriptions>`

❑ Rename element `<WXClientPrescription>` to `<PharmacyPrescription>`

❑ Remove element `<dentistName>` (the doctor's name is not to be contained in the document)

- ❑ Rename element `<quantity>` to `HowMuch` and make `HowMuch` an attribute of `<PharmacyPrescription>`

- ❑ Rename element `<medicationID>` to `MedValue` and make `MedValue` an attribute of `<PharmacyPrescription>`

- ❑ Display attribute `HowMuch` before attribute `MedValue`

A great many of the steps performed by the transform could have been achieved using an alternative technology. For example, we could have used *Source Code Style* attributes with our serialization to generate the correct XML attribute and XML element name. If we had known in advance that a consortium of pharmacies was going to develop a standard, we could have written our classes to be serialized based on the standard. The point was we didn't know and now one standard (our legacy standard) has to be converted into a newly adopted standard of the pharmacy consortium. The worst thing we could do would be to change our working code and then force all users working with the application to upgrade. It is vastly simpler to add an extra transformation step to address the new standard.

The XSLT file that facilitates the transform is named `ConvertLegacyToNewStandard.xslt`. A portion of this file is implemented as follows:

```
<xsl:template match="WXClientPrescription">
    <!-- rename <WXClientPrescription> to <PharmacyPrescription> -->
    <xsl:element name="PharmacyPrescription">
        <!-- Make element 'quantity' attribute HowMuch
            Notice attribute HowMuch comes before attribute MedValue -->
        <xsl:attribute name="HowMuch">
            <xsl:value-of select='quantity'></xsl:value-of>
        </xsl:attribute>
        <!-- Make element medicationID attribute MedValue -->
        <xsl:attribute name="MedValue">
            <xsl:value-of select='medicationID'></xsl:value-of>
        </xsl:attribute>
    </xsl:element>
    <!-- end of PharmacyPrescription element -->
</xsl:template>
```

In the previous snippet of XSLT, the following XSLT elements are used to facilitate the transformation:

- ❑ `<xsl:template match="WXClientPrescription">` — All operations in this `template` XSLT element will take place on the original document's `WXClientPrescription` node.

- ❑ `<xsl:element name="PharmacyPrescription">` — The element corresponding to the source document's `WXClientPrescription` element will be called `PharmacyPrescription` in the destination document.

- ❑ `<xsl:attribute name="HowMuch">` — An attribute name `HowMuch` will be contained in the previously specified element. The previously specified element is `<PharmacyPrescription>`. This `attribute` XSLT element for `HowMuch` comes before the `attribute` XSLT element for `MedValue`. This order was specified as part of our transform to adhere to the new standard.

- ❑ `<xsl:value-of select='quantity'>` — Retrieve the value of the source document's `<quantity>` element and place it in the destination document. This instance of XSLT element, `value-of`, provides the value associated with attribute `HowMuch`.

Two new XSLT elements have crept into our vocabulary: element and attribute. Both of these XSLT elements live up to their names. Specifying the XSLT element named element places an element in the destination XML document. Specifying the XSLT element named attribute places an attribute in the destination XML document. The XSLT transform found in ConvertLegacyToNewStandard.xslt is too long to review completely. When reading this file in its entirety, you should remember that this XSLT file contains inline documentation to specify precisely what aspect of the transformation is being performed at which location in the XSLT document. For example, the following XML code comments inform you about what the XSLT element attribute is about to do:

```
<!-- Make element 'quantity' attribute HowMuch
     Notice attribute HowMuch comes before attribute MedValue -->
<xsl:attribute name="HowMuch">
     <xsl:value-of select='quantity'></xsl:value-of>
</xsl:attribute>
```

The previous example spanned several pages but contained just three lines of code. This demonstrates that there is more to XML than learning how to use it in VB.NET and the .NET Framework. Among other things, you also need a good understanding of XSLT and XPath.

Other Classes and Interfaces in System.Xml.Xsl

We just took a good look at XSLT and the System.Xml.Xsl namespace, but there is a lot more to it than that. The other classes and interfaces exposed by System.Xml.Xsl namespace include:

❑ IXsltContextFunction—This interface accesses at runtime a given function defined in the XSLT style sheet.

❑ IXsltContextVariable—This interface accesses at runtime a given variable defined in the XSLT style sheet.

❑ XsltArgumentList—This class contains a list of arguments. These arguments are XSLT parameters or XSLT extension objects. The XsltArgumentList object is used in conjunction with the Transform method of XslTransform.

❑ XsltContext—This class contains the state of the XSLT processor. This context information allows XPath expressions to have their various components resolved (functions, parameters, and namespaces).

❑ XsltException, XsltCompileException—These classes contain the information pertaining to an exception raised while transforming data. XsltCompileException is derived from XsltException.

ADO.NET

ADO.NET allows VB.NET applications to generate XML documents and to use such documents to update persisted data. ADO.NET natively represents its DataSet's underlying data store in XML. ADO.NET also allows SQL Server-specific XML support to be accessed. In this chapter, our focus is on those features of ADO.NET that allow the XML generated and consumed to be customized. ADO.NET is covered in detail in Chapter 11.

The `DataSet` properties and methods that are pertinent to XML include `Namespace`, `Prefix`, `GetXml`, `GetXmlSchema`, `InferXmlSchema`, `ReadXml`, `ReadXmlSchema`, `WriteXml`, and `WriteXmlSchema`. An example code snippet that uses the `GetXml` method is as follows:

```
Dim adapter As New _
    SqlDataAdapter("SELECT ShipperID, CompanyName, Phone " & _
                   "FROM Shippers", _
                   "SERVER=localhost;UID=sa;PWD=sa;Database=Northwind;")
Dim ds As New DataSet

adapter.Fill(ds)
Console.Out.WriteLine(ds.GetXml())
```

The previous code uses the sample `Northwind` database (which comes with SQL Server and MSDE) and retrieves all rows from the `Shippers` table. This table was selected because it contains only three rows of data. The XML returned by `GetXml` is as follows (where . . . signifies that `<Table>` elements were removed for the sake of brevity):

```
<NewDataSet>
  <Table>
    <ShipperID>1</ShipperID>
    <CompanyName>Speedy Express</CompanyName>
    <Phone>(503) 555-9831</Phone>
  </Table>
  . . .
</NewDataSet>
```

What we are trying to determine from the previous XML document is how to customize the XML generated. The more customization we can perform at the ADO.NET level the less need there will be later. With this in mind, we notice that the root element is `<NewDataSet>` and that each row of the `DataSet` is returned as an XML element, `<Table>`. The data returned is contained in an XML element named for the column in which the data resides (`<ShipperID>`, `<CompanyName>`, and `<Phone>` respectively).

The root element, `<NewDataSet>`, is just the default name of the `DataSet`. This name could have been changed when the `DataSet` was constructed by specifying the name as a parameter to the constructor:

```
Dim ds As New DataSet("WeNameTheDataSet")
```

If the previous version of the constructor was executed, then the `<NewDataSet>` element would be renamed `<WeNameTheDataSet>`. After the `DataSet` has been constructed, we can still set property `DataSetName`, thus changing element `<NewDataSet>` to a name such as `<WeNameTheDataSetAgain>`:

```
ds.DataSetName = "WeNameTheDataSetAgain"
```

The `<Table>` element is actually the name of a table in the `DataSet`'s `Tables` property. Programmatically, we can change `<Table>` to `<WeNameTheTable>`.

```
ds.Tables("Table").TableName = "WeNameTheTable"
```

We can customize the names of the data columns returned by modifying the SQL to use alias names. For example, we could retrieve the same data but generate different elements using the following SQL:

```
SELECT ShipperID As TheID, CompanyName As CName, Phone As TelephoneNumber
FROM Shippers
```

Using the previous SQL statement the `<ShipperID>` element would become the `<TheID>` element. The `<CompanyName>` element would become `<CName>` and `<Phone>` would become `<TelephoneNumber>`. The column names can also be changed programmatically by using the `Columns` property associated with the table in which the column resides. An example of this is as follows, where the XML element `<TheID>` is changed to `<AnotherNewName>`.

```
ds.Tables("WeNameTheTable").Columns("TheID").ColumnName = "AnotherNewName"
```

This XML could be transformed using `System.Xml.Xsl`. This XML could be read as a stream (`XmlTextReader`) or written as a stream (`XmlTextWriter`). The XML returned by ADO.NET could even be deserialized and used to create an object or objects using `XmlSerializer`. What is important is to recognize what ADO.NET-generated XML looks like. If you know its format, then you can transform it into whatever you like.

ADO.NET and SQL Server's Built-In XML Features

Those interested in fully exploring the XML-specific features of SQL Server should take a look at *Professional SQL Server 2000 Programming* from Wrox Press, ISBN 0764543792. However, as the content of that book is not .NET-specific, our next example will form a bridge between *Professional SQL Server 2000 Programming* and the .NET Framework.

Two of the major XML-related features exposed by SQL Server are:

❑ FOR XML — The FOR XML clause of a SQL SELECT statement allows a rowset to be returned as an XML document. The XML document generated by a FOR XML clause is highly customizable with respect to the document hierarchy generated, per-column data transforms, representation of binary data, XML schema generated, and a variety of other XML nuances.

❑ OPENXML — The OPENXML extension to Transact-SQL allows a stored procedure call to manipulate an XML document as a rowset. Subsequently, this rowset can be used to perform a variety of tasks, such as SELECT, INSERT INTO, DELETE, and UPDATE.

SQL Server's support for OPENXML is a matter of calling a stored procedure call. A developer who can execute a stored procedure call using VB.NET in conjunction with ADO.NET can take full advantage of SQL Server's support for OPENXML. FOR XML queries have a certain caveat when it comes to ADO.NET. To understand this caveat, consider the following FOR XML query:

```
SELECT ShipperID, CompanyName, Phone FROM Shippers FOR XML RAW
```

Using SQL Server's Query Analyzer, this FOR XML RAW query generated the following XML:

```
<row ShipperID="1" CompanyName="Speedy Express" Phone="(503) 555-9831"/>
<row ShipperID="2" CompanyName="United Package" Phone="(503) 555-3199"/>
<row ShipperID="3" CompanyName="Federal Shipping" Phone="(503) 555-9931"/>
```

The same FOR XML RAW query can be executed from ADO.NET as follows:

```
Dim adapter As New _
    SqlDataAdapter("SELECT ShipperID, CompanyName, Phone " & _
                   "FROM Shippers FOR XML RAW", _
                   "SERVER=localhost;UID=sa;PWD=sa;Database=Northwind;")
Dim ds As New DataSet

adapter.Fill(ds)
Console.Out.WriteLine(ds.GetXml())
```

The caveat with respect to a FOR XML query is that all data (the XML text) is returned via a result set containing a single row and a single column named XML_F52E2B61-18A1-11d1-B105-00805F49916B. The output from the previous code snippet demonstrates this caveat (where . . . represents similar data not shown for reasons of brevity):

```
<NewDataSet>
  <Table>
    <XML_F52E2B61-18A1-11d1-B105-00805F49916B>
      &lt;row ShipperID="1" CompanyName= "Speedy Express" Phone="(503)
      555-9831"/&gt;
      . . .
    </XML_F52E2B61-18A1-11d1-B105-00805F49916B>
  </Table>
</NewDataSet>
```

The value of our single row and single column returned contains what looks to be XML, but it contains /< instead of the less-than character and /> instead of the greater-than character. The symbol < and > cannot appear inside XML data. For this reason they must be entity-encoded (that is, represented as /> and /<). The data returned in element <XML_F52E2B61-18A1-11d1-B105-00805F49916B> is not XML but is data contained in an XML document.

In order to fully utilize FOR XML queries, the data must be accessible as XML. The solution to this quandary is the ExecuteXmlReader method of the SQLCommand class. When this method is called, a SQLCommand object assumes it is executed as a FOR XML query and returns the results of this query as an XmlReader object. An example of this is as follows (again found in VBNetXML05):

```
Dim connection As New _
    SqlConnection("SERVER=localhost;UID=sa;PWD=sa;Database=Northwind;")
Dim command As New _
    SqlCommand("SELECT ShipperID, CompanyName, Phone " & _
               "FROM Shippers FOR XML RAW")
Dim memStream As MemoryStream = New MemoryStream
Dim xmlReader As New XmlTextReader(memStream)

connection.Open()
command.Connection = connection
xmlReader = command.ExecuteXmlReader()
' Extract results from XMLReader
```

The XmlReader created in this code is of type XmlTextReader, which derives from XmlReader. The XmlTextReader is backed by a MemoryStream, hence it is an in-memory stream of XML that can be traversed using the methods and properties exposed by XmlTextReader. Streaming XML generation and retrieval has been discussed earlier.

Using the ExecuteXmlReader method of the SQLCommand class it is possible to retrieve the result of FOR XML queries. What makes FOR XML style of queries so powerful is that it can configure the data retrieved. The three types of FOR XML query support the following forms of XML customization:

❑   FOR XML RAW—returns each row of a result set inside an XML element named <row>. The data retrieved is contained as attributes of the <row> element. The attributes are named for the column name or column alias in the FOR XML RAW query.

❑   FOR XML AUTO—by default returns each row of a result set inside an XML element named for the table or table alias contained in the FOR XML AUTO query. The data retrieved is contained as attributes of this element. The attributes are named for the column name or column alias in the FOR XML AUTO query. By specifying FOR XML AUTO, ELEMENTS it is possible to retrieve all data inside elements rather than inside attributes. All data retrieved must be in attribute or element form. There is no mix-and-match capability.

❑   FOR XML EXPLICIT—this form of FOR XML query allows the precise XML type of each column returned to be specified. The data associated with a column can be returned as an attribute or an element. Specific XML types, such as CDATA and ID, can be associated with a column returned. Even the level in the XML hierarchy in which data resides can be specified using a FOR XML EXPLICIT query. This style of query is fairly complicated to implement.

FOR XML queries are flexible. Using FOR XML EXPLICIT and the dental database, it would be possible to generate any form of XML medical prescription standard. The decision that needs to be made is where XML configuration takes place. Using VB.NET, a developer could use XmlTextReader and XmlTextWriter to create any style of XML document. Using the XSLT language and an XSLT file, the same level of configuration could be achieved. SQL Server and, in particular, FOR XML EXPLICIT would allow the same level of XML customization, but this customization would take place at the SQL level and may even be configured to stored procedure calls.

Typed DataSet Objects

Along with late bound access to values through weakly typed variables, the DataSet provides access to data through a strongly typed metaphor. Tables and columns that are part of the DataSet can be accessed using user-friendly names and strongly typed variables.

A *typed DataSet* is a class that derives from a DataSet. As such, it inherits all of the methods, events, and properties of a DataSet. Additionally, a typed DataSet provides strongly typed methods, events, and properties. In practice, this means you can access tables and columns by name, instead of using collection-based methods. Aside from the improved readability of the code, a typed DataSet also allows the compiler to automatically complete lines as you type. For example, when we want to reference the au_lname field in the first row of the authors table (found in the sample pubs database) we can write the following code:

```
strLastName = objDS.Tables("Authors").Rows(0).Item("au_lname").ToString()
```

But, if we were using a strongly typed DataSet, we could just write the following line of code:

```
strLastName = objDS.Authors.Rows(0).LastName
```

In this code, we are actually getting a `String` datatype at compile time instead of at runtime, since the strongly typed `DataSet` provides access to values as the correct strongly typed value at compile time. With a strongly typed `DataSet`, type mismatch errors are caught when the code is compiled rather than at runtime.

Generating Typed DataSets

Generating typed `DataSets` is done using a command-line utility called XSD that's supplied with the Framework SDK (which is installed along with Visual Studio .NET). This utility is capable of generating source code files containing a strongly typed `DataSet`, given an XML schema.

ADO.NET makes strong use of XML for data storage and manipulation. When we have a `DataSet` object, technically we can express the structure of the tables contained within that `DataSet` as an XML schema. In fact, we can use the `WriteXmlSchema` method of the `DataSet` to write the schema to a stream or to a file.

We're not going to worry too much about the structure of the schema itself, as this is a pretty advanced topic beyond the scope of this discussion. However, we don't need to know what it looks like or how it works. Simply, we get one class to generate it and ask the utility to understand it on our behalf in order to generate the VB source code containing a typed `DataSet`.

What's oddly missing from Visual Studio .NET (VS.NET) is an easy way to create typed `DataSet` from within the environment itself. Although it is possible, it involves a lot of messing around with the Design type data controls, which can be found under the Data tab in the toolbox. Personally, I'm not fond of this approach, as I prefer to programmatically access data from code rather than using the Design time controls.

What you have to do is create an untyped `DataSet` containing the data that we ultimately want in our typed `DataSet`. We'll build a simple utility that accepts a connection string and a table and automatically generates the schema file and the associated `.vb` file containing the typed `DataSet` for us.

Create a new project called `TypedDataSet`. In the Designer for `Form1`, add controls similar to what is displayed in Figure 10-5.

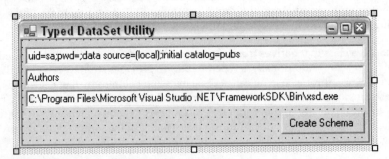

Figure 10-5

The `TextBox` controls should be called `textConnectionString`, `textTableName`, and `textXsdUtilityFilename`. The `XSD.EXE` utility should be at the location that I've specified in the screenshot. If it's not there, search for it and add in the appropriate path.

You'll also need to add a `SaveFileDialog` control to the form. Double-click the button to create a `Click` handler and add this code:

```
Private Sub buttonCreateSchema_Click(ByVal sender As System.Object, _
                                     ByVal e As System.EventArgs) _
                                     Handles buttonCreateSchema.Click
    Dim result As DialogResult = dialogSaveFile.ShowDialog()
    If result = DialogResult.OK Then
        CreateSchema(textConnectionString.Text, textTableName.Text, _
            textXsdUtilityFilename.Text, _
            dialogSaveFile.FileName)
    End If
End Sub
```

`CreateSchema` itself looks like this. Firstly, we need to connect to the database:

```
Public Sub CreateSchema(ByVal connectionString As String, _
                ByVal tableName As String, _
                ByVal xsdUtilityFilename As String, _
                ByVal xsdFilename As String)
    Dim connection As New SqlConnection(connectionString)
    Dim adapter As SqlDataAdapter
    Try
        connection.Open()
```

Then, we need to create a new `DataSet` and new `DataTable` object. The names of these objects, as specified in their constructors' parameters, will be used as the names of the newly generated classes. Here, I've used the name of the table with `DataSet` appended on the end for the name of the `DataSet` derived class, and just the name of the table for the actual `DataTable`-derived class. (This will become clearer once we have the code.) Notice as well how we used the `top 1` directive in the SQL query so that if the table is very large, we only pull back the first row:

```
adapter = New SqlDataAdapter("select top 1 * from " & _
                        tableName, connection)
Dim dataset As New DataSet(tableName & "DataSet")
Dim table As New DataTable(tableName)
dataset.Tables.Add(table)
adapter.Fill(table)
```

Once we have the `DataSet`, we can write the schema to the specified filename:

```
dataset.WriteXmlSchema(xsdFilename)
```

Now we have the slightly tricky bit. We want to run the separate XSD.EXE command line utility to generate the `.vb` file. To do this, we supply the name of the source `.xsd` file, the `/d` directive to tell it to create a `DataSet`, `/l:vb` to tell it to spit VB.NET code, and `/out` to tell the name of the directory to generate the files in

```
Dim info As New FileInfo(xsdFilename)

Dim commandLine As String = """" & xsdFilename & _
                        """ /d /l:vb /out:""" & _
                        info.DirectoryName & """"
```

```
Dim process As System.Diagnostics.Process = _
    System.Diagnostics.Process.Start(xsdUtilityFilename, commandLine)
process.WaitForExit()

MsgBox("The new typed DataSet has been created in " & _
       info.DirectoryName)
```

Finally, we catch any exceptions and tear down the connection:

```
Catch ex As Exception
  MsgBox(ex.GetType().ToString & ":" & ex.Message)

Finally

  If connection.State <> ConnectionState.Closed Then
    connection.Close()
  End If
  If Not adapter Is Nothing Then
    adapter.Dispose()
  End If
End Try
End Sub
```

If you run that, you should be able to generate new .xsd and .vb files. If you look at the .xsd file in VS.NET, it will first show you a graphical representation of the schema as illustrated in Figure 10-6.

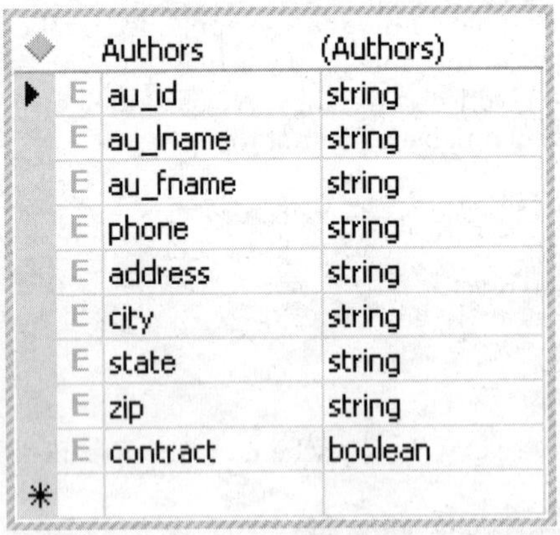

		Authors	(Authors)
◆		Authors	(Authors)
▶	E	au_id	string
	E	au_lname	string
	E	au_fname	string
	E	phone	string
	E	address	string
	E	city	string
	E	state	string
	E	zip	string
	E	contract	boolean
✱			

Figure 10-6

What's cool here is that XSD.EXE knows that the contract field in authors is a bit datatype field and therefore it needs to be handled as a Boolean variable in code.

If you click the XML button at the bottom of the editor, you'll be able to see the schema code:

```
<?xml version="1.0" standalone="yes" ?>
<xs:s,hema id="Auth_rsDataSet" xmlns="" xmlns:xs="http://www.w3.org/2001/
XMLSchema"
xmlns:msdata="urn:schemas-microsoft-com:xml-msdata">
```

```
<xs:element name="Auth_rsDataSet" msdata:IsDataSet="true" msdata:Locale=
"en-GB">
  <xs:complexType>
    <xs:choice maxO,curs="unbounded">
      <xs:element name="Authors">
        <xs:complexType>
          <xs:sequence>
            <xs:element name="au_id" type="xs:string" minOccurs="0" />
            <xs:element name="au_lname" type="xs:string" minOccurs="0" />
            <xs:element name="au_fname" type="xs:string" minOccurs="0" />
            <xs:element name="phone" type="xs:string" minOccurs="0" />
            <xs:element name="address" type="xs:string" minOccurs="0" />
            <xs:element name="city" type="xs:string" minOccurs="0" />
            <xs:element name="state" type="xs:string" minOccurs="0" />
            <xs:element name="zip" type="xs:string" minOccurs="0" />
            <xs:element name="contract" type="xs:boolean" minOccurs="0" />
          </xs:sequence>
        </xs:complexType>
      </xs:element>
    </xs:choice>
  </xs:complexType>
</xs:element>
</xs:schema>
```

Again, you don't really need to understand what that does, but with a little common sense you can see the names of the columns and the datatypes of those columns.

To test out the `DataSet`, create a new Windows Application project. Add the `Authors.vb` file to the project, add a button, and add this code to the new button control's `Click` event handler:

```
Private Sub Button1_Click(ByVal sender As System.Object, _
    ByVal e As System.EventArgs) Handles Button1.Click

    ' connect...
    Dim connection As New SqlConnection(_
        "uid=sa;pwd=;data source=(local);initial catalog=pubs")
    connection.Open()
    ' create a new authors dataset...
    Dim authorsDataSet As New AuthorsDataSet
    Dim authors As AuthorsDataSet.AuthorsDataTable = _
            authorsDataSet.Authors
    Dim adapter As New SqlDataAdapter("select * from authors", _
            connection)
    adapter.Fill(authors)
    authors.Dispose()

    ' close...
    connection.Close()

    ' walk...
    Dim builder As New StringBuilder

    For Each author As AuthorsDataSet.AuthorsRow In authors.Rows
      builder.Append(author.au_fname)
```

```
      builder.Append(" ")
      builder.Append(author.au_lname)
      builder.Append(ControlChars.CrLf)
   Next
   MsgBox(builder.ToString)

End Sub
```

You can see there how we create a new `AuthorDataSet` and, because it extends `System.Data`
`.DataSet`, we can use it anywhere where we could previously use a `DataSet`:

```
Dim authorsDataSet As New AuthorsDataSet
```

One property on this new `AuthorsDataSet` class is `Authors`. This returns a class called
`AuthorsDataSet.AuthorsDataTable`, derived from `DataTable`. We can fill that as normal:

```
Dim authors As AuthorsDataSet.AuthorsDataTable = _
            authorsDataSet.Authors
Dim adapter As New SqlDataAdapter("select * from authors", _
            connection)
adapter.Fill(authors)
authors.Dispose()
```

Once we have the `DataTable`, the `Rows` collection returns instances of `AuthorsDataSet.AuthorsRow`
objects, rather than `DataRow` objects. This class provides properties for each of the columns on the table:

```
' walk...
Dim builder As New StringBuilder

For Each author As AuthorsDataSet.AuthorsRow In authors.Rows
   builder.Append(author.au_fname)
   builder.Append(" ")
   builder.Append(author.au_lname)
   builder.Append(ControlChars.CrLf)
Next
MsgBox(builder.ToString)
```

That's it. Although typed `DataSets` seem a little more verbose and tricky to set up, what they do give
you is strongly typed access to the data in the `DataSet`.

Summary

Ultimately, XML could be the underpinnings of all electronic commerce, banking transactions, and data
exchange of almost every conceivable kind. The beauty of XML is that it isolates data representation from
data display. Technologies, such as HTML, contain data that is tightly bound to its display format. XML
does not suffer this limitation, yet at the same time has the readability of HTML. Accordingly, the XML
facilities available to a VB.NET application are vast and there are a large number of XML-related features,
classes, and interfaces exposed by the .NET Framework.

In this chapter we saw how to use `System.Xml.Serialization.XmlSerializer` to serialize classes. Source Code Style attributes were introduced in conjunction with serialization. This style of attributes allows the customization of the XML serialized to be extended to the source code associated with a class. What is important to remember about serialization classes directly is that a required change in the XML format becomes a change in the underlying source code. Developers should resist the temptation to rewrite the serialized classes in order to conform to some new XML data standard (such as the prescription format endorsed by our consortium of pharmacies). Technologies, such as XSLT, exposed via the `System.Xml.Xsl` namespace should be examined first as alternatives. We saw how to use XSLT style sheets to transform XML data using the classes found in `System.Xml.Xsl` namespace.

The most useful classes and interfaces in the `System.Xml` namespace were reviewed, including those that support document-style XML access: `XMmlDocument`, `XmlNode`, `XmlElement`, and `XmlAttribute`. The `System.Xml` namespace also contains classes and interfaces that support stream-style XML access: `XmlReader` and `XmlWriter`.

Finally, we looked at typed `DataSets`, which allow us to access tables and columns by name, instead of using collection-based methods. We saw how to create a typed `DataSet`, and then put it to use.

11

Data Access with ADO.NET

ADO.NET is the successor to *ActiveX Data Objects 2.6* (ADO). The main goal of ADO.NET is to allow you to easily create distributed, data sharing applications in the .NET Framework. ADO.NET is built upon industry standards such as XML and, like ADO, provides a data access interface to communicate with OLE DB-compliant data sources such as SQL Server and Oracle. Applications can use ADO.NET to connect to these data sources and retrieve, manipulate, and update data.

In solutions that require disconnected or remote access to data, ADO.NET uses XML to exchange data between programs or with Web pages. Any component that can read XML can make use of ADO.NET components. A receiving component does not even have to be an ADO.NET component if a transmitting ADO.NET component packages and delivers a data set in an XML file. Transmitting information in XML-formatted data sets enables programmers to easily separate the data processing and user interface components of a data-sharing application onto separate servers. This can greatly improve both the performance and maintainability of systems that support many users.

For distributed applications, the use of XML data sets in ADO.NET provides performance advantages relative to the COM marshaling used to transmit disconnected data sets in ADO. Since transmission of data sets occurs through XML streams in a simple text-based standard accepted throughout the industry, receiving components have none of the architectural restrictions required by COM. XML data sets used in ADO.NET also avoid the processing cost of converting values in the Fields collection of a `Recordset` to data types recognized by COM. Virtually, any two components from different systems can share XML data sets provided that they both use the same XML schema for formatting the data set.

ADO.NET also supports the scalability required by Web-based data-sharing applications. Web applications must often serve hundreds, or even thousands of users. By default, ADO.NET does not retain lengthy database locks or active connections that monopolize limited resources. This allows the number of users to grow with only a small increase in the demands made on the resources of a system. Although it was possible to have the same functionality in ADO 2.6, it was not a default setting for a `Recordset` object to be disconnected, which often got programmers in trouble.

In this chapter we will see that ADO.NET is a very extensive and flexible API for accessing many types of data. Also, it is similar enough to ADO that you will be able to leverage a lot of existing knowledge. In fact, to get the most out of this chapter you should have a good understanding of ADO.

In this chapter, we will understand how to use the ADO.NET object model in order to build flexible, fast, scalable data access objects and applications. Specifically, we will focus on:

❑   The ADO.NET architecture

❑   The differences between ADO and ADO.NET

❑   How to work with Managed Providers

❑   How to build a data access component

❑   How to use `DataSet` objects to bind to `DataGrid` controls

Why Do We Need ADO.NET?

You have already learned ADO, so why should you have to learn a new data access object model when the old one works OK? Well, you can use ADO in the .NET Framework if you really want to, but you will pay a performance price for going through the COM layer (for more details on this see Chapter 17). Also, the .NET Framework does not support the COM Variant data type, which is what ADO uses for the values of Field objects in a `Recordset` object. This means that if you used an ADO `Recordset` object in .NET, the CLR would have to constantly perform type-conversions for every field in order to be able to access the data. These type-conversions can become quite costly if you have to do them all of the time.

But the most significant reason for embracing ADO.NET is that you get a truly disconnected data architecture, tight integration with XML, a common data representation (utilizing .NET data types) with the ability to combine data from multiple and varied data sources, and optimized facilities for interacting with a database. Also, ADO.NET is tightly integrated with the rest of the .NET Framework, and makes use of all of the .NET Framework object hierarchy and design patterns. We saw in Chapter 10 how ADO.NET and XML are tightly integrated in the .NET Framework.

ADO.NET builds upon the foundation that was laid down by ADO, as well as offering us new tools for our data access toolset.

The ADO.NET Architecture

The main design goals of ADO.NET are to:

❑   Leverage current ADO knowledge

❑   Support the N-Tier programming model

❑   Provide support for XML

In distributed applications, the concept of working with disconnected data has become very common. A disconnected model means that once you have retrieved the data that you need, the connection to the data source is dropped—you work with the data locally. The reason why this model has become so popular is that it frees up precious database server resources, which leads to highly scalable applications. The ADO.NET solution for disconnected data is the DataSet object.

ADO.NET Components

In order to better support the disconnected model, the ADO.NET components separate data access from data manipulation. This is accomplished via two main components, the DataSet and the .NET Data Provider. Figure 11-1 illustrates the concept of separating data access from data manipulation.

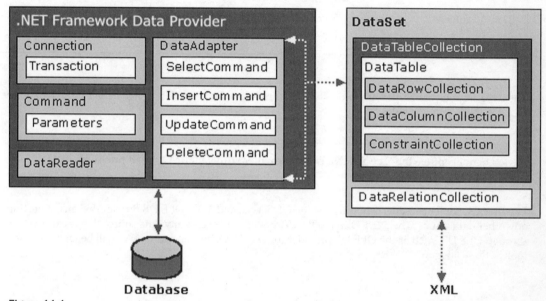

Figure 11-1

The DataSet is the core component of the disconnected architecture of ADO.NET and is basically what the Recordset object was to ADO. The DataSet is explicitly designed for data access independent of any data source. As a result it can be used with multiple and differing data sources, XML data, or even to manage data local to an application such as an in-memory data cache. The DataSet contains a collection of one or more DataTable objects made up of rows and columns of data, as well as primary key, foreign key, constraint and relation information about the data in the DataTable objects. It is basically an in-memory database, but the cool thing is that it does not care whether its data is obtained from a database, an XML file, a combination of the two, or somewhere else.

The other core element of the ADO.NET architecture is the .NET Data Provider, whose components are designed for data manipulation (as opposed to data access with the DataSet). These components are listed in the following table.

The DataAdapter uses Command objects to execute SQL commands at the data source to both load the DataSet with data, and also to reconcile changes made to the data in the DataSet back to the data source. We will take a closer look at this later when we cover the DataAdapter object in more detail.

.NET Data Providers can be written for any data source, though this is beyond the scope of this chapter.

Object	Activity
Connection	Provides connectivity to a data source
Command	Enables access to database commands to return and modify data, run stored procedures, and send or retrieve parameter information
DataReader	Provides a high-performance, read-only stream of data from the data source
DataAdapter	Provides the bridge between the `DataSet` object and the data source

The .NET Framework ships with two .NET Data Providers: The SQL Server .NET Data Provider and the OLE DB .NET Data Provider.

> **Do not confuse the OLE DB .NET Data Provider with generic OLE DB providers.**

Use the SQL Server provider when accessing SQL Server, and .NET OLE DB Provider when connecting to any other data source. The .NET OLE DB Provider is used to access any data source that is exposed through OLE DB, such as the OLE DB provider for Oracle, ODBC, and so on. We will be taking a closer look at these later on.

Differences Between ADO and ADO.NET

ADO.NET is an evolution of ADO. The following table lists several data access features and how each feature differs between ADO and ADO.NET.

Feature	ADO	ADO.NET
Memory-resident data representation	Uses the Recordset object, which holds single rows of data, much like a database table	Uses the `DataSet` object, which can contain one or more tables represented by DataTable objects
Relationships between multiple tables	Requires the JOIN query to assemble data from multiple database tables in a single result table. Also offers hierarchical recordsets, but they are hard to use	Supports the DataRelation object to associate rows in one DataTable object with rows in another DataTable object

Continues

Feature	ADO	ADO.NET
Data navigation	Traverses rows in a Recordset sequentially, by using the .MoveNext method	The DataSet uses a navigation paradigm for nonsequential access to rows in a table. Accessing the data is more like accessing data in a collection or array. This is possible because of the Rows collection of the DataTable; it allows you to access rows by index. Follows relationships to navigate from rows in one table to corresponding rows in another table
Disconnected access	Provided by the Recordset but it has to be explicitly coded for. The default for a Recordset object is to be connected via the ActiveConnection property. You communicate to a database with calls to an OLE DB provider	Communicates to a database with standardized calls to the DataAdapter object, which communicates to an OLE DB data provider, or directly to a SQL Server data provider
Programmability	All Recordset field data types are COM Variant data types, and usually correspond to field names in a database table	Uses the strongly typed programming characteristic of XML. Data is self-describing because names for code items correspond to the business problem solved by the code. Data in `DataSet` and `DataReader` objects can be strongly typed, thus making code easier to read and to write
Sharing disconnected data between tiers or components	Uses COM marshaling to transmit a disconnected record set. This supports only those data types defined by the COM standard. Requires type conversions, which demand system resources	Transmits a DataSet as XML. The XML format places no restrictions on data types and requires no type conversions
Transmitting data through firewalls	Problematic, because firewalls are typically configured to prevent system-level requests such as COM marshaling	Supported, because ADO.NET DataSet objects use XML, which can pass through firewalls
Scalability	Since the defaults in ADO are to use connected Recordset objects, database locks, and active database connections for long durations contend for limited database resources	Disconnected access to database data without retaining database locks or active database connections for lengthy periods limits contention for limited database resources

In order to make things clearer, let's look at some code to see the differences and similarities between ADO and ADO.NET. First, we will look at some familiar ADO code that grabs a Recordset of the authors table in the pubs database and traverses through it, outputting each author name as it goes:

```
'VB 6 Code
'References ADO 2.6
Private Sub TraverseRecordset()

    Dim strSQL As String
    Dim strConn As String
    Dim objRS As ADODB.Recordset
    Dim strResult As String

    'Build the SQL and Connection strings
    strConn = "Provider=SQLOLEDB;Initial Catalog=pubs;" _
        & "Data Source=(local);Integrated Security=SSPI;"
    strSQL = "SELECT * FROM authors"

    'Create an instance of the Recordset
    Set objRS = New ADODB.Recordset

    With objRS

        'Make the Recordset client-side with a static cursor
        .CursorLocation = adUseClient
        .CursorType = adOpenStatic

        'Open the Recordset
        .Open strSQL, strConn

        'Disconnect the Recordset
        Set .ActiveConnection = Nothing

        'Loop through the records and print the values
        Do Until .EOF
            strResult = .Fields("au_fname").Value _


            & " " & .Fields("au_lname").Value
            Debug.Print strResult
            .MoveNext
        Loop

    End With

    'Clean up
    Set objRS = Nothing

End Sub
```

As you can see in this code, we have to explicitly tell the ADO Recordset object that we want it to be a client-side, disconnected Recordset. Note, how we also have to clean up the memory when we are done with the object.

Now, we will look at a few ways of doing this same operation in ADO.NET. First, we will see how it is done with the DataSet component. Here is the code for traversing through a DataSet:

```
Private Sub TraverseDataSet()

    ' Build the SQL and Connection strings
    Dim sql As String = "SELECT * FROM authors"
    Dim connectionString As String = "Initial Catalog=pubs;" _
        & "Data Source=(local);Integrated Security=SSPI;"

    ' Initialize the SqlDataAdapter with the SQL
    ' and Connection strings, and then use the
    ' SqlDataAdapter to fill the DataSet with data
    Dim adapter As SqlClient.SqlDataAdapter = New _
        SqlClient.SqlDataAdapter(sql, connectionString)
    Dim authors As New Data.DataSet
    adapter.Fill(authors)

    Dim intCounter As Integer
    With authors.Tables(0)
        ' Loop through the records and print the values
        For intCounter = 0 To .Rows.Count - 1
            Console.WriteLine(.Rows(intCounter).Item("au_fname").ToString _
                & " " & .Rows(intCounter).Item("au_lname").ToString)
    Next
    End With
    ' Print the DataSet's XML
    Console.WriteLine(authors.GetXml())
    Console.ReadLine()

End Sub
```

In this code snippet, we start out the same way as before by building our SQL and connection strings. Instead of passing them directly to the DataSet object (like we do with the ADO `Recordset`), we pass them to a `SqlDataAdapter` object. This object abstracts the data access location from the `DataSet` object. After calling the `SqlDataAdapter` constructor, we call its Fill method to populate our `DataSet` object. Note how the same operation with a `DataSet` object contains fewer lines of code. This is mostly due to the fact that the `DataSet` object is already disconnected, so we do not have to write that plumbing. Also notice how there is no need to call a `MoveNext` method — a common mistake in ADO was to forget to call this method, which resulted in the computer's CPU usage skyrocketing.

We will cover the details of the `SqlCommand`, `SQLDataReader`, `SqlDataAdapter`, and the `DataSet` objects in the next section.

.NET Data Providers

.NET Data Providers are used for connecting to a database, executing commands, and retrieving results. Those results are either processed directly (via a DataReader), or placed in an ADO.NET DataSet (via a DataAdapter) in order to be exposed to the user in an ad hoc manner, combined with data from multiple sources, or passed around between tiers. The .NET Data Provider is designed to be lightweight, creating a minimal layer between the data source and the .NET programmer's code, increasing performance while not sacrificing functionality. Currently, the .NET Framework supports two data providers: the SQL Server .NET Data Provider (for Microsoft SQL Server 7.0 or later), and the OLE DB .NET Data Provider.

Connection Object

To connect to a specific data source, we use a data Connection object. To connect to Microsoft SQL Server 7.0 or later, we need to use the `SqlConnection` object of the SQL Server .NET Data Provider. We need to use the `OleDbConnection` object of the OLE DB .NET Data Provider to connect to an OLE DB data source, or the OLE DB Provider for SQL Server (SQLOLEDB) to connect to versions of Microsoft SQL Server earlier than 7.0.

Connection String Format–OleDbConnection

For the OLE DB .NET Data Provider, the connection string format is identical to the connection string format used in ADO with the following exceptions:

❏　The `Provider` keyword is required

❏　The URL, Remote Provider, and `Remote Server` keywords are not supported

Here is an example OleDbConnection connection string connecting to an Oracle database (note this is all one line):

```
Provider=msdaora;Data Source=MyOracleDB;User Id=myUsername;Password=myPassword;
```

Connection String Format–SqlConnection

The SQL Server .NET Data Provider supports a connection string format that is similar to the OLE DB (ADO) connection string format. The only thing that you need to leave off, obviously, is the Provider name-value pair, since we know we are using the SQL Server .NET provider. Here is an example of a SqlConnection connection string:

```
Initial Catalog=pubs;Data Source=(local);User ID=sa;password=;
```

Command Object

After establishing a connection, you can execute commands and return results from a data source (such as SQL Server) using a Command object. A Command object can be created using the Command constructor, or by calling the `CreateCommand` method of the Connection object. When creating a Command object using the Command constructor, you need to specify a SQL statement to execute at the data source, and a `Connection` object. The Command object's SQL statement can be queried and modified using the `CommandText` property. The following code is an example of executing a SELECT command and returning a DataReader object:

```
' Build the SQL and Connection strings
Dim sql As String = "SELECT * FROM authors"
Dim connectionString As String = "Initial Catalog=pubs;" _
    & "Data Source=(local);Integrated Security=SSPI;"

' Initialize the SqlCommand with the SQL
' and Connection strings
```

```
Dim command As SqlClient.SqlCommand = New SqlClient.SqlCommand(sql, _
    New SqlClient.SqlConnection(connectionString))
' Open the connection
command.Connection.Open()
' Execute the query, return a SqlDataReader object.
' CommandBehavior.CloseConnection flags the
' DataReader to automatically close the db connection
' when it is closed.
Dim dataReader As SqlClient.SqlDataReader = _
    command.ExecuteReader(CommandBehavior.CloseConnection)
```

Like the Command object in ADO, the `CommandText` property of the `Command` object will execute all SQL statements in addition to the standard SELECT, UPDATE, INSERT and DELETE statements. For example, you could create tables, foreign keys, primary keys, and so on, by executing the applicable SQL from the `Command` object.

The `Command` object exposes several `Execute` methods to perform the intended action. When returning results as a stream of data, `ExecuteReader` is used to return a `DataReader` object. `ExecuteScalar` is used to return a singleton value. `ExecuteNonQuery` is used to execute commands that do not return rows, which usually includes stored procedures that have output parameters and/or return values. (We'll talk about stored procedures in a later section.)

When using a DataAdapter with a DataSet, `Command` objects are used to return and modify data at the data source through the DataAdapter object's `SelectCommand`, `InsertCommand`, `UpdateCommand`, and `DeleteCommand` properties.

> Note that the DataAdapter object's SelectCommand property must be set before the Fill method is called.

The `InsertCommand`, `UpdateCommand`, and `DeleteCommand` properties must be set before the `Update` method is called. We will take a closer look at this when we look at the `DataAdapter` object.

DataReader Object

You can use the DataReader to retrieve a read-only, forward-only stream of data from the database. Using the DataReader can increase application performance and reduce system overhead because only one buffered row at a time is ever in memory. With the `DataReader` object, you are getting as close to the raw data as possible in ADO.NET; you do not have to go through the overhead of populating a `DataSet` object, which sometimes may be expensive if the DataSet contains a lot of data. The disadvantage of using a `DataReader` object is that it requires an open database connection and increases network activity.

After creating an instance of the `Command` object, a `DataReader` is created by calling `Command`
`.ExecuteReader` to retrieve rows from a data source. Here is an example of creating a DataReader and iterating through it:

```
Private Sub TraverseDataReader()

    ' Build the SQL and Connection strings
    Dim sql As String = "SELECT * FROM authors"
```

```
Dim connectionString As String = "Initial Catalog=pubs;" _
    & "Data Source=(local);Integrated Security=SSPI;"
' Initialize the SqlCommand with the SQL
' and Connection strings, and then use the
' SqlDataAdapter to fill the DataSet with data
Dim command As SqlClient.SqlCommand = New SqlClient.SqlCommand(sql, _
    New SqlClient.SqlConnection(connectionString))
' Open the connection
command.Connection.Open()
' Execute the query, return a SqlDataReader object.
' CommandBehavior.CloseConnection flags the
' DataReader to automatically close the db connection
' when it is closed.
Dim dataReader As SqlClient.SqlDataReader = _
    command.ExecuteReader(CommandBehavior.CloseConnection)

With dataReader
    ' Loop through the records and print the values
    Do While .Read = True
        Console.WriteLine(.GetString(1) & " " & .GetString(2))
    Loop
    ' Close the DataReader (and its db connection)
    .Close()
End With
Console.ReadLine()

End Sub
```

In this code snippet, we use the `SqlCommand` object to execute our query via the `ExecuteReader` method. This method returns a populated `SqlDataReader` object to us, and then we loop through it and print out the author names. The main difference with this code compared to the previous `TraverseDataSet()` example is that we have to stay connected while we loop through the data in the `DataReader` object; this is due to the fact that DataReader reads in only a small stream of data at a time in order to conserve memory space.

> At this point an obvious design question is whether to use the DataReader or the DataSet. The answer to this question really depends upon performance. If you want high performance, and you are only going to access the data that you are retrieving once, then the DataReader is the way to go. If you need access to the same data multiple times, or if you need to model a complex relationship in memory, then the DataSet is the way to go. As always, you will need to test each option thoroughly before deciding which is the best.

The `Read` method of the `DataReader` object is used to obtain a row from the results of the query. Each column of the returned row may be accessed by passing the name or ordinal reference of the column to the DataReader, or, for best performance, the DataReader provides a series of methods that allow you to access column values in their native data types (`GetDateTime`, `GetDouble`, `GetGuid`, `GetInt32`, and so on). Using the typed accessor methods when the underlying data type is known will reduce the amount of type conversion required (converting from type Object) when retrieving the column value.

The DataReader provides a nonbuffered stream of data that allows procedural logic to efficiently process results from a data source sequentially. The DataReader is a good choice when retrieving large amounts of data; only one row of data will be cached in memory at a time. You should always call the Close method when you are through using the DataReader object, as well as closing the DataReader object's database connection, otherwise the connection won't be closed until the Garbage Collector gets around to collecting the object. Note how we used the CommandBehavior.CloseConnection enumeration value on the SqlDataReader.ExecuteReader method. This tells the SqlCommand object to automatically close the database connection when the SqlDataReader.Close method is called.

> If your Command contains output parameters or return values, they will not be available until the DataReader is closed.

DataAdapter Objects

Each .NET Data Provider included with the .NET Framework has a DataAdapter object. The OLE DB .NET Data Provider includes an OleDbDataAdapter object, and the SQL Server .NET Data Provider includes a SqlDataAdapter object. A DataAdapter is used to retrieve data from a data source and populate DataTables and constraints within a DataSet. The DataAdapter also resolves changes made to the DataSet back to the data source. The DataAdapter uses the Connection object of the .NET Data Provider to connect to a data source, and Command objects to retrieve data from, and resolve changes to, the data source from a DataSet object. This differs from the DataReader, in that the DataReader uses the Connection to access the data directly, without having to use a DataAdapter. The DataAdapter essentially decouples the DataSet object from the actual source of the data, whereas the DataReader is tightly bound to the data in a read-only fashion.

The SelectCommand property of the DataAdapter is a Command object that retrieves data from the data source. The InsertCommand, UpdateCommand, and DeleteCommand properties of the DataAdapter are Command objects that manage updates to the data in the data source according to the modifications made to the data in the DataSet. The Fill method of the DataAdapter is used to populate a DataSet with the results of the SelectCommand of the DataAdapter. It also adds or refreshes rows in the DataSet to match those in the data source. We look again at our example from the TraverseDataSet() method used previously, that shows how to fill a DataSet object with information from the authors table in the pubs database:

```
Private Sub TraverseDataSet()

    ' Build the SQL and Connection strings
    Dim sql As String = "SELECT * FROM authors"
    Dim connectionString As String = "Initial Catalog=pubs;" _
        & "Data Source=(local);Integrated Security=SSPI;"

    ' Initialize the SqlDataAdapter with the SQL
    ' and Connection strings, and then use the
    ' SqlDataAdapter to fill the DataSet with data
    Dim adapter As SqlClient.SqlDataAdapter = New _
        SqlClient.SqlDataAdapter(sql, connectionString)
    Dim authors As New Data.DataSet
    adapter.Fill(authors)
```

```
            Dim intCounter As Integer
            With authors.Tables(0)
                ' Loop through the records and print the values
                For intCounter = 0 To .Rows.Count - 1
                    Console.WriteLine(.Rows(intCounter).Item("au_fname").ToString _
                        & " " & .Rows(intCounter).Item("au_lname").ToString)
                Next
            End With
            ' Print the DataSet's XML
            Console.WriteLine(authors.GetXml())
            Console.ReadLine()

        End Sub
```

Note how we use the `SqlDataAdapter`'s constructor to pass in and set the `SelectCommand`, as well as passing in the connection string in lieu of a `SqlCommand` object that already has an initialized `Connection` property. We then just call the `SqlDataAdapter` object's `Fill` method and pass in an initialized `DataSet` object. If the DataSet object is not initialized, the `Fill` method will raise an exception (`System.ArgumentNullException`). Now, let's take a look at some code in which we use a DataSet to insert data from the DataSet data to the pubs database:

```
Private Sub UpdateDataSet()

    ' Build the SQL and Connection strings
    Dim sql As String = "SELECT * FROM authors"
    Dim connectionString As String = "Initial Catalog=pubs;" _
        & "Data Source=(local);Integrated Security=SSPI;"

    ' Initialize the SqlDataAdapter with the SQL
    ' and Connection strings
    Dim adapter As SqlClient.SqlDataAdapter = _
        New SqlClient.SqlDataAdapter(sql, connectionString)

    ' Initialize the SqlCommandBuilder by passing in
    ' our DataAdapter. This will build the INSERT, UPDATE,
    ' and DELETE commands for the DataAdapter object.
    Dim commandBuilder As SqlClient.SqlCommandBuilder = New _
        SqlClient.SqlCommandBuilder(adapter)

    ' Use the SqlDataAdapter to fill the DataSet with
    ' the authors table
    Dim ds As New Data.DataSet
    adapter.Fill(ds, "Authors")

    Dim row As Data.DataRow
    ' Add a new author to the local table in memory
    row = ds.Tables("Authors").NewRow
    row("au_id") = "335-22-0707"
    row("au_fname") = "Tim"
    row("au_lname") = "McCarthy"
    row("phone") = "760-930-0075"
    row("contract") = 0
    ds.Tables("Authors").Rows.Add(row)
```

```
' Write the update back to the server
adapter.Update(ds, "Authors")

' Indicate success
Console.WriteLine("New author added!")
Console.ReadLine()

ds.WriteXmlSchema("test.txt")

Dim intCounter As Integer
With ds.Tables(0)
    ' Loop through the records and print the values
    For intCounter = 0 To .Rows.Count - 1
        Console.WriteLine(.Rows(intCounter).Item("au_fname").ToString _
            & " " & .Rows(intCounter).Item("au_lname").ToString)
    Next
End With
Console.ReadLine()

End Sub
```

This code starts out exactly the same way as the TraverseDataSet method did. It starts to differ when we use a CommandBuilder object. This is a helper object, which will internally build the INSERT, UPDATE, and DELETE commands for our DataAdapter object for us. The only caveat is that we have to make sure that our SELECT command has the primary key of the table that we are working on, in this case, the au_id field. To use the CommandBuilder object, simply pass in the initialized DataAdapter object to the CommandBuilder's constructor. We then call the Fill method of the DataAdapter, and specify that we are filling the Authors DataTable (we will cover this in more detail later).

Now comes the interesting part. In order to add the new row to the authors table, we use the DataTable's NewRow method to return an initialized DataRow object. We then reference the fields in the DataRow object by the column name, and set their respective values. Once we have finished setting the fields, we then have to add the new DataRow to the Authors DataTable. This is done by calling the Add method of the DataTable's Rows property. So far everything we have done in this update has been offline, nothing has been written to the database. In order to write the changes to the database, we simply call the Update method of our DataAdapter object, and pass in the DataSet and the name of the DataTable (Authors) to update. By doing this, the DataAdapter will implicitly invoke the INSERT command that was built for us by the CommandBuilder object. The next part of the code is the same as the TraverseDataSet method; it simply writes out the names of the authors to the screen.

SQL Server .NET Data Provider

The SQL Server .NET Data Provider uses Tabular Data Stream (TDS), to communicate with the SQL Server. This offers a great performance increase, since TDS is SQL Server's native communication protocol. As an example of how much of an increase you can expect, when I ran some simple tests accessing the authors table of the pubs database we saw the SQL Server .NET Data Provider perform about 70 percent faster than the OLE DB .NET Data Provider.

The SQL Server .NET Data Provider is lightweight and performs very well, thanks to not having to go through the OLE DB or ODBC layer. What it actually does is that it establishes a networking connection (usually sockets based) and drags data from this directly into managed code and vice versa.

> This is very important, since going through the OLE DB or ODBC layers means that the CLR has to marshal (convert) all of the COM data types to .NET CLR data types each time data is accessed from a data source. By using the SQL Server .NET Data Provider, everything runs within the .NET CLR, and the TDS protocol is faster than the other network protocols previously used for SQL Server.

To use this provider, you need to include the System.Data.SqlClient namespace in your application. Also, it will only work for SQL Server 7.0 and above. I highly recommend using SQL Server .NET Data Provider any time you are connecting to a SQL Server 7.0 and above database server. The SQL Server .NET Data Provider requires the installation of MDAC 2.6 or later.

OLE DB .NET Data Provider

The OLE DB .NET Data Provider uses native OLE DB through COM Interop (see Chapter 17 for more details) to enable data access. The OLE DB .NET Data Provider supports both manual and automatic transactions. For automatic transactions, the OLE DB .NET Data Provider automatically enlists in a transaction and obtains transaction details from Windows 2000 Component Services. The OLE DB .NET Data Provider does not support OLE DB 2.5 interfaces. OLE DB Providers that require support for OLE DB 2.5 interfaces will not function properly with the OLE DB .NET Data Provider. This includes the Microsoft OLE DB Provider for Exchange and the Microsoft OLE DB Provider for Internet Publishing. The OLE DB .NET Data Provider requires the installation of MDAC 2.6 or later. To use this provider, you need to include the System.Data.OleDb namespace in your application.

The DataSet Component

The DataSet object is central to supporting disconnected, distributed data scenarios with ADO.NET. The DataSet is a memory-resident representation of data that provides a consistent relational programming model regardless of the data source. The DataSet represents a complete set of data including related tables, constraints, and relationships among the tables; basically, like having a small relational database residing in memory.

> Since the DataSet contains a lot of metadata in it, you need to be careful about how much data you try to stuff into it, since it will be consuming memory.

The methods and objects in a DataSet are consistent with those in the relational database model. The DataSet can also persist and reload its contents as XML and its schema as XSD. It is completely disconnected from any database connections; therefore, it is totally up to you to fill it with whatever data you need in memory.

DataTableCollection

An ADO.NET DataSet contains a collection of zero or more tables represented by DataTable objects. The DataTableCollection contains all of the DataTable objects in a DataSet.

A DataTable is defined in the System.Data namespace and represents a single table of memory-resident data. It contains a collection of columns represented by the DataColumnCollection, which defines the schema and rows of the table. It also contains a collection of rows represented by the DataRowCollection, which contains the data in the table. Along with the current state, a DataRow retains its original state and tracks changes that occur to the data.

DataRelationCollection

A DataSet contains relationships in its DataRelationCollection object. A relationship (represented by the DataRelation object) associates rows in one DataTable with rows in another DataTable. The relationships in the DataSet can have constraints, which are represented by UniqueConstraint and ForeignKeyConstraint objects. It is analogous to a JOIN path that might exist between the primary and foreign-key columns in a relational database. A DataRelation identifies matching columns in two tables of a DataSet.

Relationships enable you to see what links information within one table to another. The essential elements of a DataRelation are the name of the relationship, the two tables being related, and the related columns in each table. Relationships can be built with more than one column per table, with an array of DataColumn objects for the key columns. When a relationship is added to the DataRelationCollection, it may optionally add ForeignKeyConstraints that disallow any changes that would invalidate the relationship.

ExtendedProperties

DataSet (as well as DataTable and DataColumn) has an ExtendedProperties property. ExtendedProperties is a PropertyCollection where a user can place customized information, such as the SELECT statement that was used to generate the resultset, or a date/time stamp of when the data was generated. Since the ExtendedProperties contains customized information, this is a good place to store extra user-defined data about the DataSet (or DataTable or DataColumn), such as a time when the data should be refreshed. The ExtendedProperties collection is persisted with the schema information for the DataSet (as well as DataTable and DataColumn). The following code is an example of adding an expiration property to a DataSet:

```
Private Sub DataSetExtended()

    ' Build the SQL and Connection strings
    Dim sql As String = "SELECT * FROM authors"
    Dim connectionString As String = "Initial Catalog=pubs;" _
        & "Data Source=(local);Integrated Security=SSPI;"

    ' Initialize the SqlDataAdapter with the SQL
    ' and Connection strings, and then use the
    ' SqlDataAdapter to fill the DataSet with data
    Dim adapter As SqlClient.SqlDataAdapter = _
        New SqlClient.SqlDataAdapter(sql, connectionString)
    Dim authors As New Data.DataSet
    adapter.Fill(authors)

    ' Add an extended property called "expiration"
    ' Set its value to the current date/time + 1 hour
```

```
    authors.ExtendedProperties.Add("expiration", _
        DateAdd(DateInterval.Hour, 1, Now))

    Console.Write(authors.ExtendedProperties("expiration").ToString)
    Console.ReadLine()

End Sub
```

This code starts out by filling a DataSet with the authors table from the pubs database. We then add a new extended property, called expiration, and set its value to the current date and time plus one hour. We then simply read it back. As you can see, it is very easy to add extended properties to DataSet objects. The same pattern also applies to DataTable and DataColumn objects.

Creating and Using DataSet Objects

The ADO.NET DataSet is a memory-resident representation of the data that provides a consistent relational programming model, regardless of the source of the data it contains. A DataSet represents a complete set of data including the tables that contain, order, and constrain the data, as well as the relationships between the tables. The advantage to using a DataSet over using an ADO 2.6 Recordset object is that the data in a DataSet can come from multiple sources, and it is fairly easy to get the data from multiple sources into the DataSet. Also, you can define your own constraints between the data tables in a DataSet. With ADO Recordset objects, it was possible to have data from multiple sources, but it did require a lot more work. Also, constraints were not supported in ADO Recordset objects, which made it harder to model data from a database when you were disconnected from the data source.

There are several methods of working with a DataSet, which can be applied independently or in combination. You can:

❑ Programmatically create DataTables, DataRelations and Constraints within the DataSet and populate them with data

❑ Populate the DataSet from an existing relational database management system using a DataAdapter

❑ Load and persist the DataSet using XML

Here is a typical usage scenario for a DataSet object:

1. A client makes a request to a Web service

2. Based on this request, the Web service populates a DataSet from a database using a DataAdapter and returns the DataSet to the client

3. The client can then view the data and make modifications

4. When finished viewing and modifying the data, the client passes the modified DataSet back to the Web service, which again uses a DataAdapter to reconcile the changes in the returned DataSet with the original data in the database

5. The Web service may then return a DataSet that reflects the current values in the database

6. (Optional) The client can then use the DataSet class' Merge method to merge the returned DataSet with the client's existing copy of the DataSet; the Merge method will accept successful changes and mark with an error any changes that failed

The design of the ADO.NET DataSet makes this scenario fairly easy to implement. Since the DataSet is stateless, it can be safely passed between the server and the client without tying up server resources such as database connections. Although the DataSet is transmitted as XML, Web services and ADO.NET automatically transform the XML representation of the data to and from a DataSet, creating a rich, yet simplified, programming model. In addition, because the DataSet is transmitted as an XML stream, non-ADO.NET clients can consume the same Web service as that consumed by ADO.NET clients. Similarly, ADO.NET clients can interact easily with non-ADO.NET Web services by sending any client DataSet to a Web service as XML and by consuming any XML returned as a DataSet from the Web service. One thing to be careful of is the size of the data; if there are a large number of rows in the tables of your DataSet, then it will eat up a lot of bandwidth.

Programmatically Creating DataSet Objects

Just like with the ADO Recordset object, you can programmatically create a DataSet object to use as a data structure in your programs. This could be quite useful if you have complex data that needs to be passed around to another object's method. For example, when creating a new customer, instead of passing 20arguments about the new customer to a method, you could just pass the programmatically created DataSet object with all of the customer information to the object's method.

In ADO, you could programmatically create hierarchically Recordset objects using the Shape syntax, but most people did not like dealing with the complexity of this syntax. The DataSet object offers a much richer, and easier to use model for building complex data representations. Let's take a look at some sample code to programmatically build a shaped Recordset in ADO, and then we will contrast the code with how we build the same type in ADO.NET.

Here is some (VB6) ADO code to programmatically build a shaped Recordset of data containing customer order information. This sample will build a DataSet containing customer order information for one customer and one order, and it will output the data to the screen as XML:

```vb
Sub ADOShapeSyntax()

    Dim cnShape As ADODB.Connection
    Dim rstCustomers As ADODB.Recordset
    Dim rstCustomerOrders As ADODB.Recordset
    Dim stmXML As ADODB.Stream
    Dim strRSShape As String
    Dim strXML As String

    'Initialize ADO objects
    Set cnShape = New ADODB.Connection
    Set rstCustomers = New ADODB.Recordset
    Set stmXML = New ADODB.Stream

    strRSShape = "SHAPE APPEND NEW adInteger AS CustomerID," & _
                " NEW adVarChar(100) AS FirstName," & _
                " NEW adVarChar(100) AS LastName," & _
                " NEW adVarChar(100) AS Phone," & _
                " NEW adVarChar(255) AS Email," & _
                " ((SHAPE APPEND NEW adInteger AS CustomerID," & _
                " NEW adInteger AS OrderID," & _
                " NEW adCurrency AS OrderAmount, " & _
                " NEW adDate AS OrderDate)" & _
```

```
                        " AS rstCustomerOrders RELATE CustomerID TO CustomerID) "
    cnShape.Open "Provider=MSDataShape;Data Provider=NONE;"
    rstCustomers.Open strRSShape, cnShape, adOpenStatic, adLockOptimistic

    With rstCustomers
      .AddNew
      .Fields("CustomerID").Value = 1
      .Fields("FirstName").Value = "Miriam"
      .Fields("LastName").Value = "McCarthy"
      .Fields("Phone").Value = "555-1212"
      .Fields("Email").Value = "tweety@hotmail.com"
      Set rstCustomerOrders = .Fields("rstCustomerOrders").Value
      rstCustomerOrders.AddNew
      rstCustomerOrders.Fields("CustomerID").Value = 1
      rstCustomerOrders.Fields("OrderID").Value = "12345"
      rstCustomerOrders.Fields("OrderAmount").Value = 22.22
      rstCustomerOrders.Fields("OrderDate").Value = #11/10/2001#
      rstCustomerOrders.Update
      .Save stmXML, adPersistXML
    End With

    'Get the XML string
    With stmXML
      .Type = adTypeText
      .Charset = "ascii"
      strXML = .ReadText
      Debug.Print strXML
    End With

    'Clean up
    Set cnShape = Nothing
    Set rstCustomers = Nothing
    Set rstCustomerOrders = Nothing
    Set stmXML = Nothing

End Sub
```

Notice how relatively complex the shaped provider syntax code is. Here is the code for accomplishing the exact same thing using an ADO.NET DataSet object:

```
Private Sub BuildDataSet()

    Dim customerOrders As New Data.DataSet("CustomerOrders")
    Dim customers As Data.DataTable = customerOrders.Tables.Add("Customers")
    Dim orders As Data.DataTable = customerOrders.Tables.Add("Orders")
    Dim row As Data.DataRow

    With customers
        .Columns.Add("CustomerID", Type.GetType("System.Int32"))
        .Columns.Add("FirstName", Type.GetType("System.String"))
        .Columns.Add("LastName", Type.GetType("System.String"))
```

```
            .Columns.Add("Phone", Type.GetType("System.String"))
            .Columns.Add("Email", Type.GetType("System.String"))
        End With

        With orders
            .Columns.Add("CustomerID", Type.GetType("System.Int32"))
            .Columns.Add("OrderID", Type.GetType("System.Int32"))
            .Columns.Add("OrderAmount", Type.GetType("System.Double"))
            .Columns.Add("OrderDate", Type.GetType("System.DateTime"))
        End With

        customerOrders.Relations.Add("r_Customers_Orders", _
        customerOrders.Tables("Customers").Columns("CustomerID"), _
        customerOrders.Tables("Orders").Columns("CustomerID"))

        row = customers.NewRow()
        row("CustomerID") = 1
        row("FirstName") = "Miriam"
        row("LastName") = "McCarthy"
        row("Phone") = "555-1212"
        row("Email") = "tweety@hotmail.com"
        customers.Rows.Add(row)

        row = orders.NewRow()
        row("CustomerID") = 1
        row("OrderID") = 22
        row("OrderAmount") = 0
        row("OrderDate") = #11/10/1997#
        orders.Rows.Add(row)

        Console.WriteLine(customerOrders.GetXml())
        Console.ReadLine()

End Sub
```

Here is what the resulting XML of the DataSet looks like:

```
<CustomerOrders>
  <Customers>
    <CustomerID>1</CustomerID>
    <FirstName>Miriam</FirstName>
    <LastName>McCarthy</LastName>
    <Phone>555-1212</Phone>
    <Email>tweety@hotmail.com</Email>
</Customers>
<Orders>
  <CustomerID>1</CustomerID>
  <OrderID>22</OrderID>
  <OrderAmount>0</OrderAmount>
  <OrderDate>1997-11-10T00:00:00.0000</OrderDate>
</Orders>
</CustomerOrders>
```

Notice how the ADO.NET code is much easier to read and more logical. We start out by first defining a DataSet object (objDS) named CustomerOrders. We then create two tables, one for Customers (dtCustomers), and one for Orders (dtOrders), we then define the columns of the tables. Notice how we call the Add method of the DataSet's Tables collection. We then define the columns of each of the tables, and create a relation in the DataSet between the Customers table and the Orders table on the CustomerID column. Finally, we create instances of Rows for the tables, add the data, and then append the Rows to the Rows collection of the DataTable objects. This operation contained fewer lines of code than the ADO example, was much more object-oriented, and as a result, is much easier to follow. This will usually result in code that is faster to write, easier to read, and less bug-prone.

> **If you create a DataSet object with no name, it will be given the default name of NewDataSet.**

ADO.NET DataTable Objects

A DataSet is made up of a collection of tables, relationships, and constraints. In ADO.NET, DataTable objects are used to represent the tables in a DataSet. A DataTable represents one table of in-memory relational data. The data is local to the .NET application in which it resides, but can be populated from a data source such as SQL Server using a DataAdapter.

The DataTable class is a member of the System.Data namespace within the .NET Framework class library. You can create and use a DataTable independently or as a member of a DataSet, and DataTable objects can also be used by other the .NET Framework objects including the DataView. You access the collection of tables in a DataSet through the DataSet object's Tables property.

The schema, or structure, of a table is represented by columns and constraints. You define the schema of a DataTable using DataColumn objects as well as ForeignKeyConstraint and UniqueConstraint objects. The columns in a table can map to columns in a data source, contain calculated values from expressions, automatically increment their values, or contain primary key values.

If you populate a DataTable from a database, it will inherit the constraints from the database so you do not have to do all of that work manually. A DataTable must also have rows in which to contain and order the data. The DataRow class represents the actual data contained in the table. You use the DataRow and its properties and methods to retrieve, evaluate, and manipulate the data in a table. As you access and change the data within a row, the DataRow object maintains both its current and original state.

You can create parent/child relationships between tables within a database, like SQL Server, using one or more related columns in the tables. You create a relationship between DataTable objects using a DataRelation, which can then be used to return a row's related child or parent rows.

Connection Pooling in ADO.NET

Pooling connections can significantly enhance the performance and scalability of your application. Connection pooling is a great story in ADO.NET — it comes for free! Both the SQL Client .NET Data

Provider and the OLE DB .NET Data Provider automatically pool connections using Windows 2000 Component Services and OLE DB Session Pooling, respectively. The only requirement is that you must use the exact same connection string each time if you want to get a pooled connection.

Universal Data Link (UDL) files can be used to supply OLE DB connection information to the OLE DB Provider.

> **UDL files are analogous to DSN files for ODBC connections.**

However, since UDL files can be modified externally to any ADO.NET client program, connections that use UDL files are not pooled. This is because the connection information can change without the ADO.NET client being aware of the change. As a result, for connection strings that contain UDL files, ADO.NET will parse the connection information found in a UDL file every time a connection is opened. Therefore, it is strongly suggested that you use a static connection string instead of a UDL file when using the OLE DB .NET Data Provider.

The SQL Client .NET Data Provider relies on Windows Component Services to provide connection pooling using an implicit pooling model by default.

Using Stored Procedures with ADO.NET

In this section, we'll take a quick look at how to use stored procedures, before delving into a more complex illustration of how we can build a reusable data access component that also uses stored procedures. The motivation for using stored procedures is simple. Imagine you have this code

```
SELECT au_lname FROM authors WHERE au_id='172-32-1176'
```

If you pass that to SQL Server using ExecuteReader on SqlCommand (or any execute method, for that matter), what happens is that SQL Server has to compile the code before it can run it, in much the same way that VB6 or VB .NET applications have to be compiled before they can be executed. This compilation takes SQL Server time, so it's a pretty obvious leap to deduce that if you can reduce the amount of compilation that SQL Server has to do, database performance should be increased. (Compare the speed of execution of a compiled application against interpreted code.)

That's what stored procedures are all about, we create a procedure, store it in the database and because the procedure is known of and understood ahead of time, it can be compiled ahead of time ready for use in our application.

Stored procedures are very easy to use, but the code to access them is (in my opinion) horribly verbose. In the next section, we'll see some code that can make accessing stored procedures a little more straightforward, but to make things a little clearer we'll start by building a simple application that demonstrates how to create and call a stored procedure.

Creating a Stored Procedure

To create a stored procedure, you can either use the tools in Visual Studio .NET, or you can use the tools in SQL Server's Enterprise Manager. (Although technically you can use a third party tool or do it programmatically as well.)

For our example, we'll build a stored procedure that returns all of the columns for a given author ID. The SQL to do this will look like this:

```
SELECT
      au_id, au_lname, au_fname, phone,
      address, city, state, zip, contract
FROM
      authors
WHERE
      au_id = whatever author ID we want
```

The *whatever author ID we want* part is important. When using stored procedures, we typically have to be able to provide parameters into the stored procedure and use them from within code. This isn't a book about SQL Server, so I'm only going to show you in principle how to do this. There are many resources on the Web about building stored procedures (they've been around a very long time, and they're most definitely not a .NET-specific feature).

Variables in SQL Server are prefixed by the @ symbol. So, if we have a variable called au_id, our SQL will look like this:

```
SELECT
      au_id, au_lname, au_fname, phone,
      address, city, state, zip, contract
FROM
      authors
WHERE
      au_id = @au_id
```

In SQL Server, stored procedures can be accessed using the Stored Procedures object in the management tree. In this screenshot, you'll see a number of stored procedures already loaded. Those prefixed with dt_ are the built-in SQL stored procedures. Byroyalty is a stored procedure provided by the pubs database developers. Figure 11-2 illustrates the stored procedures of the pubs database in SQL Server 2000 Enterprise Manager.

To create a new stored procedure, right-click the Stored Procedures object in the left pane and select New Stored Procedure. This will display the editor window.

A stored procedure can be either a single SQL statement, or a complex set of statements. T-SQL supports branches, loops and other variable declarations, which can make for some pretty complex stored procedure code. However, our stored procedure is just a single line of SQL. We need to declare the parameter that we want to pass in (@au_id), and the name of the procedure: usp_authors_get_by_id. Figure 11-3 illustrates this stored procedure in SQL Server 2000 Enterprise Manager.

If the screenshot isn't clear, here's the complete code:

```
CREATE PROCEDURE usp_authors_get_by_id
    @au_id varchar(11)
```

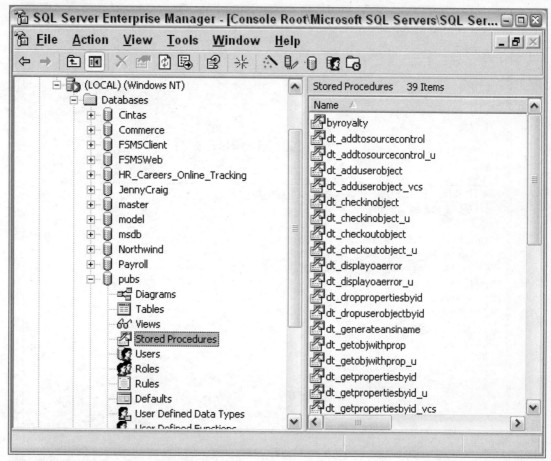

Figure 11-2

```
AS
SELECT
    au_id, au_lname, au_fname, phone,
    address, city, state, zip, contract
FROM
    authors
WHERE
    au_id = @au_id
```

Click OK to save the stored procedure in the database. We're now able to access this stored procedure from code.

Calling the Stored Procedure

Calling the stored procedure is just an issue of creating a `SqlConnection` object to connect to the database and a `SqlCommand` object to run the stored procedure.

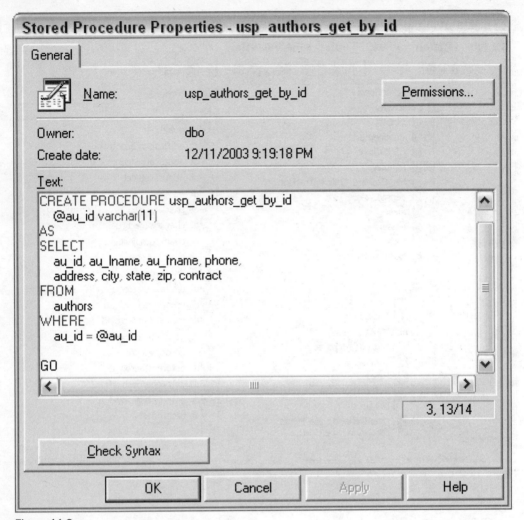

Figure 11-3

My preferred pattern for doing this is to create a separate class in the project called something like Sprocs and to add shared methods to this class to access each stored procedure. This gives me maximum potential for reuse. In addition to this, I like to create two versions of each method: one that takes a connection string and creates its own `SqlConnection` object, and one that takes a specific `SqlConnection` object.

If I'm running a complex piece of code that needs a `SqlConnection` object consistently (such as a batch reporting procedure), I'll establish a `SqlConnection` at the top of the routine and dispose of it at the end. This saves me from having to continually reopen the connection as I work through the code. However, if I'm running some code that doesn't need a `SqlConnection` object to be open all of the time, I want to create `SqlConnection` objects as I need them. The two versions of the stored procedure access method in Sprocs give me this flexibility.

Create a new project now called `LookupAuthor`. To this new project, add a new class called `Sprocs`.

Now we have to decide what we want to return out of the method. As when we supply an ID we're only going to get zero or one `DataRow` objects back, it makes sense to return either the `DataRow` that we found, or `Nothing` out of the method, which is what we'll do. However, as `SqlDataAdapter` will expect to fill a table, we'll create another helper method in Sprocs that strips out the first row and returns that or `Nothing`.

Here's the first version of the `GetAuthorById` method. The wrinkle here is that we have to tear down the connection should an exception be thrown from the other version of the method that runs the stored procedure. Notice how we don't want to handle the exception, which is why there's no Catch clause, but we do need a Finally clause to tear down the connection. Also, notice how that in addition to the connections string parameter, this method takes the same parameters as the stored procedure itself.

```
Public Shared Function GetAuthorById(ByVal connectionString As String, _
                                     ByVal authorId As String) As DataRow

    Dim connection As SqlConnection
    Dim result As DataRow
    Try
      connection = New SqlConnection(connectionString)
      connection.Open()
      result = GetAuthorById(connection, authorId)
    Finally
      If connection.State <> ConnectionState.Closed Then
        connection.Close()
      End If
    End Try
    Return result
End Function
```

Accessing the stored procedure is more verbose (but not more difficult) than accessing a normal SQL statement through the methods we've discussed thus far. The approach is:

❑   Create a `SqlCommand` object

❑   Configure it to access a stored procedure by setting the `CommandType` property

❑   Add parameters that exactly match those in the stored procedure itself

❑   Create a `SqlDataAdapter` and fill a results object of some kind (a DataTable in our case)

```
Public Shared Function GetAuthorById(ByVal connection As SqlConnection, _
                                     ByVal authorId As String) As DataRow


    Dim command As SqlCommand
    Dim adapter As SqlDataAdapter
    Dim result As DataRow
```

```
    Try
        command = New SqlCommand("GetAuthorById", connection)
        command.CommandType = CommandType.StoredProcedure

        Dim authorIdParam As SqlParameter = _
            command.Parameters.Add("@au_id", SqlDbType.VarChar)
        authorIdParam.Direction = ParameterDirection.Input
        authorIdParam.Value = authorId

        Dim datatable As New DataTable()
        adapter = New SqlDataAdapter(command)
        adapter.Fill(datatable)
        result = GetRowFromTable(datatable)

    Finally
        If Not adapter Is Nothing Then
            adapter.Dispose()
        End If
        If Not command Is Nothing Then
            command.Dispose()
        End If
    End Try

    Return result
End Function
```

Here's the method to return the top row in a table:

```
Protected Shared Function GetRowFromTable(ByVal table As DataTable) _
    As DataRow
    If table Is Nothing OrElse table.Rows.Count = 0 Then
        Return Nothing
    Else
        Return table.Rows(0)
    End If
End Function
```

There's no real need to build an impressive UI for this application, as we're about to move on to a far more interesting discussion. To Form1, add a button and add this code to its Click handler:

```
Private Sub Button1_Click(ByVal sender As System.Object, _
                          ByVal e As System.EventArgs) _
                          Handles Button1.Click

    Try
        Dim author As DataRow = Sprocs.GetAuthorById(ConnectionString, _
            "409-56-7008")
        MsgBox(author("au_fname") & " " & author("au_lname"))
    Catch ex As Exception
        MsgBox(ex.GetType().ToString() & ":" & ex.Message)
    End Try

End Sub
```

Here I've hard-coded an author ID of 409-56-7008. Run the code now and you should see the following in Figure 11-4.

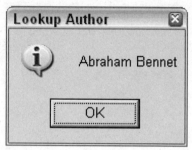

Figure 11-4

Building a Data Access Component

In order to better demonstrate what we have learned so far about ADO.NET, we are going to build a data access component. This component is designed to abstract the processing of stored procedures. The component we are building will be targeted at SQL Server, and it is assumed that all data access to the database will be through stored procedures. The idea of only using stored procedures to access data in a database has a number of advantages, such as scalability, performance, flexibility, security, etc. The only disadvantage is that you have to use stored procedures, and not SQL strings. Through the process of building this component we will see how stored procedures are implemented in ADO.NET. We will also be building on the knowledge that we have gained from the previous chapters. This component's main job is to abstract stored procedure calls to SQL Server, and one of the ways we do this is by passing in all of our stored procedure parameter metadata as XML. We will look at this XML later in this section. The other job of the component is to demonstrate the use of some of the new objects in ADO.NET.

> The code for this project is quite extensive and we will only examine the key parts of it in this chapter. The full source is available in the code download.

Let's start with the beginning of the component. The first thing we do is declare our namespace, our class, and the private members of the class:

```
Option Explicit On
Option Strict On
Imports System
Imports System.Data
Imports System.Data.SqlClient
Imports System.Xml
Imports System.Collections
Imports System.Diagnostics


Namespace IK.Data
```

```
'/ <summary>
'/ This class wraps stored procedure calls to SQL Server. It requires
'/ that all stored procedures and their parameters be defined in an XML
'/ document before calling any of its methods. The XML can be passed in as
'/ an XmlDocument instance or as a string of XML. The only exceptions to
'/ this rule are stored procedures that do not have parameters. This class
'/ also caches SqlCommand objects. Each time a stored procedure is
'/ executed, a SqlCommand object is built and cached into memory so that the
'/ next time the stored procedure is called the SqlCommand object can be
'/ retrieved from memory.
'/ </summary>
Public Class SqlServer

    Private _connectionString As String = ""
    Private _spParamXml As String = ""
    Private _spParamXmlDoc As XmlDocument = Nothing
    Private _commandParametersHashTable As New Hashtable()
    Private Const ExceptionMsg As String = "There was an error in the " _
        & "method. Please see the Windows Event Viewer Application log " _
        & "for details"
```

We start out with our `Option` statements. Note that we are using the `Option Strict` statement. This helps prevent logic errors and data loss that can occur when you work between variables of different types. Next, we import the namespaces that we need for our component. In this case, most of our dependencies are on `System.Data.SqlClient`. We declare a namespace here, `IK.Data`, but you can use any unique namespace that you wish. We will call our class `SqlServer`, to indicate that it wraps data access calls to the SQL Server. Next, we declare our private data members. We use the `ExceptionMsg` constant to indicate a generic error message for any exceptions that we throw.

Constructors

Now we get to declare our constructors for the `SqlServer` class. This is where we can really take advantage of method overloading, and it gives us a way to pass data to our class upon instantiation. First, we declare a default constructor:

```
'/ <summary>
'/ Default constructor.
'/ </summary>
Public Sub New()
End Sub
```

Since there is no code execution in this constructor we do not have to do this, but it makes the code easier to understand later on when other people have to read the code.

The next constructor we create allows for a database connection string to be passed in. By abstracting the database connection string out of this component, we give users of our component more flexibility in how they decide to store and retrieve their database connection strings. Here is the code for the constructor:

```
'/ <summary>
'/ Overloaded constructor.
```

```
'/ </summary>
'/ <param name="connectionString">The connection string to the SQL
'/ Server database.</param>
Public Sub New(ByVal connectionString As String)
    _connectionString = connectionString
End Sub
```

The only difference between this constructor and the default constructor is that we are passing in a database connection string.

In the next constructor, we pass in both a database connection string and a string of XML representing the stored procedure parameters for the stored procedures we want to call. Here is the code for the constructor:

```
'/ <summary>
'/ Overloaded constructor.
'/ </summary>
'/ <param name="connectionString">The connection string to the SQL Server
'/ database.</param>
'/ <param name="spParamXml">A valid XML string which conforms to the
'/ correct schema for stored procedure(s) and their associated
'/ parameter(s).</param>
Public Sub New(ByVal connectionString As String, ByVal spParamXml As String)
    _connectionString = connectionString
    _spParamXml = spParamXml
    _spParamXmlDoc = New XmlDocument
    Try
        _spParamXmlDoc.LoadXml(spParamXml)
    Catch e As XmlException
        LogError(e)
        Throw New Exception(ExceptionMsg, e)
    End Try
End Sub
```

This constructor sets the database connection string and then loads the stored procedure parameter configuration into a private XmlDocument instance variable. The next constructor allows you to pass in a database connection string and a valid XmlDocument instance representing the stored procedure parameters. The last constructor allows for passing in only an XmlDocument instance representing the stored procedure parameters.

Properties

Now, let's look at the properties of our object. Our object contains the following properties: ConnectionString, SpParamXml, and SpParamXmlDoc. All of the properties are provided as a courtesy in case the user of our object did not want to supply them via a constructor call. The ConnectionString property performs the same functionality as the first overloaded constructor we looked at. The SpParamXml property allows the user of the object to pass in a valid XML string representing the stored procedures parameter metadata. All of the properties are read–write. The SpParamXmlDoc property allows the user to pass in an XmlDocument instance representing the stored procedures parameter metadata.

Here is the code for the SpParamXml property:

```
'/ <summary>
'/ A valid XML string which conforms to the correct schema for
'/ stored procedure(s) and their associated parameter(s).
'/ </summary>
Public Property SpParamXml() As String
    Get
        Return _spParamXml
    End Get
    Set(ByVal Value As String)
        _spParamXml = Value
        ' Set the XmlDocument instance to null, since
        ' an XML string is being passed in.
        _spParamXmlDoc = Nothing
        Try
            _spParamXmlDoc.LoadXml(_spParamXml)
        Catch e As XmlException
            LogError(e)
            Throw New Exception(ExceptionMsg)
        End Try
    End Set
End Property
```

The interesting thing to note about this property is that it makes sure to reset the XmlDocument instance to Nothing before trying to load the document. This is in case it was already set in one of the overloaded constructors, or from a previous call to this property.

Stored Procedure XML Structure

Rather than having the user of our object be responsible for populating the Parameters collection of a Command object, in this case we will abstract it out into an XML structure. The structure is very simple; it basically allows you to store the metadata for one or more stored procedures at a time. This has a huge advantage in the fact that you can change all of the parameters on a stored procedure without having to recompile this object. Following is what the XML structure for the metadata looks like:

```
<StoredProcedures>
 <StoredProcedure name>
  <Parameters>
   <Parameter name size datatype direction isNullable value />
  </Parameters>
 </StoredProcedure>
</StoredProcedures>
```

Here is what some sample data for the XML structure looks like:

```
<?xml version="1.0"?>
<StoredProcedures>
 <StoredProcedure name="usp_Get_Authors_By_States">
  <Parameters>
```

```
    <Parameter name="@states" size="100" datatype="VarChar"
     direction="Input" isNullable="True" />
    <Parameter name="@state_delimiter" size="1" datatype="Char"
     direction="Input" isNullable="True" />
    </Parameters>
  </StoredProcedure>
</StoredProcedures>
```

The valid values for the direction attribute are Input, Output, ReturnValue, and InputOutput. These values map directly to the `System.Data.Parameter` enumeration values. The valid values for the datatype attribute are `BigInt`, `Binary`, `Bit`, `Char`, `DateTime`, `Decimal`, `Float`, `Image`, `Int`, `Money`, `NChar`, `NText`, `NVarChar`, `Real`, `SmallDateTime`, `SmallInt`, `SmallMoney`, `Text`, `Timestamp`, `TinyInt`, `UniqueIdentifier`, `VarBinary`, `VarChar`, and `Variant`. These values map directly to the `System.Data.SqlDbType` enumeration values. We will call this file *PubsStoredProcedures.xsd* and save it in the root directory of our project.

Methods

We have just finished looking at the stored procedure XML structure our class expects, as well as the public properties and public constructors for our class. Now, let's turn our attention to the public methods of our object.

ExecSpReturnDataSet

This public function executes a stored procedure and returns a DataSet object. It takes a stored procedure name (String), an optional DataSet name (String), and an optional list of parameter names and values (IDictionary). Here is the code for `ExecSpReturnDataSet`:

```
'/ <summary>
'/ Executes a stored procedure with or without parameters and returns a
'/ populated DataSet object.
'/ </summary>
'/ <param name="spName">The name of the stored procedure to execute.</param>
'/ <param name="dataSetName">An optional name for the DataSet
instance.</param>
'/ <param name="paramValues">A name-value pair of stored procedure parameter
'/ name(s) and value(s).</param>
'/ <returns>A populated DataSet object.</returns>
Public Function ExecSpReturnDataSet(ByVal spName As String, _
            ByVal dataSetName As String, _
            ByVal paramValues As IDictionary) As DataSet
    Dim command As SqlCommand = Nothing
    Try
        ' Get the initialized SqlCommand instance
        command = GetSqlCommand(spName)
        ' Set the parameter values for the SqlCommand
        SetParameterValues(command, paramValues)

        ' Initialize the SqlDataAdapter with the SqlCommand object
```

```
                Dim sqlDA As New SqlDataAdapter(command)

            ' Initialize the DataSet
            Dim ds As New DataSet()

            If Not (dataSetName Is Nothing) Then
                If dataSetName.Length > 0 Then
                    ds.DataSetName = dataSetName
                End If
            End If

            ' Fill the DataSet
            sqlDA.Fill(ds)

            ' Return the DataSet
            Return ds
        Catch e As Exception
            LogError(e)
            Throw New Exception(ExceptionMsg, e)
        Finally
            ' Close and release resources
            DisposeCommand(command)
        End Try
    End Function
```

This function uses three main objects to accomplish its mission: the `SqlCommand`, `SqlDataAdapter`, and the `DataSet` objects. We first wrap everything in a `Try-Catch-Finally` block to make sure that we trap any exceptions that are thrown and to properly close and release the `SqlCommand` and `SqlConnection` resources. The first thing we do is to call a helper method, `GetSqlCommand`, in order to get a fully initialized `SqlCommand` instance, to include any `SqlParameter` objects the `SqlCommand` may have based on our object's internal XmlDocument. Here is the code for `GetSqlCommand`:

```
'/ <summary>
'/ Initializes a SqlCommand object based on a stored procedure name.
'/ Verifies that the stored procedure name is valid, and then tries
'/ to get the SqlCommand object from cache. If it is not already in
'/ cache, then the SqlCommand object is initialized and placed into cache.
'/ </summary>
'/ <param name="spName">The name of the stored procedure to execute.</param>
'/ <returns>An initialized SqlCommand object.</returns>
Private Function GetSqlCommand(ByVal spName As String) As SqlCommand
    Dim command As SqlCommand = Nothing

    ' Get the name of the stored procedure
    If spName.Length < 1 Or spName.Length > 127 Then
        Throw New ArgumentOutOfRangeException("spName", "Stored procedure " _
            & "name must be from 1 - 128 characters.")
    End If
    ' See if the command object is already in memory
    Dim hashKey As String = _connectionString + ":" + spName
```

```
        command = CType(_commandParametersHashTable(hashKey), SqlCommand)
    If command Is Nothing Then
        ' It was not in memory
        ' Initialize the SqlCommand
        command = New SqlCommand(spName, New SqlConnection(_connectionString))

        ' Tell the SqlCommand that we are using a stored procedure
        command.CommandType = CommandType.StoredProcedure

        ' Build the parameters, if there are any
        BuildParameters(command)

        ' Put the SqlCommand instance into memory
        _commandParametersHashTable(hashKey) = command
    End If

    ' Return the initialized SqlCommand instance
    Return command
End Function
```

This method first performs a check to make sure that the stored procedure name is between 1 and 128 characters long, in accordance with the SQL Server object naming conventions. If it is not, then we throw an exception. The next step this method performs is to try to get an already initialized `SqlCommand` object from our object's private `Hashtable` variable, `_commandParametersHashTable`, using our object's database connection string and the name of the stored procedure as the key. If the `SqlCommand` was not found, then we go ahead and build the `SqlCommand` object by calling its constructor and passing in the stored procedure name and a SqlConnection instance, and then setting its `CommandType` property.

We make sure that we pass in the `CommandType.StoredProcedure` enumeration value, since we are executing a stored procedure. Once the `SqlCommand` object is properly initialized, we pass it by reference to the BuildParameters method. We will take a look at this method in more detail later. After this step, the `SqlCommand` is fully initialized, and we then place it into our object's internal cache (the `_commandParametersHashTable Hashtable` variable). Finally, the `SqlCommand` is returned to the calling code.

Getting back to the `ExecSpReturnDataSet` method, now that the `SqlCommand` object has been properly initialized, we need to set the values of the parameters. This will be done via another helper method called SetParameterValues. SetParameterValues take two arguments, a reference to a `SqlCommand` object, and an IDictionary interface. We are using an IDictionary interface instead of a class such as a Hashtable (which implements the IDictionary interface) in order to make our code more flexible. This is a good design practice and works quite well, for example, in the case where the user of our class has built their own custom dictionary object that implements the IDictionary interface. It then loops through the SqlCommand's Parameters collection and sets each SqlParameter's value based on the corresponding name-value pair in the IDictionary object as long as the parameter's direction is not Output. Following is the code for the `SetParameterValues` method:

```
'/ <summary>
'/ Traverses the SqlCommand's Parameters collection and sets the values
'/ for all of the SqlParameter(s) objects whose direction is not Output and
```

```
'/ whose name matches the name in the dictValues IDictionary that was
'/ passed in.
'/ </summary>
'/ <param name="command">An initialized SqlCommand object.</param>
'/ <param name="dictValues">A name-value pair of stored procedure parameter
'/ name(s) and value(s).</param>
Private Sub SetParameterValues(ByRef command As SqlCommand, _
                              ByVal dictValues As IDictionary)
    ' Traverse the SqlCommand's SqlParameters collection
    Dim parameter As SqlParameter
    For Each parameter In command.Parameters
        ' Do not set Output parameters
        If parameter.Direction <> ParameterDirection.Output Then
            ' Set the initial value to DBNull
            parameter.Value = TypeCode.DBNull
            ' If there is a match, then update the parameter value
            If dictValues.Contains(parameter.ParameterName) Then
                parameter.Value = dictValues(parameter.ParameterName)
            Else
                ' There was not a match
                ' If the parameter value cannot be null, throw an exception
                If Not parameter.IsNullable Then
                    Throw New ArgumentNullException(parameter.ParameterName, _
                        "Error getting the value for the " _
                        & parameter.ParameterName & " parameter.")
                End If
            End If
        End If
    Next parameter
End Sub
```

When traversing the SqlCommand's Parameters collection, if a SqlParameter's value cannot be found in the IDictionary instance, then a check is made to see whether the SqlParameter's value is allowed to be null or not. If it is allowed, then the value is set to DBNull, otherwise an exception is thrown.

After setting the values of the parameters, the next step is to pass the SqlCommand object to the SqlDataAdapter's constructor:

```
' Initialize the SqlDataAdapter with the SqlCommand object
Dim sqlDA As New SqlDataAdapter(command)
```

The next step is to try to set the name of the DataSet using the dataSetName method argument:

```
' Try to set the name of the DataSet
If Not (dataSetName Is Nothing) Then
    If dataSetName.Length > 0 Then
        ds.DataSetName = dataSetName
    End If
End If
```

After doing this, we then call the Fill method of the SqlDataAdapter to fill our DataSet object:

```
' Fill the DataSet
sqlDA.Fill(ds)
```

We then return the DataSet object back to the caller:

```
' Return the DataSet
Return ds
```

If an exception was caught, then we log the exception data to the Windows Application Log via the LogError private method, and then throw a new exception with our generic exception message. We nest the original exception inside of the new exception via the innerException constructor parameter:

```
Catch e As Exception
    LogError(e)
    Throw New Exception(ExceptionMsg, e)
```

In the Finally block, we close and release the SqlCommand object's resources via the DisposeCommand helper method:

```
Finally
    ' Close and release resources
    DisposeCommand(command)
```

The DisposeCommand helper function closes the SqlCommand's SqlConnection property and disposes of the SqlCommand object:

```
'/ <summary>
'/ Disposes a SqlCommand and its underlying SqlConnection.
'/ </summary>
'/ <param name="command"></param>
Private Sub DisposeCommand(ByVal command As SqlCommand)
    If Not (command Is Nothing) Then
        If Not (command.Connection Is Nothing) Then
            command.Connection.Close()
            command.Connection.Dispose()
        End If
        command.Dispose()
    End If
End Sub
```

BuildParameters

This private method is the heart of this object and does the most work. It is responsible for parsing the stored procedure parameter XML and mapping all of the SqlParameter objects into the Parameters property of the SqlCommand object. Here is the signature of the method:

```
'/ <summary>
'/ Finds the parameter information for the stored procedure from the
'/ stored procedures XML document and then uses that information to
'/ build and append the parameter(s) for the SqlCommand's
'/ SqlParameters collection.
'/ </summary>
'/ <param name="command">An initialized SqlCommand object.</param>
Private Sub BuildParameters(ByRef command As SqlCommand)
```

You will notice that this method's argument, `SqlCommand`, is passed in by reference. This is because we need to keep using the same instance of this `SqlCommand` object after this method has completed its work on it. The first thing we do in this method is to see if in fact there is any XML being passed in or not. Here is the code that checks for the XML:

```
' See if there is an XmlDocument of parameter(s) for the stored procedure
If _spParamXmlDoc Is Nothing Then
    ' No parameters to add, so exit
    Return
End If
```

The last code simply checks if there is an XmlDocument instance of parameter information. If the XmlDocument has not been initialized, then we exit the method. It is entirely possible that users of this object may have stored procedures with no parameters at all. We have chosen an XmlDocument object to parse the XML, as loading all of the stored procedure XML into memory will not hurt performance; it is a small amount of data. As an alternative, we could have used an XmlReader object to load in only what we needed into memory at runtime.

The next step is to clear the `SqlCommand` object's Parameters collection:

```
' Clear the parameters collection for the SqlCommand
command.Parameters.Clear()
```

We then use the name of the stored procedure as the key in our XPath query of the XML, and then execute the following XPath query to get the list of parameters for the stored procedure:

```
' Get the node list of <Parameter>'s for the stored procedure
Dim xpathQuery As String = "/StoredProcedures/StoredProcedure[@name='" _
    & command.CommandText & "']/Parameters/Parameter"
Dim parameterNodes As XmlNodeList = _spParamXmlDoc.SelectNodes(xpathQuery)
```

This query is executed off the XmlDocument object and returns an XmlNodeList object. We then start the loop through the Parameter elements in the XML and retrieve all of the mandatory Parameter attributes:

```
Dim parameterNode As XmlElement
For Each parameterNode In parameterNodes
    ' Get the attribute values for the <Parameter> element.

    ' name
    parameterName = parameterNode.GetAttribute("name")
    If parameterName.Length = 0 Then
        Throw New ArgumentNullException("name", "Error getting the 'name' " _
            & "attribute for the <Parameter> element.")
    End If

    ' size
    If parameterNode.GetAttribute("size").Length = 0 Then
        Throw New ArgumentNullException("size", "Error getting the 'size' " _
            & "attribute for the <Parameter> element.")
```

```
        Else
            parameterSize = Convert.ToInt32(parameterNode.GetAttribute("size"))
        End If

        ' datatype
        If parameterNode.GetAttribute("datatype").Length = 0 Then
            Throw New ArgumentNullException("datatype", "Error getting the " _
                & "'datatype' attribute for the <Parameter> element.")
        Else
            sqlDataType = CType([Enum].Parse(GetType(SqlDbType), _
                parameterNode.GetAttribute("datatype"), True), SqlDbType)
        End If

        ' direction
        If parameterNode.GetAttribute("direction").Length = 0 Then
            Throw New ArgumentNullException("direction", "Error getting " _
                & "the 'direction' attribute for the <Parameter> element.")
        Else
            parameterDirection = CType([Enum].Parse(GetType(parameterDirection), _
                parameterNode.GetAttribute("direction"), True), parameterDirection)
    End If
```

Since these attributes are mandatory, if any of them are missing, we throw an exception. The interesting part of this code is that we are using the `Enum.Parse` static method to convert the string value from the XML into the correct .NET enumeration data type for the `sqlDataType` and `parameterDirection` variables. This is possible because the probable values in our XML for these attributes map directly to the names of their respective enumeration data types in .NET. Next, we get the optional attributes:

```
' Get the optional attribute values for the <Parameter> element

' isNullable
Try
    If parameterNode.GetAttribute("isNullable").Length > 0 Then
        isNullable = Boolean.Parse(parameterNode.GetAttribute("isNullable"))
    Else
        isNullable = False
    End If
Catch
End Try

' precision
Try
    If parameterNode.GetAttribute("precision").Length > 0 Then
        precision = Convert.ToByte(parameterNode.GetAttribute("precision"))
    Else
        precision = 0
    End If
Catch
End Try

' scale
```

```
Try
    If parameterNode.GetAttribute("scale").Length > 0 Then
        scale = Convert.ToByte(parameterNode.GetAttribute("scale"))
    Else
        scale = 0
    End If
Catch
End Try
```

These attributes are optional mainly because of their data types. Since they are Boolean and Byte data types, we just go ahead and convert them to False and 0 if they are missing.

Now we are ready to create the `SqlParameter` object and set its `Direction` property. We do so with the following code:

```
' Create the parameter object.  Pass in the name, datatype,
' and size to the constructor.
sqlParameter = New sqlParameter(parameterName, sqlDataType, parameterSize)

' Set the direction of the parameter.
sqlParameter.Direction = parameterDirection
```

We then set the optional property values of the `SqlParameter` object:

```
' If the optional attributes have values, then set them.
If isNullable Then
    sqlParameter.IsNullable = isNullable
End If
If precision > 0 Then
    sqlParameter.Precision = precision
End If
If scale > 0 Then
    sqlParameter.Scale = scale
End If
```

Finally, we add the `SqlParameter` object to the `SqlCommand` object's Parameters collection, complete our loop, and finish the method:

```
        ' Add the parameter to the SqlCommand's parameter collection
        command.Parameters.Add(sqlParameter)
    Next parameterNode
End Sub
```

Next, we are going to look at `ExecSpReturnDataReader`. This function is almost identical to `ExecSpReturnDataSet`, except that it returns a `SqlDataReader` object instead of a DataSet object.

ExecSpReturnDataReader

This public function executes a stored procedure and returns a SqlDataReader object. Similar to the `ExecSpReturnDataSet` method, it takes a stored procedure name (String) and an optional list of parameter names and values (IDictionary). Here is the code for `ExecSpReturnDataReader`:

```
'/ <summary>
'/ Executes a stored procedure with or without parameters and returns a
'/ SqlDataReader instance with a live connection to the database. It is
'/ very important to call the Close method of the SqlDataReader as soon
'/ as possible after using it.
'/ </summary>
'/ <param name="spName">The name of the stored procedure to execute.</param>
'/ <param name="paramValues">A name-value pair of stored procedure parameter
'/ name(s) and value(s).</param>
'/ <returns>A SqlDataReader object.</returns>
Public Function ExecSpReturnDataReader(ByVal spName As String, _
    ByVal paramValues As IDictionary) As SqlDataReader

    Dim command As SqlCommand = Nothing
    Try
        ' Get the initialized SqlCommand instance
        command = GetSqlCommand(spName)

        ' Set the parameter values for the SqlCommand
        SetParameterValues(command, paramValues)

        ' Open the connection
        command.Connection.Open()

        ' Execute the sp and return the SqlDataReader
        Return command.ExecuteReader(CommandBehavior.CloseConnection)
    Catch e As Exception
        LogError(e)
        Throw New Exception(ExceptionMsg, e)
    End Try

End Function
```

This function uses two objects to accomplish its mission: the `SqlCommand` and `SqlDataReader` objects. The only part where this function differs from `ExecSpReturnDataSet` is right after we call the `SetParameterValues` private method. In this case, we have to make sure that the `SqlCommand` object's `SqlConnection` is opened. This is because the `SqlDataReader` requires an open connection. We then call the `ExecuteReader` method of the `SqlCommand` object to get our `SqlDataReader` object, passing in the `CommandBehavior.CloseConnection` value for the method's behavior argument.

Since this method returns a `SqlDataReader` object, which requires an open database connection, we do not close the connection in this method. It is up to the caller to close the `SqlDataReader` and the connection when finished. Since we used the `CommandBehavior.CloseConnection` value for the behavior argument, the user of the method only has to remember to call the SqlDataReader's `Close` method in order to close the underlying `SqlConnection` object.

The next function we are going to look at, `ExecSpReturnXmlReader`, is almost identical to the last two functions, except that it returns an XmlReader instead of a `DataSet` or a `SqlDataReader`.

ExecSpReturnXmlReader

This public function executes a stored procedure and returns an XmlReader instance. The function requires that the stored procedure contains a FOR XML clause in its SQL statement. Once again, it takes a stored procedure name (String) and an optional list of parameter names and values (IDictionary). Here is the code for ExecSpReturnXmlReader:

```
'/ <summary>
'/ Executes a stored procedure with or without parameters and returns an
'/ XmlReader instance with a live connection to the database. It is
'/ very important to call the Close method of the XmlReader as soon
'/ as possible after using it. Only use this method when calling stored
'/ procedures that return XML results (FOR XML ...).
'/ </summary>
'/ <param name="spName">The name of the stored procedure to execute.</param>
'/ <param name="paramValues">A name-value pair of stored procedure parameter
'/ name(s) and value(s).</param>
'/ <returns>An XmlReader object.</returns>
Public Function ExecSpReturnXmlReader(ByVal spName As String, _
    ByVal paramValues As IDictionary) As XmlReader
    Dim command As SqlCommand = Nothing
    Try
        ' Get the initialized SqlCommand instance
        command = GetSqlCommand(spName)

        ' Set the parameter values for the SqlCommand
        SetParameterValues(command, paramValues)

        ' Open the connection
        command.Connection.Open()

        ' Execute the sp and return the XmlReader
        Return command.ExecuteXmlReader()
    Catch e As Exception
        LogError(e)
        Throw New Exception(ExceptionMsg, e)
    End Try
End Function
```

The only difference between this method and ExecSpReturnDataReader is that we call the ExecuteXmlReader method of the SqlCommand object instead of the ExecuteReader method. Similar to the ExecSpReturnDataReader method, users of this method need to close the returned XmlReader when finished using it in order to properly release resources.

> **Note: This method will only work with SQL Server 2000 and above.**

Next, we look at the ExecSP method which only needs the SqlCommand object to get its work done. Its job is to execute stored procedures that do not return result sets.

ExecSp

This public method executes a stored procedure and does not return a value. It takes a stored procedure name (String) and an optional list of parameter names and values (IDictionary) for its arguments. Here is the code for `ExecSp`:

```vb
'/ <summary>
'/ Executes a stored procedure with or without parameters that
'/ does not return output values or a resultset.
'/ </summary>
'/ <param name="spName">The name of the stored procedure to execute.</param>
'/ <param name="paramValues">A name-value pair of stored procedure parameter
'/ name(s) and value(s).</param>
Public Sub ExecSp(ByVal spName As String, ByVal paramValues As IDictionary)
    Dim command As SqlCommand = Nothing
    Try
        ' Get the initialized SqlCommand instance
        command = GetSqlCommand(spName)

        ' Set the parameter values for the SqlCommand
        SetParameterValues(command, paramValues)

        ' Run the stored procedure
        RunSp(command)
    Catch e As Exception
        LogError(e)
        Throw New Exception(ExceptionMsg, e)
    Finally
        ' Close and release resources
        DisposeCommand(command)
    End Try
End Sub
```

It is almost identical to the other Exec* functions, except for when it executes the stored procedure. The code inside of the private RunSp method opens up the SqlCommand's `SqlConnection` object and then it calls the SqlCommand object's `ExecuteNonQuery` method. This ensures that the SqlCommand does not return any type of DataReader object to read the results. This method will be mostly used to execute INSERT, UPDATE, and DELETE stored procedures that do not return any results.

Following is the code for `RunSp`:

```vb
'/ <summary>
'/ Opens the SqlCommand object's underlying SqlConnection and calls
'/ the SqlCommand's ExecuteNonQuery method.
'/ </summary>
'/ <param name="command">An initialized SqlCommand object.</param>
Private Sub RunSp(ByRef command As SqlCommand)
    ' Open the connection
    command.Connection.Open()

    ' Execute the stored procedure
    command.ExecuteNonQuery()
End Sub
```

Finally, the last public function we are going to create is `ExecSpOutputValues`.

ExecSpOutputValues

This last public function in our component executes a stored procedure and returns an IDictionary object that contains output parameter name-value pairs. It is not meant for stored procedures that return result sets. As with the previous examples, this function takes a stored procedure name (String) and an optional list of parameter names and values (IDictionary) for its arguments. Here is the code for `ExecSPOutputValues`:

```vbnet
'/ <summary>
'/ Executes a stored procedure with or without parameters and returns an
'/ IDictionary instance with the stored procedure's output parameter
'/ name(s) and value(s).
'/ </summary>
'/ <param name="spName">The name of the stored procedure to execute.</param>
'/ <param name="paramValues">A name-value pair of stored procedure parameter
'/ name(s) and value(s).</param>
'/ <returns>An IDictionary object.</returns>
Public Function ExecSpOutputValues(ByVal spName As String, _
    ByVal paramValues As IDictionary) As IDictionary

    Dim command As SqlCommand = Nothing
    Try
        ' Get the initialized SqlCommand instance
        command = GetSqlCommand(spName)
        ' Set the parameter values for the SqlCommand
        SetParameterValues(command, paramValues)

        ' Run the stored procedure
        RunSp(command)

        ' Get the output values
        Dim outputParams As New Hashtable()
        Dim param As SqlParameter
        For Each param In command.Parameters
            If param.Direction = ParameterDirection.Output _
                Or param.Direction = ParameterDirection.InputOutput Then
                outputParams.Add(param.ParameterName, param.Value)
            End If
        Next param
        Return outputParams
    Catch e As Exception
        LogError(e)
        Throw New Exception(ExceptionMsg, e)
    Finally
        ' Close and release resources
        DisposeCommand(command)
    End Try
End Function
```

This function is almost identical to `ExecSp`, except that after the `SqlCommand.ExecuteNonQuery` method is called we iterate through the SqlCommand object's Parameters collection and look for all of the parameters that are output parameters. Next, we take the values of the output parameters and add the name-value pair to the IDictionary instance that we return.

Using DataSet Objects to Bind to DataGrids

Now that we have built our data access component, it is time to test it.

> Be sure to run the UDF.sql file—available with the code download—in SQL Server Query Analyzer before testing the data access component. This will create the necessary stored procedure and function in the pubs database.

A nice way to test it is to call the `ExecSpReturnDataSset` method, take the `DataSet` object that was created, and then bind the DataSet to a DataGrid. (You can find more about data binding in Chapter 16.) We also get to see how easily the DataSet object and the DataGrid control integrate together. To do this, create a new Windows Application project, and add references to `IK.Data`, `System`, `System.Data`, `System.Drawing`, `System.Windows.Forms`, and System.XML. Now import `IK.Data` and `System.Xml`, add a Button (named `btnTest`) and a DataGrid (named `dgdAuthors`) to your form, and bind the DataGrid to the DataSet object. Here is what your form should look like, as shown in Figure 11-5.

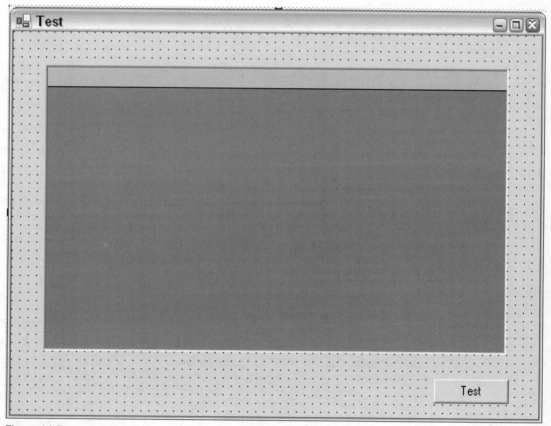

Figure 11-5

Figure 11-6 shows what your references should look like.

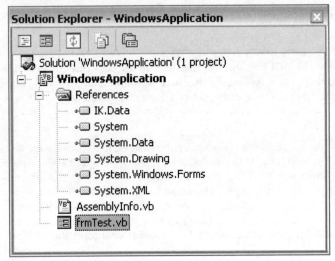

Figure 11-6

Lastly, here is the code for the test application:

```
Imports IK.Data
Imports System.Xml

Public Class frmTest

    Inherits System.Windows.Forms.Form

' Windows Form Designer generated code "

    Private Sub cmdTest_Click(ByVal sender As System.Object, _
                    ByVal e As System.EventArgs) Handles cmdTest.Click

        Dim connectionString As String
        Dim ds As DataSet
        Dim sqlServer As SqlServer
        Dim params As New Hashtable
        Dim errorMessage As String
        Dim xmlDoc As XmlDocument = New XmlDocument

        Try

            ' Set the SQL Managed Provider connection string
            connectionString = "Initial Catalog=pubs;" _
            & "Data Source=(local);Integrated Security=SSPI;"

            ' Call the SqlServer wrapper constructor and
            ' pass the db connection string
            sqlServer = New SqlServer(connectionString)
```

```
                          ' Set the SpParamXmlDoc XmlDocument property
                          xmlDoc.Load(Application.StartupPath & "\PubsStoredProcedures.xml")
                          sqlServer.SpParamXmlDoc = xmlDoc

                          ' Add the two parameter name-values
                          params.Add("@states", "CA")
                          params.Add("@delimiter", "^")

                          ' Execute the sp, and get the DataSet object back
                          ds = sqlServer.ExecSpReturnDataSet("usp_Get_Authors_By_States", _
                              "", params)

                          ' Bind the DataGrid to the DataSet object
                          dgdAuthors.SetDataBinding(ds.Tables(0), Nothing)

                     Catch ex As Exception

                          ' Display the exception message
                          errorMessage = ex.Message
                          If Not IsNothing(ex.InnerException) Then
                              errorMessage &= ex.InnerException.Message
                          End If
                          MsgBox(errorMessage)

                     End Try

                End Sub

        End Class
```

First of all, we place our XML file (PubsStoredProcedures.xml) in the path of the assembly. Next, we start out the code by supplying a database connection string to the SqlServer object constructor. We then load up an XmlDocument instance based on the PubsStoredProcedures.xml file, and then set the spParamXmlDoc property of the SqlServer object to our initialized XmlDocument instance. After that, we add two parameter name-value pairs to the Hashtable object. Next, the ExecSpReturnDataSet method of the SqlServer object is called so that a populated DataSet object is returned based upon a stored procedure that returns rows. Once we have the DataSet object, we simply call the SetDataBinding method of our DataGrid object. The SetDataBinding method takes two arguments, a data source (Object) and a data member (String). In this case, we do not have a data member, so we pass in Nothing. If you try to pass in an empty string, an exception will be thrown.

Finally, the results should look like the following in Figure 11-7.

Summary

In this chapter, we have taken a look at how ADO has evolved into ADO.NET. We have seen and used the main objects in ADO.NET that you need to quickly get up and running in order to build data access into your .NET applications. We took a fairly in-depth look at the DataSet object, since this is the core object of ADO.NET, and we also compared and contrasted ADO and ADO.NET so you could actually see the easier programming model.

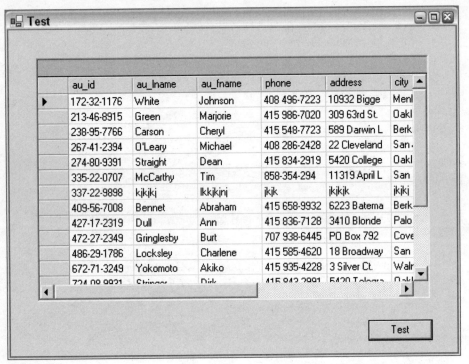

Figure 11-7

We looked at stored procedures; first by showing how to create them in SQL Server and then how to access them from our code. Finally, we built our own custom data access component, which made it easy to call stored procedures and separate data access code from the rest of business logic code in a .NET application.

12

Windows Forms

Windows Forms is the part of the .NET Framework Base Classes used to create user interfaces for local applications, often called Win32 clients. It is dramatically improved over the forms and controls available in pre-.NET versions of Visual Basic. Although some of your familiar controls have been retired, no significant functionality has been lost, and lots of new capabilities have been added. Believe me, you'll love the new world!

> While this chapter assumes you'll be writing a Windows application using Visual Studio .NET (VS.NET), it is possible to write a .NET windows application using nothing more than a text editor, and still take full advantage of everything Windows Forms have to offer.

The Importance of Windows Forms

From the way the .NET initiative has been discussed in the press and on many Web sites, it's easy to get the idea that ASP.NET and Web forms are where the action is, and that Windows Forms is just an afterthought. This seriously underestimates the importance of Windows Forms, and their importance in leading-edge applications.

As discussed in Chapter 1, "smart client" applications are likely to become more prevalent under .NET. Many applications produced with earlier tools are made browser-based just to get away from the deployment costs of client applications, in spite of the higher cost of development and a weaker user interface. But .NET changes the economics of deployment. With the XCOPY deployment of a Windows Forms-based application, the deployment and support costs of rich client or smart client applications are dramatically reduced. This should tip the scale toward a Windows Forms interface in the .NET world for many situations that today would lean toward using a browser-based user interface, even for applications distributed over the Internet.

It is just as easy to integrate Windows Forms with Web services as it is to integrate Web forms to Web services. Rich, Win32 interfaces based on Windows Forms can access and manage data on remote Internet servers through Web services just as Web forms can. This allows applications to be "Internet-enabled" without necessarily using a browser-based interface.

It's also more practical in .NET-based systems to support both browser-based and smart-client user interfaces in the same system. Middle-tier components can easily be designed to work with both. So it's not an "either-or" choice—Windows Forms interfaces may be mixed with browser-based Web forms interfaces.

The System.Windows.Forms Namespace

You've already seen how namespaces are used to organize related classes in the .NET Framework. The main namespace used for Windows Forms classes is System.Windows.Forms. The classes in this namespace are contained in the System.Windows.Forms.dll assembly.

Unlike VB6, VB.NET allows you to precisely select the assemblies you need for an application. If your application needs to have user interface support, it must contain a reference to the System.Windows .Forms.dll assembly. If you choose a Windows Application project or Windows Control Library project in VS.NET, that reference is added by default. In some other cases, such as creating a library that will work with controls, you will need to add that reference manually. (You can see more about creating controls in Windows Forms in Chapter 13.)

In either event, referring to the System.Windows.Forms.dll assembly gains you access to the System.Windows.Forms namespace. This namespace contains all the classes you need for a Windows application, from menus to message boxes.

> All languages in the .NET Framework use Windows Forms for local, Win32 interfaces. That means that Windows Forms are the replacement for several different older technologies. For Visual Basic .NET (VB.NET), Windows Forms replaces the VB forms engine. For C++, Windows Forms can be used instead of Microsoft Foundation Classes (MFC) and Active Template Library (ATL) technologies.

For a quick browse of what's in the System.Windows.Forms namespace, create a new Windows Application, and then use the Object Browser. Expand the System.Windows.Forms/System.Windows. Forms tree and you'll see all the types defined within. Figure 12-1 shows the Object Browser expanded to the Form type.

If you scroll through the namespace, you'll notice all sorts of familiar controls such as CheckBox and Button.

The System.Windows.Forms namespace makes frequent use of another namespace, System .Drawing. The System.Drawing namespace contains all the information about fonts, colors, pens, printing, and so on, and is a useful namespace if you want to start drawing your own controls. We'll cover this in Chapter 13.

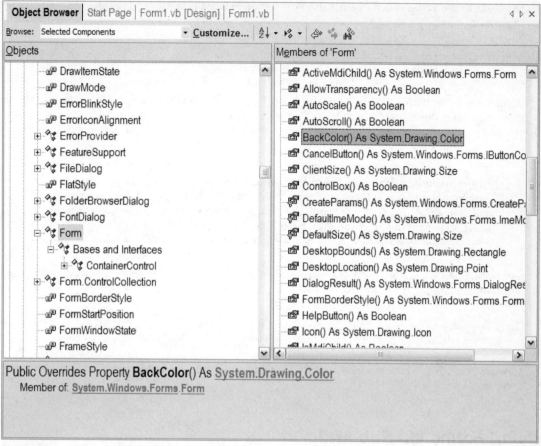

Figure 12-1

Forms as Classes

Before we explore forms in VB.NET, let's step back to VB6 for a moment. Forms and classes were considered different entities in VB6, though they shared many characteristics. Forms differed from classes in these significant ways:

❑ Only forms could contain the layout information for a Windows user interface. .FRM files contained a section at the top that detailed the controls on the form, and the initial property values for those controls.

❑ Forms had Load and Unload events. The closest equivalents for classes were the Initialize and Terminate events.

❑ Forms could be shown (instantiated) merely by referring to the form's name. Classes, on the other hand, had to be instantiated as an object before being used. That is, a form named Form1 could be shown in VB6 by using this line of code, with no preliminaries:

```
Form1.Show ' This is VB6 code!!
```

However, to use a class called `Class1` in VB6, you had to first declare a variable, and then instantiate the object as follows:

```
Dim objMyClass As Class1    ' This is VB6 code!!
Set objMyClass = New Class1 ' This is VB6 code!!
```

All of these distinctions vanish in Visual Basic .NET. In VB.NET, all forms are now true classes. All the properties are defined directly in code, instead of via a special series of settings in the `.frm` file. When you make a change to your form using the design window, you will see it appear in the code itself.

> **Pay very special attention to the fact that you no longer get a "free of charge" global variable set up for you for every form type. A form called Form1 is now a class name, *and only a class name*. If you want to use it throughout your application, you'll need to set up your own object variable to reference it.**

Since you must instantiate a form as a class before using it, typical code to create an instance of a form and show it looks like the following.

```
Dim f As New Form1
f.Show
```

However, there is one circumstance in which loading a form this way yields undesirable results. Let's cover that next.

Using Forms via Sub Main

One of the most important implications of the way forms are handled in VB.NET is that since there is no longer a default "global reference" to the form, when all object references to a form are gone, the form is disposed of, and therefore, vanishes. This is particularly apparent if you want to start your application with a `Sub Main`, and then show your first form inside `Sub Main`. You might think this code would work:

```
' This code will not work in VB.NET!!
Sub Main()

    ' Do start up work here
    ' After start up work finished, show the main form...
    Dim f As New Form1
    f.Show()

End Sub
```

What happens if you try this, however, is that `Form1` briefly appears, and then immediately vanishes, and the application quits. That's because the object variable "*f*" went out of scope, and it was the only reference to the form that was shown. So the form was destroyed because it had no references pointing to it.

You could work around this by maintaining a global reference to the form you want to show as your startup form, but it's easier to use a new built-in capability. Replace the line that shows the form, as shown in the following code:

```
' This code will not work in VB.NET!!
Sub Main()

    ' Do start up work here
    Dim f As New Form1
    Application.Run(f)

End Sub
```

Now `Sub Main` will transfer control to the form, and the form will not vanish when `Sub Main` ends.

What Is a Form in .NET?

Now that Visual Basic supports inheritance, forms take part in an inheritance structure that provides all the functionality you expect. You can also see where all that ability comes from. Forms in .NET are classes in the truest sense of the word.

In VB6, forms were saved as `.frm` files. By contrast, forms in VB.NET are saved in `.vb` files just like any other class. It's the functionality they inherit that makes a class a *form*, as opposed to just any class. In essence, calling something a "form" is just a simple way of saying a "class that has the ability to display a rich user interface."

Forms descend from the `Control` class, which gives forms their visual capabilities. Visual controls also descend from this class.

Forms at Design Time

A very nice change to VB.NET is the design time placement of controls that have no immediate user interface. The Timer control in VB6, for instance, would be sited directly on your form as a small icon. In VB.NET, these controls are placed in their own special "tray," called the *component tray*, beneath the form in the design window. A simple form with a Timer control appears, as shown in Figure 12-2.

The Design Time Grid

The design time grid is the series of small dots that appear on a form in the designer mode. In VB6 this grid was set globally. In VB.NET, each form can uniquely manage how the grid affects its controls using the following properties of a form:

❑   DrawGrid: Toggles the display of the grid

❑   SnapToGrid: Determines if child controls will automatically align and size to the nearest grid point when they are moved and resized at design time

❑   GridSize: Sets the distance, in pixels, between the dots of the grid

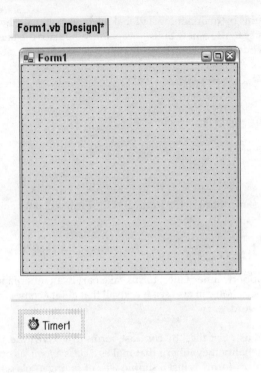

Figure 12-2

To change the default values of these settings, open the Tools ➪ Options screen and select the Windows Forms Designer section.

Setting the Startup Form

To define which form will be loaded first when your application runs, you need to open the Properties dialog box for the project and set the Startup object setting. Do this using the Project ➪ Properties menu. You can also invoke the window by right-clicking the project name in the Solution Explorer, and selecting Properties from the context menu. The Properties dialog box for a Windows Application is shown in Figure 12-3.

If the Properties menu item doesn't appear under your Project menu, open the Solution Explorer (*Ctrl-Alt-L*), highlight the project name (it will be in bold font), then try again.

Form Borders

Forms have a number of new border options in Windows Forms. The `FormBorderStyle` property is used to set the border option, and the options can affect the way a form can be manipulated by the user. The options available for `FormBorderStyle` include:

- ❑   `None` — No border, and the user cannot resize the form
- ❑   `FixedSingle` — Single 3D border, and the user cannot resize the form

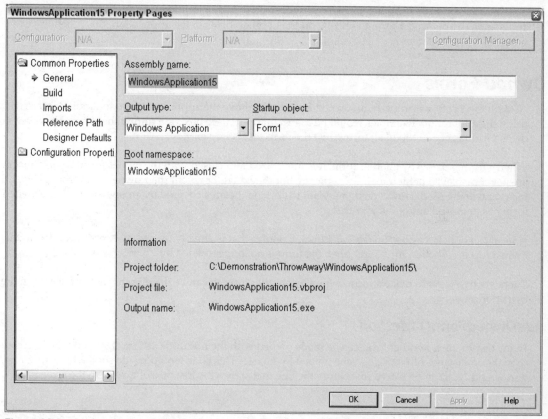

Figure 12-3

❑ `Fixed3D`—3D border, and the user cannot resize the form

❑ `FixedDialog`—Dialog box style border, and the user cannot resize the form

❑ `Sizeable`—Same as FixedSingle, except that the user can resize the form

❑ `FixedToolWindow`—Single border, and the user cannot resize the form

❑ `SizeableToolWindow`—Single border, and the user can resize the form

Each of these has a different effect on the buttons that appear in the title bar of the form. For details, check the help topic for the `FormBorderStyle` property.

Always on Top—The TopMost Property

Some applications need the ability to remain visible at all times, even when they do not have the focus. To accomplish this effect in VB6, you needed an API call. In VB.NET, forms have been given a new property called `TopMost`. Set it to `True` to have a form overlay others even when it does not have the focus.

The `TopMost` property is often used for floating toolbars, tutorial windows, and other user interface elements that must stay in the forefront of other applications.

Note that a form with `TopMost` set to `True` will be on top of *all* applications, not just the hosting application. If you need a form to only be on top of other forms in the application, this capability is provided by an *owned form*.

Owned Forms

As with the `TopMost` property, an owned form floats above the application, but does not interfere with using the application. Examples would be a search-and-replace box, or a tutorial help box. However, an owned form is not on top of all forms, just the form that is its *owner*.

When a form is *owned* by another form, it is minimized and closed with the owner form. Owned forms are never displayed behind their owner form, but they do not prevent their owner form from gaining the focus and being used. However, if you want to click on the area covered by an owned form, the owned form has to moved out of the way first.

A form can only have one "owner" at a time. If a form that is already owned by `Form1` is added to the owned forms collection for `Form2`, then the form is no longer owned by `Form1`.

There are two ways to make a form owned by another form. It can be done in the owner form, or in the owned form.

AddOwnedForm() Method

In the owner form, another form can be made owned with the `AddOwnedForm()` method. Here is code to make an instance of `Form2` become owned by `Form1`. This code would reside somewhere in `Form1`, and would typically be placed just before the line that shows the instance of `Form2` to the screen.

```
Dim frm As New Form2
Me.AddOwnedForm(frm)
```

Owner Property

The relationship can also be set up in the owned form. This is done with the `Owner` property of the form. Here is a method that would work inside `Form2` to make it owned by a form that is passed in as an argument to the function:

```
Public Sub MakeMeOwned(frmOwner As Form)
    Me.Owner = frmOwner
End Sub
```

Since this technique requires a reference to the owner inside the owned form, it is not used as often as using the `AddOwnedForm()` method in the `Owner` form.

OwnedForms Collection

The owner form can access its collection of owned forms with the `OwnedForms` property. Here is code to loop through the forms owned by a form:

```
Dim frmOwnedForm As Form
For Each frmOwnedForm In Me.OwnedForms
   Console.WriteLine(frmOwnedForm.Text)
Next
```

The owner form can remove an owned form with the RemoveOwnedForm property. This could be done in a loop like the previous one, with code like the following.

```
Dim frmOwnedForm As Form
For Each frmOwnedForm In Me.OwnedForms
   Console.WriteLine(frmOwnedForm.Text)
   Me.RemoveOwnedForm(frmOwnedForm)
Next
```

This loop would cause an owner form to stop owning all of its slaved forms. Note that those deslaved forms would not be unloaded, they would simply no longer be owned.

Startup Location

Often, you'll want a form to be centered on the screen when it first appears. VB.NET does this automatically for you when you set the StartPosition property. Here are the settings and their meanings:

StartPosition Value	Effect
Manual	Show the form positioned at the values defined by the form's Location property
CenterScreen	Show the form centered on the screen
WindowsDefaultLocation	Show the form at the windows default location
WindowsDefaultBounds	Show the form at the windows default location, with the windows default bounding size
CenterParent	Show the form centered in its owner

Making Forms Transparent and Translucent

Windows Forms goes quite a bit further than forms in Visual Basic in allowing you to make forms translucent or parts of a form transparent. You can even change the entire shape of a form.

The Opacity Property

The Opacity property measures how opaque or transparent a form is. A value of 0% makes the form fully transparent. A value of 100% makes the form fully visible. Any value between 0 and 100 makes the form partially visible, as if it was a ghost. Note that an opacity value of 0% disables the ability to click the form.

Very low levels of opacity, in the range of 1 or 2%, make the form effectively invisible, but still allow the form to be clickable. This means that the Opacity property has the potential to create mischievous applications that sit in front of other applications and "steal" their mouse clicks and other events.

> Percentage values are used to set the Opacity in the Property Window. However, if you want to set the Opacity property in code, you must use values between 0 and 1 instead, with 0 being equivalent to 0% and 1 being equivalent to 100%.

Developers are still learning how to best take advantage of this capability. Tool and dialog windows that should not completely obscure their background are one example of a usage for Opacity. Setting expiration for a "free trial" by gradually fading out the application's user interface is another.

The following block of code shows how to fade a form out and back in when the user clicks a button named Button1. You may have to adjust the Step value of the array depending on the performance of your computer:

```
Private Sub Button1_Click(ByVal sender As System.Object, _
                          ByVal e As System.EventArgs) _
                          Handles Button1.Click
    Dim i As Double
    For i = -1 To 1 Step 0.005
      ' Note - opacity is a value from 0.0 to 1.0 in code
      Me.Opacity = System.Math.Abs(i)
    Next i
End Sub
```

The TransparencyKey Property

Instead of making an entire form translucent or transparent, the TransparencyKey property allows you to specify a color that will become transparent on the form. This allows you to make some sections of a form transparent, while other sections are unchanged.

For example, if TransparencyKey is set to a red color, and some areas of the form are that exact shade of red, they will be transparent. Whatever is behind the form will show through in those areas, and if you click in one of those areas, you will actually be clicking the object behind the form.

TransparencyKey can be used to create irregularly-shaped "skin" forms. A form can its BackgroundImage property set with an image, and by just painting a part of the image with the TransparencyKey color, parts of the form will disappear.

The Region Property

Another way to gain the capability of "skins" is using the Region property of a form. The Region property allows a shape for a form to be encoded as a "graphics path," thereby changing the shape from the default rectangle to another shape. A path can contain line segments between points, curves and arcs, and outlines of letters, in any combination.

Let's do an example that will change the shape of a form to an arrow. Create a new Windows Application. Set the FormBorderStyle property of Form1 to None. Then place the following code in the Load event for Form1:

```
Dim PointArray(6) As Point
PointArray(0) = New Point(0, 40)
PointArray(1) = New Point(200, 40)
PointArray(2) = New Point(200, 0)
PointArray(3) = New Point(250, 100)
PointArray(4) = New Point(200, 200)
PointArray(5) = New Point(200, 160)
PointArray(6) = New Point(0, 160)
```

```
Dim myGraphicsPath As _
System.Drawing.Drawing2D.GraphicsPath = _
        New System.Drawing.Drawing2D.GraphicsPath

myGraphicsPath.AddPolygon(PointArray)
Me.Region = New Region(myGraphicsPath)
```

When the program is run, Form1 will appear in the shape of a right-pointing arrow. If you lay out the points in the array, you will see that they have become the vertices of the arrow.

Visual Inheritance

By inheriting from System.Windows.Forms.Form, any class automatically gets all the properties, methods, and events that a form based on Windows Forms is supposed to have. However, a class does not have to inherit directly from the System.Windows.Forms.Form class in order to become a Windows Form. It can become a form by inheriting from another form, which itself inherits from System.Windows.Forms.Form. In this way, controls originally placed on one form can be directly inherited by a second form. Not only is the design of the original form inherited, but also any code associated with these controls (the processing logic behind an Add New button, for example). This means that it is possible to create a base form with processing logic required in a number of forms, and then create other forms which inherit the base controls and functionality.

VB.NET provides an Inheritance Picker tool to aid in this process. It should be noted at this point, however, that a form must be compiled into either an .EXE or .DLL file before it can be used by the Inheritance Picker. Once that is done, the addition of a form that inherits from another form in the project can be performed via the Project ⇨ Add Inherited Form.

Setting Limits on the Form Size

In previous versions of Visual Basic, preventing a user from shrinking or expanding a form beyond a certain limit required you to check the size of the form in the Resize event, and essentially reset the height and width of the form only after it had exceeded the limits. This resulted in a terrible flickering effect. VB.NET now has MaximumSize and MinimumSize properties on the form to handle this for you. Simply set them to the sizes you desire. Use 0,0 for no limit.

Scrollable Forms

Some applications need countless (or so it seems) fields on a single screen. Try as you may, no amount of reorganizing and reducing spaces between the fields helps the situation. While you could split the data entry into multiple screens, it is often done with regret. (Imagine what the Web surfing would be like if scrolling a Web page was impossible.)

Forms in VB.NET are based on a class called ScrollableControl. This base class will give you, free of charge, scroll bars to pull controls into view that are off the edge of your forms.

The scrollable control class on which a form is based automatically gives a form scrollbars when it is sized smaller than the child controls sited on it. To enable this feature, set the AutoScroll property of your form to True. When you run your program, resize the form to make it smaller than the controls require and presto,– instant scrolling.

> You cannot have both **Autoscroll** and **IsMdiContainer** set to **True** at the same time.

Forms at Runtime

The lifecycle of a form is like that of all objects. It is created, and later destroyed. Forms have a visual component, so they use system resources, such as handles. These are created and destroyed at interim stages within the lifetime of the form. Forms can be created and will hold state as a class, but will not appear until they are activated. Likewise, closing a form doesn't destroy its state.

The following table summarizes the states of a form's existence, how you get the form to that state, the events that occur when the form enters a state, and a brief description of each.

Code	Events Fired	Description
MyForm = New Form1	None	The form's New() method will get called (as will InitializeComponent)
MyForm.Show() or	HandleCreated	Use Show() for modeless display
MyForm.ShowDialog()	Load	Use ShowDialog() for modal display
	VisibleChanged	The HandleCreated event only fires the first time the form is shown, or after it has previously been closed
	Activated	
MyForm.Activate()	Activated	A form can be activated when it is visible but does not have the focus
MyForm.Hide()	Deactivate	Hides the form (sets the Visible property to False)
	VisibleChanged	
MyForm.Close()	Deactivate	Closes the form and calls Dispose to releases the windows resources
	Closing	During the Closing event, you can set the CancelEventArgs.Cancel property to True to abort the close
	Closed	
	VisibleChanged	
	HandleDestroyed	Also called when the user closes the form using the control box or X button
	Disposed	The Deactivate event will only fire if the form is currently active

Continues

Code	Events Fired	Description
		Note: There is no longer an `Unload` event. Use the `Closing` or `Closed` event instead
`MyForm.Dispose()`	None	Use the `Close()` method to finish using your form
`MyForm = Nothing`	None	Releasing the reference to the form flags it for garbage collection. The Garbage Collector will call the form's `Finalize()` method

Controls

The controls included in Windows Forms provide the same basic functionality as those in VB6 controls, but there are many differences in how the controls are used. Some controls have been renamed, and others have been replaced. Some property names are different. This section will cover the features that all controls use (such as docking), and then address each of the standard controls available to you, as well as the important changes from previous versions of Visual Basic.

Control Tab Order

A wonderful new feature of the design environment is a tool that allows you to set the tab order of the controls on a form simply by clicking them in sequence. To activate the feature, open a form in the designer, and select the View ⇨ Tab Order menu item. This will show a small number in the upper left corner of each control on your form representing the tab index of that control.

To set the values, simply click on each control in the sequence you want the tab flow to operate. The screenshot in Figure 12-4 shows a simple form with the tab order feature enabled.

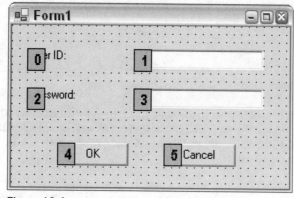

Figure 12-4

In VB.NET it is possible to have two or more controls with the same tab index value. At runtime, Visual Basic will break the tie by using the z-order of the controls. The control that is highest in the z-order will receive the focus first. The z-order can be changed by right-clicking the control and selecting Bring to Front.

Control Arrays

Control arrays, as you understood them in previous versions of Visual Basic, are gone in VB.NET. There were two capabilities for which they were needed:

❑ To have a single method handle the events of multiple controls

❑ To dynamically add new controls to your form at runtime

Both of these capabilities can also be accomplished in VB.NET, but the techniques used are different. The .NET Framework allows for any type of control to be created on the fly, and for events to be attached dynamically to controls at runtime.

Since control arrays don't exist in VB.NET, you can no longer assign the same name to multiple controls on your form. Furthermore, the Index property is gone from the standard set of control properties.

To get the control array effect, you need to connect a single method to multiple control events. Then, since you are without the Index property, your handler will need a way to determine what control fired the event. To do this, simply use the Sender parameter of the event.

A simple example is helpful to see how to set this up. First, create a new Windows application, and set the Text property of the blank Form1 to "Add Dynamic Control Demo." Then add two buttons to the form, as shown in Figure 12-5.

Figure 12-5

Double click Button1, to switch over to the code that handles the Button1.Click event. In order to make this method respond to the Button2.Click event as well, simply add the Button2.Click event handler to the end of the Handles list, and then add some simple code to display a message box indicating what button triggered the event:

```
' Note the change in the method name from Button1_Click. Since
' two objects are hooked up, it's a good idea to avoid having the
' method specifically named to a single object.
```

```
Private Sub Button_Click(ByVal sender As System.Object, _
            ByVal e As System.EventArgs) _
      Handles Button1.Click, Button2.Click
   Dim buttonClicked As Button
   buttonClicked = CType(sender, Button)
   ' Tell the world what button was clicked
   MessageBox.Show("You clicked " & buttonClicked.Text)
End Sub
```

Run the program and click the two buttons. Each one will trigger the event and display a message box, with the appropriate text from the button that was clicked.

Next, we'll enhance the program to add a third button dynamically at runtime. First, add another button to your form that will trigger the addition of Button3, as shown in Figure 12-6.

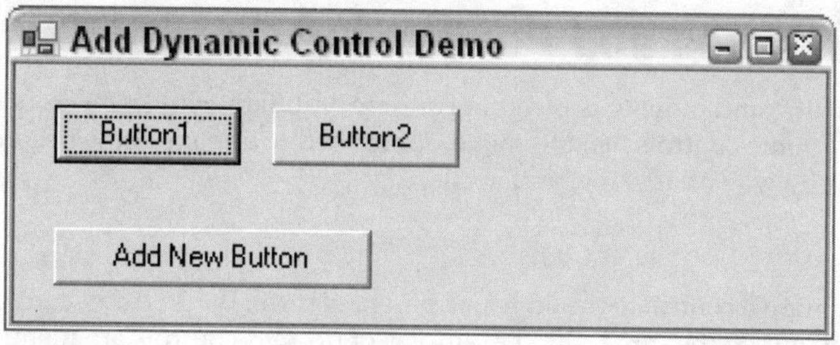

Figure 12-6

Name the new button AddNewButton and add the following code to handle its Click event:

```
Private Sub AddNewButton_Click(ByVal sender As System.Object, _
            ByVal e As System.EventArgs) _
            Handles addNewButton.Click

   Dim newButton As Button

   ' Create the new control
   newButton = New Button()

   ' Set it up on the form
   newButton.Location = New System.Drawing.Point(184, 16)
   newButton.Size = New System.Drawing.Size(75, 23)
   newButton.Text = "Button3"

   ' Add it to the form's controls collection
   Me.Controls.Add(newButton)

   ' Hook up the event handler
   AddHandler newButton.Click, AddressOf Me.Button_Click
End Sub
```

When the AddNewButton button is clicked, the code creates a new button, sets its size and position, and then does two essential things. Firstly, it adds the button to the form's controls collection, and secondly, it connects the Click event of the button to the method that will handle it.

With this done, run the program and click the `addNewButton` button. `Button3` will appear. Then, simply click Button3 to prove that the click event is being handled. You should get the result, as shown in Figure 12-7.

Figure 12-7

Automatic Resizing and Positioning Controls

If you've tried resizing and moving controls at runtime, you'll quickly come to realize that it's not as simple as it seems. Some controls need to move, some need to stretch, some need to do both. VB.NET covers these needs by way of docking, and anchoring.

Docking

Docking refers to gluing a control to the edge of a parent control. If the parent control moves or is stretched, the docked control will do the same. Good examples of docked controls are menu bars and status bars, which are typically docked to the top and bottom of a form, respectively. Docking is similar to the `Align` property of controls such as the VB6 status bar, but in VB.NET, all visual controls have a `Dock` property.

To work through an example, create a new Windows application, and place a label on a form. Then set the background color of the label to white, make its font bold, place a solid border around it, and set its `TextAlign` to `MiddleCenter`. If you also set the `Text` property of the form to "AutoResize_Demo" and the Text property of the label to "`Automatic Resizing Rocks!`", then the result when you show the form should look something like Figure 12-8.

Figure 12-8

Suppose you need to glue this label to the top of the form. To do this, view the `Dock` property of the label. If you pull it down you'll see a small graphic like Figure 12-9.

Simply click the top section of the graphic to tell the label to stick to the top of the form. The other sections give you other effects. (A status bar would use the bottom section, for example. Clicking the box in the

Figure 12-9

middle causes the control to fill the form.) The label control will immediately "stick" to the top of your form. When you run your program, and stretch the window sideways, you'll get the effect, as shown in Figure 12-10.

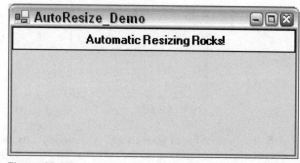

Figure 12-10

> If you attempt to dock multiple controls to the same edge, VB.NET must decide how to break the tie. Precedence is given to controls in reverse z-order. In other words, the control that is furthest back in the z-order will be the first control that is next to the edge. If you dock two controls to the same edge and want to switch them, right-click the control you want docked *first* and select Send to Back.

If you want a gap between the edge of your form and the docked controls, set the DockPadding property of the parent control. You can set a different value for each of the four directions (Left, Right, Top, Bottom). You can also set all four properties to the same value using the All setting.

Anchoring

Anchoring is similar to docking, except you can specifically define the distance each edge of your control will maintain from the edges of a parent. To see it in action, add a button to the form done in the docking example. The result should look like Figure 12-11.

Dropping down the Anchor property of the button gives you the graphic in Figure 12-12.

The four rectangles surrounding the center box allow you to toggle the anchor settings of the control. The graphic shows the default anchor setting of Top, Left for all controls.

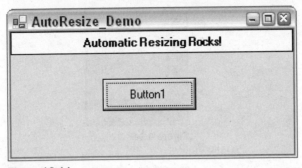

Figure 12-11

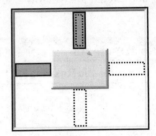

Figure 12-12

When the setting is on (dark gray), the edge of your control will maintain its starting distance from the edge of the parent as the parent is resized. If you set the anchor to two opposing edges (such as the left and right edges) the control will stretch to accommodate this, as shown in Figure 12-13.

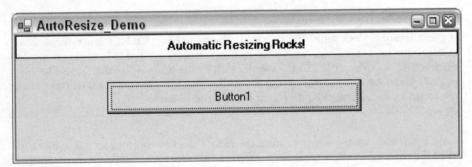

Figure 12-13

One of the most common uses of anchoring is to set the Anchor property for buttons in the lower right portion of a form. Setting Anchor property of a button to Bottom, Right will cause the button to maintain a constant distance to the bottom right corner of the form.

> Note that you should set the **Anchor** properties of your controls *after* you have designed the entire form since the anchoring effect occurs at design time as well. It can be very frustrating at design time when you need to adjust the size of your form but don't want the controls to move around.

You can also set the `Anchor` property in code. The most common time this would be needed would be for a control created on the fly. To set the Anchor property in code, you must add together the anchor styles for all the sides to which you need to anchor. For example, to set the Anchor property to `Bottom, Left` would require a line of code like this:

```
MyControl.Anchor = AnchorStyles.Bottom + AnchorStyles.Right
```

The Splitter Control

The splitter control is a great new tool that helps with resizing as well. A splitter lets a user decide the width (or height) of sections that make up a form. Windows Explorer uses a splitter to divide the folder tree view and folder content windows.

Placing a splitter on your form at design time is a bit tricky if you're new to the feature. To save yourself some frustration, follow this basic sequence of steps:

❑ Place one panel on the form that will act as the left half of the form, and set its `Dock` property to `Left`

❑ Place the splitter control on the form, it will automatically dock. Be sure the splitter is sited on the form itself, and not within the panel. Place a button in the panel, and set the button's `Anchor` property to `Top, Left, Right`

❑ Your form should now look something like Figure 12-14 (we've made the splitter extra fat and turned on their borders so you can see them).

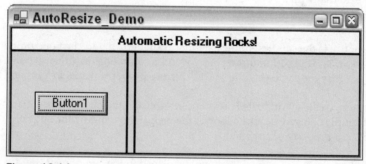

Figure 12-14

❑ Next, add another panel that will act as the right panel, and set its dock property to `Fill`. This tells it to take up the remaining space on the form

❑ Add a button to the right panel, and as with the first, set its `Anchor` property to `Top, Left, Right`

When you run the form, the splitter will automatically operate and adjust sizes of the two panels, and in turn, the size of the two buttons, as shown in Figure 12-15.

> It's a good idea to change the back color of the splitter to a bright color like red at design time. This will make it easier to see and select. At runtime, change the color to something less vibrant.

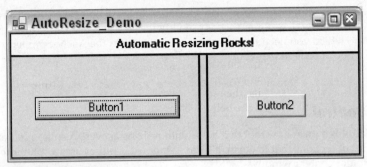

Figure 12-15

Extender Provider Controls

There is a new family of controls in Windows Forms that can only be used in association with other controls. Each of these controls, called *extender provider controls*, causes new properties to appear for every other control on the form.

Extender provider controls have no visible manifestation, so they appear in the component tray. The three extender provider controls currently available are the HelpProvider, the ToolTip, and the ErrorProvider. All three controls work in basically the same way. Each extender provider control implements the properties that are "attached" to other controls. The best way to see how this works is to go through an example, so let's do that with a `ToolTip` control.

ToolTip

The `ToolTip` control is the simplest of the extender providers. It adds just one property to each control, named `ToolTip on ToolTip1` (assuming the `ToolTip` control has the default name of `ToolTip1`). This property works exactly the same way the `ToolTipText` property works in VB6, and in fact, replaces it.

To see this in action, create a Windows Forms application. On the blank `Form1` that is created for the project, place a couple of buttons. Take a look at the properties window for `Button1`. Notice that it does not have a `ToolTip` property of any kind.

Now drag over the `ToolTip` control, which will be placed in the component tray. Go back to the properties window for `Button1`. A property named `ToolTip on ToolTip1` is now present. Set any string value you like for this property.

Now run the project, and hover the mouse pointer over `Button1`. You will see a ToolTip containing the string value you entered for the `ToolTip on ToolTip1` property.

HelpProvider

The `HelpProvider` control allows controls to have associated context-sensitive help available by pressing *F1*. When a `HelpProvider` control (named `HelpProvider1` by default) is added to a form, all controls on the form get these new properties, which show up in the controls' Properties window.

Filling in the `HelpString` property immediately causes the control to have ToolTip help when pressing *F1* while the control has the focus. The `HelpProvider` control has a property to point to a help file

Property	Usage
HelpString on HelpProvider1	Provides a pop-up ToolTip for the control when *F1* is pressed while the control has the focus. If the HelpKeyword and HelpNavigator properties (see later) are set to provide a valid reference to a help file, then the HelpString value is ignored in favor of the information in the help file.
HelpKeyword on HelpProvider1	Provides a keyword or other index to use in a help file for context-sensitive help for this control. The HelpProvider1 control has a property that indicates the help file to use. This replaces the HelpContextID property in VB6.
HelpNavigator on HelpProvider1	Contains an enumerated value that determines how the value in HelpKeyword is used to refer to the help file. There are several possible values for displaying such elements as a topic, an index, or a table of contents in the help file.
ShowHelp on HelpProvider1	Determines whether the HelpProvider control is active for this control.

(either an HTML help file or a Win32 help file), and the help topic in the HelpTopic property points to a topic in this file.

ErrorProvider

The ErrorProvider control presents a simple, visual way to indicate to a user that a control on a form has an error associated with it. The added property for controls on the form when an ErrorProvider control is used is called Error on ErrorProvider1 (assuming the ErrorProvider has the default name of ErrorProvider1). Setting this property to a string value causes the error icon to appear next to a control, and for the text to appear in a ToolTip if the mouse hovers over the error icon.

Here is a screen with several text boxes, and an error icon next to one (with a ToolTip). The error icon and ToolTip are displayed and managed by the ErrorProvider control, as shown in Figure 12-16.

Figure 12-16

The `ErrorProvider` control's default icon is the red circle with an exclamation point. When the `Error` property for the text box is set, the icon will blink for a few moments, and hovering over the icon will cause the ToolTip to appear. The code for this behavior in the example screen is explained in the next topic.

Properties of Extender Providers

In addition to providing other controls with properties, extender provider controls also have properties of their own. For example, the `ErrorProvider` control has a property named `BlinkStyle`. When it is set to `NeverBlink`, the blinking of the icon is stopped for all controls that are affected by the `ErrorProvider`.

Other properties of the `ErrorProvider` allow you to change things such as the icon used, and where the icon will appear in relation to the field that has the error. For instance, you might want the icon to show up beneath a field, instead. You can also have multiple error providers on your form. For example, you may wish to give the user a warning rather than an error. A second error provider with a yellow icon could be used to provide this feature.

Working with Extender Provider Controls in Code

Setting the Error property in the previous example can be done with the Property Window, but this is not very useful for on-the-fly error management. However, setting the Error property in code is not done with typical property syntax. By convention, extender provider controls have a method for each property they need to set, and the arguments for the method include the associated control and the property setting. To set the `Error` property in the previous example, the following code was used:

```
ErrorProvider1.SetError(txtName, "You must provide a location!")
```

The name of the method to set a property is the word `Set` prefixed to the name of the property. This line of code shows that the `Error` property is set with the `SetError()` method of the `ErrorProvider`.

There is a corresponding method to get the value of the property, and it is named with `Get` prefixed to the name of the property. To find out what the current `Error` property setting for `txtName` is, you would use the following line:

```
sError = ErrorProvider1.GetError(txtName)
```

Similar syntax is used to manipulate any of the properties managed by an extender provider control. The discussion of the ToolTip provider earlier talked about setting the ToolTip property in the Properties window. To set that same property in code, the syntax would be

```
ToolTip1.SetToolTip(Button1, "New tooltip for Button1")
```

Validating Data Entry

Most controls that you place on a form require that their content be validated in some way. A text box might require a numeric value only, or simply require that the user provide any value and not leave it blank.

The `ErrorProvider` control, covered just above, makes this task significantly easier than it was in previous versions. To illustrate the use of this control in data validation, create a new Windows application project and change the Text property for the blank Form1 to be "Validating Demo". Then place two text boxes on the form that will hold a user name and password, as shown in Figure 12-17.

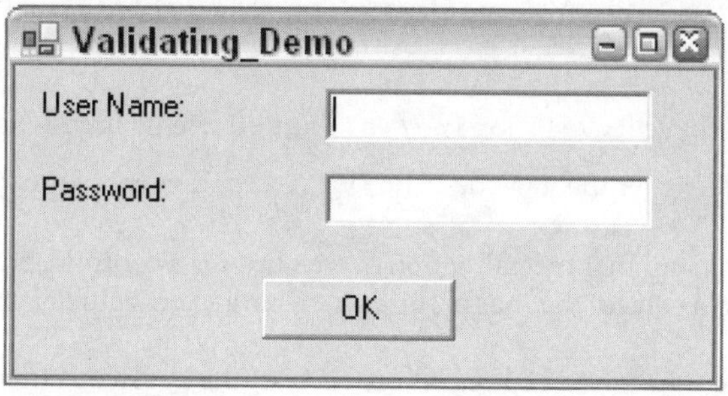

Figure 12-17

Name the first text box UserNameTextBox, and the second text box PasswordTextBox. You also need to drag an ErrorProvider control onto the form, which will cause it to appear in the Component Tray. In the next section, we'll add the code that will simply verify that the user has filled in both text boxes and given a visual indication, via the ErrorProvider, if either of the fields has been left blank.

The Validating Event

The Validating event fires when your control begins its validation. It is here that you need to place your code that will validate your control, and set a visual indication for the error. Insert the following code to see this in action:

```vb
Private Sub UserNameTextBox_Validating(ByVal sender As Object, _
                        ByVal e As System.ComponentModel.CancelEventArgs) _
                        Handles UserNameTextBox.Validating
    If userNameTextbox.Text = "" Then
        ErrorProvider1.SetError(UserNameTextBox, "User Name cannot be blank")
    Else
        ErrorProvider1.SetError(UserNameTextBox, "")
    End If
End Sub
Private Sub PasswordTextBox_Validating(ByVal sender As Object, _
                        ByVal e As System.ComponentModel.CancelEventArgs) _
                        Handles PasswordTextBox.Validating
    If passwordTextbox.Text = "" Then
        ErrorProvider1.SetError(PasswordTextBox, "Password cannot be blank")
    Else
        ErrorProvider1.SetError(PasswordTextBox, "")
    End If
End Sub
```

Run the program and the tab between the controls without entering any text to get the error message. You'll see an icon blink next to each of the textbox controls, and if you hover over an error icon, you'll see the appropriate error message.

There is also a Validated event that fires after a control's Validating event. It can be used, for example, to do a final check after other events have manipulated the contents of the control.

The CausesValidation Property

The `CausesValidation` property determines if the control will participate in the validation events on the form. A control with a `CausesValidation` setting of `True` (it is `True` by default) will have two effects:

❑ The control will have its `Validating`/`Validated` events fired when appropriate

❑ The control will trigger the `Validating`/`Validated` events for other controls

It is important to understand that the validation events fire for a control, *not when the focus is lost*, but when the focus shifts to a control that has a `CausesValidation` value of `True`.

To see this effect, set the `CausesValidation` property of the password text box in your application to `False` (be sure to leave it `True` for the username and OK button). When you run the program, tab off the username text box and again to the OK button. Notice that it isn't until the focus reaches the OK button that the validating event of the username text box fires. Also, notice that the validating event of the password field *never* fires.

Ultimately, if you determine that the control is not valid, you need to decide how to act. That may include setting the focus to the control that needs attention (as well as indicating the error with an `ErrorProvider`).

Menus

Designing menus in VB.NET is another area that has been completely redesigned. A menu is now a control that you add to your form like any other control.

The menu designer is extremely intuitive—the menu appears on your form just as it would at runtime, and you simply fill in the menu items you need.

Main Menus

Main menus are the standard menus you see that remain docked at the top of a form. Create a new Windows application and add a text box to your form. Set its `Multiline` property to `True` and stretch it out. This example will create a trivial text editor to demonstrate the use of menus.

Next, add a `MainMenu` control to your form. The menu designer will activate and you simply type your menu items and use the properties window to set the parameters.

Create the following File and Edit menu items, as shown in Figure 12-18. To set the properties of the individual menu items, simply click to select them and the properties window will show you the specific properties for that item. Set the name of the "Close" item to "closeMenuItem", the name of the "Copy" item to "copyMenuItem", and so forth, to match the names used in the code sample you'll use a bit later.

> *To create the separator in the Edit menu, enter a hyphen as the text of a menu item.*

The following code handles the menu items of our sample app. It should be inserted into the form's code.

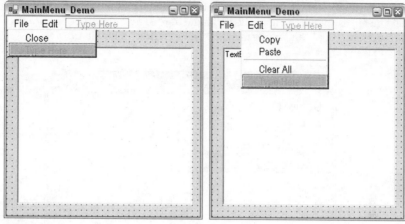

Figure 12-18

```
Private Sub copyMenuItem_Click(ByVal sender As System.Object, _
                    ByVal e As System.EventArgs) _
                    Handles copyMenuItem.Click
    TextBox1.Copy()
End Sub

Private Sub pasteMenuItem_Click(ByVal sender As System.Object, _
                    ByVal e As System.EventArgs) _
                    Handles pasteMenuItem.Click
    TextBox1.Paste()
End Sub

Private Sub closeMenuItem_Click(ByVal sender As System.Object, _
                    ByVal e As System.EventArgs) _
                    Handles closeMenuItem.Click
    Me.Close()
End Sub

Private Sub clearAllMenuItem_Click(ByVal sender As System.Object, _
                    ByVal e As System.EventArgs) _
                    Handles clearAllMenuItem.Click
    TextBox1.Text = " "
End Sub
```

Context Menus

Next, we'll add a simple context menu that will allow the user to change the color of the text box. Context menus appear as small popup menus when the user right-clicks on a form or control.

When you add a context menu to the form, it is edited in the same way a main menu is—at the top of the form. At design time, this positioning is only done to give you a place to edit the menu. At runtime, the context menu will appear in a specific location on the form, which we'll see in the code example that follows.

Double-click the ContextMenu control in the toolbox to add a new context menu to the form. Set up the context menu, as shown in Figure 12-19. Name the "Black on White" menu item "blackOnWhiteMenuItem", and name the "White on Black" menu item "whiteOnBlackMenuItem."

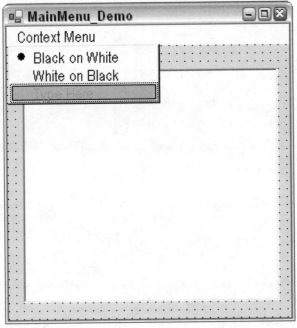

Figure 12-19

Creating the radio button indicators beside a menu item requires two properties to be manipulated. The Checked property tells Visual Basic that the menu item is "checked" and should display a checkmark indicator, while the RadioCheck property will tell Visual Basic that the indicator should be displayed as a dot instead of a checkmark. Both of these should be set to True for the Black on White option, and the RadioCheck property should be set to True for the White on Black option.

It is standard to use radio checks when the selections are mutually exclusive, and checkmarks when more than one item can be chosen at the same time. However, VB.NET will not prevent you from having two menu items with a radio check next to them at the same time. It is up to you to manage this in code.

To hook up the context menu to appear when the user right-clicks the text box, simply set the ContextMenu property of the text box to the context menu you added to the form, that's all there is to it. When you run the application and right-click the text box, you will have the result as shown in Figure 12-20.

The following code can be used when you select the items in the context menu. Note the change of the Checked property. Visual Basic will not do this for you even though it is a very common standard that radio buttons are mutually exclusive:

```
Private Sub blackOnWhiteMenuItem_Click(ByVal sender As System.Object, _
                            ByVal e As System.EventArgs) _
                            Handles blackOnWhiteMenuItem.Click
```

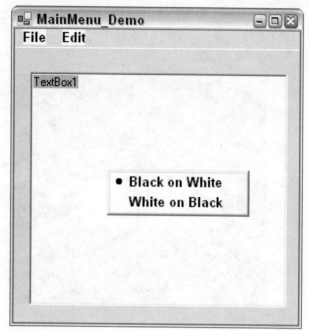

Figure 12-20

```
    TextBox1.ForeColor = System.Drawing.Color.Black
    TextBox1.BackColor = System.Drawing.Color.White

    ' toggle the radio check
    blackOnWhiteMenuItem.Checked = True
    whiteOnBlackMenuItem.Checked = False
End Sub

Private Sub whiteOnBlackMenuItem_Click(ByVal sender As System.Object, _
                                    ByVal e As System.EventArgs) _
                                    Handles whiteOnBlackMenuItem.Click
    TextBox1.ForeColor = System.Drawing.Color.White
    TextBox1.BackColor = System.Drawing.Color.Black

    ' toggle the radio check
    blackOnWhiteMenuItem.Checked = False
    whiteOnBlackMenuItem.Checked = True
End Sub
```

Run the application, right-click the text box and select the White on Black option. If you open the context menu again, you'll see that the radio check has been changed, as shown in Figure 12-21.

Dynamically Manipulating Menus at Runtime

Menus can be adjusted at runtime using code. Context menus, for instance, may need to change depending on the state of your form.

Figure 12-21

The following code shows how to add a new menu item to the context menu, and also how to clear the menu items. Although simple, it can be expanded for more advanced uses. For instance, you may want to store a list of recently accessed files in the registry. When your application loads, you could read this list back, and insert a menu item into the file menu for each item, and use the same event handler for each:

```
' Add a new menu item at the top of ContextMenu1
Private Sub AddMenuItemExample()
    Dim newMenuItem As MenuItem
    ' Create the new menu item
    newMenuItem = New MenuItem("New Menu Item!")

    ' Set up the event that will handle it's click event
    AddHandler newMenuItem.Click, AddressOf Me.NewMenuItem_Click

    ' Add it to the menu
    ContextMenu1.MenuItems.Add(0, newMenuItem)
End Sub

' This method is here to handle the click event of a new menu item that
' is added dynamically at runtime
Private Sub NewMenuItem_Click(ByVal sender As System.Object, _
                              ByVal e As System.EventArgs)
    MessageBox.Show("New menu item clicked!")
End Sub
' Remove all the menu items from ContextMenu1
Private Sub ClearMenuExample()
End Sub
```

Duplicating Menus

Another task that you can perform with menus at runtime is cloning. You may, for instance, want to have a context menu duplicate the functionality of the Edit menu in a MainMenu control. To accomplish this, use the CloneMenu() method. The following example will replace the context menu of the text box in the application above with the same edit menu from MainMenu1.

```
Private Sub CloneMenuExample()
    Dim newContextMenu As ContextMenu

    newContextMenu = New ContextMenu()
    newContextMenu.MenuItems.Add(editMenuItem.CloneMenu())

    TextBox1.ContextMenu = newContextMenu
End Sub
```

> Since CloneMenu() clones the object in its entirety, all the event handlers will be cloned as well. You don't need to copy the event handler connections for all the menu items in the cloned menu.

To switch back, simply reassign ContextMenu1 to the ContextMenu property of the text box as follows:

```
TextBox1.ContextMenu = ContextMenu1
```

Toolbars

The Toolbar control has definitely undergone some big improvements. It now hosts a collection of ToolBarButton objects, each with its own set of properties and behaviors.

As with previous examples so far, create a new Windows application to begin a simple demonstration on how to use the ToolBar control. Add a ToolBar control to your form and then expand the Buttons property to invoke the collection designer. ToolBar, as you might expect, hosts a collection of ToolBarButton objects. For now, simply add three buttons to your toolbar, using the dialog that is displayed when you press the button with three dots next to the Buttons property in the Properties window. Give the buttons the names, as seen in Figure 12-22 (notice that you must type the names in the Text property, which is blank by default). The result should look like Figure 12-22.

Next, we'll make the first button simply close the application, the second will act as a separator, and the third will be a drop-down that will invoke a context menu control. To do this, reopen the Toolbar Button collection designer and make the following changes:

❑   Change the Text property of the first button to Close

❑   Change the Style property of the second button to Separator

❑   Change the Text property of the third button to Background Color, and the Style property to DropDownButton

When you're done, your form will appear as shown in Figure 12-23.

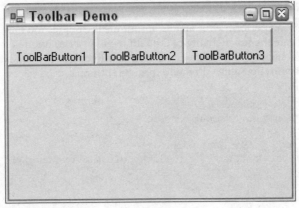

Figure 12-22

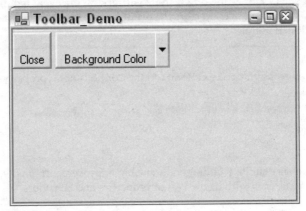

Figure 12-23

To capture the Click event of the Close button, add the following code to your form. Note the approach used to identify which button was clicked:

```
Private Sub ToolBar1_ButtonClick(ByVal sender As System.Object, _
            ByVal e As System.Windows.Forms.ToolBarButtonClickEventArgs) _
            Handles ToolBar1.ButtonClick
    Select Case ToolBar1.Buttons.IndexOf(e.Button)
        Case 0 ' Close button
            Me.Close()
    End Select
End Sub
```

When you run your application and click the Close button, your application will exit.

Next, we'll set up the drop-down button. Add a context menu to the form (see previous section) and design it to contain three items—Gray, White, and Red. If you like, assign radio checks to each as was done in the context menu sample earlier. In the form's Load event, add the following code:

```
Private Sub Form1_Load(ByVal sender As System.Object, _
                    ByVal e As System.EventArgs) Handles MyBase.Load
    ToolBarButton3.DropDownMenu = ContextMenu1
End Sub
```

That's all there is to it. You can, of course, add code similar to that shown above to handle the events of the context menu. Run the application and click the drop-down toolbar button, and you will see results similar to Figure 12-24

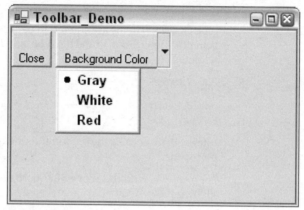

Figure 12-24

The toolbar buttons provide many other useful features to make them much nicer than the simple example shown above — images can be assigned to the buttons, the text can be aligned to the right instead of below, and the buttons themselves can appear flat, if you prefer.

While the new toolbar is certainly a big improvement over the version available in VB6, there are still a few features that it lacks. One, in particular, is that it only supports four types of buttons and separators, and so cannot include other controls such as a combo box. As a workaround, you can position a combo box or other control on top of the toolbar, but it will be necessary for you to handle the positioning of the control yourself.

Common Dialogs

VB.NET provides you with seven common dialog controls. Each is a control that will open a predefined form that is identical to the one used by the operating system. The next sections outline the use and basic properties of each control that customize their use.

OpenFileDialog and SaveFileDialog

These two controls will open the standard dialog control that allows a user to select files on the system. They are virtually identical, except for the buttons and labels that appear on the actual dialog box when it is shown to the user. Each prompts the user for a file on the system, by allowing the user to browse the files and folders available.

Use the following properties to set up the dialog boxes.

Property	Comments
InitialDirectory	Defines the initial location that will be displayed when the dialog box opens. For example: `OpenFileDialog1.InitalDirectory = "C:\Program Files"`
Filter	String that defines the "Files of type" list. Separate items using the pipe character. Items are entered in pairs with the first of each pair being the description of the file type, and the second half as the file wildcard. For example: `OpenFileDialog1.Filter = "All Files|*.*|Text Files|*.txt|Rich Text Files|*.rtf"`
FilterIndex	Integer that specifies the default filter item to use when the dialog box opens. For example, with the above filter used, default to text files as follows: `OpenFileDialog1.FilterIndex = 2`
RestoreDirectory	Boolean value that, if True, will force the system's default directory to be restored to its location as it was when the dialog box was first opened. This is False by default.
Filename	Holds the full name of the file that the user selected, including the path.
ShowDialog()	Displays the dialog.

The following code will open the standard dialog box asking the user to select a file that currently exists on the system, and simply displays the choice in a message box upon return:

```
OpenFileDialog1.InitialDirectory = "C:\ "
OpenFileDialog1.Filter = "Text files|*.txt|All files|*.*"
OpenFileDialog1.FilterIndex = 1
OpenFileDialog1.RestoreDirectory = True
OpenFileDialog1.ShowDialog()
MessageBox.Show("You selected """ & OpenFileDialog1.FileName & """")
```

ColorDialog Control

As the name obviously implies, this control gives the user a dialog box from which they can select a color. Use the following properties to set up the dialogs boxes.

Using these properties looks something like this:

```
ColorDialog1.Color = TextBox1.BackColor
ColorDialog1.AllowFullOpen = True
```

```
ColorDialog1.ShowDialog()
TextBox1.BackColor = ColorDialog1.Color
```

Property	Comments
Color	The System.Drawing.Color that the user selected. You can also use this to set the initial color selected when the user opens the dialog.
AllowFullOpen	Boolean value that, if True, will allow the user to select any color. If False, the user is restricted to the set of default colors.
ShowDialog()	Displays the dialog.

FontDialog Control

This control will display the standard dialog box allowing a user to select a font. Use the following properties to set up the dialog boxes.

Property	Comments
Font	The System.Drawing.Font that the user selected. Also used to set the initial font.
ShowEffects	Boolean value that, if True, will make the dialog box display the text effects options of underline and strikeout.
ShowColor	Boolean value that, if True, will make the dialog box display the combo box of the font colors. The ShowEffects property must be True for this to have an effect.
FixedPitchOnly	Boolean value that, if True, will limit the list of font choices to only those that have a fixed pitch (such as Courier, or Lucida console).
ShowDialog()	Displays the dialog.

Using these properties looks like this:

```
FontDialog1.Font = TextBox1.Font
FontDialog1.ShowColor = True
FontDialog1.ShowEffects = True
FontDialog1.FixedPitchOnly = False
FontDialog1.ShowDialog()
TextBox1.Font = FontDialog1.Font
```

Printer Dialog Controls

There are three more common dialog controls: PrintDialog, PrintPreviewDialog, and PageSetupDialog. They can all be used to control the output of a file to the printer. You can use these in conjunction with the PrintDocument component to run and control print jobs.

Drag and Drop

Implementing a drag-and-drop operation in the .NET Framework is accomplished using a short sequence of events. Typically, it begins in a MouseDown event of one control, and always ends with the DragDrop event of another.

To demonstrate the process, we'll begin with a new Windows Application. Add two list boxes to your form and add three items to the first using the Items property designer. This application will allow you to drag the items from one list box into the other.

The first step in making drag and drop work is specifying whether or not a control will accept a drop. By default, all controls will reject such an act and not respond to any attempt by the user to drop something onto them. In our case, set the AllowDrop property of the second list box (the one without the items added) to True.

The next item of business is to invoke the drag-and-drop operation. This is typically (although you're not restricted to it) done in the MouseDown event of the control containing the data you want to drag. The DoDragDrop method is used to start the operation. This method defines the data that will be dragged, and the type of dragging that will be allowed. In our situation, we'll drag the text of the selected list box item, and we'll permit both a move and a copy of the data to occur.

Switch over to the code window of your form and add the following code to the MouseDown event of ListBox1:

```
Private Sub ListBox1_MouseDown(ByVal sender As Object, _
                          ByVal e As System.Windows.Forms.MouseEventArgs) _
                          Handles ListBox1.MouseDown
    Dim DragDropResult As DragDropEffects
    If e.Button = MouseButtons.Left Then
        DragDropResult = ListBox1.DoDragDrop( _
                ListBox1.Items(ListBox1.SelectedIndex), _
                DragDropEffects.Move Or DragDropEffects.Copy)
        ' Leave some room here to check the result of the operation
        ' (We'll fill it in next)
    End If
End Sub
```

You'll notice the comment here about leaving room to check the result of the operation. We'll fill that in shortly. For now, calling the DoDragDrop method has got us started.

The next step involves the recipient of the data, in our case, ListBox2. There are two events here that will be important to monitor—the DragEnter and DragDrop event.

As can be predicted by the name, the DragEnter event will occur when the user first moves over the recipient control. The DragEnter event has a parameter of type DragEventArgs that contains an Effect property and a KeyState property.

The Effect property allows you to set the display of the drop icon for the user to indicate if a move or a copy will occur when the mouse button is released. The KeyState property allows you to determine the state of the *Ctrl*, *Alt*, and *Shift* keys. It is a Windows standard that when both a move or a copy can occur, a user is to indicate the copy action by holding down the *Ctrl key*. Therefore, in this event, we will check the `KeyState` property and use it to determine how to set the `Effect` property.

Add the following code to the `DragEnter` event of `ListBox2`:

```
Private Sub ListBox2_DragEnter(ByVal sender As Object, _
                            ByVal e As DragEventArgs) _
                            Handles ListBox2.DragOver
    If e.KeyState = 9 Then ' Control key
        e.Effect = DragDropEffects.Copy
    Else
        e.Effect = DragDropEffects.Move
    End If
End Sub
```

Note that you can also use the `DragOver` event if you want, but it will fire continuously as the mouse moves over the target control. In this situation, you only need to trap the initial entry of the mouse into the control.

The final step in the operation occurs when the user lets go of the mouse button to drop the data in its destination. This is captured by the `DragDrop` event. The parameter contains a property holding the data that is being dragged. It's now a simple process of placing it into the recipient control as follows:

```
Private Sub ListBox2_DragDrop(ByVal sender As Object, _
                            ByVal e As System.Windows.Forms.DragEventArgs) _
                            Handles ListBox2.DragDrop
    ListBox2.Items.Add(e.Data.GetData(DataFormats.Text))
End Sub
```

One last step — we can't forget to manipulate `ListBox1` if the drag and drop was a move. Here's where we'll fill in the hole we left in the `MouseDown` event of `ListBox1`. Once the `DragDrop` has occurred, the initial call that invoked the procedure will return a result indicating what ultimately happened. Go back to the `ListBox1_MouseDown` event and enhance it to remove the item from `Listbox1` if it was moved (and not simply copied):

```
Private Sub ListBox1_MouseDown(ByVal sender As Object, _
            ByVal e As System.Windows.Forms.MouseEventArgs) _
            Handles ListBox1.MouseDown
    Dim DragDropResult As DragDropEffects

    If e.Button = MouseButtons.Left Then
        DragDropResult = ListBox1.DoDragDrop( _
                    ListBox1.Items(ListBox1.SelectedIndex), _
                    DragDropEffects.Move Or DragDropEffects.Copy)
        ' If operation is a move (and not a copy) then remove then
        ' remove the item from the first list box
        If DragDropResult = DragDropEffects.Move Then
            ListBox1.Items.RemoveAt(ListBox1.SelectedIndex)
        End If
    End If
End Sub
```

When you're done, run your application and drag the items from Listbox1 into Listbox2. Try a copy by holding down the control key when you do it. The screenshot in Figure 12-25 shows the result after Item1 has been moved, and Item3 has been copied a few times.

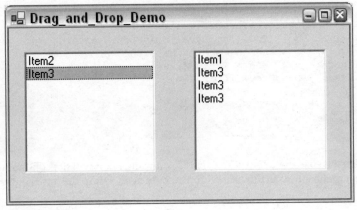

Figure 12-25

Panel and GroupBox Container Controls

In VB6, a Frame control can be used as a container to group controls. A set of option buttons (the VB6 version of radio buttons) placed in a frame control automatically becomes related as one option group. Frames are also often used in VB6 to separate areas of a form into functional areas, or to group controls for showing and hiding. If a frame is hidden, all the controls in it are hidden. Sometimes, frames in VB6 are used with a border (with or without a title for the frame), and other times without a border.

The functionality in the frame control for VB6 is divided into two controls in VB.NET. They are called the GroupBox control and the Panel control.

Each is like the VB6 frame control in the following ways:

❑ They can serve as a container for other controls

❑ If they are hidden or moved, the action affects all the controls in the container

The GroupBox control is the one that most closely resembles a frame control visually. It acts just like a VB6 frame control, with one significant exception. There is no way to remove its border. It always has a border, and it can have a title, if needed. The border is always set the same way. Figure 12-26 shows a form with a GroupBox control containing three RadioButtons.

The Panel control has three major differences from GroupBox:

❑ It has options for displaying its border in the BorderStyle property, with a default of no border.

❑ It has the capability to scroll by setting its AutoScroll property to True.

❑ It has no ability to set a title or caption (it has no Text property).

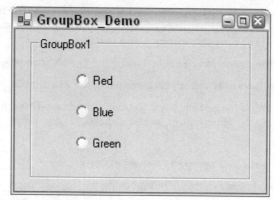

Figure 12-26

Figure 12-27 shows a form containing a Panel control with its border set to FixedSingle, with scrolling turned on, and with a CheckedListBox which is too big to display all at once (which forces the Panel to show a scroll bar).

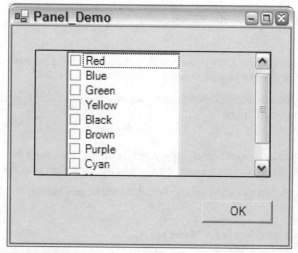

Figure 12-27

Summary of Standard Windows.Forms Controls

VB.NET of course contains most of the controls which you are accustomed to using in previous versions. The following few pages list out the basic controls that are generally quite intuitive and didn't warrant a full example to explain. Where appropriate, the important differences from previous versions of Visual Basic are stated.

❑ *Button*

    ❑ Formerly known as `CommandButton`.

    ❑ Now uses the `Text` property instead of `Caption`.

❑ Can now display both an icon and text simultaneously. The image is set using the `Image` property (instead of `Picture`). The image position can be set using the `ImageAlign` property (`left`, `right`, `center`, and so on).

❑ Text on the button can be aligned using the `TextAlign` property.

❑ Can now have different appearances using the `FlatStyle` property.

❑ No longer has the `Default` and `Cancel` properties. These are now managed by the form itself using the `AcceptButton` and `CancelButton` properties.

❑ *CheckBox*

    ❑ Now uses the `Text` property instead of `Caption`

    ❑ Can now appear as a toggle button using the `Appearance` property

    ❑ Checkbox and text can now be positioned within the defined area using the `CheckAlign` and `TextAlign` properties

    ❑ Uses the `CheckState` property instead of `Value`

    ❑ Has a `FlatStyle` property controlling the appearance of the checkbox

❑ *CheckedListBox*

    ❑ A list box that has checkboxes beside each item (see `Listbox`)

❑ *ComboBox*

    ❑ As with the new `ListBox` control, can now hold a collection of objects instead of an array of strings, (see `ListBox`)

    ❑ Now has a `MaxDropDownItems` property that specifies how many items to display when the list opens

❑ *DataGrid*

    ❑ This has been significantly upgraded from its predecessor in VB6. In essence, the DataGrid is a front-end user interface to the data objects in the .NET Framework.

    ❑ You can find more information on this control in Chapter 16.

❑ *DateTimePicker*

    ❑ Formerly known as a `DTPicker`

❑ *DomainUpDown — New!*

    ❑ A simple one line version of a list box

    ❑ Can hold a collection of objects, and will display the `ToString()` result of an item in the collection

    ❑ Can wrap around the list to give a continuous scrolling effect using the `Wrap` property

❑ *HScrollBar*

    ❑ Unchanged

❑ *ImageList*

    ❑ Same as previous versions, but with an improved window for managing the images within the list. The `MaskColor` property is now `TransparentColor`.

❏ *Label*

   ❏ Essentially the same as previous versions.

   ❏ Caption is now Text.

   ❏ Can now display an image and text.

   ❏ The TextAlign property is especially useful. The text of a label beside a text box in VB6 would always be a few pixels higher than the text in the text box. Now by setting the label's TextAlign property so that the vertical alignment is Middle, this problem is solved.

   ❏ Can now specify if a mnemonic should be interpreted (if UseMnemonic is True, the first ampersand (&) in the Text property will indicate to underline the following character and have it react to the *Alt* key shortcut, placing the focus on the next control in the tab order that can hold focus such as a text box).

❏ *LinkLabel — New!*

   ❏ Identical to a label, but behaves like a hyperlink with extra properties such as LinkBehavior (for example, HoverUnderline), LinkColor, and ActiveLinkColor

❏ *ListBox*

   ❏ A list box can now hold a collection of objects, instead of an array of strings. Use the DisplayMember property to specify what property of the objects to display in the list, and the ValueMember property to specify what property of the objects to use as the values of the list items. (This is similar to the ItemData array from previous versions) For example, the combo box can store a collection of, say employee objects, and display to the user the Name property of each, as well as retrieve the EmployeeId as the value of the item currently selected.

   ❏ Can no longer be set to display check boxes using a Style property. Use the CheckedListBox control instead.

❏ *ListView*

   ❏ Same functionality as the VB6 version but with an improved property editor that allows you to define the list view item collection *and* its subitems at design time

   ❏ Subitems can have their own font display properties

   ❏ New HeaderStyle property instead of HideColumnHeaders

❏ *MonthCalendar*

   ❏ Formerly known as MonthView

❏ *NotifyIcon — New!*

   ❏ Great new control that gives you an icon in the system tray

   ❏ Tooltip of the icon is set by the Text property of the control

   ❏ Pop-up menus are set using a ContextMenu control (see section on *Menus* earlier in chapter)

- ❏ *NumericUpDown — New!*
  - ❏ A single line text box that displays a number and up/down buttons that increment/decrement the number when clicked

- ❏ *PictureBox*
  - ❏ `Image` property defines the graphic to display instead of `Picture`
  - ❏ Use the `SizeMode` property to auto stretch, or center the picture

- ❏ *ProgressBar*
  - ❏ Now has a `Step()` method that automatically increments the value of the progress bar by the amount defined in the `Step` property

- ❏ *RadioButton*
  - ❏ Formerly known as `OptionButton`
  - ❏ Use `Checked` property to specify value (formerly `Value`)
  - ❏ Use `CheckAlign` and `TextAlign` to specify where the radio button and text appears in relation to the area of the control

- ❏ *RichTextBox*
  - ❏ Essentially the same control as before with a few new properties such as `ZoomFactor`, `WordWrap`, `DetectURLs` and `AutoWordSelection`
  - ❏ Use the `Lines()` array to get or set specific individual lines of text of the control

- ❏ *StatusBar*
  - ❏ Has a `Panels` collection and a `ShowPanels` property. If `False`, the status bar will display only the `Text` property. This would be equivalent to setting the VB6 status bar control `Style` property to `sbrSimple`.
  - ❏ The `StatusBar` control docks to the bottom of the parent control by default. (See section on *Docking*.) You could change this if you want (although we're not sure how intuitive a floating status bar would be).

- ❏ *TabControl*
  - ❏ Formerly known as the `TabStrip` control.
  - ❏ Now has a `TabPages` collection of `TabPage` objects. A `TabPage` object is a subclass of the `Panel` control specialized for use in the `TabControl`.
  - ❏ Uses the `Appearance` property to display the tabs as buttons, if desired (formerly the `Style` property of the `TabStrip` control).

- ❏ *Text box*
  - ❏ Now has a `CharacterCasing` property that can automatically adjust the text entered into upper or lower case.
  - ❏ `ReadOnly` property now used to prevent the text from being edited. This used to be the`Locked` property.

    Note: The `Locked` property now determines if the control can be moved or resized.
  - ❏ Now has `Cut`, `Copy`, `Paste`, `Undo`, and `ClearUndo` methods.

- *Timer*
  - Essentially unchanged from previous versions
  - The timer is now *dis*abled by default
  - You cannot set the interval to zero to disable it
- *TrackBar*
  - Formerly known as the Slider control, essentially unchanged
- *TreeView*
  - Same functionality as in VB6 but with a new *Node Tree Editor* that allows you to visually design the tree
- *VScrollBar*
  - Unchanged

Retired Controls

Some controls have also been "retired." The following list outlines the controls from VB6 that you won't find in VB.Net, and how to reproduce their functionality:

- *Spinner*
  - Use the `DomainUpDown` or `NumericUpDown` control
- *Line and Shape*
  - VB.NET has no line or shape control, nor any immediate equivalent. A "cheap" way of reproducing a horizontal or vertical line is to use a label control. Set its background color to that of the line you want, and then either the `Size.Height` or `Size.Width` value to 1.
  - Diagonal lines and shapes must be drawn using GDI+ graphics methods.
- *DirListBox, FileListBox, DriveListBox*
  - You would typically use these controls to create a file system browser similar to Windows Explorer. VB.NET has no equivalent controls. You can use the `OpenFileDialog` and `SaveFileDialog` (see previous section) to accomplish your needs in most circumstances.
- *Image*
  - Use the `PictureBox` control

Using ActiveX Controls

While VB.NET is optimized to use Windows Forms controls, you can certainly place an ActiveX control on your form and use it as well. You'll see how to do this in Chapter 17.

Other Handy Programming Tips

Here are some other handy programming tips for using Windows Forms:

❑ *Switch the Focus to a Control* — Use the .Focus() method. To set the focus to TextBox1, for example, use the following code

```
TextBox1.Focus()
```

❑ *Change the Cursor* — To switch the cursor to an hourglass, for example, use the Cursor object as follows

```
Cursor.Current = Cursors.WaitCursor ' hourglass Cursor.Current =
Cursors.Default ' pointer
```

❑ *Quickly Determine the Container Control or Parent Form* — With the use of group boxes and panels, controls are often contained many times removed from the ultimate form. You can now use the FindForm method to immediately get a reference to the form. Use the GetContainerControl method to access the immediate parent of a control.

❑ *Traversing the Tab Order* — Use the GetNextControl method of any control to get a reference to the next control on the form in the tab order.

❑ *Convert Client Coordinates to Screen Coordinates (and back)* — Want to know where a control is in screen coordinates? Use the PointToScreen method. Convert back using the PointToClient method.

❑ *Change the Z-Order of Controls at Runtime* — Controls now have both BringToFront and SendToBack methods.

❑ *Where is the Mouse Pointer?* — The control class now exposes a MousePosition property that returns the location of the mouse in screen coordinates.

❑ *Managing Child Control* — Container controls such as a group box or panel, can use the HasChildren property and Controls property to determine the existence of, and direct references to, child controls respectively.

❑ *Maximize, Minimize, Restore a Form* — Use the form's WindowState property.

MDI Forms

MDI (Multiple Document Interface) forms are forms that are created to hold other forms. The MDI form is often referred to as the *parent*, and the forms displayed within the MDI parent are often called *children*. Figure 12-28 shows a typical MDI parent with several children displayed within it.

Creating an MDI Parent Form

In VB.NET, a regular form is converted to an MDI parent form by setting the IsMDIContainer property of the form to True. This is normally done in the Properties window at design time.

A form can also be made into an MDI parent at runtime by setting the IsMDIContainer property to True in code. However, the design of an MDI form is usually rather different from that of a normal form, so this approach is not often needed.

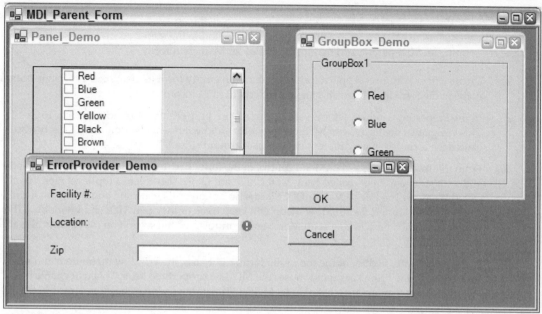

Figure 12-28

Differences in MDI Parent Forms Between VB6 and VB.NET

In VB6, an MDI parent form can only contain controls that have a property called Align. This property determines to which side of the MDI parent form the control is supposed to be docked. Typical controls like buttons and text boxes cannot be added directly to an MDI parent form. They must be added to a container control, such as a PictureBox, which has an Align property.

In VB.NET, an MDI parent can contain any control that a regular form can contain. Buttons, labels, and such can be placed directly on the MDI surface. Such controls will appear in front of any MDI child forms that are displayed in the MDI client area.

It is still possible to use controls like PictureBoxes to hold other controls on a VB.NET MDI parent, and these controls can be docked to the side of the MDI form. In fact, every control in VB.NET has the equivalent of the Align property, called Dock. The Dock property was previously discussed in the section on changes to controls in VB.NET.

MDI Child Forms

In VB.NET, a form becomes an MDI child at runtime by setting the form's MDIParent property to point to an MDI parent form. This makes it possible to use a form as either a stand-alone form or an MDI child in different circumstances. In fact, the MDIParent property cannot be set at design time—it must be set at runtime to make a form an MDI child. (Note that this is completely different from VB6, where it was necessary to make a form an MDI child at design time.)

It is possible to have any number of MDI child forms displayed in the MDI parent client area. The currently active child form can be determined with the ActiveForm property of the MDI parent form.

An MDI Example in VB.NET

To see these changes to MDI forms in action, you can do the following step-by-step exercise. It shows the basics of creating an MDI parent, and making it display an MDI child form.

1. Create a new Windows Application. It will have an empty form named Form1. Change both the name of the form and the form's Text property to MDIParentForm

2. In the Properties window, set the IsMDIContainer property for MDIParentForm to True. This designates the form as an MDI container for child windows. (Setting this property also causes the form to have a different default background color.)

3. From the Toolbox, drag a MainMenu control to the form. Create a top-level menu item called File and with submenu items called New MDI Child and Quit. Also create a top-level menu item called Window. The File ⇨ New MDI Child menu option will create and show new MDI child forms at runtime, and the Window menu will keep track of the open MDI child windows. (For more information on working with MainMenu controls, see the section on menu controls earlier in the chapter.)

4. In the menu option editor at the top of the form, right-click the Window menu item and select Properties. In the Properties window, set the MDIList property to True. This will enable the Window menu to maintain a list of open MDI child windows with a checkmark next to the active child window.

5. Now we need to create an MDI child form to use as a template for multiple instances. To do this, select Project ⇨ Add Windows Form and then Open in the Add New Item dialog box. That will result in a new blank form named Form2. Place any controls you like on the form. As an alternative, you can reuse any of the forms created in previous exercises in this chapter.

6. Now go back to MDIParentForm. In the menu editing bar, double-click the New MDI Child option under File. The code editor will appear, with the cursor in the event routine for that menu option. Place the following code in the event:

```
Protected Sub MenuItem2_Click(ByVal sender As Object,
                              ByVal e As System.EventArgs)

    ' This line may change if you are using a form with a different name.
    Dim NewMDIChild As New Form2()
    'Set the Parent Form of the Child window.
    NewMDIChild.MDIParent = Me
    'Display the new form.
    NewMDIChild.Show()

End Sub
```

7. In the menu editing bar for MDIParentForm, double-click the Quit option under File. The code editor will appear, with the cursor in the event routine for that menu option. Place the following code in the event:

```
Protected Sub MenuItem3_Click(ByVal sender As Object, _
                              ByVal e As System.EventArgs)
    End
End Sub
```

8. Now run and test the program. Use the File ⇨ New MDI Child option to create several child forms. Note how the Window menu option automatically lists them with the active one checked, and allows you to activate a different one.

Arranging Child Windows

MDI parent forms have a method called LayoutMDI that will automatically arrange child forms in the familiar cascade or tile layout. For the example above, add a menu item to your Windows menu called Tile Vertical and insert the following code into the menu item's Click event to handle it:

```
Me.LayoutMdi(MDILayout.TileVertical)
```

To see an example of the rearrangement, suppose that the MDI form in Figure 12-28 is rearranged with the MDILayout.TileVertical option. It would then look similar to the image in Figure 12-29.

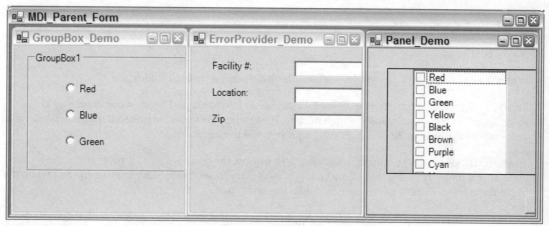

Figure 12-29

Dialog Forms

In VB6 and earlier, forms were shown with the Show method, and this technique is still used in VB.NET. In both VB6 and VB.NET, the Show method by default displays *modeless* forms, which are forms that allow the user to click off of them onto another form in the application.

In VB6, dialog boxes were displayed with the vbModal parameter (or a hardcoded value of 1) after the form's Show method. This caused the form to be a *modal* form, which meant that is was the only active form in the application until it was exited.

Showing a form modally is done differently in VB.NET. A Windows Form has a ShowDialog() method that takes the place of the Show method with the vbModal parameter. Here is code for showing a modal dialog in VB.NET:

```
Dim frmDialogForm As New DialogForm
frmDialogForm.ShowDialog()
```

DialogResult

It is common when showing a dialog form to need to get information about what action the user selected. This was often done with a custom property in VB6, but VB.NET has a built-in property for that purpose. When a form is shown with the `ShowDialog()` method, the form has a property called `DialogResult` to indicate its state.

The `DialogResult` property can take the following enumerated results:

- ❑   `DialogResult.Abort`
- ❑   `DialogResult.Cancel`
- ❑   `DialogResult.Ignore`
- ❑   `DialogResult.No`
- ❑   `DialogResult.None`
- ❑   `DialogResult.OK`
- ❑   `DialogResult.Retry`
- ❑   `DialogResult.Yes`

When the `DialogResult` property is set, as a by-product, the dialog is hidden.

The `DialogResult` property of a dialog box can be set in two ways. The most common way is to associate a `DialogResult` value with a button. Then, when the button is pressed, the associated value is automatically placed in the `DialogResult` property of the form.

To set the `DialogResult` value associated with a button, the `DialogResult` property of the button is used. If this property is set for the button, it is unnecessary to set the `DialogResult` in code when the button is pressed. Here is an example that uses this technique.

In VS.NET, start a new VB.NET Windows Application. On the automatic blank form that comes up (named `Form1`), place a single button and set its `Text` property to `Dialog`.

Property	Value for First Button	Value for Second Button
Name	BtnOK	btnCancel
Text	OK	Cancel
DialogResult	OK	Cancel

Now, add a new Windows Form using the Project ⇨ Add Windows Form . . . menu, and name it `DialogForm.vb`. Place two buttons on `DialogForm` and set the following properties for the buttons:

Do not put any code in `DialogForm` at all. The form should look like the one shown in Figure 12-30.

On the first form, `Form1`, place the following code in the `Click` event for `Button1`:

```
Private Sub Button1_Click(ByVal sender As System.Object, _
    ByVal e As System.EventArgs) Handles Button1.Click
```

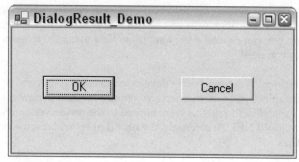

Figure 12-30

```
Dim frmDialogForm As New DialogForm()
frmDialogForm.ShowDialog()

' We're back from the dialog - check user action.
Select Case frmDialogForm.DialogResult
  Case DialogResult.OK
    MsgBox("The user pressed OK")
  Case DialogResult.Cancel
    MsgBox("The user pressed cancel")
End Select

  frmDialogForm = Nothing

End Sub
```

Now, run and test the code. When a button is pressed on the dialog form, a message box should be displayed (by the calling form) indicating the button that was pressed.

The second way to set the `DialogResult` property of the form is in code. In a `Button_Click` event, or anywhere else in the dialog form, a line like this can be used to set the `DialogResult` property for the form, and simultaneously hide the dialog form, giving control back to the calling form.

```
Me.DialogResult = DialogResult.Ignore
```

This particular line sets the dialog result to `DialogResult.Ignore`, but setting the dialog result to any of the permitted values will also hide the dialog form.

Summary

The new features and improvements to Windows Forms in VS.NET simplify development of rich client and smart client interfaces, and allow new capabilities that user interface designers did not have in earlier versions of Visual Basic. Coupled with the easy deployment of .NET applications, we can expect a resurgence in forms-based programs.

Becoming a capable Windows Forms developer requires becoming familiar with the controls that are available, and their properties, events, and methods. This takes time. If you are coming from the VB6 world, much of your expertise will continue to be useful with Windows Forms, and this chapter has highlighted the most important differences you need to know about. If you are less familiar with forms-based interfaces, you can expend a fair amount of time using the reference documentation to find the control capabilities you need.

However, many professional Windows Forms developers need to go beyond just creating forms and laying out controls. Complex applications often also require creation of new controls, or enhancement of built-in controls. The capabilities to do this were limited in the earlier versions of Visual Basic, but are much more impressive in VB.NET. Accordingly, the next chapter will discuss how to create and modify Windows Forms controls.

Creating Windows Controls

The previous chapter discussed the basics of Windows Forms, which is the library of classes for creation of local, forms-based interfaces in Visual Basic .NET (VB.NET). Windows Forms interfaces are based on using *controls*. A control is simply a special type of .NET class (just as forms are).

It's possible to write very complex Windows Forms programs using controls, such as text boxes and buttons, which are an inherent part of Windows Forms. However, as a fully object-oriented programming environment, VB.NET gives us the capability to inherit and extend classes, and controls are no exception. It is therefore, possible to create new controls that go beyond what the built-in controls can do. This chapter discusses the various techniques for creation of new controls.

Just as forms get their basic behavior from a base class called `System.Window.Forms.Form`, a control inherits (either directly or indirectly) from a base class called `System.Window.Forms.Control`. This base class ensures that certain functionality will be available to all controls in Windows Forms. It will be discussed in detail in this chapter.

The chapter will also cover the three main techniques available to developers in creating controls, namely:

❑ Inheriting from another control

❑ Building a composite control, that is, a control that combines other controls into a unit

❑ Writing a control based directly on the `System.Window.Forms.Control` class

Sources of Controls

There are four primary sources of controls for use on Windows Forms interfaces:

❑ Controls packaged with the .NET Framework (referred to in this chapter as *built-in controls*)

- Existing ActiveX controls that are imported into Windows Forms (these were mentioned in Chapter 12, and are also discussed in Chapter 17)

- Third-party .NET-based controls from a software vendor

- Custom controls that are created for a specific purpose in a particular project or organization

Built-in Controls

The set of built-in controls that comes with the .NET Framework is comparable to the set offered with the previous versions of Visual Basic (although with some changes and additions). Chapter 12, on Windows Forms, covered the basics of using these controls.

Many Windows Forms interfaces can be built completely with built-in controls. The stability and fast implementation of the built-in controls make them attractive for a wide variety of purposes.

Existing ActiveX Controls

It is relatively straightforward to use existing ActiveX controls in Windows Forms. They can be referenced in the same way as .NET controls, and a wrapper for them will be automatically created.

However, using ActiveX controls in a Windows Forms application means that the old deployment issues connected with COM-based software are still a problem. Since one of the major attractions of doing applications in Windows Forms is ease of deployment, ActiveX controls should normally be used only when it is impractical to find or create an appropriate .NET control, or when an application will not need to be distributed to many desktops.

You'll see how to use an existing ActiveX control in Chapter 17, which discusses working with classic COM.

Third-Party Controls

If the set of built-in controls proves insufficient for the needs of a particular application, another option is to acquire more visual controls from a commercial software vendor. Such third-party controls have been available in the previous versions of Visual Basic for many years, and continue to be an option for VB.NET.

A wide variety of controls from reputable vendors are available; they are often richer in functionality than the built-in controls, but just as robust.

Custom Controls

When neither built-in controls nor third-party controls are sufficient to meet our needs, the next option is to create custom controls.

This option was also possible in the previous versions of Visual Basic by developing UserControls. However, custom controls in VB.NET have several major advantages over VB6 UserControls, including simpler development, simpler deployment, and far greater flexibility.

Developing Custom Controls in .NET

As mentioned in the chapter introduction, there are three basic techniques for the creation of custom Windows Forms controls in .NET, corresponding to three different starting points. This range of options gives the flexibility to choose a technique that allows an appropriate balance between simplicity and flexibility. You can:

❑ Inherit from an existing control

❑ Build a composite control

❑ Write a control from scratch

Let's look at each of these with a view to understanding the scenarios in which each one is useful.

Inherit from an Existing Control

The simplest technique starts with a complete Windows Forms control that is already developed. A new class is created that inherits the existing control. (See Chapter 6 for a complete discussion of inheritance in .NET.) This new class has all the functionality of the base class from which it inherits and the new logic can be added to create additional functionality in this new class or, indeed, to override functionality from the parent (when permitted).

Most of the built-in Windows Forms controls can be used as the base class for such an inherited control. There are a few exceptions, such as the `NotifyIcon` control, and the `ProgressBar`. If you are in doubt about any particular control, you can check the Visual Studio Help. The declaration for a class that cannot be inherited will have the `NotInheritable` keyword included at the beginning.

Third-party controls may also be candidates for extension into new custom controls through inheritance. As with Windows Forms controls, some third party controls can be inherited and others cannot.

Here are some typical examples where it might make sense to extend an existing Windows Forms control:

❑ A text box with built-in validation for specific types of information

❑ A self-loading list box, combo box, or data grid

❑ A picture control that chooses a new image at random from a directory each time it appears on a form

❑ A menu control that varies its options based on the current user

❑ A `NumericUpDown` control that generates a special event when it reaches 80% of its maximum allowed value

Each of these scenarios starts with an existing control that simply needs some additional functionality. The more oftensuch functionality is needed in your project, the more sense it makes to package it in a custom control. If a text box that needs special validation or editing will be used in only one place, it probably doesn't make sense to create an inherited control. In that case, simply adding some logic in the form where the control is used to handle the control's events and manipulating the control's properties and methods is probably sufficient. But where such functionality is needed in many locations in an application, packaging the functionality in an inherited control can centralize the logic and facilitate reuse, thereby removing maintenance headaches.

Build a Composite Control

In some cases, a single existing control does not furnish the needed functionality, but a combination of two or more existing controls does. Here are some typical examples:

❑   A set of buttons with related logic that are always used together

❑   A set of text boxes to hold a name, address, and phone number, with the combined information formatted and validated in a particular way

❑   A set of option buttons with a single property exposed as the chosen option

❑   A data grid together with buttons that alter its appearance or behavior in specific ways

As with inherited controls, composite controls are only appropriate for situations that require the same functionality in multiple places. If the functionality is only needed once, then simply placing the relevant controls on the form and including appropriate logic right in the form is usually better.

Composite controls are the closest relative to VB6 `UserControls` and, because of that, they are sometimes referred to as UserControls. In fact, the base class used to create composite controls is the `UserControl` class in .NET.

Write a Control from Scratch

If a control needs to have special functionality not related to any existing control, then it can be written from scratch to draw its own visual interface and implement its own logic. This option requires more work, but allows us to do just about anything that is possible within .NET and Windows Forms, including very sophisticated drawing of a user interface.

To write a control from scratch, it is necessary to inherit from the `Control` class, which gives basic functionality such as properties for colors and size. With this basic functionality already built in, the main tasks to be performed to get a custom control working are to add on any specific properties and methods needed for this control, to write the rendering logic that will paint the control to the screen, and to handle mouse and keyboard input to the control.

Inheriting from an Existing Control

With this background on the options for creating custom controls, the next step is to look in depth at the procedures used for their development. First up is creating a custom control by inheriting from an existing control and extending it with new functionality. This is the simplest method for the creation of new controls, and the best way to introduce generic techniques that apply to all new controls.

After describing the general steps needed to create a custom control via inheritance, two examples will illustrate the details. It is important to understand that many of the techniques described for working with a control created through inheritance also apply to the other ways that a control can be created.

Whether inheriting from the `Control` class, the `UserControl` class, or from an existing control, a control is a .NET class. Creating properties, methods, and events, and coordinating these members with the VS.NET designers, is done in a similar fashion, regardless of the starting point.

Overview of the Process

Here are the general stages involved in the creation of a custom control via inheritance from an existing control. This is not a step-by-step recipe, but just an overview. An example follows that goes into more detail on specific steps, but those steps will carry out the following stages:

1. For the first stage, it is necessary to create or open a Windows Control Library project, and add a new `UserControl` to the project using the option on the Project menu. The class that is created will inherit from the `System.Windows.Forms.UserControl` namespace. The line that specifies the inherited class must be changed to inherit from the control that is being used as the starting point.

2. The class file then gets new logic added as necessary to add new functionality, before the project is compiled with a `Build` operation in order to create a DLL containing the new control's code.

3. The control is now ready to be used. It can be placed in the Windows Forms toolbox with the Add/Remove Items option in Visual Studio 2003 (or the Customize Toolbox option in Visual Studio 2002). From that point forward, it can be dragged onto forms like any other control.

Now, let's discuss these steps in detail by using them in a simple example.

Creating a Numeric-Only Text Box

The first example will create a text box that only allows the user to put in a numeric entry. The starting point will be a normal Windows Forms text box that allows entry of any character. The new, inherited control will have additional logic to restrict input to those characters appropriate for numeric entry.

The basic requirements for the control are to:

- Allow digits
- Allow entry of one decimal point only
- Allow a minus sign, but only at the first position in the text box
- Throw away (or ignore) all other characters entered by the user

Step-By-Step Process to Create the Control

To create the control, follow these steps:

1. Start a new Windows Control Library project in VS.NET. Give it the name NumericTextBox, rename the resulting project module `NumericTextBox.vb` (by default it will be named `UserControl1.vb`), and bring up the code window for this class.

2. The first two lines of the class will look like this.

```
Public Class UserControl1
    Inherits System.Windows.Forms.UserControl
```

3. To inherit from a text box, these lines should be changed to the following code:

```
Public Class NumericTextBox
    Inherits System.Windows.Forms.TextBox
```

4. Next, new code must be added for the new functionality. In our case, this is just one extra event routine which excludes the keys that the text box should not allow. To do that, place an event routine for the KeyPress event in the code. This is accomplished by opening the left-hand drop-down box in the code window and selecting the option NumericTextBox Events (or Base Class Events in Visual Studio 2002), before selecting the KeyPress event in the right-hand drop-down box of the code window. Figure 13-1 is a sample screen showing the KeyPress event about to be selected.

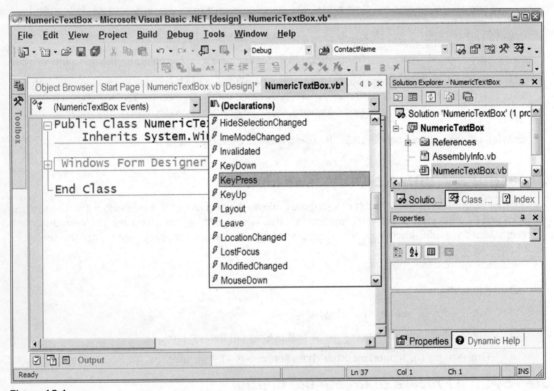

Figure 13-1

This action will cause the following code for an empty KeyPress event to be generated (the code below has line continuation characters added to facilitate readability):

```
Private Sub NumericTextBox_KeyPress(ByVal sender As Object, _
    ByVal e As System.Windows.Forms.KeyPressEventArgs) Handles _
    MyBase.KeyPress

End Sub
```

5. The following code should be added to the KeyPress event to monitor keystrokes from the user:

```
Private Sub NumericTextBox_KeyPress(ByVal sender As Object, _
    ByVal e As System.Windows.Forms.KeyPressEventArgs) _
    Handles MyBase.KeyPress

Dim KeyAscii As Integer
KeyAscii = Asc(e.KeyChar)

Select Case KeyAscii

  Case 48 To 57, 8, 13        ' these are the digits 0-9, backspace,
    ' and carriage return
    ' we're OK on these, don't do anything

  Case 45                     ' minus sign

    ' The number can only have one minus sign, so
    ' if we already have one, throw this one away
    If InStr(Me.Text, "-") <> 0 Then
      KeyAscii = 0
    End If

    ' if the insertion point is not sitting at zero
    ' (which is the beginning of the field), throw away the minus
    ' sign (because it's not valid except in first position)
    If Me.SelectionStart <> 0 Then
      KeyAscii = 0
    End If

  Case 46                     ' this is a period (decimal point)

    ' if we already have a period, throw it away
    If InStr(Me.Text, ".") <> 0 Then
      KeyAscii = 0
    End If

  Case Else
    ' provide no handling for the other keys
    KeyAscii = 0

End Select

' If we want to throw the keystroke away, then set the event
' as already handled. Otherwise, let the keystroke be handled normally.
If KeyAscii = 0 Then
  e.Handled = True
Else
  e.Handled = False
End If

End Sub
```

6. Build the project to create a DLL containing the NumericTextBox control.

7. Create a new Windows Application project to test the control. Name the new project anything you like. Now right-click the Windows Forms tab in the Toolbox, and select Add/Remove Items..., and then click the tab for .NET Framework Components. Hit the Browse button and navigate to the directory containing your NumericTextBox project, in order to select the NumericTextBox.dll file (found in the /bin subdirectory). Return to the Add/Remove Items dialog, check the box, and click the OK button.

8. Scroll to the bottom of the controls on the Windows Forms tab. The NumericTextBox control should be there.

9. Drag a NumericTextBox control onto the form as you would a normal TextBox. Start the project. Test the NumericTextBox to check that it only accepts numeric input.

Making Changes to a Custom Control

When you created a new Windows Application project to test the NumericTextBox, the Add/Remove Items operation (step 6) caused the Windows Application project to make a copy of NumericTextBox.dll in its own directory. This is necessary to run the application because of the way .NET loads DLLs. (See Chapter 25 to understand why this is the case.)

> If you change the logic in the NumericTextBox control and then build a new version of it, that new version will not be automatically supplied to the Windows Application project used to test the control. It will be necessary to remove the control from the toolbox (via Add/Remove Items) and then refer to the changed version of the control. This will cause a new copy of the control's assembly to be placed in the test application's directory.

The process required to unload and reload the control into the toolbox is tedious, and it's easy to forget to do it and then wonder why your changes don't seem to be applied. But there's a better way. It is easier to test new controls by adding a new Windows Application to the same project that is being used to create the control. Then, when new versions of the control are built, the Windows Application in the project automatically uses the new version. This is the recommended technique to use during development of any type of custom control, and it will be used for the remaining examples in the chapter.

There is one additional step needed if a new Windows Application is added to a solution to test a custom control. The Windows Application project must be set as the startup project in the solution properties (this can be done by right-clicking the project name in the Solution Explorer window and selecting Set as Startup Project). Otherwise, the default startup is the control project, and you will receive an error message if you try to execute the solution with the control still designated as the startup project.

Adding Additional Logic to a Custom Control

While the first example stated earlier is completely functional and can be useful, most custom controls are not so simple. Typically, a custom control has more complex logic to add capability to the base control.

Besides handling base class events, as in the first example, custom controls can have new logic added via any of the following:

- ❏ Overriding properties and methods in the base class
- ❏ Creating new properties and methods in the child control class
- ❏ Defining new events that the child control class will generate for handling in a Windows Form that contains the control

Overriding a property or method in the base class is used when the functionality in that property or method is not sufficient for the new class. In the overriding logic, it is often necessary to call the original property or method in the base class using the `MyBase` keyword (further details on the `MyBase` keyword can be found in Chapter 6).

More commonly, however, a custom control needs to have properties, methods, and events that the base control does not possess. The following sections discuss defining custom properties, methods, and events for an inherited control.

Creating a Property for a Custom Control

Creating a property for a custom control is just like creating a property for any other class. It is necessary to write a property procedure, and to store the value for the property somewhere, most often in a module-level variable.

Properties typically need a *default value*, that is, a value the property will take on automatically when a control is instantiated. As you might expect, you can use your own internal logic in a control to set a default value for a property. Typically, this means setting the module-level variable that holds the property value to some initial value. That can be done when the module-level variable is declared, or it can be done in the constructor for the control.

Using the constructor to initialize the value is especially useful if the default value is different for different instantiations of the control, as in the case where the default `Text` property for a button is the name of the button.

Here's the code for a typical simple property for a custom control:

```
Dim mnMaxItemsSelected As Integer = 10
Public Property MaxItemsSelected() As Integer
  Get
    Return mnMaxItemsSelected
  End Get
  Set(ByVal Value As Integer)
    If Value < 0 Then
      Throw New ArgumentException("Property value cannot be negative")
    Else
      mnMaxItemsSelected = Value
    End If
  End Set
End Property
```

Once a property is created for a control, it automatically shows up in the Properties window for the control. However, there are some additional capabilities that you can use to make the property work better with the designers and the Property window in VS.NET.

Coordinating with the Visual Studio IDE

The Visual Studio IDE needs to work with the default value of a property in two important ways:

❑　To reset the value of the property (done when a user right-clicks the property in Property Window and selects Reset)

❑　To decide whether to set the property in code. A property that is at its default value normally does not need to be explicitly set in the designer-generated code.

There are two ways to do accomplish these tasks. For properties that take simple values, such as integers, Booleans, floating point numbers, or strings, .NET provides an *attribute*. For properties that take complex types, such as structures, enumerated types, or object references, there are two methods that need to be implemented.

Attributes

You can learn more about attributes in Chapter 3. However, let's go over a couple of important notes, since this may be the first time you have needed to use them.

Attributes reside in namespaces, just as components do. The attributes used in this chapter are in the `System.ComponentModel` namespace. To use attributes, the project must have a reference to the assembly containing the namespace for the attributes. For `System.ComponentModel`, that's no problem — the project will automatically have the reference.

However, the project will not automatically have an "Imports" for that namespace. This could be done without this by using a full namespace path for each attribute. That would mean referring to a DefaultValue attribute in code like this:

```
<System.ComponentModel.DefaultValue(4)> Public Property
MyProperty() As Integer
```

This is a bit clumsy. To make it easy to refer to the attributes in code, you should put this line at the beginning of all the modules that will need to use the attributes discussed in this chapter:

```
Imports System.ComponentModel
```

Then, the preceding line can be written more simply as

```
< DefaultValue(4)> Public Property MyProperty() As Integer
```

> All of the examples in this chapter will assume that the Imports statement has been placed at the top of the class, so all attributes will be referenced by their short name. If you get a compile error on an attribute, it's likely that you've left off that line.

Finally, note that an attribute for a property must be on the same line of code as the property declaration. Of course, line continuation characters can be used so that an attribute is on a separate physical line but still on the same logical line in the program. For example, the last example could also be written as

```
< DefaultValue(4)> _
Public Property MyProperty() As Integer
```

Setting a Default Value with an Attribute

There are various attributes of the .NET Framework that can be assigned in metadata to classes, properties, and methods. The one for creating a default value is called, appropriately enough, `DefaultValue`. Let's change the last code for a simple property to include a `DefaultValue` attribute:

```
Dim mnMaxItemsSelected As Integer = 10
<DefaultValue(10)> Public Property MaxItemsSelected() As Integer
  Get
    Return mnMaxItemsSelected
  End Get
  Set(ByVal Value As Integer)
    If Value < 0 Then
      Throw New ArgumentException("Property value cannot be negative")
    Else
      mnMaxItemsSelected = Value
    End If
  End Set
End Property
```

Including the `DefaultValue` attribute allows the Property window to reset the value of the property back to the default value. That is, if you right-click the property in the Property window, and select Reset off of the pop-up context menu, the value of the property will return to 10 from any other value to which it happens to be set.

Another effect of the attribute can be seen in the code generated by the visual designer. If the property above is set to any value that is not the default, a line of code appears in the designer-generated code to set the property value. This is called *serializing* the property. (You can see this code when you expand the section of a form's code labeled `Windows Forms Designer generated code`.)

That is, if the value of `MaxItemsSelected` is set to 5, then a line of code something like this appears in the designer-generated code:

```
MyControl.MaxItemsSelected = 5
```

If the property has the default value of 10 (because it was never changed, or because it was reset to 10), the line to set the property value is not present in the designer-generated code. That is, the property does not need to be serialized in code if the value is at the default.

Alternate Techniques for Working with the IDE

The last sample property returned an `Integer`. Some custom properties return more complex types, such as structures, enumerated types, or object references. These properties cannot use a simple `DefaultValue` attribute to take care of resetting and serializing the property. An alternate technique is needed.

For complex types, designers check to see if a property needs to be serialized by using a method on the control containing the property. The method returns a Boolean value that indicates whether a property needs to be serialized (`True` if it does, `False` if it does not).

If a property is named `MyProperty`, then the method to check serialization is called `ShouldSerializeMyProperty`. It would typically look something like the following code:

```
Public Function ShouldSerializeMyProperty() As Boolean
   If mnMyProperty = mnMyPropertysDefaultValue Then
      Return False
   Else
      Return True
   End If
End Function
```

If a property in a custom control does not have a related `ShouldSerializeXXX` method or a `DefaultValue` attribute, then the property is always serialized. Code for setting the property's value will always be included by the designer in the generated code for a form. For that reason, it's a good idea to always include either a `ShouldSerializeXXX` method or a `DefaultValue` attribute for every new property created for a control.

If you include both a `DefaultValue` attribute and a `ShouldSerializeXXX` method, the `DefaultValue` attribute takes precedence and the `ShouldSerializeXXX` method is ignored.

Providing a Reset Method for a Control Property

The alternate way to reset a property's value to the default is a special reset method. As an example of this, in the case of a property named `MyProperty`, the reset method is named `ResetMyProperty`. It typically looks something like the following code:

```
Public Sub ResetMyProperty()
   mnMyProperty = mnMyPropertysDefaultValue
End Sub
```

To allow the Property window to reset the value of a property, either a `DefaultValue` attribute or a reset method must be present. If you include both a `DefaultValue` attribute and a reset method, the `DefaultValue` attribute takes precedence and the reset method is ignored.

As with the `ShouldSerializXXX` method, the default property value can be called from an attribute if one has been included with the property declaration.

Other Useful Attributes

`DefaultValue` is not the only attribute that is useful for properties. The `Description` attribute is also one that should be used with most properties. It contains a text description of the property that shows up in the Properties windows when a property is selected. To include a `Description` attribute, the declaration of the preceding property would look like the following code:

```
<DefaultValue(100), _
Description("This is a description for my property")> _
Public Property MyProperty() As Integer
```

Such a property will look like Figure 13-2 when highlighted in the Property window.

Figure 13-2

Another attribute you will sometimes need is the `Browsable` attribute. As mentioned earlier, a new property appears in the Properties window automatically. In some cases, you may need to create a property for a control that you do not want to show up in the Properties window. In that case, you use a `Browsable` attribute set to `False`. Here is code similar to the last one, making a property nonbrowsable in the Properties window:

```
<Browsable(False)> _
Public Property MyProperty() As Integer
```

Defining a Custom Event for the Inherited Control

Adding events to classes was covered in Chapter 5. In summary, the process is as follows:

❑ Declare the event in the control. The event can have any arguments that are appropriate, but they cannot have named arguments, optional arguments, or arguments that are `ParamArrays`. Here is code for declaring a generic event:

```
Public Event MyEvent(ByVal MyFirstArgument As Integer, _
                     ByVal MySecondArgument As String)
```

❑ Elsewhere in the control's code, implement code to raise the event. The location and circumstances of this code vary depending on the nature of the event, but a typical line that raises the preceding event looks like the following code:

```
RaiseEvent MyEvent(nValueForMyFirstArgument, sValueForMySecondArgument)
```

Often this code will be in a method that raises the event. This allows the raising of the event to be done in a uniform fashion. If the event will be raised from several places in your control, doing it with a method is preferred. If the event will only be raised in one place, the code to do it can just be placed in that location.

❑   The form that contains the control can now handle the event. The process for doing that is the same as handling an event for a built-in control.

You may recall that the standard convention in .NET is to use two arguments for an event — Sender, which is the object raising the event, and e, which is an object of type EventArgs or of a type that inherits from EventArgs. This is not a requirement of the syntax (you can actually use any arguments you like), but it's a consistent convention throughout the .NET Framework, so it will be followed in this chapter.

Now, it's time to illustrate the concepts on creating properties and events for a control. The following example creates a new control that contains a custom property and a custom event.

Creating a CheckedListBox that Limits the Number of Selected Items

Our next example inherits the built-in CheckedListBox control, and extends its functionality. If you are not familiar with this control, it works just like a normal ListBox control, except that selected items are indicated with a check in a checkbox at the front of the item rather than highlighting the item.

To extend the functionality of this control, the example will include creation of a property called MaxItemsSelected. This property will hold a maximum value for the number of items that a user can select. The event that fires when a user checks on an item is then monitored to see if the maximum has already been reached.

If selection of another item would exceed the maximum number, the selection is prevented, and an event is fired to let the consumer form know that the user has tried to exceed the maximum limit. The code that handles the event in the form can then do whatever is appropriate. In our case, a message box is used to tell the user that no more items can be selected.

The DefaultValue and Description attributes are placed on the MaxItemsSelected property to assist in the designer.

Here is the step-by-step construction of our example:

1.   Start a new Windows Control Library project in Visual Studio .NET (VS.NET). Give it the name LimitedCheckedListBox and name the resulting project module LimitedCheckedListBox.vb, before bringing up the code window for this class.

2.   Ensure that the following line is in the declarations at the top of the class (before the line declaring the class):

```
Imports System.ComponentModel
```

This allows us to utilize the attributes required from the `System.ComponentModel` namespace. The class declaration needs to be altered so that it reads as follows:

```
Public Class LimitedCheckedListBox
     Inherits System.Windows.Forms.CheckedListBox
```

3. Now, begin adding code specifically for this control. First, we need to implement the `MaxSelectedItems` property. A module level variable is needed to hold the property's value, so insert this line just under the two lines in step 2:

```
Private mnMaxSelectedItems As Integer = 4
```

4. Now create the code for the property itself. Insert the following code into the class just above the line that says `End Class`:

```
<DefaultValue(4), _
Description("The maximum number of items allowed to be checked")> _
Public Property MaxSelectedItems() As Integer
  Get
    Return mnMaxSelectedItems
  End Get
  Set(ByVal Value As Integer)
    If Value < 0 Then
      Throw New ArgumentException("Property value cannot be negative")
    Else
      mnMaxSelectedItems = Value
    End If
  End Set
End Property
```

This code sets the default value of the `MaxSelectedItems` property to 4, and sets a description for the property to be shown in the Properties window when the property is selected there.

5. Next, declare the event that will be fired when a user selects too many items. The event will be named `MaxItemsExceeded`. Just under the code for step 3, insert the following line:

```
Public Event MaxItemsExceeded(Sender As Object, e As EventArgs)
```

6. Next, insert code into the event routine that fires when the user clicks on an item. For the `CheckedListBox` base class, this is called the `ItemCheck` property. Open the left-hand drop-down box in the code window and select the option `LimitedCheckedListBox` Events (or Base Class Events in Visual Studio 2002). Then, select the `ItemCheck` event in the right-hand drop-down box of the code window. The following code will be inserted to handle the `ItemCheck` event:

```
Private Sub LimitedCheckedListBox_ItemCheck(ByVal sender As Object, _
        ByVal e As System.Windows.Forms.ItemCheckEventArgs) _
        Handles MyBase.ItemCheck

End Sub
```

7. The following code should be added to the ItemCheck event to monitor it for too many items:

```
Private Sub LimitedCheckedListBox_ItemCheck(ByVal sender As Object, _
        ByVal e As System.Windows.Forms.ItemCheckEventArgs) _
        Handles MyBase.ItemCheck

If (Me.CheckedItems.Count >= mnMaxSelectedItems) _
    And (e.NewValue = CheckState.Checked) Then
    RaiseEvent MaxItemsExceeded(Me, New EventArgs)
    e.NewValue = CheckState.Unchecked
End If

End Sub
```

8. Build the project to create a DLL containing the LimitedCheckedListBox control.

9. Add a new Windows Application project to the solution (using the File ⇨ Add Project ⇨ New Project... menu) to test the control. Name the new project anything you like. Right-click the solution (not the project) in the Solution Explorer, and select Properties. In the dialog box that comes up, change the drop-down box under Single Startup Project to select your new Windows Application project.

10. In the new Windows Forms project, right-click the Windows Forms tab in the Toolbox, and select Add/Remove Items (or Customize Toolbox in Visual Studio 2002). In the dialog box that appears, click the tab for .NET Framework Components, and browse to select the LimitedCheckedListBox.dll file. Return to the Add/Remove Items dialog, check the box and click the OK button.

11. Scroll to the bottom of the controls on the Windows Forms tab. The LimitedCheckedListBox control should be there.

12. The Windows Application will have a Form1 that was created automatically. Drag a LimitedCheckedListBox control onto Form1, just as you would a normal list box. Change the CheckOnClick event for the LimitedCheckedListBox to True (to make testing easier). This property was inherited from the base CheckedListBox control.

13. In the Items property of the LimitedCheckedListBox, click the button to add some items. Insert the following list of colors: Red, Yellow, Green, Brown, Blue, Pink, and Black. At this point, your Windows Application Project should have a Form1 that looks something like Figure 13-3.

14. Bring up the code window for Form1. In the left-hand drop-down box above the code window, select LimitedCheckedListBox1 to get to its events. Then, in the right-hand drop-down box, select the MaxItemsExceeded event. The empty event will look like the following code:

```
Private Sub LimitedCheckedListBox1_MaxItemsExceeded( _
        ByVal sender As System.Object, e As System.EventArgs) _
        Handles LimitedCheckedListBox1.MaxItemsExceeded

End Sub
```

15. Now insert the following code to handle the event:

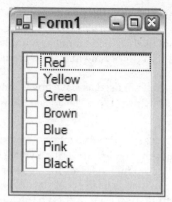

Figure 13-3

```
MsgBox("You are attempting to select more than " & _
       LimitedCheckedListBox1.MaxSelectedItems & _
       " items. You must uncheck some other item " & _
       " before checking this one.")
```

16. Now start the Windows Application project. Check and uncheck various items in the list box to see that the control works as it is supposed to. You should get a message box whenever you attempt to check more than four items. (Four items is the default maximum, and it was not changed.) If you uncheck some items, then you can check items again until the maximum is once again exceeded. When finished, close the form to stop execution.

17. Look at the code in the `Window Form Designer generated code` region and examine the properties for `LimitedCheckedListBox1`. Note, how there is no line of code that sets `MaxSelectedItems`.

18. Go back to the design mode for `Form1` and select `LimitedCheckedListBox1`. In the Properties window, change the `MaxSelectedItems` property to 3.

19. Now, return to the code window and look again at the code that declares the properties for `LimitedCheckedListBox1`. Note that there is now a line of code that sets `MaxSelectedItems` to the value of 3.

20. Go back to the design mode for `Form1` and select `LimitedCheckedListBox1`. In the Properties window, right-click the `MaxSelectedItems` property. In the pop-up menu, select Reset. The property will change back to a value of 4, and the line of code that sets the property that you looked at in the last step will be gone.

These last few steps showed that the `DefaultValue` attribute is working as it should.

The Control and UserControl Base Classes

In the earlier examples, a new control was created by inheriting from an existing control. As is standard with inheritance, this means the new control began with all the functionality of the control from which it inherited. Then new functionality was added.

This chapter didn't discuss the base classes for these new controls (Textbox and CheckedListBox), because you probably already understand a lot about the properties, methods, events, and behavior of those classes. However, you are not likely to be as familiar with the base classes used for the other techniques for control creation, so it's appropriate to discuss them now.

There are two generic base classes that are used as a starting point to create a control. It is helpful to understand something about the structure of these classes to see when the use of each is appropriate.

> The classes discussed in this chapter are all in the System.Windows.Forms namespace. There are similarly named classes for some of these in the System.Web.UI namespace (which is used for Web forms), but these classes should not be confused with anything discussed in this chapter. Chapter 15 will cover the creation of Web controls.

The Control Class

The Control class is contained within the System.Windows.Forms namespace and contains base functionality to define a rectangle on the screen, provide a handle for it, and process routine operating system messages. This gives the class the ability to perform such functions as handling user input through the keyboard and mouse. The Control class serves as the base class for any component that needs a visual representation on a Win32-type graphical interface. Besides built-in controls and custom controls that inherit from the Control class, the Form class also ultimately derives from the Control class.

In addition to these low-level windowing capabilities, the Control class also includes such visually related properties as Font, ForeColor, BackColor, and BackGroundImage. The Control class also has properties that are used to manage layout of the control on a form, such as docking and anchoring.

> The Control class does not contain any logic to paint to the screen except to paint a background color or show a background image. While it does offer access to the keyboard and mouse, it does not contain any actual input processing logic except for the ability to generate standard control events such as Click and KeyPress. The developer of a custom control based on the Control class must provide all of the functions for the control beyond the basic capabilities provided by the Control class.

Here are some of the most important members of the Control class (from the perspective of a VB developer).

The UserControl Class

The built-in functionality of the Control class is a great starting point for controls that will be built from scratch, with their own display and keyboard handling logic. However, there is limited capability in the Control class to use it as a container for other controls.

Property	Description
AllowDrop	If set to True then this control will allow drag-and-drop operations and events to be used
Anchor	Determines which edges of the control are anchored to the container's edges
BackColor Font ForeColor	Visual properties which are the same as corresponding properties in Visual Basic 6 and earlier
CanFocus	A read-only property that indicates whether the control can receive focus
Causes Validation	Indicates whether entering the control causes validation on the control itself or on controls contained by this control that require validation
Controls	A collection of child controls which this control contains
Dock	Controls to which edge of the container this control is docked to
Enabled	Property indicating whether the control is currently enabled
Handle	The HWND handle that this control is bound to
Location Size	Properties that relate to the size and position of the control
Visible	Property that indicates whether the control is currently visible on the screen
BringToFront	Brings this control to the front of the z-order
DoDragDrop	Begins a drag-and-drop operation
Focus	Attempts to set focus to this control
Hide	Hides the control by setting the visible property to False
Refresh	Forces the control to repaint itself, and to force a repaint on any of its child controls
Show	Makes the control display by setting the visible property to True
Update	Forces the control to paint any currently invalid areas

That means that composite controls do not typically use the Control class as a starting point. Composite controls combine two or more existing controls, so the starting point must be able to manage contained controls. The class that meets this requirement is the UserControl class. Since it ultimately derives from the Control class, it has all of the properties and methods listed earlier.

However, the UserControl class does not derive directly from the Control class. It derives from the ContainerControl class, which, in turn, derives from the ScrollableControl class.

As the name suggests, the ScrollableControl class adds support for scrolling the client area of the control's window. Almost all the members implemented by this class relate to scrolling. They include

Event	Description
Click DoubleClick GotFocus KeyDown KeyPress KeyUp MouseDown MouseEnter MouseMove MouseUp Resize	Same as corresponding events in Visual Basic 6 and earlier
DragDrop DragEnter DragLeave DragOver	Events relating to drag-and-drop operations
Leave	Occurs when the control is left (focus is lost)
MouseHover	New mouse event to determine when the mouse cursor has hovered over the control
Paint	Occurs when the control is forced to repaint itself to the screen
PropertyChanged	Occurs when a property of the control has changed
Validating, Validated	Occurs during the validation cycle for a control (which was discussed in Chapter 12)

AutoScroll, which turns scrolling on or off, and controlling properties such as AutoScrollPosition, which gets or sets the position within the scrollable area.

The ContainerControl class derives from ScrollableControl and adds the ability to support and manage child controls. It manages the focus and the ability to tab from control to control. It includes properties such as ActiveControl to point to the control with the focus, and Validate, which validates the most recently changed control that has not had its validation event fired.

Neither ScrollableControl nor ContainerControl are usually inherited from directly; they add functionality that is needed by their more commonly used child classes: Form and UserControl.

The UserControl class can contain other child controls, but the interface of UserControl does not automatically expose these child controls in any way. Instead, the interface of UserControl is designed to present a single, unified interface to outside clientssuch as forms or container controls. Any object interface that is needed to access the child controls must be specifically implemented in your custom control. The following example demonstrates this.

The external interface of the UserControl class consists exclusively of members inherited from other classes, though it does overload many of these members to gain functionality suitable for its role as a base class for composite controls.

A Composite UserControl

Our earlier examples showed inheriting an existing control, which was the first of the three techniques for created custom controls. The next step up in complexity and flexibility is to combine more than one existing control to become a new control. This is similar to the process of creating a UserControl in VB6, but it is easier to do in VB.NET.

The main steps in the process of creating a UserControl are:

❑ Start a new Windows Control Library project, and assign names to the project and the class representing the control.

❑ The project will contain a design surface that looks a lot like a form. You can drag controls onto this surface just as you would a form. Write logic loading and manipulating the controls as necessary, very much like you would with a form. It is usually particularly important to handle resizing when the UserControl is resized. This can be done by using the Anchor and Dock properties of the constituent controls, or you can create resize logic that will reposition and resize the controls on your UserControl when it is resized on the form containing it.

❑ Create properties of the UserControl to expose functionality to a form that will use it. This typically means creating a property to load information into and get information out of the control. Sometimes properties to handle cosmetic elements are also necessary.

❑ Build the control and refer to it in a Windows Application exactly as was done for the inherited controls discussed earlier.

> There is a key difference between this type of development and inheriting a control, as we did in the preceding examples. A UserControl will not by default expose the properties of the controls it contains. It will expose the properties of the UserControl class plus any custom properties that we give it. If you want properties for contained controls to be exposed, you must explicitly create logic to expose them.

Creating a Composite UserControl

To demonstrate the process of creating a composite UserControl, the next exercise will build one that is similar to what is shown in Figure 13-4.

This type of layout is common on wizards and in other user interfaces that require selection from a long list of items. The control has one list box holding a list of items that can be chosen (on the left), and another list box containing the items chosen so far (on the right). Buttons allow items to be moved back and forth.

Loading this control means loading items into the left list box, which we call lstSource and refer to as the source list box. Getting selected items back out will involve exposing the items that are selected in the right list box, named lstTarget and referred to in our discussion as the target list box.

The buttons in the middle that transfer elements back and forth will be called btnAdd, btnAddAll, btnRemove, and btnClear, from top to bottom respectively.

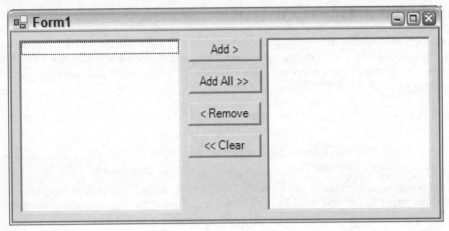

Figure 13-4

There are lots of ways to handle this kind of interface element in detail. A production-level version would have the following characteristics:

- Buttons would gray out (disable) when they are not appropriate. For example, btnAdd would not be enabled unless an item is selected in lstSource.
- Items that have been transferred from lstSource to lstTarget would not be shown in lstSource. If they are removed from lstTarget, they should show in lstSource again.
- Items could be dragged and dropped between the two list boxes.
- Items could be selected and moved with a single double-click.

Such a production-type version contains too much code to discuss in this chapter. For simplicity, the exercise will have the following limitations:

- Buttons do not gray out when they should be unavailable.
- Items transferred from lstSource will not disappear from the list. This means that it will be possible to add duplicate items to lstTarget.
- Drag-and-drop is not supported. (Implementation of drag-and-drop was discussed in Chapter 12, if you are interested in adding it to the example.)
- No double-clicking is supported.

This leaves the following general tasks to make the control work:

- Create a UserControl project.
- Add the list boxes and buttons to the UserControl design surface.
- Add logic to resize the controls when the UserControl changes size.

❑   Add logic to transfer elements back and forth between the list boxes when buttons are pressed. (More than one item may be selected for an operation, so several items may need to be transferred when a button is pressed.)

❑   Expose properties to allow the control to be loaded and selected items to be fetched by the form that contains the control.

How Does Resize Work?

The steps outlined above are fairly straightforward. Even the resize logic is made easy by using the built-in capabilities of Windows Forms controls. The list boxes can be docked to the sides to help manage their resizing, then only their width needs to be managed. The buttons need to have an area set aside for them and then be properly positioned within the area, but the sum total of this logic is far less than would be required with a similar control in VB6 (I know, I wrote one just like this in VB6 and getting the resize logic right was one of the more tedious aspects).

Setting a Minimum Size for Controls

Since we need the buttons to be always visible our UserControl needs to have a minimum size. To take care of that, it will be necessary to add logic in the Resize event to prevent the width and height of the control from dropping below certain minimums.

Exposing Properties of Sub-Controls

Most of the controls contained in the composite control in this exercise do not need to expose their interfaces to the form that will be using the composite control. The buttons, for example, are completely private to the UserControl, none of their properties or methods need to be exposed.

The easiest way to load up the control is to expose the appropriate properties of the source list box. Similarly, the easiest way to allow access to the selected items is to expose the appropriate properties of the target list box. In this way, the UserControl will expose a limited number of their properties.

As an example, the exercise also includes a Clear method that clears both list boxes simultaneously. This allows the control to be flushed and reused by a form that consumes it.

Stepping Through the Example

Here is the step-by-step procedure to build our composite UserControl:

1.   Start a new Windows Control Library project. Name it SelectComboControl.

2.   In the class file that is generated, change the name of the class to SelectCombo, and change the name of the associated VB module to SelectCombo.vb.

3.   Go to the design surface for the control. Drag two list boxes and four buttons onto the control and arrange them so that they look something like Figure 13-5.

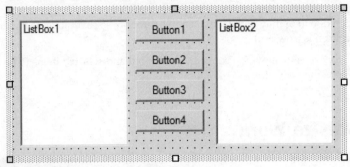

Figure 13-5

4. Change the names and properties of these controls as shown in the following table.

Original Name	New Name	Properties to Set for Control
Listbox1	LstSource	Dock = Left
Listbox2	LstTarget	Dock = Right
Button1	BtnAdd	Text = "Add >" Size = 80,24 (80 twips wide by 24 twips high)
Button2	BtnAddAll	Text = "Add All >>" Size = 80,24 (80 twips wide by 24 twips high)
Button3	BtnRemove	Text = "< Remove" Size = 80,24 (80 twips wide by 24 twips high)
Button4	BtnClear	Text = "<< Clear" Size = 80,24 (80 twips wide by 24 twips high)

5. Set up variables to hold the minimum size for the control and the size of the area for the buttons. That code should go just under the class declaration lines, and should look like the following code:

```
' Make the width of the area for the buttons 100 twips
Dim mnButtonAreaWidth As Integer = 100

' Set minimum height and width for the control
Dim mnMinControlWidth As Integer = 200
Dim mnMinControlHeight As Integer = 200
```

6. Set up resize logic to arrange these controls when the composite control is resized. Go to the code window for the class. Get an empty Resize event by selecting SelectCombo Events (or Base Class Events in Visual Studio 2002) in the left-hand drop-down box, and then Resize in the right-hand box. Place this code in the Resize event:

```
Private Sub SelectCombo_Resize(ByVal sender As Object, _
                    ByVal e As System.EventArgs) _
                    Handles MyBase.Resize
```

```
' Check for minimum width and height.
' Throw exception if new width or height too small
Dim sError As String
SError = "Attempted to make SelectCombo user control too small."

If MyBase.Size.Width < mnMinControlWidth Then
  Dim eComboException As New ApplicationException(sError)
  eComboException.Source = Me.ToString
End If
If MyBase.Size.Height < mnMinControlHeight Then
  Dim eComboException As New ApplicationException(sError)
  eComboException.Source = Me.ToString
End If

'Set source and target list boxes to appropriate width. Note that
'docking the list boxes makes their height the right size automatically.
Dim nListboxWidth As Integer
nListboxWidth = CInt(0.5 * (Me.Size.Width - mnButtonAreaWidth))
lstSource.Size = New Size(nListboxWidth, lstSource.Size.Height)
lstTarget.Size = New Size(nListboxWidth, lstSource.Size.Height)

'Now position the buttons between the list boxes.
Dim nLeftButtonPosition As Integer
nLeftButtonPosition = nListboxWidth + _
    ((mnButtonAreaWidth - btnAdd.Size.Width) \ 2)
btnAdd.Location = New Point(nLeftButtonPosition, btnAdd.Location.Y)
btnAddAll.Location = New Point(nLeftButtonPosition, _
                              btnAddAll.Location.Y)
btnRemove.Location = New Point(nLeftButtonPosition, _
                              btnRemove.Location.Y)
btnClear.Location = New Point(nLeftButtonPosition, btnClear.Location.Y)
```

End Sub

7. Put logic in the class to transfer items back and forth between the list boxes and clear the target list box when `btnClear` is pressed. This logic is surprisingly short because it involves manipulating the collections of items in the list boxes. Here are the click events for each of the buttons:

```
Private Sub btnAdd_Click(ByVal sender As Object, _
                    ByVal e As System.EventArgs) _
                    Handles btnAdd.Click
  Dim objItem As Object
  For Each objItem In lstSource.SelectedItems
    lstTarget.Items.Add(objItem)
  Next objItem
End Sub

Private Sub btnAddAll_Click(ByVal sender As Object, _
                      ByVal e As System.EventArgs) _
                      Handles btnAddAll.Click
  Dim objItem As Object
  For Each objItem In lstSource.Items
    lstTarget.Items.Add(objItem)
  Next objItem
```

```
End Sub

Private Sub btnClear_Click(ByVal sender As Object, _
                           ByVal e As System.EventArgs) _
                           Handles btnClear.Click
   lstTarget.Items.Clear()
End Sub

Private Sub btnRemove_Click(ByVal sender As Object, _
                            ByVal e As System.EventArgs) _
                            Handles btnRemove.Click
    ' Have to go through the collection in reverse
    ' because we are removing items.
   Dim nIndex As Integer
   For nIndex = lstTarget.SelectedItems.Count - 1 To 0 Step -1
      lstTarget.Items.Remove(lstTarget.SelectedItems(nIndex))
   Next nIndex
End Sub
```

The logic in the Click event for btnRemove has one oddity to take into account, the fact that items are being removed from the collection. It is necessary to go through the collection in reverse, otherwise the removal of items will cause the looping enumeration to be messed up and a runtime error will be generated.

8. Create the public properties and methods of the composite control. In our case, we need the following members.

Member	Purpose
Clear method	Clears both list boxes of their items
Add method	Adds an item to the source list box
AvailableItem property	An indexed property to read the items in the source list box
AvailableCount property	Exposes the number of items in the source list box
SelectedItem property	An indexed property to read the items in the target list box
SelectedCount property	Exposes the number of items available in the target list box

The code for these properties and methods is as follows:

```
Public ReadOnly Property SelectedItem(ByVal iIndex As Integer) As Object
   Get
      Return lstTarget.Items(iIndex)
   End Get
End Property

Public ReadOnly Property SelectedCount() As Integer
   Get
      Return lstTarget.Items.Count
   End Get
```

```
      End Property

      Public ReadOnly Property AvailableCount() As Integer
        Get
          Return lstSource.Items.Count
        End Get
      End Property

      Public Sub Add(ByVal objItem As Object)
        lstSource.Items.Add(objItem)
      End Sub

      Public ReadOnly Property AvailableItem(ByVal iIndex As Integer) As Object
        Get
          Return lstSource.Items(iIndex)
        End Get
      End Property

      Public Sub Clear()
        lstSource.Items.Clear()
        lstTarget.Items.Clear()
      End Sub
```

9. Build the control. Then create a Windows Application project to test it in. As in previous examples, it will be necessary to refer to the control using Add/Remove Items (or Customize Toolbox in Visual Studio 2002). Then, it can be dragged from the toolbox, have items added in code (via the Add method), be resized, and so on. When the project is run, the buttons can be used to transfer items back and forth between the list boxes, and the items in the target list box can be read with the SelectedItem property.

Keep in mind that you can also use the techniques for inherited controls in composite controls too. You can create custom events, apply attributes to properties, and create ShouldSerialize and Reset methods to make properties work better with the designer. (That wasn't necessary here because most of our properties were ReadOnly.)

Building a Control from Scratch

The last technique to discuss is to derive a control from the Control class. Such a control gets a fair amount of base functionality from the Control class. A partial list of properties and methods of the Control class was included earlier in the chapter. These properties arrange for the control to automatically have visual elements such as background and foreground colors, fonts, window size, and so on.

However, such a control does not automatically use any of that information to actually display anything. A control derived from the Control class must implement its own logic for painting the control's visual representation. In all but the most trivial examples, such a control also needs to implement its own properties and methods to gain the functionality it needs.

The techniques used in the earlier example for default values and the ShouldSerialize and Reset methods all work fine with the controls created from the Control class, so that capability will not be discussed again. Instead, this section will focus on the capability that is very different in the Control class — the logic to paint the control to the screen.

Painting a Custom Control with GDI+

The base functionality used to paint visual elements for a custom control is in the part of .NET called GDI+. A complete explanation of GDI+ is too complex for this chapter, but here is an overview of some of the main concepts needed.

GDI+

GDI+ is an updated version of the old GDI (Graphics Device Interface) functions provided by the Windows API. GDI+ provides a new API for graphics functions, which then takes advantage of the Windows graphics library.

The GDI+ functions can be found in the System.Drawing namespace. Some of the classes and members in this namespace will look familiar if you have used the Win32 GDI functions. Classes are available for such items as pens, brushes, and rectangles. Naturally, the System.Drawing namespace makes these capabilities much easier to use than the equivalent API functions.

The System.Drawing namespace enables you to manipulate bitmaps and indeed utilize various structures for dealing with graphics such as Point, Size, Color, and Rectangle. In addition to this, there are a number of classes available to developers, including:

❑ Cursors — contains the various cursors that you would need to set in your application, such as an hourglass or an insertion I-beam cursor

❑ Font — includes capabilities like font rotation

❑ Graphics — contains methods to perform routine drawing constructs, including lines, curves, ellipses, and so on.

❑ Icon, Pen, and Brush

❑ The Pen and Brush classes

The System.Drawing Namespace

The System.Drawing namespace includes many classes and it also includes some subsidiary namespaces. We will be using one of those in our example: System.Drawing.Text. First, let's look at important classes in System.Drawing.

The System.Drawing.Graphics Class

Many of the important drawing functions are members of the System.Drawing.Graphics class. Methods like DrawArc, DrawEllipse, and DrawIcon have self-evident actions. There are over 40 methods that provide drawing related functions in the class.

Many drawing members require one or more points as arguments. A point is a structure in the System.Drawing namespace. It has X and Y values for horizontal and vertical positions, respectively. When a variable number of points are needed, an array of points may be used as an argument. The next example uses points.

The `System.Drawing.Graphics` class cannot be directly instantiated. That is, you can't just enter code like this to get an instance of the `Graphics` class:

```
Dim grfGraphics As New System.Drawing.Graphics() ' This does not work!!
```

That's because the constructor for the class is private. It is only supposed to be manipulated by objects that can set the `Graphics` class up for themselves. There are several ways to get a reference to a `Graphics` class, but the one most commonly used in the creation of Windows controls is to get one out of the arguments in a `Paint` event. That technique is used in our example further down. For now, to understand the capabilities of GDI+ a little better, let's do a quick example on a standard Windows Form.

Using GDI+ Capabilities in a Windows Form

Here is an example of a form that uses the `System.Drawing.Graphics` class to draw some graphic elements on the form surface. The example code runs in the `Paint` event for the form, and draws an ellipse, an icon (which it gets from the form itself), and two triangles, one in outline and one filled.

Start a Windows Application project in VB.NET. On the `Form1` that is automatically created for the project, place the following code in the `Paint` event for the form:

```
Dim grfGraphics As System.Drawing.Graphics
grfGraphics = e.Graphics

' Need a pen for the drawing. We'll make it violet.
Dim penDrawingPen As New _
    System.Drawing.Pen(System.Drawing.Color.BlueViolet)

' Draw an ellipse and an icon on the form
grfGraphics.DrawEllipse(penDrawingPen, 30, 150, 30, 60)
grfGraphics.DrawIcon(Me.Icon, 90, 20)

' Draw a triangle on the form.
' First have to define an array of points.
Dim pntPoint(2) As System.Drawing.Point

pntPoint(0).X = 150
pntPoint(0).Y = 150

pntPoint(1).X = 150
pntPoint(1).Y = 200

pntPoint(2).X = 50
pntPoint(2).Y = 120


grfGraphics.DrawPolygon(penDrawingPen, pntPoint)

' Do a filled triangle.
' First need a brush to specify how it is filled.
Dim bshBrush As System.Drawing.Brush
bshBrush = New SolidBrush(Color.Blue)

' Now relocate the points for the triangle.
' We'll just move it 100 twips to the right.
```

```
pntPoint(0).X += 100
pntPoint(1).X += 100
pntPoint(2).X += 100

grfGraphics.FillPolygon(bshBrush, pntPoint)
```

Then, start the program and, when it comes up, the form will look something like this (see Figure 13-6).

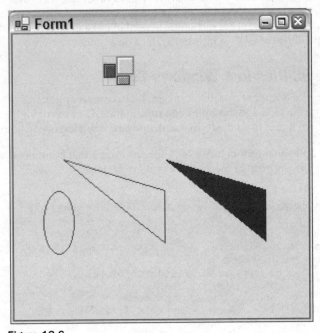

Figure 13-6

As you can see, the graphics functions are not difficult to use. The hardest part is figuring out how to initialize the objects needed, such as the graphics object itself, and the necessary brushes and pens.

For an example, you will create a custom control that displays a "traffic light", with red, yellow, and green signals that can be displayed via a property of the control. GDI+ classes will be used to draw the traffic light graphics in the control.

First, start a new project in VB.NET of the Windows Control Library type, and name it "TrafficLight". The created module will have a class in it named `UserControl1`. Rename the default class to `TrafficLight` and change the `Inherits` statement as shown:

```
Public Class TrafficLight
    Inherits System.Windows.Forms.Control
```

As with the other examples in this chapter, it is necessary to include the Imports statement for the namespace containing the attributed we will use. This line should go at the very top of the code module:

```
Imports System.ComponentModel
```

The `TrafficLight` control needs to know which "light" to display. There are three states the control can be in: red, yellow, and green. An enumerated type will be used for these states. Add the following code just below the last code:

```
Public Enum TrafficLightStatus
    statusRed = 1
    statusYellow = 2
    statusGreen = 3
End Enum
```

The example will also need a module-level variable and a property procedure to support changing and retaining the state of the light. The property will be named `Status`.

To handle the `Status` property, first place a declaration right under the last enumeration declaration that creates a module level variable to hold the current status:

```
Private mStatus As TrafficLightStatus = TrafficLightStatus.statusGreen
```

Then, insert the following property procedure in the class to create the `Status` property:

```
<DefaultValue(TrafficLightStatus.statusGreen), _
Description("Status (color) of the traffic light")> _
Public Property Status() As TrafficLightStatus
    Get
        Status = mStatus
    End Get
    Set(ByVal Value As TrafficLightStatus)
        If mStatus <> Value Then
            mStatus = Value
            Me.Invalidate()
        End If
    End Set
End Property
```

The `Invalidate` method of the control is used when the `Status` property changes, and it forces a complete redraw of the control. Ideally, this type of logic should be placed in all of the events that affect the rendering of the control.

Now, add procedures to make the property serialize and reset properly. These routines look like this:

```
Public Function ShouldSerializeStatus() As Boolean
    If mStatus = TrafficLightStatus.statusGreen Then
        Return False
    Else
        Return True
    End If
End Function

Public Sub ResetStatus()
    Me.Status = TrafficLightStatus.statusGreen
End Sub
```

Now, place code to handle the `Paint` event, that is, to draw the "traffic light" when the control repaints. We will use some code similar to that in the section on drawing with the GDI+ (above). To provide a place for this code, we override the `OnPaint` method of the `Control` base class:

```
Protected Overrides Sub OnPaint(ByVal pe As _
                        System.Windows.Forms.PaintEventArgs)
    MyBase.OnPaint(pe)

    Dim grfGraphics As System.Drawing.Graphics
    grfGraphics = pe.Graphics

    ' Need a pen for the drawing the outline. We'll make it black.
    Dim penDrawingPen As New _
        System.Drawing.Pen(System.Drawing.Color.Black)

    ' Draw the outline of the traffic light on the control.
    ' First have to define an array of points.
    Dim pntPoint(3) As System.Drawing.Point

    pntPoint(0).X = 0
    pntPoint(0).Y = 0

    pntPoint(1).X = Me.Size.Width - 2
    pntPoint(1).Y = 0

    pntPoint(2).X = Me.Size.Width - 2
    pntPoint(2).Y = Me.Size.Height - 2

    pntPoint(3).X = 0
    pntPoint(3).Y = Me.Size.Height - 2

    grfGraphics.DrawPolygon(penDrawingPen, pntPoint)

    ' Now ready to draw the circle for the "light"
    Dim nCirclePositionX As Integer
    Dim nCirclePositionY As Integer
    Dim nCircleDiameter As Integer
    Dim nCircleColor As Color

    nCirclePositionX = Me.Size.Width * 0.02
    nCircleDiameter = Me.Size.Height * 0.3
    Select Case Me.Status
        Case TrafficLightStatus.statusRed
            nCircleColor = Color.OrangeRed
            nCirclePositionY = Me.Size.Height * 0.01
        Case TrafficLightStatus.statusYellow
            nCircleColor = Color.Yellow
            nCirclePositionY = Me.Size.Height * 0.34
        Case TrafficLightStatus.statusGreen
            nCircleColor = Color.LightGreen
            nCirclePositionY = Me.Size.Height * 0.67
    End Select

    Dim bshBrush As System.Drawing.Brush
    bshBrush = New SolidBrush(nCircleColor)
```

```
    ' Draw the circle for the signal light
    grfGraphics.FillEllipse(bshBrush, nCirclePositionX, _
                nCirclePositionY, nCircleDiameter, nCircleDiameter)
End Sub
```

Now, build the control library by selecting Build from the Build menu. This will create a DLL in the /bin directory where the control library solution is saved.

Then, start a new Windows Application project and right-click the Windows Forms tab in the Toolbox. In the Add/Remove Items dialog box, first make sure that the .NET Components tab is selected, and then use the Browse button to point to the deployed DLL for the control library. The Toolbox should now contain the TrafficLight control.

Drag a TrafficLight control onto the form in the Windows Application project. Notice that its property window includes a Status property. Set that to statusYellow. Note that the rendering on the control on the form's design surface changes to reflect this new status. Also, change the background color of the TrafficLight control to a darker gray to improve its cosmetics. (The BackColor property for TrafficLight was inherited from the Control class.)

At the top of the code for the form, place the following line to make the enumerated value for the traffic light's status available.

```
Imports TrafficLight.TrafficLight
```

Add three buttons (named btnRed, btnYellow, and btnGreen) to the form to make the traffic light control display as red, yellow, and green. The logic for the buttons will look something like the following code:

```
Private Sub btnRed_Click(ByVal sender As System.Object, _
            ByVal e As System.EventArgs) Handles btnRed.Click
    TrafficLight1.Status = TrafficLightStatus.statusRed
End Sub

Private Sub btnYellow_Click(ByVal sender As System.Object, _
            ByVal e As System.EventArgs) Handles btnYellow.Click
    TrafficLight1.Status = TrafficLightStatus.statusYellow
End Sub

Private Sub btnGreen_Click(ByVal sender As System.Object, _
            ByVal e As System.EventArgs) Handles btnGreen.Click
    TrafficLight1.Status = TrafficLightStatus.statusGreen
End Sub
```

When you run the project, you can change the "signal" on the traffic light by pressing the buttons. Figure 13-7 shows a sample screen.

Of course, you can't see the color in a black-and-white screenshot, but as you might expect from its position, the circle above is yellow. The "red light" displays at the top of the control, and the "green light" displays at the bottom. These positions are all calculated in the Paint event logic, depending on the value of the Status property.

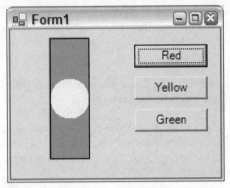

Figure 13-7

Attaching an Icon for the Toolbox

By default, the icon that appears in the toolbox next to your control's name is a gear-shaped icon. However, you can use an attribute on the class declaration that defines your control to specify a different icon to place in the toolbox.

The attribute needed is the `ToolboxBitmap` attribute. It can be used in several ways.

If the icon you want to use is already defined for another control, you can have your control get the icon out of the existing control. Suppose, for example, you want to use the icon for a `Textbox` as the icon for our `TrafficLight` control. In that case, the line that declares the class

```
Public Class TrafficLight
```

should be changed to add the attribute as follows:

```
<ToolboxBitmap(GetType(System.Windows.Forms.TextBox))> _
Public Class TrafficLight
```

You can also use an icon that resides in a graphic file. There are a lot of these included with VS.NET in the "`Common7\Graphics\Icons`" subdirectory of the VS.NET directory (which is usually under "Program Files" on your main system drive). Or, you can define your own icons in the Paint accessory of Windows by defining an image size of 16×16 pixels, and then painting the icon.

In either case, the `ToolboxBitmap` attribute is used to refer to the file containing the icon you want, as shown below.

```
<ToolboxBitmap("C:\TestData\RedLightIcon.bmp")> _
Public Class TrafficLight
```

After adding the attribute, just rebuild the control to incorporate the icon in the control's DLL. Note that you must remove the control from the toolbox and readd it to see the changed icon.

It's also possible to get a toolbox bitmap out of an arbitrary resource compiled into an assembly, but discussing all the concepts required to do that is beyond the scope of this chapter.

Summary

This chapter discussed the creation of custom controls in VB.NET, and illustrated how much easier it is to do this in comparison with the previous versions of Visual Basic. The advent of full inheritance capabilities in VB.NET means that it is a lot easier for developers to utilize functionality simply by inheriting from the namespaces built into the .NET Framework. It is probably best to start by overriding these existing controls in order to learn the basics of creating properties and coordinating them with the designer, building controls and testing them, and so on. These techniques can then be extended by the creation of composite controls, as we have illustrated with worked examples within this chapter.

You have seen how to create controls by:

❑ Inheriting from another control

❑ Building a composite control

❑ Writing a control from scratch, based on the `Control` class, although this took more work than the other two methods

In the course of writing a control from scratch, it was necessary to discuss the basics of GDI+. However, if you are going to do extensive work with GDI+, you will need to seek out additional resources to aid in that effort.

The key concept that you should take away from this chapter is that Windows Forms controls are a great way to package functionality that will be reused across many forms, and to create more dynamic, responsive user interfaces much more quickly with much less code.

14

Web Forms

Unless you have been stuck in a cave for the past year, you know that one of the biggest features in Microsoft's .NET infrastructure is the introduction of a new Web application development technology called *ASP.NET*. As a Visual Basic developer, the chances are that you are developing more and more applications that deal with the World Wide Web. Visual Basic programmers gravitated naturally to Microsoft's Active Server Pages (ASP) technology as a means to develop Web applications. This is because of the similarity between programming Visual Basic and VBScript.

Unfortunately, ASP did not have a visual metaphor for creating Web interfaces like the VB form (Visual InterDev was, at best, a poor first attempt by Microsoft). With .NET, Microsoft has bridged that gap by merging Visual InterDev within Visual Basic and has provided VB programmers with a visual ability for generating Web interfaces, using *Web Forms*.

> **This chapter explores Web forms and how you can benefit from their use but it is only meant to whet your appetite. If you want to learn more, read *Professional ASP.NET 1.0 Special Edition* (Wrox, 2002).**

Web forms are part of the new ASP.NET technology. They allow us to use one of several different languages to quickly create Web pages that combine visual HTML forms with server-side code. In a manner very similar to a VB Windows Form — which has a visual element (the form and its controls) and the code behind it — a Web form also has an HTML form, that is visible within a browser, as well as server-side code encapsulated within a code class file.

A Web Form in Action

The easiest way to learn about Web forms is to see them in action, and then take them apart to see how they are constructed. Let's look at a very simple Web form — the quintessential "Hello World" example.

Setting Up the Environment

To be able to create ASP.NET applications and Web forms, you will need to be running *Internet Information Services* (IIS). In addition, Microsoft strongly recommends that the server computer be formatted with NTFS (NT File System) rather than FAT (File Allocation Table). This results in better performance and substantially greater security, as well as offering additional options for source code control. To take full advantage of ASP.Net, it is recommended that you use Visual Studio .Net (VS.NET)

The HelloWorld Web Form

Create a new ASP.NET Web application project in VS.NET by selecting File ➪ New ➪ Project. Click "Visual Basic Projects," and then on the "ASP.Net Web application" template. Name the project HelloWorld and make sure that you select the default http://localhost/ as your location for the project, as shown in Figure 14-1.

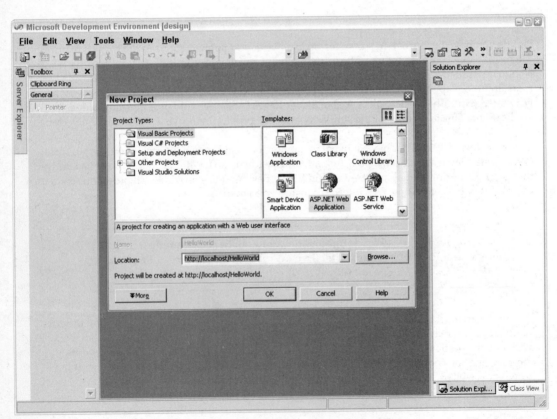

Figure 14-1

Click OK and you will be presented with a new solution. By default, VS.NET has created a new Web form for you, called `WebForm1.aspx` (`.aspx` is the new extension for ASP.NET files).

When you clicked OK, a few things happened. Apart from creating a new folder in your Visual Studio Projects directory, VS.NET also established a Web application on the target Web server (in this case, the local Web server, localhost). On the Web server, VS.NET:

❑ Creates a duplicate physical folder under the \inetpub\wwwroot directory, named after your project

❑ Marks the folder as an IIS application, allowing script to be executed

❑ Creates a FrontPage Web if you have FrontPage Server Extensions installed, allowing you to author the Web page via FrontPage

You can treat the Web form in front of you as a normal VB form, dropping controls on to it by dragging them from the toolbox. For now, drag a Label control from the toolbox and drop it onto the top left of the form. Use the Properties windows to set its caption (its Text property) to "Hello World". Your screen will look like Figure 14-2.

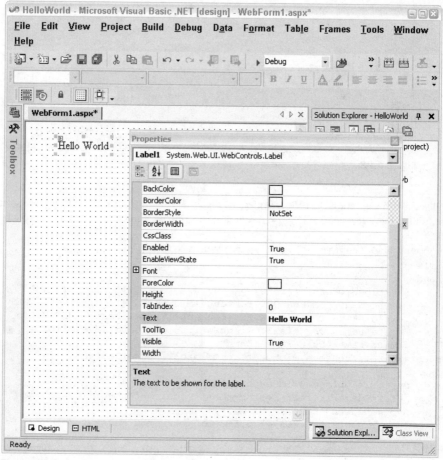

Figure 14-2

For this example, that's all you need to do. You can now execute your application. Normally, VS.NET executes applications in a special debug mode that allows you to monitor the progress of your application. For now, you simply want to execute your application in the release mode, or the production mode so change the Solution Configurations drop-down menu on your toolbar from Debug to Release. Click the Start icon on the toolbar, or select Debug ⇨ Start from the menu. If all goes well, your browser will open the WebForm1.aspx file and you will see an image similar to Figure 14-3.

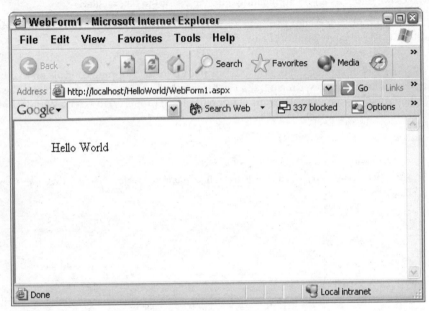

Figure 14-3

Right-click the browser and select View Source to see what the output produced by your solution looks like. You will see that it is pure HTML, generated at runtime by your aspx file (tidied up a bit here):

```
<!DOCTYPE HTML PUBLIC "-//W3C//DTD HTML 4.0 Transitional//EN">
<html>
 <head>
        <title>WebForm1</title>
        <meta name="GENERATOR" content="Microsoft Visual Studio .NET 7.1">
        <meta name="CODE_LANGUAGE" content="Visual Basic .NET 7.1">
        <meta name="vs_defaultClientScript" content="JavaScript">
        <meta name="vs_targetSchema"
content="http://schemas.microsoft.com/intellisense/ie5">
 </head>
 <body ms_positioning="GridLayout">
        <form name="Form1" method="post" action="WebForm1.aspx" id="Form1">
<input type="hidden" name="__VIEWSTATE"
 value="dDwtMTU3ODAzNTQ4MDs7PkbGgBO8kLiGvbR/u8rRCSKaxsxv" />

                <span id="Label1" style="Z-INDEX: 101; LEFT: 30px;
```

```
                    POSITION: absolute; TOP: 31px">
         Hello World
         </span>
      </form>
  </body>
</html>
```

Notice that there is an HTML `form` within your page, even though you did not ask for one. You'll look at this more closely later on in this chapter. Your label is included within the `span` tag:

```
<span id="Label1" style="Z-INDEX: 101; LEFT: 30px;
                POSITION: absolute; TOP: 31px">
         Hello World
</span>
```

The `span` tag acts as a container to hold your label and its `style` attribute defines its location and size. Close the browser and return to your VS.NET solution to see what makes this Web form tick. Web forms are very similar to Windows Forms, and you'll see how much alike they are with this next example.

Within your application, you have a single Web form, `WebForm1.aspx`. Let's create a new one with a little more to it.

From the menu, select Project ➪ Add Web form. In the Add New Item dialog box that pops up, make sure you have selected Web form and that its name is `WebForm2.aspx`. Click Open and you will have a new Web form in your solution. Add a `Label` to this new form and also add a `Button` control to the form underneath the `Label`. Widen the width of the label by clicking on it and dragging its resizing handles.

From the Properties window, set the `ID` property of the `Label` (which defines its name) to be `lblText`. Leave its `Text` property as `Label`. Then, click the `Button` and set its `ID` property to `btnSubmit` and its `Text` property to `Submit`. Now, double-click the button and watch what happens. You will be taken to the code behind the form, and your cursor is blinking within the `btnSubmit_Click` event code, just like in Visual Basic 6! Wait a minute, though. This isn't a Windows Form, so how can buttons have code behind them?

In ASP.NET, controls *do* have code behind them. As you can see, you have a subroutine called `btnSubmit_Click` that will be executed when the button is clicked. This code is executed — on the server, not the client browser — whenever the form is submitted to the server. You'll see more details later on. For now, enter the following as the code for the click event:

```
Private Sub btnSubmit_Click(ByVal sender As System.Object, _
                  ByVal e As System.EventArgs) _
                  Handles btnSubmit.Click
   lblText.Text = "Hello World"
End Sub
```

Notice how IntelliSense works when you type in this line. Although, ASP programmers had this functionality with InterDev, VS.NET's IntelliSense provides more HTML elements for use in your code.

Close the code window and return to the design mode for the form.

If you try to use the Start button to run the project, it will open up `WebForm1.aspx`, since that is the starting form for the project. In order to view the second Web form, set it to be the starting form by right-clicking its name in the Solution Explorer and selecting Set As Start Page from the pop-up menu. Then press the Start button.

The new Web form — `WebForm2.aspx` — opens up in the browser, displaying a label and a button. The label has the default caption of Label. Click the Submit button and the text "Hello World" will appear within the label as shown in Figure 14-4.

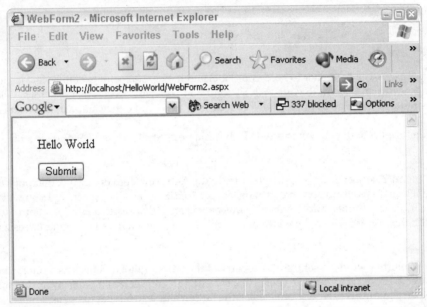

Figure 14-4

When you clicked the Submit button, the code behind the button was executed, just like a Windows Form.

The Anatomy of a Web Form

Web forms bridge the gap between VB programming and traditional ASP programming. By offering a visual technique to drag and drop controls onto a page, and code for events behind the controls, Web forms bring a very familiar metaphor to Web development.

A Web form is made up of two components: the visual elements that you can see in the design view and the code behind the controls and the page. The visual elements form the template for the presentation of the Web page in the end user's browser. The code is executed on the server when the page loads and in response to other events that you have coded for.

If you try to create a Web form by hand, using a text editor, you will probably end up creating both these components within the same physical file (this is fine as long as it has an `.aspx` extension). With VS.NET, however, the visual elements are defined in the .aspx file, while the code elements are defined in the .vb file that accompanies the Web form.

Figure 14-5 shows the two components that make up your WebForm2.aspx Web form within your example Web application.

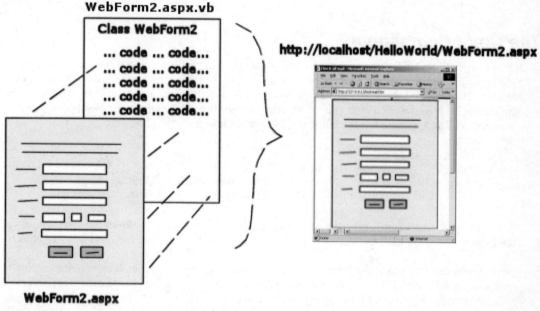

Figure 14-5

By dividing the components into separate files and, therefore, within the VS.NET environment, into separate views, Web forms provide a very familiar environment for the VB programmer. With traditional Visual Basic, you first paint the form by dragging and dropping controls, and then write the code for the events that the controls expose. When developing Web forms, you first create the look of your Web page by dragging and dropping controls onto the page, and then you write code for the events exposed by the controls.

The Template for Presentation

The .aspx file forms the User Interface component of the Web form and serves as a template for its presentation in the browser. This .aspx file is the *Page* and it contains HTML markup and Web forms specific elements. You can drag and drop several types of controls onto a Web form, including:

❑ HTML controls

❑ Web form controls

❑ Validation controls

❑   Data related controls

❑   COM and .NET components registered on your machine

❑   Items from your clipboard

❑   You'll look at these different kinds of controls later on in this chapter

The Code Component

If you code with VS.NET, the .vb file that accompanies the `.aspx` file forms the code component of your Web form. To view this file, click the Show All Files icon in the toolbar along the top of the Solution Explorer. Then, expand the `WebForm2.aspx` node, to reveal `WebForm2.aspx.vb`. This `.vb` file contains a single `Public Class` named after your Web form. In the `WebForm2.aspx` example, the `WebForm2.aspx.vb` code component has the following initial structure:

```
Public Class WebForm2
    Inherits System.Web.UI.Page
  Protected WithEvents lblText As System.Web.UI.WebControls.Label
  Protected WithEvents btnSubmit As System.Web.UI.WebControls.Button
```

Your `WebForm2` class inherits from the `System.Web.UI.Page` class. This allows the code within your Web form to access the built-in `Request`, `Response`, `Session`, `Application`, and `Server` objects.

Every control that you place on the form and, consequently, in the `.aspx` file, is represented within the `.vb` file as an event code if it exposes an event that can be handled via server-side code. This is very much reminiscent of the way that VB code-behind forms work.

In this case, you have the `Click` event of your `btnSubmit` button represented by this fragment of code:

```
Private Sub btnSubmit_Click(ByVal sender As System.Object, _
                            ByVal e As System.EventArgs) _
                            Handles btnSubmit.Click
    lblText.Text = "Hello World"
End Sub
```

Before going on to look at the processing flow of ASP.NET pages, let's take a look at another example that will drive home the point that Web forms make Web development uncannily like VB development.

A More Complex Example

Suppose that you wish to display a calendar for the current month in a Web page. Generating a dynamic calendar for a traditional ASP page involves writing at least 50 to 100 lines of code. You have to create a table to host the calendar, figure out the month and the year, and output the days of the week header. Then, you need to figure out what day the current month begins with and how many days there are in the month. Finally, you can output the days of the month starting with 1 and going on till the end of the month. When you output the days, you need to make sure that you are placing each week horizontally in one row (a <TR> tag) of a table. When you reach the end of one week, you need to close the row (a </TR> tag) and begin a new one. Finally, when you are done with the days of the month, you probably need to output a few blank days to make the table appear even and look good on the screen. All this takes up a lot of ASP code, especially if you want the calendar to be generated dynamically.

There was an alternative before Web forms. You could simply use a client-side ActiveX control—a Calendar control in your Web page. However, this had its own problems.

ActiveX controls are not supported by all browsers, in fact, only IE on Windows really supports them. The Calendar control may not exist on your user's computer, so you have to worry about distributing it. Also, an ActiveX control will only work on the Windows platform, so your Web site users on Macs, for example, will not be able to view the page properly.

> Web forms bring the ease of development with an ActiveX control to the world of ASP and Web development, but they output standard HTML on demand.

In your HelloWorld project, add a new Web form. By default, this form will be called `WebForm3.aspx`; accept the default name. Then, open up the Web form in the design view. From your toolbox, look for the `Calendar` control under the Web forms group. Double-click or drag it onto the form. That's it, you now have a fully functional calendar in your Web page, albeit a very plain looking one, as shown in Figure 14-6.

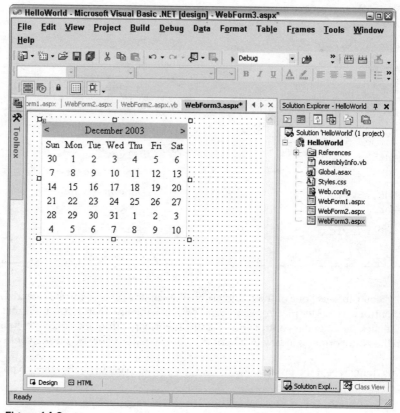

Figure 14-6

Before you run this Web form, let's make it look a little better. Using the Properties window, set the following properties as shown in the table.

Property	Setting
ID	MyCal
BackColor	A light yellow (#FFFFC0)
BorderColor	Black
BorderStyle	Solid
BorderWidth	1px
DayHeaderStyle, BackColor	Light orange (#FFC080)
DayHeaderStyle, BorderColor	Dark red (#C00000)
DayHeaderStyle, BorderStyle	Inset
DayHeaderStyle, BorderWidth	1px
DayHeaderStyle, Font, Bold	True
DayNameFormat	Short
Font, Name	Verdana
Font, Size	X-Small
NextPrevFormat	ShortMonth
OtherMonthDayStyle, ForeColor	Silver
SelectedDayStyle, BackColor	Dark blue (#0000C0)
SelectedDayStyle, ForeColor	White

Alternatively, you can select one of the predetermined formats available for the calendar. Click the `Calendar` control and, under the Properties window, click the link marked AutoFormat. (Altrernatively, you can right-click the calendar control and select AutoFormat... from the context menu.) Select an option from the AutoFormat window to inherit the same look for your `Calendar` control.

When you are done, repeat the process you did earlier, set this page to be the start up page and then run the project.

All you did was drag and drop a calendar control onto a Web page in your design environment and set a few properties to make it look different. In your browser, you should have a Web page that looks like Figure 14-7.

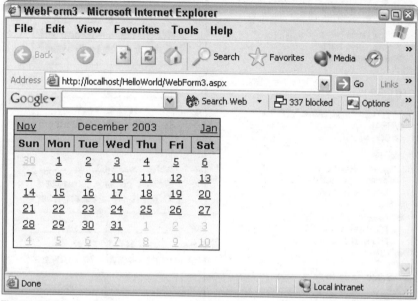

Figure 14-7

This is not a static calendar painted on the browser. It is fully interactive. Click any day and it becomes highlighted in blue. Click another day and the selection changes. Click the other months listed at the top of the calendar and the month view automatically changes. Your Web form contains the `Calendar` control that is being executed at runtime.

The `Calendar` control is a Web form server control that is outputting plain HTML to be viewed in the browser (IE and Netscape version 4.0 or above). And you developed it using Visual Basic .NET (VB.NET), just like developing and deploying a VB.NET Windows Form.

The Processing Flow of ASP.NET Web Forms

Traditional Web development, especially ASP development, has always involved generating an HTML page and adding script code to it. An ASP page in traditional ASP (ASP versions prior to ASP.NET) was therefore a plain text file separated into blocks of ASP code and HTML code. When a browser requested an ASP page from the Web server, the ASP engine kicked in and parsed the page, before its output was sent back to the browser. At runtime, the ASP engine would interpret the ASP code one line at a time. It would execute each line that contained ASP script code, and would output unchanged every line that contained plain HTML text. The traditional ASP Web development model was therefore one of HTML pages with code added to them.

Figure 14-8 shows a simplistic view of how the processing flow takes place in traditional ASP.

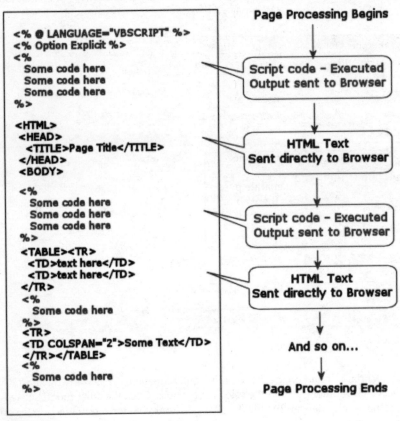

Figure 14-8

Web forms turn this paradigm of Web development upside down. With Web forms, every page is actually an executable program. The page's execution results in HTML text being outputted. You can therefore focus on developing with controls and code elements that output HTML, instead of worrying about interspersing code around HTML text.

So, what exactly is a Web form? Well, a VB.NET Web form *is* an ASP.NET page. As you've already seen, Web forms (or ASP.NET pages) are text files with an .aspx extension. On a .NET server (or indeed any IIS server where the .NET Framework has been installed), when a browser requests an .aspx file, the ASP.NET runtime parses and compiles the page. This process is similar to the way that the ASP engine in ASP 3.0 and below parsed the page. The main difference is that the ASP.NET runtime compiles the page into a .NET class file. The code is compiled and not interpreted line by line each time the page is executed using a script engine. This results in improved runtime performance since the Web page code is compiled and stored in cache for reuse.

A typical Web application project (that is, a project that contains Web forms) developed in VB.NET will have at least one .aspx file. If you incorporate controls and code on the form, the code itself is placed in the `.vb` file. That is, if your Web form is called `WebForm1`, you will end up with `WebForm1.aspx` and `WebForm1.aspx.vb`. The `.aspx` file corresponds to the traditional ASP `.asp` file and contains primarily HTML code that defines your Web page. The `.aspx.vb` file contains the code-behind-the-Web page VB code.

In addition, a Web application project usually has a `Global.asax` and a `Web.config` file. The `Global.asax` file is the .NET counterpart of the `Global.asa` file used in ASP Web applications. It contains code for event handlers that fire when the Application and the Session begin and end. A complete description of this file and its uses is available in *Professional ASP.NET 1.0 Special Edition* (Wiley, 2002).

The `Web.config` file is new to .NET. It is an XML formatted file that stores the configuration settings for your Web application. This includes features such as debug mode and compiling options.

These files are actually located in two separate places. The files need to be executed on the Web server and, therefore, their primary location is the Web server. However, VS.NET also keeps a copy in its local cache. VS.NET synchronizes the files between its local cache and the server. When you work with a file in VS.NET and then save it, VS.NET automatically updates both the local cache as well as the file on the Web server. Some local cache files serve a temporary purpose (they may be intermediary files, for example), and these are not written to the server.

When you use VS.NET to deploy your Web application, it uses the standard model for VB applications, your project is compiled and the resulting files are deployed. In the case of a Web application, all of the code files (but not the `.aspx` files) for each Web form are compiled into a DLL along with all other executable files in your project. The DLL is then deployed to the Web server as a single unit, without the source code. When the browser requests the `.aspx` file, the DLL file and the `.aspx` file are compiled into a new class and then run.

Let's take your "HelloWorld" example at the point at which you added the second Web form to your application and ran it. You had the following files in your project:

- ❑   `WebForm2.aspx`
- ❑   `WebForm2.aspx.vb`
- ❑   `Global.asax`
- ❑   `Global.asax.vb`
- ❑   `Web.config`

Remember, you did not write any code for the `Global.asax` file and its code file `Global.asax.vb`. VS.NET automatically creates them for us with placeholders for code.

When you deploy this project, by pressing the Start button, the following files are copied to the Web server with no change or compilation:

- ❑   `WebForm2.aspx`
- ❑   `Global.asax`

When you deploy this project, the following files are compiled into a single DLL called `HelloWorld`
`.dll`:

❑   `WebForm2.asax.vb`

❑   `Global.asax.vb`

At this time, your Web server contains the following three files for this Web application:

❑   `WebForm2.aspx`

❑   `Global.asax`

❑   `HelloWorld.dll`

When you request the `.aspx` file in your browser, ASP.NET dynamically generates a temporary `.cls`
class file out of the contents of the `.aspx` file. This temporary `.cls` file is then compiled into a temporary
`.dll` file. This temporary `.dll` file inherits from the `HelloWorld.dll` file and, therefore, has access to
all of the code within `HelloWorld.dll`. The temporary `.dll` file finally invokes the
`HelloWorld.dll` file that contains the compiled code from the `WebForm2.vb` file. This results in the
HTML that is rendered by the browser.

Remember, the .NET Framework exposes a number of classes from which .NET applications derive
functionality and definitions. The root class includes the `System` class that provides system level
functionality. Web forms derive their look-and-feel functionality, or UI elements, from the `System`
`.Web.UI` class. Each `.aspx` file represents one Web page in a Web application. When a browser requests
an `.aspx` file for the very first time, ASP.NET generates the temporary `.cls` class file dynamically for the
page by inheriting from the `System.Web.UI.Page` namespace. This class exposes the `Request`,
`Response`, `Server`, `Application`, and `Session` objects, properties, and methods that classic ASP
programmers are familiar with.

The above steps may seem like a lot of work. However, these steps are performed only once for each
page. When the class is dynamically generated, it is also cached in a special directory so that subsequent
requests for the same page are executed much faster. Once a page has been compiled into a class, it is
cached until the next time that you make a change to the page. Therefore, as long as a page's code does
not change, the page executes using the class file.

Figure 14-9 shows how the processing flow takes place in ASP.NET for a Web form.

The Controls Available in Web Forms

Using a paradigm very similar to the earlier versions of Visual Basic, Microsoft has introduced the concept
of adding controls on to a Web form visually. Every control you need to use in a Web form, whether it is a
text box or a button control, you can simply drag and drop from a controls toolbox. Remember, however,
that this is not the same as dragging and dropping controls in an application like FrontPage. The controls
are dragged and dropped on to a Web form, but they do not manifest themselves as ActiveX Controls in
Web pages. That would limit the Web applications you create to Internet Explorer alone, since a browser
like Netscape does not support ActiveX Controls. Instead, the ASP.Net controls you drag and drop on to a
Web form are rendered at runtime as pure HTML, allowing them to be used within all browsers.

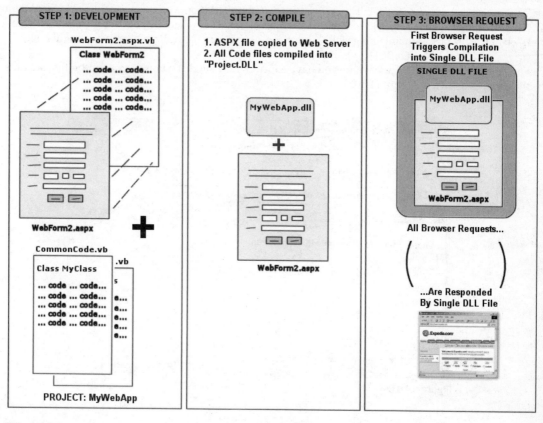

STEP 1: DEVELOPMENT

WebForm2.aspx.vb

Class WebForm2
... code ... code...
... code ... code...
... code ... code...
... code ... code...
... code ... code...

WebForm2.aspx

CommonCode.vb

Class MyClass
... code ... code...
... code ... code...
... code ... code...
... code ... code...
... code ... code...

PROJECT: MyWebApp

STEP 2: COMPILE

1. ASPX file copied to Web Server
2. All Code files compiled into "Project.DLL"

MyWebApp.dll

+

WebForm2.aspx

STEP 3: BROWSER REQUEST

First Browser Request Triggers Compilation into Single DLL File

SINGLE DLL FILE

MyWebApp.dll

WebForm2.aspx

All Browser Requests...

...Are Responded By Single DLL File

Figure 14-9

Web form controls are different to controls used in VB.NET Windows Forms. This is because Web form controls operate within the ASP.NET page framework. There are four kinds of controls for use in Web forms:

❑   HTML server controls

❑   ASP.NET server controls

❑   Validation controls

❑   User controls

Before you take a look at these types, let's examine the idea behind server-side controls.

The Concept of Server-Side Controls

Like in traditional ASP, you can use the <% and the %> tags to separate ASP code from plain HTML code. However, if you rely on these tags to delimit ASP code, you will be responsible for the maintaining state when the page is submitted back to the server.

This means that, if you want to create an interactive Web application, you will be responsible for obtaining the data from the Request object, passing it back to the browser when the page returns, and keeping track of it. This task — maintaining state — has been a big worry for ASP programmers up till now.

For example, consider the case where you have a form with a single text box and a button that submits the form, as shown in Figure 14-10.

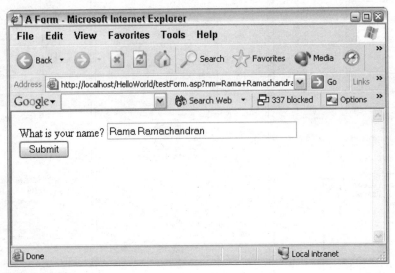

Figure 14-10

When the form is submitted, assume that it returns with the value of the text box intact. To be able to do this, you will need to code a form in this manner:

```
<html>
<head>
    <title>A Form</title>
</head>

<body>
    <form action="testForm.asp">
      What is your name?
      <input type="text" name="nm" value="<%= Request("nm") %>" size="40"
             maxlength="40"><br>
      <input type="submit" name="cmd" value=" Submit ">
    </form>
</body>
</html>
```

The programmer is responsible for maintaining the value of the text entered in the text box and returning it back to the browser

```
value="<%= Request("nm") %>"
```

You do this by obtaining the value of the text box (named "nm") from the Request object, and using that value as the value attribute of the text box. The first time around, since the Request object does not have a value named nm, it will be blank and so the user will see a blank text box. When the user enters a value and presses the Submit button, the same form is returned back but, this time, with the value of the text box filled in.

With Web forms, Microsoft has introduced a new concept that takes care of managing state automatically without having to write any incremental code. Web forms allow you to indicate that a particular form control needs to automatically maintain state when submitted by the user. You do this by using the runat="server" attribute for the form controls as well as the form. This one line change makes your form controls behave like *server-side controls* rather than just client-side controls. To take your example from above, you can change the code to the following example:

```
<html>
<head>
   <title>A Form</title>
</head>

<body>
  <form action="testForm.aspx" runat="server">
     What is your name?
     <asp:textbox runat="server" name="nm"
                   size="40" maxlength="40" /><br>
     <input type="submit" name="cmd" value=" Submit ">
   </form>
</body>
</html>
```

Save the file with an .aspx extension (to make sure that the ASP.NET runtime handles its processing correctly) and you will get automatic state maintenance without writing any further code. Notice the differences. First, it is an .aspx file. Second, the FORM tag itself has an indication runat="server":

```
<form action="testForm.aspx" runat="server">
```

This causes the ASP.NET runtime to create additional code to handle the state. This is done via a hidden form field that is appended to your form. If you chose to view the source of your file in the browser, this is what you would see in place of the form tag code:

```
<form name="_ctl0" method="post" action="testForm.aspx" id="_ctl0">
<input type="hidden" name="__VIEWSTATE"
value="dDwyMTA1NTI4MTE3Ozs++XTC7CS2N3CQ7xiWjEu4Q5P+URk=" />
```

The ASP.NET runtime has added additional code, including a form NAME and an ID, as well as a hidden field called _VIEWSTATE. ASP.NET uses this hidden field to transfer state information between the browser and the Web server. It compresses the information needed into a cryptic field value. All controls on the Web page that need their state information maintained are automatically tagged within this single hidden field value.

Notice too that, instead of using a simple INPUT tag for your text box, you used the special asp:textbox tag. This is required to make sure that the text box behaves like a server-side control.

HTML Server Controls

HTML Server Controls are HTML elements exposed to the server by using the `runat="server"` attribute. In VS.NET, HTML Server Controls are included within the Web forms group of the Toolbox. The regular HTML Form Controls (`TextBox`, `CheckBox`, `Listbox`, and so on) are available within the HTML group.

HTML Server Controls are identical to regular HTML Form controls in look, feel, and behavior, except that the presence of the `runat="server"` enables you to program them within the Web forms page framework.

HTML Server Controls are available for the HTML elements most commonly used on a Web page to make it interactive, such as the `FORM` tag, the HTML `<input>` elements (`TextBox`, `CheckBox`, `Submit` button), `ListBox` (`select`), `Table`, and `Image`. These predefined HTML Server Controls share the basic properties of the generic controls and, in addition, each control typically provides its own set of properties and its own event.

In the VS.NET environment, you can create a regular HTML control by clicking the HTML group within your toolbox and then dragging a Text Field control on to the Web form. Then give it the name `txt First_Name` by changing its `ID` property. This will result in a regular HTML control with something like the following code:

```
<input style="Z-INDEX: 102; LEFT: 221px; POSITION: absolute; TOP: 249px"
        type="text">
```

To convert a regular HTML control to an HTML Server Control (and vice versa), simply right-click the control in the design mode and select (or uncheck) the menu option Run As Server Control. If you select it, you will see the following code:

```
<input style="Z-INDEX: 102; LEFT: 221px; POSITION: absolute; TOP: 249px"
        type="text"
        id="Text1" name="Text1" runat="server">
```

Notice the difference between the above two sections of code, the final attribute that denotes that this is a server control.

HTML controls are created from classes in the .NET Framework class library's `System.Web` `.UI.HtmlControls` namespace. Regular HTML controls are parsed and rendered simply as HTML elements. For example, a regular `Text Field` HTML control will be parsed and rendered as an HTML text box.

By converting HTML controls to HTML Server Controls, you gain the ability to:

❑ Write code for events generated on the control that are executed on the server-side, rather than on the client-side. For example, you can respond with server-side code to the `Click` event of a `Button`.

❑ Write code for events in client script. Since they are displayed as standard HTML form controls, they retain the ability to handle client-side script as always.

❏ Automatically maintain the values of the control on a round-trip when the browser submits the page to the server.

❏ Bind the value of the control to a field, property, method, or expression in your server-side code.

HTML Server Controls are included for backward compatibility with existing ASP applications. They make it easier to convert traditional ASP applications to ASP.NET (Web forms) applications. However, everything that can be done with HTML Server Controls can be done — with more programmatic control — by using the new ASP.NET Server Controls.

ASP.NET Server Controls

HTML controls are just wrappers around regular HTML tags and do not offer any programmatic advantage in terms of controlling their look and feel. ASP.NET Server Controls, on the other hand, do not necessarily map to a single HTML element and provide a much richer UI output. You have already seen this with your `Calendar` ASP.NET Server Control.

VB.NET ships with over 20 ASP.NET Server Controls, ranging from simple controls like `TextBox`, `Button`, and `Label`, to more complex Server Controls such as the `AdRotator`, `Calendar`, and `DataGrid`. These controls can all be found in the `System.Web.UI.WebControls` namespace.

When you drag and drop each of these controls onto your Web form, they display their own distinctive UI. For example, a `TextBox` may simply be visible as a text box, but the `Calendar` control or the `DataGrid` control will appear as a tabular construct.

Behind the scenes, these controls are prefixed with the `asp:` tag. For example, in `WebForm1.aspx`, when you placed a `Label` on the page and set its Text property to "Hello World", your `Label` uses the following code to define it:

```
<asp:label id="Label1" style="Z-INDEX: 101; LEFT: 30px; POSITION: absolute;
TOP: 31px" runat="server">Hello World</asp:label>
```

You can view the HTML source of any control by right-clicking anywhere on the page and selecting View HTML Source from the context menu. Similarly, when you dragged a `Button` onto the form, instead of obtaining the normal HTML `INPUT TYPE="SUBMIT"` text, you get the following code:

```
<asp:button id="btnSubmit"
style="Z-INDEX: 102; LEFT: 26px; POSITION: absolute; TOP: 49px" runat="server"
text="Submit"></asp:button>
```

Notice that the code does not represent a regular HTML control, but rather, an ASP.NET control. The attributes refer to the ASP.NET control's properties. At runtime, the ASP.NET control is rendered on the Web page by using plain HTML, which depends on the browser type as well as the settings on the control. For example, the button above may be rendered on the target browser either as an `INPUT TYPE="SUBMIT"` HTML element, or as a `<BUTTON>` tag, depending on the browser type.

The following ASP Server Controls ship with VB.NET and are available for use in a Web form, and are found in the Web forms section of the Toolbox.

Control	Purpose
Label	Displays noneditable text
TextBox	Displays editable text in a box
Button	Displays a button, usually used to carry out an action
LinkButton	Behaves like a button, but appears like a hyperlink
ImageButton	Displays a button with an image rather than with text
HyperLink	Creates a hyperlink for navigation
DropDownList	Presents a list in a drop-down combo box
ListBox	Presents a list of items in a scrollable box
DataGrid	Displays information (usually from a database) in a tabular format with rows and columns
DataList	Displays information from a database, very similar to the Repeater control
Repeater	Displays information from a database using HTML elements that you specify, repeating the display once for each record
CheckBox	Displays a single check box allowing users to check on or off
CheckBoxList	Displays a set of check boxes as a group; useful when you want to bind it to data from a database
RadioButton	Displays a single radio button
RadioButtonList	Displays a group of radio buttons where only one radio button from the group can be selected
Image	Displays an image
Panel	Creates a bounding box on the Web form that acts as a container for other controls
Calendar	Displays an interactive calendar
AdRotator	Displays a sequence of images, either in predetermined or random order
Table	Creates a table

Validation Controls

Validation Controls are different from HTML or ASP.NET Server Controls in that they do not posses a visual identity. Their purpose is to provide easy client-side or server-side validation for other controls. For example, you may have a text box that you need the user to fill in, and you may need to only accept certain entries. For example, it could be a text box that requires a date in a certain format, like DD/MM/YY. Validation Controls allow you to generate validation scripts (client- or server-side) with a few clicks.

To use Validation Controls, you first attach the Validation Control to an input control and then set its parameters, so as to test for things like:

- Data entry in a required field
- Specific values or patterns of characters
- Entries between ranges

VB.NET ships with the following Validation Controls, also in the Web forms section of the Toolbox.

Control	Purpose
RequiredFieldValidator	Ensures that the user does not leave a field blank
CompareValidator	Compares the user's entry against another value—a constant, the property of another control, or even a database value
RangeValidator	Makes sure that the user's entry is between the lower and upper boundary values specified
RegularExpressionValidator	Checks to make sure that the entry matches a pattern defined by the developer
CustomValidator	Checks the user's entry against validation logic that you code

The easiest way to understand the power and capability of Validation Controls is to see them in action.

Add a new Web form to your HelloWorld solution (by default, it will be called WebForm4.aspx). Drag a TextBox control on to the Web form and change its ID property to txtName. Then drag a RequiredFieldValidator control from your toolbox onto the Web form, right next to the TextBox. Then, add a Button control onto the form, below the TextBox, and set its Text property to Submit.

Now, let's set the properties for the Validation Control. Change its ID to rfvTxtName, to signify to ourselves that it is going to be bound to the TextBox you just created. Then, click the ControlToValidate property and select the txtName TextBox from the drop-down list that appears. By doing so, you have bound the Validation Control to the txtName TextBox ASP.NET Server Control. Finally, change the ErrorMessage property to the text that you want to display if the user is in error: "Required Field. Please enter your name."

When you are done, your screen should look like Figure 14-11.

Set the WebForm4.aspx as the startup page and run the project. You should see the page in the browser with just a text box and a button visible. Do not type anything into the text box and just click the button to simulate a user submitting the form without entering a required field: your form submission is not accepted and you get a red error message reminding you that the field is required, as shown in Figure 14-12.

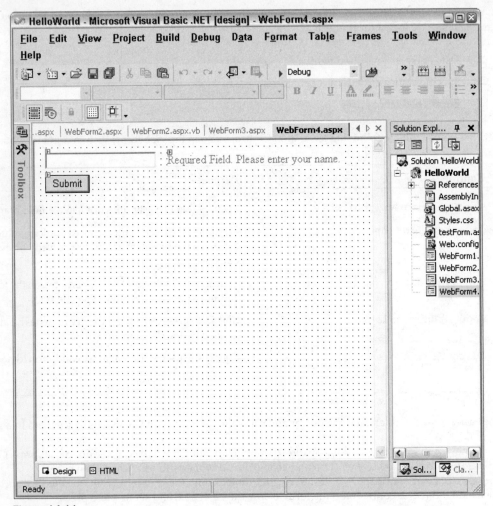

Figure 14-11

If you check the code behind this page, you will find that the Validation Controls write a lot of client-side JavaScript code to handle the data validation. However, you did not have to worry about it, you just dragged and dropped the Validation Control. The other Validation Controls also work in the same way: drop a Validation Control, attach it to a Server Control, and set the validation parameters.

User Controls

The final set of controls available is the User Controls. Similar to traditional VB User Controls, these are Web forms that you create and then use within other Web forms. This allows you to build visual components for your Web forms — useful when creating toolbars, template UI elements, and so on. (User controls are covered in Chapter 15.)

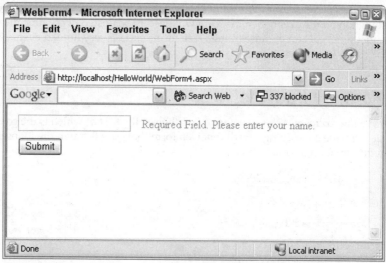

Figure 14-12

Events in Web Forms

Events in the world of Windows Forms are triggered by one of three different circumstances. An event can occur when the user makes an action: moves the mouse, uses the keyboard, and so on. An event can occur when the system makes an action: loads a page, reacts to another process or application, and so on. Finally, an event can occur without the engagement of either users or system, simply being caused by the passage of time.

In the world of the Web, however, the very stateless nature of the HTTP protocol forces Web pages to have different event handling strategies. Consider the following:

❑ A browser requests a Web page

❑ The Web server serves the page by processing its code in a linear fashion

❑ The output of the server processing is sent back to the browser as HTML

❑ The browser renders the page on the screen based on the HTML output

❑ At this point, the page no longer exists on the server

❑ The user takes some action on the Web page

❑ If the server has to react to this action, the page has to be posted back to the Web server before the Web server can react to the action

❑ This process continues over and over.

Web forms expose events to the Web developer, allowing you to write code for the events. This code is different from client-side script. The code for the event is evaluated and executed on the server.

If a Web form can trigger an event for the mouse activity on a button, for instance, in such a way that the server can take action on the event, then the form will need to be posted every time the user moves the mouse. This is not practical and because of this, Web forms expose very limited events for different controls (usually only the `Click` event).

The Web Form's Lifecycle

VB developers trying to create Web forms face a few shocks, the first of which is the concept of a Web form's lifecycle. Imagine developing a traditional VB form that goes through the following event code each time you display it on screen:

1. `Form_Initialize`: No problem.

2. `Form_Load`: No problem.

3. `Form_QueryUnload`: Huh?

4. `Form_Unload`: What?

5. `Form_Terminate`: No kidding?

This is the VB6 form's equivalent of the ASP.NET Web form's cycle. This would be nonsensical for a VB6 form because it would load itself and then unload immediately afterwards.

In the case of Web forms, when a browser requests a page, the Web form is first loaded, then its events are handled, and finally it is discarded or unloaded from memory before the HTML output is sent to the browser. So, a Web form goes through the cycle of load and unload each time that a browser makes a request for it.

Let's take a look at the stages in the life of a Web form on the Web server before its output is sent to the browser:

❑ *Configuration* — This is very similar to the `Form_Initalize` and the `Form_Load` stages of a VB6 form. This is the first stage of a Web form's lifecycle on the Web server. During this stage, the page and control state is restored and then the page's `Page_Load` event is raised.

The `Page_Load` event is built into every page. Since it occurs in the first stage of a Web form's processing, this event is a useful tool for the Web developer. The `Page_Load` event can be used to modify control properties, set up data binding or database access, and restore information from previously saved values before the page is visible on the browser.

❑ *Event handling* — If this is the first time that the browser has requested the page, no further events need to be handled. However, if this page is called in response to a form event, then the corresponding event handler in the page is called during this stage. Code within the event handler is then executed.

❑ *Cleanup* — This is the final stage in the page's lifecycle. It is the equivalent of the `Form_Unload` and `Form_Terminate` events of traditional Visual Basic. Remember, in the case of a Web form, at the end of its processing, the page is discarded. The cleanup stage handles the destruction by closing files, database connections, by invoking the `Page_Unload` event. Like the `Page_Load` event, the `Page_Unload` event is built into every page. It can be used to clean up — delete variables and arrays from memory, remove objects from memory, close database connections, and so on.

Event Categories

If you have written HTML code, you know that controls on a Web page can have events associated with them. These are client-side events raised within a browser. The controls on ASP.NET Web forms also support the HTML client-side events, but in addition expose more events that you as a developer can utilize in your code. In fact, the controls in ASP.NET Web forms expose events in a manner very similar to standard Visual Basic controls on a windows form.

Events in Web forms can be classified into different categories:

❑ Intrinsic events

❑ Client-side events versus server-side events

❑ Postback versus non-postback events

❑ Bubbled events

❑ Application and session events

Intrinsic Events

Most Web form controls support a click-type event. This is necessitated by the fact that, in order for an event to be processed, the Web form needs to be posted back to the server. Some Web form controls also support an OnChange event that is raised when the control's value changes.

Client-Side Versus Server-Side Events

ASP.NET Server Controls only support server-side events. However, the HTML elements that are outputted by these Server Controls support client-side events themselves. For example, the MouseOver event is used to change the source of an Image control and display a different image when the user rolls the mouse over the control. If you decide to use the ASP.NET ImageButton Server Control, you will be able to write code for the ImageButton's Click event, which will be processed on the server. However, you can also write client-side code for the MouseOver event of the ImageButton to handle the rollover. If you write code for both the client- and server-side event, only the server-side event will be processed.

Postback Versus Non-Postback Events

Server-side event processing happens when the form is posted back to the server. By default, these click-type events are postback events. The OnChange event is raised when a control's value changes. For example, if you write code for the OnChange event of a TextBox, when the user changes its value, the event is not fired immediately. Instead, these changes are cached by the control until the next time that a post occurs. When the Web form is posted back to the server, all the pending events are raised and processed. On the server-side, all of the OnChange events, that were cached and raised *before* the Click event that posted the form, are processed before the posting Click event.

Client-side events are automatically processed in the client browser without making a round trip to the browser. So, for example, validation client-side scripts do not need a postback to the server.

Bubbled Events

ASP.NET server controls such as the Repeater, DataList, and DataGrid controls can contain child controls that themselves raise events. For example, each row in a DataGrid control can contain one or more buttons. Events from the nested controls are *bubbled*, that is, they're sent to the container. The container in turn raises a generic event called `ItemCommand` with parameters that allow you to discover which individual control raised the original event. By responding to this single event, you can avoid having to write individual event handlers for child controls.

Application and Session Events

Continuing the tradition of ASP application and session events, VB.NET Web forms support the same high-level events. These events are not specific to a single page but, rather, work at the user and/or Web application level. These events include the `ApplicationStart` and `ApplicationEnd` events for the application level scope, and the `SessionStart` and `SessionEnd` events for the session (individual user) level scope. You can write code for these special events within the `Global.asax` file.

Web Forms Versus ASP

It is very easy to think of Web forms (ASP.NET) as the next version of ASP, that Microsoft has released a new version of ASP and is just calling it ASP.NET to equate it to the other .NET initiatives. ASP 3.0, for instance, was basically the previous version (ASP 2.0) but with new functionality, performance improvements, and one new object. This is most definitely not the case with ASP.NET and ASP 3.0.

While Web forms *are* the next version of ASP (ASP ceases to exist as a separate offering from Microsoft with the introduction of ASP.NET, though it will continue to be supported), it is not just an update. It is vastly different.

Let's consider the differences between ASP.NET and ASP 3.0:

❑   ASP was an interpreted application. This leads to poor performance, as compared to executable Windows desktop applications.

Web forms are compiled into class `.dll` files and are invoked as "applications" on the Web server. This leads to vastly improved performance. The performance drop you see when you test your application for the very first time is, in fact, indicative of this change. ASP.NET checks to see if the source code for the page has changed in any way. If it has (like in your testing mode), it recompiles the page and saves the compiled output for all subsequent requests.

❑   In ASP, you are entirely responsible for managing view state and control state via code. If you want a form control to display the value entered by the user before the form is posted, you have to obtain the value from the `Request` object and use it as part of the VALUE attribute of the control. The onus is entirely on the Web developer.

Web forms provide automatic maintenance of view state and control state. By simply using server-side controls, you automatically obtain the ability to retain state for the control during server round trips.

❑   With ASP, you can only write code with scripting languages such as VBScript and JScript. These languages do not support typed variables or early binding on objects.

Web forms support VB.NET code as well as C# code. You can use a coding language that supports typed variables (`Dim x As Integer`) as well as early binding on objects (`Dim objRS As ADODB.Recordset`). This results in additional benefits, like IntelliSense making it easier to assign property values and invoke methods on objects.

❏ With ASP, you are responsible for generating client-side validation code. When you have forms with large numbers of controls that need validation, this can be a cumbersome task, even if you have created custom routines that can simply be copied and pasted. You still need to write the code yourself to invoke these routines.

Web forms provide a very robust, drag and drop, validation control feature. Not only can you drag and drop your way to setting up validation parameters — required fields, types of accepted input, range of accepted input, and so on — Web forms also write the client-side validation routines for you.

❏ If you have used COM components with ASP applications, you know that, every time you need to change and update the COM component on the Web server, you need to release the component from the Web server (or COM+) before you can overwrite it with the new component. ASP programmers are used to bringing down the Web server or stopping and starting the COM+ services to allow such changes.

With Web forms, because of just-in-time compiling to native code, components can be updated without having to stop and start the Web services.

❏ ASP configuration settings are stored in the metabase (meta information database) of the IIS Web server. This makes it difficult to port the ASP application from one server to another. The metabase configuration settings have to be set up individually on the new Web server each time you move the ASP application.

With Web forms, all configuration settings are stored in an XML-formatted text file that can be easily moved from one Web application directory to another. The XML-formatted Config.web file allows you to create portable configuration settings.

❏ Debugging of ASP applications has always been a daunting task. The only surefire way to debug ASP applications running on a Web server is to pepper the ASP page with `response.write` statements, to output the values of variables in your code. This is similar to peppering a VB form with `Debug.Print` statements.

Web forms provide an automatic tracing capability. When you set the `Trace` and the `TraceMode` properties of a Web form, ASP.NET automatically maintains a log of actions performed, and their timestamp. When the page is rendered on the browser, ASP.NET automatically appends an HTML table listing all of the trace activity. You can also write your own tracing code to be appended to this log.

Transferring Control among Web Forms

Earlier in this chapter, it was mentioned that VB developers would get a shock when they try to create Web forms, because the familiar metaphor of VB development is turned upside down in the world of Web form development. Well, get ready for shock number two!

In a traditional VB application, suppose you have two forms, Form1 and Form2. If you want the application to transfer control from Form1 (which is currently open on the screen) to Form2, all it takes is the following code:

```
Load Form2
Form2.show
```

Of the two lines above, the first line is optional. You can use the first line if you plan to set some properties for Form2's controls, or invoke a subroutine within Form2 before showing it.

How do you do the same with a Web form? Can you "show" WebForm2 from WebForm1? The answer will surprise you. No, you can't. Not in the way that you can with traditional Visual Basic.

There are two ways to transfer control from one Web form to another:

❑ *Hyperlink*—In WebForm1, you can create a hyperlink to allow the user to navigate to WebForm2 by using a Hyperlink HTML tag (<A>). If you wish, you can pass additional arguments to the second form when navigating to it, by using the Query String (the portion of the URL that appears after the question mark in a browser's address bar). This technique of transferring control is very fast, since it transfers control to the second page directly without having to post the first page and process its events/contents.

❑ *Redirecting*—The second technique is to use the server-side Response.Redirect method to transfer control to a second page. The Response.Redirect issues an Object Moved command to the browser, forcing the browser to request the second page via a client-side request. Another similar technique is to use the Server.Transfer method to transfer control to a second page. The Server.Transfer method directly transfers control and session state to the second page without making a client round trip.

A Final Example

You'll wrap up this chapter by building a small Web forms application. Your application is a *Loan Slicer* application. Consider the scenario—you have a current home mortgage loan and you pay a certain sum of money as your monthly payment towards the loan. However, by simply making one additional payment per year towards the principal repayment, you can drastically reduce the life of the loan and pay it off faster. This is loan slicing. You want to build a Web form application that will allow an end user to figure out not only what the monthly payment for a mortgage loan will be (that would be a wimpy little application), but also to see how the loan gets sliced off if the user wishes to pay an additional sum each month towards the principal.

You begin by asking the user to enter the principal loan amount, the interest rate per annum, and the number of years for which the loan will be taken.

You then calculate the monthly payment due for the loan, and display a table of how the payments slowly eat their way through the loan till the loan is fully paid off. If the user wishes to view the "loan slicing" effect, he can specify a new monthly payment value higher than the original amount, and see how quickly the loan gets paid off.

You'll build this loan slicer using the US mortgage loan formula.

So, let's begin. Start VS.NET and select New Project. Select the project type to be ASP.NET Web application and give it the name LoanSlicer. Ensure that the target server is localhost (your own computer).

VS.NET creates a default Web form, WebForm1.aspx. Before you start adding controls to the form, right-click the Web form and select Properties to view the DOCUMENT Property Pages window (see Figure 14-13). Then change the Page Layout to FlowLayout.

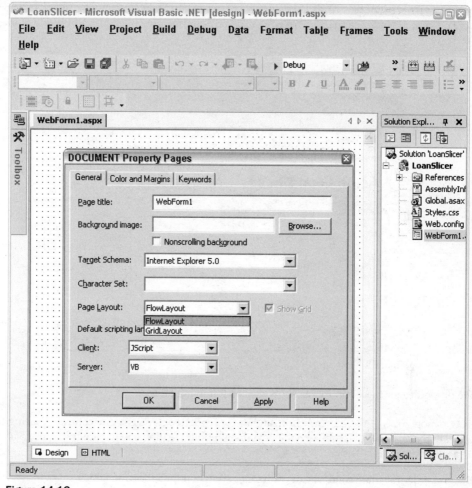

Figure 14-13

Now click OK. `FlowLayout` enables you to treat the Web form as if it were a word processing document. You can insert text and paragraph marks, and the result is translated into HTML. Controls are placed where the cursor currently is in the text.

Drag a `Label` control onto this form and position it at the top left (you can move it around by inserting or deleting paragraph marks, just as you would move an inserted object in a Microsoft Word file). Set its:

- ❏ `ID` property to be `lblTitle`
- ❏ `Text` property to be "Acme Loan Slicer"
- ❏ `Font, Size` property to `Large`
- ❏ `Font, Bold` property to `True`
- ❏ `Font, Name` property to `Verdana`

Press *Enter* to the right of the Label to create a new paragraph. Then, in sequence, insert a Label control, a TextBox control, and a RequiredFieldValidator control. Your Web form should look like Figure 14-14.

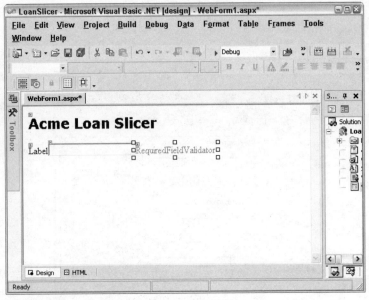

Figure 14-14

Set the properties for these controls as shown in the following table.

Insert two more rows of Label, TextBox, and RequiredFieldValidator controls, placing each set underneath the one above. To move to the next line without creating a new paragraph, use *Shift+Enter* to create a soft return (
 tag).

Set the properties for the second row of controls as shown in the following table.

Control	Property	Value
Label	ID	Leave this unchanged.
	Text	Principal amount ($)
	Font, Bold	True
	Font, Name	Verdana
TextBox	ID	TxtPrincipal
RequiredFieldValidator	ID	RfvPrincipal
	ControlToValidate	TxtPrincipal
	ErrorMessage	(Required. Please try again.)

Control	Property	Value
Label	ID	Leave this unchanged
	Text	Interest rate (%)
	Font, Bold	True
	Font, Name	Verdana
TextBox	ID	TxtInterest
RequiredFieldValidator	ID	RfvInterest
	ControlToValidate	TxtInterest
	ErrorMessage	(Required. Please try again.)

Set the properties for the third row of controls as shown in the following table.

Control	Property	Value
Label	ID	Leave this unchanged
	Text	Period (years)
	Font, Bold	True
	Font, Name	Verdana
TextBox	ID	TxtYears
RequiredFieldValidator	ID	RfvYears
	ControlToValidate	TxtYears
	ErrorMessage	(Required. Please try again.)

Underneath these three sets of controls, place another row with a Label and a TextBox control, with these properties.

Control	Property	Value
Label	ID	Leave this unchanged.
	Text	Loan slicer monthly amount ($)
	Font, Bold	True
	Font, Name	Verdana
TextBox	ID	TxtSlicerAmount

Underneath these four rows of controls, place a `Button` with these properties

Control	Property	Value
Button	ID	BtnCalculate
	Text	Calculate

Next, place a `Label` control beneath the `Button` and set its properties.

Control	Property	Value
Label	ID	LblMonthlyPayment
	Text	Monthly payment
	Font, Bold	True

Control	Property	Value
	Font, Name	Verdana
	BackColor	Light blue (#C0FFFF)

And, finally, underneath the label, place a `DataGrid` control. For the `DataGrid` control, first set the following minimal but very important properties.

Control	Property	Value
DataGrid	ID	DgValues
	Visible	False

To set the appearance of the `DataGrid` control, instead of setting individual properties, click the AutoFormat link at the bottom of the Properties window. From the list, experiment with the look you want. Figure 14-15 shows Professional 1.

Before you go any further, let's test out this Web form. You have not placed any code in it and so it shouldn't do much, but at least you can make sure that it looks fine. Before you proceed, make sure that you select Release from the Solution Configurations drop-down box on your toolbar. This will ensure that you run in the final release mode, rather than in the Debug mode.

Click the Start button to run the project. You should get the Web form displayed in a browser. The `DataGrid` and the `RequiredFieldValidator` controls should be invisible. Go ahead and click the `Calculate` button without entering any values in any of the text boxes. You should get the red error messages next to each text box as shown in Figure 14-16.

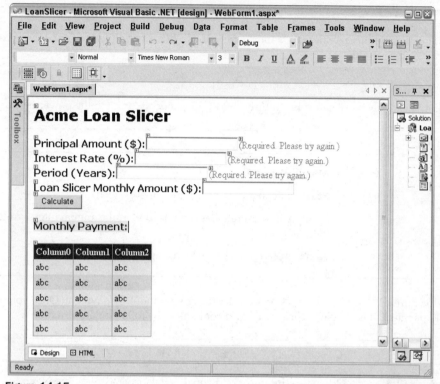

Figure 14-15

Figure 14-16

You are all set. Now let's proceed to write code for the form.

Calculating the monthly payment for a mortgage loan is a little convoluted to explain, but very simple to code. Here is the formula:

```
MP = P * ( MI / 1 -- ( 1 + MI ) ( --N ) )
```

Assuming the following (where * is multiply, / is divide, and ^ is "raise to the power of").

Variable Name	Represents
MP	Monthly payment
P	Principal loan amount (the amount borrowed)
MI	Monthly interest rate in decimals (that is, the annual interest rate divided by 1,200)
N	Number of months in the loan

This is the formula that you will be using for calculating your monthly payment. Once you calculate the monthly payment, it is simple to construct a grid containing the following information.

A	B	C	D	E	F	G	H	I
Month/ year	Loan amount	Original payment	Interest paid	Principal paid	Balance loan	New payment	New principal paid	New balance loan

Let's begin by adding code to your `Calculate` button. Double-click the button to add a call to a subroutine you will be building as part of the next step:

```
Private Sub btnCalculate_Click(ByVal sender As System.Object, _
                        ByVal e As System.EventArgs) _
                        Handles btnCalculate.Click
    CalculateValues()
End Sub
```

At the bottom of the `WebForm1` class, before the `End Class` statement, add this `CalculateValues` subroutine:

```
Private Sub CalculateValues()
    Dim dblPrincipal As Double
    Dim dblInterest As Double
    Dim lngYears As Long
    Dim dblMonthlyPayment As Double
    Dim dblMonthlyInterest As Double
```

```
Dim lngN As Long

' -- Get our values from the text boxes
dblPrincipal = CDbl(Me.txtPrincipal.Text)
dblInterest = CDbl(Me.txtInterest.Text)
lngYears = CLng(Me.txtYears.Text)
' -- Calculated intermediary values
dblMonthlyInterest = (dblInterest / (12 * 100))
lngN = lngYears * 12
' -- Monthly Payment calculation:
dblMonthlyPayment = (dblPrincipal * (dblMonthlyInterest / (1 - (1 + _
    dblMonthlyInterest) _   (-lngN))))

' -- Assign the value to the Blue label
Me.lblMonthlyPayment.Text = "Monthly Payment: " & _
    format(dblMonthlyPayment, "$#,##0.00")

End Sub
```

After declaring all the variables you will be using, you first obtain your values from the text boxes on the form, converting them to appropriate data types along the way:

```
dblPrincipal = CDbl(Me.txtPrincipal.Text)
dblInterest = CDbl(Me.txtInterest.Text)
lngyears = CLng(Me.txtYears.Text)
```

You then calculate the intermediary variable values:

```
dblMonthlyInterest = (dblInterest / (12 * 100))
lngN = lngYears * 12
```

Finally, you are ready to calculate the monthly payment:

```
dblMonthlyPayment = (dblPrincipal * (dblMonthlyInterest / (1 - (1 + _
    dblMonthlyInterest) ^ (-lngN))))
```

You store this in the variable dblMonthlyPayment. You output this value as the Text property of the blue label on the screen, performing some formatting so that it is presented as a dollar amount:

```
Me.lblMonthlyPayment.Text = "Monthly Payment: " & _
    format(dblMonthlyPayment, "$#,##0.00")
```

That was the easy part. Let's test it again by running your application. Enter the following values: Principal = 100,000, Interest Rate = 6.75, Years = 10. You should get the output shown in Figure 14-17.

Now comes the more difficult part — populating the DataGrid with your values.

Before you look at the code, let's understand what you are trying to do. You need to display a DataGrid full of rows and columns that represent your loan payouts. You want to display the current loan amount,

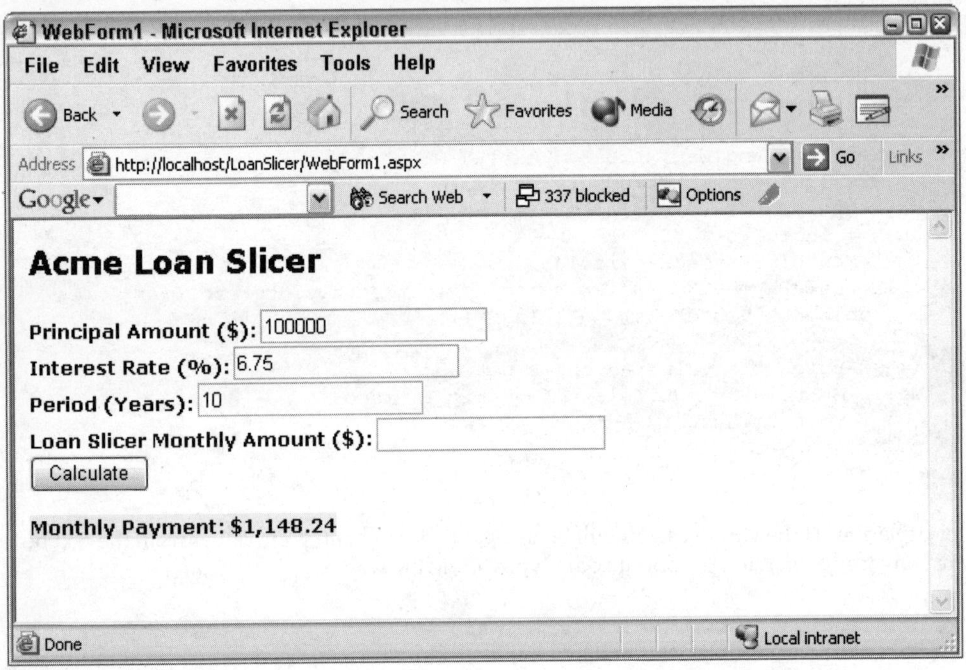

Figure 14-17

the monthly payment, the interest paid, the principal paid, and the balance loan amount for every month of every year in the loan period.

In addition, if the user has entered a Loan Slicer Monthly Amount—an amount that he/she is willing to pay that is larger than the monthly payment due—you need to also figure out how the new monthly payment will pay off the loan faster, and therefore "slice" it.

Normally, a `DataGrid` is bound to a database. You don't have a database in this scenario. You could dump the values into a database and have the `DataGrid` then read the database. But that would be very inefficient. A better way would be to create your own "database" on the fly. You can do that by creating a `DataTable` object and populating it with values. Your `DataGrid` can be bound to a `DataView` object at runtime. To do so, you need to write code as follows.

```
OurDataGridObject.DataSource = OurDataViewObject
```

A `DataView` object can be created and initialized by an existing `DataTable` object. Therefore, you can create a `DataView` object by using a `DataTable` object, as follows:

```
OurDataViewObject = New DataView(OurDataTableObject)
```

A `DataTable` object in turn consists of rows and columns, or rather `DataRow` objects and `DataColumn` objects. To create a row for a table, you use a `DataRow` object as follows:

```
OurDataTable.Rows.Add OurDataRow
```

The `DataColumn` objects can also be created at runtime by using the following code:

```
OurDataTable.Columns.Add OurDataColumn
```

And finally, you can create a `DataColumn` object by passing the `Column` definition as follows:

```
OurDataColumn = New DataColumn(strColumnName, ColumnDataType)
```

You can put all of this code together in the following `BuildPayoutGrid` subroutine. Add the following code to the bottom of the `CalculateValues` subroutine, immediately before the `End Sub`:

```
BuildPayoutGrid(dblPrincipal, dblMonthlyInterest, dblMonthlyPayment)
```

Then, add the code for the `BuildPayOutGrid` subroutine itself:

```
Private Sub BuildPayoutGrid(ByVal dblP As Double, ByVal dblMI As Double, _
                            ByVal dblM As Double)
    ' -- Variables to hold our output data
    Dim dtPayout As DataTable
    Dim drPayout As DataRow
    Dim datMonthYear As Date
    Dim dblSlicerAmount As Double
    Dim dblNewBalance As Double
    Dim dblMonthlyInterestPaid As Double

    ' -- Make sure we have the new "Loan Slicer" monthly amount
    dblSlicerAmount = CDbl(Me.txtSlicerAmount.Text)
    ' -- if the user has not entered one, add one additional payment
    ' -- per year as the new slicer amount
    If dblSlicerAmount = 0 Then
      dblSlicerAmount = dblM + (dblM / 12)
    End If
    Me.txtSlicerAmount.Text = CStr(dblSlicerAmount)
    ' -- Create a new DataTable
    dtPayout = New DataTable()
    ' -- Create nine string columns
    dtPayout.Columns.Add(New DataColumn("Month/Year", GetType(String)))
    dtPayout.Columns.Add(New DataColumn("Loan Amount", GetType(String)))
    dtPayout.Columns.Add(New DataColumn("Original Payment", _
        GetType(String)))
    dtPayout.Columns.Add(New DataColumn("Interest Paid", GetType(String)))
    dtPayout.Columns.Add(New DataColumn("Principal Paid", GetType(String)))
    dtPayout.Columns.Add(New DataColumn("Balance Amount", GetType(String)))
    dtPayout.Columns.Add(New DataColumn("New Payment", GetType(String)))
    dtPayout.Columns.Add(New DataColumn("New Principal Paid", _
        GetType(String)))
    dtPayout.Columns.Add(New DataColumn("New Balance Amount", _
        GetType(String)))
    dblNewBalance = dblP
    ' -- Populate it with values
```

```
' -- Start with current Month/Year
datMonthYear = Now()
Do While dblP > 0
   ' -- Create a new row for our table
   drPayout = dtPayout.NewRow()

   drPayout(0) = MonthName(Month(datMonthYear)) & ", " & _
      Year(datMonthYear)
   drPayout(1) = Format(dblP, "$#,##0.00")
   drPayout(2) = Format(dblM, "$#,##0.00")

   dblMonthlyInterestPaid = (dblP * dblMI)

   drPayout(3) = Format(dblMonthlyInterestPaid, "$#,##0.00")
   drPayout(4) = Format(dblM - dblMonthlyInterestPaid, "$#,##0.00")
   drPayout(5) = Format(dblP - (dblM - dblMonthlyInterestPaid), _
      "$#,##0.00")
   ' -- new values
   If dblNewBalance >= 0 Then
      drPayout(6) = Format(dblSlicerAmount, "$#,##0.00")
      drPayout(7) = Format(dblSlicerAmount - dblMonthlyInterestPaid, _
         "$#,##0.00")
      drPayout(8) = Format(dblNewBalance - (dblSlicerAmount - _
         dblMonthlyInterestPaid), "$#,##0.00")
   Else
      drPayout(6) = "PAID"
      drPayout(7) = "IN"
      drPayout(8) = "FULL"
   End If
   ' -- Add the row to the table
   dtPayout.Rows.Add(drPayout)
   ' -- Next month
   datMonthYear = DateAdd(DateInterval.Month, 1, datMonthYear)
   ' -- Starting Loan Amount is previous month's Ending balance
   dblP = (dblP - (dblM - dblMonthlyInterestPaid))
   dblNewBalance = (dblNewBalance - (dblSlicerAmount - _
      dblMonthlyInterestPaid))

Loop
' -- Create a new DataView and bind it to the DataGrid
With dgValues
   .Visible = True
   .DataSource = New DataView(dtPayout)
   .DataBind()
End With
End Sub
```

Let's examine this code piece-by-piece. You begin by declaring the variables you will need:

```
Dim dtPayout As DataTable
Dim drPayout As DataRow
Dim datMonthYear As Date
Dim dblSlicerAmount As Double
```

```
Dim dblNewBalance As Double
Dim dblMonthlyInterestPaid As Double
```

The code first makes sure that there is a valid "Loan Slicer" amount in the text box on the screen. If not, it simply adds one additional monthly payment per year to calculate a new, larger monthly payment. Finally, the text box is updated with the new "slicer" amount:

```
dblSlicerAmount = CDbl(Me.txtSlicerAmount.Text)
' -- if the user has not entered one, add one additional payment
' -- per year as the new slicer amount
If dblSlicerAmount = 0 Then
    dblSlicerAmount = dblM + (dblM / 12)
End If
Me.txtSlicerAmount.Text = CStr(dblSlicerAmount)
```

You then create a blank DataTable:

```
dtPayout  =  New  DataTable()
```

You make sure that the DataTable has the columns you will need. You do this by adding DataColumns to the DataTable. These DataColumns are created on the fly by passing column definition arguments to the DataColumn that is being created:

```
dtPayout.Columns.Add(New DataColumn("Month/Year", GetType(String)))
dtPayout.Columns.Add(New DataColumn("Loan Amount", GetType(String)))
dtPayout.Columns.Add(New DataColumn("Original Payment", _
    GetType(String)))
dtPayout.Columns.Add(New DataColumn("Interest Paid", GetType(String)))
dtPayout.Columns.Add(New DataColumn("Principal Paid", GetType(String)))
dtPayout.Columns.Add(New DataColumn("Balance Amount", GetType(String)))

dtPayout.Columns.Add(New DataColumn("New Payment", GetType(String)))
dtPayout.Columns.Add(New DataColumn("New Principal Paid", _
    GetType(String)))
dtPayout.Columns.Add(New DataColumn("New Balance Amount", _
    GetType(String)))
```

The code then stores the loan amount in a new variable to calculate the effect of the new "slicer" amount also:

```
dblNewBalance = dblP
```

You are now ready to populate the DataTable columns with values, and the DataTable with rows. To do so, you begin with the current month:

```
datMonthYear  =  Now()
```

You need to dump the output as long as there is an outstanding balance on the loan. Therefore, you use a Do...While...Loop till the loan amount reduces to zero:

```
Do While dblP > 0
```

The code then begins the process of creating a "database on the fly" by creating a new row for the `DataTable`. This new row will automatically have nine columns addressed by the column numbers 0 to 8:

```
drPayout = dtPayout.NewRow()
```

You set the values for each column in the current row. This is relatively simple. You know the initial loan amount and the monthly payment. You can then calculate the monthly interest on the outstanding loan amount and, from that, figure out how much of the monthly payment is interest and how much is the payoff of the principal itself. The balance is the amount of the loan left:

```
drPayout(0) = MonthName(Month(datMonthYear)) & ", " & _
    Year(datMonthYear)
drPayout(1) = Format(dblP, "$#,##0.00")
drPayout(2) = Format(dblM, "$#,##0.00")

dblMonthlyInterestPaid = (dblP * dblMI)

drPayout(3) = Format(dblMonthlyInterestPaid, "$#,##0.00")
drPayout(4) = Format(dblM - dblMonthlyInterestPaid, "$#,##0.00")
drPayout(5) = Format(dblP - (dblM - dblMonthlyInterestPaid), _
    "$#,##0.00")
```

The last three columns of figures are calculated based on the new "slicer" amount using the same logic as the original amount. What this means is that the first six columns will show the loan being paid out month after month, based on the bank's monthly payment figure, while the last three columns will show the loan getting sliced and paid off much faster because of the larger monthly payment. Since you know that the loan will get sliced, you also add logic to display a text "PAID IN FULL", instead of negative numbers when the loan balance reaches zero:

```
If dblNewBalance >= 0 Then
    drPayout(6) = Format(dblSlicerAmount, "$#,##0.00")
    drPayout(7) = Format(dblSlicerAmount - dblMonthlyInterestPaid, _
        "$#,##0.00")
    drPayout(8) = Format(dblNewBalance - (dblSlicerAmount - _
        dblMonthlyInterestPaid), "$#,##0.00")
Else
    drPayout(6) = "PAID"
    drPayout(7) = "IN"
    drPayout(8) = "FULL"
End If
```

Once you have filled nine columns with figures, you are ready to add the row to the `DataTable`:

```
dtPayout.Rows.Add(drPayout)
```

Since you are in a loop, you need to get your data ready for the next pass. The code increments the date by one month and updates the value of the loan amount to the balance amount remaining. You do the same for the new sliced loan balanceand then complete the loop:

```
datMonthYear = DateAdd(DateInterval.Month, 1, datMonthYear)
' -- Starting Loan Amount is previous month's Ending balance
```

```
    dblP = (dblP - (dblM - dblMonthlyInterestPaid))
    dblNewBalance = (dblNewBalance - (dblSlicerAmount - _
        dblMonthlyInterestPaid))

Loop
```

When you finish processing the loop, you will have a `DataTable` filled with values. The code then creates a `DataView` based on the `DataTable` and assigns it to the `DataSource` property of the `DataGrid`, all in one swoop. You also make sure that the `DataGrid` is visible (remember, in design mode, you had set it to be invisible). Finally, invoke the `Bind` method to actually bind the `DataGrid` to the `DataView` created on the fly:

```
With dgValues
    .Visible = True
    .DataSource = New DataView(dtPayout)
    .DataBind()
End With
```

That's it, you will get a neat HTML table filled with rows and columns of output from the `DataGrid`. Run the application and enter a Principal Amount of 100,000, an Interest Rate of 6.75, a Period value of 10 and a Loan Slicer Amount value of 1,500. (See Figure 14-18.)

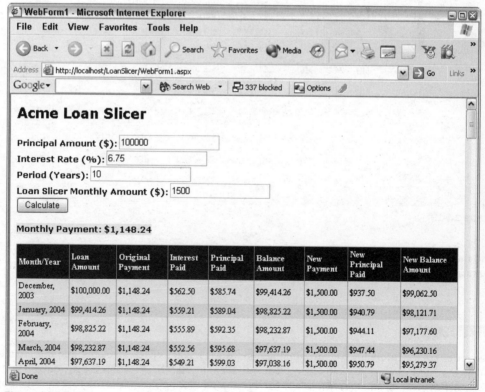

Figure 14-18

If you scroll down the page, you can see that your calculations are on the mark. At the end of 10 years, you have completely paid off your loan amount. However, because of your Loan Slicing feature, you see that, by simply paying (about) an additional $350 per month, one can cut down the loan from 10 years to around 7.5 years. The `DataGrid` ends when the principal loan amount reduces to zero. Long before that, the Loan Slicer indicates that you have PAID IN FULL your loan (see Figure 14-19).

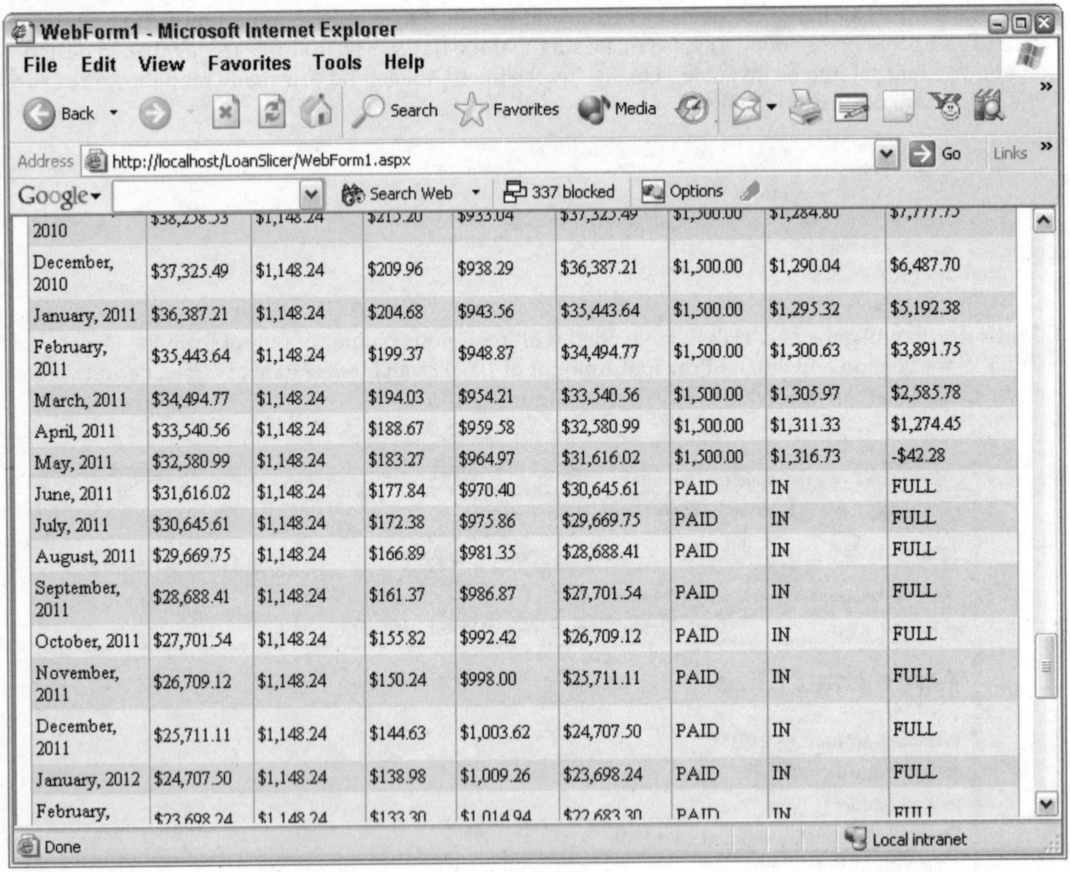

2010	$38,258.53	$1,148.24	$215.20	$933.04	$37,325.49	$1,500.00	$1,284.80	$7,777.75
December, 2010	$37,325.49	$1,148.24	$209.96	$938.29	$36,387.21	$1,500.00	$1,290.04	$6,487.70
January, 2011	$36,387.21	$1,148.24	$204.68	$943.56	$35,443.64	$1,500.00	$1,295.32	$5,192.38
February, 2011	$35,443.64	$1,148.24	$199.37	$948.87	$34,494.77	$1,500.00	$1,300.63	$3,891.75
March, 2011	$34,494.77	$1,148.24	$194.03	$954.21	$33,540.56	$1,500.00	$1,305.97	$2,585.78
April, 2011	$33,540.56	$1,148.24	$188.67	$959.58	$32,580.99	$1,500.00	$1,311.33	$1,274.45
May, 2011	$32,580.99	$1,148.24	$183.27	$964.97	$31,616.02	$1,500.00	$1,316.73	-$42.28
June, 2011	$31,616.02	$1,148.24	$177.84	$970.40	$30,645.61	PAID	IN	FULL
July, 2011	$30,645.61	$1,148.24	$172.38	$975.86	$29,669.75	PAID	IN	FULL
August, 2011	$29,669.75	$1,148.24	$166.89	$981.35	$28,688.41	PAID	IN	FULL
September, 2011	$28,688.41	$1,148.24	$161.37	$986.87	$27,701.54	PAID	IN	FULL
October, 2011	$27,701.54	$1,148.24	$155.82	$992.42	$26,709.12	PAID	IN	FULL
November, 2011	$26,709.12	$1,148.24	$150.24	$998.00	$25,711.11	PAID	IN	FULL
December, 2011	$25,711.11	$1,148.24	$144.63	$1,003.62	$24,707.50	PAID	IN	FULL
January, 2012	$24,707.50	$1,148.24	$138.98	$1,009.26	$23,698.24	PAID	IN	FULL
February,	$23,698.24	$1,148.24	$133.30	$1,014.94	$22,683.30	PAID	IN	FULL

Figure 14-19

And there you have it. A simple Web forms application with a slight twist. You also saw how to bind a `DataGrid` to a non-database source that you are calculating on the fly.

Summary

Web forms are the future for Web development in the Microsoft .NET Framework and this chapter gave you an overview of what you can accomplish with them in VB.NET. Web forms provide you with the power of Rapid Application Development for developing Web applications. They are to Web applications what Visual Basic was to Windows applications when it was first released.

Web forms are built on the common language runtime and provide all the benefits of those technologies, including a managed execution environment, type safety, inheritance, and dynamic compilation for improved performance. Web forms provide a familiar "code behind forms" design metaphor for Visual Basic programmers. They automatically manage state and values for controls when a web page is posted back to the server. Additionally, Web forms can generate an enormous amount of HTML code and client-side JavaScript code for data validation with a few clicks of your mouse.

15

Creating Web Controls

It's probably only fair to warn you that creating *Web controls* could easily be the subject of its own book, as it encompasses an entirely new form of Visual Basic control development. Custom Web controls are likely to become one of the biggest arenas for third-party control development, as various vendors vie to fill the large gap in functionality left by the controls in the basic HTML specifications. This isn't meant as a slight to the controls that Microsoft has provided, instead the attempt is to point out the contrast between the rich functionality available in the Win32 controls and the basic functionality supported by the W3C's native HTML controls.

Microsoft has actually done an excellent job of wrapping up the basic functionality of the standard HTML controls and extending the most practical into server controls for .NET. They've also added some impressive new controls (such as the Web calendar control) that take ASP Web development into areas of functionality and sophistication typically reserved for desktop applications.

However, there are times when we will want to go beyond what the W3C and Microsoft have provided for us. In this chapter we'll look at:

❑   When we should create our own controls

❑   The different types of controls that we can create

❑   How to create and use a custom control

❑   How to reuse existing code in a custom control

❑   How to expose properties and methods of a control

❑   How to create and handle events of a control

❑   How to add a custom control to the Visual Studio .NET (VS.NET) Toolbox

We'll begin by looking at why we would need to create our own controls.

Why Create Your Own Controls?

In each new Web project, we come across problems that require novel solutions, problems that range from maintaining state in an essentially stateless environment to rolling out a consistent, robust site in a short space of time. As we saw in the previous chapter, .NET has responded to the first problem by providing us with state mechanisms that are built right into the platform. .NET has responded to the second problem by providing us with an extensible set of classes to help us build reusable Web controls and components for our Web sites.

Imagine a day when Web site developers can stop worrying about which browser the client is using and which OS that browser is running on. A day, for instance, when a Web site developer can drag a menu control onto a Web form and let the control determine whether the client's browser is capable of rendering a DHTML menu or whether the menu should be output as a list of text-based hyperlinks. That's the philosophy of custom Web controls in .NET. Smart controls that abstract the vagaries of HTML (or WML and so on) and allow Web developers to focus on providing the best possible user experience, benefiting both the developer and the end user.

There are other benefits to creating custom Web controls as well. We can create controls that meet our requirements, encapsulate our code, and reuse it. For instance, you may have developed a login form at one time or another; you might have also experienced the hassle of having to redevelop that login form for successive Web sites. With .NET, we are now able to turn the login form into a class and take advantage of all of the benefits of object-oriented design, including inheritance and encapsulation.

So, the benefits of creating custom Web controls are fairly obvious in that they are centered around three of the four tenets of object-oriented design: abstraction, encapsulation, and inheritance.

> *Custom Web controls also take advantage of polymorphism, especially when participating in ASP page control management.*

When to Create Your Own Controls

According to Microsoft, there are four basic scenarios where we might want to create our own custom Web control:

❑ We have an ASP.NET page (or a portion of one) that provides a user interface (UI) or some functionality that we would like to reuse.

❑ We have an existing Web forms control that meets most of our requirements. We want to customize it by adding, altering, or removing functionality until it meets all of our requirements.

❑ We need a control that combines the functionality of two or more existing Web forms controls.

❑ We need a Web control with functionality that can't be found in an existing Web form control or even in a combination of existing Web form controls.

We should also add a fifth scenario to Microsoft's list — one that is likely to come into play in larger team development environments:

❑ We want to use the functionality of a control written in one language on an ASP.NET page that uses a different language.

Types of Custom Web Controls

ASP.NET ships with a lot of controls that you can use within your Web pages. These include server controls, HTML controls and Data Controls. In addition, ASP.NET also allows you to create your own custom controls that can, in turn, be used in your ASP.NET Web forms. .NET offers us four different types of custom Web controls that we can use to address these scenarios:

- ❑ Web User Controls
- ❑ Subclassed controls
- ❑ Composite controls
- ❑ Templated controls

Let's take a look at each type in turn and discuss where they might fit into the development scenarios.

Web User Controls

Web User Controls (WUCs) in the Web environment are different from Windows Forms User Controls. WUCs are portions of a Web page that typically combine HTML and server-side script. They have almost all of the characteristics of the ASPX page class in that they support design time HTML, code-behind, and dynamic compilation. (In fact, they are so close to ASPX pages that Microsoft originally called them *Pagelets.*) In contrast, Windows Forms User Controls are strictly class-based and, while they make use of the Windows Forms Designer, they do not allow for separation of code and content like WUCs do.

WUCs are extremely easy to create. You can build one from scratch by adding a WUC item to a Web project and working with it exactly the same way as you would an ASPX page. More frequently, though, you'll take a portion of UI and/or functionality from one of your existing ASP.NET pages, place it into a separate file with an `.ascx` extension. That's it, you've created a WUC. It really is that simple to create an abstracted, encapsulated, and reusable component!

> *A WUC may require some tweaking if you've copied certain directives (any of the @ Page directives or the @ OutputCache directive) or if you've included <HTML> or <BODY> tags. We'll discuss the necessary modifications later on.*

Of course, like most things we've seen in .NET, the ease with which we can create a WUC doesn't take away from the power and flexibility that they can offer. It's just that WUCs have been designed from the ground up to be simple yet extensible!

In previous versions of ASP, you might have used a Server-Side Include (SSI) to achieve the same effect as a WUC. In fact, in ASP.NET you could still use an SSI to encapsulate common functionality or UI elements, but WUCs provide much greater flexibility and extensibility. They offer several advantages over SSIs:

- ❑ WUCs provide their own namespace behind the scenes. This means that variables, methods, events, and constituent controls in the WUC will not conflict with identically named counterparts on the hosting page or within other instances of the same WUC.

❑ WUCs can be parameterized, which means that other developers can set properties for the control by specifying attributes in the element that inserts the WUC on the hosting page.

❑ WUCs can be written in any .NET compliant programming language, even if it's not the same server-side language used by the page that hosts it.

Once we've created our WUC, we can then choose to create or expose properties, methods, and events to the page that hosts the control — or not! A WUC can be a black box that reveals nothing of its inner workings, or it can fully expose its contents. The choice is up to us.

Subclassed Controls

Subclassed controls represent the most basic form of custom Web control development. They are created as classes and create their HTML output directly through methods of the `HtmlTextWriter` class, a utility class provided by the hosting page for writing to the HTML response stream. A fairly typical example of a subclassed control would be the `ImageButton` control, which inherits most of its functionality from the `Image` control and then adds support for a click event and a command event with associated command properties.

Don't let the phrase "the most basic form of custom Web control development" mislead you, though. Controls of this type can be very complex and detailed. "Basic" merely refers to the fact that subclassed controls do not use complex techniques like *class composition* or *templating* in rendering themselves. We'll discuss class composition and templating in the next two sections.

Typically, subclassed controls are created by inheriting from one of the following base classes in the `System.Web.UI` namespace, or from one of their derivatives:

❑ `System.Web.UI.WebControls.WebControl` — for controls with a UI

❑ `System.Web.UI.Control` — for controls without a UI

We might also choose to inherit from the `System.Web.UI.HTMLControls.HTMLControl` class to create a server control for an HTML tag that Microsoft didn't include in the `HtmlControls` namespace, but there is not much point in doing this. .NET has the `HTMLGenericControl` class if we want to create a server control for an HTML tag that isn't already represented in the `System.Web.UI` `.HTMLControls` namespace. The `HTMLGenericControl` class has a `TagName` property to determine which tag it renders, which gives us the ability to create a server control for any HTML tag that we'd like.

By inheriting from these classes, subclassed controls get all of the plumbing necessary to interact with the `Page` class, as well as the abilities to maintain state, to data bind, and to participate in server-side events.

Composite Controls

A composite control is a *container control* for other controls created by *class composition*. Class composition means that a composite control creates its child controls programmatically as classes, rather than as nested HTML or XML (the way that WUCs do) or as parameters within its element tag (the way that templated controls do). Composite controls are more or less equivalent to WUCs with the exception that they are compiled solely from a class file and persisted as part of an assembly, whereas WUCs are compiled on demand from an ASCX file (and, optionally, a Code-behind class file) and are not persisted in an assembly. Being a container control means that composite controls act as a host control for other controls. A typical example of a container class would be a `Panel` Web control.

Composite controls are created through the standard class mechanisms in .NET. They can be created either by inheriting from the controls in the `System.Web.UI` namespace or by implementing one or more of the interfaces in the `System.Web.UI` namespace.

> *While implementing interfaces is an option for creating custom Web controls, it is far too complex a subject to deal with here.*

Composite controls typically start by inheriting from the `System.Web.UI.Control` class (although you could certainly use one of its derivatives). The `Control` class provides the `Controls` collection to store child controls in and it also provides methods for rendering the child controls. All that is required of us when we develop a composite control is that we override the base class's `CreateChildControls` method to create instances of the child control classes and add them to the `Controls` collection. Once the child controls have been added to the `Controls` collection, the built-in functionality of the `Control` class will handle rendering them for us.

> *For more information on composite controls, see* Professional ASP.NET 1.1 *(Wiley, 2004).*

Templated Controls

The last of the four types, templated controls, are types of container controls also referred to in the Microsoft documentation as *lookless controls*. These are controls that separate their UI from their behavior, allowing the page author to customize the appearance of their constituent controls without the use of code. Some examples of templated controls in the `System.Web.UI.WebControls` namespace are the `Repeater` and `Datalist` classes.

The requirements for a templated control are that it implements the `INamingContainer` interface and that it exposes one or more properties of type `System.Web.UI.ITemplate`. The name of each of these *template properties* can then be mapped to the tag name of a *template element* nested inside the templated control. Then, within the template element, the page author can specify whatever they would like for the appearance of that portion of the templated control, from literal text right on up to complex combinations of nested elements.

> *For thorough coverage of templated controls, see* Professional ASP.NET 1.1 *(Wiley, 2004).*

Now that we've covered the basic types of custom Web controls, let's discuss where each type might fit in the development cycle.

When to Use Custom Web Controls

The easiest path to follow when creating custom Web controls is to develop standard ASP.NET pages and, when we determine that we have something that can be reused, separate it off into a WUC.

You could stop at this point, already having taken advantage of the abstraction and encapsulation provided by the WUC control. But if we want to use our control in multiple sites and still have a single set of source code for our control, we'll want to look at rewriting the control as one of the class-based custom

Web control types. This is because we can deploy the compiled code for a class-based control to multiple sites or to the Global Assembly Cache (GAC) for a given Web server. If we change the source code, it is a simple thing to manage versions and to redeploy the updated assembly. WUCs, on the other hand, require that their ASCX files exist locally within each Web application that uses them. This means that we would need to copy any changes to the ASCX file manually to each Web site that uses the control and, hopefully, not accidentally overwrite any other changed versions.

> **The best part of this is that the same code that you write for your ASP.NET page or your WUC will still work with minor modifications when you port it over to a subclassed, composite, or templated control.**

Aside from migrating a WUC, we could also look at developing a class-based control when we want greater control over the HTML elements that comprise a control and the behavior of those elements (as well as the behavior of the control as a whole). Subclassed controls make sense when we are building single element output, enhancing the functionality of an existing control, or generating unstructured or loosely structured output. Composite controls are excellent when we want to combine multiple controls or when we are looking at building complex or repeated combinations of other controls. Templated controls offer us a way of giving the consumer of our control a structured method for altering its appearance. Remember too that class-based custom Web controls also take advantage of much of the same framework used to create custom Windows Forms controls, so you can leverage the skills that you gain in both areas. In fact, it is one of Microsoft's stated design goals to make Web control development accessible even to developers who do not have a great deal of familiarity with HTML.

We will concentrate on WUCs and subclassed controls for the remainder of this chapter.

Creating a Web User Control

In this section you will be building a simple navigation WUC. In addition, if you take a look around the Web for any length of time you'll come across a whole host of standard UI functionality that would make for great custom Web controls. Some examples would be:

❑   Login forms

❑   Menus

❑   Search widgets

❑   Headers, footers, and copyright notices

❑   Tables of contents

❑   Site navigation elements

Building a Simple Web User Control

Let us take a quick look at building a very simple WUC. One of the simplest ones to build is a common navigation bar running on the top or on the left of every page of your Web site. For example, the Wiley.com Web site has a navigation bar on the left that we will try to mimic. You can access this navigation bar at `http://wiley.com/WileyCDA/` (see Figure 15-1).

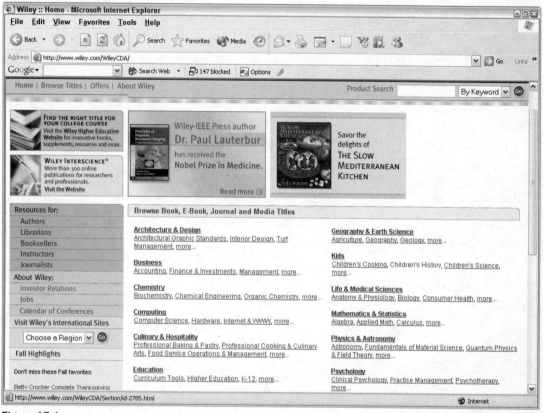

Figure 15-1

Now remember, this navigation bar appears on every page on the site. In our sample here, we will create three Web pages which will incorporate this common navigation bar using our WUC.

Create a new ASP.NET Web application project in VS.NET by selecting File ➪ New ➪ Project. Click "Visual Basic Projects," and then the "ASP.Net Web Application" template. Name the project SimpleWebUserControl and make sure that you select the default http://localhost/as your location for the project, as shown in Figure 15-2.

By default, you will get your first asp.net page called `Webform1.aspx`. Rename the file to `Authors.aspx`. Click the Web form page and in the Form Properties window, change the `pageLayout` property to `FlowLayout`. This allows you to set up the page as per the flow of the elements within it rather than based on absolute x and y positions. Also, change the `title` property to `Authors`.

In your Toolbox, click the HTML controls section. Then drag and drop a `Table` from the toolbox on to the form. By default you get a 3 rows by 3 columns table. Move your mouse to the top of the middle column and click when it becomes a downward pointing arrow to highlight the entire column. Right-click within the highlighted column and select Delete ➪ Columns to delete the middle column. Adjust the left column so that it occupies about one third of the page and widen the table to fill almost the entire page. Then, using a similar technique, select and highlight the second and third rows and delete them also. Finally,

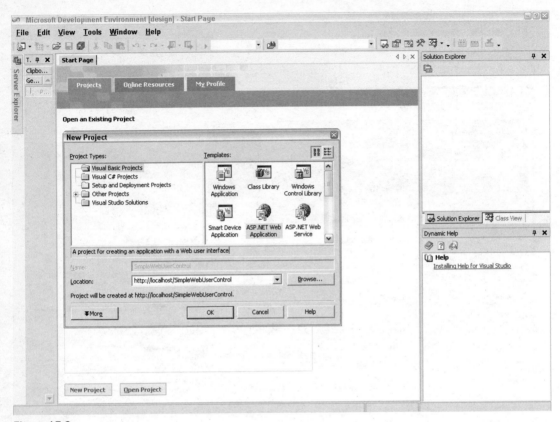

Figure 15-2

click inside the two cells remaining in the table one by one, and set their `align` property to `left` and `valign` property to `top`.

Switch back to the Web forms section within your Toolbox, and drag and drop a `Label` control on to the *right hand side* cell in the table. Change the `Text` property of the label to Resources for Authors, and select a large font size for the label. Save the page. When you are done, your page should look like Figure 15-3.

Repeat the same process twice with two new Web forms (`Librarians.aspx` and `Booksellers .aspx`). For each, begin by selecting `Project` ⇨ `Add Web Form...` from the menu. Provide the appropriate name for the aspx page and repeat the same steps as before. You will now have two new identical Web forms, each with a table within it that contains one label on the right-hand side cell with text "`Resources for Librarians`" and "`Resources for Booksellers`", respectively (see Figure 15-4).

We are now ready to create our WUC to be used in all the three asp.net pages we just built. To do so, select `ProjectAdd Web User Control...` from the menu and provide the name for the file

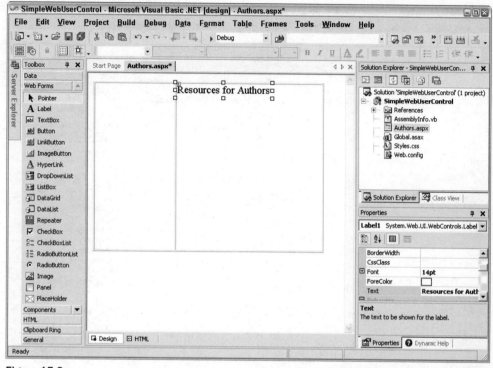

Figure 15-3

`SimpleWebUserControl.ascx`. A WUC looks and behaves just like a normal aspx page, except it has an ascx extension and it will be included within an aspx page.

In the new WUC page, switch to the HTML controls in the toolbox and add a Table control on to the WUC page. Using a technique you must be familiar with now, delete the two right columns of the table. Adjust the width of the table to be roughly the size of our navigation bar and set some of the table properties as follows.

Make sure you are setting the properties for the Table. Use the combo box at the top of the properties window to select the table (Table1 <TABLE>) before proceeding.

Property	Value
Bgcolor	#a5b2bd
Border	0
Cellpadding	0
Cellspacing	0

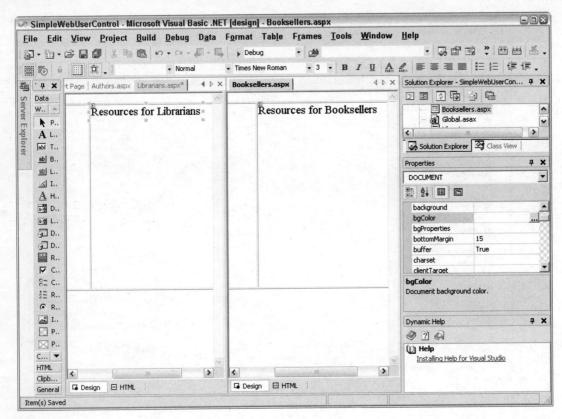

Figure 15-4

We are now set to add our images that will form the basis for our hyperlinks to different pages. Before we proceed, let's get our images in order. In the Solution Explorer, select the project by clicking it to make it active. Then select Project ⇨ New Folder from the menu to add a new child folder to our project. Name the folder images. Click the new images folder you have created. Then select Project ⇨ Add Existing Item from the menu to bring up the Add Existing Item dialog box. Change the "Files of type" option to read "Image Files". Navigate to the files accompanying this book and select the following images and click Open. (You can hold the control key down to select multiple images).

```
hp_leftnav_authors.gif

hp_leftnav_booksellers.gif

hp_leftnav_librarians.gif
```

This will add the above files to your project. Back in your project, click within the first cell in the table on your SimpleWebUserControl.ascx file. In the toolbox from the Web form section, drag and drop a

Hyperlink control into the first cell. Change the ImageURL property as follows: Click on the ImageURL property in the properties window. Then click the button with three dots (ellipses) to the far right of the properties window to bring up the Select Image dialog box. Navigate to the /images sub directory. Select the hp_leftnav_authors.gif image and click OK. The hyperlink now displays an image on screen. Change the NavigateURL property in the same fashion to point to the Authors.aspx page within the project.

Repeat the same process in the second cell of the table and add a HyperLink control with an ImageURL property pointing to the hp_leftnav_librarians.gif image file and the NavigateURL property pointing to the Librarians.aspx page. Finally, the last cell of the table needs to have a HyperLink control with an ImageURL of hp_leftnav_booksellers.gif and a NavigateURL of Booksellers.aspx. When you are done, you should have a screen that looks like Figure 15-5.

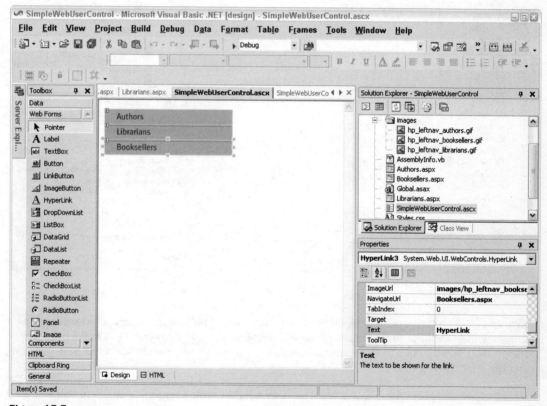

Figure 15-5

Up to now, what we have done is no different than building a simple Web Page using a WYSIWYG editor metaphor. Now, let's see how we can get the nav bar into multiple pages with a simple drag and drop. Close all active windows in your project by selecting Window ⇨ Close all documents.

Double-click the `Authors.aspx` page in the Solution Explorer to open it in design view. From the Solution Explorer, click the `SimpleWebUserControl.ascx` file and drag and drop it into the left cell of the Table within the `Authors.aspx` page. You will get a grey rectangle that reads `UserControl – SimpleWebUserControl1` (see Figure 15-6). That represents the WUC. At runtime, the Web page will render the contents of the WUC within the left cell of the Table.

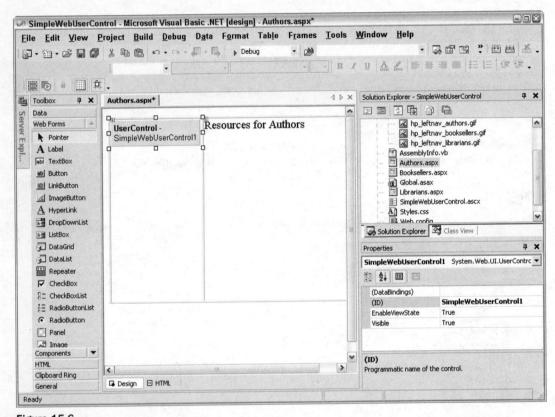

Figure 15-6

Save and close `Authors.aspx`. Open `Booksellers.aspx` and repeat the same process, dragging and dropping the ascx file onto the left cell of the table on screen to add the user control to the page (see Figure 15-7). Finally, open `Librarians.aspx` and repeat the same process once more. Save your project and run it by clicking F5.

VS.NET compiles your project and opens a browser window with `Authors.aspx` in it. You will see that the user control representing a navigation bar is now on the left-hand side of the page. Not only that, the three images point to the three pages we produced. Click the images to navigate from page to page. Notice that on each page, the left hand side navigation bar is identical, all of them being produced at runtime from our WUC.

No matter how many pages you include the WUC in, you only have to design, develop and maintain one copy of it within the `SimpleWebUserControl.ascx` file. Any changes you make in that file are immediately propagated to all files that include the user control.

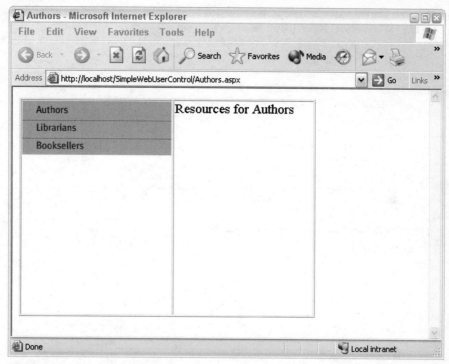

Figure 15-7

Converting a Web Page into a Web User Control

In addition to building a WUC from scratch, you can also reuse content from an existing Web page and package it up as a WUC. Let us see an example of how we can do that.

To begin with, let's take an existing Web page. We'll need a Web application to work from, so open up Visual Studio and create a new Web Application project called WebControls. Let's start with an existing Web page and work our way through creating a WUC from it. To speed things up here, instead of creating the page from scratch, we are going to paste in ready-made content from the accompanying files for this chapter.

By default, Visual Studio creates a Web Form called WebForm1.aspx. On the design surface, click the HTML tab at the bottom to view the HTML for the WebForm1.aspx page. It should look something like Figure 15-8.

```
<%@ Page Language="vb" AutoEventWireup="false" Code-behind="WebForm1.aspx.vb"
Inherits="WebControls.WebForm1"%>
<!DOCTYPE HTML PUBLIC "-//W3C//DTD HTML 4.0 Transitional//EN">
<html>
  <head>
    <title>WebForm1</title>
    <meta name="GENERATOR" content="Microsoft Visual Studio .NET 7.1">
    <meta name="CODE_LANGUAGE" content="Visual Basic .NET 7.1">
```

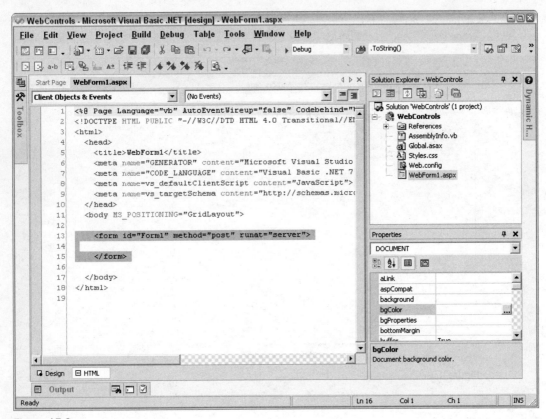

Figure 15-8

```
    <meta name=vs_defaultClientScript content="JavaScript">
    <meta name=vs_targetSchema
content="http://schemas.microsoft.com/intellisense/ie5">
  </head>
  <body MS_POSITIONING="GridLayout">

    <form id="Form1" method="post" runat="server">

    </form>

  </body>
</html>Top of Form
Bottom of Form
```

Notice the block highlighted in code. Using your mouse, carefully highlight the entire <form> block.

```
<form id="Form1" method="post" runat="server">

</form>
```

We shall now replace that entire block with ready-made content from the files accompanying this chapter's code. Making sure the above Form block is highlighted, select from the menu, Edit ➪ Insert File as Text.... In the Insert File dialog box that pops up, navigate to the WebControls project folder. Under Files of Type option at the bottom of the dialog box, select Text Files (*.txt) and click the file `WebForm1Paste.txt`. Finally, click Open to insert the contents of the file into your code. See Figure 15-9.

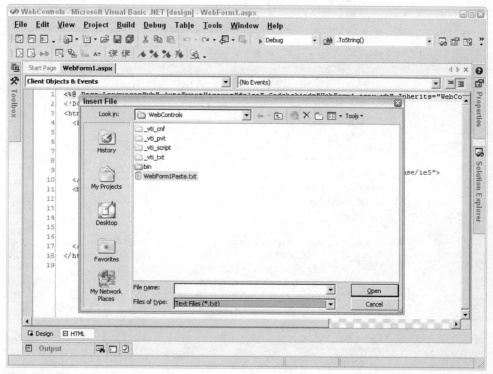

Figure 15-9

When you are finished, you should have the following code in your page:

```
<%@ Page Language="vb" AutoEventWireup="false" Code-behind="WebForm1.aspx.vb"
Inherits="WebControls.WebForm1"%>
<!DOCTYPE HTML PUBLIC "-//W3C//DTD HTML 4.0 Transitional//EN">
<html>
  <head>
    <title>WebForm1</title>
    <meta name="GENERATOR" content="Microsoft Visual Studio .NET 7.1">
    <meta name="CODE_LANGUAGE" content="Visual Basic .NET 7.1">
    <meta name=vs_defaultClientScript content="JavaScript">
    <meta name=vs_targetSchema
```

```
content="http://schemas.microsoft.com/intellisense/ie5">
  </head>
  <body MS_POSITIONING="GridLayout">

<form id="Form1" method="post" runat="server">
     <table cellspacing="10" width="99%" border="0" height="100%"
            style="font-family:verdana;font-size:10pt">
       <tr>
         <td width="200" valign="top">
           <table id="tblNavBar" bgcolor="#a5b2bd" width="100%"
                  height="100%" style="font-family:verdana;font-size:10pt"
runat="server">
             <tr>
               <td colspan="2">
                 <asp:hyperlink runat="server" id="hypHome"
                                navigateurl="/WebControls/Default.aspx"
                                font-bold="True" forecolor="white">
                 Creating Web Controls
                 </asp:hyperlink>
                 </td>
               </tr>
               <tr>
                 <td width="5px">
                    
                 </td>
                 <td>
                   <asp:hyperlink runat="server" id="hypExample1"
                           navigateurl="/WebControls/SubClassingAControl.aspx"
                           forecolor="white">
                   Sub-classing a Control
                   </asp:hyperlink>
                 </td>
               </tr>
               <tr>
                 <td>
                    
                 </td>
                 <td>
                   <asp:hyperlink runat="server" id="hypExample2"
                           navigateurl="/WebControls/ExtendingAControl.aspx"
                           forecolor="white">
                   Extending an Existing Control
                   </asp:hyperlink>
                 </td>
               </tr>
               <tr>
                 <td>
                    
                 </td>
                 <td>
                   <asp:hyperlink runat="server" id="hypExample3"
                                  navigateurl="/WebControls/Clock.aspx"
                                  forecolor="white">
```

```
                    Creating a UI-less Control
                </asp:hyperlink>
                </td>
            </tr>
            <tr>
                <td>


                     
                </td>
                <td>
                    <asp:hyperlink runat="server" id="hypExample4"
                            navigateurl="/WebControls/CompositeControl.aspx"
                            forecolor="white">
                    Creating a Composite Control
                </asp:hyperlink>
                </td>
            </tr>
            <tr>
                <td>
                     
                </td>
                <td>
                    <asp:hyperlink runat="server" id="hypExample5"
                            navigateurl="/WebControls/TemplatedControl.aspx"
                            forecolor="white">
                    Templated Control Sample
                </asp:hyperlink>
                </td>
            </tr>
            <tr>
                <td colspan="2" height="100%">
                    <!-- This row takes up any slack space at the
                        end of this table -->
                     
                </td>
            </tr>
        </table>
        </td>
        <td valign="top">
            <h3>
                Creating Custom Web Controls
            </h3>
            <p>
                The navigation bar on the left of the page is (or will be) an
                example of a User Control...
            </p>
        </td>
    </tr>
    </table>
    </form>

</body>
</html>
```

Switch to design view and you should see a nice table with a hyperlink control based navigation bar on the left, as shown in Figure 15-10. Save your project.

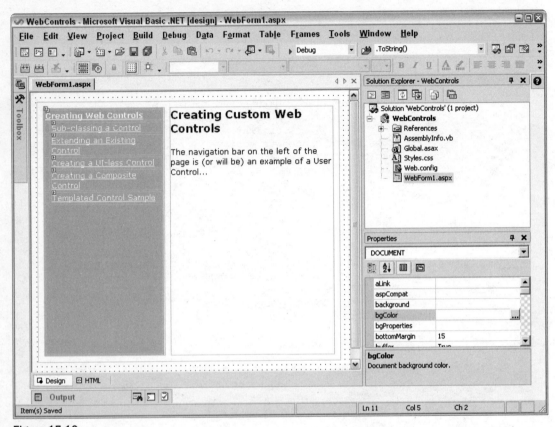

Figure 15-10

We are now ready to add some code to the Web page. Double-click the page to access the code behind for the page and insert the following code replacing the existing Page_Load event code block and save your page:

```
    Private Sub Page_Load(ByVal sender As Object, ByVal e As System.EventArgs)
Handles MyBase.Load
        Dim strPath As String = Request.Path.ToLower
        SetCurrentLink(strPath, hypHome)
        SetCurrentLink(strPath, hypExample1)
        SetCurrentLink(strPath, hypExample2)
        SetCurrentLink(strPath, hypExample3)
        SetCurrentLink(strPath, hypExample4)
        SetCurrentLink(strPath, hypExample5)

    End Sub
```

```
      Private Sub SetCurrentLink(ByVal strPath As String, _
               ByRef hypToTest As HyperLink)
         With hypToTest
            If .NavigateUrl.ToLower().IndexOf(strPath) > -1 Then
               .NavigateUrl = String.Empty
               .ForeColor = Color.Yellow
            End If
         End With
      End Sub
```

Run the project and Visual Studio displays `WebForm1.aspx` in your browser. Notice that the first hyperlink on the top is yellow in color based on our code. Don't click any of the other hyperlinks yet; those pages do not exist (see Figure 15-11).

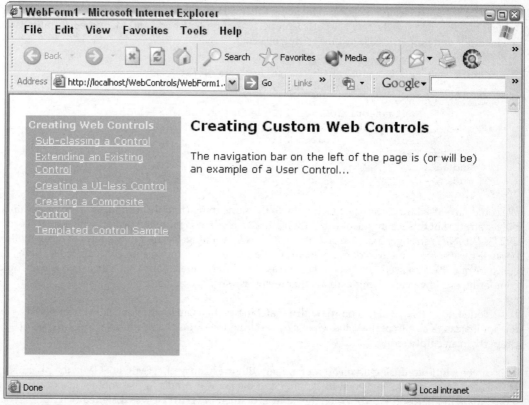

Figure 15-11

The code in this example is intentionally simplified so that we can concentrate on the specifics of creating a WUC. All the same, let's take a quick tour of the highlights.

The code works by comparing the path of the currently displayed page to the URLs specified for the `Hyperlink` server controls in our navigation bar. It does this during the `Page_Load` event by calling a helper procedure named `SetCurrentLink` and passing it the path of the currently requested page along with a reference to the hyperlink object that we want to check it against:

```
    Private Sub Page_Load(ByVal sender As Object, ByVal e As System.EventArgs)
Handles MyBase.Load
        Dim strPath As String = Request.Path.ToLower
        SetCurrentLink(strPath, hypHome)
        SetCurrentLink(strPath, hypExample1)
        SetCurrentLink(strPath, hypExample2)
        SetCurrentLink(strPath, hypExample3)
        SetCurrentLink(strPath, hypExample4)
        SetCurrentLink(strPath, hypExample5)

    End Sub
```

`SetCurrentLink` does its comparison by using the `String` object's built-in `IndexOf` method. We can write it this way because the `NavigateUrl` property is of type `String` and therefore naturally has all of the methods and properties of any other string object:

```
    Private Sub SetCurrentLink(ByVal strPath As String, _
            ByRef hypToTest As HyperLink)
    With hypToTest
        If .NavigateUrl.ToLower().IndexOf(strPath) > -1 Then
            .NavigateUrl = String.Empty
            .ForeColor = Color.Yellow
        End If
    End With
End Sub
```

We could have used the `InStr()` function to do the same thing (find the location of a string within a bigger string) but this technique of using the `IndexOf` method is more in keeping with Visual Basic .NET's (VB.NET) stronger focus on object-oriented programming. We had to use the `ToLower` method because the `IndexOf` method does not have an overloaded version that supports case-insensitive comparisons. We also used `ToLower` when we assigned the request path to `strUrl` so that we would be comparing one lowercase string with another lowercase string.

If the code finds a `Hyperlink` control with a matching path, it causes the control to be rendered as an anchor instead of as a hyperlink. It does this by resetting the `Hyperlink` control's `NavigateUrl` property to an empty string.

This can be a little confusing if you aren't familiar with the history of HTML. In SGML, the precursor to HTML, the "A" in an <A> tag stood for Anchor and the tag was used as a placeholder in a document (like a bookmark in Microsoft Word). When the tag was defined in HTML, it was assigned two duties: you could assign an anchor tag a name and use that name to refer to a given spot in a document (called an anchor), or you could specify a hyperlink reference for the tag and then click the tag to navigate to another page (in which case it's called a hyperlink). In order to differentiate between the two tasks that the <A> tag can perform, browsers typically underline hyperlinks and they leave an anchor tag's formatting alone.

When the `Hyperlink` server control goes to render itself, it takes into account that if its `NavigateUrl` property is an empty string, then it shouldn't add the `href` attribute to the <A> tag. This causes the client's browser to render the tag as an anchor instead of as a hyperlink.

If we tried to do the same thing with basic HTML, we'd have to insert an inline conditional clause in the middle of our HTML to determine whether or not to include the `href` attribute, for example

```
<% If Len(thisUrl) = 0 Then %>
<a id="hypHome">Chapter 15</a>
<% Else %>
<a id="hypHome" href="/WebControls/WebForm1.aspx">Chapter 15</a>
<% End If %>
```

This also means that we don't need to specifically turn off the text decoration for the anchor tag, as the browser will automatically turn off the underline for us.

We also want to give another visual signal that this link represents our current location in the hierarchy by setting its `ForeColor` to the `System.Drawing.Color` collection constant `Yellow`:

```
.NavigateUrl = String.Empty
.ForeColor = Color.Yellow
```

Note that we didn't have to fully qualify the reference to the `Color` collection, thanks to the `@ Import` directive that we put at the top of the page.

That's pretty much it. It's a simple example but it gives us plenty of room for enhancements later on as we look deeper into the features available in WUCs.

Now it's probably a good idea to make sure that our page works before we go through with converting it to a WUC. We could just open a browser and navigate to `http://localhost/WebControls/WebForm1.aspx`, but let's get our project set up for debugging first. Right-click `WebForm1.aspx` in the Solutions Explorer window and select the Set As Start Page option. Now, when we click the Start button, Visual Studio will compile the Web project, launch a browser window, start our Web application, and display `WebForm1.aspx`.

Adding a Web User Control Item to the Project

Hopefully, everything has worked up to now so we can go ahead and create our WUC. The first step is to add a file for the WUC to the project. Right-click the WebControls project in the Solution Explorer and choose Add ⇨ Add New Item... from the context menu. Create a new WUC named `NavBar.ascx`. The WUC file should now be open in the Design View. Switch to the HTML View.

Next, we'll want to cut the HTML and code from `WebForm1.aspx` that makes our WUC tick and paste it into our newly created `ascx` file. Add the inner table that holds our navigation elements by cutting it out of `WebForm1.aspx` and pasting it into `NavBar.ascx`:

```
<table id="tblNavBar" bgcolor="#a5b2bd" width="100%" height="100%"style="FONT-
SIZE:10pt;FONT-FAMILY:verdana"
 runat="server">
 <tr>
        <td colspan="2">
                <asp:hyperlink runat="server" id="hypHome"
```

```
navigateurl="/WebControls/WebForm1.aspx" font-bold="True"
                    forecolor="white">
              Creating Web Controls
            </asp:hyperlink>
      </td>
  </tr>
  <tr>
        <td width="5">
               
        </td>
        <td>
              <asp:hyperlink runat="server" id="hypExample1"
navigateurl="/WebControls/SubClassingAControl.aspx"
                    forecolor="white">
                Sub-classing a Control
              </asp:hyperlink>
        </td>
  </tr>
  <tr>
        <td>
               
        </td>
        <td>
              <asp:hyperlink runat="server" id="hypExample2"
navigateurl="/WebControls/ExtendingAControl.aspx"
                    forecolor="white">
              Extending an Existing Control
              </asp:hyperlink>
        </td>
  </tr>
  <tr>
        <td>
               
        </td>
        <td>
              <asp:hyperlink runat="server" id="hypExample3"
navigateurl="/WebControls/Clock.aspx" forecolor="white">
                Creating a UI-less Control
              </asp:hyperlink>
        </td>
  </tr>
  <tr>
        <td>
               
        </td>
        <td>
              <asp:hyperlink runat="server" id="hypExample4"
navigateurl="/WebControls/CompositeControl.aspx"
                    forecolor="white">
              Creating a Composite Control
              </asp:hyperlink>
        </td>
  </tr>
```

```
    <tr>
        <td>
               
        </td>
        <td>
              <asp:hyperlink runat="server" id="hypExample5"
navigateurl="/WebControls/TemplatedControl.aspx"
                      forecolor="white">
            Templated Control Sample
          </asp:hyperlink>
        </td>
    </tr>
    <tr>
        <td colspan="2" height="100%">
              <!-- This row takes up any slack space at the
                      end of this table -->
               
        </td>
    </tr>
</table>
```

This next step is very important, so do not forget to do it. Switch to the design view for the `NavBar.ascx` Web control and save your project. This enables Visual Studio to update the code-behind page for this control with all the server controls placed on the page. By this time your screen should look like Figure 15-12.

Double-click the Web control to expose its code-behind page. Move the code from `WebForm1.aspx.vb` to `NavBar.ascx.vb`:

```
    Private Sub Page_Load(ByVal sender As Object, ByVal e As System.EventArgs)
Handles MyBase.Load
        Dim strPath As String = Request.Path.ToLower
        SetCurrentLink(strPath, hypHome)
        SetCurrentLink(strPath, hypExample1)
        SetCurrentLink(strPath, hypExample2)
        SetCurrentLink(strPath, hypExample3)
        SetCurrentLink(strPath, hypExample4)
        SetCurrentLink(strPath, hypExample5)

    End Sub

    Private Sub SetCurrentLink(ByVal strPath As String, _
            ByRef hypToTest As HyperLink)
        With hypToTest
            If .NavigateUrl.ToLower().IndexOf(strPath) > -1 Then
                .NavigateUrl = String.Empty
                .ForeColor = Color.Yellow
            End If
        End With
    End Sub
```

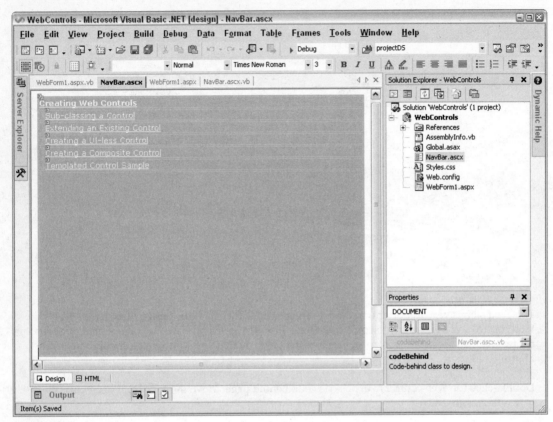

Figure 15-12

All that should be left in the `WebForm1.aspx` page are the `html`, `head`, and `body` tags, and the outer table.

```
<%@ Page Language="vb" AutoEventWireup="false" Code-behind="WebForm1.aspx.vb"
Inherits="WebControls.WebForm1"%>
<!DOCTYPE HTML PUBLIC "-//W3C//DTD HTML 4.0 Transitional//EN">
<html>
 <head>

        <title>WebForm1</title>
        <meta name="GENERATOR" content="Microsoft Visual Studio .NET 7.1">
        <meta name="CODE_LANGUAGE" content="Visual Basic .NET 7.1">
        <meta name="vs_defaultClientScript" content="JavaScript">
        <meta name="vs_targetSchema"
content="http://schemas.microsoft.com/intellisense/ie5">
 </head>
 <body ms_positioning="GridLayout">
        <form id="Form1" method="post" runat="server">
                <table cellspacing="10" width="99%" border="0" height="100%"
```

```
style="FONT-SIZE:10pt;FONT-FAMILY:verdana">
                    <tr>
                            <td width="200" valign="top">
                            </td>
                            <td valign="top">
                                    <h3>
                                            Creating Custom Web Controls
                                    </h3>
                                    <p>
                                            The navigation bar on the left of
    the page is (or will be) an example of a User
                                            Control...
                                    </p>
                            </td>
                    </tr>
            </table>
        </form>
    </body>
</html>
```

Reusing Code in a Web User Control

We only need to make a few modifications to get code from an ASP.NET Web form to work in a WUC. The differences between the two are:

- ❑ WUCs don't allow the @page directive, which is aimed specifically at pages.

- ❑ It isn't recommended to include <html>, <head>, or <body> elements in a WUC. It isn't forbidden, but it will make your WUC unfriendly to any page that already contains these elements.

- ❑ It is also recommended not to put <form> tags in a WUC. The reason for this is that your WUC could not then be placed inside a form on the hosting page (ASP.NET doesn't allow for nested server forms).

- ❑ You may optionally change any page event handlers from Page_EventName to Control_EventName. The WUC will still work whether you change this or not though.

You may wish to ignore the third recommendation if you are creating a login form or a self-contained search form. You know that you won't be nesting the control in another form, and you want the action and other attributes of the form to remain consistent throughout every instance of the control.

The @ Control Directive

The @ Control directive supports all of the same attributes that the @ Page directive does, with the exception of the AspCompat attribute and the tracing attributes (trace and traceMode). ASP compatibility and tracing can only be set at the page or Web site level. We haven't included either of these attributes in our navigation bar example so we don't need to make any other modifications to the @ Control directive.

As a point of interest, ASP.NET will actually interpret any `<%@ %>` directive that does not specify the directive name as an `@ Page` or an `@ Control`, based on whether it is in an ASPX or an ASCX file, respectively. So, the following statement would work in both file types without modification:

```
<%@ Language="vb" AutoEventWireup="true" %>
```

The question, of course, is whether this will continue to be supported in future versions of ASP.NET!

That's it. You've created your first WUC and, yes, they can really be that easy. Let's head back to the `WebForm1.aspx` page and add our new WUC to it.

Web User Controls and the @ Register Directive

We'll need to register our new control with the page before we'll be able to add it to the page. Place the following line at the top of `WebForm1.aspx` just under the `<%@ Page %>` directive:

```
<%@ Register TagPrefix="WebControlsuc" TagName="NavBar" src="NavBar.ascx"%>
```

Your page code will look like this:

```
<%@ Page Language="vb" AutoEventWireup="false" Codebehind="WebForm1.aspx.vb"
Inherits="WebControls.WebForm1"%>
```

```
<%@ Register TagPrefix="WebControlsuc" TagName="NavBar" src="NavBar.ascx"%>
```

```
<!DOCTYPE HTML PUBLIC "-//W3C//DTD HTML 4.0 Transitional//EN">
```

The `@ Register` directive tells the compiler how to identify the element tags for our custom controls and where to locate their code. The `TagPrefix` and `TagName` attributes tell the compiler the syntax we'll use when we create elements for our WUC. The `src` attribute identifies the file that contains the code for the WUC and can be either a relative or an absolute reference. So the page now knows that it should create any tag of the form `<tagprefix:tagname runat="server">` as an instance of the WUC found at the location specified in `src`.

In the left cell of the two cell table that we used to contain our original navigation bar elements, type in the following XML-style element declaration:

```
        <form id="Form1" method="post" runat="server">
                <table cellspacing="10" width="99%" border="0" height="100%"
style="FONT-SIZE:10pt;FONT-FAMILY:verdana">
                        <tr>
                                <td width="200" valign="top">
                                <Webcontrolsuc:navbar id="MyNavBar" runat="server"/>
                                </td>
                                <td valign="top">
                                        <h3>
                                                        Creating Custom Web Controls
                                        </h3>
                                        <p>
                                                        The navigation bar on the left
of the page is (or will be) an example of a User
```

```
                                            Control...
                                </p>
                    </td>
                </tr>
            </table>
        </form>
```

You could alternatively write the highlighted line as

```
<WebControlsuc:navbar id="MyNavBar" runat="server">
```

```
</WebControlsuc:navbar>
```

The page will accept either empty tags or tag pairs but, since the control that we've created isn't meant to contain nested text or HTML elements, the former is more appropriate. It's a strong indicator to anyone else who looks at our page that they aren't expected to include any additional content within our element.

Switch to the design view, save the project, and run it. You should get the same effect as before except now, the navigation bar is being served from our WUC.

As we've seen previously, WUCs are very simple to create. Creating one doesn't even require writing any additional code. They don't have to remain simple, though. In the following sections, we'll take a look at some of the more advanced techniques that we can use when creating WUCs.

Reaching Into a Web User Control

The way our WUC stands now, it is pretty much a black box as far as our page is concerned. Well, that's not entirely true. By virtue of being a WUC, it inherits the standard methods, properties, and events of the `System.Web.UI.UserControl` class, but there is no direct way to access the controls or the code it contains. It could contain nothing but the literal text "Hello World!" or it could contain a highly complex collection of elements and script but, without exposing any custom properties, methods, or events, the hosting page would never know.

So how do we expose custom properties, methods, and events? Pretty much the same way as we would for any other class. Any members of a WUC marked as `Public` will be available to the hosting page. It means that we can expose any variables, property statements, functions, procedures, and events we choose in a manner consistent with the rest of the VB.NET architecture.

Exposing Custom Properties

As an example, let's expose a custom property on our WUC that sets the background color of our navigation bar's table. We'll call it `BackColor` to keep it consistent with the rest of the ASP.NET server controls:

```
Protected _BackColor As Color = ColorTranslator.FromHtml("#a5b2bd")
Public Property BackColor() As String
    Get
        Return ColorTranslator.ToHtml(_BackColor)
    End Get
```

```
      Set(ByVal Value As String)
          _BackColor = ColorTranslator.FromHtml(Value)
      End Set
  End Property
```

When the WUC is rendered, we want the table containing the navigation elements to use this `BackColor` property. Therefore, in the `NavBar.ascx.vb` code-behind, add the following code to the `Page_PreRender` event:

```
      Private Sub Page_PreRender(ByVal sender As Object, ByVal e As System.
      EventArgs)
  Handles MyBase.PreRender
          Me.tblNavBar.BgColor = Me.BackColor
      End Sub
```

Finally, to actually see the effect of this background color, modify the WUC tag within the `WebForm1.aspx` from

```
  <td width="200" valign="top">
   <Webcontrolsuc:navbar id="MyNavBar" runat="server" />
  </td>
```

to

```
  <td width="200" valign="top">

  <Webcontrolsuc:navbar id="MyNavBar" runat="server" backcolor="red" />

  </td>
```

Save and run your project. The WUC displays the navigation bar with a background color of red (see Figure 15-13).

What we've done is to create a protected variable of type `System.Drawing.Color` and initialize it with a teal background color. Why not just create a variable of type string, though? By using the `Color` type, we're allowing our user to specify any of the named colors known to .NET, an RGB (Red-Green-Blue) value, a hex value, or an ARGB (Alpha-RGB) value. The `Color` class will also ensure that only valid named colors and color values can be assigned to our property. For instance, trying to assign either `PurpleHaze` or `#gg0000` to `BackColor` will generate runtime exceptions because they don't represent valid colors.

When we go to initialize the `BackColor` property, or to make use of it in an HTML tag, we run into a bit of a wrinkle, though. The `Color` class is based on 32-bit ARGB values while HTML uses 24-bit RGB or named colors. Now, if we were using `BackColor` to set the color on an ASP.NET server control, this wouldn't be a problem at all! The server controls automatically render any property that uses the `Color` type in an HTML friendly fashion, as either a hex value or a known color name. The HTML controls are another matter though. In order to have them render correctly, we need to convert from the ARGB values of the `Color` class to HTML friendly values manually.

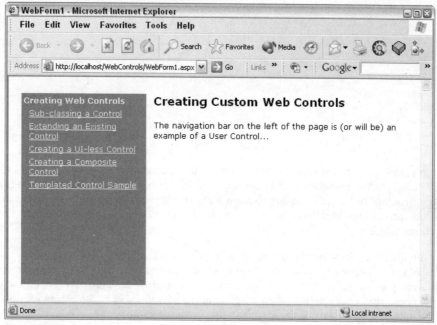

Figure 15-13

To do this, we can use the System.Drawing.ColorTranslator class like so:

```
Return ColorTranslator.ToHtml(_BackColor)
```

To set the BackColor property in our hosting page, we specify it as an attribute in the element for the control:

```
<WebControlsuc:navbar id="MyNavBar" runat="server"
                      backcolor="red" />
```

Next, let's set up a property that will allow the consumer of our control to specify the current link directly. We'll add a little spice to the example by exposing the property complete with an enumeration of the available controls. Then we'll finish it up by modifying our existing code to make use of the new property. We'll start by putting in a couple of private, module-level variables to help us maintain and control the use of the new property:

```
Private mblnLinksHaveBeenChecked As Boolean
Private mlclCurrentLink As LinkControlList = LinkControlList.Default
```

We've declared mlclCurrentLink as a variable of type LinkControlList and initialized it to one of LinkControlList's members. LinkControlList is the enumeration type representing the

`Hyperlink` controls in the WUC that we're going to create next:

```
Public Enum LinkControlList
   [Default] = -1
   Home
   Example1
   Example2
   Example3
   Example4
   Example5
End Enum
```

If you aren't familiar with it already, then the code for the enumeration type will probably seem pretty strange. The square brackets around the name of the first member of the enumeration (`Default`) allow us to take advantage of VB.NET's ability to allow us to use keywords and reserved words for the names of properties, procedures, and variables. That's probably not the most bizarre-looking portion of the enumeration though.

The only member that we've specifically assigned a value to is `Default`. That's because any enumeration member that is not specifically set *automatically* takes on a value of one plus the previous member's value. So `Home` is one plus the value of `Default`, `Example1` is one plus the value of `Home`, and so on. This behavior comes in extremely handy when we go to add a new member to the list, as we don't have to waste time manually renumbering the members that come afterwards.

> **If we were willing to start the enumeration list at zero, we wouldn't even have to assign a value to the first member.**

Now on to the property definition:

```
Public Property CurrentLink() As LinkControlList
    Get
        Return Me.mlclCurrentLink
    End Get
    Set(ByVal Value As LinkControlList)
        ' -- do some exception checking
        If Me.mblnLinksHaveBeenChecked Then
            ' -- already rendered
            Throw New Exception("The current link has already been rendered.")
        ElseIf Not System.Enum.IsDefined(Me.mlclCurrentLink.GetType, Value)
Then
            ' -- wrong format
            Throw New ArgumentOutOfRangeException("CurrentLink", _
                    Value, "Not a valid CurrentLink value! " & _
                    "Please select a member from the LinkControlIndex
enumeration.")
        Else
            ' -- all ok
            Me.mlclCurrentLink = Value
        End If
    End Set
End Property
```

In the `Set` portion of the property declaration, we do a little exception checking before setting the internal variable to the new property value:

```
If Me.mblnLinksHaveBeenChecked Then
    ' -- already rendered
    Throw New Exception("The current link has already been rendered.")
```

The first section of the `If` statement checks to see if our control has already called the `SetCurrentLink` method or not. If it has, then we throw an exception to alert the consumer of our control that it is too late in the control's lifecycle to set the current link.

In the next section, the `ElseIf` statement checks to make sure that the value that has been passed in to us is actually a member of the `LinkControlIndex` enumeration:

```
        ElseIf Not System.Enum.IsDefined(Me.mlclCurrentLink.GetType, Value)
Then
            ' -- wrong format
            Throw New ArgumentOutOfRangeException("CurrentLink", _
                Value, "Not a valid CurrentLink value! " & _
                "Please select a member from the LinkControlIndex
enumeration.")
```

> Even though the **System** namespace has been imported by default, we still have to qualify the reference to the **System.Enum** class to distinguish it from the Enum keyword.

If the hosting page has tried to set the index to an unacceptable value, for example 5, then this will cause our property to throw one of the standard system exception types. We use one of the constructor methods of the `ArgumentOutOfRangeException` class to expose as much information about the exception as possible.

This constructor takes three arguments. The first is the name of the argument that caused the exception, which we'll use to pass back the name of the property. The second passes in a reference to the invalid argument itself and exposes it through the `ActualValue` property of the exception. The third argument is a custom message that we'll use to give back an exception message that's slightly more informative than the default one.

If the new value makes it past our validation code, we set our internal variable equal to it:

```
Else
    ' -- all ok
    Me.mlclCurrentLink = Value
End If
```

At this point, the property is available to the hosting page but it doesn't do much yet. We'll need to make some changes to the rest of the code to implement it and, while we're at it, we might as well make a few optimizations. We can start by switching from using the `Load` event to making use of the `PreRender` event, instead. Just like with an ASPX `Page` object, the `PreRender` event happens well after the `Load` event and just before the controls on the WUC are actually written to the HTML output stream.

Cut all the code from the `Page_Load` event and paste it into the `Page_PreRender` event. When you are done, your `Page_Load` and `Page_PreRender` code will look like the following:

```
    Private Sub Page_Load(ByVal sender As Object, ByVal e As System.EventArgs)
Handles MyBase.Load

    End Sub

    Private Sub Page_PreRender(ByVal sender As Object, ByVal e As System.
EventArgs)
Handles MyBase.PreRender
        Me.tblNavBar.BgColor = Me.BackColor
        Dim strPath As String = Request.Path.ToLower
        SetCurrentLink(strPath, hypHome)
        SetCurrentLink(strPath, hypExample1)
        SetCurrentLink(strPath, hypExample2)
        SetCurrentLink(strPath, hypExample3)
        SetCurrentLink(strPath, hypExample4)
        SetCurrentLink(strPath, hypExample5)
    End Sub
```

It's time to implement the functionality behind the property. We're going to be replacing most of the existing code in the `PreRender` event procedure. Modify the code so that it looks like the following:

```
    Private Sub Page_PreRender(ByVal sender As Object, ByVal e As System.
EventArgs)
Handles MyBase.PreRender

        Dim strPath As String
        Dim i As Integer
        Dim mLinkControls() As HyperLink = {hypHome, _
                                            hypExample1, _
                                            hypExample2, _
                                            hypExample3, _
                                            hypExample4, _
                                            hypExample5}
        If mlclCurrentLink = LinkControlList.Default Then
            strPath = Request.Path.ToLower
            For i = 0 To mLinkControls.GetUpperBound(0)
                If SetCurrentLink(strPath, mLinkControls(i)) Then
                    mlclCurrentLink = CType(i, LinkControlList)
                    Exit For
                End If
            Next
        Else
            strPath = mLinkControls(mlclCurrentLink).NavigateUrl.ToLower
            SetCurrentLink(strPath, mLinkControls(mlclCurrentLink))
        End If
        mblnLinksHaveBeenChecked = True

        Me.tblNavBar.BgColor = Me.BackColor
    End Sub
```

The If statement expects a return value from the SetCurrentLink procedure. We'll be converting SetCurrentLink to a function shortly.

The first major change is that we need to be able to access our `Hyperlink` controls via the indices created in the `LinkControlList` enumeration. To do that we create the `mLinkControls()` array of type `Hyperlink` and initialize it with references to our `Hyperlink` server controls:

```
Dim mLinkControls() As HyperLink = {hypHome, _
                                    hypExample1, _
                                    hypExample2, _
                                    hypExample3, _
                                    hypExample4, _
                                    hypExample5}
```

The next step is to check and see if the `CurrentLink` property has been set, by comparing it to the `LinkControlList.Default` member. If it hasn't been set, then we loop through the array calling `SetCurrentLink` for each of the hyperlink objects, until we find one whose `NavigateURL` property matches the request path:

```
If mlclCurrentLink = LinkControlList.Default Then
   strPath = Request.Path.ToLower
   For i = 0 To mLinkControls.GetUpperBound(0)
      If SetCurrentLink(strPath, mLinkControls(i)) Then
         mlclCurrentLink = CType(i, LinkControlList)
         Exit For
      End If
   Next
```

This differs from the original code that we had because we are now using a `For` loop to walk an array of controls, where previously we had hard coded the calls for each control. This is obviously more flexible than the previous technique. All we need to do to add a new control to the list is to add it to the array and add a corresponding entry in the `LinkControlList` enumeration. This automatically includes the new control in the `For` loop. It also allows us to make an easy optimization by giving us a simple way to stop checking the rest of the hyperlink objects once a matching path has been found.

We'll do one more thing once we've found the current link and that is to set the internal variable for the `CurrentLink` property. Now if code in the container cares to inquire as to which link was actually set, it will be able to get the value back out.

If it turns out that the `CurrentLink` property has been set, we'll skip looping through the controls and call `SetCurrentLink` directly for the indicated control:

```
Else
   strPath = mLinkControls(mlclCurrentLink).NavigateUrl.ToLower
   SetCurrentLink(strPath, mLinkControls(mlclCurrentLink))
End If
```

We needed to force the path comparison to be equal in `SetCurrentLink`, so we set the `strPath` variable equal to the path of the control that we are passing in. It's a bit of a hack, but it keeps the example simple.

Finally, we have to set the `mblnLinksHaveBeenChecked` flag so that we can prevent any attempts to set the current link after this code has finished:

```
mblnLinksHaveBeenChecked = True
```

We do need to go back and change one more thing before we can test our new code. We've added an `If` statement up above that looks for a return value from `SetCurrentLink` to determine whether the item being tested is actually the current link. Since `SetCurrentLink` is defined as a sub procedure and not a function, we need to change its declaration and modify it so that it returns a value of `True` when it finds the current link:

```
Private Function SetCurrentLink(ByVal strPath As String, _
          ByRef hypToTest As HyperLink) As Boolean

    With hypToTest
        If .NavigateUrl.ToLower().IndexOf(strPath) > -1 Then
            .NavigateUrl = String.Empty
            .ForeColor = Color.Yellow

            Return True

        End If
    End With

End Function
```

To test our changes, add the following code to the `WebForm1.aspx.vb` code-behind page in the `Page_Load` event:

```
    Private Sub Page_Load(ByVal sender As Object, ByVal e As System.EventArgs)
Handles MyBase.Load
        MyNavBar.CurrentLink = MyNavBar.LinkControlList.Example3
    End Sub
```

If you get a compile error (a red squiggly line) under the text `MyNavBar`, it means that the code-behind page does not recognize the presence of our WUC. In that case, add the following line of code to the declarations section at the top of the code-behind page `NavBar.ascx.vb`:

```
    Protected WithEvents MyNavBar As NavBar
```

When you run the project, the current link will be set to `Example3` and you'll get a page that looks like Figure 15-14.

Exposing a Custom Method

Exposing a custom method is again a matter of taking a private sub or function and marking it as available to other objects outside of the current class. Let's try it out by creating a subprocedure that sets the style of all of the `Hyperlink` controls in our WUC. Here is the code for the procedure:

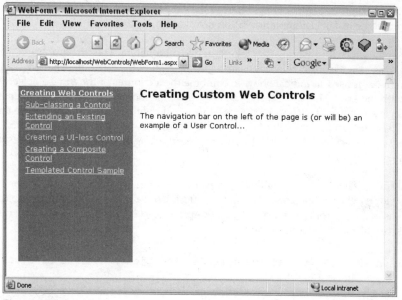

Figure 15-14

```
Public Sub SetLinkStyle(ByRef MasterStyle As Style, _
                    Optional ByVal Merge As Boolean = True)

    Dim mLinkControls() As HyperLink = {hypHome, _
                                        hypExample1, _
                                        hypExample2, _
                                        hypExample3, _
                                        hypExample4, _
                                        hypExample5}
    Dim hl As HyperLink
    For Each hl In mLinkControls
        If Merge Then
            hl.MergeStyle(MasterStyle)
        Else
            hl.ApplyStyle(MasterStyle)
        End If
    Next
End Sub
```

> The goal of an example is to illustrate the topic at hand clearly, and not necessarily to write examples that are fully optimized for performance. Considering how important efficient code is to Web application scalability, though, I would like to point out that, while having the If statement in the For loop is easier to read, it is not very efficient. In production grade code, this should be written with a top level If statement that determines whether to branch off and run a loop that merges the style or to run a loop that applies the style.

The important part for us right now is declaring the subprocedure as `Public`. After that, we've exposed the method and the rest is just implementation details.

The way that the procedure works is by taking in two parameters. The first is a `System.Web.UI .WebControls.Style` object that has been set up with all of the attributes that we want to apply. The second parameter is used to indicate how to combine the attributes of the `Style` object that has been passed in with the `Style` object of each of our `Hyperlink` controls. If we want to keep all of the nonblank style attributes of each `Hyperlink` control and only add attributes from the passed in `Style` object, we'll set the `Merge` parameter to `True`. If, instead, we want to copy all of the nonblank attributes of the `NewStyle` object over to each `Hyperlink`, overwriting any matching attributes, then we'll want to set the `Merge` parameter to `False`.

The procedure itself cycles through all of the server controls in our WUC looking for ones of the `Hyperlink` type. When it finds one, it casts the generic `Control` type to the `Hyperlink` type so that it can get access to the appropriate `MergeStyle` or `ApplyStyle` method. Test our new method by adding this to the script block in `Default.aspx`:

```
    Private Sub Page_Load(ByVal sender As Object, ByVal e As System.EventArgs)
Handles MyBase.Load
        MyNavBar.CurrentLink = MyNavBar.LinkControlList.Example3
        Dim objStyle As New Style
        objStyle.Font.Italic = True
        MyNavBar.SetLinkStyle(objStyle, False)

    End Sub
```

The resulting form should look like Figure 15-15 — notice that all the hyperlinks are now italic in style.

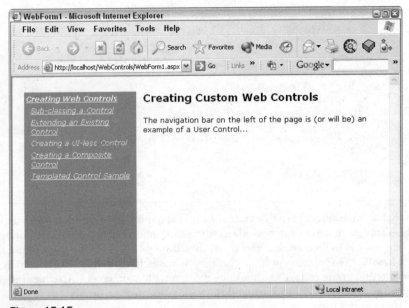

Figure 15-15

Creating an Event

At its most basic, creating a new event in a WUC is a fairly simple task. All it takes is a declaration of the event and then you raise the event from somewhere in the code.

> **Although, not strictly a requirement for creating an event, it is a strongly encouraged convention to provide a protected overridable OnEventName method that is called internally to raise the event rather than raising it directly. This convention makes our control easier to work with when it is inherited from, by allowing other developers to modify the event raising logic (that is, adding their own code or events that run before, after, or instead of our event).**

Add the following in the declarations section of NavBar.ascx:

```
Public Event CurrentLinkProcessed(ByVal Sender As System.Object, _
                           ByVal e As System.EventArgs)
```

This declares a new event called CurrentLinkProcessed, which we'll raise at the end of the Page_PreRender code. It's a good idea to keep the event signature (the parameter declarations) consistent with the ASP.NET standard for Web control events. That standard is to pass the object that triggered the event and an instance of a class that gives information about the event itself to the event handler. Typically, that class is the EventArgs class or a class that derives from it. You may use any class you like, but it really is the best practice to at least inherit from the EventArgs class.

Now, let's add the event raising method mentioned earlier:

```
Protected Overridable Sub OnCurrentLinkProcessed( _
                    ByVal e As System.EventArgs)
  RaiseEvent CurrentLinkProcessed(Me, e)
End Sub
```

Remember that, by marking the method as Protected, we are making this method available only to code within our class and to classes that inherit from it. By marking it as Overridable, we are allowing any classes that derive from this to sink, modify, or replace the event.

We use the RaiseEvent syntax to differentiate this from a call to an ordinary procedure. Having declared the event, we still need to call our event raising method from somewhere in our code. Add this line at the end of the Page_PreRender event:

```
    mblnLinksHaveBeenChecked = True
    Me.tblNavBar.BgColor = Me.BackColor

    OnCurrentLinkProcessed(EventArgs.Empty)
End Sub
```

Here we pass in an `EventArgs` object and we let the `OnCurrentLinkProcessed` method pass along the reference to the current instance of our WUC. Since we don't have any additional information about the event that we want to include, we use the shared `Empty` field (a public variable) of the `EventArgs` object to return an `EventArgs` object with its `ExtendedInfo` property set to `Nothing`.

So now that we've created the `CurrentLinkProcessed` event, let's see what it takes for the hosting container to respond to it.

Handling Web User Controls' Events

When we work with controls that have been created via tags in an ASPX page, creating event handlers is an exceptionally simple process. If we create a control programmatically, the process is a bit more involved but still reasonably simple. The good news with custom Web controls and WUCs is that nothing is different with event handling. We can use the exact same techniques.

So, for our example, we only need to write the procedure that we want to use to respond to the event:

```
      Private Sub MyNavBar_CurrentLinkProcessed(ByVal Sender As Object, ByVal e
As System.EventArgs) Handles MyNavBar.CurrentLinkProcessed
          Dim strMessage As String = "CurrentLink is: " & _
                                      CStr(CType(Sender, NavBar).CurrentLink) &
"<BR>"
          Response.Write(strMessage)

      End Sub
```

Notice that Visual Studio can automatically wire the code to the `CurrentLinkProcessed` event by using the `Handles` statement.

```
      Private Sub MyNavBar_CurrentLinkProcessed(ByVal Sender As Object, ByVal e
As System.EventArgs) _

Handles MyNavBar.CurrentLinkProcessed
```

If you omit that, then you will need to manually wire it up by specifying it in an `OnEventName` attribute of the given element:

```
<WebControlsuc:navbar id="MyNavBar" runat="server"
  onCurrentLinkProcessed="MyNavBar_CurrentLinkProcessed" />
```

The `UserControl` class that our control is inherited from takes care of delegating the event handler for us and all we need to do is sit back and watch.

> If you are used to the way that Internet Explorer wires up client-side events for us, it might surprise you to discover that you can't just create a procedure for a server event called **MyNavBar-OnCurrentLinkProcessed** and have it wired up automatically. While you can call the procedure whatever you want, if you're not using code-behind, you will always need to specify the name of the handling function in the OnEventName attribute of the element tag. If you are using a Code-behind class, then you can keep with the .NET standard and use the Handles statement.

We've essentially finished our WUC demo now and all that remains is to test it out. View the `WebForm1.aspx` page in your browser and you should get results like Figure 15-16.

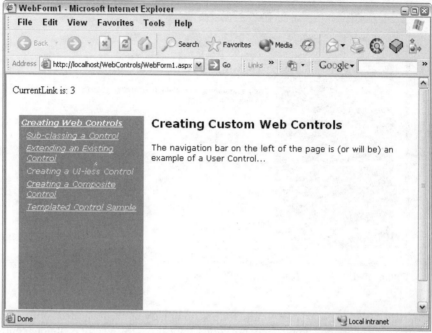

Figure 15-16

If you look at the top of the page, you'll see the `Response.Write` output indicating that the `CurrentLinkProcessed` event has fired. Since we've specifically set the current link to `Example3`, the index value for the `CurrentLink` property is 3, of course.

Comment out the line in the `Page_Load` event that sets the current link, so that the `NavBar` control will go back to determining the link based on the current location:

```
'MyNavBar.CurrentLink = MyNavBar.LinkControlList.Example3
```

Now view the page and you should get the output in Figure 15-17, instead.

As expected, the `CurrentLinkProcessed` event fires whether we manually set the current link or not. Here, we get the index value 0 indicating that `hypHome` is the current link.

> If you've used previous versions of ASP, you may be wondering why the
> `Response.Write` output is at the top of the page. This happens because the
> `CurrentLinkProcessed` event is firing before any HTML has actually been written
> to the output stream.

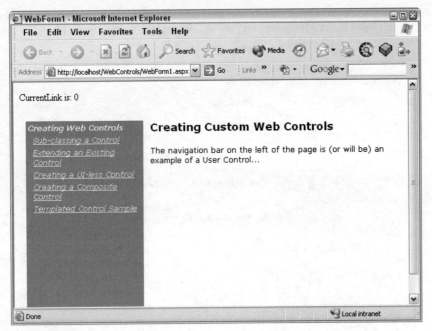

Figure 15-17

ASP.NET provides the `PlaceHolder` control for positioning dynamically added controls. The `PlaceHolder` control has no UI of its own but serves only as a light-weight container control for other server controls.

To use a `PlaceHolder` control, add the control from the Toolbox to the Design View of an ASPX page. Position the control where you want your dynamically added controls to go. Then, in code, call the `Add` or `AddAt` methods of the `PlaceHolder.Controls` collection.

The next couple of sections cover some additional topics that should be of interest to you as you continue to work with WUCs, before we move on to discuss subclassed custom Web controls.

Reaching Out of a Web User Control

Reaching out of a WUC can be a fairly simple process if all you are looking for is the standard members of the hosting page or parent control (if our custom control is nested inside of other server controls). The `UserControl` class that our control inherits from exposes a `Page` field and a `Parent` field, respectively, for accessing the container hierarchy above us. So, if you want to know what the value of the hosting page's `IsValid` property is, refer to it with the following syntax:

```
If Me.Page.IsValid Then
 'Code to use if the host page passed validation
 ...
Else
```

```
'Code to use if the host page did not pass validation
...
End If
```

Similarly, if you want access to one or more of the controls on a host container (maybe you're looking for other instances of your WUC), remember that you have access to the container's `FindControl` method and the `Controls` collection.

Casting to the Hosting Container's Type at Runtime

Be forewarned that if you want to access a variable, property, or method that you've added to a page or a hosting container, you'll need to cast the object returned by the `Page` or `Parent` fields to the appropriate type first. In other words, the `Page` and `Parent` fields return objects of the base class `Page` and `Control` types. Any custom members of the specific instance of the page or control in question are not directly available through these objects. If you want to get access to, say, a public variable on the hosting page called `strTestVar`, you can't just use the following code:

```
Response.Write(Me.Page. strTestVar)
```

If you do, you'll get a compiler error telling you that, "The name 'strTestVar' is not a member of 'System.Web.UI.Page'." So, in order to get to `strTestVar`, we need to get a reference to the class of the ASP.NET page itself instead of the reference to its base class, `System.Web.UI.Page`. We can't use the `CType` function to convert between the two because we would need the type name from the current ASP page. Since that type name changes whenever our control is hosted by another page, we need a method to convert one object to another type — one that works even if we don't know the type until runtime. The shared method `ChangeType()`, from the `System.Convert` class, can do this for us:

```
Dim objPageInstance as Object = System.Convert.ChangeType(Me.Page, _
                                                Me.Page.GetType)
```

`ChangeType` takes two arguments — the object you want to convert and the type that you want to convert it to. In this case, we get the object from `Me.Page` and we use the same object's `GetType` method to get at the type that the object was originally instanced from. Now we have access to *all* of the public members of the hosting page. We can rewrite our `Response.Write` statement as

```
Response.Write(objPageInstance. strTestVar)
```

As long as the hosting page actually has an `strTestVar` string field or property, we'll get the value back.instead of an error.

Other Web User Control Features

WUCs offer a wealth of features and functionality; more, really, than we could expect to cover even in an entire chapter dedicated solely to their use and development. So, to give the other control types their fair share of discussion we'll close off this section with a brief overview of some of the more salient topics.

Web User Control Namespaces

In the section that introduced WUCs, it was mentioned that they provide their own namespace. This means that we'll never have a naming conflict with any of the child controls created in a WUC. If you take a look at the source code from the example we've been working with, you'll find that each named element from our custom control has been given a new ID, one that is unique throughout the hosting page. This is accomplished by concatenating the unique ID of our WUC with the ID of the constituent element, creating a new unique ID!

To illustrate this, take a look at this portion of the source code that our WUC sample generates:

```
<a id="MyNavBar_hypHome"
    style="color:Yellow;font-weight:bold;font-style:italic;">
  Creating Web Controls
</a>
```

Notice that the client side ID generated for this element is the ID of the WUC, an underscore, and the ID of the hyperlink server control from within the WUC. This combination should guarantee us a unique ID on the client side for each of the server controls in the WUC, no matter how many instances of the WUC are added to the page.

This happens because the base `UserControl` class implements the `INamingContainer` interface, a tagging interface that instructs the hosting container to create a separate naming scope for each instance of a WUC. This interface will also come in handy later as we develop other types of container controls, since its use is not limited to WUCs.

Adding Web User Controls Programmatically

WUCs can also be added programmatically. Because they don't reside in class files there is a special method used to load them, though. The method is called `LoadControl` and it is available in every page and container control. The `LoadControl` syntax is as follows:

```
HostingContainer.LoadControl("SomePath/MyUserControl.ascx")
```

Where `HostingContainer` is the page or other container object that we want to add the WUC to, and where `SomePath/MyUserControl.ascx` is the virtual path to the file where the WUC is saved.

The important thing to keep in mind as you read the remainder of the chapter is that WUCs share almost all of the features and functionality of the class-based forms of custom Web control development. So, if you see something cool in the remaining portion of this chapter, chances are it applies to WUCs as well.

Creating a Subclassed Control

There are actually a couple of variations on basic subclassed controls that we can create. We can roll our own by inheriting from the `System.Web.UI.WebControl` class (custom Web controls), we can inherit from one of the controls in the `System.Web.UI.Webcontrols` or `System.Web.UI.HTMLcontrols` (extending an existing control), or we can inherit from the `System.Web.UI.Control` class (creating a control without a UI). We'll discuss them all, but let's cover a little bit of setup first.

Setting Up a Test Bed Project

Let's start off our class-based examples by setting up our Web control library and adding a test bed project to it. Create a new Web Control Library named `SubClassedControls` (see Figure 15-18).

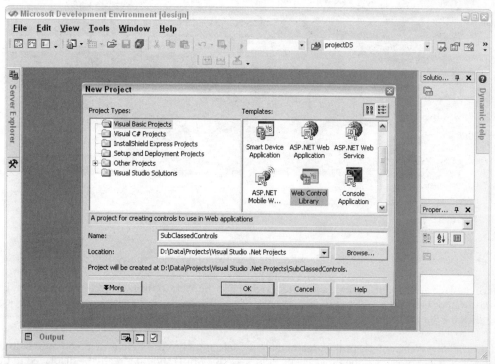

Figure 15-18

We're going to use the default namespace (which is the same as the project name) so we don't need to change any of the project settings. If you wanted to change the namespace though, you could right-click the project in the Solution Explorer and select Properties. In the General properties section of the SubClassedControls Property Pages dialog box is the text box for the Root Namespace of the project.

Select File ⇨ Add Project ⇨ Existing Project From Web from the menu bar. Enter the URL of the server that is currently hosting the `WebControls` Web application (although the dialog box only asks to enter the URL of the server, you can type in the full address of the application if you prefer). See Figure 15-19.

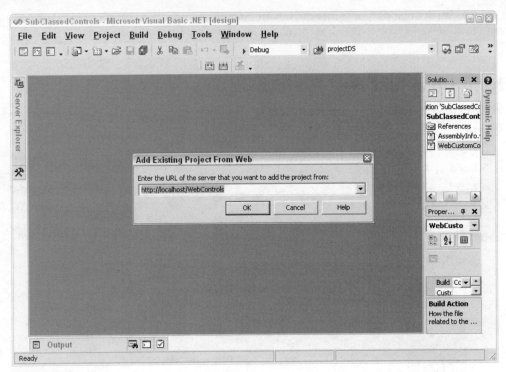

Figure 15-19

Open the `WebControls.vbproj` file when the Add Existing Project dialog box displays.

Once the Web application project has loaded, right-click the WebControls project in the Solution Explorer window and select Set as Startup Project. We need to do this so that we'll have an executable project when we click the Start button.

Right-click the WebControls project again, this time selecting the Add Reference menu option. In the Add Reference dialog box, go to the Projects tab. SubClassedControls should already be displayed in the list box (see Figure 15-20).

Double-click the SubClassedControls project to add it to the Selected Components list box and then click OK. We've now made it so that the two projects will be built together when the project is run and that the `SubClassedControls.dll` will be copied to the `WebControls` Web application's `Bin` folder.

Now that we've set up our test bed project, let's move into the next section and start authoring our first subclassed control.

Subclassed Controls and the Web Custom Control Template

To become familiar with the basics of class-based custom Web control development in VB.NET, let's start off by examining the custom Web control template provided with .NET.

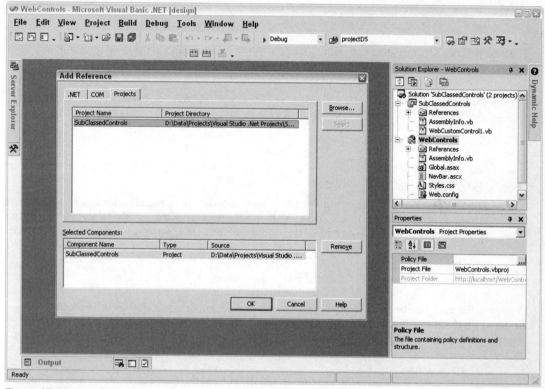

Figure 15-20

First, change the name of the class file that was created for us to `SubClassedControl.vb`. If the file isn't open already, double-click it to open it up in the code editor window. Now do a search for `WebCustomControl1` and replace each occurrence with `SubClassedControl`.

Now let's take a look at the code that has been created for us. Believe it or not, this is all the code we need to build a custom Web control. We could compile this code right now and it would work just fine. It might be a bit boring, but it would work.

These first two lines import some namespaces that will be of value to us as we develop our custom Web control:

❑ `System.ComponentModel` — contains classes for implementing and licensing components, including the `MemberAttribute` class that allows us to describe properties of our class like the default property and how our class should appear in the design environment. While it is possible to write a custom Web control that doesn't draw on this namespace, it would seriously hamper its use in development environments like Visual Studio.

❑ `System.Web.UI` — contains the ASP.NET classes, including the state management classes, enumerations for attributes, styles, tags, output caching, and persistence, and the text writer classes that we'll be using to write our control's output to the response stream.

```
Imports System.ComponentModel
Imports System.Web.UI
```

The next line declares our class and defines some attributes that tell the design environment how to represent our control:

```
<DefaultProperty("Text"), ToolboxData("<{0}:SubClassedControl
runat=server></{0}:SubClassedControl>")> Public Class SubClassedControl
```

Let's review these attributes:

❑   `DefaultProperty`—tells the design environment which property to highlight in the property window when a control based on our class is selected.

❑   `ToolboxData`—this attribute gives the design environment a template for inserting the element tags of our control when it is added to an ASP.NET page from the toolbox. If we are writing a control that is intended as an empty tag—like the `<br>` or `<img>` tags—then we would change this attribute to something like

```
ToolboxData("<{0}:SubClassedControl runat=server/>")>.
```

Changing the `ToolboxData` attribute to insert a self-closing tag does not change the output that is rendered for the client. If you need to override your control's closing tag characteristics, you should create a new control builder class for your control. For more information see *Professional ASP.NET 1.1* (Wiley, 2004).

Following our class declaration is the instruction to inherit from the base class `WebControl`. This one line gives us access to all of the properties, methods, and events that will facilitate the creation of the UI for our control, and it provides all of the plumbing necessary for the control to be hosted by an ASP.NET page:

```
Inherits System.Web.UI.WebControls.WebControl
```

> **Next comes a block of code to define a custom property for our control, its attributes, and the internal variable to store the property value in. It could just as easily have been called the `Message` property, but Text is more consistent with the naming conventions for control properties.**

```
Dim _text As String
```

The first portions of the property declaration are again attributes (or metadata) to help with the proper use of our control:

❑   `Bindable`—is used by the compiler to determine whether or not this property can participate in data binding.

❑   `Category`—is intended for the design environment and tells it how to group the property in the Properties window.

❑ DefaultValue—is metadata that identifies what the default value of the property is supposed to be. It is typically used by the design environment to identify when the value of the property has been changed.

> **DefaultValue** does *not* set the value of the property! It only describes what that value should be.

```
    <Bindable(True), Category("Appearance"), DefaultValue("")> _
    Property [Text]() As String
      Get
        Return _text
      End Get

      Set(ByVal Value As String)
        _text = Value
      End Set
    End Property

    Protected Overrides Sub Render(_
        ByVal output As System.Web.UI.HtmlTextWriter)
      output.Write([Text])
    End Sub
End Class
```

The Render Method

The interesting part is what happens when we override the Render method. The hosting container calls the Render method of our control when it is ready to insert our control into the *output stream*. The output stream is a buffer for holding the characters that will form our HTML response to the client browser. The page passes the Render method an HtmlTextWriter object in its output argument, which we use as the mechanism for writing to the output buffer (we'll come back to the HtmlTextWriter class in a moment).

Generally, you'll end up overriding one or more of the rendering methods of the base class (Render, RenderBeginTag, RenderContents, RenderChildren, or RenderEndTag) in most of the subclassed controls that you create. Overriding the control's rendering methods gives us the opportunity to create our own custom content; otherwise we'd end up with the base control's rendering of the control. In the template, the version of the Render method supplied overrides the base Render method to write literal text output. By doing so it prevents the WebControl from rendering the tags that it normally produces, and prevents any of the attributes that would normally be added to that tag from being rendered as well:

```
Protected Overrides Sub Render( _
    ByVal output As System.Web.UI.HtmlTextWriter)
  output.Write([Text])
End Sub
```

So, now we have a control that writes its `Text` property directly to the output stream without adornment or modification.

> This is not a recommended practice! Although you'll frequently see examples and demos that write directly to the output stream like this, it is a gross simplification. In real-world code development, you should only use this technique for outputting literal text. For any other output, especially outputting beginning and ending tags, use the specialized writing and rendering methods of the **`HtmlTextWriter`** class.

Writing a control where all of the output is done through the `HtmlTextWriter.Write()` method will either prevent or seriously hamper your control from enjoying the benefits of the ASP.NET framework. Specifically, this approach would mean that:

❑ The control would require its own attribute writing and style handling logic

❑ It would require its own client-side naming and namespace handling conventions

❑ It could introduce nonstandard behavior when working with other controls or ASP.NET pages

❑ It could even prevent the control from being properly rendered in browsers that support upcoming versions of the HTML standard

The temptation always exists to resort to using `HtmlTextWriter.Write` when outputting a simple set of tags or text. After all, if all you want to do is write a simple `<br>` or `<hr>` tag, it's easier to type

```
output.Write("<br>")
```

than it is to type

```
output.RenderBeginTag(HtmlTextWriterTag.Hr)
output.RenderEndTag()
```

It's a false economy, though. Aside from the fact that the utility methods of `HtmlTextWriter` can take care of so much of the coding, if you use them, you can count on having controls that will render correctly in browsers that are compliant with new HTML standards.

ASP.NET Delivers Different Code for Different Standards

We've already seen in the previous chapter that ASP.NET server controls change how they are rendered based on the version of HTML supported by the client's browser. The `Page` class manages this automatic process with assistance from classes that derive from `HtmlTextWriter`. When a request comes in from a client, the ASP.NET page determines the type of browser that the client has and uses that to decide which type of `HtmlTextWriter` object to create. Currently, if the client is considered to be *downlevel*, then the page creates an `Html32TextWriter` object to render HTML 3.2 compliant mark up. Otherwise, it creates an `HtmlTextWriter` object that will render HTML 4.01 compliant output.

So, as browsers come out with support for new standards, Microsoft (or third-party vendors) will supply new HTML text writers that override the utility methods and shared constants of the `HtmlTextWriter` base class to comply with those standards. Once the `Page` class has been updated to be aware of new subclasses of `HtmlTextWriter`, a control created with the utility methods will, in most cases, automatically render output that is compliant with the new standard.

The Rendering Methods Subset

When we look at examples illustrating custom Web control development, frequently the only output method of a control that gets customized is the `Render` method. While this technique works for keeping demonstrations simple, it can leave something to be desired when we want to start developing professional quality controls. To create a subclassed control that takes better advantage of the controls in the `WebControls` namespace, we need to examine the subset of rendering methods that the base class provides.

The Web control architecture is designed to allow fine-grained control of how we want to inherit rendering behavior. It's designed so that we can choose exactly the parts of the rendering process that we want to customize. The way that the Web control architecture works is that the base `WebControl` class (and all of the controls derived from it) provides five separate methods that correspond to the various stages of control rendering. In order of execution they are:

❑ `RenderBeginTag` — responsible for outputting the opening character of the tag and the tag name, this method also calls `AddAttributesToRender`. It uses the read-only `TagName` property of the control to determine which tag to output and uses it in a call to the `HtmlTextWriter`'s `RenderBeginTag` method.

❑ `AddAttributesToRender` — this method adds the identification, style, and standard tag attributes to the `HtmlTextWriter`'s internal attribute collections by repeatedly calling the `HtmlTextWriter`'s `AddAttribute` and `AddStyleAttribute` methods. Note that none of the `AddAttributesToRender`, `AddAttribute`, or `AddStyleAttribute` methods actually produce output; instead they prepare the attributes for later rendering, by the `HtmlTextWriter.RenderBeginTag` method, by adding items to the `HtmlTextWriter`'s internal collections.

❑ `RenderContents` — produces the content after the beginning tag and before the ending tag. If the tag contains nested server controls then this method will, instead, call the `RenderChildren` method and let it handle creating the inner content. It will not call `RenderChildren` if the tag does not support nested controls (for example, controls like the `Image` control).

❑ `RenderChildren` — handles creating the child control content, by cycling through this control's Controls collection and calling each `Render` method of each child control in the collection.

❑ `RenderEndTag` — outputs the closing tag if necessary through a call to the `HtmlTextWriter.RenderEndTag` method. Typically, whether the control requires a closing tag or not is determined by the `HtmlTextWriter` and the control builder class associated with the control. Whether your control requires a closing tag or not, it should either implement the `RenderEndTag` behavior or inherit it from its base class.

> The control's rendering methods are only responsible for invoking the associated methods of the **HtmlTextWriter** object. In all of the control's rendering methods, it is only the **HtmlTextWriter** object that actually adds to the output stream.

All of the methods in the rendering subset take the HtmlTextWriter instance for the control as their only argument. With the exception of RenderChildren, they each make use of public constants from the HtmlTextWriter class to determine how their tag is written (that is, HtmlTextWriter.TagLeftChar for the opening chevron of the opening and closing tags, HtmlTextWriter.SelfClosingTagEnd for the forward slash and closing chevron of a self-closing element, etc.).

As for the Render method itself, it acts as a wrapper for the other five methods. Its main purpose is typically not to produce the control's output but, instead, to invoke the RenderBeginTag, RenderContents, and RenderEndTag methods (with RenderBeginTag and RenderContents calling AddAttributesToRender and RenderChildren in turn).

Developing Subclassed Controls

We've been working with the Web Custom Control template so far, but now that we've examined the rendering methods in greater detail, why don't we redevelop the template to take advantage of them?

By overriding the Render method directly and not invoking the rest of the Web control rendering method subset members, or calling the HtmlTextWriter's rendering methods directly, the template creates a literal text control (for example, the Text property without any surrounding tags). If we want to create a label control, we need to modify the template's code to have it create tags and attributes, as well as output the contents of the Text property. The best way to do this is to override the RenderContents method and move the output write statement there. So remove the Render method override from the SubClassedControl class and replace it with the following code:

```
Protected Overrides Sub RenderContents( _
        ByVal writer As System.Web.UI.HtmlTextWriter)
   writer.Write([Text])
End Sub
```

With this one change, we go from a literal text control to a control that outputs a complete tag — including support for the full set of tag and style attributes. To see which tag we get from the default WebControl implementation, let's add a host page to out project and check out the results.

Creating a Hosting Page

Right-click the WebControls project and select Add ⇨ Add Web Form from the context menu. Call the new Web form SubClassingAControl.aspx. Then right-click SubClassingAControl.aspx in the Solution Explorer and select Set As Start Page.

To keep from adding a whole bunch of positioning attributes to our control when we add it to the design surface, right-click the design surface and select Properties. Now change the page layout property to FlowLayout.

Now we're ready to add our control.

Adding a Custom Web Control to the Toolbox

Our control's class declaration includes metadata that tells the Toolbox how to write the control's element tags to the page. It would be nice to see that in action, so let's add our control to the Toolbox.

We can only add compiled components to the Toolbox, so we need to build SubClassedControls into a DLL before we can add the SubClassedControl. Right-click the SubClassedControls project and select Build.

In the Toolbox, select the tab that you want to display the control on. Since it should still be relatively uncluttered, let's choose the General tab. Right-click anywhere on the General tab's surface and pick Add/Remove Items from the context menu.

In the Customize Toolbox dialog box, select the .NET Framework Components tab. Click the Browse button and locate SubClassedControls.dll in the SubClassedControls\Bin folder. Check its box, then click OK (see Figure 15-21).

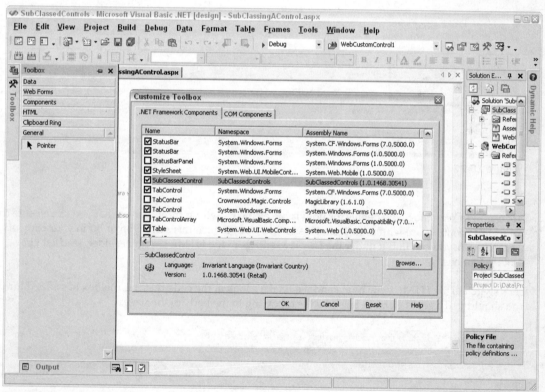

Figure 15-21

The SubClassedControl should now be displayed in the Toolbox. Drag it onto the SubClassingAControl.aspx page. The control should now appear on the page, looking as though we have added an empty literal text server control, as shown in Figure 15-22.

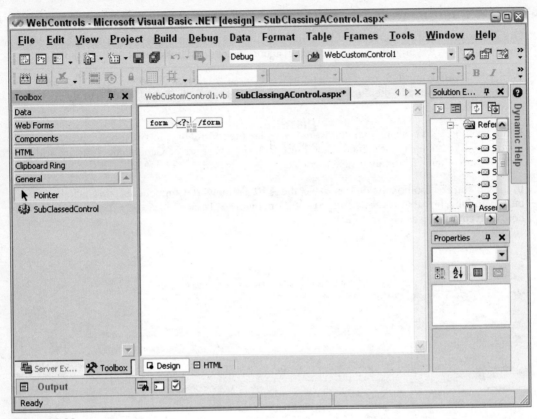

Figure 15-22

It is useful to keep the Show details for nonvisible elements setting turned on so that you can be sure that your server controls are within the form tags. If you want to turn this setting on or off in your copy of Visual Studio, you can find it under the Display settings in the HTML Designer folder, reached via Tools ➪ Options.

Let's switch to the HTML view mode and we'll take a look at the code that the Toolbox has added for us. You should find a set of element tags like the following in the body of the page:

```
<form id="Form1" method="post" runat="server">
  <cc1:subclassedcontrol id="SubClassedControl1" runat="server">
  </cc1:subclassedcontrol>
</form>
```

The element tag is based on the template provided in the `ToolboxData` attribute for the class. It looks essentially the same as the template, except that Visual Studio has substituted a tag prefix for the [0] placeholder and has assigned a unique ID to the element.

Of course, if you dragged the control onto the page and the page is set up for grid layout, you'll also have a bunch of positioning attributes.

> The Toolbox does not get updated with the latest value of your control's ToolboxData attribute when you rebuild your solution. If you change the ToolboxData attribute between builds, you'll need to remove the control from the Toolbox and then readd it before you'll see your changes.

Custom Controls and the @ Register Directive

Just below the @ Page directive at the top of the file, you'll also find an @ Register directive like the following code:

```
<%@ Register TagPrefix="cc1" Namespace="SubClassedControls"
             Assembly="SubClassedControls" %>
```

This version of the @ Register directive is a little different from the one that we saw in the WUCs section. For one thing, it doesn't have an src attribute—it has an Assembly attribute instead. The src and Assembly attributes serve the same purpose, though, and that is to identify the location of the controls in the namespace to the compiler and to the design environment. In the case of a WUC, that location was a file but, in the case of our subclassed control, the location is an assembly containing the compiled code for our control.

Earlier, we discussed why the compiler needs to know the location of our control, but why does the design environment need to know it? When we first open the page, Visual Studio puts us into a graphical design mode. Now, when we add a custom control to the page, Visual Studio wants to be able to provide a graphical representation of our control in the Design view. So, when we first enter Design view, Visual Studio actually instantiates our control and asks it to render itself—which is why the design environment also needs to know where to find our control.

The second reason that we need the @ Register directive is to define a tag prefix so that we can uniquely identify the controls that belong to any given namespace in an assembly. Visual Studio has picked a tag prefix for us, although it's not very informative. Let's use the tag prefix WebControlscwc (which stands for Custom Web Controls) instead.

We'll need to change it in two places. First, in the @ Register directive:

```
<%@ Register TagPrefix="WebControlscwc" Namespace="SubClassedControls"
             Assembly="SubClassedControls" %>
```

And then in the element tags:

```
<WebControlscwc:subclassedcontrol id=SubClassedControl1 runat="server">
</WebControlscwc:subclassedcontrol>
```

Don't forget to make the tag prefix change in both the opening and closing tags.

Specifying a Default TagPrefix for the Assembly

If you don't like the default tag prefix that the design environment provides, we can instruct it to use a default TagPrefix value. We can assign a default tag prefix for each namespace in our assembly through the use of the `TagPrefix` attribute. The `TagPrefix` attribute can be added to the `AssemblyInfo.vb` file and it uses the following syntax:

```
<Assembly: System.Web.UI.TagPrefix("NamespaceName", "TagPrefix")>
```

So, in our case, we would add the following to the `AssemblyInfo.vb` file for the `SubClassedControls` project:

```
<Assembly: System.Web.UI.TagPrefix("SubClassedControls", "WebControlscwc")>
```

If you don't want to have to fully qualify `TagPrefix`, you can add a statement to import `System.Web.UI` at the top of the `AssemblyInfo.vb` file.

Save the file, close it, and compile the project. The next time that a control from `SubClassedControls` is added to a new page from the Toolbox, it will also add an `@ Register` directive with its `TagPrefix` attribute set to `WebControlscwc`.

Using the Control

All right, so we've written our control and we've put it on a hosting page. All that is left to do is to give it some text to display. In the opening tag of our control, add some content in the `Text` attribute (feel free to type in "Hello world" if you're a traditionalist):

```
<WebControlscwc:subclassedcontrol id=SubClassedControl1 runat="server"
    text="Sub-classed control with attribute text!">
</WebControlscwc:subclassedcontrol>
```

Now start the application and see what we get in the browser. Your page should look very similar to Figure 15-23.

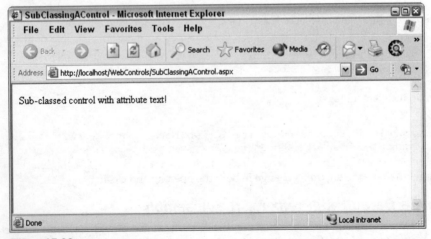

Figure 15-23

Now let's see what kind of tag the `WebControl` base class created for us. Right-click the page and select View Source. You shouldn't need to look too far to find our control's output. When you do, it should look something like this

```
<span id="SubClassedControl1">Sub-classed control with attribute text!</span>
```

So `<span>` is the default tag name for the `WebControl` class, but what if we had wanted our control to use a `<div>` or an `<h1>` tag instead? If we were subclassing from any other control, we would want to override the `RenderBeginTag` method and call the `HtmlTextWriter`'s `RenderBeginTag` method with the appropriate tag name. Since we are inheriting directly from the `WebControl` class, we can take advantage of the extra constructors that `WebControl` has to offer.

The WebControl Constructors

`WebControl` offers two additional constructors over and above the basic constructor. They are:

❑ `New(ByVal tag As HtmlTextWriterTag)`: this constructor takes a member from the `HtmlTextWriterTag` enumeration and uses that value to initialize the read-only `TagKey` and `TagName` properties

❑ `New(ByVal tag As String)`: this constructor takes in the tag name as a string and uses that value to initialize the read-only `TagKey` and `TagName` properties

So, if we want to render a control that inherits directly from `WebControl` as any tag other than a `<span>`, we should override the default class constructor and supply the appropriate tag to the constructor of our base class. To have our control rendered as a `<div>`, we'll supply the following constructor:

```
Public Sub New()
    MyBase.New(HtmlTextWriterTag.Div)
End Sub
```

We call the base class' tag key constructor instead of its tag name constructor because using a tag key offers the greatest extensibility. Should our control be hosted in any other form of output stream, we can supply it with a customized `HtmlTextWriter` class that maps any unsupported tag keys to an equivalent tag name. With a tag name, what we supply is always what we'll get!

Start the application again and let's see if we get the results that we want. The screen output should look pretty much the same but, when we view the source, we should see that the control has now been output as a `<div>` element:

```
<div id="SubClassedControl1">
  Sub-classed control with attribute text!
</div>
```

So far, so good. Earlier, when we set the display text for our new control, we used the `text` attribute to pass in the value to our control. Take a moment and change the control tags so that the text is now nested between them instead:

```
<WebControlscwc:subclassedcontrol id=SubClassedControl1 runat="server">
Sub-classed control with nested text!

</WebControlscwc:subclassedcontrol>
```

Now try running the application. You should get a parser error, as shown in Figure 15-24.

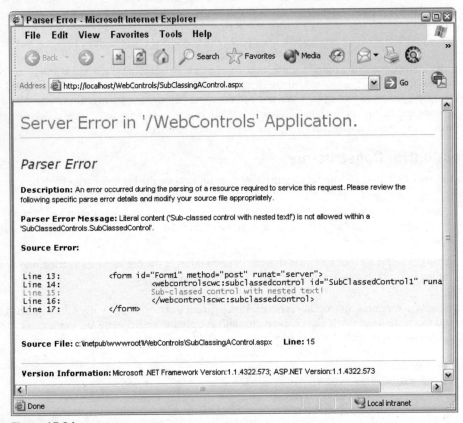

Figure 15-24

This is because Microsoft has disallowed nesting in the base WebControl class by default. It seems to be a bit of an odd choice, considering that most people who are familiar with HTML will expect to be able to nest content within our tags, rather than specifying content through attributes. Since we'd probably like to give them the choice to use either technique, let's see how we can change the default behavior of our control in this regard.

Allowing/Disallowing Nested Controls

If we want to allow controls or literal text to be nested within our control, there is an attribute that can be added to the class declaration. The attribute that we want is the ParseChildren attribute. We add it to the class declaration like so:

```
<DefaultProperty("Text"), ToolboxData( _
        "<{0}:SubClassedControl runat=server></{0}:SubClassedControl>"), _

        ParseChildren(False)> _

Public Class SubClassedControl
```

We are telling the compiler to add the attribute to the metadata for the class so that the page parser can determine at runtime whether the control is allowed to have nested (child) controls or not. Now, by default the `WebControl` class has its `ParseChildren` attribute set to `True`, which means it does not allow nested elements unless they correspond to properties of the control (typically this setting would be used in a data bound control like the `Repeater` control).

By setting it to `False` in our class, we are instructing the parser to convert any nested text into `LiteralText` controls, to instantiate any nested server controls, and to add everything to a collection of child controls for our control. After that, it is up to us as control developers to determine whether to render some, none, or all of the child controls in the collection.

> **Any nested tags that are not marked with the runat="server" attribute will be treated as literal text and will not be instantiated as HTML server controls. In other words, the elements will still be output on the client-side, but we won't have access to them in server-side script.**

Special Cases in Rendering Content

So now, by adding the `ParseChildren(False)` attribute to our class definition, nested content will no longer cause a parser error. Since we've overridden the method in the base control that would call the `RenderChildren` method, we still need to add code to our method to actually render that content. We need to go back to the `RenderContents` method and make use of some of the collections and state properties that we have inherited from the `System.Web.UI.Control` class.

The `Control` class, which `WebControl` inherits from, includes a collection to contain child controls, as well as two properties that indicate special states for that collection. The collection is (not surprisingly) called `Controls` and the two properties are `HasControls` and `IsLiteralContent`. The purpose of the `Controls` collection has already been discussed earlier, so we'll just take a look at the two properties here. `HasControls` and `IsLiteralContent` are essentially shortcuts that avoid the overhead associated with having to call upon the `Controls` collection directly. `HasControls` indicates whether we have any nested controls and it is equivalent to the following code:

```
Controls.Count > 0
```

`IsLiteralContent` checks for the special case where we have nested content, but where none of that content defines server controls. In other words, we have either plain text or client-side HTML (which server-side code treats as though it were literal text) between the beginning and ending tags of our control. To give us access to the content on the server-side, ASP.NET stores it all in a single `LiteralControl` and adds that control to our `Controls` collection. So `IsLiteralControl` is shorthand for the following code:

```
Controls.Count = 1 And TypeOf Controls(0) Is LiteralControl
```

It's more efficient to call `HasControls` and `IsLiteralContent` because they have already been evaluated during the parsing stage.

So, to decide what to do with nested elements in our control, we'll add the following to our overridden `RenderContents` method:

```
Protected Overrides Sub RenderContents( _
        ByVal writer As System.Web.UI.HtmlTextWriter)

    If Not HasControls Then
      writer.Write([Text])
    ElseIf IsLiteralContent Then
      writer.Write(CType(Controls(0), LiteralControl).Text)
    Else
      MyBase.RenderChildren(writer)
    End If

End Sub
```

The conditional statements above first check to see if we have any nested content. If we don't then, as before, we output the value of the `Text` property. If we *do* have nested content, then we check for the special case where the content doesn't have any nested server controls and output the `Text` property of the `LiteralText` control directly. Finally, if we have more than one control in the collection or we have one control but it isn't a `LiteralText` control, then we call on the `RenderChildren` method of our base control to walk through our `Controls` collection and render each child control in turn.

We haven't chosen to output the Text attribute when we have nested content because that is the way that the .NET server controls with a Text property generally behave.

When the only nested content that we have is literal text or client-side HTML, it's good practice to expose that content on the server-side by setting the `Text` property equal to the nested content. So we'll go back to the `Text` property procedures and modify them to make them aware of the `IsLiteralText` special case:

```
<Bindable(True), Category("Appearance"), DefaultValue("")> _
Property [Text]() As String
  Get
    If IsLiteralContent Then
      Return CType(Controls(0), LiteralControl).Text
    Else
      Return _text
    End If
  End Get

  Set(ByVal Value As String)
    If IsLiteralContent Then
      CType(Controls(0), LiteralControl).Text() = Value
    Else
      _text = Value
    End If
  End Set
End Property
```

This way, if code in the hosting container retrieves or changes the `Text` property it will get access to the text that will actually be displayed on the page.

Summary

In this chapter, we've taken a long look at the various forms of custom Web control development that are available in the .NET Framework. We've seen how the Web development process has been designed, from the ground up, to leverage existing skill sets and to take full advantage of the powerful new object-oriented features in VB.NET.

We've examined the basic structure of Web user and subclassed controls, and covered some best practices for control design. We also took a brief look at composite and templated controls.

This chapter should act as a good starting point for your exploration of the wealth of Web control development options that .NET has to offer.

Data Binding

One extremely common requirement of applications is the ability to extract data from a data source (a database, Web service, XML file, or whatever) and display it on the screen. Once there, the user expects to be able to use user interface controls to manipulate and change the data, potentially to save any changes back to a data source.

.NET provides *data binding* to make this process a little easier for the programmer. It allows the automatic population of controls with data from an underlying data source and also provides a mechanism for updating the underlying data source in response to any changes the user might make. In this chapter, we're going to specifically take a look at Windows Forms data binding.

Presenting Data

One basic way of presenting database data is in a tabular format. You've probably already seen tools such as SQL Server Enterprise Manager display information in this way as shown in Figure 16-1.

au_id	au_lname	au_fname	phone	address	city	state	zip	contract
172-32-1176	White	Johnson	408 496-7223	10932 Bigge Rd.	Menlo Park	CA	94025	1
213-46-8915	Green	Marjorie	415 986-7020	309 63rd St. #411	Oakland	CA	94618	1
238-95-7766	Carson	Cheryl	415 548-7723	589 Darwin Ln.	Berkeley	CA	94705	1
267-41-2394	O'Leary	Michael	408 286-2428	22 Cleveland Av. #	San Jose	CA	95128	1
274-80-9391	Straight	Dean	415 834-2919	5420 College Av.	Oakland	CA	94609	1
341-22-1782	Smith	Meander	913 843-0462	10 Mississippi Dr.	Lawrence	KS	66044	0
409-56-7008	Bennet	Abraham	415 658-9932	6223 Bateman St.	Berkeley	CA	94705	1
427-17-2319	Dull	Ann	415 836-7128	3410 Blonde St.	Palo Alto	CA	94301	1
472-27-2349	Gringlesby	Burt	707 938-6445	PO Box 792	Covelo	CA	95428	1
486-29-1786	Locksley	Charlene	415 585-4620	18 Broadway Av.	San Francisco	CA	94130	1
527-72-3246	Greene	Morningstar	615 297-2723	22 Graybar House I	Nashville	TN	37215	0
648-92-1872	Blotchet-Halls	Reginald	503 745-6402	55 Hillsdale Bl.	Corvallis	OR	97330	1
672-71-3249	Yokomoto	Akiko	415 935-4228	3 Silver Ct.	Walnut Creek	CA	94595	1

Figure 16-1

We can replicate that view more or less instantly by using the DataGrid Windows Forms control.

To start by showing an example of this, we'll need a new Windows Application project. Name the project `DataGridDemo`. In the default `Form1` form, add a `DataGrid` control from the toolbox. Set its name property to `datagridAuthors` and its `Dock` property to `Fill`. Your form should appear as illustrated in Figure 16-2.

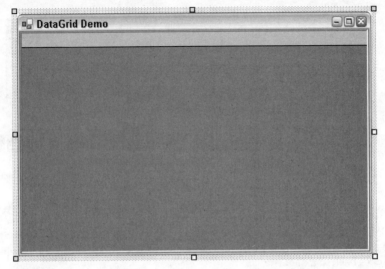

Figure 16-2

Add a `MainMenu` control to the form. Set its `Name` property to `menuMain`. Add a single top-level menu item to this menu. Set its `Name` property to `menuRefresh` and set its `Text` property to `&Refresh`. Your form should now appear as shown in Figure 16-3.

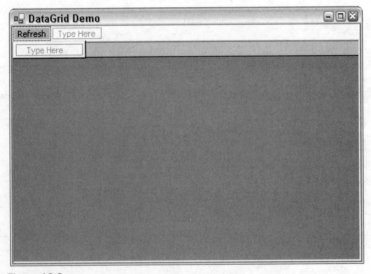

Figure 16-3

Double-click the new menu item to create a new event handler. Add this code:

```
Private Sub menuRefresh_Click(ByVal sender As System.Object, _
        ByVal e As System.EventArgs) Handles menuRefresh.Click
    RefreshData()
End Sub
```

Now, add a new Load event handler for the form itself and add this code:

```
Private Sub Form1_Load(ByVal sender As System.Object, _
        ByVal e As System.EventArgs) Handles MyBase.Load
    RefreshData()
End Sub
```

The RefreshData method itself simply connects to the database and populates a DataSet object. Before that, we need to add some constants to Form1. The first defines the SQL Server connection string and you'll need to modify this to suit your own needs. The second defines the SQL string that will be used to return a list of the authors back from the SQL Server sample database pubs.

```
Imports System.Data.SqlClient

Public Class Form1
    Inherits System.Windows.Forms.Form

    Public Const ConnectionString As String = _
        "integrated security=sspi;initial catalog=pubs;data source=localhost"
    Protected Const GetAllAuthorsSqlString As String = "select au_id,
        au_lname, au_fname, phone, address, city, state, zip, contract
        from authors order by au_lname, au_fname"
```

Once RefreshData has established a connection to the database and populated the DataSet, we assign the DataTable to the DataGrid control in setting the DataGrid control's DataSource property. This results in the data within the assigned table being added to the DataGrid so that the user can see the data:

```
Public Sub RefreshData()
    Dim connection As New SqlConnection(ConnectionString)
    connection.Open()
    Dim adapter As New SqlDataAdapter(GetAllAuthorsSqlString, connection)
    Dim dataset As New DataSet
    adapter.Fill(dataset)
    adapter.Dispose()
    connection.Close()
    Dim table As DataTable = dataset.Tables(0)
    datagridAuthors.DataSource = table
End Sub
```

Run the project now and the DataGrid will duly display the data as shown in Figure 16-4.

As you can see, using data binding to display a table of information in a Windows Form application is very simple indeed.

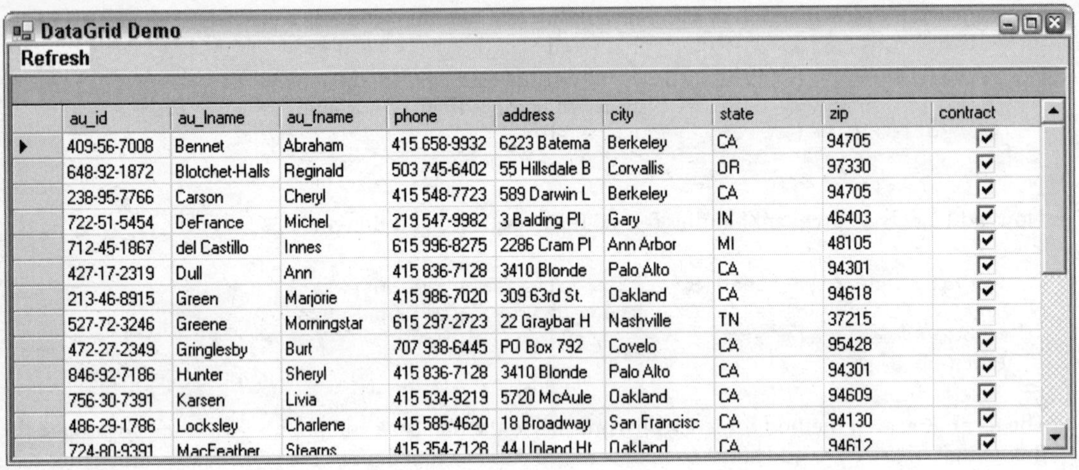

au_id	au_lname	au_fname	phone	address	city	state	zip	contract
409-56-7008	Bennet	Abraham	415 658-9932	6223 Batema	Berkeley	CA	94705	☑
648-92-1872	Blotchet-Halls	Reginald	503 745-6402	55 Hillsdale B	Corvallis	OR	97330	☑
238-95-7766	Carson	Cheryl	415 548-7723	589 Darwin L	Berkeley	CA	94705	☑
722-51-5454	DeFrance	Michel	219 547-9982	3 Balding Pl.	Gary	IN	46403	☑
712-45-1867	del Castillo	Innes	615 996-8275	2286 Cram Pl	Ann Arbor	MI	48105	☑
427-17-2319	Dull	Ann	415 836-7128	3410 Blonde	Palo Alto	CA	94301	☑
213-46-8915	Green	Marjorie	415 986-7020	309 63rd St.	Oakland	CA	94618	☑
527-72-3246	Greene	Morningstar	615 297-2723	22 Graybar H	Nashville	TN	37215	☐
472-27-2349	Gringlesby	Burt	707 938-6445	PO Box 792	Covelo	CA	95428	☑
846-92-7186	Hunter	Sheryl	415 836-7128	3410 Blonde	Palo Alto	CA	94301	☑
756-30-7391	Karsen	Livia	415 534-9219	5720 McAule	Oakland	CA	94609	☑
486-29-1786	Locksley	Charlene	415 585-4620	18 Broadway	San Francisc	CA	94130	☑
724-80-9391	MacFeather	Stearns	415 354-7128	44 Upland Ht	Oakland	CA	94612	☑

Figure 16-4

The `DataGrid` has functionality built in that enables it to understand the `DataTable`. Although we can bind all sorts of data (which is a topic we'll look at later in this chapter), what it's really doing here is getting a `DataTable` and saying, "OK, I know what to do with that. I know that I can get a list of columns from the `Columns` collection in the `DataTable`, and I also know how to iterate through the rows and display them."

However, at present with our application, what we can't do is change the data. Or rather, we can, but we cannot marshal the changes back into the database. What happens is if you change the data on this view, the column in the underlying `DataRow` does indeed get changed, because the `DataGrid` knows that when changes are made to the UI, those changes need to be passed back to the underlying, in-memory store of the data. What we need to do is copy the changes out of the in-memory store and put it back into SQL Server.

Saving Changes

When we load the data inside `RefreshData`, we disconnect the database connection after it is read:

```
Public Sub RefreshData()
    Dim connection As New SqlConnection(ConnectionString)
    connection.Open()
        '...
    connection.Close()
        '...
End Sub
```

This is great from a scalability perspective, but presents a slight problem when we want to save the data back. When we need to save, we establish a connection to the database again and give a new `SqlDataAdapter` to the rows that have changed (we'll see how to tell which rows have changed in a moment).

Before we do this though, we need a way of telling the application that the data does need to be saved. We'll do this by adding a menu item. What would be cool though is if we only enabled this menu item when the data had actually changed. First off though, we need the menu item, so add a new menu item to menuMain. Set its Name property to menuSaveChanges, its Text property to &Save Changes and its Enabled property to False. This is illustrated in Figure 16-5.

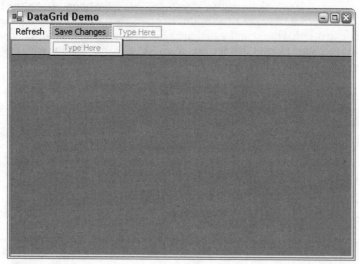

Figure 16-5

We can detect when the user changes the data by listening for an event on the DataTable object itself! DataTable raises these events: ColumnChanged, ColumnChanging, RowChanged, RowChanging, RowDeleted, and RowDeleting.

We'll hook into the ColumnChanged event, which will be sent when the user changes a value in any column. Add this code to RefreshData:

```
Public Sub RefreshData()
    ' ...
    connection.Close()
    Dim table As DataTable = dataset.Tables(0)
    AddHandler table.ColumnChanged, _
        New DataColumnChangeEventHandler(AddressOf ColumnChanged)
    datagridAuthors.DataSource = table
End Sub
```

Now, add the ColumnChanged method:

```
Protected Sub ColumnChanged(ByVal sender As Object, _
                ByVal e As DataColumnChangeEventArgs)
    menuSaveChanges.Enabled = True
End Sub
```

Add this handler to menuSaveChanges.

```
Private Sub menuSaveChanges_Click(ByVal sender As System.Object, _
                    ByVal e As System.EventArgs) Handles _
                    menuSaveChanges.Click
    SaveChanges()
End Sub
```

The job of `SaveChanges` is to look through every `DataRow` on the bound `DataTable` examining the `State` property. If this is not `DataRowState.Unchanged`, then we need to ask a new `SqlDataAdapter` to marshal the changes back into the database. First off, when we start walking the collection we add any changed rows that we find to an `ArrayList`. If at the end of walking the collection we find that there are no changed rows, we return:

```
Public Sub SaveChanges()
    Dim table As DataTable = CType(datagridAuthors.DataSource, DataTable)
    Dim changedRows As New ArrayList

    For Each row As DataRow In table.Rows
        If row.RowState <> DataRowState.Unchanged Then
            changedRows.Add(row)
    End If
Next

If changedRows.Count = 0 Then
    Return
End If
```

Once we have the list, we connect to the database:

```
Dim connection As New SqlConnection(ConnectionString)
connection.Open()
```

We used a `SqlDataAdapter` to get the data out of the database and into a `DataSet`, and so now we're going to do the reverse — that is, we're going to use a `SqlDataAdapter` to put data back into the database. To do this, we only need the original SELECT SQL statement that we used to retrieve the data (this technique only works if we select a single table at a time). We can use a `System.Data` `.SqlClient.SqlCommandBuilder` object to examine that SELECT SQL statement and build us a new UPDATE SQL statement (which, if you ask me, is pretty smart!). The object will also build us new INSERT and DELETE statements too. To do this, we just create a new `SqlCommandBuilder` and pass the `SqlDataAdapter` into the constructor:

```
Dim adapter As New SqlDataAdapter(GetAllAuthorsSqlString, connection)
Dim builder As New SqlCommandBuilder(adapter)
```

We use the `Update` method on `SqlDataAdapter` to provide the data that should be updated (somewhat confusingly, this "Update" method will also "Insert" and "Delete" rows as appropriate). If we give it an entire `DataSet`, what the adapter actually does is look through all the rows on all the tables in much the same way as we've done in the first part of this method. Instead, we'll use the alternative version of this method that takes an array of `DataRow` objects:

```
Dim rows() As DataRow = _
            CType(changedRows.ToArray(GetType(DataRow)),DataRow())
adapter.Update(rows)
```

Finally, we close the connection and disable the menu item:

```
        ' close...
        adapter.Dispose()
        connection.Close()

        ' flag...
        menuSaveChanges.Enabled = False
    End Sub
```

Now try running the project again. In this screen shot, I've changed Cheryl Carson's city from `Berkeley, CA` to `Tempe, AZ` as shown in Figure 16-6.

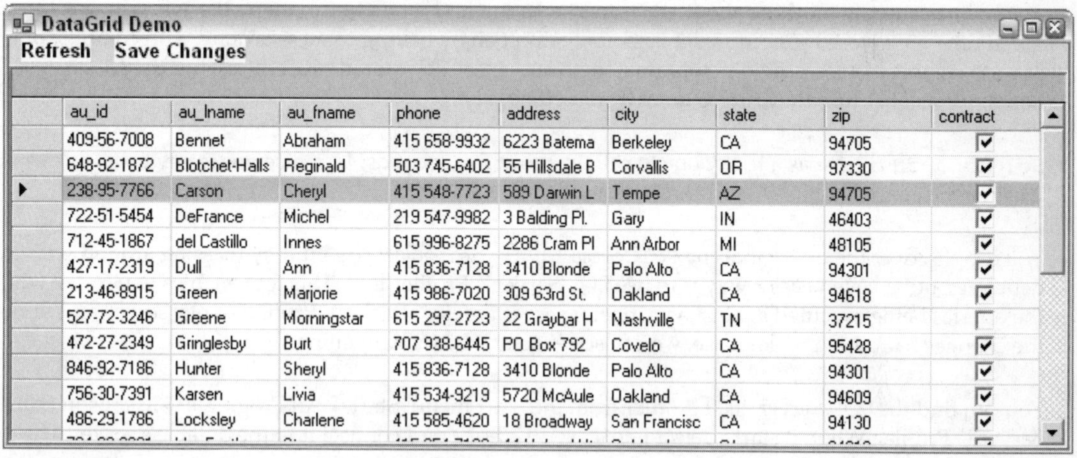

au_id	au_lname	au_fname	phone	address	city	state	zip	contract
409-56-7008	Bennet	Abraham	415 658-9932	6223 Batema	Berkeley	CA	94705	✓
648-92-1872	Blotchet-Halls	Reginald	503 745-6402	55 Hillsdale B	Corvallis	OR	97330	✓
238-95-7766	Carson	Cheryl	415 548-7723	589 Darwin L	Tempe	AZ	94705	✓
722-51-5454	DeFrance	Michel	219 547-9982	3 Balding Pl.	Gary	IN	46403	✓
712-45-1867	del Castillo	Innes	615 996-8275	2286 Cram Pl	Ann Arbor	MI	48105	✓
427-17-2319	Dull	Ann	415 836-7128	3410 Blonde	Palo Alto	CA	94301	✓
213-46-8915	Green	Marjorie	415 986-7020	309 63rd St.	Oakland	CA	94618	✓
527-72-3246	Greene	Morningstar	615 297-2723	22 Graybar H	Nashville	TN	37215	
472-27-2349	Gringlesby	Burt	707 938-6445	PO Box 792	Covelo	CA	95428	✓
846-92-7186	Hunter	Sheryl	415 836-7128	3410 Blonde	Palo Alto	CA	94301	✓
756-30-7391	Karsen	Livia	415 534-9219	5720 McAule	Oakland	CA	94609	✓
486-29-1786	Locksley	Charlene	415 585-4620	18 Broadway	San Francisc	CA	94130	✓

Figure 16-6

If you click the Save Changes button, the data will then be saved back into the database. You need to select another row in the `DataGrid` in order for the changes to be made to the `DataSet`, so if you don't do this Save Changes will have no effect. If you click Refresh, this will prove that the data has indeed been changed, but the skeptical amongst you may wish to look in the database itself using the SQL Server Enterprise Manager, as displayed in Figure 16-7.

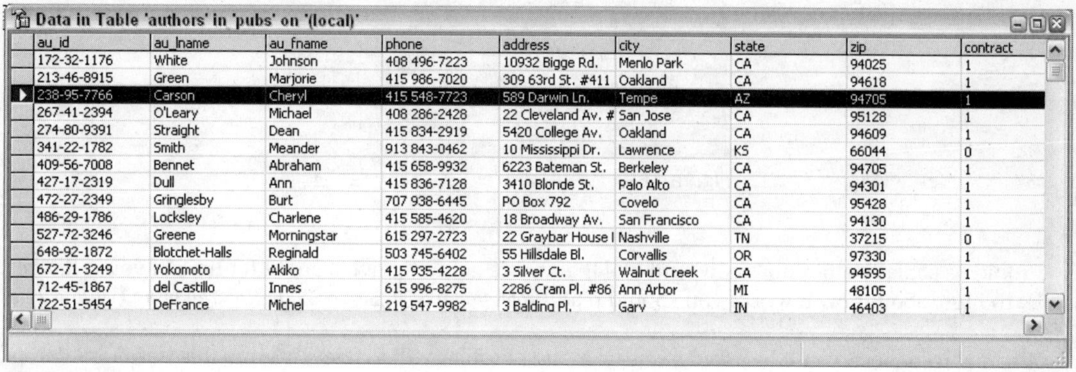

au_id	au_lname	au_fname	phone	address	city	state	zip	contract
172-32-1176	White	Johnson	408 496-7223	10932 Bigge Rd.	Menlo Park	CA	94025	1
213-46-8915	Green	Marjorie	415 986-7020	309 63rd St. #411	Oakland	CA	94618	1
238-95-7766	Carson	Cheryl	415 548-7723	589 Darwin Ln.	Tempe	AZ	94705	1
267-41-2394	O'Leary	Michael	408 286-2428	22 Cleveland Av. #	San Jose	CA	95128	1
274-80-9391	Straight	Dean	415 834-2919	5420 College Av.	Oakland	CA	94609	1
341-22-1782	Smith	Meander	913 843-0462	10 Mississippi Dr.	Lawrence	KS	66044	0
409-56-7008	Bennet	Abraham	415 658-9932	6223 Bateman St.	Berkeley	CA	94705	1
427-17-2319	Dull	Ann	415 836-7128	3410 Blonde St.	Palo Alto	CA	94301	1
472-27-2349	Gringlesby	Burt	707 938-6445	PO Box 792	Covelo	CA	95428	1
486-29-1786	Locksley	Charlene	415 585-4620	18 Broadway Av.	San Francisco	CA	94130	1
527-72-3246	Greene	Morningstar	615 297-2723	22 Graybar House I	Nashville	TN	37215	0
648-92-1872	Blotchet-Halls	Reginald	503 745-6402	55 Hillsdale Bl.	Corvallis	OR	97330	1
672-71-3249	Yokomoto	Akiko	415 935-4228	3 Silver Ct.	Walnut Creek	CA	94595	1
712-45-1867	del Castillo	Innes	615 996-8275	2286 Cram Pl. #86	Ann Arbor	MI	48105	1
722-51-5454	DeFrance	Michel	219 547-9982	3 Balding Pl.	Gary	IN	46403	1

Figure 16-7

Profiling the Update Statement

I personally get a little concerned when I ask .NET to do something for me and I have no idea what it's doing behind the scenes. This is particularly important when thinking about database access. For example, when I ask `SqlDataAdapter` to fill a `DataSet` for me, I give it the SQL statement to use or (better yet) I give it a stored procedure to use. However, when I ask `SqlDataAdapter` to persist the changes back into the database, I'm using `SqlCommandBuilder` and, frankly, the fact that I don't know what that's doing concerns me.

Database access is one of those things in commercial software development that's both absolutely necessary, but can cause a tremendous amount of problems. A badly formed SQL query has the potential to kill the performance of an otherwise well-written application, and it's for this reason that we spend so much time carefully thinking about what queries to run and when to run them. It's also why we spend so much time with stored procedures. I personally don't enjoy having to mess around with complex blocks of code responsible for providing parameters to and executing stored procedures, but they are a necessary evil because they run so quickly and efficiently.

`SqlCommandBuilder` is a tricky one to call. In about five seconds, I can use one in my code, but what is it actually doing?

You can discover the query that the `SqlCommandBuilder` object has built by messing around with the debugger, but an even easier way is to use SQL Server's Profiler tool. This tool enables you to see what the queries being executed against a particular server are. By attaching Profiler to our server and saving the changes back into the database, we can see exactly what is happening.

You can find the SQL Server 2000 Profiler from the Start menu: Start ⇨ All Programs ⇨ Microsoft SQL Server ⇨ Profiler. When it starts, select File ⇨ New ⇨ Trace and connect it to the database server. The dialog box is shown in Figure 16-8.

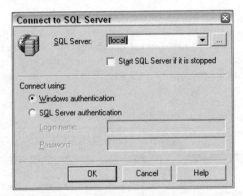

Figure 16-8

Profiler is actually a far more powerful tool than we're going to give it credit for here. If you'd like to learn more about how it works you should read *Professional SQL Server 2000 Programming* (Wiley, 2000).

When you connect, you'll be asked to create a *trace*. Profiler will save events into this trace for later use, although in our case we're just going to watch the events unfold on the display as we run our application.

Click Run. A ton of stuff will be displayed on the screen, which we can ignore. Select Edit ➪ Clear Trace Window.

Run the DataGrid application. At this point, the application will connect to the database and query for the authors. If you look at the Profiler (shown in Figure 16-9), you'll find some trace events. You can ignore the ones coming from SQLAgent ➪ Alert Engine.. But, the ones coming from .Net SqlClient Data Provider are important. These are the ones from our application.

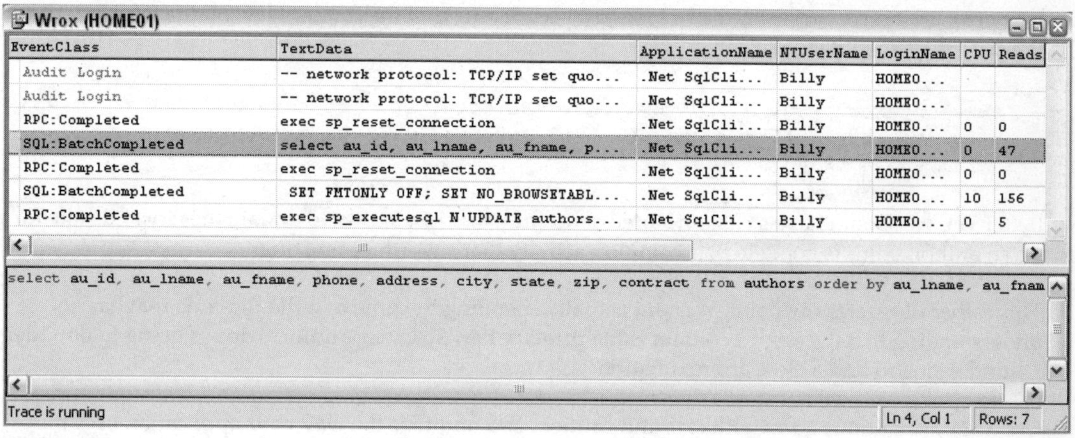

EventClass	TextData	ApplicationName	NTUserName	LoginName	CPU	Reads
Audit Login	-- network protocol: TCP/IP set quo...	.Net SqlCli...	Billy	HOMEO...		
Audit Login	-- network protocol: TCP/IP set quo...	.Net SqlCli...	Billy	HOMEO...		
RPC:Completed	exec sp_reset_connection	.Net SqlCli...	Billy	HOMEO...	0	0
SQL:BatchCompleted	select au_id, au_lname, au_fname, p...	.Net SqlCli...	Billy	HOMEO...	0	47
RPC:Completed	exec sp_reset_connection	.Net SqlCli...	Billy	HOMEO...	0	0
SQL:BatchCompleted	SET FMTONLY OFF; SET NO_BROWSETABL...	.Net SqlCli...	Billy	HOMEO...	10	156
RPC:Completed	exec sp_executesql N'UPDATE authors...	.Net SqlCli...	Billy	HOMEO...	0	5

```
select au_id, au_lname, au_fname, phone, address, city, state, zip, contract from authors order by au_lname, au_fnam
```

Trace is running   Ln 4, Col 1   Rows: 7

Figure 16-9

Look at the second .NET event. It'll look like the following code:

```
exec sp_executesql N'select au_id, au_lname, au_fname, phone,
address, city, state, zip, contract from authors order by au_lname,
au_fname'
```

That's exactly the statement that we supplied, with the curious exception that SQL Server appears to be running a built-in stored procedure called sp_executesql and passing in our SQL statement as a parameter. This is "one of those things" and nothing to worry about.

Change some data in the DataGrid application and select Save Changes. You'll find an UPDATE statement that looks like this:

```
exec sp_executesql N'UPDATE authors SET city = @p1, state = @p2 WHERE
((au_id = @p3) AND ((au_lname IS NULL AND @p4 IS NULL) OR (au_lname =
@p5)) AND ((au_fname IS NULL AND @p6 IS NULL) OR (au_fname = @p7))
AND ((phone IS NULL AND @p8 IS NULL) OR (phone = @p9)) AND ((address IS NULL
AND @p10 IS NULL) OR (address = @p11)) AND ((city IS NULL AND @p12 IS NULL)
OR (city = @p13)) AND ((state IS NULL AND @p14 IS NULL) OR (state = @p15))
AND ((zip IS NULL AND @p16 IS NULL) OR (zip = @p17)) AND ((contract IS NULL
AND @p18 IS NULL) OR (contract = @p19)) )', N'@p1 varchar(5),@p2 char(2),@p3
varchar(11),@p4 varchar(6),@p5 varchar(6),@p6 varchar(6),@p7 varchar(6),@p8
char(12),@p9 char(12),@p10 varchar(14),@p11 varchar(14),@p12 varchar(7),@p13
varchar(7),@p14 char(2),@p15 char(2),@p16 char(5),@p17 char(5),@p18 bit,@p19
bit', @p1 = 'Tempe', @p2 = 'AZ', @p3 = '238-95-7766', @p4 = 'Carson', @p5 =
```

```
'Carson', @p6 = 'Cheryl', @p7 = 'Cheryl', @p8 = '415 548-7723', @p9 = '415
548-7723', @p10 = '589 Darwin Ln.', @p11 = '589 Darwin Ln.', @p12 =
'Berkley', @p13 = 'Berkley', @p14 = 'CA', @p15 = 'CA', @p16 = '94705', @p17 =
'94705', @p18 = 1, @p19 = 1
```

That's a long SQL statement! The first line is telling us that SqlCommandBuilder is only changing the values for city and state, which is right because when I ran this statement I changed city from Berkeley to Scottsdale and state from CA to AZ. However, the rest of the statement is a bit of mishmash. It appears that SqlCommandBuilder couldn't work out what the primary key on the table was, because the statement should look like this:

```
exec sp_executesql N'UPDATE authors SET city=@p1, state=@p2 WHERE au_id=@p3,
N'@p1 varchar(10), @p2 char(2), @p3 varchar(11), @p1 = 'Scottsdale', @p2 =
'AZ', @p3 = '238-95-7766'
```

Better yet, we should have a custom stored procedure that just knows to update the city and state for a given author, if this is going to be a common activity that's worth optimizing.

This rather illustrates my point. Without actually spending the time to write the code that has an understanding that the au_id column is the primary key, SqlCommandBuilder is going to flounder around trying to find a close approximation.

Use SqlCommandBuilder with care and caution, and optimize the way your application uses the database to precisely fit your needs!

Master/Details Data Binding

A very common design pattern in data-centric applications is the "master/details" view. In this kind of view, the "top-level" data is shown in one UI element (for example, a list of books published). When this UI element is manipulated, another element or a set of elements showing the detail is updated to display the detail "within" the top-level data (for example, the sales for the selected book).

There are two ways of doing this: one relatively ugly and quite difficult to use from the user's perspective (although very easy to code), the other being a slightly more elegant solution (but slightly more difficult to code).

Multiple, Related Tables in a Single DataGrid

The first solution we'll look at (although ugly) shows some functionality of the DataGrid related to the fact that a DataSet can, in fact, contain multiple tables of data. For example, if we wanted, we could create a single DataSet that loads data from a collection of different databases, and loads data from XML files, and even holds data created programmatically. This is illustrated in Figure 16-10.

In the previous example, we gave the DataGrid control just the table that we had bound to through the DataSource member. We could have given it the entire DataSet, in which case, the control would have provided a list of tables for us to choose from. As there was only one table in the list, the list would have contained just one item.

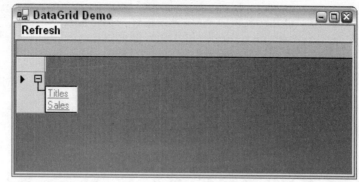

Figure 16-10

In this next section, we'll take a look at using the `titles` table to retrieve a list of books that the publisher has published and we'll combine this with the `sales` table so that for a given book we can see what sales have been made.

We can use the same VS .NET project, as the code to drive this example will be similar to the previous one. First off, we need SQL statements to load all of the data from the `titles` table and from the `sales` table:

```
Public Class Form1
    Inherits System.Windows.Forms.Form
    ' const...
    Public Const ConnectionString As String = "integrated security=sspi;initial
        catalog=pubs;data source=corrado"
    Protected Const GetAllAuthorsSqlString = "select au_id, au_lname, au_fname,
        phone, address, city, state, zip, contract from authors
        order by au_lname, au_fname"
    Protected Const GetAllTitlesSqlString As String = "select title_id, title,
        type, pub_id, price, advance, royalty, ytd_sales, notes, pubdate from
        titles"
    Protected Const GetAllSalesSqlString As String = "select stor_id, ord_num,
        ord_date, qty, payterms, title_id from sales"
```

To load the data this time round, we want to explicitly create the `DataTable` objects and use the `SqlDataAdapter` to fill the table. Previously, we didn't create the tables and told the `SqlDataAdapter` to fill the `DataSet`. All that happened here was that `SqlDataAdapter` discovered no tables in the `DataSet` and created a new one for its purposes. Notice as well how we specifically give the `DataSet` a name of `Book Sales` and how we do the same with the two tables. Finally, notice how we bind `datagridTitles` (I've changed the name from `datagridAuthors`) to the `DataSet`, not to an individual table:

```
Public Sub RefreshData()

    ' connect...
    Dim connection As New SqlConnection(ConnectionString)
    connection.Open()
```

```
' create a dataset...
Dim dataset As New DataSet("Book Sales")

' manually create a titles table...
Dim titlesTable As New DataTable("Titles")
dataset.Tables.Add(titlesTable)

' get the titles back...
Dim adapter As New SqlDataAdapter(GetAllTitlesSqlString, connection)
adapter.Fill(titlesTable)
adapter.Dispose()

' do the same for the sales table...
Dim salesTable As New DataTable("Sales")
dataset.Tables.Add(salesTable)

' get the sales back...
adapter = New SqlDataAdapter(GetAllSalesSqlString, connection)
adapter.Fill(salesTable)
adapter.Dispose()

' close...
connection.Close()

' bind...
datagridTitles.DataSource = dataset
End Sub
```

Run the project and you'll see a view with a plus button. Click this plus button and you'll see a list of tables as shown in Figure 16-11.

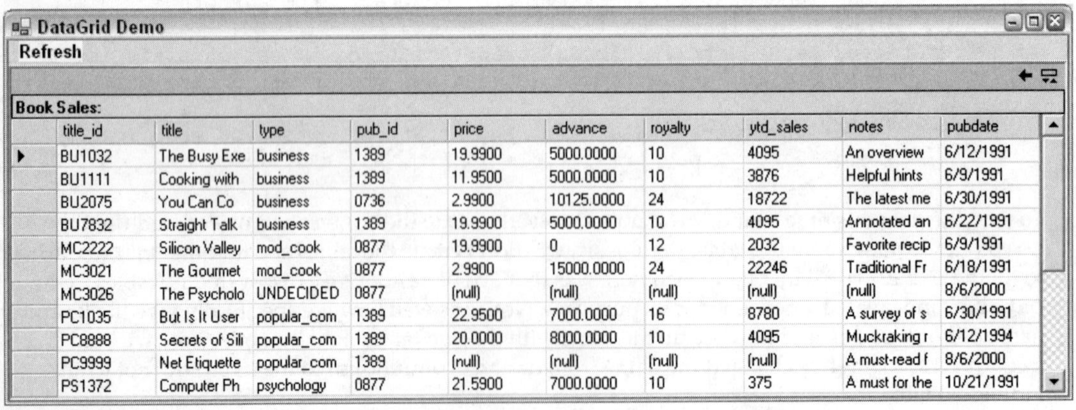

Book Sales:

	title_id	title	type	pub_id	price	advance	royalty	ytd_sales	notes	pubdate
▶	BU1032	The Busy Exe	business	1389	19.9900	5000.0000	10	4095	An overview	6/12/1991
	BU1111	Cooking with	business	1389	11.9500	5000.0000	10	3876	Helpful hints	6/9/1991
	BU2075	You Can Co	business	0736	2.9900	10125.0000	24	18722	The latest me	6/30/1991
	BU7832	Straight Talk	business	1389	19.9900	5000.0000	10	4095	Annotated an	6/22/1991
	MC2222	Silicon Valley	mod_cook	0877	19.9900	0	12	2032	Favorite recip	6/9/1991
	MC3021	The Gourmet	mod_cook	0877	2.9900	15000.0000	24	22246	Traditional Fr	6/18/1991
	MC3026	The Psycholo	UNDECIDED	0877	(null)	(null)	(null)	(null)	(null)	8/6/2000
	PC1035	But Is It User	popular_com	1389	22.9500	7000.0000	16	8780	A survey of s	6/30/1991
	PC8888	Secrets of Sili	popular_com	1389	20.0000	8000.0000	10	4095	Muckraking r	6/12/1994
	PC9999	Net Etiquette	popular_com	1389	(null)	(null)	(null)	(null)	A must-read f	8/6/2000
	PS1372	Computer Ph	psychology	0877	21.5900	7000.0000	10	375	A must for the	10/21/1991

Figure 16-11

If you click in the `Titles` table, you'll see all of the titles as shown in Figure 16-12.

The small left arrow button on the `DataGrid` control's toolbar acts as a back button, so you can use this to go back and see the `Sales` table.

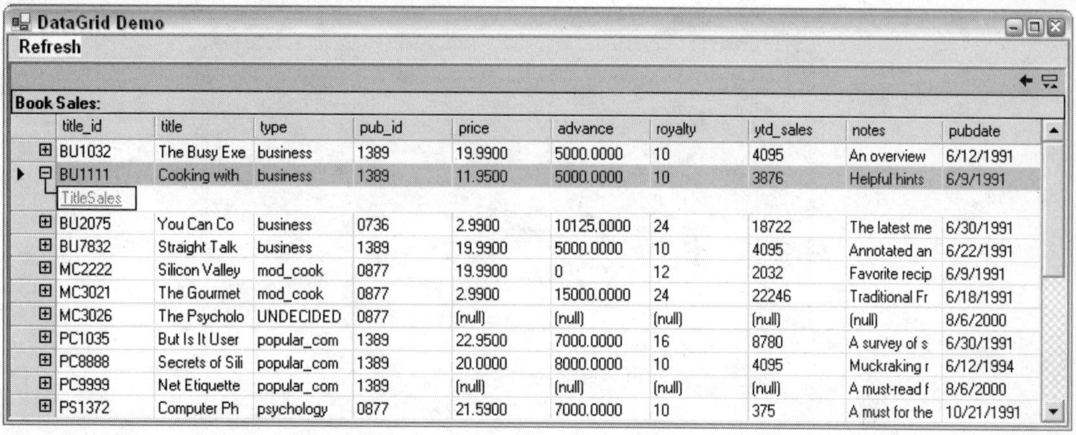

Figure 16-12

This does show the data from the tables, but it doesn't really solve our problem, as we can't see which sales *specifically relate* to titles in the database. To solve this, we have to add a relation to the `DataSet` that defines how `titles` and `sales` are related. We do this by creating a new `System.Data` `.DataRelation` instance and adding it to the `Relations` collection of the `DataSet`. All we need to know is the name of the column from the master table and the name of the matching column in the details table. Here's the code:

```
' close...
connection.Close()

' relate the tables...
Dim relation As New DataRelation("TitleSales", _
    titlesTable.Columns("title_id"), salesTable.Columns("title_id"))
dataset.Relations.Add(relation)

' bind...
datagridTitles.DataSource = dataset
End Sub
```

Now if you look at the `titles` table, you'll find that small plus buttons appear next to each of the rows. Expanding one of these buttons gives you the option to view the sales, as shown here in Figure 16-13.

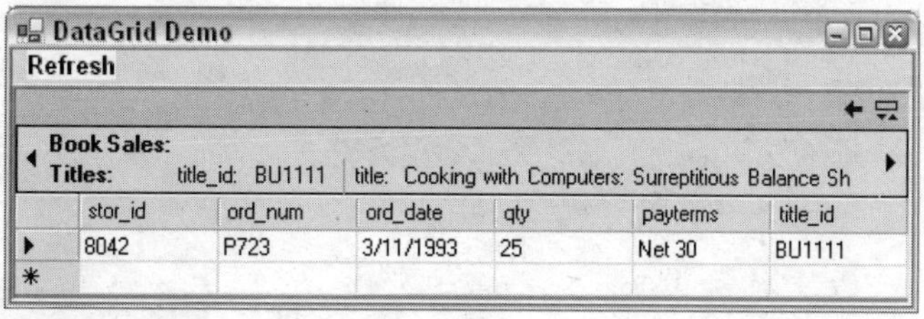

Figure 16-13

Clicking the link displays the related data as illustrated in Figure 16-14.

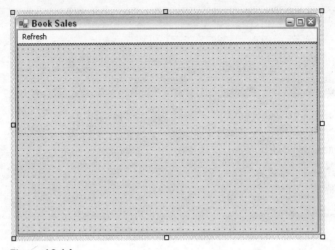

Figure 16-14

Personally, I feel that using this view for day-to-day use is pretty useless. The master data displayed in the headers is squashed at best, unreadable at worst. Plus, you have to keep using the back button to go back to the master rows if you want to see sales for another book. Here's a better solution.

A More Usable Solution

A better solution is to have two `DataGrid` controls. The master list is always visible and changing the selection on this row leads to the selection being changed on the details list.

To do this, delete the `DataGrid` from `Form1` and add a new `Panel` control. Set the `Panel` control's `Dock` property to `Top`. Then, add a `Splitter` control, setting its `Dock` property to `Top` as well. Finally, add a new `Panel` control to the blank region at the bottom of the form and set its `Dock` property to `Fill`. Your form should now appear as shown here in Figure 16-15.

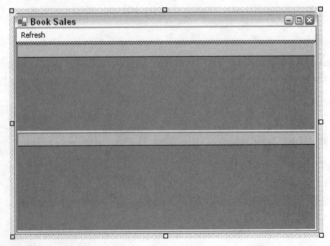

Figure 16-15

Then, add two new `DataGrid` controls to each of the two panels. Call the top one `datagridTitles` and the bottom one `datagridSales`. Set the `Dock` property of each to `Fill`. This is shown in Figure 16-16.

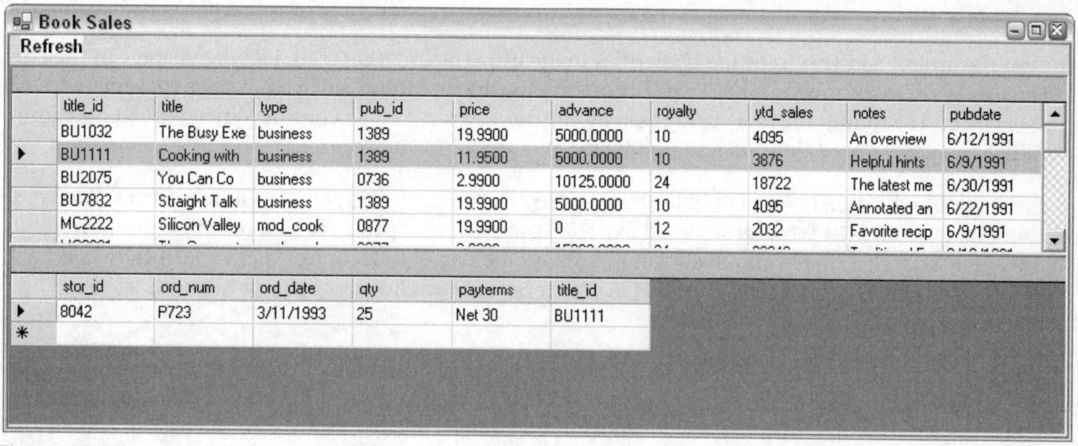

title_id	title	type	pub_id	price	advance	royalty	ytd_sales	notes	pubdate
BU1032	The Busy Exe	business	1389	19.9900	5000.0000	10	4095	An overview	6/12/1991
BU1111	Cooking with	business	1389	11.9500	5000.0000	10	3876	Helpful hints	6/9/1991
BU2075	You Can Co	business	0736	2.9900	10125.0000	24	18722	The latest me	6/30/1991
BU7832	Straight Talk	business	1389	19.9900	5000.0000	10	4095	Annotated an	6/22/1991
MC2222	Silicon Valley	mod_cook	0877	19.9900	0	12	2032	Favorite recip	6/9/1991

stor_id	ord_num	ord_date	qty	payterms	title_id
8042	P723	3/11/1993	25	Net 30	BU1111

Figure 16-16

One of the issues with using the first ("ugly") approach was that not only did we have to load the entire `titles` table into memory, but we also had to load the entire `sales` table. This isn't particularly elegant if you consider that not only might this `sales` table be very large, but also that we don't need all of the data in that table to be loaded. It would be better to use an on-demand approach where the relevant sales data is loaded only when a title is selected.

However, our first job is to load the titles (these are the "master" records). To do this, remove the lines of code from `RefreshData` that query data from `sales` and change the binding statement so that `datagridTitles` is bound to `tableTitles`. You'll also need to remove the line that creates the `DataRelation`:

```
Public Sub RefreshData()

    ' connect...
    Dim connection As New SqlConnection(ConnectionString)
    connection.Open()

    ' create a dataset...
    Dim dataset As New DataSet("Book Sales")

    ' manually create a titles table...
    Dim titlesTable As New DataTable("Titles")
    dataset.Tables.Add(titlesTable)

    ' get the titles back...
    Dim adapter As New SqlDataAdapter(GetAllTitlesSqlString, connection)
    adapter.Fill(titlesTable)
    adapter.Dispose()

    ' close...
    connection.Close()
```

```
' bind...
datagridTitles.DataSource = titlesTable

End Sub
```

Run the project and you'll see the book titles in the uppermost DataGrid. However, you can't see the sales data yet in the lower DataGrid. To correct this, the first thing we need to do is to listen for CurrentCellChanged events being sent by the datagridTitles control. When we receive those messages, we can load the data and update the datagridSales control.

Finding out what title is selected in the datagridTitles control is actually quite difficult. You would think that the DataGrid control would expose a CurrentRow property that returned the current DataRow. In fact, it doesn't do this, mainly because the DataGrid control is not specifically tied to displaying data from a DataTable, and of course, a CurrentRow property only makes sense if you do have a list containing DataRow objects.

What we have to do instead is find out what title is selected by actually examining the row information loaded into the control. We are told when the selection changes what row number we're looking at. However, this does not map to a row number in the underlying DataTable as the user may have used the header of the DataGrid to resort the data by the columns (in which case the data won't marry up; originally row 16 in the DataTable would have matched row 16 in the DataGrid, but after the sort this may not be true). If we have the row number, we can look for the cell at column 0 at that row number, which will contain the title ID, providing the user hasn't changed its value (you can set the 'DataGrid to be read-only by using the ReadOnly property):

```
Private Sub datagridTitles_CurrentCellChanged(ByVal sender As Object, _
    ByVal e As System.EventArgs) Handles _
    datagridTitles.CurrentCellChanged

    ' what row?
    Dim titleId As String = _
    datagridTitles.Item(datagridTitles.CurrentCell.RowNumber, 0)

    ' form the sql...
    Dim sql As String = "select stor_id, ord_num, ord_date, qty, payterms, _
    title_id from sales where title_id='" & titleId & "'"

    ' connect...
    Dim connection As New SqlConnection(ConnectionString)
    connection.Open()

    ' fill...
    Dim adapter As New SqlDataAdapter(sql, connection)
    Dim dataset As New DataSet
    adapter.Fill(dataset)
    adapter.Dispose()

    ' close...
    connection.Close()

    ' show...
    datagridSales.DataSource = dataset.Tables(0)

End Sub
```

With that code in place, run the application. You'll find that when you select titles from the master list (Figure 16-17), the matching sales information is displayed in the details list:

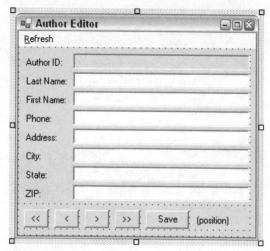

Figure 16-17

Forms

We've seen how data can be bound and displayed as tables. We've also seen how we can save the data back into the database once the user has changed it. What we haven't seen is how we can work with data that's displayed using a form.

Using forms in this way is a very common design pattern, and also gives rise to expectations in the user as to how the form should work. Typically, such forms use VCR (or in this day and age, DVD) buttons to allow the user to move through the records. Typically we have "first," "previous," "next," and "last" buttons. The user also expects to be told when the data has been changed, and have the opportunity to save or to discard the data when they change the selection.

To keep track of things, we need to hold a `DataTable` containing the authors, and the index of the record that they are currently looking at. We also need to know whether they have changed the data in the underlying `DataTable` by changing the text in the form's `TextBox` controls so that we can prompt the user to save or discard the changes.

For this, you can either create a new project or use the existing one. Either way, you'll need to create a new form and add a number of `TextBox`, `Label` and `Button` controls. Also, if you are using a new project add a Refresh menu item again as before, otherwise keep the existing item. This is illustrated in Figure 16-18.

Name the `TextBox` controls like this: `textAuthorId`, `textLastName`, `textFirstName`, `textPhone`, `textAddress`, `textCity`, `textState`, and `textZip`. I've made the `textAuthorId` control read-only as it's unlikely the user will want to change this, or rather the user may potentially "break" the data if this is changed.

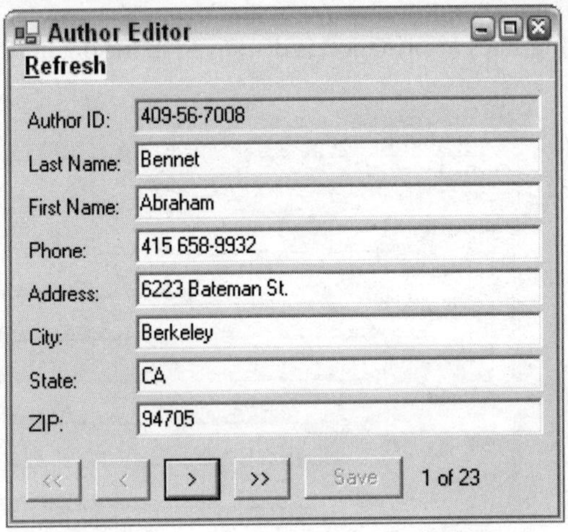

Figure 16-18

Name the `Button` controls like this: `buttonFirst`, `buttonPrevious`, `buttonNext`, `buttonLast`, and `buttonSave`. `buttonSave` should have its `Enabled` property set to `False`. Finally, set the `Name` property of the `Label` control in the bottom-right to `labelPosition`:

As a private field of `Form1`, create `_authors`:

```
Imports System.Data.SqlClient
Public Class Form1
    Inherits System.Windows.Forms.Form

    Private _authors As DataTable
```

When the form loads, call `RefreshData`. This method loads the entire `authors` table into a new `DataTable` and sets the `Authors` property (we'll build this property in a moment):

```
Private Sub Form1_Load(ByVal sender As System.Object, _
            ByVal e As System.EventArgs) Handles MyBase.Load

    RefreshData()
End Sub

Public Sub RefreshData()

    ' connect...
    Dim connection As New SqlConnection(ConnectionString)
    connection.Open()

    ' create and fill...
    Dim table As New DataTable
    Dim adapter As New SqlDataAdapter(GetAllAuthorsSqlString, connection)
    adapter.Fill(table)
    adapter.Dispose()
```

```
     ' close...
     connection.Close()

     ' bind...
     Authors = table
End Sub
```

The `Authors` property is not only responsible for setting the `_authors` field, but is also responsible for establishing the data binding. Add this code:

```
Public Property Authors() As DataTable
    Get
        Return _authors
    End Get
    Set(ByVal Value As DataTable)

        ' set it...
        _authors = Value

        ' update the bindings...
        UpdateBindings()
    End Set
End Property
```

The Windows Forms data binding is very flexible, but I find it a little hard to get my head around, so try and fully understand the next few points before moving on. The idea is that if you have a control, you can use data binding to "tie" a property on that control together with an "item" in the underlying data source. In our case, the "item" we want to tie into is a specific column on the current row of the underlying `DataTable`. Without getting too far ahead, there is a mechanism for discovering and changing the current row, which is how we'll move through the records, but we're going to do that in the next section.

You can nominate pretty much any property on a control to data bind to, provided that the property can accept the data type you're trying to use. (For example, you can't put a `varchar` field into a `Boolean` property.) In our case, we're going to use the `Text` property. So, when we start data binding we're going to set the `Text` property to the associated value, the result of which is the value that will appear on the screen. When the user changes this value, the `Text` property will be read and the underlying `DataRow` will have the relevant column changed. Likewise, as we move through the rows in the table, the properties will be automatically updated.

The `DataBindings` property is defined on the `System.Windows.Forms.Control` class. All of the .NET Framework controls (including `Form`) extend this class, so `DataBindings` is pretty much universally available on all the controls. It's by manipulating this property that we can control the data binding. The first step is to remove any existing data bindings, and then add new data bindings that associated the `Text` property of each control with the relevant column from the `_authors DataTable`.

```
Protected Sub UpdateBindings()

    ' remove the bindings...
    textAuthorId.DataBindings.Clear()
    textLastName.DataBindings.Clear()
```

```
        textFirstName.DataBindings.Clear()
        textPhone.DataBindings.Clear()
        textAddress.DataBindings.Clear()
        textCity.DataBindings.Clear()
        textState.DataBindings.Clear()
        textZip.DataBindings.Clear()

        ' do we have an author?
        If Not _authors Is Nothing Then

            ' bind the data to the text boxes...
            textAuthorId.DataBindings.Add("Text", _authors, "au_id")
            textLastName.DataBindings.Add("Text", _authors, "au_lname")
            textFirstName.DataBindings.Add("Text", _authors, "au_fname")
            textPhone.DataBindings.Add("Text", _authors, "phone")
            textAddress.DataBindings.Add("Text", _authors, "address")
            textCity.DataBindings.Add("Text", _authors, "city")
            textState.DataBindings.Add("Text", _authors, "state")
            textZip.DataBindings.Add("Text", _authors, "zip")

        End If
    End Sub
```

Run the project now and you'll find the first record displayed in the form as shown in Figure 16-19.

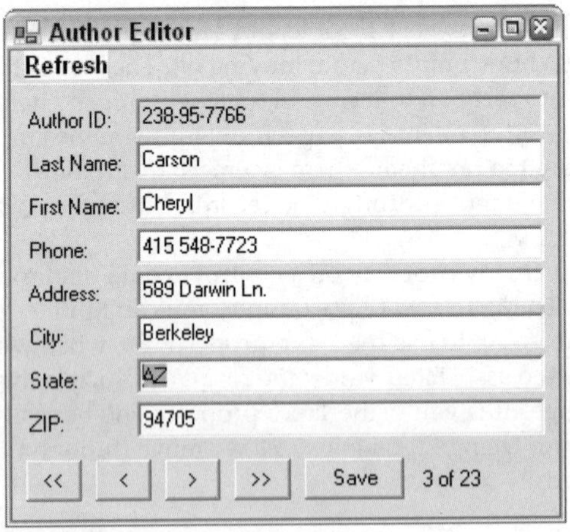

Figure 16-19

What's happening here is that after we've loaded the data in, when we establish the data bindings the `TextBox` control is dredging the data from the underlying `DataTable` and using it to set the `Text` properties against each control.

Moving Through the Records

Now that we can display a record, we need to configure our form so that the user can move through the records. Although getting it to do this is remarkably easy, actually understanding what's happening behind the scenes is a little strange.

When working with data binding in this way, we're in a situation where all the eight TextBox controls have to be synchronized to the same data source. In our case, we've bound the Text properties of each to different "items" (in our specific case, "columns") on the same underlying data source (in our specific case again, a "DataTable"). However, a table has two dimensions, which means that something has to keep track of which row is actually selected. That same "something" also has to be manipulatable from code so that we can change the row when the user clicks the VCR buttons.

The form maintains a collection of *binding managers*, which keep the various bindings synchronized. The base class is System.Windows.Forms.BindingManagerBase and there are two default derivations from this defined in the .NET Framework: CurrencyManager and PropertyManager .CurrencyManager is a slightly odd name, because it refers to "that which is current" and has absolutely nothing to do with "money"!

The form itself is asked by the control for a binding manager through the BindingContext property. This property is implemented on System.Windows.Forms.Control and returns a BindingContext object. This object in turn supports an Item property, and if we give this property the data source that we want to bind to, it will either return a new binding manager or give us one that's already in use. So, in our case, when we bind textAuthorId for the first time, the collection is empty so a new CurrencyManager is created, configured to work with the authors DataTable and is added to the collection. When we bind to textLastName, because the same underlying data source is used, that *same* CurrencyManager is used, and therefore *both controls are bound to the same binding manager*.

To see this in action, we need to wire up the buttons. These buttons will be responsible for changing the value of the AuthorIndex property, which will in turn be responsible for manipulating the data bindings such that a different record is displayed. Add new handlers for the four navigation buttons:

```
Private Sub buttonFirst_Click(ByVal sender As System.Object, _
        ByVal e As System.EventArgs) Handles buttonFirst.Click
    If CheckSave() = True Then
        AuthorIndex = 0
    End If
End Sub


Private Sub buttonPrevious_Click(ByVal sender As System.Object, _
        ByVal e As System.EventArgs) Handles buttonPrevious.Click
    If AuthorIndex <> 0 Then
        If CheckSave() = True Then
            AuthorIndex -= 1
        End If
    End If
End Sub

Private Sub buttonNext_Click(ByVal sender As System.Object, _
        ByVal e As System.EventArgs) Handles buttonNext.Click
    If AuthorIndex < AuthorCount - 1 Then
        If CheckSave() = True Then
            AuthorIndex += 1
        End If
    End If
End Sub
Private Sub buttonLast_Click(ByVal sender As System.Object, _
        ByVal e As System.EventArgs) Handles buttonLast.Click
```

```
            If CheckSave() = True Then
                AuthorIndex = AuthorCount - 1
            End If
        End Sub
```

The `CheckSave` method will eventually check to see if the user wants to save any changes, but for now add this stub implementation:

```
Protected Function CheckSave() As Boolean
    Return True
End Function
```

`AuthorCount` will return the number of `DataRow` objects in the `DataTable`. If we don't have a `DataTable` available, we return zero:

```
Public ReadOnly Property AuthorCount() As Integer
    Get
        If Not _authors Is Nothing Then
            Return _authors.Rows.Count
        End If
        Return 0
    End Get
End Property
```

When we set the `Authors` table, we want to show the first record, which we will do by setting the to-be-built `AuthorIndex` to 0:

```
Public Property Authors() As DataTable
    Get
        Return _authors
    End Get
    Set(ByVal Value As DataTable)

        ' set it...
        _authors = Value

        ' update the bindings...
        UpdateBindings()

        ' position at zero...
        AuthorIndex = 0
    End Set
End Property
```

`AuthorIndex` is responsible for enabling and disabling the navigation buttons (we don't want to display the "previous" button if we're at the first record in the table, for example) and also for setting the `Position` property of the `CurrencyManager` that's associated with the `DataTable`. When we change this value, the values in the `TextBox` controls will magically update. In effect, they detect when the position has changed and rebind themselves to the new values.

To access the binding manager, we'll add a new property called `AuthorBindingContext`. This will cast the return value to a `CurrencyManager` and also check to make sure that we do have a `DataTable` of authors loaded:

```
Protected ReadOnly Property AuthorBindingContext() As CurrencyManager
    Get
        If Not _authors Is Nothing Then
            Return CType(BindingContext(_authors), CurrencyManager)
        Else
            Return Nothing
        End If
    End Get
End Property
```

Now the `AuthorIndex` code. This is mostly UI stuff, but take note of the point at which we set the `Position` property of the binding manager, because this is the point at which the actual record is changed. If the index is the first record (0), we disable the buttons that allow the user to move back. If the index is the last record (`AuthorCount - 1`) we disable the buttons that allow the user to move forward:

```
Public Property AuthorIndex() As Integer
    Get
        If Not AuthorBindingContext Is Nothing Then
            Return AuthorBindingContext.Position
        End If
    End Get
    Set(ByVal Value As Integer)

        ' do we have anything loaded?
        If _authors Is Nothing Then
            buttonFirst.Enabled = False
            buttonPrevious.Enabled = False
            buttonNext.Enabled = False
            buttonLast.Enabled = False
            labelPosition.Text = ""
            Return
        End If

        ' do the buttons...
        Dim enableBack As Boolean = False
        If Value > 0 Then
            enableBack = True
        End If
        Dim enableForward As Boolean = False
        If Value < AuthorCount - 1 Then
        enableForward = True
        End If
        buttonFirst.Enabled = enableBack
        buttonPrevious.Enabled = enableBack
        buttonNext.Enabled = enableForward
        buttonLast.Enabled = enableForward
```

```
            ' get the binding manager...
            Dim manager As CurrencyManager = AuthorBindingContext
            If Not manager Is Nothing Then

                ' have we actually changed?
                If manager.Position <> Value Then
                    manager.Position = Value
                End If
            End If

            ' position...
            labelPosition.Text = _
                    String.Format("{0} of {1}", Value + 1, AuthorCount)
        End Set
    End Property
```

Run the project now and you'll be able to page through the records.

Saving Changes

To save the changes back into the database, we have to do virtually what we did before. When the user changes information in the form, we need to listen for ColumnChanged events coming off of the DataTable and at some point prompt them to save the data. This prompt will either be overt, that is, when they try to move off of a modified record, we'll pop up a message box asking if they want to save the changes, or we'll give them the opportunity to click the Save button to explicitly save the changes.

When the record needs to be saved, we'll keep a flag on the form itself that records the record to be "dirty." We'll simply use the Enabled state of buttonSave to do this. When the button is enabled, the form is dirty. When disabled, it is not. Here's the property:

```
Public Property IsDirty() As Boolean
    Get
        Return buttonSave.Enabled
    End Get
    Set(ByVal Value As Boolean)
        buttonSave.Enabled = Value
    End Set
End Property
```

When the authors are first loaded by setting the Authors property, we need to signal that the record is "clean" by setting IsDirty to False (which will also disable the Save button):

```
Public Property Authors() As DataTable
    Get
        Return _authors
    End Get
    Set(ByVal Value As DataTable)

        ' set it...
        _authors = Value
```

```
                ' update the bindings...
                UpdateBindings()

                ' position at zero...
                AuthorIndex = 0

                ' reset "isdirty"...
                IsDirty = False
        End Set
End Property
```

We've already said that when the data is changed we'll get a `ColumnChanged` event fired. This would seem like a good point to set `IsDirty` to `True`. However, there's a strange wrinkle in the .NET Framework that we have to consider.

We mentioned before that each row has a `RowState` property that returns an enumeration value indicating if the row is unchanged (`DataRowState.Unchanged`), or if the row is new (`DataRowState.Added`), deleted (`DataRowState.Deleted`), modified (`DataRowState.Modified`) or "detached" (`DataRowState.Detached`) (This last one means that the row is not associated with a collection, typically a state indicating that it has just been created.)

`SqlDataAdapter` will ignore any row with a state of `Unchanged` (as you would expect). However, when `ColumnChanged` is fired `RowState` remains `Unchanged` even though data has been changed. `RowState` is a read-only property, so you can't just say "Your state is now *whatever*". Instead, we have to call `EndEdit` on the row to make the change permanent in memory and change the `RowState` value to `Modified`:

```
Protected Sub ColumnChanged(ByVal sender As Object, _
                      ByVal e As DataColumnChangeEventArgs)

        ' accept the change...
        e.Row.EndEdit()
End Sub
```

> We didn't have to worry about this problem before, because the **DataGrid** already has the proper behavior built in. In this example, we start from scratch, so we have to replicate the behavior for our own purposes.

Of course, we have to actually add the handlers for this event. This should also be done in the `Authors` property:

```
Public Property Authors() As DataTable
    Get
        Return _authors
    End Get
    Set(ByVal Value As DataTable)

        ' set it...
        _authors = Value
```

```
        ' update the bindings...
        UpdateBindings()

        ' position at zero...
        AuthorIndex = 0

        ' listen for data changes...
        AddHandler _authors.ColumnChanged, _
            New DataColumnChangeEventHandler(AddressOf ColumnChanged)

        ' reset "isdirty"...
        IsDirty = False
    End Set
End Property
```

If you run the project now, you'll find that if you change the value of a field the button will change (displayed in Figure 16-20). The events are only fired when the keyboard focus moves off of the TextBox control that you are editing. For example, change a value, press *Tab* and the Save button will become enabled as the IsDirty property is set to True:

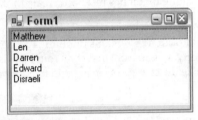

Figure 16-20

To save the changes, we need to wire up the buttonSave control and also implement a proper version of CheckSave. Here's the Click event handler for buttonSave:

```
Private Sub buttonSave_Click(ByVal sender As System.Object, _
            ByVal e As System.EventArgs) Handles buttonSave.Click
    SaveChanges()
End Sub
```

CheckSave will return False if the user wants to cancel the navigation. For example, if the user changes a record, clicks buttonNext and when prompted, "Do you want to save changes?" presses *Cancel*, then the navigation needs to be stopped:

```
Protected Function CheckSave() As Boolean    ' do we need to save?
    If IsDirty = False Then
        Return True
    End If

    ' ask the user?
    Dim result As DialogResult = _
        MsgBox("Do you want to save changes to this record?", _
        MsgBoxStyle.YesNoCancel Or MsgBoxStyle.Question)
```

```
        If result = DialogResult.Cancel Then
            Return False
        End If

        ' do we want to save?
        If result = DialogResult.Yes Then
            SaveChanges()
        Else
            IsDirty = False
        End If

        ' return...
        Return True

    End Function
```

SaveChanges is very similar to the last SaveChanges method we built. However, this time rather than breaking out the rows that need to be saved, we pass the entire DataTable object over to the new SqlDataAdapter and ask it to work out what rows actually need to be saved:

```
    Public Sub SaveChanges()

        ' do we have authors?
        If _authors Is Nothing Then
            Return
        End If

        ' connect...
        Dim connection As New SqlConnection(ConnectionString)
        connection.Open()

        ' create an adapter...
        Dim adapter As New SqlDataAdapter(GetAllAuthorsSqlString, connection)
        Dim builder As New SqlCommandBuilder(adapter)
        adapter.Update(_authors)
        adapter.Dispose()

        ' close...
        connection.Close()

        ' flag...
        IsDirty = False
    End Sub
```

And that's it!

What Data Can Be Data Bound?

To round off this chapter, I'm going to talk about what kinds of data can be data bound. We've dealt exclusively with binding to DataSet, DataTable, and DataRow objects. In fact, data binding can be done with pretty much any form of data.

Lists of Items

First off, we'll think about lists of objects. Although DataTable contains a list of DataRow objects, we can actually bind to any form of list, providing that they give us the correct interfaces.

With .NET, the two most common ways to represent lists of objects is by using the "array" or the "collection," An array is always derived from System.Array, whereas we have a bit more flexibility when it comes to the collection. System.Array supports these interfaces:

❑ System.ICloneable — provides a mechanism for copying the array

❑ System.Collections.IEnumerable — provides a mechanism for walking all of the objects contained within the array in turn, typically with a For Each loop

❑ System.Collections.ICollection — derived from IEnumerable, provides a mechanism for returning the number of objects contained within the array and also some other functionality for synchronizing the array for use in multiple threads

❑ System.Collections.IList — derived from ICollection, IList provides mechanisms for adding and removing items from the array

By and large, with the built-in controls, if the object supports IEnumerable you can data bind to it. Although I won't go through this in much detail, if we add a ListBox control to a form, we can bind an array of string objects to it as shown:

```
Private Sub Form1_Load(ByVal sender As System.Object, _
                        ByVal e As System.EventArgs) Handles MyBase.Load

    ' create an array of names...
    Dim names() As String = {"Matthew", "Len", "Darren", "Edward", "Disraeli"}

    ' bind the list to the array...
    listNames.DataSource = names
End Sub
```

The display of each name sequentially happens because the array supports one of the interfaces needed by the control. In this case, IEnumerable is used to walk each of the objects in turn. ToString is called on each one to get a string representation and the string value is added to the Items collection of the control itself.

In this case, the DataSource property is inherited from System.Windows.Forms.ListControl, the base class of both ListBox and ComboBox. This tells us that both of these controls will bind to a list of data in the same way.

Properties of Objects

We mentioned way back that DataBindings is implemented on System.Windows.Forms.Control, and as most of the Windows Forms controls are derived from this, it makes sense that most of the Windows Forms controls support data binding. However, this is not the form of data binding that we've just seen where a list is automatically iterated and presented. It's the kind of data binding where a property on the control is bound to a value on some other object.

Earlier, we saw how this kind of data binding could be used to bind a `TextBox` control's `Text` property to a column in a row of a `DataTable`. The other object doesn't have to be a `DataRow`, it can be anything that exposes a property.

Imagine we have the following class:

```
Public Class Customer

    ' members...
    Private _id As Integer
    Private _firstName As String
    Private _lastName As String
    Public Property Id() As Integer
        Get
            Return _id
        End Get
        Set(ByVal Value As Integer)
            _id = Value
        End Set
    End Property
    Public Property FirstName() As String
        Get
            Return _firstName
        End Get
        Set(ByVal Value As String)
            _firstName = Value
        End Set
    End Property
    Public Property LastName() As String
        Get
            Return _lastName
        End Get
        Set(ByVal Value As String)
            _lastName = Value
        End Set
    End Property
End Class
```

We can bind any *property* (it must be a property, not just a public member) of that class to another property on a control, providing that the data types are compatible, as shown in the following example:

```
Public Sub UpdateBindings()

    ' create the customer object...
    Dim customer As New Customer()
    customer.Id = 27
    customer.FirstName = "Bill"
    customer.LastName = "Evjen"

    ' bind it...
    buttonBind.DataBindings.Add("Text", customer, "FirstName")
End Sub
```

If we call `UpdateBindings`, what happens is that the text of the button will display the value stored in `FirstName` of the bound object.

Summary

In this chapter, we took a look at how to use data binding in our Windows Forms application and saw some important design patterns that are common when building data-centric applications.

We started by examining the DataGrid control. This is a sophisticated control for presenting tables of data in applications. We found that binding a DataTable to this control was very easy, resulting in the table being displayed to the user. We then saw how we could save changes made back to the database.

We also discussed two ways to build the classic master/detail view, at first using a single DataGrid control bound to a DataSet containing two related tables, and then using two separate DataGrid controls. We also saw how we could discover what SQL statements were actually being executed against the database by our application.

Finally, we looked at how to present data to the user in a form, offering them the classic VCR navigation buttons so common to form-entry applications. Finally, we looked at the various list interfaces supported by the .NET Framework and saw how we were not limited to just working with DataSet objects and its associates when data binding.

Working with Classic COM and Interfaces

However much as we try, we just can't ignore the vast body of technology surrounding Microsoft's Component Object Model, or COM. Over the years, this model has been the cornerstone of so much Microsoft-related development that we have to take a long, hard look at how we are going to integrate all that stuff into the new world of .NET.

In this chapter, we're going to start by taking a brief backward glance at COM. We're then going to compare it with how components interact in .NET, and see what tools Microsoft have provided us with to help link the two together. Having looked at the theory, we'll then try it out by building a few example applications. Firstly, we'll take a legacy basic COM object and run it from a Visual Basic .NET (VB.NET) program. Then we'll repeat the trick with a full-blown ActiveX control. Finally, we'll turn things around and try running some VB.NET code in the guise of a COM object.

> More information on how to make COM and VB6 code interoperate with the .NET platform can be found in *Professional Visual Basic Interoperability: COM and VB6 to .NET* (Wiley, 2002).

As we do all this, try to remember one thing: COM is, to a large extent, where .NET came from. In evolutionary terms, COM's kind of like Lucy, the *Australopithecus* from ancient Ethiopia. So, if it seems a little clunky at times, let's not to be too hard on it. In fact, let's not refer to it as "Nasty, tired, clunky old COM" at all. Let's simply call it "Classic COM."

Classic COM

Before we look into COM-.NET interoperability, we should make sure that we are aware of the main points about COM itself. We won't attempt to do anything more than skim the surface here, however. While the basic concepts are fundamentally simple, the underlying technology is anything but.

Some of the most impenetrable books on software that have ever been written have COM as their subject, and I have no wish to add to these.

COM was Microsoft's first full-blown attempt at creating a language-independent standard for programming. The idea was that interfaces between components would be defined according to a binary standard. This would mean that you could, for the first time, invoke a VB component from a VC++ application, and vice versa. It would also be possible to invoke a component in another process or even on another machine, via Distributed COM (DCOM). We won't be looking at out-of-process servers here, however, as the vast majority of components developed to date are in-process. To a large extent, DCOM was fatally compromised by bandwidth, deployment, and firewall problems and never achieved a high level of acceptance.

A COM component implements one or more *interfaces*, some of which are standard ones provided by the system and some of which are custom interfaces defined by the component developer. An interface defines the various methods that an application may invoke. Once specified, an interface definition is supposed to be inviolate so that, even if the underlying code changes, applications that use the interface don't need to be rebuilt. If the component developers find that they have left something out, they should define a new interface containing the extra functionality in addition to that in the original interface. This has, in fact, happened with a number of standard Microsoft interfaces. For example, the `IClassFactory2` interface extends the `IClassFactory` interface by adding features for managing the creation of licensed objects.

The key to getting applications and components to work together is *binding*. COM offers two forms of binding, early and late:

❑   In *early binding*, the application uses a *type library* at compile time to work out how to link in to the methods in the component's interfaces. A type library can either come as a separate file, with extension `.tlb`, or as part of the DLL containing the component code.

❑   In *late binding*, no connection is made between the application and its components at compile time. Instead, the COM runtime searches through the component for the location of the required method when the application is actually run. This has two main disadvantages: it's slower and it's unreliable. If a programming error is made (for example, the wrong method is called, or the right method with the wrong number of arguments), it doesn't get caught at compile time.

If a type library is not explicitly referred to, there are two ways to identify a COM component, by *class ID*, which is a GUID, and by *ProgID*, which is a string and looks like `"MyProject.MyComponent"`. These are all cross-referenced in the registry. In fact, COM makes extensive use of the registry to maintain links between applications, their components, and their interfaces. All experienced COM programmers know their way around the registry blindfold.

VB6 has a lot of COM features embedded into it, to the extent that many VB6 programmers aren't even aware that they are developing COM components. For instance, if you create a DLL containing an instance of a VB6 class, you will in fact have created a COM object without even asking for one. We'll see how easy this is during the course of this chapter.

There are clearly similarities between COM and .NET. So, to a large extent, all we've got to do to make them work together is put a wrapper around a COM object to make it into an assembly, and vice versa.

COM and .NET in Practice

It's time to get serious and see if all this seamless integration really works. In order to do this, we're going to have to simulate a legacy situation. Let's imagine that our enterprise depends on a particular COM object that was written for us a long time ago by a wayward genius (who subsequently abandoned software development and has gone to live in a monastery in Tibet). Anyway, all we know is that the code works perfectly and we need it for our .NET application.

We have one, or possibly two, options here. If we have the source (which is not necessarily the case) and we have sufficient time (or, to put it another way, money), we can upgrade the object to .NET and continue to maintain it under Visual Studio .NET (VS.NET). For the purist, this is the ideal solution for going forward. However, maintaining the source as it is under VS.NET isn't really a viable option. VS.NET does offer an upgrade path, but it doesn't cope well with COM objects using interfaces specified as abstract classes.

If upgrading to .NET isn't an option, all we can do is simply take the DLL for our COM object, register it on our .NET machine, and use the .NET interoperability tools. This is the path that we're going to take.

So, what we need is a genuine legacy COM object, and what we're going to have to use is genuine legacy VB6. For the next section, then, we're going to be using VB6. If you've already disposed of VB6, or never had it in the first place, feel free to skip this section. The DLL is available as part of the code download, in any case.

A Legacy Component

For our legacy component, we're going to imagine that we have some kind of analytics engine that requires a number of calculations. Because of the highly complex nature of these calculations, their development has been given to specialists, while the user interface for the application has been given to UI specialists. A COM interface has been specified that all calculations must confirm to. This interface has the name `IMegaCalc` and has the following methods.

Method	Description
`Sub AddInput (InputValue as Double)`	Add input value to calculation
`Sub DoCalculation ()`	Do calculation
`Function GetOutput () as Double`	Get output from calculation
`Sub Reset ()`	Reset calculation for next time

Step 1: Defining the Interface

The first thing we have to do is define our interface. In VB6, the way to do this is to create an abstract class, that is, one without any implementation. So, let's create an ActiveX DLL project called `MegaCalculator`. We do this by creating a new project and then changing its name to

`MegaCalculator` by means of the Project ➪ Project1 Properties dialog box. Having done that, let's create a class called `IMegaCalc`. This is what the code looks like:

```
Option Explicit

Public Sub AddInput(InputValue As Double)
End Sub

Public Sub DoCalculation()
End Sub

Public Function GetOutput() As Double
End Function

Public Sub Reset()
End Sub
```

From the main menu, select File ➪ Make MegaCalculator.dll to define and register the interface.

Step 2: Implementing Our Component

For the purposes of this demonstration, the actual calculation that we're going to perform is going to be fairly mundane: in fact, we're going to calculate the mean of a series of numbers. So let's create another ActiveX DLL project, called `MeanCalculator` this time. We need to add a reference to the type library for the interface that we're going to implement, so select the MegaCalculator DLL via the References dialog box that appears when you select Project ➪ References.

Having done that, we can go ahead and write the code for the mean calculation. We do this in a class called `MeanCalc`:

```
Option Explicit

Implements IMegaCalc

Dim mintValue As Integer
Dim mdblValues() As Double
Dim mdblMean As Double

Private Sub Class_Initialize()
  IMegaCalc_Reset
End Sub

Private Sub IMegaCalc_AddInput(InputValue As Double)
  mintValue = mintValue + 1
  ReDim Preserve mdblValues(mintValue)
  mdblValues(mintValue) = InputValue
End Sub

Private Sub IMegaCalc_DoCalculation()
  Dim iValue As Integer
  mdblMean = 0#
```

```
    If (mintValue = 0) Then Exit Sub

    For iValue = 1 To mintValue
      mdblMean = mdblMean + mdblValues(iValue)
    Next iValue

    mdblMean = mdblMean / mintValue

End Sub

Private Function IMegaCalc_GetOutput() As Double
  IMegaCalc_GetOutput = mdblMean
End Function

Private Sub IMegaCalc_Reset()
  mintValue = 0
End Sub
```

As before, we select File ⇨ Make MeanCalculator.dll to build and register the component. It has a default interface called MeanCalc (which contains no methods, and is thus invisible to the naked eye), plus an implementation of IMegaCalc.

Step 3: Registering Our Legacy Component

We now have our legacy component. If we're developing our new .NET application on the same machine, we don't need to do anything more, because our component would already have been registered by the build process. However, if we're working on an entirely new machine, we'll need to register it there. The easiest way to do this is to open up a command box, and register it with the following command:

```
regsvr32 MeanCalculator.dll
```

Then we should see the result shown in Figure 17-1.

Figure 17-1

Because MeanCalculator implements an interface from MegaCalculator, we'll also have to repeat the trick with that DLL

```
regsvr32 MegaCalculator.dll
```

and here's what we see (see Figure 17-2).

We're now ready to use our component from a .NET application.

Figure 17-2

The .NET Application

For our .NET application, all we're going to do is instantiate a `MeanCalc` object, and get it to work out a mean for us. So let's create a Windows Application project in VB.NET called `CalcApp`. This is what the form looks like (see Figure 17-3).

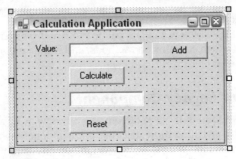

Figure 17-3

The two text boxes are called `txtInput` and `txtOutput`, respectively; the second one is not enabled for user input. The three command buttons are `btnAdd`, `btnCalculate`, and `btnReset`, respectively.

Referencing the Legacy Component

Before we dive into writing the code behind those buttons, we need to make our new application aware of the `MeanCalculator` component. So we have to add a reference to it, via the Project ➪ Add Reference menu item. This brings up a dialog box with three tabs: .NET, COM, and Projects. Select MeanCalculator and MegaCalculator in turn from the COM tab (see Figure 17-4).

Now, hit the OK button. Notice that, in the list of references in the Solution Explorer, we can now see both MeanCalculator and MegaCalculator (see Figure 17-5).

Inside the .NET Application

Now that we've successfully got our component referenced, we can go ahead and finish coding our application. First of all, we add a global variable (`mobjMean`) to hold a reference to an instance of the mean calculation component.

```
Public Class Form1
    Inherits System.Windows.Forms.Form

Dim mobjMean As MeanCalculator.MeanCalc
```

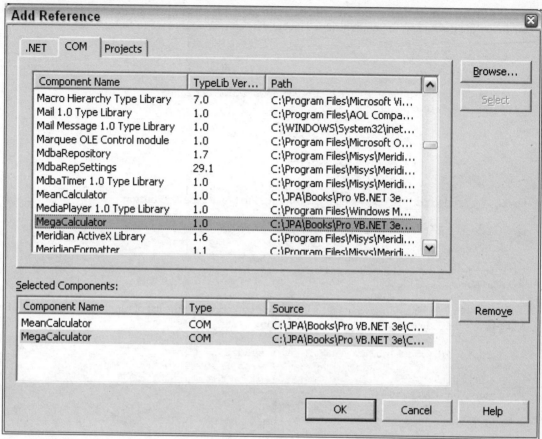

Figure 17-4

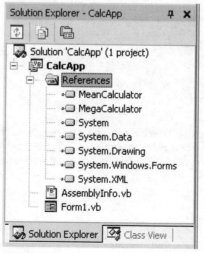

Figure 17-5

Next, we need to open up the section labeled Windows Form Designer generated code, and add the following instruction to New, which will create the component that we're going to use.

```
Public Sub New()
    MyBase.New()

    'This call is required by the Windows Form Designer.
    InitializeComponent()

    'Add any initialization after the InitializeComponent() call

    mobjMean = New MeanCalculator.MeanCalc()
End Sub
```

Finally, we need to add the code behind the buttons. First of all, the Add button:

```
Private Sub btnAdd_Click(ByVal sender As Object, _
                         ByVal e As System.EventArgs) _
                         Handles btnAdd.Click
    mobjMean.AddInput(CDbl(txtInput.Text))
End Sub
```

All we're doing here is adding whatever's in the input text box into the list of numbers for the calculation. Next, here's the code behind the Calculate button:

```
Private Sub btnCalculate_Click(ByVal sender As Object, _
                               ByVal e As System.EventArgs) _
                               Handles btnCalculate.Click
    mobjMean.DoCalculation()
    txtOutput.Text = mobjMean.GetOutput()
End Sub
```

This performs the calculation, retrieves the answer, and puts it into the output text box. Finally, the code behind the Reset button simply resets the calculation.

```
Private Sub btnReset_Click(ByVal sender As Object, _
                ByVal e As System.EventArgs) Handles btnReset.Click
    mobjMean.Reset()
End Sub
```

Trying It All Out

Of course, the proof of the pudding is in the eating, so let's see what happens when we run our application. First of all, let's put one value in, say 2, and click Add. Now, enter another value, say 3, and click Add once more. When you click Calculate, you'll get the mean of the two values (2.5 in this case; see Figure 17-6).

Using TlbImp Directly

In the preceding example, there's actually quite a lot going on under the covers. Every time we import a COM DLL into VS.NET, it's creating a *default interop assembly*, which is basically a .NET assembly that acts

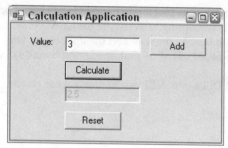

Figure 17-6

as a wrapper for the COM object. If we're doing this a lot, it might be better to do the wrapping once and for all, and then let our application developers import the resulting .NET assembly instead. Let's see how we might do that.

The process that creates the default interop assembly on behalf of VS.NET is called `TlbImp.exe`. The name stands for *Type Library Import*, and that's pretty much what it does. It comes as part of the .NET Framework SDK, and you might find it convenient to extend the `PATH` environment variable to include the `\bin` directory of the .NET Framework SDK.

`TlbImp` takes a COM DLL as its input and generates a .NET assembly DLL as its output. By default, the .NET assembly has the same name as the type library, which will — in the case of VB6 components — always be the same as the COM DLL. This means that we'll have to explicitly specify a different output file. We do this by using the `/out:` switch. So that we can see what's going on at each step in the process, we'll also specify `/verbose`:

```
tlbimp MeanCalculator.dll /out:MeanCalculatorNet.dll /verbose
```

Let's see what happens (see Figure 17-7).

```
C:\WINDOWS\System32\cmd.exe                                          _ □ ×

C:\JPA\Books\Pro UB.NET 3e\Chapter 17\MeanCalculator>tlbimp MeanCalculator.dll /
out:MeanCalculatorNet.dll /verbose
Microsoft (R) .NET Framework Type Library to Assembly Converter 1.1.4322.573
Copyright (C) Microsoft Corporation 1998-2002.  All rights reserved.

Type _MeanCalc imported.
Resolving reference to type library 'MegaCalculator'.
Auto importing 'MegaCalculator' to 'C:\JPA\Books\Pro UB.NET 3e\Chapter 17\MeanCa
lculator\MegaCalculator.dll'.
Type _IMegaCalc imported.
Type IMegaCalc imported.
Type MeanCalc imported.
Type library imported to C:\JPA\Books\Pro UB.NET 3e\Chapter 17\MeanCalculator\Me
anCalculatorNet.dll

C:\JPA\Books\Pro UB.NET 3e\Chapter 17\MeanCalculator>_
```

Figure 17-7

Notice that `TlbImp` has encountered a reference to another COM type library, `MegaCalculator`, and it has very kindly imported that one as well. Note that the imported DLL retains the name

MegaCalculator.dll. This means that if you happen to be storing both DLLs in the same place, TlbImp is going to find itself attempting to overwrite the COM version of MegaCalculator.dll with .NET one (it won't actually do this, by the way, and the import will fail). The way around this is to explicitly run TlbImp on MegaCalculator first, specifying MegaCalculatorNet.dll as your output.

Having converted our COM DLLs into .NET assemblies, we can reference them in an application as we would any other .NET DLL.

Late Binding

We've seen that we can successfully do early binding on COM components within a .NET application. But what if we want to do late binding? What if we don't have access to a type library at application development time? Can we still make use of the COM components? Does the .NET equivalent of late binding even exist?

The answer is that, yes, it does, but, no, it's nothing like as transparent as with VB6. Let's take a look at what we used to do in VB6. If we wanted to do early binding, what we would do is this.

```
Dim myObj As MyObj
Set myObj = New MyObj

MyObj.MyMethod (...)
```

For late binding, it would look like this instead.

```
Dim myObj As Object
Set myObj = CreateObject ("MyLibrary.MyObject")

MyObj.MyMethod (...)
```

There's actually an enormous amount of stuff going on under the covers here; if you're interested in looking into this further, try *VB COM: Visual Basic 6 Programmer's Introduction to COM*.

An Example for Late Binding

For our sample, let's extend the calculator to a more generic framework that can feed inputs into a number of different calculation modules rather than just the fixed one. We'll keep a table in memory of calculation ProgIDs and present the user with a combo box to select the right one.

The Sample COM Object

The first problem we encounter with late binding is that you can only late-bind to the default interface, which, in our case, is MeanCalculator.MeanCalc, not MeanCalculator.IMegaCalc. So we're going to have to redevelop our COM object as a standalone library, with no references to other interfaces.

As before, we'll build a DLL under VB6, copy it over to our .NET environment and reregister it there. We'll call this VB6 DLL MeanCalculator2.dll, and the code in the class (called MeanCalc) should look like this:

```
Option Explicit

Dim mintValue As Integer
Dim mdblValues() As Double
Dim mdblMean As Double

Private Sub Class_Initialize()
  Reset
End Sub

Public Sub AddInput(InputValue As Double)
  mintValue = mintValue + 1
  ReDim Preserve mdblValues(mintValue)
  mdblValues(mintValue) = InputValue
End Sub

Public Sub DoCalculation()
  Dim iValue As Integer
  mdblMean = 0#

If (mintValue = 0) Then Exit Sub

For iValue = 1 To mintVal
  mdblMean = mdblMean + mdblValues(iValue)
Next iValue

mdblMean = mdblMean / mintValue

End Sub

Public Function GetOutput() As Double
  GetOutput = mdblMean
End Function

Public Sub Reset()
  mintValue = 0
End Sub
```

As before, we'll need to move this across to our .NET machine and register it using `RegSvr32`.

The Calculation Framework

For our generic calculation framework, we'll create a new application in VB.NET called `CalcFrame`. We'll basically use the same dialog box as last time, but with an extra combo box at the top (see Figure 17-8).

The new combo box is called `cmbCalculation`. We've also disabled the controls `txtInput`, `btnAdd`, `btnCalculate`, and `btnReset`, until we know if the selected calculation is valid.

We'll start off by importing the `Reflection` namespace; we'll need this for handing all the latebinding.

```
Imports System.Reflection
```

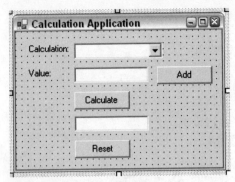

Figure 17-8

Then we add a few member variables:

```
Public Class Form1
    Inherits System.Windows.Forms.Form

    Private mstrObjects() As String
    Private mnObject As Integer
    Private mtypCalc As Type
    Private mobjcalc As Object
```

Next, we need to add a few lines to New:

```
Public Sub New()
    MyBase.New()

    'This call is required by the Windows Form Designer.
    InitializeComponent()

    'Add any initialization after the InitializeComponent() call

    mnObject = 0
    AddObject("Mean", "MeanCalculator2.MeanCalc")
    AddObject("StdDev", "StddevCalculator.StddevCalc")

    If (mnObject > 0) Then
        cmbCalculation.SelectedIndex = 0
    End If

End Sub
```

What we're doing here is building up a list of calculations. Once we've finished, we select the first one in the list. Let's just take a look at that subroutine AddObject:

```
Private Sub AddObject(ByVal strName As String, ByVal strObject As String)
    cmbCalculation.Items.Add(strName)
    mnObject = mnObject + 1
    ReDim Preserve mstrObjects(mnObject)
    mstrObjects(mnObject - 1) = strObject
End Sub
```

In this code segment, we're adding the calculation name to the combo box and its `ProgID` to an array of strings. Neither of these is sorted, so we get a one-to-one mapping between them. Let's see what happens when we select a calculation via the combo box:

```
Private Sub cmbCalculation_SelectedIndexChanged(ByVal sender As Object,_
                                    ByVal e As System.EventArgs) _
                        Handles cmbCalculation.SelectedIndexChanged
    Dim intIndex As Integer
    Dim bEnabled As Boolean

    intIndex = cmbCalculation.SelectedIndex
    mtypCalc = Type.GetTypeFromProgID(mstrObjects(intIndex))

    If (mtypCalc Is Nothing) Then
        mobjcalc = Nothing
        bEnabled = False
    Else
        mobjcalc = Activator.CreateInstance(mtypCalc)
        bEnabled = True
    End If

    txtInput.Enabled = bEnabled
    btnAdd.Enabled = bEnabled
    btnCalculate.Enabled = bEnabled
    btnReset.Enabled = bEnabled
End Sub
```

There are two key calls here. The first is to `Type.GetTypeFromProgID`. This takes the incoming `ProgID` string and converts it to a `Type` object. This may either succeed or fail; if it fails, we disable all controls and let the user try again. If it succeeds, however, we go on to create an instance of the object described by the type. We do this in the call to the static method `Activator.CreateInstance`.

So let's assume that our user has selected a calculation that we can successfully instantiate. What next? The next thing is that the user enters a number and clicks the Add button.

```
    Private Sub btnAdd_Click(ByVal sender As Object, ByVal e As
System.EventArgs) Handles btnAdd.Click
        Dim objArgs() As [Object] = {CDbl(txtInput.Text)}
        mtypCalc.InvokeMember("AddInput", BindingFlags.InvokeMethod, Nothing,
mobjcalc, objArgs)
    End Sub
```

The important call here is to `InvokeMember`. Let's take a closer look. There are five parameters here:

❑ The first parameter is the name of the method that we want to call: `AddInput` in this case. So instead of going directly to the location of the routine in memory, we ask the .NET runtime to find it for us.

❑ The value from the `BindingFlags` enumeration tells it that we want it to invoke a method for us.

❑ The next parameter is to provide language-specific binding information, which isn't needed in this case.

❑   The fourth parameter is a reference to the COM object itself (the one that we instantiated using `Activator.CreateInstance`).

❑   Finally, the fifth parameter is an array of objects representing the arguments for the method. In this case, there's only one argument, the input value.

Something very similar to this is going on underneath VB6 late binding, except that here it's exposed to us in all its horror. In some ways, that's no bad thing, because it should bring it home to you that late binding is something to avoid, if at all possible. Anyway, let's carry on and complete the program. Here are the remaining event handlers:

```
Private Sub btnCalculate_Click(ByVal sender As Object, _
            ByVal e As System.EventArgs) Handles btnCalculate.Click
    Dim objResult As Object
    mtypCalc.InvokeMember("DoCalculation", BindingFlags.InvokeMethod, _
                    Nothing, mobjcalc, Nothing)
    objResult = mtypCalc.InvokeMember("GetOutput", _
                BindingFlags.InvokeMethod, Nothing, mobjcalc, Nothing)
    txtOutput.Text = objResult
End Sub
Private Sub btnReset_Click(ByVal sender As Object, _
            ByVal e As System.EventArgs) Handles btnReset.Click
    mtypCalc.InvokeMember("Reset", BindingFlags.InvokeMethod, Nothing,
mobjcalc, Nothing)

End Sub
```

Running the Calculation Framework

OK, let's quickly complete the job by running the application. Here's what happens when we select the nonexistent calculation StdDev (see Figure 17-9).

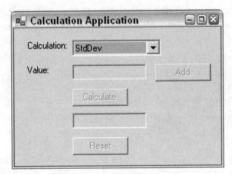

Figure 17-9

As we can see in the screenshot, the input fields have been disabled, as we wanted.

And, here's what happens when we repeat our earlier calculation using Mean (see Figure 17-10).

This time, the input fields are enabled, and we can carry out our calculation as before.

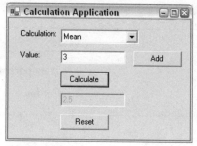

Figure 17-10

One final word about late binding. We took care to ensure that we checked to see that the object was successfully instantiated. In a real-life application, we would also need to take care that the method invocations were successful, ensuring that all exceptions were caught—we don't have the luxury of having the compiler find our bugs for us.

ActiveX Controls

Let's move on from basic COM objects to ActiveX controls. These are still COM objects, with the crucial extension that they have to implement a whole further set of interfaces relating to user interface characteristics. We're going to do pretty much the same as we did with the basic COM component (apart from late binding, which has no relevance to ActiveX controls)—build a legacy control using VB6 and then import it into a VB.NET project.

A Legacy ActiveX Control

For our legacy control, we're going to build a simple button-like object that is capable of interpreting a mouse click and can be one of two colors according to its state. We do this by taking a second foray into VB6; once again, if you don't have VB6 handy, feel free to skip the next section, download the OCX file, and pick it up when we start developing our .NET application.

Step 1: Create the Control

This time, we need to create an ActiveX Control project. We'll call the project `Magic`, and the control class `MagicButton`, so as to give a proper impression of its remarkable powers. From the toolbox, we select a `Shape` control and place it on the `UserControl` form that VB6 provides us with. Rename the shape to `shpButton`, and change its properties as follows.

Property	Value
FillStyle	0—Solid
Shape	4—Rounded Rectangle
FillColor	Gray (&H00808080&)

Add a label on top of the shape control and rename this to lblText. Change its properties as follows.

Property	Value
BackStyle	0 — Transparent
Alignment	2 — Center

Switch to the code view of MagicButton.

Now we need to add two properties called Caption and State, and an event called Click, as well as code to handle the initialization of the properties and persisting them, to ensure that the shape resizes correctly and that the label is centered. We also need to handle mouse clicks. The code in MagicButton should look like this:

```
Option Explicit

Public Event Click()

Dim mintState As Integer

Public Property Get Caption() As String
  Caption = lblText.Caption
End Property

Public Property Let Caption(ByVal vNewValue As String)
  lblText.Caption = vNewValue
  PropertyChanged ("Caption")
End Property

Public Property Get State() As Integer
  State = mintState
End Property

Public Property Let State(ByVal vNewValue As Integer)
  mintState = vNewValue
  PropertyChanged ("State")

  If (State = 0) Then
    shpButton.FillColor = &HFFFFFF&
  Else
    shpButton.FillColor = &H808080&
  End If
End Property

Private Sub UserControl_InitProperties()
  Caption = Extender.Name
  State = 1
End Sub

Private Sub UserControl_ReadProperties(PropBag As PropertyBag)
  Caption = PropBag.ReadProperty("Caption", Extender.Name)
```

```
    State = PropBag.ReadProperty("State", 1)
End Sub

Private Sub UserControl_WriteProperties(PropBag As PropertyBag)
  PropBag.WriteProperty "Caption", lblText.Caption
  PropBag.WriteProperty "State", mintState
End Sub

Private Sub UserControl_Resize()
  shpButton.Move 0, 0, ScaleWidth, ScaleHeight
  lblText.Move 0, (ScaleHeight - lblText.Height) / 2, ScaleWidth
End Sub

Private Sub lblText_Click()
  RaiseEvent Click
End Sub

Private Sub UserControl_MouseUp(Button As Integer, Shift As Integer, _
                        X As Single, Y As Single)
  RaiseEvent Click
End Sub
```

If we build this, we'll get an ActiveX control called `Magic.ocx`.

Step 2: Registering Our Legacy Control

We now have our legacy control. As before, if we're developing our new .NET application on the same machine, we don't need to do anything more, because our control will already have been registered by the build process. However, if we're working on an entirely new machine, we'll need to register it there. As before, we need to open up a command box and register it with the following command:

```
regsvr32 Magic.ocx
```

Having done that, we're ready to build our .NET application.

A .NET Application, Again

This .NET application is going to be even more straightforward than the last one. All we're going to do this time is show a button that will change color whenever the user clicks it. Let's create a Windows Application project in VB.NET called `ButtonApp`. Before we start to develop it, however, we need to extend the toolbox to incorporate our new control. We do this via the Tools ⇨ Add/Remove Toolbox Items menu item (see Figure 17-11).

When we click the OK button, we can see that our magic button class is now available to us in the toolbox (see Figure 17-12).

Let's add one to our form (see Figure 17-13).

Notice that references to `AxMagic` and `Magic` have just been added to the project, in the Solution Explorer window (see Figure 17-14).

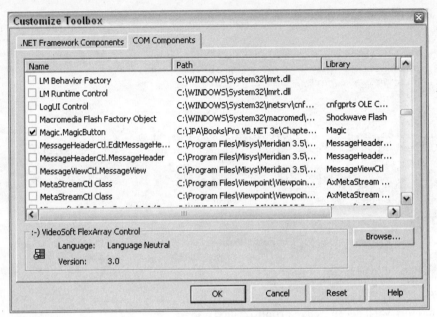

Figure 17-11

Figure 17-12

Figure 17-13

Figure 17-14

All we need to do now is initialize the `Caption` property to `ON`, change the `Text` of the form to `Button Application`, and code up a handler for the mouse click event:

```
Private Sub AxMagicButton1_ClickEvent(ByVal sender As Object, _
        ByVal e As System.EventArgs) Handles AxMagicButton1.ClickEvent
    AxMagicButton1.CtlState = CType(1 - AxMagicButton1.CtlState, Short)
    If (AxMagicButton1.CtlState = 0) Then
        AxMagicButton1.Caption = "OFF"
    Else
        AxMagicButton1.Caption = "ON"
    End If
End Sub
```

Something slightly peculiar happened here. In the course of importing our control into .NET, the variable `State` mutated into `CtlState`. This happened because there is already a class in the `AxHost` namespace called `State`, which is used to encapsulated the persisted state of an ActiveX control. (So maybe we should have called it something else.)

Trying It All Out, Again

So what happens when we run this one? First of all, we see the control in the "ON" position (see Figure 17-15).

And if we click the control, it changes to the "OFF" position (see Figure 17-16).

Using .NET Components in the COM World

So, we've established beyond all doubt that we can use our COM legacy components in the brave new .NET world. We don't have to throw everything out *quite* yet. It's now time to consider the opposite question: Can we run .NET components in the COM world?

Figure 17-15

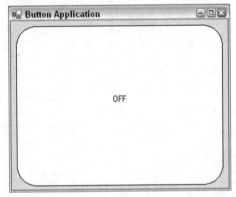

Figure 17-16

Actually, the question we should first be asking is probably this one: Why on earth should we want to run .NET components in the COM world? It's not immediately obvious, in fact, because migration to .NET would almost certainly be application-led in most cases, rather than component-led. However, it's possible (just) to imagine a situation where a particularly large application remains non-.NET while component development moves over to .NET. Well, let's pretend that that's the case for the next section. The technology's quite cool, anyway.

A .NET Component

Let's take a look at our definitely nonlegacy component. We'll implement an exact copy of the functionality that we did earlier with MegaCalculator and MeanCalculator, except using VB.NET rather than VB6.

Start off by creating a Class Library project called MegaCalculator2. This is the entire code of the class library:

```
Public Interface IMegaCalc

    Sub AddInput(ByVal InputValue As Double)
```

```
    Sub DoCalculation()
    Function GetResult() As Double
    Sub Reset()

End Interface
```

Next, we create another Class Library project, called `MeanCalculator3`. This will contain a class called `MeanCalc` that is going to implement the `IMegaCalc` interface, in a precise analog of the `MeanCalc` in our original VB6 `MeanCalculator` project. As before, we'll need to add a reference to `MegaCalculator2` first, although this time it will be a true .NET Framework reference, and we'll have to browse for it (see Figure 17-17).

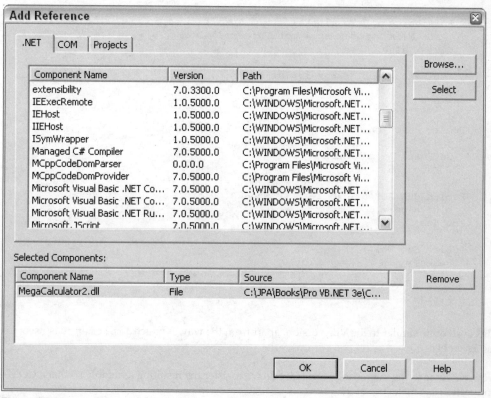

Figure 17-17

This is what the code looks like:

```
Public Class MeanCalc
    Implements MegaCalculator2.IMegaCalc

    Dim mintValue As Integer
    Dim mdblValues() As Double
    Dim mdblMean As Double
```

```
  Public Sub AddInput(ByVal InputValue As Double) _
      Implements MegaCalculator2.IMegaCalc.AddInput
    mintValue = mintValue + 1
    ReDim Preserve mdblValues(mintValue)
    mdblValues(mintValue - 1) = InputValue
  End Sub
  Public Sub DoCalculation() _
      Implements MegaCalculator2.IMegaCalc.DoCalculation
    Dim iValue As Integer

    mdblMean = 0

    If (mintValue = 0) Then Exit Sub

    For iValue = 0 To mintValue - 1 Step 1
      mdblMean = mdblMean + mdblValues(iValue)
    Next iValue

    mdblMean = mdblMean / iValue

  End Sub

  Public Function GetResult() As Double Implements _
                  MegaCalculator2.IMegaCalc.GetResult
    GetResult = mdblMean
  End Function

  Public Sub Reset() Implements MegaCalculator2.IMegaCalc.Reset
    mintValue = 0
  End Sub

  Public Sub New()
    Reset()
  End Sub

End Class
```

This is all quite similar to the VB6 version, apart from the way in which Implements is used. Let's build the assembly.

Now we come to the interesting part: How do we register the resulting assembly so that a COM-enabled application can make use of it?

RegAsm

The tool provided with the .NET Framework SDK to register assemblies for use by COM is called RegAsm. RegAsm and is very simple to use. If all you're interested in is late binding, then you simply run it like this (see Figure 17-18).

The only problem with RegAsm, in fact, is finding the thing. It's usually to be found lurking in %SystemRoot%\Microsoft.NET\Framework\<version>, where <version> is the current .NET Framework version number. You might find it useful to add this to your path in the system environment.

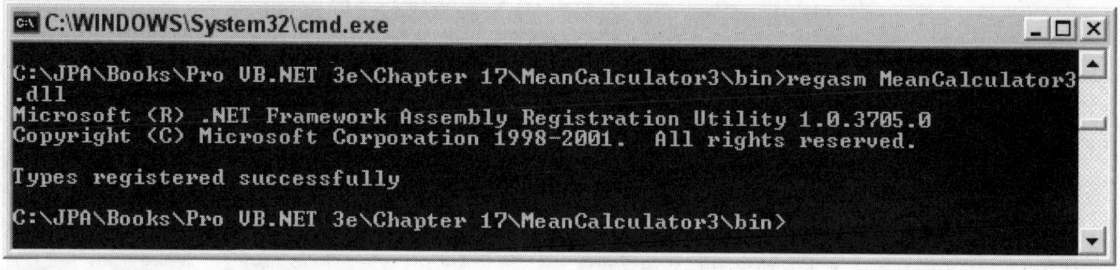

Figure 17-18

However, there's probably even less reason for late binding to an exported .NET component than there is for early binding, so we'll move on to look at early binding. For this, we need a type library, so we need to add another parameter, /tlb (see Figure 17-19).

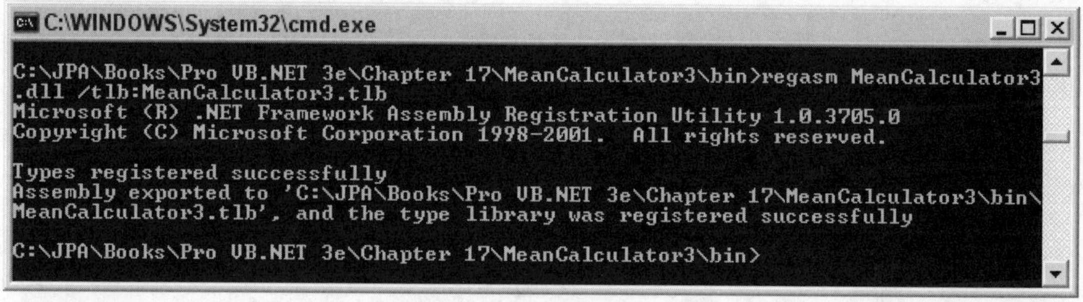

Figure 17-19

If we now take a look in our target directory, we see that not only do we have the original MeanCalculator3.dll, but we've also acquired a copy of the MegaCalculator2.dll and two type libraries: MeanCalculator3.tlb and MegaCalculator2.tlb. We'll need both of these, so it was good of RegAsm to provide them for us. We need the MegaCalculator2 type library for the same reason as .NET needed the MegaCalculator assembly because it contains the definition of the IMegaCalc interface that MeanCalculator is using.

Testing with a VB6 Application

Turning the tables again, we need to build a VB6 application to see if this is really going to work. Let's copy the type libraries over to our pre-.NET machine (if that's where VB6 is running) and create a Standard EXE project in VB6. We'll call this CalcApp2. We'll need to create references to our two new type libraries, so we go to the References dialog box, browse to find them and select them (see Figure 17-20).

Now we've got all we need to create our application. Let's create the same as we did for the VB.NET CalcApp (see Figure 17-21).

As before, the text boxes are txtInput and txtOutput, respectively, and the command buttons are btnAdd, btnCalculate, and btnReset. Here's the code behind it:

```
Option Explicit

Dim mobjCalc As MeanCalculator3.MeanCalc
Dim mobjMega As MegaCalculator2.IMegaCalc
```

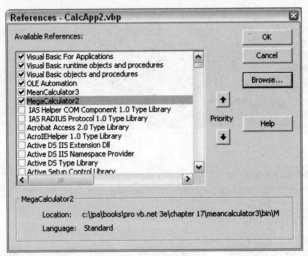

Figure 17-20

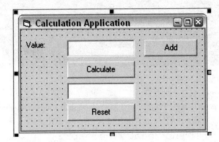

Figure 17-21

```
Private Sub btnAdd_Click()
  mobjMega.AddInput (txtInput.Text)
End Sub

Private Sub btnCalculate_Click()
  mobjMega.DoCalculation
  txtOutput.Text = mobjMega.GetResult
End Sub

Private Sub btnReset_Click()
  mobjMega.Reset
End Sub

Private Sub Form_Load()
  Set mobjCalc = New MeanCalculator3.MeanCalc
  Set mobjMega = mobjCalc
End Sub
```

Notice that, this time, we have to explicitly get hold of a reference to the interface `IMegaCalc`. The default interface of the component, `MeanCalc`, is entirely empty.

We make the executable via the File ➪ Make CalcApp2.exe menu item, and then we can move it back to our .NET machine (unless, of course, we're already there). Let's run it up and see what happens (see Figure 17-22).

Figure 17-22

Well, that's not *quite* what we expected. What's happened here?

In COM, the location of the DLL containing the component is available via the registry. In .NET, the assembly always has to be either in the current directory or the global assembly. All the registry is doing for us here is converting a COM reference to a .NET one; it's not finding the .NET one for us.

But it's easy to sort out. All we have to do to resolve matters is move the two assemblies, for `MegaCalculator3` and `MeanCalculator2`, to our current directory, and try again (see Figure 17-23).

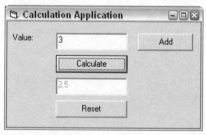

Figure 17-23

That's better. So we've established that in the unlikely event of having to run .NET from a COM-oriented application, Microsoft have provided us with the tools.

TlbExp

In fact, Microsoft has provided us with not one, but *two* alternative tools. The other one is `TlbExp`, which, as its name suggests, is the counterpart of `TlbImp`. This is how we can use `TlbExp` to achieve the same result as `RegAsm` in the previous section (see Figure 17-24).

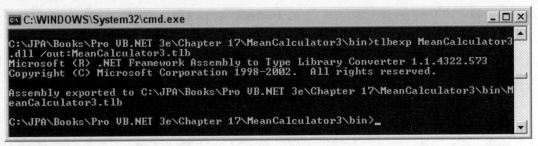

Figure 17-24

Summary

COM isn't going to go away for quite some time yet, so .NET applications have to interoperate with COM, and they have to do it well. In this chapter, we have looked at how all this works in practice.

- ❑ We managed to make a .NET application early bind to a COM component, using the import features available in VB.NET

- ❑ We looked at the underlying tool, Tlbimp

- ❑ We managed to make it late bind as well, although it wasn't a pleasant experience

- ❑ We incorporated an ActiveX control into a .NET user interface, again using the features of VB.NET

- ❑ We looked at using Regasm and TlbExp to export type libraries from .NET assemblies, so as to enable VB6 applications to use .NET assemblies as if they were COM components

18

Component Services

In Chapter 17, we explored the vast hinterland of legacy software known as COM. We're now going to look at "what COM did next" and how it fits into the world of .NET, in the shape of *.NET Component Services*. You would be forgiven for thinking that Component Services is yet another version of legacy software, except that much of it hasn't been around for long enough to be considered as legacy. However, there is more to it than that. The end result is something of a compromise between the old COM world and .NET.

To understand Component Services, we need to go back in time to around 1997. Microsoft had, by this time, become by far the dominant supplier to the PC market, and was looking for something else to do. The obvious thing was to move into the enterprise server market, and a number of initiatives began to emerge from Microsoft. Amongst these, in no particular order, were *Microsoft Transaction Server* (MTS), *Microsoft Message Queuing* (MSMQ), and *Microsoft Clustering Services*. The aim of these developments was to bring something that had previously been esoteric, specialized, and generally mainframe-based within the scope of standard PC technology.

Handling transactions involved a considerable extension to the NT/COM runtime. It also involved the introduction of several new standard COM interfaces, some to be used or implemented by transactional components and some to be used or implemented by the underlying resource managers, such as SQL Server. These additions, along with some other innovations relating to areas like asynchronous COM, came to be known as *COM+*.

There must have been considerable debate as to whether this vast infrastructure should be completely reimplemented within .NET or whether it should be tacked onto the side. In the event, pragmatism seems to have won the day because, under .NET, the *Component Services* (as they have been renamed) sit slightly uneasily between pure .NET and the kind of legacy COM stuff that we saw in the previous chapter. The end result is perfectly acceptable from an operational point of view, although it's debatable as to how elegant it is.

In this chapter, we're going to explore the .NET Component Services. In particular, we're going to look at transaction processing and queued components. This is an enormous subject that could easily fill a whole book by itself. In this chapter, we will only be able to scratch the surface of it. However, by the end of the chapter, you will understand how all the various pieces fit together.

Let's start by looking at what transactions are, and how they fit into Visual Basic .NET (VB.NET).

> You can find more information about transactions in .NET in *Professional VB.NET Transactions* (Wiley, 2002).

Transactions

A *transaction* is one or more linked units of processing placed together as a single unit of work, which either succeeds or fails. If the unit of work succeeds, the work is then committed. If the unit fails, then every item of processing is rolled back and the process is placed back to its original state.

The standard transaction example involves transferring money from account A to account B. The money must either end up in account B (and nowhere else), or — if something goes wrong — stay in account A (and go nowhere else). We don't want the case in which we have taken money from account A but haven't put it in account B.

The ACID Test

Transaction theory starts with *ACID*. According to the ACID theory, all transactions should have the following properties:

- ❑ *Atomicity* — A transaction is *atomic*; that is, everything is treated as one unit. However many different components the transaction involves, and however many different method calls on those components there are, the system treats it as a single operation that either entirely succeeds or entirely fails. If it fails, the system is left in a state as if the transaction had never happened.

- ❑ *Consistency* — All changes are done in a consistent manner. The system goes from one valid state to another.

- ❑ *Isolation* — Transactions that are going on at the same time are isolated from each other. If transaction A changes the system from state 1 to state 2, transaction B will see the system in either state 1 or 2, but not some half-baked state in between the two.

- ❑ *Durability* — If a transaction has been committed, the effect will be permanent, even if the system fails.

Let's illustrate this with a concrete example. Imagine that, having spent a happy afternoon browsing in your favorite bookstore, you decide to shell out some of your hard-earned dollars for a copy of, yes, *Professional VB.NET 3rd Edition* (wise choice). You take the copy to the checkout, and you ask if they happen to have a less dog-eared one. A transaction is going on here: you pay money, and the store provides you with a book.

There are only two reasonable outcomes, either you get the book and the store gets their money or you don't get the book and the store doesn't get their money. If, for example, there is insufficient credit on your card, you'll walk out of the shop without the book. If, on the other hand, there are no more copies of the book in the stockroom, you don't hand over your card at all. In either case, the transaction doesn't happen. The only way for the transaction to complete is for you to get the book and the store to get their money. This is the principle of atomicity.

If, on the other hand, the store decides to provide you with a copy of, say, Neal Stephenson's *Cryptonomicon* instead, you might reasonably feel that you have ended up with an outcome that wasn't originally on the agenda. This would be a violation of the principle of consistency.

Let's now imagine that there is one copy of the book in the storeroom. However, another potential buyer has gone up to the till next to you. As far as the person at the next till is concerned, your respective transactions are isolated from each other (even though you are competing for the same resource). Either your transaction succeeds or the other person's does. What very definitely *doesn't* happen is that the bookstore decides to exert the wisdom of Solomon and give you half each.

Once you have taken the book home, let's imagine that the bookstore calls you up and asks you if they could have the book back. Apparently, some important customer (well, far more important than you, anyway) needs a copy. You would feel that this was a tad unreasonable, and a violation of the principle of durability.

At this point, it's worth considering what implications all this is likely to have on the underlying components. How can you ensure that all of the changes in the system can be unwound if the transaction is aborted at some point? Perhaps you're in the middle of updating dozens of database files, and something goes wrong.

There are three aspects to rescuing this situation with transactions. First of all, we have to know that something has gone wrong. Secondly, we need to know how to perform the recovery. Thirdly, we need to coordinate the process of recovery. The middle part of the process is handled by the resource managers themselves; the likes of SQL Server and Oracle are fully equipped to deal with two-phase commit and rollback (even if the resource manager in question is restarted part-way through a transaction), and we don't need to worry about any of that. The last part of the process, coordination, is handled by the .NET runtime (or at least the Component Services part of it). The first part, knowing that something is wrong, is shared between the components themselves and the .NET runtime. This isn't at all unusual: Sometimes a component can detect that something has gone wrong itself and signal that recovery is necessary whilst, on other occasions, it may not be able to do so, because it has crashed.

We'll see how all this works as we build our first transactional application. However, before we do that, we need to look at how transactions are implemented within .NET component services.

Transactional Components

But what actually are the components that are managed by Component Services? What purpose do they serve? To answer that, we need to consider what a typical real-world *n*-tier application looks like. The bottom tier is the persistent data store, typically an industry-standard database such as SQL Server or Oracle. The software here is concerned with maintaining the integrity of the application's data and providing rapid and efficient access to it. The top tier is the user interface. This is a completely different specialization, and the software here is concerned with presenting a smooth, easy to follow front-end to the end user. This layer shouldn't actually do any data manipulation at all, apart from whatever formatting is necessary to meet each user's presentational needs. The interesting stuff is in the tiers in between, in particular, the business logic. In the .NET/COM+ transactional model, the software elements that implement this are components running under the control of the Component Services runtime.

Typically, these components are called into being to perform some sort of transaction and then, to all intents and purposes, disappear again. For example, a component might be called into play to transfer information from one database to another in such a way that the information was either in one database or the other, but not both. This component might have a number of different methods, each of which did a different kind of transfer. However, each method call would carry out a complete transfer:

```
Public Sub TransferSomething()
   TakeSomethingFromA
   AddSomethingToB
End Sub
```

Crucially, this means that most transaction components have no concept of *state*, there are no properties that hold values between method calls. Persistence is left to the outside tiers in this model. This takes a little bit of getting used to at first, because it runs counter to everything that we learnt in first grade object-orientation classes, so let's take a minute or two to consider what we're actually gaining from this.

The business logic is the area of the system that requires all the transactional management. Anything that happens here needs to be monitored and controlled to ensure that all the ACID requirements are met. The neatest way to do this in a component-oriented framework is to develop the business logic as components that are required to implement a standard interface. The transaction management framework can then use this interface to monitor and control how the logic is implemented from a transactional point of view. The transaction interface is a means for the business logic elements to talk to the transaction framework and for the transaction framework to talk back to the logic elements.

So what's all this about not having state? Well, if we maintain state inside our components, then we've immediately got ourselves a scaling problem. The middle tiers of our application are now seriously resource-hungry. If you want an analogy from another area of software, consider why the Internet scales so well. The reason that it does is because HTTP is a stateless protocol. Every HTTP request stands in isolation, so no resources are tied up in maintaining any form of session. It's the same with transactional components.

This is not to say that you can't ever maintain state inside your transactional components. You can. However, it's not recommended, and we certainly won't be doing it in the examples in this chapter.

Before we move on into some practical examples, there's one other thing we need to talk about. We said earlier that transactional components are called into being, do their thing, and then disappear. This isn't the most efficient way of doing things, as instantiating a component takes a fair amount of effort. It would be better if we had a whole pool of components sitting there waiting to be used. In fact, it turns out that we can do just this. We'll see how it works in practice later.

An Example of Transactions

For our transaction example, we're going to build a simple business logic component that transfers data from one bank account (Wrox's, in fact) to another one (mine, of course). Wrox's bank account will be represented by a row in one database (BankOfWrox), whilst mine will be represented by a row in another one (BankOfJon, it's kind of a sideline).

There's one important point that we should make right from the start. You can't have transactions without any resource managers. It's very tempting to think that you can experiment with transactional component services without actually involving, say, a database, because (as we shall see) none of the methods in the transactional classes makes any explicit references to one. However, if you do try to do this, you will find that your transactions don't actually trouble the system's statistics. Fortunately, you don't need to go out and lay out your hard-earned cash for a copy of SQL Server (nice though that is), because Visual Studio .NET (VS.NET) comes with a stripped-down (but fully functional) copy of SQL Server, which goes under the name of *Microsoft Database Engine*, or *MSDE*. If for some reason, you don't have MSDE installed, you can download it from Microsoft's Web site.

Creating Our Databases

The first thing we have to do, then, is set up our databases. Check to see if the Server Explorer tab is visible in VS.NET. If it isn't, you may need to connect to your server. You can do this by selecting Tools, and then Connect to Server from the menu. The Server Explorer tab should become visible now, and you'll see the start of a tree of servers. Your computer should be in there; open up this node, and you should see SQL Servers. Open this up, and you should see your instance of SQL Server listed (see Figure 18-1).

Figure 18-1

The next thing to do is right-click this, and select New Database from the menu. A further dialog box will appear (see Figure 18-2).

We enter our database name (BankOfWrox), and elect to use Windows NT Integrated Security (which means that it uses the same security as Windows itself). You should now see BankOfWrox in the tree below your instance of SQL Server (see Figure 18-3).

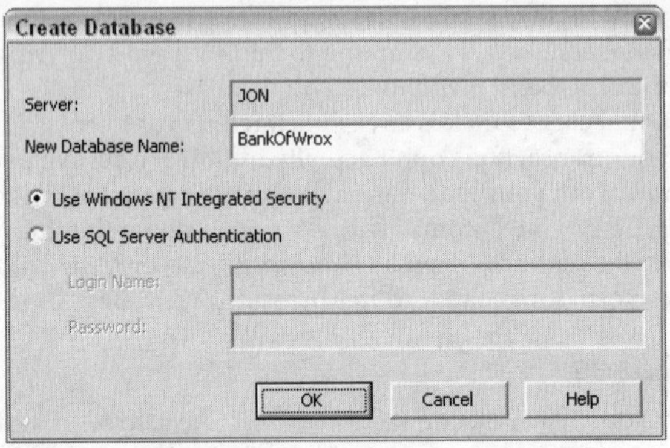

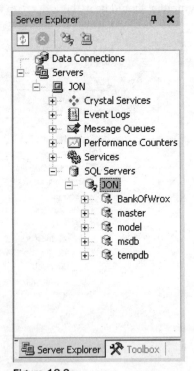

Figure 18-2

Figure 18-3

The next thing to do is set up the database. If you open up the new node, you should see a number of other nodes, including Tables. Right-click this, then select New Table from the menu. A further dialog box should appear (see Figure 18-4).

Create two columns, Name and Amount, as shown. Make sure that Name is set up to be the primary key. When you click the close box, you'll be asked if you want to save changes to Table1. Select Yes, and another dialog box will appear (see Figure 18-5).

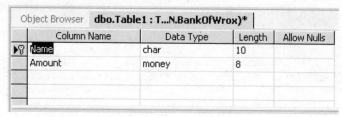

Figure 18-4

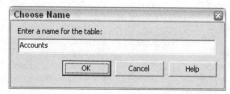

Figure 18-5

As suggested, use the name Accounts for the table. You should now see a child node called Accounts below Tables in the tree.

OK, that's BankOfWrox created. Repeat the whole process for BankOfJon. The structure is exactly the same (although it doesn't need to be for the purposes of this example). Don't forget to set Name as the primary key.

Populating Our Databases

The next thing we need to do is populate our databases. If we right-click over Accounts for either database, and select Retrieve Datafrom Table from the menu, we will see a grid which will enable us to add rows and initialize the values of their columns (see Figure 18-6).

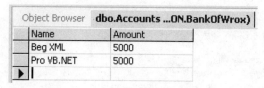

Figure 18-6

Enter two accounts in BankOfWrox, Pro VB.NET and Beg XML, and allocate $5,000 to each. Now repeat the process for BankOfJon, setting up one account, Jon, with $0 in it. (So Jon is either (a) broke or (b) wise enough not to leave any cash lying around in this sort of account. Go figure this out!)

The Business Logic

The next step is to create our transactional component to support our business logic. Create a new Class Library project called TransSample. Then, add a reference to System.EnterpriseServices (see Figure 18-7).

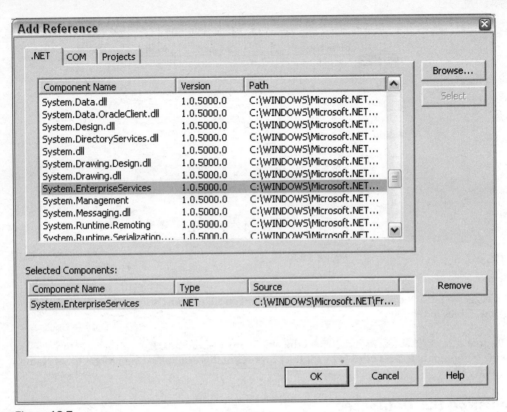

Figure 18-7

We're going to need this reference because, in order to come under the control of the Component Services runtime, our component needs to inherit from the `System.EnterpriseServices` `.ServicedComponent` class:

```
Imports System.EnterpriseServices

Public Class TransSample
  Inherits ServicedComponent
```

Here's the main function in our component, `TransferMoney`:

```
Public Function TransferMoney(ByVal intDollars As Integer) As Boolean
    If TakeFromWrox(intDollars) = True Then
      If AddToJon(intDollars) = True Then
        ContextUtil.SetComplete()
        TransferMoney = True
      Else
        ContextUtil.SetAbort()
        TransferMoney = False
      End If
    Else
```

```
        ContextUtil.SetAbort()
        TransferMoney = False
    End If
  End Function
End Class
```

Ignoring, for the moment, the references to `ContextUtil`, we can see that we have effectively divided up the logic into two halves, the half that takes money from the Wrox account (represented by the private function `TakeFromWrox`), and the half that adds it to Jon's account (represented by the private function `AddToJon`). For the function to complete successfully, each of the two halves must complete successfully.

So what does `ContextUtil` do? The `ContextUtil` class represents the context of the transaction. Within that context, there are basically two bits that control the behavior of the transaction from the point of view of each participant: the *consistent* bit and the *done* bit. The done bit determines whether or not the transaction is finished, so that resources can be reused (we'll have more to say on this later, when we talk about Just-In-Time Activation and Object Pooling). The consistent bit determines whether or not the transaction was successful from the point of view of the participant. This is established during the first phase of the two-phase commit process. In complex distributed transactions involving more than one participant, the overall consistency and doneness are voted on, so that a transaction is only consistent or done when everyone agrees that it is. If a transaction completes in an inconsistent state, it is not allowed to proceed to the second phase of the commit.

In this case, we only have a single participant, but the principal remains the same. We can determine the overall outcome by setting these two bits, and we do this via `SetComplete` and `SetAbort`, which are static methods in the `ContextUtil` class. Both of these set the done bit to `True`. `SetComplete` also sets the consistent bit to `True`, whereas `SetAbort` sets the consistent bit to `False`. In our example, `SetComplete` is only set if both halves of the transaction are successful.

The First Half of the Transaction

Now let's see what's going on in the two halves of the transaction itself.

1. First of all, here's the function that takes the money out of the Wrox account:

```
Private Function TakeFromWrox(ByVal intDollars As Integer) As Boolean
   Dim strConn As String
   Dim strCmd As String

   Dim objConn As SqlClient.SqlConnection
   Dim objAdapter As SqlClient.SqlDataAdapter
   Dim objBuilder As SqlClient.SqlCommandBuilder

   Dim objDataset As DataSet
   Dim objTable As DataTable
   Dim objRow As DataRow

   Dim intBalance As Integer
```

2. We start off by establishing a connection to our database, and extracting the entire table from it:

```
strConn = "DATABASE=BankOfWrox;SERVER=(local);UID=sa;PWD=;"
strCmd = "Select * From Accounts"
```

```
objConn = New SqlClient.SqlConnection(strConn)
objAdapter = New SqlClient.SqlDataAdapter(strCmd, objConn)
objBuilder = New SqlClient.SqlCommandBuilder(objAdapter)
```

3. The call to `SqlCommandBuilder` sets up the default SQL commands that will be used when we update the database. Next, we extract the second row (which should be Pro VB.NET) into a `DataRow` object:

```
objDataset = New DataSet()
objAdapter.Fill(objDataset)
objTable = objDataset.Tables(0)
objRow = objTable.Rows(1)
```

4. We get the current balance, and see if we can afford to transfer the amount that we've asked for. If not, we set the result of the function to `False`:

```
intBalance = CInt(objRow("Amount"))

If intDollars > intBalance Then
    TakeFromWrox = False
```

5. Otherwise, we subtract the amount, and update the table accordingly, setting the result to `True`:

```
Else
    intBalance = intBalance - intDollars

    objRow("Amount") = intBalance
    objAdapter.Update(objTable)

    TakeFromWrox = True
End If
```

6. Finally, we close the database:

```
    objConn.Close()
End Function
```

The Second Half of the Transaction

The second half of the transaction is similar, except that the failure conditions are slightly different. First of all, Jon has stipulated that he doesn't want fiddly bits of loose change from Wrox, and so won't accept any transfer of less than $500. Secondly, we've inserted a bug such that an attempt to transfer a negative amount will cause a divide by zero. We'll see why we did this rather bizarre act of sabotage in a little while. Here's the code:

```
Private Function AddToJon(ByVal intDollars As Integer) As Boolean
    Dim strConn As String
    Dim strCmd As String
```

```
    Dim objConn As SqlClient.SqlConnection
    Dim objAdapter As SqlClient.SqlDataAdapter
    Dim objBuilder As SqlClient.SqlCommandBuilder

    Dim objDataset As DataSet
    Dim objTable As DataTable
    Dim objRow As DataRow

    Dim intBalance As Integer

    If intDollars < 0 Then
      intDollars = intDollars / 0
    ElseIf intDollars < 500 Then
      AddToJon = False
    Else
      strConn = "DATABASE=BankOfJon;SERVER=(local);UID=sa;PWD=;"
      strCmd = "Select * From Accounts"
      objConn = New SqlClient.SqlConnection(strConn)
      objAdapter = New SqlClient.SqlDataAdapter(strCmd, objConn)
      objBuilder = New SqlClient.SqlCommandBuilder(objAdapter)

      objDataset = New DataSet()
      objAdapter.Fill(objDataset)

      objTable = objDataset.Tables(0)
      objRow = objTable.Rows(0)

      intBalance = CInt(objRow("Amount"))

      intBalance = intBalance + intDollars

      objRow("Amount") = intBalance
      objAdapter.Update(objTable)

      objConn.Close()

      AddToJon = True
    End If
  End Function
End Function
```

Our business logic component is complete. Let's see how we bring it under the control of Component Services. First of all, of course, we need to build our DLL in VS.NET.

The RegSvcs Tool

Because the Component Services infrastructure is COM-oriented, we need to use a tool that does two things: it needs to expose the .NET component as a COM component, and it then needs to register that COM component with Component Services . Component Services handles all transaction coordination. In other words, you only have to declare your required scripts and components, and then Component Services tracks any changes and restores the data should the transaction fail. The tool to do this is called RegSvcs. It's part of the .NET Framework, like the other tools (such as RegAsm) that we encountered in the previous chapter. There are a number of different options associated with the RegSvcs tool and they are outlined in the following table.

Option	Description
/appname:(name)	Specifies the name of the target application
/c	Creates the target application or gives an error message if it already exists
/componly	Configures components only, without methods or interfaces
/exapp	Expects an existing application
/extlb	Uses an existing type library
/fc	Finds or creates the target application (default)
/help or /?	Displays a usage message containing tool options and command syntax
/nologo	Suppresses the Microsoft logo output
/noreconfig	Doesn't reconfigure the existing target application
/parname:(name)	Specifies the name or ID of the target partition
/quiet	Specifies quiet mode; suppresses the logo and success output
/reconfig	Reconfigures an existing target application (default)
/tlb:(typelibrary file)	Specifies the filename for the type library to install
/u	Uninstalls the target application

This is what happens when we run with the following command (see Figure 18-8).

```
regsvcs TransSample.dll
```

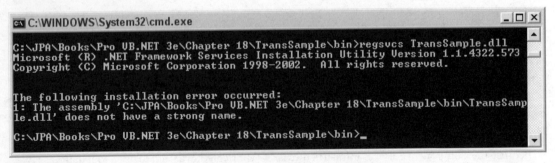

Figure 18-8

Actually, that wasn't really what we wanted to see. RegSvcs is telling us that our DLL doesn't have a strong name.

In Chapter 25, you can find more information about strong names and assemblies in general.

The problem that we are facing is that the assembly that we've just created is a private assembly. In order to make it available to the transaction framework, we need to turn it into a shared assembly. To do this, we need to give the assembly a *cryptographically strong name*, generally referred to as its *shared name*.

Cryptographically strong means that the name has been signed with the private key of a dual key pair. This isn't the place to go into a long discussion on dual key cryptography, but the essence of this is as follows: A pair of keys are generated, one public and one private. If something is encrypted using the private key, it can only be decrypted using the public key from that pair

This means that it is an excellent tool for preventing tampering with information. If, for example, the name of an assembly were to be encrypted using the private key of a pair, then the recipient of a new version of that assembly could verify the origin of that new version, and be confident that it was not a rogue version from some other source. This is because only the original creator of the assembly retains access to its private key.

This is slightly scary stuff, because we don't usually expect to get involved in cryptography unless we're either (a) paranoid or (b) routinely working in the field of security. However, it's not a big deal in .NET, because Microsoft has helpfully provided us with a tool to generate key pairs. The tool is called sn, which stands for strong name.

The sn Tool

sn is another of those command line tools that come as part of the .NET package. This one is located in the \bin subdirectory from the .NET Framework SDK path. It's a very simple tool to use if all we want to do is generate a key pair. We use the -k command line option, plus the name of the key file that we want to create, as shown in the following example:

```
sn -k sgKey.snk
```

Let's run it and see what happens (see Figure 18-9).

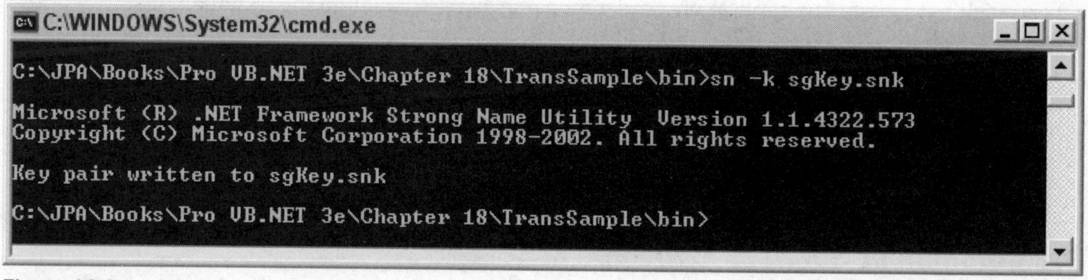

```
C:\WINDOWS\System32\cmd.exe                                          _ □ X

C:\JPA\Books\Pro UB.NET 3e\Chapter 18\TransSample\bin>sn -k sgKey.snk

Microsoft (R) .NET Framework Strong Name Utility  Version 1.1.4322.573
Copyright (C) Microsoft Corporation 1998-2002. All rights reserved.

Key pair written to sgKey.snk

C:\JPA\Books\Pro UB.NET 3e\Chapter 18\TransSample\bin>
```

Figure 18-9

Giving the Assembly a Strong Name

We now have to make sure that our assembly uses the strong name. Add the following (adjusted appropriately for your configuration) to Assembly.vb:

```
<Assembly: AssemblyKeyFile("C:\JPA\Books\Pro VB.NET 3e\Chapter
18\TransSample\sgKey.snk")>
```

This new line tells .NET where to find the file containing the strong name that the assembly should be signed with.

Registering with Component Services

Once we've built the DLL again, we can run `RegSvcs` once more (see Figure 18-10).

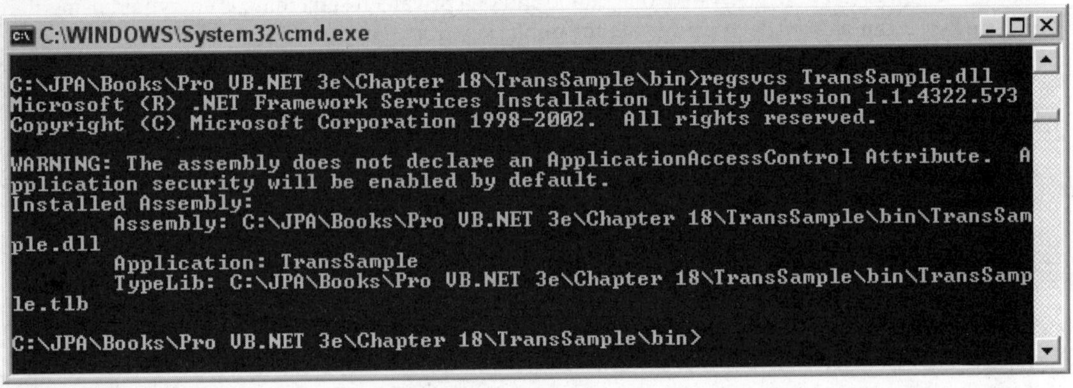

Figure 18-10

Note that `RegSvcs` has rapped us on the knuckles slightly, by pointing out that we haven't explicitly stated how we want security to operate for this application. COM+ security is outside the scope of this chapter, but suffice to say that it is controlled by the settings of an attribute called `ApplicationAccessControl`. If we don't explicitly declare this attribute in `AssemblyInfo.vb`, `RegSvcs` supplies default settings for us, the effect of which is the same as if we had added the following line:

```
<Assembly: ApplicationAccessControl(True)>
```

We could have given our application a different name by passing it into the command line:

```
regsvcs TransSample.dll TransSampleApp
```

We could also have changed the name of the type library that it generated as well by passing this as the third parameter. The type library, of course, is only there because Component Services talks COM, and not native .NET.

The Component Services Console

The *Component Services Console* is the control interface for Component Services. This is an MMC snap-in, which you can find (on Windows 2000 and XP) by selecting Control Panel ⇨ Administrative Tools ⇨ Component Services. If you open it up, you'll see something like this (see Figure 18-11).

Hey! That's the name of our sample, under COM+ Applications. A COM+ application is a set of related COM+ components that have been packaged together. `RegSvcs` creates a new application for every component that it registers. If you want to bundle together a series of components from separate DLLs, you can do this, but you can only do it by creating a new application via the Component Services Console (try right-clicking COM+ Applications and then selecting New). We'll explore the console a little more as we go on.

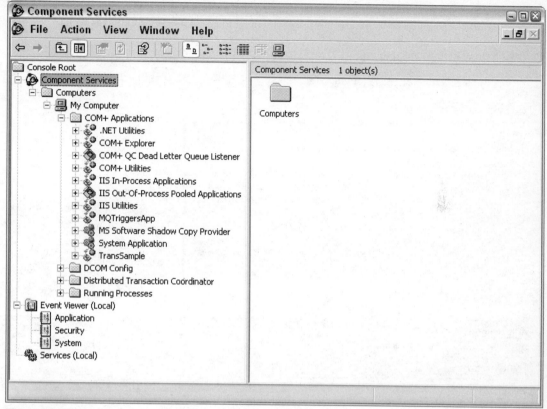

Figure 18-11

That's all very nice, but we're missing a couple of things. First of all, we need a test application. Secondly, and more importantly, we need to tell Component Services that we're interested in transactions.

A Test Application

Let's deal with the first problem straight away. We'll create a Windows Application project called `TransApp` and make a very simple form (see Figure 18-12).

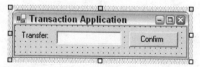

Figure 18-12

The text field is called `txtDollars` and the command button is called `btnConfirm`.

In order to access our transactional component, we need to add references to a couple of DLLs. First of all, we need to add a reference to the transactional component DLL itself. We'll need to browse for this, as it isn't currently in the global assembly cache.

Secondly, in order to access the objects in this DLL, we'll also need to make our application aware of the `System.EnterpriseServices` assembly, so we'll need to add a reference to that as well.

Having done that, we need to import `TransSample` into our application:

```
Imports TransSample.TransSample

Public Class Form1
    Inherits System.Windows.Forms.Form
```

Here's the code behind our `Confirm` button:

```
Private Sub btnConfirm_Click(ByVal sender As System.Object, _
                             ByVal e As System.EventArgs) _
                             Handles btnConfirm.Click
    Dim objTrans As TransSample.TransSample
    objTrans = New TransSample.TransSample()

    If objTrans.TransferMoney(CInt(txtDollars.Text)) = True Then
      MsgBox("Transfer complete")
    Else
      MsgBox("Transfer failed")
```

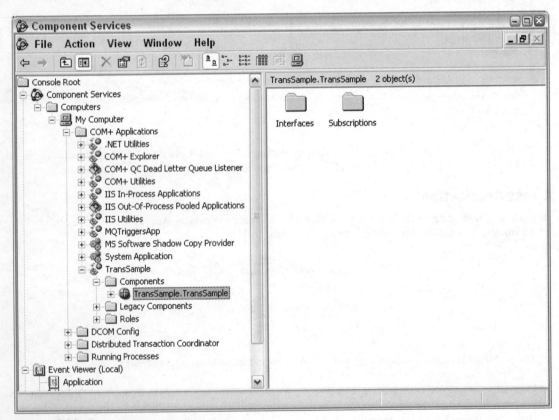

Figure 18-13

```
End If

    objTrans = Nothing
End Sub
```

The Transaction Attribute

We now need to tell Component Services how we wish our component to enter a transaction. There are two ways of doing this. Firstly, we can do it via the Component Services Console. First of all, we need to open up the explorer tree to locate the `TransSample` component (see Figure 18-13).

Next, we right click over this, and select Properties from the menu, then the Transactions tab (see Figure 18-14).

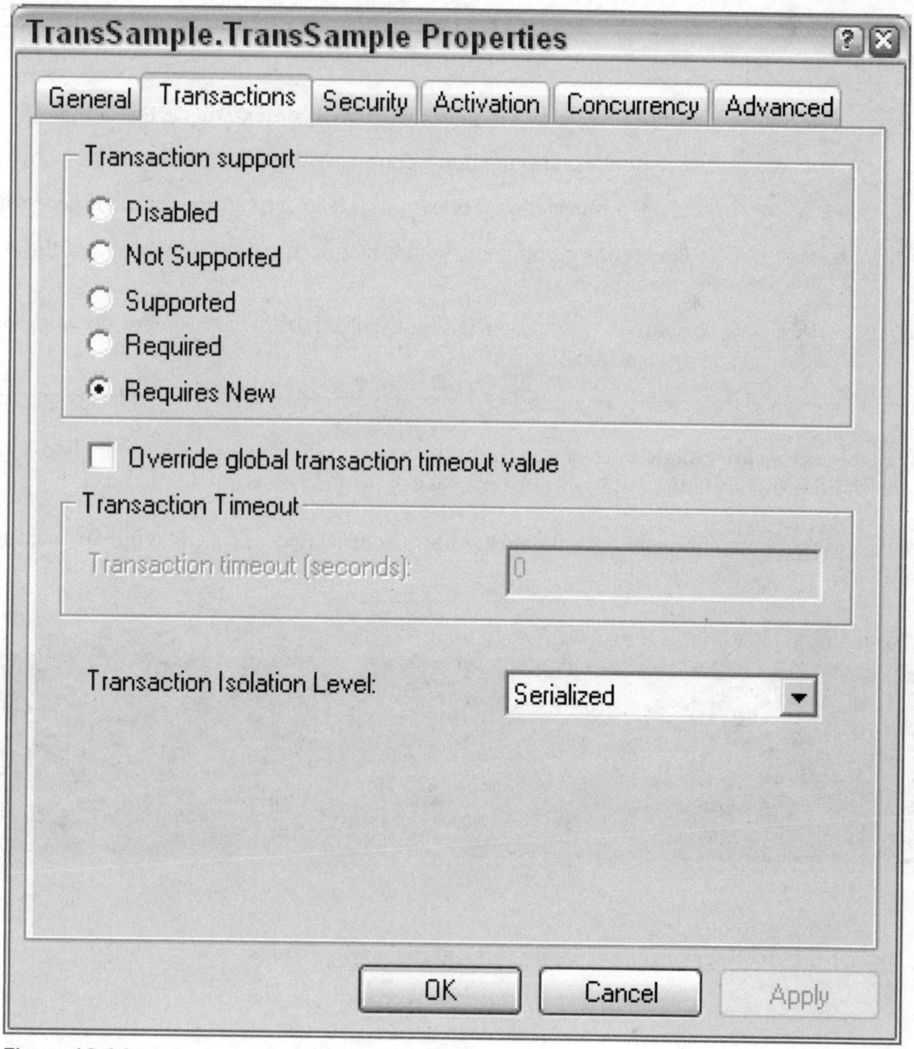

Figure 18-14

We can then select one of the available options; we'll discuss what these all mean in a moment.

However, it's a little tiresome to require our system manager to do this every time, especially if we already know that our component is always going to have the same transaction characteristics. So there's an alternative mechanism available to us: we can explicitly set up an attribute in the code for our component.

Attributes are items of declarative information that can be attached to the elements of code, such as classes, methods, data members, and properties. Anything that uses these can query their values at runtime. One such attribute is called `TransactionAttribute`, and, unsurprisingly, this is used for specifying the transaction characteristics of a component class. The value of this attribute is taken from an enumeration called `TransactionOption`. Both `TransactionAttribute` and `TransactionOption` are found within the `System.EnterpriseServices` namespace. That enumeration can take the following values.

Value	Description
Disabled	Ignore any transaction in the current context; this is the default.
NotSupported	Create the component in a context with no governing transaction
Required	Share a transaction if one exists; create a new transaction if necessary
RequiresNew	Create the component with a new transaction, regardless of the state of the current context
Supported	Share a transaction if one exists. If it doesn't, create the component in a transaction-free context

The available values are exactly the same as the ones shown in the `Transaction` tab. In our case, we've got a stand-alone transaction, so either `RequiresNew` or `Required` is equally valid.

Before we change our component, let's deregister the current version, so as to avoid any confusion (see Figure 18-15).

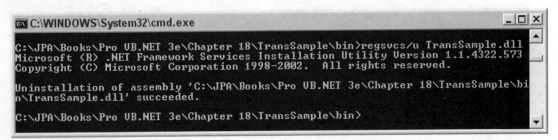

Figure 18-15

Now let's go back to our `TransSample` project and make the change:

```
<Transaction(TransactionOption.RequiresNew)> _
Public Class TransSample
    Inherits ServicedComponent
```

Having made our change, we can rebuild `TransSample` and then reregister it as we did before.

Before we start running our application, open up the section of the explorer tree in the Component Services Console labeled DistributedTransaction Coordinator, and select Transaction Statistics. You should see something like this (see Figure 18-16).

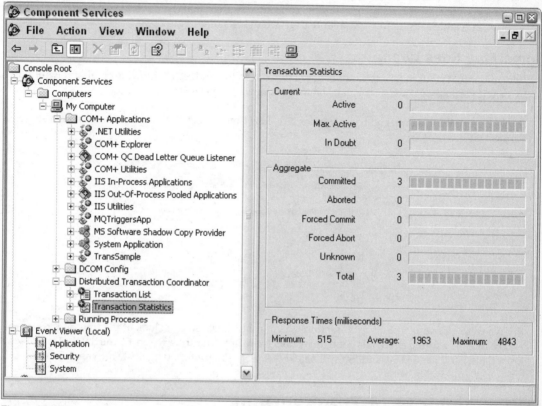

Figure 18-16

Now run the application.

Enter 1000 and hit the Confirm button. You should see the number of current active transactions briefly go from none to one, followed by the number of committed transactions and the total both going up by one. Great, we've implemented our first transaction. And if we check the two databases, we can see that the amount in `BankOfWrox`'s Pro VB.NET account has been reduced to $4,000, whereas Jon's account in `BankOfJon` has been increased by $1,000. ("Because I'm worth it", says Jon.)

Invalid Data

So what happens if we enter a value that we know is invalid? There are two options here: Either we try to transfer more money than there is in the Pro VB.NET account, or we try to transfer less than Jon will accept. Let's run the application again and try to transfer $100. As expected, the transaction will fail, and no changes will be made to the accounts. Pro VB.NET still has $4,000, and Jon still has $1,000. This isn't too much of a big deal, because the invalid condition is spotted before any database manipulation is carried out. If we look at the transaction statistics, we can see that the number of *aborted* transactions has been incremented this time.

However, let's try to transfer $10,000. This time around, the first part of the transaction is successful, but the *second* part fails. Again, the number of aborted transactions is incremented. But what's happened to the database? Well, fortunately for everyone concerned, we see that there is still $4,000 in the Pro VB.NET account, and still $1,000 in Jon's. The *entire* transaction has failed.

Something Goes Wrong

Remember that bit of mindless vandalism that we did to the `AddToJon` function, so that it would divide by zero if we entered a negative value? Here's where we get to try it out.

Run the application again, and try to transfer $-1. This time we get a rather unpleasant response (see Figure 18-17).

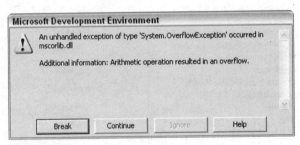

Figure 18-17

But we were halfway through a transaction! Never mind, because if we look at the transaction statistics, we see that the aborted count has gone up by one. More importantly, if we check the databases, we see that Pro VB.NET *still* has $4,000, and Jon still has $1,000. So we're protected against software failures as well.

Other Aspects of Transactions

There are a number of other things that we can do with transactions that we should briefly cover here. We will first of all discuss how manual transactions differ from automatic ones, and then look at Just-In-Time activation and Object Pooling.

Manual Transactions

So far in this chapter, we have, in fact, been talking about *automatic transactions*. That is, transactions where Component Services determines when a transaction is about to start, according to the transaction attributes of the components taking part. In most cases, this is the sort of transaction that we'd be using by choice. However, there are also *manual transactions*, which are transactions that are started whenever we want them to. For example, within ADO.NET, you can use the `BeginTransaction` method on the `Connection` object to start a manual transaction. This returns a reference to a `Transaction` object, and you can use the `Commit` or `Rollback` methods on this to determine its outcome.

Just-In-Time

Creating and deleting components takes time. So, instead of discarding the component when we've finished with it, why not keep it around in case another instance is required? The mechanism by which we do this is called *Just-In-Time* (JIT) *activation*, and it's set by default for all automatic transactional components (it's unset by default for all other COM+ components, however).

We know by now that all good transactional components are entirely stateless. However, real life dictates differently, because, for example, we might want to maintain a link to our database, one that would be expensive to set up every time. The JIT mechanism provides us with a couple of methods that we can override in the `ServicedComponent` class in this case.

The method that gets invoked when a JIT component gets activated is called `Activate`, and the component that gets invoked when it is deactivated is called, unsurprisingly, `Deactivate`. In `Activate` and `Deactivate` you should put the things that you would normally put in your constructor and deconstructor. In addition, JIT can be activated by adding the `JustInTimeActivation` attribute to any class within `ServicedComponent`.

Object Pooling

We can, if we want, take this a stage further and maintain a pool of objects already constructed and prepared to be activated whenever required. When the object is no longer required or deactivated, it is returned to the pool until the next time it is required. By retaining objects, we do not have to continually create them from new, which in turn reduces the performance costs of our application. We can use the `ObjectPooling` attribute within our class to determine how the pool is to operate:

```
<Transaction(TransactionOption.RequiresNew), _
ObjectPooling(MinPoolSize:=5, MaxPoolSize:=20, _
                    CreationTimeOut:=30)> Public Class TransSample
```

Holding Things Up

A JIT-activated component will be deactivated whenever the current method call returns, unless we tell it otherwise. The way that we control this is by means of methods in the `ContextUtil` class. The `ContextUtil` is the favored method to obtain information about the context of the COM+ object.

If we invoke `ContextUtil.DisableCommit`, we are effectively telling Component Services that we are not finished yet; in other words, we're setting the consistency and done bits of the transaction to `False`. The transaction is in an indeterminate state for the time being. Once we are happy that everything is complete, we can call `ContextUtil.EnableCommit`, setting the consistency to `True` and the done bit to `False`. This says that we are happy for the component to be deactivated at the end of the current method call. However, it doesn't say whether or not the transaction is complete or not. It's up to us to invoke either `SetComplete`, setting both the consistency and done parts to true, or `SetAbort`, which sets the consistency to false and done to true, in other words, aborting the call.

As has been shown, `ContextUtil` allows us to control the activity of the object and retrieve any information about its context.

Queued Components

The traditional component programming model is very much a *synchronous* one. Put simply, you invoke a method and you get a result. However, a little thought reveals the unfortunate fact that an awful lot of real-world problems are inherently *asynchronous*. You can't always wait for a response to your request before moving on to the next task. So, if we are to be able to tackle everything that the real world throws at us, we need to introduce an asynchronous component model.

Actually, it's a little more complicated than that. The synchronous model is quite simple to manage, because the three possible outcomes of a request are quite straightforward to handle. First of all, the request can be successful. Secondly, the software can crash. Finally, the software can simply not respond at all; in which case, we will have to time it out. However, if we are dealing with asynchronous requests, we have to handle all manner of unusual conditions. For example, the target system may not currently be operational, so we will have to take a decision on how long to wait before it comes back up again. Each outstanding request will take up system resources, so we will have to manage these resources carefully. We need to be able to know when the response comes back. And so on.

We are, in fact, dealing with a whole new infrastructure here, an infrastructure to handle reliable messaging. Microsoft's product to tackle this type of problem is MSMQ, or Microsoft Message Queue.

The idea behind reliable messaging is that once you have sent a message to a given target, you can effectively forget about it. The system will handle storing and forwarding of messages to their target, and will handle retries and timeouts for you, eventually giving up and returning messages to your dead letter queue if all else fails. MSMQ is, in fact, a whole technology in itself, but we're not going to cover it in any great detail here. However, we are going to look at where it impinges on .NET Component Services — welcome to *queued components*.

The principle behind queued components is quite simple. With standard component technology, every method call is entirely synchronous. You invoke the method and you wait for the response. If something fails along the way, you may have to wait a long time, but the system will eventually time you out. This is, generally speaking, all well and good if we are dealing with a single, self-contained system. However, once we get out into the distributed computing world, things get a little messier. We have to consider the possibility that it isn't sensible to wait for a response before moving on to the next task. This is where queued components come in. The idea is that you just invoke the method and then continue processing.

Naturally, this places some restrictions on the kind of component that we can use for this kind of thing. For example, we can't have any output arguments, and we can't have any return value. However, there are some cool things that we can do, and we're going to explore them in the next section.

> In order to run the Queued Components examples, MSMQ is needed, which comes with Windows 2000 and XP.

An Example of Queued Components

We're going to write a very simple logging component that takes a string as its input, and writes it out to a sequential file, as well as outputting it in a message box. For the purposes of a simple example, the client and the server will be on the same machine; however, in a production scenario they would be separate. So let's create a Class Library project called `Reporter`. As usual with component services, we need to add a reference to the `System.EnterpriseServices` namespace. The first thing we do is define an interface:

```
Imports System.IO
Imports System.EnterpriseServices

Public Interface IQReporter
  Sub Log(ByVal strText As String)
End Interface
```

We need to separate out the interface from the implementation because the implementation, residing on the server, is going to be sitting on another machine somewhere. The client isn't the slightest bit interested in the details of this; all it needs to know is how to interface to it.

Let's take a look at the actual implementation. As with our transactional component, we inherit from `ServicedComponent`, and we also implement the interface that we have just defined. However, notice the `<InterfaceQueuing()>` attribute that indicates to the component services runtime that the interface can be queued (we did the same for the interface):

```
<InterfaceQueuing(Interface:="IQReporter")> Public Class ImplReporter
  Inherits ServicedComponent
  Implements IQReporter
```

In the logging method, all we do is output a message box, open up a `StreamWriter` component to append to our log file, and then close it again:

```
  Sub Log(ByVal strText As String) Implements IQReporter.Log

    MsgBox(strText)

    Dim objStream As StreamWriter
    objStream = New StreamWriter("D\VB.NET\Chapter 18\account.log", True)

    objStream.WriteLine(strText)
    objStream.Close()

  End Sub

End Class
```

And that's it for the code for the component. Let's take a look at what we have to do to the assembly definition:

```
Imports System.Reflection
Imports System.Runtime.InteropServices
Imports System.EnterpriseServices

' General Information about an assembly is controlled through the following

...

<Assembly: AssemblyTitle("")>
<Assembly: AssemblyDescription("")>
```

```
<Assembly: AssemblyCompany("")>
<Assembly: AssemblyProduct("")>
<Assembly: AssemblyCopyright("")>
<Assembly: AssemblyTrademark("")>
<Assembly: AssemblyKeyFile("D:\VB.NET\Chapter 18\Reporter\sgKey.snk")>
<Assembly: ApplicationQueuing(Enabled:=True, QueueListenerEnabled:=True)>
<Assembly: ApplicationAccessControl(Value:=False, _
                Authentication:=AuthenticationOption.None)>
<Assembly: ApplicationActivation(ActivationOption.Server)>
<Assembly: ApplicationName("Reporter")>
<Assembly: CLSCompliant(True)>
```

The first addition is a reference to the `EnterpriseServices` namespace. In the actual assembly code, the first reference we need to make is to our old friend, the strong name key file. Next, we ensure that queuing is correctly enabled for this component. The next line is a special line to enable message queuing to work correctly in a workgroup environment, by switching off authentication. If we didn't do this, we would need to set up an entire domain structure. (In a production scenario, that's exactly what we would use, so you would need to remove this line.) Finally, we ensure that the component runs as a server, rather than as a library. This was optional in the case of transactional components, but it's mandatory for queued components. We'll soon see why.

Consoles Again

We're ready to build our component. As before, we register it using `RegSvcs` (see Figure 18-18).

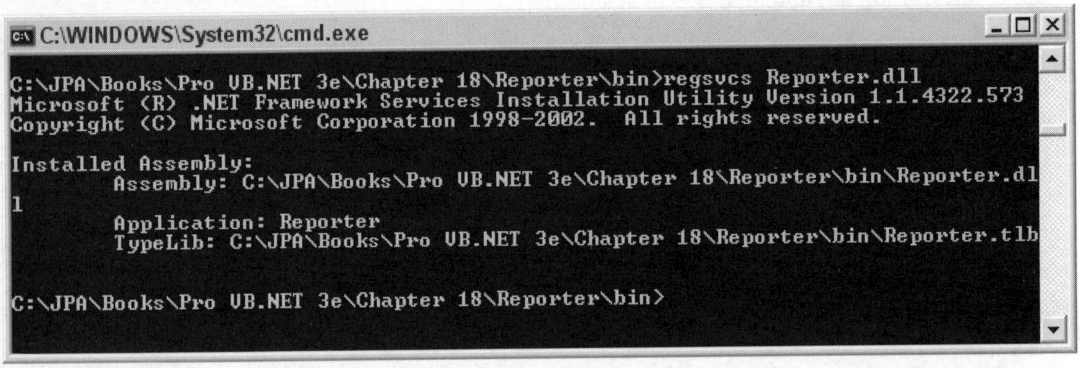

Figure 18-18

Let's take a look at the Component Services Console to see how we're doing (see Figure 18-19).

That looks fine, but there's one other console that we should be looking at right now. This is the *Computer Management Console*. You can get to this either from the system console, or by right-clicking the My Computer icon, and selecting Manage from the menu (see Figure 18-20).

Tucked away, right at the bottom, is the part we're interested in. You'll need to open up Services and Applications to find it. Let's take a closer look (see Figure 18-21).

Excellent, Component Services has set up some queues for us. There are five queues feeding into the main one, so we've got our infrastructure ready. Remember, by the way, that all this would be running on the server machine in a production scenario, not the client.

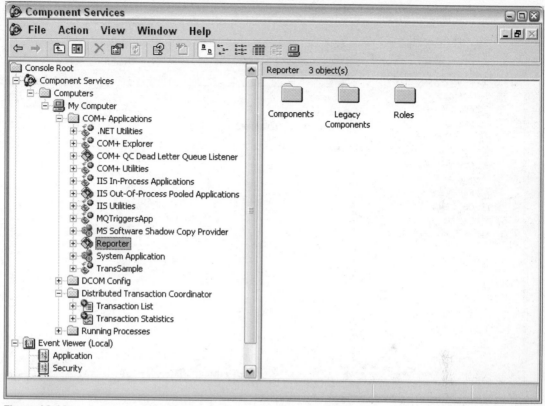

Figure 18-19

The Client

Let's build our client now. This is where it gets unexpectedly messy, so hang on to your hats. The problem is that all of this is built on top of the MSMQ infrastructure, which is, inevitably, a COM infrastructure. Worse, the kind of things that we are going to do involve *marshaling* COM objects into a stream suitable for inserting into a queued message. For the purposes of this discussion, we can think of marshaling as basically intelligently serializing the contents of a method invocation on an interface. We do this in such a way that they can then be deserialized at the other end and turned into a successful invocation of the same method in a remote implementation of the interface. We get COM to do this for us by constructing a *moniker*, which is basically an intelligent name.

We'll start by creating a Windows Application project called `QueuedApp`. We need to add a reference to our `Reporter` component, in the usual manner. Here's the form (see Figure 18-22).

The text box is called `txtMessage`, and the button is called `btnSend`. Here's the code:

```
Imports System.Runtime.InteropServices
Imports Reporter

Public Class Form1
  Inherits System.Windows.Forms.Form
```

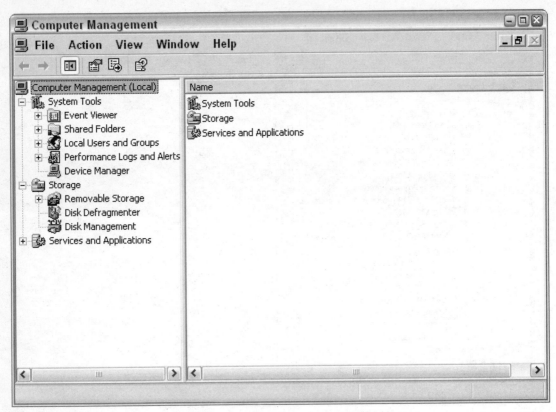

Figure 18-20

```
Private Sub btnSend_Click(ByVal sender As System.Object, _
                          ByVal e As System.EventArgs) _
                          Handles btnSend.Click
```

Here's the crucial line. The important things to note are the references to our interface and its implementation. Everything else remains the same:

```
Dim iQReporter As Reporter.Reporter.IQReporter
iQReporter = CType(Marshal.BindToMoniker( _
                "queue:/new:Reporter.ImplReporter"), _
                Reporter.IQReporter)
```

Here's the queued call:

```
iQReporter.Log(txtmessage.text)
```

Finally, we have to release the reference to the underlying COM object:

```
    Marshal.ReleaseComobject(iQReporter)
  End Sub
  '...
End Class
```

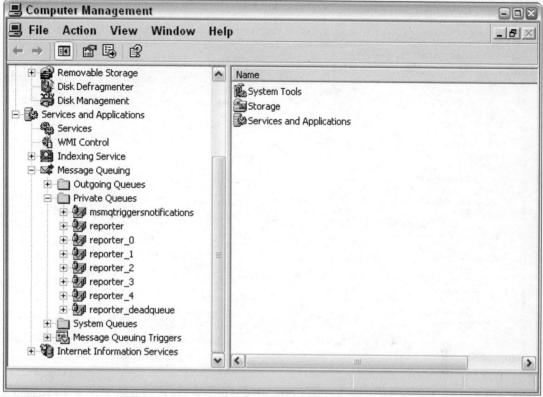

Figure 18-21

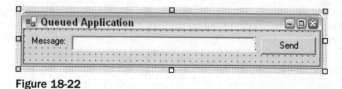

Figure 18-22

Like I said, it's not pretty, but you only have to do it once to be able to do it many times over.

Queuing Invocations

Let's try using this application to put a message onto our queue. So let's run it up and and enter a suitable message (see Figure 18-23).

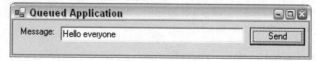

Figure 18-23

We click the Send button and nothing happens. Let's take a look at our message queue (see Figure 18-24).

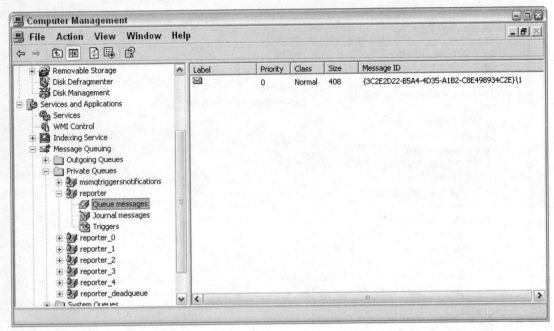

Figure 18-24

We've definitely created a message. So that represents our invocation. If we were to be able to read it, we would see "Hello everyone" embedded somewhere in it. (Unfortunately, the console only allows us to inspect the start of the message, but if we do so, we can see the name of our component in there.)

But why hasn't it been actioned? The answer is that we haven't actually started our server. Remember, we said that our component had to run as a server? This is why. The server has to sit there all the time, serving the incoming queue. So let's go to the Component Services Console, right-click Reporter, select Start from the menu, and we're off. Lo and behold, there's our message box (see Figure 18-25).

Figure 18-25

Now that our message has been delivered, let's go back to the Component Services Console. If we right-click over the message queue, and select Refresh, we can see that the message has indeed been removed from the queue (see Figure 18-26).

If we look in `account.log` we can see that it has been updated as well. Now, if we run our application, we'll see the message boxes popping up straight away.

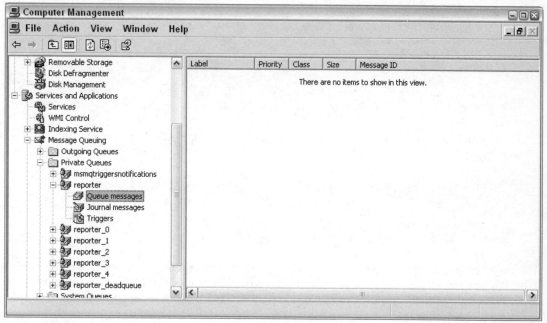

Figure 18-26

Transactions with Queued Components

Now, why did we call that file `account.log`? The thing is that MSMQ is, like SQL Server, a resource manager, and it can take part in transactions. At first, this is a little counter-intuitive, because how on earth can anything so asynchronous as MSMQ have anything to do with transactions? The point is that it is *reliable*. If we take the transaction to go up to the point at which a message is securely in the queue, we have definitely got something that can participate. What happens at the other end of the queue is an entirely separate transaction. Of course, if something goes wrong there, we may need to look at setting up a compensating transaction coming back the other way to trigger some kind of rollback.

For our final example, then, we're going to take our original transactional component, and add in a queued element, so that not only does the transfer of money take place, but the fact also gets logged to a remote file. We'll use exactly the same queued component as last time. And that's why we called the file `account.log`.

We start off by making a clone of `TransSample`, called `TransSample2`. We need to add a reference to `Reporter` and a couple more imports:

```
Imports System.EnterpriseServices
```

```
Imports System.Runtime.InteropServices
Imports Reporter
```

We also need a new private subroutine:

```
Private Sub ReportTransfer(ByVal intDollars As Integer)
  Dim iQReporter As Reporter.IQReporter
```

```
    iQReporter = _
      CType(Marshal.BindToMoniker("queue:/new:Reporter.ImplReporter"), _
      Reporter.IQReporter)

    iQReporter.Log("Transferring $" + CStr(intDollars))

    Marshal.ReleaseComobject(iQReporter)
End Sub
```

This may look kind of familiar to the previous queued component example application. Finally, we add a call to this:

```
Public Function TransferMoney(ByVal intDollars As Integer) As Boolean
    ReportTransfer(intDollars)

    If TakeFromWrox(intDollars) = True Then
        If AddToJon(intDollars) = True Then
```

So we're including a queued component into our transaction. It's been deliberately placed at the start to see if it genuinely takes part in the two-phase committal. If the transaction fails, we shouldn't see any messages come through. Once we've built our `TransSample2` component, we need to register it using `regsvcs` in the usual manner.

We also need to make a small change to our `Reporter` component. However, we need to shut it down via the Component Services Console first. The change is very simple. To ensure that the queued component takes part in the transaction it must be marked with the `Transaction` attribute:

```
<InterfaceQueuing(Interface:="Reporter.IQReporter"), _
Transaction(TransactionOption.Required)> _
Public Class ImplReporter
```

Finally, we'll need a clone of `TransApp`, called `TransApp2`, which uses the `TransSample2` version of the transaction component instead of the `TransSample` version.

If we now transfer $1,000, we see the usual "Transfer complete" message box. And if we now start up the Reporter component, we also see the message box from our queued component (see Figure 18-27).

Figure 18-27

If we try it again, we see the queued message coming through first. So we know it's OK for valid transfers. What happens if we try to transfer $100? As we know from the earlier example, this will fail, and indeed, we see the "Transfer failed" message box from the main component. But not a peep out of the queued component.

Summary

In this chapter, we have looked at the .NET Component Services, those parts of .NET that address issues required for serious enterprise computing. To begin with, we looked at transactions, what they are and the ACID (Atomicity, Consistency, Isolation, Durability) theory that describes the properties of transactions. This was followed by an example showing how transactions are controlled and monitored via the Component Services Console. We also introduced and described the `RegSvcs` tool used to register components with Component Services.

After we had finished our transactional components example, we then went on to look at some of the other activities that could be carried out with transactions including manual transactions, just-in-time attributes, object pooling, and the `ContextUtil` class.

We also looked at how the two-phase commit is organized so that the failure of a single participant in the transaction causes the entire transaction to be abandoned. Then, we looked at queued components, and how these can be used for asynchronous method invocations. Finally, we looked at how these could be combined with transactions.

19

Threading

One of the things that the move from 16-bit to 32-bit computing gave us was the ability to write code that made use of threads, but although Visual C++ developers have been able to use threads for some time, Visual Basic developers haven't had a really reliable way to do so, until now. Previous techniques involved accessing the threading functionality available to Visual C++ developers. Although this worked, without adequate debugger support in the Visual Basic environment, actually developing multithreaded code was nothing short of a nightmare.

This chapter will introduce you to the various objects in the .NET Framework that enable any .NET language to be used to develop multithreaded applications.

What Is a Thread?

The term *thread* is short for *thread of execution*. When your program is running, the CPU is actually running a sequence of processor instructions, one after another. You can think of these instructions, one after another, as forming a thread which is being executed by the CPU. What we call a thread is, in effect, a pointer to the currently executing instruction in the sequence of instructions that make up our application. This pointer starts at the top of the program and moves through each line, branching and looping when it comes across decisions and loops and, at a time when the program is no longer needed, the pointer steps outside of the program code and the program is effectively stopped.

Most applications have only one thread, so they are only executing one sequence of instructions. Some applications have more than one thread, so they can simultaneously execute more than one sequence of instructions.

It is important to realize that each CPU in your computer can only execute one thread at a time. This means that if you only have one CPU, then your computer can only execute one thread at a time. Even if an application has several threads, only one can run at a time in this case. If your computer has two or more CPUs then each CPU will run a different thread at the exact same time. In this case, more than one thread in your application may run at the same exact time, each on a different CPU.

Of course, we know that when we have a computer with only one CPU that several programs can actively be running at the same time, so the statements in the previous paragraph fly in the face of visual evidence. However, it is true that only one thread can execute at a time on a single-CPU machine. What you may *perceive* to be simultaneously running applications is really an illusion created by the Windows operating system through a technique called timesharing. We'll discuss this later in the chapter.

All applications have at least one thread — otherwise they couldn't do any work, as there'd be no pointer to the thread of execution.

The principle of a thread is that it allows your program to perform multiple actions, potentially at the same time. Each sequence of instructions is executed independently of other threads.

The classic example of *multithreaded* functionality is Microsoft Word's spell checker. When the program starts, the execution pointer starts at the top of the program and eventually gets itself into a position where you're able to start writing code.

However, at some point Word will start another thread and create another execution pointer. As you type, this new thread examines the text and flags any spelling errors as you go, underlining them with a red wavy line (see Figure 19-1).

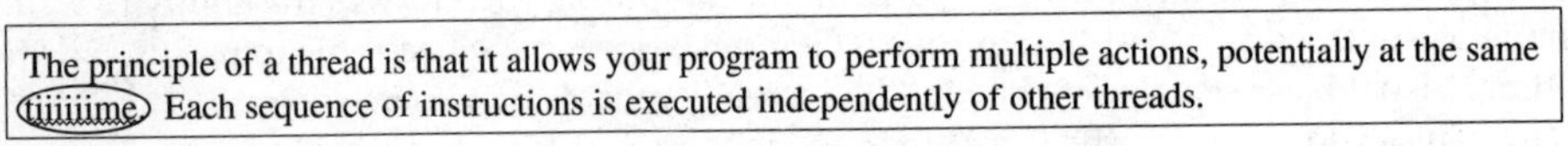

The principle of a thread is that it allows your program to perform multiple actions, potentially at the same tiiiiiime. Each sequence of instructions is executed independently of other threads.

Figure 19-1

Every application has one primary thread. This thread serves as the main process thread through the application. Imagine you have an application that starts up, loads a file from disk, performs some processing on the data in the file, writes a new file, and then quits. Functionally, it might look like Figure 19-2.

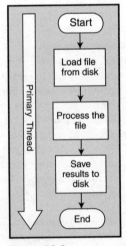

Figure 19-2

In this simple application, we need to use only a single thread. When the program is told to run, Windows creates a new process and also creates the *primary thread*. To understand more about exactly what it is that a thread does, we need to understand a little more about how Windows and the computer's processor deal with different processes.

Processes, AppDomains, and Threads

Windows is capable of keeping many programs in memory at once and allowing the user to switch between them. These programs manifest themselves as applications and services. The difference between applications and services is the user interface — services don't usually have a user interface that allows the user to interact with them, whereas applications do. (In this way Microsoft Word is an example of an application, whereas Internet Information Server is an example of a service.) The ability to run many programs at once is called *multitasking*.

Each of these programs that your computer keeps in memory runs in a single *process*. A process is an isolated region of memory that contains a program's code and data. All programs run within a process, and code running in one process can not access the memory within any other process. This prevents one program from interfering with any other program.

The process is started when the program starts and exists for as long as the program is running. When a process is started, Windows sets up an isolated memory area for the program and loads the program's code into that area of memory. It then starts up the main thread for the process, pointing it at the first instruction in the program. From that point, the thread runs the sequence of instructions defined by the program.

Windows supports *multithreading*, so the main thread might execute instructions that create more threads within the same process. These other threads run within the same memory space as the main thread — all sharing the same memory. Threads within a process are not isolated from each other. One thread in a process can tamper with data being used by other threads in that same process. However, a thread in one process can not tamper with data being used by threads in any other processes on the computer.

At this point you should understand that Windows loads program code into a process and executes that code on one or more threads. The .NET Framework adds another concept to the mix: the *AppDomain*. An AppDomain is very much like a process in concept. Each AppDomain is an isolated region of memory, and code running in one AppDomain can not access the memory of another AppDomain.

The .NET Framework introduced the AppDomain to make it possible to run multiple, isolated programs within the same Windows process. It turns out to be relatively expensive to create a Windows process in terms of time and memory. It is much cheaper to create a new AppDomain within an existing process.

Remember that Windows has no concept of an AppDomain, it only understands the concept of a process. The only way to get *any* code to run under Windows is to load it into a process. This means that each .NET AppDomain exists within a process. The end result is that all .NET code runs within an AppDomain *and* within a Windows process (see Figure 19-3).

In most cases, a Windows process will contain one AppDomain, which will contain our program's code. The main thread of the process will execute our program's instructions. The end result is that the existence of the AppDomain is largely invisible to our program.

In some cases, most notably ASP.NET, a Windows process will contain multiple AppDomains, each with a separate program loaded (see Figure 19-4).

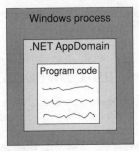

Figure 19-3

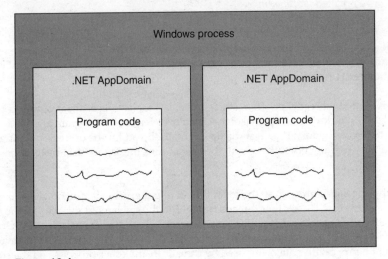

Figure 19-4

ASP.NET uses this technique to isolate Web applications from each other without having to start an expensive new Windows process for each virtual root on the server.

Note that AppDomains do not change the relationship between a process and threads. Each process has a main thread and may have other threads. This means that even in the ASP.NET process, with multiple AppDomains, there is only one main thread. Of course, ASP.NET creates other threads so multiple Web applications can execute simultaneously, but there's only a single main thread in the entire process.

Thread Scheduling

Earlier in the chapter we noted that visual evidence tells us that multiple programs, and thus multiple threads, execute simultaneously even on a single-CPU computer. This is an illusion created by the operating system through the use of a concept called time slicing or time sharing.

The reality is that only one thread runs on each CPU at a time. In a single-CPU machine this means that only one thread is ever executing at any one time. To provide the illusion that many things are happening at the same time, the operating system never lets any one thread run for very long, giving other threads a chance to get a bit of work done as well. The end result is that it *appears* that the computer is executing several threads at the same time.

The length of time each thread gets to run is called a *quantum*. Although a quantum can vary, it is typically around 20 milliseconds. Once a thread has run for its quantum, the operating system stops the thread and allows another thread to run. When that thread reaches its quantum, yet another thread gets to run and so forth.

Because the length of time each thread gets to run is so short, we never notice that the threads are getting started and stopped constantly behind the scenes. This is the same concept animators use when creating cartoons or other animated media. As long as the changes happen faster than we can perceive them, we are given the illusion of motion, or, in this case, of simultaneous execution of code.

The technology used by Windows is called *preemptive multitasking*. It is preemptive because no thread is ever allowed to run beyond its quantum. The operating system always intervenes and allows other threads to run. This helps ensure that no single thread can consume all the processing power on the machine to the detriment of other threads.

It also means that we can never be sure when our thread will be interrupted and another thread allowed to run. This is the primary source of the complexity of multithreading, as it can cause race conditions when two threads access the same memory. If we attempt to solve a race condition with a lock, it can cause deadlock conditions when two threads attempt to access the same lock. We'll discuss these concepts more later, the point you should take away now is that writing multithreaded code can be exceedingly difficult.

The entity that executes code in Windows is the thread. This means that the operating system is primarily focused on scheduling threads to keep the CPU or CPUs busy at all times. The operating system does not schedule processes, nor does it schedule AppDomains. Processes and AppDomains are merely regions of memory that contain our code—threads are what execute the code.

Threads have priorities, and Windows always allows higher priority threads to run before lower priority threads. In fact, if a higher priority thread is ready to run, Windows will cut short a lower priority thread's quantum to allow the higher priority thread to execute sooner. The end result is that Windows has a bias towards threads of higher priority.

Setting thread priorities can be useful in situations where you have a process that requires a lot of processor muscle, but it doesn't matter how long the process takes to do its work. An example of this is the Intel/United Devices Cancer Research Project. This project is based on having thousands of computers around the world running an algorithm that tries to match drug molecules with target proteins associated with the spread of cancer. This program runs continuously, but the actual calculations involve a great deal of math that tends to use a lot of processor power. However, this process runs at a very low priority, so if we need to use Word or Outlook or another application, Windows gives more processor time to these applications and less time to the research application. This means the computer can work smoothly when the user needs it to, letting the research application take up the slack.

> You can learn more about the Intel/United Devices Cancer Research Project at www.ud
> .com/.

Threads may also voluntarily suspend themselves before their quantum is complete. This happens frequently, for instance, when a thread attempts to read data from a file. It takes some significant time for the IO subsystem to locate the file and start retrieving the data. We can't have the CPU sitting idle during that time, especially when there are probably other threads that could be running. So what happens is that the thread enters a wait state to indicate that it is waiting for an external event. The Windows scheduler immediately locates and runs the next ready thread, keeping the CPU busy while the first thread waits for its data.

Windows also automatically suspends and resumes our threads depending on its perceived processing needs, the various priority settings, and so on. Say we're running one AppDomain containing two threads. If we can somehow mark the second thread as dormant (in other words, tell Windows that it has nothing to do), there's no need for Windows to allocate time to it. Effectively, the first thread will receive 100 percent of the processor horsepower available to that process. When a thread is marked as dormant we say it's in a *wait state*.

Windows is particularly good at managing processes and threads. It's a core part of Windows' functionality and so its developers have spent a lot of time making sure that it's super-efficient and as bug-free as software can be. This means that creating and spinning up threads is very easy to do and happens very quickly. Threads also only take up a small amount of system resources. However, there is a caveat you should be aware of.

The activity of stopping one thread and starting another is called *context switching*. This switching happens relatively quickly, but only if you're relatively careful with the number of threads you create. Remember that this happens for each active thread at the end of each quantum (of not before) — so after at most 20 milliseconds. If you spin up too many threads, the operating system will spend all of its time switching between different threads, perhaps even getting to a point where the code in the thread doesn't get a chance to run because as soon as you've started the thread it's time for it to stop again.

Creating thousands of threads is not the right solution. What you need to do is find a balance between the amount of threads that your application needs and the amount of threads that Windows can handle. There's no magic number or right answer to the question of "How many threads should I create?" You just need to be aware of context switching and experiment a little.

Take the Microsoft Word spell check example. The thread that performs the spell check is around all the time. Imagine you have a blank document containing no text. At this point, the spell check thread is in a wait state. Imagine you type a single word into the document and then pause. At this point, Word will pass the word over to the thread and signal it to start working. The thread will use its own slice of the processor power to examine the word. If it finds something wrong with the word, it will tell the primary thread that a spelling problem was found and that the user needs to be alerted. At this point, the spell check thread drops back into a wait state until more text is entered into the document. Word doesn't spin up the thread whenever it needs to perform a check — rather the thread runs all the time but, if it has nothing to do, it drops into this efficient wait state. (We'll talk about how the thread starts again later.)

Again, this is an oversimplification. Word will "wake up" the thread at various times. However, the principle is sound — the thread is given work to do, it reports the results and then it starts waiting for the next chunk of work to do.

So why is all this important? If you plan to author multithreaded applications, it is important to realize how the operating system will be scheduling our threads as well as the threads of all other processes on the system. Most importantly, you need to recognize that your thread can be interrupted at any time so that another thread can run.

Thread Safety and Thread Affinity

Most of the .NET Framework base class library is not *thread safe*. Thread safe code is code that can be called by multiple threads at the same time without negative side effects. If code is not thread-safe, then calling that code from multiple threads at the same time will result in unpredictable and undesirable side effects, potentially even blatantly crashing our application. When dealing with objects that are not thread safe we must ensure that multiple threads never simultaneously interact with the same object.

To find out if any specific method in the .NET Base Class Library is thread safe refer to the online help. If there is no mention of threading in association with the method then the method is *not* thread safe.

The Windows Forms subset of the .NET Framework is not only not thread safe, but also has *thread affinity*. Thread affinity means that objects created by a thread can only be used by that thread. Other threads should never interact with those objects. In the case of Windows Forms, this means that we must ensure that multiple threads never interact with Windows Forms objects (like forms and controls). This is important, because when we are creating interactive multithreaded applications we must ensure that only the thread that created a form interacts directly with that form.

As we'll see, Windows Forms includes technology by which a background thread can safely make method calls on forms and controls by transferring the method call to the thread that owns the form.

When to Use Threads

If we regard computer programs as being either application software or service software, we find there are different motivators for each one.

Application software uses threads primarily to deliver a better user experience. Common examples are:

❑   Microsoft Word — background spell checker

❑   Microsoft Word — background printing

❑   Microsoft Outlook — background sending and receiving of e-mail

❑   Microsoft Excel — background recalculation

You can see that in all of these cases, threads are used to do "something in the background." This provides a better user experience. For example, I can still edit a Word document while Word is spooling another to the printer. Or, I can still read e-mails while Outlook is sending my new e-mail. As an application developer, you should use threads to enhance the user experience. Figure 19-5 shows the threads involved when the Word spell checker is utilized.

At some point during the application startup, code running in the primary thread would have spun up this other thread to be used for spell checking. As part of the "allow user to edit the document" process, we give the spell checker thread some words to check. This thread separation means that the user can continue to type, even though spell checking is still taking place.

Service software uses threads to deliver scalability and improve the service offered. For example, imagine I had a Web server that receives six incoming connections simultaneously. That server needs to service

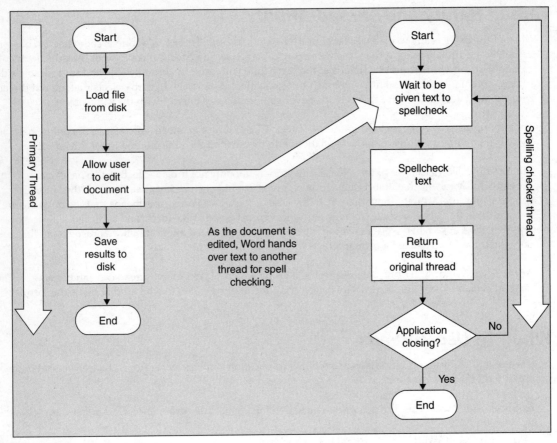

Figure 19-5

each of the requests in parallel, otherwise the sixth thread would have to wait for me to finish threads one through five before it even got started. Figure 19-6 shows how IIS might handle incoming requests.

The primary motivation for multiple threads in a service like this is to keep the CPU busy servicing user requests even when other user requests are blocked waiting for data or other events. If we have six user requests, odds are high that some, or all of them, will read from files or databases and thus will spend many milliseconds in wait states. While some of the user requests are in wait states, other user requests will need CPU time and can be scheduled to run. The end result is higher scalability because we keep the CPU, IO and other subsystems of the computer as busy as possible at all times.

Designing a Background Task

The specific goals and requirements for background processing in an interactive application are quite different from a server application. By interactive application, I am talking about Windows Forms or Console applications. While a Web application might be somewhat interactive, the fact is that all our code runs on the server, and so Web applications are server applications when it comes to threading.

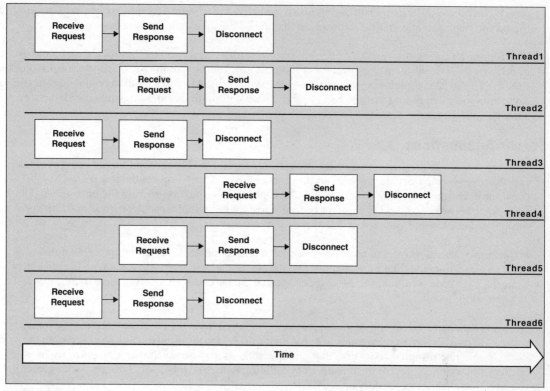

Figure 19-6

Interactive Applications

In the case of interactive applications (typically Windows Forms applications), our design must center around having the background thread do useful work, but also interact appropriately (and safely) with the thread that is managing the UI. After all, we'll typically want to let the user know when the background process starts, stops and does interesting things over its life. We can summarize these to the following basic requirements for the background thread:

❑   Indicate that the background task has started

❑   Provide periodic status or progress information

❑   Indicate that the background task has completed

❑   Allow the user to request that the background task cancel

While every application is different, these four requirements are typical for background threads in an interactive application.

As we noted earlier, most of the .NET Framework is not thread safe, and Windows Forms is even more restrictive by having thread affinity. We know that we want our background task to be able to notify the user when it starts, stops and provide progress information. The fact that Windows Forms has thread affinity complicates this, since our background thread can never directly interact with Windows Forms

679

objects. Fortunately, Windows Forms provides a formalized mechanism by which code in a background thread can send messages to the UI thread, so that the UI thread can update the display for the user.

This is done by calling the Invoke or BeginInvoke method on a Form or Control object. Invoke is used to run a method on the form or control synchronously — meaning that the background thread is blocked until the UI thread completes the method. BeginInvoke is used to run a method on the form or control asynchronously — meaning that the background thread will continue running, while the UI thread simultaneously runs the invoked method.

Server Applications

In the case of server programs, our design must center around the background thread being as efficient as possible. Server resources are precious, so the quicker the task can complete the less resource we'll consume over time. Interactivity with a UI isn't a concern, since our code is running on a server, detached from any UI. The key to success in server coding is to avoid or minimize locking, thus maximizing throughput becaue our code never gets stopped by a lock.

For example, Microsoft went to great pains to design and refine ASP.NET to minimize the number of locks required from the time a user request hits the server to the time an ASPX page's code is running. Once the page code is running, no locking occurs, so the page code can just run, top to bottom, as fast and efficiently as possible.

Avoiding locking means avoiding shared resources or data. This is the dominant design goal for server code — we must design our programs to avoid scenarios where multiple threads need access to the same variables or other resources. Any time that multiple threads may access the same resource we need to implement locking to prevent the threads from colliding with each other. We'll discuss locking later in the chapter, as sometimes it is simply unavoidable.

Implementing Threading

At this point you should have a basic understanding of threads and how they relate to the process and AppDomain concepts. You should also realize that for interactive applications multithreading is not a way to improve performance, but rather is a way to improve the end user experience by providing the illusion that the computer is executing more code simultaneously. In the case of server-side code, multithreading enables higher scalability by allowing Windows to better utilize the CPU along with other subsystems such as IO.

A Quick Tour

When a background thread is created, it points to a method or procedure that will be executed by the thread. Remember that a thread is just a pointer to the current instruction in a sequence of instructions to be executed. In all cases, the first instruction in this sequence is the start of a method or procedure.

It is also important to realize that this method can't be a Function. There is no mechanism by which a method running on one thread can return a result directly to code running on another thread. This means that any time we design a background task, we'll start by creating a Sub in which we write the code to run on the background thread.

Also, because the goals for interactive applications and server programs are different, our design for implementing threading in these two environments are different. This means that the way we design and code the background task will vary.

By way of explanation, let's work with a simple method that calculates prime numbers. This implementation is naïve, and so can take quite a lot of time when run against larger numbers, so it makes for a useful example of a long-running background task. Do the following:

1. Create a new Windows Forms Application project named `Threading`

2. Add a `Button` and `ListBox` control to Form1

3. Add the following to the form's code.

```
Private mMin As Integer
Private mMax As Integer
Private mResults As New ArrayList

Private Sub FindPrimes()

  mResults.Clear()

  For count As Integer = mMin To mMax Step 2
    Dim isPrime As Boolean = True

    For x As Integer = 1 To count / 2
      For y As Integer = 1 To x
        If x * y = count Then
          ' the number is not prime
          isPrime = False
          Exit For
        End If
      Next
      ' short-circuit the check
      If Not isPrime Then Exit For
    Next

    If isPrime Then
      mResults.Add(count)
    End If

  Next

End Sub
```

Notice that the method is a `Sub`, so it returns no value. Instead, it stores its results into a variable, in this case, an ArrayList. The idea is that once the background task is complete we can do something useful with the results.

Also notice that the method accepts no parameters. Just as there's no way to return a value from a background task, there's also no way to directly pass parameters to a method on a new thread. This means that we must initialize any data values before launching the background thread, so the assumption here is that the mMin and mMax variables will be set properly before the task is started.

To call this method on a background thread, we need to import the System.Threading namespace:

```
Imports System.Threading
```

Then we can write code behind the button to run the task on a background thread:

```
Private Sub Button1_Click(ByVal sender As System.Object, _
        ByVal e As System.EventArgs) Handles Button1.Click

    ' intialize the tasks's data
    mMin = 10001
    mMax = 12000

    ' run the task
    Dim worker As New Thread(AddressOf FindPrimes)
    worker.Start()

    ' wait for the task to complete
    worker.Join()

    ' process the results
    For Each value As Integer In mResults
      ListBox1.Items.Add(value)
    Next

End Sub
```

First we initialize the data for our background task, providing the min and max values. Then we create a Thread object, setting it up so it points at our method:

```
Dim worker As New Thread(AddressOf FindPrimes)
```

This means that the thread starts with the first instruction in that method and will run subsequent instructions in order. When all instructions in the method are complete the thread will automatically terminate.

Once the thread is created, we need to start it before it will become active and do work. This is done by calling the Start method on the Thread object.

Of course, we want to display the results of the background task, and this is where things get tricky. We can't loop through the list of results until the background task is complete, and we need some way to know when it is complete. In this code example, we've taking the simplest possible approach, by calling the Join method on the thread.

The Join method blocks our main thread until the background thread completes. In other words, the background thread gets to run, but our main foreground thread is stopped cold until the task is done. If we run the project and click the button we'll find that the UI is totally locked until the values have been calculated. See Figure 19-7.

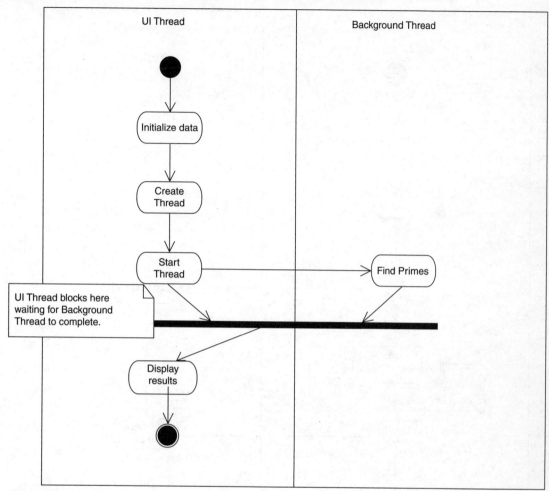

Figure 19-7

What we've accomplished here is to run the task on a background thread, but with the same end result as if we'd run it on the main UI thread. Obviously, we have more work to do. There are numerous possible solutions that would allow the UI thread to remain active while the background task is running. Typically, the best solution is to change the way we handle the results so we don't process them until the background thread *tells us* that it is complete. This means we'll have the background thread call us back when it is done. See Figure 19-8.

To do this we first need to change our calling code a bit:

```
Private Sub Button1_Click(ByVal sender As System.Object, _
        ByVal e As System.EventArgs) Handles Button1.Click

  ' intialize the tasks's data
  mMin = 10001
  mMax = 12000
```

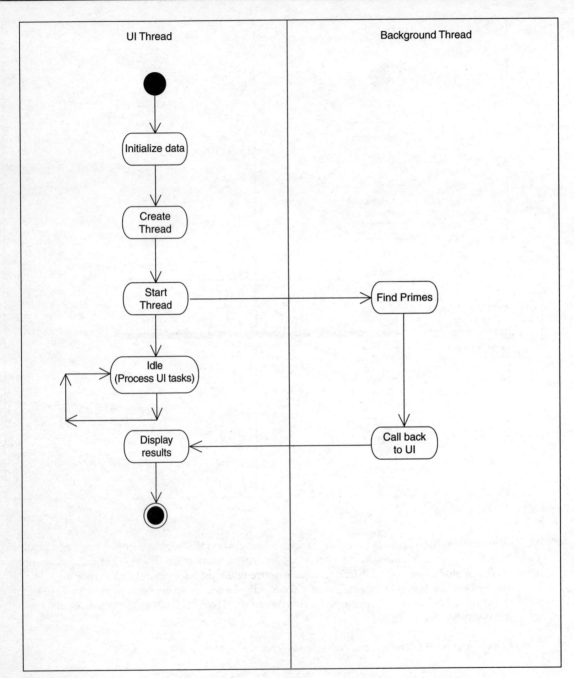

Figure 19-8

```
' run the task
Dim worker As New Thread(AddressOf FindPrimes)
worker.Start()

End Sub
```

```
Private Sub DisplayResults()

  ' process the results
  For Each value As Integer In mResults
    ListBox1.Items.Add(value)
  Next

End Sub
```

Notice how we have moved the processing of the results out of the click event handler and into its own method. This way we don't need the UI thread to wait until the background thread completes. After we call `Start` to start the thread, the UI thread can keep running because it doesn't immediately try to display the results.

The next thing we need to do is have the background thread call `DisplayResults` when it is complete. You might expect that the `FindPrimes` method could just directly call `DisplayResults`, but that would lead to disaster. Remember that `FindPrimes` is running on a background thread. Any methods it directly calls will also run on that background thread. If `FindPrimes` calls `DisplayResults` directly, the `DisplayResults` code will run on the background thread. Since `DisplayResults` directly interacts with Windows Forms objects (namely the `ListBox` control) this will cause our application to fail.

> *Note that doing this might not cause the application to fail reliably. You might not see the failure in many, many tests, but it will fail — probably when rolled out in production to hundreds of workstations, or right when your boss is demonstrating the application to the VP...*

Fortunately, there is a safe way for the background task to call methods such that they actually end up running on the UI thread. This is done through the use of the `Invoke` method on our `Form` object. All `Form` and `Control` objects have an `Invoke` method that can be used to transfer a method call from a background thread to the UI thread.

To do this we first need a delegate with a method signature that matches the `DisplayResults` method:

```
Private Delegate Sub Display()
```

Then we can change `FindPrimes` to use this delegate to invoke the `DisplayResults` method:

```
Private Sub FindPrimes()

  mResults.Clear()

  For count As Integer = mMin To mMax Step 2
    Dim isPrime As Boolean = True

    For x As Integer = 1 To count / 2
      For y As Integer = 1 To x
        If x * y = count Then
```

```
            ' the number is not prime
          isPrime = False
          Exit For
             End If
          Next
          ' short-circuit the check
          If Not isPrime Then Exit For
        Next

        If isPrime Then
          mResults.Add(count)
        End If

      Next

      Dim display As New Display(AddressOf DisplayResults)
      Me.Invoke(display)

    End Sub
```

When we call the form's `Invoke` method the background thread is automatically blocked, and the method pointed to by the delegate (`DisplayResults`) is run on the UI thread. When it is complete, the background thread continues processing — in this case, it immediately falls off the end of the `FindPrimes` method and so is terminated.

If we now run the code we'll see that the UI remains entirely responsive while the background task is running, and the results are displayed when available.

Now that we've explored the basics of threading in an interactive application, let's discuss the various threading options that are at our disposal.

Threading Options

The .NET Framework offers two ways to implement multithreading. Regardless of which approach we use, we must specify the method or procedure that the thread will execute when it starts.

First, we can use the thread pool provided by the .NET Framework. The thread pool is a managed pool of threads that can be reused over the life of our application. Threads are created in the pool on an as-needed basis and idle threads in the pool are reused, thus keeping the number of threads created by our application to a minimum. This is important because threads are an expensive operating system resource.

> **The thread pool should be your first choice in most multithreading scenarios.**

Many built-in .NET Framework features already use the thread pool. Any time we do an asynchronous read from a file, URL or TCP socket the thread pool is used on our behalf. Any time we implement a remoting listener, a Web site or a Web service the thread pool is used. Because the .NET Framework itself relies on the thread pool, we can have a high degree of confidence that it is an optimal choice for most multithreading requirements.

Second, we can create our own thread object. This can be a good approach if we have a single, long-running background task in our application. It is also useful if we need fine-grained control over the background thread. Examples of such control include setting the thread priority or suspending and resuming the thread's execution.

Using the Thread Pool

The .NET Framework provides a thread pool in the System.Threading namespace. This thread pool is self-managing. It will create threads on demand and, if possible, will reuse idle threads that already exist in the pool.

The thread pool won't create an unlimited number of threads. In fact, it will create at most 25 threads per CPU in the system. If we assign more work requests to the pool than it can handle with these threads, our work requests will be queued until a thread becomes available. This is typically a good feature, as it helps ensure that our application won't overload the operating system with too many threads.

There are four primary ways to use the thread pool: through BeginXYZ methods, via Delegates, manually via the ThreadPool.QueueUserWorkItem method, or by using a System.Timers.Timer control. Of the four, the easiest and most common is to use delegates.

Using BeginXYZ Methods

Many of the .NET Framework objects support both synchronous and asynchronous invocation. For instance, we can read from a TCP socket by using the Read method or the BeginRead method. The Read method is synchronous, so we are blocked until the data is read.

The BeginRead method is asynchronous, so we are not blocked. Instead, the read operation occurs on a background thread in the thread pool. We provide the address of a method that is called automatically when the read operation is complete. This *callback* method is invoked by the background thread, and so the result is that our code also ends up running on the background thread in the thread pool.

Behind the scenes, this behavior is all driven by delegates. Rather than exploring TCP sockets or some other specific subset of the .NET Framework class library, let's move on and discuss the underlying technology itself.

Using Delegates

A delegate is a strongly typed pointer to a function or method. Delegates are the underlying technology used to implement events within Visual Basic .NET (VB.NET), and they can be used directly to invoke a method given just a pointer to that method.

We've already seen how delegates allow us to transfer a method call from a background thread to the UI thread. We can also use them to launch a background task on a thread in the thread pool. To adapt our prime application to use delegates, we need to define a delegate for the FindPrimes method:

```
Private Delegate Sub Task()
```

The only requirement here is that the delegate signature match the function signature. This means that we could simplify `FindPrimes` to accept the `min` and `max` values as parameters and provide those parameters via the delegate:

```
Private Delegate Sub Task(ByVal min As Integer, ByVal max As Integer)

Private Sub FindPrimes(ByVal min As Integer, ByVal max As Integer)

  mResults.Clear()

  For count As Integer = min To max Step 2
    Dim isPrime As Boolean = True

    For x As Integer = 1 To count / 2
      For y As Integer = 1 To x
        If x * y = count Then
          ' the number is not prime
          isPrime = False
          Exit For
        End If
      Next
      ' short-circuit the check
      If Not isPrime Then Exit For
    Next

    If isPrime Then
      mResults.Add(count)
    End If

  Next

End Sub
```

Running background tasks via delegates allows us to pass strongly typed parameters to the background task, thus clarifying and simplifying our code.

Also, notice that we've removed the code that invoked the `DisplayResults` method. We won't need that now either, because there's a simpler alternative at our disposal as we'll see in a moment.

Now that we have a delegate defined, we can change our click event handler code to use it to run `FindPrimes` on a background thread:

```
Private Sub Button1_Click(ByVal sender As System.Object, _
        ByVal e As System.EventArgs) Handles Button1.Click

  ' run the task
  Dim worker As New Task(AddressOf FindPrimes)
  worker.BeginInvoke(10001, 12000, AddressOf TaskComplete, Nothing)

End Sub
```

First we create an instance of the delegate, setting it up to point to the `FindPrimes` method. Then we call `BeginInvoke` on the delegate to invoke the method.

The `BeginInvoke` method is the key here. `BeginInvoke` is an example of the `BeginXYZ` methods we discussed earlier, and as you'll recall, they automatically run the method on a background thread in the thread pool. This is true for `BeginInvoke` as well, meaning that `FindPrimes` will be run in the background and the UI thread is not blocked, so it can continue to interact with the user.

Notice all the parameters we're passing to `BeginInvoke`. The first two correspond to the parameters we defined on our delegate—the `min` and `max` values that should be passed to `FindPrimes`.

The next parameter is the address of a method that will be automatically invoked when the background thread is complete. The final parameter (to which we've passed `Nothing`), is a mechanism by which we can pass a value from our UI thread to the method that is invoked when the background task is complete.

This means that we need to implement the `TaskComplete` method. This method is invoked when the background task is complete. It will run on the background thread, not on the UI thread, so we need to remember that this method can't interact with any Windows Forms objects. Instead it will contain the code to invoke the `DisplayResults` method on the UI thread via the form's `Invoke` method:

```
Private Sub TaskComplete(ByVal ar As IAsyncResult)

  Dim display As New Display(AddressOf DisplayResults)
  Me.Invoke(display)

End Sub
```

Now when we run the application we'll have a responsive UI, with the `FindPrimes` method running in the background within the thread pool. Better still, we've simplified our code because we are able to pass parameter values to `FindPrimes` rather than resorting to the use of shared variables as in our previous examples.

Manually Queuing Work

The final option for using the thread pool is to manually queue items for the thread pool to process. This is done by calling `ThreadPool.QueueUserWorkItem`. This is a `Shared` method on the `ThreadPool` class that directly places a method into the thread pool to be executed on a background thread.

This technique doesn't allow us to pass arbitrary parameters to the worker method. Instead it requires that the `worker` method accept a single parameter of type object, through which we can pass an arbitrary value. We can use this to pass multiple values by declaring a class with all our parameter types. Add the following class *inside* the `Form4` class:

```
Private Class params
  Public min As Integer
  Public max As Integer

  Public Sub New(ByVal min As Integer, ByVal max As Integer)
    Me.min = min
    Me.max = max
  End Sub

End Class
```

Then we can make `FindPrimes` accept this value as an Object:

```
Private Sub FindPrimes(ByVal state As Object)
  Dim params As params = DirectCast(state, params)
  mResults.Clear()

  For count As Integer = params.min To params.max Step 2
    Dim isPrime As Boolean = True

    For x As Integer = 1 To count / 2
      For y As Integer = 1 To x
        If x * y = count Then
          ' the number is not prime
          isPrime = False
          Exit For
        End If
      Next
      ' short-circuit the check
      If Not isPrime Then Exit For
    Next

    If isPrime Then
      mResults.Add(count)
    End If

  Next

  Dim display As New Display(AddressOf DisplayResults)
  Me.Invoke(display)

End Sub
```

Also notice that we've reinstated the code to call `DisplayResults` on the UI thread when the task is complete. When we manually put a task on the thread pool, there is no automatic callback to a method when the task is complete, so we must do the callback here.

Now that `FindPrimes` accepts a parameter of type `Object` we can manually queue it to run in the thread pool within our click event handler:

```
Private Sub Button1_Click(ByVal sender As System.Object, _
        ByVal e As System.EventArgs) Handles Button1.Click

  ' run the task
  ThreadPool.QueueUserWorkItem(AddressOf FindPrimes, New params(10001, 12000))

End Sub
```

The `QueueUserWorkItem` method accepts the address of the worker method — in this case `FindPrimes`. This worker method must accept a single parameter of type Object or we'll get a compile error here.

The second parameter to `QueueUserWorkItem` is the object that is to be passed to the worker method when it is invoked on the background thread. In our case, we're passing a new instance of the `params` class we defined earlier. This allows us to pass our parameter values to `FindPrimes`.

When we run this code we'll again find that we have a responsive UI, with `FindPrimes` running on a background thread in the thread pool.

Using System.Timers.Timer

Beyond `BeginXYZ` methods, delegates and manually queuing work items there are various other ways to get our code running in the thread pool. One of the most common is through the use of a special `Timer` control. The `Elapsed` event of this control is raised on a background thread in the thread pool.

This is different from the `System.Windows.Forms.Timer` control, where the `Tick` event is raised on the UI thread. The difference is very important to understand, since we can't directly interact with Windows Forms objects from background threads. Code running in the `Elapsed` event of a `System.Timers.Timer` control must be treated like any other code running on a background thread.

The exception to this is if we set the `SynchronizingObject` property on the control to a Windows Forms object such as a Form or Control. In this case, the `Elapsed` event will be raised on the appropriate UI thread rather than on a thread in the thread pool. The end result is basically the same as using `System.Windows.Forms.Timer` instead.

Manually Creating a Thread

When we took our first quick look at creating a background thread we directly created and used a `Thread` object:

```
' run the task
Dim worker As New Thread(AddressOf FindPrimes)
worker.Start()
```

While this seems like the obvious way to do multithreading, the thread pool is typically the preferred approach. This is because there is a cost to creating and destroying threads, and the thread pool helps avoid that cost by reusing threads when possible. When we manually create a thread as shown here, we must pay the cost of creating the thread each time or implement our own scheme to reuse the threads we create.

However, manual creation of threads can be useful. The thread pool is designed to be used for background tasks that run for a while and then complete, thus allowing the background thread to be reused for subsequent background tasks. If we need to run a background task for the entire duration of our application, the thread pool is not ideal, because that thread would never become available for reuse. In such a case, we are better off creating the background thread manually.

An example of this is the aforementioned spellchecker in Word, which runs as long as we are editing a document. Running such a task on the thread pool would make little sense, since the task will run as long as the application, so instead it should be run on a manually created thread, leaving the thread pool available for shorter running tasks.

The other primary reason for manual creation of threads is where we want to be able to interact with the `Thread` object as it is running. We've already seen the `Join` method, which allows our main thread to block until the background thread is complete. There are various other methods on the `Thread` object we can use to interact with and control the background thread. These are as shown in the following table.

`Abort`	Stops the thread (not recommended, as no cleanup occurs — this is not a graceful shutdown of the thread)
`ApartmentState`	Sets the COM apartment type used by this thread — important if we're using COM interop in the background task
`Join`	Blocks our current thread until the background thread is complete
`Priority`	Allows us to raise or lower the priority of the background thread so Windows will schedule it to get more or less CPU time relative to other threads
`Sleep`	Causes the thread to be suspended for a specified period of time
`Suspend`	Suspends a thread — temporarily stopping it without terminating the thread
`Resume`	Restarts a suspended thread

There are many other methods available on the `Thread` object as well, consult the online help for more details.

We can use these methods to control the behavior and lifetime of the background thread, which can be useful in advanced threading scenarios.

Shared Data

In most multithreading scenarios, we have data in our main thread that needs to be used by the background task on the background thread. Likewise, the background task typically generates data that is needed by the main thread. These are examples of *shared data*, or data that is used by multiple threads.

Remember that multithreading means that we have multiple threads within the same process, and in .NET within the same AppDomain. Because memory within an AppDomain is common across all threads in that AppDomain, it is very easy for multiple threads to access the same objects or variables within our application.

For example, in our prime examples thus far the background task has needed the min and max values from the main thread, and has provided an `ArrayList` of results back to the main thread when the task was complete. These are examples of shared data. Note that we didn't do anything special to make the data shared — our variables were shared by default.

When we're writing multithreaded code, the hardest issue is that of managing access to shared data within our AppDomain. You don't, for example, want two threads writing to the same piece of memory at the same time. Equally, you don't want a group of threads reading memory that another thread is in the process of changing. This management of memory access is called *synchronization*. It's properly managing synchronization that makes writing multithreaded code difficult.

When multiple threads want to simultaneously access a common bit of shared data, we use synchronization to control things. This is typically done by blocking all but one thread, so only one thread can access the shared data. All other threads are put into a wait state by using a blocking operation of some sort. Once the nonblocked thread is done using the shared data it will release the block, allowing another thread to resume processing and to use the shared data.

The process of releasing the block is often called an event. When we say "event" we are *not* talking about a VB.NET event. Although the naming convention is unfortunate, the principle is the same — something happens and we react to it. In this case, the nonblocked thread causes an event, which releases some other thread so it can access the shared data.

Although blocking can be used to control the execution of threads, it's primarily used to control access to resources, including memory. This is the basic idea behind synchronization — if we need something, we block until we can access it.

Synchronization is expensive and can be complex. It is expensive because it stops one or more threads from running while another thread uses the shared data. The whole point of having multiple threads is to do more than one thing at a time, and if we're constantly blocking all but one thread then we lose this benefit.

It can be complex because there are many ways to implement synchronization. Each technique is appropriate for a certain class of synchronization problem, and using the wrong one in the wrong place will increase the cost of synchronization.

It is also quite possible to create *deadlocks*, where two or more threads end up *permanently* blocked. You've undoubtedly seen examples of this. Pretty much any time a Windows application totally locks up and must be stopped by the Task Manager you are seeing an example of poor multithreading implementation. The fact that this happens even in otherwise high-quality commercial applications (such as Microsoft Outlook) is confirmation that synchronization can be very hard to get right.

Avoid Sharing Data

Since synchronization has so many downsides in terms of performance and complexity, the best thing we can do is avoid or minimize its use. If at all possible, we should design our multithreaded applications to avoid reliance on shared data, and to maintain tight control over the usage of any shared data that is required.

Typically, some shared data is unavoidable, so the question becomes how to manage that shared data to avoid or minimize synchronization. There are two primary schemes we can use for this purpose, so let's discuss them now.

Transferring Data Copies

The first approach is to avoid sharing of data by always passing copies of the data between threads. If each thread has its own copy of the data, then no thread needs access to data being used by any other threads.

This is exactly what we did in our prime example where we started the background task via a delegate:

```
Dim worker As New Task(AddressOf FindPrimes)
worker.BeginInvoke(10001, 12000, AddressOf TaskComplete, Nothing)
```

The min and max values are passed as ByVal parameters, meaning that they are copied and provided to the FindPrimes method. No synchronization is required here, because the background thread never tries to access the values from the main thread.

We passed copies of the values a different way when we manually started the task in the thread pool:

```
ThreadPool.QueueUserWorkItem(AddressOf FindPrimes, New params(10001, 12000))
```

In this case, we created a `params` object into which we put the `min` and `max` values. Again, those values were copied before they were used by the background thread. The `FindPrimes` method never attempted to access any data being used by the main thread.

These are examples of passing copies of the data *into* a background thread. What about passing copies *out of* a background thread? In particular, what if we want to get results from the background thread as it is running, rather than waiting until it has completed?

We can enhance our prime application to provide the prime numbers to the UI thread as it finds them, rather than in a batch at the end of the process. To do this, we'll start with the code where we called `FindPrimes` via a delegate. That is the easiest and typically the best way to start a background task, and so we'll use it as a base implementation.

This means that our click event handler looks like this:

```
Private Sub Button1_Click(ByVal sender As System.Object, _
        ByVal e As System.EventArgs) Handles Button1.Click

  ' run the task
  Dim worker As New Task(AddressOf FindPrimes)
  worker.BeginInvoke(10001, 12000, Nothing, Nothing)

End Sub
```

Note that we've slightly changed the `BeginInvoke` call so it no longer points to a method that will run when the background task is complete. Since we'll be handling the results value by value, we no longer need to do any work when the task is complete. This means we can remove the `TaskComplete` method as well.

If we're going to return the results value by value rather than in an `ArrayList` at the end, we can also remove the declaration of `mResults`. Then we can change the `Display` delegate and `DisplayResults` method to display single values:

```
Private Delegate Sub Display(ByVal value As Integer)

Private Sub DisplayResults(ByVal value As Integer)

  ' process the results
  ListBox1.Items.Add(value)

End Sub
```

We still need to use the delegate from the background thread to safely invoke the `DisplayResults` method on the UI thread. The `DisplayResults` method interacts with a Windows Forms object, so it must run on the UI thread, not on the background thread.

All we need to do now is update the `FindPrimes` method to pass its results to the UI thread by value:

```
Private Sub FindPrimes(ByVal min As Integer, ByVal max As Integer)

  Dim display As New Display(AddressOf DisplayResults)
```

```
   For count As Integer = min To max Step 2
     Dim isPrime As Boolean = True

     For x As Integer = 1 To count / 2
       For y As Integer = 1 To x
         If x * y = count Then
           ' the number is not prime
           isPrime = False
           Exit For
         End If
       Next
       ' short-circuit the check
       If Not isPrime Then Exit For
     Next

     If isPrime Then
       Me.Invoke(display, New Object() {count})
     End If

   Next

 End Sub
```

Rather than invoking `DisplayResults` at the end of the process, we're now invoking it each time we get a prime value. When we call a method using the `Invoke` method, we need some way to pass parameters to that method. This is done by putting the parameters into an array of type `Object`, and then passing that array to the `Invoke` method. The `Invoke` method uses the elements of the array as parameters when it actually calls the method. This is why we are declaring such an array and initializing it with the newly found prime number.

The result is that the prime number is copied by value into the array. This means that a copy of the value is provided to the UI thread, so the UI thread is never attempting to access memory being used by the background thread.

If we run the code, at this point we'll find that not only is our UI continually responsive, but the results from the background task are displayed as they are discovered rather than in a batch at the end of the process.

Note that the `Invoke` method of our display delegate is synchronous. This means that the background thread is blocked while the UI thread updates the display with each new value. While this works, it is not ideal, as it means our background task is frequently being blocked. In fact, if we do a lot of dragging and resizing of the form we should see a visible slow-down in the generation and display of the results.

Since we're passing the result by value, we can change this to use `BeginInvoke` instead:

```
If isPrime Then
  Me.BeginInvoke(display, New Object() {count})
End If
```

As you run the application, resize and move the form while the prime numbers are being found. Although the *displaying* of the data may be slowed down as we interact with the form (because the UI thread can only do so much work), the *generation* of the data continues independently in the background and is not blocked by the UI thread's work.

Transferring Data Ownership

What we've done so far works great for variables that are *value types*, such as `Integer` and *immutable objects*, such as `String`. It won't work for *reference types*, such as a regular object, because reference types are never passed by value, only by reference.

To see how this works, suppose we decide to return our results in small batches rather than value-by-value. This is a good idea anyway, since using the form's `Invoke` or `BeginInvoke` method incurs quite a bit of overhead and we should minimize the number of times these methods are called. The overhead occurs due to the way the `Invoke` and `BeginInvoke` methods are implemented.

First, they are late-bound. Notice how they accept the parameter values as an array of type `Object`. This array of objects is transferred to the UI thread, where it is translated to a set of actual parameters when the method is finally called. That's a lot of overhead all by itself.

Second, the way that the method call moves from the background thread to the UI thread is by sending a Windows message to the form. Windows messages are normally things like mouse movements, mouse clicks, key presses and so forth. Creating and sending a Windows message is relatively inexpensive, but is far more expensive than a normal method call.

The end result is that calling the form's `Invoke` or `BeginInvoke` method for every prime number is highly inefficient and we'd be better off returning the values in small groups. For instance, we might return a set of five values at a time in an `ArrayList`. Since `ArrayList` is a reference type, it won't be automatically copied when returned from the background thread—even if we pass the parameter `ByVal`. Let's explore how we can address this issue.

To handle getting a batch of results for display in the UI, we need to modify `DisplayResults`:

```
Private Delegate Sub Display(ByVal list As ArrayList)

Private Sub DisplayResults(ByVal list As ArrayList)

  ' process the results
  For Each value As String In list
    ListBox1.Items.Add(value)
  Next
End Sub
```

Next, we need to modify `FindPrimes` to return the values in batches rather than singly:

```
Private Sub FindPrimes(ByVal min As Integer, ByVal max As Integer)

  Dim display As New Display(AddressOf DisplayResults)
  Dim results As New ArrayList

  For count As Integer = min To max Step 2
    Dim isPrime As Boolean = True

    For x As Integer = 1 To count / 2
      For y As Integer = 1 To x
        If x * y = count Then
```

```
            ' the number is not prime
            isPrime = False
            Exit For
        End If
    Next
    ' short-circuit the check
    If Not isPrime Then Exit For
  Next

  If isPrime Then
    results.Add(count)
    If results.Count > 4 Then
      Me.Invoke(display, New Object() {results})
      results.Clear()
    End If
  End If

Next

If results.Count > 0 Then
  Me.Invoke(display, New Object() {results})
End If

End Sub
```

We create an `ArrayList` object, and then put each prime number into it as we find the new number. Any time the ArrayList contains five values we invoke the `DisplayResults` method in the UI to display the values. We also check at the very end of the method to see if there are any prime numbers we haven't sent to the UI, and if so we send them by invoking `DisplayResults`.

If you run the code now, you'll see that the data shows up in blocks of five values. You should also see that the application is a bit more responsive, because we've reduced the overhead due to the form's `Invoke` method being called.

This only works because we're using Invoke. If we used the form's `BeginInvoke` method we'd get some truly unpredictable results. Why? Because the ArrayList is shared data.

Since we're using the form's `Invoke` method the background thread is blocked while the UI thread uses the `ArrayList` object. What we've done here is transferred ownership of the ArrayList from the background thread to the UI thread for the duration of the `DisplayResults` method call. We are using a basic form of synchronization to ensure that only one thread has access to the `ArrayList` object at a time.

If we switched the code to use the form's `BeginInvoke` method then *both* the UI and background thread would be using it at the same time. The UI thread would be looping through to display the results as the background thread calls the `Clear` method. Sometimes we'd display all the data, sometimes none of it, sometimes some of it. Sometimes we'd just plain crash and burn.

When we rely on transferring data ownership we are ensuring that only one thread can access the data at any given time by blocking one of the threads via a synchronous method call. We can also share ownership of the data by using more advanced synchronization techniques, so let's discuss them now.

Sharing Data with Synchronization

So far, we've seen ways to avoid or tightly control the sharing of data. If at all possible, those are the best approaches to sharing data. However, sometimes we will have a requirement for more advanced data sharing, in which case we'll be faced with the complex world of synchronization.

As we discussed earlier, incorrect implementation of synchronization can cause performance issues, deadlocks and application crashes. Success is dependent on serious attention to detail. Problems may not manifest in testing, but when they happen in production they are often catastrophic. You can't *test* to ensure proper implementation, you must prove it in the same way mathematicians prove mathematical truths — by careful logical analysis of all possibilities.

Built-in Synchronization Support

Some objects in the .NET Framework have built-in support for synchronization, so we don't need to write it ourselves. In particular, most of the collection oriented classes have optional support for synchronization. These include: Queue, Stack, Hashtable, ArrayList, and more.

Rather than transferring ownership of our `ArrayList` from the background thread to the UI thread as we did in the last example, it might seem that we could use the synchronization provided by the `ArrayList` object to help mediate between the two threads. Although this won't actually work, let's walk through the process to illustrate just how insidious threading bugs can be.

To use a synchronized `ArrayList`, we need to change how we create the `ArrayList` itself:

```
Private Sub FindPrimes(ByVal min As Integer, ByVal max As Integer)

  Dim display As New Display(AddressOf DisplayResults)
  Dim results As ArrayList = ArrayList.Synchronized(New ArrayList)
```

What we're doing here is creating a normal `ArrayList`, and then having the `ArrayList` class "wrap" it with a synchronized wrapper. The end result is an `ArrayList` object that is thread safe and automatically prevents multiple threads from interacting with the data in invalid ways.

That's all we need to do in the `FindPrimes` method. All the usage of the `ArrayList` within `FindPrimes` just became thread safe.

Unfortunately, the `For..Each` construct can not be made thread safe by adding a synchronized wrapper around a collection object. This means we need to change the `DisplayResults` method to accommodate the fact that the `ArrayList` is now synchronized:

```
Private Sub DisplayResults(ByVal list As ArrayList)

  ' process the results
  SyncLock list.SyncRoot
    For Each value As String In list
      ListBox1.Items.Add(value)
    Next
  End SyncLock

End Sub
```

The `SyncLock` statement in VB.NET is used to provide an exclusive lock on an object. We'll discuss `SyncLock` more later, but here it is being used to get an exclusive lock on the ArrayList object's `SyncRoot`. This means that all our code within the `SyncLock` block can be sure that it is the only code that is interacting with the contents of the `ArrayList`. No other threads can access the data while our code is in this block.

If we run the code, at this point it will work fine, though you'll probably notice that it is visibly slower than it was before we switched to a synchronized `ArrayList` object. This is because all the extra blocking code causes overhead and slows down our application. But everything will work fine.

That's because we are still transferring ownership of the `ArrayList` from the background thread to the UI thread. Change `FindPrimes` to use the form's `BeginInvoke` method:

```
Private Sub FindPrimes(ByVal min As Integer, ByVal max As Integer)

  Dim display As New Display(AddressOf DisplayResults)
  Dim results As ArrayList = ArrayList.Synchronized(New ArrayList)

  For count As Integer = min To max Step 2
    Dim isPrime As Boolean = True

    For x As Integer = 1 To count / 2
      For y As Integer = 1 To x
        If x * y = count Then
          ' the number is not prime
          isPrime = False
          Exit For
        End If
      Next
      ' short-circuit the check
      If Not isPrime Then Exit For
    Next

    If isPrime Then
      results.Add(count)
      If results.Count > 4 Then
        Me.BeginInvoke(display, New Object() {results})
        results.Clear()
      End If
    End If

  Next

  If results.Count > 0 Then
    Me.BeginInvoke(display, New Object() {results})
  End If

End Sub
```

Now run the code. You might have to run it a few times, but if you watch closely you'll see that we're losing prime numbers. The end result is that the UI doesn't get all the numbers to display. You may also find some duplicate values listed in the display. If you interact with the UI while the code is running, or if you are running on a multiCPU machine the problems will be worse.

The reason this happens is because we've introduced a *race condition* into our code. A race condition is a situation where the order in which threads are scheduled can affect the outcome of the code. In our case, we can't tell for sure whether the background thread will call `results.Clear()` before or after the UI thread enters the `SyncLock` block to display the data.

If the UI thread enters the `SyncLock` first, then the background thread will be blocked when it tries to do the `results.Clear()` call. This happens because the `ArrayList` object is synchronized.

On the other hand, if the background thread reaches the `results.Clear()` call first, then by the time the UI thread enters the `SyncLock` block the `ArrayList` is already empty and there's no data to display.

Or, the background thread might not only do `results.Clear()`, but it could already have found one or more *new* prime values and put them into the `ArrayList`. When the UI thread finally gets to running `DisplayResults` it might not only miss the original batch of values, but it might display data from the *next* batch. It could easily end up displaying those values twice, again depending on the timing of the threads.

Race conditions are incredibly hard to spot and debug. This particular one is quite obvious if you look for it, though you might not notice it on casual inspection. After all, the code compiles and runs without any visible errors, and data is generated. The only way you'd catch this is by checking to ensure that you really did get all the values you expected. Worst of all, *sometimes* this code will run perfectly, while other times it will provide invalid results.

We can avoid this race condition by switching from an ArrayList to a different type of collection object — a `Queue`. The `Queue` object allows us to put items into the queue and then take them out one by one in the order in which they were inserted. Like `ArrayList`, the `Queue` class has a `Shared Synchronized` method so we can create a synchronized wrapper around the `Queue` object. To use a `Queue`, change `DisplayResults`:

```
Private Delegate Sub Display(ByVal list As Queue)

Private Sub DisplayResults(ByVal list As Queue)

  ' process the results
  While list.Count > 0
    ListBox1.Items.Add(CInt(list.Dequeue))
  End While

End Sub
```

Now we accept a `Queue` as a parameter. As long as there are items in the `Queue` (its `Count` value is greater than zero) we remove values from the `Queue`. This is done by calling the `Dequeue` method, which returns an `Object`. We convert the value to an `Integer` and add it to the `ListBox` control for display.

One notable difference here is that we're no longer using a `For..Each` construct, so we no longer need to use `SyncLock`. This is beneficial because it simplifies our code, and as we'll see our code will run faster. The `Queue` object has an efficient locking mechanism that helps avoid blocking either the UI or background thread in many cases.

Now we need to update `FindPrimes` to use a `Queue` instead of an `ArrayList`:

```
Private Sub FindPrimes(ByVal min As Integer, ByVal max As Integer)

  Dim display As New Display(AddressOf DisplayResults)
```

```
Dim results As Queue = Queue.Synchronized(New Queue)

For count As Integer = min To max Step 2
  Dim isPrime As Boolean = True

  For x As Integer = 1 To count / 2
    For y As Integer = 1 To x
      If x * y = count Then
        ' the number is not prime
        isPrime = False
        Exit For
      End If
    Next
    ' short-circuit the check
    If Not isPrime Then Exit For
  Next

  If isPrime Then
    results.Enqueue(count)
    If results.Count > 4 Then
      Me.BeginInvoke(display, New Object() {results})
    End If
  End If

Next

If results.Count > 0 Then
  Me.BeginInvoke(display, New Object() {results})
End If

End Sub
```

With these code changes, we first create a `Queue` object and then wrap it within a synchronized wrapper object. The result is a `Queue` object that is thread safe and automatically ensures that multiple threads can safely add and remove items from the queue without collision.

Then we change the code to call the `Enqueue` method to add each new prime value to the queue. Any time the queue has five items we call `BeginInvoke` so the UI thread will run the `DisplayResults` method. Notice that we're using `BeginInvoke` here, so the UI thread and background thread will both run simultaneously, virtually assuring that both with interact with the Queue object at the same time. That's fine though, because this is a synchronized `Queue` object.

With this change we've eliminated our race condition. It no longer matters in what order each thread runs. If the background thread gets ahead of the UI thread, it just means that the UI thread will read more items from the queue. If the UI thread gets ahead of the background thread it just means that the UI thread will stop processing items until the next time `DisplayResults` is invoked. It is no longer possible to lose items or to get duplicate items.

Synchronization Objects

While many collection objects optionally provide support for synchronization, most objects in the .NET Framework or in third-party libraries are not thread safe. To safely share these objects and classes in a multithreaded environment, we must manually implement synchronization.

To manually implement synchronization, we must rely on help from the Windows operating system. The .NET Framework includes classes that wrap the underling Windows operating system concepts however, so we don't need to call Windows directly. Instead we use the .NET Framework synchronization objects.

Synchronization objects have their own special terminology. Most of these objects can be acquired and released. In other cases, we wait on an object until it is signaled. Let's explore these terms.

For objects that can be acquired, the idea is that when we have the object we have a lock. Any other threads trying to acquire the object are blocked until we release the object. These type of synchronization objects are like a hot potato, only one thread has it at a time and other threads are waiting for it. No thread should hold onto such an object any longer than necessary, since that slows down the whole system.

The other class of objects are ones where we wait on the object — which means our thread is blocked. Some other thread will signal our object, which releases us so we become unblocked. Many threads can be waiting on the same object, and when the object is signaled all the blocked threads are released. This is basically the exact opposite of an acquire/release type object.

The following table lists the primary synchronization objects in the .NET Framework.

Object	Model	Description
AutoResetEvent	Wait/Signal	Allows a thread to release other threads that are waiting on the object
Interlocked		Allows multiple threads to safely increment and decrement values that are stored in variables accessible to all the threads
ManualResetEvent	Wait/Signal	Allows a thread to release other threads that are waiting on the object
Monitor	Acquire/Release	Defines an exclusive application-level lock where only one thread can hold the lock at any given time
Mutex	Acquire/Release	Defines an exclusive systemwide lock where only one thread can hold the lock at any given time
ReaderWriterLock	Acquire/Release	Defines a lock where many threads can read data, but provides exclusive access to one thread for writing data

Exclusive Locks and the SyncLock Statement

Perhaps the easiest type of synchronization to understand and implement is an *exclusive lock*. When one thread holds an exclusive lock, no other thread can obtain that lock. Any other thread attempting to obtain the lock is blocked until the lock becomes available.

There are two primary technologies for exclusive locking: the monitor and mutex objects. The *monitor* object allows a thread in a process to block other threads in the same process. The *mutex* object allows a thread in any process to block threads in the same process or in other processes. Because a mutex has systemwide scope, it is a more expensive object to use and should only be used when cross-process locking is required.

VB.NET includes the SyncLock statement, which is a shortcut to access a monitor object. While it is possible to directly create and use a System.Threading.Monitor object, it is far simpler to just use the SyncLock statement, so that is what we'll do here. We already used SyncLock earlier when we were using a synchronized ArrayList object.

Exclusive locks can be used to protect shared data so only one thread at a time can access the data. They can also be used to ensure that only one thread at a time can run a specific bit of code. This exclusive bit of code is called a *critical section*. While critical sections are an important concept in computer science, it is far more common to use exclusive locks to protect shared data, and that's what we'll focus on in this chapter.

If we want, we can use an exclusive lock to lock virtually any shared data. As an example, we can change our code to use the SyncLock statement instead of using a synchronized queue object. See Figure 19-9.

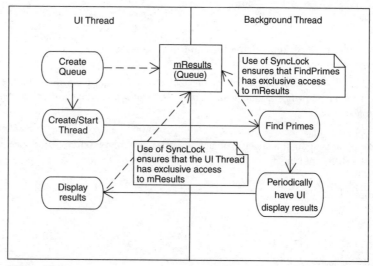

Figure 19-9

Change the declaration of the queue so it is global to the form, and is no longer synchronized:

```
' shared data
Dim mResults As New Queue
```

Then we can change the DisplayResults method to use the SyncLock statement to get a lock on the queue object any time we use it:

```
Private Delegate Sub Display()

Private Sub DisplayResults()

  Dim resultCount As Integer
```

```
  ' process the results
  SyncLock mResults
    resultCount = mResults.Count
  End SyncLock
  While resultCount > 0
    SyncLock mResults
      ListBox1.Items.Add(CInt(mResults.Dequeue))
      resultCount = mResults.Count
    End SyncLock
  End While

End Sub
```

Notice how our code structure is changed. Any time we access the mResults variable we must be inside a SyncLock block, thus ensuring that no other thread can be accessing mResults at the same time:

```
SyncLock mResults
  resultCount = mResults.Count
End SyncLock
```

The SyncLock statement acts against an object, in this case mResults.

The trick to making this work is to ensure that all code throughout our application wraps any access to mResults within a SyncLock statement. If any code doesn't follow this protocol we will have conflicts between threads!

Because SyncLock acts against a specific object, we can have many active SyncLock statements, each working against a different object:

```
SyncLock obj1
  ' blocks against obj1
End SyncLock

SyncLock obj2
  ' blocks against obj2
End SyncLock
```

Note that neither obj1 nor obj2 are altered or affected by this at all. The only thing we're saying here is that while we're within a SyncLock obj1 code block, any other thread attempting to execute a SyncLock obj1 statement will be blocked until we've executed the End SyncLock statement.

In the end, we need to make sure than any time we access mResults we are inside a SyncLock mResults code block. For example, this means that our While statement must change to use a variable rather than using mResults directly. While we could wrap the entire method in a single SyncLock statement, that would block the background thread unnecessarily. By blocking and unblocking on each element in the queue, we give the background thread the opportunity to run even while we're updating the UI.

We also must update FindPrimes to safely use mResults, again making sure to wrap each usage of mResults within a SyncLock block:

```
Private Sub FindPrimes(ByVal min As Integer, ByVal max As Integer)

  Dim resultCount As Integer
  Dim display As New Display(AddressOf DisplayResults)

  For count As Integer = min To max Step 2
    Dim isPrime As Boolean = True

    For x As Integer = 1 To count / 2
      For y As Integer = 1 To x
        If x * y = count Then
          ' the number is not prime
          isPrime = False
          Exit For
        End If
      Next
      ' short-circuit the check
      If Not isPrime Then Exit For
    Next

    If isPrime Then
      SyncLock mResults
        mResults.Enqueue(count)
        resultCount = mResults.Count
      End SyncLock
      If resultCount > 4 Then
        Me.BeginInvoke(display, Nothing)
      End If
    End If

  Next

  SyncLock mResults
    resultCount = mResults.Count
  End SyncLock
  If resultCount > 0 Then
    Me.BeginInvoke(display, Nothing)
  End If

End Sub
```

It doesn't matter if we're reading or changing values in mResults, we can never access the queue object unless we're in a SyncLock block.

At this point our code is using shared data, the mResults queue object. Before either the UI thread or background thread use mResults they always obtain an exclusive lock against mResults. This means that only one thread or the other can ever be accessing mResults at any given time.

Reader–Writer Locks

While exclusive locks are an easy way to protect shared data, they are not always the most efficient. In many cases, our application will contain some code that is updating shared data, and other code that is only reading from shared data. Some applications do a great deal of data reading, and only periodic data changes.

Since reading data doesn't change anything, there's nothing wrong with having multiple threads read data at the same time, as long as we can ensure that no threads are *updating* data while we're trying to read. Also, we typically only want one thread updating at a time.

What we have then, is a scenario where we want to allow many concurrent readers, but if the data is to be changed then one thread must temporarily gain exclusive access to the shared memory. This is the purpose behind the *ReaderWriterLock* object.

Using a `ReaderWriterLock`, we can request either a read lock or a write lock. If we obtain a read lock, we can safely read the data. Other threads can simultaneously also obtain read locks and can safely read the data.

Before we can update data, we must obtain a write lock. When we request a write lock any other threads requesting either a read or write lock will be blocked. If there are any outstanding read or write locks in progress, we'll be blocked until they are released. Once there are no outstanding locks (read or write), we'll be granted the write lock. No other locks are granted until we release the write lock, so our write lock is an exclusive lock.

Once we release the write lock, any pending requests for other locks are granted, allowing either another single writer to access the data, or allowing multiple readers to simultaneously access the data. We can adapt our sample code to use a `System.Threading.ReaderWriterLock` object. Start by using the code we just created based on the `SyncLock` statement with a `Queue` object as shared data.

First, we need to create an instance of the `ReaderWriterLock` in a form-wide variable:

```
' lock object
Dim mRWLock As New ReaderWriterLock
```

Since a `ReaderWriterLock` is just an object, we can have many lock objects in an application if needed. We could use each lock object to protect different bits of shared data.

Then we can change the `DisplayResults` method to make use of this object instead of the `SyncLock` statement:

```
Private Sub DisplayResults()

  ' process the results
  mRWLock.AcquireReaderLock(100)
  While mResults.Count > 0
     Dim cookie As LockCookie = mRWLock.UpgradeToWriterLock(100)
     ListBox1.Items.Add(CInt(mResults.Dequeue))
     mRWLock.DowngradeFromWriterLock(cookie)
  End While
  mRWLock.ReleaseLock()

End Sub
```

The first thing our code does is reads the `Count` property of the queue object. Before we can read data from the shared queue we need a read lock:

```
mRWLock.AcquireReaderLock(100)
```

We are telling the system that we'll wait 100 milliseconds before giving up on trying to get the lock. In production code, we'd need to wrap this in a `Try..Catch` block in case a timeout occurs.

Once we have the read lock, we can read the `Count` property. Assuming there's data in the queue, the next thing we want to do is remove an item from the queue. As this alters the queue's data, we need a write lock. The best way to get a write lock when we already have a read lock is to upgrade the read lock to a write lock:

```
Dim cookie As LockCookie = mRWLock.UpgradeToWriterLock(100)
```

This upgrade process gives us a cookie that we will use later when we're done updating the shared data. Note that we'll be blocked until there are no other threads holding read or write locks, so when the next line of code runs we'll know we have an exclusive lock.

Once we've removed the item from the queue, we downgrade our write lock back to a read lock:

```
mRWLock.DowngradeFromWriterLock(cookie)
```

Since we're still in the `While` loop, the next thing our code will do is read the `Count` property, so the read lock is important.

Once we exit the `While` loop, we're done interacting with `mResults` so we release the lock entirely:

```
mRWLock.ReleaseLock()
```

This ensures that we are no longer holding either a read or write lock.

> **It is critical that we always release locks we're holding.**

Failure to release a lock will almost certainly block other threads, possibly forever — causing a deadlock situation. The alternate fate is that the other threads will request a lock and will time out, throwing an exception and causing the application to fail. Either way, if we don't release our locks we'll cause application failure.

Now that `DisplayResults` has been updated to use the `ReaderWriterLock`, we need to update `FindPrimes` so the background thread uses the same locking scheme:

```
Private Sub FindPrimes(ByVal min As Integer, ByVal max As Integer)

  Dim display As New Display(AddressOf DisplayResults)

  For count As Integer = min To max Step 2
    Dim isPrime As Boolean = True

    For x As Integer = 1 To count / 2
      For y As Integer = 1 To x
        If x * y = count Then
          ' the number is not prime
          isPrime = False
          Exit For
        End If
```

```
        Next
        ' short-circuit the check
        If Not isPrime Then Exit For
    Next

    If isPrime Then
      mRWLock.AcquireWriterLock(100)
      mResults.Enqueue(count)
      mRWLock.ReleaseWriterLock()
      mRWLock.AcquireReaderLock(100)
      If mResults.Count > 4 Then
        mRWLock.ReleaseReaderLock()
        Me.BeginInvoke(display, Nothing)

      Else
        mRWLock.ReleaseReaderLock()
      End If
    End If

  Next

  mRWLock.AcquireReaderLock(100)
  If mResults.Count > 0 Then
    mRWLock.ReleaseReaderLock()
    Me.BeginInvoke(display, Nothing)

  Else
    mRWLock.ReleaseReaderLock()
  End If

End Sub
```

Again, before reading from mResults we always get a reader lock, and before changing the queue object we get a writer lock. In each case, we make certain that we've released the lock before moving on.

AutoReset Events

Both Monitor (SyncLock) and ReaderWriterLock objects follow the acquire/release model, where threads are blocked until they can acquire control of the appropriate lock.

We can flip the paradigm by using AutoResetEvent and ManualResetEvent objects. With these objects, threads voluntarily wait on the event object. While waiting, they are blocked and do no work. When another thread signals (raises) the event, any threads waiting on the event object are released and do work.

Signaling an event object is done by calling the object's Set method. To wait on an event object, a thread calls that objects WaitOne method. This method blocks the thread until the event object is signaled (the event is raised).

Event objects can be in one of two states: signaled or not signaled. When an event object is signaled, threads waiting on the object are released. If a thread calls WaitOne on an event object that is signaled then the thread isn't blocked, and continues running. However, if a thread calls WaitOne on an event object that is not signaled then the thread is blocked until some other thread calls that object's Set method, thus signaling the event.

AutoResetEvent objects automatically reset themselves to the not signaled state as soon as any thread calls the WaitOne method. In other words, if an AutoResetEvent is not signaled and a thread calls WaitOne then that thread will be blocked. Another thread can then call the Set method, thus signaling the event. This both releases the waiting thread and immediately resets the AutoResetEvent object to its not signaled state.

We can use an AutoResetEvent object to coordinate the use of shared data between threads. Change the ReaderWriterLock declaration to declare an AutoResetEvent instead:

```
' wait object
Dim mWait As New AutoResetEvent(False)
```

By passing False to the constructor we are telling the event object to start out in its not signaled state. Were we to pass True, it would start out in the signaled state, and the first thread to call WaitOne would *not* be blocked, but would trigger the event object to automatically reset its state to not signaled.

Next we can update DisplayResults to use the event object. Remember that DisplayResults is invoked by FindPrimes when there's data to display. By using an event object, we can allow the FindPrimes background task to resume processing before we're done displaying the data to the user. To do this, we'll copy the queue data, then release the background thread, and then update the UI by using the data we copied:

```
Private Sub DisplayResults()

  ' copy the data
  Dim temp As Queue = mResults.Clone()
  mResults.Clear()

  ' release the background thread
  mWait.Set()

  ' process the results
  While temp.Count > 0
    ListBox1.Items.Add(CInt(temp.Dequeue))
  End While

End Sub
```

As soon as we've copied the data from mResults, we clear the shared data. With that done, there's no reason that the background thread couldn't continue to find prime numbers while we update the UI with our copy of the data. To release the background thread, we call Set on the event object:

```
' release the background thread
mWait.Set()
```

Then the UI is updated by using our local copy of the data. In the meantime, the background thread is already busily looking for more prime numbers.

Of course, this means that the `FindPrimes` method must also use the `AutoResetEvent` object:

```
Private Sub FindPrimes(ByVal min As Integer, ByVal max As Integer)

  Dim display As New Display(AddressOf DisplayResults)

  For count As Integer = min To max Step 2
    Dim isPrime As Boolean = True

    For x As Integer = 1 To count / 2
      For y As Integer = 1 To x
        If x * y = count Then
          ' the number is not prime
          isPrime = False
          Exit For
        End If
      Next
      ' short-circuit the check
      If Not isPrime Then Exit For
    Next

    If isPrime Then
      mResults.Enqueue(count)
      If mResults.Count > 4 Then
        Me.BeginInvoke(display)
        ' wait for the display to update
        mWait.WaitOne()
      End If
    End If

  Next

  If mResults.Count > 0 Then
    Me.BeginInvoke(display)
  End If

End Sub
```

The UI thread won't attempt to access `mResults` until we invoke the `DisplayResults` method by calling the form's `BeginInvoke` method:

```
Me.BeginInvoke(display)
```

As soon as we do this, we must ensure that `FindPrimes` is blocked until the UI thread is done interacting with `mResults`. Remember that `mWait` is not signaled until the UI thread calls the `Set` method, so we can just call `WaitOne` to block against the nonsignaled event object:

```
mWait.WaitOne()
```

This line blocks the background thread until the UI thread calls `mWait.Set`, which it only does after it is done using the `mResults` object. This not only releases the background thread to resume running, but automatically resets the `mWait` object to its nonsignaled state so the next time the background thread calls `WaitOne` it will be blocked.

What this means though, is that if the UI thread get scheduled such that mResults is copied and cleared and mWait.Set called before the background thread even gets to the WaitOne method, then the background thread may never be blocked. While unlikely in this example, the point is that proper use of event objects can create highly optimized multithreaded code by minimizing blocking, or at least reducing the amount of time threads are blocked.

ManualReset Events

A ManualResetEvent object is very similar to the AutoResetEvent we just used. The difference is that with a ManualResetEvent object we are in total control over whether the event object is set to its signaled or not signaled state. The state of the event object is never altered automatically.

This means that we must manually call the Reset method rather than relying on it to occur automatically. To see how this works, change the declaration to create a ManualResetEvent:

```
' wait object
Dim mWait As New ManualResetEvent(False)
```

Then change FindPrimes to reset the event object to nonsignaled after the WaitOne call:

```
If isPrime Then
  mResults.Enqueue(count)
  If mResults.Count > 4 Then
    Me.BeginInvoke(display)
    ' wait for the display to update
    mWait.WaitOne()
    mWait.Reset()
  End If
End If
```

The end result is the same as with the AutoResetEvent, but here we have control over whether the event is reset to its nonsignaled state.

Canceling a Background Task

At this point, we've explored basic threading, techniques to work with shared data and synchronization objects. The one remaining question is how to cancel a background task. This isn't as easy as it might appear, since the background task should be allowed to close itself gracefully.

On the surface, it might seem we could do something like this:

```
Private mThread As Thread

Private Sub StartTask()
  mThread = New Thread(AddressOf Worker)
  mThread.Start()
End Sub

Private Sub CancelTask()
  mThread.Abort()
End Sub
```

```
Private Sub Worker()
   ' do work here
End Sub
```

The problem with this is that calling the `Abort` method on a thread simply stops the thread dead in its tracks. If our worker code was in the middle of using an expensive resource, such as a database connection, it wouldn't get an opportunity to release the resource. In general, the `Abort` method should be used as a last resort, if at all. It certainly shouldn't be part of our design for canceling a background task.

Instead, what we need to do is develop a protocol by which the user can tell the UI that a cancel is desired. The UI should pass this request on to the background task, which should honor the request at the first opportunity.

This leaves it up to the background task to notice that a cancel has been requested and to properly shut itself down. The benefit to this is that the background task can clean up any resources it was using and can exit gracefully.

Of course, in the meantime, the UI thread can't exit either, nor can the user restart the task until the original has completed.

In reality it would be possible to allow the user to restart the task before the previous one was complete, but to do that we'd have to develop a locking protocol by which the second task and first task didn't conflict in their use of any shared data. As that can be quite complex, it is typically best to prevent restarting the task until the first one has canceled.

All these requirements are part of our cancel protocol.

There are a variety of ways to pass the cancel request to the background task. The simplest is to use a bit of shared data — a Boolean — that is updated by the UI thread and read by the background thread. For instance,

```
Private mCancel As Boolean

Private Sub StartTask()
  mCancel = False
  mThread = New Thread(AddressOf Worker)
  mThread.Start()
End Sub

Private Sub CancelTask()
  mCancel = True
End Sub

Private Sub Worker()
   ' do work here
  If mCancel Then
     ' do cleanup here
     Exit Sub
  End If
   ' do more work here
End Sub
```

Before starting the background task, we make sure the cancel flag, mCancel, is False. While the background task is running, it periodically checks the flag to see if it is True. If it is True, then the background task does any cleanup it might need to do and gracefully exits. Any time we want to request a cancel, we simply set mCancel to True.

Note that even though mCancel is shared across threads that there is no synchronization for the variable. It turns out that we don't need synchronization in this case. A Boolean is a value type, which means it is stored in a single area of memory. Reading and changing a value type is relatively straightforward, and as long as only one thread *updates* the value, we can get away without synchronization.

> *Avoiding synchronization when possible is a good thing. Remember back to our earlier discussions — use of synchronization objects decreases performance. The less synchronization we do the better for performance and overall throughput of our application.*

Notice that only the UI thread updates the value. The background thread only reads the value. If both threads updated the value we'd need synchronization. Or, if mCancel was a reference type we'd need synchronization. But that is not the case, so we can get away without it.

However, you should realize what's going on behind the scenes when we update a value type. When we set mCancel to True it seems like a single operation:

```
mCancel = True
```

However, in reality the following steps occur:

1. The mCancel value is moved from memory to a CPU register
2. The value in the register is updated to the new value
3. The value is moved from the CPU register back to the mCancel memory location

None of this is atomic. In other words, the background thread could run at any point during this process. Note that the background thread reads the value in *memory*, so if the value is in the middle of being updated in the CPU register, the background thread will get the *old* value, not the new value. The new value isn't available until after step 3 has completed.

For our purposes, using mCancel as a simple flag, this isn't a problem. In other cases, where both threads may be updating the value, this can be a serious problem. The worst case scenario for us is that the background thread might run a bit longer because it read the old value as mCancel was being set to True — which is not a big deal.

The other piece of the puzzle is that we must prevent restarting the task if it is still running. To do this, we'll use another Boolean to indicate the background task's state. Again, this is a simple value type, and it will only be updated by the background thread and read by the UI thread. Because we meet these conditions, we can get away without the use of synchronization:

```
Private mCancel As Boolean
Private mRunning As Boolean

Private Sub StartTask()
  If Not mRunning Then
```

```
         mCancel = False
         mThread = New Thread(AddressOf Worker)
         mThread.Start()
     End If
End Sub

Private Sub CancelTask()
   mCancel = True
End Sub

Private Sub Worker()
   mRunning = True
   ' do work here
   If mCancel Then
       ' do cleanup here
     mRunning = False
     Exit Sub
   End If
   ' do more work here
   mRunning = False
End Sub
```

The mRunning variable is used to prevent restarting the task if it is already running. The UI thread, in the StartTask method, checks this value to see if the background task is active. If it is, we prevent another task from being started.

In the Worker method, which is the background task on the background thread, we first set mRunning to True to indicate that the task is active. Then, whether we exit due to a cancel request or exit normally, we set mRunning to False to indicate that the task is no longer running.

Let's see how this works in our sample application. We can implement this strategy in any of the models, but to keep things flowing we'll implement it in the most recent code where we used the ManualResetEvent for synchronization of the shared queue object.

First, rename Button1 to StartButton and add a new button named CancelButton. This will help keep things clear as we start and stop the background task.

Then declare the two flags at the form level:

```
' cancel flag
Dim mCancel As Boolean = False
' background task state
Dim mRunning As Boolean = False
```

Now in the click event of StartButton we need to do some setup before starting the background task:

```
Private Sub StartButton_Click(ByVal sender As System.Object, _
        ByVal e As System.EventArgs) Handles StartButton.Click

    ' disable start button while running
    StartButton.Enabled = False
```

```
    ' reset display and shared data
    ListBox1.Items.Clear()
  mResults.Clear()
```

```
  ' reset cancel flag
  mCancel = False
```

```
  ' run the task
  Dim worker As New Task(AddressOf FindPrimes)
  worker.BeginInvoke(10001, 12000, Nothing, Nothing)
```

```
End Sub
```

First, we disable the StartButton control so the user can't click it while the task is active. This is better than a simple If..Then check, because it gives the user a visual cue that the task is active.

Then we clear the ListBox and Queue objects. Since we could be restarting after a canceled operation, there could be leftover data in those objects and we want to make sure we're starting with a clean slate.

Finally we make sure that mCancel is set to False. Since we're about to start the background task, we want to make sure it isn't flagged to be canceled before it even gets going. With this done, we can add code behind the CancelButton control so the user can request a cancel:

```
' user requested a cancel
Private Sub CancelButton_Click(ByVal sender As System.Object, _
      ByVal e As System.EventArgs) Handles CancelButton.Click

  ' set cancel flag
  mCancel = True

End Sub
```

This is simply a matter of setting the mCancel flag to True, indicating to the background task that it should stop running as soon as possible.

Notice that we don't reenable the StartButton control here. All we've done at this point is *requested* that the background task stop — we didn't actually stop it. Some time may pass before the task stops, and we don't want to reenable the StartButton control until the background task is done.

We can tell when the task is done by checking the mRunning flag in the DisplayResults method:

```
Private Sub DisplayResults()

  ' copy the data
  Dim temp As Queue = mResults.Clone()
  mResults.Clear()

  ' release the background thread
  mWait.Set()

  ' process the results
  While temp.Count > 0
    ListBox1.Items.Add(CInt(temp.Dequeue))
  End While
```

```
   If Not mRunning Then
     ' if the background task is done, reset
     ' the start button to enabled
     StartButton.Enabled = True
   End If

 End Sub
```

As long as the background task sets `mRunning` before invoking `DisplayResults`, we'll be able to tell whether the background task is done or not.

Finally, we need to update `FindPrimes` to both honor the cancel request via `mCancel` and to set `mRunning` appropriately:

```
Private Sub FindPrimes(ByVal min As Integer, ByVal max As Integer)

  Dim display As New Display(AddressOf DisplayResults)

  ' indicate we're running
  mRunning = True

  For count As Integer = min To max Step 2
    Dim isPrime As Boolean = True

    For x As Integer = 1 To count / 2
      For y As Integer = 1 To x
        If x * y = count Then
          ' the number is not prime
          isPrime = False
          Exit For
        End If
      Next
      ' short-circuit the check
      If Not isPrime Then Exit For
    Next

    ' see if user wants us to stop
    If mCancel Then
      ' indicate we're stopped
      mRunning = False
      ' flush any data to display
      Me.BeginInvoke(display)
      ' exit the task
      Exit Sub
    End If

    If isPrime Then
      mResults.Enqueue(count)
      If mResults.Count > 4 Then
        Me.BeginInvoke(display)
        ' wait for the display to update
        mWait.WaitOne()
        mWait.Reset()
      End If
    End If
```

```
Next

' indicate we're stopped
mRunning = False
Me.BeginInvoke(display)

End Sub
```

As the task starts up, the first thing we do is set `mRunning` to `True`. Notice that we set it to `False` before using the form's `BeginInvoke` method to call `DisplayResults`, both in the case of a cancel request and in the case that the background task completes normally. This clearly communicates to `DisplayResults` whether the task is still running or not each time the UI is updated.

Periodically, we check the `mCancel` flag to see if a cancel has been requested. In this case, we're checking as each number is evaluated. In very processor intensive work, we might check less often, since even checking the value of a Boolean isn't entirely free and we don't want this check to noticeably slow down the background task.

If `mCancel` turns out to be `True`, then we gracefully stop working and exit the `FindPrimes` method. This ends the background task, honoring the user's request to cancel. Notice that in the case of a cancel we still invoke `DisplayResults` one last time. This not only displays any final data we've found, but also allows the UI to notice that `mRunning` is now `False`.

Summary

In this chapter, we took a fairly involved look at the subject of threading in .NET and how VB.NET developers now have access to a rich set of threading functionality. We started off by defining the nature of threads and how they relate to processes AppDomain objects in .NET. We also discussed the reasons for using multithreading in both interactive and server-side applications.

We then created a simple threading example to calculate and display prime numbers. While the simple example manually created a `Thread` object, we should typically look first to use the built-in `ThreadPool` object in the .NET Framework. Most of our examples in the chapter used the `ThreadPool` object — launching our background task using an asynchronous delegate.

Using the prime number example, we explored ways to avoid or minimize shared data. Assuming we can't avoid shared data, we also examined the key synchronization objects available in the .NET Framework and explored how each is used.

Finally, we explored the issues around canceling background tasks. Background tasks can't be simply stopped on demand, we must request that they stop themselves in a graceful and controlled manner. This allows the background task to clean up any expensive resources that were in use and to notify the main thread when the task is done running.

20

Remoting

Remoting is the .NET technology that allows code in one application domain to call into the methods and properties of objects running in another application domain. A major use of remoting is in the classic three-tier desktop approach where presentation code on the desktop needs to access objects running on a server somewhere on the network. Another primary use for remoting is when code in ASP.NET Web forms or Web services need to call objects running on an application server somewhere on the network. In short, remoting is the technology to use when our *n*-tier code needs to talk to our business or data tier that is running on an application server.

In terms of code, remoting is related to Web services. Although these two technologies share a lot of the same classes and principles, Remoting is designed to be an extensible technology that's not bound by the limitations of the SOAP/HTTP approach.

SOAP's biggest problem is that it is not lightweight. It's designed with maximum platform interoperability in mind, and this puts certain limits on how data can be transferred. For example, imagine that Platform A stores Integer variables as a four-byte block of memory, with the lowest-value byte appearing first. Now imagine that Platform B also uses a four-byte block of memory, but this time the highest-value byte appears first. Without some form of conversion, if we copy that block of bytes from Platform A to Platform B, because the encoding of the value is different, the platforms won't be able to agree on what the number actually is. In this scenario, one platform will think it's got the number 4, whereas the other thinks that the number is actually 536870912.

SOAP gets around this problem by representing numbers (and everything else) as strings of ASCII characters—as ASCII is a text-encoding standard that most platforms can understand. However, this means that the native binary representations of the numbers have to be converted to text each time the SOAP document has to be constructed. In addition, the values themselves have to be packaged in something that we can read (with a little bit of effort). This leads to two problems: massive bloat (a four-byte value starts taking hundreds of bytes to store) and wasted CPU cycles in converting from native encoding to text encoding and back again.

We can live with all these problems if we only want to run our Web service on, say, Windows 2000, and have it accessed through a client running on a cell phone. SOAP is designed to do this kind of thing.

However, if we have a Windows XP desktop application that wants to use objects hosted on a Windows 2000 server (using the same platform), the bloated network traffic and wastage in terms of conversion is suboptimal at best, and ridiculous at worst.

Remoting lets us enjoy the same power of Web services but without the downside. If we want, we can connect directly to the server over TCP and send binary data without having to do any conversions. If one Windows computer has a four-byte block of memory holding a 32-bit integer value, we can safely copy the bit pattern to another Windows computer and both will agree on what the number is. In effect, network traffic sanity is restored and we're not wasting processor time doing conversions.

Now that you know what Remoting is, we're ready to understand its architecture.

Remoting Overview

Before we go on, we need to understand several basics about remoting, including the basic terms and related objects.

Basic Terminology

A normal object is not accessible via remoting. By default, .NET objects are only accessible to other code running within the same .NET AppDomain.

A *remote object* is an object that's been made available over Remoting by inheriting from `System.MarshalByRefObject`. These objects are often also called `MBR`s. Remote objects are the same kinds of objects that you build normally, with the single condition that they inherit from `MarshalByRefObject` and that we register them with the `Remoting` subsystem to make them available to clients. Remote objects are anchored to the machine and AppDomain where they were created, and we communicate with them over the network.

A *serializable* object is an object that's been made available over Remoting by marking the class with the `<Serializable()>` attribute. These objects will move from machine to machine or AppDomain to AppDomain. They are not anchored to any particular location, so they are unanchored objects. A common example of a serializable object is the `DataSet`, which can be returned from a server to a client across the network. The `DataSet` physically moves from server to client via the serialization technology in the .NET Framework.

A *remoting host* is a server application that configures remoting to listen for client requests. Remoting runs within the host process, using the memory and threads of the host process to handle any client requests. The most common remoting host is IIS. We can create custom remoting hosts, which are typically created as a Windows service, so they can run even when no user is logged into the server. It is also possible to have any .NET application be a remoting host, which can allow us to emulate ActiveX EXE behaviors to some degree. This last technique is most commonly used when creating peer-to-peer style applications.

A *channel* is a way of communicating between two machines. Out-of-the-box, .NET comes with two channels: TCP and HTTP. The TCP channel is a lightweight channel designed for transporting binary data between two computers. (You need to think of the "TCP channel" as being different to the TCP protocol that HTTP also uses.) It works using sockets, something we talk about in much more detail in Chapter 23. HTTP is, as you already know, the protocol that Web servers use. In typical use, you'd expect to see clients connecting to remote objects over TCP when they are behind the firewall of a private network. It's likely you'd use HTTP when the client is outside of the network and on the public Internet, perhaps using a VPN connection into the private network, or just using an open port on your firewall. You can build your own networks to suit your own needs.

A *formatter* is how an object is "crunched" into a format so that it can be squirted down the channel. This is serialization and deserialization, which we'll talk more about later. Out-of-the-box, we have two formatters: Binary and SOAP. Binary is typically used in combination with the TCP channel, whereas SOAP is typically used in combination with the HTTP channel. You can also build your own formatters for your own needs. In fact, you can mix and match channels, so if you want to use the SOAP formatter with the binary channel you can, and so on. However, the HTTP/SOAP and TCP/Binary combinations are recommended by Microsoft.

A *message* is a communication between the client and server. It holds the information about the remote object and the method or property that's being invoked, as well as any parameters.

A *proxy* is used on the client-side to call into the remote object. To use Remoting, you don't typically have to worry about creating the proxy, .NET can do it all for you. However, there's a slightly confusing split between something called a *transparent proxy* and a *real proxy*. A transparent proxy is so called because "you can't see it." When you request a remote object, a transparent proxy is what you get. It looks like the remote object (that is, it has the same properties and methods as the original), which means that your client code can use the remote object or a local copy of the would-be-remote object without you having to make any changes, and without you knowing that there is any difference. The transparent proxy defers the calls to the real proxy. The real proxy is what actually constructs the message, sends it to the server, and waits for the response. You can think of the transparent proxy as a "fake" object that contains the same methods and properties that the real object contains.

The real proxy is effectively a set of helper functions that manage the communications. You don't use the real proxy directly, instead, the transparent proxy calls into the real proxy on your behalf.

A *message sink* is an "interceptor object." Before messages go into the channel, these are used to do some further processing on them, perhaps to attach more data, reformat data before it is sent, route debugging information or perform security checking. On the client-side, we have an "envoy sink." On the server-side, we have a "server context sink" and an "object context sink." In typical use, you can ignore these.

Message sinks are a pretty advanced topic that allow for some powerful extensions to the Remoting model. Unfortunately, they're out of the scope of this book.

Figures 20-1 and 20-2 show how these concepts fit together.

Figure 20-1 shows how a client calls the `Hello` method of a transparent proxy object. The transparent proxy looks just like the real object, so the client doesn't even realize that remoting is involved. The transparent proxy then invokes the real proxy, which converts the method call into a generic remoting message.

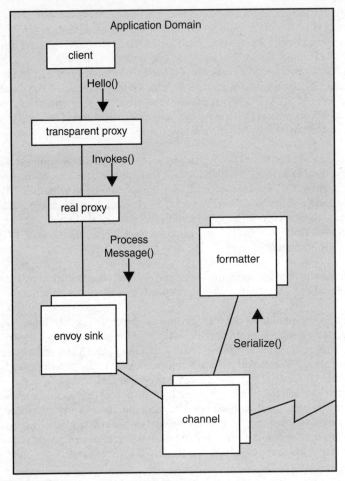

Figure 20-1

This message is sent through any messaging sinks configured on the client. These messaging sinks may transform the message in various ways, including adding encryption or compression of the data.

The message is then serialized by the formatter object. The result is a byte stream that is sent to the server by using the channel configured for use on the client.

Figure 20-2 shows how the server handles the message. The message comes into the server via a channel. The message is then deserialized by the formatter object and run through any messaging sinks configured on the server. These messaging sinks typically mirror those on the client, unencrypting or decompressing the data as appropriate.

Finally, the message is decoded by the object context sink, which uses the information in the message to invoke the method on the actual object. The object itself has no idea that it was invoked via remoting, since the method call was merely relayed from the client.

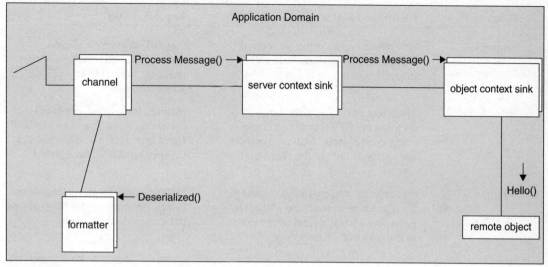

Figure 20-2

SingleCall, Singleton, and Activated Objects

The next step is to look at the way that Remoting treats objects. In Remoting, objects are divided into three camps: *wellknown* objects, *client-activated* objects and *serializable* objects.

❏ Wellknown objects run on the server and perform a service for the remote application, such as *give me a list of all the customers* or *create and invoice*. They can be configured to act similar to a Web service or using what's called a singleton pattern (which we'll discuss shortly).

❏ Client-activated objects are created for each client and maintain state on the server over time. In many ways, these objects act similar to COM objects we accessed via DCOM in the past.

❏ Serializable objects can move from machine to machine as needed. For instance, a serializable object can be created on the server (by a wellknown or client-activated object), and then returned to a client. When the object is returned to the client, it is physically copied *to the client machine* where it can be used by client code.

Service objects are further divided into two types: *singleton* and *single* call. The following table summarizes the types of object.

Type	Calling semantics	Key Attributes
SingleCall	An object is created for each client method call made to the server	Stateless, per-method lifetime, atomic methods, no threading issues, anchored to AppDomain where created

Continues

Type	Calling semantics	Key Attributes
Singleton	One object exists on the server and is used to handle all method calls from all clients	Stateful, long-lived, shared instance, thread synchronization required, anchored to AppDomain where created
Activated	The client creates activated objects on the server. The client can create many such objects. Activated objects are available only to the client that created the object	Stateful, long-lived, per-client instances, threading issues only if client is multithreaded, anchored to AppDomain where created
Serializable	The object is automatically copied from machine to machine when it is passed as a parameter or returned as the result of a function	Stateful, long-lived, no threading issues, nonanchored (moves across network automatically)

Let's discuss each in a bit more detail.

SingleCall Objects

SingleCall objects act much like typical Web service objects. Each time a client calls a method on a SingleCall object, an object is created specifically to handle that method call. Once the method call is complete, the object is not reused and is garbage collected by the .NET runtime.

SingleCall objects also work the way a JIT (just-in-time) activated object does in COM+, and matches the way most people use MTS or COM+ objects. In those environments we typically create a server-side object, make a method call and then release the object.

These objects must inherit from System.MarshalByRefObject, so they are MBRs. This means that they always run in the AppDomain and Windows process where they are created. If they are created on a server in a host process that is where they live and run. Clients interact with them across the network.

The most commonly used type of service object in remoting is the SingleCall object. Not only do they provide semantics similar to Web services, MTS and COM+, but they also provide the simplest programming model.

Since an object is created for each method call, these objects are inherently stateless. Even if an object tried to keep state between calls, it would fail because the object is destroyed after each method is complete. This helps ensure that no method call can be affected by previous method calls or can contaminate subsequent method calls.

Each method call runs on its own thread (from the .NET thread pool as discussed in Chapter 19). However, since each method call also gets its very own object, there's typically no contention between threads. This means we don't need to worry about writing synchronization or locking code in our SingleCall code.

Technically, it is possible to encounter synchronization issues if we have shared stateful objects on the server. This requires substantial work on our part to create and access such shared objects and is outside the scope of this book. Typically, this type of model is not used, and so threading is a nonissue with SingleCall objects.

Due to the automatic isolation, statelessness and threading simplicity `SingleCall` objects are the preferred technology for creation of server code in remoting.

Singleton Objects

Singleton objects are quite different from `SingleCall` objects. Only one `Singleton` object exists at a time, and it may exist for a long time and maintain state. All client method calls from all users are routed to this one `Singleton` object. This means that all clients have equal, shared access to any state maintained by the `Singleton` object.

These objects must inherit from `System.MarshalByRefObject`, so they are MBRs. This means that they always run in the AppDomain and Windows process where they are created. If they are created on a server in a host process that is where they live and run. Clients interact with them across the network.

As with the `SingleCall` scenario, all method calls are run on threads from the .NET thread pool. This means that multiple simultaneous method calls can be running on different threads at the same time. As we discussed in Chapter 19, this can be complex since we'll have to write multithreaded synchronization code to ensure that these threads don't collide as they interact with our `Singleton` object.

`Singleton` objects have a potentially unpredictable lifespan. When the first client makes the first method call to the object, it is created. From that point forward it remains in memory for an indeterminate period of time. As long as it remains in memory, all method calls from all the clients will be handled by this one object. However, if the object is idle for a long time, remoting may release it to conserve resources. Also, some remoting hosts may recycle their `AppDomain` objects, which automatically causes the destruction of all our objects.

Because of this, we can never be certain that the data stored in memory in the object will remain available over time. This means that any long-term state data must be written to a persistent store like a database, since we can't rely on the object always remaining in memory.

Due to the complexity of shared memory, thread synchronization and dealing with object lifetime issues, `Singleton` objects are more complex to design and code than `SingleCall` objects. While they can be useful in specialized scenarios, they aren't as widely used as `SingleCall` objects.

Activated Objects

Client-activated, or just activated, objects are different from both `SingleCall` and `Singleton` objects. `Activated` objects are created by a client application, and they remain in memory on the server over time. They are associated with just that one client, so they are not shared between clients. Also, they are stateful objects, meaning that they can maintain data in memory during their lifetime.

These objects must inherit from `System.MarshalByRefObject`, so they are MBRs. This means that they always run in the AppDomain and Windows process where they are created. If they are created on a server in a host process that is where they live and run. Clients interact with them across the network.

A client can create multiple activated objects on the server. The objects will remain on the server until the client releases the objects or the server AppDomain is reset (which can happen with some types of remoting host). Also, if the client doesn't contact the server for several minutes the server will assume the client abandoned the objects and it will release them.

`Activated` objects typically don't have any threading issues. The only way multiple threads will be running in the same activated object is if the client is multithreaded and multiple client threads simultaneously make method calls to the same server-side activated object. If this is the case in your application, then you'll have to deal with shared data and synchronization issues as discussed in Chapter 19.

While long-lived, stateful, per-client objects can be useful in some specialized scenarios, they are not commonly used in most client/server or n-tier application environments.

Serializable Objects

While `SingleCall, Singleton` and `Activated` objects are always anchored to the AppDomain, Windows process and machine where they are created, this is not the case with serializable objects.

`Serializable` objects can move from machine to machine as needed. The classic example of this is the ADO.NET DataSet, which can be returned as a result of a function on a server. The `DataSet` physically moves to the client machine, where it can be used by client code. When the client wants to update the `DataSet` it simply passes the object to the server as a parameter, causing the `DataSet` to physically move to the server machine.

These objects *do not* inherit from `System.MarshalByRefObject`. Instead, they are decorated with the `<Serializable()>` attribute and may optionally implement the `ISerializable` interface. This means that they are not anchored to the AppDomain or Windows process where they were created. The remoting subsystem will automatically serialize these objects' data and transfer it across the network to another machine. On that other machine, a new instance of the objects will be created and loaded with the data, effectively cloning the objects across the network.

When working with serializable objects, we'll typically use a `SingleCall` object on the server to create the serializable object and call any server-side methods (such as ones to load the object with data from a database). The `SingleCall` object will then return the serializable object to the client as a function result, so the client can then interact with the object. The `SingleCall` object's method might look like the following:

```
Public Function GetCustomer(ByVal ID As Integer) As Customer

    Dim cust As New Customer()
    cust.Load(ID)
    Return cust

End Function
```

The client code might look like this:

```
Dim cust As Customer

cust = myService.GetCustomer(123)
TextBox1.Text = cust.Name()
```

Note that both server and client code have direct, local access to the `Customer` object, because it is automatically copied from the server to the client as a result of the `GetCustomer` method call.

Serializable objects can be very useful in many client/server scenarios, especially if the application is created using object-oriented application design principles.

Implementing Remoting

When we implement an application using remoting, we'll have three key components to the application.

Client	The application calling the server
Server Library	The DLL containing the objects to be called by the client
Host	The application running on the server that hosts remoting and the Server Library

Basically, we create our server-side objects in a Visual Basic .NET Class Library project. Then, we expose the classes in that DLL from our server-side remoting host application. With the objects exposed on the server, we can then create client applications that call the objects in the Server Library DLL.

We might also have some other optional components to support various scenarios.

Interface	A DLL containing interfaces that are implemented by the objects in the Server Library
Proxy	A DLL containing generated proxy code based on the objects in the Server Library
Shared Library	A DLL containing serializable objects that must be available to both the Server Library and the client

We'll discuss these in detail as we use them later in the chapter. For now, let's get into some code and see how remoting works.

A Simple Example

To start with, let's create a simple remoting application. It will consist of a library DLL that contains the server-side code, a remoting host application, and a client to call the library DLL on the server.

The first thing we need to realize is that both the host and the client need access to the type information that describes the classes in the library DLL. The type information includes the name of the classes in the DLL and the methods exposed by those classes.

The host needs the information because it will be exposing the library DLL to clients via remoting. However, the client needs the information in order to know which objects to create and what methods are available on those objects.

Since we know that the library DLL will be on the server, it is easy enough for the host application to just reference the DLL to get the type information. The client is a bit trickier though, since the library DLL won't necessarily be on the client machine. There are three options for getting the type information to the client.

Reference the library DLL	This is the simplest approach, since the client just references the DLL directly and thus, has all the type information. The drawback is that the DLL must be installed on the client along with the client application
Use an interface DLL	This approach is more complex. The classes in the library DLL must implement formal interfaces as defined in this interface DLL. The client can then reference just the interface DLL, so the library DLL doesn't need to be installed on the client machine. The way the client invokes the server is different when using interfaces
Generate a proxy DLL	This approach is of moderate complexity. The server must expose the objects via HTTP so we can run the soapsuds.exe command line utility. The utility creates an assembly containing the type information for the library DLL classes exposed by the server. The client then references this proxy assembly rather than the library DLL

We'll implement all three options in this chapter, starting with the simplest — referencing the library DLL directly from the client application.

Library DLL

To begin, let's create the library DLL. This is just a regular `Class Library` project, so open Visual Studio .NET (VS.NET) and create a new Class Library named `SimpleLibrary`. Remove `Class1.vb` and add a new class named `Calculator`. Since we're creating a wellknown remoting object, it must inherit from `MarshalByRefObject`:

```
Public Class Calculator
  Inherits MarshalByRefObject

End Class
```

That's really all there is to it. At this point the `Calculator` class is ready to be exposed from a server via remoting. Of course, we need to add some methods that clients can call.

Any and all `Public` methods we write in the `Calculator` class will be available to clients. How we design the methods depends entirely on whether we plan to expose this class as `SingleCall` `Singleton`, or `Activated`. For `SingleCall` we know that an instance of `Calculator` will be created for *each method call*, so there's absolutely no point in using any class-level variables. After all, they'll be destroyed along with the object when each method call is complete.

It also means that we can't have the client call a sequence of methods on our object. Since each method call gets its own object, each method call is entirely isolated from any previous or subsequent method calls. In short, each method must stand alone.

For illustration purposes, we need to prove that the server-side code is running in a different process from the client code. The easiest way to prove this is to return the `thread ID` where the code is running. We can compare this `thread ID` to the `thread ID` of the client process. If they are different, then we are sure that the server-side code really is running on the server (or at least in another process on our machine).

Add the following method:

```
Public Function GetThreadID() As Integer

  Return AppDomain.GetCurrentThreadId

End Function
```

You can add other `Public` methods as well if you'd like, for instance:

```
Public Function Add(ByVal a As Integer, ByVal b As Integer) As Integer

  Return a + b

End Function
```

Since this is a calculator class, it only seems appropriate that it should do some calculations.

At this point, we have a simple, but functional, `Calculator` class. Build the solution to create the DLL. Our remoting host application will use this DLL to provide the calculator functionality to clients.

Host Application

With the server-side library complete, we can create a remoting host. Most applications use IIS as a remoting host, but it is quite possible to create a custom host as well. We'll use IIS later in the chapter, but for now let's see how we can create a custom host in a `Console` Application for testing.

Most custom hosts are created as a Windows service so the host can run on the server even when no user is logged into the machine. However, for testing purposes a Console Application is easier to create and run.

The advantage to a custom host is that we can host a remoting server on any machine that supports the .NET Framework. This includes Windows 98 and up. If we use IIS as a host, we can only host on Windows 2000 and up, which is a bit more restrictive.

The drawback to a custom host is that it isn't as robust and capable as IIS, at least, not without a lot of work on our part. For our example, in this chapter we're not going to attempt to make our host as powerful as IIS. We'll just stick with the basic process of creating a custom host.

Setting up the Project

Create a new solution in VS.NET, with a Console Application named `SimpleServer`.

Since the remoting host will be interacting with remoting, we need to reference the appropriate framework DLL. Use the `Add Reference` dialog box to add a reference to `System.Runtime.Remoting.dll`, as in Figure 20-3.

Then, in Module1 we need to import the appropriate namespace:

```
Imports System.Runtime.Remoting
```

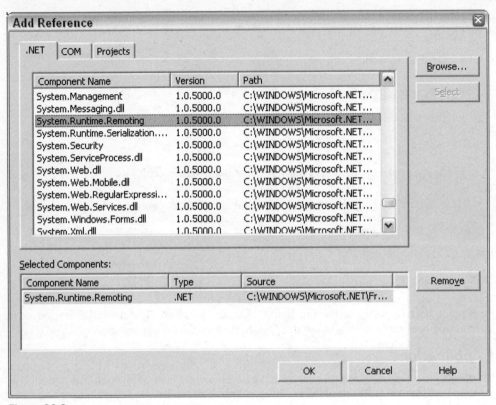

Figure 20-3

At this point we can configure and use remoting. However, before we do that, we need to have access to the DLL containing the classes we plan to expose via remoting—in our case this is `SimpleLibrary` `.dll`.

Referencing the Library DLL

There are two ways to configure remoting, via a configuration file or via code. If we opt for the configuration file approach then the only requirement is that `SimpleLibrary.dll` be in the same directory as our host application. We don't even need to reference `SimpleLibrary.dll` from the host. However, if we opt to configure remoting via code then our host must reference `SimpleLibrary.dll`.

Even if we go with the configuration file approach, referencing `SimpleLibrary.dll` from the host project allows VS.NET to automatically keep the DLL updated in our project directory, and it means that any setup project we might create will automatically include `SimpleLibrary.dll`. In general, it is a good idea to reference the library DLL from the host and that's what we'll do here.

Add a reference to `SimpleLibrary.dll` by clicking the Browse button in the Add References dialog box and navigating to the `SimpleLibrary\bin` directory, as shown in Figure 20-4.

All that remains now is to configure remoting.

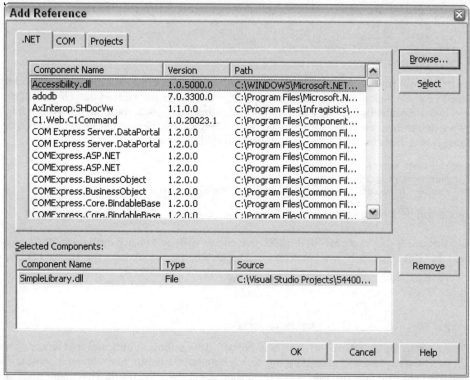

Figure 20-4

Configuring Remoting

The typical way to do this is with a configuration file. Using the Project ⇨ Add New Item menu option, add a new Application Configuration File. Make sure to use the default name of App.config. That will ensure that VS.NET can automatically copy the file into our bin directory and rename it to SimpleServer.exe.config so the .NET runtime can find it.

In this config file we'll add a section to configure remoting. Remember that XML is case-sensitive, so the slightest typo here will prevent remoting from being properly configured:

```xml
<?xml version="1.0" encoding="utf-8" ?>
<configuration>
  <system.runtime.remoting>
    <application>
      <!-- the following section defines the classes we're
           exposing to clients from this host -->
      <service>
        <wellknown mode="SingleCall"
            objectUri="Calculator.rem"
            type="SimpleLibrary.Calculator, SimpleLibrary" />
      </service>

      <channels>
        <channel ref="tcp" port="49341" />
```

```
      </channels>

    </application>
  </system.runtime.remoting>
</configuration>
```

Notice that all our configuration is within the `<system.runtime.remoting>` element, and then within an `<application>` element. The real work happens first inside the `<service>` element. The `<service>` element tells remoting that we're configuring server-side components. Within this block is where we define the classes we want to make available to clients. We can define both wellknown and activated classes here. In our case we're defining a wellknown class:

```
<wellknown mode="SingleCall"
    objectUri="Calculator.rem"
    type="SimpleLibrary.Calculator, SimpleLibrary" />
```

The mode will be either `SingleCall` or `Singleton` as we discussed earlier in the chapter.

The `objectUri` is the "end part" of the URL that clients will use to reach our server. We'll revisit this in a moment, but this is basically how it fits (depending on whether we're using the TCP or HTTP protocol):

```
tcp://localhost:12345/ Calculator.rem
```

or

```
http://localhost:12345/ Calculator.rem
```

The ".rem" extension on the `objectUri` is important. This extension indicates that remoting should handle the client request, and is used by the networking infrastructure to route the request to the right location. We can optionally use the ".soap" extension to get the same result. The ".rem" and ".soap" extensions are totally equivalent.

Finally, the type defines the full type name and assembly where the actual class can be found. Remoting uses this information to dynamically load the assembly and create the object when requested by a client.

We can have many `<wellknown>` blocks here to expose all the server-side classes we want to make available to clients.

The other key configuration block is where we specify which remoting channel (protocol) we want to use. We can choose between the TCP and HTTP channels.

| TCP | Slightly faster than HTTP, defaults to the faster binary serialization of data, can be hard to test |
| HTTP | Slightly slower than TCP, defaults to the slower SOAP serialization of data, is more easily tested |

Since we'll look at the HTTP channel later, we're using the TCP channel now. Either way, we need to specify the IP port number on which we'll listening for client requests. When choosing a port for a server we should keep the following port ranges in mind:

❑ *0-1023*— Wellknown ports reserved for specific applications such as Web servers, mail servers, and so on

❑   *1024-49151* — Registered ports that are reserved for various widely used protocols such as DirectPlay

❑   *49152-65535* — Intended for dynamic or private use, such as for applications that might be performing remoting with .NET

We're setting remoting to use a TCP channel, listening on port 49341:

```
<channels>
  <channel ref="tcp" port="49341" />
</channels>
```

With the config file created, the only thing remaining is to tell remoting to configure itself based on this information. To do this we need to add code to `Sub Main`:

```
Sub Main()
  RemotingConfiguration.Configure( _
    AppDomain.CurrentDomain.SetupInformation.ConfigurationFile)
  Console.Write("Press <enter> to exit")
  Console.Read()
End Sub
```

The `Console.Write` and `Console.Read` statements are there to ensure that the application stays running until we are ready for it to terminate. The line that actually configures remoting is:

```
RemotingConfiguration.Configure( _
  AppDomain.CurrentDomain.SetupInformation.ConfigurationFile)
```

We are calling the `Configure` method, which tells remoting to read a config file and to process the `<system.runtime.remoting>` element in that file. We want it to use our application configuration file, so we pass that path as a parameter. Fortunately, we can get the path from our AppDomain object so we don't have to worry about hard-coding the filename.

Configuring Remoting via Code

Our other option is to configure the remoting host via code. To do this we'd write different code in `Sub Main`:

```
Sub Main()
  RemotingConfiguration.RegisterWellKnownServiceType( _
    GetType(SimpleLibrary.Calculator), _
    "Calculator.rem", _
    WellKnownObjectMode.SingleCall)

  System.Runtime.Remoting.Channels.ChannelServices.RegisterChannel( _
    New System.Runtime.Remoting.Channels.Tcp.TcpServerChannel(49341))

  Console.Write("Press <enter> to exit")
  Console.Read()
End Sub
```

You can see that we're providing the exact same information here as we did in the config file, only via code. We call `RegisterWellKnownServiceType`, passing the mode, `objectUri` and type data just as we did in the config file. Then, we call `RegisterChannel`, passing a new instance of the `TcpServerChannel` configured to use the port we chose earlier.

The end result is the same as using the config file. Most server applications use a config file to configure remoting, as it allows us to change things like the channel and port without having to recompile the host application.

Build the solution. At this point our host is ready to run. Open a Command Prompt window, navigate to the `bin` directory and run `SimpleServer.exe`.

Client Application

The final piece of the puzzle is to create a client application that calls the server.

Setting up the Project

Here's how to create a new VS.NET solution with a Windows Application named `SimpleClient`. As we discussed earlier, the client needs access to the type information for the classes it wants to call on the server. The easiest way to get this type information is to have it reference `SimpleLibrary.dll`. Since we'll be configuring remoting, we also need to reference the remoting dll. Do both via the Add References dialog as shown in Figure 20-5.

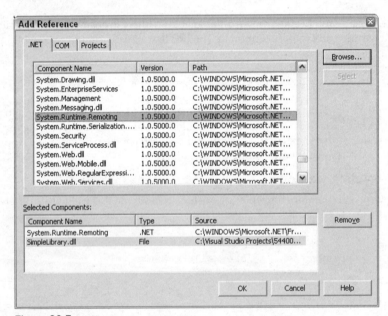

Figure 20-5

We also need to import the remoting namespace in Form1:

```
Imports System.Runtime.Remoting
```

Now, we can write code to interact with the `Calculator` class. Add controls to the form as shown in Figure 20-6.

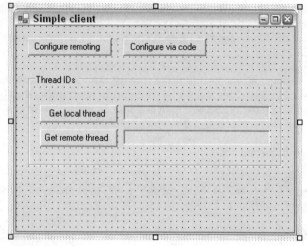

Figure 20-6

Name the controls (in order): `ConfigureButton`, `CodeConfigureButton`, `LocalThreadButton`, `LocalThread`, `RemoteThreadButton`, `RemoteThread`. First, let's write the code to get the `thread ID` values for each object:

```
Private Sub LocalThreadButton_Click( _
  ByVal sender As System.Object, ByVal e As System.EventArgs) _
  Handles LocalThreadButton.Click

  LocalThread.Text = CStr(AppDomain.GetCurrentThreadId)

End Sub

Private Sub RemoteThreadButton_Click( _
    ByVal sender As System.Object, ByVal e As System.EventArgs) _
    Handles RemoteThreadButton.Click

  Dim calc As New SimpleLibrary.Calculator

  RemoteThread.Text = CStr(calc.GetThreadID)

End Sub
```

Displaying the thread ID of the local process is easily accomplished. More interesting though, is that our code to interact with the `Calculator` class doesn't look special in any way. Where's the remoting code?

It turns out that there's this idea of *location transparency*, where it is possible to write "normal" code that interacts with an object whether it is running locally or remotely. This is an important and desirable trait for distributed technologies, and remoting supports the concept. Looking at the code we've written you can't tell if the `Calculator` object is local or remoting, its location is transparent.

All that remains is to configure remoting so it knows that the `Calculator` object should, in fact, be created remotely. As with the server, we can configure clients either via a config file or through code.

Before we configure remoting, we need to realize something important. If remoting is not configured before our first usage of `SimpleLibrary.Calculator`, then the `Calculator` object will be created locally. If that happens, configuring remoting won't help and we'll never create remote `Calculator` objects.

To prevent this from happening, we need to make sure we can't interact with the class until after remoting is configured. Typically, this is done by configuring remoting as the application starts up, either in `Sub Main` or in the first form's `Load` event. In our case, however, we're going to configure remoting behind some buttons, so we need to take a different approach.

In `Form_Load` add the following code:

```
Private Sub Form1_Load( _
  ByVal sender As System.Object, ByVal e As System.EventArgs) _
  Handles MyBase.Load

  RemoteThreadButton.Enabled = False

End Sub
```

This prevents us from requesting the remote thread. We won't enable this button until after remoting has been configured either through the config file or code.

Configuring Remoting

To configure remoting via a config file, we first need to add a config file to the project. Use the Project ➪ Add New Item menu to add an Application Configuration File. Make sure to keep the default name of `App.config`. In this file add the following code:

```xml
<?xml version="1.0" encoding="utf-8" ?>
<configuration>
  <system.runtime.remoting>
    <application>
      <!-- the following section defines the classes we're
           getting from the remote host -->
      <client>
        <wellknown mode="SingleCall"
            type="SimpleLibrary.Calculator, SimpleLibrary"
            url="tcp://localhost:49341/Calculator.rem" />
      </client>
    </application>
  </system.runtime.remoting>
</configuration>
```

In this case, we're not using the `<service>` element, instead we're using the `<client>` element, telling remoting that we're configuring ourselves as a client. Within the `<client>` block we define the classes that should be run on a remote server, both wellknown and activated. In our case we have a wellknown class:

```xml
<wellknown
    type="SimpleLibrary.Calculator, SimpleLibrary"
    url="tcp://localhost:49341/Calculator.rem" />
```

On the client we only need to provide two bits of information. We need to tell remoting the class and assembly that should be run remotely. This is done with the type attribute, which specifies the full type name and assembly name for the class, just as we did on the server. We also need to provide the full URL for the class on the server.

We defined this URL when we created the server, though it might not have been clear that we did so. When we defined the class for remoting on the server we specified an `objectUri` value (`Calculator.rem`). Also, on the server we specified the channel (TCP) and port (49341) on which the server will listen for client requests. Combined with the server name itself, we have a URL:

```
tcp://localhost:49341/Calculator.rem
```

The channel is tcp://, the server name is localhost (or whatever your server name might be), the port is 49341 and the object's URI is `Calculator.rem`. This is the unique address of our `SimpleLibrary`.`Calculator` class on the remote server.

As with the server configuration, we might have many <wellknown> and <activated> elements in the config file, one for each server-side object we wish to use.

With the configuration set up, we just need to tell remoting to read the file. We'll do this behind the `ConfigureButton` control:

```
Private Sub ConfigureButton_Click( _
   ByVal sender As System.Object, ByVal e As System.EventArgs) _
   Handles ConfigureButton.Click

   RemotingConfiguration.Configure( _
      AppDomain.CurrentDomain.SetupInformation.ConfigurationFile)

   ConfigureButton.Enabled = False
   CodeConfigureButton.Enabled = False
   RemoteThreadButton.Enabled = True

End Sub
```

Once remoting is configured in an application we can't configure it again, so we're disabling the two configuration buttons. Also, we're enabling the button to retrieve the remote thread ID. Now that remoting has been configured it is safe to interact with `SimpleLibrary.Calculator`.

The line of code that configures remoting is the same as it was in the server:

```
RemotingConfiguration.Configure( _
   AppDomain.CurrentDomain.SetupInformation.ConfigurationFile)
```

Again, we're telling remoting to read our application configuration file to find the <system.runtime .remoting> element and process it.

Configuring Remoting via Code

Another option for configuring remoting is to do it via code. We must provide the same information in our code as we did in the config file. Put this behind the `CodeConfigureButton` control:

```
Private Sub CodeConfigureButton_Click( _
   ByVal sender As System.Object, ByVal e As System.EventArgs) _
   Handles CodeConfigureButton.Click
```

```
    RemotingConfiguration.RegisterWellKnownClientType( _
      GetType(SimpleLibrary.Calculator), "tcp://localhost:49341/Calculator.rem")

    ConfigureButton.Enabled = False
    CodeConfigureButton.Enabled = False
    RemoteThreadButton.Enabled = True

  End Sub
```

The `RegisterWellKnownClientType` method requires that we specify the type of the class to be run remotely, in this case `SimpleLibrary.Calculator`. It also requires that we provide the URL for the class on the remote server, just like we did in the config file.

Regardless of whether we configure via code or the config file, the end result is that the .NET runtime now knows that any attempt to create a `SimpleLibrary.Calculator` object should be routed through remoting so the object will be created on the server.

Compile and run the application. Try configuring remoting both ways. In either case, you should discover that the local thread ID and the remote thread ID are different, proving that the Calculator code is running on the server, not locally in the Windows application, as shown in Figure 20-7.

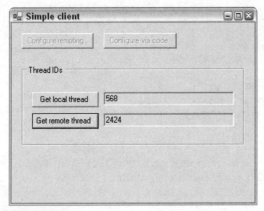

Figure 20-7

Note that your specific thread ID values will vary from those shown here. The important part is that they are different from each other, establishing that our local code and remote code are running in different places.

Using IIS as a Remoting Host

We've seen how to create a very basic custom host. In most production environments however, such a basic host isn't directly useful. We'd need to create a Windows service, add management and logging facilities, implement security and so forth.

Or, we could just use IIS as the host and get all those things automatically. Due to this, it is often better to use IIS as a remoting host than to try to create your own.

Creating the Host

Using IIS as a host is a straightforward exercise. The first thing to do is create a virtual root and get it properly configured for ASP.NET. To do this, create a new solution in VS.NET with an Empty Web Project named `SimpleHost` as shown in Figure 20-8.

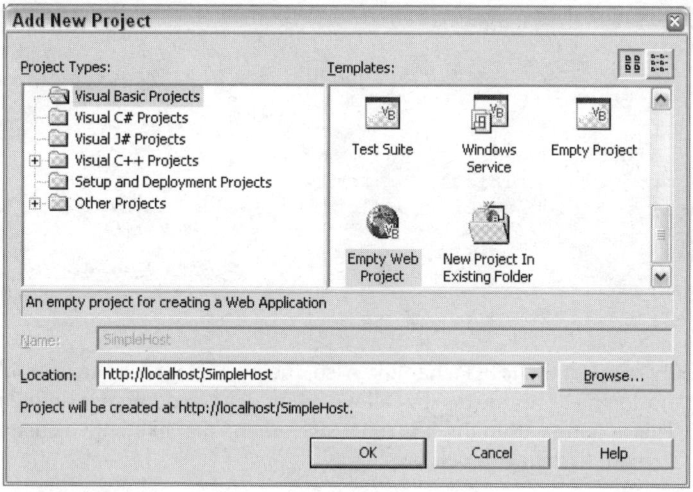

Figure 20-8

When we click OK, VS.NET will properly create and configure the virtual root on our server.

Next, we need to ensure that the `SimpleLibrary.dll` is in the `bin` directory under the virtual root. While we could copy the DLL there by hand, it is often easier to simply add a reference to the DLL from our project. This allows VS.NET to automatically copy the DLL to the right location, and has the added side-benefit that if we create a deployment project the DLL will be automatically included as part of the setup.

Add a reference to `SimpleLibrary.dll` using the Add References dialog box as we did in the SimpleServer and SimpleClient projects previously. This way VS.NET will ensure that the DLL is available to us as needed.

All that remains now is to configure remoting. The only thing we need to do within an IIS host is add the `<system.runtime.remoting>` section to the `web.config` file. Remoting is automatically configured based on `web.config` by ASP.NET.

Use the Project ➪ Add New Item menu to add a Web Configuration File. Make sure to use the default name of `web.config`. This adds a `web.config` file to the project with a series of default settings. You may opt to change some of these settings for your environment. In particular, these settings allow you to control security options and so forth. Since we won't be using ASP.NET Session, we probably do want to turn that off:

```
<sessionState
    mode="Off"
```

This reduces the overhead of session management for our remoting calls. More importantly however, we need to add the remoting configuration to the file:

```
<?xml version="1.0" encoding="utf-8" ?>
<configuration>

  <system.runtime.remoting>
    <application>
      <!-- the following section defines the classes we're
           exposing to clients from this host -->
      <service>
        <wellknown mode="SingleCall"
            objectUri="Calculator.rem"
            type="SimpleLibrary.Calculator, SimpleLibrary" />
      </service>

    </application>
  </system.runtime.remoting>
</configuration>
```

An IIS host can only support the HTTP channel. Also, the port on which the host listens is defined by IIS, not by our configuration file. This means that all we really need to do here is define the classes we want to expose to clients. This is done within the `<service>` element, just like with a custom host. Again, we use a `<wellknown>` element to define our class:

```
<wellknown mode="SingleCall"
    objectUri="Calculator.rem"
    type="SimpleLibrary.Calculator, SimpleLibrary" />
```

The `<wellknown>` element shown here is the exact same definition as with the custom host, and we'll get the same end result.

The primary difference between our custom host and the IIS host is that IIS cannot use the TCP channel, but only uses the HTTP channel. This means that the URL for our server-side class is different:

```
http://localhost/SimpleHost/Calculator.rem
```

The channel defines the protocol, which is http://. The server name is localhost (or whatever your server name might be). The virtual root within IIS is SimpleHost, named just like it is with any Web project. And finally, the `objectUri` value for our class (`Calculator.rem`) rounds out the URL.

Again note that the ".rem" extension is important. This extension (or the equivalent ".soap" extension) tells IIS to route the client request to ASP.NET, and it tells ASP.NET to route the request to remoting so it can be properly handled by invoking our `Calculator` class.

At this point, the remoting host is done and ready to go. Since it is using the HTTP protocol we can test it with the browser by navigating to the following URL:

```
http://localhost/SimpleHost/Calculator.rem?wsdl
```

This should return an XML description of the host service and all the classes exposed from the host.

Updating the Client Application

With a new host set up, we can change the client application to use this IIS host instead of the custom host. To do this, all we need to do is change the URL for the object when we configure remoting.

If we're using the config file to configure remoting we'd make the following change:

```xml
<?xml version="1.0" encoding="utf-8" ?>
<configuration>
  <system.runtime.remoting>
    <application>
      <!-- the following section defines the classes we're
           getting from the remote host -->
      <client>
        <wellknown
            type="SimpleLibrary.Calculator, SimpleLibrary"
            url="http://localhost/SimpleHost/Calculator.rem" />
      </client>
    </application>
  </system.runtime.remoting>
</configuration>
```

Once making this change to App.config make sure to rebuild the project so VS.NET copies the new config file to the bin directory and renames it to SimpleClient.exe.config.

If we're configuring remoting via code, change the code to the following:

```vb
Private Sub CodeConfigureButton_Click( _
  ByVal sender As System.Object, ByVal e As System.EventArgs) _
  Handles CodeConfigureButton.Click

  RemotingConfiguration.RegisterWellKnownClientType( _
    GetType(SimpleLibrary.Calculator), _
    "http://localhost/SimpleHost/Calculator.rem")

  ConfigureButton.Enabled = False
  CodeConfigureButton.Enabled = False
  RemoteThreadButton.Enabled = True

End Sub
```

In either case, we're simply changing the URL so remoting now routes our calls to the IIS host instead of our custom host.

Using the Binary Formatter in IIS

One thing to note about using IIS as a host is that it always uses the HTTP channel. The HTTP channel defaults to using the SoapFormatter instead of the BinaryFormatter to encode the data that is sent across the network. While SOAP is a fine format, it is extremely verbose. The BinaryFormatter generates about 1/3 the number of bytes as the SoapFormatter to send the same data.

For production code, we'll typically want to use the `BinaryFormatter` to reduce the amount of data sent across the network and to improve performance. The formatter is controlled by the client, so we'll need to update the client configuration of remoting.

To change the config file do as follows:

```xml
<?xml version="1.0" encoding="utf-8" ?>
<configuration>
  <system.runtime.remoting>
    <application>
      <!-- the following section defines the classes we're
           getting from the remote host -->
      <client>
        <wellknown
            type="SimpleLibrary.Calculator, SimpleLibrary"
            url="http://localhost/SimpleHost/Calculator.rem" />
      </client>
  <!-- use the binary formatter over the
       http channel -->
  <channels>
    <channel ref="http">
      <clientProviders>
        <formatter ref="binary" />
      </clientProviders>
    </channel>
  </channels>

    </application>
  </system.runtime.remoting>
</configuration>
```

The highlighted XML shown above configures remoting so when it initializes the HTTP channel, it does so with a `BinaryFormatter` instead of the default `SoapFormatter`.

To do the equivalent to the XML configuration in code, we'll want to import a couple namespaces into Form1:

```vb
Imports System.Runtime.Remoting.Channels
Imports System.Runtime.Remoting.Channels.Http
```

Then, when we configure remoting we need to add the following:

```vb
Private Sub CodeConfigureButton_Click( _
  ByVal sender As System.Object, ByVal e As System.EventArgs) _
  Handles CodeConfigureButton.Click

  RemotingConfiguration.RegisterWellKnownClientType( _
    GetType(SimpleLibrary.Calculator), _
    "http://localhost/SimpleHost/Calculator.rem")

  ' use the binary formatter with the
  ' http channel
  Dim clientFormatter As New BinaryClientFormatterSinkProvider
```

```
Dim channel As New HttpChannel(Nothing, clientFormatter, Nothing)
ChannelServices.RegisterChannel(channel)

ConfigureButton.Enabled = False
CodeConfigureButton.Enabled = False
RemoteThreadButton.Enabled = True
```

```
End Sub
```

As with the config file approach, we're specifically creating the `HttpChannel` object, specifying that it should use a `BinaryFormatter` rather than the default.

At this point we've explored the basic use of remoting. We've created a library DLL, a client that uses the library DLL and two different types of remoting host so the library DLL can run on the server.

There are many other facets of remoting to explore, more than we can fit into this single chapter. However, for the remainder of the chapter I want to explore some of the more common features that you might encounter or use in your applications. We'll have to take them pretty fast, but the complete code for each of them is available in the code download for the book so you can get the complete picture there.

Using Activator.GetObject

In our simple client we configured remoting so that all attempts to use `SimpleLibrary.Calculator` were automatically routed to a specific server via remoting. If we want more control and flexibility, we can take a different approach by using the `System.Activator` class. The full code for this example is in the `ActivatorClient` project.

Instead of configuring remoting to always know where to find the remote class, we can specify it as we create the remote object. Since we won't be configuring remoting, we don't need a reference to `System.Runtime.Remoting.dll`, nor do we need any of the remoting configuration code we had in the client to this point.

All we do is replace the use of the `New` keyword with a call to `Activator.GetObject`. To use the custom host we'd use the following code to retrieve the remote thread ID:

```
Private Sub RemoteThreadButton_Click( _
  ByVal sender As System.Object, ByVal e As System.EventArgs) _
  Handles RemoteThreadButton.Click

  Dim calc As SimpleLibrary.Calculator

  calc = CType(Activator.GetObject( _
    GetType(SimpleLibrary.Calculator), _
    "tcp://localhost:49341/Calculator.rem"), _
    SimpleLibrary.Calculator)

  RemoteThread.Text = CStr(calc.GetThreadID)

End Sub
```

For this to work, the `SimpleServer` application must be running before the `RemoteThread` button is clicked.

The `Activator.GetObject` method accepts the type of object to create (`SimpleLibrary` `.Calculator`) and the URL where the object can be found. To use the IIS host we'd change the URL:

```
calc = CType(Activator.GetObject( _
  GetType(SimpleLibrary.Calculator), _
  "http://localhost/SimpleHost/Calculator.rem"), _
  SimpleLibrary.Calculator)
```

Using this approach we lose location transparency, because it is quite obvious looking at our code that we're using a remote object. However, we gain explicit control over where the remote object will be created. This can be useful in some cases, where we want to programmatically control the URL on a per-call basis.

Interface-Based Design

One drawback to the simple implementation we've used thus far is that the library DLL (`SimpleLibrary.dll`) must be installed on the client machine. Sometimes this is not desirable, as we don't want clients to have access to the server-side code. There are a couple of solutions to this problem: using an interface DLL or using a generated proxy. Let's look first at the interface DLL approach.

Interface DLL

To use this approach we need to create a new DLL that contains interface definitions for our server-side classes and their methods. For instance, in the `SimpleInterface` project we have the following interface defined:

```
Public Interface ICalculator
  Function GetThreadID() As Integer
  Function Add(ByVal a As Integer, ByVal b As Integer) As Integer
End Interface
```

This interface defines the methods on our `Calculator` class. We need to update the `Calculator` class to implement this interface. The `SimpleLibrary` project must reference the `SimpleInterface` DLL, then we can do the following in our `Calculator` class:

```
Public Class Calculator
  Inherits MarshalByRefObject

Implements SimpleInterface.ICalculator
Public Function GetThreadID() As Integer _
  Implements SimpleInterface.ICalculator.GetThreadID

  Return AppDomain.GetCurrentThreadId

End Function

Public Function Add(ByVal a As Integer, ByVal b As Integer) As Integer _
  Implements SimpleInterface.ICalculator.Add

  Return a + b

End Function

End Class
```

At this point our `SimpleLibrary.Calculator` class can be invoked either directly or via the `ICalculator` interface.

Make sure to rebuild the custom and IIS host projects so the new `SimpleLibary` and the `SimpleInterface` DLLs are both copies to the host directories. Note that since `SimpleLibrary.Calculator` is still available natively, our existing client applications (`SimpleClient` and `ActivatorClient`) will continue to run just fine.

Updating the Client Application

The `InterfaceClient` project only references `SimpleInterface.dll`, not `SimpleLibrary.dll`. This means that the client machine doesn't need to install `SimpleLibrary.dll` for the client to run, meaning that the client has no access to the actual server-side code.

Since we don't have access to the types in `SimpleLibrary`, we can't use them in our code. The only types we can use come from `SimpleInterface`. This means that our code to retrieve the remote thread ID is a bit different. To use the custom host we do the following:

```
Private Sub RemoteThreadButton_Click( _
  ByVal sender As System.Object, ByVal e As System.EventArgs) _
  Handles RemoteThreadButton.Click

  Dim calc As SimpleInterface.ICalculator

  calc = CType(Activator.GetObject( _
    GetType(SimpleInterface.ICalculator), _
    "tcp://localhost:49341/Calculator.rem"), _
    SimpleInterface.ICalculator)

  RemoteThread.Text = CStr(calc.GetThreadID)

End Sub
```

Note that the `calc` variable is now declared as type `ICalculator` rather than `Calculator`. Also notice that we're using `Activator.GetType`. This is required when using interfaces, as we can't use the `New` keyword at all. We can't do the following:

```
calc = New SimpleInterface.ICalculator()
```

The result is a compiler error because it isn't possible to create an instance of an interface. Because of this, we can't just configure remoting and use location transparency, we must use `Activator.GetObject` to have remoting create an instance of the object on the server.

Remoting knows how and where to create the object based on the URL we provide. It then converts the object to the right type (`SimpleInterface.ICalculator`) based on the type we provide in the `GetObject` call. If the remote object doesn't implement this interface then we'll get a runtime exception.

Using Generated Proxies

Another way to create a client that doesn't reference the library DLL is to use the `soapsuds.exe` command line utility to create a proxy assembly for the service and the classes it exposes. This proxy assembly is then referenced by the client application, giving the client access to the server type information so it can interact with the server objects.

Proxy DLL

To create the proxy DLL we just run the `soapsuds.exe` utility with the following command line:

```
> soapsuds -url:http://localhost/SimpleHost/Calculator.rem -oa:SimpleProxy.dll
```

Note that we're going against the IIS host here because it uses the HTTP protocol. This won't work against our current custom host, as the `soapsuds.exe` utility doesn't understand the `tcp://` prefix. To use this against a custom host, we'd have to make sure the custom host used the HTTP protocol.

Creating the Client Application

In the code download there's a `ProxyClient` project. This is a Windows Application that references only `SimpleProxy.dll`. There is no reference to `SimpleLibrary.dll` or `SimpleInterface.dll` — this client relies entirely on the generated proxy assembly to interact with the server.

The best part of this is that the generated proxy contains the same namespace and class names as the service on the server. In other words, it appears that we are working with `SimpleLibrary.Calculator`, because the proxy is set up with that same namespace and class name. To get the remote thread ID we write the following code:

```
Private Sub RemoteThreadButton_Click( _
  ByVal sender As System.Object, ByVal e As System.EventArgs) _
  Handles RemoteThreadButton.Click

  Dim calc As New SimpleLibrary.Calculator()

  RemoteThread.Text = CStr(calc.GetThreadID)

End Sub
```

Note that this is the same code as we used in our original simple example. We've come full circle at this point, but now the client application doesn't directly reference our library DLL.

Summary

Remoting is a powerful technology that provides many of the capabilities of Web services and DCOM plus some new capabilities of its own. Using remoting we can create both Windows and Web applications that interact with objects on an application server across the network.

On the server we can create `SingleCall`, `Singleton`, and `Activated` objects. These three object types provide a great deal of flexibility in terms of n-tier application design and should be able to meet almost any need. `SingleCall` gives us behavior similar to Web services or typical COM+ objects. Activated gives us objects that act similar to COM objects exposed via DCOM. `Singleton` objects are unique to remoting and allow all our clients to share a single stateful object on the server.

We can also create serializable objects, which can move from machine to machine as needed. Using this type of object allows us to easily move data and business logic from server to client and back again. This technology is particularly exciting for object-oriented development in a distributed environment.

In this chapter, we created a library DLL and exposed it to clients from both a custom and IIS remoting host. We then created client applications to use our server-side code by referencing the library DLL directly, using an interface DLL and using the `soapsuds.exe` utility to create a proxy DLL. These techniques apply not only to `SingleCall` objects, but also to `Singleton` and `Activated` objects, so you should have a good grounding in the techniques available for using remoting in your environment.

21

Windows Services

Modern, multitasking operating systems often need to run applications that operate in the background and which are independent of the user who is logged in. In Windows NT, Windows 2000, Windows XP, and Windows Server 2003, such applications are called *Windows Services* (formerly known as NT Services). The tasks carried out by Windows Services are typically long running and have little or no direct interaction with a user (so they don't usually have user interfaces). Such applications may be started when the computer is booted, and often continue to run until the computer is shut down.

In this chapter we're going to look at:

❑ The characteristics of a Windows Service

❑ How we can interact with a Windows Service using VS.NET and the management applets in the Windows Control Panel

❑ How we can create, install, and communicate with a Windows Service using VB.NET

❑ How we can debug a Windows Service from within VS.NET

As VB6 did not offer direct support for the creation of Windows Services, you might be unfamiliar with such applications. So, to help understand the variety of such applications, we'll examine some scenarios in which a Windows Service application is a good solution.

Example Windows Services

Microsoft SQL Server, Exchange Server, Internet Information Server (IIS), and antivirus software all use Windows Services to perform tasks in response to events that occur on the system overall. Only a background service, or Windows Service, which runs no matter which user is logged in, could perform such operations.

Consider these potential Windows Services:

❏ *A File Watcher*—Suppose we are running an FTP server that places files it receives in a particular directory. We could use a Windows Service to monitor and process files within that directory as they arrive. The service would run in the background and detect when files are changed or added within the directory, and then extract information from these files in order to process orders, or update address and billing information. We'll see an example of such a Windows Service later in this chapter.

❏ *An Automated Stock Price Reporter*—We could build a system that extracts stock prices from a Web site and then e-mails the information to users. We could set thresholds so that an e-mail is only sent out if the stock price reaches a certain price. This Windows Service could be automated to extract the information every 10 minutes, every 10 seconds, or whatever we wish. Because a Windows Service can contain any logic that does not require a user interface, we have a lot of flexibility in constructing such applications.

❏ *Microsoft Transaction Server (MTS)*—This (part of COM+ Services in Windows 2000 and later) is an object broker that manages instances of components and is used regularly by professional developers. This service runs constantly in the background and manages components as soon as the computer is booted, just like IIS or Exchange Server.

Characteristics of a Windows Service

To properly design and develop a Windows Service, it's important to understand how a Windows Service differs from a typical Windows program. Here are the most important characteristics of a Windows Service:

❏ A Windows Service can start before a user logs on. The system maintains a list of Windows Services and they can be set to start at boot time. Services can also be installed so that they require a manual startup and will not start at boot.

❏ A Windows Service can run under a different account from that of the current user. Most Windows Services provide functionality that needs to be running all the time and some load before a user logs on, so they cannot depend on a user being logged on to run.

❏ A Windows Service has its own process. It does not run in the process of a program communicating with it (Chapter 20 has more information on processes).

❏ A Windows Service typically has no user interface. This is because the service may be running under a different account from that of the current user, or the service may start at boot time, which would mean that the calls to put up a user interface might fail because they are out of context (it is possible to create a Windows Service with a user interface, but Visual Basic .NET (VB.NET) cannot be used to do it; we'll discuss why later on).

❏ A Windows Service requires a special installation procedure; just clicking on a compiled EXE won't run it. The program must run in a special context in the operating system, and a specific installation process is required to do the configuration necessary for a Windows Service to be run in this special context.

❏ A Windows Service works with a *Service Control Manager* (which we'll discuss shortly). The Service Control Manager is required to provide an interface to the Windows Service. External programs that want to communicate with a Windows Service (for example, to start or stop the service) must go through the Service Control Manager. The Service Control Manager is an operating-system-level program, but it has a user interface that can be used to start and stop services, and this interface can be accessed through the Computer Management section of the Control Panel.

Interacting with Windows Services

You can view the services that are used on your computer by opening the Services Control Manager user interface. This can be done in Windows 2000 via Administrative Tools ➪ Services in the Control Panel, and in Windows XP Professional via All Programs ➪ Administrative Tools ➪ Services from the Start button. Using the Services Control Manager, a service can be set to automatically start up when the system is booted, or a service can be started manually. Services can also be stopped or paused. The list of services contained in the Services Control Manager includes the current state for each service. Figure 21-1 shows the Services Control Manager in Windows XP.

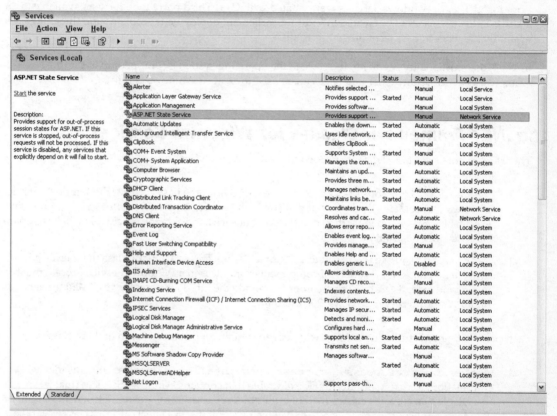

Figure 21-1

The Status column indicates the current state of the service. If this column is blank, the service has not been started since the last time the computer was booted. Other possible values for Status are Started, Stopped, and Paused. You can get access to additional settings and details concerning a service by double-clicking it.

When a service is started, it can automatically log into the system using either a user or system account:

❑ The user account is a regular NT account that allows the program to interact with the system — in essence, the service will impersonate a user

❑ The system account is not associated with a particular user

The Services Control Manager seen in Figure 21-1 is part of the operating system (which is what supports Windows Services); it is not a part of .NET. Any service run by the operating system is exposed through the Services Control Manager, no matter how the service was created or installed. We can also interact with Windows Services via the Server Explorer in Visual Studio .NET (VS.NET). We'll cover this technique later on.

Creating a Windows Service

Prior to .NET, most Windows Services were created with C++. Third party toolkits were available to allow Windows Services to be created in VB6 and earlier, but deployment problems and threading issues meant that few developers went down this route.

In .NET, the functionality needed to interface to the operating system is wrapped up in the .NET Framework classes, so any .NET language can be used to create a Windows Service.

The .NET Framework Classes for Windows Services

There are several base classes that are needed to create a Windows Service:

❑ `System.ServiceProcess.ServiceBase` — Provides the base class for the Windows Service. The class that contains the logic that will run in the service inherits from `ServiceBase`. A single executable can contain more than one service, but each service in the executable will be a separate class that inherits from `ServiceBase`.

❑ `System.Configuration.Install.Installer` — This is a generic class that performs the installation chores for a variety of components. One class in a Windows Service process must inherit and extend `Installer` in order to provide the interface necessary to install the service under Windows Server 2003, XP, 2000, and NT.

Each class that inherits from `Installer` will need to contain an instance of each of these classes:

❑ `System.ServiceProcess.ServiceProcessInstaller` — This class contains the information needed to install a .NET executable that contains Windows Services (that is, an executable that contains classes that inherit from `ServiceBase`). The .NET installation utility for Windows Services (`InstallUtil.exe`, which we will discuss later) calls this class to get the information it needs to perform the installation.

❑ `System.ServiceProcess.ServiceInstaller` — This class also interacts with the `InstallUtil.exe` installation program. Whereas `ServiceProcessInstaller` contains information needed to install the executable as a whole, `ServiceInstaller` contains information on a specific service in the executable. If an executable contains more than one service, an instance of `ServiceInstaller` is needed for each one.

For most Windows Services we develop, we can let VS.NET take care of `Installer`, `ServiceProcessInstaller`, and `ServiceInstaller`. We'll just need to set a few properties. The class we need to thoroughly understand is `ServiceBase`, as this is the class that contains the functionality of a Windows Service and therefore must inherit from it.

The ServiceBase Class

ServiceBase contains several useful properties and methods, but initially it's more important to understand the events of ServiceBase. Most of these events are fired by the Service Control Manager when the state of the service is changed. The most important events are as follows.

Event	How and When the Event is Used
OnStart	Occurs when the service is started. This is where the initialization logic for a service is usually placed.
OnStop	Occurs when the service is stopped. Cleanup and shutdown logic is generally placed here.
OnPause	Occurs when the service is paused. Any logic required to suspend operations during a pause goes here.
OnContinue	Occurs when a service continues after being paused.
OnShutdown	Occurs when the operating system is being shut down.
OnPowerEvent	Occurs when the system's power management software causes a change in the power status of the system. Usually used to change the behavior of a service when a system is going in or out of a "suspended" power mode. This is more frequent with end users who are working on a laptop.
OnCustomCommand	Occurs when an external program has told the Service Control Manager that it wishes to send a command to the service. The operation of this event is covered in *Communicating with the Service*.

The events used most frequently are OnStart, OnStop, and OnCustomCommand. The OnStart and OnStop events are used in almost every Windows Service written in VB.NET, and the OnCustomCommand is used if any special configuration of the service needs to be done while the service is running.

All of these are Protected events, so they are only available to classes that inherit from ServiceBase. Because of the restricted context in which it runs, a Windows Service component that inherits from ServiceBase often lacks a public interface. While we can add public properties and methods to such a component, they are of limited use because outside programs cannot obtain an object reference to running Windows Service component.

To be active as a Windows Service, an instance of ServiceBase must be started via the shared Run method of the ServiceBase class. However, normally we don't have to write code to do this because the template code generated by VS.NET places the correct code in the Main subroutine of the project for us.

The most commonly used property of ServiceBase is the AutoLog property. This Boolean property is set to True by default. If True, then the Windows Service automatically logs the Start, Stop, Pause, and Continue events to an event log. The event log used is the Application Event Log and the Source in the log entries is taken from the name of Windows Service. This automatic event logging is stopped by setting the AutoLog property to False.

The following File Watcher example goes into more detail about the automatic logging capabilities in a Windows Service, and about event logs in general.

Installation-Oriented Classes

The `Installer`, `ServiceProcessInstaller`, and `ServiceInstaller` classes are quite simple to build and use if you are employing VS.NET. After you create your Windows Service project, VS.NET will create a class file called `Service1.vb` for you. To add the `Installer`, `ServiceProcessInstaller`, and `ServiceInstaller` classes to your project, simply right-click the design surface of this `ServiceBase` class, `Service1.vb`, and select Add Installer. This creates the code framework necessary to use them.

The `Installer` class (named `ProjectInstaller` by default in a Windows Service project) generally needs no interaction at all—it is ready to use when created by VS.NET. However, it may be appropriate to change some properties of the `ServiceProcessInstaller` and `ServiceInstaller` classes. You can do this by simply highlighting these objects on the design surface and changing their properties directly in the Properties window of VS.NET. The properties that are typically modified for `ServiceProcessInstaller` include:

❑   `Account`—This specifies the type of account under which the entire service application will run. Different settings give the services in the application different levels of privilege on the local system. We'll use the highest level of privilege, `LocalSystem`, for most of the examples in this chapter in order to keep it simple. If this property is set to `User` (which is the default), then we must supply a username and password, and that user's account is used to determine privileges for the service. If there is any possibility that a service could access system resources that should be "out-of-bounds," then using the `User` setting to restrict privileges is a good idea. Besides `LocalSystem` and `User`, other possible settings for the `Account` property include `NetworkService` and `LocalSystem`.

❑   `Username`—If Account is set to `User`, then this property determines the user account to use in determining the privileges the system will have and how it interacts with other computers on the network. If this property is left blank, it will be requested when the service is installed.

❑   `Password`—This property determines the password to access the user account specified in the `Username` property. If the password is left blank, it will be requested when the service is installed.

❑   `HelpText`—The information about the service that will be displayed in certain installation options.

If the `Account` property is set to `User` it is good practice to set up a special user account for the service, rather than relying on some existing account that is intended for a live user. The special account can be set up with exactly the appropriate privileges for the service. It also is not as vulnerable to having its password or its privileges inadvertently changed in a way that would cause problems in running the service.

For the `ServiceInstaller` class, the properties we might change include:

❑   `DisplayName`—The name of the service as displayed in the Service Manager or the Server Explorer can be different from the class name and the executable name if desired, though it's a good convention to make this name the same as the class name for the service.

❑   `StartType` — This specifies how the service is started. The default is `Manual`, which means we must start the service manually as it won't start by itself after the system boots. If we want the service to always start when the system starts, we can change this property to `Automatic`. The Service Manager can be used to override the `StartType` setting.

❑   `ServiceName` — The name of the service that this `ServiceInstaller` handles during installation. If we changed the class name of the service after using the Add Installer option, we would need to change this property to correspond to the new name for the service.

We don't normally need to understand or manipulate the methods of either `ServiceProcessInstaller` or `ServiceInstaller`. They are used as necessary during the installation process.

Multiple Services Within One Executable

It is possible to place more than one class that inherits from `ServiceBase` in a single Windows Service executable. Each such class then allows for a separate service that can be started, stopped, and so on, independently of the other services in the executable.

If a Windows Service executable contains more than one service, it needs to contain one `ServiceInstaller` for each service. Each `ServiceInstaller` is configured with the information used for its associated service, such as the displayed name and the start type (automatic or manual). However, the executable still only needs one `ServiceProcessInstaller`, which works for all the services in the executable. It is configured with the account information that will be used for all the services in the executable.

The ServiceController Class

Another important .NET Framework class for working with Windows Services is the `System.ServiceProcess.ServiceController` class. This class is not used when constructing a service. It is used by external applications to communicate with a running service, allowing operations such as starting and stopping the service. The `ServiceController` class is described in detail in *Communicating with the Service*.

Other Types of Windows Service

The `ServiceBase` and `ServiceController` classes can be used to create typical Windows Services that work with high-level system resources such as the file system or performance counters. However, some Windows Services need to interact at a deeper level. For example, a service may work at the kernel level, fulfilling functions such as that of a device driver.

Presently, the .NET Framework classes for Windows Services cannot be used to create such lower-level services, which rules out both VB and C# as tools to create them. C++ is typically the tool of choice for these types of services. If .NET version of C++ is used, the code for such services would typically run in unmanaged mode.

Another type of service that cannot be created with the .NET Framework classes is one that interacts with the Windows Desktop. Again, C++ is the preferred tool for such services.

We'll look at the types of services that *are* possible again when we cover the `ServiceType` property of the `ServiceController` class, in *Communicating with the Service*.

General Instructions to Create a Windows Service with VB.NET

Let's create and use a Windows Service with VB.NET, using the .NET Framework classes we discussed. We will demonstrate these tasks later in a detailed example. Here is a high-level description of the necessary tasks:

1. Create a new project of the type Windows Service. By default, the service will be in a module named `Service1.vb`. The service can be renamed as with any other .NET module. (The class that is automatically placed in `Service1.vb` will be named `Service1` by default, and it will inherit from `ServiceBase`.)

2. Place any logic needed to run when the service is started in the `OnStart` event of the service class. You can find the code listing for the `Service1.vb` file by double-clicking this file's design surface.

3. Add any additional logic that the service needs to carry out its operation. Logic can be placed in the class for the service, or in any other class module in the project. Such logic is typically called via some event that is generated by the operating system and passed to the service, such as a file changing in a directory, or a timer tick.

4. Add an installer to the project. This module provides the interface to Windows Server 2003, Windows XP, Windows 2000, or Windows NT to install the module as a Windows Service. The installer will be a class that inherits from `System.Configuration.Install.Installer`, and it will contain instances of the `ServiceProcessInstaller` and `ServiceInstaller` classes.

5. Set the properties of the installer modules as necessary. The most common settings needed are the account under which the service will run and the name the service will display in the Service Control Manager.

6. Build the project. This will result in an EXE file. If the service were named `WindowsService1`, then the executable file would be named `WindowsService1.exe`.

7. Install the Windows Service with a command line utility named `InstallUtil.exe`. (As previously mentioned, a service cannot be started by just running the EXE file.)

8. Start the Windows Service with the Service Control Manager (available in the Control Panel ➪ Administrative Tools folder in Windows 2000, or the Start ➪ All Programs ➪ Administrative Tools folder in Windows XP) or with the Server Explorer in VS.NET.

You can also start a service from the command console if the proper paths to .NET are set. The command is "NET START <servicename>". Note that the <servicename> used in this command is the name of the service, not the name of the executable in which the service resides. Depending on the configuration of your system, a service being started with any of the aforementioned methods will sometimes fail with an error message that says the service did not start in a timely fashion. This may be because the .NET libraries and other initialization tasks did not finish fast enough to suit the Service Control Manager. If this happens, attempt the start the service again, and it will usually succeed the second time.

Note that steps 2 through 5 can be done in a different order. It doesn't matter if the installer is added and configured before or after the logic that does the processing for the service is added.

At this point, a service is installed and running. The Service Manager or the Server Explorer can stop the service, or it will be automatically stopped when the system is shut down. The command to stop the service in a command console is "NET STOP <servicename>".

The service will not automatically start up the next time the system is booted unless the service is configured for that. This can be done by setting the StartType property for the service to Automatic when developing the service or it can be done in the Service Manager. Right-clicking the service in the Service Manager gives access to this capability.

This process is superficially similar to doing most other VB.NET projects. There are a few important differences, however:

❑   We cannot debug the project in the environment as you normally would any other VB.NET program. The service must be installed and started before it can be debugged. It is also necessary to attach to the process for the service to do debugging. Details about this are included in *Debugging the Service*.

❑   Even though the end result of the development is an EXE, we should not include any message boxes or other visual elements in the code. The Windows Service executable is more like a component library in that sense, and should not have a visual interface. If you include visual elements such as message boxes, the results can vary. In some cases, the UI code will have no effect. In others cases, the service may hang when attempting to write to the user interface.

❑   Finally, we should be especially careful to handle all errors within the program. Since the program is not running in a user context, a runtime error has no place to report itself visually. We should handle all errors with structured exception handling, and use an event log or other offline means to record and communicate runtime errors.

Creating a Counter Monitor Service

To illustrate the steps we outlined, we'll create a simple service. The service we'll create will check the value of a performance counter, and when the value of the counter exceeds a certain value, the service will beep every three seconds. This is a good example for stepping through the process of creating, installing, and starting a Windows Service. It contains very little logic, and we can easily tell when it is working.

In the first phase of the example, we'll create a service that always beeps. Then in the second phase, we'll add logic to monitor the performance counter and only beep when the counter exceeds a specific value:

1.   Start a new Windows Service project using VS.NET. Name the project CounterMonitor.

2.   In the Solution Explorer, rename Service1.vb to CounterMonitor.vb.

3.   Click the design surface for CounterMonitor.vb. In the Properties window, change the (Name) property to CounterMonitor, and change the ServiceName property from Service1 to CounterMonitor (the (Name) property changes the name of the class on which the service is based, while the ServiceName property changes the name of the service as known to the Service Control Manager).

4. Right-click the project for the service (not the solution, but the project found directly below the solution node in the Solution Explorer), and select Properties. You will then be presented with the CounterMonitor Property Pages dialog box. Under Startup Object (found on the General tab within the Common Properties node), select CounterMonitor.

5. The Designer fails to change one reference to the old Service1. This is intentional. The Sub Main for the project can start multiple services, so the Designer cannot be sure when to change the name of the service or services being started. Consequently, you will need to change your service name manually in one line. Looking at the code view of the CounterMonitor.vb file in VS.NET, open the Component Designer generated code section by clicking the plus sign next to it. This will open a large section of VS.NET generated code. Within this code block, look for the following line:

```
ServicesToRun = New System.ServiceProcess.ServiceBase() {New Service1}
```

Change the name "Service1" at the end of the line to "CounterMonitor". The line will then look like the following:

```
ServicesToRun = New System.ServiceProcess.ServiceBase() {New CounterMonitor}
```

6. Go back to the CounterMonitor.vb file's design view and open the VS.NET Toolbox. Click on the Components (not the Windows Forms) tab. Drag a Timer control from the Toolbox onto the CounterMonitor design surface. It will appear on the design surface with the name Timer1.

7. In the Properties window for Timer1, change the Interval property to a value of 3000 (that's 3,000 milliseconds, which will cause the timer to fire every 3 seconds).

8. Go to the code for CounterMonitor.vb. Inside the OnStart event handler (which is already created for you in the code), enter the following code:

```
Timer1.Enabled = True
```

9. In the OnStop event for the class, enter the following code:

```
Timer1.Enabled = False
```

10. Create an Elapsed event for the timer by highlighting Timer1 in the left-hand drop-down box at the top of the code editor window, and then selecting the Elapsed event in the right-hand drop-down box.

11. In the Elapsed event, place the following line of code:

```
Beep()
```

12. Now add an installer to the project. Go back to the design surface for CounterMonitor and right-click it. Select Add Installer. A new file called ProjectInstaller1.vb is created and added to the project. The ProjectInstaller1.vb file will have two components added to its design surface, named ServiceProcessInstaller1 and ServiceInstaller1. This is shown in Figure 21-2.

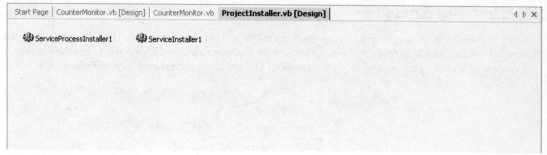

Figure 21-2

13. On the `ProjectInstaller1` design surface, highlight the `ServiceProcessInstaller1` control. In its Properties window, change the `Account` property to `LocalSystem`.

14. Highlight the `ServiceInstaller1` control. In its Properties window, change the `DisplayName` property to `CounterMonitor`.

15. Now build the project. An EXE for the service will be created named `CounterMonitor.exe`.

Installing the Service

Now we are ready to install the service. The utility for doing this must be run from a command line. The utility is called `InstallUtil.exe`, and it is located in the .NET utilities directory, which will be found at `C:\WINNT\Microsoft.NET\Framework\v1.1.4322` on Windows 2000 and NT systems, or `C:\Windows\Microsoft.NET\Framework\v1.1.4322` on Windows XP.

You can easily access this utility (and all the other .NET utilities in that directory) using an option off of the Programs menu that is installed with VS.NET. Choose Microsoft Visual Studio .NET 2003 ➪ Visual Studio .NET Tools ➪ Visual Studio .NET 2003 Command Prompt. This will result in display of a command window. Change to the directory that contains `CounterMonitor.exe`. By default, when using Visual Studio .NET 2003, you'll find this executable at `C:\Documents and Settings\`*your name*`]\My Documents\Visual Studio Projects\CounterMonitor\obj\Debug`. Once found, run the following command:

```
InstallUtil CounterMonitor.exe
```

You should look at the messages generated by `InstallUtil.exe` to make sure that the installation of the service was successful. The utility will generate several lines of information, and if it is successful, the last two lines will be

```
The Commit phase completed successfully.

The transacted install has completed.
```

If these two lines do not appear, you will need to read all the information generated by the utility to find out why the install did not work. Reasons might include a bad path name for the executable, or trying to install the service again when it is already installed [it must be uninstalled before it can be reinstalled (see later)].

Starting the Service

Later in this chapter, we will create our own "control panel" screen to start and stop the service. But for now, to test our new Windows Service, we will use the Server Explorer in VS.NET. Open the Server Explorer in VS.NET and expand the Services node. The resulting screen is shown in Figure 21-3.

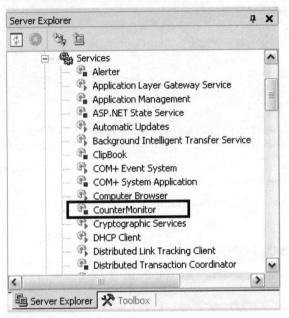

Figure 21-3

If the `CounterMonitor` service does not appear in the list, the installation was unsuccessful. Try the installation again and check the error messages.

Right-click the `CounterMonitor` service. Select the Start menu option. You will hear the service beep every 3 seconds. You can stop the service by right-clicking it again, and selecting the Stop menu option.

You can also use the Service Control Manager built into Windows to start the `CounterMonitor` service. This is illustrated in Figure 21-4.

Start `CounterMonitor` by right-clicking it and selecting Start. As before, you will hear your computer beep every three seconds. You can stop the service by right-clicking `CounterMonitor` and selecting Stop. Note that if you already started the service via the Server Explorer (as discussed earlier), then it will be in a Started state when you go into the Service Control Manager program.

Uninstalling the Service

Uninstalling the service is very similar to installing it. The service must be in a stopped state before it can be uninstalled, but the uninstall operation will attempt to stop the service if it is running. The uninstall operation is done in the same command window (with the Visual Studio .NET 2003 Command Prompt) as the install operation, and the command used is the same as the one for installation, except that the option /u is included just before name of the service. Remember that you will need to navigate to

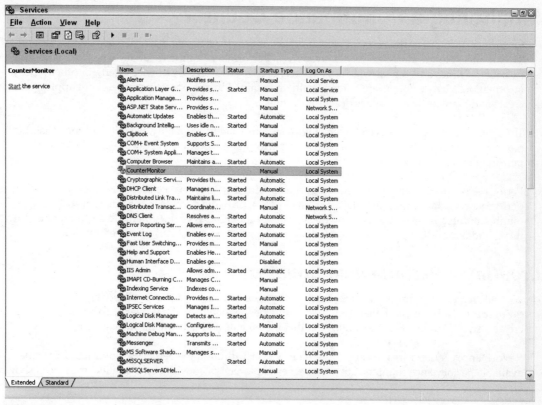

Figure 21-4

C:\Documents and Settings\[your *name*]\My Documents\Visual Studio Projects\ CounterMonitor\obj\Debug to run this command.

```
InstallUtil.exe /u CounterMonitor.exe
```

You can tell that the uninstall was successful if the information displayed by the utility contains the following line:

```
Service CounterMonitor was successfully removed from the system.
```

If the uninstall is unsuccessful, you should read the rest of the information to find out why. Besides typing in the wrong path name, another common reason for failure is trying to uninstall a service that is in a running state and could not be stopped in a timely fashion.

Once you have uninstalled CounterMonitor, it will no longer show up in the list of available services to start and stop (at least after a refresh it won't).

> A Windows Service must be uninstalled and reinstalled every time you make changes to it. You should uninstall **CounterMonitor** now because we're about to add new capabilities to it.

Monitoring a Performance Counter

Performance counters are a system-level function of Windows Server 2003, Windows 2000, XP, and NT. They are used to track usage of system resources. Performance counters can be expressed as counts (number of times a Web page was hit), or percentages (how much disk space is left), or other types of information. Many counters are automatically maintained by the operating system, but applications can create and manage their own performance counters.

To demonstrate how services can interact with system-level functionality, we will add the capability to our `CounterMonitor` to monitor a particular performance counter, and only beep when the performance counter exceeds a certain value.

Performance counters can be monitored by a user with the Performance Monitor. There are a variety of performance counters built into the operating system, providing access to information such as the number of threads currently active on the system, or the number of documents in a print queue. Any of these, and any custom performance counters, can be graphed in the Performance Monitor.

Creating a Performance Counter

We will create a performance counter named `ServiceCounter`. Then we will change `CounterMonitor` to check that counter and only beep when its value is over 5. To test it, we will also create a small Windows Forms application that increments and decrements the counter.

Performance counters are typically accessed in VS.NET through the Server Explorer tab. To see the available performance counters, open the Server Explorer, which will look much like the screen shown in Figure 21-5.

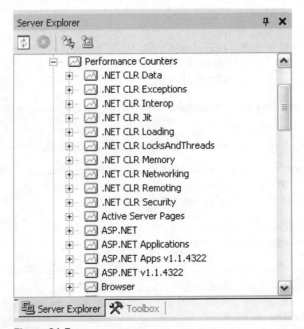

Figure 21-5

To see the categories of performance counters, click the plus sign next to the Performance Counters option in the Server Explorer. Several dozen categories will be shown. You can look at the counters in any particular category by clicking the plus sign next to the category.

You can also create new categories and new counters. For this example, you need to create a new category for our counter called `Service Counters`. To do that, right-click the Performance Counters option in the Server Explorer and select the Create New Category option. In the resulting Performance Counter Builder dialog box, enter the name of the category as `Service Counters`, and create a new counter by clicking the New button and entering `TestCounter` for the name. Once that is complete, click the OK button in the dialog box and VS.NET will then create a new category called `Service Counters` that contains a single performance counter called `TestCounter`.

Integrating the Counter into the Service

Using a performance counter in the `CounterMonitor` service we created earlier is straightforward. Open the `CounterMonitor` project, and go to the design surface for `CounterMonitor`. Then open the Server Explorer so that it shows the `TestCounter` performance counter we created. Click `TestCounter` from within the Server Explorer and drag it onto the `CounterMonitor.vb` design surface.

A new visual control named `PerformanceCounter1` will now be shown on the page's design surface. The performance counter is now ready to use. Change the logic in the `Elapsed` event for `Timer1` to look like this:

```
If PerformanceCounter1.RawValue > mnMaxValue Then
    Beep()
End If
```

The `RawValue` property being used in this code fetches the unformatted value of the counter. For counters that track whole numbers (such as the number of times a Web page is hit), the `RawValue` property is normally used to get the value of the counter for testing or display. Some other types of counters use a `NextValue` method to get a formatted value. See the `CounterType` property of the `PerformanceCounter` class for more on the types of performance counters available.

Next, put this statement in the code module just under the line that begins with `Inherits`:

```
Dim mnMaxValue As Integer = 5
```

Now build the service again, and install it as we did before. Start the service. It should not beep at this point, because the value in the performance counter is zero. You can leave the counter running at this point, because we will now create a program to change the value in the performance counter, and thus make the service begin beeping.

Changing the Value in the Performance Counter

To manipulate the performance counter, we will build a small forms-based application. Close the `CounterMonitor` solution in Visual Studio, and start a new Windows Application Project named `CounterTest`. Place two buttons on `Form1` and change their properties as shown in the following table.

Name	Text
BtnIncrement	Increment Counter
BtnDecrement	Decrement Counter

Then, open the Server Explorer and drag the `TestCounter` performance counter onto the form itself, just as you did earlier with the `CounterMonitor` project. As with all nonvisible components from the toolbox, the counter will appear in the component tray (just under the form) rather than on the form design surface.

The `PerformanceCounter1` control for `CounterTest` needs one property change. The `ReadOnly` property of the control needs to be set to `False`. This will allow the application to manipulate the counter. (This change was unnecessary for the `CounterMonitor` Windows Service project, because that project only reads the value of the performance counter and does not change it.)

Now double-click `btnIncrement` to get to its click event. Place the following code in the event:

```
PerformanceCounter1.Increment()
```

Double-click the `btnDecrement` to get to its click event. Place the following code in the event:

```
PerformanceCounter1.Decrement()
```

Build and run the program and click the increment button six times. If the `CounterMonitor` service is running, on the sixth click it will begin beeping because the value in the counter has exceeded five. Then click the decrement button a couple of times, and the beeping will stop.

If you want to monitor the current value of the counter, select Control Panel ⇨ Administrative Tools ⇨ Performance. This program, the Performance Monitor, allows the value of counters to be graphed. You add a counter for display by clicking the New Counter Set button and right-clicking the right-hand portion of the Performance Monitor, and adding a counter in the dialog box that pops up. Change the Performance Object drop-down list to `Service Counters` and add the `TestCounter` performance counter to the list. When completed, press the *Close* button. The counter that you created will then be monitored by the dialog box. You can use the help for this program for more details on displaying counters in the Performance Monitor.

Communicating with the Service

Up to this point, we've seen how to:

❑   Create a Windows Service using VB.NET

❑   Start and stop a service with the Server Explorer in VS.NET or the Service Control Manager in the control panel

❑   Make a service work with a system level function such as a performance counter

If it is sufficient to start, stop, and check on the service through the Server Explorer or Service Control Manager, and there is no need to do any other communication with the service, then these procedures are all you need. But it is often times helpful to create a specialized application to manipulate your service. This application will typically be able to start and stop a service, and to check on its status. The application may also need to communicate with the service to change its configuration. Such an application is often referred to as a *control panel* for the service, even though it does not necessarily reside in the operating system's Control Panel. A commonly-used example of such an application is the SQL Server Service Manager, whose icon appears in the tray on the Taskbar (normally in the lower right section of the screen) if you have SQL Server 2000 installed.

Such an application needs a way to communicate with the service. The .NET Framework base class that is used for such communication is the `ServiceController` class. It is in the `System.ServiceProcess` namespace. You need to add a reference to `System.ServiceProcess.dll` (which contains this namespace) before a project can use the `ServiceController` class.

The `ServiceController` class provides an interface to the Service Control Manager, which coordinates all communication with Windows Services. However, we don't have to know anything about the Service Control Manager to use the `ServiceController` class. We just manipulate the properties and methods of the `ServiceController` class, and any necessary communication with the Service Control Manager is accomplished on our behalf behind the scenes.

It's a good idea to use exactly *one* instance of the `ServiceController` class for each service you are controlling. Multiple instances of `ServiceController` that are communicating with the same service can have timing conflicts. Typically, that means using a module-level object variable to hold the reference to the active `ServiceController`, and instantiating the `ServiceController` during the initialization logic for the application. The following example uses this technique.

The ServiceController Class

The constructor for the `ServiceController` requires the name of the Windows Service with which it will be communicating. This is the same as the name that was placed in the `ServiceName` property of the class that defined the service. We'll see how to instantiate the `ServiceController` class shortly.

The `ServiceController` class has several members that are useful in manipulating services. Here are the most important methods.

Method	Purpose
Start	A method to start up the service.
Stop	A method to stop the service.
Refresh	A method to make sure the ServiceController object contains the latest state of the service (needed because the service might be manipulated from another program).
ExecuteCommand	A method used to send a custom command to the service. We will cover this method in the section on *Custom Commands*.

Here are the most important properties.

Property	Purpose
CanStop	A property indicating whether the service can be stopped.
ServiceName	A property containing the name of the associated service.
Status	An enumerated property that indicates whether a service is stopped, started, in process of being started, and so on. The ToString method on this property is useful for getting the status in a string form for text messages. The possible values of the enumeration are:
	ContinuePending — The service is attempting to continue
	Paused — The service is paused
	PausePending — The service is attempting to go into a paused state
	Running — The service is running
	StartPending — The service is starting
	Stopped — The service is not running
	StopPending — The service is stopping
ServiceType	A property that indicates the type of service. The result is an enumerated value. The enumerations are:
	Win32OwnProcess — The service uses its own process (this is the default for a service created in .NET).
	Win32ShareProcess — The service shares a process with another service (this advanced capability is not covered here).
	Adapter, FileSystemDriver, InteractiveProcess, KernelDriver, RecognizerDriver — These are low-level service types that cannot be created with VB.NET because the ServiceBase class does not support the types. However, the value of the ServiceType property may still have these values for services created with other tools.

Integrating a ServiceController into the Example

To manipulate the service, we'll enhance the CounterTest program we created earlier. Here are step-by-step instructions to do that:

1.   Add three new buttons to the CounterTest form, with the following names and text labels.

Name	Text
BtnCheckStatus	"Check Status"
BtnStartService	"Start Service"
BtnStopService	"Stop Service"

2. Add a reference to the DLL that contains the `ServiceController` class. To do this, select Project ➪ Add Reference. On the .NET tab, highlight the `System.ServiceProcess.dll` option, and press the *Select* button. Then press the OK button.

3. Add this line at the top of the code for `Form1`:

```
Imports System.ServiceProcess
```

4. As we discussed, the project needs to use only one instance of the `ServiceController` class. Create a module-level object reference to a `ServiceController` class by adding the following line of code within the `Form1` class:

```
Dim myController As ServiceController
```

5. Create a `Form Load` event in `Form1`, and place the following line of code in it to instantiate the `ServiceController` class:

```
myController = New ServiceController("CounterMonitor")
```

We now have a `ServiceController` class named `myController` that we can use to manipulate the `CounterMonitor` Windows Service. In the click event for `btnCheckStatus`, place the following code:

```
Dim sStatus As String
myController.Refresh()
sStatus = myController.Status.ToString

MsgBox(myController.ServiceName & " is in state:" & sStatus)
```

In the click event for `btnStartService`, place the following code:

```
Try
    myController.Start()
Catch exp As Exception
    MsgBox("Could not start service")
End Try
```

In the click event for `btnStopService`, place the following code:

```
If myController.CanStop Then
    myController.Stop()
Else
    MsgBox("Service cannot be stopped")
End If
```

Run and test the program. The service may already be running because of one of your previous tests. Make sure the performance counter is high enough to make the service beep, and then test starting and stopping the service.

More About ServiceController

ServiceController classes can be created for *any* Windows Service, not just those created in .NET. For example, you could instantiate a ServiceController class that was associated with the Windows Service for Internet Information Server (IIS), and use it to start, pause, and stop IIS. The code would look just like the code used earlier for the application that controlled the CounterMonitor service. The only difference is that the name of the service would need to be changed in the line that instantiates the ServiceController (step 5).

It's also useful to emphasize that the ServiceController is not communicating directly with the service. It is working through the Services Control Manager. That means the requests from the Service Controller to start, stop, or pause a service do not behave synchronously. As soon as the ServiceController has passed the request to the ServicesControlManager, it continues to execute its own code without waiting for the Service Control Manager to pass on the request, or for the service to act on the request.

Custom Commands

Some services need additional operations besides starting and stopping. For example, for our CounterMonitor Windows Service, we might want to set the threshold value of the performance counter that causes the service to begin beeping, or we might want to change the interval between beeps.

With most components, we would implement such functionality through a public interface. That is, we would put public properties and methods on the component. However, we cannot do this with a Windows Service, because it has no public interface that we can get to from outside the service.

To deal with this need, the interface for a Windows Service contains a special event called OnCustomCommand. The event arguments include a numeric code that can service as a command sent to the Windows Service. The code can be any number in the range 128 to 255. (Those numbers under 128 are reserved for use by the operating system.)

To fire the event and send a custom command to a service, the ExecuteCommand method of the ServiceController is used. The ExecuteCommand method takes the numeric code that needs to be sent to the service as a parameter. When this method is accessed, the ServiceController class tells the Service Control Manager to fire the OnCustomCommand event in the service, and to pass it the numeric code.

To see this process in action, let's go through an example. Suppose we want to be able to change the interval between beeps for our CounterMonitor service. We cannot directly send the beep interval that we want, but we can pick various values of the interval, and associate a custom command numeric code with each.

Suppose we want to be able to set intervals of one second, three seconds (the default), or 10 seconds. We could set up the following correspondence.

Custom Command Numeric Code	Beep Interval
201	One second (1,000 milliseconds)
203	Three seconds (3,000 milliseconds)
210	Ten seconds (10,000 milliseconds)

The correspondence between code and times we have chosen is completely arbitrary. We could use any codes between 128 and 255 to associate with our beep intervals. The ones shown in the table were chosen because they are easy to remember.

First, we need to change the `CounterMonitor` service so that it is able to accept the custom commands for the beep interval. To do that, first make sure the `CounterMonitor` service is uninstalled from any previous installs. Then open the VS.NET project for the `CounterMonitor` service.

Create an `OnCustomCommand` event in the service. To do this, first open the code window for `CounterMonitor.vb`. Then select (Overrides) in the left drop-down box above the code window, and select OnCustomCommand in the right drop-down box. This will generate the shell event. Notice how it only accepts a single Integer as a parameter. In the `OnCustomCommand` event, place the following code:

```
Timer1.Enabled = False
Select Case command
    Case 201
        Timer1.Interval = 1000
    Case 203
        Timer1.Interval = 3000
    Case 210
        Timer1.Interval = 10000
End Select
Timer1.Enabled = True
```

Now build the `CounterMonitor` service, reinstall it, and start it.

Now we can enhance our `CounterTest` application that we created earlier to set the interval. To allow the user to pick the interval, we will use radio buttons. On the `CounterTest` program `Form1` (which currently contains five buttons), place three radio buttons. Set their text labels as follows:

```
RadioButton1 - "1 second"
RadioButton2 - "3 seconds"
RadioButton3 - "10 seconds"
```

Then, place a button directly under these option buttons. Name it `btnSetInterval`, and set its text to `Set Interval`. In the click event for this button, place the following code:

```
Dim nIntervalCommand As Integer = 203
If RadioButton1.Checked Then
    nIntervalCommand = 201
End If
```

```
    If RadioButton2.Checked Then
        nIntervalCommand = 203
    End If
    If RadioButton3.Checked Then
        nIntervalCommand = 210
    End If
    myController.ExecuteCommand(nIntervalCommand)
```

At this point, `Form1` should look something like the sample screen shown in Figure 21-6.

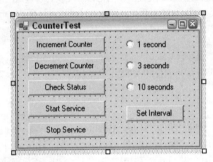

Figure 21-6

Start the `CounterTest` control program, and test the ability to change the beep interval. Remember to make sure the performance counter is high enough so that the `CounterMonitor` service beeps. Also remember that every time you stop and restart the service, it will reset the beep interval to 3 seconds.

Passing Strings to a Service

Since the `OnCustomCommand` event only takes numeric codes as input parameters, we cannot directly pass strings to the service. For example, if we wanted to reconfigure a directory name for a service, we could not just send the directory name over.

Instead it would be necessary to place the information to be passed to the service in a file in some known location on disk. Then a custom command for the service could instruct it to look at the standard file location, and read the information in the file. What the service did with the contents of the file would, of course, be customized for the service.

Creating a File Watcher

Now let's step through another example to illustrate what a Windows Service can do and how to construct one. We will build a service that monitors a particular directory, and reacts when a new or changed file is placed in the directory. The example Windows Service application waits for those files, extracts information from them, and then logs an event to a system log to record the file change.

As before, we create a Windows Service from the built-in template named Windows Service in the New Project screen. Start by creating a new project and selecting the Windows Service template. Name this project FileWatcherService and click OK. This will create a new service class called `Service1.vb`. Rename this to `FileWatcherService.vb`. Then right-click the design surface, select Properties, and set the `ServiceName` property to `FileWatcherService`.

As in the first example, you will need to reset the project's start object to `FileWatcherService`, and to change the name `Service1` to `FileWatcherService` in the designer code that starts the service. All of this is illustrated earlier in this chapter.

Writing Events Using an Eventlog

We will make sure the service is doing its job by having it write events to a system event log. Event logs are available under Windows NT, Windows 2000, Windows XP, and Windows Server 2003. As with many other system-level features, the use of event logs is simplified in .NET because a .NET Framework base class does most of the work for you.

There are three event logs on the system: `Application`, `Security`, and `System`. Normally, your applications should only write to the `Application` log. A property of a log entry called `Source` identifies the application writing the message. This property does not have to be the same as the executable name of the application, but is often given that name to make it easy to identify the source of the message.

You can look at the events in the event log by using the Event Viewer. It is in Control Panel ⇨ Administrative Tools ⇨ Event Viewer on Windows 2000, and Start ⇨ All Programs ⇨ Administrative Tools ⇨ Event Viewer on Windows XP. We will use the event viewer in our example below to make sure our service is generating events.

The AutoLog Property

Early in the chapter, we briefly mentioned that the `AutoLog` property of the `ServiceBase` class determines whether the service automatically writes events to the Application log. The `AutoLog` property instructs the service to use the Application event log to report command failures, as well as information for `OnStart`, `OnStop`, `OnPause`, and `OnContinue` events on the service. What is actually logged to the event log is an entry saying Service started successfully and Service stopped successfully, and any errors that might have occurred. If you look in the Application event log now, you will notice these logged events for the CounterMonitor Windows Service that you created and ran earlier in the chapter.

We can turn off the event log reporting by setting the `AutoLog` property to `False` in the Properties window for the service. However, we will leave it set to `True` for our example. That means some events will be logged automatically (without us including any code for them). Then, we will add some code to our service to log additional events not covered by the AutoLog property.

First, though, we need to implement a file monitoring control into our project.

Creating a FileSystemWatcher

For performance reasons, we should do all of our work on a separate thread to our main application thread. We want to leave our main application free to accept any requests from the user or the operating system. We can do this by using some of the different components that create their own threads when they are launched. The `Timer` component and the `FileSystemWatcher` component are two examples. When the `Timer` component fires its `Elapsed` event, a thread is spawned and any code placed within that event will work on that newly created thread. The same thing happens when the events for the `FileSystemWatcher` component fire.

You can learn more about threading .NET in Chapter 19.

The FileSystemWatcher Component

The `FileSystemWatcher` component is used to monitor a particular directory. The component implements `Created`, `Changed`, `Deleted`, and `Renamed` events, which are fired when files are placed in the directory, changed, deleted or renamed, respectively.

The operation that takes place when one of these events is fired is up to the application developer. Most often, logic is included to read and process the new or changed files. However, we are just going to write a message to a log file.

To implement the component in the project, drag and drop a `FileSystemWatcher` control from the Components tab of the Toolbox onto the designer surface of `FileWatcherService.vb`. This control will automatically be called `FileSystemWatcher1`.

The EnableRaisingEvents Property

The `FileSystemWatcher` control should not generate any events until the service is initialized and ready to handle them. To prevent this, set the `EnableRaisingEvents` property to `False`. This will prevent the control from firing any events. We will enable it during the `OnStart` event in the service.

These events fired by the `FileSystemWatcher` are controlled using the `NotifyFilter` property, discussed later.

The Path Property

Next, the path that we want to monitor is the `TEMP` directory on the C: drive, so set the `Path` property to `C:\TEMP` (be sure to check that there is a `TEMP` directory on your C: drive). Of course, this path can be changed to monitor any directory depending on your system, including network or removable drives.

The NotifyFilter Property

We only want to watch for when a file is freshly created, or the last modified value of a file has changed. To do this we set the `NotifyFilter` property to FileName, LastWrite. We could also watch for other changes such as attributes, security, size, and directory name changes as well, just by changing the `NotifyFilter` property. Note that we specify multiple changes to watch for by including a list of changes separated by commas.

The Filter Property

The types of files that we will look for are text files. This is done by setting the `Filter` property to `*.txt`. Notice that if you were going to watch for all file types, then the value of the `Filter` property needs to be set to `*.*`.

The IncludeSubdirectories Property

If we wanted to watch subdirectories, we would set the `IncludeSubdirectories` property to `True`. In this sample, we're leaving it as `False`, which is the default value.

You should have the following properties set as illustrated in Figure 21-7.

Figure 21-7

Adding FileSystemWatcher Code to OnStart and OnStop

Now that we have some properties set, let's add some code to the `OnStart` event. We need to start the `FileSystemWatcher1` component so it will start triggering events when files are created or copied into the directory we're monitoring, so we set the `EnableRaisingEvents` property to `True`:

```
Protected Overrides Sub OnStart(ByVal args() As String)

    ' Start monitoring for files
    FileSystemWatcher1.EnableRaisingEventst = True
End Sub
```

Once our file monitoring properties are initialized, we are ready to start the monitoring.

When the service stops we need to stop the file monitoring process. Add this code to your `OnStop` event:

```
Protected Overrides Sub OnStop()
    ' Stop monitoring for files
    FileSystemWatcher1.EnableRaisingEvents = False

End Sub
```

The EventLog Component

Now we are ready to place an `EventLog` component in the service to facilitate logging of events. Drag and drop an `EventLog` control from the Components tab of the Toolbox onto the designer surface of `FileWatcherService.vb`. This control will automatically be called `EventLog1`.

Set the Log property for Eventlog1 to Application, and set the Source property to FileWatcherService.

The Created Event

Next, we will place some logic in the Created event of our FileSystemWatcher component to log when a file has been created. This event will fire when a file has been placed or created in the directory that we are monitoring. This event fires because the last modified information on the file has changed.

Select FileSystemWatcher1 from the Class Name drop-down and select Created from the Method Name drop-down, and the Created event will be added to your code. Add code to the Created event as follows:

```
Public Sub FileSystemWatcher1_Created(ByVal sender As Object, _
        ByVal e As System.IO.FileSystemEventArgs) _
        Handles FileSystemWatcher1.Created

    Dim sMessage As String
    sMessage = "File created in directory - file name is " + e.Name
    EventLog1.WriteEntry(sMessage)

End Sub
```

Notice that the event arguments object (the object named "e" in the event parameters) includes a property called Name. This property holds the name of the file that generated the event.

At this point, we could add the other events for FileSystemWatcher (Changed, Deleted, Renamed) in a similar way and create corresponding log messages for those events. To keep the example simple, we'll just do the Created event in this service.

We need to add an Installer class to this project to install the application. This is done as it was in the earlier CounterMonitor example, by right-clicking the design surface for the service and selecting Add Installer. Don't forget to change the Account property to LocalSystem, or set it to User and fill in the Username and Password properties.

As before, you must install the service using InstallUtil.exe. Then you can start it with the Server Explorer or the Service Manager.

Upon successful compilation of these steps, we will get a message logged for any file with a .txt extension that we copy or create in the monitored directory. So, after dropping some sample text files into our monitored directory, we can use the Event Viewer to check and make sure the events are present.

Figure 21-8 shows the Event Viewer with several example messages created by our service.

If you right-click one of the events for FileWatcherService, you'll see a detail screen. Notice that the message corresponds to the event log message we constructed in the Created event of the FileSystemWatcher control in the service as shown in Figure 21-9.

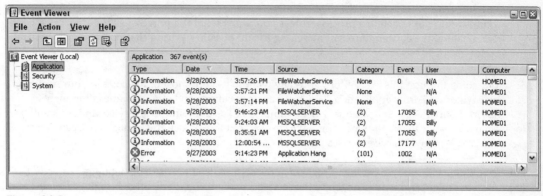

Figure 21-8

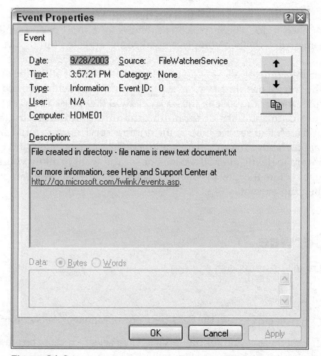

Figure 21-9

Debugging the Service

Because a service must be run from within the context of the Services Control Manager rather than from within VS.NET, debugging a service is not as straightforward as debugging other VS.NET application types. To debug a service, we must start the service and then attach a debugger to the process in which it is running. We can then debug your application using all of the standard debugging functionality of VS.NET.

> You should not attach to a process unless you know what the process is and understand the consequences of attaching to and possibly killing that process.

To avoid going through this extra effort, you may want to test out most of the code in your service in a standard Windows Forms application. This test-bed application can have the same components (FileSystemWatchers, EventLogs, Timers, and so on) as the Windows Service, and thus will be able to run the same logic in events. Once you have checked out the logic in this context, you can just copy and paste it into a Windows Service application.

However, there will be some occasions for which the service itself needs to be debugged directly. So it's important to understand how to attach to the service's process and do direct debugging. The rest of this section explains how to do that.

The only time you can debug a service is when it's running. When you attach the debugger to the service, you are interrupting the service. The service is suspended for a short period while you attach to it. The service will also be interrupted when you place breakpoints and step through you code.

Attaching to the service's process allows you to debug most, but not all, of the service's code. For instance, because the service has already been started, you cannot debug the code in the service's OnStart method this way, or the code in the Main method that is used to load the service. To debug the OnStart event or any code under the Component Designer generated code region, you have to add a dummy service and start that service first. In the dummy service, you would create an instance of the service that you want to debug. You can place some code in a Timer object and create the new instance of the object that you want to debug after 30 seconds or so. You want to allow yourself enough time to attach to the debugger before the new instance is created. Meanwhile, you can place breakpoints in your startup code to debug those events.

To Debug a Service

Follow these steps to debug a service

1. Install your service.

2. Start your service, either from the Services Control Manager, Server Explorer, or from code.

3. In VS.NET, load the solution for the service. Then select Processes from the Debug menu. The Processes dialog box appears (see Figure 21-10).

4. For a Windows Service, the process you want to attach to is not a foreground process, so you must check the check box next to the Show system processes option.

5. In the Available Processes section, click the process indicated by the executable name for your service, and then the Attach button. The Attach to Process dialog box appears. This is shown in Figure 21-11.

6. Make sure that just the common language runtime option is selected and then click OK. You will return to the Processes dialog box. Before you close the Processes dialog box, you have the option to select either Detach from this process or Terminate this process from the drop-down

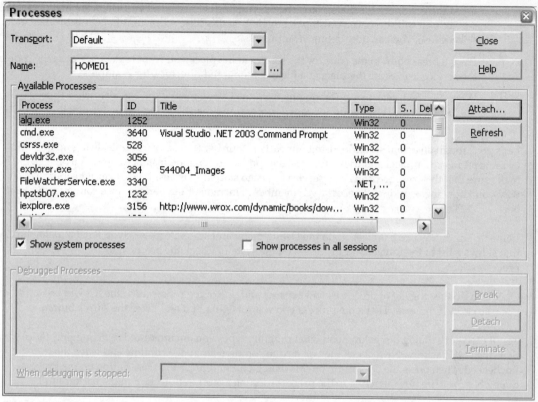

Figure 21-10

Figure 21-11

list at the bottom of the dialog box, once debugging is finished. If you select the first option, your service will still run once you stop debugging. In this case, select Terminate this process and select Close. You can now debug your process.

7. Place a breakpoint in the code for the service at the place you want to debug. Cause the code in the service to execute (by placing a file in a monitored directory, for example).

8. When finished, select Stop Debugging from the Debug menu. You can also select Processes from the Debug menu, click your debugged process, and then click Detach or Terminate.

Let's go through an actual scenario, using our earlier `CounterMonitor` example. Bring up both the `CounterMonitor` project and the `CounterTest` project in separate instances of the VS.NET IDE. Then make sure that the `CounterMonitor` service has been started. It is best if you hear it beeping—that way you know it is working. If necessary, remember to increment the performance counter to make it beep.

In the `CounterMonitor` project, go to the Debug menu and select Processes, you'll get a dialog box that shows a list of the foreground processes on the system. Check the box next to "Show system processes."

Once you do this, the list of processes will expand, and one of the processes in the list will be `CounterMonitor.exe`. That's the process you want. Highlight it and press the *Attach* button.

You'll then get a dialog box asking you what program types you are interested in debugging. Since we are working solely within .NET, check the box next to common language runtime and leave the rest unchecked. Then press the *OK* button on this dialog box, and press the *Close* button on the Processes dialog box. You are now attached to the process running `CounterMonitor` in the background.

Place a breakpoint on the first line of the `OnCustomCommand` event:

```
Timer1.Enabled = False
```

Now we are ready to check debugging. Bring up the `CounterTest` program, and start it. Press one of the radio buttons to change the beep interval. You will hear the beeping stop, because `CounterMonitor.exe` has entered debugging mode. Switch back to the `CounterMonitor` project, and the cursor will be on the breakpoint line in `OnCustomCommand`. You can use the normal commands at this point to step through the code.

Summary

In this chapter, we have seen a general overview of what a Windows Service is and how to create one with VB.NET. The techniques in this chapter can be used for many different types of background service. A few examples are:

❑ Automatically moving statistical files from a database server to a Web server

❑ Pushing general files across computers and platforms

❑   A watchdog timer to ensure that a connection is always available

❑   An application to move and process FTP files, or indeed files received from any source

While VB.NET cannot be used to create every type of Windows Service, it is effective at creating many of the most useful ones. The .NET Framework classes for Windows Services make this creation relatively straightforward. The designers generate much of the routine code needed, and you as a developer can concentrate on the code that is specific to your particular Windows Service.

22

Web Services

To start this chapter, we're going to dive into a short history of multitier architecture and network operating systems. We'll discuss the early days of the network-as-the-computer, and some of the future. The reason for this diversion is to make us understand the rationale behind *Web services*.

We'll go on to look at a sample Web service, make it accessible to the Internet, and access it from a client application—both with the Visual Studio .NET IDE and using command line tools. From there we'll move on to a key feature of Web services, the *Service Repository*, *discovery* and *Universal Description, Discovery, and Integration* (UDDI), features which allow remote programmers to correctly access Web services.

We'll get into more in-depth topics when we discuss the four namespaces found in the .NET Framework class library (`System.Web.Services`, `System.Web.Description`, `System.Web.Services.Discovery`, and `System.Web.Services.Protocols`) that deal with Web services, and how to access them with Visual Basic .NET (VB.NET). Then, we will move to a discussion of the serious topics, such as security, transactions, and the downsides of any distributed architecture (including Web services). Finally, we'll wrap up with a short discussion of where we go from here, and how we get there.

Introduction to Web Services

A Web service is a means of exposing application logic or data via standard protocols such as XML and SOAP. A Web service comprises one or more functions, packaged together for use in a common framework throughout a network. This is shown in Figure 22-1, where Web services provide access to information through standard Internet Protocols. By using a WSDL (Web Services Description Language) contract, consumers of the Web service can learn the structure of the data the Web service provides as well as all the details on how to actually consume it.

This simple concept provides for a very wide variety of potential uses by developers of Internet and enterprise applications alike, as shown in Figure 22-1.

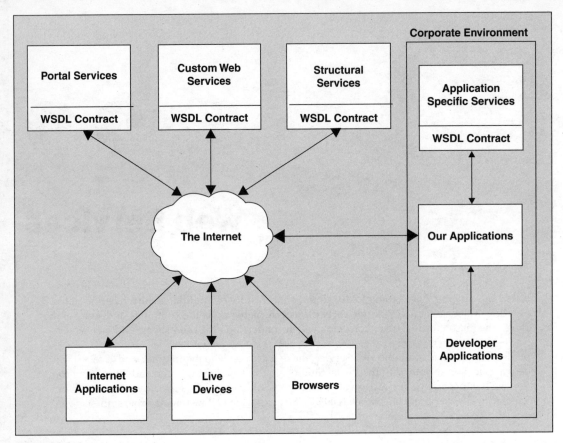

Figure 22-1

Web services are going to be the heart of the next generation of systems architecture because they are:

❏ Architecture neutral — Web services don't depend on a proprietary wire format, schema description, or discovery standard.

❏ Ubiquitous — Any service that supports the standards can support the service.

❏ Simple — Creating Web services is easy, quick, and can be free. The data schema is human readable. Any language can participate.

❏ Interoperable — Since the Web services all speak the same standards, they can all speak to one another.

In basic terms, a Web service is an object with an XML document describing all of the methods, properties, and events sitting between the code and the caller. Any body of code written in just about any programming language can be described with this XML document, and then any application that understands SOAP (*Simple Object Access Protocol*) can access the object. That's because the parameters you'd type after the function name are passed via XML to the Web service and because SOAP is an open standard.

Microsoft has put a wrapper around all of the XML schemas that support Web services (including SOAP and WSDL) so that they look like .NET or COM objects. Next, we'll talk about how the world views a Web service, then how Microsoft views Web services.

Early Architectural Designs

An understanding of the history of the search for a decent *remote method invocation* (RMI) protocol is imperative to our understanding of why Web services are so important. Each of the RMI systems created before Web services solved a particular set of problems, and we will see how Web services represents the next evolution of these ideas and cross platform boundaries to solve the problems these other technologies tried to address.

The Network Angle

Throughout the history of computing, the networking operations were largely handled by the operating system. UNIX, the networking host of early computing, featured a body of shell operations that gave remarkable user control over the operations of the network. Personal computing was slower to catch up: Microsoft and Apple software didn't inherently support networking protocols until the mid 1990s. Third party add-ons by Novell and Banyan were available earlier, but they were only an adjunct to the operating system. The concept of the network being the computer didn't fully infiltrate the development community until the expansion of the World Wide Web.

Application Development

Let's break from networking for a minute and look at how application development progressed through this time. Early time-sharing operation systems allowed several people to use the same application with its built-in data. These single tier systems didn't allow for growth in the system size, and data redundancy became the standard, with nightly batch jobs synchronizing the data becoming commonplace through the seventies and early eighties.

Eventually, the opportunity presented by networks became the overriding factor in systems development, and enterprise network developers began offering the loosely termed *Object Request Brokers* (ORBs) on their systems: Microsoft's MTS, *Common Object Request Broker Architecture* (CORBA), and the like. These ORBs allowed for the separation of the user interface from the business logic using tightly coupled method pooling. This three-tier architecture brings us to the present in development terms, so let's step back for a second and let networking catch up.

Merging the Two with the Web

The HTTP protocol was born in 1990. There had been several other information delivery protocols before, such as Gopher, but what made HTTP different were the extensibility of the related language, HTML, and the flexibility of the transport layer, TCP/IP. Suddenly movement of many formats of data was possible in a stateless, distributed way. Software-as-a-service was on its way.

Over the next decade, low-level protocols supported by network systems and the Internet became a staple in applications, with SMTP and FTP providing file and information transfer among distributed servers. *Remote procedure calls* (RPC) took things to the next level, but were platform specific, with UNIX implementations in CORBA and Microsoft's *Distributed COM* (DCOM) leading the pack.

Enterprise development took a clue from the emerging technologies in WAN networking and personal computing, and development for these large-scale business systems began to mature. As usage of networks grew, developers began to solve problems of scalability, reliability, and adaptability, with the traditional flat-format programming model. Multitier development began to spread the data, processing, and user interface of applications over several machines connected by local area networks.

This made applications more scalable and reliable by allowing for growth and providing redundancy. Gradually, vendor compliance and the Java programming language provided adaptability, allowing the applications to run in a variety of circumstances on a variety of platforms.

However, there was a dichotomy between the capabilities of the network and the features of the programming environment. Specifically, after the introduction of XML there still existed no "killer app" using its power. XML is a subset of Standard Generalized Markup Language (SGML), an international standard that describes the relationship between a document's content and its structure. It allows developers to create their own tags for hierarchical data transport in an HTML-like format. With HTTP as a transport and SOAP as a protocol, there still needed to be an interoperable, ubiquitous, simple, broadly supported system for the execution of business logic throughout the world of Internet Application development.

The Foundations of Web Services

The hunt began with a look at the existing protocols. As has been the case for years, the Microsoft versus Sun Alliance debate was heating up among RPC programmers. CORBA versus DCOM was, and continues to be, a source of continuing argument for developers using those platforms for distributed object development. After Sun added Remote Method Invocation to Java with Java-RMI, we had three distributed object protocols that fit none of the requirements we set out.

First, let's focus on DCOM and RMI, because they are manufacturer-specific. CORBA is centrally managed by the Object Management Group, so it is a special case and should be considered separately.

RMI and DCOM provide distributed object invocation for their respective platforms — extremely important in this era of distributed networks. Both allow for the enterprise-wide reuse of existing functionality, which dramatically reduces cost and time-to-market. Both provide encapsulated object methodology, preventing changes to one set of business logic from affecting another. Finally, similar to ORB-managed objects, maintenance and client weight are reduced by the simple fact that applications using distributed objects are by nature multitier.

DCOM

DCOM's best feature is the fact that it is based on COM, surely one of the most prevalent desktop object models in use today. COM components are shielded from one another, and calls between them are so well-defined by the OS-specific languages that there is practically no overhead to the methods. Each COM object is instantiated in its own space, with the necessary security and protocol providers. If an object in one process needs to call an object in another process, COM handles the exchange by intercepting the call and forwarding it through one of the network protocols.

When you use DCOM, all you are doing is making the wire a bit longer. In NT4 Microsoft added the TCP/IP protocol to the COM network architecture and essentially made DCOM Internet-savvy. Aside from the setup on the client and server, the inter-object calls are transparent to the client, and even to the programmer.

Any Microsoft programmer can tell you, though, that DCOM has its problems. First, there is a customer wire transport function, so most firewalls will not allow DCOM calls to get through, even though they are by nature quite benign. There is no way to query DCOM about the methods and properties available, unless you have the opportunity to get the source code or request the remote component locally. In addition, there is no standard data transfer protocol (though that is less of a problem since DCOM is mostly for Microsoft networks).

Remote Method Invocation in Java

RMI is Sun's answer to DCOM. Java relies on a really neat, but very proprietary, protocol called Java Object Serialization, which protects objects marshaled as a stream. The client and server both need to be constructed in Java for this to work, but it simplifies remote method invocation even more, as Java doesn't care if the serialization takes place on one machine or across a continent. Similar to DCOM, RMI allows the object developer to define an interface for remote access to certain methods.

CORBA

CORBA uses Internet Inter-ORB Protocol to provide remote method invocation. It is remarkably similar to Java Object Serialization in this regard. Since it is only a specification, though, it is supported by a number of languages on diverse operating systems. With CORBA, the ORB does all the work, such as finding the pointer to the parent, instantiating it so that it can receive remote requests, carrying messages back and forth, and dispute arbitration and trash collection. The CORBA objects use specially designed sub-ORB objects balled Basic or Portable Object Adapters to communicate with remote ORBs, allowing developers more leeway in code reuse.

At first sight, it seems CORBA is our ace-in-the-hole. There is only one problem, it doesn't really work that way. CORBA suffers from the same thing the Web browsers do — poor implementations of the standards, causing lack of interoperability between Object Request Brokers. With IE and Netscape, a little differential in the way the pages display is written off as cosmetic. If there is a problem with the CORBA standard though, it is a *real* problem. Not just looks are affected, but network interactions too, as if there were 15 different implementations of HTTP.

The Problems

The principal problem of the DCOM/CORBA/RMI methods is the complexity of the implementation. The transfer protocol of each of these is based on manufacturers' standards, generally preventing interoperability. In essence, the left hand has to know what the right hand is doing. This prevents a company using DCOM from communicating with a company using CORBA, emphasizing platform as a reason for doing business with one another.

First, we have the problem of wire format. Each of these three methods uses an OS-specific wire format that encompasses information only supplied by the operating system in question. The problem with this is that two diverse machines cannot usually share information. The benefit is security; since the client and server can make assumptions about the availability of functionality, data security can be managed with API calls to the operating system.

The second problem is the number of issues associated with describing the format of the protocol. Apart from the actual transport layer, we have to have a schema or layout for the data that moves back and forth. Each of the three contemporary protocols makes great assumptions between the client and server. DCOM, for instance, provides ADO/RDS for data transport, whereas RMI has JDBC. While we can endlessly argue the benefits of one over the other, we'll agree on the fact that they don't play well together.

The third problem is how to know where to find broadly available services, even within your own network. We've all faced the problem of having to call up the COM+ MMC panel so we could remember how to spell this component or that method. When the method is resident on a server 10 buildings over and we don't have access to the MMC console, the next step is digging through the text documentation, if there is any.

The Other Players

On a path to providing these services, we stumble across a few other technologies. While *Java Applets* and Microsoft's *client-side ActiveX* aren't technically distributed object invocation, they do provide distributed computing and provide important lessons. Fortunately, we can describe both in the same section since they are largely the same, with different operating systems as their backbone.

Applets and client-side ActiveX are both attempts to use the HTTP protocol to send thick clients to the end user. In a circumstance where a user can provide a platform previously prepared to maintain a thicker-than-HTML client base to a precompiled binary, the ActiveX and Applet protocols pass small applications to the end user, usually running a Web browser. These applications are still managed by their servers, at least loosely, and usually provide custom data transmission, utilizing the power of the client to manage the information distributed, as well as display it.

This concept was taken to the extreme with *Distributed Applet-based Massively Parallel Processing*, a strategy that used the power of the Internet to complete processor-intense tasks like 3D rendering or massive economic models with a small application installed on the user's computer. If you view the Internet as a massive collection of parallel processors, sitting mostly unused, you have the right idea. An example of this type of processing is provided by United Devices (`http://www.ud.com`).

What we learned here is that HTTP can provide distributed computing. The problem we discovered is that the tightly coupled connection between the client and server had to go, given the nature of today's large enterprises. The HTTP angle did show developers that using an industry recognized transport method did solve problem number one, that is wire format. Using HTTP meant that no matter what the network, the object could communicate. The client still had to know a lot about the service being sent, but the network didn't.

The goal is *Distributed Object Invocation Meets the World Wide Web*. The problems that face us are wire format, protocol, and discovery. The solution is a standards-based, loosely-coupled method invocation protocol with a huge catalog. Microsoft, IBM, and Ariba set out in 1999 to create just that, and generated the RFC for Web services.

What All the Foundations Missed

You may notice that in reviewing the majority of the earlier services we have not mentioned much about language. This is because it was a problem that was overlooked by the foundations. Even RMI didn't see reality that you can't make everyone use the same language, even if it is a great language.

HTTP — A Language Independent Protocol

What we really need is a language independent protocol that allows for a standard wire transfer, protocol language, and catalog service. Java and Remote Scripting and ActiveX taught us that HTTP is the wire transfer of choice.

Why is this? What does HTTP do that is so great? First, it is simple. The header added to a communication by HTTP is straightforward enough that a power user could type it at a command prompt if he had to. Second, it doesn't require a special data protocol, it just uses ASCII text. Finally, it is extensible. Additional headers can be added to the HTTP header for application specific needs, and intermediary software just ignores it.

XML — Cross-Language Data Markup

Now that we have the standard wire transfer protocol that we know works, we need a language and a transport mechanism. Existing languages don't really have data description functions, aside from the data management object models like ADO. XML fits the bill because it is self-describing. There's no need for the left hand to know what the right hand is doing. An XML file transported over HTTP doesn't need to know the answering system's network protocol or its data description language. The concepts behind XML are so light and open; everyone can agree to support them. In fact, almost everyone has. XML has become the ASCII of the Web.

XML is important to Web services because it provides a universal format for information to be passed from system to system. We knew that, but Web services actually uses XML as the object invocation layer, changing the input and output to tightly formatted XML so to be platform and language independent.

SOAP — The Transfer We Need

Enter Simple Object Access Protocol (SOAP), which uses HTTP to package essentially one-way messages from service to service in such a way that business logic can interpolate a request/response pair. In order for your Web page to get the above listing, for instance, a SOAP request would look something like this:

```
POST /Directory HTTP/1.1
Host: Ldap.companyname.com
Content-Type: text/xml;
charset="utf-8"
Content-Length: 33
SOAPAction: "Some-URI"

<SOAP-ENV:Envelope
 xmlns:SOAP-ENV="http://schemas.xmlsoap.org/soap/envelope/"
 SOAP-ENV:encodingStyle="http://schemas.xmlsoap.org/soap/encoding/">
  <SOAP-ENV:Body>
    <m:FindPerson xmlns:m="Some-URI">
      <NAME>sempf</NAME>
    </m: FindPerson>
  </SOAP-ENV:Body>
</SOAP-ENV:Envelope>
```

This is an HTTP page request, just like you'd see for an HTML page except the `Content-Type` specifies XML and there is the addition of the `SOAPAction` header. SOAP has made use of the two most powerful parts of HTTP — content neutrality and extensibility. Here is the response statement from the server:

```
HTTP/1.1 200 OK
Content-Type: text/xml;
```

```
charset="utf-8"
Content-Length: 66

<SOAP-ENV:Envelope
 xmlns:SOAP-ENV="http://schemas.xmlsoap.org/soap/envelope/"
 SOAP-ENV:encodingStyle="http://schemas.xmlsoap.org/soap/encoding/"/>
  <SOAP-ENV:Body>
    <m:FindPersonResponse xmlns:m="Some-URI">
      <DIRECTORY>Employees
      <PERSON>
         <NAME>Bill Gates</NAME>
         <FUNCTION>Architect
            <TYPE>Web Services</TYPE>
         </FUNCTION>
         <CONTACT>
            <PHONE TYPE=CELL>123-456-7890</PHONE>
            <PHONE TYPE=HOME>555-111-2222</PHONE>
         </CONTACT>
      </PERSON>
      </DIRECTORY>
    </m: FindPersonResponse >
  </SOAP-ENV:Body>
</SOAP-ENV:Envelope>
```

SOAP allows us to send the XML files back and forth among remote methods. It is tightly similar to XML-RPC, a protocol developed by Dave Winer in parallel with the SOAP protocol. Both protocols provide similar structures, but it is the official SOAP protocol that is used by VB.NET and the entire .NET platform.

SOAP isn't specific to .NET, either. The SOAP Toolkit is another set of tools that Microsoft's Web Services Team provides free of charge. It contains a wonderful WSDL editor, retrofit objects for Windows 2000 and NT4 boxes, and more. You can find it at http://msdn.microsoft.com/webservices.

Web Services Description Language

A Web Services Description Language (WSDL) document is a set of definitions. Six elements are defined and used by the SOAP protocol: types, message, portType, binding, port, and service. Essentially adding another layer of abstraction, the purpose of WSDL is to isolate remote method invocations from their wire transport and data definition language. Once again, it is a specification, not a language, so it is much easier to get companies to agree to its use.

As WSDL is just a set of descriptions in XML; it has not so much a protocol as a grammar. Following is the sample service contract for the UpdateRemote Web service we'll be building later in the chapter. You will be able to see this file by visiting http://localhost/WebService1/Service1.asmx?WSDL using your Web browser after you install the samples:

```
<?xml version="1.0" encoding="utf-8" ?>
<definitions xmlns:s="http://www.w3.org/2001/XMLSchema"
  xmlns:http="http://schemas.xmlsoap.org/wsdl/http/"
  xmlns:mime="http://schemas.xmlsoap.org/wsdl/mime/"
  xmlns:tm="http://microsoft.com/wsdl/mime/textMatching/"
```

```
     xmlns:soap="http://schemas.xmlsoap.org/wsdl/soap/"
     xmlns:soapenc="http://schemas.xmlsoap.org/soap/encoding/"
     xmlns:s0="http://Localhost/WebService1"
     targetNamespace="http://Localhost/WebService1"
     xmlns="http://schemas.xmlsoap.org/wsdl/">
<types>
 <s:schema attributeFormDefault="qualified" elementFormDefault="qualified"
     targetNamespace="http://Localhost/WebService1">
  <s:import namespace="http://www.w3.org/2001/XMLSchema" />
   <s:element name="AcceptUpdate">
    <s:complexType>
     <s:sequence>
      <s:element minOccurs="1" maxOccurs="1" name="dsDataSet"
                nillable="true">
       <s:complexType>
        <s:sequence>
       <s:element ref="s:schema" />
       <s:any />
      </s:sequence>
     </s:complexType>
    </s:element>
   </s:sequence>
  </s:complexType>
 </s:element>
 <s:element name="AcceptUpdateResponse">
  <s:complexType>
   <s:sequence>
    <s:element minOccurs="1" maxOccurs="1" name="AcceptUpdateResult"
      type="s:boolean" />
   </s:sequence>
  </s:complexType>
 </s:element>
</s:schema>
  </types>
<message name="AcceptUpdateSoapIn">
 <part name="parameters" element="s0:AcceptUpdate" />
</message>
<message name="AcceptUpdateSoapOut">
 <part name="parameters" element="s0:AcceptUpdateResponse" />
</message>
<portType name="Service1Soap">
 <operation name="AcceptUpdate">
  <input message="s0:AcceptUpdateSoapIn" />
  <output message="s0:AcceptUpdateSoapOut" />
 </operation>
</portType>
<portType name="Service1HttpGet" />
 <portType name="Service1HttpPost" />
  <binding name="Service1Soap" type="s0:Service1Soap">
   <soap:binding transport="http://schemas.xmlsoap.org/soap/http"
     style="document" />
   <operation name="AcceptUpdate">
   <soap:operation soapAction="http://Localhost/WebService1/AcceptUpdate"
     style="document" />
```

```
   <input>
    <soap:body use="literal" />
   </input>
   <output>
    <soap:body use="literal" />
   </output>
  </operation>
 </binding>
 <binding name="Service1HttpGet" type="s0:Service1HttpGet">
  <http:binding verb="GET" />
   </binding>
 <binding name="Service1HttpPost" type="s0:Service1HttpPost">
  <http:binding verb="POST" />
 </binding>
 <service name="Service1">
  <port name="Service1Soap" binding="s0:Service1Soap">
   <soap:address location="http://localhost/WebService1/Service1.asmx" />
  </port>
  <port name="Service1HttpGet" binding="s0:Service1HttpGet">
   <http:address location="http://localhost/WebService1/Service1.asmx" />
  </port>
  <port name="Service1HttpPost" binding="s0:Service1HttpPost">
   <http:address location="http://localhost/WebService1/Service1.asmx" />
  </port>
 </service>
 </definitions>
```

This is what makes it all work. You'll notice that each of the inputs and outputs of the `AcceptUpdateResponse` function are defined as elements in the schema. .NET uses this to build library files that understand how best to format the outgoing requests, so no matter what operating system develops the WSDL, as long as it is well formed, a Windows application can consume it with SOAP and .NET.

In fact, IIS with the .NET Framework is set up to use the WSDL to provide a great user interface for developers and consumers to check out and test Web services. If you remove the *?wsdl* from the preceding URL, you'll see a very nicely formatted documentation screen for the service. Click the function name and you'll get the screen shown in the following figure. This is all dynamically generated from the WSDL document, which is dynamically generated from ASP.NET code. Abstraction makes it all work, as shown here in Figure 22-2.

The benefit to knowing how WSDL works is being able to define your own descriptions. More documentation would be available on the listing of functions screen before this one, had we added it to the WSDL. Also, we could manually define HTTP POST and GET schemas, though it wouldn't do much good since the sole function of this particular service is to pass a Microsoft-specific DataSet.

Building a Web Service

Building Web services with Visual Studio .NET (VS.NET) is *incredibly* easy. Microsoft has made it a cakewalk to put together a new Web service application and expose methods off of that Web service.

To get started, all you need is an ASP.NET Web service application. Visual Studio will ask you for the location of the Web server. Enter this as `http://localhost/MyWebService`.

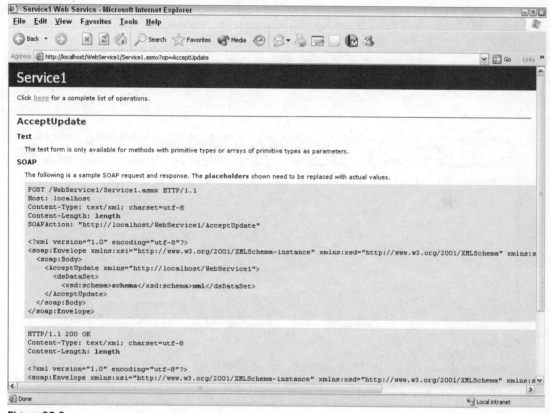

Figure 22-2

Unlike an ASP.NET Web Aaplication project, Visual Studio will create an `.asmx` file rather than an `.aspx` file. .asmx is short for Active Server Methods, and its name comes from the fact that what we're going to do is add methods that will be exposed through the Web service.

By default, the Designer for the new Service1.asmx file will appear. Right-click the Designer and select View Code; you'll notice a commented out `HelloWorld` method. You'll also notice that this method is decorated with `<WebMethod()>`. This attribute (`System.Web.Services.WebMethodAttribute`) is what we use to tell ASP.NET that we want to expose this method over the Web service.

Uncomment the `HelloWorld` method, leaving the `WebMethod` attribute in place:

```
<WebMethod()> _
  Public Function HelloWorld() As String
    HelloWorld = "Hello World"
  End Function
```

Next, add a new method called `GoodbyeWorld`, without a `WebMethod` attribute:

```
Public Function GoodbyeWorld() As String
  GoodbyeWorld = "Goodbye World"
End Function
```

Run the project and VS .NET will open the `Service1.asmx` file. By default, Web services display a test interface (see Figure 22-3) that lets you see which methods are available, and also lets you execute the methods.

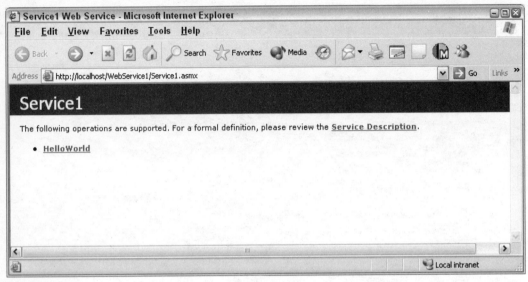

Figure 22-3

Notice, how we can only see the `HelloWorld` method. This is the only method decorated with the `WebMethod` attribute, hence the reason why `GoodbyeWorld` and all of the inherited methods on the `Service1` class were not displayed.

If you click the link, you'll be given the option to invoke the method, as shown in Figure 22-4.

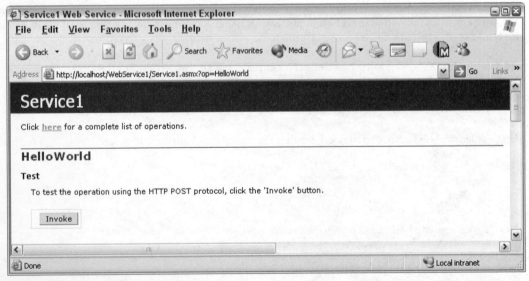

Figure 22-4

If you do this, the URL http://localhost/MyWebService/Service1.asmx/HelloWorld? will be requested, which happens to be the URL for this specific method. You'll then see the payload of the SOAP document directly in the browser which contains the results of the call as illustrated in Figure 22-5.

Figure 22-5

That's pretty much all there is to Web services from an implementation perspective in .NET. .NET deals with all of the plumbing that we discussed in the first part of this chapter (SOAP, WSDL, and so on), which means that all we have to do is add properly decorated methods to the service.

A Realistic Example

Although the example we saw before was very easy to implement, it doesn't demonstrate a real world application of Web services. Let's look at a more realistic example by building a Web service that updates a Web site from the data in an intranet. For the sake of example, we'll imagine that a third party provider hosts the site. Our SQL Server and the hosting company's SQL Server are behind firewalls, and the Internet Information Server is in a demilitarized zone—a safe, though exposed, network position. This is illustrated in Figure 22-6.

In order to get the data from our site to the remote site, we'll call a Web service on the remote Web server from our intranet. Since the SOAP envelope is sent via HTTP, our firewall will allow it through, and ADO.NET on the IIS box will handle the actual database manipulation. The remote firewall will allow database calls only from the IIS box, and our data will be updated safely through the security.

In real life, the class file `UpdateRemote` would be local to our intranet server, and the database file would be a SQL Server on a second PC. Across the Internet, as shown in the diagram, the Web service would be on an IIS box sitting outside the network firewall. The DLL that actually provides the data functions would be on an application server inside the firewall and the database would again be on a separate machine.

For our application, though, we'll have two SQL Server databases (called `ItemsLocal` and `ItemsRemote`) on the same server. Both databases will have a single table, `Items`. This will have fields called `ItemId`, `Description`, and `Quantity`. Open the `ItemsLocal` file and add a few sample items.

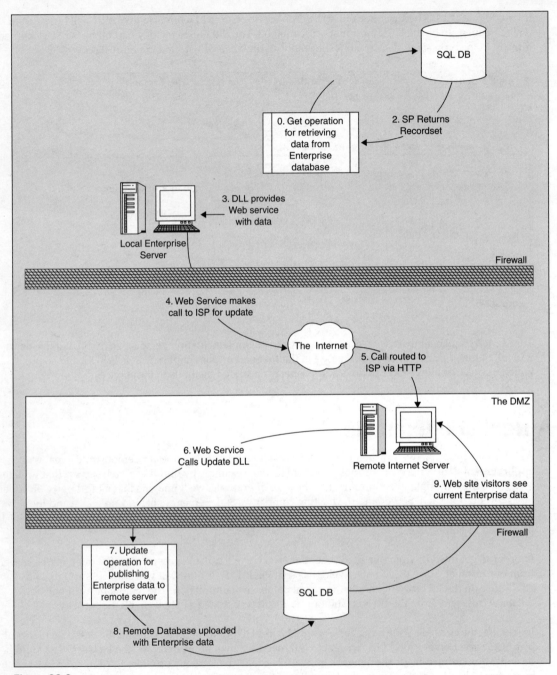

Figure 22-6

Using Visual Studio .NET to Build Web Services

The VS.NET IDE shows a marked improvement from the add-ins provided for Visual Studio 6 in the SOAP Toolkit. For instance, Web services are shown as references on a project, rather than in a separate dialog box. The discovery process, discussed later, is used to its fullest, providing much more information to the developer. In short, it is nearly as easy to consume a Web service with VB.NET as it is to use DLLs.

After providing a URL, VB.NET creates four new files, including a blank `.asmx` file called `Service1.asmx`, a `Global.asax` file, an `AssemblyInfo.vb` file, and a `Web.config` file.

Make a DataSet

For simplicity, we'll use the DataSet Designer feature of VS.NET. The DataSet Designer will allow us to quickly and easily create the data access we need, without having to dig through lots of ADO.NET code.

Right-click the WebService1 project in the Solution Explorer and select Add ⇨ Add New Item. One of the options is a new DataSet, accept the default name of `Dataset1.xsd`. This creates a new DataSet schema on the fly, and it's already strongly typed for us.

In the Server Explorer window, right-click Data Connections and select Add Connection. Make sure you select the Microsoft OLE DB Provider for SQL Server from the Provider tab (this is the default setting), and your server's name and login information in the Connection tab. Select ItemsRemote as the database to which we want to connect and click OK.

If it's not already open; double-click the `Dataset1.xsd` file in the Solution Explorer. Then, go back to the Server Explorer, expand the data connection we just made and drag the `Items` table on to the designer surface of `Dataset1.xsd`.

The layout of our table appears in the schema file, and we have access to the data we need. This database should be empty of data, since we didn't put anything in it, but we'll change that when we consume the service.

Build the Service

Right-click `Service1.asmx` from within the Solution Explorer of VS.NET and select View Code. Rename the `HelloWorld` function to `AcceptUpdate` and have it take a `DataSet` as a parameter. Then, we simply add code to merge the DataSet in the class file, which we just added, to the DataSet passed to the method. The block of IDE code in the `#Region` segment remains unchanged:

```
Imports System.Web.Services

<System.Web.Services.WebService(Namespace := _
    "http://tempuri.org/MyWebService/Service1")> _
Public Class Service1
    Inherits System.Web.Services.WebService

'...

<WebMethod()> _
Public Function AcceptUpdate(ByVal dsDataSet As DataSet) As Boolean

  Dim dsRemoteDataset As New Dataset1
```

```
        dsRemoteDataset.Merge(dsDataSet)
        dsRemoteDataset.AcceptChanges()
        dsRemoteDataset = Nothing

    End Function

    End Class
```

Right-click the `Service1.asmx` file in the Solution Explorer and select Build With. If there are no errors, you'll see a simple screen listing `AcceptUpdate` as the sole method of the service. Click AcceptUpdate and you'll get a screen like that earlier shown in the *Web Services Description Language* section. No HTTP form is provided because our service doesn't support HTTP POST or GET. Complex objects are only served by SOAP and are therefore, not testable from this autogenerated page.

Consuming the Service

For our consuming application, we will provide a class file called `UpdateRemote`, so create a new Class Library project and the class within it both with that name. For now, we'll have a single function called `sendData`. This time we'll code the DataSet by hand, since we need to use the `DataAdapter` to fill it with data from the local database.

Add a Web Reference

The only bit of magic here is the adding of a Web reference to the project with the VS.NET IDE. As we'll see later, we are really creating a proxy DLL with the WSDL file of the service and referencing it in the project, but the IDE makes it very easy.

Right-click the UpdateRemote project in the Solution Explorer and select Add Web Reference. You'll see a simple form that advertises Microsoft UDDI services. Enter the URL of our service in the Address bar, this would be at the ISP in our real life scenario, but if you've been following along it'll be `http://localhost/webservice1/service1.asmx`. The dialog box should appear as displayed in Figure 22-7.

The service description page we've just seen when we built our service appears in the left pane, with .NET specific information in the right. Click the Add Reference button at the bottom of the window to add this to the project. The service appears in a new folder in the Solution Explorer, Web References, as illustrated in Figure 22-8.

One Line of Code

The COM architecture continually promised "one line of code" to generate great results. Web services live up to the promise, minus the declarations. We now need only call the referenced Web service and pass the generated DataSet, and we are done. Compared to the scores of lines of XML we would have to write to pass the DataSet in the existing Microsoft technologies, this is a breeze.

To accomplish this, let's add the `sendData` function to the `UpdateRemote` class:

```
    Public Class UpdateRemote
```

```
    Function sendData() As Boolean
        Dim wsRemoteUpdate As New localhost.Service1
        Dim dsLocalData As DataSet = New DataSet
        Dim strSQL As String
```

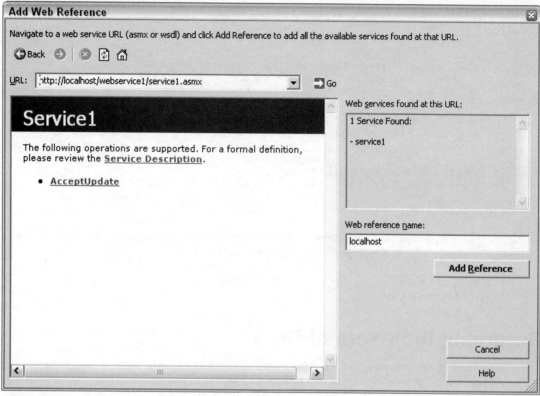

Figure 22-7

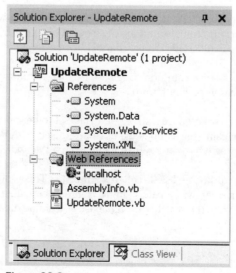

Figure 22-8

```
       Dim strConn As String
       Dim objDA As SqlClient.SqlDataAdapter

       strConn = "Data Source=(local);User ID=sa;password=;" & _
                 "Initial Catalog=ItemsLocal"
       strSQL = "SELECT * FROM Items"

       objDA = New SqlClient.SqlDataAdapter(strSQL, strConn)
       objDA.Fill(dsLocalData, "Items")

       'Call the Web Service, passing the DataSet
       wsRemoteUpdate.AcceptUpdate(dsLocalData)
    End Function
```

```
End Class
```

Right-click the UpdateRemote project and select Build. If there are no errors, generate a test container and the `UpdateRemote.dll`. You'll need to use the following lines of code:

```
Dim objRemote As New UpdateRemote.UpdateRemote()
objRemote.sendData()
```

Returning Rich Sets of Data

So far we've seen that we can return something as simple as a string (as in our first example) and that we can also return and pass more complicated objects around, like a DataSet.

> **Web services can handle any type of data that can be serialized.**

In Chapter 21 we spent some time talking about serialization. Specifically, we were talking about how the process can take a rich object and transform it into a string of bytes for transmission down a wire. We also spoke about the HTTP/SOAP and TCP/Binary channel/formatter combinations.

Remoting and Web services share a common code base (in fact, Remoting is like an extensible, semiproprietary Web services implementation).

What actually happens when we prepare a string or a DataSet to be sent from client to server or from server to client is that we're using the same SOAP formatter used with Remoting. Therefore, any object that can be serialized can be sent back as a return value from a Web service.

Create a solution in Visual Studio .NET 2003 called `RichData`. This will contain the single `.asmx` page called `Service1.asmx`. We will create a single WebMethod called `GetCutomers` which will return the Customers table from the Northwind database as a single dataset. This is illustrated here in the following code listing:

```
Imports System.Web.Services
Imports System.Data
Imports System.Data.SqlClient
```

```
<System.Web.Services.WebService(Namespace="http//RichData/Service1")> _
Public Class Service1
    Inherits System.Web.Services.WebService


    <WebMethod()> _
    Public Function GetCustomers() As DataSet
        Dim conn As SqlConnection
        Dim da As SqlDataAdapter
        Dim cmdString As String = "Select * From Customers"
        Dim ds As DataSet = New DataSet


        conn = New SqlConnection _
          ("Server=localhost;uid=sa;pwd=password;database=Northwind")
        da.Fill(ds)


        Return ds
    End Function
End Class
```

Run the project and click the GetCustomers method link. Click the Invoke button and you will see the following results as shown in Figure 22-9.

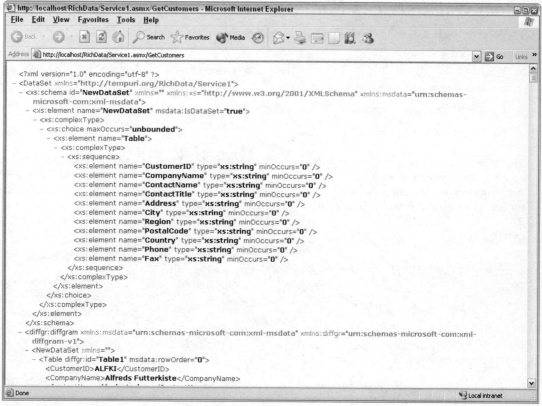

Figure 22-9

By compiling and running the XML Web service, you are able to pull out of the database the entire Customers table. A returned DataSet contains a wealth of information, including:

❑   An XSD definition of the XML that is contained in the DataSet

❑   All the customer information from the Customers table of the Northwind database

Then on the consumption side, consumers of this XML Web service can easily use the XSD definition and the XML that is contained within the DataSet within their own applications. If consumers are then consuming this DataSet into .NET applications, they can easily bind this data to a DataGrid and use it within their applications with minimal lines of code.

VB .NET and System.Web.Services

The SOAP toolkit provided a number of wizards to accomplish most of the obstacle course required to set up a Web service, but the .NET Framework class library provides the abstract classes. The System.Web.Services namespace provides four classes and three other namespaces that allow programmatic exposure of methods to the Web.

System.Web.Services Namespace

The System.Web.Services namespace includes these component classes:

❑   WebService

❑   WebMethodAttribute

❑   WebServiceAttribute

❑   WebServicesBindingAttribute

The WebService class is the base class from which all the ASP.NET services are derived, and includes access to the public properties for Application, Context, Server, Session, Site, and User. ASP programmers will recognize these objects from the ASP namespace. Web services can access the IIS object model from the WebService class, such as application-level variables:

```
<%@ WebService Language="VB" Class="Util"%>

Imports System.Web.Services

Public Class Util
    Inherits WebService

<WebMethod(Description = "Application Hit Counter", _
         EnableSession = "False")> _
Public Function HitCounter() As String

    If (Application("HitCounter") = null) Then
      Application("HitCounter") = 1
    Else
```

```
        Application("HitCounter") = Application("HitCounter") + 1
    End If
    HitCounter = Application("HitCounter")

End Function

End Class
```

WebService is an optional base class. If you don't need access to ASP.NET objects, you don't have to use it. The WebMethodAttribute class, however, is a necessity if you want your class to be available over the Web.

The WebServiceAttribute class is similar to the WebMethodAttribute class in that it allows you to add the description string to an entire class, rather than method by method. We'd add it before the previous class declaration:

```
<WebService(Description="Common Server Variables")> _
Public Class ServerVariables
    Inherits WebService
```

Instead of using WSDL in the contract to describe these services, the System.Web.Services namespace provides programmatic access to these properties. IIS Service Discovery will use these descriptions when queried. This way we have removed the necessity to struggle with the myriad of protocols surrounding Service Contract Language and SOAP.

System.Web.Services.Description Namespace

The System.Web.Services.Description namespace provides a host of classes that provide total management of the WSDL Descriptions for your Web service. This object manages every element in the WSDL schema as a class property.

Let's look at an example. In our preceding discussion on the benefits of WSDL description, we mentioned the benefits of being able to query a Web service about its methods and parameters. The System.Web.Services.Description namespace provides methods for the discovery of methods and parameters, gathering the information from the service contract and providing it to the object model in our VB.NET code.

If we are working on the HTTP-GET protocol (as opposed to SOAP, for instance), the HttpGetRequestResponseInfo class provides access to the information we can find in the contract in the <requestResponse> element. In the serviceDescription element, we find all parameter info for all three protocols, including HTTP GET.

```
<httpget xmlns="urn:schemas-xmlsoap-org:get-sdl-2000-01-25">
  <service>
   <requestResponse name="IsValidEmail"
      href="http://aspx.securedomains.com/sempf/validate.asmx/IsValidEmail">
   <request>
    <param name="sEmail"/>
   </request>
   <response>
```

```
        <mimeXml ref="s0:boolean"/>
      </response>
    </requestResponse>
  </service>
</httpget>
```

The parameter, sEmail, is shown in the schema as a request element. This is available to us in our
VB.NET code through the Request property of the HttpGetRequestResponseInfo object:

```
Imports System.Web.Services.Description

ReadOnly Property ExpectedParameters() As String
  Get
    ExpectedParameters = HttpGetRequestResponseInfo.Request
  End Get
End Property
```

System.Web.Services.Discovery Namespace

The System.Web.Services.Discovery namespace provides access to all of the wonderful features of
the .disco files on a dynamic basis. Since Microsoft is currently trying to integrate Web services as a
remoting protocol and not pushing the public service side as much, we don't see the use of .disco files
as often in the Microsoft side of things. Your business partner might be using them, though, so this
namespace proves useful. For instance, you can access the DiscoveryDocument using the Discovery
class:

```
Imports System.Web.Services.Discovery

ReadOnly Property DiscoveryDocument(strURL As String) As DiscoveryDocument
  Get
    DiscoveryDocument = DiscoveryClientProtocol.Discover(strURL)
  End Get
End Property
```

Like the System.Web.Services.Description namespace, the System.Web.Services
.Discovery namespace provides many tools to build a .disco document on the fly.

System.Web.Services.Protocols Namespace

All of the wire service problems we solved with HTTP and SOAP are handled here in the
System.Web.Services.Protocols namespace. Handling references to classes also referenced in
other Web services namespaces, the System.Web.Services.Protocols namespace will prove to be a
handy tool. The objects referenced by the System.Web.Services.Protocols namespace include
(among others):

❑   Cookies per RFC 2019

❑   HTML forms

❑   HTTP request and response

❑   MIME

- ❏ Server

- ❏ SOAP, including SOAPException, our only error handling mechanism

- ❏ URI and URLs

- ❏ XML

The `System.Web.Services.Protocols` namespace is particularly handy for managing the connection type by a client. A consumer of a Web service can use HTTP GET or HTTP POST to call a service, as well as HTTP SOAP. Microsoft's .NET initiative focuses on SOAP. The `System.Web.Services.Protocols.SoapDocumentMethodAttribute` class allows the developer to set special attributes of a public method for when a client calls it using SOAP:

```vb
<%@ WebService Language="VB" class="MyUser" %>

Imports System
Imports System.Web.Services
Imports System.Web.Services.Protocols

Public Class MyUser
    Inherits WebService

  <SoapDocumentMethod(Action="http://MySoapmethod.org/Sample", _
   RequestNamespace="http://MyNameSpace.org/Request", _
   RequestElementName="GetUserNameRequest", _
   ResponseNamespace="http://MyNameSpace.org/Response", _
   ResponseElementName="GetUserNameResponse") _
   WebMethod(Description="Obtains the User Name")> _
  Public Function GetUserName()
    '...
  End Function
End Class
```

Architecting with Web Services

Web services impart two remarkable benefits to users — one more obvious, another less so. First, they will replace common binary RPC formats, such as DCOM, CORBA, and RMI. Since these use a proprietary communication protocol, they are significantly less architecturally flexible than Web services. With appliances utilizing more and more of the Internet, platform neutrality will be a great advantage.

Less obvious but more importantly, Web services will be used to transfer structured business communication in a secure manner, potentially ending the hold Sterling has had on the EDI market. HTTPS with 128-bit SSL can provide the security necessary for intra-company information transfer. In addition to this, Microsoft has recently released Web Services Enhancements (WSE) which allows you to easily use WS-Security to apply credentials, encryption and digital signing to your SOAP messages in an easy and straightforward manner.

Why Web Services?

So why Web services? First, they are remarkably easy to deploy with VB.NET. The key to remoting with Web services is the SDL contract — written in the dense WSDL protocol we looked at earlier.

IIS 5.0 and 6.0 does that for you in conjunction with the .NET Framework, analyzing your VB code, and dynamically generating the WSDL code for the contract.

Also, they are inherently cross-platform, even if created with Microsoft products. Yes, we've heard this before, but so far this seems to be true. Since the standard XML schemas are centrally managed, and IBM mostly built the WSDL specification, Microsoft seems to have toed the line on this one.

Finally, they best represent where the Internet is going — toward an architecturally neutral collection of appliances, rather than millions of PCs surfing the World Wide Web. Encapsulating code so that you can simply and easily allow cell phones to use your logic is a major boon to developers, even if they don't know it yet.

How This All Fits Together

It is important to note that Web services are not a feature of the .NET Framework per se. In fact, Web services run fine on Windows NT4 SP6, with SOAP Toolkit installed. You can do most anything we are doing here with VB6 and IIS 4.0.

However, the .NET Framework encapsulates the Web services protocol into objects. It is now an integrated part of the strategy, rather than an add-on. If you are currently working in a VB6 environment, take a look at the SOAP toolkit, and understand that the services you build are available not only to different flavors of Windows, but to IBM and Sun platforms as well.

The goal of Web services is to provide a loosely coupled, ubiquitous, universal information exchange format. Toward that end, SOAP is not the only mechanism for communicating with Web services — HTTP GET and HTTP POST are also supported by .NET. Response is via HTTP, just like normal RPCs with SOAP. This allows legacy Web applications to make use of Web services without the benefit of the .NET Framework.

Web Service Proxies

When you make a Web reference to an XML Web service using VS.NET, it will automatically create a proxy class for you within the project. To actually see the proxy class for yourself, you simply need to click the Show All Files button within the Solution Explorer and drill down into the Web reference that VS.NET created for you. Here you will find a `Reference.vb` file. This is the proxy class itself.

You can create proxy classes either by using VS.NET, by hand, or by using the .NET Framework's `wsdl.exe` utility.

State Management for XML Web Services

The Internet is *stateless* by nature. Many of the same techniques that you would use for managing state in your ASP.NET Web applications is the same techniques you can use within your XML Web services that you build on the .NET platform. Remember that XML Web services are part of the ASP.NET model and both application types have the same objects at their disposal.

So, just like an ASP.NET application, your XML Web services can also use the `Application` object, or the `Session` object. These sessions can also be run in the same process as the XML Web service application itself, out-of-process, using the .NET StateServer, or by storing all the sessions within SQL Server.

In order to use sessions within your XML Web services that you will build on the .NET platform, you actually have to turn on this capability within the WebMethod attribute by using the EnableSession property. By default, the EnableSession property is set to False, so if you want to use the HTTPSessionState object, you will have to set this property to True. You would do this as shown here:

```
Imports System.Web.Services

<System.Web.Services.WebService(Namespace := _
  "http://tempuri.org/WebService1/Service1")
Public Class Service1
   Inherits System.Web.Services.WebService

   <WebMethod(EnableSession:=True)> _
   Public Function SessionCounter() As Integer
      If Session("Counter") Is Nothing Then
         Session("Counter") = 1
      Else
         Session("Counter") = CInt(Session("Counter")) + 1
      End If

      Return CInt(Session("Counter"))
   End Function
End Class
```

The EnableSession property goes directly in the parenthesis of the WebMethod declaration. This property takes a Boolean value and needs to be set to True in order to work with the Session object.

Using DNS as a Model

How does any computer know where to find a Web page? Every machine doesn't know every location of every page. Rather, there is a big catalog called *DNS* that is replicated by most Internet Service Providers, which translates domain names (like yahoo.com) into IP numbers (like 204.71.200.74).

The benefit of the DNS system is that it offers a further level of abstraction between the marketing and the wires. It's a lot easier to remember yahoo.com than 204.71.200.74. With Web services, it becomes even more important, as there is not only a function name, but also the parameters that we must remember.

Three things make up the *Web Service Repository*: a standard format, a language, and a database. We have already discovered the language, WSDL. This can be used to layout the discovery information we need to publicize our Web services. The format of choice is called *DISCO* (short for DISCOvery of all things). Finally, and most exciting is the Web services answer to DNS—*UDDI* (*Universal Description, Discovery, and Integration*). Let's talk about DISCO first.

DISCO

One way to enable a repository is to have applications that look for services. In order to implement this, we drop a DISCO document into the Web service directory—a file that an application can look for that enables the discovery of the Web services present in that directory, or on that machine. Alternatively, we can mark each particular service we would like to enable.

Web service discovery is the process of locating and interrogating Web service descriptions, which is a preliminary step for accessing a Web service. It is through the discovery process that Web service clients learn that a Web service exists, what its capabilities are, and how to properly interact with it.

Dynamic Discovery with IIS

Admittedly not as fun as it sounds, *dynamic discovery* is Web services' answer to the `robots.txt` file. Dynamic discovery automatically exposes Web services beneath a given URL on a Web site. By placing this document at the root of your service's directories you give a prospective consumer the opportunity to obtain information about all services contained in that directory or subdirectories.

To enable dynamic discovery for your Web services, you'll create a `<filename>.disco` document at the root of your Web services directory.

This XML file contains the *excluded* directories within the hierarchy, so that the dynamic discovery process knows where not to go to gather information about Web services:

```
<?xml version="1.0" ?>
<dynamicDiscovery xmlns="urn:schemas-dynamicdiscovery:disco.2000-03-17">
    <exclude path="_vti_cnf"/>
    <exclude path="_vti_pvt"/>
    <exclude path="_vti_log"/>
    <exclude path="_vti_script"/>
    <exclude path="_vti_txt"/>
</dynamicDiscovery>
```

In order for the dynamic discovery to be noticed by visiting consumers, you should refer to it in the `<head>` of your default HTML or ASP document.

```
<head>
  <link type='text/xml' rel='alternate' href='Default.disco'/>
  <title></title>
</head>
```

Or, if you have an XML page as your default:

```
<?xml-stylesheet type="text/xml" alternate="yes" href="default.disco" ?>
```

Dynamic discovery is the way to go with IIS; the discovery process is very well tuned. If you work with another Web server, though, or are a hands-on sort, you can roll-your-own discovery documents for each Web service.

A *discovery document* is just an XML file with references listed in the `discovery` hierarchy. Within the hierarchy, you can add as many service contracts as you have services, and references to other DISCO documents throughout the server:

```
<?xml version="1.0" ?>
<disco:discovery xmlns:disco="http://schemas.xmlsoap.org/disco"
                 xmlns:scl="http://schemas.xmlsoap.org/disco/scl">
  <scl:contractRef ref="http://ServerName/ServiceName.asmx?SDL"/>
  <scl:contractRef ref="http://ServerName/AnotherName.asmx?SDL"/>
```

```
    <scl:contractRef ref="http://ServerName/ThirdName.asmx?SDL"/>
    <disco:discoveryRef ref="Folder1/default.disco"/>
    <disco:discoveryRef ref="Folder2/default.disco"/>
    <disco:discoveryRef ref="Folder3/default.disco"/>
  </disco:discovery>
```

This is essentially what IIS will do for you using Dynamic Discovery.

The DISCO concept depends on the client knowing where to start. If you don't know that a business offers a particular Web service, you won't know where to look for a DISCO document. UDDI is all about changing that.

The UDDI Project

The DISCO format allows crawlers to index Web services just as they index Web sites. The robots.txt approach, however, is dependent on the ability of a crawler to locate each Web site and the location of the service description file on that Web site. The current system relies upon the interlocking nature of Web sites to crawl from site to site — there is no such visible connection between Web services. This leaves the programmer having to know where to begin looking for a Web service before he starts.

UDDI (*Universal, Description, Discovery, and Integration*) takes an approach that relies upon a distributed registry of businesses and their service descriptions implemented in a common XML format. You can learn all about UDDI at www.uddi.org, but we'll give you an introduction to it here and talk about how it relates to Microsoft in general and VB.NET in particular.

UDDI can be thought of as the Yellow Pages for Web services. UDDI is a means of defining a standard way to publish and discover information about Web services, so businesses can provide descriptions of their Web services in terms of an XML file with white, yellow, and green pages:

❑ The *white pages* include how and where to find the service

❑ The *yellow pages* include ontological classifications and binding information

❑ The *green pages* include the technical specification of the service

In the XML schema for UDDI, this breaks into four elements: businessEntity, businessService, bindingElements and metadata, or tModels. The tModels provide additional important technical information that falls outside the bindingElements element, but that is necessary for the consumption of the service once bound.

You can find the XML schema for this at http://www.uddi.org/schema/uddi_1.xsd but you don't have to understand it because UDDI provided an API that is built into the .NET Framework, as we'll see in the next section. Generally, though, each API function represents a publicly accessible SOAP message used to get or place information about a registry entry. For instance, the findService SOAP message lists available services based on the conditions specified in the arguments:

```
<find_service businessKey="uuid_key" generic="1.0" [ maxRows="nn" ]
              xmlns="urn:uddi-org:api" >
  [<findQualifiers/>]
  <name/> |  <categoryBag/> |  <tModelBag/>
</find_service>
```

The parameters it accepts include `maxRows`, `businessKey`, `findQualifiers`, `name`, `categoryBag`, and `tModelBag`. On success, it returns a `serviceList` as a SOAP response object. On the whole, it's not that much different from what we are used to in the COM world, except it is entirely an open standard.

Using UDDI

The best thing about UDDI is how easy it is to use. Many of us who started early in the Internet field remember filling out the InterNIC's domain add/change forms, and having our own representative at the NIC to help us when we were stuck. Now, though, the Web handles registration of services — you only need to really have a grasp of the discovery schema if you are going to build a registration site.

In fact, Microsoft has a UDDI mirror if its own at `http://uddi.microsoft.com/` where you can register your Web services, just like adding them to DNS or a search engine. Of course, you'll have to have a Microsoft Passport (another UDDI registered Web service) to do it, but it is a rather simple task. After registering against your Passport, you enter business and contact information that is stored in your UDDI registry. Then you can add your Web services.

Where UDDI is Headed

UDDI is the invisible fourth layer in the stack of protocols that represent Web services. Like DNS and HTTP, UDDI provides a needed interface between the SOAP messaging and the ubiquity of the service that is so important, but difficult to achieve.

Going forward, UDDI as an organization sees itself being a global provider of discovery services for the business-to-business Web services market, hosted throughout the world. For instance, software companies can build applications that customize themselves based on services information in the UDDI registry on installation. Online marketplaces can back their market sites with UDDI technology; to better serve the growing needs of B2B value-added services.

Future services planned by UDDI include extension of the technology far beyond the specifications in the Open Draft. Eventually, regional and hierarchical searches will be accomplished through simple, effective conventions. Their goal is much farther reaching than InterNICs was at the beginning — truly using the lessons learned in the past to shape the future.

Microsoft's commitment to UDDI is apparent from its use within Windows Server 2003. If you have Windows Server 2003 Enterprise Edition, you can enable your server to be a UDDI server as well as there is a UDDI database built right in.

Security in Web Services

When you open up a procedure call to remoting, you have the potential to fall prey to accidents, poor end-user implementation, and crackers. Any application design needs to include some level of security. Web services demand inclusion of security.

Security problems with Web services fall into two categories — that of interception, and that of unauthorized use. SOAP messages intercepted by crackers potentially expose private information like account numbers and passwords to the public. Unauthorized use at best costs money and at worst wreaks havoc within a system.

Very few of the concepts we are discussing here are things we would like to see in the hands of those wearing the black hats. Even the simple validation service handles e-mail addresses — a valuable commodity in this world of "opt in" spamming. If you add Social Security or account numbers to the service, then this becomes even more of a concern. Fortunately, the wire transport of choice — HTTPS — provides a 128-bit solution to our problems.

Also, as mentioned earlier, now by using Microsoft's Web Services Enhancements (WSE) capabilities, you can easily apply security standards such as WS-Security to your SOAP messages.

The Secure Sockets Layer

The Secure Sockets Layer, or SSL, is a protocol consumed by HTTP in the transfer of Internet data from the Web server to browser. On the Web, the process works like this:

1. The user calls a secure Web document, and a unique public key is generated for the client browser, using the server's root certificate

2. A message, encrypted with the server's public key, is sent from the browser

3. The server can decrypt the message using its private key

The protocol in the URI represents HTTP; if it were changed to HTTPS:

```
<address uri="https://aspx.securedomains.com/evjen/Validate.asmx" />
```

Then the service would make an SSL call to the server. Remember that SSL is significantly slower than HTTP, so you will suffer a performance hit. Given the sensitivity of much of the information passing over Web services, it is probably worth the slowdown.

Directory Level Security

We also have the option to code security into our applications. This solves different problems from SSL, and in fact you may wish to combine the two services for a complete security solution.

Unauthorized access is a potential problem for any remote system, but for Web services even more so. The open architecture of the system provides crackers with all the information they need to plan an attack. Fortunately, simplicity is often the best defense. Use of the NT security options already on your server is your best bet to defend against unauthorized users.

You can use NTFS permissions for individual directories within an application, and require users to provide a valid username and password combination if they wish to access the service.

Web service security is a large area to cover. For more information you should refer to the documentation included with the .NET Framework SDK.

The best approach to security is to use SSL and directory level security together. Though slow and at times inconvenient, it is a small price to pay for the heightened level of security. Though this is different from the traditional role-based COM+ security, it is still very effective for running information across the wire.

Other Types of Security

The Windows platform also provides for other forms of security. For instance, the Windows CryptoAPI supplies access to most of the commonly used encryption algorithms—outside from the protocols used in Secure Sockets Layer. Digital Certificates (sort of a personal form of SSL ServerCertificates) is now rapidly becoming a powerful force in security.

The Down Side

There is a down side to any distributed architecture. We've covered most of them in this chapter and suggested workarounds—security, state, speed, and connectivity. Let's go over them once more to help make sure that Web services are the way to go.

Security

The issue and solution of security problems is the management of client expectations. If Web services are built securely to begin with, there will be no instances to draw concern or scrutiny. Consider the security of everything you write. It's fairly easy, and the payoff is great.

State

State is less of a problem because in Windows DNA, Microsoft has been saying for years that n-tier statefulness has to go. Most developers are used to the idea and if you aren't then you need to get on the boat with the rest of us. Architect your solutions to be loosely coupled. That's what Web services are made to do.

Transactions

Web services are not made for transactional systems. If our Web server at MyCompany.com were to access a database at UPS for example, and the connection dropped in the middle, the lock on the database would remain without giving the network system at UPS a chance to solve the problem. Web services are by nature loosely coupled. They are not designed for tight transactional integration.

A common use of Web services, communication between differing systems, prompted a number of technology architects to design a number of XML transaction protocols like 2PC. These packages provide for a code of understanding between two systems that can assume that the network link will remain stable.

Speed and Connectivity

Speed and connectivity is going to be a continuing problem until we have the ubiquitous bandwidth George Gilder talks about in Telecosm. Right now, the majority of Internet devices that could really benefit from Web services—cell phones, PDAs—are stuck at the paltry 14,000-bits per second currently supported by most wireless providers.

For application development, this is a concern because when the router goes down, the application goes down. Right now, our intranets continue to function when our ISP drops the ISDN. With Web services running the links to our customers and suppliers, that ISDN line becomes the company lifeline. Redundancy of connections and a firm partnership with your service provider are the only solution.

Where We Go from Here

The cell phone is a listening device. It listens for a call to its network address from the cell network. When it receives one, it follows some logic to handle the call. Sound familiar? This works just like the RPC architecture, and will be the format for a new host of devices that listen for our Web services calls over the G3 wireless network.

The first lines of the W3C XML group's charter says:

> "Today, the principal use of the World Wide Web is for interactive access to documents and applications. In almost all cases, such access is by human users, typically working through Web browsers, audio players, or other interactive front-end systems. The Web can grow significantly in power and scope if it is extended to support communication between applications, from one program to another."

New business communication will be via XML and Web services, rather than EDI and VANs. Micropayment may actually become a reality. There are scores of promises that the Internet made since its inception that can be fulfilled with Web services and XML. It won't stop there, though. The power of listening devices will bring Web services development into user-to-user markets from business-to-business.

It sounds far-fetched, I know, but I hope you can see how the power of Web services on .NET could make it possible. SOAP isn't just about replacing the RPC architecture already out there. It is a fundamentally different way to think about the network as the platform.

Summary

In this chapter, we've looked at the need for an architecturally neutral, ubiquitous, easy-to-use, and interoperable system to replace DCOM, RMI, and CORBA. We've discussed how Web services fill the gaps successfully because HTTP is used as the language independent protocol, XML is its language (in WSDL) and transport mechanism, and SOAP allows us to package up messages for sending over HTTP.

Then, we moved on to look at how to create and consume our Web services programmatically using VB.NET. We discussed the abstract classes provided by the .NET Framework class library to set up and work with Web services. In particular, we looked at the `WebService`, `WebServiceAttribute`, `WebMethodAttribute`, and `WebServiceBindingAttribute` component classes of the `System.Web.Services` namespace, in addition to the `System.Web.Services.Description`, `System.Web.Services.Discovery`, and `System.Web.Services.Protocols` namespaces.

Next, we took a high-level look at some of the technologies supporting Web services — namely DISCO and UDDI — before briefly covering security in Web services.

Finally, we talked about some of the downsides to using any distributed architecture (Web services included) but we finished with an optimistic note on where Web services might take us in the future.

VB.NET and the Internet

In today's network-centric world, it's very likely that our applications will need to work with other computers over a private network, the public Internet, or both.

In this chapter, we'll be looking at how we can:

❑ Download resources from the Web

❑ Design our own communication protocols

❑ Reuse Internet Explorer in our applications

A good place to start working with network resources is to look at how we can download content from the Web.

Downloading Internet Resources

Downloading content from the Web is very easy, so we'll throw together a basic application before getting onto some more meaty topics. Our application will download HTML from a Web page and display it in a text box. Later on, we'll look at how we can display HTML properly by hosting Internet Explorer (IE) directly in our Windows Forms applications, but for now we'll just use plain text.

In order to download a Web page, we need to be able to identity the remote page that we wish to download, make a request of the Web server that can provide that page, listen for the response, and download the data for the resource.

The classes we're interested here are `System.Uri`, `System.Net.WebRequest`, `System.Net` `.HttpWebRequest`, and `System.Net.HttpWebResponse`:

❑ `System.Uri` is a useful general-purpose class for expressing a *Uniform Resource Identifier* (URI). A *Uniform Resource Locator* (URL) is a type of URI (although in reality the terms are so confused that they are often used interchangeably). A URI, however is "more than" a URL, which is why this .NET class is `Uri` and not `Url`. `System.Uri` has many properties for decoding a URI. For example, if we had a string like `www.pretendcompany.com:8080/myservices/myservice.asmx?WSDL`, we could use the `Port` property to extract the port number, the `Query` property to extract the query string, and so on.

❑ A `WebRequest` expresses some kind of Internet resource (so in my opinion a better name for this class would be `InternetRequest`, as the classes aren't specifically related to the Web protocol).

❑ Protocol-specific descendants of `WebRequest` carry out the actual request: `HttpWebRequest` expresses an HTTP download and `FileWebRequest` expresses a file download, for example `file:///c:/MyFile.txt`.

❑ An `HttpWebResponse` is returned once a connection to the Web server has been made and the resource is available to download.

There are another two major classes related to working with the Internet in the .NET Framework. One is `System.Net.WebClient` and the other is `System.Net.WebProxy`. `WebClient` is basically a helper class that wraps the request and response classes I've just mentioned. As this is a Professional level book, I'm going to show you what to do behind the scenes, in effect, reengineer what `WebClient` can do. I'll talk about `WebProxy` later, which allows us to explicitly define a proxy server to use for Internet communications.

Let's use these classes to build an application. Create a new Windows Application, create a new form, and add controls to it as shown in Figure 23-1.

Figure 23-1

The control names are: `textUrl`, `buttonGo`, and `textData`. The `Anchor` properties of the controls are set so that the form resizes properly. `textUrl` should be set to `Top, Left, Right`, `buttonGo` to `Top, Right`, and `textData` to `Top, Left, Bottom, Right`.

Add these namespace import declarations to the form's code:

```
Imports System.IO
Imports System.Net
Imports System.Text
```

To keep our code simple, we'll include all the functionality into the `Click` handler of `buttonGo`. In an ideal world, you want to break the code in the handler out to a separate method. This enriches the interface of the object and promotes good reuse.

The first thing we do here is create a new `System.Uri` based on the URL that the user enters into the text box:

```
Private Sub buttonGo_Click(ByVal sender As System.Object, _
    ByVal e As System.EventArgs) Handles buttonGo.Click
    Dim uri As New Uri(textUrl.Text)
```

Then, we'll illustrate some of the useful properties of `System.Uri`:

```
Dim builder As New StringBuilder
builder.Append("AbsolutePath: " & uri.AbsolutePath & ControlChars.CrLf)
builder.Append("AbsoluteUri: " & uri.AbsoluteUri & ControlChars.CrLf)
builder.Append("Host: " & uri.Host & ControlChars.CrLf)
builder.Append("HostNameType: " & uri.HostNameType.ToString() & _
               ControlChars.CrLf)
builder.Append("LocalPath: " & uri.LocalPath & ControlChars.CrLf)
builder.Append("PathAndQuery: " & uri.PathAndQuery & ControlChars.CrLf)
builder.Append("Port: " & uri.Port & ControlChars.CrLf)
builder.Append("Query: " & uri.Query & ControlChars.CrLf)
builder.Append("Scheme: " & uri.Scheme)
MsgBox(builder.ToString())
```

The shared `Create` method of `System.Net.WebRequest` is used to create the actual object that we can use to download the Web resource. Notice how we don't create an instance of `HttpWebRequest`; we're working with a return object of type `WebRequest`. However, we'll actually be given `HttpWebRequest` object, `WebRequest` chooses the most appropriate class to return based on the URI. This allows us to build our own handlers for different network resources that can be used by consumers who simply supply an appropriate URL.

To make the request and get the response back from the server (so ultimately we can access the data), we call the `GetResponse` method of `WebRequest`. In our case, we'll get an `HttpWebResponse` object — once more it's up to the implementation of the `WebRequest`-derived object, in this case `HttpWebRequest`, to return an object of the most suitable type.

If the request is not OK, we'll get an exception (which for the sake of simplicity we won't bother processing). If the request is OK, we can get the length and the type of the response using properties of the `WebResponse` object:

```
Dim request As WebRequest = WebRequest.Create(uri)
Dim response As WebResponse = request.GetResponse()
builder = New StringBuilder
builder.Append("Request type: " & request.GetType().ToString() & _
               ControlChars.CrLf)
builder.Append("Response type: " & response.GetType().ToString() & _
               ControlChars.CrLf)
builder.Append("Content length: " & response.ContentLength & _
               " bytes" & ControlChars.CrLf)
```

```
builder.Append("Content type: " & response.ContentType & _
            ControlChars.CrLf)
MsgBox(builder.ToString())
```

It just remains for us to download the information. We can do this through a stream (WebResponse objects return a stream by overriding GetResponseStream), and what's more, we can use a System.IO.StreamReader to download the whole lot in a single call by calling the ReadToEnd method. This method will only download text, so if you want to download binary data you'll have to use the methods on the Stream object directly, or use a System.IO.BinaryReader.

```
Dim stream As Stream = response.GetResponseStream()
Dim reader As New StreamReader(stream)
Dim data As String = reader.ReadToEnd()
reader.Close()
stream.Close()
textData.Text = data
End Sub
```

If you run the application, enter a URL of www.wrox.com, and click the Go button, you'll see debugging information about the URL as shown in Figure 23-2.

Figure 23-2

This is a simple URL. Our application tells us that the scheme is http, and the host name type is Dns. If, for example, we enter an IP into the URL to be requested rather than a host name, this type will come back as IPv4. This tells us where the host name came from, in this case, it's a general Internet hostname.

Next, our application as shown in Figure 23-3 provides information about the response.

Figure 23-3

Finally, we get to see the response data itself as illustrated in Figure 23-4.

Figure 23-4

Perhaps the most important exception to be aware of when using these classes is the `System.Net`
`.WebException` exception. If anything goes wrong on the `WebRequest.GetResponse` call, this
exception will be thrown. Among other things, this exception provides access to the `WebResponse` object
through the `Response` property. The `StatusCode` property of `WebResponse` tells you what actually
happened through the `HttpStatusCode` enumeration. For example, `HttpStatusCode.NotFound` is
the equivalent of the HTTP 404 status code.

Sockets

There may be times when you need to transfer data across a network (either a private network or the
Internet) when the existing techniques and protocols don't exactly suit your needs. For example, you
wouldn't be able to download resources using the techniques discussed at the start of this chapter; and
you can't use Web services (as described in Chapter 22) or Remoting (as described in Chapter 20). When
this happens, the best course of action is to roll your own protocol using *sockets*.

TCP/IP, and therefore, the Internet itself, is based on sockets. The principle is simple, establish a port at
one end and allow clients to "plug in" to that port from the other end. Once the connection is made,
applications can send and receive data through a stream. For example, HTTP nearly always operates
on port 80. So, a Web server opens a socket on port 80 and waits for incoming connections (Web
browsers, unless told otherwise, attempt to connect to port 80 in order to make a request of that Web
server).

In .NET, sockets are implemented in the `System.Net.Sockets` namespace, and use classes from
`System.Net` and `System.IO` to get the stream classes. Although working with sockets can be a little
tricky outside of .NET, the Framework includes some superb classes that enable you to open a socket for
inbound connections (`System.Net.TcpListener`) and for communication between two open sockets
(`System.Net.TcpClient`). These two classes, in combination with some threading shenanigans, allow
us build our own protocol, through which we can send any data we like. With our own protocol, we have
ultimate control over the communication.

To demonstrate these techniques we're going to build Wrox Messenger, a very basic instant messenger
application similar to MSN Messenger.

Building the Application

We'll wrap all the functionality of our application into a single Windows Application. This application will act as both a server that waits for inbound connections and as a client that established outbound connections.

Create a new project called WroxMessenger. Change the title of Form1 to Wrox Messenger and add a TextBox control called textConnectTo and a Button control called buttonConnect. Your form should appear as shown in Figure 23-5.

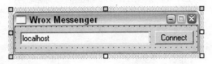

Figure 23-5

We'll talk about this in more detail in a little while, but for now you need to know that it's very important that all of our UI code runs in the same thread, and that the thread is actually the main application that creates and runs Form1.

To keep track of what's happening, we'll add a field to Form1 that allows us to store the ID of the startup thread, and also report that ID on the caption. This will help our understanding of the thread/UI issues that we will discuss later. We'll also need some namespace imports and a constant specifying the ID of the default port. Add this code to Form1:

```
Imports System.Net
Imports System.Net.Sockets
Imports System.Threading
Public Class Form1
    Inherits System.Windows.Forms.Form

    Private Shared _mainThreadId As Integer

    Public Const ServicePort As Integer = 10101
```

Next, open the Windows Form Designer generated code region and add this code to the constructor that populates the field and changes the caption:

```
Public Sub New()
    MyBase.New()

    'This call is required by the Windows Form Designer.
    InitializeComponent()

    'Add any initialization after the InitializeComponent() call
    _mainThreadId = Thread.CurrentThread.GetHashCode()
    Text &= "-" & _mainThreadId.ToString()

End Sub
```

To listen for incoming connections, we'll create a separate class called Listener. This class will use an instance of System.Net.Sockets.TcpListener to wait for incoming connections. Specifically, this will open a TCP port that *any* client can connect to—sockets are absolutely not platform specific. Although connections are always made on a specific, known port, the actual communication takes place on a port of the TCP/IP subsystems choosing, which means you can support many inbound connections at once, despite the fact that each of them connects to the same port. Sockets are an open standard available on pretty much any platform you care to mention. For example, if we publish the specification for our protocol, developers working on Linux would be able to connect to our Wrox Messenger service.

When we detect an inbound connection, we'll be given a `System.Net.Sockets.TcpClient` object. This is our gateway to the remote client. To send and receive data, we need to get hold of a `System.Net.NetworkStream` object (returned through a call to `GetStream` on `TcpClient`), which returns us a stream that we can use.

Create a new class called `Listener`. This thread needs members to hold an instance of a `System.Threading.Thread` object, and also a reference back to the `Form1` class that is the main form in the application. We won't go into a discussion of how to spin up and spin down threads, nor are we going to talk about synchronization. (You should refer back to Chapter 19 if you need more information on this.)

Here's the basic code for our `Listener` class:

```
Imports System.Net.Sockets
Imports System.Threading

Public Class Listener

  Private _main As Form1
  Private _listener As TcpListener
  Private _thread As Thread

  Public Sub New(ByVal main As Form1)
    _main = main
  End Sub

  Public Sub SpinUp()

    ' create and start the new thread...
    _thread = New Thread(AddressOf ThreadEntryPoint)
    _thread.Start()
  End Sub
End Class
```

The obvious missing method here is `ThreadEntryPoint`. This is where we need to create the socket and wait for inbound connections. When we get them, we'll be given a `TcpClient` object, which we need to pass back to `Form1` where the conversation window can be created.

To create the socket, we create an instance of `TcpListener` and give it a port. In our application, the port we're going to use is `10101`. This port should be free on your computer, but if your debugger breaks on an exception when you instantiate `TcpListener` or call `Start`, try another port. Once we've done that and called `Start` to configure the object to listen for connections, we drop into an infinite loop and call `AcceptTcpClient`. This method will block until the socket is closed, or a connection becomes available. If we get `Nothing` back, either the socket is closed or there's a problem, so we drop out of the thread. If we get something back, then we pass the `TcpClient` over to `Form1` through a call to (not yet built) `ReceiveInboundConnection` method:

```
' ThreadEntryPoint...
Protected Sub ThreadEntryPoint()

    ' create a socket...
    _listener = New TcpListener(Form1.ServicePort)
    _listener.Start()

    ' loop infinitely, waiting for connections...
    Do While True

        ' get a connection...
        Dim client As TcpClient = _listener.AcceptTcpClient()
        If client Is Nothing Then
            Exit Do
        End If
        ' process it...
        _main.ReceiveInboundConnection(client)
    Loop
End Sub
```

It's in the `ReceiveInboundConnection` method that we'll create the Conversation form that the user can use to send messages.

Creating Conversation Windows

When we build Windows Forms applications that support threading, we can run into a problem with the Windows messaging subsystem. This is a very old part of Windows (the idea has been around since version 1.0 of the platform, although the implementation on modern Windows versions is far removed from the original) that powers the Windows user interface.

Even if you're not familiar with old school Windows programming, such as MFC, Win32, or even Win16 development, you should be familiar with events. When we move a mouse over a form, we get `MouseMove` events. When we close a form, we get a `Closed` event. There's a mapping between these events and the messages that Windows passes around to support the actual display of the windows. For example, whenever we receive a `MouseMove` event, a message called `WM_MOUSEMOVE` is sent to the window, by Windows, in response to the mouse driver. In .NET, and in other RAD development environments like VB and Delphi, this message is converted into an event that we can write code against.

Although this is getting way off the topic — we know how to build Windows Forms applications by now and don't need to get into the details of messages like `WM_NCHITTEST` or `WM_PAINT` — it has an important implication. In effect, Windows creates a message queue for each thread into which it posts the messages that the thread's windows have to work with. This queue is looped on a virtually constant basis, and the messages are distributed to the appropriate window (remember, small controls like buttons and text boxes are also windows). In .NET, these messages are turned into events, but unless the message queue still gets looped the messages don't get through.

Imagine that Windows needs to paint a window. It will post a `WM_PAINT` message to the queue. A message loop implemented on the main thread of the process containing the window detects the message and dispatches it on to the appropriate window where it is processed. Now, imagine that the queue isn't looped. The message never gets picked up, and the window will never get painted.

In a Windows application, a single thread is usually responsible for message dispatch. This thread is usually (although it doesn't have to be) the main application thread, the one that's created when the process is first created. If we create windows in a different thread then that new thread has to support the message dispatch loop so that messages destined for the windows get through. However, with `Listener`, we have no code for processing the message loop and there's little point in writing any because the next time we call `AcceptTcpClient` we're going to block and everything will stop working.

The trick then is to create the windows only in the main application thread, which is the thread that created `Form1` and that is processing the messages for all the windows created in this thread. We can pass calls from one thread to the other by calling the `Invoke` method of `Form1`.

This is where things start to get complicated. We have to write an awful lot of code to get to a point where we can see that the socket connection has been established and get conversation windows to appear. Here's what we need to do:

❑ Create a new Conversation form. This form will need controls for displaying the total content of the conversation, plus a `TextBox` control for adding new messages.

❑ The Conversation window will need to be able to send and receive messages through its own thread.

❑ `Form1` needs to be able to initiate new connections. This will be done in a separate thread that is managed by the thread pool. When the connection has been established, a new Conversation window needs to be created and configured.

❑ `Form1` also needs to receive inbound connections. When it gets one of these, a new Conversation needs to be created and configured.

Let's look at these problems one at a time.

Creating the Conversation Form

The simplest place to start is to build the new Conversation form. This needs three `TextBox` controls (`textUsername`, `textMessages`, and `textMessage`) and a `Button` control (`buttonSend`). Here's the form (see Figure 23-6).

Figure 23-6

This class requires a number of fields and an enumeration. It needs fields to hold the username of the user (which we'll default to `Evjen`), the underlying `TcpClient`, the `NetworkStream` returned by that client. The enumeration indicates the direction of the connection (which will help us when debugging):

```
Imports System.Net
Imports System.Net.Sockets
Imports System.Text
Imports System.Threading
Imports System.Runtime.Serialization.Formatters.Binary
Public Class Conversation
   Inherits System.Windows.Forms.Form
   Private _username As String = "Evjen"
   Private _client As TcpClient
   Private _stream As NetworkStream
   Private _direction As ConversationDirection

   Public Enum ConversationDirection As Integer
      Inbound = 0
      Outbound = 1
   End Enum
```

We won't look into the issues of establishing a thread for exchanging messages at this stage, but we will look at implementing the `ConfigureClient` method. This method will eventually do more work than this, but, for now, it sets a couple of fields and calls `UpdateCaption`:

```
Public Sub ConfigureClient(ByVal client As TcpClient, _
                           ByVal direction As ConversationDirection)
   ' set it up...
   _client = client
   _direction = direction

   ' update the window...
   UpdateCaption()
End Sub

Protected Sub UpdateCaption()

   ' set the text...
   Dim builder As New StringBuilder(_username)
   builder.Append(" - ")
   builder.Append(_direction.ToString())
   builder.Append(" - ")
   builder.Append(Thread.CurrentThread.GetHashCode())
   builder.Append(" - ")
   If Not _client Is Nothing Then
      builder.Append("Connected")
   Else
      builder.Append("Not connected")
   End If
   Text = builder.ToString()
End Sub
```

One debugging issue that we have is that if we're connecting to a conversation on the same machine, we need a way of changing the name of the user sending each message, otherwise things will get confusing.

That's what the top-most `TextBox` control is for. In the constructor, set the text for the `textUsername` `.Text` property:

```
Public Sub New()
  MyBase.New()

  'This call is required by the Windows Form Designer.
  InitializeComponent()

  'Add any initialization after the InitializeComponent() call
  textUsername.Text = _username
End Sub
```

On the `TextChanged` event for this control, update the caption and the internal _username field:

```
Private Sub textUsername_TextChanged(ByVal sender As System.Object, _
                                ByVal e As System.EventArgs) _
                                Handles textUsername.TextChanged
  _username = textUsername.Text
  UpdateCaption()
End Sub
```

Initiating Connections

`Form1` needs to be able to both initiate connections and receive inbound connections — the application is both a client and a server. We've already created some of the server portion by creating `Listener` and now we'll look at the client side.

The general rule when working with sockets is that any time we send anything over the wire, we must perform the actual communication in a separate thread. Virtually all calls to send and receive do so in a blocking manner, that is, they block until data is received, block until all data is sent and so on.

If threads are used well, the UI will keep running as normal, irrespective of the problems that may occur during transmit and receive. This is why in the `InitiateConnection` method on `Form1` we defer processing to another method called `InitiateConnectionThreadEntryPoint` that is called from a new thread:

```
Public Sub InitiateConnection()
  InitiateConnection(textConnectTo.Text)
End Sub
Public Sub InitiateConnection(ByVal hostName As String)

  ' give it to the threadpool to do...
  ThreadPool.QueueUserWorkItem(AddressOf _
  Me.InitiateConnectionThreadEntryPoint, hostName)
End Sub
Private Sub buttonConnect_Click(ByVal sender As System.Object, _
                        ByVal e As System.EventArgs) _
                        Handles buttonConnect.Click

  InitiateConnection()
End Sub
```

Inside the thread, we try to convert the host name that we're given into an IP address (`localhost` is used as the host name in the demonstration, but it could be the name of a machine on the local network or a hostname on the Internet). This is done through the shared `Resolve` method on `System.Net.Dns` and returns a `System.Net.IPHostEntry` object. As a hostname can point to multiple IP addresses, we'll just use the first one that we're given. We take this address expressed as an IP (for example, `192.168.0.4`) and combine it with the port number to get a new `System.Net.IPEndPoint`. We create a new `TcpClient` from this `IPEndPoint` and try to connect.

If at any time an exception is thrown (which can happen because the name couldn't be resolved, or the connection could not be established), we'll pass the exception over to `HandleInitiateConnectionException`. If it succeeds, we'll pass it to `ProcessOutboundConnection`. Both of these methods will be implemented shortly:

```
Private Sub InitiateConnectionThreadEntryPoint(ByVal state As Object)

  Try

    ' get the host name...
    Dim hostName As String = CStr(state)

    ' resolve...
    Dim hostEntry As IPHostEntry = Dns.Resolve(hostName)
    If Not hostEntry Is Nothing Then

      ' create an end-point for the first address...
      Dim endPoint As New IPEndPoint(hostEntry.AddressList(0), _
          ServicePort)

      ' create a tcp client...
      Dim client As New TcpClient
      client.Connect(endPoint)

      ' create the connection window...
      ProcessOutboundConnection(client)
    Else
      Throw New ApplicationException("Host '" & hostName & _
          "' could not be resolved.")
    End If
  Catch ex As Exception
    HandleInitiateConnectionException(ex)
  End Try
End Sub
```

When it comes to `HandleInitiateConnectionException` we start to see the inter-thread UI problems that were mentioned earlier. When there is a problem with the exception, we need to tell the user, which means that we need to move the exception from the thread pool managed thread into the main application thread. The principle for this is the same, we need to create a delegate and call that delegate through the `Invoke` method of the form. This method does all the hard work in marshaling the call across to the other thread.

Here's what the delegates look like. They have the same parameters of the calls themselves. As a naming convention I tend to use the same name as the method and tack the word `Delegate` on the end:

```
Public Class Form1
    Inherits System.Windows.Forms.Form
```

```
Private Shared _mainThreadId As Integer

' delegates...
Protected Delegate Sub HandleInitiateConnectionExceptionDelegate( _
                                        ByVal ex As Exception)
```

In the constructor for `Form1`, we capture the thread callers thread ID and store it in `_mainThreadId`. Here's a method that compares the captured ID with the ID of the current thread:

```
Public Shared Function IsMainThread() As Boolean
   If Thread.CurrentThread.GetHashCode() = _mainThreadId Then
      Return True
   Else
      Return False
   End If
End Function
```

The first thing we do at the top of `HandleInitiateConnectionException` is to check the thread ID. If it doesn't match, we create the delegate and call it. Notice how we set the delegate to call back into the same method, as the second time it's called we would have moved to the main thread, therefore `IsMainThread` will return `True` and we can process the exception properly:

```
Protected Sub HandleInitiateConnectionException(ByVal ex As Exception)

   ' main thread?
   If IsMainThread() = False Then

      ' create and call...
      Dim args(0) As Object
      args(0) = ex
      Invoke(New HandleInitiateConnectionExceptionDelegate(AddressOf _
         HandleInitiateConnectionException), args)
      ' return...
      Return
   End If

   ' show it...
   MsgBox(ex.GetType().ToString() & ":" & ex.Message)
End Sub
```

The result is that when the call comes in from the thread pool managed thread, `IsMainThread` returns `False`, and the delegate is created and called. When the method is entered again as a result of the delegate call, `IsMainThread` returns `True` and we see the message box.

When it comes to `ProcessOutboundConnection`, we have to again jump into the main UI thread. However, the magic behind this method is implemented in a separate method called `ProcessConnection`, which can handle either inbound or outbound connections. Here's the delegate:

```
Public Class Form1
    Inherits System.Windows.Forms.Form

    Private Shared _mainThreadId As Integer
```

```
Private _listener As Listener

Protected Delegate Sub ProcessConnectionDelegate(ByVal client As _
        TcpClient, ByVal direction As Conversation.ConversationDirection)
Protected Delegate Sub HandleInitiateConnectionExceptionDelegate(ByVal _
        ex As Exception)
```

Here's the method itself, which creates the new Conversation form and calls the `ConfigureClient` method:

```
Protected Sub ProcessConnection(ByVal client As TcpClient, _
    ByVal direction As Conversation.ConversationDirection)

    ' do we have to move to another thread?
    If IsMainThread() = False Then

        ' create and call...
        Dim args(1) As Object
        args(0) = client
        args(1) = direction
        Invoke(New ProcessConnectionDelegate(AddressOf ProcessConnection), _
            args)

        Return
    End If


    ' create the conversation window...
    Dim conversation As New Conversation
    conversation.Show()
    conversation.ConfigureClient(client, direction)
End Sub
```

Of course, `ProcessOutboundConnection` needs to defer to `ProcessConnection`:

```
Public Sub ProcessOutboundConnection(ByVal client As TcpClient)
    ProcessConnection(client, Conversation.ConversationDirection.Outbound)
End Sub
```

Now that we can connect to something on the client-side, let's look at how to receive connections (on the server-side).

Receiving Inbound Connections

We've already built `Listener`, but we haven't created an instance of it, nor have we spun up its thread to wait for incoming connections. To do this, we need a field in `Form1` to hold an instance of the object, and we also need to tweak the constructor. Here's the field:

```
Public Class Form1
    Inherits System.Windows.Forms.Form

    Private _mainThreadId As Integer
    Private _listener As Listener
```

Here is the new code that needs to be added to the constructor:

```
Public Sub New()
  MyBase.New()

  'This call is required by the Windows Form Designer.
  InitializeComponent()

  'Add any initialization after the InitializeComponent() call
  _mainThreadId = Thread.CurrentThread.GetHashCode()
  Text &= " - " & _mainThreadId.ToString()

  ' listener...
  _listener = New Listener(Me)
  _listener.SpinUp()
End Sub
```

When inbound connections are received, we'll get a new `TcpClient` object. This is passed back to `Form1` through the `ReceiveInboundConnection` method. This method, like `ProcessOutboundConnection`, defers to `ProcessConnection`. As `ProcessConnection` already handles the issue of moving the call to the main application thread, `ReceiveInboundConnection` looks like this:

```
Public Sub ReceiveInboundConnection(ByVal client As TcpClient)
  ProcessConnection(client, Conversation.ConversationDirection.Inbound)
End Sub
```

If you run the project now, you should be able to click the Connect button and see two windows — one inbound and one outbound as shown in Figure 23-7.

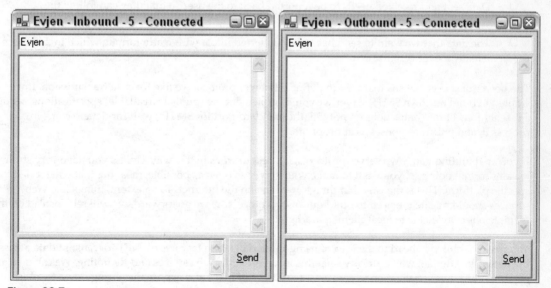

Figure 23-7

If you close all three windows, the application will keep running because we haven't written code to close down the listener thread, and having an open thread like this will keep the application open. Use the Debug ⇨ Stop Debugging menu option in VS.NET to close the application down by killing all running threads.

By clicking the Connect button, we're calling `InitiateConnection`. This spins up a new thread in the pool that resolves the given host name (`localhost`) into an IP address. This IP address, in combination with a port number, is then used in the creation of a `TcpClient` object. If the connection can be made, `ProcessOutboundConnection` is called, which results in the first of the conversation windows being created and marked as "outbound."

Our example is somewhat artificial, as the two instances of Wrox Messenger should be running on separate computers. On the remote computer (if we're connecting to `localhost` this will be the same computer) a connection is received through the `AcceptTcpClient` method of `TcpListener`. This results in a call to `ReceiveInboundConnection`, which, in turn, results in the creation of the second conversation window, this time marked as "inbound."

Sending Messages

Next, we have to work out how to exchange messages between the two Conversation windows. We already have a `TcpClient` in each case so all we have to do is squirt binary data down the wire on one side and pick it up at the other end. As the two Conversation windows act both as client and server, both need to be able to send and receive.

We have three problems to solve:

❑   We need to establish one thread to send and another thread to receive data

❑   Data sent and received needs to be reported back to the user so that they can follow the conversation

❑   The data that we want to send has to be converted into a wire-ready format, which in .NET terms usually means serialization

The power of sockets means that we can define whatever protocol we like for data transmission. If we wanted to build our own SMTP server we could implement the (publicly available) specifications, set up a listener to wait for connections on port 25 (the standard port for SMTP), wait for data to come in, process it, and return responses as appropriate.

If you are building your own server protocols, it's best to work in this way. Unless you have very strong reasons for not doing so, you want to make your server as open as possible, meaning that it's not tied to a specific platform. This is the way that things are done on the Internet. To an extent, things like Web services should negate the need to build our own protocols; as we go forward, we will rely instead on the "remote object available to local client" paradigm.

You may be thinking ahead to the idea of using the serialization features of .NET to transmit data across the network. After all, we've already seen this in action with Web services and Remoting. We can take an object in .NET, use serialization to convert it to a string of bytes and expose that string down to a Web service consumer, or Remoting client, or even to a file.

In Chapter 20, we learned about the `BinaryFormatter` and `SoapFormatter` classes. We could use either of those classes, or create our own custom formatter, to convert data for transmission and reception. In this case, we're going to create a new class called `Message` and use `BinaryFormatter` to crunch it down into a wire-ready format and convert it back again for processing.

This approach isn't ideal from the perspective of interoperability, as the actual protocol used is lost in the implementation of the .NET Framework, rather than being under our absolute control.

If we want to build an open protocol, this is *not* the best way to do it. Unfortunately, the best way to do it is out of the scope of this book but a good place to start is to look at existing protocols and standards and model any protocol on their approach. `BinaryFormatter` is quick and dirty, which is why we're going to use it.

The Message Class

The `Message` class contains two fields, _username and _message, which form the entirety of the data that we want to transmit. The code for this class follows; notice how the `Serializable` attribute is applied to it so that `BinaryFormatter` can change it into a wire-ready form, also notice how we've provided a new implementation of `ToString`:

```
Imports System.Text
<Serializable()> Public Class Message

  Private _username As String
  Private _message As String

  Public Sub New(ByVal name As String)
    _username = name
  End Sub
  Public Sub New(ByVal name As String, ByVal message As String)
    _username = name
    _message = message
  End Sub

  Public Overrides Function ToString() As String
    Dim builder As New StringBuilder(_username)
    builder.Append(" says:")
    builder.Append(ControlChars.CrLf)
    builder.Append(_message)
    builder.Append(ControlChars.CrLf)
    Return builder.ToString()
  End Function
End Class
```

Now, all we have to do is spin up two threads, one for transmission and one for reception, updating the display. We need two threads per *conversation*, so if we have 10 conversations open, we'll need 20 threads plus the main UI thread, plus the thread running `TcpListener`.

Receiving messages is pretty easy. When we call `Deserialize` on `BinaryFormatter`, we give it the stream returned to us from `TcpClient`. If there's no data, this blocks. If there is data, it's decoded into a `Message` object that we can display. If we have multiple messages coming down the pipe,

`BinaryFormatter` will keep processing them out until the pipe is empty. Here's the method for doing this, and this should be added to `Conversation`. Remember, we haven't implemented `ShowMessage` yet:

```
Protected Sub ReceiveThreadEntryPoint()

    ' create a formatter...
    Dim formatter As New BinaryFormatter
    ' loop...
    Do While True

        ' receive...
        Dim message1 As Message = formatter.Deserialize(_stream)
        If message1 Is Nothing Then
            Exit Do
        End If

        ' show it...
        ShowMessage(message1)
    Loop
End Sub
```

Transmitting messages is a touch more complex. What we want is a queue (managed by a `System.Collections.Queue`) of outgoing messages. Every second, we'll examine the state of the queue and if we find any messages, we'll use `BinaryFormatter` to transmit them. As we'll be accessing this queue from multiple threads, we'll use a `System.Threading.ReaderWriterLock` to control access. To minimize the amount of time we spend inside locked code, we'll quickly transfer the contents of the shared queue into a private queue that we can process at our leisure. This allows the client to continue to add messages to the queue through the UI, even though existing messages are being sent by the transmit thread.

First, add these members to `Conversation`:

```
Public Class Conversation
    Inherits System.Windows.Forms.Form

    Private _username As String = "Evjen"
    Private _client As TcpClient
    Private _stream As NetworkStream
    Private _direction As ConversationDirection
    Private _receiveThread As Thread
    Private _transmitThread As Thread
    Private _transmitQueue As New Queue()
    Private _transmitLock As New ReaderWriterLock()
```

Now, add this method again to `Conversation`:

```
Protected Sub TransmitThreadEntryPoint()

    ' create a formatter...
    Dim formatter As New BinaryFormatter
    Dim workQueue As New Queue
```

```
    ' loop...
    Do While True

      ' wait for the signal...
      Thread.Sleep(1000)

      ' go through the queue...

      _transmitLock.AcquireWriterLock(-1)
      Dim message As Message
      workQueue.Clear()
      For Each message In _transmitQueue
        workQueue.Enqueue(message)
      Next
      _transmitQueue.Clear()
      _transmitLock.ReleaseWriterLock()

      ' loop the outbound messages...
      For Each message In workQueue

        ' send it...
        formatter.Serialize(_stream, message)

      Next

    Loop

End Sub
```

When we want to send a message, we call one version of the `SendMessage` method. Here are all of the implementations, and the `Click` handler for `buttonSend`:

```
Private Sub buttonSend_Click(ByVal sender As System.Object, _
  ByVal e As System.EventArgs) Handles buttonSend.Click
  SendMessage(textMessage.Text)
End Sub

Public Sub SendMessage(ByVal message As String)
  SendMessage(_username, message)
End Sub

Public Sub SendMessage(ByVal username As String, ByVal message As String)
  SendMessage(New Message(username, message))
End Sub

Public Sub SendMessage(ByVal message As Message)

  ' queue it...
  _transmitLock.AcquireWriterLock(-1)
  _transmitQueue.Enqueue(message)
  _transmitLock.ReleaseWriterLock()

  ' show it...
  ShowMessage(message)
End Sub
```

ShowMessage is responsible for updating textMessages so that the conversation remains up-to-date (notice how we add the message both when we send it and when we receive it so that both parties have an up-to-date thread). This is a UI feature, so it is good practice to pass it over to the main application thread for processing. Although, the call in response to the button click comes off of the main application thread, the one from inside ReceiveThreadEntryPoint does not. Here's what the delegate looks like:

```
Public Class Conversation
   Inherits System.Windows.Forms.Form

   ' members...
   Private _username As String = "Evjen"
   Private _client As TcpClient
   Private _stream As NetworkStream
   Private _direction As ConversationDirection
   Private _receiveThread As Thread
   Private _transmitThread As Thread
   Private _transmitQueue As New Queue()
   Private _transmitLock As New ReaderWriterLock()

   Public Delegate Sub ShowMessageDelegate(ByVal message As Message)
```

Here's the method implementation:

```
Public Sub ShowMessage(ByVal message As Message)

   ' thread?
   If Form1.IsMainThread() = False Then

      ' run...
      Dim args(0) As Object
      args(0) = message
      Invoke(New ShowMessageDelegate(AddressOf ShowMessage), args)

      ' return...
      Return
   End If

   ' show it...
   textMessages.Text &= message.ToString()
End Sub
```

All that remains now is to spin up the threads. This should be done from within ConfigureClient. Before the threads are spun up, we need to get hold of the stream and store it in the private _stream field. After that, we create new Thread objects as normal:

```
Public Sub ConfigureClient(ByVal client As TcpClient, _
    ByVal direction As ConversationDirection)

   ' set it up...
   _client = client
   _direction = direction

   ' update the window...
   UpdateCaption()
```

```
' get the stream...
_stream = _client.GetStream()
' spin up the threads...
_transmitThread = New Thread(AddressOf TransmitThreadEntryPoint)
_transmitThread.Start()
_receiveThread = New Thread(AddressOf ReceiveThreadEntryPoint)
_receiveThread.Start()
End Sub
```

At this point, if you run the application you should be able to connect and exchange messages as shown in Figure 23-8.

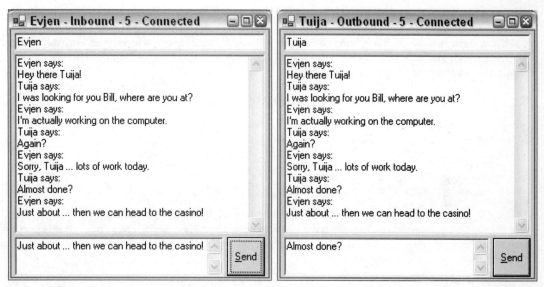

Figure 23-8

Notice how in these screenshots I've changed the username of the inbound connection to `Tuija` using the `textUsername` text box so that I can follow which half of the conversation comes from where.

Shutting Down the Application

We've yet to solve the problem of neatly closing the application, or, in fact, dealing with one person in the conversation closing down their window indicating that they wish to end the conversation. When the process ends (whether "neatly" or forcefully), Windows automatically mops up any open connections and frees up the port for other processes.

If we close our window (imagine, if you will, that we have two computers, one window per computer as we would in a production environment), we're indicating that we want to end the conversation. We need to close the socket and spin down the transmission and reception threads. At the other end, we should be able to detect that the socket has been closed, spin down the threads and tell the user that the other user has terminated the conversation.

This all hinges on being able to detect when the socket has been closed. For some reason, Microsoft has actually made this very hard, thanks to the design of the `TcpClient` class. `TcpClient` effectively encapsulates a `System.Net.Sockets.Socket` class, providing methods for helping to manage the connection lifetime and communication streams. However, `TcpClient` does not have a method or property that answers the question, "Am I still connected?" What we need to do is get hold of the `Socket` object that `TcpClient` is wrapping and then we can use its `Connected` property to find out if the connection has been closed.

`TcpClient` does support a property called `Client` that returns a `Socket`. However, this property is protected, meaning that we can only access it by inheriting a new class from `TcpClient`. But, there is another way, we could use Reflection to get at the property and call it without having to inherit a new class.

Microsoft claims that this is a legitimate technique, even though it appears to violate every rule in the book about encapsulation. Reflection is designed not only for finding out which types are available, and learning which methods and properties each type supports, but also for invoking those methods and properties whether they're protected or public.

So, in `Conversation` we need to store the socket:

```
Public Class Conversation
   Inherits System.Windows.Forms.Form

   Private _username As String = "Evjen"
   Private _client As TcpClient
   Private _socket As Socket
```

In `ConfigureClient`, we need to use `Reflection` to peek in to the `Type` object for `TcpClient` and dig out the `Client` property. Once we have a `System.Reflection.PropertyInfo` for this property, we can retrieve its value by using the `GetValue` method. Here's the code. You'll also need to import the `System.Reflection` namespace:

```
Public Sub ConfigureClient(ByVal client As TcpClient, _
                           ByVal direction As ConversationDirection)


   ' set it up...
   _client = client
   _direction = direction

   ' update the window...
   UpdateCaption()

   ' get the stream...
   _stream = _client.GetStream()

   ' get the socket through reflection...
   Dim propertyInfo As PropertyInfo = _
      _client.GetType().GetProperty("Client", _
      BindingFlags.Instance Or BindingFlags.NonPublic)
   If Not propertyInfo Is Nothing Then
     _socket = propertyInfo.GetValue(_client, Nothing)
   Else
     Throw New Exception("Couldn't retrieve Client property from TcpClient")
   End If
```

```
' spin up the threads...
_transmitThread = New Thread(AddressOf TransmitThreadEntryPoint)
_transmitThread.Start()
_receiveThread = New Thread(AddressOf ReceiveThreadEntryPoint)
_receiveThread.Start()
End Sub
```

Applications are able to check the state of the socket either by detecting when an error occurs because we've tried to send data over a closed socket, or by actually asking if the socket is connected. If we either don't have a `Socket` available in `_socket` (that is, it is `Nothing`), or if we have one and it tells us we're disconnected, we give the user some feedback and exit the loop. By exiting the loop, we effectively exit the thread, which is a neat way of quitting the thread. Notice as well that we might not have a window at this point (we might be the one that closed the conversation by closing the window), so we wrap the UI call in a `Try...Catch` (the other side will see a `<disconnect>` message):

```
Protected Sub TransmitThreadEntryPoint()

    ' create a formatter...
    Dim formatter As New BinaryFormatter
    Dim workQueue As New Queue

    ' name...
    Thread.CurrentThread.Name = "Tx-" & _direction.ToString()

    ' loop...
    Do While True
    ' wait for the signal...
    Thread.Sleep(1000)

    ' disconnected?
    If _socket Is Nothing OrElse _socket.Connected = False Then
      Try
        ShowMessage(New Message("Debug", "<disconnect>"))
      Catch
      End Try
      Exit Do
    End If

    ' go through the queue...
```

`ReceiveThreadEntryPoint` also needs some massaging. When the socket is closed, the stream will no longer be valid and so `BinaryFormatter.Deserialize` will throw an exception. Likewise, we quit the loop and therefore neatly quit the thread:

```
Protected Sub ReceiveThreadEntryPoint()

    ' create a formatter...
    Dim formatter As New BinaryFormatter

    ' loop...
    Do While True

      ' receive...
      Dim message As Message = Nothing
      Try
        message = formatter.Deserialize(_stream)
```

835

```
        Catch
        End Try
        If message Is Nothing Then
          Exit Do
        End If

        ' show it...
        ShowMessage(message)
    Loop
  End Sub
```

So, how do we deal with actually closing the socket? Well, we tweak the Dispose method of the form itself (you will find this method in the Windows Generated Code section of the file) and if we have a _socket object we close it:

```
Protected Overloads Overrides Sub Dispose(ByVal disposing As Boolean)
   If disposing Then
     If Not (components Is Nothing) Then
       components.Dispose()
     End If
   End If

   ' close the socket...
   If Not _socket Is Nothing Then
     _socket.Close()
     _socket = Nothing
   End If

   MyBase.Dispose(disposing)
End Sub
```

Now, you'll be able to start a conversation and if you close one of the windows, <disconnect> will appear in the other. This is illustrated in Figure 23-9. In the background, the four threads (one transmit, one receive per window) will spin down properly.

Figure 23-9

However, the application itself will still not close properly, even if you close all the windows. That's because we need to stop the Listener when Form1 closes. To do this, we'll make Listener implement Idisposable:

```
Public Class Listener
    Implements IDisposable
  Public Sub Dispose() Implements System.IDisposable.Dispose

    ' stop it...
    Finalize()
    GC.SuppressFinalize(Me)

  End Sub

  Protected Overrides Sub Finalize()

    ' stop the listener...
    If Not _listener Is Nothing Then
      _listener.Stop()
      _listener = Nothing
    End If

    ' stop the thread...
    If Not _thread Is Nothing Then
      _thread.Join()
      _thread = Nothing
    End If

    ' call up...
    MyBase.Finalize()

  End Sub
```

Now all that remains is to call `Dispose` from within `Form1`. A good place to do this is in the `Closed` event handler:

```
Protected Overrides Sub OnClosed(ByVal e As System.EventArgs)
  If Not _listener Is Nothing Then
    _listener.Dispose()
    _listener = Nothing
  End If
End Sub
```

After you compile again, you'll find that you'll now be able to properly close down the application.

Using Internet Explorer in Your Applications

A common requirement of modern applications is to display HTML files and other files commonly used with Internet applications. Although, the .NET Framework has considerable support for common image formats (such as GIF, JPEG and PNG), working with HTML is a touch trickier.

We don't want to have to write our own HTML parser so using an existing component to display HTML pages is, in most cases, your only option. Microsoft's Internet Explorer was implemented as a standalone component comprising a parser and a renderer, all packaged up in a neat COM object. The Internet

Explorer application that we all use "simply" hosts this COM object. There's nothing to stop us using this COM object in our own applications, and in this section that's exactly what we're going to do.

Yes, I said COM object. There is no managed version of Internet Explorer for use with .NET. If you consider the issue that writing an HTML parser is extremely hard, and writing a renderer is extremely hard you'll come to the conclusion that I'd rather use interop to get to Internet Explorer in my .NET applications than have Microsoft try and rewrite a managed version of it just for .NET. I'm confident that we will see "Internet Explorer .NET" within the next year or two, but for now we do have to use Interop.

Internet Explorer Interop Design Pattern

My preferred design pattern for using IE in Windows Forms applications is to create a separate library containing a "mini browser." This is a separate control that contains the Internet Explorer COM control, a toolbar and a status bar in one. I can just drop this into my applications as and when I need it. I'll demonstrate how to build this mini browser control in the following sections. In some cases, you might want to display HTML pages without giving the user the UI widgets like toolbar or the ability to enter their own URLs. An extension to this pattern (which we're not going to see here), would include properties to turn off the toolbar and status bar and route status bar text change messages through to a control of your choosing.

Creating the Project

Create a new Windows Control Library. In the library, we need a new MiniBrowser control class. Delete the default UserControl1 and create a new user control called MiniBrowser.

To gain access to the IE COM object, we need to create a COM wrapper for the object. Visual Studio can do this for us, which makes our lives a bit easier. With the Designer open, right-click the Toolbox and select Add/Remove Items; then with the COM Components tab selected, scroll down until you find Microsoft Web Browser, check it on, and press the *OK* button.

You may be prompted to create a new interop wrapper for the control, in which case indicate that you do. This will result in the control being added to the Toolbox, as shown in Figure 23-10.

Open the Designer for MiniBrowser. Drag and drop a new Microsoft Web Browser control onto it. As well as the new control appearing on the surface of the Designer, new assemblies will be added to the list of references for the project. These references point to assemblies that VS.NET has created to host the control. In fact, AxSHDocVw (implemented in the new AxInterop.ShDocVw.dll assembly, which you can find in the project's bin folder) contains a class called WebBrowser. This class is inherited from System.Windows.Forms.AxHost (shown in the Solution Explorer in Figure 23-11), a class that understands how to host ActiveX, or rather "COM" components. (Again, this is a curious .NET nomenclature issue. ActiveX is actually a deprecated name, the proper name is now COM. More properly, this class should be called ComControlHost.) This class contains the same methods and properties that the contained COM component implements, and the class itself maps the calls into the managed methods and properties and into the unmanaged COM object.

To the Designer, add a StatusBar control. This will automatically dock at the bottom of the design surface and you should ensure that the bar does not obscure the WebBrowser control. The StatusBar usually looks better if we use the panels, so set the ShowPanels property to True. Using the Panels

Figure 23-10

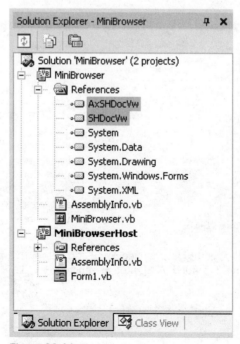

Figure 23-11

property, add a new Panel. Set the `Text` property of the Panel to `Ready`, the `Name` property to `panelStatus` and `AutoSize` to `Spring`. Your form should now appear as shown in Figure 23-12.

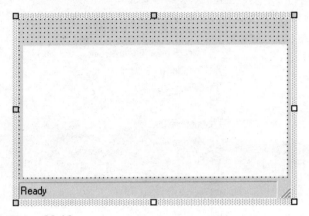

Ready

Figure 23-12

We'll build the toolbar buttons a bit later, but for now we need an address bar. To the top of the control, add a TextBox control. Clear its `Text` property, set its `Name` property to `textUrl` and set its `Anchor` property to `Top, Left, Right`.

Finally, to implement the resizing set the `Anchor` property of the `WebBrowser` control to `Left, Right, Top, Bottom`. In addition, set its `Name` property to `Ie`. Your form should now appear as shown in Figure 23-13.

Ready

Figure 23-13

To test the control we need to get it to load a page. We'll add a `HomeUrl` property and make it navigate to that location when the control is loaded. Add these members to `MiniBrowser`:

```
Public Class MiniBrowser
    Inherits System.Windows.Forms.UserControl

    Private _url As String
    Private _homeUrl As String = "http://www.wrox.com/"
```

When the `HomeUrl` property is set, we'll just update the `_homeUrl` field. However, when the `Url` is set we'll take the opportunity to ask the `WebBrowser` control to navigate to the URL:

```
Public Property HomeUrl() As String
  Get
    Return _homeUrl
  End Get
  Set(ByVal Value As String)
    _homeUrl = Value
  End Set
End Property

Public Property Url() As String
  Get
    Return _url
  End Get
  Set(ByVal Value As String)
    Ie.Navigate(Value)
  End Set
End Property
```

Notice, how we can just call the `Navigate` method on `WebBrowser`. This will call straight through to the matching `Navigate` method on the underlying COM control. Also, notice how we don't update the `_url` field whenever we set the `Url` property. We'll do this later, once IE tells us that navigation is complete.

So that we can navigate to the URL of our choice, we need to tweak the `textUrl` control. Set the `AcceptsReturn` property of this control to `True`. Add a handler for the `KeyPress` event of `textUrl` and add this code to check whether the user has hit the return key whilst editing the text in the control:

```
Private Sub textUrl_KeyPress(ByVal sender As Object, _
  ByVal e As System.Windows.Forms.KeyPressEventArgs) _
  Handles textUrl.KeyPress
  If e.KeyChar = Chr(13) Then
    Url = textUrl.Text
  End If
End Sub
```

To test the control we need a host application. Create a Windows Application project in the same solution called `MiniBrowserHost` *and, to the newly created* `Form1` *form, add a* `MiniBrowser` *control. Set its* `Dock` *property to* `Fill`.

Run the project and enter a URL into the text box. Be sure that you right-click the Windows Form project and select Set as StartUp Project. Press the *return* key and IE will navigate to the URL that you supplied as demonstrated in Figure 23-14.

Updating the Text Property of textURL

You'll notice that when you click around the links, the text in `textUrl` is not updated and also the status bar doesn't update itself. We can fix this by listening for events coming off of the IE control and adding handlers to the control.

Figure 23-14

Updating the status bar text is easy. We just have to listen for the `StatusTextChange` event and update the `Text` property on `panelStatus`:

```
Private Sub Ie_StatusTextChange(ByVal sender As Object, _
  ByVal e As AxSHDocVw.DWebBrowserEvents2_StatusTextChangeEvent) _
  Handles Ie.StatusTextChange
  panelStatus.Text = e.text
End Sub
```

When IE has finished opening a resource, the `DownloadComplete` event will be fired. We can listen for this and update the `_url` field and the text on `textUrl`. That way when the user clicks through the links, her position on the site will be properly updated. However, this event doesn't return the URL through as a parameter. We have to use the `LocataionURL` property of `WebBrowser` to return this information:

```
Private Sub Ie_DownloadComplete(ByVal sender As Object, _
                                ByVal e As System.EventArgs) _
                                Handles Ie.DownloadComplete


  _url = Ie.LocationURL
  textUrl.Text = Url
End Sub
```

Now, if you run the application you'll find that the status bar and address bar work as they do in IE, as demonstrated in Figure 23-15.

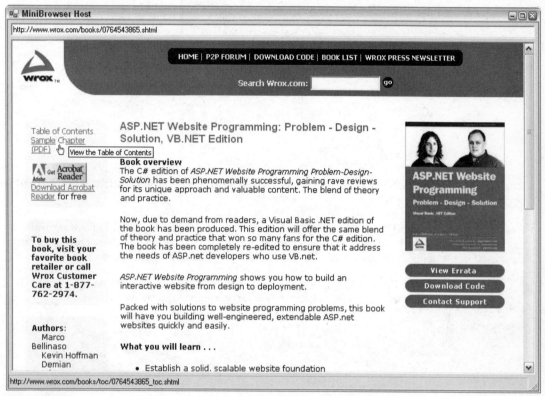

Figure 23-15

The Toolbar

To round off our discussion on building the mini browser, we'll add a simple toolbar to the top of the control that gives us the usual features we'd expect from a Web browser, that is back, forward, stop, refresh, and home.

Rather than using the `ToolBar` control, we'll add a set of button controls at the top of the control where we've currently got the address bar. Add five buttons to the top of the control as illustrated in Figure 23-16.

I've just changed the text on the button to indicate their function. Of course, you can use a screen capture utility to "borrow" button images from IE and use those. The buttons should be named `buttonBack`, `buttonForward`, `buttonStop`, `buttonRefresh`, and `buttonHome`. To get the resizing to work properly, make sure you set the `Anchor` property of the three buttons on the right to `Top`, `Right`.

On startup, `buttonBack`, `buttonForward`, and `buttonStop` should be disabled. The IE COM control will tell us explicitly when to enable and disable the Back and Forward buttons, depending on where the user is in the page stack. We'll enable the Stop button whenever the download starts, and disable again

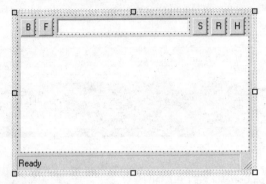

Figure 23-16

when it stops. Curiously, the Refresh button has to be enabled when the Stop button is disabled and vice versa.

First off though, we'll add the functionality behind the buttons. It's good practice to have separate methods for each of the handlers rather than coding directly into the event handlers. The `WebBrowser` class itself implements the methods that we need, so this is all very straightforward:

```
Private Sub buttonBack_Click(ByVal sender As System.Object, _
  ByVal e As System.EventArgs) Handles buttonBack.Click
  GoBack()
End Sub

Public Sub GoBack()
  Ie.GoBack()
End Sub

Private Sub buttonForward_Click(ByVal sender As System.Object, _
  ByVal e As System.EventArgs) Handles buttonForward.Click
  GoForward()
End Sub

Public Sub GoForward()
  Ie.GoForward()
End Sub

Private Sub buttonStop_Click(ByVal sender As System.Object, _
  ByVal e As System.EventArgs) Handles buttonStop.Click
  StopDownload()
End Sub

Public Sub StopDownload()
  Ie.Stop()
End Sub

Private Sub buttonRefresh_Click(ByVal sender As System.Object, _
  ByVal e As System.EventArgs) Handles buttonRefresh.Click
  RefreshBrowser()
End Sub
```

```
Public Sub RefreshBrowser()
  Ie.Refresh2()
End Sub

Private Sub buttonHome_Click(ByVal sender As System.Object, _
  ByVal e As System.EventArgs) Handles buttonHome.Click
  Ie.GoHome()
End Sub
```

To manage the enable and disabling of the buttons, we have to key into a couple of events. As we mentioned before, whenever downloading begins, we need to enable Stop and disable Refresh. Add an event handler for the `DownloadBegin` event of `Ie` that contains code to enable and disable the buttons:

```
Private Sub Ie_DownloadBegin(ByVal sender As Object, _
                             ByVal e As System.EventArgs) _
                             Handles Ie.DownloadBegin
  buttonStop.Enabled = True
  buttonRefresh.Enabled = False
End Sub
```

We already have a handler for `DownloadComplete`, but we need to add a call to switch the buttons around when this is received:

```
Private Sub Ie_DownloadComplete(ByVal sender As Object, _
  ByVal e As System.EventArgs) Handles Ie.DownloadComplete
  _url = Ie.LocationURL
  textUrl.Text = Url
  buttonStop.Enabled = False
  buttonRefresh.Enabled = True
End Sub
```

The `CommandStateChange` event lets IE tell us when we should update the enabled or disabled states of our buttons. This event provides an ID so we know which button and a `Boolean` flag indicating whether or not we should enable it or disable it. Here's the code:

```
Private Sub Ie_CommandStateChange(ByVal sender As Object, _
    ByVal e As AxSHDocVw.DWebBrowserEvents2_CommandStateChangeEvent) _
    Handles Ie.CommandStateChange

  ' do what?
  Dim control As Control = Nothing
  Select Case e.command
    Case 1
      control = buttonForward
    Case 2
      control = buttonBack
  End Select

  ' set it...
  If Not control Is Nothing Then
    control.Enabled = e.enable
End Sub
```

Run the project now and visit a Web page and click through a few links. You should also be able to use the toolbar to enhance your browsing experience.

Summary

In this chapter, we kicked off by looking at just how easy it is to download resources from a Web server using classes built into the .NET Framework. `System.Uri` lets us express a URI, and `System.Net.WebRequest`, in combination with `System.Net.HttpWebRequest` and `System.Net.HttpWebResponse`, lets us physically get hold of the data.

In the second section, we took a look at how we could build our own network protocol by using sockets, implemented in the `System.Net.Sockets` namespace. We looked at how `TcpListener` and `TcpClient` make it relatively easy to work with sockets. We also spent a lot of time working with threads and the various UI issues that such kind of work throws up in order to make the application as usable as possible.

Finally, we looked at how we could reuse the COM-based Internet Explorer control in our own Windows Form application through .NET's interop layer.

Security in the .NET Framework

This chapter will cover the basics of security and cryptography. We'll begin with a brief discussion of the .NET Framework's security architecture, because this will have an impact on the solutions that we may choose to implement.

The .NET Framework provides us with additional tools and functionality with regard to security. We now have the System.Security.Permissions namespace, which allows us to control code access permissions along with role-based and identity permissions. Through our code, we can control access to objects programmatically, as well as receive information on the current permissions of objects. This security framework will assist us in finding out if we have permissions to run our code, instead of getting half way through execution and having to deal with permission-based exceptions. In this chapter we will cover:

❑ Concepts and definitions

❑ Permissions

❑ Roles

❑ Principals

❑ Code access permissions

❑ Role based permissions

❑ Identity permissions

❑ Managing permissions

❑ Managing policies

❑ Cryptography

Cryptography is the cornerstone of .NET Web services security model, so in the second half of this chapter we discuss the basis of cryptography and how to implement it. Specifically, we will cover:

Chapter 24

- ❏ Hash algorithms
- ❏ SHA
- ❏ MD5
- ❏ Secret key encryption
- ❏ Public key cryptography standard
- ❏ Digital signatures
- ❏ Certification
- ❏ Secure Sockets Layer communications

Let's begin the chapter by taking a look at some security concepts and definitions.

> As always, the code for this chapter is available for download from www.wrox.com, which you'll need in order to follow along.

Security Concepts and Definitions

Before going on, let's detail the different types of security that we will be illustrating in this chapter and how they can relate to real scenarios.

Security Type	Related Concept in Security.Permissions Namespace or Utility	Purpose
NTFS	None	Lock down specific files on any given machine
Security Policies	`Caspol.exe` utility, `PermView.exe` utility	Set up overall security policy for a machine or user from an operating system level.
Cryptographic	Strong name and assembly, generation, `SignCode.exe` utility	Use of Public key infrastructure and Certificates
Security Type	Related concept in Security.Permissions namespace or utility	Purpose
Programmatic	Groups and permission sets	For use in pieces of code that are being called into. Provides extra security to prevent users of calling code from violating security measures implemented by the program that are not provided for on a machine level

There are many approaches to providing security on our machines where our shared code is hosted. If multiple shared code applications are on one machine, each piece of shared code can get called from many front-end applications. Each piece of shared code will have its own security requirements for accessing environment variables — such as the registry, the file system, and other items — on the machine that it is running on. From an NTFS perspective, the administrator of our server can only lock down those items on the machine that are not required to be accessed from *any* piece of shared code running on it. Therefore, some applications will want to have additional security built in to prevent any calling code from doing things it is not supposed to do. The machine administrator can further assist the programmers by using the utilities provided with .NET to establish additional machine and/or user policies that programs can implement. As a further step along this line, the .NET environment has given us programmatic security through *Code Access* security, *Role Based* security, and *Identity* security. As a final security measure, we can use the cryptographic methods provided to require the use of certificates in order to execute our code.

Security in the .NET infrastructure has some basic concepts that we will discuss here. Code security is managed and accessed in the .NET environment through the use of security policies. Security policies have a relationship that is fundamentally tied to either the machine that code is running on, or to particular users under whose context the code is running. To this end, any modifications to the policy are done either at the machine or user level.

We establish the security policy on a given set of code by associating it with an entity called a *group*. A group is created and managed within each of the machine and user-based policies. These group classifications are set up so that we can place code into categories. We would want to establish new code groups when we are ready to categorize the pieces of code that would run on a machine, and assign the permissions that users will have to access the code. For instance, if we wanted to group all Internet applications and then group all non-Internet applications together, we would establish two groups and associate each of our applications with its respective group. Now that we've got the code separated into groups, we can define different permission sets for each group. If we wanted to limit our Internet applications' access to the local file system, we could create a permission set that limits that access and associates the Internet application group with the new permission set. By default, the .NET environment gives us one code group named `All Code` that is associated with the `FullTrust` permission set.

Permission sets are unique combinations of security configurations that determine what each user with access to a machine can do on that machine. Each set determines what a user has access to, for instance, whether they can read environment variables, the file system, or execute other portions of code. Permission sets are maintained at the machine and user levels through the utility `Caspol.exe`. Through this utility, we can create our own permission sets, though there are seven permission sets that ship with the .NET infrastructure that are also useful, as shown in the following table.

Permission Set	Explanation
FullTrust	Allows full access to all resources — adds assembly to a special list that has FullTrust access
Everything	Allows full access to everything covered by default named permission sets, only differs from FullTrust in that the group does not get added to the FullTrust Assembly List
Nothing	Denies all access including Execution
Execution	Allows execution-only access

Continues

Permission Set	Explanation
SkipVerification	Allows object to bypass all security verification
Internet	Grants default rights that are normal for Internet applications
LocalInternet	Grants rights that are not as restricted as Internet, but not full trust

Security that is used within the programming environment also makes use of permission sets. Through code we can control access to files in a file system, environment variables, file dialogs, isolated storage, reflections, registry, sockets, and UI. Isolated storage and virtual file systems are new operating system level storage locations that can be used by programs and are governed by the machine security policies. These file systems keep a machine safe from file system intrusion by designating a regulated area for file storage. The main access to these items is controlled through code access permissions.

Although many methods that we use in Visual Basic .NET (VB.NET) give an identifiable return value, the only return value that we will get from security methods is if the method fails. If a security method succeeds, it will not give a return value. If it fails, it will return an exception object reflecting the specific error that occurred.

Permissions in the System.Security.Permissions Namespace

The System.Security.Permissions namespace is the namespace that we will use in our code to establish and use permissions to access many things such as the file system, environment variables, and the registry within our programs. The namespace controls access to both operating system level objects as well as code objects. In order to use the namespace in our project, we need to include the Imports System.Security.Permissions line with any of our other Imports statements in our project. Using this namespace gives us access to using the CodeAccessPermissions, and PrincipalPermissions classes for using role-based permissions and also utilizing information supplied by Identity permissions. CodeAccessPermission is the main class that we will use as it controls access to the operating system level objects our code needs in order to function. Role-based permissions and Identity permissions grant access to objects based on the identity that the user of the program that is running carries with them.

In the following table, those classes that end with Attribute, such as EnvironmentPermissionAttribute, are the classes that allow us to modify the security level at which our code is allowed to interact with each respective object. The attributes that we can specify reflect either Assert, Deny, or PermitOnly permissions.

If permissions are asserted, we have full access to the object, while if we have specified Deny permissions we are not allowed to access the object through our code. If we have PermitOnly access, only objects within our program's already determined scope can be accessed, and we cannot add any more resources beyond that scope. In our table, we also deal with security in regard to *Software Publishers*. A Software Publisher is a specific entity that is using a digital signature to identify itself in a Web-based application. The following is a table of the namespace members that apply to Windows Forms programming with an explanation of each.

Class	Description
CodeAccessSecurityAttribute	Specifies security access to objects such as the registry and file system
EnvironmentPermission	Controls ability to see and modify system and user environment variables
EnvironmentPermissionAttribute	Allows security actions for environment variables to be added via code
FileDialogPermission	Controls ability to open files via a file dialog
FileDialogPermissionAttribute	Allows security actions to be added for File Dialogs via code
FileIOPermission	Controls ability to read and write files in the file system
FileIOPermissionAttribute	Allows security actions to be added for file access attempts via code
IsolatedStorageFilePermission	Controls ability to access a private virtual file system within the isolated storage area of an application
IsolatedStorageFilePermission Attribute	Allows security actions to be added for private virtual file systems via code
IsolatedStoragePermission	Controls ability to access the isolated storage area of an application
IsolatedStoragePermission Attribute	Allows security actions to be added for the isolated storage area of an application
PermissionSetAttribute	Allows security actions to be added for a permission set
PrincipalPermissionAttribute	Allows for checking against a specific user. Security principals are a user and role combination used to establish security identity
PublisherIdentityPermission	Allows for ability to access based on the identity of a software publisher
PublisherIdentityPermission Attribute	Allows security actions to be added for a software publisher
ReflectionPermission	This controls the ability to access nonpublic members of a given type
ReflectionPermissionAttribute	Allows for security actions to be added for public and nonpublic members of a given type
RegistryPermission	Controls the ability to access registry keys and values

Continues

851

Class	Description
RegistryPermissionAttribute	Allows security actions to be added for registry keys and values
SecurityAttribute	Controls which security attributes are representing code, used to control the security when creating an assembly
SecurityPermission	The set of security permission flags for use by .NET; this collection is used when we want to specify a permission flag in our code
SecurityPermissionAttribute	Allows security actions for the security permission flags
UIPermission	Controls ability to access user interfaces and use the windows clipboard
UIPermissionAttribute	Allows security actions to be added for UI Interfaces and the use of the clipboard

Code Access Permissions

Code access permissions are controlled through the CodeAccessPermissions class within the System.Security namespace, and its members make up the majority of the permissions we'll use in our attempt to secure our code and operating environment. The following is a table of the class methods and an explanation of their use.

Method	Description
RevertAll	Reverses all previous assert, deny or permit-only methods
RevertAssert	Reverses all previous assert methods
RevertDeny	Reverses all previous deny methods
RevertPermitOnly	Reverses all previous permit-only methods
Assert	Sets the permission to full access so that the specific resource can be accessed even if the caller hasn't been granted permission to access the resource
Copy	Copies a permission object
Demand	Returns whether or not all callers in the call chain have been granted the permission to access the resource in a given manner
Deny	Denies all callers access to the resource

Continues

Method	Description
Equals	Determines if a given object is the same instance of the current object
FromXml	Establishes a permission set given a specific XML encoding. This parameter is an XML encoding
GetHashCode	Returns a hash code associated with a given object
GetType	Returns the type of a given object
Intersect	Returns the permissions two permission objects have in common
IsSubsetOf	Returns result of whether the current permission object is a subset of a specified permission
PermitOnly	Determines that only those resources within this permission object can be accessed even if code has been granted permission to other objects
ToString	Returns a string representation of the current permission object
ToXml	Creates an XML representation of the current permission object
Union	Creates a permission that is the union of two permission objects

Role-Based Permissions

Role-based permissions are permissions granted based on the user and the role that code is being called with. Users are generally authenticated within the operating system platform and hold a *Security Identifier* (SID) that is associated within a security context. The SID can further be associated with a role, or a group membership that is established within a security context. The .NET role functionality supports those users and roles associated within a security context and also have support for generic and custom users and roles through the concept of principals. A principal is an object that holds the current caller credentials, which is termed the identity of the user. Principals come in two types: *Windows* principals and *non-Windows* principals. Windows-based Principal objects are objects that store the Windows SID information regarding the current user context associated with the code that is calling into the module where we are using role-based permissions. NonWindows Principals are principal objects that are created programmatically via a custom login methodology which are made available to the current thread.

Role-based permissions are not set against objects within our environment like code access permissions. They are instead a permission that is checked within the context of the current user and role that a user is part of. Within the System.Security.Permissions namespace, the concept of the principals and the PrincipalPermission class of objects are used to establish and check permissions. If a programmer passes the user and role information during a call as captured from a custom login, the PrincipalPermission class can be used to verify this information as well. During the verification, if the user and role information is Null then permission is granted, regardless of the user and role. The

`PrincipalPermission` class does not grant access to objects, but has methods that determine if a caller has been given permissions according to the current permission object through the `Demand` method. If a security exception is generated then the user does not have sufficient permission.

The following is the table of the methods in the `PrincipalPermission` class and a description of each.

Method	Description
Copy	Copies a permission object
Demand	Returns whether or not all callers in the call chain have been granted the permission to access the resource in a given manner
Equals	Determines if a given object is the same instance of the current object
FromXml	Establishes a permission set given a specific XML encoding
GetHashCode	Returns a hash code associated with a given object
GetType	Returns the type of a given object
Intersect	Returns the permissions two permission objects have in common specified in parameter
IsSubsetOf	Returns result of whether the current permission object is a subset of a specified permission
IsUnrestricted	Returns result of whether the current permission object is unrestricted
ToString	Returns a string representation of the current permission object
ToXml	Creates an XML representation of the current permission object
Union	Creates a permission that is the union of two permission objects

As an example of how we might use these, here is a code snippet which captures the current Windows principal information and displays it on the screen in the form of a message box output. Each element of the principal information could be used in a program to validate against, and thus, restrict code execution based on the values in the principal information. In our example, we have inserted an `Imports System.Security.Principal` line at the top of our module so we could use the identity and principal objects:

```
Imports System.Security.Principal
Imports System.Security.Permissions

...
```

```
Private Sub btnRoleBasedPermissions_Click(ByVal sender As System.Object, _
    ByVal e As System.EventArgs) Handles btnRoleBasedPermissions.Click

    Dim objIdentity As WindowsIdentity = WindowsIdentity.GetCurrent
    Dim objPrincipal As New WindowsPrincipal(objIdentity)
    MessageBox.Show(Str(objPrincipal.Identity.IsAuthenticated))
    MessageBox.Show(Str(objIdentity.IsGuest))
    MessageBox.Show(objIdentity.ToString)
    objIdentity = Nothing
    objPrincipal = Nothing

End Sub
```

In this code we have illustrated a few of the properties that could be used to validate against when a caller wants to run our code. Sometimes we want to make sure that the caller is an authenticated user, and not someone who bypassed the security of our machine with custom login information. This is achieved through the following line of code:

```
MessageBox.Show(Str(objPrincipal.Identity.IsAuthenticated))
```

and will output in the MessageBox as either True or False.

Another piece of information to ensure that our caller is not bypassing system security would be to check and see if the account is operating as a guest. We do this by the following line of code:

```
MessageBox.Show(Str(objIdentity.IsGuest))
```

Once again, the IsGuest returns either True or False, based on whether the caller is authenticated as a guest.

The final MessageBox in our example displays the ToString value for the identity object. This is a value that tells us what type of identity it is, either a Windows Identity or non-Windows Identity. The line of code that executes it is:

```
MessageBox.Show(objIdentity.ToString)
```

The output from the IsString method is shown in the following screenshot in Figure 24-1.

Figure 24-1

Again, the principal and identity objects are used in verifying the identity or aspects of the identity of the caller that is attempting to execute our code. Based on this information, we can lock down or release certain system resources. We will show how to lock down and release system resources through our code access permissions examples coming up.

Identity Permissions

Identity permissions are pieces of information, also called *evidence*, by which a piece of code can be identified. Examples of the evidence would be the strong name of the assembly or the digital signature associated with the assembly.

> *A strong name is a combination of the name of a program, its version number, and its associated cryptographic key and digital signature files.*

Identity permissions are granted by the runtime based on information received from the trusted host, or someone who has permission to provide the information. Therefore, they are permissions that we don't specifically request. Identity permissions provide additional information to be used by the runtime when we configure items in the Caspol.exe utility. The additional information that the trusted host can supply includes the digital signature, the application directory, or the strong name of the assembly.

Managing Code Access Permissions

In this section, we'll be looking at the most common type of permissions — that of programmatic access — permissions, and how they are used. As our example, we created a Windows Form and placed four buttons on it. This Windows Form will be used to illustrate the concept we previously mentioned, namely that, if a method fails, an exception object is generated which contains our feedback. Note at this point, that in the case of a real-world example we would be setting up permissions for a calling application. In many instances we don't want a calling application to be able to access the registry, or we want a calling application to be able to read memory variables, but not change them. However, in order to demonstrate the syntax of our commands, in our examples that follow, we have placed the attempts against the objects we have secured in the same module. In our examples, we first set up the permission that we want and grant the code the appropriate access level we wish it to be able to utilize. Then we use code that accesses our security object to illustrate the effect our permissions have on the code that accesses the objects. We'll also be tying together many of the concepts discussed so far by way of these examples.

To begin with, let's look at an example of trying to access a file in the file system, which will illustrate the use of the FileIOPermission class in our Permissions namespace. In the first example, the file C:\testsecurity\testing.txt has been secured at the operating system level so that no one can access it. In order to do this, the system administrator would set the operating system security on the file to no access:

```
Imports System.Security.Principal
Imports System.Security.Permissions
Imports System.IO

...
```

```
Private Sub btnFileIO_Click(ByVal sender As System.Object, _
                          ByVal e As System.EventArgs) Handles btnFileIO
                       .Click
Dim oFp As FileIOPermission = New _
  FileIOPermission(FileIOPermissionAccess.Write, "C:\testsecurity\testing.txt")

oFp.Assert()
Try
    Dim objWriter As New IO.StreamWriter _
        (File.Open("C:\testsecurity\testing.txt", IO.FileMode.Open))
    objWriter.WriteLine("Hi there!")
    objWriter.Flush()
    objWriter.Close()
    objWriter = Nothing
Catch objA As System.Exception
    MessageBox.Show(objA.Message)
End Try

End Sub
```

Let's walk through the code. In this example, we are going to attempt to open a file in the C:\testsecurity directory called testing.txt. We set the file access permissions within our code so that the method, irrespective of who called it, should be able to get to it with the following lines:

```
Dim oFp As FileIOPermission = New _
  FileIOPermission(FileIOPermissionAccess.Write, "C:\testsecurity\testing.txt")

oFp.Assert()
```

We used the Assert method, which declares that the resource should be accessible even if the caller has not been granted permission to access the resource. However, in this case, since the file is secured at the operating system level (by the system administrator), we get the following error as illustrated in Figure 24-2 that was caught in our exception handling.

Figure 24-2

Now, let's look at that example again with full operating system rights, but the code permissions set to Deny:

```
Protected Sub btnFileIO_Click(ByVal sender As Object, _
    ByVal e As System.EventArgs)
Dim oFp As FileIOPermission = New _
  FileIOPermission(FileIOPermissionAccess.Write, "C:\testsecurity\testing.txt")

oFp.Deny()
```

```
Try

      Dim objWriter As New IO.StreamWriter _
      (File.Open("C:\testsecurity\testing.txt", _
      IO.FileMode.Open))
      objwriter.WriteLine("Hi There")
      objWriter.Flush()
      objWriter.Close()
      objWriter = Nothing

Catch objA As System.Exception
      messagebox.Show(objA.Message)

End Try
End Sub
```

The Deny method denies all callers access to the object, regardless of whether the operating system granted them permission. With the Deny method, we catch the following error in our exception handler as shown in Figure 24-3.

Request for the permission of type System.Security.Permissions.FileIOPermission, mscorlib, Version=1.0.5000.0, Culture=neutral, PublicKeyToken=b77a5c561934e089 failed.

OK

Figure 24-3

As you can see, this error differs from the first by reflecting a Security.Permissions .FileIOPermission failure as opposed to an operating system level exception.

Now, let's look at an example of how we would use the EnvironmentPermission class of the namespace to look at EnvironmentVariables.

```
Protected Sub btnTestEnvironmentPermissions_Click _
    (ByVal sender As Object, ByVal e As System.EventArgs) _
    Handles btnTestEnvironmentPermissions.Click

    Dim oEp As EnvironmentPermission = New EnvironmentPermission _
       (environmentpermissionaccess.read, "Temp")

    Dim sEv As String
    oEp.assert()

    Try
        sEv = environment.GetEnvironmentVariable("Temp")
        MessageBox.Show("Assert was a success")

    Catch objA As System.Exception
        MessageBox.Show("Assert failed")
```

```
      End Try
      oEp.revertassert()
      oEp.Deny()

      Try
          sEv = environment.GetEnvironmentVariable("Temp")
        MessageBox.Show("Deny was a success")

      Catch objA As System.Exception
          MessageBox.Show("Deny failed")

      End Try

      MessageBox.Show(oEp.ToString)

    End Sub
```

There is a lot going on in this example, so let's look at it carefully. We first establish an environment variable permission and use the `assert` method to ensure access to the code that follows:

```
Dim oEp As EnvironmentPermission = New EnvironmentPermission _
    (environmentpermissionaccess.read, "Temp")

Dim sEv As String
oEp.assert()
```

We then try to read the environment variable into a string. If the string read succeeds we pop up a message box to reflect the success. If the read fails, a message box is shown reflecting the failure:

```
Try
    sEv = environment.GetEnvironmentVariable("Temp")
    MessageBox.Show("Assert was a success")

Catch objA As System.Exception
    MessageBox.Show("Assert failed")

End Try
```

Next, we revoke the assert we previously issued by using the `RevertAssert` method and establish Deny permissions:

```
oEp.RevertAssert()
oEp.Deny()
```

We then try again to read the variable, and write the appropriate result to a message box:

```
Try
    sEv = environment.GetEnvironmentVariable("Temp")
    MessageBox.Show("Deny failed")
Catch objA As System.Exception
    MessageBox.Show("Deny was a success")
End Try
```

We finally write the `ToString` of the method to another message box. Following is the output of all three message boxes as a result of running our subroutine. The first two message box messages give us the feedback from our `Assert` and `Deny` code, followed by the output of our `ToString` method:

Assert was a success

Deny failed

<IPermission class="System.Security.Permissions.EnvironmentPermission, mscorlib,
Version=1.0.5000.0, Culture=neutral, PublicKeyToken=b77a5c561934e089"

version="1"

Read="Temp"/>

As you can see, the `ToString` method is an XML representation of the permission object that is currently in effect. The first and second message boxes that are output are the system information of the version of the VB.NET security environment that was running at the time the button was clicked. The third message box is the environment variable name surrounded by the `Read` tags, which was the permission in effect at the time the `ToString` method was executed.

Let's look at one more example of where the permissions would affect us in our program functionality, that of accessing the registry. We would generally access the registry on the computer that was the central server for a component in our Windows Forms application.

When we use the `EventLog` methods to create entries in the machine event logs, we access the registry. To illustrate this concept, in the following code example we'll deny permissions to the registry and see the result:

```vb
Protected Sub btnTestRegistryPermissions_Click(ByVal sender As Object, _
                                ByVal e As System.EventArgs) _
                                Handles btnTestRegistryPermissions.Click

Dim oRp As New _
    RegistryPermission(Security.Permissions.PermissionState.Unrestricted)
oRp.Deny()

Dim objLog As New EventLog
Dim objLogEntryType As EventLogEntryType

Try
    Throw (New EntryPointNotFoundException)
    Catch objA As System.EntryPointNotFoundException
    Try
      If Not objLog.SourceExists("Example") Then
        objLog.CreateEventSource("Example", "System")
      End If
      objLog.Source = "Example"
      objLog.Log = "System"
```

```
        objLogEntryType = EventLogEntryType.Information
        objLog.WriteEntry("Error: " & objA.message, objLogEntryType)
    Catch objB As System.Exception
        MessageBox.Show(objB.Message)
    End Try
End Try

End Sub
```

As we walk through our code, we start with setting up registry permission and setting it to Deny access:

```
Dim oRp As New _
    RegistryPermission(Security.Permissions.PermissionState.Unrestricted)
oRp.Deny()
```

Next, we set up to Throw an exception on purpose in order to set up writing to an event log:

```
Throw (New EntryPointNotFoundException)
```

When the exception is caught, it checks the registry to make sure a specific type of registry entry source is already in existence:

```
If Not objLog.SourceExists("Example") Then
    objLog.CreateEventSource("Example", "System")
End If
```

And at this point our code fails with the following error message as shown in Figure 24-4:

Figure 24-4

These examples can serve as a good basis for use in developing classes that access the other objects within the scope of the Permissions namespace, such as reflections and UI permissions.

Managing Security Policy

As we stated in the introduction to the chapter, we have two new command line utilities (Caspol.exe and Permview.exe) that help us configure and view security policy at both machine and user levels. When we manage security policy at this level we are doing so as an administrator of a machine or user policy for a machine that is hosting code that will be called from other front-end applications. Caspol.exe is a command line utility that has many options to give us the ability to configure our security policies (Caspol stands for Code Access Security Policy). User and machine policy are associated with groups and permission sets. There is one group that is provided for us, the AllCode Group.

The `Caspol` utility has two categories of commands for us to review. The first category listed in the following table is the set of commands that give us feedback on the current security policy.

Command	Short Command	Parameters	Effect
-List	-l	None	This lists the combination of the following three options
-ListGroups	-lg	None	This will list only groups
-ListPset	-lp	None	This will list only permission sets
-ListFulltrust	-lf	None	This will list only assemblies which have full trust privileges
-Reset	-rs	None	This will reset the machine and user policies to the default for .NET. This is handy if a policy creates a condition that is not recoverable. Use this command carefully as you will lose all changes made to the current policies
-ResolveGroup	-rsg	Assembly File	This will list what groups are associated with a given assembly file
-ResolvePerm	-rsp	Assembly File	This will list what permission sets are associated with a given assembly file

This is not the list in its entirety, but a listing of some of the more important commands. Now let's look at some examples of output from our previous listed commands.

If we wanted to list the groups active on our local machine at the Visual Studio .NET 2003 Command Prompt, we would type the following:

```
Caspol -Machine -ListGroups
```

The output will look similar to the following, as illustrated in Figure 24-5 (though will differ slightly depending upon the machine you are working on).

Let's talk about the previous screen, so that we know some of the other things that are listed besides what we specifically requested. On the third line, we see that code access security checking is ON. On the

```
Visual Studio .NET 2003 Command Prompt                          _ □ ×
C:\>caspol -machine -listgroups
Microsoft (R) .NET Framework CasPol 1.1.4322.573
Copyright (C) Microsoft Corporation 1998-2002. All rights reserved.

Security is ON
Execution checking is ON
Policy change prompt is ON

Level = Machine

Code Groups:

1.  All code: Nothing
    1.1.   Zone - MyComputer: FullTrust
       1.1.1.   StrongName - 00240000004800000094000000060200000024000052534131300040
0000010001000D7D1FA57C4AED9F0A32E84AA0FAEFD0DE9E8FD6AEC8F87FB03766C834C99921EB23BE
79AD9D5DCC1DD9AD23613210290B723CF980957FC4E177108FC607774F29E8320E92EA05ECE4E82
1C0A5EFE8F1645C4C0C93C1AB99285D622CAA652C1DFAD63D745D6F2DE5F17E5EAF0FC4963D261C8
A12436518206DC093344D5AD293: FullTrust
       1.1.2.   StrongName - 0000000000000000000400000000000000: FullTrust
    1.2.   Zone - Intranet: LocalIntranet
       1.2.1.   All code: Same site Web.
       1.2.2.   All code: Same directory FileIO - Read, PathDiscovery
    1.3.   Zone - Internet: Internet
       1.3.1.   All code: Same site Web.
    1.4.   Zone - Untrusted: Nothing
    1.5.   Zone - Trusted: Internet
       1.5.1.   All code: Same site Web.
Success

C:\>
```

Figure 24-5

following line we see that the machine is checking for the user's right to execute the `Caspol` utility, since Execution checking is ON. The Policy change prompt is on, so if the user executes a `Caspol` command that will change system policy there will be an "Are You Sure?" style prompt which appears to confirm that this is really intentional.

The level is also listed on our screen prior to our requested output, which is detailed at the bottom listing the groups present on the machine. There are two levels that the policies pertain to, those being the machine and the user. When changing policy, if the user is not an administrator, the user policy is affected unless the user specifically applies the policy to the machine through use of the `-machine` switch, as illustrated in our screenshot. If the user is an administrator the machine policy is affected unless the user specifically applies the policy to the user level through the use of the `-user` switch.

Let's now look at another request result example. This time we will ask for a listing of all of the permission sets on our machine. At the Command Prompt we would type the following:

```
Caspol -machine -listpset
```

And we would see the output similar to the following screenshot. The following output has been shortened for space considerations, but the output would contain a listing of all of the code explicitly set to execute against the seven permission sets that we mentioned in our definitions section. Also, note that the output is an XML representation of a permission object. The listing details the named permission sets and what each one has as active rights. For instance, the fifth permission set is named `LocalIntranet`, while the next lines detail the `Permission` class, being an environment permission with read access to the environment variable – `USERNAME`. The next class detail is regarding `FileDialogpermissions`, and it lists those as being unrestricted. The screenshot shown in Figure 24-6 then goes on to detail the effective settings for `IsolatedStorage` and others.

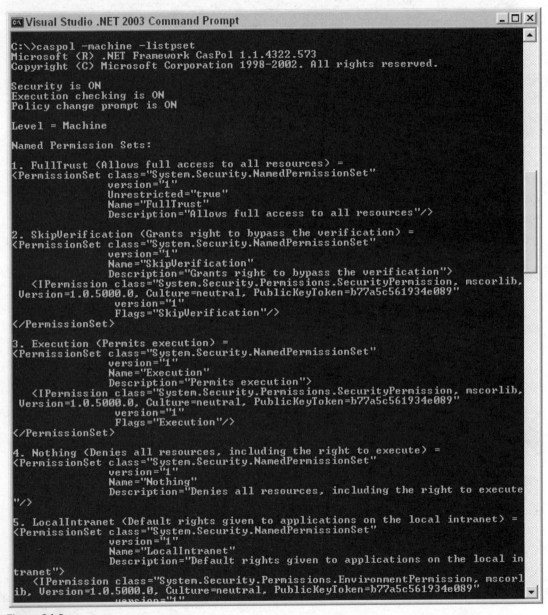

Figure 24-6

Let's now look at the second category of commands that go with the `Caspol` utility as shown in the following table. These commands are those that we will use to actually modify policy.

Command	Short Command	Parameters	Effect
-AddFullTrust	-af	Assembly File Name	Adds a given Assembly file to the full trust permission set
-AddGroup	-ag	Parent Label, Membership, Permission Set Name	Adds a code group to the code group hierarchy
-AddPSet	-ap	Permission Set Path, Permission Set Name	Adds a new named permission set to the policy; the permission set should be an XML file
-ChgGroup	-cg	Membership, Permission Set Name	Changes a code group's information
-ChgPset	-cp	File Name, Permission Set Name	Changes a named permission set's information
-Force	-f		This option is not recommended. It forces `Caspol` to accept policy changes even if the change could cause `Caspol` itself not to be able to be executed
-Recover	-r		Recovers policy information from a backup file that is controlled by the utility
-RemFullTrust	-rf	Assembly File Name	Removes a given Assembly file from the full trust permission set
-RemGroup	-rg	Label	Removes a code group
-RemPSet	-rp	Permission Set Name	Removes a permission set. The seven default sets cannot be removed

Again, this is not a comprehensive list of all the available commands, therefore you should consult the MSDN documentation for the complete listing, if needed. Let's begin our discussion of these commands with a few more definitions that will help us understand the parameters that go with our commands. An *assembly file* is created within VB.NET each time we do a build where our version is a release version. An assembly needs to have a strong name associated with it in order to be used in our permissions groupings. An assembly gets a strong name from being associated with a digital signature uniquely identifying the assembly. We carry out this association in addition to providing other pieces of evidence to be used with the strong name within the `AssemblyInfo.vb` file of our project.

To do this, open up the `AssemblyInfo.vb` file within Visual Studio .NET (VS.NET). This file is automatically created for you by VS.NET when you create a project. Simply add a new assembly attribute to the list as shown here:

```
<Assembly: AssemblyKeyFileAttribute("myKey.snk")>
```

This associates our assembly with an existing originating key file in order for VS.NET to generate a strong name during the build process. Be sure that you place the key file in the project directory as this is where VS.NET will be looking for it during the build process. During the build, VS.NET has generated the strong name, and then we can add our assembly to our security configuration. Place the executable, `SecurityApp.exe` (your executable will be the name of your project), which was created from our build, into the `C:\testsecurity` directory on the local machine for use with our policy method illustrations.

If we wanted to add our assembly to the `fulltrust` permission set, we would type

```
Caspol -addfulltrust C:\testsecurity\SecurityApp.exe
```

The following is a screenshot of the outcome of our command (Figure 24-7).

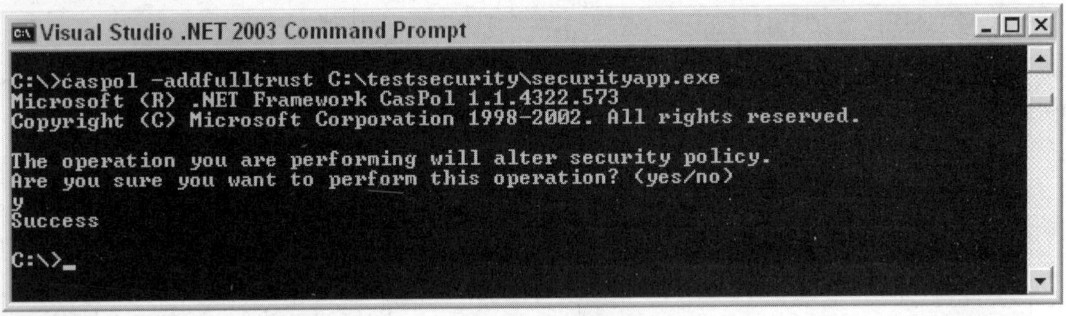

Figure 24-7

As we can see, we were prompted before our command altered our security policy, and then our new application was added to the `fulltrust` assembly list. We can confirm it was added by issuing the following command:

```
Caspol -listfulltrust
```

The excerpt of output from our command that includes our new assembly would look like what is shown in Figure 24-8.

In the screenshot, we can see our application name, version, and key information that was associated with our `.exe` file when we did our build.

Now, let's look at the creation and addition of a permission set to our permission sets in our security policy. Permission sets can be created by hand, in any text editor, in an XML format and saved as an `.xml` file (for this example I have saved it as `securityexample.xml`). Following is a listing from one such file that was created for this example:

Figure 24-8

```
<PermissionSet class="System.Security.NamedPermissionSet" version="1">
<Permission class="System.Security.Permissions.FileIOPermission, mscorlib, _
          SN=03689116d3a4ae33" version="1">
   <Read> C:\TestSecurity </Read>
</Permission>
<Permission class="System.Security.Permissions.EnvironmentPermission, _
```

```
              mscorlib, SN=03689116d3a4ae33" version="1">
    <Read> [TEMP] </Read>
</Permission>
    <Name>SecurityExample</Name>
    <Description>Gives Full File Access</Description>
</PermissionSet>
```

The listing has multiple permissions within the permission set. The listing sets up read file permissions within one set of tags as shown:

```
<Permission class="System.Security.Permissions.FileIOPermission, mscorlib, _
            SN=03689116d3a4ae33" version="1">
    <Read> C:\TestSecurity </Read>
</Permission>
```

We then set up read access to our Temp environment variable in the second set of permission tags:

```
<Permission class="System.Security.Permissions.EnvironmentPermission, _
            mscorlib, SN=03689116d3a4ae33" version="1">
    <Read> [TEMP] </Read>
</Permission>
```

The listing also gives our custom permission set the name of `SecurityExample` with a description:

```
<Name>SecurityExample</Name>
<Description>Gives Full File Access</Description>
```

When we want to add our permission set to our policy, we would type the following command:

```
Caspol -addpset C:\testsecurity\securityexample.xml securityexample
```

In the last command, we are issuing the `-addpset` flag to indicate that we want to add a permission set, followed by the XML file containing our permission set, followed finally by the name of our permission set. The outcome of our command looks like the following screenshot (Figure 24-9).

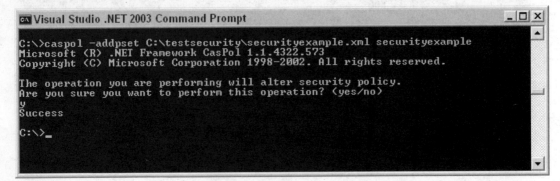

Figure 24-9

We can then list our security permission sets by typing `Caspol-listpset`. Here is the excerpt (Figure 24-10) that shows our new security permission set.

Figure 24-10

As you can see, typing `Caspol -listpset` gives a listing of just the permission sets within our policy. Our named permission set `SecurityExample` shows up under the `Named Permission Sets` heading, and its description is listed just after its name.

Now that we have a permission set, we can add a group that our assembly object fits into and which enforces our new permission set. We add this group by using the `AddGroup` switch in `Caspol`. The `AddGroup` switch has a couple of parameters that need more explanation. The first parameter is `parent_label`. When we look at the group screenshot that follows, we can see our `All` code group has a `1.` before it. The labels within code groups have a hierarchy that gets established when we add groups, and so we need to specify what our parent label would be. In our case, since the only one that exists is 1., that is what we'll be designating.

Since we designate 1, the new group will become a child of 1. The second parameter is membership. The membership parameter has a certain list of options that we can put in based on the following table. Each option designates a piece of information we are providing about the pieces of code that we will add to our group. For instance, we would state that we will only be adding code that had a specific signature with the -Pub option, or add only code in a certain application directory with the -AppDir option.

Option	Description
-All	All code
-Pub	Code that has a specific signature on a certificate file
-Strong	Code that has a specific strong name, as designated by a file name, code name, and version
-Zone	Code that fits into the following zones: MyComputer, Intranet, Trusted, Internet, or Untrusted
-Site	Originating on a Web site
-Hash	Code that has a specific assembly hash
-AppDir	A specific application directory
-SkipVerif	Code that requests the skipverification permission
-URL	Originating at a specific URL
-Custom	Code that requires a custom membership condition.

The third parameter to the AddGroup command is the permission set name that we want to be associated with our group. The group that we will create will be under parent label 1, and we will designate the -Zone parameter as being MyComputer since our code lives on a local drive. We will also associate the new group with our SecurityExample permission set by typing the following command:

```
Caspol -addgroup 1. -Zone MyComputer SecurityExample
```

We can see that our output from the command was successful in the following screenshot shown in Figure 24-11.

In our screenshot (Figure 24-12), we use the -listgroups command to list our new group.

In the screenshot we can see that a 1.6 level was added with our SecurityExample permission set attached to all code that fits into the MyComputer Zone. Now, let's verify that our assembly object fits into the MyComputer Zone by using our resolveperm command. This is illustrated in Figure 24-13.

As we can see at the bottom of the screenshot, it lists which ZoneIdentityPermission the assembly object has been associated with—MyComputer. In addition, each assembly will get an URLIdentityPermission specifying the location of the executable.

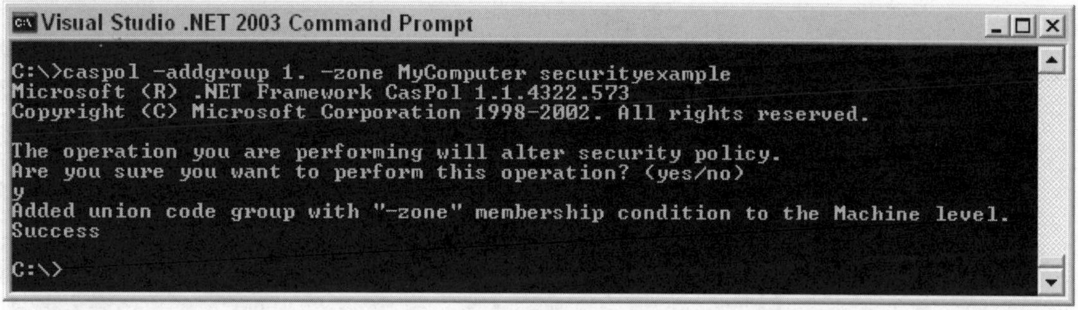

Figure 24-11

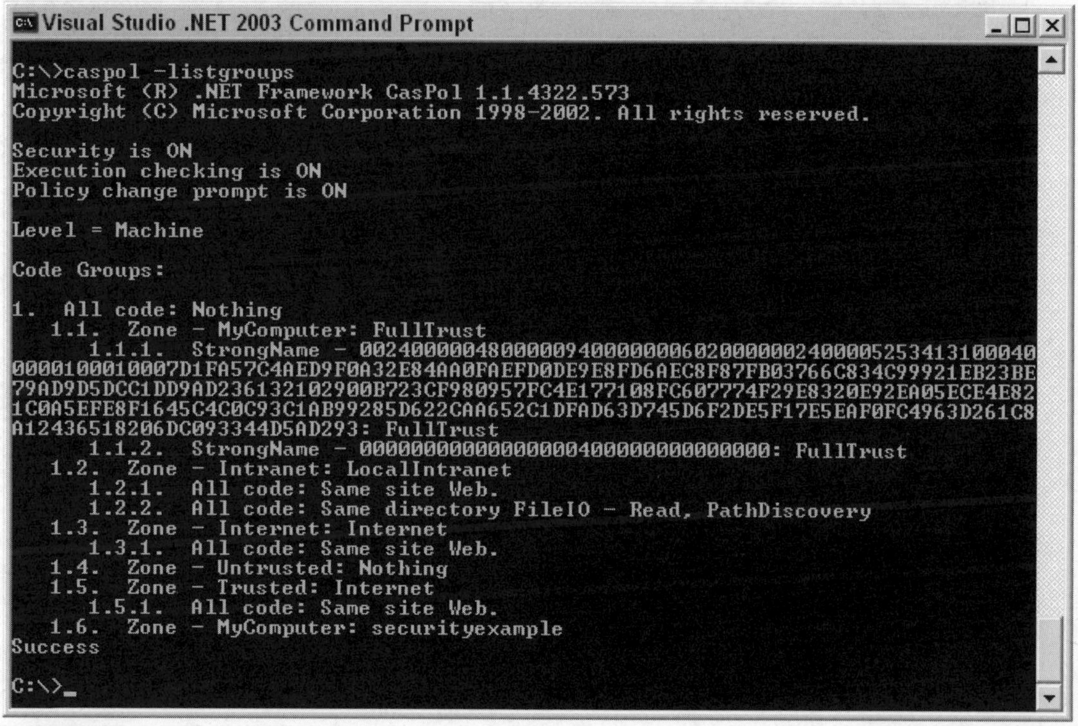

Figure 24-12

Not only do we have the utility that helps us with managing security permission sets and groups, but we also have a utility that views the security information regarding an assembly called `Permview.exe`. (`Permview` stands for Permissions Viewer.)

`Permview` is not as complex as `Caspol` because its main purpose is to give a certain type of feedback regarding the security requests of assemblies. In fact, the `Permview` utility only has two switches, one for the output location, and one for declarative security to be included in the output. In order to specify an output location the switch is `/Output` and then a file path is appended to the command line after the switch. The `Permview` utility brings up another concept we have yet to cover, that of declarative security.

Figure 24-13

Declarative security is displayed in the `Permview` utility with the `/Decl` switch, and is security that a piece of code requests at an assembly level. Since it is at the assembly level, the line which requests the security is at the top of the VB.NET module, even before our `Imports` statements. We can request one of three levels of security, as shown in the following table.

Level	Description
`RequestMinimum`	Permissions the code must have in order to run
`RequestOptional`	Permissions that code may use, but could run without
`RequestRefused`	Permissions that you want to ensure are never granted to the code

Requesting permissions at the assembly level will help ensure that the code will be able to run, and not get permission-based security exceptions. Since we have users calling our code, the declarative security ensures the callers have proper security to do all that our code requires, otherwise a security exception will be thrown. The following is an example of the syntax of how we would request minimum permissions, and the code would be placed at the top of our procedure. This example also illustrates syntax as described in the table at the beginning of our chapter regarding permissions in the `Security.Permissions` namespace. It also illustrates the use of a security constant, `SecurityAction.RequestMinimum` for the type of security we are requesting:

```
<Assembly: SecurityPermissionAttribute(SecurityAction.RequestMinimum)>
```

Once this line is added to our assembly by means of the `AssemblyInfo.vb` file, `Permview` will report on what the assembly requested by listing minimal, optional, and refused permission sets, including our security permission set under the minimal set listing.

Security Tools

Microsoft provides many security tools in its .NET SDK. Most of these tools are console-based utility applications. These can be used to help implement the security processes outlined above. We won't be discussing the use of these tools in great detail.

There are two groups of tools provided with the SDK:

❑   Permissions and assembly management tools

❑   Certificate management tools

Permissions and Assembly Management Tools

Program Name	Function
Caspol.exe	Stands for Code Access Security Policy tool. Lets you view and modify security settings
Signcode.exe	File signing tool; lets you digitally sign your executable files
Storeadm.exe	Administration tool for isolated storage management. Restricts code access to filing system
Permview.exe	Displays assembly's requested access permissions
Peverify.exe	Checks if the executable file will pass the runtime test for type safe coding
Secutil.exe	Extracts a public key from a certificate and puts it in a format that is usable in your source code
Sn.exe	Creates assemblies with strong names; that is, digitally signed namespace and version info

Certificate Management Tools

Program Name	Function
`Makecert.exe`	Creates a X.509 certificate for testing purposes
`Certmgr.exe`	Assembles certificates into a CTL (Certificate Trust List). Can also be used for revoking
`Chktrust.exe`	Validates a signed file containing data, its PKCS#7 hash and a X.509 certificate
`Cert2spc.exe`	Creates an SPC (Software Publisher Certificate) from a X.509 certificate

Now that we've covered the permissions side of .NET security, let's take a look at cryptography.

Cryptography Basics

Rather than being a general exposition of cryptography, this section is meant to familiarize you with basic techniques required to deal with .NET security and protecting your Web services through encryption. The three building blocks we need are hashing algorithms, secret key encryption, and an understanding of the Public Key Cryptographic System (PKCS).

Hashing algorithms digest long sequences of data into short *footprints*, the most popular being 64-bit hash keys. The two most popular hashing algorithms are SHA (Secured Hash Algorithm) and MD5 (Message Digest version 5). These hash keys are used for signing digital documents, in other words, the hash is generated and encrypted using a *private key*.

Secret key encryption is commonly used to protect data through passwords and pass phrases (long phrases that would be difficult to guess). Secret key encryption is suitable for situations where the encrypted data needs to be accessed by the same person who protected it.

Public Key Cryptography is most widely used in protecting the data through encryption. It is also used for digital signatures. Public Key Cryptography is based on asymmetric keys. This means that you always have a pair of keys. One is known to all and is called the *public key*. The other key of the pair is kept secret and is known only to the owner. This is called the *private key*. If we use the public key to encrypt data, it can only be decrypted using the corresponding private key of the key pair, and vice versa.

The public key is known to all, so any one can decrypt the information. However, the private key is known only to the owner, so this process acts as a *digital signature*. In other words, if the public key decrypts the message, we know that the sender was the owner of the private key. As we hinted, rather than encrypting the whole document using the private key, a hash algorithm is used to digest the data into a compact form, and this is then encrypted using the private key. The result of this process is called the digital signature of the digital document.

If the data is encrypted using the public key, it can then only be decrypted by the corresponding private key, which means that only the owner of the private key will be able to read the unencrypted data. This can be used for encryption purposes.

The cryptographic namespace of the .NET Framework is `System.Security.Cryptography`.

Hash Algorithms

Hash algorithms are also called *one-way functions*. This is because of their mathematical property of nonreversibility. The hash algorithms reduce large binary strings into a fixed length binary byte array. This fixed length binary array is used for computing digital signatures, as explained earlier.

To verify a piece of information, the hash is recomputed and compared against a previously computed hash value. If both the values match, the data has not been altered. The cryptographic hashing algorithms map a large stream of binary data to a much shorter fixed length, so it is theoretically possible to have two different documents having the same hash key.

Although, in theory, it is possible that two documents may have the same MD5 hash key and a different check sum, it is computationally impossible to create a forged document having the same hash key as the original hash value. Take the case of a virus attack on an executable code. In the late eighties, the state-of-art was to create a check sum or a CRC (Cyclic Redundancy Check) as a protection measure against accidental or malicious damage to the code integrity.

> Virus makers drew cunning designs to create viruses that added padding code to the victim's files so that the check sum and CRC remained unchanged in spite of the infection. However, using MD5 hash values, this kind of stealth attack is rendered unfeasible.

Windows Meta Files (WMF), still use check sums in the file header. For example, the .NET Framework class `System.Drawing.Imaging.WmfPlaceableFileHeader` has a read/write property of type `short` called `Checksum`. However, due to ease of computation, this check sum is used as a cheap mode of protection against accidental damage rather than against malicious attacks.

Here is a simple program to calculate a check sum:

```
' Cryptography/Checksum.vb

Imports System
Imports System.IO

Module Module1
```

This is the entry point for the program. Here, we check to see if we've received the correct argument from the command line to run the program, and stop the program if we haven't:

```
Public Sub Main(ByVal CmdArgs() As String)
    If (CmdArgs.Length <> 1) Then
        Console.WriteLine("usage: Checksum <filename>")
        End
    End If
```

First, we open the file for which the check sum is to be computed:

```
Dim fs As FileStream = File.OpenRead(CmdArgs(0))
```

We then compute the check sum and close the file, and then output the result to the screen:

```
    Dim sum As Short = compute(fs)
    fs.Close()
    Console.WriteLine(sum)
End Sub
```

The following method computes the check sum:

```
Function compute(ByVal strm As Stream)
        Dim sum As Long = 0
        Dim by As Integer
        strm.Position = 0
        by = strm.ReadByte
        While (by <> -1)
            sum = (((by Mod &HFF) + sum) Mod &HFFFF)
            by = strm.ReadByte
        End While
        Return CType((sum Mod &HFFFF), Short)
    End Function
End Module
```

Compile this program with:

```
vbc Checksum.vb
```

and run it with:

```
Checksum <filename>
```

Due to their unsafe nature, check sum and CRC are sometimes termed as poor cousins of cryptographic hash algorithms. We will now look into classes provided by the .NET Framework to cater for cryptographic grade algorithms.

Cryptographic Hash Algorithms

The abstract class `System.Security.Cryptography.HashAlgorithm` represents the concept of cryptographic hash algorithms within the .NET Framework. The framework provides seven classes which extend the `HashAlgorithm` abstract class. These are:

❑ `MD5CryptoServiceProvider` (extends abstract class `MD5`)

❑ `SHA1CryptoServiceProvider` (extends abstract class `SHA1`)

❑ `SHA256Managed` (extends abstract class `SHA256`)

❑ `SHA384Managed` (extends abstract class `SHA384`)

❑ `SHA512Managed` (extends abstract class `SHA512`)

❑ `HMACSHA1` (extends abstract class `KeyedHashAlgorithm`)

❑ `MACTripleDES` (extends abstract class `KeyedHashAlgorithm`)

The last two classes belong to a class of algorithm called *keyed hash algorithms*. The keyed hashes extend the concept of cryptographic hash with the use of a shared secret key. This is used for computing the hash of a data transported over an unsecured channel.

The following is an example of computing a hash value of a file:

```
' Cryptography/TestKeyHash.vb

Imports System
Imports System.IO
```

```
Imports System.Security.Cryptography
Imports System.Text
Imports System.Runtime.Serialization.Formatters

Module Module1
    Public Sub Main(ByVal CmdArgs() As String)
        If (CmdArgs.Length <> 1) Then
            Console.WriteLine("usage: TestKeyHash <filename>")
            End
        End If
```

Here, we create the object instance of the .NET SDK Framework class, with a salt (a random secret to confuse a potential snooper):

```
Dim key() As Byte = Encoding.ASCII.GetBytes( _
"My Secret Key".ToCharArray())
Dim hmac As HMACSHA1 = New HMACSHA1(key)
Dim fs As FileStream = File.OpenRead(CmdArgs(0))
```

The next four lines compute the hash, convert the binary hash into a printable base 64 format, close the file, and then print the base 64 encoded string as the result of hashing to the screen:

```
        Dim hash() As Byte = hmac.ComputeHash(fs)
        Dim b64 As String = Convert.ToBase64String(hash)
        fs.Close()
        Console.WriteLine(b64)
    End Sub
End Module
```

The code can be compiled at the command line using the following:

```
vbc TestKeyHash.vb
```

To execute the code, give the following command at the console prompt:

```
TestKeyHash TestKeyHash.vb
```

This should produce a hashed output:

```
IOEj/D0rOxjEqCD8qHoYm+yWw6I=
```

The previous example uses an instance of the HMACSHA1 class. The output displayed is a Base64 encoding of the binary hash result value. Base64 encoding is widely used in MIME and XML file formats to represent binary data. To recover the binary data from a Base64 encoded string, we could use the following code fragment:

```
Dim orig() As Byte = Convert.FromBase64String(b64)
```

The XML parser, however, does this automatically. We will come across this in later examples.

SHA

SHA (Secured Hashing Algorithm) is a block cipher and operates on a block size of 64 bits. However, the subsequent enhancements of this algorithm have bigger key values, thus increasing the value range and therefore enhancing the cryptographic utility. We must note that the bigger the key value sizes, the longer it takes to compute the hash. Moreover, for relatively smaller data files, smaller hash values are more secure. To put it another way, the hash algorithm's block size should be less than or equal to the size of the data itself.

The hash size for the SHA1 algorithm is 160 bits. Here is how to use it, which is similar to the HMACSHA1 code discussed previously:

```vb
' Cryptography/TestSHA1.vb

Imports System
Imports System.IO
Imports System.Security.Cryptography
Imports System.Text
Imports System.Runtime.Serialization.Formatters

Module Module1
    Public Sub Main(ByVal CmdArgs() As String)
        If (CmdArgs.Length <> 1) Then
            Console.WriteLine("usage: TestSHA1 <filename>")
            End
        End If
        Dim fs As FileStream = File.OpenRead(CmdArgs(0))

        Dim sha As SHA1 = New SHA1CryptoServiceProvider
        Dim hash() As Byte = sha.ComputeHash(fs)
        Dim b64 As String = Convert.ToBase64String(hash)
        fs.Close()
        Console.WriteLine(b64)
    End Sub
End Module
```

The .NET Framework provides bigger key size algorithms as well, namely SHA256, SHA384, and SHA512. The numbers at the end of the name indicate their block size.

The class SHA256Managed extends the abstract class SHA256, which in turn extends the abstract class HashAlgorithm. The Forms Authentication module of ASP.NET security (System.Web.Security .FormsAuthenticationModule) uses SHA1 as one of its valid formats to store and compare user passwords.

MD5

MD5 stands for Message Digest version 5. It is a cryptographic, one-way hash algorithm. The MD5 algorithm competes well with SHA. MD5 is an improved version of MD4, devised by Ron Rivest of RSA fame. In fact, FIPS PUB 180-1 states that SHA-1 is based on similar principles to MD4. The salient features of this class of algorithms are:

❑ It is computationally unfeasible to forge an MD5 hash digest

❑ MD5 is not based on any mathematical assumption such as the difficulty of factoring large binary integers

❑ MD5 is computationally cheap, and therefore suitable for low latency requirements

❑ It is relatively simple to implement

The MD5 is the de facto standard for hash digest computation, due to the popularity of RSA.

The .NET Framework provides an implementation of this algorithm through the class `MD5CryptoServiceProvider` in the `System.Security.Cryptography` namespace. This class extends the `MD5` abstract class, which in turn extends the abstract class `HashAlgorithm`. This class shares a common base class with SHA1, so the examples previously discussed can be modified easily to accommodate this:

```
Dim fs As FileStream = File.OpenRead(CmdArgs(0))

Dim md5 As MD5 = New MD5CryptoServiceProvider
Dim hash() As Byte = md5.ComputeHash(fs)

Dim b64 As String = Convert.ToBase64String(hash)
fs.Close()
Console.WriteLine(b64)
```

Secret Key Encryption

Secret key encryption is widely used to encrypt data files using passwords. The simplest technique is to seed a random number using a password, and then encrypt the files with an XOR operation using this random number generator.

The .NET Framework represents the secret key by an abstract base class `SymmetricAlgorithm`. Four concrete implementations of different secret key algorithms are provided by default:

❑ `DESCryptoServiceProvider` (extends abstract class `DES`)

❑ `RC2CryptoServiceProvider` (extends abstract class `RC2`)

❑ `RijndaelManaged` (extends abstract class `Rijndael`)

❑ `TripleDESCryptoServiceProvider` (extends abstract class `TripleDES`)

Let's explore the `SymmetricAlgorithm` design. As will be clear from the following example code, two separate methods are provided to access encryption and decryption. Here is a console application program that encrypts and decrypts a file given a secret key:

```
' Cryptography/SymEnc.vb

Imports System.Security.Cryptography
Imports System.IO
Imports System.Text
Imports System

Module Module1
    Public Sub Main(ByVal CmdArgs() As String)
        If (CmdArgs.Length <> 4) Then
            UsageAndExit()
        End If
```

Here, we compute the index of the algorithm that we'll use:

```
Dim algoIndex As Integer = CmdArgs(0)
If (algoIndex < 0 Or algoIndex >= algo.Length) Then
    UsageAndExit()
End If
```

We open the input and output files (the file name represented by CmdArgs(3) is the output file, and CmdArgs(2) is the input file):

```
Dim fin As FileStream = File.OpenRead(CmdArgs(2))
Dim fout As FileStream = File.OpenWrite(CmdArgs(3))
```

We create the symmetric algorithm instance using the .NET Framework class SymmetricAlgorithm. This will use the algorithm name indexed by the CmdArgs(0) parameter. After this, we'll set the key parameters, and display them on-screen for information:

```
Dim sa As SymmetricAlgorithm = _
    SymmetricAlgorithm.Create(algo(algoIndex))
sa.IV = Convert.FromBase64String(b64IVs(algoIndex))
sa.Key = Convert.FromBase64String(b64Keys(algoIndex))
Console.WriteLine("Key " + CType(sa.Key.Length, String))
Console.WriteLine("IV " + CType(sa.IV.Length, String))
Console.WriteLine("KeySize: " + CType(sa.KeySize, String))
Console.WriteLine("BlockSize: " + CType(sa.BlockSize, String))
Console.WriteLine("Padding: " + CType(sa.Padding, String))
```

At this point, we check to see which operation is required, and execute the appropriate static method:

```
    If (CmdArgs(1).ToUpper().StartsWith("E")) Then
        Encrypt(sa, fin, fout)
    Else
        Decrypt(sa, fin, fout)
    End If
End Sub
```

Here is where the encryption itself takes place:

```
Public Sub Encrypt(ByVal sa As SymmetricAlgorithm, _
                   ByVal fin As Stream, _
                   ByVal fout As Stream)
    Dim trans As ICryptoTransform = sa.CreateEncryptor()
    Dim buf() As Byte = New Byte(2048) {}
    Dim cs As CryptoStream = _
        New CryptoStream(fout, trans, CryptoStreamMode.Write)
    Dim Len As Integer
    fin.Position = 0
    Len = fin.Read(buf, 0, buf.Length)
    While (Len > 0)
        cs.Write(buf, 0, Len)
        Len = fin.Read(buf, 0, buf.Length)
    End While
```

```
        cs.Close()
        fin.Close()
    End Sub
```

Here's the decryption method:

```
    Public Sub Decrypt(ByVal sa As SymmetricAlgorithm, _
                       ByVal fin As Stream, _
                       ByVal fout As Stream)
        Dim trans As ICryptoTransform = sa.CreateDecryptor()
        Dim buf() As Byte = New Byte(2048) {}
        Dim cs As CryptoStream = _
            New CryptoStream(fin, trans, CryptoStreamMode.Read)
        Dim Len As Integer
        Len = cs.Read(buf, 0, buf.Length)
        While (Len > 0)
            fout.Write(buf, 0, Len)
            Len = cs.Read(buf, 0, buf.Length)
        End While
        fin.Close()
        fout.Close()
    End Sub
```

This next method prints usage information:

```
    Public Sub UsageAndExit()
        Console.Write("usage SymEnc <algo index> <D|E> <in> <out> ")
        Console.WriteLine("D =decrypt, E=Encrypt")
        For i As Integer = 0 To (algo.Length - 1)
            Console.WriteLine("Algo index: {0} {1}", i, algo(i))
        Next i
        End
    End Sub
```

The static parameters used for object creation are indexed by CmdArgs(0). How we arrive at these magic numbers will be discussed shortly:

```
        Dim algo() As String = {"DES", "RC2", "Rijndael", "TripleDES"}
        Dim b64Keys() As String = { _
            "YE32PGCJ/g0=", _
            "vct+rJ09WuUcR61yfxniTQ==", _
            "PHDPqfwE3z25f2UYjwwfwg4XSqxvl8WYmy+2h8t6AUg=", _
            "Q1/lWoraddTH3IXAQUJGDSYDQcYYuOpm"}
        Dim b64IVs() As String = { _
            "onQX8hdHeWQ=", _
            "jgetiyz+pIc=", _
            "pd5mgMMfDI2Gxm/SKl5I8A==", _
            "6jpFrUh8FF4="}
    End Module
```

After compilation, this program can encrypt and decrypt using all four of the symmetric key implementations provided by the .NET Framework. The secret keys and their initialization vectors (IV) have been generated by a simple source code generator, which we will examine shortly.

The following commands encrypt and decrypt files using the DES algorithm. With the first command, we take a text file, 1.txt, and use the DES algorithm to create an encrypted file calle 2.bin. The next command decrypts this file back and stores it into 3.bin:

```
SymEnc 0 E 1.txt 2.bin
SymEnc 0 D 2.bin 3.bin
```

The first parameter of the SymEnc program is an index to the string array, which determines the algorithm to be used:

```
Dim algo() As String = {"DES", "RC2", "Rijndael", "TripleDES"}
```

The string defining the algorithm is passed as a parameter to the static Create method of the abstract class SymmetricAlgorithm. This class has an abstract factory design pattern:

```
Dim sa As SymmetricAlgorithm = _
    SymmetricAlgorithm.Create(algo(algoIndex))
```

To encrypt, we get an instance of the ICryptoTransform interface by calling the CreateEncryptor method of the SymmetricAlgorithm class extender:

```
Dim trans As ICryptoTransform = sa.CreateEncryptor()
```

Similarly, for decryption, we get an instance of the ICryptoTransform interface by calling the CreateDecryptor method of the SymmetricAlgorithm class instance:

```
Dim trans As ICryptoTransform = sa.CreateDecryptor()
```

We use the class CryptoStream for both encryption and decryption. However, the parameters to the constructor differ. For encryption we use the following code:

```
Dim cs As CryptoStream = _
    New CryptoStream(fout, trans, CryptoStreamMode.Write)
```

Similarly, for decryption we use the following code:

```
Dim cs As CryptoStream = _
    New CryptoStream(fin, trans, CryptoStreamMode.Read)
```

We call the Read and Write methods of the CryptoStream for decryption and encryption, respectively. For generating the keys we use a simple code generator listed as follows:

```
' Cryptography/SymKey.vb

Imports System.Security.Cryptography
Imports System.Text
Imports System.IO
Imports System
Imports Microsoft.VisualBasic.ControlChars
```

```
Module Module1
    Public Sub Main(ByVal CmdArgs() As String)
        Dim keyz As StringBuilder = New StringBuilder
        Dim ivz As StringBuilder = New StringBuilder
        keyz.Append("Dim b64Keys() As String = { _" + crlf)
        ivz.Append(crlf + "Dim b64IVs() As String = { _" + crlf )
```

The algorithm names for symmetric keys used by .NET SDK are given the correct index values here:

```
Dim algo() As String = {"DES", "RC2", "Rijndael", "TripleDES"}
```

For each of the algorithms, we generate the keys and IV:

```
Dim comma As String = ", _" + crlf
For i As Integer = 0 To 3
    Dim sa As SymmetricAlgorithm = _
        SymmetricAlgorithm.Create(algo(i))
    sa.GenerateIV()
    sa.GenerateKey()
    Dim Key As String
    Dim IV As String
    Key = Convert.ToBase64String(sa.Key)
    IV = Convert.ToBase64String(sa.IV)
    keyz.AppendFormat(tab + """" + Key + """" + comma)
    ivz.AppendFormat(tab + """" + IV + """" + comma)
    If i = 2 Then comma = " "
Next i
```

Here, we print or emit the source code:

```
        keyz.Append("}")
        ivz.Append("}")
        Console.WriteLine(keyz.ToString())
        Console.WriteLine(ivz.ToString())
    End Sub
End Module
```

The preceding program creates a random key and an initializing vector for each algorithm. This output can be inserted directly into the SymEnc.vb program. The simplest way to do this is to type

```
SymKey > keys.txt
```

This will redirect the information into a file called keys.txt, which you can then use to cut and paste the values into your program. We use the StringBuilder class along with the control character crlf (carriage return and line feed) to format the text so that it can be inserted directly into your program. We then convert the binary data into Base64 encoding using the public instance method ToBase64String of the class Convert. Kerberos, the popular network authentication protocol supported by Windows Server 2003, Windows 2000 and all of the UNIX flavors, uses secret key encryption for implementing security.

In this next section, we will look into public key encryption.

PKCS

The Public Key Cryptographic System is a type of asymmetric key encryption. This system uses two keys, one private and the other public. The public key is widely distributed whereas the private key is kept secret. One cannot derive or deduce the private key by knowing the public key, so the public key can be safely distributed.

The keys are different, yet complementary. That is, if you encrypt data using the public key, only the owner of the private key can decipher it, and vice versa. This forms the basis of PKCS encryption.

If the private key holder encrypts a piece of data using their private key, any person having access to the public key can decrypt it. The public key, as the name suggests, is available publicly. This property of the PKCS is exploited along with a hashing algorithm, such as SHA or MD5, to provide a verifiable digital signature process.

The abstract class `System.Security.Cryptography.AsymmetricAlgorithm` represents this concept in the .NET Framework. Two concrete implementations of this class are provided by default, and they are:

❑   `DSACryptoServiceProvider` which extends the abstract class `DSA`.

❑   `RSACryptoServiceProvider` which extends the abstract class `RSA`.

DSA (Digital Signature Algorithm) was specified by NIST (National Institute of Standards and Technology) in January 2000. The original DSA standard was, however, issued by NIST, way back in August 1991. DSA cannot be used for encryption and is good for only digital signature. We will discuss digital signature in more detail in the next subsection.

RSA algorithms can also be used for encryption as well as digital signatures. RSA is the de facto standard and has much wider acceptance than DSA. RSA is a tiny bit faster than DSA as well.

RSA algorithm is named after its three inventors: Rivest, Shamir, and Adleman. It was patented in the USA, but the patent expired on September 20, 2000. RSA can be used for both digital signature and data encryption. It is based on the assumption that large numbers are extremely difficult to factor. The use of RSA for digital signatures is approved within the FIPS PUB 186-2 and defined in the ANSI X9.31 standard document.

To gain some practical insights into RSA implementation of the .NET Framework, consider the following code:

```
' Cryptography/TestRSAKey.vb

Imports System.Security.Cryptography.Xml

Module Module1
    Sub Main()
        Dim RSA As RSAKeyValue = New RSAKeyValue
        Dim str As String = RSA.Key.ToXmlString(True)
        System.Console.WriteLine(str)
    End Sub
End Module
```

This code creates a pair of private and public keys and prints it out at the command line in XML format. To compile the preceding code, simply open a console session, run `corvar.bat` (if necessary) to set the

.NET SDK paths, and compile the program by typing the following command:

```
vbc /r:System.Security.dll TestRSAKey.vb
```

This should produce a file called `TestRSAKey.exe`. Execute this program and redirect the output to a file such as `key.xml`:

```
TestRSAKey > key.xml
```

The file `key.xml` contains all the private and public members of the generated RSA key object. You can open this XML file in Internet Explorer 5.5 or above. If you do so, you will notice that the private member variables are also stored in this file. The binary data representing the large integers is encoded in `Base64` format.

The program listed above uses an `RSAKeyValue` instance to generate a new key pair. The class `RSAKeyValue` is contained in the `System.Security.Cryptography.Xml` namespace. This namespace can be thought of as the XML face of the .NET cryptographic framework. It contains a specialized, lightweight implementation of XML for the purpose of cryptography, and the model allows XML objects to be signed with a digital signature.

The `System.Security.Cryptography.Xml` namespace classes depend upon the classes contained in the `System.Security.Cryptography` namespace for the actual implementation of cryptographic algorithms.

The `key.xml` file, generated by redirecting the output of the VB.NET test program `TestRSAKey`, contains both private and public keys. However, we need to keep the private key secret while making the public key widely available. Therefore, we need to separate out the public key from the key pair. Here is the program to do it:

```vb
' Cryptography/TestGetPubKey.vb

Imports System.Text
Imports System.Security.Cryptography
Imports System.IO
Imports System.Security.Cryptography.Xml
Imports System

Module Module1
    Public Sub Main(ByVal CmdArgs() As String)
        If (CmdArgs.Length <> 1) Then
            Console.WriteLine("usage: TestGetPubKey <key pair xml>")
            End
        End If
        Dim xstr As String = File2String(CmdArgs(0))
```

The following code creates an instance of the RSA implementation and reinitializes the internal variables through the XML formatted string:

```vb
        Dim rsa As RSACryptoServiceProvider = New RSACryptoServiceProvider
        rsa.FromXmlString(xstr)
```

```
            Dim x As String = rsa.ToXmlString(False)
            Console.WriteLine(x)
        End Sub

        Public Function File2String(ByVal fname As String)
            Dim finfo As FileInfo = New FileInfo(fname)
            Dim buf() As Byte = New Byte(finfo.Length) {}
            Dim fs As FileStream = File.OpenRead(fname)
            fs.Read(buf, 0, buf.Length)
            Return (New ASCIIEncoding).GetString(buf)
        End Function
End Module
```

This program is logically similar to TestRSAKey.vb, except that it has to read the key file and pass a different parameter in the ToXmlString method.

The cryptography classes use a lightweight XML implementation, thus avoiding the elaborate ritual of parsing the fully-formed generic XML data containing serialized objects. This has another advantage of speed because it bypasses the DOM parsers. To compile the previous code, type:

```
vbc /r:System.Security.dll TestGetPubKey.vb
```

This should produce the file TestGetPubKey.exe. Run this file, giving key.xml as the name of the input file, and redirect the program's output to pub.xml. This file will contain an XML formatted public key. The binary data, basically binary large integers, are Base64 encoded. You may recall that key.xml contains both the public and private key pairs, and was generated by redirecting the output of TestRSAKey.exe. The following line will redirect key.xml's public key to pub.xml:

```
TestGetPubKey key.xml > pub.xml
```

Now, let's write a program to test the encrypt and decrypt feature of the RSA algorithm:

```
' Cryptography/TestCrypt.vb

Imports System
Imports System.IO
Imports System.Security.Cryptography.Xml
Imports System.Security.Cryptography
Imports System.Text

Module Module1
    Public Sub Main(ByVal CmdArgs() As String)
        If (CmdArgs.Length <> 4) Then
            Console.WriteLine("usage: TestCrypt <key xml> <E|D> <in> <out>")
            Console.WriteLine(" E= Encrypt, D= Decrypt (needs private key)")
            End
        End If
```

Here, we read the public or private key into memory:

```
Dim xstr As String = File2String(CmdArgs(0))
```

We create an instance of an RSA cryptography service provider and initialize the parameters based on the XML lightweight file name passed in `CmdArgs(0)`:

```
Dim RSA As New RSACryptoServiceProvider
RSA.FromXmlString(xstr)
```

We display the key file name:

```
Console.WriteLine("Key File: " + CmdArgs(0))
Dim op As String= "Encrypted"
```

We read the input file and store it into a byte array:

```
Dim info As FileInfo = New FileInfo(CmdArgs(2))
Dim inbuflen As Integer = CType(info.Length, Integer)
Dim inbuf() As Byte = New Byte(inbuflen-1) {}
Dim outbuf() As Byte
Dim fs As FileStream = File.OpenRead(CmdArgs(2))
fs.Read(inbuf, 0, inbuf.Length)
fs.Close()
```

We either encrypt or decrypt depending on `CmdArgs(1)` option:

```
If (CmdArgs(1).ToUpper().StartsWith("D")) Then
    op = "Decrypted"
    outbuf = rsa.Decrypt(inbuf, False)
Else
    outbuf = rsa.Encrypt(inbuf, False)
End If
```

We'll write back the result in the output buffer into the file and display the result:

```
    fs = File.OpenWrite(CmdArgs(3))
    fs.Write(outbuf, 0, outbuf.Length)
    fs.Close()
    Console.WriteLine(op + " input [" + CmdArgs(2) + "] to output [" _
                    + CmdArgs(3) + "]")
End Sub
```

Here's a helper method to read the file name passed as an argument and convert the content to string:

```
    Public Function File2String(ByVal fname As String)
        Dim finfo As FileInfo = New FileInfo(fname)
        Dim buf() As Byte = New Byte(finfo.Length) {}
        Dim fs As FileStream = File.OpenRead(fname)
        fs.Read(buf, 0, buf.Length)
        fs.Close()
        Return (New ASCIIEncoding).GetString(buf)
    End Function
End Module
```

This test program encrypts or decrypts a short file depending on the parameters supplied to it. It takes four parameters, the XML formatted private or public key file, option E or D standing for encrypt or decrypt options, respectively, and input and output file names.

This program can be compiled with the following command.

```
vbc /r:System.Security.dll TestCrypt.vb
```

The previous command will produce a PE file `TestCrypt.exe`. To test the encrypt and decrypt functions, we'll create a small plain text file called `1.txt`. Recall that we had also created two other files `key.xml` and `pub.xml`. The file `key.xml` contains a key pair and `pub.xml` contains the public key extracted from the file `key.xml`.

Let's encrypt the plain text file `plain.txt`. To do so, use the following command:

```
TestCrypt pub.xml E 1.txt rsa.bin
```

Note that we have used the public key file to encrypt it. You can type the output on the console, but this won't make any sense to us because it contains binary data. You could use a binary dump utility to dump out the file's content. If you do this, you will notice that the total number of bytes is 128 compared to the input of 13 bytes. This is because the RSA is a block cipher algorithm and the block size equals the key size, so the output will always be in multiples of the block size. You may wish to rerun the preceding examples with larger files to see the resulting encrypted file length.

Let us now decrypt the file to get back the original text. Use the following command to decrypt:

```
TestCrypt key.xml D rsa.bin decr.txt
```

Note that we used the `key.xml` file, which also contains the private key, to decrypt. That's because we use the public key to encrypt and private key to decrypt. In other words, anyone may send encrypted documents to you if they know your public key, but only you can decrypt the message. The reverse is true for digital signatures, which we will cover in the next section.

Digital Signature Basics

Digital signature is the encryption of a hash digest (for example, MD5 or SHA-1) of data using a public key. The digital signature can be verified by decrypting the hash digest and comparing it against a hash digest computed from the data by the verifier.

As noted earlier, the private key is known only to the owner, so the owner can sign a digital document by encrypting the hash computed from the document. The public key is known to all, so anyone can verify the signature by recomputing the hash and comparing it against the decrypted value, using the public key of the signer.

The .NET Framework provides DSA and RSA digital signature implementations by default. We will consider only DSA, as RSA was covered in the previous section. Both of the implementations extend the same base class, so all programs for DSA discussed below will work for RSA as well.

We will go through the same motions of producing a key pair and a public key file and then sign and verify the signature:

```
' Cryptography/GenDSAKeys.vb

Imports System
Imports System.Security.Cryptography
Imports FileUtil
Module Module1
    Public Sub Main(ByVal CmdArgs() As String)
        Dim dsa As DSACryptoServiceProvider = New DSACryptoServiceProvider
        Dim prv As String = dsa.ToXmlString(True)
        Dim pub As String = dsa.ToXmlString(False)
        Dim fileutil As FileUtil = New FileUtil
        fileutil.SaveString("dsa-key.xml", prv)
        fileutil.SaveString("dsa-pub.xml", pub)
        Console.WriteLine("Created dsa-key.xml and dsa-pub.xml")
    End Sub
End Module
```

This code generates two XML formatted files `dsa-key.xml` and `dsa-pub.xml`, containing private and public keys respectively. Before we can run this, however, we need to create the `FileUtil` class used to output our two files:

```
' Cryptography/FileUtil.vb

Imports System.IO
Imports System.Text

Public Class FileUtil
    Public Sub SaveString(ByVal fname As String, ByVal data As String)
        SaveBytes(fname, (New ASCIIEncoding).GetBytes(data))
    End Sub

    Public Function LoadString(ByVal fname As String)
        Dim buf() As Byte = LoadBytes(fname)
        Return (New ASCIIEncoding).GetString(buf)
    End Function

    Public Function LoadBytes(ByVal fname As String)
        Dim finfo As FileInfo = New FileInfo(fname)
        Dim length As String = CType(finfo.Length, String)
        Dim buf() As Byte = New Byte(length) {}
        Dim fs As FileStream = File.OpenRead(fname)
        fs.Read(buf, 0, buf.Length)
        fs.Close()
        Return buf
    End Function

    Public Sub SaveBytes(ByVal fname As String, ByVal data() As Byte)
        Dim fs As FileStream = File.OpenWrite(fname)
        fs.SetLength(0)
        fs.Write(data, 0, data.Length)
        fs.Close()
    End Sub
End Class
```

The following code signs the data:

```
' Cryptography/DSASign.vb

Imports System
Imports System.IO
Imports System.Security.Cryptography
Imports System.Text
Imports FileUtil

Module Module1
    Public Sub Main(ByVal CmdArgs() As String)
        If CmdArgs.Length <> 3 Then
            Console.WriteLine("usage: DSASign <key xml> <data> <sign>")
            End
        End If
        Dim fileutil As FileUtil = New FileUtil
        Dim xkey As String = fileutil.LoadString(CmdArgs(0))
        Dim fs As FileStream = File.OpenRead(CmdArgs(1))
```

The DSA provider instance is created and the private key is reconstructed from the XML format using the following two lines of code:

```
Dim dsa As DSACryptoServiceProvider = New DSACryptoServiceProvider
dsa.FromXmlString(xkey)
```

The next line signs the file:

```
        Dim sig() As Byte = dsa.SignData(fs)
        fs.Close()
        fileutil.SaveString(CmdArgs(2), Convert.ToString(sig))
        Console.WriteLine("Signature in {0} file", CmdArgs(2))
    End Sub
End Module
```

To verify the signature, we'll use the following sample code:

```
' Cryptography/DSAVerify.vb

Imports System
Imports System.IO
Imports System.Security.Cryptography
Imports System.Text
Imports FileUtil

Module Module1
    Public Sub Main(ByVal CmdArgs() As String)
        If CmdArgs.Length <> 3 Then
            Console.WriteLine("usage: DSAVerify <key xml> <data> <sign>")
            End
        End If
```

```
            Dim fileutil As FileUtil = New FileUtil
            Dim xkey As String = fileutil.LoadString(CmdArgs(0))
            Dim data() As Byte = fileutil.LoadBytes(CmdArgs(1))
            Dim xsig As String = fileutil.LoadString(CmdArgs(2))
            Dim dsa As DSACryptoServiceProvider = New DSACryptoServiceProvider
            dsa.FromXmlString(xkey)
            Dim xsigAsByte() As Byte = New Byte(xsig) {}
            Dim verify As Boolean
            verify = dsa.VerifyData(data, xsigAsByte)
            Console.WriteLine("Signature Verification is {0}", verify)
        End Sub
    End Module
```

The actual verification is done using the highlighted code fragment.

The next four commands listed compile the source files:

```
    vbc /target:library FileUtil.vb
    vbc /r:FileUtil.dll GenDSAKeys.vb
    vbc /r:FileUtil.dll DSASign.vb
    vbc /r:FileUtil.dll DSAVerify.vb
```

There are many helper classes within the System.Security.Cryptography, and the System.Security.Cryptography.Xml namespaces, which provide many features to help deal with digital signatures and encryption and, at times, provide overlapping functionality. Therefore, there is more than one way of doing the same thing.

X509 Certificates

X509 is a public key certificate exchange framework. A public key certificate is a digitally signed statement by the owner of a private key, trusted by the verifier (usually a certifying authority) that certifies the validity of the public key of another entity. This creates a trust relationship between two unknown entities. This is an ISO standard specified by the document ISO/IEC 9594-8. X.509 certificates are also used in SSL (Secure Sockets Layer), which is covered in the next section.

There are many certifying authority services available over the Internet. VeriSign (www.verisign.com) is the most popular one. This company was also founded by the RSA trio themselves. You can also run your own Certificate Authority (CA) service over an Intranet using Microsoft Certificate Server.

The Microsoft .NET Framework SDK also provides tools for generating certificates for testing purposes.

```
    makecert -n CN=Test test.cer
```

This command generates a test certificate. You can view it by double clicking the test.cer file from Windows Explorer. The certificate is shown in Figure 24-14.

From the same dialog box, you could also install this certificate on your computer by clicking the Install Certificate button at the bottom of the dialog box.

Three classes dealing with X509 certificates are provided in the .NET Framework in the namespace System.Security.Cryptography.X509Certificates. Here is a program that loads and manipulates the certificate created earlier:

Figure 24-14

```
' Cryptography/LoadCert.vb

Imports System
Imports System.Security.Cryptography.X509Certificates

Module Module1
    Public Sub Main(ByVal CmdArgs() As String)
        If CmdArgs.Length <> 1 Then
            Console.Write("usage loadCert <cert file> ")
            End
        End If
        Dim cert As X509Certificate = _
            X509Certificate.CreateFromCertFile(CmdArgs(0))
        Console.WriteLine("hash= {0}", cert.GetCertHashString())
        Console.WriteLine("effective Date= {0}", _
                        cert.GetEffectiveDateString())
        Console.WriteLine("expire Date= {0}", _
                        cert.GetExpirationDateString())
        Console.WriteLine("Isseued By= {0}", cert.GetIssuerName())
        Console.WriteLine("Issued To= {0}", cert.GetName())
        Console.WriteLine("algo= {0}", cert.GetKeyAlgorithm())
        Console.WriteLine("Pub Key= {0}", cert.GetPublicKeyString())
    End Sub
End Module
```

The static method loads CreateFromCertFile the certificate file and creates a new instance of the class X509Certificate.

The next section deals with SSL, which uses X509 certificates for establishing the trust relationship.

Secure Sockets Layer

SSL (Secure Sockets Layer) protocol provides privacy and reliability between two communicating applications over the Internet. SSL is built over the TCP layer. In January 1999, IETF (Internet Engineering Task Force) adopted an enhanced version of SSL 3.0 and called it TLS, which stands for Transport Layer Security. TLS is backwardly compatible with SSL, and is defined in RFC 2246. However, the name SSL stayed due to wide acceptance of this Netscape protocol name.

SSL provides connection-oriented security and has the following four properties:

❑   Connection is private and encryption is valid for that session only.

❑   Symmetric key cryptography, like DES, is used for encryption. However, the session secret key is exchanged using public key encryption.

❑   Digital certificates are used to verify the identities of the communicating entities.

❑   Secure hash functions, like SHA and MD5, are used for message authentication code (MAC).

The SSL protocol sets the following goals for itself:

❑   *Cryptographic security*—Uses symmetric key for session and public key for authentication

❑   *Interoperability*—Interpolates OS and programming languages

❑   *Extensibility*—Adds new protocols for encrypting data which are allowed within the SSL framework

❑   *Relative efficiency*—Reduces computation and network activity by using caching techniques

The following is a simplified discussion of the SSL algorithm sequence.

Two entities communicating using SSL protocols must have a public–private key pair, optionally with digital certificates validating their respective public keys.

At the beginning of a session, the client and server exchange information to authenticate each other. This ritual of authentication is called the *Handshake Protocol*. During this, a session ID, the compression method and the cipher suite to be used are negotiated. If the certificates exist, they are then exchanged. Although certificates are optional, either the client or the server may refuse to continue with the connection and end the session in the absence of a certificate.

After receiving each other's public keys, a set of secret keys based on a randomly generated number is exchanged by encrypting it with each other's public keys. After this, the application data exchange can commence. The application data will be encrypted using a secret key, and a signed hash of the data is sent to verify the data integrity.

Microsoft implements the SSL client in the .NET Framework classes. However, the server-side SSL can be used by deploying your service through the IIS Web server.

The following code fragment can be used to access SSL protected Web servers from the .NET platform:

```
Dim req As WebRequest = WebRequest.Create("https://www.reuters.com")
Dim result As WebResponse = req.GetResponse()
```

Note that the preceding URL starts with `https`, which signals the `WebRequest` class (part of `System.Net`) to use SSL protocol. Interestingly, the same code is useful for accessing unsecured URLs as well.

The following is a program for accessing a secured URL. It takes care of the minor details such as encoding for us:

```vb
' Cryptography/GetWeb.vb

Imports System
Imports System.IO
Imports System.Net
Imports System.Text

Module Module1
    Public Sub Main(ByVal CmdArgs() As String)
        If CmdArgs.Length <> 1 Then
            Console.WriteLine("usage: GetWeb url")
            Console.WriteLine("example: GetWeb https://www.reuters.com")
            End
        End If
        Dim ms As String
```

We call the `Create()` method (which we'll see in a moment) with a URL and an encoding format:

```vb
    Try
        ms = Create(CmdArgs(0), "utf-8")
    Catch x As Exception
        Console.WriteLine(x.StackTrace)
        Console.WriteLine("Bad URL: {0}", CmdArgs(0))
    End Try
    Console.WriteLine(ms)
End Sub
```

Now, we come to the `Create()` method. Using the .NET Framework `WebRequest` object, we create an HTTP secured request object and get its response stream:

```vb
Function Create(ByVal url As String, ByVal encod As String) As String
    Dim req As WebRequest = WebRequest.Create(url)
    Dim result As WebResponse = req.GetResponse()
    Dim ReceiveStream As Stream = result.GetResponseStream()
```

We create an encoding instance from the .NET Framework object, `Encoding`:

```vb
Dim enc As Encoding = System.Text.Encoding.GetEncoding(encod)
```

Here, we'll create the stream reader:

```vb
Dim sr As StreamReader = New StreamReader(ReceiveStream, enc)
```

We read the stream fully—the entire Web page or serialized object is read into the `response` `String`:

```
         Dim response As String = sr.ReadToEnd()
         Return response
      End Function
      Dim MaxContentLength As Integer = 16384 ' 16k
   End Module
```

The preceding console application gets a secured (SSL) protected URL and displays the content on the console. To compile the code, give the following command:

```
vbc /r:System.dll GetWeb.vb
```

Summary

In this chapter we covered the basics of security and cryptography. We started with an overview of the security architecture of the .NET Framework, and looked at four types of security: NTFS, security policies, cryptographic, and programmatic.

We went on to examine the security tools and functionality that the .NET Framework provides. We examined the System.Security.Permissions namespace, and learned how we can control code access permissions, role-based permissions, and identity permissions. We looked at how we can manage code access permissions and manage security policies for our code. We used two tools—Caspol.exe and Permview.exe—that help us to configure and view security at both the machine and user levels.

In the second half of the chapter, we turned our attention to cryptography, both the underlying theory and how it can be applied within our applications. We looked at the different types of cryptographic hash algorithms, including SHA, MD5, Secret Key Encryption, and PKCS. We also understood how we can use digital certificates (specifically, X509 certificates) and Secure Socket Layers.

25

Assemblies and Deployment

When you create Windows applications for end users, you can be pretty sure that people will need to install the application in order to use it. However, all sorts of errors can occur when we try to run an application we've just created (and which worked perfectly on the developer machine) on another machine during the development or Quality Assurance process. Even more infuriating are problems that occur months later when an end user has installed another piece of software that is totally unrelated to the one that you developed. You'll be pleased to hear that there are many new features in Visual Studio .NET (VS.NET) and the common language runtime that make application deployment easier.

This chapter is going to look at what VS.NET and the CLR have to offer to help us. For many years, application deployment wasn't treated as an integral part of the development lifecycle of an application. It was often treated as an afterthought, not thought of until the application had been finished. With the increasing componentization of products, the deployment of applications has led to a number of problems for end users. This is not to say that it's the developer's fault that these problems occur. Often, they could be attributed to a form of growing pains as we moved toward a more component-based software architecture.

Specifically, in this chapter, we're going to look at:

❑   What assemblies are and how they are used

❑   How assemblies can be versioned

❑   The different ways that an application can be deployed

❑   How we can use VS.NET to create deployment projects for our applications

Assemblies

The assembly is used by the CLR as the smallest unit for:

❑   Deployment

- ❏ Version control
- ❏ Security
- ❏ Type grouping
- ❏ Code reuse

An assembly can be thought of as a logical DLL (assemblies can also be contained with an EXE file). It must contain a *manifest* (also referred to as the *assembly metadata*) and (optionally) any of the following three sections:

- ❏ Type metadata
- ❏ Microsoft Intermediate Language (MSIL) code
- ❏ Resources

An assembly can be just one file. Figure 25-1 details the contents of an assembly.

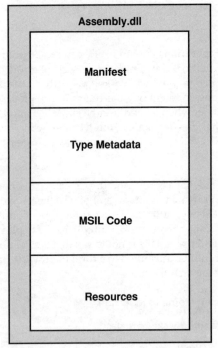

Figure 25-1

Alternatively, the structure can be split across multiple files as shown in Figure 25-2 (or any other combination that you would want).

An assembly can only have one manifest section across all the files that make up the assembly. There is nothing stopping you, however, from having a resource section (or any of the other sections of Type Metadata, and MSIL code) in each of the files that make up an assembly. The ability to split an assembly across multiple files can help with deployment and specifically on-demand downloading. The section of assemblies of most interest to us is the manifest.

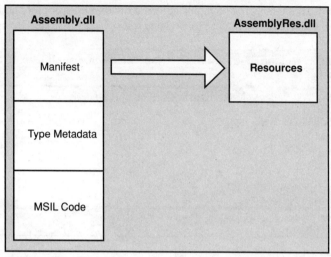

Figure 25-2

The Manifest

The *manifest* is a part of the mechanism by which an assembly is self-describing. The manifest includes the following sections (which will be covered later) as displayed in Figure 25-3.

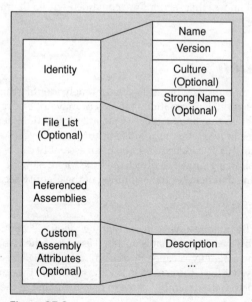

Figure 25-3

To look at what the manifest contains for a particular assembly, we can use the *IL Disassembler* (Ildasm.exe) that is part of the .NET Framework SDK. When Ildasm.exe loads up, you can browse for an assembly to view by selecting Open from the File menu. Once an assembly has been loaded into

`Ildasm.exe`, it will disassemble the metadata contained within the assembly and present you with a treeview view of the data that you can use to navigate through, as illustrated in Figure 25-4.

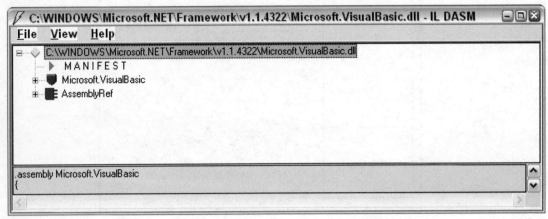

Figure 25-4

The full path of the assembly you are viewing will represent the root node. You will notice that the first node below the root is called M A N I F E S T and, as you probably have guessed, it contains all the information about the assembly's manifest. If you double-click this node, a new window will be displayed containing the information contained within the manifest as shown in Figure 25-5.

However, it's all very well know what sections are contained within the manifest and how to view them, but what are they used for?

The Identity Section

The *identity* section of the manifest is what is used to uniquely identify this particular assembly. This section can contain some optional information that may or may not be present. There are certain restrictions on the information that must appear in the identity section, depending on the type of assembly. Assemblies come in two types: *application-private* and *shared*. (We will cover the differences between the two types shortly.) The identity section of an assembly can be found by looking for the `.assembly` (without a following `extern`) directive in the Manifest window of `Ildasm.exe`. In the previous screenshot the line that denotes the beginning of the identity section is:

```
.assembly Microsoft.VisualBasic
```

From the earlier figure of the manifest, we can see that the identity section can contain a number of subsections. Every assembly has a name that is declared as part of the `.assembly` directive; in the case of the last line, we can see the assembly is called `Microsoft.VisualBasic`. The name of the assembly is very important, as this is what the CLR uses to locate the actual file that contains the assembly. The extension `.dll` is appended to the assembly name to give the name of the file that contains the assembly manifest.

The Version Number

The identity section must also contain an entry that describes what version of the assembly it is. A version number for an assembly is presented by the `.ver` directive in `Ildasm.exe` and by looking

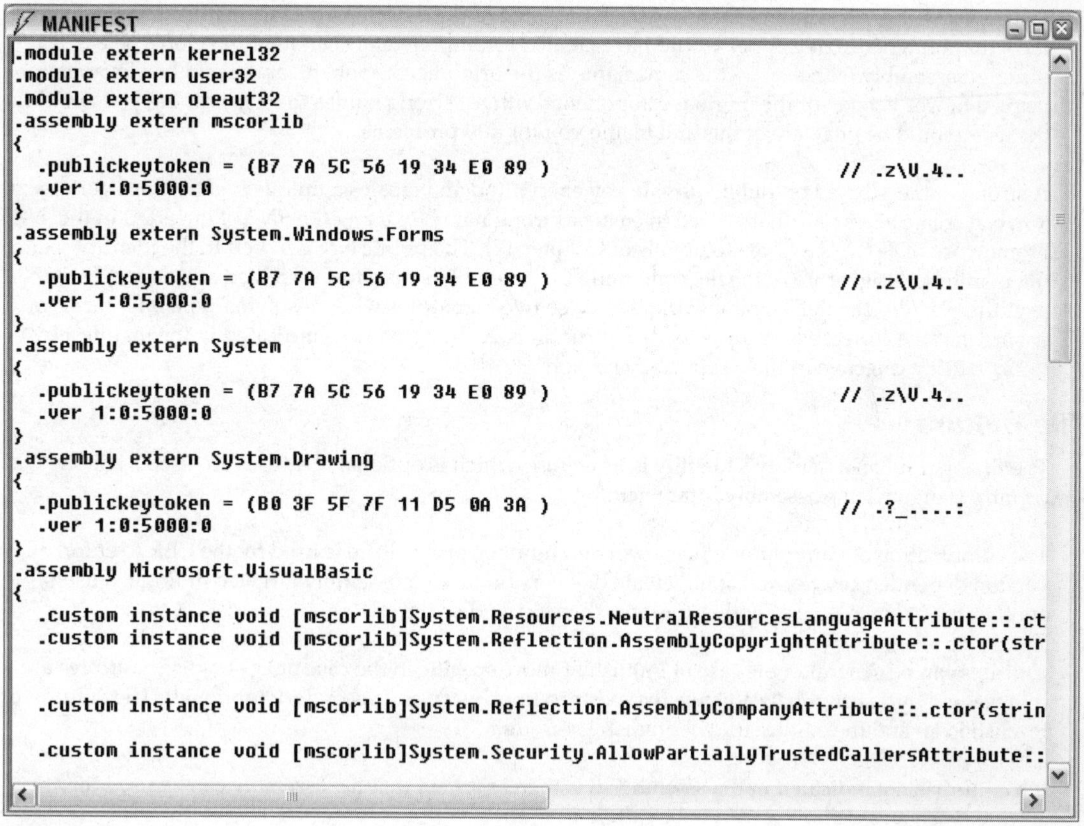

```
MANIFEST                                                                    _ □ ☒
.module extern kernel32
.module extern user32
.module extern oleaut32
.assembly extern mscorlib
{
  .publickeytoken = (B7 7A 5C 56 19 34 E0 89 )                    // .z\U.4..
  .ver 1:0:5000:0
}
.assembly extern System.Windows.Forms
{
  .publickeytoken = (B7 7A 5C 56 19 34 E0 89 )                    // .z\U.4..
  .ver 1:0:5000:0
}
.assembly extern System
{
  .publickeytoken = (B7 7A 5C 56 19 34 E0 89 )                    // .z\U.4..
  .ver 1:0:5000:0
}
.assembly extern System.Drawing
{
  .publickeytoken = (B0 3F 5F 7F 11 D5 0A 3A )                    // .?_....:
  .ver 1:0:5000:0
}
.assembly Microsoft.VisualBasic
{
  .custom instance void [mscorlib]System.Resources.NeutralResourcesLanguageAttribute::.ct
  .custom instance void [mscorlib]System.Reflection.AssemblyCopyrightAttribute::.ctor(str

  .custom instance void [mscorlib]System.Reflection.AssemblyCompanyAttribute::.ctor(strin

  .custom instance void [mscorlib]System.Security.AllowPartiallyTrustedCallersAttribute::
```

Figure 25-5

through the output you can see that the `Microsoft.VisualBasic` assembly has a version number of 7:0:0:0 as indicated by the following entry in the `.assembly` section:

```
.ver 7:0:0:0
```

As you can see, there are four parts to a version number:

```
Major : Minor : Build : Revision
```

Assemblies that have the same name but different version numbers are treated as completely different assemblies. If you have an assembly on your machine that has a version number of 1.5.2.3 and another version of the same assembly with a version number of 1.6.0.1, then the CLR will treat them as different assemblies. The version number of an assembly is part of what is used to define dependencies between assemblies.

Strong Names

The identity section can also contain an optional *strong name*. The strong name is not a name as such but is, in fact, a public key that has been generated by the author of the assembly in order to uniquely identify the assembly. A strong name is what is used to ensure that your assembly has a unique signature compared to other assemblies that may have the same name. Strong names were introduced to combat the situation where a developer would have created a component and another developer releases a different assembly with exactly the same name as the original component, and could be mistaken for being a newer version of the original component. Without strong names there is nothing you could do, the user would be unaware of this and blame you for any problems.

A strong name is based on public-private key encryption and creates a unique identity for your assembly. You can create a key pair that is used to create a strong name by using the *SN tool* included in the .NET Framework SDK (we saw how to do this in Chapter 17). The public key is stored in the identity section of the manifest. A signature of the file containing the assembly's manifest is created and stored in the resulting PE file. The .NET Framework uses these two signatures when resolving type references to ensure that the correct assembly is loaded at runtime. A strong name is indicated in the manifest by the `.publickey` directive in the `.assembly` section.

The Culture

The final part of an assembly's identity is its *culture*, which is optional. Cultures are used to define what country/language the assembly is targeted for.

The combination of name, strong name, version number, and culture is used by the CLR to enforce version dependencies. So, you could create one version of your assembly targeted at English users, another for German users, another for Finnish users, and so on.

Cultures can be general in the case of English or more specific in the case of US-English. Cultures are represented by a string that can have two parts to it: primary and secondary (optional). The culture for English is `en` and the culture for US-English is `en-us`.

If a culture is not indicated in the assembly, it is then assumed that the assembly can be used for any culture. Such an assembly is said to be *culture-neutral*.

A culture can be assigned to an assembly by including the attribute `AssemblyCulture` from the `System.Reflection` namespace in your assembly's code (usually within the `AssemblyInfo.vb` file):

```
<Assembly: AssemblyCulture("en")>
```

The culture of an assembly is represented in the manifest by the `.locale` directive in the `.assembly` section:

```
.locale = (65 00 6E 00 00 00)                          // e.n...
```

Referenced Assemblies

The next section of the manifest that we are going to look at is the *referenced assemblies* section. As the name suggests, this section is where information is recorded about all the assemblies that are referenced by us. An assembly reference is indicated in the manifest by the use of the `.assembly extern` directive, as shown in Figure 25-6.

You can see from the preceding screenshot that various pieces of information are stored about an assembly when it is referenced. The first piece of information stored is the name of the assembly. This is included as part of the `.assembly extern` directive. The screenshot shows a reference to the `mscorlib`

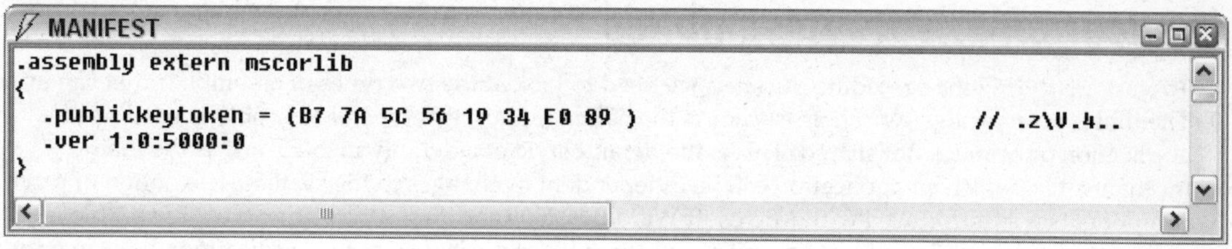

```
MANIFEST                                                          _ □ ⊠
.assembly extern mscorlib
{
  .publickeytoken = (B7 7A 5C 56 19 34 E0 89 )              // .z\V.4..
  .ver 1:0:5000:0
}
```

Figure 25-6

assembly. This name of the reference is used to determine the name of the file that contains the implementation of the assembly. The CLR takes the name of the assembly reference and appends .dll. So, in the last example, the CLR will look for a file called mscorlib.dll when it resolves the type references. The assembly mscorlib is a special assembly in .NET that contains all the definitions of the base types used in .NET and is referenced by all assemblies. We will talk about the process that the CLR goes through to resolve a type reference later on in this chapter.

The .publickeytoken Directive

If the assembly being referenced contains a strong name, then a *hash* of the public key of the referenced assembly is stored as part of the record to the external reference. This hash is stored in the manifest using the .publickeytoken directive as part of the .assembly extern section. The assembly reference shown in Figure 25-6 contains a hash of the strong name of the mscorlib assembly. The stored hash of the strong name is compared at runtime to a hash of the strong name (.publickey) contained within the referenced assembly to help ensure that the correct assembly is loaded. The value of the .publickeytoken is computed by taking the low 8 bytes of a hash (SHA1) of the strong name of the referenced assemblies.

The .Ver Directive

The version of the assembly being referenced is also stored in the manifest. This version information is used with the rest of the information stored about a reference to ensure the correct assembly is loaded; this will be discussed later. If an application references version 1.1.0.0 of an assembly, it will not load version 2.1.0.0 of the assembly unless a version policy (discussed later) exists to say otherwise. The version of the referenced assembly is stored in the manifest using the .ver directive as part of a .assembly extern section.

The .Locale Directive

If an assembly that is being referenced has a culture, then the culture information will also be stored in the external assembly reference section using the .locale directive. The combination of name, strong name (if it exists), version number, and culture are what make up a unique version of an assembly.

Assemblies and Deployment

So we've looked at the structure of assemblies, in particular we've looked at the contents of the assembly manifest and how this is used to help provide a mechanism of self-description for the assembly. But how does the concept of assemblies help with deployment and the issues of versioning as well as DLL Hell? We'll take a look at this issue in this next section.

Application-Private Assemblies

To start answering the preceding question we need to look at the two types of assemblies that can exist. The first is an *application-private assembly*. As the name implies, this type of assembly is used by one application only and is not shared. This is the default style of assembly in .NET and is the main mechanism by which an application can be independent of changes to the system. The notion of private components was introduced with Microsoft Windows 2000 and the .local file. If a .local file is created in an application's directory and a component is requested from the application, the search for the component would be started in the application's directory first. If the component is found in the application's directory then it is used. If the component could not be found locally, then it would be searched for in the system path.

Application-private assemblies are deployed into the application's own directory. As application-private assemblies are not shared, they do not need a strong name. This means, at a minimum, they only need to have a name and version number in the identity section of the manifest. As the assemblies are private to the application, the application does not perform version checks on the assemblies, as the application developer has control over the assemblies that are deployed to the application directory. If strong names exist, however, the CLR will check that they match. If all the assemblies that an application uses are application-private and the CLR is already installed on the target machine, it is possible to simply copy the application's directory to the target machine, assuming there are no other dependencies that need to be created (such as databases, message queues, file associations, and shortcuts). This can be accomplished due to the fact that assemblies are self-describing and contain all the information that is needed to resolve references. Therefore, there is no need to copy and then register any components. The self-describing aspect of assemblies removes the dependency on the registry, which means that applications can be backed up and copied much more easily. This is a form of XCOPY deployment and cannot be used if an application uses shared assemblies (which are described next) or requires any other dependencies that cannot be simply copied.

Shared Assemblies

The second type of assembly is the *shared assembly* and as the name suggests, this type of assembly can be shared amongst several different applications that reside on the same server. This type of assembly can be used in situations where it is not necessary to install a version of an assembly for each application that uses it. For instance, it is not necessary to install the System.Windows.Forms.dll assembly for each application that uses it, it is far better to install a shared version of the assembly.

There are certain requirements that are placed upon shared assemblies. The assembly needs to have a globally unique name, which is not a requirement of application-private assemblies. As mentioned earlier, strong names are used to create a globally unique name for an assembly. As the assembly is shared, all references to the shared assembly are checked to ensure the correct version is being used by an application. Shared assemblies are stored in the *Global Assembly Cache* (GAC), which is usually located in the assembly folder in the Windows directory (for example in Windows XP, C:\Windows\assembly).

There need be no other changes to the code of the assembly to differentiate it from that of an application-private assembly. In fact, just because an assembly has a strong name does not mean it has to be deployed as a shared assembly; it could just as easily be deployed in the application directory as an application-private assembly.

You must have administrator rights to the machine you are installing a shared assembly on, which rules out the form of XCOPY deployment mentioned earlier.

The Global Assembly Cache (GAC)

Each computer that has the .NET runtime installed has a GAC. If you have both the .NET Framework 1.0 and 1.1 on your server, you will only find a singe `assembly` folder that is shared by both runtimes. The strong name of an assembly is used when the shared assembly is placed into the GAC. A hash of the assembly is created using the public key stored as part of the metadata, which is then compared to the hash that was created when the component was compiled. If they differ, the component has been modified (since it was compiled) and it will not be installed.

> *An assembly must have a strong name to be placed in the GAC.*

The strong name is also used when an application resolves a reference to an external assembly. It checks that the public key stored in the assembly is equal to the hash of the public key stored as part of the reference in the application. If the two do not match then the application knows that the external assembly has not been created by the original author of the assembly.

You can view the assemblies that are contained within the GAC by navigating to the directory using the Windows Explorer. This is shown in Figure 25-7.

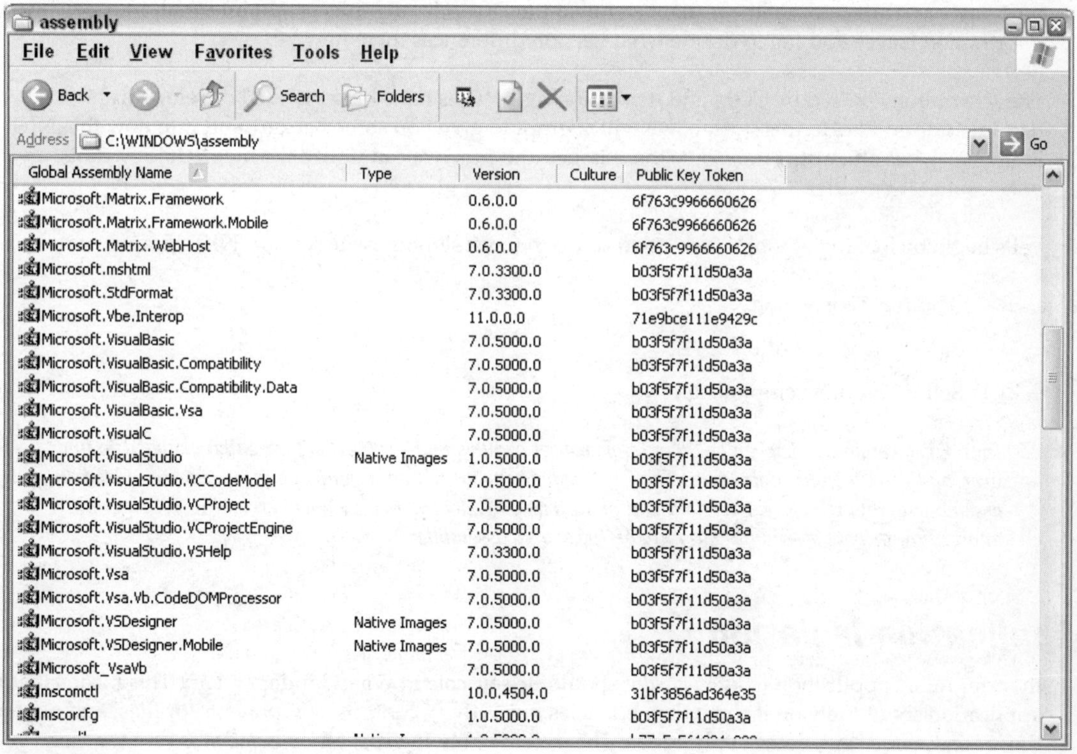

Figure 25-7

The `gacutil.exe` utility that ships with .NET is used to add and remove assemblies from the GAC. To add an assembly into the GAC using the `gacutil.exe` tool, use the following command line:

```
gacutil.exe /i myassembly.dll
```

To remove an assembly, use the /u option like this:

```
gacutil.exe /u myassembly.dll
```

Versioning Issues

Although COM was a landmark achievement in Windows programming history, it left much to be desired when it came to maintaining backward compatibility. COM used type libraries to describe its interfaces and each interface was represented by a GUID. Each interface ID was stored in the registry along with other related entries which made for a complex set of interrelated registry entries. The separation between the registry entries and the actual DLL on disk made it extremely easy for things to go wrong. A wrong registry entry or simply a mismatched GUID rendered the DLL useless. We were sometimes left with manual registry entry deletion or modification, which, at its best, was somewhat tedious.

The problem described here is that COM DLLs are not self-describing as they rely heavily on the registry having the correct entries. Another problem lies with the operating system not being able to best resolve differences between different DLL versions. Prior versions of Visual Basic relied on the `Server.coClass` and not the actual version of the DLL. Having the version information purely as information leaves nothing to decide what version differences there may be.

The frustrations caused by COM and its versioning policies have long plagued developers and administrators alike. In this section, we will attempt to give you some background into how the .NET Framework has attempted to resolve these issues and how we can utilize the methodology, tools, and policies that it provides.

Let's begin by looking at topics for a good solution to versioning issues of our .NET components:

❑ Application isolation

❑ Side-by-side execution

❑ Self-describing components

In .NET, a version policy can be thought of as a set of rules that the CLR enforces that enable it to find, load, and execute your component. The CLR policy sets out to find if you have the authority to load an assembly, to find the correct version, and more. The CLR does not enforce its versioning policies onto application-private assemblies but only on the shared assemblies.

Application Isolation

In order for an application to be *isolated* it should be self-contained and independent. This means that the application should rely on its own dependencies for ActiveX controls, components, or files, and not have those files shared with other applications. The option of having *application isolation* is essential for a good solution to versioning problems.

If an application is isolated, components are owned, managed by, and used by the parent application alone. If a component is used by another application, even if it is the same version, it should have its very own copy. This ensures that each application can install and uninstall dependencies and not have it interfere with other applications.

Does this sound familiar? This is what most early Windows and DOS applications did until the emphasis was put into registering DLLs into the system directory. The wheel surely does turn! Also at that time, the registry started to replace our need for INI files, and now we will be moving back to the separate configuration file (which we will discuss later in this chapter) like the INI file, as it lends itself well to application isolation.

The .NET Framework caters to application isolation by allowing us to create application-private assemblies that are for individual applications and are repeated physically on disk for each client. This means that each client is independent from the other. This nonsharing attitude works best for some scenarios.

Side-by-Side Execution

However, it is not always a good idea for an application to be completely isolated as sometimes code sharing is more beneficial and/or logical. If this is the case, the .NET Framework allows us to create and distribute shared assemblies. These assemblies must have versioning policies enforced as well as the ability to run side-by-side.

Side-by-side execution occurs when multiple versions of the same assembly can run at the same time. There are two side-by-side execution models. They are defined as being single machine execution in different processes and then more particularly within the same process.

The CLR is responsible for ensuring that assemblies are able to execute side-by-side. However side-by-side execution is not a CLR mechanism alone, as you can easily make unmanaged code execute side-by-side within the normal COM environment (known as *DLL/COM redirection*). Components that are to execute side-by-side must be installed within the application directory or a subdirectory of it. This ensures application isolation (as we discussed earlier).

Self-Describing

Many problems that we have had with COM components with regard to backward compatibility, resolving references, and versioning incompatibilities have largely been due to the way in which COM has traditionally stored information about the components it describes. Although, the interfaces for a class are described together within a type library, the mechanism to find the owner of the class is left to registry entries. This means that the registry entries are often separate from the actual class and thus, become misaligned. Therefore, one of the most important must-haves for good versioning policies is that the component must describe itself completely. The assembly contains all the code (MSIL) and information the runtime requires to enforce a good versioning policy.

Version Policies

We discussed earlier that a version number is comprises four parts: major, minor, build, and revision. The version number is used as part of the identity of the assembly. The combination of the major and minor parts of a version number indicates if a version is compatible with a previous version or not. When the version number of a component only changes by its build and revision parts, it is compatible. This is often referred to as *Quick Fix Engineering* (QFE).

When an application comes across a type that is implemented in an external reference, the CLR has to determine what version of the referenced assembly to load. What steps does the CLR go through to ensure the correct version of an assembly is loaded? To answer this question, we need to look at *version polices* and how they affect what version of an assembly is loaded.

The Default Versioning Policy

We will start by looking at the *default versioning policy*. This policy is what is followed in the absence of any configuration files on the machine that modify the versioning policy. The default behavior of the runtime is to consult the manifest for the name of the referenced assembly and the version of the assembly to use.

If the referenced assembly does not contain a strong name, it is assumed that the referenced assembly is application-private and is located in the application directory. The CLR takes the name of the referenced assembly and appends `.dll` to create the filename that contains the referenced assembly's manifest. The CLR then searches in the application's directory for the filename and, if found, it will use the version that was found even if the version number is different from the one specified in the manifest. Therefore, the version numbers of application-private assemblies are not checked as the application developer, in theory, has control over which assemblies are deployed to the applications directory. If the file can not be found, the CLR will raise a `System.IO.FileNotFoundException`.

Automatic Quick Fix Engineering Policy

If the referenced assembly contains a strong name, the process by which an assembly is loaded is different:

1. The three different types of assembly configuration files (discussed later) are consulted, if they exist, to see if they contain any settings that will modify which version of the assembly the CLR should load.

2. The CLR will then check to see if the assembly has been requested and loaded in a previous call. If it has, it will use the loaded assembly.

3. If the assembly is not already loaded, the GAC is then queried for a match. If a match is found, then this assembly will be used by the application.

4. If any of the configuration files contain a `codebase` (discussed later) entry for the assembly, the assembly is looked for in the location specified. If the assembly cannot be found in the location specified in the `codebase`, a `TypeLoadException` is raised to the application.

5. If there are no configuration files or if there are no `codebase` entries for the assembly, the CLR then moves on to probe for the assembly starting in the application's base directory.

6. If the assembly still hasn't been found, the CLR will ask the Windows Installer service if it has the assembly in question. If it does, then the assembly is installed and the application uses this newly installed assembly. This is a feature called *on-demand installation*.

If the assembly hasn't been found by the end of this entire process, a `TypeLoadException` will be raised.

Although a referenced assembly contains a strong name, this does not mean it has to be deployed into the GAC. This allows application developers to install a version with the application that is known to work. The GAC is consulted to see if it contains a version of an assembly with a higher *build.revision* number to enable administrators to deploy an updated assembly without having to reinstall or rebuild the application. This is known as *Automatic Quick Fix Engineering Policy*.

Configuration Files

The default versioning policy described earlier may not be the most appropriate policy for our requirements. Fortunately, we can modify this policy with the use of XML configuration files to meet our specific needs. There are three types of configuration files that can be created:

❑ The first is an *application configuration file* and is created in the application directory. As the name implies, this configuration file applies to a single application only. To do this, you need to create the application configuration file in the application directory with the same name as the application filename and appending .config. For example, suppose we have a Windows Forms application called HelloWorld.exe installed in the C:\HelloWorld directory. The application configuration file would be: C:\HelloWorld\HelloWorld.exe.config.

❑ The second type of configuration file is called the *machine configuration file*. It is named machine.config and can be found in the C:\Windows\Microsoft.NET\ Framework\v1.1.4322\CONFIG directory. The machine.config file overrides any other configuration files on a machine and can be thought of as containing global settings.

❑ The third type of configuration file is the *security configuration file* and it contains information regarding the code access security system. The code access security system allows us to grant/deny access to resources by an assembly. This configuration file must be located within the Windows directory.

The main purpose of the configuration file is to provide binding-related information to the developer or administrator that wishes to override the default policy handling of the CLR.

Specifically, the configuration file, as it's written in XML, has a root node named <configuration> and must have the end node of </configuration> present in order to be syntactically correct.

The configuration file is divided into specific types of nodes that represent different areas of control. These areas are:

❑ Startup

❑ Runtime

❑ Remoting

❑ Crypto

❑ Class API

❑ Security

Although all of these areas are important, in this chapter we will look only at the first two.

The settings that we are going to discuss can be added to the application configuration file. Some of the settings (these will be pointed out) can also be added to the machine configuration file. If a setting in the application configuration file conflicts with that of one in the machine configuration file, then the setting in the machine configuration is used. When we talk about assembly references in the following discussion of configuration settings, we are talking about shared assemblies (in other words, assemblies that have a strong name).

Startup Settings

The `<startup>` node of the application and machine configuration files has a `<requiredRuntime>` node that specifies the runtime version required by the application. This is because different versions of the CLR can run on a machine side-by-side. The following example shows how we would specify the version of the .NET runtime inside the configuration file:

```
<configuration>
  <startup>
    <requiredRuntime version="1.1.4322" safemode="true"/>
  </startup>
</configuration>
```

Runtime Settings

The runtime node, which is written as `<runtime>` (not to be confused with `<requiredRuntime>`), specifies the settings that manage how the CLR handles garbage collection and versions of assemblies. With these settings, we can specify which version of an assembly the application requires or redirect it to another version entirely.

Loading a Particular Version of an Assembly

The application and machine configuration files can be used to ensure that a particular version of an assembly is loaded. You can indicate whether this version should be loaded all the time or only to replace a specific version of the assembly. This functionality is supported through the use of the `<assemblyIdentity>` and `<bindingRedirect>` elements in the configuration file. For example:

```
<configuration>
  <runtime>
    <assemblyBinding xmlns="urn:schemas-microsoft-com:asm.v1">
      <dependentAssembly>
        <assemblyIdentity name="AssemblyName"
                          publickeytoken="b77a5c561934e089"
                          culture="en-us"/>
          <bindingRedirect oldVersion="*"
                          newVersion="2.0.50.0"/>
      </dependentAssembly>
    </assemblyBindings>
  </runtime>
</configuration>
```

The `<assemblyBinding>` node is used to declare settings for the locations of assemblies and redirections via the `<dependentAssembly>` node and also the `<probing>` node (which we will look at shortly).

In the last example, when the CLR resolves the reference to the assembly named `AssemblyName`, it will load version 2.0.50.0 instead of the version that appears in the manifest. If you would like to only load version 2.0.50.0 of the assembly when a specific version is referenced, then you can replace the value of the `oldVersion` attribute with the version number that you would like to replace (for example, 1.5.0.0). The `publickeytoken` attribute is used to store the hash of the strong name of the assembly to replace. This is used to ensure that the correct assembly is identified. The same is true of the `culture` attribute.

Defining the Location of an Assembly

The location of an assembly can also be defined in both the application and machine configuration files. We can use the `<codeBase>` element to inform the CLR of the location of an assembly. This enables us to distribute an application and have the externally referenced assemblies downloaded the first time they are used. This is called on-demand downloading. For example:

```
<configuration>
  <runtime>
    <assemblyBinding xmlns="urn:schemas-microsoft-com:asm.v1">
      <dependentAssembly>
        <assemblyIdentity name="AssemblyName"
                          publickeytoken="b77a5c561934e089"
                          culture="en-us"/>
        <codeBase version="2.0.50.0"
                  href="http://www.wrox.com/AssemblyName.dll/>
      </dependentAssembly>
    </assemblyBindings>
  </runtime>
</configuration>
```

From the previous example, we can see that whenever a reference to version 2.0.50.0 of the assembly `AssemblyName` is resolved (and the assembly isn't already on the users computer), the CLR will try to load the assembly from the location defined in the `href` attribute. The location defined in the `href` attribute is a standard URL and can be used to locate a file across the Internet or locally.

If the assembly cannot be found or the details in the manifest of the assembly defined in the `href` attribute do not match those defined in the configuration file, the loading of the assembly will fail and you will receive a `TypeLoadException`. If the version of the assembly in the preceding example is actually 2.0.60.0 then the assembly will load, as the version number is only different by build and revision number.

Providing the Search Path

The final use of configuration files that we will look at is that of providing the search path for use when locating assemblies in the application's directory. This setting only applies to the application configuration file. By default, the CLR will only search for an assembly in the application's base directory, it will not look in any subdirectories. We can modify this behavior by using the `<probing>` element in an application configuration file. For example:

```
<configuration>
  <runtime>
    <assemblyBinding xmlns="urn:schemas-microsoft-com:asm.v1">
      <probing privatePath="regional"/>
    </assemblyBinding>
  </runtime>
</configuration>
```

The `privatePath` attribute can contain a list of directories relative to the application's directory (separated by a semi-colon) that you would like the CLR to search in when trying to locate an assembly. The `privatePath` attribute cannot contain an absolute pathname.

As part of an assembly reference being resolved, the CLR will check in the application's base directory for it. If it cannot find it, it will look through in order all the subdirectories specified in the `privatePath` variable, as well as looking for a subdirectory with the same name as the assembly. If the assembly being resolved is called `AssemblyName`, the CLR will also check for the assembly in a subdirectory called `AssemblyName`, if it exists.

This isn't the end of the story, though. If the referenced assembly being resolved contains a culture setting, the CLR will also check for culture specific subdirectories in each of the directories it searches in. For example, if the CLR is trying to resolve a reference to an assembly named `AssemblyName` with a culture of `en`, a `privatePath` equal to that in the last example, and the application being run has a home directory of `C:\ExampleApp`, the CLR will look in the following directories to find the assembly (in the order they are shown):

- ❑ `C:\ExampleApp`
- ❑ `C:\ExampleApp\en`
- ❑ `C:\ExampleApp\en\AssemblyName`
- ❑ `C:\ExampleApp\regional\en`
- ❑ `C:\ExampleApp\regional\en\AssemblyName`

As you can see, the CLR can probe quite a number of directories to locate an assembly.

When an external assembly is resolved by the CLR it consults the configuration files first to see if it needs to modify the process by which it resolves an assembly. As we discussed, the resolution process can be modified to suit your needs.

Now that we understand assemblies, we are going to start discussing the problems that occur when we deploy applications, along with a number of terms that are used when talking about application deployment. We will then move to look at what the CLR contains that helps us alleviate some of the deployment issues discussed previously. The remainder of the chapter will then focus on the practical aspects of creating deployment projects in VS.NET, which will include a number of walkthroughs.

> *Deployment in .NET is a huge topic and we couldn't hope to cover every aspect in the pages that we have for this chapter. What this chapter should give you is the understanding, basic knowledge, and the desire to learn more about the options available to you.*

Application Deployment

We are going to start this section by discussing the main issues associated with application deployment and defining a few common terms that are used. We will then move on to discuss the deployment options available prior to .NET. Hopefully, this will give you an understanding of the issues to be overcome when considering deployment in .NET.

First, what do we mean by the term "application deployment"? In the context of this chapter, it means the process of taking an application, packaging it up, and installing it on another machine. This includes installing the application on a machine that already doesn't have the application on it, reinstalling the application or upgrading it. It applies to traditional Windows-based applications or Web-based applications that will need to be installed within the confines of another Web server, as well as any of the other Visual Basic project templates.

DLL Hell

These two small words "DLL" and "Hell" describe what can be a very large problem for application developers. If you are aware of the problems that *DLL Hell* encompasses, then please feel free to skip this section.

What does DLL Hell mean? The term is actually used to describe a number of problems that can arise when multiple applications share a common component. The common component is usually a `.dll` or a COM component. The problems usually arise for one of three following reasons:

❑ The first common cause of DLL Hell is when you install a new application that overwrites a shared component with a version that is not compatible with the version that already resides on the computer. Any applications that relied on the previous version of the component could well be rendered unusable. This is often caused when you install an application that overwrites a system file (for example, `MFC42.dll`) with an older version. Any application that relied on the functionality of the newer version will stop working. When installing the application on the computer the installer should check that it is not overwriting a newer version of the component. However, not all installations do this check.

❑ The second cause occurs when a new version of a shared component is installed that is binary compatible (the public interface matches exactly) with the previous version, but in updating the functionality, a new bug has been introduced into the component which could cause any application that depends on the component to misbehave or stop working. This type of error can be very hard to diagnose.

❑ The third common cause occurs when an application uses a feature of a common component that is actually an undocumented and unexpected behavior of the component: a side effect. When this shared component is updated with a newer version the side effect may well have disappeared, breaking any applications that depended on it. There are many undocumented API calls available in DLLs; the problem is that, because they are undocumented, they may well disappear in a subsequent version without warning.

As the discussion indicates, DLL Hell can be caused by a variety of reasons and the effects can be wide ranging. Applications may stop working but worse still, it could introduce subtle bugs that may lie undetected for some time. It may be some time before you realize an application has stopped working, which can make it significantly harder to detect the cause of the problem.

Microsoft has tried to address some of these issues with the latest versions of Windows by introducing Windows File Protection and private DLLs:

❑ As the name suggests Windows File Protection is a mechanism by which the OS protects a list of system DLLs from being overwritten with a different version. Normally, only service packs and other OS updates can update the DLLs that are protected, although this can be overridden by changing some registry keys. This should reduce some of the causes of DLL Hell that are caused by the overwriting of system DLLs.

❑ The second feature introduced is that of private DLLs. Private DLLs are used by one particular application only and are not shared amongst different applications. If an application relies on a specific version of a `.dll` or COM component then it can be installed in the application directory and a `.local` file created in the directory to inform that OS to look for private DLLs first and then move on to look for shared DLLs.

You will be pleased to hear that Microsoft has incorporated new features into the CLR and the .NET Framework that will help to overcome DLL Hell and make deployment easier. These new features will be discussed throughout the remainder of this chapter.

XCOPY Deployment

The term *XCOPY deployment* was coined to describe an ideal deployment scenario. Its name derives from the DOS xcopy command that is used to copy an entire directory structure from one location to another. XCOPY deployment relates to a scenario where all you have to do to deploy an application is to copy the directory (including all child directories) to the computer that you would like to run the program.

Why can't we use XCOPY deployment at present for older Windows applications? The main reason is that the process of installing an application currently is a multistep process. For example, any application that uses a COM component will require a number of steps to install it on another computer. First, the component needs to be copied to the machine, and then the component must be registered on the machine, creating a dependency between the component and the registry. The application requires the entry in the registry to activate the component. Because of this coupling between the component and the registry, it is not possible to install the component by simply copying it from one machine to another.

All but the simplest of applications also require other dependencies (such as databases, message queues, document extensions) to be created on the new computer. The CLR tries to overcome the problem of the coupling between the registry and components, but at present it cannot help with the dependencies that are required by more advanced applications. We are closer to XCOPY deployment with .NET and in some cases we may actually be able to achieve a form of it.

The issue of what runtime files need to be on a computer to run an application should also be addressed. For a .NET application to run on a computer it needs to have the necessary core CLR files installed, as well as any files required by the application. Some people argue that if you need to install a runtime prior to installing an application then this can never be classed as true XCOPY deployment. To start with, the CLR will be distributed as a downloadable installation routine (or distributed as part of an applications setup routine), but we can expect it to be included in future service packs and natively included as part of the operating system in future versions of Microsoft Windows as it is with Windows Server 2003. Once the CLR has been installed it will not need to be installed again, therefore we can define one requirement of an application to be that a particular version of the CLR is installed.

Deployment Options Prior to .NET

Prior to VS.NET there were a number of deployment options available to the developer, some supplied by Microsoft and others supplied by third party companies, each trying to ease the pain of deploying applications. In this section, we will take a brief look at some of these options.

Manual Installation

As the name suggests, the *manual installation* method involves copying all the files manually into the correct place and then completing any other steps that are required to complete the installation of the software, for example, registering any COM components and adding any other registry entries. It could also mean setting up database connections, and so on. There is no automation in this deployment method and the steps have to be repeated on every computer that the application needs to be installed on. This installation method is time consuming and is not feasible for most applications, as it often requires advanced knowledge that perhaps the typical user of the application cannot be expected to have or learn. This is the installation method most commonly used when COM+ components are installed onto a server.

Custom Installer

The second deployment method we will look at is the use of a *custom installation program*. We can use the installation program to define the steps and actions that are required to install the application on a computer. The program then packages up all the required files, including the instructions into an application the users can use to install the application on their machines.

The *Package and Deployment Wizard*, which was provided with VB6, is an example of such an application. You run the wizard, selecting the files that need to be copied and where they need to be copied. The wizard then creates an installation that can be run on another computer.

Another variant often used to create an installation program is script based (for example, InstallShield). It packages up any files that need to be copied and allows us to write a script to define what needs to be done when the installer is run. The script-based approach is very flexible in that we can easily incorporate any additional processing that needs to be done when installing an application (for example, creating a new database).

There are many other variants on this theme of creating an installation program. As you can see, there is no consistency between the installation programs; each program can offer different functionality (or lack of). Microsoft acknowledged this inconsistency and tried to come up with a solution, which we will discuss next.

Windows Installer

Microsoft introduced the *Windows Installer* service as part of Windows 2000 as the solution to the shortcomings of the existing installation programs. Although the Windows Installer service was released as part of Windows 2000, it can also be installed on previous versions of Windows and is automatically installed with several Microsoft applications (such as Microsoft Office). The Windows Installer service is what Microsoft calls an *operating system component*. The service implements all the required rules that a setup needs (for instance, *do not overwrite a system file with an older version*).

Instead of creating an executable that contains all the rules to install the application, you create a file, called a *Windows Installer package file* (.msi), which describes what needs to be done to install your application. An application is described in the resulting Windows Installer package as being made up of three parts: components, features, and products. Each part is made up of any number of the previous parts. For example, a product is made up of several features, and a feature may contain one or more components. The component is the smallest part of the installation and contains a group of files and other resources that need to be installed together. We will not be going into the underlying details of the Windows Installer architecture. If you are interested then you should take a look at the Windows Installer SDK documentation on MSDN.

The files that make up a product can be packaged externally in a number of cabinet files or the files can be packaged up into the resultant .msi file. As you will see later, there are a number of options within the deployment project templates that allow us to specify how the product's files are packaged. When the user requests that a particular application needs to be installed they can just double-click the .msi file (assuming the Windows Installer service is installed). If the Windows Installer service is not installed there is usually a `Setup.exe` file that will install the Windows Installer service first. The service will read the file and determine what needs to be done (such as which files need to be copied and where they need to be copied to) to install the application. All the installation rules are implemented centrally by the service and do not need to be distributed as part of a setup executable. The Windows Installer package file contains a list of actions (such as *copy file mfc40.dll to the windows system folder*) and what rules need to be applied to these actions. It does not contain the implementation of the rules.

The Windows Installer service also provides a rich API that developers can use to include features, such as on-demand installing, into their applications. One of the biggest complaints about previous installers is that if the installation fails, the user's computer is often left in an unstable state. The Windows Installer service overcomes this by providing a rollback method. If the installation fails for some reason, the Windows Installer service will rollback the computer to its original state, so we could say that the installation is transactional.

You can manually create a Windows Installer package file using the Windows Installer SDK tools. However, this is not very user-friendly, so Microsoft released the *Visual Studio Installer* (VSI) as an add-on for Visual Studio 6. The VSI integrated into the development environment and made the development of the Windows Installer package files easier. Three out of the four actual deployment/setup templates in VS.NET use Windows Installer technology. We will look at these in more detail later in the chapter.

Application Deployment in Visual Studio .NET

We've just looked at some background issues relating to application deployment and some of the deployment options that have been previously available to developers. We're now going to turn our attention to looking at how the CLR and the .NET Framework can help with deployment and resolve the issue of DLL Hell. Finally, we will take a look at the deployment project templates that are available within VS.NET.

Visual Studio .NET Deployment Projects

So you have decided that you need to package your application in some way so that it can be installed on other machines. The option of just zipping up the application directory is not satisfactory or not possible. What can you do? You will be pleased to hear that VS.NET provides a set of project templates that can be used to help package your application and deploy it. The remainder of this chapter will focus on these project templates. We will start by taking a look at the different templates and what they should be used for, after which we will take a practical look at their creation.

Project Templates

Visual Studio .NET includes five project templates that can be used for setup and deployment in .NET. Before we discuss the project templates, we need to define the difference between setup and deployment. A *setup* is an application/process that you create which packages your application up and provides an easy mechanism by which it can be installed on another machine. *Deployment* is the process of taking an application and installing it on another machine, usually by the use of a setup application/process.

The five project templates available within VS.NET can be created by the same means as any other project in VS.NET, by using the New Project dialog box as shown in Figure 25-8.

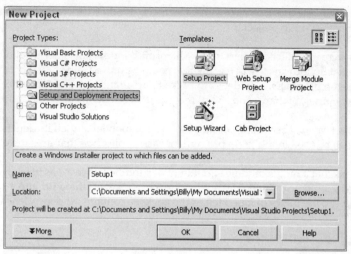

Figure 25-8

As you can see from the Figure 25-8, you need to select the Setup and Deployment Projects node from the treeview of project types to the left of the dialog box. Out of the five available project templates there are four actual project templates:

- ❑   Cab project
- ❑   Merge module project
- ❑   Setup project
- ❑   Web setup project

and one wizard that can be used to help create one of the four project templates listed:

- ❑   Setup wizard

Let's now consider each of the project types in turn.

The Cab Project Template

As its name implies, the Cab Project template is used to create a *cabinet file*. A cabinet file (`.cab`) can contain any number of files. It is usually used to package components into a single file that can then be placed on a Web server so that the cab file can be downloaded by a Web browser.

Controls hosted within Internet Explorer are often packaged into a cabinet file and a reference added to the file in the Web page that uses the control. When Internet Explorer encounters this reference, it will check that the control isn't already installed on the user's computer, at which point it will download the cabinet file, extract the control, and install it to a protected part of the user's computer.

Cabinet files can be compressed to reduce their size and consequently the time it takes to download them.

The Merge Module Project Template

The Merge Module Project template is used to create a *merge module*, which is similar to a cabinet file in that it can be used to package a group of files. The difference is that a merge module file (`.msm`) cannot be used by itself to install the files that it contains. The merge module file created by this project template can be used within another setup project.

Merge modules were introduced as part of the Microsoft Windows Installer technology to enable a set of files to be packaged up into an easy to use file that could be reused and shared between Windows Installer-based setup programs. The idea is to package up all the files and any other resources (for example, registry entries, bitmaps, and so on) that are dependent on each other into the merge module.

This type of project can be very useful for packaging a component and all its dependencies. The resulting merge file can then be used in the setup program of each application that uses the component.

Microsoft suggests that a merge module should not be modified once it has been distributed, which means a new one should be created. The notion of packaging everything up into a single redistributable file can help alleviate the issues of DLL Hell as the package contains all dependencies.

The Setup Project Template

The Setup Project template is used to create a standard Windows Installer setup for an application. This type of project will probably be familiar to you if you have used the Visual Studio Installer add-on for Visual Studio 6. The Setup Project template can be used to create a setup package for a standard Windows application, which is normally installed in the `Program Files` directory of a user's computer.

The Web Setup Project Template

The Web Setup Project template is used to create a Windows Installer setup program that can be used to install a project into a virtual directory of a Web server. It is intended to be used to create a setup program for a Web application.

The Setup Wizard

The Setup Wizard can be used to help guide you through the creation of one of the above four setup and deployment project templates. The steps that the wizard displays to you depend on whether the wizard was started to add a project to an existing solution or started to create a totally new project.

Creating a Deployment Project

A deployment project can be created in exactly the same way as any other project in VS.NET by using the New ➪ Project option from the File menu or by using the New Project button on the VS.NET start page.

You can also add a deployment project to an existing solution by using the Add Project item from the File menu. You will then be presented with the Add New Project dialog box where you can select the deployment template of choice.

Walkthroughs

Now that we have looked at how we can create a deployment project, the next two sections are going to contain practical walkthroughs of the creation of two deployment projects. The two walkthroughs are going to cover:

❑   A Windows application

❑   An ASP.NET Web application

Each these scenarios will detail a different deployment project template. They have been chosen as they are the most common deployment scenarios. You will be able to use the walkthroughs and apply or modify them to your own needs. We will not use the wizard to create the deployment projects in the walkthroughs. This decision has been taken so that you will be able to understand what is required to create a deployment project. The wizard can be used to help guide you through the creation of a deployment project and therefore, hide from you some of the steps that we will be taking in the walkthroughs. However, the wizard can be very useful in providing the base for a deployment project.

A Windows Application

The first deployment scenario that we are going to look at is that of a Windows application where a user installs and runs an application on his local machine. In deploying this application, we will need to ensure that everything the application needs is distributed with the application's executable. This type of deployment scenario is one of the most typical that you will come across.

In this deployment scenario, the package needs to be created in such a way that it will guide the user through the process of installing the application on his or her machine. The best deployment template for this scenario is the Setup Project and this is what we will be using throughout this section.

Before we start getting into the specifics of this project type, we need to create an application that will serve as our desktop application that we want to deploy. For this example, we are going to use the Windows Application project type. Create a new project and choose WindowsApplication from the list of available Visual Basic project templates. We will not add any code to the project and will use it just as the new project wizard originally created it. Following this, we should have a solution with just one project.

After this, add a new project to the solution and choose Setup Project from the list of available Setup and Deployment Project templates. You will now have a VS.NET solution containing two projects as shown in Figure 25-9.

Figure 25-9

919

The deployment project does not contain any files at present, just a folder called Detected Dependencies, which we will discuss later. Notice also the buttons that appear along the top of the Solution Explorer. These are used to access the editors of this deployment project template and will be discussed later in this chapter.

Next, we need to add files to the setup project and in particular we need to look at how we can add the file created by the Windows application project. We can add files to the setup deployment project in two ways. The first is to make sure the setup project is the active project and then choose the Add item from the Project menu. The second method is to right-click the setup project file in the Solution Explorer and choose Add from the popup menu. Both these methods enable you to choose from one of four options:

❑　If you select File from the submenu, you will be presented with a dialog box that will allow you to browse for and select a particular file to add to the setup project. This method is sufficient if the file you are adding is not the output from another project within the solution. This option is very useful in Web setup projects as it allows you include external business components (if they are used) and so on.

❑　The Merge Module option allows us to include a merge module in the deployment project. If you select this option, you will be presented with a dialog box that you can use to browse for and select a merge module to include in your project. Third-party vendors can supply merge modules or we can create our own with VS.NET.

❑　The Assembly option can be used to select a .NET component (assembly) to be included in the deployment project. If you select this option you will be presented with a window that you can use to select an assembly to include from those that are installed on your machine.

❑　If the deployment project is part of a solution (as in this walkthrough) you can use the Project ➪ Add ➪ Project Output submenu item. As the name implies, this allows you to add the output from any of the projects in the solution to the setup project.

We want to add the output of the Windows application project to the setup project. So we need to select the Project Output menu item to bring up the dialog box (shown in Figure 25-10) that will enable us to accomplish this task.

The Add Project Output Group dialog box is split into several parts:

❑　The combo box at the top contains a list of the names of all the nondeployment projects in the current solution. In our case there is only one project — WindowsApplication.

❑　Below the combo box is a list box containing a list of all the possible outputs from the selected project. If you click a possible output, a description of the selected output appears in the Description box at the bottom. We are interested in the Primary output so make sure this is selected. The different types of output are summarized in the following table.

❑　Below the list of possible outputs is a combo box that allows us to select the Configuration to use for the selected project. We will use the (Active) option as this will use whatever configuration is in effect when the project is built. The combo box will also contain all the possible build configurations for the selected project.

Click OK to return to the solution.

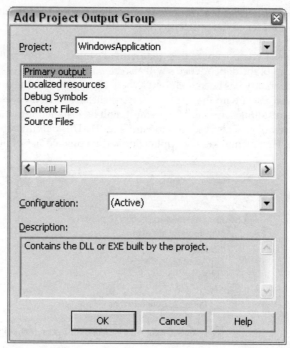

Figure 25-10

Project Output	Description
Primary output	The primary output of a project is the resulting DLL or EXE that is produced by building the particular project
Localized resources	The localized resource of a project is a DLL that contains only resources. The resources within the DLL are specific to a culture or locale. This is often called a satellite DLL
Debug Symbols	When the particular project in question is compiled a special file is created that contains special debugging information about the project. These are called *debug symbols*. The debug symbols for a project have the same name as the primary output but with an extension of .pdb. The debug symbols provide information to a debugger when an application is being run through it
Content Files	This project output is used only with ASP.NET Web applications. The content files of a Web application are the HTML files, image files and so on that form the content of the Web site
Source Files	This will include all the source files for the selected project including the project file. The solution file is NOT included

Now, not only has the output from the Windows application been added to the Setup project but the Detected Dependencies folder contains an entry.

Whenever you add a .NET component to this deployment project, its dependencies are added to this folder. The dependencies of the dependencies will also be added and so on until all the required files have been added. This functionality has been included to help ensure that all the dependencies of an application are deployed along with the application. The files listed in the Detected Dependencies folder will be included in the resulting setup and, by default, will be installed into the application's directory as application-private assemblies. This is shown in Figure 25-11. This default behavior helps reduce the possible effects of DLL Hell by making the application use its own copies of dependent files.

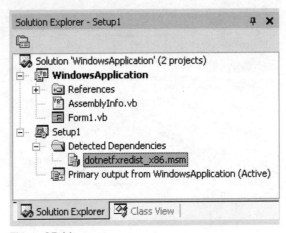

Figure 25-11

If you do not want a particular dependency file to be included in the resulting setup, you can exclude it by right-clicking the particular entry under Detected Dependencies and selecting Exclude from the popup menu. The dependency will now have a little blue stop sign before its name to indicate that it has been excluded, as illustrated in Figure 25-12.

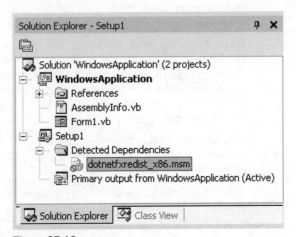

Figure 25-12

Dependencies can also be excluded by selecting the particular dependency and using the Properties window to set the Exclude property to True. The listed dependencies will be refreshed whenever a .NET file is added to or removed from the setup project taking into account any files that have already been excluded.

You may decide that you want to exclude a detected dependency from the setup of an application because you know that the dependency is already installed on the target computer. This is fine if you have tight control over what is installed on a user's machine. If you don't and you deploy the application with the missing dependency, your application could well be rendered unusable. In the previous screenshot you can see that there is one entry in the folder. The `dotnetfxredist_x86.msm` file is a merge module dependency. As mentioned previously, a merge module is used to package a group of files that are dependent on each other. This merge module contains a redistributable version of the CLR and will be installed on the user's computer when the installation is run.

We can select an item in the setup project in the Solution Explorer and that particular item's properties will be displayed in the Properties window. For example, if we select the root node of the setup project (Setup), the Properties window will change to show us the details of the setup project as illustrated in Figure 25-13.

Figure 25-13

As with any other project in VS.NET, there are a set of project properties that can also be modified. The project properties are accessed by right-clicking the project file and choosing Properties from the popup menu. These properties will be covered later.

We are not going to include a discussion of every single property of all the different project items as we could probably fill a whole book on the subject. Instead, we will take a look at the properties from the root setup node and each of the two different project items. We are going to start with the root setup node (Setup). Before we start our discussion, make sure that the node is selected and take some time to browse the list of available properties. The root setup node represents the resulting output from this deployment project type: Windows Installer package (.msi). Therefore, the Properties window contains properties that will affect the resulting .msi that is produced.

Properties of the Root Setup Node

The first property we are going to look at is `ProductName`. This property, as the name tells us, is used to set the textual name of the product that this Windows Installer package is installing. By default, it is set to the name of the setup project (in our case `Setup1`). The value of this property is used throughout the steps of the resulting setup. For instance, it is used for the text of the title bar when the resulting .msi file is run. The property is used along with the `Manufacturer` property to construct the default installation directory:

```
C:\Program Files\<Manufacturer>\<ProductName>
```

The `ProductName` property is also used by the Add/Remove Programs control panel applet (Figure 25-14) to show that the application is installed.

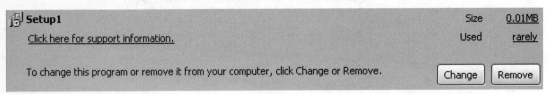

Figure 25-14

From this screenshot in Figure 25-15, you can see there is a link that you can click to get support information about the selected application.

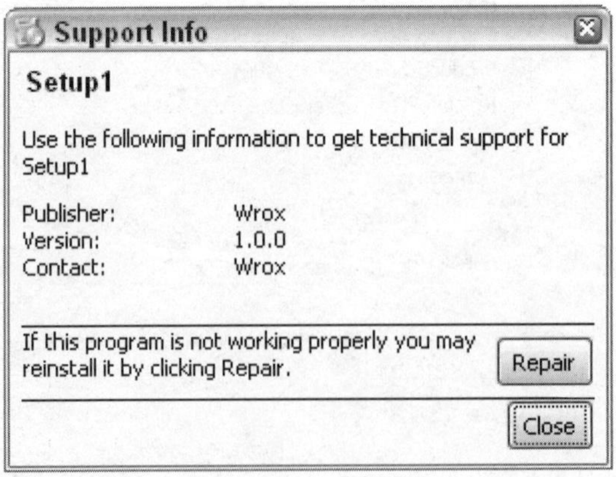

Figure 25-15

A number of the properties of the setup project can be used to customize the support information that is shown. The following table contains details of how the properties relate to the support information that is shown.

Support Information	Related Properties	Description
Publisher	Manufacturer	The Manufacturer property is used to help create the default installation directory for the project and provide a textual display of the manufacturer of the application contained within the Windows Installer package
Version	ManufacturerUrl	This property is used in conjunction with the Manufacturer property to make a hyperlink for the Publisher part of the support information. If a value is entered, the name of the Publisher will be underlined, which can then be clicked to allow you to visit the publisher's Web site. If a value is not included the publisher's name does not act as a hyperlink
	Version	This is the version number of the Windows Installer package. It can be changed to match the version number of the application that thepackage installs. But this has to be done manually
Contact	Author	This property is used to hold the name of the company/person that created the Windows Installer package. By default this has the same value as the Manufacturer property
Support Information	SupportPhone	This property can be used to provide a support telephone number for the application.
	SupportUrl	This property can be used to provide a URL for the product's support Web site. The value of this property will be represented as a hyperlink in the support information window.
Comments	Description	This property can be used to include any information that you would like to appear in the support information window. For instance, it could be used to detail the opening hours of your support department.

The next property that we are going to look at for the root setup node is called AddRemoveProgramsIcon. As you can probably guess, this property allows us to set the icon that appears in the Add/RemovePrograms control panel applet for the application contained within this Windows Installer package. We can select (None) from the drop-down list, which means that we do not want to change the icon and the default icon will be used. Alternatively, we have the option to (Browse) for an icon, which brings up a window that allows us to find and select the particular icon we would like to use. We do not have to use a stand-alone icon file; we can use an icon from an executable or DLL that is contained within the project. The last option, the Icon option is used when an icon has been selected and will then be used in the Add/Remove Programs list.

The remainder of the properties for the root setup node are summarized in the following table.

Property	Description
DetectNewerInstalledVersion	If this property is set to True and a newer version of the application is found on the machine then the installation will not continue. If the property is set to False then this check will not occur and the application will install even if there is a newer version on the computer already
Keywords	This property enables you to set a number of keywords that can be used to locate this installer
Localization	This property is used to set which locale this installer has been designed to run in. The values of this property will affect what string resources are used within the installation
PackageCode	This property is a GUID that is used to uniquely identify this installer. This property is used to link the installer with a specific version of the application that it installs
ProductCode	This property is a GUID that is used to uniquely identify the particular version of the application contained within it
RemovePreviousVersion	If this property is set to True and an older version of the application is found on the machine then the installation will remove the old version and continue on with the installation. If the property is set to False then this check is not done
SearchPath	This property is used to specify a search path that VS.NET uses when it builds the setup project and needs to find the detected dependencies
Subject	This property is used to provide an additional text string of what the installation is used for.
Title	This property is used to set the textual title of the application that is installed. By default, this property will have the same name as the setup project
Upgrade Code	This property is a GUID and is used to uniquely identify a product. This property should stay the same for all versions of the same application. The ProductCode and PackageCode properties change depending on the specific version of the product

Properties of the Primary Output Project Item

We are now going to move on and take a quick look at the properties of the primary output project item in the following table.

Property	Description
Condition	This enables you to enter a condition that will be evaluated when the installation is run. If the condition evaluates to `True` then the file will be installed; likewise, if the condition evaluates to `False` then the file won't be installed. If we only wanted a particular file to be installed if the installation was being run on Microsoft Windows 2000 or better, we could enter the following for the condition: `VersionNT >= 5`
Dependencies	Selecting this property will display a window that shows all the dependencies of the selected project output
Exclude	You can use this property to indicate whether you want the project output to be excluded from the resulting Windows Installer package
ExcludeFilter	This property enables you to exclude files from the project output using wildcards. For example, if you enter a wild card of `*.txt`, then all files that are part of the project output that have an extension of `.txt` will be excluded from the resulting Windows Installer package. Selecting this property will display a window that will allow you to enter any number of wildcards
Folder	As mentioned previously, this property allows you to select the target folder for the project outputs
Hidden	This property allows you to install the files that make up the project output as hidden files. This property basically toggles on/off the hidden attribute of the files
KeyOutput	This property expands to provide information about the main file that makes up the project output. In our case, it will show information of the `WindowsApplication.exe` file
Outputs	Selecting this property will display a window that lists all the files that are part of the project output and where these files are located on the development machine
PackageAs	This property can be used to indicate whether the project output should be packaged according to what is defined in the project properties (`vsdpaDefault`) or externally (`vsdpaLoose`) to the resulting Windows Installer package. The default is to use the project properties setting
Permanent	This property is used to indicate whether the files that make up the project output should be removed when the application is uninstalled (`False`) or left behind (`True`). It is advisable that all the files that are installed by an application be removed when the application is uninstalled. Therefore, this property should be set to `False`, which it is the default
ReadOnly	This property is used to set the read-only file attribute of all the files that make up the project output. As the name suggests, this makes the file read-only on the target machine

Continues

Property	Description
Register	This property allows you to instruct the Windows Installer to register the files contained within the project output as COM objects. This only really applies to projects (for example, Class Library project template) that have been compiled with the Register for COM Interop project property set
SharedLegacy	This property indicates whether the files that make up the project output are to be reference counted, once installed. This really only applies to files that are going to be shared across multiple applications. When the installation is removed the files will only be uninstalled if their reference count is equal to zero
System	This property indicates that the files contained within the project output are to be treated as system files and protected by Windows file protection
Transitive	This property indicates whether the condition specified in the condition property is reevaluated when the installation is rerun on the computer at a later date. If the value is True then the condition is checked on each additional run of the installation. A value of False will cause the condition only to be run the first time the installation is run on the computer. The default value is False
Vital	This property is used to indicate that the files contained within the project output are vital to the installation — if the installation of these files fails then the installation as a whole should fail. The default value is True

Properties of the Detected Dependency Items

We are now going to take a brief look at the properties of the dotnetfxredist_x86_enu.msm file in the DetectedDependencies folder. This file is a merge module dependency and the second is an assembly dependency. We will only cover the properties that are different to those of the project output item (discussed earlier). Most of the additional properties are read-only and cannot be changed. They are used purely to provide information to the developer.

Property	Description
MergeModuleProperties	A merge module can contain a number of custom configurable properties. If the selected merge module contains any they will appear here. In the case of our example, there are no custom properties.
Author	This property stores the name of the author of the merge module. [Read-only]
Description	This property is used to store a textual description of the merge module. [Read-only]

Continues

Property	Description
LanguageIds	This property is used to indicate what language the selected merge module is targeted at. [Read-only]
ModuleDependencies	Selecting this property will show a window that lists all the dependencies of the selected merge module. [Read-only]
ModuleSignature	This property will display the unique signature of the merge module. [Read-only]
Subject	This property is used to display additional information about the merge module [Read-only]
Title	This property is used to simply state the title of the merge module. [Read-only]
Version	This property is used to store the version number of the selected merge module. The version number of the merge module usually changes as the version number of the files it contains changes. [Read-only]

Of course, some projects will also contain other .dll files in this folder. In this case, some of the additional properties that may be encountered for these files are as follows.

Property	Description
DisplayName	This contains the filename of the selected assembly. Read only
Files	Selecting this property will display a window that will list all the files that make up the selected assembly. Read only
HashAlgorithm	This property shows what hash algorithm was used by the manifest in hashing the files contents (to stop tampering). Read only
Language	This property will show what language this assembly is targeted at. This property relates to the culture of an assembly. If the property is empty, then the assembly is culture (language) independent. [Read only]
PublicKey PublicKeyToken	These two properties are used to show information about the strong name of the selected assembly. If an assembly has a strong name then either of these two properties will contain a value (other than all 0s). One or the other of these properties are used and not normally both. [Read only]
SourcePath	This property contains the location of where the selected assembly can be found on the development computer. [Read-only]
TargetName	This property contains the filename of the assembly, as it will appear on the target machine. [Read-only]
Version	This property shows you the version number of the selected assembly. [Read only]

This has been a brief look at the Setup Project template. It uses all the project defaults and provides a standard set of steps to the user when they run the Windows Installer package. More often than not, this simple approach of including a single application file and its dependencies is not good enough. Fortunately, the setup project can be customized extensively to meet our needs. We can create shortcuts, directories, registry entries and so on. These customizations and more can be accomplished using the set of built-in editors, which will be covered after the next walkthrough.

An ASP.NET Web Application

The other deployment scenario we are going to look at is that of a Web application that has been created using the ASP.NET Web application project template. We are assuming that the Web application is being developed on a development Web server and that we will need to create a deployment project to transfer the finished application to the production Web server. Although the previous deployment scenario is one of the most typical, this scenario has to come a very close second.

From the simple requirements defined earlier, we can see that the best deployment template to use is the Web Setup Project template. There is one major difference between this template and the previous Setup Project template, in that the Web Setup Project will by default deploy the application to a virtual directory of the Web server on which the setup is run, whereas a Setup Project will deploy the application to the `Program Files` folder on the target machine by default. There are obviously some properties that differ between the two project templates, but other than that they are pretty similar. They both produce a Windows Installer package and have the same set of project properties discussed later in the chapter.

As with the other walkthroughs, we need to create an application that we can use to deploy. Start a new project and make sure you select ASP.NET Web Application from the list of available project templates. We are not going to add any code to the project that we just created, as it is being used purely as a base for the deployment project. Now add a Web Setup Project template. Our solution should now contain two projects.

As with the previous walkthroughs, the deployment project does not contain any files at present. There is also a folder called `Detected Dependencies` in the Solution Explorer (shown in Figure 25-16) that acts in exactly the same way as in the previous walkthrough.

Figure 25-16

The next step that we need to look at is adding the output of the Web application to the deployment project. This is accomplished in pretty much the same way as the previous walkthrough. So to start with, add the Primary output from the Web application to the deployment project using the method described in the previous walkthroughs.

If we built the solution now and tried to deploy the application onto the production Web server it would not work. When adding the Primary output from a Web application, only the compiled code of the Web application, including its detected dependencies, are added to the deployment project. All the other files that make up a Web application (HTML files, style sheets, and so on) are not included as part of the Primary output of the project.

To include these files in the deployment project, we need to add another project output to the deployment project. This time we need to include the Content Files of the Web application. The resulting project should look like what is displayed in Figure 25-17.

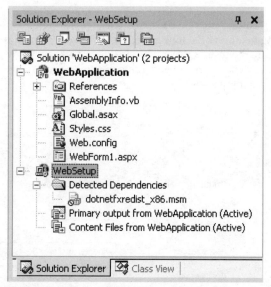

Figure 25-17

Now if we build the solution, the resulting Windows Installer package will include the compiled code of the Web application along with its dependencies, as well as the other files that make up a Web application, ASP.NET files, style sheets, and so on.

Most of the topics discussed in the last walkthrough apply to this walkthrough. As mentioned earlier, the Setup Project and Web Setup projects are very similar and are only really different in where they install the application by default.

Modifying the Deployment Project

In the last two walkthroughs, we created the default Windows Installer package for the particular project template. We didn't customize the steps or actions that were performed when the package was run. What if we had wanted to add a step into the installation process that displayed a ReadMe file to the user? Or what if we needed to create registry entries on the installation computer? The walkthroughs did not cover how to customize the installation to our needs, which is what this section is going to focus on. There are six editors that we can use to customize a Windows Installer-based deployment project:

- ❑ File System editor
- ❑ Registry editor
- ❑ File Types editor
- ❑ User Interface editor
- ❑ Custom Actions editor
- ❑ Launch Conditions editor

The editors are accessible through the View ➪ Editor menu option or by using the corresponding buttons at the top of the Solution Explorer.

We can also modify the resulting Windows Installer package through the project properties window. In this section, we are going to take a brief look at each of the six editors and the project properties, and how they can be used to modify the resulting Windows Installer package. We will only be able to cover the basics of each of the editors, enough to get you going. We will use the project created in the Windows application walkthrough in this section.

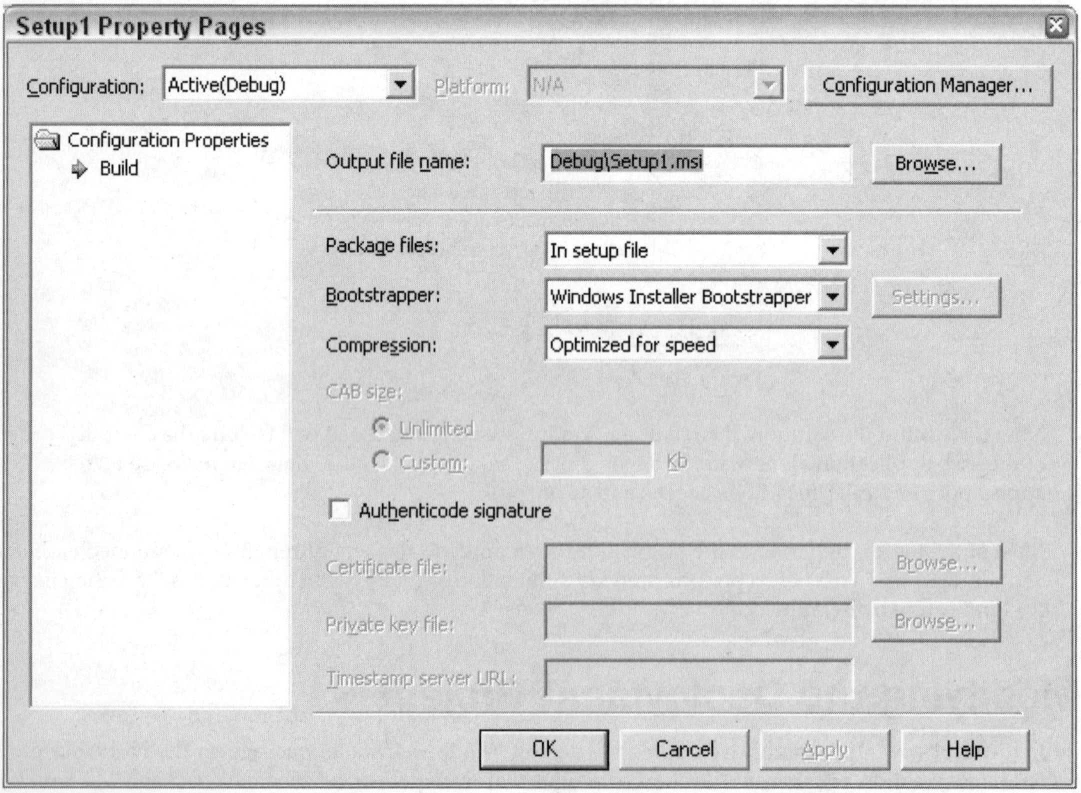

Figure 25-18

Project Properties

The first step we can take in customizing the Windows Installer package is to use the project properties. The project properties dialog box is accessed by right-clicking the root of the setup project and selecting Properties from the popup menu or by selecting the Properties item from the Project menu when the setup project is the active project. Both of these methods will bring up the project properties dialog box as illustrated in Figure 25-18.

As you can see from the preceding screenshot, there is only one page that we can use to set the properties of the project: Build.

The Build Page

We will now take a look at the Build page and how the options can be used to affect how the resulting Windows Installer package is built.

Build Configurations

The first thing to notice is that like most other projects in VS.NET we can create different build configurations. We can modify the properties of a project for the currently active build configuration or we can modify the properties for all the build configurations. We use the Configuration combo box to change what build configuration we want to change the properties for. In the previous screenshot, notice that we are modifying the properties for the currently active build configuration: Debug. The button labeled Configuration Manager allows us to add, remove, and edit the build configurations for this project.

Moving on, we can see an option called Output file name, which can be used to modify where the resulting Windows Installer package (.msi) file will be created. We can modify the filename and path directly or we can press the *Browse* button.

Package Files

By using the next setting, Package files, we can specify how the files that make up the installation are packaged up. The following table describes the possible settings.

Package	Description
As loose uncompressed files	When we build the project, the files that are to be included as part of the installation are copied to the same directory as the resulting Windows Installer package (.msi) file. As mentioned earlier, this directory can be set using the Output file name setting
In setup file	When the project is built, the files that are to be included as part of the installation are packaged up in the resulting Windows Installer package (.msi) file. By using this method, we only have one file to distribute. This is the default setting
In cabinet file(s)	With this option, when the project is built, the files that are to be included as part of the installation are packaged up into a number of cabinet files. The size of the resulting cabinet files can be restricted by the use of a number of options, which will be discussed later in this section. This option can be very useful if you want to distribute the installation program on a set of floppy disks

What happens if we try to install the resulting Windows Installer package on a machine that does not have the Windows Installer services running on it? Not a great deal. Luckily, there is a project option that will help us overcome this problem: Bootstrapper. There are three options available from the combo box:

❑ None

❑ Windows Installer bootstrapper

❑ Web bootstrapper

If None is selected, then only the Windows Installer package file will be produced when the setup project is built. If you select Windows Installer Bootstrapper, then some additional files will be placed in the output directory when the setup project is built. These additional files will install the Windows Installer services on the machine that it is run on. With this option selected, four additional files will be added to the directory that contains the resulting Windows Installer package file. The following table details the additional files.

File	Description
Setup.exe	If a user does not have the Windows Installer service installed on his machine, he can use this file to install the application. When running this file the Windows Installer services will be installed onto the machine (if it is not already installed) and then the .msi file will be run and the installation will continue as normal
Setup.ini	This is a configuration file that is used by Setup.exe after it has installed the Windows Installer services (if needed) and contains one setting — the name of the .msi file to run
InstMsiA.exe	This file is the installation for the Windows Installer services for a Windows 95 or 98 based machine
InstMsiW.exe	This file is the installation for the Windows Installer services for a Windows NT, 2000, XP, or Windows Server 2003 based machine

The final option is Web Bootstrapper. This option allows you produce a number of additional files that can be used to allow the application to be installed over the Internet. When you select this option a window (shown in Figure 25-19) will be presented to you.

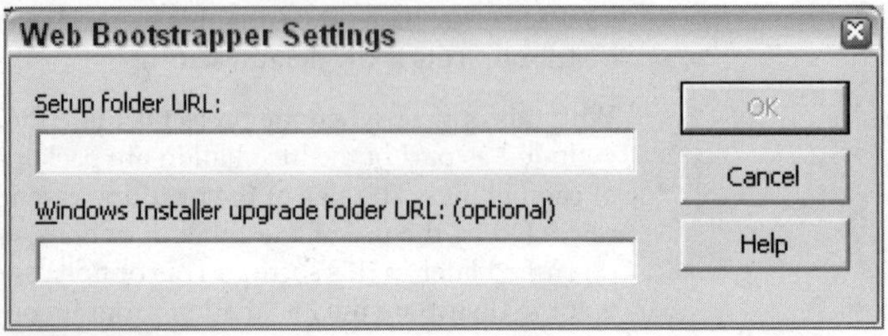

Figure 25-19

This window is used to set two options of the Web bootstrapper:

❑ The Setup folder URL setting is used to define the location of where the Windows Installer package file produced will be located when deployed. This setting needs to be the URL of a folder.

❑ The Windows Installer upgrade folder URL setting is where you can optionally set the location of where the two Windows Installer service installer files (InstMsiA.exe and InstMsiW.exe) are located. This setting (if used) needs to be the URL of a folder. If this setting is not used, it is assumed that the two files are located at the URL specified by the Setup folder URL setting.

When we build the setup project with this option, three additional files are created in the output directory: Setup.exe, InstMsiA.exe, and InstMsiW.exe. The only file that has a different function from that discussed previously is the Setup.exe file, which we will discuss later in this section. The Windows Installer package (.msi) file that was created by the build needs to be copied to the Web server so that it is available via the URL specified in the Setup folder URL setting. The InstMsiA.exe and InstMsiW.exe files need to be copied to the Web server so they are accessible via the URL specified in the Windows Installer upgrade folder URL setting. If no value was specified for this property, then they need to be copied to the same location as the Windows Installer package file. The Setup.exe file can then be distributed to anyone who wants to install your application.

When the user executes the Setup.exe file, it first checks that the correct version of the Windows Installer service is installed. If it is not, then the required setup (InstMsiA.exe or InstMsiW.exe) file is downloaded from the URL specified in the above settings and then installed. Once the correct version of the Windows Installer service is installed, the Setup.exe file then downloads the package file (.msi) from the location specified. Once the package has been downloaded, the installation continues as normal by executing this Windows Installer package. If the package file cannot be downloaded, then you will receive an error informing you that it could not be downloaded. The installation will then end.

The advantage of using this technique is that you do not have to deploy the Windows Installer setup files to each of the clients; they are available centrally from one location over the Web. Several installers can share the same download location. The Windows Installer package file that contains your application is also not distributed to each client. They download it from a central location. This allows you to change the package and have the client pick up this change automatically when they install the application. The disadvantage to this approach is that anyone who installs your application will need to have an Internet connection and if the files are large, it could take a long time to download them.

Compression

We also have the option to modify the compression used when packaging up the files that are to be contained within the installation program. The three options (Optimized for speed, Optimized for size, and None) are pretty self-explanatory and will not be covered in this book. The default, however, is Optimized for speed.

Setting the Cabinet File Size

If we want to package the files in cabinet files, then we have the option to specify the size of those resulting cabinet file(s):

❑ The first option we have is to let the resulting cabinet file be of an unlimited size. What this effectively means is that all the files will be packaged into one big cabinet file. The resulting size of the cabinet file will also be dependent on the compression method selected.

❑ If, however, creating one large cabinet file is not practical, especially if you want to distribute your application on floppy disks (1440KB of space per floppy), you can use the second option to specify the maximum size of the resulting cabinet file(s). If you select this option, you need to fill in the maximum size that a cabinet file can be (this figure is in KB). If all the files that need to be contained within this installation exceed this size then multiple cabinet files will be created.

Using the Solution Signing Options

The final set of options are concerned with signing the resulting Windows Installer package using Authenticode. To enable Authenticode signing you must make sure the checkbox is checked. This will enable you to set the three settings that are required to sign the package file.

Setting	Description
Certificate file	This setting is used to define where the Authenticode certificate file can be found. This file is used to sign the package
Private key file	This setting is used to define where the private key file is. This file contains what we call an encryption key that is used to sign the package
Timestamp server URL	This setting allows you to optionally specify the URL of a timestamp server. The timestamp server will be used to get the time of when the package was signed

We will not be covering Authenticode signing in this chapter. If you are interested in this option you should consult the MSDN documentation.

The File System Editor

Now that we have taken a look at the project properties, we are going to move on to look at the editors that are available for us to use to customize the resulting Windows Installer package. You will need to make sure that the current active project is the setup project.

We are going to start by taking a look at the File System Editor. This editor is automatically displayed for you in VS.NET's Document Window when you first created the Setup project. Though, you can get at this editor and the other editors that are available to you via the View ➪ Editor menu option in the VS.NET IDE. The first editor we will look at, the File System Editor, is used to manage all the file system aspects of the installation including:

❑ Creating folders on the user's machine
❑ Adding files to the folders defined
❑ Creating shortcuts

Basically, this is the editor we use to define what files need to be installed and where they are installed on the user's machine.

The File System Editor is split into two panes in the Document Window as shown in Figure 25-20.

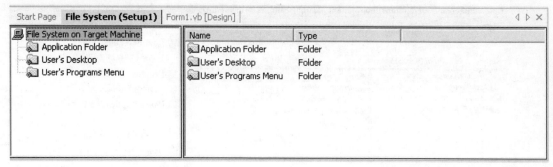

Figure 25-20

The left-hand pane shows a list of the folders that have been created automatically for the project (discussed earlier in the chapter). When you select a folder in the left pane, two things happen: firstly, the right-hand pane of the editor displays a list of the files that are to be installed into the selected folder, and secondly, the Properties windows will change to show you the properties of the currently selected folder.

Adding Items to a Folder

To add an item that needs to be installed to a folder, we can either right-click the folder in the left-hand pane and choose Add from the popup menu, or we can select the required folder and right-click in the right-hand pane and again choose Add from the popup menu. You will be presented with four options, three of which have been discussed earlier in the walkthroughs:

❑ Project output

❑ File

❑ Assembly

The fourth option (Folder) allows us to add a subfolder to the currently selected folder. This subfolder then becomes a standard folder that can be used to add files. If we add any .NET components or executables, the dependencies of these components will also be added to the installation automatically.

Adding Special Folders

When we create a new deployment project, a set of standard folders will be created for us (listed in the desktop application section). What if the folders created do not match our requirements? Well, we can also use the File System editor to add special folders. To add a special folder, right-click anywhere in the left-hand pane (other than on a folder) and you will be presented with a popup menu that has one item: Add SpecialFolder. Alternatively, it's also available through the Action ⇨Add Special Folder menu option. This menu item (shown in Figure 25-21) expands to show you a list of folders that you can add to the installation (folders already added to the project will be grayed out).

As you can see from the screenshot, there are a number of system folders that we can choose from. They are summarized in the following table.

If none of the built-in folders match your requirements, you can even use the item at the bottom of the list to create your own custom folder. This is where the Windows Installer property column of the preceding table comes. Suppose, we wanted to create a new directory in the user's favorites folder called Wrox

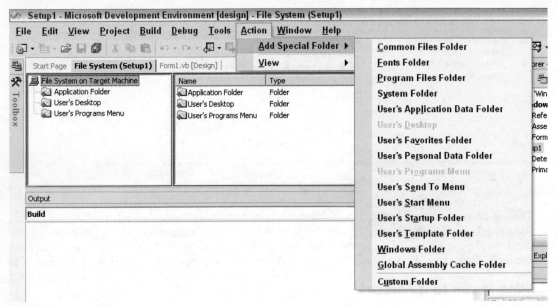

Figure 25-21

Name	Description	Windows Installer Property
Common Files Folder	Files (nonsystem) that are shared by multiple applications are usually installed to this folder.	[CommonFilesFolder]
Fonts Folder	This folder is used to contain all the fonts that are installed on the computer. If your application used a specific font you want to install it into this folder.	[FontsFolder]
Program Files Folder	Most applications are installed in a directory below the program files folder. This acts as root directory for installed applications.	[ProgramFilesFolder]
System Folder	This folder is used to store shared system files. The folder typically holds files that are part of the OS.	[SystemFolder]
User's Application Data Folder	This folder is used to store data on a per-application basis that is specific to a user.	[CommonAppDataFolder]
User's Desktop	This folder represents the user desktop. This folder could be used to create and display a shortcut to your application that a user could use to start your application.	[DesktopFolder]

Continues

Name	Description	Windows Installer Property
User's Favorite Folder	This folder is used as a central place to store links to the user's favorite Web sites, documents, folders, and so on.	[FavoritesFolder]
User's Personal Data Folder	This folder is where a user will store their important files. It is normally referred to as "My Documents."	[PersonalFolder]
User's Programs Menu	This folder is where shortcuts are created to applications that appear on the user's program menu. This would be an ideal place to create a shortcut to your application.	[ProgramMenuFolder]
User's Send To Menu	This folder stores all the user's send to shortcuts. A send to shortcut is displayed when you right-click a file in the Windows Explorer and choose Send To. The send to shortcut usually invokes an application passing in the pathname of the files it was invoked from.	[SendToFolder]
User's Start Menu	This folder can be used to add items to the user's start menu. This is not often used.	[StartMenuFolder]
User's Startup Folder	This folder is used to start applications whenever the user logs into the computer. If you would like your application to start every time the user logs in, then you could add a shortcut to your application in this folder.	[StartupFolder]
User's Template Folder	This folder contains templates specific to the logged in user. Templates are usually used by applications like Microsoft Office 2000.	[TemplateFolder]
Windows Folder	This folder is the windows root folder. This is where the OS is installed.	[WindowsFolder]
Global Assembly Cache Folder	This folder is used to store all the shared assemblies on the user's computer.	

Press, we could accomplish this by adding the correct special folder and then adding a subfolder to it. Another way to accomplish this is to create a custom folder, the process of which we will discuss now.

Right-click in the left-hand pane of the file editor and choose Custom Folder from the popup menu.

The new folder will be created in the left-hand pane of the editor. The name of the folder will be edit mode, so enter the text Wrox Press and press *Enter*.

The folder will now be selected and the Properties window will have changed to show the properties of the new folder. The properties of a folder are summarized in the following table.

Property	Description
(Name)	This is the name of the selected folder. The name property is used within the setup project as the means by which you select a folder.
AlwaysCreate	This property is used to indicate whether this folder should be created on installation even if it's empty (True). If the value is False and there are no files to be installed into the folder, then the folder will not be created. The default is False.
Condition	This enables you to enter a condition that will be evaluated when the installation is run. If the condition evaluates to True then the folder will be created, likewise if the condition evaluates to False then the folder won't be created.
DefaultLocation	This is where we define where the folder is going to be created on the target machine. We can enter a literal folder name (such as C:\Temp), or we can use a Windows Installer property, or a combination of the two. A Windows Installer property contains information that is filled in when the installer is run. In the last table of special folders, there was a column called Windows Installer property. The property defined in this table would be filled in with the actual location of the special folder at runtime. Therefore, if we entered [WindowsFolder] as the text for this property, the folder created would represent the Windows special folder.
Property	This property is used to define a Windows Installer property that can be used to override the DefaultLocation property of the folder when the installation is run.
Transitive	This property indicates whether the condition specified in the condition property is reevaluated on subsequent (re)installs. If the value is True then the condition is checked on each additional run of the installation. A value of False will cause the condition only to be run the first time the installation is run on the computer. The default value is False.

Set the DefaultLocation property to [FavoritesFolder]\Wrox Press.

We could now add some shortcuts to this folder using the technique described below. When the installation is run, a new folder will be added to the user's favorite folder called Wrox Press.

Creating Shortcuts

The final aspect of the File System Editor that we are going to look at is that of creating shortcuts. The first step in creating a shortcut is to locate the file that is to be the target of the shortcut. Select the target file and right-click it. The popup menu that appears will include an option to create a shortcut to the selected file, which will be created in the same folder. Select this option.

To add the shortcut to the user's desktop, we need to move this shortcut to the folder that represents the user's desktop. Likewise, we could move this shortcut to the folder that represents the user's programs menu. Cut and paste the new shortcut to the User's Desktop folder in the left-hand pane of the editor. The shortcut will now be added to the user's desktop when the installation is run. You will probably want to rename the shortcut, which can be accomplished easily via the Rename option of the popup menu.

We have only taken a brief look at the File System Editor. I would encourage you to explore what can be accomplished by using the editor.

The Registry Editor

The next editor that we are going to look at is the Registry Editor, which is used to:

❑ Create registry keys

❑ Create values for registry keys

❑ Import a registry file

Like the File System Editor, the Registry Editor is split into two panes as illustrated in Figure 25-22.

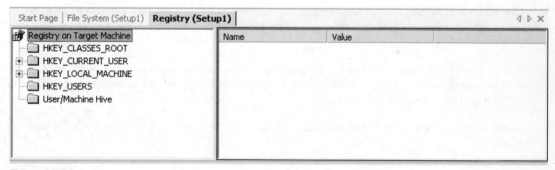

Figure 25-22

The left-hand pane of the editor represents the registry keys on the target computer. When you select a registry key, two things happen: the right-hand pane of the editor will be updated to show the values that are to be created under the selected registry key, and if the registry key selected is not a root key in the left-hand pane, the Properties window will be updated with a set of properties for this registry key.

When you create a new deployment project, a set of registry keys will be created for you that correspond to the standard base registry keys of Windows. Notice in the screenshot that there is a key defined with a name of [Manufacturer]. When the installation is run, this will be replaced with the value of the Manufacturer property that we discussed earlier in the chapter. [Manufacturer] is a property of the installation and can be used elsewhere within the installation. There are a number of these properties defined that can be used in much the same way (you should consult the *Property Reference* topic in the MSDN documentation for a full list).

Adding a Value to a Registry Key

So, what do we need to do to add a value to a registry key? We must first select the required registry key (or create it) that is going to hold the registry values and then there are a number of ways that we can add the registry value:

❑ We can right-click the registry key and use the resulting popup menu

❑ We can right-click in the right-hand pane and use the resulting popup menu

❑ We can use the Action menu

The menu items contained within the Action menu will depend on where the current focus is. For illustrational purposes here, select one of the Software registry keys. The Action menu will contain one item, New, which contains a number of menu items:

❑ Key

❑ String value

❑ Environment string value

❑ Binary value

❑ DWORD value

Using this menu, we can create a new registry key below the currently selected key (via Key), or we can create a value for the currently selected registry key using one of the four Value types: String, Environment String, Binary, and DWORD.

So let's take a look at how we can create a registry entry that informs the application whether or not to run in the debug mode. The registry value must be applicable to a particular user, must be called Debug, and must contain the text True or False.

The first step that needs to be completed is to select the following registry key in the left-hand pane of the editor:

```
HKEY_CURRENT_USER\Software\[Manufacturer].
```

The registry key HKEY_CURRENT_USER is used to store registry settings that apply to the currently logged in user.

Now, we want to create a value so that it is applicable to only this application and not all applications created by us. What we need to do is create a new registry key below the HKEY_CURRENT_USER\Software\[Manufacturer] key that is specific to this product, so select the Action ⇨ New ⇨ Key menu item.

When the key is created, the key name will be editable, so give it a name of [ProductName] and press *Enter*. This will create a key that is given the name of the product contained within this Windows Installer package. The ProductName property of the setup was discussed earlier in this chapter.

Now that we have created the correct registry key, we need to create the actual registry value. Make sure that our new registry key is selected and choose String Value from the Action ⇨ New menu and give the new value a name of Debug.

Once the value has been created, we can set a default value for it, in our case `False`. Make sure that the new value is selected; the Properties window will have changed to show you the details for this value. Notice that there is a property called `Value`, which we will use to set the initial value. Enter `False` as the value for the `Value` property and that's it. The end result is displayed in Figure 25-23.

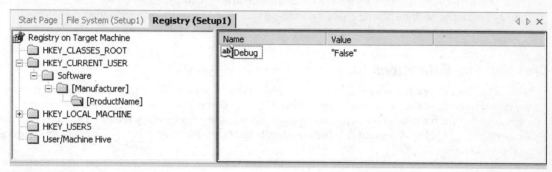

Figure 25-23

When the Windows Installer package is run the Debug registry, value will be created. As you can see, manipulating the Windows Registry is straightforward.

We can move most keys and values in the Registry Editor around by using cut-and-paste or simply by dragging and dropping the required item.

> *If a value already exists in the registry, the Windows Installer package will overwrite the existing value with that defined in the Registry Editor.*

Importing Registry Files

If you already have a registry file that contains the registry settings that you would like to be created, you can import the file into the Registry Editor, which saves you having to manually enter the information. To import a registry file, you need to make sure the root node (Registry onTarget Machine) is selected in the left-hand pane of the editor. You can then use the Import item of the Action menu to select the registry file to import.

> *Registry manipulation should be used with extreme caution. Windows relies heavily on the registry and as a result of this you can cause yourself a great deal of problems if you delete/overwrite/change registry values and keys without knowing the full consequences of the action.*

If you want to create the registry entries that are required to create file associations, you can use the editor covered next.

The File Types Editor

The File Types Editor can be used to create the required registry entries to establish a *file association* for the application being installed. A file association is simply a link between a particular file extension and a particular application. For example, the file extension `.doc` is normally associated with Microsoft WordPad or Microsoft Word.

When we create a file association, not only do we create a link between the file extension and the application, we also define a set of actions that can be performed from the context menu of the file with the associated extension. Looking at our Microsoft Word example, if we right-click a document with an extension of .doc, we get a context menu that can contain any number of actions, for example, Open and Print. The action in bold (Open, by default) is the default action to be called when we double-click the file, so in our example double-clicking a Word document will start Microsoft Word and load the selected document.

Creating File Extensions

So, how do we create a file extension using the editor? We will answer this question by walking through the creation of a file extension for our application. Let's say that our application uses a file extension of .set and that the file is to be opened in the application when we double-click the file. To accomplish this, we need to start the FileTypes editor, which unlike the last two editors, only has one pane to its interface as shown in Figure 25-24.

Figure 25-24

To add a new file type we need to make sure the root element (File Types on Target Machine) is selected in the editor. We can then choose Add File Type from the Action menu. Give the new file type the name, Example File Type.

Before we continue, we must set the extension and application that this file type uses. These are both accomplished using the Properties window (shown in Figure 25-25).

Enter .set as the value for the Extensions property.

To associate an application with this file type, we need to use the Command property. The ellipsis button for this property presents us with a dialog box where we can select an executable file contained within any of the folders defined in the File System Editor. In our case, we'll select the Primary Output from WindowsApplication (active) from the Application Folder as the value for Command.

When we first created this new file type, a default action was added for us called &Open — select it. Now take a look at the Properties window again. Notice the Arguments property: we can use this to add command line arguments to the application defined in the last step. In the case of the default action that has been added for us, the arguments are "%1", where the value %1 will be replaced by the filename that invoked the action. We can add our own hardcoded arguments (such as /d). An action is set to be the default by right-clicking it and selecting Set as Default from the popup menu.

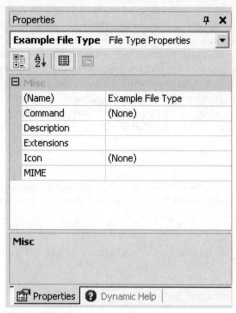

Figure 25-25

The User Interface Editor

The User Interface Editor is used to manage the interface that the user uses to proceed through the installation of the application. The editor allows us to define the dialog boxes that are displayed to the user and in what order they are shown. The User Interface Editor looks like this (see Figure 25-26).

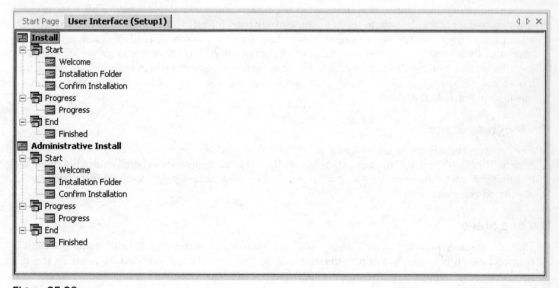

Figure 25-26

The editor uses a treeview with two root nodes: Install and Admin. Below each of these nodes there are three nodes that represent the stages of installation: Start, Progress, and End. Each of the three stages can contain a number of dialog boxes that will be displayed to the user when the resulting Windows Installer package is run. A default set of dialog boxes is predefined when we create the deployment project. The default dialog boxes that are present depend on the type of deployment project: Setup Project or Web Setup Project. The previous screenshot shows the dialog boxes that were added by default to a Setup Project. However, if you are creating a Web Setup Project the Installation Folder dialog box will be replaced by an Installation Address dialog box. Using the previous screenshot, we will discuss the two modes that the installer can be run in and what the three stages of the installation are.

Installation Modes

We'll start by taking a look at the two modes that the installation runs: Install and Admin. These basically distinguish between an end user installing the application and a system administrator performing a network setup.

> *To use the Admin mode of the resulting Windows Installer package you can use* `msiexec.exe` *with the/a command line parameter:*
>
> `msiexec.exe /a <PACKAGE>.msi`

The Install mode will be the one that is most used and is what we will use in this discussion. As mentioned earlier, the steps the installation goes through can be split into three stages and are represented as subnodes of the parent installation mode.

The Start Stage

The Start stage is the first stage of the installation and contains the dialog boxes that need to be displayed to the user before the actual installation of the files begins. The Start stage should be used to gather any information from the user that may affect what is installed and where it is installed. This stage is commonly used to ask the user to select the base installation folder for the application and to ask the user what parts of the system he would like to install. Another very common task of this stage is to ask the user what their name is and what organization they work for. At the end of this stage the Windows Installer service will determine how much disk space is required on the target machine and check that this amount of space is available. If the space is not available, the user will receive an error and the installation will not continue.

The Progress Stage

The Progress stage is the second stage of the installer and is where the actual installation of the files occurs. There isn't usually any user interaction in this stage of installation. There is normally one dialog box that indicates the current progress of the installation. The current progress of the installation is calculated automatically.

The End Stage

Once the actual installation of the files has finished, the installer moves into the End stage. The most common use of this stage is to inform the user that the installation has completed successfully. It is often used to provide the option of running the application straight away or to view any release notes.

Customizing the Order of Dialog Boxes

The order in which the dialog boxes appear within the treeview determines the order in which they are presented to the user when the resulting Windows Installer package is run. Dialog boxes cannot be moved between different stages.

The order of the dialog boxes can be changed by dragging the respective dialog boxes to the position in which we want them to appear. We can also move a particular dialog box up or down in the order in which it is shown by right-clicking the dialog box and selecting either Move Up or Move Down.

Adding Dialog Boxes

A set of predefined dialog boxes have been added to the project for us, but what happens if these do not match our requirements? As well as being able to modify the order in which the dialog boxes appear, we can also add or remove dialog boxes from any of the stages.

When adding a dialog box, we have the choice of using a built-in dialog box or importing one. To illustrate how to add a dialog box, we will look at an example of adding a dialog box to display a ReadMe file to the user of Windows Installer package. The ReadMe file will need to be displayed before the actual installation of the files occurs.

The first step is to determine the mode in which the dialog box is to be shown: Install or Admin. In our case, we are not interested in the Admin mode so we will use the Install mode. After this, we need to determine the stage at which the dialog box is to be shown. In our example, we want to display the ReadMe file to the user before the actual installation of the files occurs, which means we will have to show the ReadMe file in the Start stage. Make sure the Start node is selected below the Install parent node.

We are now ready to add the dialog box. Using the Action menu again, select the Add Dialog menu item, which will display a dialog box (Figure 25-27) where you can choose from the built-in dialog boxes.

As you can see from the screenshot, there are a number of built-in dialog boxes to choose from. Each dialog box has a short description that appears at the bottom of the window to inform you of its intended function. In the case of our example, we want to use the Read Me dialog box, so select it and click on OK.

New dialog boxes are always added as the last dialog box in the stage that they are added to, so now we need to move it into the correct position. In our case, we want the Read Me dialog box to be shown immediately after the Welcome dialog box, so drag and drop it into position.

Properties of the Dialog Boxes

Like most other project items in VS.NET, dialog boxes have a set of properties that we can change to suit our needs using the Properties window. If you make sure a dialog box is selected, you will notice that the properties window changes to show the properties of the selected dialog box. The properties that appear depend on the dialog box selected. Details of all the properties of the built-in dialog boxes can be found by looking at the *Properties of the User Interface Editor* topic in the MSDN documentation.

The Custom Actions Editor

The Custom Actions Editor is used for fairly advanced installations and allows us to define actions that are to be performed due to one of the following installation events: Install, Commit, Rollback, and

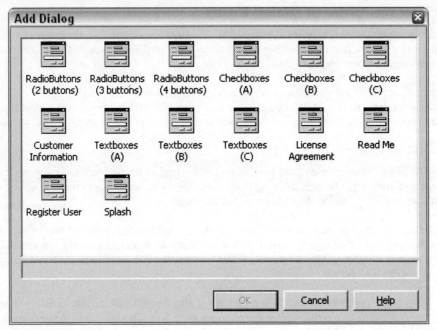

Figure 25-27

Uninstall. For example, we can use this editor to define an action that creates a new database when the installation commits.

The custom actions that are added using this editor can be windows script-based or compiled executables or DLLs.

Before we continue with our discussion of this editor, make sure that it is loaded. Once loaded, you will notice that it uses a treeview to represent the information, much like the User Interface Editor. There are four nodes that represent each of the four installation events that you can add custom actions to. This is displayed in Figure 25-28.

Figure 25-28

As with the User Interface Editor, the order in which the actions appear determines the order in which they are run and this can be modified by simply dragging and dropping the actions, or by using the context menus of the actions to move them up or down.

Adding a Custom Action

To add a custom action we must select the node of the event into which we want to install the action. You can then use the Action menu to select the executable, DLL or script that implements the custom action. The four actions that are defined in the editor are defined in the following table.

Event	Description
Install	The actions defined for this event will be run when the installation of the files has finished, but before the installation has committed
Commit	The actions defined for this event will be run when the installation has been committed and has therefore been successful
Rollback	The actions defined for this event will be run when the installation fails and rolls back the machine to the same state as before the install was started
Uninstall	The actions defined for this event will be run when the application is being uninstalled from the machine

Suppose, we wanted to start our application up as soon as the installation had been completed successfully. We could use the following process to accomplish this.

First, we need to decide when the action must occur. Using the preceding table we can see that the Commit event will be run when the installation has been successful. Make sure this node is selected in the editor. We are now ready to add the actual action we would like to happen when the commit event is called. Using the Action menu again, select the Add Custom Action menu item, which will display a dialog box that we can use to navigate for and select a file (exe, .dll or windows script) from any that are included in the File System Editor. In the case of our example select Primary output from WindowsApplication (Active), which is contained within the Application Folder.

As with most items in the editors that we are discussing, the new custom action has a number of properties that we can use. These properties are summarized in the following table.

Property	Description
(Name)	This is the name given to the selected custom action
Arguments	This property allows you to pass command line arguments into the executable that makes up the custom action. This only applies to custom actions that are implemented in executable files (.exe). By default, the first argument passed in can be used to distinguish what event caused the action to run. The first argument can have the following values: /Install /Commit /Rollback /Uninstall

Continues

949

Property	Description
Condition	This enables you to enter a condition that will be evaluated before the custom action is run. If the condition evaluates to True then the custom action will run, likewise if the condition evaluates to False then the custom action will not run
CustomActionData	This property allows you to pass additional information to the custom action
EntryPoint	This property is used to define the entry point in the .dll that implements the custom action. This only applies to custom actions that are implemented in dynamic linked libraries (.dll). If no value is entered then the installer will look for an entry point in the selected DLL with the same name as the event that caused the action to run (Install, Commit, Rollback, Uninstall)
InstallerClass	If the custom action is implemented by an Installer class (consult the MSDN documentation for more information) in the selected component then this property must be set to True. If not it must be set to False
SourcePath	This property will show the path to the actual file on the developer's machine that implements the custom action

Set the InstallClass property to equal False as our application does not contain an installer class.

That's it. When we run the Windows Installer package and the installation is successful, our application will automatically start. The custom action that we implemented earlier is very simple, but custom actions can be used to accomplish any customized installation actions that you could want. I suggest that you take some time to play around with what can be accomplished using custom actions.

The Launch Conditions Editor

The Launch Conditions Editor can be used to define a number of conditions for the target machine that must be met before the installation will run. For example, if your application relies on the fact that the user must have Microsoft Word 2000 installed on their machine to run your application, you can define a launch condition that will check this.

You can define a number of searches that can be performed to help create launch conditions:

❑ File search

❑ Registry search

❑ Windows Installer search

As with the Custom Actions Editor, the Launch Conditions Editor (shown in Figure 25-29) uses a treeview to display the information contained within it.

Figure 25-29

There are two root nodes: the first (Search Target Machine) is used to display the searches that have been defined, the second (Launch Conditions) contains a list of the conditions that will be evaluated when the Windows Installer package is run on the target machine.

As with many of the other editors, the order in which the items appear below these two nodes determines the order in which the searches are run and the order in which the conditions are evaluated. If we wish, we can modify the order of the items in the same manner as previous editors.

> *The searches are run and then the conditions are evaluated as soon as the Windows Installer package is run, before any dialog boxes are shown to the user.*

We are now going to look at an example of adding a file search and launch condition to a setup project. For argument's sake, let's say that we want to make sure that our users have Microsoft Word 2000 installed on their machine before they are allowed to run the installation for our application.

Adding a File Search

To add a file search, we begin by searching for the Microsoft Word 2000 executable.

Making sure the Search Target Machine node is currently selected in the editor, add a new file search by selecting the Add File Search item from the Action menu. The new item will need to be given a meaningful name, so enter Word2KSearch. The end result is shown in Figure 25-30.

Figure 25-30

Modifying the File Search Properties

Like most items contained within the editors mentioned in this chapter, the new file search item has a set of properties that we can modify using the Properties window. The properties of the file search item determine the criteria that will be used when searching for the file. Most of the properties are self-explanatory and have been covered in previous sections and will not be covered in this chapter.

In our example here, we need to search for the Microsoft Word 2000 executable, which means that a number of these properties will need to be modified to match our own search criteria.

The first property that we need to modify is `FileName`, which is used to define the name of the file that the search will look for. In our case, we need to search for Microsoft Word 2000 executable, so enter `winword.exe` as the value for this property. Previous versions of Microsoft Word used the same filename.

There is no need for us to search for the file from the root of the harddrive. The `Folder` property can be used to define the starting folder for the search. By default, the value is `[SystemFolder]`, which indicates that the search will start from the Windows `system` folder. There are a number of these built-in values that we can use; if you are interested then you can look up what these folders correspond to in *Adding Special Folders* section.

In our example, we do not want to search the Windows `system` folder as Microsoft Word is usually installed in the `Program Files` folder, so set the value of the `Folder` property to `[ProgramFilesFolder]` to indicate that this should be our starting folder.

When the search starts it will only search the folder specified in the `Folder` property as indicated by the default value (0) of the `Depth` property. The `Depth` property is used to specify how many levels of subfolders the search will look in from the starting folder specified above for the file in question. There are performance issues relating to the `Depth` property. If a search is performed for a file that is very deep in the file system hierarchy, it can take a long time to find the file. Therefore, it is advisable that, wherever possible, you should use a combination of the `Folder` and `Depth` properties to decrease the possible search range. The file that we are searching for in our example will probably be at a depth of greater than 1, so change the value to 3.

There may be different versions of the file that we are searching for on a user's machine. We can use the remaining properties to specify a set of requirements for the file that must be met for it to be found, for example, minimum version number, minimum file size.

We are searching for the existence of Microsoft Word 2000; this means that we will need to define the minimum version of the file that we want to find. To search for the correct version of `winword.exe` we need to enter `9.0.0.0` as the value for the `MinVersion` property. This will ensure that the user has Microsoft Word 2000 or later installed and not an earlier version.

The result of the file search will need to be assigned to a Windows Installer property so that we can use it to create a launch condition later. This is going to be a bit of a tongue-twister. We need to define the name of the Windows Installer property that is used to store the result of the file search using the `Property` property. Enter `WORDEXISTS` as the value for the `Property` property. If the file search is successful, the full path to the found file will be assigned to this Windows Installer property, otherwise it will be left blank as shown in Figure 25-31.

Creating a Launch Condition

A file search alone is pretty useless. Which takes us on to the second step of the process of ensuring the user has Microsoft Word 2000 installed, creating a launch condition. We can use the results of the file search described earlier to create a launch condition.

Make sure the Launch Conditions node is selected in the editor and add a new launch condition to the project by selecting Add Launch Condition from the Action menu. We need to give this new item a meaningful name and in the case of our example (Figure 25-32) we will give it a name of `Word2KExists`.

Figure 25-31

Figure 25-32

This new item has a number of properties that we will need to modify. The first property we will change is called `Message` and is used to set the text of the message box that will appear if this condition is not met. Enter any meaningful description that describes why the installation cannot continue.

The next property that we will need to change is called `Condition` and is used to define a valid deployment condition that is to be evaluated when the installation runs. The deployment condition entered must evaluate to `True` or `False`. When the installer is run, the condition will be evaluated, if the result of the condition is `False` then the message defined will be displayed to the user and the installation will stop.

For our example, we need to enter a condition that takes into account if the `winword.exe` file was found. We can use the Windows Installer property defined earlier (`WORDEXISTS`) as part of the condition. As the property is empty if the file was not found and nonempty if the file was found, we can perform a simple test on whether the property is empty to create the condition. Enter `WORDEXISTS <> " "` as the value for the `Condition` property.

Hopefully, from the preceding discussion of this search you will be able to apply the knowledge gained, to understand how to use the other searches and create your own launch conditions.

We have now finished our brief discussion of the editors that we can use to modify the resulting Windows Installer package to our needs. We have only looked briefly at the functionality of the editors, but they are extremely powerful so I advise you to spend some time playing around with them.

Building

The final step is concerned with how to build the deployment or setup project you have created. There is basically no difference between how you build a Visual Basic .NET application and deployment/setup project. If the project is the only project contained within the solution then you can just use the Build item from the Build menu, which will cause the project to be built. As with the other projects, you will be informed of what is happening during the build through the Output window.

The deployment/setup project can also be built as part of a multiproject solution. If the Build Solution item is chosen from the Build menu, all the projects in the solution will be built. Any deployment or setup projects will be built last. This is to ensure that if they contain the output from another project in the solution that they pick up the latest build of that project.

As with most other project templates in VS.NET, you can set the current build configuration to be used when building the project. This will not be covered in this chapter as it has been covered previously in the book. As you can see, building a setup/deployment project is basically the same as building any other project template.

Summary

We started by looking at the structure of an assembly and how it contains metadata that enables it to describe itself. This mechanism of self-description will help us when we come to deploy our applications by removing dependencies on the registry, unlike COM components. If a machine has the CLR installed on it, it is more feasible that an application can be deployed to a machine simply by copying the files (although this does not apply if the application must install shared assemblies).

We also looked at how the identity of an assembly is used to allow multiple versions of an assembly to be installed on a machine and how this aids the side-by-side use of assemblies. We covered how an assembly is versioned and the process by which the CLR resolves an external assembly reference and how we can modify this process through the use of configuration files.

We also looked at how an assembly stores information such as version number, strong name, and culture, about any external assemblies that it references. We also looked at how this information is checked at runtime to ensure that the correct version of the assembly is referenced and how we can use versioning policies to override this in the case of a buggy assembly. The assembly is the single biggest aid in reducing the errors that can occur due to DLL Hell and in helping with deployment.

We also covered a number of topics relating to deployment and deployment issues, including:

- How assemblies are used as the foundations of deployment in .NET
- How assemblies are structured to help reduce the problems of deployment, known as DLL Hell
- How assemblies move us towards the goal of true XCOPY deployment
- VS.NET setup and deployment project types
- Setup/deployment project editors

26

Mobile Application Development

One of the most visible changes that accompanied Visual Studio .NET 2003 has been the inclusion of more tools to support the development of applications that target the hand-held device market. These devices are starting to take a larger role in the lives of users as varied as delivery men and doctors. As a category of applications this will probably be one of the fastest growing markets and at some point you are bound to need or want to make your application available to a mobile user.

The focus of mobile applications will take you into two additional project types for Visual Basic .NET. The first is the ASP.NET Mobile Web Application. Applications created using this template are Web based applications which run on a server, but which are accessed from a mobile device. The second project type is the Smart Device application. These applications are where you work with the .NET Compact Framework, and understanding how to build mobile applications with VB.NET is a surprisingly simple process.

In order to walk you through some of the special limitations of these applications this chapter will touch on the following areas:

❑ Mobile Web Applications

❑ Differences of Mobile Web and .NET Compact Framework Applications

❑ Introducing the .NET Compact Framework

❑ Limitations of the .NET Compact Framework

❑ Mobile Device Emulators

❑ A First .NET Compact Framework Application

This chapter isn't going to cover everything about creating mobile applications, but will provide you a solid understanding of how you can create applications that operate on any device. The goal is to expose some of the special concerns for creating applications that will function in a mobile world.

Accordingly, this means that the .NET Compact Framework will be covered in more detail since to a large extent, mobile Web applications have very few differences from other Web applications.

Mobile Web Applications

When Visual Studio .NET 2002 was originally released there was a separate package available for mobile Web applications. You had to be aware of the Microsoft Mobile Internet Toolkit (MMIT) in order to download and install it as part of your environment. Visual Studio .NET 2003 has fully integrated this toolkit, now encapsulated as an additional project template. The ASP.NET Mobile Web Template is the simplest way of limiting a new project to the appropriate user interface elements.

The key to mobile Web applications is that at their core they are only different from other Web applications at runtime. A traditional browser can be used to navigate throughout the screens of a mobile Web application. Not that this is meant to suggest you would design your Web applications for the UI limitations of the mobile device, but that behind the scenes you have the full power of the .NET Framework running on the Web server. The differentiating factor for a mobile Web application is its user interface limitations. Other areas such as components and services which are not related to the interface can be the same as those used for traditional ASP.NET applications.

You have heard that developing a multi-tiered application can have advantages in several common computing areas such as scalability, reliability and maintainability. When you are building applications with the mobile device market in mind a more important consideration is reusability. Building a defined layer to manage your business logic means that since a mobile Web application is server based you can reuse the exact same classes for your mobile application.

Web Services for Mobile Applications

One of the limitations of running .NET on a mobile device is that you can't have it provide a Web service. This discussion is better handled as part of the discussion of the limitations of the .NET Compact Framework, but what about consuming Web services. As was just noted, the only real limitations for mobile devices on the Web are related to the user interface. By definition an XML Web service is designed to act as a component used by other applications. The result is that while you are probably not going to create a "mobile Web service," yet at the same time you will probably create several Web services for use by mobile applications.

The result is that the story of Web services for mobile devices is very short and simple. You can't host a Web service on a mobile device. However, a mobile device can be used to connect to a Web service and a .NET Compact Framework application can be used to leverage a Web service as part of a rich user interface.

Limitations of the Mobile Web Template

Limitations of the user interface are the primary difference between mobile web applications and desktop web applications. The result is that developers are forced to focus on ways to provide the user with a effective interface that is limited to a display area that is a fraction of the area that an application was designed to use. The second biggest challenge in adjusting the user interface to fit a smaller display area is the consistency, or lack of, for the various devices that fall under the category of mobile. As a developer you are by now familiar with the fact that in the desktop world minor differences between the ways that Internet Explorer and Netscape work can cause significant challenges. Even with .NET there to help smooth out these differences you wouldn't think of creating an application that needed to support both browsers without testing it on both browsers. As challenging and time consuming as this can be for the relatively small number of browsers on the desktop, consider that the Microsoft's mobile Web handler has to deal with literally hundreds of different devices each of which can have a separate way of doing the same thing.

For you the developer there is almost no chance that you have the time or means to test your application on every possible device, the result is that more then ever before when you are developing a mobile Web application you want a feature set which will be stable across every device. Even more challenging then the browser wars on the desktop is that fact that mobile phone Web standards have evolved over time. Originally there was WML for managing mobile devices, while newer devices tend to rely more on a subset of traditional HTML. To put this in perspective, the table shown below lists the user interface elements available by default as part of the mobile Web tool suite. The list separates out the validators and page elements so that you get a feel for the limited number of actual controls, there are really only a dozen controls in a classic UI sense.

Control Name	Description
Ad Rotator	The ad rotator works as you might expect allowing your site to place a varying graphic as part of your page. There are image limitations as noted in the Image control.
Calendar	Similar to the ASP.NET calendar control, allows the user to select a date.
Command	Commands are displayed as buttons on your forms. The Command control supports the post back of a form to your server.
Image	Provides support for images in your Web page. Remember that not all devices support images. Also consider the potential for a limited display area and remember that HTML and WML based devices expect different image formats, so you will need multiple images.
Label	Works similarly to the ASP.NET label control
Link	A Label control that encapsulates hyper-link behavior.
List	Mobile Web applications may only have a dozen controls, but three of them are list controls. The List control is the most generic way to display a list of items. You can create a list based on a data bound set, and when an item is selected send a message to your server to indicate the user's selection.
ObjectList	The second option for listing items the ObjectList supports some alternative behaviors. The ObjectList is strictly a data-bound control unlike the list, which is programmatic. The ObjectList can be customized to display multiple items in something closer to a grid display.
PhoneCall	As you might imagine this is oriented toward mobile phones. Not all mobile devices support a phone, but for those which do, this control allows a user to select and dial a phone number in a single step.

Continues

Control Name	Description
SelectionList	A selection list is the third type of list. It varies from a list control in that it does not trigger an event to the server when the user selects an item. As such it is good for supporting a small list of choices which are part of a larger form.
TextBox	The mobile TextBox is limited to a single line of text. Note you should use this with care as many mobile devices do not have good keyboard support and most users would prefer to pick an item from a list.
TextView	A label of course can be programmatically changed, but is limited in that it doesn't support a lengthy string. The TextView is most closely related to the Label control, but the TextView is designed to support an unlimited amount of text which the device can then scroll through. It is very similar to having static text on a page, but the text in a TextView control is set when the page is requested from the server.

Other UI Elements	Description
Form	There can be only a single form on each page, and every control must be contained within a form.
MobilePage	As the name indicates this object represents a mobile page.
Panel	Allows you to separate your page or form into different control areas. This allows you to group common controls within your display
StyleSheet	This element doesn't really have a display component of its own, but is used to control the custom look of other controls and text on your mobile page.
ValidationSummary	Just as with other ASP.NET applications it is possible to add validation elements to your mobile forms. The Validation Summary displays a summary list of the errors which are found by the individual validators associated with the various controls on your form.
CompareValidator	Compares the value of two controls based on a specific condition. For example is the start date earlier then the stop date.
CustomValidator	Provides a handle from which you can call a custom method in order to validate a control's data.
RangeValidator	Validates that a numeric value is within a certain range.
RegularExpressionValidator	Validates that the entered text passes a specified regular expression.
RequiredFieldValidator	Ensures that a control has data when the form is submitted.

When working with mobile applications is that given the wide range of devices you are going to find yourself working with a much smaller subset of available controls. However don't let the limited options fool you, the mobile interface is powerful in that these controls will automatically recognize and adapt to the device's limitations. The advantage of using the mobile Web template for your project is that Microsoft has handled recognizing and the programmatic changes associated with responding to different devices. When a request is received the .NET framework interprets the request header and looks for information to determine the user's current device. This information is then used by the rendering engine to adjust the layout and behavior of the mobile controls to fit within the limitations of the calling device.

While you may need to provide alternate image formats and text replacements for image files, you do not need to include logic to detect a particular device. This auto detection also means that while you can test the basic feel of your application from your desktop browser, you need to keep in mind that the framework might behave very differently from your cell phone. The result is you need to test at least a subset of devices to get a feel for how your application behaves on WML vs. HTML or on different size displays from phone to smart device.

Creating a Mobile Web Application

The process of creating a new mobile Web application starts with the creation of a new project. This process has been covered several times previously; for a Mobile Web application you need to select an "ASP.NET Mobile Web" application template. Notice that the project is created similarly to any other ASP.NET project as a virtual directory on your local IIS server. Once you have named and created your new application you will have a display similar to the one shown in Figure 26-1.

The figure illustrates how with a mobile Web application you are working with a limited display area. The template has automatically positioned an initial form on the page, and if you attempt to resize the form you'll see that there is no support for changing the design area. The fact is that the design area associated with your display is just an approximation. To get a better feel for what this means first open the Toolbox to select a control. As Figure 26-2 illustrates a separate section is available which lists only those controls that are appropriate for a mobile Web application.

You can select a Label control and drop it on your design template outside the form. The control which is not within a form displays an error message in place of its default display place holder. The design UI for Mobile Web applications is a more controlled and limited environment then the default Web design interface. You can then either drag the current control into the confines of the form or add a second label inside the form.

Next you should attempt to place a text box next to the label. You'll notice this second control is automatically placed below your first. Try as you might the default logic is going to force you to use an entire row of your display area for each control. Thus if you now add a command button next to your text box, it is placed at the bottom of the list of controls. As shown in Figure 26-3 the display options when working with a mobile Web application are far more restrictive then any other application type.

If you still have that first label in your design surface be certain to remove it. The result is a fairly simple for with three controls inside of a form. Take a few minutes to notice the reduced list of properties associated with your controls and then double click on your command button. This will add a click handler to the code view for your form as shown in Figure 26-4. Even though the design surface has

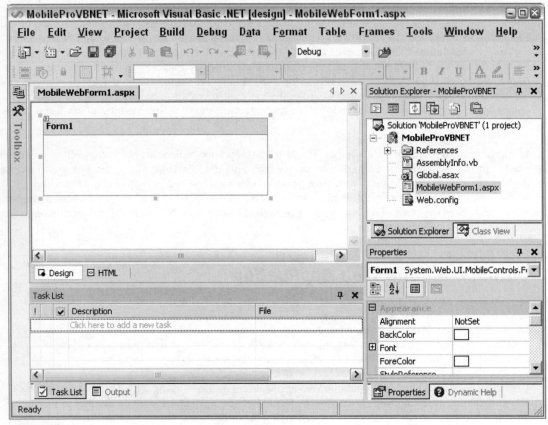

Figure 26-1

limitations it's important to note as you move to the next display area that the coding for a Mobile Web application is no different from any other ASP.NET application.

As illustrated in Figure 4, you can combine the elements of your application to get behavior that is essentially the same as what you would expect from any ASP.NET application. Even though there are fewer elements available to design your user interface, those elements which are available tend to work on the same principles as their ASP.NET equivalents. The challenge in working with Mobile Web applications occurs in managing that limited user interface experience and in testing.

Testing is a challenge because as a rule of thumb if you are running code in an environment that isn't the same as your release environment you aren't getting a trully valid test. Hitting F-5 or the Play button in Visual Studio will launch your mobile Web application in your desktop browser. Unlike the .NET Compact Framework which ties in with a pair of emulators Mobile Web applications are by default tested against your desktop environment. Thus running your application results in a desktop based browser display similar to the one seen in Figure 26-5. Not that there's anything wrong with that, after all your business logic will execute on a server. However, this testing doesn't reflect your interface's usability on the latest phone or in an environment where there isn't a keyboard.

Figure 26-2

It's really unfortunate that unlike the .NET Compact Framework which is supported by a pair of emulators that you aren't given the opportunity to automatically switch to one of the environments for testing Mobile Web applications. Being forced to input a string for a text box takes on a whole new meaning when you no longer have a keyboard available. Of course the testing environment is only one of the differences between Mobile Web applications and .NET Compact Framework Applications.

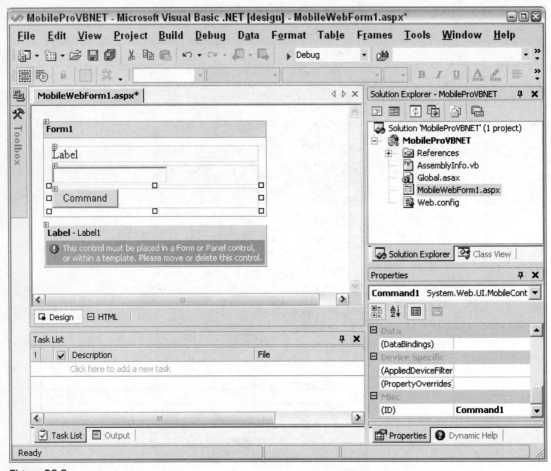

Figure 26-3

Differences of Mobile Web and .NET Compact Framework Applications

While Mobile Web applications are server based applications which host only a dumb user interface on the client, a .NET Compact Framework application can run entirely on a mobile device. As a result in many ways a .NET Compact Framework application is both a more limited environment and a richer environment then is a Mobile Web application. A good example is the number of devices supported. The Mobile Web supports well in excess of 150 different devices, while the .NET Compact Framework supports a limited number of "Smart" devices that run one of the following versions of either the Pocket PC or Windows CE operating system.

❑   Pocket PC2000

❑   Pocket PC 2002

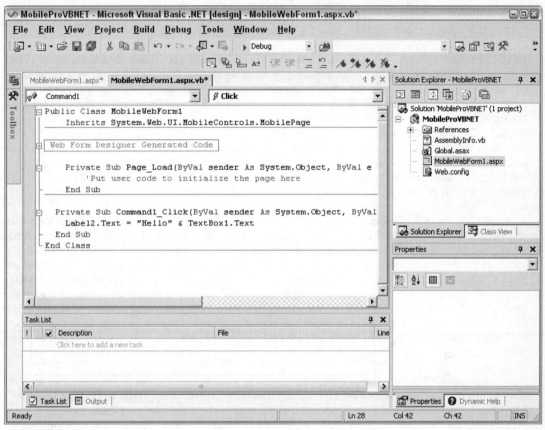

Figure 26-4

Figure 26-5

❑   Windows Mobile 2003 Pocket PC

❑   Windows CE.NET (aka Windows CE version 4.1) or later

Of note this list doesn't include Microsoft's Smart Phone. While this is a Smart device the Smart Phone is being supported by an add-on toolkit targeting its far more limited Framework support. This toolkit is currently available as a free download from Microsoft.com. This is a quick reminder that not all devices are created equally even for the .NET Compact Framework and as you'll see later in this chapter, the Pocket PC supports a richer user interface then does Windows CE. They both have the same version of the .NET Compact Framework but just as with Mobile Web Applications there are device specific user interface limitations. As a result when you want to target both default platforms, build your application against the more limiting Windows CE environment and then do additional testing against the Pocket PC. If you install the SmartPhone SDK, then this is the most limiting environment and the one you should target for your application.

As for the Mobile Web, the key difference is that the .NET Compact Framework is about having a version of .NET that runs locally on these devices. You can create a .NET Compact Framework application which communicates with a SQL Server database local to the device it is running on. The fully functioning application may run even when the mobile device is running without any connectivity to the Internet. You can also use the .NET Compact Framework to create an application which communicates with Web Services and simply provides a richer user experience while still operating against the same business objects which are used by your mobile Web application. As a .NET Compact Framework developer you have a full set of tiered application architectures available. You can create a business layer that lives on the handheld device, cache data locally and create a common data access layer for data stored in a local SQL CE database.

Thus while the .NET Compact Framework limits you to a smaller number of targeted devices, and you have to install the actual Framework on those devices along with your application code, but in return you have the ability to create much more powerful applications. The .NET Compact Framework is a replacement for tools such as Embedded C++ and Embedded VB which were used to develop applications for early versions of Windows CE. The remainder of this Chapter focuses on using the version of the .NET Compact Framework which ships with Visual Studio .NET 2003. As has been noted there is an additional SDK available for working with Smart Phones but this is beyond the baseline provided by Visual Studio .NET 2003 and thus beyond the scope of this Chapter.

Introducing the .NET Compact Framework

Yes the .NET Compact Framework is for what most of us think of as compact devices. However, it gets its name from the fact that the .NET Compact Framework does not include everything which makes up the .NET Framework. According to the Microsoft's documentation the .NET framework redistributable requires about 110 MB of space on your hard drive. Let's face it most mobile devices don't have that much space to spare. So in order to account for a smaller disk, slower processor and reduced memory the developers of the .NET Compact Framework took out many of the features of the .NET Framework to reduce the footprint of the .NET Framework.

The .NET Compact Framework 1.0 SP1 Redistributable comes in at a much slimmer 62 megabytes in size. The framework didn't shrink in half magically, this was done by leaving out many of the classes that are available as part of the .NET Framework. Not only are entire Classes and Namespaces omitted, but even the classes which are included have been placed on the equivalent of a logic diet losing many of the extra methods and properties that provide enhanced but not truly necessary functionality. A quick way to verify this is to open the help for a class such as the System.Windows.Forms.DataGrid and examine which methods included the statement "Supported by the .NET Compact Framework." It is a surprisingly small number, yet when you look at the DataGrid most of the key capabilities are still supported. In part this is because one of the areas where Microsoft put .NET on a diet was in the area of method overloads. Overloaded methods make for convenient interfaces for developers; however they also amount to bloat in the library. As a result it is common for a method which had several overloads to have only one or two supported options under the Compact Framework.

The key to developing with the .NET Compact Framework is understanding what is available. The .NET Compact Framework was created to help you write applications, not drivers, not reusable business components or Web servers. Additionally when given two ways to carry out a task the engineers picked what was arguably the more robust or open option. For example you can consume a XML Web Service, but the .NET Compact Framework does not support Remoting. Both Remoting and Web Services are ways to implement support for distributed components, but by choosing Web Services over Remoting the engineers choose the more open standard.

Microsoft also had experience in the compact device environment. Just as VB.NET is a replacement for Visual Basic 6.0, the .NET Compact Framework is a replacement for Embedded Visual Basic 3.0 (eVB). While Embedded C++ is still available to support some low level functions that the Compact Framework omits, when working with building applications, the Compact Framework provides .NET developers (both VB and C#) a familiar environment for creating applications for the mobile world.

If you are an experience VB.NET developer then when you first start working with the .NET Compact Framework you will be tempted to reuse code that was designed for desktop applications. Unfortunately this will reference a class or method which isn't available as part of the .NET Compact Framework and you will find yourself rewriting and reconsidering decisions. The good news is that if you take this route, most such errors are exposed quickly as compile errors and when you test you can choose one of two possible emulators and see how your code will actually execute on the targeted platform(s).

Limitations of the .NET Compact Framework

Remoting has already been mentioned as a casualty of the engineer's knife. What are some of the other key areas that you are going to run into? To be honest there are some such as overloaded methods are too numerous to try and cover in detail but many others can be categorized. For example the .NET Framework does not support the System.Web namespace except as it relates to consuming Web services. At first this might sound a little drastic but think about it. The Compact Framework is about creating windows applications. These applications might consume a Web service but they don't need to create a Web interface. Let's face it although the performance of say WROX.COM might sometimes seem like it must be running on someone's Pocket PC, the reality is you don't expect to host a Web application from your hand-held device.

The Web isn't the only thing limited, data access has been limited. Not just for databases, but also for XML. The .NET Framework provides a rich set of classes to support the XML Document Object Model (DOM), XPath and XSLT for querying and transforming XML. Unfortunately the Compact Framework only supports the XML DOM. If you need to manipulate XML you are either going to be forced to work within the limitations of the DOM or plan to make use of a call to a remote Web Service.

The story for databases is also a bit limiting. If you were an avid eVB developer you may have gotten accustomed to Pocket Access. Unfortunately the .NET Compact Framework doesn't provide support for this legacy database structure. The .NET Compact Framework comes equipped to work with SQL CE, a more robust handheld database. However, if you are looking to migrate an application that was written under eVB, you are going to need to either migrate your data source or consider a third party adapter such as the one from InTheHand Software to access your existing database. As for SQL CE it provides an excellent tool for creating tables and setting up a replication model with its big brother SQL Server. As for working with SQL CE one it's limitations is that it doesn't support stored procedures. The result is that when you are planning your application; take a few moments to think about creating a data access layer that will encapsulate your SQL Queries to replace this missing capability.

The other surprising limitation of the .NET Compact Framework's database access implementation is that it does not support the System.Data.OleDB namespace. Of course the System.Data.SqlClient namespace is supported, as is the System.Data.SqlServerCe namespace required to support working with SQL CE. However, while you may be tempted to use the SQL CE version of the System.Data.SqlClient libraries to access SQL Server, and certainly this is a supported activity we recommend you avoid doing so. If there is data that you need from a central server and you aren't using SQL CE replication to manage a local copy, consider creating a Web service interface for managing data access. The .NET Compact Framework's System.Data.SqlClient support for Integrated Windows Authentication is weak and you don't want to risk exposing your central database directly, instead use a XML Web Services layer to validate input received from handheld applications.

Security as it just so happens is one of the areas where the framework holds some limitations by design. While the .NET Framework has a rich set of Cryptographic classes to support encrypting data none of the available implementations were included with the .NET Compact Framework. This is truly unfortunate since these might have been useful for working with XML Web Services. There are other options such as the API's that exist as part of the device OS, but these have their own limitations both in ease of use and portability.

The .NET Compact Framework has also omitted support for role based security. This actually makes sense when you consider the handheld operating model. The fact is there isn't much need to manage different user groups across a handheld device, given that part of any security model is physical security; a handheld device is fully controlled by the person physically holding it. After all while you can secure a SQL CE database, there is still only a single user with a single password available to the database.

That's right a single password for the database, the good news as a developer is that you won't be putting a bunch of passwords into application configuration files. The bad news is that this is in part because the System.Configuration namespace hasn't been included. This is the namespace which supports reading application settings from a *.config file. The common alternative to such files of course is to save information to the registry.

While all of the operating systems which are supported by the .NET Compact Framework support a version of the system registry, the rich set of classes for accessing the registry have also not been included. The result is that when it comes to working application settings you are going to be writing a handler more or less from scratch. One solution is to leverage the ease of the System.Data.Dataset class to create a settings table and then use the ReadXML and WriteXML methods to retrieve and persist your application's settings.

Alternatively you can look at accessing machine specific capabilities such as the registry via PInovke. The PInvoke capabilities are particularly important when working with a Windows CE application since most of low level features require PInvoke calls for access. These calls are embedded within the

System.Runtime.INteropServices namespace. Unfortunately not everything available in the full version of this namespace is part of the .NET Compact Framework. In particular another limitation of the Compact Framework is that it doesn't provide automatic support COM interoperability.

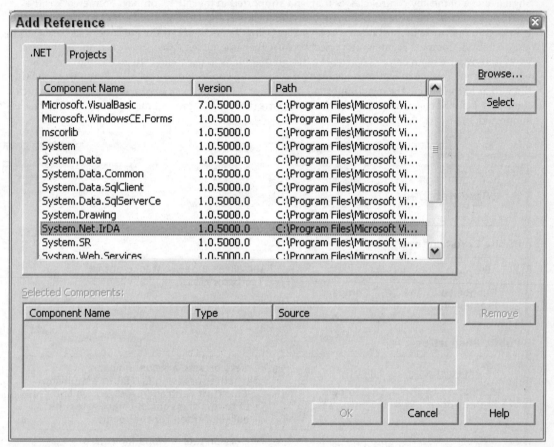

Figure 26-6

Figure 26-6 shows that when you open the Add Reference dialog as part of a Compact Framework project, there isn't a tab for COM components. The good news is that you can still interop it's just that instead of having a friendly auto-generated class, you need to create a custom Interop wrapper using Embedded Visual C++ 4.0. Don't trivialize this, if C++ programming was easy there wouldn't have an environment like .NET that abstracts the operating system and C++ layer away from your applications. The result is that in most cases unless a class has some serious business logic that just can't be reproduced you will spend less time implementing the class using the .NET Compact Framework then you will spend creating the necessary interop assemblies.

As you can tell many limitations are associated with the way that handheld devices operate, but there are also limitations caused solely by size considerations. And a good example of these are many of the User Interface elements which are not supported. Foremost among these is the System.Windows.Forms.Design namespace. This is the namespace which provides support for design-time support for Windows Forms, things like Control Anchoring, the component tray for those controls without a UI element and several other design time elements.

Similarly one of the key control classes that isn't supported in the .NET Compact Framework is the UserControl class. There are in fact many individual classes and methods that aren't supported by the Compact Framework. In most cases when you are using Visual Studio these are easy to recognize from within a .NET Compact Framework project because they are not available. However, one of the best ways to recognize them before you create a design that plans to use them is to go through the help system. As you can see in Figure 7, the methods which are supported by the .NET Framework include a disclaimer to this effect. The most important disclaimer is the one associated with the class constructor. If there isn't a public constructor avaiable that supports the .NET Compact Framework, then the class isn't supported.

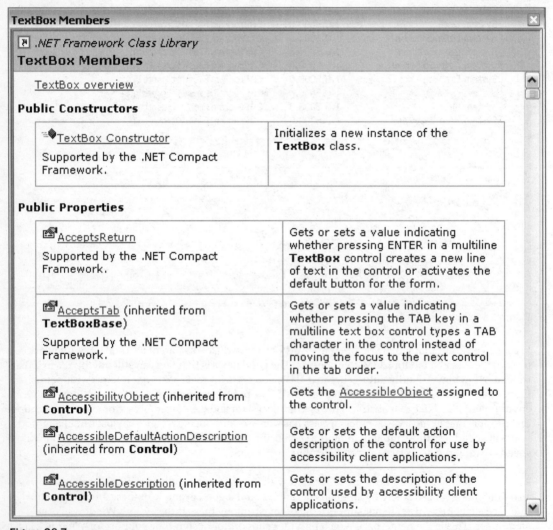

Figure 26-7

As Figure 26-7 illustrates, the TextBox control is a supported control since it's constructor is supported. The AcceptsReturn method is supported, as is the AcceptsTab method which is inherited from its parent class. However The accessibility methods are not supported on the .NET Compact Framework. This mixture of supported and unsupported methods and properties is common across every namespace and class which is supported by the .NET Compact Framework. The rule is that if it isn't documented as being supported, it isn't supported.

.NET Compact Framework Specific Namespaces

After all that discussion of limitations you are probably beginning to doubt if the .NET Compact Framework can do anything. It is a very powerful tool suite, and even has a couple of unique namespaces stuffed in. The first of these System.Data.SqlServerCe is relatively self explanatory. This is the namespace that is associated with accessing a SQL CE database. The class has the necessary methods and logic to create connections to either a local or remote SQL CE database.

However beyond this namespace there are two other DLLs available from the references list that deserve some specific coverage. The first of these is the System.Net.IrDAEndPoint class. You won't find this class in a normal .NET application, the IrDA stands for Infrared Data Association. The IrDA is a consortium that sets up common standards for Infrared data access. The IrDAEndPoint class handles the management of the infrared network interface. This namespace is only available to .NET Compact Framework applications. Even for .NET Compact Framework applications you need to explicitly reference this class from the System.Net.IrDA reference listing. The class then provides two methods. The first Create is used to create a new connection via the Infrared port. This is where the second method, Serialize comes in. The Serialize method allows for the creation of a SocketAddress. In short the only time that you are likely to use an instance of this class is when you are creating a custom network communication object, but the class was necessary to support other classes which encapsulate this capability.

The remaining DLL that you can import is System.SR. The reference for System.SR doesn't actually provide any classes. Open up the Object Browser and take a look at the reference, you'll see there aren't any classes or methods, yet there it is under the list of .NET references. This class is there to help you as a developer by providing robust error handling. One of the potential limitations of the .NET Compact Framework which wasn't mentioned was the fact that by default error objects which are created don't include a meaningful text message.

Textual error messages take up quite a bit of space, so what the System.SR class provides are the hooks to retrieve those error messages. By including this reference in your project you are increasing the footprint of your application, but during debugging sessions you will be able to get full error messages. Then when ready to build the release version of your application you can remove this reference.

Mobile Device Emulators

One of the better features of Visual Studio .NET 2003's environment for developing .NET Compact Framework applications is the inclusion of device emulators. The environment ships with two different emulators, one for the PocketPC and one for WindowsCE. While an emulator isn't the same as an actual device, having these emulators available makes the testing process for your application a much more manageable process.

Which emulator you select will generally be determined by the target for your application. The emulators are normally started by selecting them as part of the application testing process. When you run your application you will be asked to select where to run the application. The list normally includes one or both of the emulators along with one or more targeted devices. If you intend to use the emulator for the majority of your testing one of the items to be aware of is how to customize the emulator's environment. This isn't normally a big deal for the Pocket PC based emulator but can be important when targeting Windows CE.

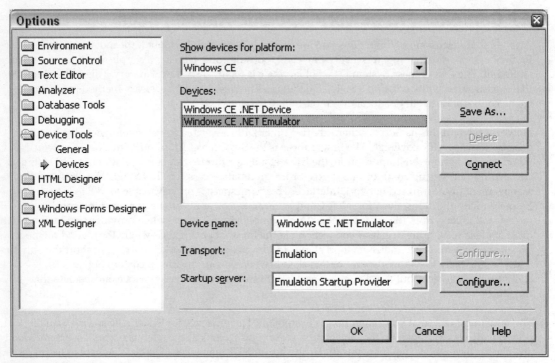

Figure 26-8

From the Tools menu select options and then within the Options dialog select the Device Tools ➪ Devices item to get the display shown in Figure 26-8. From this screen you can select to work with either the Windows CE or Pocket PC emulator settings. However, before going into the device settings take a moment to start the device using the Connect button. This will give you an idea of how long it takes to start each device while you are attempting to test your application. You'll notice that the startup can be rather slow, the side effect of this is that unlike a typical .NET application where you will code a little then test, with a Compact Framework application you are going to find the testing process far more time consuming.

However, this screen is about settings, so use the Configure button in the lower right corner of the display to open the dialog shown in Figure 26-9. You should note that there are two Configure buttons, but only one will ever be enable. The top button is associated with setting the deployment characteristics of an actual device. The lower button is associated with the emulator package. The first tab of the Configure Emulator Settings dialog is dedicated to the display resolution. For most Pocket PC applications these values tend to be constant. However, Windows CE can be installed on devices which have widely varying user interfaces.

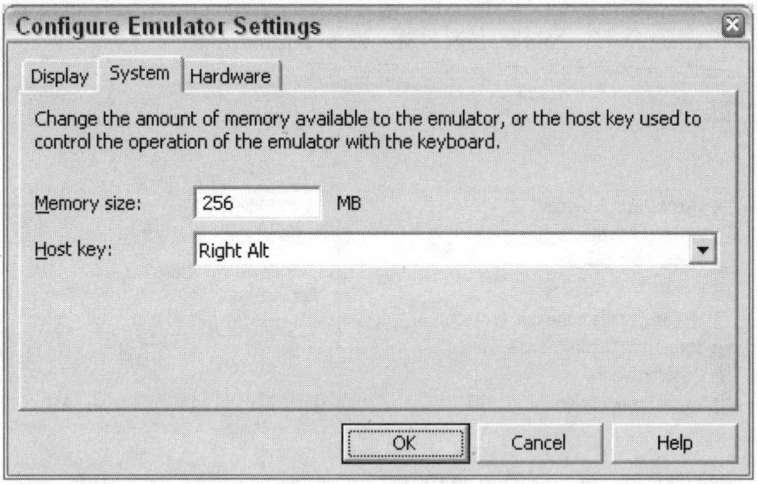

Figure 26-9

The second tab of this display allows you to define simulated system's memory and keyboard Host key. The Emulator will automatically simulate a limited memory range to help determine your applications performance on the actual device, unfortunately the emulator doesn't have anyway of reflecting what might be the actual performance. In order to support database applications you will want to change the memory setting shown in Figure 26-9 to 256 MB. The Host key is the key that is used to allow you to enter keyboard commands into your application's user interface. I prefer to avoid doing this since the idea of designing a hand-held application is to ensure that it will be usable when it is deployed to a device without a keyboard.

The final tab in this display is associated with various ports that are available from the device. Although the .NET Compact Framework doesn't provide native support for any print capabilities odds are good that over time your users will be connecting printers, barcode scanners, modems and any number of other similar add-ons to their hand held devices. While you could arrange to repeatedly send your code to a device with the appropriate equipment the framework also supports attaching that same device to your development desktop and then mapping the emulator so that it can see the physical device attached to your workstation.

All in all the emulators provide an excellent pair of tools for preparing your code for deployment. They are implemented based on Microsoft's Virtual PC environment so when your run one of the emulators the software runs just as if it was running on a handheld device. While they won't serve as a final test bed, they more then meet the needs of a Unit Test environment which can be available to every developer's desktop. After all just because you are building a compact application doesn't mean you won't still be working in a team environment and leveraging all of the same skills that you've created in working on .NET desktop applications. One warning, if you use VMWare you may find that the VPC emulator and VMWare clash preventing you from building your application within a virtual environment.

A First .NET Compact Framework Application

Having talked quite a bit about the limitations of a .NET Compact Framework application now seems to be the time to look at creating your first .NET Compact Framework application. So the first step after opening up Visual Studio is to select to create a new project. In this case you will select the Visual Basic template labeled Smart Device Application as shown in Figure 26-10.

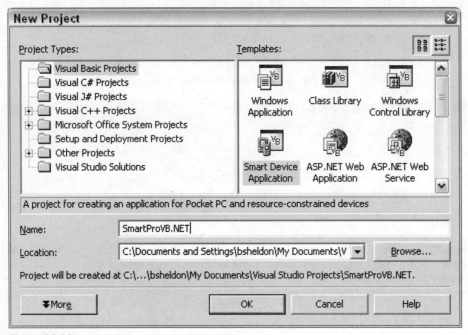

Figure 26-10

For this first demonstration you can name the application something like SmartProVBNET. What you are going to notice upon selecting the OK button is that unlike a traditional application you are not taken into the Visual Studio IDE. Instead you are taken to what is essentially the Project Selection dialog for Compact Framework applications. Of course the correct title as shown in Figure 26-11 is the Smart Device Application Wizard, but you might notice that this wizard doesn't include a Next button nor a finish button. Instead this dialog allows you to select a target platform and then the type of project for that platform.

As shown in Figure 26-11, by default Visual Studio .NET supports two broad categories of device. The first is the Pocket PC based application. This platform accounts for the various versions of the Pocket PC, and when you target the Pocket PC you are creating an application which might not be compatible with a Windows CE device. Switching between the Pocket PC and Windows CE platform results in changes across the other dialog windows. As you can see in Figure 26-11, selecting a Windows CE device means that Visual Studio will allow you to run this application on either the Windows CE or Pocket PC emulators. This also means that certain special functions associated with the keypad of a Pocket PC device will not be available.

Additionally as you switch between the WindowsCE and Pocket PC platform you'll notice that the available project types change. The Pocket PC doesn't have a console environment. As a result instead of being able to create a Console Application you are offered an opportunity to create a Non-graphical Application. The key difference is that unlike console applications where you can open message windows and send output to the screen, with a non-graphical application there is no support for any UI. These

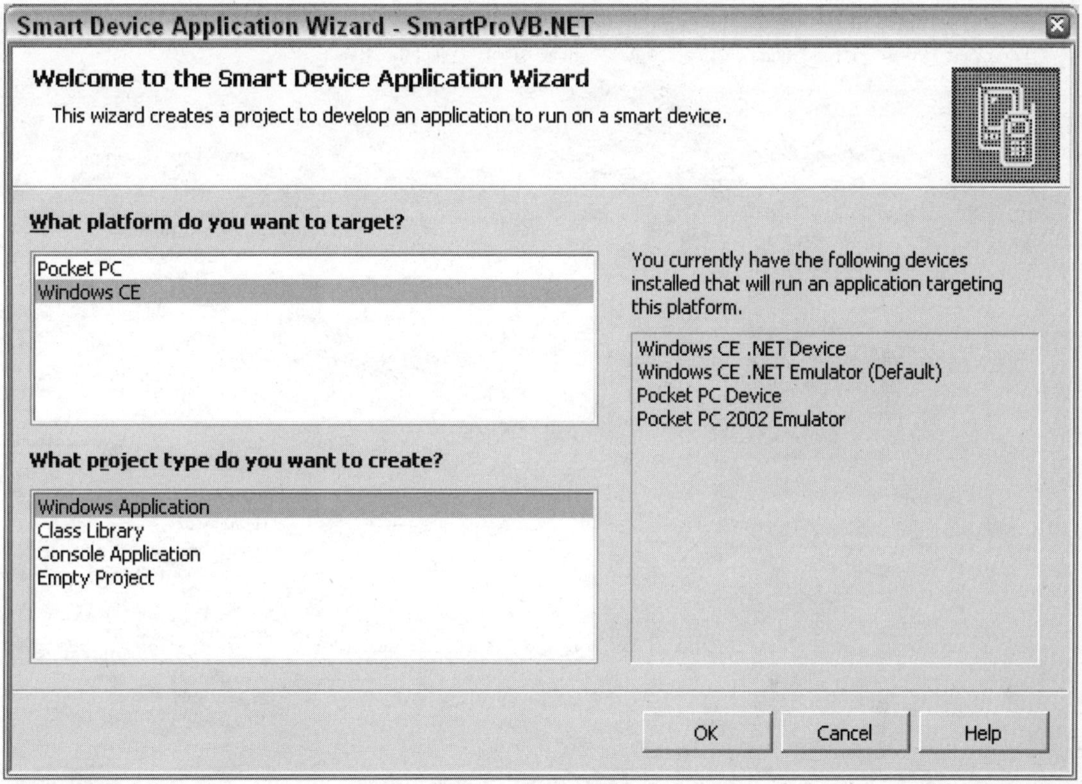

Figure 26-11

applications are good for setting up background tasks, but keep in mind that most hand-held devices are under-powered to begin with.

Once you have accepted a targeted platform, the Visual Studio IDE will open. Since this example is going to be based on a Windows CE platform you will see a display similar to the one shown in Figure 26-12, only empty. So what are the steps for getting to what is shown in Figure 26-12?

1. Resize the default form for a smaller interface.
2. Add a button to the form.
3. Rename it as 'CmdBuild' and change the Text to "Build It"
4. Add a second button to the form.
5. Rename it as 'cmdRead' and change the text to "Read It"
6. Add a Datagrid control to the center of the form.
7. Add a Label to the form
8. Add a TextBox to the form

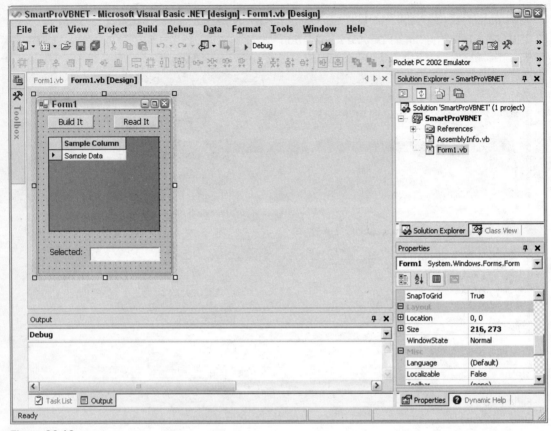

Figure 26-12

The layout of the elements is up to you, however I highly recommend a display area similar to the one shown in Figure 26-12. With all of these controls positioned, the next step is to start adding code. The goal of this project will be to introduce you to SQL CE. As you'll see even if this is the first time you've used the Compact Framework Visual Studio makes it easy to work with SQL CE. Having designed the form double click on the cmdBuild button to add a handler. This will open the code window and brings you to the next step, adding references to the project.

In order to work effectively with SQL CE you are going to want to add a reference to the SQL CE Libraries. Additionally whenever you start working with a database you'll find that you want to add a reference to the System.Data.Common namespace. Once you have added a reference you can optionally import these namespaces into your code module with the following two lines. The import statements aren't required in your code, and for instructional purposes the fully qualified namespace on each of the database elements has been included.

```
Imports System.Data.Common
Imports System.Data.SqlServerCe
```

Once you have referenced the required assemblies the next step is to create a new database. This is a fairly straightforward process and you can use the cmdBuild Click event handler to do this. When you create a

SQL CE database what you need is a file location on the device where the actual data will live. For now you can create an instance of this temporary database in the C:\Temp directory. The database below will be called kids and so the first step is to create an instance of the SQL CE database engine. This class provides methods associated with managing SQL CE databases.

The first part of the cmdBuild_Click handler creates a new instance of the database engine and then has it reference a datasource. Of course you would tend to have error handling and check for the previous creation of your datasource in a production application. But for demonstration purposes the code below will start up the database engine and reference the database source file. It then calls the CreateDatabase method to create an instance of a SQL CE database. Optionally you could add a password to your database if you wanted to have a 'secure' data store. To do this you would include "Password=not4you" as part of the datasource definition used to create an instance of the SQL CE Engine.

```
Private Sub cmdBuild_Click(ByVal sender As System.Object, ByVal e As
  System.EventArgs) Handles cmdBuild.Click

  'First create a new database
  Dim sqlEngine As New _
      System.Data.SqlServerCe.SqlCeEngine("Data Source = \Temp\Kids.sdf")
  sqlEngine.CreateDatabase()

  'Connect to it.
  Dim conn As New _
      System.Data.SqlServerCe.SqlCeConnection("Data Source = \Temp\Kids.sdf")
  conn.Open()
```

Once you have a database the next step is to create a connection to your database. Here again you are going to reference the file which holds the data as the source of your data. This string should by definition match the string used to create your database. So if you do place a password on your database this call will also need to use that password.

Once the database has been created and you have an active connection the next step is to create a database object. Of course the first item any database needs is a table. The code below starts by creating a SQL Command object which has been associated with the database connection. This command object can then be used to execute T-SQL statements against it's connection. What you see in the code below is a typical table creation statement that defines a new table with three columns. The first column is an identity column which starts with an index of zero (just like arrays in .NET) and automatically increments by one. This column is also designated as the primary key for the table. The second column is a text column which is called name. The final column is an integer and represents the age of the named individual.

```
'Create a table
Dim sqlCmd As System.Data.SqlServerCe.SqlCeCommand = conn.CreateCommand()
sqlCmd.CommandText = _
    "CREATE TABLE NeicenNephew(kid_id int IDENTITY(0,1) PRIMARY KEY, _
    name ntext, age int)"
sqlCmd.ExecuteNonQuery()
```

Once you have defined your SQL statement the next step is to execute it against the database. There are several different ways to execute SQL statements. In those situations where you don't expect to receive a data table in return it is more efficient to use the ExecuteNonQuery method on the SQL Command object.

977

The next block of code then adds some values into this table. The code takes advantage of the fact that the identity column automatically increments for each new entry. All that needs to occur is a new statement is defined for the same SQL Command object and then it is executed against the database. Once you have added some data, more then a single row, you can close the database connection and then let the user know that the handler has finished it's work.

```
    'Insert some values
    sqlCmd.CommandText = "INSERT INTO NeicenNephew(name, age)
VALUES('Nikita', 3)"
    sqlCmd.ExecuteNonQuery()
    sqlCmd.CommandText = "INSERT INTO NeicenNephew(name, age)
VALUES('Elena', 2)"
    sqlCmd.ExecuteNonQuery()
    conn.Close()

    MessageBox.Show("DB Creation Complete")
End Sub
```

At this point the database is ready to go. If you want to start your testing in stages you can skip ahead and attempt to run your application for the first time. Or you can carry out the next two steps for the application code. After all .NET makes it fairly obvious if you have any compilation errors in your code so it's much easier to write up a lot of code, and given the cost of starting up your emulator its often more satisfying to complete the coding process.

The next step is to add a handler for the click event of the cmdRead button. This can be done either by returning to the design screen and double clicking on the button or from the code window by selecting the cmdRead object from the upper left drop down list and then selecting it's click event from the upper right drop down list. Regardless of how you add it, the job of the read handler will be to open a connection to the database, read the contents of your table and then bind that data to the datagrid in your display. Most of these steps you've already done for desktop and Web based applications. This is the power of .NET you are writing code which you are already familiar with. The first step is to again create and open a database connection.

```
    Private Sub cmdRead_Click(ByVal sender As System.Object, ByVal e As
    System.EventArgs) Handles cmdRead.Click

        Dim conn As New System.Data.SqlServerCe.SqlCeConnection
("Data Source = \Temp\People.sdf")
        conn.Open()
        Dim sqlCmd As System.Data.SqlServerCe.SqlCeCommand = conn.CreateCommand()
        sqlCmd.CommandText = "Select * from NeicenNephew"
        Dim da As New System.Data.SqlServerCe.SqlCeDataAdapter(sqlCmd)
        Dim dtKids As New System.Data.DataTable

        da.Fill(dtKids)
        DataGrid1.DataSource = dtKids
        conn.Close()

    End Sub
```

Once you have the connection you repeat the process of associating it with a new SQL command object and then you add a simple select statement to retrieve your data. The process continues to work in the same manner as what you've undoubtedly done before by creating a Data Adapter to execute your query and a Data Table object to hold the disconnected results. The Fill method of your Data Adapter populates the data table object.

Now that you have a collection of elements you can apply a custom data view, or for the purposes of this demo associate that Data Table with the Data Grid. One quick note on the use of Data Sets. One of the minor changes in the .NET Compact Framework is that the overload which allows you to associated the Data Source of a Data Grid with a Data Set isn't available. This doesn't mean you can't use the Data Set object, but rather that when you are ready to bind to a table in the Data Set you need to reference the specific table which should be used as the Data Source.

The final portion of this demonstration is capturing the selected cell in the data grid. Most people are very familiar with finding the currently selected row. So you are going to go a step further and copy the contents of the current cell into the text box. This is some of the simplest code you will ever write. Once again it is triggered by an event handler, this time a handler on the DataGrid object. When the user selects a cell within the grid the CurrentCellChanged event is fired, so using the drop downs in the code view you can add a handler for this event.

```
Private Sub DataGrid1_CurrentCellChanged(ByVal sender As Object, _
    ByVal e As System.EventArgs) Handles DataGrid1.CurrentCellChanged

  TextBox1.Text = DataGrid1.Item(DataGrid1.CurrentRowIndex, _
    DataGrid1.CurrentCell.ColumnNumber)
End Sub
```

Within that CurrentCellChanged event handler you want to reset the current value of Textbox1's Text property. The new value should be the current cell. The DataGrid object keeps each cell in a two dimensional array of items. To access the current cell you can use the CurrentCell property of the Datagrid object and retrieve the ColumnNumber associated with the Current Cell to pass in as the index for the correct item. Thus you only need a single line of code to associate that currently selected cell with your Textbox control.

So now that you have written all of this code it is time to start up the emulator and take a look at it in action. The first time your run the code it is a good idea to add a breakpoint into each of your handlers so that you can step through each line of code and watch how local variables are being updated as your code executes. You will also get a better feel for how easy the emulator makes it to debug your Compact Framework application. There aren't any special instructions here associated with debugging because there really aren't any special steps needed for debugging to work.

So when your application starts the first step will be the dialog box shown in Figure 26-13. This dialog box is optional, so if you are trying to debug the same application on only a single targeted platform you can clear the checkbox and automatically head into your runtime environment. For the purposes of this application you should leave that checkbox since you will want to see it run both on the Windows CE and Pocket PC emulator. For the first attempt however let's select the Windows CE environment.

So the first step in this process is for Visual Studio to populate your emulator with all of the elements of the .NET framework, SQL CE and your assemblies. This is not a quick process and so when you are looking at the display shown in Figure 26-14, the key rule is don't panic. This is a great time to leave the room and see if it's raining outside or if the mail has been delivered or whatever, eventually your application will appear as shown in Figure 26-15.

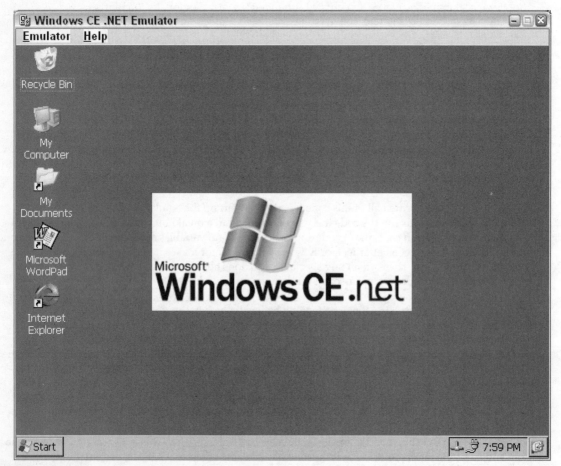

Figure 26-13

Figure 26-14

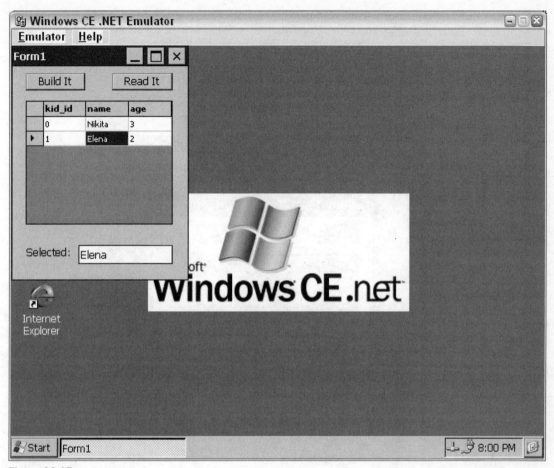

Figure 26-15

What you should take away from this is that starting up the emulator is painful, why is this important because once you've gone through this pain the first time — Don't Turn Off the Emulator. Whether your application throws an error or you just plain are finished with your current testing, close your application and leave the emulator running. It may take a second for Visual studio to respond, after all it is communicating with your application running on a different operating system, but it will exit debug mode with the emulator still running.

So once Visual Studio has completed its initial deployment of your application the application will start up as shown in Figure 26-15. You can now start testing your application out. Create that database the first time. If your database creation only partially completes then after your application has shut down, simply go to the C:\Temp directory where you created the database and delete it from the emulator. Remember you don't want to shut down the emulator once you have it running. In fact if you are successful in starting up and running through your application on the first try, you should exit the application and then restart just to get a feel for how much faster it is to work with an emulator that is already running and primed with your referenced assemblies.

Of course testing this application on Windows CE meets the first criteria for saying it works, but what about on the Pocket PC. Once you have things running on Windows CE restart the application and this time start up the Pocket PC emulator. Notice you don't have to shut down the Windows CE emulator to start up the Pocket PC emulator, they can run side by side on your desktop. Figure 26-16 shows how the Pocket PC user interface has very different default characteristics.

Figure 26-16

The first thing you should notice is that your application is going to fill the entire display. Notice that the sample design shown here doesn't actually fill the screen, so the Pocket PC just expanded the right hand side of the window to fill the Pocket PC display. The second thing to note is that the Pocket PC has some additional buttons as part of it's hardware. Most of them are tied to specific built in capabilites associated with the Pocket PC, but in the center is a directional toggle. After you have the application up and running you can click on the up, down and left, right buttons on that center toggle shown in Figure 16. Notice how without needing to write any additional custom code your application navigates in the datagrid and your event handler automatically updates the text box with the currently selected cell's value.

Summary

This chapter provides a basic introduction to some of the idiosyncrasies associated with creating an application for the mobile world. Whether that application is a Mobile Web application which is hosted on your server or a .NET Compact Framework application running on a hand held device Visual Studio .NET 2003 provides a robust environment for enabling the mobile user. This chapter has introduced several key elements related to mobile applications including:

- ❏ Building Mobile Web applications
- ❏ Differences between Mobile Web and .NET Compact Framework applications
- ❏ Limitations of the .NET Compact Framework
- ❏ Mobile Device Emulators
- ❏ Running a Compact Framework application on both the Pocket PC and Win CE emulators

No single chapter can completely cover these complex new project types. Becoming an expert developer for mobile applications takes months as you learn to adjust your approach to application design. However, this chapter gives you more then enough knowledge to allow you to become effective with these new project types. Remember when you are planning for a major implementation using the Compact Framework that this is a rapidly growing and changing market. Many of the lessons from the early days of Visual Basic where different drivers would step on each other and conflict seem to be replaying with the array of available devices. Ensure you plan for this cutting edge environments quirks when you are estimating the time required to complete a project. For the future, both the .NET Compact Framework and Mobile Web applications are going to become even more integrated with Visual Studio .NET in future versions. . . and you can expect more and more applications will target both desktop and handheld user interfaces.

Upgrading: Using the Visual Basic Compatibility Library

There has been much said about the newest version of VB, and how to handle legacy code. Many are saying that anything new should be started in the latest version, and anything old should be rewritten from ground up. Other insist that while new projects can begin in the new language existing components should first be run through a conversion to quickly make them compatible and then only rewritten if the list of exceptions is extreme. Regardless of which approach you take for your VB6 code, the compatibility library will come in handy along the way. The idea is that there is a lot of code out there written in VB6 and manually converting every line isn't the most realistic option if you are on a tight schedule. The solution in the short term is to consider converting that code converted automatically and then evaluated by an experienced engineer.

The Visual Basic Compatibility Library is provided in the .NET environment in order to assist in the conversion of existing code. Secondarily it claims to provide backward compatibility and support for developers who are transitioning to .NET, but that is open to debate. While the compatibility library is there to support the migration not only of your VB6 applications but your VB6 developers, the only time you should ever encounter it is when using the code migration wizard. The elements of the compatibility library aren't simple language elements such as the Msgbox function which is now encapsulated in the MessageBox class, but rather functions that are no longer supported by the .NET Framework class libraries such as BaseOcxArray or which are difficult to automatically convert, such as Format statements.

Don't misinterpret this, the compatibility library is a very useful tool, but you should limit its use in your design to managing conversion issues for the short term. The main goal should be to use it as a temporary solution to the learning curve presented by new software revisions. Please also keep in mind that the compatibility library is not all-inclusive and therefore will not assist in every instance where a programmer is undergoing the task of converting code to VB.NET. When you run the various conversion tools certain statements in particular graphic statements will cause problems and require manual intervention. As a general rule the less User Interface code in a project the easier it will be to convert that project code to VB.NET.

Converting to VB.NET

The compatibility library is referenced automatically in any project that has run through the Visual Basic Upgrade Wizard. You can start the wizard either by opening an existing VB6 project in Visual Studio .NET, or manually using the `VBUpgrade.exe` program included with the Visual Studio .NET installation. During the conversion, if a function is no longer supported, the converter will place a comment by it and the VB6 compatibility library equivalent, if available, is used. The first step in this process is understanding what exactly the compatibility library is and how your project references it.

What Is the Compatibility Library?

The compatibility library is a library made up of the VB6 functions that have been replaced in VB.NET due to reorganization into different libraries, syntax changes or just that they weren't deemed necessary anymore. At the end of the chapter is a list, including information about what these functions were replaced with in .NET. The library is used by the conversion tools and can also be used by adding a reference to it within a VB.NET project.

The compatibility library is primarily for transitioning to the new environment. The key is that there are a few major changes to the language which drive most of the changes in syntax with regard to the functions. In particular the change to a true object oriented development language, use of the common .NET Framework libraries and inclusion of ASP.NET within Visual Basic tend to drive many of the changes. As mentioned before, the conversion tools automatically put the reference into a converted project, but you'll want to clean up your projects and remove the reference both for improved performance and long term maintainability.

Referencing the Compatibility Library

The compatibility library can be added as a reference, and is located under the .NET tab of the Add Reference dialog. It is listed as Microsoft VisualBasic .NET Compatibility Runtime, as illustrated in Figure A-1. It is important to note that the other .NET library labeled for compatibility Microsoft VisualBasic .NET Compatibility Data Runtime is a collection of elements associated with ADO data binding. This library works in a similar fashion to the baseline library and if your project has ADO data access logic you will see both of these references added to your project.

Once a reference is added to the project you can begin to reference this library by name. Of note when working with the Visual Basic upgrade wizard, it will automatically add a global reference to the compatibility library when the upgrade is run. If you are working to only convert a limited amount of VB6 code then instead of having this reference used across your entire assembly, after you add the project reference you can import the compatibility library directly into the effected project files using the following line.

```
Imports Microsoft.VisualBasic.Compatibility
```

In either case, having the library available makes the certain key functions which are associated with Visual Basic 6 available. Keep in mind however, that these libraries are designed to support your transition to standard Visual Basic .NET code during the upgrade process.

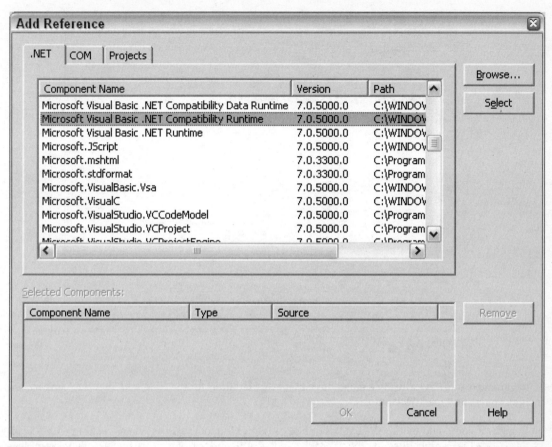

Figure A-1

Upgrade Tools

Visual Studio .NET ships with several upgrade tools. Not only those associated with Visual Basic, but for example a Visual J++ upgrade wizard. However, this book is going to focus on the two options for upgrading VB 6 code. The first which will be briefly discussed is the code upgrade window. The second, which is more common for projects is the upgrade wizard.

Using Visual Basic Code Converter

The Visual basic code converter is a dialog window which allows you to enter some VB6 code. When you select the convert button, as shown in Figure A-2 the conversion engine transforms your code into its .NET equivalent and then inserts the updated code into your project.

To open the dialog shown in Figure A-2, you need to be in a Visual Basic project. Then from the Tools menu in Visual Studio .NET you can select the Upgrade Visual Basic 6 code . . . menu option. The goal of this converter isn't to convert an entire project, but rather to allow you to transform a limited amount of code copied for example from an ASP page. Keep in mind that whether you are converting a VB Script file or an ASP page, un-typed variable declarations will be converted to object declarations, so it is often

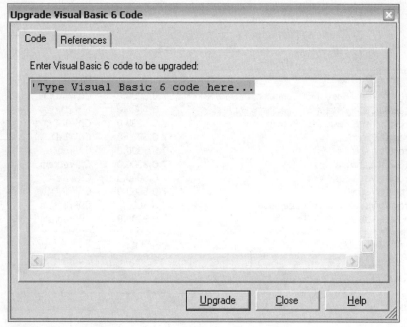

Figure A-2

advantageous to have already created the variable declarations for the code you intend to convert, and not convert un-typed declarations.

In general you'll find that the Visual Basic code converter is a tool you use when working with Visual Basic code that is embedded in other places. As noted ASP and Script files are two excellent examples, but you may also find it useful for working with old VBA code which you are now transitioning to Visual Studio Tools for Office (VSTO). The idea is that not every upgrade involves a complete set of project source files, such as what you will feed the Upgrade Wizard.

Using the Upgrade Wizard

The Visual Basic Upgrade Wizard was the original and is still the best tool for converting Visual Basic 6 projects. Note that the tool works for project files not solution files, if you have a VB6 solution with multiple projects, you will need to convert each project independently. When you are working with the upgrade wizard there are a couple of simple rules you should follow.

The first is that you should really have Visual Studio 6.0 installed on your machine prior to installing it with Visual Studio .NET 2003. There are a couple reasons for this, starting with the fact that you are going to probably find that you either want to make changes to the VB6 code before it is converted, to reduce errors. Secondly the upgrade wizard modifies your source code to match the syntax of VB.NET, however it does not change out your project references. This means you are going to want to have all of the COM objects currently referenced by your VB6 project available for your new project.

The good news here is that if you have a solution where the projects reference each other, start with the dependent project and convert each project in turn. You will then need to open each project and remove the references to the original COM components and create new references to your other converted projects. You don't need to change any code as part of this project, because Visual Studio .NET will automatically map the calls to your object to the new reference. The fact that .NET has removed the GUID underpinnings in references makes this possible.

Another key issue is that you should ensure the project will compile in Visual Studio 6.0. If the VB6 project you want to convert won't compile, it won't convert. This simple rule of thumb means that you can't take a partial project and run it through the conversion wizard. Fortunately the addition of the Visual Basic Code Converter in Visual Studio .NET 2003 allows for a workaround when you are trying to work with a new project.

The final bit of advice is that if you have installed Visual Studio .NET 2003 alongside Visual Studio 2002, be aware that there is only a single copy of the Visual Basic Upgrade Wizard on your system. Unlike other elements of Visual Studio the newer version of the upgrade wizard which ships with Visual Studio .NET 2003 does in fact replace the original upgrade wizard.

Once you have met the basic prerequisites you are ready to try out the upgrade wizard. The great thing about the upgrade wizard is that it is a non-destructive upgrade. You've been there in the past, with Visual Studio 2003 in fact, where you open a project with a new tool and it becomes inaccessible to the original tool which created it. The Visual Basic Upgrade wizard differs from this in that it creates an entirely new project directory and then recreates your entire project in this new location. The result is that if you need to return to your original project files you can do so.

Upgrading Your Project

To start the upgrade wizard you can call it from the command line, or simple open any VB6 project file (.vbp) using Visual Studio .NET. Note using the open dialog you will have to change the file type for project files from solution file to All Project types. When you open a VB6 project file the upgrade wizard will automatically start. A good place to start if you want to get a feel for the time required to convert a project is to start with a sample that ships with Visual Studio .NET. If you navigate to you installation directory then go under the subdirectory SDK\v1.1\Samples\Technologies\Interop\Applications you will find several subdirectories which contain VB6 projects that you can upgrade. Of course if you don't have any VB6 projects to convert then count your blessings and go back to learning about .NET and the way that development will be done on future projects.

Alternatively you can create a simple VB6 project. Create a standard executable and then in the Visual Basic 6 IDE, add a text field called 'txtCreate' and a command button called 'cmdCreateFile' to the new form. Then double click on your command button to create a new handler for the button's click event. To that event add the sample code below which simply opens a file, writes two lines to it and closes the file, populating a text box with status while working.

```
'This is VB6 code
Private Sub cmdCreateFile_Click()
    Dim Handle As Integer
    Handle = FreeFile
Open "c:\Testing.txt" For Output As Handle
    txtCreate = "Writing File"
Write #Handle, "This is line 1"
Write #Handle, "This is line 2"
Close #Handle
    txtCreate = "File Written"
End Sub
```

At this point test run your project and save off your project files to a directory. Once you are comfortable that the code works, open Visual Studio .NET 2003 and choose to open a project. Adjust the file open dialog so that you can see all project types and navigate to the directory where you have saved your sample project. Once you select your project the Visual Basic Upgrade Wizard will automatically start.

When the Upgrade Wizard starts up it will recognize whether the project you are upgrading is an executable or a dynamic link library. The wizard will then prompt you for the target directory for the converted files. Ideally you will see a warning similar to the one shown in Figure A-3. This warning means that you are going to create the new project in a new directory and won't be overwriting any existing files. If you don't see this warning after accepting the location for your new project you might want to use the back button and enter a new location.

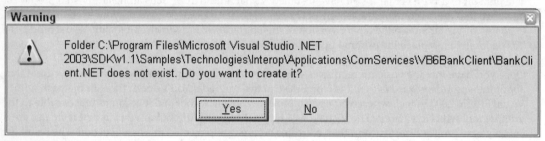

Figure A-3

After you have entered the location for the new files the next step is to carry out the actual conversion. The conversion itself should complete fairly quickly if you are using a sample project. After Visual Studio .NET has converted the project it will place you inside of Visual Studio and in your new project. In addition to your project files you will find a new HTML page that has been generated to document any errors that were encountered during the conversion process. There are several levels of error, there is code which simply can't be converted, code which is converted but for which there may be new or unexpected behavior.

```
Private Sub cmdCreateFile_Click(ByVal eventSender As System.Object, ByVal
eventArgs As System.EventArgs) Handles cmdCreateFile.Click

 'UPGRADE_NOTE: Handle was upgraded to Handle_Renamed. Click for more: 'ms-
help://MS.VSCC/commoner/redir/redirect.htm?keyword="vbup1061"'
 Dim Handle_Renamed As Short

 Handle_Renamed = FreeFile
 FileOpen(Handle_Renamed, "c:\Testing.txt", OpenMode.Output)
 txtCreate.Text = "Writing File"
 WriteLine(Handle_Renamed, "This is line 1")
 WriteLine(Handle_Renamed, "This is line 2")
 FileClose(Handle_Renamed)
 txtCreate.Text = "File Written"
 End Sub
```

There are interesting alterations in this code that should give you a feel of what to expect from the conversion process. The first is that it has added a note that it has renamed one of the variable names used in your original code. The term handle matches the name of a windows data type. Since the conversion engine sees this as a potential conflict it has automatically renamed every instance of this variable in your code to match this new name. It then added this note so that you could quickly recognize this change, and within Visual Studio .NET you should find that the associated link in your code takes you to a help page explaining this change.

The next thing it did to your code wasn't documented but is almost as important. The conversion tool changed the variable Handle_Renamed to Short instead of Integer. This is because the conversion engine is looking for compatibility and a short value is directly compatible to the VB6 Integer type. For those cases where you have previously used Hungarian notation such as 'intMyNumber' to namespace variables, this change will impact your ability to identify the correct type of the variable. Accordingly you might want to make a change to your variable name by manually replacing variables prefaced with int to be prefaced with short throughout your project.

Next you'll note that the Open function from VB6 has changed to FileOpen. The conversion wizard has automatically updated the original syntax of

```
Open "c:\Testing.txt" For Output As Handle
```

to use the updated syntax of:

```
FileOpen(Handle_Renamed, "c:\Testing.txt",OpenMode.Output)
```

As you can see, there is a syntactical difference between the two lines, changing to a function that has the `OpenMode` parameter within it. This is still not what would be considered the standard method of working with files in VB.NET but this is a compatible method.

The conversion tool has also identified what was the default property assignment associated with the text box txtCreate. .NET does not use default properties so when it can recognize the default property of an object, .NET will automatically spell out the actual property which is being assigned. A common place where this will trigger a note instead of just being handled as part of the conversion is for objects which were declared as variants or functions where the return type was not specified. For your code however the wizard has automatically handled the translation.

Another change that the upgrade wizard handled automatically involved the write statement. The following line of code from VB6

```
Write #Handle, "This is line 1"
```

Was modified for VB.NET to use an updated function which reads

```
WriteLine(Handle_Renamed, "This is line 1")
```

How the Code Could Read

The key is that the wizard has looked at the code and worked to update it with minimal changes to maintain compatibility. On the other hand, what it hasn't done is refactor the code to truly leverage .NET. What I mean by this is that while the preceding function and statements will work in .NET they do not reflect the way that you would normally accomplish this task in VB.NET. For an example of that you can review the following VB.NET code:

```
Private Sub cmdCreateFile_Click(ByVal sender As System.Object, _
        ByVal e As System.EventArgs) Handles
cmdCreateFile.Click
Dim objWriter As New IO.StreamWriter(File.Open& _
```

```
    ("c:\Testing.txt",FileMode.OpenOrCreate))
txtcreate.Text = "Writing File"
objWriter.Write("This is Line 1")
objwriter.Write("This is Line 2")
objWriter.Flush()
objWriter.Close()
txtCreate.Text = "File Written"
objWriter = Nothing
End Sub
```

In this example the file is opened using a Stream writer and the write statements are then executed against that specific object. This is a more appropriate method of working with files from .NET as it allows you to control the details of opening and closing your file handle. The Streamwriter object and other similar file handles are located within the System.IO namespace. There are differences in the preferred way of doing things. These include, using stream writers to create, read, and write files as well as having the open and close functions embedded within the stream writer instead of having a file handle.

The key is that the upgrade wizard didn't give you the best possible solution when it converted your code. Instead it looked for a simple and compatible migration, and in the long run you are responsible for updating that migrated code to work using the framework classes. Of course in this sample example all of the code you wrote was easily converted by the wizard. Unfortunately the real world is rarely so simple. It is likely that in a large project you will have literally hundreds of conversion issues that will need to be resolved before your code will actually work. Conversion issues are especially common with graphic elements that are embedded within your forms, and any object which is tightly coupled to COM+.

Another good example of code which can't be fully converted involves the use of Declare statements. The Declare statement allows you to specify a parameter as of type Any. In VB6 this allowed you to pass different types sting vs integer to the same call and VB handled the mapping of the data. .NET is a strongly typed language and it does not provide support for the Any type. The wizard however isn't smart enough to find each location where the declared method is used and then map the actual object types used in each call. Instead it will flag the statement using As Any and it is your job to now go through the code and find all of these references and convert them manually. The good news is that this is a relatively simple correction.

In the big picture this need to follow up your automated conversion with what can be a significant amount of work to rewrite code is the biggest drawback to the upgrade wizard. This section has only touched on the actual issues involved but has hopefully spelled out how you can make use of the hyper linked references generated as part of the conversion process to help in correcting issues with your converted code. For business components that don't do a lot of UI, the amount of time needed to convert your object using the upgrade wizard can provide results in significantly less time then starting from scratch.

Compatibility Library Reference Listing

Once you have converted code over time you will want to remove many of the compatibility references contained in your code. To help in this goal, the following section provides a listing of the compatibility functions and a where possible a suggestion of where to look to resolve these items in Visual Basic.NET. As mentioned before, the .NET replacements fall into several categories. The categories referenced here include declaration syntax changes, elements replaced by methods, data type change, Boolean operator changes, and class and interface changes.

Declaration Syntax Changes

Declaration syntax changes mainly encompass declaring multiple variables on one line. For instance, where in VB6 the following statement requires you to repeat the integer keyword in order to evaluate both variables as integers:

```
Dim A as Integer, B as Integer
```

in VB.NET you can do the same thing without repeating the As Integer keywords:

```
Dim A, B as Integer
```

Additionally it was considered not only poor style but based on knowledge base articles was known to be incompatible with COM+ to use a statement such as:

```
Dim myObj as New MyObject
```

However under .NET this practiced is not only considered appropriate but encouraged over moving the creation of a new instance to a following line.

In VB6, references to external procedures can include a variable of the 'As Any' type. The As Any keywords were used to disable type checking. Visual Basic .NET does not support the As Any declaration. To support type safety you must specifically declare the data type of every argument. Fortunately VB.NET supports procedure overloading so you can declare a separate call for each type which you need to pass to an external procedure.

Elements Replaced by Methods

At Times in Visual Basic you might work with language elements that were commonly available. Under .NET everything is now associated with a class. The table below lists a few of the commonly referenced elements which are now referenced as methods on a class.

Converted properties	New Method, Property or Class
CopyArray	Use the Copy method of the Array class in the System namespace.
FontChangeBold	Use the Bold property of the Font class in the System.Drawing namespace.
FontChangeItalic	Use the Italic property of the Font class.
FontChangeName	Use the Name property of the Font class.
FontChangeSize	Use the Size property of the Font class.
FontChangeStrikeOut	Use the StrikeOut property of the Font class.
FontChangeUnderline	Use the Underline property of the Font class.
FontChangeWeight	Use the Size property of the Font class.

Continues

Converted properties	New Method, Property or Class
Math	Moved to Math class in System
Oct	Moved to Math class in System
PixelstoTwipsX	See Point Converter class in the System.Drawing namespace.
PixelstoTwipsY	See Point Converter class in the System.Drawing namespace.
TwipsPerPixelX	Duplicates the VB6 Screen.TwipsPerPixelX property. See Point Converter class in the System.Drawing namespace.
TwipsPerPixelY	Duplicates the VB6 Screen.TwipsPerPixelY property. See Point Converter class in the System.Drawing namespace.
TwipsToPixelsX	See Point Converter class in the System.Drawing namespace.
TwipsToPixelsY	See Point Converter class in the System.Drawing namespace.

Data Type Changes

The data type changes that affect us most in the VB.NET environment surround the date and time functions, integer data type changes and the universal data type changes. The changes to date and time functionality are mainly data type changes to 8 byte formats. The Integer data types have been expanded and changed. What used to be an Integer in VB6 was a 16 bit size, and is now a 32 bit size. The 16 bit size has been changed to the Short data type. The previous Long data type was a 32 bit size, and is now a 64 bit size. Constant usage and support for the standard VB constants has changed as well. Constants from VB6, such as the familiar VBOK, used for message box feedback, have changed to be supported within the objects they relate to. For instance, as illustrated in the previous examples, what was once simply VBOK is now declared as a DialogResult.OK. A couple additional changes associated with this new behavior are listed in the following table:

Converted Methods	New Behavior
Constants	Constants can now be defined as part of Structures or as Properties on Shared classes.
FixedLengthString	Data type change the Strings does not have a fixed length property, but you can implement fixed length strings as a custom class
Format	Use the ToString() method of objects in the System namespace, such as Decimal.format
ZorderConstants	Support changed for constants, shared properties can be created in a static fashion, but are still associated with a class.

Boolean Operator Changes

In VB6 the And, Or, Not were used for Bitwise and Boolean operations. In the new version of VB they have added specific Bitwise operators. This was done because the older And, Or, Not and Xor are interpreted exclusively as Boolean operatiors. The next table lists some of the common operators from VB6 and their replacement:

Converted action	Replacement
And	And as well as `BitAnd`
Imp	Replaced by = operator
EQV	Replaced by = operator
Or	Or as well as `BitOr`
Not	Not as well as `BitNot`
Xor	Xor as well as `BitXOr`

Class and Interface Changes

There are new classes which encompass the majority of our changes from generic VB6 functions to class-based functions in VB.NET. The `System.Windows.Forms` namespace holds all of the classes that make up the objects that you place on your forms and the properties of those controls. The table which follows indexes many such objects now associated with the `System.Windows.Forms` namespace.

Converted Call	New Class or Method
`ButtonArray`	Use the Button class in the System.Windows.Forms `namespace`
`ComboBoxArray`	Use the CheckBox class
`CheckBoxArray`	Use the CheckBox class
`CheckedListBoxArray`	Use the CheckBox class
`GetCancel`	CancelButton property of `Form`
`GetDefault`	`Default` button has moved to be the `Accept` button property
`GetItemData`	Use `ItemData` property of each object
`GetItemString`	Use `GetItemText` method
`GroupBoxArray`	`Group Box Collection` of the `GroupBox` class
`HscrollBarArray`	Use the `HscrollBar` class in System.Windows.Forms.Scrollbar

Continues

Converted Call	New Class or Method
LabelArray	Use the Label class
ListBoxArray	Use the Listbox class
ListBoxItem	Use the Listbox class
MenuItemArray	Replaced in the new menu classes
PanelArray	New Panel classes
PictureBoxArray	Use the PictureBox class methods
SendKeys	Use the SendKeys class
ShowForm	Changed to Form.Show
SetAppearance	Choose appropriate appearance property of object
SetBorderStyle	Use appropriate BorderStyle property for object
SetCancel	CancelButton property of Form
SetDefault	Default button has moved to be the Accept button property
SetDefaultProperty	DefaultPropertyattribute of field object
SetItemData	Use ItemDate property of object
SetItemString	Use SetItemText method
SetListBoxColumns	Columns property of listbox class
TabControlArray	Use the TabControl class
TabLayout	Use the TabControl class
TextBoxArray	Use the TextBox class
TimerArray	Use the Timer class
VScrollBarArray	Use the VscrollBar class in System.Windows.Forms.Scrollbar
WhatsThisMode	Use the cursor class associated with windows forms
Zorder	Use the LayoutMDI method on the Form class

Many other common user interface elements have been moved into the System.IO namespace. The next table contains an alphabetic listing of other VB6 objects and their new namespace if it varies from the System.IO parent namespace:

Converted Method	New Class or Method
BaseControlArray	Parent class for Visual Basic 6.0 control array emulation, no direct replacement, use from the compatibility library.

Continues

Converted Method	New Class or Method
BaseOcxArray	Parent class for emulated arrays of ActiveX controls, no direct replacement, use from the compatibility library.
BOF	Moved to the `File` class in the `System.IO` namespace
Close	Use the File class in the System.IO namespace
CreateObject	Replace with usage of `New`
DirDrive	Use the OpenFileDialog and SaveFileDialog methods
DirListBox	Use the OpenFileDialog and SaveFileDialog methods
DirListBoxArray	Use the OpenFileDialog and SaveFileDialog methods
DriveListBox	Use the OpenFileDialog and SaveFileDialog methods
DriveListBoxArray	Use the OpenFileDialog and SaveFileDialog methods
FileListBox	Use the OpenFileDialog and SaveFileDialog methods
FileListBoxArray	Use the OpenFileDialog and SaveFileDialog methods
EOF	Use the Length and Position properties of the System.IO.FileStream object to check for the End of File.
FileAttr	Use the File class in the System.IO namespace
FileGet	Use the File class in the System.IO namespace
FileGetObject	Use the File class in the System.IO namespace
FilePut	Use the File class in the System.IO namespace
FilePutObject	Use the File class in the System.IO namespace
FileSystem	Use System.IO.FileSystemInfo
GetActiveControl	Moved into ContainerControl class ActiveControl property
GetEXEName	Use the GetExecutingAssembly method of the Assembly class in the System.Reflection namespace
GetFileDescription	`FileVersionInfo.FileDescription` property
GetHInstance	Moved to the Marshal class in the System.Runtime.Interopservices namespace
GetPath	Moved to the File class in the System.IO namespace
LineInput	Use the Stream classes in System.IO
Open	Replaced by class methods in the System.IO namespace
OpenAccess	Replaced by class methods in the System.IO namespace
OpenforAppend	Replaced by class methods in the System.IO namespace

Continues

Converted Method	New Class or Method
OpenforInput	Replaced by class methods in the System.IO namespace
OpenforOutput	Replaced by class methods in the System.IO namespace
OpenMode	Replaced by class methods in the System.IO namespace
OpenShare	Replaced by class methods in the System.IO namespace
Write	Use the Stream classes in System.IO
WriteLine	Use the Stream classes in System.IO

Index

SYMBOLS

(-) symbol, 167
(+) symbol, 167
.aspx file, 485
.disco files, 802
.Focus() method, 436
.Locale directive, 903
.MSI installations, 63
.NET AppDomain, 720
.NET application, 618, 629
.NET application, elements of, 60
  assemblies, 60
  classes, 60
  modules, 60
.NET channel, 721
.NET class libraries, 32
.NET Compact Framework application, 973
.NET Compact Framework specific namespaces, 971
.NET Compact Framework, introduction, 966
.NET Compact Framework, limitations of, 967
.NET component, 632
.NET components in COM world, using, 631
.NET Data Provider, components of, 351
  Command, 352
  Connection, 352
  DataAdapter, 352
  DataReader, 352
.NET Data Providers, 352, 355
  OLE DB .NET Data Provider, 352
  SQL Server .NET Data Provider, 352
.NET Framework, 1
.NET Framework class library namespaces, 781
  System.Web.Description, 781
  System.Web.Services, 781
  System.Web.Services.Discovery, 781
  System.Web.Services.Protocols, 781
.NET Framework SDK, 2, 634
.NET Framework version 1.0, advantages of, 106
.NET Framework, testing, 50

.NET Framwework classes for Windows Services, 752
  System.Configuration.Install.Installer, 752
  System.ServiceProcess.ServiceBase, 752
.NET system class library, 136
  EventArgs object, 136
  sender, 136
.NET/COM+ transactional model, 642
.publickeytoken directive, 903
.vb extension, 124
.vb file, 486
.Ver directive, 903
@ control directive, 547
@ symbol, 370
'>' command prompt, 55
'>' command prompt, 55
+,, 97
=, 97

A

Abort method, 712
abstract base class, creating, 210
abstract base classes, 211
abstract method, 211
AbstractBaseClass, 211
abstraction, 221
AcceptTcpClient method, 828
AcceptUpdateResponse function, 790
Access Control Lists (ACLs), 63
ACID test, 640
  atomicity, 640
  consistency, 640
  durability, 640
  isolation, 640
Activate method, 659
activated objects, 725
Activator.GetObject, using, 743
active configuration drop-down list, 49
  Configuration Manager, 49
  Debug, 49
  Release, 49

Active Server Pages (ASP), 479

ActiveForm property, 437

ActiveX control, 613

ActiveX controls, 627

ActiveX controls, using, 435

ActiveX Data Objects (ADO), 349

Add method, 108, 361

Add References dialog box, 32

Add Server dialog box, 56

Add Server option, 56

AddHandler method, 137

additional logic to custom control, adding, 450

AddOwnedForm() method, 402

AddRef method, 64

AddressOf operator, 156

ADO and ADO.NET, differences between, 352

ADO.NET, 337
  architecture, 350
  significance of, 350

ADO.NET and SQL Server's built-in features, 339
  FOR XML, 339
  OPENXML, 339

ADO.NET components, 351
  .NET Data Provider, 351
  DataSet, 351

ADO.NET DataTable objects, 368

advanced concepts, 145
  combining overloading and optional parameters, 147
  constructor methods, overloading, 148
  method signatures, 146
  methods, overloading, 145

Age method, 128

aliasing namespaces, 266

Align property, 437

AllowDrop property, 428

AmbientAllergens property, 134

Anchor property, 411

anchoring, 411

AppDomain, 673

AppDomans, 673

Append method, 108

application and session events, 504

application configuration file, 909

application deployment, 912

application deplyment in Visual Studio .NET, 916

application development, 783

application isolation, 906

application software, 677
  Microsoft Excel; 677
  Microsoft Outlook, 677
  Microsoft Word, 677

application versus framework inheritance, 241

application, building, 818

ApplicationAccessControl attribute, 652

ApplicationException class, 274

application-private assemblies, 904

applications, building, 50
  Build, 50
  Rebuild, 50

arbitrary elements, shadowing, 186

ArgumentException, 278

ArrayList, 105

ArrayList collection class, 105

arrays, 101

Asc method, 92

ASCII, 91

ASMX page, 30

ASP page, 489

ASP.NET, 479

ASP.NET server controls, 497
  AdRotator, 497
  Button, 497
  Calendar, 497
  DataGrid, 497
  Label, 497
  TextBox, 497

ASP.NET Web application, 930

ASPX page, 30

assemblies, 60

assemblies and deployment, 903

assemblies, application of, 897
  code reuse, 898
  deployment, 897
  security, 898
  type grouping, 898
  version control, 898

assemblies, types of, 900
  application-private, 900
  shared, 900

assembly (component) level scoping, 112
  Friend method, 112
  Private method, 112
  Protected method, 112
  Public method, 112

assembly a strong name, giving, 651

assembly attributes, 40

Assembly class, 77

assembly file, 865
assembly files, 60
.ASPX, 60
.config, 60
images, 60
assembly manifest, 60
.DLL, 60
.EXE, 60
assembly metadata, types of, 898
Microsoft Intermediate Language (MSIL), 898
resources, 898
type metadata, 898
assembly modifier, 40
AssemblyInfo.vb, 39, 40
attribute blocks, 40
attributes, 40, 75, 115, 452
Attributes method, 329
audit type entries, 290
Failure audit, 290
Success audit, 290
AuthorBindingContext property, 605
AutoLog property, 753
AutoLog Property, 771
automatic quick fix engineering policy, 908
AutoReset events, 708
AutoResetEvent object, 709
AutoResetEvent objects, 708
AutoScroll property, 405
AxHost namespace, 631

B

background task, canceling, 711
background task, designing, 678
BackgroundImage property, 404
base class, 81, 165
base class, creating, 166
base class, interacting with, 191
base Object class, 81
BeginInvoke method, 680
BeginTransaction method, 658
BeginXYZ methods, 689
BeginXYZ methods, using, 687
behavior See object, composition of, 114
binary formatter in IIS, using, 741
BinaryFormatter, 741
Bind method, 519
Bindable, 568
binding managers, 603
BlinkStyle property, 416

boolean operator changes, 995
And, 995
EQV, 995
Imp, 995
Not, 995
Or, 995
Xor, 995
Boolean property, 753
Boolean type, 85
False, 85
True, 85
Bootstrapper, 934
boxing, 107
BringToFront method, 436
btnAdd, button, 463
btnAddAll button, 463
btnClear button, 463
btnRemove button, 463
btnSubmit_Click event, 483
bubbled events, 503
Build Configurations, 933
Build menu, 50
Build Page, 933
BuildParameters method, 383
business logic, 645
Button class, 46
Button_Click event, 441
ByRef keyword, 129
Byte data types, 386
ByVal keyword, 129

C

C#, 1
Cab Project template, 917
cabinet file size, setting, 935
CalculateDistance method, 231
calculation framework, 623
calculation framework, running, 626
Calendar control, 488
callback method, 687
CanDeserialize method, 307
Category, 568
CausesValidation property, 418
CCyclicalRef class, 65
Central Processing Unit (CPU), 671
Certificate Authority (CA) service, 891
certificate management tools, 874
changes to custom control, making, 450
ChangeType method, 563

channel, 721

char and byte, 91

Checked property, 420

CheckedListBox base class, 457

CheckedListBox control, 456

CheckedListBox that limits the number of selected
    items, creating, 456

child windows, arranging, 439

ChildNodes method, 326

Chr method, 91

ChrW method, 91

CInt method, 95

class, 112

class and interface changes, 995

class composition, 526

Class keyword, 123

class library, 30

class module, 38

Class View window, 125

Class_Initialize event, 141

Class_Terminate method, 67, 79

classes, 123
  basic, 123
  creating, 123

classes and interfaces in System.XMI.Xsl, other,
    337

classes versus components, 158

classic COM, 613

classic COM and interfaces, working with, 613–15

classic three-tier desktop, 719

client application, 734

client application, creating, 746

client application, updating, 741, 745

client, building, 663

client-side versus server-side events, 503

CloneMenu() method, 423

Close method, 68, 315, 387

CloseAndSend, 321

Closed event, 820

CLR garbage collector, 65

Code Access permissions, managing, 856

Code Access security, 849

code component, 486

code editor window, 33

code in Web User Control, reusing, 547

code, customizing, 43

code, reviewing, 45

CodeAccessPermissions class, methods of, 852
  Assert, 852
  Copy, 852

Demand, 852

Deny, 852

Equals, 853

FromXml, 853

GetHashCode, 853

GetType, 853

Intersect, 853

IsSubsetOf, 853

PermitOnly, 853

RevertAll, 852

RevertAssert, 852

RevertDeny, 852

RevertPermitOnly, 852

ToString, 853

ToXml, 853

Union, 853

code-editing environment, 124

Collect method, 71

Collections, 104

Collections namespace, 104

ColorDialog control, properties of, 426
  AllowFullOpen, 427
  Color, 427
  ShowDialog(), 427

COM, 2, 784

COM and .NET in practice, 614–15

COM Interop, 362

COM object, 622

COM+, 639

ComboBox Windows Forms control, 327

command lines tools, 2

Command object, 356

Command Window, 55

Command.ExecuteReader, 357

CommandText property, 356

Commit method, 658

common binary RPC formats, 803
  CORBA, 803
  DCOM, 803
  RMI, 803

common dialogs, 425

common image formats, 837
  GIF, 837
  JPEG, 837
  PNG, 837

common implementation, reusing, 218

common language runtime (CLR), 2, 28,
    59–60
  features, 59
  functionality, 59

common language runtime (CLR), features of, 59
  implementation inheritance, 59
  objects, marshaling, 59
  operator overloading, 59
  threading, 59
common namespaces, 261
Common Object Request Broke Architecture
    (CORBA), 783
Common Type System (CTS), 72, 81
communicating with Service, 764
Compare method, 208
Compatibility Library, 986
Compatibility Library reference listing, 992
compile time, 614
Component Deployment tool, 63
Component Object Model (COM), 613
Component Services, 639
Component Services Console, 652, 662
Component Services, registering with, 652
component tray, 399
component, implementation of, 616
component-based language, 112
composite controls, 526
composite UserControl, creating, 463
Computer Management Console, 662
configuration file, specific node of, 909
  class API, 909
  crypto, 909
  remoting, 909
  runtime, 909
  security, 909
  startup, 909
configuration files, 909
Configuration Manager, 49
configurations, building, 47
Configure method, 733
ConfigureClient method, 822, 826
configuring remoting, 736
configuring remoting via code, 737
Connection object, 356
connection oriented features of SSL, 893
connection pooling in ADO.NET, 368
  OLE DB Session Pooling, 369
  Windows 2000 Component Services, 369
connection string format, 356
  OleDbConnection, 356
  SqlConnection, 356
Console object, 53
Console.Out, 305
Console.Read statement, 733

Console.Write statements, 733
Const keyword, 85
constructor method, overloading, 148
constructor methods, 141
constructors, 96, 197, 376
constructors with parameters, 199
constructors with parameters, more, 201
constructors, detailed, 198
constructors, overloading and variable
    initialization, 200
Container class object, 160
container control, 526
ContainsKey method, 132
context switching, 676
ContextMenu control, 420
ContextUtil class, 647, 659
ContextUtil.DisableCommit, 659
ContextUtil.EnableCommit, 659
control among Web forms, transferring, 505
  hyperlink, 506
  redirecting, 506
control and event handler, adding, 42
control and UserControl base classes, 459
control arrays, 408
control class, events of, 462
  Click, 462
  DoubleClick, 462
  DragDrop, 462
  DragEnter, 462
  DragLeave, 462
  DragOver, 462
  GotFocus, 462
  KeyDown, 462
  KeyPress, 462
  KeyUp, 462
  Leave, 462
  MouseDown, 462
  MouseEnter, 462
  MouseHover, 462
  MouseMove, 462
  MouseUp, 462
  Paint, 462
  PropertyChanged, 462
  Resize, 462
  Validating, Validated, 462
control class, methods of, 460
  BringToFront, 461
  DoDragDrop, 461
  Focus, 461
  Hide, 461

control class, methods of, *(continued)*
Refresh, 461
Show, 461
Update, 461
control class, properties of, 460
AllowDrop, 461
Anchor, 461
BackColor, 460
BackGroundImage, 460
CanFocus, 461
Causes Validation, 461
Controls, 461
Dock, 461
Enabled, 461
Font, 460
ForeColor, 460
Handle, 461
Location Size, 461
Visible, 461
control from scratch, building,
    469
control tab order, 407
control, use of, 576
controls, 407
controls available in Web forms, 492
ASP.NET server controls, 493
HTML server controls, 493
user controls, 493
validation controls, 493
Controls property, 436
conversation form, creating, 821
conversation windows, creating,
    820
conversion methods, 95
CBool(), 95
CByte(), 95
CChar(), 95
CDate(), 95
CDbl(), 95
CDec(), 95
CInt(), 95
CLng(), 95
CObj(), 95
CShort(), 95
CSng(), 95
CStr(), 95
Convert class, 96
Convert.MethodName method, 95
Copy Local property, 260
CORBA, 785

core Value types, 83
Boolean, 83
Byte, 83
Char, 83
DateTime, 84
Decimal, 84
Double, 84
Guid, 84
Int16, 84
Int32, 84
Int64, 84
SByte, 84
Single, 84
TimeSpan, 84
Count property, 707
counter monitor service, creating, 757
Create method, 815
Create() method, 894
CreateChildControls method, 527
CreateCommand method, 356
Created event, 774
CreateEventSource method, 291
CreateInstance method, 233
CreateObject statement, 117
creating thread, manually, 691
critical section, 703
cross-language data markup, 787
cross-language integration, 2, 72
cryptographic hash algorithms, 876
cryptographically strong name, 651
cryptography basics, 874
CTS methods, 73
Boolean Equals(Object), 73
Int32 GetHashCode(), 73
String ToString(), 73
Type GetType(), 73
CType function, 563
CType function, use of, 121
CType method, 92, 96
CurrentCellChanged event, 598
CurrentLinkProcessed event, 561
custom action events, 949
Commit, 949
Install, 949
Rollback, 949
Uninstall, 949
Custom Actions editor, 932
Custom Actions Editor, 947
adding, 949
custom commands, 768

custom control with GDI+, painting, 470
custom controls and the @ register directive, 575
custom controls in .NET, developing, 445
  composite control, building, 446
  control from scratch, creating, 446
  from an existing control, inheriting, 445
custom event for inherited control, defining, 455
custom installation, 915
custom method, exposing, 556
custom properties, exposing, 549
custom Web control to toolbox, adding, 573
custom Web controls, types of, 525
  composite controls, 525
  subclassed controls, 525
  templated controls, 525
  Web User Controls, 525
custom Web controls, using, 527
Customizing the order of dialog boxes, 946–47
cyclical references, 64

D

Data Access Component (DAC), building, 375
Data access with ADO.NET, 349–50
data binding, 583
data copies, transfering, 693
data entry, validating, 416
data ownership, transfering, 696
data type changes, 994
  Constants, 994
  FixedLengthString, 994
  Format, 994
  ZorderConstants, 994
DataAdapter object, properties of, 357
  DeleteCommand, 357
  InsertCommand, 357
  SelectCommand, 357
  UpdateCommand, 357
DataAdapter objects, 359
DataAdapter, properties of, 359
  DeleteCommand, 359
  InsertCommand, 359
  SelectCommand, 359
  UpdateCommand, 359
database access, 1
databases, creating, 643
Datalist class, 527
DataReader class, methods of, 358
  GetDateTime, 358
  GetDouble, 358

  GetGuid, 358
  GetInt32, 358
DataReader object, 357
DataRelationCollection, 363
DataSet component, 362
DataSet constraint objects, 363
  ForeignKeyConstraint, 363
  UniqueConstraint, 363
DataSet object, 221, 325
DataSet objects, 364
  creating, 364
  using, 364
DataSet objects to bind DataGrids, using, 391
DataSet, making, 795
DataTable events, 587
  ColumnChanged, 587
  ColumnChanging, 587
  RowChanged, 587
  RowChanging, 587
  RowDeleted, 587
  RowDeleting, 587
DataTableCollection, 362
datatype attributes, valid values, 379
  BigInt, 379
  Binary, 379
  Bit, 379
  Char, 379
  DateTime, 379
  Decimal, 379
  Float, 379
  Image, 379
  Int, 379
  Money, 379
  NChar, 379
  NText, 379
  NVarChar, 379
  Real, 379
  SmallDateTime, 379
  SmallInt, 379
  SmallMoney, 379
  Text, 379
  Timestamp, 379
  TinyInt, 379
  UniqueIdentifier, 379
  VarBinary, 379
  VarChar, 379
  Variant, 379
Date keyword, 92
DateDiff, 183
DateTime, 92

DBNull class, 101
DCOM, 784
Deactivate method, 659
deadlocks, 693
debug a service, process to, 776
Debug class interface, 293
debug listeners, 293
Debug mode, 52
Debug object, methods of, 293
  Assert, 294
  Close, 294
  Fail, 294
  Flush, 294
  Write, 294
  WriteIf, 294
  WriteLine, 294
  WriteLineIF, 294
Debug objects, 53
debugging, 757
debugging and measuring performance, 295
debugging the service, 775
debug-related Windows, 52
  Autos, 53
  Breakpoints, 53
  Call, 53
  Locals, 53
  Output, 53
  Watch, 54
Decimal, 91
decimal types, 89
  Currency, 89
  Decimal, 89
  Double, 89
  Single, 89
declaration syntax changes, 993
DeclaringType property, 77
default interop assembly, 620
Default keyword, 134
default property, 134
default TagPrefix for assembly, specifying, 575
default value, 451
default value with attribute, setting, 453
DefaultProperty, 568
DefaultTraceListener, 293
DefaultValue, 569
DefaultValue attribute, 456
dehydratingan See XML serialization, 304
Delegate keyword, 154
delegate method, implementing, 155

delegates, 154
  declaring, 154
  delegate data type, using, 155
delegates, using, 687
Delete method, 291
DeleteEventSource method, 291
Demo type, 75
DemoDispose class, 68
deploying .NET applications, 1
deployment, 63
deployment options prior to .NET, 914
deployment project, creating, 918
deployment project, modifying, 931
Dequeue method, 700
dereferencing objects, 119
deriving, 166
Description attribute, 456
Deserialize method, 306
design time grid, properties of, 399
  DrawGrid, 399
  GridSize, 399
  SnapToGrid, 399
detected dependency items, 928
DetectNewerInstalledVersion property, 926
DHTML, 524
dialog boxes, 38
dialog boxes, adding, 947
dialog forms, 439
DialogResult property, 440
different ASP.NET code for different standards, delivery of, 570
digital signature, 874
Digital Signature Algorithm (DSA), 884
digital signature basics, 888
DirectCast function, use of, 123
directory level security, 809
DISCO (short for DISCOvery of all things), 805
DisplayResults, 685
DisplayResults method, 688, 694, 698, 701
Dispose method, 67, 143, 836
DisposeCommand helper method, 383
DistanceTo method, 228
Distributed Applet-based Massively Parallel Processing, 786
Distributed COM (DCOM), 614
DLL Hell, 260, 913
DNA architectural model, 2
DNS as model, using, 805
Dock property, 410, 437

docking, 410
DockPadding property, 411
Document Object Model (DOM), 324
Document Type Definition (DTD), 309
DoDragDrop method, 428
DOM traversing raw XML elements, 325
DOM traversing XML attributes, 328
DOM-specific classes, 324
  XmlAttribute, 325
  XmlDocument, 324
  XmlElement, 325
  XmlNode, 324
DoOtherStuff, 211
DoSomething, 211
DoSomething method, 118
DoSort routine, 157
Double, 90
DownloadComplete event, 842
drag and drop, 428
DragDrop event, 428
DragEnter event, 428
DragEventArgs, 428
DragOver event, 429
duplicating menus, 423
dynamic discovery with IIS, 806
Dynamic Help, 37
Dynamic Help window, categories, 37
  Getting Started, 37
  Samples, 37
  top category, 37
dynamic link library (DLL), 60

E

early binding, 120, 614
Effect property, 428
Elapsed event, 771
element See XMI stream, reading, 315
elements of VB6 removed in VB.NET, 108
  As Any, 109
  Atn function, 109
  Calendar property, 109
  Circle statement, 109
  Currency, 109
  Date function and statement, 109
  Date $ function, 109
  Debug.Assert method, 109
  Debug.Print method, 109
  DefType, 109
  DoEvents function, 109

  Empty, 109
  Eqv operator, 109
  GoSub statement, 109
  Imp operator, 109
  Initialize event, 109
  Instancing property, 109
  IsEmpty function, 109
  IsMissing function, 109
  IsNull function, 109
  IsObject function, 109
  Let statement, 109
  Line statement, 109
  Lset, 109
  Now function, 109
  Null key word, 109
  On ... GoSub, 109
  On ... GoTo, 109
  Option Base, 109
  Option Private Module, 109
  properties (Get, Let and Set), 109
  PSet method, 109
  Rnd function, 109
  Round function, 109
  Rset, 109
  Scale method, 109
  Set statement, 109
  Sgn function, 109
  Sqr function, 109
  String function, 109
  Terminate event, 109
  Time function and statement, 109
  Time $ function, 109
  Timer function, 109
  Type statement, 109
  Variant data type, 109
  VarType function, 109
  Wend key word, 109
elements replaced by methods, 993
  CopyArray, 993
  FontChangeBold, 993
  FontChangeItalic, 993
  FontChangeName, 993
  FontChangeSize, 993
  FontChangeStrikeOut, 993
  FontChangeUnderline, 993
  FontChangeWeight, 993
  Math, 994
  Oct, 994
  PixelstoTwipsX, 994

elements replaced by methods, *(continued)*
PixelstoTwipsY, 994
TwipsPerPixelX, 994
TwipsPerPixelY, 994
TwipsToPixelsX, 994
TwipsToPixelsY, 994
e-mail, 321
EmailStream class, 321
Employee class, 189
EnableRaisingEvents property, 772
encapsulation, 224–26
End Namespace command, 266
End SyncLock statement, 704
enhanced event handling capabilities, 96
Enqueue method, 701
enterprise software development, role of
  namespaces in, 269
EntryWritten event, 291
Enum keyword, 171
Enum.Parse static method, 385
Equals method, 78, 286
Err object, 272
Err.Raise, 277
error handling, 271
error handling in VB6, 271
error logging, 288
ErrorProvider control, 415
event categories, 503
  application and session events, 503
  bubbled events, 503
  client-side versus server-side events, 503
  intrinsic events, 503
  postback versus nonpostback events,
    503
event handler, customizing, 44
Event keyword, 136
event log entries, 289
  audit type entries, 289
  event type entries, 289
event logs, 289, 771
  application, 289
  security logs, 289
  system, 289
event type entries, 289
  Error, 290
  Information, 289
  Warning, 289
event, creating, 559
EventLog component, 291, 773
EventLog method, 860

events, 135
  Click, 135
  TextChanged, 135
events and inheritance, 204
events from subclasses, raising, 205
events using Eventlog, writing, 771
  Application, 771
  Security, 771
  System, 771
events with AddHandler, raising, 139
events, inheriting, 204
Exception class, methods of, 274
  Equals, 274
  GetBaseException, 274
  GetHashCode, 274
  GetObjectData, 274
  GetType, 274
  ToString, 274
Exception class, properties of, 273
Exception classes, 274
  ApplicationException, 275
  ArgumentNullException, 275
  DivideByZeroException, 275
  MissingFieldException, 275
  MissingMemberException, 275
  OutofMemoryException, 275
  OverflowException, 275
  SystemException, 275
  Vb6Exception, 275
exception properties, using, 281
exception types, 274
  InteropServices, 275
  Protocols, 275
  System, 275
  System.Data, 275
  System.IO, 275
  System.Runtime, 275
  System.Web.Services, 275
  System.XML, 275
exception, properties of
  HelpLink, 273
  InnerException, 273
  Message, 273
  Source, 273
  StackTrace, 273
  TargetSite, 273
exceptions and Err object in VB6, difference
  between, 274
Exchange Server, 750
exclusive lock, 702

exclusive locks and SyncLock statement, 702

ExecSp, 388

ExecSp method, 388

ExecSpOutputValues function, 390

ExecSpReturnDataReader function, 386

ExecSpReturnDataSet function, 379
  DataSet objects, 380
  SqlCommand, 380
  SqlDataAdapter, 380

ExecSpReturnDataSet method, 381, 386, 393

ExecSpReturnDataSset method, 391

ExecSpReturnXmlReader function, 388

executable (EXE), 60

Execute methods, 357

ExecuteCommand method, 768

ExecuteNonQuery method, 389

ExecuteReader method, 358

ExecuteXmlReader method, 340

Exists method, 291

Exit Try statement, 279

explicit conversions, 92

ExtendedProperties property, 363

extender provider controls, 414

extender provider controls in code, working with, 416

extender providers, properties of, 416

Extensible Markup Language (XML), 301

Extensible Stylesheet Language (XSL), 301

F

fields, 115

File Allocation Table (FAT), 480

file extensions, creating, 944

file search properties, modifying, 951

file search, adding, 951

File System editor, 932

File System Editor, 936
  items to folder, adding, 937
  special folders, adding, 937

File Types editor, 932

File Types Editor, 943

file watcher, 750

file watcher, creating, 770

Filename property, 426

FileSystemObject, 64

FileSystemWatcher code to OnStart and OnStop, adding, 773

FileSystemWatcher component, 772
  Changed event, 772
  Created event, 772
  Deleted event, 772
  Renamed event, 772

FileSystemWatcher, creating, 771

Fill method, 361, 979

Filter property, 426, 772

FilterIndex property, 426

Finalize method, 67, 120

finalizers, 96

FindControl method, 563

FindForm method, 436

FindPrimes method, 685, 687, 694

Flush method, 314

FontDialog control, properties of, 427
  FixedPitchOnly, 427
  Font, 427
  ShowColor, 427
  ShowDialog, 427
  ShowEffects, 427

FOR XML query, 341
  FOR XML AUTO, 341
  FOR XML EXPLICIT, 341
  FOR XML RAW, 341

form borders, 400

Form Designer, 33

form properties set in code, 38

form size, setting limits, 405

formatter, 721
  binary, 721
  SOAP, 721

FormBorderStyle property, 400
  Fixed3D, 401
  FixedDialog, 401
  FixedSingle, 400
  FixedToolWindow, 401
  None, 400
  Sizeable, 401
  SizeableToolWindow, 401

forms, 38, 599–602

forms as classes, 397

forms at design time, 399

forms at runtime, 406

forms in .NET, 399

forms via Sub Main, using, 398

fragile base class, 250

Friend keyword, 113

Friend scope, 114, 203

FromOADate method, 92

FrontPage, 492
Function keyword, 127
Function routine, 113
functions, 106

G

GAC assembly features, 62
  automatic QFE (hotfix) support, 62
  side-by-side versioning, 62
Garbage Collection, 64
Garbage Collector (GC), 63, 65
garbage collector optimizations, 70
GDI+, 470
GDI+ capabilities in Windows form, using, 471
generalization, 165
Generated Code Region, 38
generated proxies, using, 745
generations, 70
Get...End Get block, 130
GetAuthorById method, 373
GetAverage function, 281
GetBaseException method, 286
GetContainerControl method, 436
GetElementsByTagName method, 326
GetEventLogs method, 291
GetExecutingAssembly method, 77
GetHashCode method, 286
GetMembers method, 77
GetNextControl method, 436
GetResponse method, 815
GetType method, 168, 563
GetTypes method, 77
GetUserName, 72
GetValue method, 219, 834
GetXml method, 325
Global Assembly Cache (GAC), 62, 528, 905
globally unique identifier (Guid), 222–23
GoTo statement, 271
Graphic Device Interface (GDI) function, 470
Graphics class, 471
GreaterThan parameter, 155
Greenwich Mean Time, 92

H

Handles keyword, 135
handling events, 135
handling exceptions, 319
Handshake protocol, 893

handy programming tips, 436
  child controls, managing, 436
  client coordinates to screen coordinates (and back),
    converting, 436
  container control or parent form, determining,
    436
  cursor, 436
  focus to a control, using, 436
  maximizing, minimizing and restoring form, 436
  mouse pointer, 436
  tab order, traversing, 436
  Z-order of controls at runtime, changing, 436
HasChildren property, 436
hash algorithms, 875
Hashcode generation, 286
Hashtable class, 131
HelloWorld Web form, 480
Help Filter, 28
HelpLink property, 287
HelpProvider control, properties of, 414
  HelpKeyword, 415
  HelpNavigator, 415
  HelpString, 415
  ShowHelp, 415
HKEY_CURRENT_USER, 942
host application, 729
host, creating, 739
hosting container's type at runtime, casting,
    563
hosting page, creating, 572
HTML, 346
HTML server controls, 496
HtmlTextWriter class, 526
HTTP, 721, 732, 787
HTTP GET protocol, 801
HttpWebResponse class, 814
hyperlink server controls, 541

I

icon for toolbox, attaching, 476
IDE windows, 51
  Autos, 51
  Breakpoints, 52
  Call Stack, 52
  Command, 52
  Locals, 51
  Output, 52
  Watch, 51
identity permissions, 856

identity section, 900
Identity security, 849
IDisposable interface, 66, 143
IIS as remoting host, using, 738
IL disassembler, 78
IL Disassembler, 2
ildasm.exe, 78
ImageButton control, 526
ImageURL property, 533
IMegaCalc interface, methods of, 615
    Function GetOutput () as Double, 615
    Sub ADDInput (InputValue as Double),
        615
    Sub DoCalculation (), 615
    Sub Reset (), 615
immutable class, 100
implementation, 202
implementation changes, 252
implementation See methods, 127
implementation See objects, composition of, 114
Implements keyword, 212
implicit dereferencing, 143
importing and aliasing namespaces, 263
importing namespaces, 264
Imports Microsoft.Win32, 265
Imports statement, 265
Imports statement, working with, 43
Imports System.Diagnostics statement, 291
INamingContainer interface, 527
inbound connections, receiving, 826
IncludeSubdirectories property, 772
IndexOf method, 542
inheritance, 164, 237
inheritance and multiple interfaces, 242
inheritance and multiple interfaces, applying, 244
inheritance, implementing, 166
inheritance, preventing, 211
InitialDirectory property, 426
Initialize method, 65
InitializeComponent procedure, 39, 46
InitiateConnection method, 823, 828
initiating connections, 823
InnerException object, 284
InnerException property, 282
installation modes, 946
    end stage, 946
    progress stage, 946
    start stage, 946
installation oriented classes, 754
installing the Service, 759

InstallUtil.exe, 756
instance, 112
instance methods, 149
InstMsiA.exe file, 934
InstMsiW.exe file, 934
InStr() function, 542
intCount, 108
Integer, 88
Integer array, 102
integer parameter, 138
integer types, 88
    Integer, 88
    Int32, 88
    UInt32, 88
    Long, 88
    Int64, 88
    UInt64, 88
    Short, 88
    Int16, 88
    UInt16, 88
Integrated Development Environment (IDE), 28
integrating counter into Service, 763
IntelliSense, 35
interactive applications, 679
interface, 113, 727
interface changes, 250
interface DLL, 744
interface DLL, using, 728
interface keyword, 214
Interface keyword, 211
interface, defining, 615
interface, using, 215
interface-based design, 744
interfaces, 212, 614
    defining, 214
    implementing, 216
    multiple, 212
    object, 212
    secondary, 213
interfaces and inheritance, combining, 219
Internet Engineering Task Force (IETF), 893
Internet Explorer, 492
Internet Explorer (IE), 813
Internet Explorer in applications, using, 837
Internet Explorer interop design pattern, 838
Internet Information Server (IIS), 480, 673
Internet Information Services (IIS), 2
internet protocols, 781
Internet resources, downloading, 813
Inter-ORB protocol, 785

intrinsic events, 503
invalid data, 657
Invalidate method, 473
Invoke method, 155, 680, 685, 824
IO subsystem, 676
IPrintableObject interface, 214, 217
IPrintableObject, implementing, 245
is comparison operator, 101
IsDBNull, 261
IsDBNull(), 101
IsEmpty function, 101, 108
ISerializable interface, 726
IShared interface, 231
IsMainThread, 825
IsMDIContainer property, 436
IsNull function, 101, 108
IsObject function, 108
IsString method, 855
ItemCheck event, 457
ItemCheck property, 457
ItemOf property, 329
ITheInterface, 117
IUnknown interface, 64
IValues interface, 220
IXsltContextFunction interface, 337
IXsltContextVariable variable, 337

J

Java Applets, 786
Join method, 682
Just-In-Time (JIT) activation, 659
just-in-time (JIT) compiler, 61
JustInTimeActivation attribute, 659

K

key.xml file, 885
Keyboard Layout, 28
KeyState property, 428
keywords and methods, retired, 108
    Currency type, 108
    DefType statement, 108
    Left function, 108
    Lset function, 108
    Mid function, 108
    Right function, 108
    Rset function, 108
    String function, 108
Keywords property, 926

keywords that control the scope of variables,
    126
    Friend, 126
    Private, 126
    Protected, 126
    Protected Friend, 126
    Public, 126

L

late binding, 120, 614, 622
    features of, 120
    implementing, 120
launch condition, creating, 952
Launch Conditions editor, 932
Launch Conditions Editor, 950
    file search, 950
    Registry search, 950
    Windows Installer search, 950
LayoutMDI method, 439
LBound function, 103
legacy ActiveX control, 627
legacy component, referencing, 618
legacy component, registering, 617
legacy control, registering, 629
levels of inheritance, 188
library DLL, 728
library DLL, referencing, 728, 730
LimitedCheckedListBox control, 458
ListBox control, 456
ListDictionary class, 106
LngLong.MaxValue, 95
Load event, 153, 736
Load method, 324
LoadFrom method, 77
Loan Slicer application, 506
local registry values, 55
local variables, advantages of, 263
Localization property, 926
location of assembly, defining, 911
Location property, 46
location transparency, 735
locks, 705
    reader, 705
    writer, 705
Log property, 291
LogError private method, 383
Long, 89
lookless controls, 527
LSet statement, 99

M

machine configuration file, 909
Macro Explorer, 57
macros, 56
Macros in VS.NET, recording and using, 56
MainMenu control, 418
Major.Minor.Build.Revision, 62
manifest, 899
manipulating menus at runtime, dynamically, 421
manual installation, 914
ManualReset events, 711
ManualResetEvent object, 708
marshaling COM objects, 663
master/details data binding, 592
MaximumSize property, 405
MaxItemsSelected property, 456
MaxValue method, 95
MDAC, 362
MDI child forms, 437
MDI example in VB.NET, 438
MDI parent form, creating, 436
MDI parent forms between VB6 and VB.NET,
    differences in, 437
MDI-based interface, 34
MDIParent property, 437
Me keyword, 39, 192
Me Keyword, 191
member or instance variables, 115
member variables, 126
memory allocation, 71
memory allocation for objects, 68
memory management, 2, 63
memory management and garbage collection, 59
MemoryStream, 320
MemoryStream object, using, 320
menus, 418
    context, 419
    main, 418
Merge Module Project template, 917
message, 721
Message class, 829
    message, 829
    username, 829
Message Digest version 5 (MD5), 878
Message property, 282
message sink, 721
MessageBox, 43
MessageBox.Show, 44
MessageBoxButtons, 43

messages, sending, 828
metadata, 2, 73
method parameters, 128
method scope, indicating, 128
method signatures, 227
methods, 106, 126, 215, 379
    imperative methods, 127
    interrogative methods, 127
methods that return values, 127
methods, overloading, 171
methods, overriding, 173
Microsoft Clustering Services, 639
Microsoft Database Engine (MSDE), 643
Microsoft Message Queue (MSMQ), 660
Microsoft Message Queuing (MSMQ), 639
Microsoft Mobile Internet Toolkit (MMIT),
    958
Microsoft Outlook, 693
Microsoft SQLXML website, 302
Microsoft Transaction Server (MTS), 639, 750
Microsoft Word, 676
Microsoft.VisualBasic.Compatibility.Data.dll,
    258–59
minimum size for controls, setting, 465
MinimumSize property, 405
MinValue method, 95
MMC snap-in, 652
mobile application development, 957
mobile device emulators, 971
mobile Web and .NET Compact Framework
    applications, differences between, 964
mobile Web application, creating, 961
mobile Web applications, 958
mobile Web template, limitations of, 958
mobile Web tool suite, interface elements,
    959
    Ad Rotator, 959
    Calendar, 959
    Command, 959
    Image, 959
    Label, 959
    Link, 959
    List, 959
    ObjectList, 959
    PhoneCall, 959
    SelectionList, 960
    TextBox, 960
    TextView, 960
modal form, 439
modeless forms, 439

modules, 60
  assembly manifest, 60
  associated metadata, 60
  Microsoft Intermediate Language (MSIL), 60
monitor object, 702
MouseDown event, 428
MouseMove event, 820
MousePosition property, 436
MoveNext method, 355
MoveToNextAttribute method, 315
moving through records, 602
mscorlib.dll, 78
MSDE (Microsoft Data Engine), 2
MSMQ, 2
multidimensional arrays, 103
multilevel inheritance, 189
multiple configurations, advantages of, 48
Multiple Document Interface (MDI), 436
multiple events, handling, 136
multiple inheritance, 188
multiple interfaces, 163
multiple services within one executable, 755
multiple, related tables in single DataGrid, 592
multitasking, 673
multithreaded functionality, 672
multithreading, 673
MustInherit KeywWord, 210
MustOverride keyword, 236
MustOverride Keyword, 210
mutex object, 702
My Profile page, 28
MyBase keyword, 451
MyBase Keyword, 176, 195
MyBase.Finalize(), 67
MyBase.New(), 198
MyClass Keyword, 196
MyCSharpClass, 87
MyMetaNamespace namespace, 266

N

Name method, 192
Name property, 47
NameChanged event, 205
namespace crowding, 265
namespaces, 31, 255, 256
namespaces and references, 259
namespaces for Windows applications, default, 33
  System, 33
  System.Data, 33
  System.Drawing, 33
  System.Windows.Forms, 33
  System.XML, 33
namespaces, creating, 266
native interface, 112, 163
native interface, using, 213
  DoSomething method, 213
  DoSomethingElse method, 213
native OLE DB, 362
Navigate method, 841
NavigateUrl property, 542
nested controls, allowing/disallowing, 578
Netscape, 492
New Code Window, 33
New Exception statement, 284
new exception, throwing, 278
New keyword, 117, 743
NewRow method, 361
NextValue method, 763
NodeType property, 317
nondeterministic finalization, 66
nonvirtual methods, 182
NonVirtual methods, overriding, 182
NotifyFilter property, 772
NotInheritable keyword, 445
Now() method, 92
NT File System (NTFS), 480
NT Services, 749
N-Tier programming model, 350
numeric-only text box, creating, 447

O

object, 112
Object Browser, 31, 263
Object class, 97
Object data type, 120
object interfaces, 108
object orientation, 111, 221
  abstraction, 111, 221
  encapsulation, 111, 221
  inheritance, 112
  inheritance, 221
  polymorphism, 111, 221
object orientation, concepts of, 112
  assembly (component) level scoping, 112
  multiple interfaces, 112
object pooling, 659
Object Request Brokers (ORBs), 783
object syntax, introduction of, 111–12

object, composition of, 113
object-oriented programming, 221, 250
objects, 116
  declaration, 117
  instantiation, 117
  working with, 116
objects and components, applying, 221
objects, properties of, 610
ODBC layer, 361
OfficeEmployee, 189
OLE DB .NET Data Provider, 362
On Error GoTo . . . statement, 272
On_Click event handler, 43
OnChange event, 503
OnClosed method, 144
OnCustomCommand event, 770
OnLoad method, 144
OnPaint method, 474
OnStart event, 773
OnStop event, 773
OnWalk method, 138
oObject references, 119
Opacity property, 403
OpenFileDialog property, 425
operating system component, 915
Option Base statement, 101
Option Base This = statement, 102
Option Compare, 94
Option Explicit, 92, 93
Option statement, 376
Option Strict, 93
Optional keyword, 106, 145
Oracle, 349
other UI elements, 960
  CompareValidator, 960
  CustomValidator, 960
  Form, 960
  MobilePage, 960
  Panel, 960
  RangeValidator, 960
  RegularExpressionValidator, 960
  RequiredFieldValidator, 960
  StyleSheet, 960
  ValidationSummary, 960
Output window, 50
OverflowException, 274
overloaded methods, overriding, 180
Overloads keyword, 171
Overridable Keyword, 174
Overrides keyword, 67, 174, 220

owned forms, 402
OwnedForms collection, 402
owner property, 402

P

Package and Deployment Wizard, 915
Package files, 933
PackageCode property, 926
PadLeft method, 99
PadRight method, 99
Page_Load event, 502, 541
Pagelets, 525
Paint event, 471
panel and GroupBox container controls, 430
parameter passing, 106
parameterized constructors, 141
parameterized properties, 131
particular version of assembly, loading, 910
passing strings to Service, 770
Path property, 772
performance counter, creating, 762
performance counter, monitoring, 762
performing Explicit conversions, 94
permission sets, creating, 849
  Everything, 849
  Execution, 849
  FullTrust, 849
  Internet, 850
  LocalInternet, 850
  Nothing, 849
  SkipVerification, 850
permissions and assembly management tools, 873
Person base class, creating, 244
PictureBoxes control, 437
PointToClient method, 436
PointToScreen method, 436
polymorphism, 226–27
polymorphism through .NET reflection, 231
Polymorphism through .NET reflection and multiple
    interfaces, 233
polymorphism through late binding, 228
polymorphism with inheritance, 235
polymorphism with multiple interfaces, 230
polymorphism, implementation, 227
  .NET reflection, 227
  inheritance, 227
  late binding, 227
  multiple interfaces, 227
polymorphism, techniques for, 237

populating databases, 645
port ranges, 732
   0-1023, 732
   1024-49151, 733
   49152-65535, 733
postback versus nonpostback events, 503
preemptive multitasking, 675
PreRender event, 553
Preserve Keyword, 104
primary interface, 112
primary output project item, properties, 926
primary synchronization objects, 702
   AutoResetEvent, 702
   Interlocked, 702
   ManualResetEvent, 702
   Monitor, 702
   Mutex, 702
   ReaderWriterLock, 702
primary thread, 672
Primitive Type, 84
   Boolean, 84
   Byte, 84
   Char, 84
   Date, 84
   Decimal, 84
   Double, 84
   Integer, 84
   Long, 84
   Short, 84
   Single, 84
   String, 84
primitive types, 82, 84
primitive types, keywords for, 84
   Integer, 84
   Long, 84
   String, 84
PrincipalPermission class, methods of, 854
   Copy, 854
   Demand, 854
   Equals, 854
   FromXml, 854
   GetHashCode, 854
   GetType, 854
   Intersect, 854
   IsSubsetOf, 854
   IsUnrestricted, 854
   ToString, 854
   ToXml, 854
   Union, 854
Print method, 245

printer dialog controls, 427
   PageSetupDialog, 427
   PrintDialog, 427
   PrintPreviewDialog, 427
PrintPage event, 246
PrintPreview method, 245
private key, 874
Private method, 113
Private scope, 203
procedures, 106
process See threading, 673
processes, 673
processing flow of ASP.NET Web forms, 489
ProductCode property, 926
Professional VB.NET, 2
programmatic identifier (ProgID) values, 255
Project properties, 933
project templates, 916
project, setting up, 729, 734
properties, 115, 129
Properties dialog box, attributes, 40
   AssemblyCompany, 41
   AssemblyCopyright, 41
   AssemblyDescription, 41
   AssemblyProduct, 41
   AssemblyTitle, 41
   AssemblyTrademark, 41
   AssemblyVersion, 41
   CLSCompliant, 41
   Guid, 41
properties of dialog boxes, 947
properties of sub-controls, exposing, 465
Properties Window, 36
property for custom control, creating, 451
Property keyword, 212
Property method, 132
Property Pages, 48
Property routine, 113
protected methods, 96
Protected scope, 201, 203
Protected variables, 203
ProVB.NET, 40
proxy, 721, 727
proxy DLL, 746
proxy DLL, generating, 728
public key, 874
Public Key Cryptographic System (PKCS), 874, 883
Public key cryptography, 874
Public method, 111, 112, 728

Public scope, 114, 203
pure virtual function, 211

Q

quantity attribute, 329
quantum, 675
queued components, 660
queued components, example of, 660
QueueUserWorkItem method, 690
queuing invocations, 665
queuing work, manually, 689

R

RadioCheck property, 420
RaiseEvent keyword, 137
RaiseEvent method, 205
raising events, 136
Read method, 315, 316, 358, 687
ReadElementString method, 319
ReaderWriterLock object, 706
ReadInnerXml, 319
ReadLine method, 319
ReadOnly keyword, 133
read-only properties, 133
ReadOuterXml, 319
ReadToEnd method, 816
real proxy, 721
receiving events with WithEvents, 137
Record Temporary Macro, 57
Recordset object, 111, 350
ReDim statement, 103
reference types, 81, 83, 696
reference types (classes), 96
referenced assemblies, 902
referenced memory, 100
Referencing the Compatibility Library, 986
Reflection API, 76
RefreshData method, 585
RegAsm tool, 634
Region property, 404
RegisterWellKnownClientType method, 738
Registry editor, 932
Registry Editor, 941
    registry file, importing, 941
    registry keys, creating, 941
    values for registry keys, creating, 941
Registry files, importing, 943
RegSvcs, 652

RegSvcs tool, options for, 649
    /appname
        (name), 650
    /c, 650
    /componly, 650
    /exapp, 650
    /extlb, 650
    /fc, 650
    /help or /?, 650
    /nologo, 650
    /noreconfig, 650
    /parname
        (name), 650
    /quiet, 650
    /reconfig, 650
    /tlb
        (typelibrary, 650
    /u, 650
RegularExpressions, 256
Release method, 64
remote method invocation (RMI), 783
remote method invocation in Java, 785
remote object, 720
remote procedure calls (RPC), 784
remoting, 719
remoting host, 720
remoting objects
    client-activated object, 723
    serializable object, 723
    wellknown object, 723
remoting overview, 720
Remoting subsystem, 720
remoting via code, configuring, 733
remoting, configuring, 731
remoting, implementing, 727
    client, 727
    host, 727
    server library, 727
RemoveHandler method, 139
RemovePreviousVersion property, 926
Render method, 569
RenderChildren method, 579
rendering content, special cases, 579
rendering methods subset, 571
RenderPage method, 245
Repeater class, 527
Request property, 802
Reset method, 469, 711
reset method for control property, providing, 454
ResetMyProperty method, 454

Resize event, 405
resize logic, 465
resizing and positioning controls, automatic, 410
Resolve method, 824
ResourceWriter type, 75
Response.Redirect method, 506
RestoreDirectory property, 426
results.Clear(), 700
retired controls, 435
   DirListBox, FileListBox, DriveListBox, 435
   Image, 435
   Line and Shape, 435
   Spinner, 435
Return keyword, 127
Role Based security, 849
role-based permissions, 853
Rollback method, 658
RSet statement, 99
Run method, 753
runtime settings, 910

S

sample application, enhancing, 41
Save method, 324
SaveFileDialog property, 425
saving changes, 586
scope options, 202
   Friend, 202
   Private, 202
   Protected, 202
   Protected Friend, 202
   Public, 202
Scripting.FileSystem object, 64
scrollable forms, 405
ScrollableControl class, 461
search path, providing, 911
SearchPath property, 926
secret key encryption, 879
Secure Sockets Layer (SSL), 809, 893
Secured Hash Algorithm (SHA), 874
Secured Hashing Algorithm (SHA), 877
security concepts and definitions, 848
security configuration file, 909
Security Identifier (SID), 853
security level, 872
   RequestMinimum, 872
   RequestOptional, 872
   RequestRefused, 872
security policy, managing, 861

security tools, 873
security, other types, 810
SELECT command, 356
self-describing, 907
sEmail parameter, 802
sendData function, 796
SendMessage method, 831
SendToBack method, 436
Serializable attribute, 75
serializable object, 720
serializable objects, 726
SerializableAttribute attribute, 321
Serialize method, 305, 971
serializing, 453
server applications, 680
Server Explorer, 55–56
Server Object, 55
Server.Transfer method, 506
server-side controls, concept of, 493
Server-Side Include (SSI), 525
server-side library, 729
Service Control Manager, 750
service object, 723
   Activated, 724
   Serializable, 724
   SingleCall, 723
   Singleton, 724
service software, 677
Service software, 677
service, consuming, 796
ServiceBase class, 755
ServiceBase class, events of, 753
   OnContinue, 753
   OnCustomCommand, 753
   OnPause, 753
   OnPowerEvent, 753
   OnShutdown, 753
   OnStart, 753
   OnStop, 753
ServiceController, 768
ServiceController class, 755
ServiceController class, methods of, 765
   ExecuteCommand, 765
   Refresh, 765
   Start, 765
   Stop, 765
ServiceController class, properties of, 765
   CanStop, 766
   ServiceName, 766
   Status, 766

ServiceController into example, integrating, 766
ServicedComponent class, 659
ServiceInstaller class, properties of, 754
DisplayName, 754
ServiceName, 755
StartType, 755
ServiceInstaller classes, 754
ServiceProcessInstaller, properties of, 754
Account, 754
HelpText, 754
Password, 754
Username, 754
Services Control Manager, 751
SET command, 296
Set method, 710
Set statement, 119
Set...End Set block, 131
SetAbort, 659
SetComplete, 659
SetDataBinding method, 393
SetParameterValues method, 381
SetParameterValues, arguments of, 381
IDictionary interface, 381
SqlCommand object, 381
Setup Project template, 918
Setup Wizard, 918
Setup.exe file, 934
shadowing, 182
Shadows keyword, 182
shared assembly, 651, 904
shared data, 692
shared events, 152, 209
Shared keyword, 149
shared library, 727
shared methods, 151, 207
shared methods, overloading, 208
shared methods, shadowing, 208
shared methods, variables and events, 149
shared name, 651
shared properties, 152
Shared Synchronized method, 700
shared variables, 149
sharing data, avoiding, 693
Short, 88
Short.MaxValue, 95
shortcuts, creating, 940
ShouldSerialize method, 469
ShouldSerializeMyProperty property, 454
ShouldSerializeXXX method, 454

Show method, 439
ShowDialog() method, 439
ShowDialog() property, 426
ShowDistance method, 230
shutting down the application, 833
side-by-side execution, 907
simple constructors, 197
simple object access protocol (SOAP), 787
simple Web User Control, building, 528
Single, 90
SingleCall objects, 724
SingleCall, Singleton and Activated objects, 722–23
singleton objects, 725
Sleep method, 61
Smalltalk, 249
Smart Client deployment, 63
SMTP server, 828
sn tool, 651
SOAP, 719
SOAP (Simple Object Access Protocol), 782
SoapFormatter, 741
sockets, 817
Solution Explorer, 93
Solution Explorer Window, 30
solution signing options, solution, 936
Certificate file, 936
Private key file, 936
Timestamp server URL, 936
SortedList collection, 108
Source Code Style, 336
source code style attributes, 308
Source property, 285, 290, 291
SourceExists method, 290, 291
sources of controls, 443
ActiveX controls, existing, 444
built-in controls, 444
custom controls, 444
spaghetti code, 249
span tag, 483
speed and connectivity, 810
splitter control, 413
SQL database, 55
SQL Enterprise Manager, 55
SQL Server, 2, 349, 639
SQL Server .NET Data Provider, 361
SQL Server database, 55
SQL Server Enterprise Manager, 370, 589
SQL Server Query Analyzer, 339

SQL statements, 357
  DELETE, 357
  INSERT, 357
  SELECT, 357
  UPDATE, 357
SQLCommand class, 340
SqlDataReader.Close method, 359
SqlDataReader.ExecuteReader method, 359
SQLXML, 302
SSL protocol, 893
  cryptographic security, 893
  extensibility, 893
  interoperability, 893
  relative efficiency, 893
StackTrace properties, 285
standard COM interfaces, 639
Standard Generalized Markup Language (SGML),
      302, 784
standard Windows.Forms controls, 431
  Button, 431
  Check Box, 432
  CheckedListBox, 432
  Combo box, 432
  DataGrid, 432
  DateTimePicker, 432
  DomainUpDown, 432
  HScrollBar, 432
  ImageList, 432
  Label, 433
  LinkLabel, 433
  ListBox, 433
  ListView, 433
  NotifyIcon, 433
  NumericUpDown, 434
  PictureBox, 434
  ProgressBar, 434
  RadioButton, 434
  RichTextBox, 434
  StatusBar, 434
  TabControl, 434
  Text box, 434
  Timer, 435
  TrackBar, 435
  TreeView, 435
  VScrollBar, 435
Start method, 332, 682
StartPosition property, 403
  CenterParent, 403
  CenterScreen, 403
  Manual, 403

  WindowsDefaultBounds, 403
  WindowsDefaultLocation, 403
StartTask method, 714
startup location, 403
startup settings, 910
state, 810
state management for XML Web services, 804
Status property, 473
Step-By-Step process to create control, 447
stock price reporter, automated, **750**
stored procedure, 370
  accessing, 373
  calling, 371
  creating, 370
stored procedure XML structure, 378
stored procedures with ADO.NET, using, 369
StreamWriter component, 661
StreamWriter interface, 293
StreamWriter object, methods, 293
  Close, 293
  Flush, 293
  Write, 293
  WriteLine, 293
streamwriters, 293
String class, 98, 100
String class, shared methods, 98
  Compare, 99
  CompareOrdinal, 99
  Concat, 99
  Copy, 99
  Empty, 99
  Equality operator (=), 99
  Equals, 99
  Inequality operator (op Inequality), 99
String objects, 97, 99
String() method, 98
StringBuilder class, 83, 101
StringCollection class, 105
StringDictionary class, 105
strMyString variable, 100
strong names, 901
structured exception handling, 273
structured exception handling keywords in VB.NET,
      275
  Catch, 275–76
  Finally, 276
  Throw, 276
  Try, 275
Sub routines, 113
subclass, creating, 167

subclassed control, creating, 564

subclassed controls, 526

subclassed controls and the Web custom control template, 566

subclassed controls, developing, 572

subclassing, 166

subclassing Person, 244

Subject property, 926

SubString method, 99

switch class interface, properties of, 296
  TraceError, 296
  TraceInfo, 296
  TraceVerbose, 296
  TraceWarning, 296

synchronization, 692

synchronization objects, 701

synchronization support, built in, 698
  ArrayList, 698
  Hashtable, 698
  Queue, 698
  Stack, 698

synchronization, sharing data, 698

SyncLock block, 700

SyncLock statement, 699, 703

system account, 751

System namespace, 78, 256

System.Array class, 102

System.Array interfaces, 610
  System.Collections.ICollection, 610
  System.Collections.IEnumerable, 610
  System.Collections.IList, 610
  System.ICloneable, 610

System.Collections namespace, objects of, 104
  ArrayList, 104
  BitArray, 104
  Hashtable, 104
  Queue, 104
  SortedList, 104
  Stack, 104

System.Collections.Specialized namespace, 105

System.ComponentModel, 567

System.Data.OleDb, 362

System.Data.SqlClient, 362

System.Data.SqlClient namespace, 265

System.Diagnostics namespace, 291

System.DirectoryServices namespace, 257

System.Drawing namespace, 83, 470

System.Drawing Namespace, 31

System.Drawing.DLL, 31

System.Drawing.Graphics class, 470

System.Drawing.Graphics class, methods of, 470
  DrawArc, 470
  DrawEllipse, 470
  DrawIcon, 470

System.Drawing.Point, 83

System.EnterpriseServices namespace, 266, 656, 661

System.GC.Collect method, 66

System.IO class, 817

System.IO namespace, 256
  classes, 256
  interfaces, 256
  structures, 256

System.IO.FileStream, 320

System.IO.MemoryStream class, 320

System.MarshalByRefObject, 720

System.Math library, 108

System.Net class, 817

System.Net. WebProxy class, 814

System.Net.HttpWebRequest class, 813

System.Net.HttpWebResponse class, 813

System.Net.Sockets namespace, 817

System.Net.Sockets.NetworkStream, 320

System.Net.WebClient class, 814

System.Net.WebRequest class, 813

System.Object, 248

System.Object class, 73

System.Security.Permissions namespace, 847

System.Security.Permissions namespace, permissions in, 850

System.ServiceProcess namespace, 765

System.ServiceProcess.ServiceInstaller class, 752

System.ServiceProcess .ServiceProcessInstaller class, 752

System.Text namespace, 83, 256

System.Text.StringBuilder class, 83

System.Text.StringBuilder object, 100

System.Threading namespace, 687

System.Threading.Monitor object, 703

System.Timers.Timer, using, 691

System.Uri classes, 813

System.Web.Mail namespace, 321

System.Web.Services namespace, component classes of, 800
  WebMethodAttribute, 800
  WebService, 800
  WebServiceAttribute, 800
  WebServicesBindingAttribute, 800

System.Web.Services.Description namespace, 801
System.Web.Services.Discovery namespace, 802
System.Web.Services.Protocols namespace, 802
cookies per RFC 2019, 802
HTML forms, 802
HTTP request and response, 802
MIME, 802
Server, 803
SOAP, 803
URI and URLs, 803
XML, 803
System.Web.UI, 567
System.Web.UI namespace, 527
System.Web.UI.HtmlControls namespace, 496
System.Web.UI.WebControls namespace, 527
System.Windows.Forms namespace, 46, 260, 396, 995
System.Windows.Forms.dll assembly, 396
System.Xml document support, 309
System.Xml namespaces, 311
XmlNameTable, 311
XmlResolver, 311
XmlUrlResolver, 311
System.Xml.Serialization namespace, 304
System.Xml.XmlException, 320

T

TabIndex property, 47
Tabs versus MDI Interface, 34
Tabular Data Stream (TDS), 361
TargetSite property, 283
Task List, 54–55
Task List window, 50
Task Manager, 693
TaskComplete method, 689, 694
TCP, 720, 721, 732
TCP/IP, 783
template element, 527
template for presentation, 485
template properties, 527
templated controls, 527
templating, 526
termination and cleanup, 142
test bed project, setting up, 565
TestTrue() method, 35, 87

text property of textURL, updating, 841
thread, 671, 677
affinity, 677
safety, 677
thread object, methods of, 691
Abort, 692
ApartmentState, 692
Join, 692
Priority, 692
Resume, 692
Sleep, 692
Suspend, 692
thread pool, using, 687
thread scheduling, 674
threading, 671
threading options, 686
threading, implementation, 680
ThreadPool class, 689
ThreadPool.QueueUserWorkItem, 689
threads, using, 677
Throw Keyword, 277
Throw statement, 277
Titleproperty property, 926
TlbExp tool, 637
TlbImp, using, 620
Today() method, 92
TODO keyword, 54
ToOADate method, 92
Toolbar control, 423
ToolboxBitmap attribute, 476
ToolboxData, 568
ToolTip property, 414
TopMost property, 401
ToString method, 95, 191, 281
trace, 590
Trace class, 293
trace files, writing to, 292
Trace objects, 53
trace switches, 295
BooleanSwitch, 296
TraceSwitch, 296
TrafficLight control, 475
transaction, 640
transaction attribute, 655
transactional components, 641
TransactionAttribute attribute, 656
TransactionOption enumeration, 656
Disabled, 656
NotSupported, 656
Required, 656

RequiresNew, 656
Supported, 656
transactions, 810
transactions with queued components, 667
transactions, automatic, 658
transactions, example of, 642
transactions, manual, 658
transactions, other aspects, 658
Transform method, 332
TransparencyKey property, 404
transparent and translucent forms, making, 403
transparent proxy, 721
Transport Layer Security (TLS), 893
TransSample Class Library project, 645
TravelingEmployee classes, 189
TraverseDataSet method, 361
TraverseDataSet(), 358
tree-control interface, 53
Try structures, nested, 280
Try, Catch and Finally keywords, 276
type, 61
   fields, 61
   methods, 61
   properties, 61
type library, 614
Type Library Import, 621
type system, 61
typed DataSet, 341
   events, 341
   methods, 341
   properties, 341
typed DataSet objects, 341
typed DataSets, generating, 342
TypeOf operator, 96
types
   reference, 61
   value, 61
types of security, different, 848
   Cryptographic, 848
   NTFS, 848
   Programmatic, 848
   Security Policies, 848
   Security Type, 848

U

UBound function, 102
UDDI (Universal, Description, Discovery, and Integration), 807
   green pages, 807

   white pages, 807
   yellow pages, 807
UDDI project, 807
UDDI, using, 808
UI thread, 690
Unicode, 91
Uniform Resource Identifier (URI), 333, 813
Uniform Resource Locator (URL), 813
uninstalling the Service, 760
Universal Coordinated Time, 92
Universal Data Link (UDL), 369
Universal Modeling Language (UML), 164
unsigned types, 89
Update method, 588
Update statement, profiling, 590
Upgrade property, 926
upgrade tools, 987
Upgrade Wizard, using, 988
useful attributes, other, 454
user account, 751
user controls, 500
User Defined type (UDT), 108
User Defined Type (UDT), 84
   integers, 84
   strings, 84
User Interface editor, 932
User Interface Editor, 945
UserControl class, 460
UserControl composite, 463
UtcNow() method, 92

V

validating event, 417
validation controls, 498
   CompareValidator, 499
   CustomValidator, 499
   RangeValidator, 499
   RegularExpressionValidator, 499
   RequiredFieldValidator, 499
value and reference types, difference between, 82
value in performance counter, changing, 763
Value method, 218
Value property, 329
value to Registry key, adding, 941
value types, 81, 83, 696
Value types, 83
ValueType namespace, 78

VAN, 811

variable, 177

variable types, 81

   reference, 81

   value, 81

variables and types, 81–82

variant type, 97

VB.NET, 1

VB.NET and System.Web.Services, 800

VB.NET applications, 2

VB.NET namespaces, 262

   `System.Collections`, 262

   `System.Data`, 262

   `System.Diagnostics`, 262

   `System.Drawing`, 262

   `System.EnterpriseServices`,
     262

   `System.IO`, 262

   `System.Text`, 263

   `System.Threading`, 263

   `System.Web`, 263

   `System.Web.Services`, 263

   `System.Windows.Forms`, 263

VB.NET Object, 97

VB6 application, testing, 635

vbModal parameter, 439

VBNetXML02, 314

version number, 900

version policies, 907

versioning and deployment, 2, 59, 61

versioning issues, 906

versioning policy, default, 908

versioning, managing, 62

View Designer, 33

View Menu, 31

virtual class, 211

virtual methods, 177

Visual, 916

Visual Basic .NET, 1

Visual Basic code converter, using, 987

Visual Basic Compatibility Library, 985

Visual Basic, importance of, 1

Visual Basic.NET, 38

   code, 38

   working with, 38

Visual C#, 28

Visual C++, 28

visual inheritance, 38, 405

Visual Interdev, 55

Visual InterDev, 479

Visual Studio .NET, 2, 27

Visual Studio .NET deplyment projects, 916

Visual Studio .NET IDE, 57

Visual Studio .NET to build Web services, using,
   795

Visual Studio IDE, coordinating with, 452

Visual Studio Installer (VSI), 916

Visual Studio menu, 34

   Hide Selection, 34

   Stop Outlining, 34

VS.NET, 2

VS.NET, features of, 54

   Command window, 54

   Macros, 54

   Server Explorer, 54

   Task List, 54

W

W3C Extensible Markup Language (XML) 1.0,
   311

wait state See threading, 676

WaitOne method, 708

Walk method, 128

WAN networking, 784

Web application project, 491

   Global.asa file, 491

   Global.asax file, 491

   Web.config file, 491

Web controls, creating, 523

Web development, 2

Web form, anatomy of, 484

Web forms, 479

Web form's lifecycle, 502

   cleanup, 502

   configuration, 502

   event handling, 502

Web forms versus ASP, 504

Web forms, events in, 501

Web page into Web User Control, converting,
   535

Web reference, adding, 796

Web service, 30

Web service proxies, 804

Web service repository, components of, 805

   database, 805

   language, 805

   standard format, 805

Web services, 781
Web Services Description Language (WSDL), 788
  binding, 788
  message, 788
  port, 788
  portType, 788
  service, 788
  types, 788
Web Services Enhancements (WSE), 803
Web services for mobile applications, 958
Web services, architecturing with, 803
Web services, building, 790
Web services, features of, 781, 782
  architecture neutral, 782
  discovery, 781
  interoperable, 782
  Service Repository, 781
  simple, 782
  ubiquitous, 782
  UDDI (Universal Description, Discovery and
    Integration), 781
Web Services, foundations of, 784
Web services, introduction to, 781
Web services, security in, 808
Web Setup Project template, 918
Web sites, 395
Web User Control events, handling, 560
Web User Control item to project, adding, 543
Web User Control namespaces, 564
Web User Control programmatically, adding, 564
Web User Control, creating, 528
Web User Control, features of, 563
Web User Control, reaching into, 549
Web User Control, reaching out for, 562
Web User Controls (WUC), 525
Web User Controls and the @ register directive,
    548
WebControl class, methods of, 571
  AddAttributesToRender, 571
  RenderBeginTag, 571
  RenderChildren, 571
  RenderContents, 571
  RenderEndTag, 571
WebControl constructors, 577
WebRequest class, 814, 894
While statement, 704
whitespace, 315
Win32 controls, 523
Window Layout, 28

Windows 2000, 749
Windows 2000 Professional, 2
Windows 2003 Server, 2
Windows API, 72
Windows application, 45, 919
Windows controls, creating, 443
  third-party controls, 444
Windows Explorer, 40
Windows Form Designer Generated Code, 33
Windows Forms, 395
  application, 395
  importance of, 395
Windows Installer, 915
Windows Installer package (.msi), 915
Windows Meta Files (WMF), 875
Windows NT, 749
Windows platform, 27
Windows Server 2003, 749
Windows Service, 750
  characteristics of, 750
  creating, 752
  interacting with, 751
Windows Service with VB.NET, general instructions
    to create, 756
Windows Service, other types of, 755
Windows Services, 749
Windows XP, 2, 749
WindowState property, 436
WithEvents key word, 46
WithEvents Keyword, 136
worker method, 689
Worker method, 714
working with IDE, alternate techniques, 453
WriteAttributeString method, 313
WriteComment method, 312
WriteEntry method, 291
WriteLine method, 293
WriteOnly keyword, 134
write-only properties, 133
WriteRaw method, 314
WriteStartDocument method, 312
WriteStartElement method, 312
WriteToLog, 64
WriteXmlSchema method, 342
WSDL (Web Services Description Language), 781
WXClientMultiPrescription, 306
WXClientPrescription class, 304
WXPotilasResepti class, 311
WXShowXMLNode subroutine, 316

X

X509 certificate, classes, 891
X509 certificates, 891
XCopy applications, 63
XCOPY deployment, 904, 914
XML, 1
XML DataSet properties and methods, 338
  GetXml, 338
  GetXmlSchema, 338
  InferXmlSchema, 338
  Namespace, 338
  Prefix, 338
  ReadXml, 338
  ReadXmlSchema, 338
  WriteXml, 338
  WriteXmlSchema, 338
XML Document Object MOdel (DOM), 967
XML document, components of, 311
  attributes, 311
  elements, 311
  schema, 311
XML documents, generating and navigating, 310
  Document Object Model (DOM), 310
  Stream-based, 310
XML in VB.NET, using, 301–2
XML namespaces, 309
XML schemas, 309
XML serialization, 303
XML stream, reading, 314
XML stream, writing, 311
XML stream-style parsers, 310
XML using XmlTextReader, traversing, 317
XML, introduction, 302
XmlAttributeCollection data type, 329
XmlDocument class, self-documenting methods of, 324
  CreateAttribute, 324
  CreateCDataSection, 324
  CreateComment, 324
  CreateDocumentFragment, 324
  CreateDocumentType, 324
  CreateElement, 324
  CreateEntityReference, 324
  CreateNode, 324
  CreateProcessingInstruction, 324
  CreateSignificantWhitespace, 324
  CreateTextNode, 324
  CreateWhitespace, 324
  CreateXmlDeclaration, 324
XmlException class, properties of, 320
  LineNumer, 320
  LinePosition, 320
  Message, 320
XmlException, properties, 320
  LineNumber, 320
  LinePosition, 320
  Message, 320
XMLNode class, methods and properties, 324
  AppendChild, 325
  CloneNode, 325
  InsertAfter, 325
  InsertBefore, 325
  PrependChild, 325
  RemoveAll, 325
  RemoveChild, 325
  ReplaceChild, 325
XmlReader class, 310
XML-related namespaces, 301
  System.Xml, 301
  System.Xml.Schema, 301
  System.Xml.Serialization, 301
  System.Xml.XPath, 301
  System.Xml.Xsl, 301
XML-related technologies, 301
  ADO, 301–2
  ADO.NET, 302
  SQL Server 2000, 302
XmlSerializer, 304
XmlTextReader class, 314
XmlTextReaderClass, methods of, 318
  ReadEndElement(), 318
  ReadStartElement(String), 318
XmlTextWriter class, 311
XmlTextWriter class, methods of, 314
  WriteBinHex, 314
  WriteCData, 314
  WriteString, 314
  WriteWhiteSpace, 314
XmlUrlResolver class, 333
XmlWriter class, 310
XPath, 309, 337, 967
XQuery, 302
XSD, 342
XSL Transformations (XSLT), 301
XSL/T, 309
XSLT, 967

XSLT elements, 330
for-each, 330
stylesheet, 330
template, 330
value-of, 330
XSLT transforming between XML standards, 334
XSLT transforms, 330
XsltArgumentList class, 337

XsltCompileException class, 337
XsltContext class, 337
XsltException class, 337
XslTransform, 311
XslTransform class, methods and properties, 333
Load, 333
Transform, 334
XmlResolver, 333